DOCTRINE
AND
COVENANTS
REFERENCE
COMPANION

DOCTRINE
AND
COVENANTS
REFERENCE
COMPANION

DENNIS L. LARGEY
GENERAL EDITOR

LARRY E. DAHL
SENIOR EDITOR

ASSOCIATE EDITORS
SUSAN EASTON BLACK, SCOTT C. ESPLIN, CRAIG J. OSTLER,
CHARLES D. TATE, AND ROBERT J. WOODFORD

GRAPHICS EDITOR
SCOTT C. ESPLIN

DESERET BOOK COMPANY
SALT LAKE CITY, UTAH

Library of Congress Cataloging-in-Publication Data

Doctrine and Covenants reference companion / Dennis L. Largey, general editor ; Larry E. Dahl, senior editor ; associate editors: Susan Easton Black, Scott C. Esplin, Craig J. Ostler, Charles D. Tate, and Robert J. Woodford.
     pages cm
  Includes bibliographical references and index.
    ISBN 978-1-59038-599-9 (hardbound : alk. paper) 1. Doctrine and Covenants—Dictionaries. 2. The Church of Jesus Christ of Latter-day Saints—Doctrines—Dictionaries. 3. Mormon Church—Dictionaries. I. Largey, Dennis L., editor. II. Dahl, Larry E., editor. III. Black, Susan Easton, editor. IV. Esplin, Scott C. (Scott Clair), 1974– editor. V. Ostler, Craig J., 1954– editor. VI. Tate, Charles D., editor. VII. Woodford, Robert J. (Robert John), editor.
  BX8628.D639 2012
  289.3'2—dc23   2012019694

Printed in China
Through Four Colour Print Group, Louisville, Kentucky

10 9 8 7 6 5 4 3 2 1

CONTENTS

MAPS

PREFACE

WHEN I FIRST HEARD THE MESSAGE OF The Church of Jesus Christ of Latter-day Saints as a young college student in Hawaii, I was intrigued by the teaching that the gospel and Church of Jesus Christ established in New Testament times was lost through apostasy but restored in modern times through a chosen prophet—Joseph Smith. I came to know the truth of that claim through the power of the Holy Ghost as I searched, studied, and prayed for answers.

The Church of Jesus Christ of Latter-day Saints, like the Church established in ancient times by Jesus Christ, is "built upon the foundation of the apostles and prophets, Jesus Christ himself being the chief corner stone" (Eph. 2:20). Words of Jesus Christ to his latter-day servants are recorded in the Doctrine and Covenants. That book of scripture contains revelations with instructions concerning the organization of the Church; its sacred saving ordinances; the priesthood and its keys; and principal doctrines of the gospel of Jesus Christ such as the fall of Adam and Eve, the atonement of the Lord Jesus Christ, kingdoms of glory in the hereafter, eternal marriage, and salvation for the dead.

The revelations in the Doctrine and Covenants not only add another testimony to the teachings of the Lord and his servants recorded in the Holy Bible but they expand upon doctrines that are mentioned or taught but not fully explained in the Bible. The revelations recorded in the Doctrine and Covenants tell of the renewed effort by called and authorized servants to take the gospel to "every nation, and kindred, and tongue, and people" (133:37); they admonish all people to prepare for the great day of the Lord's return to earth; and they contain a multitude of prophecies and promises that the Lord himself attests will come to pass: "Search these commandments, for they are true and faithful, and the prophecies and promises which are in them shall all be fulfilled" (1:37).

The message of the Doctrine and Covenants is one of hope and victory through Jesus Christ. He is the Savior and Redeemer of the world. The Lord's words in the Doctrine and Covenants, although many times first spoken to specific individuals, may be read and applied as if the Lord were speaking directly to each of us. In an 1829 revelation the Lord offered these comforting and reassuring words: "Look unto me in every thought; doubt not, fear not. Behold the wounds which pierced my side, and also the prints of the nails in my hands and feet; be faithful, keep my commandments, and ye shall inherit the kingdom of heaven" (6:36–37).

I am grateful to have had the opportunity to work on the *Doctrine and Covenants Reference Companion*. The Doctrine and Covenants does contain the voice of Jesus Christ, a voice that readers may discern through the Holy Ghost as they sincerely seek wisdom and instruction within its pages. Jesus said to his servants: "These words are not of men nor of man, but of me; wherefore, you shall testify they are of me and not of man; for it is my voice which speaketh them unto you; for they are given by my Spirit unto you, and by my power you can read them one to another; and save it were by my power you could not have them; wherefore, you can testify that you have heard my voice, and know my words" (18:34–36).

It is my testimony that the Doctrine and Covenants is scripture, a gift from the Lord containing instructions, light, and truth, which can bring joy in this life and exaltation in the life to come.

—Dennis L. Largey
General Editor

ACKNOWLEDGMENTS

THIS VOLUME IS THE RESULT OF THE EFFORTS of many individuals, and we express our appreciation to them.

Contributors. One hundred and twenty-seven authors wrote the articles in this volume.

Associate editors. The associate editors—Susan Easton Black, Scott C. Esplin, Craig J. Ostler, Charles D. Tate, and Robert J. Woodford—worked many hours over several years, applying their knowledge of the Doctrine and Covenants and the history of the Church. We are thankful for their efforts and endurance over the course of the project.

Graphics editor. Scott C. Esplin gathered the images, secured permissions for their use, and wrote the captions.

Office staff. The following individuals made various helpful contributions: Ben Berlin, Kalie Clark, Kelsie Douglas, Nathan Fox, Meara Glazebrook, Darcy Hill, KateLyn Jenkins, Sarah Juchau, Tacy LeBaron, Tyson Lies, Laura McAllister, Becky McCarty, Suzie Skinner, Chelsea Slade, Ashley Thompson, Emma Watkins, and Rachel Williams. Special recognition should be given to Jeanine Ehat and Kristene Largey for their important editorial work.

Reviewers. In addition to the editors, the following individuals reviewed articles in the book: Filip Askerlund, Alexander Baugh, Andrew Hedges, Steven Harper, Judy Tolman, D. Kelly Ogden, and Clyde Williams.

Special assistants. Sincere appreciation is extended to Suzanne Brady, managing editor at Deseret Book, for applying to this volume her exceptional skill, drawn from years of editorial experience, and for her coordination with others at Deseret Book to complete the project: Richard Erickson, art director; Scott Eggers and Shauna Gibby, designers; and Rachael Ward, typographer.

ABOUT THIS VOLUME

THE *DOCTRINE AND COVENANTS REFERENCE COMPANION* (DCRC) addresses more than 850 topics on the Doctrine and Covenants—people, places, words, phrases, doctrines, historical context and overview of each section, and much more—in a single volume. The entries have been prepared by some of the finest scholars in the Church: faculty members from Brigham Young University, BYU–Idaho, and BYU–Hawaii; teachers from Seminaries and Institutes; researchers from the Church Historical Department; and others—a total of 127 authors.

This volume offers readers a unique approach to better understanding the revelations recorded in the Doctrine and Covenants. It brings together all that is in that wonderful book of scripture about a particular topic, augmented with references from other scriptures and teachings of latter-day prophets. Having this reference work at hand is as helpful to the seasoned student of the scriptures as it is to the investigator or new convert studying the Doctrine and Covenants for the first time.

Style and Format

Like the *Book of Mormon Reference Companion* (BMRC; Deseret Book, 2003) and encyclopedic Bible dictionaries, the topics in the *DCRC* are listed alphabetically in a split-column format. Subheadings within articles assist the reader in finding desired subjects. *See also* cross-references at the end of entries and *See* references and words in SMALL CAPITALS within entries direct the reader to related articles.

The revelations recorded in the Doctrine and Covenants are discussed individually and in numerical order in the section following the alphabetical listing of topics.

The first sentence of each entry in the *DCRC* contains a concise explanation of the topic addressed, providing basic knowledge as introductory information. Helpful elaborations follow and are augmented by examples and additional references.

Citations to the Doctrine and Covenants within the text are by section and verse number only. "Doctrine and Covenants" is omitted.

Throughout the *DCRC* the original spelling, grammar, and punctuation of nineteenth-century sources has been retained, unless noted otherwise.

Brief Biographical Sketches

This volume contains an entry for every person named in the revelations. The purpose of these biographical sketches is two-fold: To discuss individuals in relation to the verses in which they are mentioned and to provide a brief summary of their lives and contributions. The biographical information does not include their families because the focus of this volume is on the scriptures themselves. Other published works on individuals in the Doctrine and Covenants include information on the faith, strengths, and contributions of spouses and children who also sustained the work of the Restoration.

The contributors to individual biographical sketches examined both primary and secondary sources, which are generally not cited unless quoted directly. The following works provided useful background or other source materials:

Susan Easton Black. *Who's Who in the Doctrine and Covenants*. Salt Lake City: Deseret Book, 1997.

Donald Q. Cannon and Lyndon W. Cook, eds. *Far West Record: Minutes of The Church of Jesus Christ of Latter-day Saints, 1830–1844*. Salt Lake City: Deseret Book, 1983.

Lyndon W. Cook. *The Revelations of the Prophet Joseph Smith*. Salt Lake City: Deseret Book, 1985.

Andrew Jenson. *Latter-day Saints' Biographical Encyclopedia*. 4 vols. 1901–36. Reprint, Salt Lake City: Western Epics, 1971.

Dean C. Jessee, Mark Ashurst-McGee, and Richard L. Jensen, eds. *Journals, Volume 1: 1832–1839*. Vol. 1 of the Journals series of *The Joseph Smith Papers*, edited by Dean C. Jessee, Ronald K. Esplin, and Richard Lyman Bushman. Salt Lake City: Church Historian's Press, 2008.

Dean C. Jessee, ed. *The Papers of Joseph Smith*. 2 vols. Salt Lake City: Deseret Book, 1989–92.

Joseph Smith. *History of The Church of Jesus Christ of Latter-day Saints*. Edited by B. H. Roberts. 7 vols. 2d ed. rev. Salt Lake City: The Church of Jesus Christ of Latter-day Saints, 1932–51.

Places

Each place name given in the revelations is discussed concisely in the *DCRC*. Entries will be found, for example, on Council Bluffs, Iowa; Hiram, Ohio; and Nauvoo, Illinois. Several such articles are accompanied by maps pinpointing precise locations. *See* List of Maps, page vii.

Doctrinal Topics

The *DCRC* contains articles on principal doctrines of the gospel of Jesus Christ. These entries include both what the Doctrine and Covenants teaches about the doctrine as well as references to other scriptures and teachings of latter-day prophets that explain the doctrine more fully.

Historical Context and Overview of the Sections of the Doctrine and Covenants

Following the alphabetical list of topics are discussions of the historical context and overview of the revelations recorded in the Doctrine and Covenants, arranged in numerical order by section number. Because other articles address the principal doctrines, key words, phrases, and topics found within each section, readers are pointed to them from these more general articles by the volume's cross-referencing system. For example, in the article entitled "Historical context and overview of Doctrine and Covenants 132," the word MARRIAGE directs readers to that topic. The article on the historical context and overview of Doctrine and Covenants 29 has a *See* reference within it to the separate article entitled "Fall of Adam and Eve, the." Likewise, the article on the historical context and overview of Doctrine and Covenants 45 has a *See also* cross-reference at the end to direct readers to a separate article on the second coming of Jesus Christ.

We note that Robert J. Woodford contributed to many of the articles that are focused on individual sections of the Doctrine and Covenants. Dr. Woodford is part of a team of scholars who have prepared volumes 1 through 3 of the Documents series of *The Joseph Smith Papers* for publication beginning in 2013. His work on the *DCRC* benefited from prepublication drafts of those volumes, which will provide transcripts and detailed historical treatment of the early revelations.

Articles on Periods of Latter-day Saint Church History

The *DCRC* contains individual articles for each major period of early Church history: the New York period, the Ohio period, the Missouri period, and the Illinois period. These articles, placed in alphabetical order among the alphabetically arranged topics, discuss the travels, struggles, and successes of members of the Church in each area as the Restoration unfolded and the Saints were eventually driven west to the Salt Lake Valley.

Appendixes

The *DCRC* has five appendixes to further assist readers in their study and appreciation of the Doctrine and Covenants.

Appendix A is Joseph Smith's poetic rendering of Doctrine and Covenants 76.

Appendix B contains comparative section numbers of principal editions of the Doctrine and Covenants/Book of Commandments.

Appendix C shows the order in which the Doctrine and Covenants was first published in languages other than English.

Appendix D is a list of prophecies and promises recorded in the Doctrine and Covenants. In the Lord's preface to his revelations, he challenged readers to "search these commandments, for they are true and faithful, and the *prophecies and promises* which are in them shall all be fulfilled" (1:37; emphasis added).

Appendix E contains selected excerpts of definitions from Webster's 1828 *American Dictionary of the English Language,* featuring words contained in the Doctrine and Covenants, some of which may be unfamiliar to modern readers.

CONTRIBUTORS

KLA   Kenneth L. Alford—Church History and Doctrine; Brigham Young University, Provo, Utah

JBA   James B. Allen—History, retired; Brigham Young University, Provo, Utah

PAA   Philip Andrew Allred—Religious Education; Brigham Young University–Idaho, Rexburg, Idaho

KRA   Karl Ricks Anderson—Seminaries and Institutes; Cincinnati, Ohio

RLA   Richard Lloyd Anderson—Research historian and review editor for *The Joseph Smith Papers;* Ancient Scripture, retired; Brigham Young University, Provo, Utah

DWB   Danel W. Bachman—Seminaries and Institutes, retired

MVB   Milton V. Backman—Church History and Doctrine, retired; Brigham Young University, Provo, Utah

TBB   Terry B. Ball—Ancient Scripture; Brigham Young University, Provo, Utah

CWB   Cory William Bangerter—Seminaries and Institutes, retired

RB   Ronald Bartholomew—Seminaries and Institutes; Orem, Utah

ALB   Alexander L. Baugh—Church History and Doctrine; Brigham Young University, Provo, Utah; Coeditor of volumes in the Documents series of *The Joseph Smith Papers*

JMB   John M. Beck—Seminaries and Institutes, retired

DLB   Daniel Lee Belnap—Ancient Scripture; Brigham Young University, Provo, Utah

REB   Richard E. Bennett—Church History and Doctrine; Brigham Young University, Provo, Utah

RAB   RoseAnn Benson—Provo, Utah

SEB   Susan Easton Black—Church History and Doctrine; Brigham Young University, Provo, Utah

DFB   David F. Boone—Church History and Doctrine; Brigham Young University, Provo, Utah

RLB   Randy L. Bott—Church History and Doctrine, retired; Brigham Young University, Provo, Utah

DEB   Douglas E. Brinley—Church History and Doctrine, retired; Brigham Young University, Provo, Utah

SKB   S. Kent Brown—Ancient Scripture, retired; Brigham Young University, Provo, Utah

CMC   C. Max Caldwell—Church History and Doctrine, retired; Brigham Young University, Provo, Utah

TWC   Terry W. Call—Religious Education; Brigham Young University–Idaho, Rexburg, Idaho

DQC   Donald Q. Cannon—Church History and Doctrine, retired; Brigham Young University, Provo, Utah

JRC   Jeffrey R. Chadwick—Church History and Doctrine; Brigham Young University, Provo, Utah

JC   Jack Christianson—Seminaries and Institutes; Salt Lake City, Utah

DCC   D. Cecil Clark—Teacher Education, retired; Brigham Young University, Provo, Utah

RC   Rachel Cope—Church History and Doctrine; Brigham Young University, Provo, Utah

ROC   Richard O. Cowan—Church History and Doctrine; Brigham Young University, Provo, Utah

RHC   Richard H. Cracroft—English, retired; Brigham Young University, Provo, Utah

PC   Peter Crawley—Mathematics, retired; Brigham Young University, Provo, Utah

LED   Larry Evans Dahl—Church History and Doctrine, retired; Brigham Young University, Provo, Utah

DRD   Dee R. Darling—Seminaries and Institutes, retired

JFD   Joseph F. Darowski—Historian and web editor for *The Joseph Smith Papers,* Salt Lake City, Utah

KD   Kay Darowski—Web editor for *The Joseph Smith Papers*, Salt Lake City, Utah

GLD   Guy L. Dorius—Church History and Doctrine; Brigham Young University, Provo, Utah

RDD   Richard D. Draper—Ancient Scripture, retired; Brigham Young University, Provo, Utah

BLD   Bryce Lane Dunford—Seminaries and Institutes; Salt Lake City, Utah

RIE   Robert I. Eaton—Religious Education; Brigham Young University–Idaho, Rexburg, Idaho

SCE   Scott C. Esplin—Church History and Doctrine; Brigham Young University, Provo, Utah

JSF   J. Spencer Fluhman—History; Brigham Young University, Provo, Utah

KWF Kristine Wardle Frederickson—Provo, Utah

RCF Robert C. Freeman—Church History and Doctrine; Brigham Young University, Provo, Utah

AKG Arnold K. Garr—Church History and Doctrine, retired; Brigham Young University, Provo, Utah

HDG Henry Dean Garrett—Church History and Doctrine, retired; Brigham Young University, Provo, Utah

ALG Alonzo L. Gaskill—Church History and Doctrine; Brigham Young University, Provo, Utah

DJG Douglas James Geilman—Seminaries and Institutes; Salt Lake City, Utah

TLG Ted L. Gibbons—Seminaries and Institutes, retired

MAG Michael Allen Goodman—Church History and Doctrine; Brigham Young University, Provo, Utah

CDG Cynthia Doxey Green—Winston-Salem, North Carolina

RLH Randall L. Hall—Seminaries and Institutes; Salt Lake City, Utah

SCH Steven C. Harper—Historian/Writer, Church History Department, The Church of Jesus Christ of Latter-day Saints, Salt Lake City, Utah.

WGH William G. Hartley—Coeditor of volumes in the Documents series of *The Joseph Smith Papers*; History, retired; Brigham Young University, Provo, Utah

BMH Brian Michael Hauglid—Ancient Scripture; Brigham Young University, Provo, Utah

AHH Andrew H. Hedges—Historian/Writer, Church History Department, The Church of Jesus Christ of Latter-day Saints, Salt Lake City, Utah

JLH John Levi Hilton III—Ancient Scripture; Brigham Young University, Provo, Utah

RNH Richard Neitzel Holzapfel—Church History and Doctrine; Brigham Young University, Provo, Utah

AOH Andrew O Horton—Seminaries and Institutes; Salt Lake City, Utah

PYH Paul Y. Hoskisson—Ancient Scripture; Brigham Young University, Provo, Utah

EDH Eric D. Huntsman—Ancient Scripture; Brigham Young University, Provo, Utah

KPJ Kent P. Jackson—Ancient Scripture; Brigham Young University, Provo, Utah

RCJ Ryan Craig Jenkins—Seminaries and Institutes; Salt Lake City, Utah

RLJ Richard Louis Jensen—Senior writer, research historian, and review editor for *The Joseph Smith Papers*; Church History Department of The Church of Jesus Christ of Latter-day Saints, Salt Lake City

DKJ Daniel K Judd—Ancient Scripture; Brigham Young University, Provo, Utah

FFJ Frank F. Judd Jr.—Ancient Scripture; Brigham Young University, Provo, Utah

NEL   Neal Elwood Lambert—English, retired; Brigham Young University, Provo, Utah

JCL   Jennifer C. Lane—Religious Education; Brigham Young University–Hawaii, Laie, Hawaii

ZLL   Zachary Lee Largey—Orem, Utah

DLL   Dean L. Larsen—Provo, Utah

EDL   E. Dale LeBaron—Church History and Doctrine, retired; Brigham Young University, Provo, Utah

GML   Glen M. Leonard—Church History Museum, retired

JPL   John P. Livingstone—Church History and Doctrine; Brigham Young University, Provo, Utah

JWL   Jared Warner Ludlow—Ancient Scripture; Brigham Young University, Provo, Utah

REL   Robert E. Lund—Seminaries and Institutes; Salt Lake City, Utah

CCM   Carol Cornwall Madsen—History, retired; Brigham Young University, Provo, Utah

TGM   Truman G. Madsen—Philosophy, retired; Brigham Young University, Provo, Utah

WJM   W. Jeffrey Marsh—Ancient Scripture; Brigham Young University, Provo, Utah

RJM   Robert J. Matthews—Ancient Scripture, retired; Brigham Young University, Provo, Utah

JFM   Joseph Fielding McConkie—Ancient Scripture, retired; Brigham Young University, Provo, Utah

BRM   Byron R. Merrill—Ancient Scripture; Brigham Young University, Provo, Utah

RLM   Robert L. Millet—Ancient Scripture; Brigham Young University, Provo, Utah

RGM   Richard G. Moore—Seminaries and Institutes; Orem, Utah

BEM   Barbara Elaine Morgan—Church History and Doctrine; Brigham Young University, Provo, Utah

RHM   Richard Henrie Morley—Seminaries and Institutes, retired

MMM   Maren M. Mouritsen—Ancient Scripture, retired; Brigham Young University, Provo, Utah

KMM   Kerry Miles Muhlestein—Ancient Scripture; Brigham Young University, Provo, Utah

RLN   Reid L. Neilson—Managing Director of the Church History Department, The Church of Jesus Christ of Latter-day Saints, Salt Lake City, Utah

LDN   Lloyd D. Newell—Church History and Doctrine; Brigham Young University, Provo, Utah

MSN   Monte Stephen Nyman—Ancient Scripture, retired; Brigham Young University, Provo, Utah

DKO D. Kelly Ogden—Ancient Scripture; Brigham Young University, Provo, Utah

CFO Camille Fronk Olson—Ancient Scripture; Brigham Young University, Provo, Utah

TDO Terry D. Olson—School of Family Life; Brigham Young University, Provo, Utah

CJO Craig James Ostler—Church History and Doctrine; Brigham Young University, Provo, Utah

LGO Leaun G. Otten—Church History and Doctrine, retired; Brigham Young University, Provo, Utah

KWP Keith W. Perkins—Church History and Doctrine, retired; Brigham Young University, Provo, Utah

PHP Paul H. Peterson—Church History and Doctrine, retired; Brigham Young University, Provo, Utah

DMP Dana M. Pike—Ancient Scripture; Brigham Young University, Provo, Utah

LCP Larry C. Porter—Church History and Doctrine, retired; Brigham Young University, Provo, Utah

GP Gary Purse—Religious Education; Brigham Young University–Idaho, Rexburg, Idaho

MOR Matthew O. Richardson—Church History and Doctrine; Brigham Young University, Provo, Utah

DJR David John Ridges—Seminaries and Institutes, retired

EPR Eric Paul Rogers—Seminaries and Institutes; Missoula, Montana

BKS Bruce K. Satterfield—Religious Education; Brigham Young University–Idaho, Rexburg, Idaho

DRS David Rolph Seely—Ancient Scripture; Brigham Young University, Provo, Utah

JHS Jo Ann H. Seely—Provo, Utah

ACS Andrew C. Skinner—Ancient Scripture; Brigham Young University, Provo, Utah

BLS Brian Lewis Smith—Seminaries and Institutes; Orem, Utah

JS Jonathan Stephenson—Seminaries and Institutes; New York, New York

BGS Bruce G. Stewart—Seminaries and Institutes; Salt Lake City, Utah

GS Gaye Strathearn—Ancient Scripture; Brigham Young University, Provo, Utah

CS Charles Swift—Ancient Scripture; Brigham Young University, Provo, Utah

CDT Charles D. Tate Jr.—English and Ancient Scripture, retired; Brigham Young University, Provo, Utah

JCT John C. Thomas—Religious Education; Brigham Young University–Idaho, Rexburg, Idaho

JST John S. Thompson Jr.—Seminaries and Institutes; Orem, Utah

BLT Brent L. Top—Church History and Doctrine; Brigham Young University, Provo, Utah

RT Rodney Turner—Ancient Scripture, retired; Brigham Young University, Provo, Utah

TRV Thomas Roy Valletta—Seminaries and Institutes; Salt Lake City, Utah

TAW Thomas A. Wayment—Ancient Scripture, Brigham Young University, Provo, Utah

JWW John W. Welch—J. Reuben Clark Law School; Brigham Young University, Provo, Utah

DMW David M. Whitchurch—Ancient Scripture; Brigham Young University, Provo, Utah

GBW Gregory B. Wightman—Religious Education; Brigham Young University–Idaho, Rexburg, Idaho

CJW Clyde J. Williams—Assistant director of Correlation Evaluation, The Church of Jesus Christ of Latter-day Saints, Salt Lake City, Utah

FGW Frederick G. Williams III—Spanish and Portuguese; Brigham Young University, Provo, Utah

NHW Nathan Homer Williams—Religious Education; Brigham Young University–Idaho; Rexburg, Idaho

KJW Keith J. Wilson—Ancient Scripture; Brigham Young University, Provo, Utah

RJW Robert John Woodford—Coeditor of volumes in the Documents series of *The Joseph Smith Papers;* Seminaries and Institutes, retired

MJW Mary Jane Woodger—Church History and Doctrine; Brigham Young University, Provo, Utah

DAW Dennis A. Wright—Church History and Doctrine; Brigham Young University, Provo, Utah

EDS. Editors

ABBREVIATIONS

OLD TESTAMENT

Gen.	Genesis
Ex.	Exodus
Lev.	Leviticus
Num.	Numbers
Deut.	Deuteronomy
Josh.	Joshua
Judg.	Judges
Ruth	Ruth
1 Sam.	1 Samuel
2 Sam.	2 Samuel
1 Kgs.	1 Kings
2 Kgs.	2 Kings
1 Chr.	1 Chronicles
2 Chr.	2 Chronicles
Ezra	Ezra
Neh.	Nehemiah
Esth.	Esther
Job	Job
Ps.	Psalms
Prov.	Proverbs
Eccl.	Ecclesiastes
Song.	Song of Solomon
Isa.	Isaiah
Jer.	Jeremiah
Lam.	Lamentations
Ezek.	Ezekiel
Dan.	Daniel
Hosea	Hosea
Joel	Joel
Amos	Amos
Obad.	Obadiah
Jonah	Jonah
Micah	Micah
Nahum	Nahum
Hab.	Habakkuk
Zeph.	Zephaniah
Hag.	Haggai
Zech.	Zechariah
Mal.	Malachi

NEW TESTAMENT

Matt.	Matthew
Mark	Mark
Luke	Luke
John	John
Acts	Acts
Rom.	Romans
1 Cor.	1 Corinthians
2 Cor.	2 Corinthians
Gal.	Galatians
Eph.	Ephesians
Philip.	Philippians
Col.	Colossians
1 Thes.	1 Thessalonians
2 Thes.	2 Thessalonians
1 Tim.	1 Timothy
2 Tim.	2 Timothy
Titus	Titus
Philem.	Philemon
Heb.	Hebrews
James	James
1 Pet.	1 Peter
2 Pet.	2 Peter
1 Jn.	1 John
2 Jn.	2 John
3 Jn.	3 John

Jude — Jude
Rev. — Revelation

BOOK OF MORMON

1 Ne. — 1 Nephi
2 Ne. — 2 Nephi
Jacob — Jacob
Enos — Enos
Jarom — Jarom
Omni — Omni
W of M — Words of Mormon
Mosiah — Mosiah
Alma — Alma
Hel. — Helaman
3 Ne. — 3 Nephi
4 Ne. — 4 Nephi
Morm. — Mormon
Ether — Ether
Moro. — Moroni

DOCTRINE AND COVENANTS

D&C — Doctrine & Covenants
OD — Official Declaration

PEARL OF GREAT PRICE

Moses — Moses
Abr. — Abraham
JS–M — Joseph Smith–Matthew
JS–H — Joseph Smith–History
A of F — Articles of Faith

OTHER REFERENCES

BC — Book of Commandments
CR — Conference Report
EMS — The Evening and the Morning Star
FWR — Far West Record
JD — Journal of Discourses
JH — Journal History of the Church
JI — Juvenile Instructor
JST — Joseph Smith Translation of the Bible
KCMB — Kirtland Council Minute Book

KJV — King James Version of the Bible
KRB — Kirtland Record Book
MA — Messenger and Advocate
MH — Manuscript History of the Church
MS — Millennial Star
NIV — New International Version of the Bible
TS — Times and Seasons

GENERAL

A.D. — anno domini (in the year of our Lord)
B.C. — before Christ
ca. — about, approximately
cf. — compare, confer
comp[s]. — compiler, compilers
ed. — edition, editor
eds. — editors
e.g. — for example
et al. — and others
etc. — and so on
ff — and following
i.e. — that is
n or n. — note
n.p. — no publisher
pro tem, pro tempore — for the time being
s.v. — under the word
v. — verse
vv. — verses
// — parallel passage(s)

Listen to him who is the **advocate** with the Father, who is pleading your cause before him—Saying: Father, behold the sufferings and death of him who did no sin, in whom thou wast well pleased; behold the blood of thy Son which was shed, the blood of him whom thou gavest that thyself might be glorified; wherefore, Father, spare these my brethren that believe on my name, that they may come unto me and have everlasting life. 45:3–5

Aaron

Moses' older brother and descendant of Levi (Ex. 6:16–20; 7:7). His name appears twenty-seven times in the Doctrine and Covenants, generally in connection with the PRIESTHOOD (8:6, 7; 13:1; 27:8; 28:3; 68:15–20; 84:18–34; 107:13, 16–17, 69–70, 73, 76, 87; 132:59). Revelations in the Doctrine and Covenants and in the teachings of Joseph Smith clarify many items of priesthood authority and administration pertaining to Aaron and his sons that were divinely established during Israel's forty years in the wilderness (e.g., Smith, *History,* 5:257–58; 6:249–51; *Joseph Smith,* 84–85, 93). Though Aaron's life is chronicled in the books of Exodus through Deuteronomy, latter-day revelation restores a focus on Aaron beyond the present biblical account.

Aaron is an example of one "called of God" by revelation through a living prophet and ordained to the priesthood with particular assignments in the Lord's work (Heb. 5:4; cf. D&C 27:8; 28:3; 132:59). He served in positions of leadership among the elders of Israel, including spokesman for Moses, and he, with Moses, Nadab, Abihu, and seventy elders, saw the God of Israel (Ex. 4:10–16; 24:9–11). Later, when most of Israel "hardened their hearts," the Lord took away the Melchizedek Priesthood from the general population and appointed Aaron and his sons as priests to administer in a lesser authority known as the "Priesthood of Aaron," or the Aaronic Priesthood. This priesthood continued "with the house of Aaron among the children of Israel until John" the Baptist (84:18–28, 30; 107:13–14).

Aaron was the presiding priest, the high priest of the Aaronic Priesthood, comparable to the presiding bishop in the Church today. Originally the latter-day position was to be hereditary, but in the absence of a qualified "literal descendant of Aaron," a high priest of the Melchizedek Priesthood may be appointed to hold the keys of that office (68:16–21; 107:13–17, 69–76).

The Aaronic Priesthood was restored to the earth in this dispensation by John the Baptist on 15 May 1829 (13:1). The unspecified "gift of Aaron," promised to Oliver Cowdery in 8:6–9, appears to be some object to be held in his hands as an aid to revelation. In a "revelation on priesthood" (84, headnote), the Lord indicates that faithful priesthood holders "become the sons of Moses and of Aaron and the seed of Abraham, and the church and kingdom, and the elect of God" (84:33–34).

Notable descendants of Aaron include Jeremiah, Ezekiel, Ezra, Zacharias, Elisabeth, and John the Baptist.

See also Bishop(s); Gift of Aaron; Rod(s).

BIBLIOGRAPHY

Smith, Joseph. *History of The Church of Jesus Christ of Latter-day Saints.* Edited by B. H. Roberts. 7 vols. 2d ed. rev. Salt Lake City: The Church of Jesus Christ of Latter-day Saints, 1932–51.

———. *Joseph Smith.* Teachings of Presidents of the Church series. Salt Lake City: The Church of Jesus Christ of Latter-day Saints, 2007.

RJM

Aaron, gift of. *See* Gift of Aaron.

Aaronic Priesthood. *See* Priesthood.

Abase. *See* Appendix E.

Abel

Faithful son of Adam and Eve, notable for significant righteous accomplishments but perhaps best remembered for being murdered by his older brother Cain, thereby becoming mankind's first martyr (84:16). Revelations in the Doctrine and Covenants note that Abel was ordained to the priesthood by his father, Adam, and that he was among the righteous spirits to whom Jesus ministered in the spirit world between his crucifixion and resurrection (84:16; 138:36–40).

Abel was a relatively early child of Adam and Eve but not the second child as implied in Genesis 4:2 (Moses 5:1–3, 16–17). A keeper of sheep, he offered the firstlings of his flock as sacrifices in similitude of the future sacrifice of Jesus Christ (Moses 5:6–7, 17, 20). He walked in holiness and received personal revelation of the Lord's approval. By contrast, Cain's offering was rejected by the Lord because it was not done properly or in faith (Moses 5:26; Heb. 11:4; Smith, *History,* 2:15–16; 4:208–9; *Joseph*

Smith, 93); whereupon, Cain, moved with jealousy and desire to have Abel's flocks, conspired with SATAN and slew his younger brother (84:16; Moses 5:21–36).

An apostate belief in Abraham's day held that Abel's blood (rather than Christ's) was shed for remission of man's sins (JST Gen. 17:3–7; cf. Heb. 12:24). As a resurrected being and holding the keys of his dispensation, Abel ministered as an angel to Paul (*Joseph Smith,* 169).

BIBLIOGRAPHY

Smith, Joseph. *History of The Church of Jesus Christ of Latter-day Saints.* Edited by B. H. Roberts. 7 vols. 2d ed. rev. Salt Lake City: The Church of Jesus Christ of Latter-day Saints, 1932–51.

————. *Joseph Smith.* Teachings of Presidents of the Church series. Salt Lake City: The Church of Jesus Christ of Latter-day Saints, 2007.

RJM

Abraham

Abraham, son of Terah and father of Ishmael and Isaac (Gen. 11:26; 16:15; 21:3), is a principal figure in the Bible and in the Doctrine and Covenants. He grew up in Ur of the Chaldees (Gen. 11:26–28; Abr. 1:1; 2:1) but moved to Haran and then to the land of Canaan at the command of the Lord (Gen. 12:1–6; Abr. 2:1–15). He and his wife, Sarah, also resided in Egypt for an unspecified time (Gen. 12:10–13:1; Abr. 2:21). Abraham's original name was Abram. The name Abraham, given to him by the Lord (Gen. 17:5), means "father of a multitude."

Abraham appears thirty-seven times in thirteen sections of the Doctrine and Covenants. Nine sections (27, 98, 101, 103, 109, 110, 133, 137, 138) mention him once; one section (124) refers to him twice; two sections (84, 136) three times; and one section (132) twenty times.

Many references to Abraham in the Doctrine and Covenants add information not reflected in the Genesis account. In one section, the faithful receive a promise that they will someday partake of the sacrament with Abraham and other ancient prophets (27:10). In another, Abraham's Melchizedek Priesthood lineage is outlined (84:13). In still another, the law of retribution revealed in Kirtland receives divine endorsement

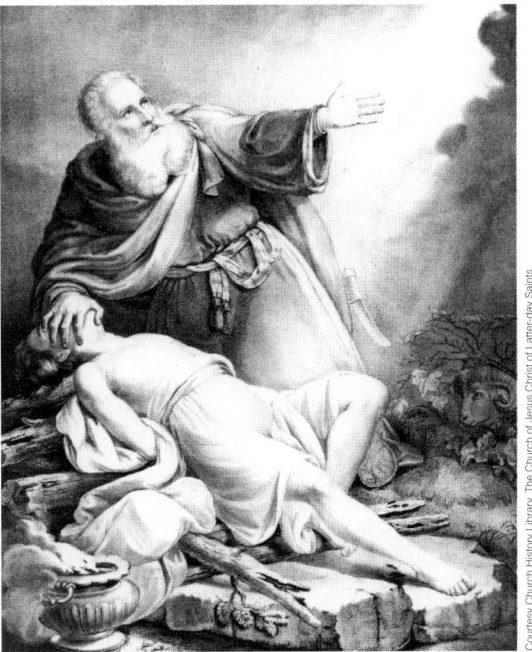

Abraham Commanded Not to Sacrifice Isaac; *print by C. Forgen. "Therefore, they must needs be chastened and tried, even as Abraham, who was commanded to offer up his only son" (D&C 101:4).*

as the same law that was given to Abraham and all the ancient prophets (98:32).

Furthermore, the Doctrine and Covenants reminds those who experience persecutions that "they must needs be chastened and tried, even as Abraham" (101:4; 132:51). It establishes the faithful as the seed of Abraham (84:34; 103:17) and part of the ABRAHAMIC COVENANT (110:12; 124:58) and as those who will be in the presence of the Lord after the resurrection with Abraham and all the redeemed (133:55–56). A prophetic pronouncement declares that Judah will return to the land given to Abraham (109:64).

A little over a year after the death of his father, Joseph Smith Sr., the Prophet received a revelation that his father sits at the right hand of Abraham (124:19). This presaged another revelation in which the Lord sealed up Joseph Smith Jr. to sit with Abraham (132:49) at some time in the future because, as with Abraham, God had accepted Joseph Smith's sacrifices and offerings (132:50). God revealed to Joseph Smith that He was with him as He was with Abraham (132:57).

The Genesis account mentions Abraham's plural wives; the Doctrine and Covenants explains the practice (132:1, 29–37) and the law of Sarah (132:64–65). The faithful should obey the words of God from Adam to Abraham, to Moses, to Jesus and his apostles, and to Joseph Smith (136:37), keeping themselves from evil (136:21). In October 1918 Church president Joseph F. Smith saw Abraham in the spirit world (138:41).

BMH

Abraham, seed of. *See* Seed of Abraham.

Abrahamic covenant

A sacred agreement between the Lord and Abraham and his descendants. For faithfulness to the terms of the covenant, which are centered in the gospel of Jesus Christ, the Lord assures Abraham and his descendants of great promises regarding (1) their posterity, (2) their rights to the priesthood, (3) their opportunity to bless all the nations of the earth with the gospel, and (4) an inheritance of land, both in time and eternity (Gen. 13:13–14; 17:1–7; 22:15–18; Abr. 2:9–11). This covenant applies to the literal seed of Abraham as well as to all those who become the seed of Abraham by accepting the GOSPEL (Gal. 3:7–9; Abr. 2:19).

Revelations in the Doctrine and Covenants verify the restoration of the Abrahamic covenant in latter days. On 3 April 1836, in the Kirtland Temple, an ancient prophet named Elias "committed the dispensation of the gospel of Abraham" to Joseph Smith and Oliver Cowdery (110:12). Thus, the promises made to Abraham were restored to the Saints.

1. Promises of eternal seed. Speaking of eternal MARRIAGE as "the law of my Holy Priesthood, as was ordained by me and my Father before the world was" (132:28), the Lord explained the promises Abraham received "concerning his seed, and of the fruit of his loins . . . which were to continue so long as they were in the world . . . and out of the world should they continue as innumerable as the stars; or, if ye were

9 And I will make of thee a great ᵃnation, and I will ᵇbless thee above measure, and make thy name great among all nations, and thou shalt be a blessing unto thy seed after thee, that in their hands they shall bear this ministry and ᶜPriesthood unto all nations;

10 And I will ᵃbless them through thy name; for as many as receive this ᵇGospel shall be called after thy ᶜname, and shall be accounted thy ᵈseed, and shall rise up and bless thee, as their ᵉfather;

11 And I will ᵃbless them that bless thee, and ᵇcurse them that curse thee; and in thee (that is, in thy Priesthood) and in thy ᶜseed (that is, thy Priesthood), for I give unto thee a promise that this ᵈright shall continue in thee, and in thy seed after thee (that is to say, the literal seed, or the seed of the body) shall all the families of the earth be blessed, even with the blessings of the Gospel, which are the blessings of salvation, even of life eternal.

Abraham 2:9–11.

to count the sand upon the seashore ye could not number them" (132:30–31). This covenant comprises the promise of "eternal lives," the blessing of rising in the resurrection clothed with the power to beget spirit children, to those whose marriages are performed by proper authority and "sealed unto them by the Holy Spirit of promise" (132:19–24).

2. Promise of the PRIESTHOOD. The Lord referred to those who receive and faithfully magnify their callings in the Aaronic and Melchizedek priesthoods as "the seed of Abraham" (84:34). Further, the Lord spoke of those who receive the priesthood "through the lineage of your fathers" as "lawful heirs, according to the flesh," and assured them, "Blessed are ye if ye continue in my goodness, a light unto the Gentiles, and through this priesthood, a savior unto my people Israel" (86:8–11).

3. Promise of blessing all nations. Concerning the promise that the seed of Abraham would bless all the nations of the earth by sharing the gospel with them, the Lord, in the beginning of this dispensation, reiterated his command to his meridian-day apostles to preach the gospel to the "uttermost parts of the earth" (58:64; cf. Acts 1:8). He instructed the leaders of the Church to send "forth the elders of my church unto the nations which are afar off; unto the islands of the sea; send forth unto foreign lands; call upon all nations, first upon the Gentiles, and then upon the Jews" (133:8), thus fulfilling the promise to Abraham that his seed "shall bear this ministry and Priesthood unto all nations" and that through his seed—that is, his priesthood seed and his literal seed—"shall all the families of the earth be blessed, even with the blessings of the Gospel, which are the blessings of salvation, even of life eternal" (Abr. 2:9–11; cf. 1 Ne. 15:18).

4. Promise of land. An important aspect of the Abrahamic covenant is the promise of land as an inheritance. In the biblical record, the Lord covenanted with Abraham that he and his posterity would receive the land of Canaan as an inheritance (Gen. 13:14–17). In the Book of Mormon and the Doctrine and Covenants the Lord promised the land of America as an inheritance for the "remnant of Jacob" (52:2), more specifically, the "remnant of the house of Joseph" (3 Ne. 15:12–13; 16:16). The descendants of Lehi, through Ephraim and Manasseh, the sons of Joseph, are a "remnant of Jacob" and therefore heirs to the land of America (Alma 10:3; 2 Ne. 3:1–11; Snow, 23:184). In the last days, as preparations are made for the return of the Savior to the earth, special responsibilities and blessings are assigned to the birthright tribe, "Ephraim and his fellows," in this land (133:34; cf. vv. 17–34). Ultimately, the righteous will inherit the earth for an eternal abode (88:17–26). God's promises in the Abrahamic covenant are sure for anyone who fulfills his or her commitment to the terms of the covenant—"obedience to the laws and ordinances" of the fulness of the gospel of Jesus Christ, which includes taking the gospel to the world (A of F 3; D&C 66:2).

See also Inheritance; Lawful heirs according to the flesh.

BIBLIOGRAPHY

Snow, Erastus. *Journal of Discourses.* 26 vols. London: Latter-day Saints' Book Depot, 1854–86.

CJO

Abridgment. *See* Appendix E.

Acceptable day of the Lord/acceptable year of the Lord

A divinely appropriate time for something significantly beneficial to happen. Two passages in the Doctrine and Covenants employ this phrase. In section 93 the Lord commissioned Sidney Rigdon to "proclaim the acceptable year of the Lord, and the gospel of salvation" (93:51). In this latter-day context, the expression denotes the time of restoration as well as redemption through Christ. In section 138, President Joseph F. Smith recorded a vision in which he observed the Savior authorize and organize righteous spirits to proclaim the gospel to those spirits who were "in darkness" (138:30). President Smith saw that these "chosen messengers went forth to declare the acceptable day of the Lord and proclaim liberty to the captives who were bound" (138:31). The "acceptable day" refers to the time and opportunity for the spirits of the dead to receive the message of salvation through Jesus Christ. *See* Salvation for the dead.

Both passages in the Doctrine and Covenants reflect the language of the messianic prophecy in Isaiah 61:1–2, which declares that the Lord's "anointed" would preach, heal, liberate the captives, and "proclaim the acceptable year of the Lord." The Hebrew noun translated here as "acceptable" means "favorable, that which is pleasing" (e.g., Ps. 69:13; Isa. 49:8; 58:5; 61:2). Jesus announced during his mortal ministry that he was the one who fulfilled Isaiah's prophecy (Luke 4:16–21). Thus, Christ, the Anointed One, proclaimed the pleasing or favorable time of the Lord, which was his coming to redeem the world.

DMP

Accountability

Responsibility to AUTHORITY for one's behavior or worthiness; an eternal principle inseparably entwined with the exercise of AGENCY. The principle of accountability is evident in several contexts in the Doctrine and Covenants, all indicating mankind's accountability to God and/or his servants:

Accountability based on age and capability to repent

Several revelations teach that little CHILDREN are not guilty of sin "until they begin to become accountable" before God (29:46–47). They are to be baptized only after they have "arrived unto the years of accountability before God, and [are] capable of repentance" (20:71; cf. 18:42). The appropriate age for baptism is given by the Lord as "eight years old" (68:25–27). The phrase "capable of repentance" excludes the need for baptism of anyone "that hath no understanding," regardless of chronological age (29:50). Joseph Smith's vision of the celestial kingdom also reveals that "all children who die before they arrive at the years of accountability are saved in the celestial kingdom of heaven" (137:10). *See* Celestial kingdom, vision of.

Accountability of everyone for sins

In instructing the Saints who had been "scattered by their enemies" in Jackson County, Missouri, in 1833, the Lord told them to "continue to importune for redress" to every level of government, "according to the laws and constitution of the people, which I have suffered to be established . . . that every man may act . . . according to the moral agency which I have given unto him, that every man may be accountable for his own sins in the day of judgment" (101:76–78; cf. 1:33; 19:15–18; 82:23).

Accountability for all earthly blessings

When the Lord directed that the group-held properties of the United Order/United Firm be divided into individual stewardships, he said: "It is expedient that I, the Lord, should make every man accountable, as a steward over earthly blessings, which I have made and prepared for my creatures. . . . For the earth is full, and there is enough and to spare; yea, I prepared all things, and have given unto the children of men to be agents unto themselves. Therefore, if any man shall take of the abundance which I have made, and impart not his portion, according to the law of my gospel, unto the poor and the needy, he shall, with the wicked, lift up his eyes in hell, being in torment" (104:11–18).

Accountability for actions in relation to governments

Section 134 is a "declaration of belief" of the Church "regarding governments and laws in general" (134, headnote). "We believe that governments were instituted of God for the benefit of man; and that he holds men accountable for their acts in relation to them" (134:1). In other revelations, the Lord said he "established the Constitution of this land [the United States], by the hands of wise men whom [he] raised up unto this very purpose, and redeemed the land by the shedding of blood" (101:80). He enjoined the Saints to "diligently" seek for and uphold "honest men and wise men" to be their leaders in GOVERNMENT (98:10). Latter-day Saints cannot escape the responsibility to be appropriately involved in issues of government.

Accountability to priesthood leaders for worthiness and standing in the Church

When the Church in the 1830s had two main centers of activity—Kirtland, Ohio, and Missouri—the Lord made it clear that members in each center were to give accounts of their stewardships, under the principles of CONSECRATION, to their respective bishops. Those going from one branch of the Church to another were to carry certificates of worthiness and good standing in the Church, signed by the bishop or other priesthood leaders who were acquainted with them (72:15–25; cf. 20:64, 84). Anyone who could not do so was not "accounted as a wise steward" (72:26). *See* License/certificate(s).

The Lord warned of rather severe punishments for those who broke their sacred covenants to live by the principles of consecration, whether they were individual members or members of the United Order/United Firm or the Literary Firm (51:5; 78:12; 82:21).

LED

Adam

"The first man" on earth (84:16), also known as "Michael, the prince, the archangel" (107:54), "the father of all . . . the ancient of days" (27:11). He, along with "our glorious Mother Eve," became a principal benefactor to all mankind through the Fall, which brought about the conditions of mortality, made possible man's mortal probation, and laid the foundation for the redemption of mankind through Jesus Christ (138:39; 29:39–44; cf. 2 Ne. 2:19–23; Moses 5:11).

The Doctrine and Covenants affirms Adam's important role in the history of this EARTH and adds significant insight not found in other scriptures. He was given "the keys of salvation under the counsel and direction of the Holy One" (78:16). All those who hold the "Holy Priesthood" can trace their authority back to Adam (84:6–17), and Adam personally ordained to the patriarchal order of the PRIESTHOOD each PATRIARCH from Seth to Methuselah, making an unbroken line of righteous men who had personal knowledge of Adam's greatness from the beginning to the Flood (107:41–52). After the Fall, Adam dwelt in the land of ADAM-ONDI-AHMAN in northern Missouri (117:8). Three years before his death, Adam called the seven patriarchs (from Seth to Methuselah), "with the residue of his posterity who were righteous, into the valley of Adam-ondi-Ahman, and there bestowed upon them his last blessing." The Lord appeared and confirmed eternal blessings upon Adam, and Adam, "being full of the Holy Ghost, predicted whatsoever should befall his posterity unto the latest generation" (107:53–56). "These things were all written in the book of Enoch, and are to be testified of in due time" (107:57). Adam (Michael) was one of many ancient patriarchs and prophets who visited Joseph Smith in establishing the restoration of the fulness of the gospel on the earth in the latter days (128:20–21). And his "voice" was heard "on the banks of the Susquehanna, detecting the devil when he appeared as an angel of light" (128:20).

Before the end of the world Adam will come again to Adam-ondi-Ahman "to visit his people" (116:1) and "hold a council with them to prepare them for the coming of the Son of Man. . . .

All that have had the KEYS must stand before him in this grand council" (Smith, 3:386–87). He was among the righteous who met with Jesus in the postmortal spirit world when the Savior visited between his crucifixion and resurrection to organize extended missionary efforts to the spirits of the dead (138:38). Adam was seen by the Prophet Joseph Smith in vision as being in the celestial kingdom with "the Father and the Son," Abraham, Joseph's parents, and his brother Alvin (137:1–5). He will lead "the hosts of heaven" in the final triumph over the devil and his armies in "the battle of the great God," which will take place at the end of the "little season" following the MILLENNIUM (88:110–16). And the sound of Adam's TRUMP will herald the final RESURRECTION (29:26).

In addition to what is revealed in the Doctrine and Covenants, other scriptures and the inspired teachings of latter-day prophets provide more particulars about Adam. Known as Michael in the premortal life, he helped create the earth (McConkie, 16, 17) and led the righteous spirits in opposition to Lucifer's rebellion in the "war in heaven" (Rev. 12:7–9). He is the great high priest, under Christ, who "presides over the spirits of all men" as well as "angels," has "dominion given him over every living creature," and holds the keys of the priesthood for all dispensations (Smith, 3:386–87; 4:xl). "The Priesthood was first given to Adam; he obtained the First Presidency, and held the keys of it from generation to generation. He obtained it in the Creation, before the world was formed. . . . The keys have to be brought from heaven whenever the Gospel is sent. When they are revealed from heaven, it is by Adam's authority" (Smith, 3:385–86). God "set the ordinances to be the same forever and ever, and set Adam to watch over them, to reveal them from heaven to man, or to send angels to reveal them" (Smith, 4:xl).

Truly, Adam—Michael, the prince, the archangel—holds preeminent status in many aspects of the plan of salvation in addition to being the first man on the earth.

See also Fall of Adam and Eve, the.

BIBLIOGRAPHY

McConkie, Bruce R. *Mormon Doctrine.* 2d ed. Salt Lake City: Bookcraft, 1966.

Smith, Joseph. *History of The Church of Jesus Christ of Latter-day Saints.* Edited by B. H. Roberts. 7 vols. 2d ed. rev. Salt Lake City: The Church of Jesus Christ of Latter-day Saints, 1932–51.

RJM

Adam, Fall of. *See* Fall of Adam and Eve, the.

Adam-ondi-Ahman

On 19 May 1838, while visiting Lyman Wight at SPRING HILL, DAVIESS COUNTY, MISSOURI, Joseph Smith revealed that the area was formerly the homeland of Adam and his posterity and was known anciently as Adam-ondi-Ahman (78:15–16; 116; 117:8). The area was sometimes referred to as "Diahman" by Latter-day Saint settlers.

Three years before his death, Adam called his righteous posterity into the valley of Adam-ondi-Ahman "and there bestowed upon them his last blessing." The Lord appeared and "administered comfort unto Adam," declaring him to be a prince over his posterity forever. "Adam stood up in the midst of the congregation; and, notwithstanding he was bowed down with age, being full of the Holy Ghost, predicted whatsoever should befall his posterity unto the latest generation" (107:50–56). The Doctrine and Covenants affirms that Adam will again come to Adam-ondi-Ahman to "visit his people" (116:1). Of that meeting, the Prophet Joseph Smith said: "Daniel in his seventh chapter speaks of the Ancient of Days; he means the oldest man, our Father Adam, Michael, he will call his children together and hold a council with them to prepare them for the coming of the Son of Man. He (Adam) is the father of the human family, and presides over the spirits of all men, and all that have had the keys must stand before him in this

© Intellectual Reserve, Inc.

Aerial view of the valley of Adam-ondi-Ahman, on a bend of the Grand River in northern Missouri. In the late 1830s, the site was known as Spring Hill, and Latter-day Saints settled there in 1838. Three years before his death, Adam called "the residue of his posterity who were righteous, into the valley of Adam-ondi-Ahman, and there bestowed upon them his last blessing. And the Lord appeared unto them" (D&C 107:53–54). In the last days, this encounter will be repeated. Before the Savior's return, Adam-ondi-Ahman "is the place where Adam shall come to visit his people" (D&C 116:1).

grand council. . . . The Son of Man stands before him, and there is given him glory and dominion. Adam delivers up his stewardship to Christ, that which was delivered to him as holding the keys of the universe, but retains his standing as head of the human family" (*History*, 3:386–87).

By early 1838, a number of Latter-day Saint settlers had moved into the area of Spring Hill and Adam-ondi-Ahman. On 28 June 1838, a stake was created with John Smith, Joseph Smith's uncle, as stake president and Reynolds Cahoon and Lyman Wight as counselors. Vinson Knight was appointed bishop. Heber C. Kimball reported that a temple site at Adam-ondi-Ahman was chosen and the plot dedicated by Brigham Young. Although Elder Kimball did not state when this occurred, his narrative suggests that it occurred sometime in October 1838. Where the temple was to be situated is not now known.

By the fall of 1838, Adam-ondi-Ahman was the most populated community in Daviess County, with between 600 and 750 people. When hostilities erupted in mid-October and forced many Latter-day Saints living in outlying areas to move to Diahman for safety and protection, the settlement's population may have swelled to as many as 1,200 to 1,500. After the Mormon surrender to Missouri authorities in November, the Saints were forced to evacuate the area, and most temporarily relocated in Caldwell County before making their way out of the state in early 1839. Following the departure of the Saints, Adam-ondi-Ahman became known as Cravensville, after John Cravens. By the early 1870s, most of the inhabitants had moved away, and the community ceased to exist.

Considerable confusion exists surrounding certain discoveries and statements made by Joseph Smith and his contemporaries about Adam-ondi-Ahman and more specifically the site known as Tower Hill. On Joseph Smith's 19 May 1838 visit to the area, his secretary, George Robinson, indicated in the Prophet's "Scriptory Book" that they discovered "the remains of an old Nephitish Alter an[d] Tower" (Smith, *Papers*, 2:244). This statement may suggest that the company came across ruins dating to the Nephite civilization; however, it may be that

Joseph Smith meant that he and his party had located the remains of an Indian ("Nephitish") altar or tower. Such an interpretation is supported by a 1980 archaeological excavation of the top of the hill, which showed that the knoll had been a Native American burial mound.

In the past few decades, the LDS Church has purchased land at Adam-ondi-Ahman, including the Saints' original settlement site. Church labor missionaries live and work there to beautify and improve the property. *See* maps, pp. 414 and 710.

BIBLIOGRAPHY

Britton, Rollin J. "Adam-ondi-Ahman." *Missouri Historical Review* 20 (January 1926): 236–46.

Gentry, Leland H. "Adam-ondi-Ahman: A Brief Historical Survey." *BYU Studies* 13 (Summer 1973): 553–76.

———. "The Land Question at Adam-ondi-Ahman." *BYU Studies* 26 (Spring 1986): 45–56.

———. "Was a Temple Site Ever Dedicated at Adam-ondi-Ahman?" *Ensign* 4 (April 1974): 16.

Matthews, Robert J. "Adam-ondi-Ahman." *BYU Studies* 13 (Autumn 1972): 27–35.

Smith, Joseph. *History of The Church of Jesus Christ of Latter-day Saints*. Edited by B. H. Roberts. 7 vols. 2d ed. rev. Salt Lake City: The Church of Jesus Christ of Latter-day Saints, 1932–51.

———. *The Papers of Joseph Smith.* Vol. 2, *Autobiographical and Historical Writings*. Edited by Dean C. Jessee. Salt Lake City: Deseret Book, 1992.

ALB

Administrations to the sick and dying. *See* Priesthood.

Adultery

Sexual relations between a man or a woman with someone other than his or her spouse. In a figurative sense, a person individually or a people collectively commit spiritual adultery when they turn from worshiping the true God and instead worship false gods of one kind or another. The Lord said to ancient Israel: "I am married unto you" (Jer. 3:14), "but thou hast played the harlot with many lovers" (Jer. 3:1); "surely as a wife treacherously departeth from her husband, so have ye dealt treacherously with me" (Jer. 3:20).

The revelations in the Doctrine and Covenants speak of adultery only in the sense of sexual immorality (42:22–26, 74–77, 80–83; 59:6; 63:14–16; 66:10; 76:103; 132:41–44, 61–63).

In section 42, known as "the law of the Church" (42, headnote), the Lord commanded against adultery (42:24; cf. 59:6; 66:10) and directed that unrepentant adulterers be "cast out," or excommunicated. A first offender who repents with all his heart is to be forgiven; "but if he doeth it again, he shall not be forgiven, but shall be cast out" (42:24–26). It should be noted that these instructions were given before temple covenants were available. Violating sacred temple covenants by committing adultery may result in excommunication for a first offense. Mercifully, after excommunication and upon complete REPENTANCE, one may be rebaptized and have one's blessings restored.

The Lord cautioned against admitting unrepentant adulterers into the Church (42:76–77) and gave instructions concerning adultery and divorce. Innocent spouses who DIVORCE or separate because their husband or wife commits fornication are not subject to Church discipline (42:74). Those guilty of adultery, however, are to be "cast out" (42:75). In this context, the word FORNICATION in verse 74 is most likely synonymous with *adultery*. Verses 80–82 outline disciplinary proceedings against those who are guilty of adultery—they are to be tried before two or more elders of the Church, with the testimony of at least two witnesses, and, "if it can be, it is necessary that the bishop be present also." Moreover, the elders are to "lay the case before the church, and the church shall lift up their hands against" them. Again, it should be noted that these instructions were given early in the history of the organization of the Church, before the establishment of disciplinary councils in wards and stakes. Therefore, both policies and procedures in the Church today may differ somewhat from what is contained in section 42. Currently, a bishop's council and/or a stake presidency and high council carefully examine transgressions and circumstances of an offender, and decisions concerning that person's church status are made in accordance with policies and procedures established by the First Presidency of the Church and after the council

earnestly and prayerfully seeks heavenly inspiration. These modern councils do not "lay the case before the church" (42:81), and, in almost all cases, their decisions are not publicly announced. *See* Church discipline.

In 63:14–16, the Lord declared that there were adulterers and adulteresses among the early Saints and admonished them to repent. He also repeated a warning given earlier (42:23) that "he that looketh on a woman to lust after her, or if any shall commit adultery in their hearts, they shall not have the Spirit, but shall deny the faith and shall fear" (63:16). Furthermore, unrepentant guilty parties are warned that "the fearful," along with "the whoremonger, and the sorcerer, shall have their part in that lake which burneth with fire and brimstone" (63:17). "Their part," if they do not receive "the gospel, neither the testimony of Jesus," will consist of their being "cast down to hell" and suffering the "wrath of Almighty God, until the fulness of times," at which time they will be brought out of hell and placed in the telestial kingdom (76:98–107).

In 132:61–63, the Lord explained that the same laws of fidelity and moral purity spoken of in earlier sections pertain to participants in authorized plural MARRIAGE.

See also Virtue.

LED

Adversary. *See* Satan.

Adversity. *See* Affliction(s).

Advocate

One who defends, pleads, intercedes, or speaks in behalf of another. By virtue of the ATONEMENT, JESUS CHRIST is the advocate with the Father for all mankind (29:5; 38:4; 110:4). Having conquered sin and death, only he is able to intercede on behalf of humankind to provide a place for them in the kingdom of the Father (45:3–5; cf. 2 Ne. 2:9; Mosiah 15:8; Moro. 7:27–28). More than just an authoritative arbitrator of JUSTICE, Christ in his role of advocate embodies divine MERCY by protecting, succoring, and pleading for the righteous (32:3; 45:3–5; 62:1).

MOR

Affliction(s)

Tribulation, distress, oppression, hardship. Affliction is a notable theme in the Doctrine and Covenants. Shortly after the Church was organized, Joseph Smith was tried and acquitted twice on trumped-up charges of disorderly conduct (Smith, 1:88–96). Soon thereafter, in June 1830, at Harmony, Pennsylvania, the Prophet received a revelation that declared: "Be patient in afflictions . . . for, lo, I am with thee" (24:8; cf. 31:9; 66:9). At the same time, Emma Smith was instructed to comfort Joseph in his afflictions (25:5), and Peter Whitmer was told, "Be you afflicted in all [Joseph's] afflictions, ever lifting up your heart unto me in prayer and faith, for his and your deliverance" (30:5–6; cf. 124:16; 133:53).

Antagonists in Harmony continued to persecute Joseph Smith, so he moved to Fayette, New York, in August 1830 (Smith, 1:109). There the Prophet received a revelation concerning gathering in the last days; the revelation proclaimed that the unrighteous will suffer afflictions and "tribulation and desolation" because of their sinful ways (29:8–9).

The theme of affliction is prominent in the Doctrine and Covenants during the Missouri period in the 1830s. On 20 July 1831, the Prophet received a revelation that designated Independence, Missouri, as the "center place" of Zion (57:3). Soon thereafter hundreds of Saints began to gather at Independence and other places in Jackson County. Little did they realize that they would experience tremendous affliction over the next few years (109:47–49). In section 58, however, the Lord revealed an important principle: If individuals are faithful during times of adversity, they will be rewarded for their obedience, "for after much tribulation come the blessings" (v. 4). The Lord also indicated that he had "suffered the affliction" in 1833 to come upon the Saints "in consequence of their transgressions" but reassured them that he would "not utterly cast them off" (101:2–9). The Lord had earlier promised that ultimately "all things wherewith you have been afflicted shall work together for your good, and to my name's glory" (98:3).

In 1834, when the Church was in debt to New York lenders, the Lord promised that he would soften hearts, "that it shall be taken away out of their minds to bring affliction upon you" (104:81).

The revelations in the Doctrine and Covenants contain several reasons why afflictions come: failure to teach children "light and truth" (93:42), difficulty imposed by nonbelieving family members (31:2), failure to forgive others (64:8), and disobedience (97:26; 101:2; 105:1–2). Moreover, Saints are to "remember in all things the poor and the needy, the sick and the afflicted, for he that doeth not these things, the same is not my disciple (52:40; cf. 105:1–4).

A significant truth concerning affliction was revealed to Joseph Smith while he was imprisoned in the LIBERTY JAIL during the winter of 1838–39. There the Prophet learned that his adversity and afflictions would "be but a small moment" and that if he endured them well, God would "exalt [him] on high" (121:7–8).

BIBLIOGRAPHY

Smith, Joseph. *History of The Church of Jesus Christ of Latter-day Saints.* Edited by B. H. Roberts. 7 vols. 2d ed. rev. Salt Lake City: The Church of Jesus Christ of Latter-day Saints, 1932–51.

AKG

Affrighted. *See* Appendix E.

Age of accountability. *See* Accountability.

Agency

The ability and freedom to choose among alternatives; an eternal and foundational principle in God's plan of salvation for all mankind. The Doctrine and Covenants and the Pearl of Great Price use the terms *agent, agency,* or *moral agency* to refer to this principle; the Bible and the Book of Mormon employ or imply variations of the word *choose.* The scriptures do not use the term *free agency,* although that term has often been used by members of the Church. Agency is made possible through the ATONEMENT of Jesus Christ (2 Ne. 2:24–29), and it is fully operational only when certain conditions exist: opposing, enticing alternatives (29:39; cf. 2 Ne. 2:11–13); awareness, or light and truth concerning the alternatives (93:31–32); and unrestricted freedom of choice (58:27–28; cf. 2 Ne. 2:26–27).

Agency is an eternal principle: "Man was also in the beginning with God. Intelligence, or the light of truth, was not created or made, neither indeed can be. All truth is independent in that sphere in which God has placed it, to act for itself, as all intelligence also; otherwise there is no existence" (93:29–30). In the premortal councils, the devil was able to turn "a third part of the hosts of heaven . . . away from [God] because of their agency" (29:36–39; cf. Moses 4:1–4; Rev. 12:7–11).

On earth, every person is given the LIGHT OF CHRIST that he may know GOOD from EVIL and is given the right to choose whether to follow, ignore, or rebel against that light. A person who chooses to follow this light "cometh unto God, even the Father," and to the restored gospel of Jesus Christ, whereas those who choose not to "receive" the light, even when it is "plainly manifest unto them," remain in the "bondage of sin" and "under condemnation" (84:46–53; 93:31–32; cf. John 1:9; Moro. 7:16–19).

Very early in this DISPENSATION, the Lord encouraged the Saints to use their agency to be "anxiously engaged in a good cause, and do many things of their own free will, and bring to pass much righteousness; for the power is in them, wherein they are agents unto themselves" (58:27–28).

When speaking of those who persecuted the Saints and drove them from Jackson County, Missouri, in 1833, the Lord instructed the Saints to "continue to importune for redress" to the government officials, "according to the laws and constitution of the people . . . that every man may act in doctrine and principle . . . according to the moral agency which I have given unto him, that every man may be accountable for his own sins in the day of judgment" (101:76–78).

The Lord honors the agency given to mankind throughout their mortal lives but will require an accounting from each one concerning his or her use of it when he comes again to reign on earth in the Millennium: "Behold, here is wisdom, and let every man choose for himself until I come" (37:4; cf. 38:22; 58:22; 98:8; 2 Ne. 2:26–27). The Lord has sent the gospel,

his "everlasting covenant," into the world through the instrumentality of the Prophet Joseph Smith. Eventually everyone, including the "nations of the earth," will acknowledge and submit to its rightful and righteous governance, either by choice or by the power of God (49:9–10).

The use of agency and the accounting for its use have not been forced upon anyone. Everyone who has lived or who will live on this earth was in attendance in the premortal councils and sustained the plan of salvation, of which agency is a critical part. Joseph Smith explained, "At the first organization in heaven we were all present and saw the Savior chosen and appointed, and the plan of salvation made and we sanctioned it" (Ehat and Cook, 60).

See also Accountability, Agent(s), Fall of Adam and Eve, the; Premortal existence.

BIBLIOGRAPHY

Ehat, Andrew F., and Lyndon W. Cook, comps. and eds. *The Words of Joseph Smith.* Provo, Utah: Religious Studies Center, Brigham Young University, 1980.

LED

Agent(s)

Term with two meanings:

1. A person choosing and acting for oneself. God provided that man "should be an agent unto himself" (29:35)—to act and not be acted upon (2 Ne. 2:16, 26). "It must needs be that the devil should tempt the children of men, or they could not be agents unto themselves" (29:39); that is, "let every man choose for himself" (37:4), "for the power [to choose] is in them, wherein they are agents unto themselves" (58:28; cf. 104:17).

2. One authorized to act for another. Appointed leaders among the Saints are the Lord's agents, and as such they "are on the Lord's errand," to do the Lord's business according to the will of the Lord (64:29). The bishop or his agent was to be appointed to handle money for food and clothing for the Saints (51:8, 12). Sidney Gilbert was to be an "agent unto the church, to buy land" (57:6; cf. 58:49, 51, 55). Bishop Newel K. Whitney, busy serving "among all the churches," was to "employ an agent to take charge and to do his secular business"

(84:112–13). Joseph Smith, while hiding from Missouri and Illinois officials to avoid unjust arrest, assured the Saints that he had "left [his] affairs with agents and clerks who will transact all business in a prompt and proper manner" (127:1).

A significant contribution of the restored gospel of Jesus Christ pertains to SALVATION FOR THE DEAD. Essential ordinances, such as baptism, are valid for the dead when performed as authorized by a living agent (128:8).

See also Agency.

DKO

Ahman. *See* Son Ahman.

Albany, Boston, and New York City

Albany and Boston are each mentioned once in the Doctrine and Covenants (84:114), and New York City is mentioned twice (84:114; 104:81).

On 22–23 September 1832, in a "revelation on priesthood" (84, headnote), Bishop Newel K. Whitney was instructed to go to the cities of New York, Albany, and Boston and "warn the people . . . with the sound of the gospel, with a loud voice, of the [eventual] desolation and utter abolishment which await them if they do reject these things" (84:114). In response to that revelation, Bishop Whitney, accompanied by Joseph Smith, visited the three cities in October 1832 (Smith, *History,* 1:295). There is no known record of their public preaching in any of the cities while they were there; however, in a letter from Joseph Smith to his wife, Emma, written from New York City on 13 October 1832, the Prophet expressed both dismay and compassion for the people of New York City and his determination to "lift up [his] voice" to them. He wrote, "When I reflect upon this great city like Nineveh, not discerning their right hand from their left, yea, more than two hundred thousand souls, my bowels are filled with compassion towards them, and I am determined to lift up my voice in this City and leave the event with God" (*Writings,* 278–79; spelling, grammar, and punctuation modernized). Joseph Smith returned to Kirtland on 6 November 1832.

Other reported purposes for the visit to these eastern cities was for Bishop Whitney to procure goods to stock the shelves of the Newel K. Whitney and Company store in Kirtland and the Gilbert, Whitney & Company store that was to operate in Zion (Missouri), as well as to negotiate a loan for $15,000 in behalf of the United Firm (or United Order; *see* Consecration). In his letter to Emma, Joseph praised Bishop Whitney for his endurance in "stand[ing] on the feet all day to select goods" (*Writings,* 279). Bishop Whitney was authorized in April 1832 by Joseph Smith, "in council with the brethren," to secure the loan (Smith, *History,* 1:269–70). Such debts to eastern lenders posed a problem for the United Firm over the next two years, at the end of which time they had more debts than assets. In April 1834, they were obliged to divide "the properties of the order" into individual stewardships, as directed by the Lord (104:1–46), and appeal to their New York creditors for patience until they could repay their debts. The one other mention of New York City in the Doctrine and Covenants is in connection with this situation. The Prophet was instructed to "write speedily to New York and write according to that which shall be dictated by my Spirit; and I will soften the hearts of those to whom you are in debt, that it shall be taken away out of their minds to bring affliction upon you" (104:81). The Saints were instructed to "pay all [their] debts" and promised that if they were diligent and humble and exercised "the prayer of faith," the Lord would "soften the hearts" of those to whom they owed money until he sent "means unto [them] for [their] deliverance" (104:78–80).

BIBLIOGRAPHY

Smith, Joseph. *History of The Church of Jesus Christ of Latter-day Saints.* Edited by B. H. Roberts. 7 vols. 2d ed. rev. Salt Lake City: The Church of Jesus Christ of Latter-day Saints, 1932–51.

———. *Personal Writings of Joseph Smith.* Compiled and edited by Dean C. Jessee. Rev. ed. Salt Lake City: Deseret Book, 2002.

DQC & LCP

All eternity to all eternity. *See* Eternity.

Alms

Almost always the term *alms* is used in the scriptures to refer to gifts that are given to the

POOR (e.g., 3 Ne. 13:1–4 // Matt. 6:1–4; Luke 11:41; Acts 3:2–3, 10). In the Doctrine and Covenants, however, the Lord refers to prayer itself as a type of almsgiving. In 1832 in Kirtland, Ohio, the Lord praised those who prayed to know his will concerning them: "The alms of your prayers have come up into the ears of the Lord" (88:2). In 1837, also in Kirtland, the Lord similarly praised Thomas B. Marsh, president of the Quorum of the Twelve, who petitioned him concerning the mission of the apostles to England: "I have heard thy prayers; and thine alms have come up as a memorial before me, in behalf of those, thy brethren, who were chosen to bear testimony of my name and to send it abroad" (112:1; cf. Acts 10:4).

FFJ

Alpha and Omega

The first and last letters of the Greek alphabet, employed by the Savior many times in the Doctrine and Covenants as a title for himself (19:1; 35:1; 38:1; 45:7; 54:1; 61:1; 63:60; 68:35; 75:1; 81:7; 84:120; 112:34; 132:66), with the variants "Alphus" and "Omegus" occurring an additional time in 95:17. Since letters in both Greek and Latin are neuter nouns, this alternate seems to be emphasizing Jesus as the personification of the beginning and the end through its use of masculine forms.

Reminiscent of the self-designation used by Christ in Revelation 1:8, 11; 21:6; and 22:13, this title appears in some sections that have clear associations with events at the Lord's final coming (e.g., 19:2–3; 84:96–103) and deal with apocalyptic themes such as judgment and the destruction of the wicked. In the Bible, however, the title is an example of a "merism," or statement of polar opposites, that describes not just that Jesus is "the Beginning and the End" but also highlights everything between—that is, that Jesus is sovereign throughout history (Beale, 199). This fact may help explain why some sections in the Doctrine and Covenants refer to the Savior's impending or threatened judgment upon the contemporary subjects of various revelations, such as Leman Copley in 54, Thomas Marsh in 112, or Emma Smith in 132:51–66.

See also Jesus Christ.

BIBLIOGRAPHY

Beale, G. K. "The Book of Revelation: A Commentary on the Greek Text." *The New International Greek Testament Commentary.* Grand Rapids, Mich.: Eerdmans, 1999.

Kittel, Gerhard. "Alpha and Omega," 1:1–3. In *Theological Dictionary of the New Testament.* Edited by Gerhard Kittel and Gerhard Friedrich. Translated by Geoffrey W. Bromiley. 10 vols. Grand Rapids: Eerdmans, 1964–76.

Reddish, Mitchell G. "Alpha and Omega," 1:161–62. In *The Anchor Bible Dictionary.* Edited by David Noel Freedman. 6 vols. New York: Doubleday, 1992.

Robinson, Stephen E., and H. Dean Garrett. *A Commentary on the Doctrine and Covenants,* 1:112; 3:211. 4 vols. Salt Lake City: Deseret Book, 2000–2005.

EDH

Amen. *See* Appendix E.

Amenable. *See* Appendix E.

Amherst, Ohio

A township in Lorain County, Ohio, about fifty miles southwest of Kirtland. Amherst was in the area where Parley P. Pratt "first settled in the wilderness" after his marriage. In the fall of 1830 Pratt and other missionaries to the LAMANITES introduced the gospel to residents of Amherst, resulting in "a church of about sixty members" (Pratt, 48–51; cf. Perkins and Cannon, 66). In September 1831 Joel Johnson was appointed president of the Amherst Branch, which consisted of 100 members (Johnson, 2–4). At a general conference of the Church held in Amherst, 25 January 1832, Joseph Smith was "sustained and ordained President of the High Priesthood," and "considerable business was done to advance the kingdom" (75, headnote; Smith, 1:243). At the same conference Joseph Smith received a revelation assigning missionary companionships and assuring that faithful elders, who proclaim the "truth according to the revelations and commandments" that the Lord has given, "shall be laden with many sheaves, and crowned with honor, and glory, and immortality, and eternal life" (75:1–5; cf. vv. 6–36). *See* map, p. 355.

See also Historical context and overview of Doctrine and Covenants 75 (p. 779).

BIBLIOGRAPHY

Johnson, Joel Hills. Autobiography. Typescript. L. Tom Perry Special Collections, Harold B. Lee Library, Brigham Young University, Provo, Utah.

Perkins, Keith W., and Donald Q. Cannon. *Ohio and Illinois*. Vol. 3 of *Sacred Places: A Comprehensive Guide to Early LDS Historical Sites*. Edited by LaMar C. Berrett. Salt Lake City: Deseret Book, 2002.

Pratt, Parley P. *Autobiography of Parley P. Pratt*. Edited by Parley P. Pratt Jr. Salt Lake City: Deseret Book, 1976.

Smith, Joseph. *History of The Church of Jesus Christ of Latter-day Saints*. Edited by B. H. Roberts. 7 vols. 2d ed. rev. Salt Lake City: The Church of Jesus Christ of Latter-day Saints, 1932–51.

MVB

Ancient of Days. *See* Adam.

Angel of light. *See* Satan.

Angel(s)

Servants, ministers, and messengers of God. Angels serve both in heaven and on earth. Those angels who minister for God on this earth may be resurrected beings (129:1), TRANSLATED BEINGS (7:1–8; Smith, 4:425), or spirits (cf. 29:42). In whatever form, however, "there are no angels who minister to this earth but those who do belong or have belonged to it" (130:5). Examples noted in the Doctrine and Covenants include Michael (Adam), Gabriel, and Raphael (128:20–21); Moroni (27:5); John the Baptist (13:1), Peter, James, and John (27:12); and Moses, Elias, and Elijah (110:11–13).

The work of angels who are God's ministers on earth includes ministering for "heirs of salvation" (7:5–6); teaching and revealing the gospel and God's will to mortals, especially prophets (20:5–10, 35; 27:16; 29:42; 43:25; 77:8; 133:17, 36, 136:37; cf. Moro. 7:29–32); and restoring lost KEYS and authority (13:1; 110:11–13; 84:26–28; 128:20–21). Some are "given . . . charge" concerning specific individuals, suggesting a protecting, nurturing, and guiding role (84:42, 88; 103:19–20; 109:22; 121:27; 133:53). Some ordain "high priests" commissioned to "administer the everlasting gospel" before the second coming of Christ (77:9–11). Some act as heralds sounding "trump[s]" as various dispensations and portions of God's plan and work progress (29:26; 45:44–45; 49:23;

77:9, 12; 88:92–112). Some cleanse the earth by reaping and destroying the wicked when God commands them to do so (38:11–12; 63:54; 86:5; 89:21; cf. 77:8). All holy angels reside in the presence of God (130:4–7) and will accompany Christ at his second coming, though they do not know the day or the hour of the event (45:44; 49:7; cf. 76:63–67). They may appear in a glorified state to mortals (20:6), and some spiritual preparation is apparently necessary to "abide" their presence (67:13). The Aaronic Priesthood "holds the keys of the ministering of angels" (13:1; 84:26; 107:20).

The activities of angels in heaven include attending to and worshiping God (76:21) and ministering in the telestial realm (76:88). Heirs to the celestial realm who choose not to enter into eternal marriage become angels who serve exalted beings (132:16–17). Some angels appear to have a stewardship over heavenly records and rejoice over the penitent and faithful (62:3; cf. 88:2; 90:34).

Some personages who are designated *angels* are not God's servants. SATAN was once "an angel of God who was in authority in the presence of God" who fell through rebellion (76:25–29). He may still attempt to deceive by appearing as an "angel of light" (128:20; 129:4–9). Those who follow Satan are called his "angels" and will suffer with him for eternity (e.g., 29:28, 37; 76:33, 36, 44).

See also Ministering spirits.

BIBLIOGRAPHY

Smith, Joseph. *History of The Church of Jesus Christ of Latter-day Saints*. Edited by B. H. Roberts. 7 vols. 2d ed. rev. Salt Lake City: The Church of Jesus Christ of Latter-day Saints, 1932–51.

TBB

Anger

God's divine displeasure with those who are "wicked and rebellious" (63:2); also an emotion man is to overcome. The most frequent scriptural use of the term relates to an emotion expressed by God (Num. 32:10; Hel. 11:12). Following this pattern, the Doctrine and Covenants vividly describes the anger felt by God toward his rebellious children (19:15; 133:51). It warns of a day of JUDGMENT when "the anger

The Angel Moroni, Delivering the Gold Plates to Joseph Smith; *painting by Lewis Ramsey, 1923.*

of the Lord" will "fall upon the inhabitants of the earth" (1:13). Specifically, "the anger of God kindleth against the inhabitants of the earth . . . for all have gone out of the way" (82:6). In this context, God's anger becomes an expression of his JUSTICE as he prepares to cleanse the earth at his second coming. See Jesus Christ, second coming of.

God's anger or wrath is against the "unbelieving and stiffnecked" (5:8), "the rebellious" (56:1), those "who confess not his hand in all things, and obey not his commandments" (59:21), any who "hide the talent which [he had] given unto them" (60:2), and those who seek signs but not by faith (63:11). He expresses anger because of his LOVE for his children. "God's anger is kindled not because we have harmed him but because we have harmed ourselves" (Maxwell, 85).

Joseph Smith was cautioned that SATAN "stirreth up . . . hearts to anger" (10:24, 32; 63:27) and that Saints are to avoid wrath or anger in preaching the gospel (60:7, 14).

See also God, nature of.

BIBLIOGRAPHY

Maxwell, Neal A. *Sermons Not Spoken.* Salt Lake City: Bookcraft, 1985.

DAW

Animals

Various animals are mentioned in both literal and figurative contexts in the Doctrine and Covenants. Literally, animals are frequently listed as part of God's creation and are often identified as acceptable to use for food, raiment, or work "with judgment" and "not to excess" nor "by extortion" (59:16–20; 29:24; 49:18–19; 89:12–17; 101:24–26; 117:6). Animal care and diet are touched upon in the WORD OF WISDOM (89:8, 14, 17). As a sign of God's power, promised to those who exercise faith, the righteous may enjoy divine protection from serpents (84:72; 124:98–99), but in the destruction of the wicked at the second coming of Christ, many of the unrepentant are to be plagued or devoured by flies, beasts, and fowls (29:17–20).

Figuratively, Christ likens himself to a shepherd and his people to his flock (6:34; 10:59–60; 35:27; 50:44; 88:72; 112:14). He also offers

protection "as a hen gathereth her chickens" (10:65; 29:2). Because of his atoning sacrifice, Christ is often referred to as the "Lamb" of God (65:3; 76:119; 88:106; 133:56). Human traits are often likened to those of animals. Thus some of the brethren were counseled to be "as wise as serpents" (111:11), and the incarcerated Joseph Smith was promised that eventually his voice would be "more terrible . . . than the fierce lion" among enemies (122:4). Later he would go to Carthage "like a lamb to the slaughter" (135:4; cf. 122:6). Lyman Wight was assured that the Lord would "bear him up as on eagles' wings" as he continued preaching (124:18), and William Law was assured that if he were humble and without guile, "he shall mount up in the imagination of his thoughts as upon eagles' wings" (124:97, 99). In contrast, SATAN and other enemies of the Saints are likened to serpents, vipers (76:28; 121:23), and bloodthirsty wolves (122:6), while the unworthy or spiritually unappreciative are compared to dogs and swine (41:6). The four worshipful beasts of John's Revelation are described as "figurative expressions . . . shown to John, to represent the glory of the classes of beings in their destined order or sphere of creation, in the enjoyment of their eternal felicity" (77:2–3).

In the Doctrine and Covenants the Lord has made clear that the flesh of animals is to be used for food sparingly and is not to be wasted (49:18–21; 59:16–20; 89:11–15).

TBB

Anointed, anointing(s)

Terms used in the Doctrine and Covenants as a title, as a noun, and as a verb to refer to individuals, temple ordinances, priesthood ordinations or appointments, and special callings or privileges.

The title "Anointed" is identified with several individuals and groups. Jesus Christ is referred to as "thine Anointed," an expression of the Father's mercy as he looks upon Jesus as the ADVOCATE of repentant souls (109:53; cf. 45:3–5). The Lord's servants, his prophets and faithful Saints, are referred to as "anointed ones" (109:80; 121:16). In giving his life as a martyr, Joseph Smith is compared to "the Lord's anointed in ancient times" (135:3).

Anointings are among the sacred TEMPLE ordinances to be administered in the Nauvoo Temple (124:39). In the dedicatory prayer of the Kirtland Temple, the Prophet prayed, "Let the anointing of thy ministers be sealed upon them with power from on high" (109:35).

Anointed refers to priesthood ordinations or appointments in the following instances: the descendants of Aaron being anointed to the office of bishop (68:20–21); William Law being anointed to be a member of the First Presidency (124:91, 126); Joseph Smith being singularly anointed to hold the sealing power, making effectual all gospel covenants, including eternal marriage (132:7, 18, 19, 41); and Jesus Christ being "anointed . . . to bind up the brokenhearted, to proclaim liberty to the captives, and the opening of the prison to them that are bound," as prophesied by Isaiah (Isa. 61:1) and seen by President Joseph F. Smith in the vision of the redemption of the dead (138:42).

Anointed and *anointing* are used in reference to special callings or privileges. For example, the Lord says of Vinson Knight (if he obeys the instruction about putting stock in the Nauvoo House): "I have chosen him and anointed him, and he shall be honored in the midst of his house, for I will forgive all his sins" (124:74–76). Also, Joseph Smith and his posterity received an "anointing" to "have place" in the Nauvoo House when it was constructed (124:55–61).

JWL

Antiquities. *See* Appendix E.

Apocrypha

Title given by Jerome, an early church father (ca. A.D. 347–420), to a group of texts included in the early manuscripts of the Septuagint, the Greek version of the Old Testament used by some in the early Christian Church but not included in the Hebrew Bible. *Apocrypha* comes from the Greek *apokrypha,* which means "the hidden things." The apocryphal texts included the Epistle of Jeremiah, 1 and 2 Esdras, Judith, Tobit, Additions to Esther, 1 and 2 Maccabees,

Wisdom of Solomon, Ben Sira, Susanna, Bel and the Dragon, 1 Baruch, Prayer of Manasses, the Prayer of Azariah and the Song of the Three Young Men, and others. In the Septuagint, the apocryphal texts are interspersed with the other Old Testament texts. Martin Luther was the first to separate them and place them in a separate section between the Old and New Testaments, although he left out 1 and 2 Esdras. This practice of separating the Apocrypha was followed in the 1611 King James Version of the Bible, although it included 1 and 2 Esdras, but the section was omitted in copies of the Bible published by the British and Foreign Bible Society after 1826 because of a decision to withdraw funding for printing any books of the Apocrypha (Howsam, *Bibles,* 14).

When Joseph Smith was translating the Old Testament, he came across the Apocrypha in a copy of the King James Bible and sought the Lord's direction about whether to translate it. He was informed that although "there are many things contained therein that are true," there are also "interpolations by the hands of men" (91:1–2). Therefore, he was directed that "it is not needful" for the apocryphal texts to be translated, but that if a person is "enlightened by the Spirit" he or she "shall obtain benefit therefrom" (91:3–6).

In addition, a number of noncanonical Christian texts are often gathered under the title New Testament Apocrypha. These include gospels, treatises, apocalypses, acts of the apostles, letters, and liturgical materials. These texts were not included in Joseph Smith's inquiry to the Lord that resulted in Doctrine and Covenants 91.

See also Historical context and overview of Doctrine and Covenants 91 (p. 797).

BIBLIOGRAPHY

Howsam, Leslie. *Cheap Bibles: Nineteenth-Century Publishing and the British and Foreign Bible Society.* Cambridge: Cambridge University Press, 1991.

Schneemelcher, Wilhelm, ed. *New Testament Apocrypha.* Translated by R. M. Wilson. 2 vols. Louisville, Ky.: John Knox Press, 1991–93.

GS

Apocryphal Text	Approximate Date of Writing	Genre of Literature	Description of the Text
1 Esdras	Written sometime between the 2nd century B.C. and 1st century A.D.[1]	Rewritten Bible	Retells the story of 2 Chronicles 35–36, Ezra and Nehemiah 8. Describes the contemporary history of the Jews from Josiah's religious reforms in 640 B.C. until the destruction of the temple in 588 B.C. 1 Esdras 3:1–5:6 (the contest of the three bodyguards) is not found in the biblical account. Also highlights and elevates the work of Zerubbabel, who absorbs some of the achievements of Nehemiah in the biblical text.[2]
2 Esdras	Written sometime within the 1st century A.D.	Apocalypse	Narrative of seven revelations given to Ezra as he grieves over the afflictions of his people by Gentile nations. Wrestles with the question of why God would allow covenant Israel to be overcome by a wicked nation such as Rome. Also seeks to reaffirm the importance of living the covenant even in the face of disaster. The beginning two chapters and final two chapters are Christian additions to the Jewish apocalypse.
Tobit	ca. 200 B.C.	Historical fiction	Narrative that discusses how to maintain covenant fidelity during the threat of cultural and religious assimilation. It emphasizes that adherence to God's commandments brings integrity and will eventually result in God's favor.
Judith	ca. 150 B.C.	Historical fiction	Tale of a female military hero who uses her wiles to save her people and the temple from an invading Assyrian army. The message of Judith centers on the efficacy of prayer and emphasizes that God helps those who have a proactive trust in him.
Additions to Esther	Additions written in parts anywhere between 160 B.C. to A.D. 70.	Historical narrative	Emphasizes the active role of God in the story of Esther that is absent in the Hebrew version. Esther and Mordecai are portrayed as role models of covenant fidelity for Jews living in the diaspora.
Wisdom of Solomon	ca. 1st century B.C.	Wisdom literature	Promotes the active pursuit of wisdom, which is understood to be reverence for God and his commandments. Heavily influenced early Christian writers.
Ben Sira	Written in Jerusalem ca. 196–175 B.C.	Wisdom literature	Written around the time of the Maccabean revolt. Emphasizes that the path to attaining wisdom is living the commandments: "If you desire wisdom, keep the commandments, and the Lord will lavish her upon you" (1:26). Heavily influenced early Christian writers.
1 Baruch	200–100 B.C.	Mixed genre including, historical narrative, wisdom literature, penitential prayers, and prophecy of deliverance	Claims to be written by Jeremiah's scribe, Baruch (Jer. 36:4), a few years after Judah was taken into Babylonian exile. Written as a response to the theological challenge of the exile. The text emphasizes that restoration is possible through a wholehearted return to living by their covenantal obligations.

1. Dates are in accordance with David A. deSilva, *Introducing the Apocrypha* (Grand Rapids: Baker Academic, 2002); James H. Charlesworth, *The Old Testament Pseudepigrapha* (2 vols; New York: Doubleday, 1983–1985); James H. Charlesworth, *Old Testament Apocrypha* (*The Anchor Bible Dictionary*, 6 vols.; ed. David Noel Freedman et al.; New York: Doubleday, 1992), 1:294–94.

2. Descriptions of the texts are from deSilva, *Introducing the Apocrypha*.

Apocryphal Text	Approximate Date of Writing	Genre of Literature	Description of the Text
Epistle of Jeremiah	ca. 300 B.C.	Polemical literature	This epistle is often attached to the Book of Baruch and claims to be from Jeremiah. The text is a polemic against the worship of idols, which is the primary challenge of living in the diaspora.
Prayer of Azariah and the Song of the Three Young Men	ca. 2nd century B.C.	Mixed genre including, prayer, narrative, and psalm of praise	An addition to the canonical book of Daniel between Daniel 3:23 and 24 including a prayer offered by Shadrach, Meshach, and Abed-nego as they are thrown into the fiery furnace; and a psalm of praise. "Both are liturgical pieces that were probably composed for worship and only later inserted into the biblical narrative."[3] Its purpose is to glory in the worship of God.
Susanna	Perhaps written in the 2nd century B.C.	Historical fiction	Another addition to the canonical book of Daniel. The narrative depicts a virtuous woman who is falsely accused by two elders because she would not sleep with them. Daniel is sent by God to intervene. Highlights the importance of remaining loyal to God and his commandments even in the face of danger. It is a reminder that God will vindicate those who walk uprightly and eventually punish the sinner.
Bel and the Dragon	Perhaps written in the 2nd century B.C.	Historical fiction	Another addition to the canonical book of Daniel. Composed of two narratives where the king of Babylon presents Daniel with challenges to prove that idols are not real gods. The purpose of this text is to critique idolatry and prove that the God of Israel is the one true God.
Prayer of Manasses	Written sometime between 200 B.C. and A.D. 50.	Prayer	Manasseh was the king of Judah from 687 to 642 B.C. who promoted idol worship in the Jerusalem temple. 2 Chronicles 33:11–18 tells how he was taken captive into Assyria, prays and repents, then returns to Israel and destroys his idols. This text purports to be the repentant prayer Manasseh offered in Assyria.
1 Maccabees	ca. 100 B.C.	Historical narrative	Glorifies the Maccabean revolt against the Hellenization crisis under Antiochus IV and successors from 175 B.C. to 135 B.C. in which Israel became an independent nation and rededicated the temple. Emphasizes the political importance of the Hasmonean family. Focuses on the question of how to maintain covenant fidelity in the midst of the pressures and allures of the secular world. Influential work in shaping Jewish nationalism and political messianic aspirations.
2 Maccabees	ca. 100 B.C.	Historical narrative	Overlaps the time period of 1 Maccabees, but emphasizes the role of the Jewish high priests and aristocracy in fostering the adoption of Hellenistic cultural practices. Like 1 Maccabees, it focuses on the question of how to maintain covenant fidelity in the midst of the pressures and allures of the secular world, but it does so from a more theologically oriented perspective, with themes of martyrdom, miracles and the resurrection.

3. deSilva, *Introducing the Apocrypha*, 226.

Apollos

A man identified in the Doctrine and Covenants as one whose followers are typical of groups that claim allegiance to one or another Church leader or missionary but do not receive "the gospel, neither the testimony of Jesus, neither the prophets, neither the everlasting covenant" (76:98–102). These are designated as those who receive the telestial kingdom (76:99).

Apollos was a Jew "born at Alexandria" in New Testament times and was "an eloquent man, and mighty in the scriptures." An enthusiastic missionary, he traveled throughout the Mediterranean area, where "he mightily convinced the Jews, and that publickly, shewing by the scriptures that Jesus was Christ" (Acts 18:24–28). Apollos, like Paul, was a true follower of Christ, but some among the Corinthian Saints who claimed to follow him were rebuked by Paul for causing "divisions" and "contentions" among the Saints (1 Cor. 1:10–13; 3:4–7, 20–23).

RJM

Apostasy, of early dissenters from restored Church

The falling away from the Church, its leaders and its doctrines, by members of the Church in the 1830s and 1840s. Many revelations in the Doctrine and Covenants contain warnings about apostasy, both to individuals and to the Church as a body—warnings which, as the early history of the Church and the revelations themselves demonstrate, often went unheeded. Joseph Smith received his first lesson on apostasy after the loss of the 116 pages of Book of Mormon manuscript, when the Lord warned him that "although a man may have many revelations, and have power to do many mighty works, yet if he boasts in his own strength, and sets at naught the counsels of God, and follows after the dictates of his own will and carnal desires, he must fall and incur the vengeance of a just God upon him" (3:4). Joseph later reiterated this caution to the Church membership, warning them of the very real possibility that "even . . . those who are sanctified" can "fall from grace and depart from the living God" (20:32, 34), thereby forfeiting an "inheritance among the saints" (85:11). By

1839, Joseph had learned "by sad experience" how significant these warnings were (121:39), having watched hundreds of his fellow Saints set their hearts "so much upon the things of this world, and aspire to the honors of men" to such a degree that they had left the Church "to kick against the pricks, to persecute the saints, and to fight against God" (121:35, 38). Such is the inevitable end for any who "undertake to cover [their] sins, or to gratify [their] pride, [their] vain ambition, or to exercise control or dominion or compulsion upon the souls of the children of men, in any degree of unrighteousness" (121:37).

One of the first individuals to accept the message of the Restoration and then to apostatize was James Covill, who "returned to his former principles and people" (40, headnote) in January 1831—less than one month after having covenanted to "obey any command that the Lord would give" (39, headnote) to him through Joseph Smith (Smith, *Papers*, 1:346; cf. D&C 39; 40). Heman Basset (52:37) and Northrop Sweet also left the Church in 1831, the latter to found the short-lived "Pure Church of Christ" (Smith, *JD*, 7:114; 11:4).

Not all of the early apostates left quietly. Ezra Booth, for example, who apostatized during his mission to Jackson County, Missouri, in the summer of 1831, returned to Ohio to publish a series of nine articles against the Church, its leaders, and its members in a local newspaper (Smith, *Papers*, 1:363–64). Of Booth's apostasy Joseph Smith wrote: "He went up to Missouri as a companion of Elder Morley; but when he actually learned that faith, humility, patience, and tribulation go before blessing . . . he was disappointed" (Smith, *History*, 1:216). Another apostate, Symonds Ryder, allegedly led the mob that tarred and feathered Joseph Smith in March 1832 (Smith, *Papers*, 1:374–77).

Rising materialism among Church members in Kirtland, combined with the failure of the Church-sponsored bank there in 1837, resulted in some two hundred to three hundred individuals in the Kirtland area (representing 10 to 15 percent of Church membership there) apostatizing from the Church between 1837 and 1838. This "Kirtland apostasy" affected all levels of Church membership and leadership. Several members of the Quorum of the Twelve Apostles spoke out to one degree or another against Joseph and the Church at this time, resulting in the eventual excommunication of four of them: William E. McLellin, Luke Johnson, Lyman Johnson, and John Boynton. Frederick G. Williams, second counselor in the First Presidency, left the Church during this period as well, as did Joseph's private secretary Warren Parrish and longtime friends of the Prophet and Book of Mormon witnesses Oliver Cowdery and Martin Harris. Cowdery's and Harris's fellow Book of Mormon witness, David Whitmer, who was serving as president pro tem of the Church in Missouri, was also excommunicated during this time, as were his two counselors W. W. Phelps and John Whitmer, the latter of whom was one of the Eight Witnesses to the Book of Mormon. Two more of the Eight Witnesses, Jacob Whitmer and Hiram Page, also left the Church at this time (Backman, 310–41). *See* Presidents of thy Church.

As the number of apostates increased in Kirtland, so did the threats against Joseph's life, requiring him to flee Kirtland in January 1838 for the relative safety of Missouri. This safety was short-lived, as by the end of the year and largely on the sworn testimony of apostates, Joseph and five others were incarcerated in LIBERTY JAIL for treason and related charges. Those testifying against Joseph Smith included such earlier dissenters as W. W. Phelps and John Whitmer, as well as more recent apostates, including Thomas B. Marsh, president of the Quorum of the Twelve; apostle Orson Hyde; George Hinkle, an officer in the Caldwell County militia; and Sampson Avard, leader of the secretive Danites. In a revelation given to Joseph after he had spent five months in confinement, the Lord underscored the gravity of the apostates' actions in the strongest possible terms: "Cursed are all those that shall lift up the heel against mine anointed . . . and cry they have sinned when they have not sinned before me," he told the Prophet. "A generation of vipers shall not escape the damnation of hell" (121:16, 23; cf. vv. 11–15, 17–22, 24–25). He also told Joseph of the ultimate futility of the apostates' agenda:

"Thy people shall never be turned against thee by the testimony of traitors," he declared. "And although their influence shall cast thee into trouble, and into bars and walls, thou shalt be had in honor" (122:3–4).

Apostasy and dissent continued to plague Joseph and the Church in Nauvoo. One vocal and influential apostate in Nauvoo was John C. Bennett, Nauvoo's first mayor, a general in the Nauvoo legion, and one-time member of the First Presidency. Others apostatized during this time as well—often, it appears, over the issue of plural marriage. Evidence suggests that at least part of Sidney Rigdon's and George Robinson's estrangement at this time was over this issue, as was Orson Pratt's excommunication in 1842. By the time William Law (who had been serving as second counselor in the First Presidency) was excommunicated in March 1844, several hundred apostates lived in the vicinity of Nauvoo. Many of these, led by Law and others, entered into a covenant to destroy the Prophet and were prevented from doing so only through the vigilance of Joseph's friends and supporters. When other means of assassination failed, Law's and other apostates' idea to publish slander against Joseph in the *Nauvoo Expositor* put events into motion that ultimately led to Joseph's murder at Carthage.

See also Apostasy, the great; Deception; Hyde, Orson; Martyrdom of Joseph and Hyrum Smith; Phelps, William W.

BIBLIOGRAPHY

Backman, Milton V., Jr. *The Heavens Resound: A History of the Latter-day Saints in Ohio, 1830–1838.* Salt Lake City: Deseret Book, 1983.

Smith, George A. *Journal of Discourses.* 26 vols. London: Latter-day Saints' Book Depot, 1854–86.

Smith, Joseph. *History of The Church of Jesus Christ of Latter-day Saints.* Edited by B. H. Roberts. 7 vols. 2d ed. rev. Salt Lake City: The Church of Jesus Christ of Latter-day Saints, 1932–51.

———. *The Papers of Joseph Smith.* Vol. 2. *Autobiographical and Historical Writings.* Edited by Dean C. Jessee. Salt Lake City: Deseret Book, 1992.

AHH

Apostasy, the great

The period following the deaths of Jesus Christ and the meridian apostles during which specific doctrines, covenants, and ordinances were corrupted and priesthood AUTHORITY was taken from the earth. That Joseph Smith was called by God to be an instrument in restoring the fulness of the everlasting gospel necessarily affirms that there was an apostasy, or falling away, from the faith sometime after the death of Christ.

The word *apostasy* means, literally, "away from standing" and implies more than just wandering or drifting from the principles of truth; rather, the word suggests a mutiny, revolution, or rebellion against the faith. There are two kinds of apostasy—apostasy *within* the Church (individual apostasy) and apostasy *of* the Church (institutional apostasy). There have been many apostasies and restorations throughout the centuries (e.g., Moses 5:12–13; 6:27–28; 8:22–30). With the call of Joseph Smith in the spring of 1820 and the opening of the dispensation of the fulness of times, latter-day prophets have testified that there will never again be an apostasy of the Church and that the fulness of the gospel of Jesus Christ will remain upon the earth until the second coming of the Son of Man (138:44; cf. 65:1–6; Dan. 2:44).

The apostasy following the ministry of the Savior is often called the Great Apostasy. Warnings about this falling away can be found in the Old and the New Testaments (e.g., Isa. 24:5–6; Amos 8:11–12; Acts 20:28–31; 2 Thes. 2:1–7; 1 Tim. 4:1–3; 2 Tim. 4:1–4; 1 Jn. 2:18–19). The apostasy was universal (Jacob 5:29–32, 40); the Savior declared that his vineyard had "become corrupted every whit; and there is none which doeth good save it be a few; and they err in many instances because of priestcrafts, all having corrupt minds" (33:4). Such a state prevents many from accepting the truth, for their minds become clouded and deceived by the precepts of men (45:29; cf. 2 Ne. 28:14). Others are honest in heart and are "only kept from the truth because they know not where to find it" (123:12).

The Doctrine and Covenants confirms the reality of the Great Apostasy. The Lord declared, "They have strayed from mine ordinances, and have broken mine everlasting covenant . . . every man walketh in his own way, and after the image of his own god" (1:15–16). The revelation in section 86 acknowledged that after the early apostles had "fallen asleep," Satan drove "the church into the wilderness" (86:1–3; cf. 5:14; 109:73).

Nephi was shown in vision that many "plain and precious" truths, as well as "many covenants of the Lord," would be taken from the Bible and the gospel, thus causing many to stumble and fall (1 Ne. 13:20–29; D&C 76, headnote). Examples of plain and precious truths that were lost or corrupted include the following:

• The nature of GOD THE FATHER. Joseph Smith declared that "the Father has a body of flesh and bones as tangible as man's" (130:22). *See* God the Father; God, nature of.

• The GOSPEL of Jesus Christ as a NEW AND EVERLASTING COVENANT. Scriptures of the Restoration reveal Christ's eternal gospel, the profound truth that Christian prophets have declared Christian doctrine and administered Christian ordinances since the days of Adam (20:26–27; 49:9; 66:2; cf. Alma 39:17–19). "We cannot believe," Joseph Smith affirmed, "that the ancients in all ages were so ignorant of the system of heaven as many suppose, since all that were ever saved, were saved through the power of this great plan of redemption, as much before the coming of Christ as since; if not, God has had different plans in operation (if we may so express it), to bring men back to dwell with Himself; and this we cannot believe, since there has been no change in the constitution of man since he fell" (Smith, 2:16–17). Also, "now taking it for granted that the scriptures say what they mean, and mean what they say, we have sufficient grounds to go on and prove from the Bible that the gospel has always been the same; the ordinances to fulfil its requirements, the same; and the officers to officiate, the same; and the *signs* and *fruits* resulting from the promises, the same" (*TS*, 904; cf. Smith, 5:423).

• The relationship of God the Father, his Beloved Son Jesus Christ, and the Holy Ghost. After the deaths of the apostles and the loss of divine authority, men sought to harmonize revealed doctrine with Greek philosophy, which resulted in the corruption of fundamental and foundational truths, such as the distinct and separate natures and beings of the Father, the Son, and the Holy Ghost. *See* Godhead, the.

Elder Dallin H. Oaks explained: "Many Christians reject the idea of a tangible, personal God and a Godhead of three separate beings. They believe that God is a spirit and that the Godhead is only one God. In our view, these concepts are evidence of the falling away we call the Great Apostasy. We maintain that the concepts identified by such nonscriptural terms as 'the incomprehensible mystery of God' and 'the mystery of the Holy Trinity' are attributable to the ideas of Greek philosophy. These philosophical concepts transformed Christianity in the first few centuries following the deaths of the Apostles. . . . The consequences persist in the various creeds of Christianity, which declare a Godhead of only one being and which describe that single being or God as 'incomprehensible' and 'without body, parts, or passions.' One of the distinguishing features of the doctrine of The Church of Jesus Christ of Latter-day Saints is its rejection of all of these postbiblical creeds" (84–85).

• Examples of other vital doctrines that were lost include the identity of JESUS CHRIST as JEHOVAH; the necessity of the ORDINANCES of salvation, both the proper authority and the specific manner in which they are to be performed; the eternal significance of TEMPLES, temple ordinances, and sealing powers; man as a literal child of God, the PREMORTAL EXISTENCE of man, the innocence and salvation of little CHILDREN, and the age of ACCOUNTABILITY; degrees of glory in the hereafter (*see* Kingdoms of glory and perdition, vision of); and the capacity of man to become, through the transforming power of the ATONEMENT of Jesus Christ, a partaker of the divine nature (2 Pet. 1:4), a joint heir with Christ (Rom. 8:16–17); even to become like the Father (1 Jn. 3:1–2; Moro. 7:48).

After the death of the Savior and the apostles, not only were doctrines and ordinances changed but the KEYS of the PRIESTHOOD (the right of presidency or directing powers) were taken from the earth. Because these keys are essential in authorizing, directing, and overseeing the ordinances (baptism, confirmation, ordination, sealing,

and so forth) and the work of the Lord's kingdom, there was no one on earth with the divine authority to perpetuate those covenants and ordinances found only in the Church of Jesus Christ. It would, however, be a serious misrepresentation to suggest that Latter-day Saints believe all of Christian practice and doctrine since the time of the original apostles has been apostate. Noble and God-fearing men and women who lived through the period that many have termed the "dark ages" sought to do good and maintain the tenets of Christianity to the best of their ability, but the world was without the full light of heaven.

President John Taylor taught that there were persons during medieval times who "could commune with God, and who, by the power of faith, could draw aside the curtain of eternity and gaze upon the invisible world" (16:197). President Brigham Young explained that many good men before the time of Joseph Smith's call enjoyed "the spirit of revelation" and specifically noted that John Wesley, the father of Methodism, was as good a man as lived on earth (6:170; 7:5; 11:126).

In speaking of the Primitive Church, President Boyd K. Packer observed that "the flame flickered and dimmed. . . . But always, as it had from the beginning, the Spirit of God inspired worthy souls. We owe an immense debt to the protestors and the reformers who preserved the scriptures and translated them. They knew something had been lost. They kept the flame alive as best they could. Many of them were martyrs" ("Cloven," 8). On another occasion President Packer taught: "The line of priesthood authority was broken. But mankind was not left in total darkness or completely without revelation or inspiration. The idea that with the crucifixion of Christ the heavens were closed and that they opened in the First Vision is not true. The Light of Christ would be everywhere present to attend the children of God; the Holy Ghost would visit seeking souls. The prayers of the righteous would not go unanswered" ("Light," 11). Similarly, Elder Oaks explained, "We are indebted to the men and women who kept the light of faith and learning alive through the centuries to the present day. We have only to contrast the lesser light that exists among peoples unfamiliar with the names of God and Jesus Christ to realize the great contribution made by Christian teachers through the ages. We honor them as servants of God" (Oaks, 85).

God's divine authority was not to be found in the Old World by the middle of the second century A.D. and in the New World by the middle of the fifth century A.D. The Roman Church essentially had control of the Christian faith in western Europe until the sixteenth century, when courageous men objected to, opposed, and broke away from Catholicism. Through the tenacity of such individuals as John Hus, Martin Luther, John Calvin, Roger Williams, John Wesley, and others, what is known as the Protestant Reformation came to pass. The Reformers focused attention on the need for personal study of the Bible, the sovereignty of God, the fallen nature of man (a belief shared with Catholicism), salvation by grace alone, and a "priesthood of all believers." The Reformation was vitally important and was God-inspired, inasmuch as it prepared the way for the complete Restoration of the gospel.

Joseph Smith was called upon to bring the fulness of the gospel "out of obscurity and out of darkness" (1:30); that is, to lead "out of the wilderness" the Lord's Church "clear as the moon, and fair as the sun, and terrible as an army with banners" (5:14). The Church of Jesus Christ of Latter-day Saints is the custodian of the fulness of the gospel of Jesus Christ and is the only church on earth possessing the Melchizedek and Aaronic Priesthoods. Without such authority, labors or activities or sacred ordinances are merely "dead works" (22:2–3).

See also Church of Jesus Christ of Latter-day Saints, The; Historical context and overview of Doctrine and Covenants 86 (p. 790); Parable of the wheat and the tares; Priesthood, restoration of priesthood and priesthood keys.

BIBLIOGRAPHY

Oaks, Dallin H. "Apostasy and Restoration." *Ensign* 25 (May 1995): 84–86.

Packer, Boyd K. "The Cloven Tongues of Fire." *Ensign* 30 (May 2000): 7–9.

———. "The Light of Christ." *Ensign* 35 (April 2005): 8–14.

Smith, Joseph. *History of The Church of Jesus Christ of Latter-day Saints.* Edited by B. H. Roberts. 7 vols. 2d ed. rev. Salt Lake City: The Church of Jesus Christ of Latter-day Saints, 1932–51.

Taylor, John. *Journal of Discourses.* 26 vols. London: Latter-day Saints' Book Depot, 1854–86.

Times and Seasons 3 (1 September 1842): 904.

Young, Brigham. *Journal of Discourses.* 26 vols. London: Latter-day Saints' Book Depot, 1854–86.

RLM

Apostle(s)

"Special witnesses of the name of Christ in all the world" (107:23).

The Doctrine and Covenants contains dozens of references to apostles. Many of those references are to the apostles who served in the Savior's dispensation in the meridian of time, two thousand years ago (e.g., 18:9; 29:12; 35:6; 49:11; 63:21; 66:2; 74:2, 5; 84:63–64, 108; 95:9; 98:32; 136:37; 138:5). Early in the current dispensation, "the dispensation of the fulness of times," "a dispensation of the gospel for the last times; and for the fulness of times" (138:48; 27:13), the Lord called apostles to serve, as he did in days of old.

In June 1829, the Lord told Oliver Cowdery and David Whitmer that they had been called with the same calling as the apostle Paul (18:9). The Lord then told them that "there are others who are called to declare my gospel, . . . yea, even twelve. . . . And if they desire to take upon them my name with full purpose of heart, they are called to go into all the world to preach my gospel unto every creature" (18:26–28). These future apostles were promised by the Lord, "Behold, my grace is sufficient for you; you must walk uprightly before me and sin not" (18:31). They were to be "ordained" to baptize in Christ's name, "to ordain priests and teachers; to declare my gospel, according to the power of the Holy Ghost which is in [them]" (18:29, 32; cf. 20:39; 107:58). Oliver Cowdery and David Whitmer were instructed to "search out the Twelve . . . and by their desires and their works you shall know them" (18:37–38). Martin Harris was later added to assist in the search (Smith, 2:186–87).

In a revelation directing the organization of the Church in 1830, the Lord said Joseph Smith and Oliver Cowdery had been "called of God, and ordained [apostles] of Jesus Christ" and were to be the first and second elders of the Church (20:2–5). That same revelation teaches that "an apostle is an elder, and it is his calling to baptize; and to ordain other elders, priests, teachers, and deacons; and to administer bread and wine—the emblems of the flesh and blood of Christ—and to confirm those who are baptized into the church, by the laying on of hands for the baptism of fire and the Holy Ghost, according to the scriptures; and to teach, expound, exhort, baptize, and watch over the church . . . and to take the lead of all meetings" (20:38–44).

Section 27:12–13 (cf. 107:23) states that Peter, James, and John were sent to ordain Joseph Smith and Oliver Cowdery apostles and to confer upon them the keys of Christ's kingdom. Oliver Cowdery, David Whitmer, and Martin Harris (these men having been honored to be the Three Witnesses of the Book of Mormon) chose twelve apostles in February 1835, as instructed in Doctrine and Covenants 18 (Smith, 2:181–89). At first the Twelve were designated as a "Traveling Presiding High Council" (107:33; cf. 102:30; 107:33–36; 124:127, 139), administering the affairs of the Church in areas other than organized stakes (the first stakes were organized in Kirtland, Ohio, and Clay County, Missouri, in 1834; the Twelve were called in 1835). Soon, however, they took their place as a presiding quorum, under the direction of the First Presidency, over the whole Church.

Section 107 explains that as a quorum, the Twelve Apostles "officiate in the name of the Lord, under the direction" of the Quorum of the First Presidency in the government of the Church, "to build up the church, and regulate all the affairs of the same in all nations" (107:33). "They form a quorum, equal in authority and power" to the Quorum of the First Presidency in the event that the First Presidency is dissolved (107:24). The Quorum of the Twelve functions as a quorum of unanimity in that "every decision made . . . must be by the unanimous voice of the same; that is, every member . . . must be agreed to its decisions, in

order to make their decisions of the same power or validity one with the other" (107:27). It is the responsibility of the Quorum of the Twelve "holding the keys" of the priesthood "to open the door by the proclamation of the gospel of Jesus Christ, and first unto the Gentiles and then unto the Jews" (107:35; cf. 124:128). They are to be assisted in that endeavor by the SEVENTY (107:34, 38; 124:139). "It is the duty of the Twelve . . . to ordain evangelical ministers" (i.e., PATRIARCHS; Smith, 3:381) and "to ordain and set in order all the other officers of the church" (107:39, 58).

In a revelation through the Prophet Joseph Smith to Thomas B. Marsh, the president of the first Quorum of the Twelve, the Lord affirmed that the Twelve, along with the First Presidency, hold the keys of the "dispensation of the fulness of times," a power held "in connection with all those who have received a dispensation at any time from the beginning of the creation" (112:30–32). Speaking to the Twelve in this revelation, the Lord said: "Arise and gird up your loins, take up your cross, follow me, and feed my sheep. Exalt not yourselves; rebel not against my servant Joseph; for verily I say unto you, I am with him, and my hand shall be over him; and the keys which I have given unto him, and also to youward, shall not be taken from him till I come" (112:14–15). "Cleanse your hearts and your garments, lest the blood of this generation be required at your hands. Be faithful" (112:33–34).

In section 118, the Lord called the Twelve to leave on a mission "over the great waters" (118:4). He also called John Taylor, John E. Page, Wilford Woodruff, and Willard Richards to replace "those who [had] fallen" (118:6). Sadly, William E. McClellin, Lyman Johnson, Luke Johnson, and John Boynton, members of the first Quorum of the Twelve, had apostatized by this time. The Twelve left on 26 April 1839 from Far West, Missouri. See Apostasy, of early dissenters from restored Church.

President Thomas B. Marsh having become disaffected from the Church, the Lord in section 124 called Brigham Young as the new "president over the Twelve traveling council; which Twelve hold the keys to open up the authority of my kingdom upon the four corners of the earth, and after that to send my word to every creature" (124:127–28).

The Quorum of the Twelve Apostles is a quorum of seniority and is presided over by the senior member of the quorum. When a vacancy occurs, revelation is received for another to be called by the president of the Church to fill that vacancy (118:6; cf. 124:130).

At Winter Quarters, Brigham Young received a revelation that directed the organization of the "Camp of Israel" for their "journeyings to the West" into companies of tens, fifties, and hundreds, which were organized "under the direction of the Twelve Apostles" (136:1–3).

The Quorum of the Twelve Apostles functions in harmony with the instructions from the Lord in the Doctrine and Covenants, acting under the direction of the First Presidency, in regulating "all the affairs" of the Church "in all nations" (107:33). Missionaries and all members of the Church are instructed to teach "none other things than that which the prophets and apostles have written, and that which is taught them by the Comforter through the prayer of faith" (52:9, 36). That which the Holy Ghost teaches will be in harmony with the apostles, the "special witnesses of the name of Christ in all the world" (107:23); they are "God's high priests" and his "friends" (84:63).

See also Apostles, the first Twelve of latter days; Apostles, the Twelve, mission to Great Britain; Succession, apostolic; Traveling high council/bishops/elders/high priests/ministers/ presiding high council.

BIBLIOGRAPHY

Smith, Joseph. *History of The Church of Jesus Christ of Latter-day Saints.* Edited by B. H. Roberts. 7 vols. 2d ed. rev. Salt Lake City: The Church of Jesus Christ of Latter-day Saints, 1932–51.

HDG

Apostles, the first Twelve of latter days

The office of APOSTLE was restored in the latter days when Joseph Smith and Oliver Cowdery were ordained to that office by Peter, James, and John even before the Church was organized. It carried with it a distinctive spiritual mission. As explained in a revelation given to Joseph Smith shortly after the Quorum of the Twelve was organized in this dispensation, the Twelve are "special witnesses of the name of Christ in all the world—thus differing from other officers in the church in the duties of their calling" (107:23).

When the Church was organized on 6 April 1830, its governing body consisted of Joseph Smith and Oliver Cowdery, who had previously been ordained as apostles by Peter, James, and John (27:12). At that point they were simply called the first and second elders of the Church (20:2–3). As the Church grew, other offices were gradually added to the presiding hierarchy, including the Quorum of the Twelve Apostles in 1835.

A revelation to Joseph Smith in June 1829, ten months before the Church was organized, foreshadowed the calling of twelve apostles and the organization of the Quorum of the Twelve. The Quorum's full range of administrative duties was not spelled out at this time, but what the revelation did state must have been both awe-inspiring and humbling to the young men who were eventually called. They were to "take upon them [the Lord's] name with full purpose of heart [and] . . . go into all the world to preach [the] gospel unto every creature." They were also to "walk uprightly before [the Lord] and sin not," baptize converts, ordain priests and teachers, and "declare [the] gospel, according to the power of the Holy Ghost" (18:26–36). Oliver Cowdery and David Whitmer, two of the Three Witnesses to the Book of Mormon, were initially given the responsibility of seeking out the Twelve, and the other witness, Martin Harris, was later asked to assist (18:37; Smith, *History,* 2:186–87).

The Quorum of the Twelve was organized at a special meeting called for that purpose on 14 February 1835 in Kirtland, Ohio. Among those at the meeting were former members of ZION'S CAMP, who in 1834 had marched to Missouri to help the Saints who had been driven from their homes. This march of a thousand miles was a kind of baptism by fire for them as they endured numerous hardships that tested their faith and their willingness to follow the Prophet. The meeting to identify the Twelve was a long

Joseph Smith addressing Church leaders in Nauvoo; painting by William Major, 1844. Left to right: Hyrum Smith, Willard Richards, Joseph Smith (standing), Orson Pratt, Parley P. Pratt, Orson Hyde, Heber C. Kimball, and Brigham Young. The five men pictured on the right are five of the original apostles in this dispensation.

one and included various expressions from the elders present about their willingness to have the Spirit of the Lord dictate who they chose, prayers by each of the Three Witnesses, and a blessing of the Witnesses by the Presidency of the Church. The Witnesses then proceeded to choose the apostles, laid their hands on the first three, blessed them, and ordained them to their new office. Another six were ordained the following day. Parley P. Pratt was ordained on 21 February, and Thomas B. Marsh and Orson Pratt, who had just returned from missions, were ordained on 26 April (Smith, *History*, 2:186–200). Shortly thereafter, Thomas B. Marsh was named president of the Twelve because the order of seniority among members of the first Quorum of the Twelve was determined by age and he was the oldest. With that arrangement, the order of seniority became Thomas B. Marsh (35), David W. Patten (35), Brigham Young (33), Heber C. Kimball (33), Orson Hyde (30), William E. McLellin (29), Parley P. Pratt (27), Luke S. Johnson (27), William B. Smith (23), Orson Pratt (23), John F. Boynton (23), and Lyman E. Johnson (23). Seniority within the Quorum was later determined by date of ordination (Top et al., 80). Interestingly, the original Quorum included two sets of brothers, the Pratts and the Johnsons, as well as a brother of Joseph Smith.

Over the next several days, the newly ordained apostles received instruction from Joseph Smith and Oliver Cowdery. On 27 February, Joseph Smith defined their responsibility to include not only missionary work throughout the world but also presiding over the churches of the Saints everywhere outside the established stakes. In addition, they were to "unlock the door of the Kingdom of heaven unto all nations, and to preach the Gospel to every creature." Joseph Smith's *History* indicates that the apostles were to preside "where there is a presidency established" (2:200). The word "a" in this context may be a typographical error, however, for the sentence should read, "where there is no presidency [i.e., stake presidency] established." This policy was clarified by Joseph Smith on 26 April 1835, when he taught that the Twelve could not regulate the affairs of the Church within any of the organized stakes where there was a standing high council (*History*, 2:220). A few years later the authority of the Quorum was considerably expanded, placing the Twelve next to the First Presidency in administering the affairs of the Church.

The new apostles went about their work quickly. On 4 May 1835 they left Kirtland, bound for New York on their first mission as a quorum. The mission lasted slightly more than four months, and during that time they conscientiously did what they had been instructed to do: preach the gospel, organize churches, conduct conferences, and set in order the affairs of the various branches they visited. During the next few years they continued in that activity and made regular reports to the First Presidency about Church affairs in the areas they visited. In 1837 Elders Heber C. Kimball and Orson Hyde went by assignment to England, where they opened the first mission of the Church outside North America.

These were troubled times, however, as the Church faced formidable problems both from within and without. Persecution in Ohio and Missouri, serious economic difficulties, internal tensions over programs and policies, and various human weaknesses all contributed to heavy difficulties for the struggling young Church and its hardworking young leaders. Sadly, even the Quorum of the Twelve suffered internal tensions, and some of its members were found to be in open opposition to the Prophet. In fact, all but two, Brigham Young and Heber C. Kimball, at one time or another found fault with Joseph. Eight left the Church or were excommunicated; four of them returned to the Church, and two

of those four were reinstated as members of the Twelve.

Thomas B. Marsh was deeply devoted to his calling but had a difficult time as leader of the Quorum of the Twelve. He led his quorum on two missions (1835 and 1836) and also found himself settling differences among Quorum members, reconciling differences between the Quorum and the First Presidency, and sometimes disagreeing with the Prophet. It appears that he was prideful of his position, perhaps jealous of Joseph Smith's power, and this, together with his dissatisfaction with the way his wife was treated when she was accused of violating an agreement with Lucinda Harris concerning the sharing of milk strippings (Dudley, 18–20), led him to leave the Church in October 1838. He signed an affidavit accusing Joseph Smith of hostility toward Missouri. He was officially excommunicated in March 1839. In 1857, full of remorse for his actions, he was rebaptized in Florence, Nebraska. He joined the main body of the Church in Utah that same year and died in January 1866.

David W. Patten was one of the Twelve who on 3 November 1835 was chastised by the Lord for not being sufficiently humble and, along with Elders Hyde and McLellin, for other things (Smith, *Papers*, 1:120–21). The reason for the rebuke is unclear, but he did not hold a grudge and continued faithful in his position, sometimes helping Elder Marsh to reconcile disgruntled Quorum members. In 1837 he had a brief disagreement with the Prophet but was soon reconciled (Dudley, 30–32). In October 1838 Elder Patten led a body of militia from Caldwell County, Missouri, in an effort to rescue several kidnapped Saints. During this excursion he was killed at the Battle of Crooked River, thus becoming the first modern apostolic martyr.

Brigham Young was the senior member of the Quorum of the Twelve after the apostasy of Thomas B. Marsh and the death of Elder David W. Patten. He led out in helping the Saints endure the continuing Missouri persecutions and undertake their subsequent evacuation from the state while Joseph Smith remained imprisoned. In response to a call by revelation, the Twelve went to England on a mission, and it was during that mission on 14 April 1840 that Elder Young was sustained as president of the Quorum. After the death of Joseph Smith in 1844, he led the Church as president of the Quorum of the Twelve, organizing the exodus to Utah and settlement there. The First Presidency was reorganized 5 December in Hyde Park, Iowa, and Brigham Young was sustained as president of the Church at a special conference of the Church in Kanesville, Iowa, on 27 December 1847. After leading the Church as president for thirty years, he died in Salt Lake City in 1877.

Heber C. Kimball went with others of the Twelve on their 1840–41 mission to the British Isles. This was his second mission to that area, he and Orson Hyde having opened the British Mission in 1837. He was an effective leader in the organization of the westward movement, became first counselor to President Brigham Young in December 1847, and died in Salt Lake City in 1868.

Orson Hyde first expressed his dissatisfaction with Church leadership in 1835, when he and William E. McLellin objected to some of Sidney Rigdon's activities in Kirtland. The two were disfellowshipped by the Kirtland high council for speaking against a member of the First Presidency, but after they confessed their error, they were quickly restored to fellowship. Their dissatisfaction still festered, however, and on 3 November 1835, the two of them as well as other members of the Twelve were chastised by the Lord in a revelation to Joseph Smith (Smith, *Papers*, 1:120–21). It is unclear exactly what they were chastised for, but in the case of Elder Hyde, it may have been his criticism of William Smith, the Prophet's brother and a fellow member of the Quorum, or continued criticism of Sidney Rigdon, a member of the First Presidency (Dudley, 41–44). In 1837 Elder Hyde went with Heber C. Kimball to England to open the mission there, but after his return he joined with Thomas B. Marsh in criticizing the Prophet and signing an affidavit against him. Elder Hyde soon began to feel deep anguish for his actions, and though he was temporarily suspended from his activities as an apostle, he was not excommunicated. By mid-1839 he was back in full fellowship. During 1840 and 1841, while most others of his quorum were doing missionary work in England, he traveled to England and then to Palestine, by appointment, where he dedicated that land for the return of the Jews. He became president of the Quorum of the Twelve when Brigham Young became president of the Church. He died in Utah in 1878.

William E. McLellin worked diligently with the other apostles when they were sent out on their early missions, though at times he was critical of Church leaders. In August 1835 he, along with Orson Hyde, was disciplined by the Kirtland high council. Like Elder Hyde, however, he quickly confessed his error and was forgiven. On 3 November 1835 he and other members of the Twelve were again chastised by the Lord. In 1836 he went on a second mission, proselytizing for a few months in Ohio and Kentucky. He soon became disaffected again and in August wrote a letter of withdrawal from the Church. His withdrawal was not accepted, however, and for a time he even continued as a member of the Quorum. He was finally excommunicated in May 1838 and later joined the mobs that eventually drove the Saints from Missouri. After that he associated with various offshoot groups, apparently having never lost his confidence in the Book of Mormon or the events that led to the foundation of the Church. He believed, however, that the original leaders, including Joseph Smith, had gone astray. At one time he tried to organize his own church. He died in Independence, Missouri, in 1883.

Parley P. Pratt was a faithful, well-published proponent of the restored gospel from the time of his ordination as an apostle and his call to the Quorum of the Twelve in February 1835 until his death in 1857, except for a brief period of disaffection in 1837. Pratt first expressed his discontent with Joseph Smith in the spring of 1837, when he joined with his brother Orson and others in writing accusatory letters about the Prophet. The apostles involved were brought before the Kirtland high council for trial, which ended in confusion over the question of whether the high council had the right to try members of the Twelve. No official action was taken by the council. With help from Elders Thomas B. Marsh and John Taylor, Elder Pratt acknowledged his error and made an impassioned, tearful confession to Joseph Smith. After his plea for forgiveness was accepted, he never wavered, continuing diligently in his labors as an apostle until he was murdered in 1857 while serving a mission in Arkansas (Dudley, 86–91).

Luke S. Johnson was dropped from the apostleship and the Church in December 1837 (Dudley, 171). His apostasy, as well as that of his brother Lyman and John F. Boynton, was related to the serious financial difficulties of the Church in Kirtland; the runaway speculative spirit that captured many of the Saints; the collapse of the Kirtland Safety Society, which led some to look on Joseph Smith as a fallen prophet; and the efforts of Warren Parrish to set up a rival church. Details of this turbulent time are complex. Suffice it to say that Luke and Lyman Johnson and John Boynton were caught up in economic speculation, and all three participated in the Parrish movement. Unlike the other two, however, Luke Johnson did not show any continuing hostility to the Church and continued to help and support Joseph Smith through some of his difficulties. In March 1846 he was rebaptized in Nauvoo by Orson Hyde, his brother-in-law. He went with the Church to Utah, where he was called as a bishop. He died in 1861.

William B. Smith, Joseph Smith's younger brother, found fault with his brother and was estranged from him almost from the beginning of his appointment to the Quorum. He frequently abused Joseph verbally, and although he expressed remorse for his actions and sought forgiveness at times, he seemed unable to completely overcome his antagonism. He continued as a member of the Quorum, however, and occasionally seemed to get along well with the Prophet. Being less than diligent in his quorum duties from May to October 1839, however, he was suspended from acting in his office. Pleading poverty, he refused to go with the Twelve on their mission to the British Isles. In 1844, after further disagreement with Joseph, he left Nauvoo with his family. After Joseph's death he came into conflict with the rest of the apostles over the question of leadership, even claiming that it was his right to lead the Church.

He was excommunicated in 1845 and never returned to the Church. He died in 1893.

Orson Pratt was also involved in the Kirtland dissensions of 1837, but no action was taken against him, as he quickly repented of his criticism of the Prophet and promised to devote himself fully to the work of the Church. He provided strength in Missouri when other members of the Twelve fell away. He was among those of the Twelve who filled their mission to the British Isles. Following his return from that mission, however, he became troubled over the issue of plural marriage, which had recently been introduced into the Church by Joseph Smith, and particularly over stories he heard of possible advances by the Prophet or John C. Bennett toward his wife. What really happened is not clear, but Orson Pratt believed the worst and became so incensed that he made serious public accusations against Joseph Smith, for which he was excommunicated in August 1842. Nevertheless, Orson continued to maintain his faith in the truth of Mormonism, and his attitude toward Joseph soon softened. In January 1843, five months after his excommunication, he returned to the Church, was reinstated in the Quorum of the Twelve, and remained steadfast thereafter. He died in Utah in 1881.

John F. Boynton was cut off from the Church in December 1837 and never renewed his association with the Church. He did, however, maintain contact with Latter-day Saint friends. He once traveled to Utah and denounced the persecution the members of the Church received because of plural marriage. He died in New York in 1890.

Lyman E. Johnson was excommunicated on 13 April 1838 at Far West, Missouri. Like Boynton, he never returned to the Church but did remain friendly with many members of it, often visiting Saints in Nauvoo. He was drowned in the Mississippi River in December 1856.

It must be stated that these stories of dissent and excommunication do not do justice to the members of the first Quorum of the Twelve in this dispensation. Most of them also made important contributions to the Church through missionary work, establishing Church communities in Ohio and Missouri, and helping to uplift the Saints through their preaching and Church service. Their estrangement is, in part, only one illustration of how difficult it was for Joseph Smith to establish the Church in the turbulent environment of the 1830s. Each of the original Twelve was a young, strong-willed man, and tension was inevitable as they were thrown suddenly into new positions in a quorum whose duties were not fully defined. Their challenge was not only to do missionary work and help set in order the affairs of the Church but also to learn how to function, both spiritually and administratively, as a unit. It was in this capacity that they struggled to succeed. A different kind of trial or challenge, it seems, was needed to establish a pattern for a more unified, successful quorum. That challenge came when the successors of those who fell away joined with those who stayed faithful and successfully carried out the all-important mission of the Quorum to the British Isles in 1840 and 1841.

See also articles on each of the original Twelve Apostles; Church of Jesus Christ of Latter-day Saints, The; Apostles, the Twelve, mission to Great Britain.

BIBLIOGRAPHY

Dudley, L. Todd. "All But Two: The Disaffection of Ten of the Original Twelve Modern Apostles." Honors thesis, Brigham Young University, 1994.

Esplin, Ronald K. "Brigham Young and the Transformation of the 'First' Quorum of the Twelve." In *Lion of the Lord: Essays on the Life and Service of Brigham Young.* Edited by Susan Easton Black and Larry C. Porter. Salt Lake City: Deseret Book, 1995.

———. "The Emergence of Brigham Young and the Twelve to Mormon Leadership, 1830–1841." Ph.D. dissertation, Brigham Young University, 1981.

Smith, Joseph. *History of The Church of Jesus Christ of Latter-day Saints.* Edited by B. H. Roberts. 7 vols. 2d ed. rev. Salt Lake City: The Church of Jesus Christ of Latter-day Saints, 1932–51.

———. *The Papers of Joseph Smith.* Vol. 2, *Autobiographical and Historical Writings.* Edited by Dean C. Jessee. Salt Lake City: Deseret Book, 1992.

Smith, Joseph Fielding. *Doctrines of Salvation.* Compiled by Bruce R. McConkie. 3 vols. Salt Lake City: Bookcraft, 1954–56.

Top, Brent L., Larry E. Dahl, and Walter D. Bowen. *Following the Living Prophets.* Salt Lake City: Bookcraft, 1993.

JBA

Apostles, the Twelve, mission to Great Britain

Members of the Quorum of the Twelve Apostles served missions to Great Britain from 1839 to 1841. The story of that mission began several years earlier.

On 4 June 1837, the Prophet Joseph Smith announced to Heber C. Kimball of the Quorum of the Twelve, "The Spirit of the Lord has whispered to me, 'let my servant Heber go to England and proclaim my gospel and open the door of salvation to that nation'" (Kimball). This was astonishing, for the Church was in deep crisis caused by serious financial problems, intense persecution, criticism of the Prophet even from within the Church, and the apostasy or disaffection of several members of the original Quorum of the Twelve. To send a faithful apostle so far away during such troubled times could hardly seem to help, but Joseph Smith had been told by the Lord that "something new must be done for the salvation of His Church" (Smith, 2:489). That "something" was Elder Kimball's mission to England and the subsequent mission to the British Isles of the Quorum itself.

Elder Kimball left Kirtland nine days after Joseph extended the call, accompanied by Elder Orson Hyde of the Quorum of the Twelve, Willard Richards, and Joseph Fielding. They were joined in New York by three other missionaries: John Goodson, John Snyder, and Isaac Russell. They began their work in Preston, England, where they preached their first sermons on Sunday, 23 July 1837. The next Sunday afternoon nine converts were baptized. Not unexpectedly, their work was dogged by bitter opposition, especially from Protestant ministers. Nevertheless, the gospel message caught on quickly, and by the time Elders Kimball and Hyde completed their mission and sailed for America on 20 April 1838, there were around 1,600 members of the Church in the towns and villages of Lancashire. The apostles left the new converts in the charge of a mission presidency that consisted of Joseph Fielding, Willard Richards, and William Clayton.

Sadly, the apostles found the Church in America even more distressed than when they had left. Joseph Smith had fled Kirtland for

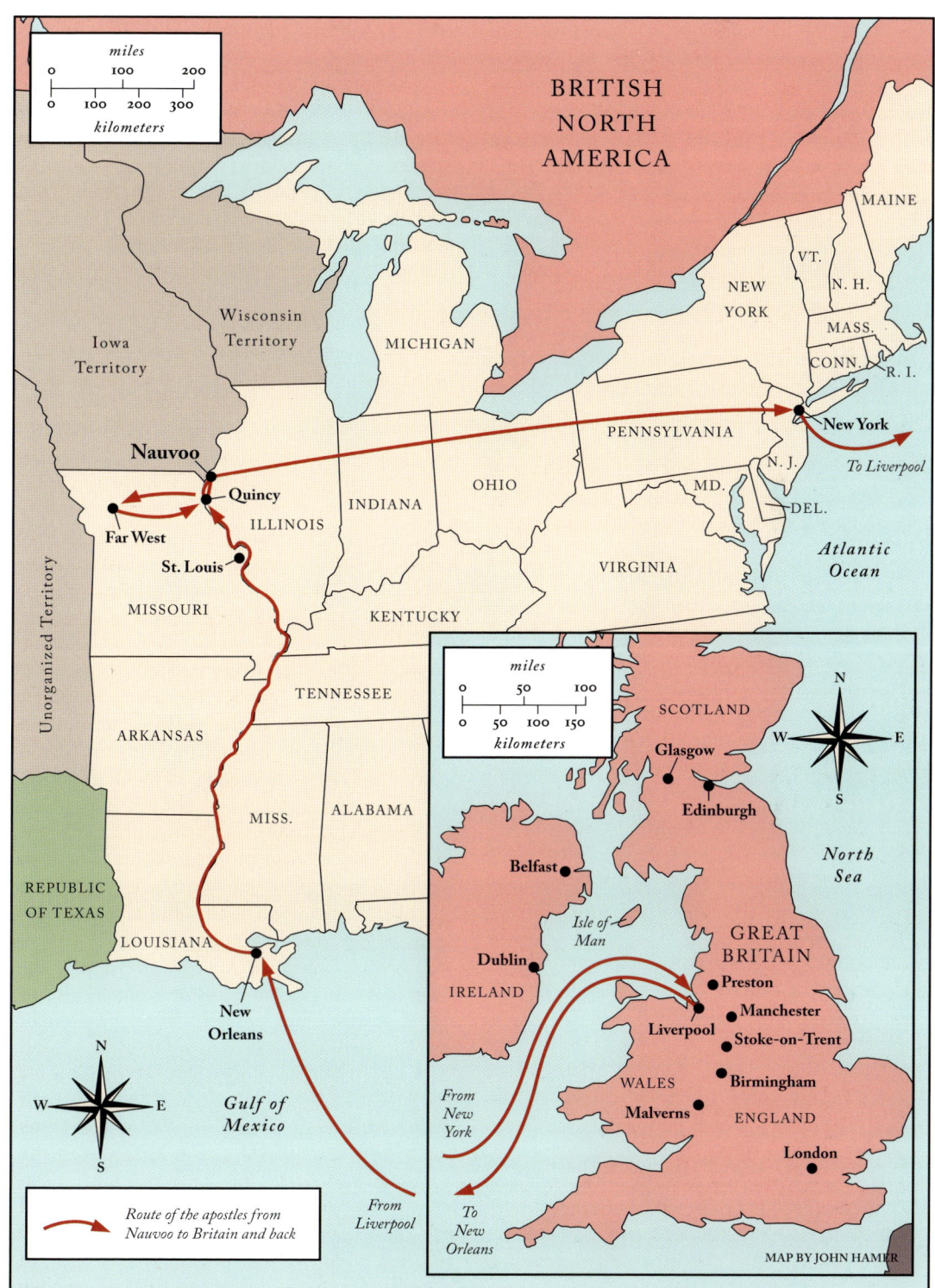

Mission of the Twelve Apostles to Great Britain, 1839–1841.

Missouri. The Quorum of the Twelve was still struggling with internal dissent. But the Prophet Joseph Smith still had the inspired, far-reaching vision that would soon send the apostles back to England. On 8 July 1838, he received a revelation concerning the Twelve: "Next spring let them depart to go over the great waters, and there promulgate my gospel, the fulness thereof, and bear record of my name. Let them take leave of my saints in the city of Far West, on the twenty-sixth day of April next, on the building-spot of my house, saith the Lord." The revelation also named four new Quorum members: "Let my servant John Taylor, and also my servant John E. Page, and also my servant Wilford Woodruff, and also my servant Willard Richards, be appointed to fill the places of those who have fallen" (118:4–6). See Historical context and overview of Doctrine and Covenants 118 (p. 828).

Before that revelation could be fulfilled, the Church faced an incredible challenge—in October 1838 the governor of Missouri issued his infamous extermination order, the Saints were brutally driven from the state, and Joseph Smith and other Church leaders languished in jail at Liberty, Missouri. But the apostles, under the leadership of Brigham Young, Quorum president, were determined to fulfill the precise terms of the revelation, despite the dangers of returning to Missouri. Early in the morning on the appointed day and at the appointed spot in Far West, five apostles and several other Church members met. They held a short service, placed cornerstones for a temple, and ordained two more apostles: Wilford Woodruff and George A. Smith. Then they left quickly before they could be discovered.

Eight members of the Quorum of the Twelve fulfilled the mission to the British Isles: Brigham Young, Heber C. Kimball, Parley P. Pratt, Orson Pratt, John Taylor, Wilford Woodruff, George A. Smith, and Willard Richards (who was ordained in March 1840 in England). Another, Orson Hyde, went first to England and then was sent by revelation to Palestine to dedicate that land for the return of the Jews. There were only eleven Quorum members at the time, and two

of them, John E. Page and William Smith, declined the call.

When the apostles left for England, beginning in August 1839, some were seriously ill, some were nearly penniless, and some left families who were ill and without money. Nevertheless, sustained by members of the Church as they traveled, they made their way to New York City and from there across the Atlantic.

First to reach England were Wilford Woodruff and John Taylor, arriving at Liverpool on 11 January 1840. Elder Taylor and Joseph Fielding set up headquarters there. On 4 February they baptized their first ten converts in the ice-cold waters of the Irish Sea. They faced bitter opposition, however, and after three months there were only twenty-eight members in Liverpool.

Meanwhile, Elder Woodruff began his work in the Staffordshire Potteries, where he baptized about forty converts by the end of February. At that point he was inspired to go to Herefordshire, where he was immediately invited by John and Jane Benbow to preach in their home. The next day the Benbows and four others were baptized. The Benbows belonged to a group known as the United Brethren, which had broken away from the Primitive Methodists. The United Brethren taught principles that, in many respects, were similar to those taught by the Latter-day Saints, so it was not difficult for them to accept the message of the Restoration. Area residents flocked to hear Elder Woodruff, and by mid-April he had baptized 158 people, including forty-eight United Brethren preachers. Many of the converted preachers were so well prepared that they were quickly given the priesthood and sent back to their own congregations, this time to preach the fulness of the restored gospel. They also made available to the Church forty-two places legally licensed for preaching. The promise in the Doctrine and Covenants that "the field is white already to harvest" (4:4) was never more true than in Herefordshire.

The other five apostles landed in Liverpool on 6 April 1840. Eight days later, in Preston, the Quorum held a council meeting in which Willard Richards was ordained as one of its members. Humbled and very much aware of the dissension that had plagued the Quorum earlier, the new apostle prayed fervently that he would be able to carry out his duties in righteousness and that the members of his quorum might "be of one heart and one mind in all things" (Allen et al., 134). This prayer was answered fully. Under the leadership of Brigham Young, the apostles developed a genuine love for each other as well as for the people they worked with, resulting in a unified and effective quorum. They were assisted in their work by other missionaries, including recent converts; however, the challenges confronting them were manifold. Most had little or no money and often relied on local Saints for food, clothing, and housing. They also needed funds to publish the Book of Mormon, a hymnal, and other Church literature. Again, they relied on the donations of the Saints. They faced constant harassment, often fomented by angry ministers. It was not uncommon for them to be subjected to threats of arrest and for stones, bricks, and verbal abuse to be hurled at them. On a few occasions the apostles even experienced direct confrontations with the forces of Satan, who was trying to halt their activities.

After the April conference in Preston, Heber C. Kimball returned to Lancashire, where he saw many more converts join the Church. Wilford Woodruff returned to Herefordshire, taking with him Brigham Young and Willard Richards, though Elder Young soon left for Manchester to take charge of publishing the Book of Mormon and the hymnal. Conversions in Herefordshire continued apace, and by mid-June the Church there had grown to thirty-three congregations and 534 members. Near the end of June, Elder Richards returned to Manchester, where he continued to live and do missionary work, though at times his work was hampered by the continuing illness of his wife and their newborn son.

Manchester and Liverpool became the Church's administrative and publishing centers, and Brigham Young spent most of his time there. He himself had little time for proselytizing but was effective in organizing and directing the work of other missionaries.

John Taylor remained in Liverpool, where he directed many new converts in missionary work,

leading to many baptisms. At the end of July, he went briefly to Ireland, where he had minimal personal success; the missionaries he left behind, however, soon began harvesting more souls. In mid-September, he sailed to the Isle of Man, the childhood home of his wife, Leonora. There he faced bitter challenges from ministers, but by the time he left in mid-November, he had organized a branch of the Church. He spent most of the rest of his mission preaching and proselytizing in and around Liverpool. He also visited Wales and other places while working closely with Brigham Young on Church publications and organizing emigration.

George A. Smith's first assignment was in Staffordshire, where he found abject poverty, but his deep sensitivity and humility helped him win the hearts of everyone he met. He also seemed tireless, despite his ill health. One Sunday, for example, he preached in one place in the morning and another in the afternoon, where he confirmed seven people. After that he walked back to the earlier location, where he baptized two people. Still wet because he had no change of clothes, he preached in the evening and then walked ten miles to Burslem with his clothes still drying on his body (Allen et al., 160).

Parley P. Pratt spent most of his time in Manchester, where he founded the Church's first official periodical in England, the *Latter-day Saints' Millennial Star*. In July he returned briefly to America to get his family, for it had been decided that he should remain in England after the rest of his quorum left.

Orson Pratt spent his entire mission in Scotland, living in Edinburgh, where he set a goal of gaining 200 converts in that city alone. At first he had only moderate success, partly because the intellectual milieu of Edinburgh resulted in polite curiosity rather than the intense opposition faced by his colleagues elsewhere. He actually craved opposition, for only that, he felt, could attract the kind of attention that would result in greater interest. In December, opposition finally came from angry pastors. Converts were soon baptized in the frigid waters of the North Sea. By the time Elder Pratt left Scotland at the end of March 1841, there were 203 members in Edinburgh, as well as many more in Glasgow and other parts of Scotland.

In August 1840, Heber C. Kimball, Wilford Woodruff, and George A. Smith went to London, where they experienced the most discouraging period of their mission. Their first baptism was finally performed in a public bath on 31 August, but by the end of September there were still only eleven members of the Church in England's capital city. After attending a conference in Manchester in October, Elders Smith and Woodruff returned to London, but the heavy fog and the thick, black smoke from coal-burning stoves and fireplaces exacerbated Elder Smith's already poor health to the degree that he was forced to leave early in November and return to Staffordshire.

Three weeks later Elders Young and Kimball arrived in London, though Elder Young stayed for only eleven days. Elder Kimball soon baptized several people, and as the months went on, baptisms steadily increased. On 14 February 1841 the apostles organized the London Conference, consisting of a branch in London and three small branches in nearby towns. "This is a day I have long desired to see," Wilford Woodruff wrote in his journal, "for we have laboured exceding hard to esstablished the work in this city, & in several instances it seemed as though we should have to give it up but by claiming the promises of God & holding on to the word of God, the rod of Iron we have been enabled to overcome, & plant a church & esstablish a conference which we are enabled through the grace of God to leave in a Prosperous Situation which has the appearance of a great increase" (Journal, 14 February 1841).

It was inevitable that the British converts should develop an overwhelming desire to gather with the Saints in America under the leadership of the Prophet Joseph Smith. The apostles were delighted, but "the gathering," as the movement was known, soon placed additional burdens on some of them. Planning, organizing, and coordinating the emigration program became a large and complex enterprise, and Brigham Young, John Taylor, and Willard Richards did much of the work. They contracted ships, negotiated the cost of passage, and

helped to purchase food and other provisions. They also organized each emigrant company as a Church unit under the direction of a presidency so that the company would cross the Atlantic in an orderly and efficient manner. In addition, they coordinated by mail with the other apostles to bring together at the right moment all the emigrants, money, supplies, and ships.

In December 1840 the Prophet wrote to the apostles, instructing them to return to Nauvoo the following spring. On 1 April 1841 they met in Manchester and were joined by Orson Hyde on his way to Palestine. By then there were 5,864 members of the Church in the British Isles, a dramatic increase of more than 250 percent from the 1,600 members Elders Woodruff and Taylor had found when they arrived in England fifteen months earlier. This was in addition to nearly 1,000 members who had already emigrated.

Seven of the nine apostles, along with a company of emigrating Saints, sailed for America on 20 April 1841. Parley P. Pratt remained in Great Britain, and Orson Hyde continued on to Palestine. Brigham Young arrived in Nauvoo on 1 July. Eight days later everything he had done seemed ratified by a revelation given through the Prophet Joseph Smith:

"Dear and well-beloved brother, Brigham Young, verily thus saith the Lord unto you: My servant Brigham, it is no more required at your hand to leave your family as in times past, for your offering is acceptable to me. I have seen your labor and toil in journeyings for my name. I therefore command you to send my word abroad, and take especial care of your family from this time, henceforth and forever. Amen" (126:1–3).

Joseph Smith's 1837 inspiration that the British mission would be the salvation of the Church was literally fulfilled. As a result of the gathering, begun under the direction of the Twelve, more than 4,800 British Saints arrived in Nauvoo before the city was abandoned in 1846, and by the end of the nineteenth century, well over 50,000 had emigrated to America. These Saints swelled the ranks of the main body of the Church just at the time it was needed most. British immigrants also played a vital role in providing Church leadership at both the general and the local levels in the nineteenth and early twentieth centuries. In addition, England became the base for extending missionary work to much of the world, including the European continent, South Africa, India, Australia, and Asia.

The Quorum's publishing activities also had long-range positive consequences. The British hymnal became the basis for all subsequent Latter-day Saint hymnals published in that century. The British edition of the Book of Mormon likewise influenced succeeding editions. Liverpool, where Parley P. Pratt moved his publishing office in 1842, became the center for Latter-day Saint publishing and the supply depot for the world. This office sent missionary literature to the United States, Hawaii, Australia, India, and South Africa. It also published several Church books, including the first edition of the *Pearl of Great Price* in 1851. The widely distributed *Latter-Day Saints' Millennial Star,* which did not cease publication until 1970, became tremendously important because of the doctrinal and historical information that filled its pages.

One of the most important consequences of the mission of the apostles to Great Britain was its effect on the Quorum of the Twelve itself and, as a result, on the Church as an institution. Previously, the divided and at times contentious quorum had few administrative responsibilities, nor did it seem capable of handling them, despite the fact that an 1835 revelation declared the Quorum "equal in authority" to the First Presidency in the hierarchy of the Church (107:24). Under the leadership of Brigham Young, however, those who filled their foreign mission assignments became a remarkably humble, unified, and effective quorum, ready to take the reins of leadership when called upon. John E. Page and William Smith, who did not fill that missionary assignment, never caught the spirit of their calling and eventually left the Church.

After the apostles returned to Nauvoo, the Quorum was given important new leadership responsibilities. For the first time since its organization, the Quorum of the Twelve Apostles

was given authority over organized stakes. Other responsibilities were soon added. The Prophet told a special conference of the Church on 10 August 1841 that the time had come when the Twelve should stand in their place next to the First Presidency. For several months before he was killed, the Prophet Joseph Smith met regularly with the Twelve, giving them their "endowments," teaching them "those glorious principles which God had revealed to him," and bestowing upon them "all the keys and authority of the Holy Priesthood which he had received" (*Wilford Woodruff,* 18–21). They now had the "keys of the kingdom of God" (65:2; cf. Matt. 16:19; D&C 27:12–13; 81:2; 112:30–32). Finally, in an extraordinary meeting in March 1844, two months before his death, Joseph Smith told the apostles that the kingdom was about to rest on their shoulders and that they were to assume the burden of leadership should anything happen to him. All of this had enormous consequences for the future, for it was more clear than ever before that the Quorum of the Twelve should be his successors in the leadership of the Church and that the apostles held all the keys and authority necessary to administer the affairs of the Church in all the world. The strengthening of the Quorum resulting from the 1837 and 1840–41 missions of the Twelve did, indeed, contribute much to the salvation of the Church.

See also Apostles, the first Twelve of latter days.

BIBLIOGRAPHY

Allen, James B., Ronald K. Esplin, and David J. Whittaker. *Men with a Mission, 1837–1841: The Quorum of the Twelve Apostles in the British Isles.* Salt Lake City: Deseret Book, 1992.

Bloxham, V. Ben, James R. Moss, and Larry C. Porter, eds. *Truth Will Prevail: The Rise of The Church of Jesus Christ of Latter-day Saints in the British Isles, 1837–1987.* Salt Lake City: The Church of Jesus Christ of Latter-day Saints, 1987.

Kimball, Heber C. "Synopsis of the History of Heber Chase Kimball." Serially in *Deseret News,* 31 March–28 April 1858.

Smith, Joseph. *History of The Church of Jesus Christ of Latter-day Saints.* Edited by B. H. Roberts. 7 vols. 2d ed. rev. Salt Lake City: The Church of Jesus Christ of Latter-day Saints, 1932–51.

Woodruff, Wilford. Journal. Wilford Woodruff Collection, Church History Library, The Church of Jesus Christ of Latter-day Saints.

———. *Wilford Woodruff.* Teachings of Presidents of the Church series. Salt Lake City: The Church of Jesus Christ of Latter-day Saints, 2004.

JBA

Appendage. *See* Appendix E.

Archangel. *See* Adam.

Ark of God, steady the

Jehovah commanded Moses to make the ark of the covenant (Ex. 25), an oblong chest of acacia wood overlaid with gold, as a repository for sacred artifacts: "the golden pot that had manna, and Aaron's rod that budded, and the tables of the covenant" (Heb. 9:4). Doctrine and Covenants 85:8 refers to the ark of God. The top of the ark served symbolically as Jehovah's earthly seat. The ark usually resided in the tabernacle in the Holy of Holies. Solemnity surrounded the ark, and Jehovah reserved the privilege of touching it only to those he designated; others touched it upon penalty of death (Num. 4:15). Uzzah, therefore, was slain for his unauthorized steadying of the ark, as recorded in 2 Samuel 6:6–7. "Steadying the ark" thereafter became a metaphor for meddling in affairs beyond one's God-given stewardship.

Joseph Smith wrote to William Phelps in Missouri on 27 November 1832; section 85 is contained in that letter (Smith, *Writings*, 285–86). It prophesies in verse 8 that the man "who was called of God and appointed, that putteth forth his hand to steady the ark of God, shall fall by the shaft of death, like as a tree that is smitten by the vivid shaft of lightning." Oliver Cowdery sought clarification from Joseph Smith on this prophecy, and Joseph told him that the prophecy "does not mean that any one had" steadied the ark "at the time, but it was given as a caution to those in high standing to beware, lest they should fall by the vivid shaft of death as the Lord had said" (Cowdery to John Whitmer).

Bishop Edward Partridge and other Church

Replica of the ark of the covenant; photograph by Welden C. Andersen.

leaders in Missouri failed to heed the warning fully. Joseph subsequently wrote to them that "men should not attempt to steady the ark of God!" (Smith, *Writings,* 337). Edward Partridge repented. President Joseph F. Smith stated in 1906 that Edward's faithfulness "procure[d] for him a mitigation of the severe judgment decreed against him" (938–39).

See also Historical context and overview of Doctrine and Covenants 85 (p. 789).

BIBLIOGRAPHY

Cowdery, Oliver. Oliver Cowdery to John Whitmer, 1 January 1834. Huntington Library, San Marino, California.

Smith, Joseph. *Personal Writings of Joseph Smith.* Compiled and edited by Dean C. Jessee. Rev. ed. Salt Lake City: Deseret Book, 2002.

Smith, Joseph F. "One Mighty and Strong." *Improvement Era* 10 (October 1907): 929–43.

SCH

Arm of the Lord

Symbol of the POWER, AUTHORITY, and JUDGMENT of the Lord. The phrase "arm of the Lord" appears four times in the Doctrine and Covenants: "the arm of the Lord shall be revealed" (1:14; 90:10) and shall fall "upon the nations" (45:45, 47). References to the Lord's arm as "his arm," "my arm," "mine arm," and so forth appear many times.

The Lord explains that his arm is over the entire earth (15:2); is an arm of mercy (29:1) and love (6:20); is "not shortened" (35:8; 133:67); is "stretched out" to save his Saints (103:17; 136:22); will support the righteous and judge "the rebellious" (3:8; 35:13–14; 56:1); will with power convince nations of the gospel (90:10); will judge mankind (56:1; 123:6); and will be revealed—"make bare"—to the inhabitants of the earth (109:51–52; 123:17; 133:3). The "arm of the Lord" is also contrasted with the "arm of flesh" (1:14–19) and the "puny arm" of man (121:33).

The phrase "arm of the Lord" appears also in Isaiah (51:9; 53:1) and in both the Book of Mormon (2 Ne. 8:9; Mosiah 14:1) and the New Testament (John 12:38). References to the power of God through his "arm" appear in numerous places throughout the scriptures.

For example, the Lord delivered Moses and ancient Israel by his "stretched out arm" (Ex. 6:6); he led Lehi and his family out of Jerusalem by "mine arm" (Jacob 2:25); and he preserved the Book of Mormon "by the power of his holy arm" (Enos 1:13).

KLA

Armor of God

Protective gear covering parts of the physical body, symbolic of safeguarding critical elements of spirituality (27:15–18; cf. Eph. 6:11–17).

In a letter to the Saints in 1842, Joseph Smith wrote, "Behold, the great day of the Lord is at hand; and who can abide the day of his coming, and who can stand when he appeareth?" (128:24). According to an earlier revelation, on August 1830, the Savior said it will be those who have taken upon themselves the "whole armor" of God, enabling them to "withstand the evil day . . . until I come" and "be caught up, that where I am ye shall be also" (27:15, 18).

The physical armor of a man protects areas of the body that, if wounded, could result in death. In like manner, the symbolic armor of God protects spiritual areas that, if wounded, could result in spiritual death.

God's armor protects four spiritually vulnerable areas symbolically represented by the loins, heart, head, and feet. The loins, which in religious and scriptural settings typically refer to reproduction and symbolize virtue or chastity, are to be "girt about" or protected with truth (27:16)—the true purpose and proper use of the power of procreation (42:22–26; 49:16–17; 132:63). The heart, considered to be the source of desires, motivation, and conduct, is protected by a "breastplate of righteousness" (27:16). If people "love darkness rather than light, because their deeds are evil," it follows that righteous deeds will help people to love light rather than darkness (10:21; John 3:19). The head, symbolizing thoughts, is to be protected by "the helmet of salvation" (27:18), salvation that comes only through Jesus Christ (Mosiah 3:17). Throughout the Doctrine and Covenants the Lord instructs the Saints to govern and channel their thoughts: "Look unto me in every thought" (6:36); "cast away your idle thoughts"

(88:69); "let virtue garnish thy thoughts unceasingly" (121:45); "[consider] the end of your salvation" (46:7); and "let the solemnities of eternity rest upon your minds" (43:34). The feet, symbolic of movement or direction in life, are to be "shod with the preparation of the gospel of peace" (27:16), firmly planted in "gospel sod" (McConkie).

As Satan attempts to dilute standards of virtue and chastity with lies and deceit, to challenge appropriate motives, desires, and power with temptations toward unacceptable behavior, and to derail progression by promoting ignorance of how disciples must act, the Saints can protect themselves with truth by educating their desires, properly channeling their thoughts, and consistently obeying the gospel. The Lord revealed additional elements of God's armor to be used as protection as well as weapons in opposing evil—"the shield of faith wherewith ye shall be able to quench all the fiery darts of the wicked," the "sword of my Spirit," and "my word which I reveal unto you" (27:17–18). See Sword.

The Lord's instruction about the armor of God came in a revelation about the sacrament. Partaking of the sacrament with real intent can strengthen the armor of God we have put on: thoughts are protected through promises to "always remember him" and conduct is directed toward righteousness as pledges are made to take his name by representing him in all that is done and to "keep his commandments." Finally, there is the promise that if the Saints measure up to the conditions in the sacrament prayers, they will "always have his Spirit to be with them" (20:77–79). Such an endowment of truth and guidance is a supernal gift to those living in a deceitful and sinful world.

BIBLIOGRAPHY

McConkie, Bruce R. "I Believe in Christ," no. 134. *Hymns of The Church of Jesus Christ of Latter-day Saints.* Salt Lake City: The Church of Jesus Christ of Latter- day Saints, 1985.

MOR

Army, armies

A group of individuals organized for a purpose, often with military objectives. Three kinds of armies are referred to in the Doctrine and Covenants:

1. The Lord's Church/Saints (5:14; 88:112; 105:26, 30–31; 109:73–74), including ZION'S CAMP, an armed group of approximately two hundred who went from Kirtland, Ohio, to Missouri to assist the Saints there who had been driven from their homes (103:21–34).

2. Followers of Jesus Christ (88:112–13; cf. 105:26, 30, 31) or Satan (88:111, 113–14).

3. Armies of men (60:4; 117:6; 136:8). Doctrine and Covenants 136:8, for example, references Church members who enlisted in the United States Army in 1846 as soldiers in the Mormon Battalion and instructed that their families should be taken care of in their absence.

Three times in the Doctrine and Covenants (5:14; cf. 105:31; 109:73) the Lord described his Church as "clear as the moon, and fair as the sun, and terrible as an army with banners," indicating that the kingdom of God will eventually prevail over all enemies and "the kingdoms of this world" (105:32; 65:5–6; cf. Dan. 2:44; 1 Ne. 14:14–15).

KLA

Articles and Covenants. *See* Doctrine and Covenants, historical development of.

Ashery

Asheries were used in the early 1800s to make potash and the more refined pearl ash, produced when hardwood trees were burned into ash and then mixed with water under intense heat. Potash and pearl ash were used in making soaps and glass, in cleaning wool, and in preparing some medicines of the day. Clearing trees from the land made hardwood for burning very plentiful.

The ashery in Kirtland played an important role in the early history of the Church. The Whitney family owned an ashery there before they became members of the Church. When the United Order was established in 1831, the Whitneys consecrated their store and their ashery to the Church. These became principal business properties of the Church in Kirtland. The ashery produced sufficient potash and pearl ash for the needs of the Saints as well as for

Interior of the rebuilt ashery at Kirtland, Ohio; photograph by Welden C. Andersen. At an ashery, hardwood ashes were converted into potash and pearl ash.

commercial sales that brought revenue into the order. In a revelation given through the Prophet Joseph Smith in which the properties of the order were given to the private ownership of individual members, the ashery was assigned to Newel K. Whitney (104:39). *See* map, p. 345.

See also Consecration.

HDG

Ashley, Major N.

Birth: 3 March 1798, Sheffield, Berkshire County, Massachusetts

Death: Unknown

Major Noble Ashley had been baptized and ordained a high priest by 1831. During the Amherst, Ohio, conference of January 1832, in which the Prophet Joseph Smith "was sustained and ordained President of the High Priesthood," Ashley was among "certain elders" who sought out the Lord's will concerning their duties (75, headnote). He was subsequently commanded through revelation to lift up his voice "as with the sound of a trump, proclaiming the truth according to the revelations and commandments" (75:4). The revelation called him to preach in the "south country" with his companion, Burr Riggs (75:17). Nothing further is known concerning his mission.

Ashley lived in Jackson County, Missouri, from 1832 to 1833. He worked there as a tanner and was among the members of the Colesville Branch who were driven out of the county in 1833 by a mob (Porter, 303n49). Ashley had "left the Church by 1838" (Cannon and Cook, 246), and census records show him living in Tallmadge, Summit County, Ohio, in 1840.

BIBLIOGRAPHY

Cannon, Donald Q., and Lyndon W. Cook, eds. *Far West Record: Minutes of The Church of Jesus Christ of Latter-day Saints, 1830–1844.* Salt Lake City: Deseret Book, 1983.

Porter, Larry C. "The Colesville Branch in Kaw Township, Jackson County, Missouri, 1831–1833." In *Missouri,* edited by Arnold K. Garr and Clark V. Johnson, 281–311. Regional Studies in Latter-day Saint Church History series. Provo, Utah: Department of Church History, Brigham Young University, 1994.

ZLL

Asia

An important geographic area of New Testament times, mentioned in Doctrine and Covenants 138:5, citing 1 Peter 1:1. The New Testament uses *Asia* twenty-one times, referring to only one Roman province called Asia in the extreme western end of what is today called Turkey (Acts 2:9; 19:10; Rev. 1:4, 11). In a much larger sense, the entire Turkish peninsula is today called Asia Minor (a term never employed in the New Testament). In New Testament times several Roman provinces were organized in Asia Minor, including Asia, Bithynia, Cappadocia, Galatia, and Pontus, each having important branches of the Church. It is in the larger sense of Asia Minor that the word *Asia* is used in 138:5.

RJM

Assembly. *See* Solemn assembly.

Atonement, the

The infinite sacrifice of Jesus Christ. The fall of Adam and Eve brought physical and spiritual DEATH. The atonement of Christ overcomes physical death through the universal RESURRECTION of mankind, and it overcomes spiritual death through Jesus' suffering for sin, thus enabling the truly repentant to return to God the Father, cleansed of all sin. "For, behold, the Lord your Redeemer suffered death in the flesh; wherefore he suffered the pain of all men, that all men might repent and come unto him" (18:11; cf. Alma 7:11–13). Revelations in the Doctrine and Covenants emphasize that the Atonement is the very heart of the GOSPEL of JESUS CHRIST.

The Savior's sacrifice encompasses not only those who live on this earth but also those who live on other earths created by him (76:24). The Prophet Joseph Smith's poetic rendering of this verse reads:

> And I heard a great voice, bearing record from heav'n,
> He's the Saviour, and only begotten of God—
> By him, of him, and through him, the worlds were all made,
> Even all that career in the heavens so broad,
> Whose inhabitants, too, from the first to the last,
> Are sav'd by the very same Saviour of ours;
> And, of course, are begotten God's daughters and sons,
> By the very same truths, and the very same pow'rs. (TS, 82–83)

Latter-day scripture teaches that the power of the Atonement was efficacious long before the actual events of the Atonement were accomplished (e.g., Mosiah 3:13; Enos 1:8; Alma 36:18–21). The Doctrine and Covenants also teaches that the spirit and power of the Atonement reaches back into premortal life. This is evident in that "every spirit of man was innocent in the beginning; and God having redeemed man from the fall, men became *again*, in their infant state, innocent before God" (93:38; emphasis added; cf. Rev. 12:7–11). The Atonement is more than awe-inspiring; it is overwhelming. That one individual, even a God, can absorb the sin and guilt and pain of countless numbers of mortals is beyond human comprehension. Nevertheless, it is true.

And it resolves a seeming divine dilemma— how can God, being morally perfect, excuse or justify sin? "For I the Lord cannot look upon sin

with the least degree of allowance" (1:31). His divine integrity will not permit him to do so if the moral foundations of the demands of justice are to be sustained. At the same time, the Father loves his children with a perfect love and has provided for their salvation, even though they sin. The revelation continues: "Nevertheless, he that repents and does the commandments of the Lord shall be forgiven" (1:32). The Prophet Joseph Smith explained, "God does not look on sin with allowance, but when men have sinned, there must be allowance made for them" (*History*, 5:24). This allowance is made possible "through Jesus the mediator of the new covenant, who wrought out this perfect atonement through the shedding of his own blood" (76:40–42, 69), which satisfies the demands of divine JUSTICE and enables God to grant MERCY to repentant sinners (54:6; 61:2; 109:53; Alma 34:15–17; 42:13–15) without compromising his divine integrity.

No mortal can begin to plumb the depths of the divine atonement, and no one ever came into this world with so dreadful, so terrifying, and yet so glorious a mission as did the Son of God. "He came into the world, even Jesus, to be crucified for the world, and to bear the sins of the world, and to sanctify the world, and to cleanse it from all unrighteousness; that through him all might be saved whom the Father had put into his power and made by him" (76:41–42). He accomplished his mission at an incomprehensible price. In a revelation through the Prophet Joseph Smith, directed to Martin Harris, the Lord described his sufferings in behalf of mankind: "For behold, I, God, have suffered these things for all, that they might not suffer if they would repent; but if they would not repent they must suffer even as I; which suffering caused myself, even God, the greatest of all, to tremble because of pain, and to bleed at every pore, and to suffer both body and spirit—and would that I might not drink the bitter cup, and shrink" (19:16–19; cf. 29:17). He suffered "even more than man can suffer, except it be unto death" (Mosiah 3:7).

Having paid the debt for all mankind, atoning for the sins of countless men and women, the Redeemer was empowered to be their

Gethsemane; *painting by Liz Lemon Swindle.* "*Listen to him who is the advocate with the Father, who is pleading your cause before him—saying: Father, behold the sufferings and death of him who did no sin, in whom thou wast well pleased; behold the blood of thy Son which was shed, the blood of him whom thou gavest that thyself might be glorified; wherefore, Father, spare these my brethren that believe on my name, that they may come unto me and have everlasting life*" (D&C 45:3–5).

Advocate at the throne of divine justice. There he pleads for the salvation of all the truly repentant: "Father, behold the sufferings and death of him who did no sin, in whom thou wast well pleased; behold the blood of thy Son which was shed, the blood of him whom thou gavest that thyself might be glorified; wherefore, Father, spare these my brethren that believe on my name, that they may come unto me and have everlasting life" (45:4–5; cf. 29:5; 32:3; 62:1; 110:4). In his divine selflessness, Jesus "so loved the world that he gave his own life, that as many as would believe might become the sons of God" (34:3), demonstrating the ultimate example of consecration.

Little CHILDREN have special claim on the blessings of the Atonement. The innumerable children who have died before reaching the age of accountability are redeemed by the Atonement. The Lord declared, "Behold, I say unto you, that little children are redeemed from the foundation of the world through mine Only Begotten; wherefore, they cannot sin, for power is not given unto Satan to tempt little children, until they begin to become accountable before me" (29:46–47; cf. 18:42; 20:71; 74:7; 137:10).

Provision is also made in the Atonement for those "who have died without a knowledge of this gospel." Those "who would have received it if they had been permitted to tarry, shall be heirs of the celestial kingdom of God" (137:7–9;

cf. 2 Ne. 9:26; Mosiah 3:11). Even those who did not take full advantage of gospel knowledge here on earth will be taught the gospel in the postmortal spirit world and have the opportunity to repent, suffer for their sins, and receive "a reward according to their works, for they are heirs of salvation," all by virtue of the atonement of Jesus Christ (138:30–37, 57–59). Eventually, "every knee shall bow, and every tongue shall confess" that Jesus is the Christ and that his judgments are just (88:104; cf. Mosiah 27:31; Philip. 2:10–11). Thus, the Atonement is efficacious for all who will repent and receive the gospel—enter into a covenant with Jesus Christ in the waters of baptism, whether personally, or vicariously (through baptism for the dead), and obey eternal law. It opens the gate to salvation, to all three degrees of glory. In every case, however, the degree of spiritual maturity and worthiness and the timely response of the individual will determine his or her ultimate standing before the Lord and the glory he or she will receive (76; 88:16–24). Jesus Christ, and he alone, is the final judge as to which gate each soul will enter (19:1–3; 77:12; 2 Ne. 9:41; John 5:22). *See* Kingdoms of glory and perdition, vision of.

See also Advocate; Born of me; Fall of Adam and Eve, the; Forgiveness; Grace; Jesus Christ, merits of; Jesus Christ, sons and daughters of; Repentance; Sin, transgression.

BIBLIOGRAPHY

Smith, Joseph. *History of The Church of Jesus Christ of Latter-day Saints.* Edited by B. H. Roberts. 7 vols. 2d ed. rev. Salt Lake City: The Church of Jesus Christ of Latter-day Saints, 1932–51.

———. "A Vision." *Times and Seasons* 4, no. 6 (1 February 1843): 82–85.

RT

Authority

Power to represent, act, or officiate. The Doctrine and Covenants contains numerous passages that emphasize the importance of authority in the Church. Nearly every time the word *authority* appears in the Doctrine and Covenants, it is associated with the PRIESTHOOD. For example, on one occasion Elias Higbee asked Joseph Smith what Isaiah meant when he wrote, "Put on thy strength, O Zion." Joseph replied

that the passage had reference to Zion putting on "the authority of the priesthood" (113:7–8; cf. Isa. 52:1). The concepts of priesthood and authority are further connected in section 121, where the Lord used the phrase "priesthood or the authority of that man" (121:37). Authority is often linked with priesthood "power" (107:8, 18, 20, 24; 138:26, 30). In other instances, it is equated with priesthood "keys" (68:17; 107:15).

President Joseph F. Smith defined priesthood as "divine authority committed unto man from God" (3). A fundamental teaching of The Church of Jesus Christ of Latter-day Saints is that the Lord always gives priesthood authority to his prophets, and through that authority the prophets organize and lead the Church on earth. Soon after the death of Jesus Christ, his Church fell into apostasy and priesthood authority was taken from the earth. In 1829, heavenly messengers with divine keys appeared to Joseph Smith and Oliver Cowdery and restored that authority. Section 13 contains an account of John the Baptist conferring the Aaronic Priesthood on these two men. There is no record of the date of the restoration of the Melchizedek Priesthood, but when John the Baptist conferred the Aaronic Priesthood, he declared "that he acted under the direction of Peter, James and John, who held the keys of the Priesthood of Melchizedek, which Priesthood, he said, would in due time be conferred on" them (JS–H 1:72). Doctrine and Covenants 27:12–13 affirms that Peter, James, and John did ordain and confirm Joseph Smith and Oliver Cowdery as apostles, committing unto them the KEYS of the kingdom.

On 10 April 1830, shortly after Joseph Smith organized the Church, the Lord revealed to him the Articles and Covenants of the Church, now in section 20. In part, the Articles give instructions on how to baptize new members of the Church, explaining that to perform a legitimately recognized baptism one must be "called of God" and have "authority from Jesus Christ" (20:73). A person receives this authority by the laying on of hands by another who already has priesthood authority. As the Church's fifth article of faith declares, "We believe that a man must be called of God, by prophecy, and by the laying on of hands by those who are in authority, to preach the Gospel and administer in the ordinances thereof." An excellent example of this teaching is found in section 36, in which the Lord declares to Edward Partridge through Joseph Smith, "I will lay my hand upon you by the hand of my servant Sidney Rigdon" (36:2).

The Doctrine and Covenants emphasizes that authority is necessary to serve. "It shall not be given to any one," the Lord declared, "to go forth to preach my gospel, or to build up my church, except he be ordained by some one who has authority, and it is known to the church that he has authority and has been regularly ordained by the heads of the church" (42:11).

One great truth concerning priesthood authority is that there is no power in the priesthood unless the person who bears that authority is living worthily: "The rights of the priesthood are inseparably connected with the powers of heaven, and . . . the powers of heaven cannot be controlled nor handled only upon the principles of righteousness" (121:36).

A use of the term not associated with priesthood is in the preface to the Doctrine and Covenants, wherein the Lord gives Joseph Smith and others "authority" to publish the commandments or revelations they had received (1:6). Another general use of the term includes a reference to the authority of government leaders (101:76).

BIBLIOGRAPHY

Smith, Joseph F. "Opening Address." Conference Report, April 1904, 1–5.

AKG

Avail[eth]. *See* Appendix E.

Avails. *See* Appendix E.

Avenge. *See* Appendix E.

Ax is laid at the root of the trees

Biblical metaphor drawn from the agricultural practice of destroying trees that do not bear good fruit (Matt. 3:10; 7:19; Luke 3:9). The single use of this metaphor in the Doctrine and Covenants appears in a revelation to the Prophet Joseph Smith in Kirtland, Ohio, dated 2 August 1833: "There are those that must needs be chastened, and their works shall be made known. The ax is laid at the root of the trees; and every tree that bringeth not forth good fruit shall be hewn down and cast into the fire" (97:6–7).

Less than two weeks after antagonistic Missourians destroyed the Church's printing office and press in Independence, Missouri, and then forced Church leaders to agree to leave Jackson County, the Lord warned in the revelation that a symbolic ax would cut off Church members who did not bear good fruit. The implication was that some of the Missouri Saints had failed to keep their covenants and would face punishment if they failed to repent. The Lord used the metaphor as a warning to those unfaithful Church members. Rather than follow the Lord's commandments for the building up of ZION, some Saints had moved to Missouri without the certificate described in 72:24–26, and some disregarded the law of CONSECRATION when they arrived there (66; Robinson and Garrett, 3:220–21). *See* License/certificate(s).

These Saints did not keep the covenants necessary for the establishment of Zion. Like the tree in the metaphor, they did not bear good fruit and therefore faced destruction by the Lord's ax. The Book of Mormon uses the phrase to describe a judgment upon the unrepentant because of their unrighteous behavior (Alma 5:52).

BIBLIOGRAPHY

Robinson, Stephen E., and H. Dean Garrett. *A Commentary on the Doctrine and Covenants.* 4 vols. Salt Lake City: Deseret Book, 2000–2005.

Wilcox, S. Michael. "Eyes That See Afar." In *Doctrines for Exaltation: The 1989 Sperry Symposium on the Doctrine and Covenants,* edited by Susan Easton Black. Salt Lake City: Deseret Book, 1989.

DAW

Yea, let the cry go forth among all people: Awake and arise and go forth to meet the **Bridegroom;** behold and lo, the Bridegroom cometh; go ye out to meet him. Prepare yourselves for the great day of the Lord. 133:10

Babbitt, Almon Whiting

Birth: 1 October 1812, Cheshire, Berkshire County, Massachusetts

Death: September 1856, approximately 120 miles northwest of Fort Kearny, Nebraska

Almon Babbitt was baptized and moved to Kirtland, Ohio, in 1833. Throughout his life he struggled to comply with directives of Church leaders. After marching with ZION'S CAMP in 1834 and being ordained in 1835 to the First Quorum of the Seventy, Babbitt was rebuked by the Kirtland high council for "not keeping the Word of Wisdom; for stating the Book of Mormon was not essential to our salvation, and that we have no articles of faith except the Bible" (Smith, 2:252). In December 1835 he was charged by Joseph Smith with "traducing my character" (2:346). In 1838 he led a company of Canadian Saints to Missouri contrary to counsel (Smith, 3:62). And in 1840 he was reprimanded for encouraging Latter-day Saints to settle in Kirtland rather than in Nauvoo (Smith, 4:166).

Babbitt confessed to wrongdoing and was forgiven. On 19 October 1840 he was called to be president of the Kirtland Stake. Joseph and Hyrum Smith admonished the Kirtland Saints to "hold up the hands of our beloved brother [Almon Babbitt], and unite with him in endeavoring to promote the interests of the kingdom" (4:226). Three months after that appointment, the Lord revealed to the Prophet Joseph Smith: "With my servant Almon Babbitt, there are many things with which I am not pleased; behold, he aspireth to establish his counsel instead of the counsel which I have ordained . . . ; and he setteth up a golden calf for the worship of my people" (124:84). According to Benjamin Johnson, Babbitt was "hurt by the rebuke in the revelation, and he was in great temptation to complain, and to turn his heel upon the Prophet" (Johnson, 87).

At the October general conference of 1841, Babbitt was disfellowshipped for "counteracting the efforts of the presidency to gather the Saints" (Smith, 4:424). Upon moving from Kirtland to Illinois in 1843, he was restored to full fellowship and appointed to be the presiding elder of the branch at Ramus, Illinois. In May 1844 he

was called on a mission to France but did not fulfill the call.

Babbitt went west to the Salt Lake Valley in 1849. He was later selected to convey a memorial to the U.S. Congress requesting statehood for Deseret. In 1852 he was appointed secretary of the territory of Utah. In 1856 he traveled to Washington, D.C., to obtain supplies for the statehouse in Salt Lake City. He was killed by Cheyenne Indians while journeying back to the Salt Lake Valley.

BIBLIOGRAPHY

Johnson, Benjamin F. *My Life's Review*. Independence, Mo.: Zion's Printing and Publishing, 1947.

Smith, Joseph. *History of The Church of Jesus Christ of Latter-day Saints*. Edited by B. H. Roberts. 7 vols. 2d ed. rev. Salt Lake City: The Church of Jesus Christ of Latter-day Saints, 1932–51.

SEB

Babylon

Powerful and important ancient city on the Euphrates River, near modern Baghdad, Iraq. Babylon was politically and culturally important in the ancient Near East, especially in the time of Hammurabi (1792–1750 B.C.), who reigned during the Old Babylonian Empire (1894–1595 B.C.), and in the time of Nebuchadnezzar II (604–562 B.C.), who reigned during the Neo-Babylonian Empire (626–539 B.C.). Nebuchadnezzar II, a contemporary of Jeremiah, Ezekiel, Daniel (who lived in Babylon most of his life), and Lehi, presided over the conquest (597 B.C.) and destruction (586 B.C.) of Jerusalem, including the temple, as well as the death or deportation of thousands of Israelites (2 Kgs. 24:10–25:21).

Because of its influence in antiquity and its devastating effect on Jerusalem and God's covenant people, Babylon, "the mother of harlots and abominations," became a symbol in the New Testament of worldly power and wickedness (Rev. 17:5; 19:2; cf. 1 Pet. 5:13). The prophecy that "Babylon the great is fallen" (Rev. 18:2; cf. 14:8) can be understood in relation to Rome and to the whole world at Jesus' second coming. Babylon thus became a typological representation of the "great and abominable church" that "was founded by the devil and his children . . . which is the mother of abomina-tions; and she is the whore of all the earth" (1 Ne. 14:3, 10).

The symbolic use in the book of Revelation of the name Babylon and its associated values often parallels the usage in the Doctrine and Covenants. It is always connected with the fi-nal, divine judgment of the wicked inhabitants and powers of the world. In 133:14 the wick-edness of the fallen world is aptly defined as "spiritual Babylon." Therefore, the Lord's "voice of warning" (1:4) in 1:16 includes a condemna-tion of those who seek their "own god," for they and their possessions "shall perish in Babylon . . . which shall fall" (cf. 35:11; Rev. 14:8). In teaching that those who are "tithed shall not be burned at his [second] coming" (64:23), the Lord reminds the Saints that when he comes, "the proud and they that do wickedly" will be destroyed, because he "will not spare any that remain in Babylon" (64:24).

Not surprisingly, the revelation explaining the parable of the wheat and tares in 86:3 re-fers to "Babylon" as the "great persecutor of the church, the apostate, the whore, . . . even Satan" (cf. Rev. 17:5). Consequently, the Lord commands Latter-day Saints to separate them-selves spiritually (and originally also physically) from the world: "Go ye out from Babylon. Be ye clean. . . . Go ye out of Babylon . . . from among the nations, even from Babylon, from the midst of wickedness, which is spiritual Babylon" (133:5, 7, 14).

See also Great and abominable church; Idumea; Jesus Christ, second coming of; Parable of the wheat and the tares; Wicked, the/wicked-ness; World(s), world's, worldliness.

DMP

Baker, Jesse

Birth: 23 January 1778, Charlestown, Washington County, Rhode Island

Death: 1 November 1846, Mills County, Iowa

Jesse Baker was about fifty-eight years old when he was baptized into the Church some-time between 1835 and 1837. He moved to Missouri with the Kirtland Camp in 1838. Expelled from Missouri with other Saints under

then-Governor Lilburn W. Boggs's extermina-tion order, Baker moved to Illinois. He settled in Nauvoo to help the Saints build up a new Church headquarters (*Kirtland*, 70). On 19 January 1841, Joseph Smith received the reve-lation now recorded in Doctrine and Covenants 124. In this revelation the Lord called Baker, John A. Hicks, and Samuel Williams "to preside over the quorum of elders" (124:137). Baker was at first a counselor to Hicks and later served as president of that quorum from 1841 to 1844 (Adams, 15).

BIBLIOGRAPHY

Adams, Williams. Autobiography. Typescript. L. Tom Perry Special Collections, Harold B. Lee Library, Brigham Young University, Provo, Utah.

Kirtland Elders' Quorum Record, 1836–1841. Edited by Lyndon W. Cook and Milton V. Backman Jr. Provo, Utah: Grandin, 1985.

ZLL

Baldwin, Wheeler

Birth: 7 March 1793, Albany County, New York

Death: 11 May 1887, Stewartsville, DeKalb County, Missouri

Wheeler Baldwin learned of the Restoration late in 1830 while he was laying flooring for Levi Hancock in a home near Rome, New York (Hancock, 25–26). Shortly thereafter he was baptized and moved to Kirtland, Ohio. On 7 June 1831 the Lord called Wheeler Baldwin and William Carter to serve as missionaries together (52:31). Carter refused the call, leaving Baldwin without a missionary companion. As a result, he labored in the Kirtland area to strengthen local congregations. Church historian John Whitmer recorded that "many mighty miracles were wrought by elders" during this period. For example, Baldwin, in company with other el-ders, gave a blessing to a woman who had been confined to bed for years. "She was immediately made whole and magnified and praised God, and is now enjoying perfect health" (Whitmer, 80–81).

Baldwin moved to Jackson County, Missouri, by October 1832 and later to Caldwell County. When the Saints were expelled from Missouri in 1839, he moved to Lee County, Iowa, across the river from Nauvoo, Illinois. In 1840 the high council appointed Baldwin "to obtain affidavits and other documents to be forwarded to the city of Washington" for REDRESS for the wrongs the Saints experienced in Missouri (Smith, 4:94).

Baldwin did not go with the Saints when they migrated west. About 1853 or 1854, he joined Alpheus Cutler's apostate group called the "True Church of Jesus Christ" and moved with them to Manti, Iowa. In 1863 he joined the Reorganized Church of Jesus Christ of Latter Day Saints.

BIBLIOGRAPHY

Hancock, Levi. Autobiography. L. Tom Perry Special Collections, Harold B. Lee Library, Brigham Young University, Provo, Utah.

Smith, Joseph. *History of The Church of Jesus Christ of Latter-day Saints.* Edited by B. H. Roberts. 7 vols. 2d ed. rev. Salt Lake City: The Church of Jesus Christ of Latter-day Saints, 1932–51.

Whitmer, John. *An Early Latter Day Saint History: The Book of John Whitmer.* Edited by F. Mark McKiernan and Roger D. Launius. Independence, Mo.: Herald Publishing House, 1980.

RC

Banner(s)

A standard, ensign, flag, or sign that affirms principles and is used as a means of rallying support. The word *banners* (plural) is used three times in the Doctrine and Covenants, all in reference to the restored Church "coming forth . . . out of the wilderness—clear as the moon, and fair as the sun, and terrible as an army with banners" (5:14; 105:31; 109:73; cf. 1 Ne. 14:12–14). *Banner* (singular) is used once, in connection with the martyrdom of Joseph and Hyrum Smith. John Taylor testified that "their *innocent blood* [would be] on the banner of liberty" (135:7). Here the "banner of liberty" is symbolic of the constitutionally guaranteed rights these prophets were denied.

See also Army, armies.

MJW

Baptism by water

A GOSPEL ordinance essential for a remission of sins and salvation, performed by immersion in water by proper AUTHORITY. This ordinance was restored through the Prophet Joseph Smith on 15 May 1829. While translating the Book of Mormon, Joseph and his scribe, Oliver Cowdery, went into the woods to pray concerning baptism for the remission of sins. John the Baptist appeared as a resurrected being and laid his hands upon their heads, stating, "Upon you my fellow servants, in the name of Messiah I confer the Priesthood of Aaron, which holds the keys of . . . baptism by immersion for the remission of sins" (13:1). Having received authority, Joseph and Oliver followed John's instruction and baptized each other (JS–H 1:68–71). *See* Priesthood, restoration of priesthood and priesthood keys.

The authority to baptize is further discussed in later revelations (20:38, 46, 58; 107:20; cf. 3 Ne. 11:21–27). One must be baptized by the proper authority, or it "availeth him nothing" (22:2). Candidates for baptism must have "arrived unto the years of accountability" (20:71), designated by the Lord as eight years old (68:25), and be "capable of repentance" (20:71; cf. Moro. 8:8–24). *See* Children.

The attitude and qualifiers for those coming unto Christ through baptism are given as "all those who humble themselves before God, and desire to be baptized, and come forth with broken hearts and contrite spirits, and witness before the church that they have truly repented of all their sins, and are willing to take upon them the name of Jesus Christ, having a determination to serve him to the end, and truly manifest by their works that they have received of the Spirit of Christ unto the remission of their sins, shall be received by baptism into his church" (20:37; cf. Moro. 6:2–3). The method of baptism and the prayer for the ordinance are recorded in the Doctrine and Covenants. "Baptism is to be administered in the following manner unto all those who repent— the person who is called of God and has authority from Jesus Christ to baptize, shall go down into the water with the person who has presented himself or herself for baptism, and shall say, calling him or her by name: Having been commissioned of Jesus Christ, I baptize you in the name of the Father, and of the Son, and of the Holy Ghost. Amen" (20:72–73). Baptism with water is to be done by "immersion for the remission of sins" (13:1) and is always followed "by the laying on of hands for the baptism of fire and the Holy Ghost" (20:41; cf. 33:11; 39:6; 2 Ne. 31:12–14). The revelations make it clear that believers are to come unto Christ through baptism for the remission of sins (e.g., 20:25; 33:11; 39:5–6, 10; 55:1–2), and they come to an understanding of "all things concerning the church of Christ" after baptism (20:68).

The need for baptism is not limited to those who are living. Everyone, whether living or dead, must be saved by the same principles and ordinances. As part of the restoration of all things, the Lord revealed the doctrine of baptism for the dead to Joseph Smith and subsequent prophets, with precise procedures and instructions for record keeping (124:27–29; 127–28; 138). *See* Salvation for the dead.

Baptism by immersion is also a symbolic representation of resurrection from the dead (128:12).

See also Baptism of fire and the Holy Ghost; Gift of the Holy Ghost; Laying on of hands; Repentance.

GLD

Baptism for the dead. *See* Salvation for the dead.

Baptism of fire and the Holy Ghost

The cleansing, sanctifying power of the HOLY GHOST, promised to those who believe in Christ, repent of their sins, are baptized by water, and receive the GIFT OF THE HOLY GHOST by the LAYING ON OF HANDS (19:31; 20:41–43; 33:11). It is an integral part of being "born of the Spirit," "born of God," and "born again," becoming spiritual sons and daughters of Jesus Christ. This baptism of the Spirit brings forgiveness of sins, peace of conscience, joy, expanded spiritual knowledge, a mighty change of heart, and a desire to obey God's commandments (5:16; 2 Ne. 31:17; Mosiah 4:3; 5:1–7; 27:24–26; Alma 36:4–22; 3 Ne. 27:20; John 3:3–5). The baptism of fire and the Holy Ghost is not necessarily a once-in-a-lifetime experience (Alma 5:14, 26). Having to constantly battle against sin and needing ongoing FORGIVENESS, the Saints of God are afforded the opportunity to renew

their covenants and receive renewal of the promised blessings attached thereto each week through partaking of the SACRAMENT. Those who, with renewed commitment, "always remember [the Savior]" and "keep his commandments" are promised to "always have his Spirit to be with them" (20:77, 79). In addition to the blessings promised, the Spirit, associated with the baptism of fire and the Holy Ghost, "showeth all things, and teacheth the peaceable things of the kingdom" (39:6).

See also Baptism by water; Born of me.

CFO

Basset, Heman

Birth: 1814, Guildhall, Essex County, Vermont

Death: 1876, Philadelphia, Philadelphia County, Pennsylvania

Heman Basset was baptized in 1830 in Kirtland, Ohio, where he lived with about one hundred others on the Isaac Morley farm as part of a communal "family." Unfortunately, soon after his baptism, he claimed to have received a revelation "from the hand of an angel" (Hancock, 27) that called him to "go into the world and preach" (in Black, 11). As Levi Hancock recalled, Basset's preaching consisted of reading the revelation and showing "pictures of a course of angels declared to be Gods." Then he "would testify of the truth of the work," to which Hancock lamented, "I believed it all, like a fool" (Hancock, 27). Because of this, on 4 June 1831 Joseph Smith told Basset to "sit still [for] the Devil wants to sift you" (Hancock, 33).

On 7 June 1831 Joseph Smith received a revelation for the elders, declaring that Basset, "in consequence of transgression," would have that "which was bestowed upon [him] be taken from him, and placed upon the head of Simonds Ryder" (52:37); that is, Ryder would serve a mission, whereas Basset would not (Black, 11–12). That same day Ryder was ordained an elder (JH, 7 June 1831). Basset was seventeen years old at the time he was mentioned in the revelation recorded in section 52, making him the youngest person named in the Doctrine and Covenants. He died in 1876, having left the Church years before in Ohio because he believed Mormonism was a "hoax" (Cook, 72).

BIBLIOGRAPHY

Black, Susan Easton. *Who's Who in the Doctrine and Covenants.* Salt Lake City: Deseret Book, 1997.

Cook, Lyndon W. *The Revelations of the Prophet Joseph Smith.* Salt Lake City: Deseret Book, 1985.

Hancock, Levi. Autobiography. Typescript. L. Tom Perry Special Collections, Harold B. Lee Library, Brigham Young University, Provo, Utah.

Journal History of the Church, 7 June 1831. Church History Library, The Church of Jesus Christ of Latter-day Saints, Salt Lake City, Utah.

ZLL

Battle of the great God. *See* Millennium, the.

Be still and know that I am God

The directive to "be still and know that I am God" (101:16) can be viewed as instruction to refrain from murmuring or seeking to counsel God (22:4), as well as an invitation to be patient, to trust in God, to carry on despite trials, believing that he knows all circumstances, is firmly in control, and will see to it that all his purposes are fulfilled.

This directive came from the Lord to the Saints in 1833 after they had been "afflicted, and persecuted, and cast out from the land of their inheritance" (101:1). Two years before, the Lord had designated Jackson County, Missouri, as "the land which I have appointed and consecrated for the gathering of the saints. Wherefore, this is the land of promise, and the place for the city of Zion." The Saints were told to buy up the land, establish businesses "for the good of the saints," and gather "as it shall be counseled by the elders of the church" (57:1–2, 8; 58:56). Hundreds of Saints did as instructed but ran into serious difficulties with the local citizens, who drove them from their homes and lands in Jackson County. Understandably, their hearts were anxious about why they had been driven out and how the commandments of the Lord concerning ZION were to be fulfilled. The Lord responded with a revelation answering their concerns. After telling them that he had "suffered the affliction to come upon them . . . in consequence of their [own] transgressions" (101:2–8), the Lord gave them counsel

and reassurance about Zion: "Let your hearts be comforted concerning Zion; for all flesh is in mine hands; *be still and know that I am God.* Zion shall not be moved out of her place, notwithstanding her children are scattered. They that remain, and are pure in heart, shall return, and come to their inheritances, they and their children, with songs of everlasting joy, to build up the waste places of Zion." That day will come in the Lord's own time, after the Saints are truly prepared (101:16–18; emphasis added; cf. 101; 103; 105).

"Stand still," a directive similar to "be still and know that I am God," is employed twice in the Doctrine and Covenants. Joseph Smith was told by the Lord to "stand still until I command thee" to move forward with the translation of the Book of Mormon (5:34). And from LIBERTY JAIL, the Prophet wrote to the Saints, "Therefore, dearly beloved brethren, let us cheerfully do all things that lie in our power; and then may we stand still, with the utmost assurance, to see the salvation of God, and for his arm to be revealed" (123:17; cf. Ex. 14:13).

President Gordon B. Hinckley, while a counselor in the First Presidency and carrying much of the responsibility for administering the affairs of the Church because of the illness of other members of the First Presidency, said: "Recently while wrestling in my mind with a problem I thought to be of serious consequence I went to my knees in prayer. There came into my mind a feeling of peace and the words of the Lord, 'Be still and know that I am God.' . . . God is weaving his tapestry according to his own grand design. All flesh is in his hands. It is not our prerogative to counsel him. It is our responsibility and our opportunity to be at peace in our minds and in our hearts, and to know that he is God, that this is his work, and that he will not permit it to fail. We have no need to fear. We have no need to worry" (6).

See also Historical context and overview of Doctrine and Covenants 101 (p. 806).

BIBLIOGRAPHY

Hinckley, Gordon B. "He Slumbers Not, nor Sleeps." *Ensign* 13 (May 1983): 5–8; paragraphing altered.

LDN

Behoov[eth]. *See* Appendix E.

Belief, believing

Acceptance of, or TRUST and confidence in, something or someone. Belief and FAITH are terms often used interchangeably in the Doctrine and Covenants. Obedience to the injunctions "believe on the name of Jesus Christ" and "endure in faith on his name to the end" results in SALVATION in the kingdom of God (20:29). The Lord frequently encourages his followers to ask for spiritual knowledge with faith, believing that they will receive (8:1; 14:8; 18:18; Matt. 21:22). This suggests that belief is a step towards faith and then knowledge. Belief is a necessary component of true faith. "In faith believing" is a common description of the process leading to discovery or revelation of spiritual truth and of receipt of the HOLY GHOST (11:14; 14:8).

Considerable results and rewards are given by the Lord for belief in him. "Be believing, and all things shall work together for your good" (90:24). Whoever believes on the Lord's words will receive a manifestation, or confirmation, of the Spirit and be spiritually reborn (5:16). Believing in the gospel and the words of the prophets leads to salvation, even to eternal life (10:50; 20:25–26). "He that believeth and is baptized shall be saved" (68:9). The opposite is also true: Those who refuse to believe and will not be baptized shall be damned (84:74; 112:29). Those who believe on the name of Christ may come unto him and have everlasting life (45:5); they will "be raised in immortality unto eternal life" (29:43; cf. 45:8). Even those who believe on the words of others who know that Jesus Christ is the Son of God "also might have eternal life if they continue faithful" (46:13–14).

Another result and reward for believing souls is that those who believe on the name of Jesus Christ are given "power to become the sons of God" (11:30; cf. 34:3; 35:2), that is, to be spiritually born of Christ and "become his sons and his daughters" (Mosiah 5:7). *See* Born of me.

Furthermore, those who believe on his name may see miracles, signs, and wonders (35:8); signs will follow them that believe (58:64;

68:10; 84:65–72). Additionally, the Savior will plead before the Father for those who believe on his name (38:4).

The revelations in the Doctrine and Covenants reprove the lack of belief. If individuals will not believe the Lord's words, they will not believe Joseph Smith (5:7). As in the past, the Lord remonstrates, "Ye believed not my servants" (133:71; cf. Matt. 21:33–41).

The text also declares that all should be free to exercise their own religious beliefs (134:7).

DKO

Benighted. *See* Appendix E.

Benjamin, king

A righteous Book of Mormon king (W of M 1:10–18; Mosiah 1–6; ca. 120 B.C.). He is named in the Doctrine and Covenants in connection with the Lord's instructions to Joseph Smith concerning the translation of the Book of Mormon (10:41).

See also Book of Mormon lost manuscript (116 pages); Historical context and overview of Doctrine and Covenants 3 (p. 716) and 10 (p. 720).

DKO

Bennett, John C.

Birth: 3 August 1804, Fairhaven, Bristol, Massachusetts

Death: 5 August 1867; burial in Poke City, Poke County, Iowa

John C. Bennett had joined the Church by 1840. On 19 January 1841 Joseph Smith received a revelation directing Bennett to help him send "my word to the kings and people of the earth" and to stand by him in his "hour of affliction" (124:16). For so doing, the Lord promised to crown Bennett "with blessings and great glory" (124:17). *See* Solemn proclamation.

On 1 February 1841 Bennett was elected the first mayor of Nauvoo and appointed chancellor of the University of Nauvoo. Three days later, he was elected major-general of the Nauvoo Legion. One month later, in March 1841, Joseph Smith learned that Bennett, who had touted himself as a bachelor, actually had a wife and three children. Despite the cloud cast upon his integrity,

John C. Bennett, 1804–1867.

at the April 1841 general conference he was appointed assistant to the First Presidency of the Church.

On 7 May 1842 when the Nauvoo Legion fought a sham battle, Bennett tried to coax Joseph Smith into unprotected positions on the battlefield. Joseph refused, for the Spirit whispered that there was "mischief concealed in that sham battle" (Smith, 5:4). Bennett resigned as mayor of Nauvoo on 17 May 1842. Two days later, the hand of fellowship was withdrawn from him and he was pronounced "an impostor and base adulterer" (Smith, 5:35).

In mid-June 1842 Bennett embarked on a speaking tour addressing the perceived evils of Joseph Smith and Mormonism. In November 1842 he published *The History of the Saints; or, An Exposé of Joe Smith and Mormonism*. After the martyrdom of Joseph Smith, Bennett returned to Nauvoo, claiming that Sidney Rigdon was the next leader of the Church. By 1846 he was the chief advisor to James Strang. After leaving Strangism, Bennett pursued such vocations as practicing medicine and dentistry, breeding poultry, lecturing, and writing. At his death, he was reported to be "a miserable pauper" (Stevenson, 88).

BIBLIOGRAPHY

Smith, Joseph. *History of The Church of Jesus Christ of*

Latter-day Saints. Edited by B. H. Roberts. 7 vols. 2d ed. rev. Salt Lake City: The Church of Jesus Christ of Latter-day Saints, 1932–51.

Stevenson, Edward. *Selections from the Autobiography of Edward Stevenson, 1820–1897*. Edited by Joseph Grant Stevenson. Provo, Utah: Stevenson's Genealogical Center, 1986.

SEB

Benson, Ezra T.

Birth: 22 February 1811, Mendon, Worcester County, Massachusetts

Death: 3 September 1869, Ogden, Weber County, Utah

Growing up, Ezra Taft Benson worked in various occupations, including hotel keeping, farming, and cotton manufacturing. At age twenty he married Pamelia Andrus; they had several children, most of whom died very young. Benson joined the Church in 1840, having found the Mormons "by conversation . . . very agreeable." In his autobiography he wrote that "their spirits amalgamated with mine" and that he sympathized with those who had been expelled from Missouri (Benson, 55–56). After listening to Orson Hyde, John E. Page, and other elders of the Church and comparing their preaching to that of other ministers, he became "convinced that the Latter-day Saints were believers and observers of the truths of the Bible." He requested baptism for himself and his wife. They were baptized in the Mississippi River near Quincy, Illinois, in July 1840 in the presence of roughly three hundred people. "The cry was among the crowd, 'the Mormons have got them'" (Benson, 101–2).

Before moving from Quincy to Nauvoo in 1841, Benson was ordained an elder and a high priest and served in the Quincy stake presidency. After completing three missions in the east, he returned to Nauvoo, where he worked on the temple before fleeing west with the Saints. Of the event he said, "I had no property, but a good brick house. . . . I asked Bro. Brigham what I should do to get away, not having a team nor any means to purchase one. He said, go out in the streets and enquire of every brother you meet till you pick up one." He followed that counsel and was successful in

Ezra T. Benson, 1811–1869.

obtaining what he needed (JH, 16 July 1846). By early 1846 he had left Nauvoo. On 16 July 1846, Benson was ordained a member of the Quorum of the Twelve Apostles (JH, 16 July 1846).

Elder Benson's name appears in a revelation received by Brigham Young in preparation for the Saints' journey to the Salt Lake Valley. He and Erastus Snow were to "organize a company" for the trek west (136:12).

Over the next twenty-three years Elder Benson served in various Church and civic leadership roles: He presided with Orson Pratt over the British Mission in 1856 and 1857, was a member of the Utah Territorial House of Representatives from 1859 to 1869, and was a principal organizer in "the construction of homes, mills, schools, canals, and churches" in Cache Valley (Black, 19).

BIBLIOGRAPHY

Benson, Ezra Taft. "An Autobiography." *Instructor* 80 (1945): 55–56, 101–3, 162–64, 213–15.

Black, Susan Easton. *Who's Who in the Doctrine and Covenants.* Salt Lake City: Deseret Book, 1997.

Journal History of the Church, 16 July 1846. L. Tom

Perry Special Collections, Harold B. Lee Library, Brigham Young University, Provo, Utah.

ZLL

Bent, Samuel

Birth: 19 July 1778, Barre, Worcester County, Massachusetts

Death: 16 August 1846, Garden Grove, Decatur County, Iowa

Samuel Bent was the first man to receive the priesthood in Pontiac, Michigan, being baptized and ordained an elder in January 1833. He left immediately to serve a mission in Huron, Michigan. There, he presided over a branch of the Church (Littlefield, 28–29). In spite of many trials, Bent remained faithful until his death. He was a member and presiding officer of ZION'S CAMP (JH, 8 June 1834; cf. Bradley, 33) and upon his return served another mission. Following this mission he returned to Kirtland, attended the School of the Prophets, and was present at the KIRTLAND TEMPLE DEDICATION. After moving to Missouri he served on the high council in Far West in 1838, and when the Saints were expelled from Missouri he relocated to Nauvoo, Illinois, in 1839. His name appears in Doctrine and Covenants 124, wherein he was named a member of the Nauvoo "high council, for the cornerstone of Zion" (vv. 131–32). Bent also served as a colonel in the Nauvoo Legion and later as a captain of the exodus of the Saints from Nauvoo in 1846. He once told the high council in Far West that "his faith is as ever and that he feels to praise God in prisons and in dungeons and in all circumstances" (Cannon and Cook, 222).

Bent started west with the Saints and presided over Church members at Garden Grove, Iowa, one of the temporary settlements of the Saints along the trail west.

BIBLIOGRAPHY

Bradley, James L. *Zion's Camp 1834: Prelude to the Civil War.* Logan, Utah: James L. Bradley, 1990.

Cannon, Donald Q., and Lyndon W. Cook, eds. *Far West Record: Minutes of the Church of Jesus Christ of Latter-day Saints, 1830–1844.* Salt Lake City: Deseret Book, 1983.

Journal History of the Church, 8 June 1834. Church History Library, The Church of Jesus Christ of Latter-day Saints, Salt Lake City, Utah.

Littlefield, Lyman Omer. *Reminiscences of Latter-day Saints, Giving an Account of Much Individual Suffering Endured for Religious Conscience*. Logan, Utah: The Utah Journal Co., 1888; L. Tom Perry Special Collections, Harold B. Lee Library, Brigham Young University, Provo, Utah.

ZLL

Bespeak[eth]. *See* Appendix E.

Betimes. *See* Appendix E.

Bible. *See* Doctrine and Covenants, what it says about the Bible.

Billings, Titus

Birth: March 1793, Greenfield, Franklin County, Massachusetts

Death: 6 February 1866, Provo, Utah County, Utah

One of the first converts in Kirtland, Ohio, Titus Billings was baptized there in November 1830 by the missionaries traveling through Ohio on their way to preach the gospel to the Lamanites (28; 30; 32). His name appears in Doctrine and Covenants 63. Part of this revelation included instructions for Billings to "dispose of the land" he had care of in Kirtland that he might "be prepared in the coming spring to take his journey up unto . . . Zion" (63:39). Billings was obedient; he consecrated to the Church his money, bedding, clothing, "farming utensils," and livestock (Smith, 1:365).

Billings's service to the Church also included an 1833 calling as counselor to Bishop Edward Partridge in Jackson County, Missouri, which he could not fulfill until moving to Far West because of persecution. Later, Billings participated in the Battle of Crooked River, where David Patten, an apostle, was martyred. According to his son, Billings "said the bullets were flying all around him but he had no fear until he saw brother Patten fall" (Billings, 17). Billings subsequently moved his family to Lima, Illinois, and served in the Lima Branch as president from 1839 to 1845 (Billings, 17). After persecution drove Billings and his family from Lima, he moved to Nauvoo, but more "threats of violence . . . compelled [Billings] to leave Illinois for the unknown rigors of the Iowa wilderness" (Black, 25). Ultimately, Billings traveled west with the

Saints and fulfilled a mission to assist in settling the Sanpete Valley.

BIBLIOGRAPHY

Billings, Melvin, ed. "Titus Billings, Early Mormon Pioneer." L. Tom Perry Special Collections, Harold B. Lee Library, Brigham Young University, Provo, Utah.

Black, Susan Easton. *Who's Who in the Doctrine and Covenants*. Salt Lake City: Deseret Book, 1997.

Smith, Joseph. *History of The Church of Jesus Christ of Latter-day Saints*. Edited by B. H. Roberts. 7 vols. 2d ed. rev. Salt Lake City: The Church of Jesus Christ of Latter-day Saints, 1932–51.

ZLL

Bishop(s)

An office in the Aaronic PRIESTHOOD having both temporal and spiritual duties. The Doctrine and Covenants teaches that "the office of a bishop is in administering all temporal things" (107:68). A bishop is a "judge in Israel" (107:72), president of the Aaronic Priesthood, and president of the PRIESTS quorum (107:87–88). As president "over the Priesthood of Aaron," a bishop is to "preside over forty-eight priests, and sit in council with them, to teach them the duties of their office, as is given in the covenants" (107:87). Beyond these fundamental duties, the responsibilities of a bishop have changed throughout the years. For example, in the 1830s the bishop administered the law of CONSECRATION (42:30–31) but did not preside over a WARD. It was not until the 1840s, during the Nauvoo period, that wards were first established and bishops charged to preside over them (Smith, *History*, 5:119). Eventually, a system of local bishops presiding over wards developed, while a presiding bishop served as a Church general authority. The passages in the Doctrine and Covenants explaining the duties of the office of bishop were revealed in the 1830s before bishops had the responsibility of presiding over congregations, serving as the presiding high priest in a ward, administering the Church welfare program, and overseeing finances, records, and the use and security of the meetinghouse.

On 4 February 1831 the Lord called Edward Partridge to serve as the "bishop unto the church," the Church's first bishop (41:9). A few days later, on 9 February, the Lord revealed to Joseph Smith the "law," which is now section 42. The law included principles pertaining to the law of consecration (42:30–39). Bishop Partridge's responsibility was to administer the law.

Over time, the specific duties of a bishop concerning this law were revealed. The Saints were told that if they loved the Lord, served him, and kept his commandments, they would "remember the poor, and consecrate of [their] properties" to the Church to help them. These possessions were to be donated "with a covenant and a deed" and "laid before the bishop" (42:30–31). The bishop was to keep these properties in a "storehouse, to administer to the poor and the needy" (42:34). It was also the bishop's responsibility to "divide the lands" (58:17) of the Church among the Saints and make them stewards over the property they received (42:32). These transactions were to be formalized in writing and legalized with a deed (51:3–5).

On 1 August 1831 the Lord called Bishop Partridge to serve in Missouri (58:14), which had recently been designated by revelation as a gathering place for the Church (57:1). This left the Saints in Kirtland without a bishop. On 4 December 1831 the Lord filled that need by calling Newel K. Whitney as the second bishop of the Church (72:2, 8). Joseph Smith received a revelation that extended the call to Whitney and outlined the duties of a bishop for him. He was to (1) "keep the Lord's storehouse," (2) "receive the funds of the church," (3) "take an account of the elders," (4) administer to the wants of the elders and "the poor and needy," and (5) issue a certificate (or recommend), which verified to the bishop in Zion, Bishop Partridge, the worthiness of the Saints moving from Ohio to Missouri (72:10–17). In a subsequent revelation, Bishop Whitney was told to be proactive in meeting the needs of the poor: "And the bishop, Newel K. Whitney, also should travel round about and among all the churches, searching after the poor to administer to their wants by humbling the rich and the proud" (84:112). Later, in Nauvoo, George Miller (124:20–21) and Vinson Knight (124:141), who had previously served as a

bishop at Diahman, Missouri, were likewise called as bishops.

Sections 68 and 107 speak of the possibility of a firstborn literal descendant of Aaron serving as the bishop of the Church, provided he is "designated by [the First] Presidency, and found worthy, and anointed, and ordained under the hands of [the First] Presidency"; he could even serve "independently, without counselors" (68:16–20; 107:69–70, 76). President Joseph Fielding Smith explained: "This has reference only to one who *presides over the Aaronic Priesthood* [the Presiding Bishop]. *It has no reference whatever to bishops of wards*" (3:92–93). Presiding Bishops who are not literal descendants of Aaron are provided for in the same revelations: "But, as a high priest of the Melchizedek Priesthood has authority to officiate in all the lesser offices he may officiate in the office of bishop when no literal descendant of Aaron can be found, provided he is called and set apart and ordained unto this power, under the hands of the First Presidency of the Melchizedek Priesthood" (68:19; cf. 107:69–71).

The bishop of the Church was designated in 1835 as a "judge in Israel, to do the business of the church, to sit in judgment upon transgressors . . . , by the assistance of his counselors. . . . Thus shall he be a judge, even a common judge among the inhabitants of Zion, . . . until the borders of Zion are enlarged and it becomes necessary to have other bishops or judges in Zion or elsewhere. And inasmuch as there are other bishops appointed they shall act in the same office" (107:72–75). Today, the borders of Zion have been enlarged, and thousands of bishops have been called to preside over wards and serve as common judges "among the inhabitants of Zion" worldwide (107:74). *See* Church discipline.

Although the duty to serve as "a judge in Israel" generally falls to local bishops (107:72), provision is made for the Presiding Bishop to judge a case involving a "President of the High Priesthood" (that is, a member of the First Presidency; 107:76, 81–84). *See* Common council of the Church.

The Doctrine and Covenants makes it clear that only the First Presidency may discipline a Presiding Bishop (68:22–24).

An additional reference in the revelations to bishops is in section 120 and relates to the Presiding Bishop's responsibilities in administering the general tithing funds of the Church. On 8 July 1838 Joseph Smith received a revelation commanding the Saints to put "all their surplus property . . . into the hands of the bishop" as a "beginning of the tithing of my people. And after that, those who have thus been tithed shall pay one-tenth of all their interest annually; and this shall be a standing law unto them forever" (119:1–4). On that same day the Lord revealed that the tithing monies thus donated "shall be disposed of by a council, composed of the First Presidency of my Church, and of the bishop and his council, and by my high council; and by mine own voice unto them" (120:1). Today this council "is composed of the First Presidency, the Quorum of the Twelve Apostles, and the Presiding Bishopric" (Cantwell, 28).

BIBLIOGRAPHY

Cantwell, Robert W. "Church Auditing Department Report, 2010." *Ensign* 41 (May 2011): 28.

Smith, Joseph. *History of The Church of Jesus Christ of Latter-day Saints.* Edited by B. H. Roberts. 7 vols. 2d ed. rev. Salt Lake City: The Church of Jesus Christ of Latter-day Saints, 1932–51.

Smith, Joseph Fielding. *Doctrines of Salvation.* Compiled by Bruce R. McConkie. 3 vols. Salt Lake City: Bookcraft, 1954–56.

AKG

Bishops' storehouse. *See* Consecration.

Blasphemy against the Holy Ghost/sin against the Holy Ghost. *See* Innocent blood; Sons of perdition

Blood

Fluid consisting of plasma and life-sustaining cells that circulate through a body, essential to vertebrate life in this world. The words *blood* and *life* often occur together in scripture, as in "the life of the flesh is in the blood" (Lev. 17:11). Blood also represents the Lord's saving power, extended through covenant to his children. The Doctrine and Covenants uses the term *blood* forty-seven times, in both literal and symbolic ways.

The most significant occurrences refer to the atoning blood of Jesus Christ, symbolized originally by sacramental wine and, later, by water (20:40, 79; 27:2; cf. Deut. 32:14, in which wine is described as the "blood of the grape"). Saints partake of this emblem in remembrance of the Savior's blood (20:79). Christ repeatedly taught that he mediates between sinners and Heavenly Father "by the virtue of the blood" he shed in atoning for sin (38:4; 45:3–4; 76:69), the suffering for which caused him to "bleed at every pore" (19:18). He warns, however, that his atoning blood will not cleanse the unrepentant (29:17).

Several references to blood occur in the context of phenomena related to Christ's second coming (45:41). The Lord revealed that the moon will become as blood (29:14; 34:9; 45:42; 88:87). He also described the red apparel he will wear, signifying the shed lifeblood of the unrepentant: "I have trampled them in my fury, and I did tread upon them in mine anger, and their blood have I sprinkled upon my garments" (133:48–51). At Jesus' second coming, an angel will announce that the GREAT AND ABOMINABLE CHURCH is ready to be burned because it shed the blood of the Saints (88:94).

When the "innocent blood" of Saints is shed by the wicked, it figuratively cries out to the Lord for justice as a witness against persecutors (87:7; 109:49). This includes the INNOCENT BLOOD of Joseph and Hyrum Smith (135:7; 136:36), whose martyred blood sealed the truth of their testimonies (135:3; 136:39). Section 132 describes shedding innocent blood as a damning sin (132:26–27).

Blood also symbolizes guilt and violence, from which the Saints need to be cleansed and which are often referred to as "the blood of this generation" (88:75, 85, 138; 109:42; 112:33; 135:5).

Blood can represent the price paid for promised land. Section 101 explains that the blood shed during the American Revolution "redeemed the land" (101:80); however, other passages contain the Lord's directive against shedding blood to obtain the land of Zion (63:28–31; cf. 58:53).

Additional occurrences of *blood* include a curse upon those who needlessly shed the blood of animals (49:21). Also, the Lord declared that the rebellious in Zion "are not of the blood of Ephraim" (64:36), because they forfeit the blessings promised to the house of Israel. And with a vivid simile, the Lord compares Joseph Smith's enemies to wolves prowling for the blood of a lamb (122:6).

See also Atonement, the; Murder, murderers; Sacrament, the.

DMP

Blood, shed innocent. *See* Blood; Innocent blood.

Boggs, Lilburn W.

Birth: 14 December 1796, Lexington, Fayette County, Kentucky

Death: 14 March 1860, Napa, Napa County, California, burial in Tulocay Cemetery

Around 1816, Lilburn W. Boggs moved to Missouri, eventually settling in Independence in 1826, where he operated a mercantile business. An ardent Jacksonian Democrat, Boggs was active in Missouri politics, being elected to three state offices by 1842: state senator (1826–32

Lilburn W. Boggs, 1796–1860.

and 1842–46), lieutenant governor (1832–36), and governor (1836–40).

During his four years as the state's chief executive, he spearheaded the chartering of the state bank, established the University of Missouri at Columbia, organized a public school system, and procured funding to construct a new state capitol building. Despite these achievements, his administration was not popular. Merchants were generally opposed to the state bank; the state borrowed heavily to pay for the capitol building; and Boggs's political appointments caused in-fighting within the Democratic Party. He was highly criticized in the press and by his political opponents for his handling of the Honey War (a boundary dispute between Missouri and Iowa) and the 1838 Mormon War, including the "Extermination Order," which led to the driving of the Saints out of Missouri. By the end of his term in 1840, public and party support for him and his policies had waned, so he chose not to run for reelection.

In 1842 Boggs again sought political office, this time as a candidate for the state senate. On 6 May 1842, however, an unknown assailant shot Boggs at his home in Independence. His wounds were severe, but he recovered. Orrin Porter Rockwell was suspected of the attack, and Joseph Smith was accused as an accessory to the crime. Missouri governor Thomas Reynolds petitioned Illinois governor Thomas Carlin to extradite Joseph Smith and Orrin Porter Rockwell back to Missouri to stand trial for the attempted assassination. The two men were subsequently arrested on 8 August 1842 and taken before the municipal court of Nauvoo, which released them both. Rockwell went east while Joseph went into hiding temporarily. During this time Joseph received instructions, now canonized as Doctrine and Covenants 127 and 128, regarding the purposes and proper procedures for performing the ordinance of baptism for the dead.

Missouri officials questioned the legality of the Nauvoo court, and two additional attempts were made to bring Joseph and Rockwell to answer charges. In December 1842, Illinois governor Thomas Ford (who succeeded Carlin) encouraged Joseph to stand trial in Springfield, assuring him the court would rule in his favor. Confident he would be acquitted, Joseph submitted. Following a four-day trial beginning 4 January 1843, Judge Nathaniel Pope ruled in favor of the Mormon leader.

In June 1843 Missouri authorities made a final attempt to secure Joseph Smith. On this occasion Governor Ford gave permission to Joseph H. Reynolds, sheriff of Jackson County, to serve a warrant for the Prophet's arrest. Reynolds and a force of more than one hundred men searched out Joseph Smith at Dixon, Illinois, and then escorted him to Nauvoo. There, through the instrumentality of his attorney, Cyrus Walker, the Prophet was once again acquitted. After the court's decision, Ford refused to allow Missouri authorities to take any further action and sent word to Governor Thomas Reynolds of Missouri that Joseph Smith had been duly tried in the Illinois courts and found not guilty.

Rockwell was not as fortunate. On 5 March 1843, while in St. Louis, he was arrested in connection with the Boggs incident. He was jailed in Missouri in Independence and in Liberty until 11 December 1843, when fifth circuit court judge Austin King finally released him.

In 1846 Boggs left Missouri and journeyed to northern California, eventually settling in Napa.

See also Missouri period.

BIBLIOGRAPHY

Baugh, Alexander L. "Missouri Governor Lilburn W. Boggs and the Mormons." *John Whitmer Historical Association Journal* 18 (1998): 111–32.

Gayler, George R. "The Attempts of the State of Missouri to Extradite Joseph Smith, 1841–1843." *Missouri Historical Review* 58 (October 1963): 21–36.

Gordon, Joseph F. "The Political Career of Lilburn W. Boggs." *Missouri Historical Review* 52 (January 1958): 111–22.

McLaws, Monte B. "The Attempted Assassination of Missouri's Ex-Governor, Lilburn W. Boggs." *Missouri Historical Review* 60 (October 1965): 50–62.

ALB

Bondage

Absence of freedom of body, mind, or spirit. In the Doctrine and Covenants, *bondage* is used in a number of contexts:

1. Bondage of sin. Those who do not come unto Christ through the promptings of the universally available "Spirit of Jesus Christ," or the LIGHT OF CHRIST, are "under the bondage of sin" (84:45–51; cf. 88:5–13; 93:31–32). They will remain under the bondage of sin until they accept the GOSPEL of Jesus Christ, repent, are baptized, and receive the Holy Ghost (39:5–10; cf. 3 Ne. 27:13–21).

2. Bondage of financial DEBT. The Lord instructed Martin Harris to "pay the debt thou hast contracted with the printer. Release thyself from bondage" (19:35; cf. 104:83–84). Harris had used part of his farm as collateral to guarantee the cost of printing the Book of Mormon. After this instruction from the Lord, Harris sold eighty acres of his farm to pay the debt.

3. Slavery. The Lord revealed, "It is not right that any man should be in bondage one to another. And for this purpose have I established the Constitution of this land [United States of America], by the hands of wise men whom I raised up unto this very purpose" (101:79–80). *See* Constitution.

4. Unjust imprisonment. To "those who swear falsely against my servants, that they might bring them into bondage and death," the Lord said, "Wo unto them; because they have offended my little ones they shall be severed from the ordinances of mine house" (121:18–19).

5. Bondage felt by spirits who have been separated from their physical bodies. The Lord reassured his original apostles, who "looked upon the long absence of [their] spirits from [their] bodies to be a bondage" (evidently anticipating an extended period of time in the postmortal spirit world after their deaths) concerning "how the day of [their] redemption shall come" (45:17; cf. 138:50).

Liberation from the bondage of sin comes by accepting Christ and his gospel. Freedom from financial bondage comes by avoiding incurring debts or by paying them if they are incurred. Freedom from imprisonment comes, for the most part, by obeying constitutional laws. Some cases of bondage, however, may occur, and they require the help of the Lord, as in the case of ancient and modern Israel (103:15–20; cf. 109:60–67). RESURRECTION releases the feeling of bondage felt by disembodied spirits (138:50–51).

See also Chains.

RCF

Book(s)

The words *book* or *books* are used in the Doctrine and Covenants in three senses: reference to books of scripture; Church records, including records of people's works; and published sources of knowledge.

1. *Book* is typically the way the Lord refers to one of the volumes of SCRIPTURE, although the Old and New Testaments are specifically referred to as the "Bible" in one verse (42:12) and as the "holy scriptures" (20:11, 35, 69; 33:16). In one verse, *book* also refers specifically to the last book of the Bible (20:35). The "book of Enoch" (107:57) is not in our present scriptural canon.

Book appears in references to the Nephite scriptures. The Lord testifies that the "Book of Mormon" was translated "by the power of God" (1:29) and the "book," therefore, is "true" (17:6). Because the Book of Mormon contains "the fulness of the gospel" (20:9; cf. 27:5) and witnesses that the Bible and latter-day revelation are true (20:11), the Saints were to teach from it (33:16; 42:12). The Lord later chastised the Saints for neglecting the Book of Mormon and the "former commandments" he had given them (the revelations; 84:54–57). Several revelations refer to the coming forth of the Book of Mormon (24:1; 27:5; 128:20). Martin Harris was to pay for the printing of this book (19:26), and faith in it was a requirement for investing in the Nauvoo House (124:119). The Lord first referred to the collection of his latter-day revelations as "the book of my commandments" (1:6), perhaps prompting the original title of the published volume (cf. 67:6). In a later revelation, the Lord referred to "the book of Doctrine and Covenants" (124:141). In his tribute to Joseph Smith, Elder John Taylor affirmed that the Prophet had sealed with his blood his testimony of these books of modern scripture (135:1–3).

2. John the Revelator saw how the dead were judged out of "the books" and that "the book of life" was also opened (Rev. 20:12). Commenting on this passage in an 1842 epistle, the Prophet Joseph Smith explained that the "books" were "the records which are kept on the earth," whereas "the book of life" was "the record which is kept in heaven" and that a thing must be recorded on earth in order to be recorded in heaven (128:6–9). In this same epistle, therefore, the Prophet gave careful instructions about keeping accurate records to be compiled in the "general church book" (128:3–4; cf. 20:82). He concluded the epistle by challenging the Saints as individuals and as a Church to prepare a book containing a worthy record of their dead (128:24). Elder Bruce R. McConkie wrote that the books from which the dead would be judged include "the Standard Works of the Church, the holy scriptures wherein the law of the Lord is recorded and the instruction given as to how men should walk in this mortal probation" (3:578).

As the Saints were attempting to establish Zion in Missouri, the Lord directed that a record of their deeds be kept in what was called "the book of the law of God" (85:1, 5). This same name had been used by Joshua for a record when the Israelites were about to enter the promised land (Josh. 24:26). "Apparently [in section 85], the terms 'book of the law of God' (vv. 5, 7), 'book of remembrance' (v. 9), and 'book of the law' (v. 11) all refer to the same record of those who have entered the covenant of consecration and are to receive inheritances in Zion" (Robinson and Garrett, 3:73; cf. 88:2).

3. *Books* also refer to a source of knowledge (55:4). Significantly, the Lord admonished care in selecting "good books" (90:15) or "the best books" (88:118).

BIBLIOGRAPHY

McConkie, Bruce R. *Doctrinal New Testament Commentary*. 3 vols. Salt Lake City: Bookcraft, 1965–73.

Robinson, Stephen E., and H. Dean Garrett. *A Commentary on the Doctrine and Covenants*. 4 vols. Salt Lake City: Deseret Book, 2000–2005.

ROC

Book of Commandments. *See* Doctrine and Covenants, historical development of.

Book of Enoch

The book of Enoch, noted once in the Doctrine and Covenants (107:57), contains the prophecy of Adam that he uttered in "the valley of Adam-ondi-Ahman" about "whatsoever should befall his posterity unto the latest generation" (107:53–56). The record may include more than Adam's prophecy, perhaps incorporating a larger record from Adam, a portion of which evidently lies in Moses 6:51–68. At a minimum, the book of Enoch likely incorporates Enoch's calling, visions, preaching, and prophesying (Moses 6:26–8:1; Jude 1:14–15). The pseudepigraphal books of Enoch (writings claiming to be from Enoch but which are not canonized) are known from antiquity and may derive from Enoch's original record, although that remains uncertain.

SKB

Book of Lehi

"An account abridged from the plates of Lehi, by the hand of Mormon" (Smith, 1:56). The book of Lehi is mentioned by name only in the headnotes to Doctrine and Covenants 3 and 10, indicating that the translation of the book of Lehi was contained in the 116 manuscript pages lost by Martin Harris. The Lord revealed that the information found on the plates of Nephi (1 Nephi, 2 Nephi, Jacob, Enos, Jarom, and Omni), covering the same time period as the book of Lehi, were "more particular concerning the things which, in my wisdom, I would bring to the knowledge of the people" than what was written in Mormon's abridgement of the plates of Lehi (10:40).

See also Book of Mormon, lost manuscript of (116 pages); Doctrine and Covenants, what it says about the Book of Mormon; Plates.

BIBLIOGRAPHY

Smith, Joseph. *History of The Church of Jesus Christ of Latter-day Saints.* Edited by B. H. Roberts. 7 vols. 2d ed. rev. Salt Lake City: The Church of Jesus Christ of Latter-day Saints, 1932–51.

CJW

Book of Life. *See* Book(s).

Book of Mormon. *See* Doctrine and Covenants, what it says about the Book of Mormon.

Book of Mormon, lost manuscript (116 pages) of

The loss of the first 116 pages of the Book of Mormon manuscript occurred during the time in which Martin Harris served as scribe for Joseph Smith. Beginning around 12 April 1828, Harris worked as scribe at Harmony (now Oakdale), Pennsylvania, until 14 June of the same year, during which time the first 116 pages of manuscript, containing the book of Lehi, were translated. At some point during this two-month period, Harris began asking Joseph if he could take home to Palmyra, New York, the manuscript to show to a few others, including his wife. Joseph inquired through the URIM AND THUMMIM and was told no. Because of continued family pressure, Harris requested a second time and received the same response. After the third query, the answer was yes but with conditions. Harris was not to show the manuscript to anyone other than his wife, Lucy; his brother Preserved; his mother and father; and Polly Cobb, his wife's sister. Joseph was responsible for the safety of the manuscript. Joseph and Martin entered into a covenant concerning the custody of the manuscript, and Harris left for Palmyra on Saturday, 14 June.

The next day, Joseph's wife, Emma, gave birth to a baby boy they named Alvin, but he died the same day. Emma had a difficult recovery, and for the next two weeks Joseph's attention was on his wife's health. During that time he heard nothing from Harris, causing him to worry about the manuscript. It appears Joseph still trusted his friend, but Emma finally convinced him to travel to Palmyra to check on the manuscript. The trip most likely occurred during the first week of July 1828 and was about 135 miles, at least two days' travel by stage. Upon his arrival at his parents' home, Joseph immediately sent for Harris. Though expected in the morning, Harris approached the Smith home shortly after noon, "walking with a slow and measured tread . . . , his eyes fixed thoughtfully upon the ground" (Smith, 164). After they sat down to eat, Martin cried out, "Oh! I have lost my soul. I have lost my soul." Upon hearing this and obviously knowing the answer, Joseph asked, "Oh! Martin, have you lost that manuscript?" (Smith, 164–65).

What happened to the manuscript pages is unknown. In her account, Joseph's mother stated that Harris had shown it to many others besides those to whom God had expressly given him permission to show it. She suggested that Mrs. Harris eventually stole the manuscript to discredit the Book of Mormon at a later date; Lucy Harris never admitted to doing so, however. Interestingly, though obviously concerned with God's response, according to his mother, Joseph's thoughts went to his wife and her fragile health: "'Then must I,' said Joseph, 'return to my wife with such a tale as this? I dare not do it lest I should kill her at once'" (Smith, 166). Joseph left the next morning, probably 4 or 5 July, Friday or Saturday, respectively, to return home to Harmony.

The consequences were, understandably, severe. Two sections of the Doctrine and Covenants discuss the event. Section 3 was received upon Joseph's return to Harmony in July 1828. In the revelation Joseph was rebuked for his failure to follow the Lord's instructions because he feared man more than God. He was told, "Although men set at naught the counsels of God, and despise his words—yet you should have been faithful" (3:7–8). He was warned that if he did not repent, he would lose completely the opportunity to translate the Book of Mormon. As it was, both the PLATES and the Urim and Thummim were taken from the Prophet, though he was promised that if he repented he could receive again the two items, which he did on 22 September 1828. Later, the revelation now recorded in section 10 was received. It outlined the devil's plan for the manuscript and instructed Joseph not to retranslate the missing portion. A summary of the information in section 10 was included as part of a note to the reader at the beginning of the original Book of Mormon publication.

Though this event was certainly traumatic for the young prophet, the Lord himself makes it clear that the eventual publication of the Book of Mormon was never in jeopardy. In section 3,

when he rebuked Joseph, the Lord stated, "Nevertheless, my work shall go forth, . . . even so shall the knowledge of a Savior come unto my people—and to the Nephites, and the Jacobites, and the Josephites, and the Zoramites, through the testimony of their fathers" (3:16–17). Later, in section 10, the Lord declared, "Verily, I say unto you, that I will not suffer that Satan shall accomplish his evil design in this thing. . . . I will not suffer that they shall destroy my work" (10:14, 43). Thus, the effect that it had on the Restoration was negligible, but its effect on the Prophet was immense. Both Joseph Smith and Martin Harris apparently learned their lesson: the Prophet repented and received again the gift to translate (10:3); Harris, for his part, also repented and was later chosen to be one of the special Three Witnesses of the Book of Mormon.

See also Book of Lehi; Doctrine and Covenants, what it says about the Book of Mormon; Historical context and overview of Doctrine and Covenants 3 (p. 716), 5 (p. 717), and 10 (p. 720).

BIBLIOGRAPHY

Smith, Lucy Mack. *The Revised and Enhanced History of Joseph Smith by His Mother.* Edited by Scot Facer Proctor and Maurine Jensen Proctor. Salt Lake City: Bookcraft, 1996.

DLB

Book of Remembrance. *See* Book(s).

Book of the Law of God. *See* Book(s).

Book of the Names of the Sanctified. *See* Book(s).

Books, judged out of. *See* Judgment(s).

Booth, Ezra

Birth: 14 February 1792, Newton, Fairfield County, Connecticut

Death: January 1873, Cuyahoga Falls, Summit County, Ohio

Ezra Booth and his family resided at Nelson, Ohio, until 1835, when they moved a few miles to Mantua, where they lived for more than thirty years. Booth and his wife, Dorcas, had only one child, Almeda Ann. Almeda never married and was a faculty member of Hiram College. She died on 15 December 1875. Her close friend and fellow faculty member, James A. Garfield, future president of the United States, delivered an extensive summary of her life on 22 June 1876 at Hiram College. In his discourse, Garfield reminisced about Almeda's father, Ezra Booth: "He was a man of more than ordinary powers of mind,—gentle, affectionate, impressible, and deeply religious. His early intellectual training did not go beyond the rudiments taught in the common schools of Connecticut; but he was an inveterate reader of books, and the armful of choice volumes that lay on the shelves of his little library was probably a greater number than could have been found in one house out of every thousand on the Reserve. Possessed of slender means, he adopted a profession which rendered the acquirement of wealth well nigh impossible. He early entered the ministry of the Methodist Episcopal Church, and was assigned to a circuit of nearly a thousand miles, embracing in its range the township of Nelson; and there, in 1819, he married Dorcas Taylor, and fixed his home. Soon after entering the ministry, he sent eleven silver dollars to England to purchase a Greek lexicon; and he so far mastered the language as to read the Greek Testament with ease. He used to say that, in the early days of his ministry, he and a Mr. Charles Elliott were the only Methodist preachers west of the Alleghanies who were able to read Greek" (294–95).

Ezra Booth is first named as a circuit preacher in Methodist records in 1816. He labored until 1824 in the Erie Circuit, which extended from Lake Erie to the Allegheny and Ohio Rivers. During that time, the Erie Circuit contained twenty appointments, requiring a minister to travel four hundred miles every four weeks to fill them. Having married in 1819 and with a baby less than a month old, Booth evidently located at Nelson, Ohio, in 1824, for his name does not appear in the records as a circuit preacher after that.

Marinda Johnson Hyde, daughter of John and Ilsa Johnson, recorded: "In the winter of 1831, Ezra Booth, a Methodist minister, procured a copy of the Book of Mormon and brought it to my father's house. They sat up all night reading it, and were very much exercised over it. As soon as they heard that Joseph Smith had arrived in Kirtland, Mr. Booth and wife and my father and mother went immediately to see him. They were convinced and baptized before they returned. They invited the prophet and Elder Rigdon to accompany them home, which they did, and preached several times to crowded congregations, baptizing quite a number" (Tullidge, 403–4). Luke Johnson, Marinda's brother, observed that during their first visit with the Prophet his "mother had been laboring under an attack of chronic rheumatism in the shoulder, so that she could not raise her hand to her head for about two years; [and] the Prophet laid hands upon her, and she was healed immediately" (Johnson, 834). Experiencing this miracle gave further reason for all of them to be baptized.

By June 1831 Booth had been ordained a high priest and called by revelation to travel with Isaac Morley (his missionary companion) and several others to Missouri to hold the next conference of the Church (52:23). Some events during this journey were disagreeable to Booth, and by the time he returned to Ohio in early September, he no longer desired to continue as a member of the Church. But Ezra Booth was not without fault in the matter; his own actions during the summer had angered the Lord (64:15–16). At a conference held at Nelson, Ohio, on 6 September 1831, "upon testimony satisfactory to this conference it was voted that Ezra Booth be silenced from preaching as an Elder in this Church" (Cannon and Cook, 12). Later that same month, Booth and Symonds Ryder, another disgruntled Church member, formally renounced Mormonism at a camp meeting at Shalersville, Ohio ("Renunciation," 3).

Between 12 September and 6 December 1831, Ezra Booth sent a series of nine letters to a fellow Methodist minister, Ira Eddy, denouncing the Church and the Prophet Joseph Smith. These letters were widely published and became the first extensive anti-Mormon literature in print. The adverse influence of these letters was such that the Lord instructed Joseph Smith and Sidney Rigdon to preach in the areas nearby and "confound your enemies; call upon them to meet you both in public and in private; and inasmuch as ye are faithful their shame shall be made manifest" (71:7). They began their preaching mission on 3 December 1831 and formally ended it during the second week of the following January.

Booth's short time as a member of the Church was not the only instance of his pursuing spiritual fulfillment outside of Methodism. James A. Garfield said of him that his "enthusiastic temperament led him to study any new phases of religious opinion, with a somewhat impressible credulity. The Mormon movement of 1830–32 swept him for a time into its turbulent current; ten or fifteen years later, he was interested in the socialistic theories of the Shakers, with whom, as I understand, he united for a short time; later still, he paid much attention to the Spiritualistic philosophy" (317).

Toward the end of 1865, Ezra Booth and his wife, Dorcas, had become "old and feeble" and needed care. Their daughter, Almeda, gave up her teaching position at Hiram College to tend to their needs. Ezra "had so far failed in body and mind as to need those tender personal services which none but she could render" (Garfield, 311). She moved her parents to Cuyahoga Falls, Summit County, Ohio, and cared for them there. Ezra Booth rallied for a short time but died in early January 1873 and is buried in the Oakwood Cemetery at Cuyahoga Falls. The Oakwood cemetery records have 12 January 1873 as the date of his burial. The only words still discernible on his tombstone are his name. Almeda moved to Cleveland in November 1875 and died there a month later on 15 December 1875. Dorcas outlived both her husband and daughter and passed away 9 September 1887 at the age of eighty-seven. Dorcas and Almeda are buried next to Ezra in the Oakwood Cemetery.

BIBLIOGRAPHY

Burial Records for Oakwood Cemetery, Cuyahoga Falls Historical Society, Cuyahoga Falls, Ohio.

Cannon, Donald Q., and Lyndon W. Cook, eds. *Far West Record: Minutes of The Church of Jesus Christ of Latter-day Saints, 1830–1844.* Salt Lake City: Deseret Book, 1983.

Garfield, James A. *The Works of James Abram Garfield.* Vol. 2. Edited by Burke A. Hinsdale. Boston: James R. Osgood & Co., 1883.

Johnson, Luke. "History of Luke Johnson." *The Latter-day Saints' Millennial Star* 26 (1864): 834–36; 27 (1865): 5–7.

"Renunciation of Mormonism." *[Hudson, Ohio] Observer and Telegraph,* 29 September 1831, [3].

Tullidge, Edward W. *Women of Mormondom.* New York: Tullidge & Crandall, 1877.

RJW

Borders of the Lamanites

In the 1830s the line dividing Missouri from Indian territory to the west. In September 1830, section 28 revealed that the city of Zion would be built "on the borders by the Lamanites" (28:9). In June 1831 the Lord commanded Saints migrating from Colesville, New York, to Ohio to continue their journey "into the regions westward, unto the land of Missouri, unto the borders of the Lamanites" (54:8). *See* Lamanites.

After a heated debate, the United States Congress had passed the Indian Removal Act just a few weeks before the Church was organized in April 1830, and President Andrew Jackson signed it into law in May. The new law empowered the president to trade land west of the Mississippi River, but not then part of any state, with Native American nations for their land within the states. The law further empowered the president to relocate Native Americans to the western lands. The Indian Removal Act of 1830 thus led to the creation of Indian Territory west of Missouri in what is now Kansas and Oklahoma. The Lord referred to the border between this land and the state of Missouri. Moreover, Jackson County, Missouri, in which the Lord located "the place for the city of Zion" centered in Independence, shared a western border with Missouri and thus with Indian Territory, or "the borders of the Lamanites" (57:2; 54:8).

SCH

Born of me

A phrase, used once in the Doctrine and Covenants (5:16), referring to being spiritually born again and becoming by regeneration and adoption the sons and daughters of Jesus Christ (Mosiah 5:7). Because of the Fall, all men and women are lost and fallen and hardened (Alma

34:9; cf. 1 Ne. 10:4–6), subject to spiritual death, living without God in the world (Alma 41:11). Being spiritually born again reverses those conditions. In March 1829, just before the restoration of the Aaronic and Melchizedek priesthoods and the Church of Jesus Christ, the Lord proclaimed, "Whosoever believeth on my words, them will I visit with the manifestation of my Spirit; and they shall be born of me, even of water and of the Spirit" (5:16). All who are baptized by water and the Spirit by one authorized to perform these ordinances take upon themselves the name of Jesus Christ by covenant, being thus born of him and becoming his sons and daughters.

See also Baptism by water; Baptism of fire and the Holy Ghost.

RLM

Boston. *See* Albany, Boston, and New York City.

Box (box-tree). *See* Appendix E.

Boynton, John F.

Birth: 20 September 1811, Bradford, Essex County, Massachusetts

Death: 20 October 1890, Syracuse, Onondaga County, New York

John Farnham Boynton was schooled in New York City during his teens and had entered medical school in St. Louis by age twenty. His scholastic achievements surpassed those of many of his contemporaries. His acceptance of baptism by the Prophet Joseph Smith went against conventional norms. By age twenty-one, Boynton was ordained an elder and served his first mission in the eastern states and Canada.

On 15 February 1835 he was ordained an apostle. The name of John F. Boynton appears with the "Testimony of the Twelve Apostles to the Truth of the Book of Doctrine and Covenants" (Explanatory Introduction). In that testimony, the Twelve affirmed that the revelations and commandments in the Doctrine and Covenants were "given by inspiration of God, and are profitable for all men and are verily true." *See* Doctrine and Covenants, testimony of the Twelve Apostles to the truth of.

After Boynton's ordination to the Twelve, his enthusiasm for the latter-day work was evident as he labored again in the eastern states. In 1837, however, when Boynton entered into a scheme of trafficking merchandise for quick wealth, he lost the Spirit of the Lord. Heber C. Kimball recorded, "Two of the Twelve, Lyman E. Johnson and John F. Boynton, went to New York and purchased the amount of $20,000 worth of goods, and entered into the mercantile business, borrowing considerable money" (Whitney, 99). Failure of the Kirtland Safety Society served as Boynton's excuse for failure to repay his debts.

Dubbing himself a "reformer" and claiming Joseph Smith was a fallen prophet, Boynton and other dissidents claimed ownership of the Kirtland Temple. Armed with a pistol and a bowie knife, Boynton entered the temple to press his claim, but help was called, and he and the others were removed from the temple. In December 1837 he was expelled from the Twelve and excommunicated on 12 April 1838.

Boynton did not return to Church activity. He established himself as a respected farmer and

John F. Boynton, 1811–1890; portrait by Lynne Millman-Weidinger.

a renowned scientist in Syracuse, New York. He invented a fluid and light apparatus for extinguishing small fires, a soda fountain, a method for extracting gold from ore by a vacuum process, electrical appliances, a process for converting cast iron into malleable steel, and a method for coloring buttons and glassware. He had over thirty patents to his name.

A. H. Hale wrote about Boynton's later life: "Since the Nauvoo days Boynton has resided in Syracuse, N. Y., where he still lives. He has always been considerate to his former friends and colaborers in the ministry, and never said or done anything against the Church." After leaving the Church, Boynton never "joined himself to any other denomination and does not believe in any religion whatever. He says, however, that if anything is right, 'Mormonism' is" (Jenson, 53–54). Boynton died at age seventy-nine at his home. Those at his bedside said he was "not depressed at the thought of death and with his characteristic zeal in the cause of science he expressed a willingness to have his body examined before the students of the Medical college to determine the cause of death" ("Boynton," 1–2).

See also Apostasy, of early dissenters from restored Church; Apostles, the first Twelve of latter days.

BIBLIOGRAPHY

Jenson, Andrew. "The Twelve Apostles." *The Historical Record* 5, no. 4 (April 1886): 49–54.

"John Farnham Boynton: Death of This Brilliant and Versatile Man." *Syracuse [New York] Evening Herald* 14 (20 October 1890): 2.

Whitney, Orson F. *Life of Heber C. Kimball.* 3d ed. Salt Lake City: Bookcraft, 1967.

SEB

Branch

A term used in scripture in different contexts and with different meanings:

1. Groups or individuals. The Lord and his prophets often compared the covenant people, the people of Israel, to an olive tree (1 Ne. 10:12; Jacob 5) or a vine (Alma 16:17). Groups or individuals are referred to as branches of the tree or the vine. The Savior used the image of "other sheep" while teaching both Jews and Nephites/Lamanites (John 10:16; 3 Ne. 15:17,

21). He again used the image in latter-day scripture, explaining that the other sheep were "a branch of the house of Jacob" (10:59–60).

2. A unit of the latter-day Church. "No person is to be ordained to any office in this church, where there is a regularly organized branch of the same, without the vote of that church" (20:65). A bishop was a common judge in "any branch of the church" where he was set apart to that ministry (107:74).

3. Ancestors and descendants. In the dedicatory prayer of the Kirtland Temple, a curse was invoked on the Saints' enemies: "May thine anger be kindled, and thine indignation fall upon them, that they may be wasted away, both root and branch, from under heaven" (109:52). The malediction of Malachi regarding the Second Coming was reissued in the revealed appendix of the Doctrine and Covenants: "For, behold, the day cometh that shall burn as an oven, and all the proud, yea, and all that do wickedly, shall be stubble; and the day that cometh shall burn them up . . . that it shall leave them neither root nor branch" (133:64)—the wicked would continue into the next life with no ancestry and no posterity, that is, no eternal family connections.

DKO

Breastplate. *See* Urim and Thummim.

Breastwork. *See* Appendix E.

Bride

Figurative expression for the restored Church of Jesus Christ used by Joseph Smith in his dedicatory prayer of the Kirtland Temple. The Prophet petitioned the Lord that the Church might "be adorned as a bride" for the day when Christ (the BRIDEGROOM) comes again (109:74).

Although there is only one reference to "bride" in the Doctrine and Covenants, there are six references to "Bridegroom." All of these references point to the second coming of the Lord and exhort hearers to prepare for the coming of the Bridegroom and become worthy to participate in the wedding celebration, including the "supper of the Lord," or "supper of the Lamb" (33:17–18; 58:7–11; 65:3; 88:92; 133:10, 19). *See* Marriage of the Lamb.

In ancient times the children of Israel,

collectively, were considered the Lord's bride, and the relationship between bride and bridegroom is frequently highlighted in the standard works of the Church (e.g., Isa. 61:10; JST Isa. 62:5; Jer. 3:1–22; Matt. 25:1–13; John 3:29; Rev. 21:2, 9).

This divinely revealed metaphor emphasizes Christ's feelings toward and his relationship with his covenant people, in addition to their obligations toward him.

See also Jesus Christ, second coming of.

ALG

Bridegroom

A symbolic title for Christ, characterizing his covenant relationship with his Church, which is referred to as the "bride" (109:73–74). This metaphorical identification of the Savior as the "Bridegroom" is used six times in the Doctrine and Covenants (33:17–18; 65:3; 88:92; 133:10, 19), always in reference to his second coming. Section 33:17–18 represents Christ as the bridegroom whose coming the "ten virgins" were to anticipate and prepare for (Matt. 25:1–13). In Hebrew culture the bride's party would await and then go out to meet the arriving bridegroom and his entourage on the night of the wedding feast. Thus, by using the symbolic titles of BRIDE and Bridegroom in anticipation of a wedding celebration, the Lord is emphasizing the need for his covenant people to anticipate and prepare for his return to the earth at his second coming. Additionally, as a groom loves, protects, and provides for his bride, Christ loves, protects and provides for his Saints. So also, just as a bride is expected to have love, fidelity, and trust in her spouse, the Church is called to exhibit these same attributes toward its Savior. As the bride and bridegroom keep their covenant responsibilities, the relationship between them becomes eternal. Such is the case between a groom and bride, and it is also true of Christ and his Church.

See also Jesus Christ, second coming of.

ALG

Broken heart and contrite spirit

An expression that first appears in Doctrine and Covenants 20:37 as an important qualification for baptism, illustrating the state of the HEART that is required of those who have truly repented and come unto Christ. Four subsequent references connect the condition of one's heart to the nature of the sacrifices that he or she makes for the gospel. For instance, in June 1831 the Lord contrasted the sacrifices of the poor who were pure in heart with the greedy poor of Thompson, Ohio, whose hearts were not broken and whose spirits were not contrite (56:17–18). More positively, in two revelations regarding the qualities and sacrifices demanded of the saved in Zion, the resurrected Jesus Christ used this phrase: "thou shalt offer a sacrifice unto the Lord thy God in righteousness, even that of a broken heart and a contrite spirit" (59:8); "all . . . who know their hearts are honest, and are broken, and their spirits contrite, and are willing to observe their covenants by sacrifice—yea, every sacrifice which I, the Lord, shall command—they are accepted of me" (97:8).

The phrases "broken heart" and "contrite spirit" appear in the King James Version of Psalm 34:18, with a variant in Psalm 51:17; both poems traditionally attributed to David. The feature of Hebrew poetry known as synonymous parallelism suggests that "contrite spirit" is a restatement of the same idea as "broken heart" (Peterson and Richards, 24–31). In this instance, "contrite" (*dk'* for "crushed") is a rarer, poetic way of expressing the more common word "broken" (*šbr,* for "shatter, smash") (Koehler and Baumgartner, 1:221; 4:1402–4). Psalm 34:18 suggests that the Lord is near to one whose pride, ambition, and haughtiness have been shattered; Psalm 51:17–19 has much in common with the critiques that later Old Testament prophets leveled against the Mosaic sacrificial system: more important than the thing offered to the Lord was the attitude and heart of the one sacrificing (Amos 5:22; Isa. 1:11; Jer. 6:20; see Kraus, 506; Thomas, 172).

For these passages from Psalms, the Greek Septuagint rendered *šbr* with a form of the verb *syntribō,* which likewise meant "smashed, crushed," but interpreted *dk'* with forms of *tapeinos* and *tapeinoō,* meaning "lowly, undistinguished" or "abase, make humble" (Bauer et al., 976, 989–90). Surprisingly, however, the expression does not appear in the Greek New Testament. Further, the English word *contrite* comes from the Latin *contero,* which returned to the original Hebrew sense of "crush, grind, or pound to pieces," making this the meaning to which readers of the Book of Mormon and the Doctrine and Covenants should look to understand the absolute destruction of pride and individual will that the Lord requires as a personal sacrifice (cf. 2 Ne. 2:7; 4:32; 3 Ne. 9:19–20; 12:19; Moro. 6:2).

Indeed, it is the voice of the Savior, who used these words in 3 Nephi, that echoes in 59:8 and 97:8, where he speaks to modern Saints about both their hearts and their sacrifices.

See also Humble, humility; Meek, meekness.

BIBLIOGRAPHY

Bauer, Walter, William F. Arndt, F. Wilbur Gingrich, and Frederick W. Danker. *A Greek-English Lexicon of the New Testament and Other Early Christian Literature.* 3d ed. Chicago: University of Chicago Press, 2000.

Koehler, Ludwig, and Walter Baumgartner. *The Hebrew and Aramaic Lexicon of the Old Testament.* 5 vols. Leiden: E. J. Brill, 1994–2000.

Kraus, Hans-Joachim. *Psalms 1–59: A Commentary.* Minneapolis: Augsburg Publishing House, 1988.

Peterson, David L., and Kent Harold Richards. *Interpreting Hebrew Poetry.* Minneapolis: Fortress Press, 1992.

Thomas, M. Catherine. "Broken Heart and Contrite Spirit." In *Book of Mormon Reference Companion,* edited by Dennis L. Largey et al., 172–73. Salt Lake City: Deseret Book, 2003.

EDH

Broome County. *See* Colesville, Broome County, New York.

Brunson, Seymour

Birth: 18 September 1799, Orwell, Addison County, Vermont

Death: 10 August 1840, Commerce, Hancock County, Illinois

Seymour Brunson was baptized into the Church in January 1831 by Solomon Hancock and ordained an elder by John Whitmer on 25 January that same year. Brunson's name occurs twice in the Doctrine and Covenants. During the Amherst, Ohio, 25 January 1832 conference, he

was commanded to serve in the "ministry" with Daniel Stanton (75:30, 33), which resulted in the baptisms of fifty-three people in Windsor, Ohio ("Progress," 100).

Brunson died on 10 August 1840 after becoming ill while herding cattle in July. The next year Joseph Smith received section 124, in which the Lord said, "Seymour Brunson I have taken unto myself; no man taketh his priesthood, but another may be appointed unto the same priesthood in his stead" (124:132). He had been appointed to the Nauvoo high council in October 1839 (Smith, 4:12) and was remembered by the Lord when a new high council was appointed in this 1841 revelation.

Of Seymour Brunson, Joseph Smith said: "He has always been a lively stone in the building of God and was much respected by his friends and acquaintances. He died in the triumph of faith, and in his dying moments bore testimony to the Gospel that he had embraced" (Smith, 4:179). Notably, it was during Brunson's funeral on 15 August 1840 that Joseph Smith first publicly taught the doctrine of baptism for the dead (Smith, 4:231; MH, 19 October 1840).

BIBLIOGRAPHY

Manuscript History of the Church, 19 October 1840. Church History Library, The Church of Jesus Christ of Latter-day Saints, Salt Lake City, Utah.

Smith, Joseph. *History of The Church of Jesus Christ of Latter-day Saints.* Edited by B. H. Roberts. 7 vols. 2d ed. rev. Salt Lake City: The Church of Jesus Christ of Latter-day Saints, 1932–51.

"The Progress of the Church of Christ." *The Evening and the Morning Star,* June 1833, 100–101.

ZLL

Buckler. *See* Appendix E.

Buffetings of Satan

The mental, emotional, spiritual, and even physical suffering for sins of those who reap the "wrath of Almighty God" on earth and/or in the spirit world (76:104–6), being "tormented with the pains of hell" (Alma 36:13). The Prophet Joseph Smith equated being delivered to the "buffetings of Satan" with being "sealed . . . unto the damnation of hell" (6:252). To buffet means to treat badly, to strike or knock again and again, or incessantly. A person delivered to the buffetings of Satan must endure the constant taunting, belittling, burning anxiety, darkness, and hopelessness inflicted by the spirit and power of the devil. Such buffeting includes fueling the flames of conscience, one's self-condemnation for sins, and fearful anticipation of God's JUDGMENT, all likened in the scriptures to a "lake which burneth with fire and brimstone" (63:17; cf. Mosiah 2:38; Alma 12:17), a FIRE that is extremely hot and uninterrupted. Those who appear cavalier and defiant in their wickedness will one day be brought to a "perfect knowledge" of their "guilt," "uncleaness," and "nakedness" (2 Ne. 9:14; Alma 11:43). When they are "brought to see . . . the glory of God, and the holiness of Jesus Christ, it will kindle a flame of unquenchable fire upon" them. They will acknowledge that all God's judgments are just (Morm. 9:1–5; Alma 12:13–15).

The Doctrine and Covenants is the only volume of scripture among the standard works of the Church that employs the term "buffetings of Satan." The idea of Satan's buffeting, however, is evident in Paul's statement in the New Testament that "there was given to me a thorn in the flesh, the messenger of Satan to buffet me" (2 Cor. 12:7). It seems in Paul's case that the buffeting was intended to keep him humble rather than to punish him for his sins, a different application from those in the Doctrine and Covenants references, where the term "buffetings of Satan" appears five times (78:12; 82:21; 104:9; 104:10; 132:26). The first four of these have to do with the consequences for any who violated sacred covenants in connection with the United Firm, sometimes referred to as the United Order, an organization that briefly owned and managed Church properties and operated under the law of CONSECRATION in Kirtland and in Missouri, 1832 to 1834. Covenant-breaking members of the Firm were to be "delivered over to the buffetings of Satan until the day of redemption" (78:12). The fifth reference (132:26) refers to those who have entered into the new and everlasting covenant of MARRIAGE and been sealed by the Holy Spirit of promise to come forth "in the first resurrection; and if it be after the first resurrection, in the next resurrection" to their exaltation, and who

then sin seriously, but do not deny the HOLY GHOST. They may "enter into their exaltation; but they shall be destroyed in the flesh, and shall be delivered unto the buffetings of Satan unto the day of redemption" (132:19–27). And that is "after severe and humble repentance!" (Smith, *Doctrines,* 2:96–97). This interpretation is in harmony with the statement of Joseph Smith that "this spirit of Elijah was manifest in the days of the apostles, in delivering certain ones to the buffetings of Satan, that they might be saved in the day of the Lord Jesus" (*History,* 6:252). The hopeful phrase "unto the day of redemption" indicates there will be an end to the buffetings, at least for all except the SONS OF PERDITION. For those suffering the buffetings of SATAN on the earth, that day of redemption can come when they exercise FAITH in Jesus Christ and his ATONEMENT, and genuine REPENTANCE. Alma explains both the suffering and the relief and commitments that come with FORGIVENESS (Alma 36:12–25). For those suffering the buffetings in the spirit world, perhaps the buffetings will end for some of them when they have paid the uttermost farthing; for others, their day of redemption will not come until "the last resurrection, until the Lord . . . shall have finished his work" (76:85; see also vv. 106–7).

The Prophet Joseph Smith spoke of being delivered over to the buffetings of Satan (e.g., 1:323–24; 2:204, 271; 3:232; 5:392). On two occasions he named individuals who were so delivered: In June 1833, Ziba Peterson was delivered (by the First Presidency of the Church) "over to the buffetings of Satan, in the name of the Lord, that he may learn not to transgress the commandments of God" (Smith, 1:367); and in December 1835, concerning a Brother Draper, the Prophet indicated, "I was constrained by the Spirit to deliver him over to the buffetings of Satan, until he should humble himself and repent of his sins, and make satisfactory confession before the Church" (2:326). In July 1839, in speaking to the apostles and some of the seventies who were about to leave on missions to Great Britain, Joseph Smith lamented that several members of the original Quorum of the Twelve Apostles had gone "wallowing through the mud and mire and darkness, Judas like, to the buffetings of Satan," and hoped the newly called brethren who replaced them would not follow that path (3:384). One of the original Twelve who was excommunicated was Lyman E. Johnson. Of his subsequent buffetings, he was quoted by Brigham Young as saying: "Brethren—I will call you brethren—I will tell you the truth. If I could believe 'Mormonism' . . . as I did when I traveled with you and preached, if I possessed the world I would give it. I would give anything, I would suffer my right hand to be cut off, if I could believe it again. Then I was full of joy and gladness. My dreams were pleasant. When I awoke in the morning my spirit was cheerful. I was happy by day and by night, full of peace and joy and thanksgiving. But now it is darkness, pain, sorrow, misery in the extreme. I have never since seen a happy moment" (19:41).

See also Hell.

BIBLIOGRAPHY

Smith, Joseph. *History of The Church of Jesus Christ of Latter-day Saints*. Edited by B. H. Roberts. 7 vols. 2d ed. rev. Salt Lake City: The Church of Jesus Christ of Latter-day Saints, 1932–51.

Smith, Joseph Fielding. *Doctrines of Salvation*. Compiled by Bruce R. McConkie. 3 vols. Salt Lake City: Bookcraft, 1954–56.

Young, Brigham. *Journal of Discourses*. 26 vols. London: Latter-day Saints' Book Depot, 1854–86.

LED

Burlington, Iowa

A city on the west side of the Mississippi River, approximately thirty miles north and west of Nauvoo (Brown et al., map 25). Burlington was referred to in a revelation when William Law was commanded to "proclaim my everlasting gospel with a loud voice . . . unto the inhabitants of Warsaw, . . . Carthage, . . . Burlington, and . . . Madison" (124:88). It is not known whether Law fulfilled the assigned mission.

BIBLIOGRAPHY

Brown, S. Kent, Donald Q. Cannon, and Richard H. Jackson, eds. *Historical Atlas of Mormonism*. New York: Simon and Schuster, 1994.

DQC

Burnett, Stephen

Birth: 1814, Ohio
Death: unknown

After Stephen Burnett's baptism in late November 1830, his confirmation brought an "outpouring of the spirit so that [his] strength was taken from [him]" (Murdock, 10). On 25 October 1831, Burnett, then only seventeen years old, was ordained a high priest by Oliver Cowdery; the next day Burnett was among those rebuked "because of their indifference to be ordained to [the] office" of "the High priesthood" (Cannon and Cook, 26). Burnett was called to "be united in the ministry" with Ruggles Eames on 25 January 1832 (75:30, 35), but two months later he was called to "go . . . into the world and preach the gospel to every creature" with Eden Smith (80:1–2). On the date of this call Eden Smith became ill and his father, John Smith, went with Burnett for a time. Burnett fulfilled his mission call with Smith but apparently did not serve with Eames.

By 1837 Burnett had grown disillusioned with Joseph Smith. He joined with Warren Parrish, Luke S. Johnson, Lyman E. Johnson, and John F. Boynton in opposing the Prophet after the failure of the Kirtland bank (Roberts, 1:404–5). In 1838 he wrote a letter to Luke Johnson, in which he recalled hearing Martin Harris say "that he [Martin] never saw the [golden] plates with his natural eyes" (Anderson, 155–56). Burnett officially left the Church in 1838.

BIBLIOGRAPHY

Anderson, Richard Lloyd. *Investigating the Book of Mormon Witnesses*. Salt Lake City: Deseret Book, 1981.

Cannon, Donald Q., and Lyndon W. Cook, eds. *Far West Record: Minutes of The Church of Jesus Christ of Latter-day Saints, 1830–1844*. Salt Lake City: Deseret Book, 1983.

Murdock, John. Journal. Typescript. L. Tom Perry Special Collections, Harold B. Lee Library, Brigham Young University, Provo, Utah.

Roberts, B. H. *A Comprehensive History of The Church of Jesus Christ of Latter-day Saints, Century One*. 6 vols. Salt Lake City: The Church of Jesus Christ of Latter-day Saints, 1930. Reprint, Provo, Utah: Brigham Young University Press, 1965.

ZLL

Burroughs, Philip

Birth: 1801, New Jersey

Death: Between 1860 and 1870, Portage, Livingston County, New York

In a revelation received on September 1830, the Lord directed John Whitmer to "proclaim my gospel . . . at [his] brother Philip Burroughs', and in that region round about" (30:9–10). It is not known whether John Whitmer preached to Burroughs, but it is clear that during the same month the revelation was given, Parley P. Pratt addressed a congregation gathered in the Burroughs's home. He recalled: "The Holy Ghost came upon me mightily. I spoke the word of God with power, reasoning out of the Scriptures and the Book of Mormon. The people were convinced, overwhelmed in tears, and four heads of families came forward expressing their faith, and were baptized" (42).

Samuel Smith and Orson Hyde visited the Burroughs family in 1832 and their journal entries note Sister Burroughs's commitment to the faith as well as their attempt to convince her husband to move to Zion. It is uncertain, however, whether Philip was baptized a member of the Church (Smith; Hyde).

BIBLIOGRAPHY

Hyde, Orson. Journal, 1831–1832. Microfilm. Church History Library, The Church of Jesus Christ of Latter-day Saints, Salt Lake City, Utah.

New York Federal Census 1860.

Pratt, Parley P. *Autobiography of Parley P. Pratt*. Edited by Parley P. Pratt Jr. Salt Lake City: Deseret Book, 1985.

Smith, Samuel H. Journal, 1831–1833. Microfilm. Church History Library, The Church of Jesus Christ of Latter-day Saints, Salt Lake City, Utah.

RC

Butterfield, Josiah

Birth: 13 March 1795, Dunstable, Middlesex County, Massachusetts

Death: 3 March 1871, Watsonville, Santa Cruz County, California

Josiah Butterfield was baptized on 1 October 1833 in Maine. He moved to Kirtland, Ohio, in about 1834, worked on the Kirtland Temple, and attended the dedication in 1836. In 1838, he helped lead the Kirtland Camp to Missouri, afterwards settling in Daviess County. When he was driven from Missouri with the rest of the Saints, he moved to Nauvoo, Illinois. Butterfield's name appears in section 124 as one of the presidents of the seventy in Nauvoo (124:138), which by January 1841 had been established as Church headquarters. Butterfield's service in the quorum ended with his excommunication in 1844 "for neglect of duty and for other causes" (Jenson 1:192). Joseph Smith once wrote that Butterfield "insulted me so outrageously that I kicked him out of the house, across the yard, and into the street" (5:316). Butterfield was later rebaptized and received his temple endowment in the Nauvoo Temple in January 1846. He did not go west with the Saints, electing to remain in the Midwest until the early 1850s. By 1853 he had moved to California, where he was baptized into the Reorganized Church of Jesus Christ of Latter Day Saints on 1 May 1865 (Black, *Early*, 1:784–85). Nonetheless, "several years after his excommunication his nephew, Thomas Butterfield, heard him explain to relatives in the Salt Lake Valley that his faith in Mormonism was as strong as ever" (Black, *Who's Who*, 45).

BIBLIOGRAPHY

Black, Susan Easton. *Early Members of the Reorganized Church of Jesus Christ of Latter Day Saints*. 6 vols. Provo, Utah: Religious Studies Center, Brigham Young University, 1993.

———. *Who's Who in the Doctrine and Covenants*. Salt Lake City: Bookcraft, 1997.

Jenson, Andrew. *Latter-day Saints' Biographical Encyclopedia*. 4 vols. Salt Lake City: The Andrew Jenson History Company, 1901–36. Reprint, Salt Lake City: Western Epics, 1971.

Smith, Joseph. *History of The Church of Jesus Christ of Latter-day Saints*. Edited by B. H. Roberts. 7 vols. 2d ed. rev. Salt Lake City: The Church of Jesus Christ of Latter-day Saints, 1932–51.

ZLL

But behold, I say unto you, that little **children** are re-deemed from the foundation of the world through mine Only Begotten, wherefore, they cannot sin, for power is not given unto Satan to tempt little children, until they begin to become accountable before me. 29:46–47

Caesar

Title of Roman emperors; used in the Doctrine and Covenants to represent the civil law. While explaining that the land of Zion (Jackson County) must be properly acquired by purchase in order to avoid legal entanglements with the other residents, the Lord described the appropriate course with his ancient biblical teaching to "render unto Caesar the things which are Caesar's" (63:26; cf. Matt. 22:21; Luke 20:25). God recognizes that the laws and conventions of civil governments, here represented by "Caesar," should be honored, thereby establishing the Saints as law-abiding citizens.

DKO

Cahoon, Reynolds

Birth: 30 April 1790, Cambridge, Washington County, New York

Death: 29 April 1861, South Cottonwood, Salt Lake County, Utah

Reynolds Cahoon was baptized on 12 October 1830 after accepting the message taught by the four missionaries who had been sent to preach to the Lamanites. In June 1831 the Lord called Cahoon to travel with Samuel Smith as a missionary to Missouri (52:30). Six days after the revelation, they left Kirtland and preached from town to town. They arrived in Independence, Missouri, on 4 August 1831. During this time, Joseph Smith received a revelation in which Cahoon and Samuel Smith were told to "be not separated until they return to their homes" (61:35). They were obedient to this counsel. During their journey home, they discovered many who were intrigued by the Book of Mormon and wanted to hear them preach. As a result, they performed several baptisms before arriving home on 28 September 1831.

Cahoon was later called to serve on the Kirtland Temple building committee, along with Jared Carter and Hyrum Smith (94:13–15). On 1 June 1833, the three men issued a circular, urging the Saints to help "bring about the fulfillment of the command of the Lord concerning the establishing, or preparing a house, wherein the Elders, who have been commanded of the Lord so to do, may gather themselves together, and prepare all things, and call a solemn assembly, and treasure up words of wisdom, that they may go forth to the Gentiles for the last time" (Smith, 1:349).

Elder George Reynolds reported that "while residing in Kirtland Elder Reynolds Cahoon had a son born to him. One day when President Joseph Smith was passing his door he called the Prophet in and asked him to bless and name the baby. Joseph did so and gave the boy the name of Mahonri Moriancumer. When he had finished the blessing he laid the child on the bed, and turning to Elder Cahoon he said, the name I have given your son is the name of the brother of Jared; the Lord has just shown [or revealed] it to me. . . . This was the first time the name of the brother of Jared was known in the Church in this dispensation" (JI, 282; brackets in original).

Reynolds Cahoon moved to Missouri in 1838 and served as a counselor in the stake presidency at Adam-ondi-Ahman. Expelled from Missouri with the other Saints in 1839, he moved to Lee County, Iowa, across the river from Nauvoo. He served on the building committees for the Mansion House, the Nauvoo House, and the Nauvoo Temple. He went west and arrived in the Salt Lake Valley in September 1848. There he served as a "supervisor of road repair, manager of the Church farm, superintendent of the armory construction, and sergeant-at-arms of the Utah territorial legislature" (Black, 48).

BIBLIOGRAPHY

Black, Susan Easton. *Who's Who in the Doctrine and Covenants*. Salt Lake City: Deseret Book, 1997.

Cahoon, Reynolds. Diaries, 1831–1832. Church History Library, The Church of Jesus Christ of Latter-day Saints, Salt Lake City, Utah.

Reynolds, George. "The Jaredites." *Juvenile Instructor* 27 (May 1, 1892): 282–85.

Smith, Joseph. *History of The Church of Jesus Christ of Latter-day Saints*. Edited by B. H. Roberts. 7 vols. 2d ed. rev. Salt Lake City: The Church of Jesus Christ of Latter-day Saints, 1932–51.

RC

Cain

Son of Adam and Eve who murdered his younger brother Abel. Cain is mentioned by name once in the Doctrine and Covenants relative to his unacceptable sacrifice (124:75). Abel's murder is described as a "conspiracy of his brother" (84:16), which by definition means a secret planning and action for an unlawful purpose; that is, Satan and Cain plotted the death of Abel for material gain, and they did it by a secret combination of oaths and promises (Moses 5:29–33). *See* Secret Combinations.

Cain's sacrificial offering was not acceptable because it was done without faith in the atonement of Christ (Smith, 2:15–16) and was not performed in the proper manner, which required the shedding of blood. Cain had been ordained to the priesthood and knew the right way to offer sacrifice, but he willfully rebelled (Smith, 4:208–9).

BIBLIOGRAPHY

Smith, Joseph. *History of The Church of Jesus Christ of Latter-day Saints.* Edited by B. H. Roberts. 7 vols. 2d ed. rev. Salt Lake City: The Church of Jesus Christ of Latter-day Saints, 1932–51.

RJM

Cainan

HIGH PRIEST, an ordained PATRIARCH, and a great-grandson of Adam; he lived 910 years (Moses 6:10–19). Little is said of Cainan in the Bible (Gen. 5:9–14). In the Doctrine and Covenants, however, a revelation specifying the lineal descent of the patriarchal order of the priesthood, provides a few details concerning him. When Cainan was forty years old, God "called upon [him]" in the wilderness, and he, Cainan, met Adam while journeying to the place called Shedolamak. The significance of the meeting and the place is unknown. Cainan was ordained in the patriarchal order of the priesthood, presumably by Adam, at age eighty-seven (107:39–52).

Cainan was present when seven generations of patriarchs and the "residue of [Adam's] posterity who were righteous" met at ADAM-ONDI-AHMAN, three years before the death of Adam. In that gathering Adam bestowed his last blessing upon those present. The Lord appeared, "and they rose up and blessed Adam, and called him Michael, the prince, the archangel" (107:53–54).

RJM

Calamity. *See* Disasters, calamities; Appendix E.

Caleb

Melchizedek Priesthood bearer who lived between the time of Abraham (ca. 2000 B.C.) and Moses (ca. 1260 B.C.). In modern revelation, Caleb was identified in Moses' priesthood lineage: Caleb received the priesthood "under the hand of Elihu," and ordained Jethro, father-in-law to Moses (84:7–8). Nothing more is known of him. He is not to be confused with the Caleb of the Old Testament books of Numbers, Deuteronomy, Joshua, and Judges.

RJM

Call, calling

To invite, request, or ask, and also to be chosen or selected, to perform a duty. God's children are to "call upon [him] in mighty prayer" (29:2; cf. 20:76; 24:5; 39:10, 16; 75:10; 133:40; 136:32). His Saints are "called to bring to pass the gathering of [God's] elect" (29:7) and to "call upon the nations to repent" (43:20). The Lord laments when his children reject a call from his servants to repent and gather to him: "How oft have I called upon you by the mouth of my servants . . . and would have saved you with an everlasting salvation, but ye would not!" (43:25).

All persons are called or invited to come unto Christ and his Church. This call or calling does not require specific PRIESTHOOD authorization. Those with a desire to be witnesses of Jesus Christ are "called to the work" (4:3; 12:4; 14:4). In the latter days, in "the dispensation of the fulness of times" (112:30), the coming forth of the Book of Mormon is evidence that God calls men "to his holy work in this age and generation, as well as in generations of old" (20:9–11).

More formally, individuals are called to perform an official duty at a ward, stake, or general level in priesthood or auxiliary programs. When members are asked to perform such duties, they are called of God. The Church is administered by individual volunteers who are asked by inspired Church leaders to work in various assignments for an indefinite time. Those "called to the work of the ministry in all their several callings and offices" (97:13) are called through an orderly selection process. Referring to this meaning of *called,* the Doctrine and Covenants instructs, "You need not suppose that you are called to preach until you are called" (11:15).

As it relates to priesthood, *call* also refers to the selection of worthy male Church members age twelve and older to receive the Aaronic and later the Melchizedek Priesthood and subsequent ordinations to priesthood offices (20:60; 18:32). Responsibilities associated with a certain office are assigned after a calling, setting apart, and ordination (107:17; 68:19). Great blessings are promised to priesthood holders who magnify their callings (84:33; cf. 88:80).

Unfortunately, some individuals reject calls. The scripture "Behold, there are many called, but few are chosen" (121:34; cf. 95:5) suggests that many were foreordained in the premortal life to priesthood office, who felt the call or desire to serve, but then chose not to continue.

MJW

Calling and election made sure. *See* More sure word of prophecy.

Camp of Israel, camp of the Lord

Eighteen months after the death of Joseph Smith Jr., the Latter-day Saints began their exodus westward from Nauvoo, Illinois, in early February 1846 to some yet undetermined valley in the Rocky Mountains. Under the direction of Brigham Young, the vanguard "Company of the Twelve [Apostles]" or "Camp of Israel," consisting of 2,500 of the city's best prepared residents, crossed over the Mississippi River in the hope of reaching the Missouri River by mid-April. From there a small "pioneer company" or "pioneer Camp of Israel" would set out to find a suitable location "far away in the West." Inclement weather and organizational difficulties so impeded their progress that they had to establish "way stations," or farms, first at Garden Grove and later at Mt. Pisgah, Iowa Territory, to sustain both themselves and those several thousands following after them. Consequently, they did not reach Council Bluffs until mid-June, too late to make a start for the Rockies that year. With the permission of the United States government, which had asked for a Mormon Battalion of five hundred of their best men to fight in the Mexican War, President Young established their "Winter Quarters" on the west side of the Missouri River in what is today Florence, Nebraska, so as to provide for departure for the West in the early spring. Meanwhile, the rest of the Saints had begun leaving Nauvoo in May 1846 and continued to do so throughout the summer. By year's end, about 7,500 Mormons were settling in on both sides of the Missouri River with another 5,000 to 6,000 scattered across Iowa.

The Saints chose the term "Camp of Israel" in deliberate reference to the biblical Exodus, or "camp of Israel" (Ex. 14:19), that fled from Egypt into the wilderness. Believing themselves to be modern Israel and that they, too, would find their place if they followed their God, the Mormon exodus was unlike any other American migration before or since. It was a large-scale movement of a church and people, with their wagons, animals, and livelihoods, in search of a place where they could live and worship in peace. Although "Camp of Israel" described the headquarters of the leaders of the Church while in transit westward, the term was loosely applied to all the settlements and way stations they established by the winter of 1846–47. Hence, "The Word and Will of the Lord," though given at Winter Quarters, was addressed to the "Camp of Israel in their journeyings to the West" (136:1); in other words, it was given to all the scattered settlements of the Church on the move west, including those at the Missouri River, along the Iowa Mormon trail, and even to other smaller groups found along the Mississippi as far south as St. Louis. *See* map, p. 857.

See also Historical context and overview of Doctrine and Covenants 136 (p. 856).

BIBLIOGRAPHY

Bennett, Richard E. *Mormons at the Missouri, 1846–52: "And Should We Die."* Norman: University of Oklahoma Press, 1987.

Journal History of the Church, 2 February 1846–31 December 1847. Church History Library, The Church of Jesus Christ of Latter-day Saints, Salt Lake City, Utah.

Kimball, Heber C. Journals, 7 June 1846. Church History Library, The Church of Jesus Christ of Latter-day Saints, Salt Lake City, Utah.

On the Mormon Frontier: The Diary of Hosea Stout, 1844–1861, 1:142, entry of 23 March 1846. Edited by Juanita Brooks. 2 vols. Salt Lake City: University of Utah Press and Utah State Historical Society, 1982.

Pratt, Orson. *The Orson Pratt Journals,* 7 April 1847, 375–76. Edited by Elden J. Watson. Salt Lake City: E. J. Watson, 1975.

Young, Brigham. Manuscript History of Brigham Young. Church History Library, The Church of Jesus Christ of Latter-day Saints, Salt Lake City, Utah.

REB

Capital punishment

Penalty of death inflicted on a murderer. God's law in ancient times required that a murderer be executed: "Whoso sheddeth man's blood, by man shall his blood be shed" (Gen. 9:6). The Lord said to Moses, "He that killeth any man shall surely be put to death" (Lev. 24:17). *See* Murder, murderers.

A latter-day revelation known as the law of the Church reiterates the old law: "Thou shalt not kill; but he that killeth shall die" (42:19). Unlike in Old Testament times, however, the modern separation of church and state precludes the Church from administering capital punishment (134:10). Therefore, the Church is instructed: "If any persons among you shall kill they shall be delivered up and dealt with according to the laws of the land; for remember that he hath no forgiveness; and it shall be proved according to the laws of the land" (42:79).

DKO

Cappadocia. *See* Asia.

Capstone. *See* Doctrine and Covenants, as capstone scripture.

Carmel. *See* Dews of Carmel.

Carnal, sensual, and devilish

Although sometimes used in the scriptures independently, the words *carnal, sensual,* and

View of the Missouri River and Council Bluffs, from an Elevation; *engraving by Frederick Hawkins Piercy, 1855.* *"The Word and Will of the Lord concerning the Camp of Israel in their journeyings to the West" was received by Brigham Young in nearby Winters Quarters, Nebraska, in January 1847 (D&C 136:1).*

Courtesy Church History Library

devilish are usually linked together to describe the characteristics and disposition of fallen mankind—lustful, worldly, wicked, and contrary to God and his ways. The Doctrine and Covenants teaches that by reason of the fall of Adam, "man became sensual and devilish, and became fallen man" (20:20), and that one cannot comprehend God, see him, or abide his presence in such a fallen state (67:10–12). Joseph Smith was told, upon the loss of the 116 pages of the Book of Mormon manuscript, that one who "boasts in his own strength, and sets at naught the counsels of God, and follows after the dictates of his own will and carnal desires . . . must fall and incur the vengeance of a just God upon him" (3:4).

One who is "carnal, sensual, and devilish" (Alma 42:10) is a fallen man, or as the Book of Mormon teaches, a "natural man," who is "an enemy to God" (Mosiah 3:19), who is "without God in the world," and whose desires and deeds are "contrary to the nature of God" (Alma 41:11). As the Book of Mormon extensively teaches, only through faith in the Lord Jesus Christ and obedience to the ordinances and principles of the GOSPEL are people "changed from their carnal and fallen state, to a state of righteousness" (Mosiah 27:25–26), wherein they "have no more disposition to do evil, but to do good continually" (Mosiah 5:2).

The Doctrine and Covenants affirms that God's "commandments are spiritual; they are not natural nor temporal, neither carnal nor sensual" (29:35). Nonetheless, the Lord indicates that the law of Moses, given to the ancient Israelites, constitutes a "law of carnal commandments" (84:27). In this instance *carnal* means earthly, temporal, having to do with daily life: "a very strict law . . . a law of performances and of ordinances, a law which they were to observe strictly from day to day, to keep them in remembrance of God and their duty towards him" (Mosiah 13:29–30). *See* Law of carnal commandments.

See also Fall of Adam and Eve, the.

BLT

Carter, Gideon

Birth: 1798, Killingworth, Middlesex County, Connecticut

Death: 25 October 1838, Crooked River, Missouri

Gideon Hayden Carter was a faithful member of the kingdom from the time of his baptism by Joseph Smith in Orange, Ohio, on 25 October 1831, until seven years later, when he became one of the first martyrs of the Church in 1838. On the day of his baptism by Oliver Cowdery, Carter was ordained a priest and three months later, in January 1832, was ordained an elder. In a revelation given at Amherst, Ohio, dated 25 January 1832, Carter was called to serve a mission with Sylvester Smith (75:34). They were instructed to "ask and they shall receive, knock and it shall be opened unto them, and be made known from on high, even by the Comforter, whither they shall go" (75:27). Their brief mission included work in Pennsylvania, New York, and Vermont.

After his missionary service, Carter joined the Saints in Kirtland, where he served on the high council. In 1838, he moved to Far West, Missouri, with his family. When he learned of mob activity against the Saints, he took up arms with other brethren at the Battle of Crooked River and was killed in the fighting.

KWF

Carter, Jared

Birth: 14 June 1801, Killingworth, Middlesex County, Connecticut

Death: 6 July 1849, DeKalb, DeKalb County, Illinois

At age twenty-nine, Jared Carter was converted to the Church through reading the Book of Mormon. After being baptized by Hyrum Smith, Carter testified, "I felt the influence of the spirit of God, for as I stepped out of the water I was wrapped in the spirit, both soul and body" (1). Some of Carter's early Church activities are chronicled in the revelations recorded in the Doctrine and Covenants. In June 1831 the Lord instructed that Carter be ordained a priest (52:38). By September 1831 he had been ordained an elder and left to serve a mission to the East. In March 1832, Carter was told that he "should go again into the eastern countries [eastern states, where he had lived in Benson, Vermont], from place to place . . . in the power of [his] ordination . . . proclaiming glad tidings of great joy, even the everlasting gospel." After promising him success and the enlightenment of the Holy Ghost in his missionary labors, the Lord admonished: "Let your heart be glad, my servant Jared Carter, and fear not, saith your Lord, even Jesus Christ" (79:1–4). Carter's missionary labors in New York, Ohio, Pennsylvania, Vermont, and Michigan between 1831 and 1834 proved successful: seventy-nine people were baptized.

In 1833 Carter was appointed to serve on the building committee to oversee construction of the Kirtland Temple (Smith, 2:333), a printing house, and an office building for the First Presidency. Heber C. Kimball recorded that the committee "used every exertion in their power to forward the work" (868). Jared Carter was assigned a building lot just north of the temple as an inheritance (94:1–15) and served as a member of the Kirtland high council (102:3, 34).

By the fall of 1835, Carter had begun a cycle of apostasy and repentance that continued for the next ten years. In September 1835, for example, he was brought before a Church court (now known as a disciplinary council) for rejecting the advice and counsel of the First Presidency. He confessed and was forgiven. Thereafter, Jared served on the Kirtland high council, participated in the dedication services of the Kirtland Temple, and became a charter member of the Kirtland Safety Society Bank.

The Carter family left Kirtland for Far West, Missouri, in September 1837, where Jared again served on the high council, before being expelled from the state and moving to Nauvoo with the rest of the Saints in 1839. In 1843 and again in 1844, he became disaffected, conspiring with others against the Prophet Joseph Smith. Both times he confessed his error, promised to return to faithfulness, and was reconciled. When the Saints left Nauvoo, however, he did not go west but instead moved his family to Chicago (he was listed as a member of the Yoree branch of the Church) and later to DeKalb County, Illinois.

BIBLIOGRAPHY

Carter, Jared. Journal. Typescript. Church History Library, The Church of Jesus Christ of Latter-day Saints, Salt Lake City.

Kimball, Heber C. "Extracts from H. C. Kimball's Journal." *Times and Seasons* (15 April 1845): 866–69.

Smith, Joseph. *History of The Church of Jesus Christ of Latter-day Saints.* Edited by B. H. Roberts. 7 vols. 2d ed. rev. Salt Lake City: The Church of Jesus Christ of Latter-day Saints, 1932–51.

KWF

Carter, John S.

Birth: 1796, Killingworth, Middlesex County, Connecticut
Death: 26 June 1834, Clay County, Missouri

John S. Carter was baptized and ordained an elder and high priest in 1832. Soon afterward, he departed on a mission to Vermont, subsequently leading those he had taught to Kirtland, Ohio. On 17 February 1834 he was called to the Kirtland high council, and he and others "answered that they accepted their appointments, and would fill their offices according to the grace of God bestowed upon them" (102:3–4). Only three days later he was called to serve a mission in the east (Smith, 2:35). Upon his return he responded to the Prophet's call to join Zion's Camp.

During the march of Zion's Camp, Joseph Smith warned its members that "a scourge would come upon the camp in consequence of the fractious and unruly spirits . . . and they should die like sheep with the rot" (*History*, 2:80). Although he was the first to die from cholera in Zion's Camp, Carter was a faithful Saint. The Prophet Joseph explained, "When the cholera made its appearance, Elder John S. Carter was the first man who stepped forward to rebuke it, and upon this, was instantly seized, and became the first victim in the camp" (*History*, 2:115). In 1836, two years after Carter's death, his daughter Marietta received her patriarchal blessing. It affirmed, "Thy father laid down his life for the redemption of Zion—his spirit watches over thee" (Smith, *Papers*, 2:166).

BIBLIOGRAPHY

Smith, Joseph. *History of The Church of Jesus Christ of Latter-day Saints.* Edited by B. H. Roberts. 7 vols. 2d

ed. rev. Salt Lake City: The Church of Jesus Christ of Latter-day Saints, 1932–51.

———. *The Papers of Joseph Smith*. Edited by Dean C. Jessee. 2 vols. Salt Lake City: Deseret Book, 1989–92.

KWF

Carter, Simeon

Birth: 7 July 1794, Killingworth, Middlesex County, Connecticut

Death: 3 February 1869, Brigham City, Box Elder County, Utah

From the time of his baptism on 22 February 1831 until his death, Simeon Carter served faithfully as a missionary, follower, and leader in the Church. In 1830 Parley P. Pratt left behind a "Book of Mormon in Carter's house" in Amherst, Ohio, when Parley was arrested and escorted to court (Pratt, 36). Carter read the book, believed it to be true, and traveled fifty miles to Kirtland to seek baptism. He was baptized and ordained an elder and a high priest in 1831.

In Amherst, he preached, baptized, and organized a branch of about sixty members. Twice, as recorded in the Doctrine and Covenants, he was called to be a missionary (52:27; 75:30), and saw many become converted to the gospel, explaining that "the Lord has kept me and supported me" ("Extracts," 70). He exercised the gift of healing when he blessed the daughter of his brother Jared. Although his niece was close to death, she was healed when Simeon commanded her in the name of Jesus Christ to rise and walk.

Simeon Carter marched with ZION'S CAMP, oversaw branches of the Church, served on high councils in Clay County and Far West, Missouri, and was wounded at the Battle of Crooked River. He later testified that Joseph was a prophet and that he, Carter, was "determined to persevere and act in righteousness in all things, so that he might at last gain a crown of glory, and reign in the kingdom of God" (Smith, 3:225). Carter served a mission in England from 1846 to 1849, crossed the plains, and was called by Brigham Young in 1851 to settle in Box Elder County, Utah.

BIBLIOGRAPHY

"Extracts of Letters from the Elders Abroad." *The Evening and the Morning Star* 1, no. 9 (February 1833): 138–39.

Pratt, Parley Jr. *Autobiography of Parley P. Pratt*. Edited by Parley P. Pratt Jr. Salt Lake City: Deseret Book, 1985.

Smith, Joseph. *History of The Church of Jesus Christ of Latter-day Saints*. Edited by B. H. Roberts. 7 vols. 2d ed. rev. Salt Lake City: The Church of Jesus Christ of Latter-day Saints, 1932–51.

KWF

Carter, William

Birth: Unknown

Death: Unknown

Although several men by the name of William Carter are known in early Church history, there is little information about the William Carter mentioned in Doctrine and Covenants 52. It is known that he was baptized and ordained an elder before June 1831 and that he was blind. Notwithstanding this handicap, he was called with Wheeler Baldwin (52:31) to preach "the word by the way" (52:22) as they traveled to Missouri. Carter failed to respond to the call (Black, 60), and by 1 September 1831 he and Edison Fuller were "silenced from holding the office of Elders in this Church" (Cannon and Cook, 11). After visiting with him, his uncle Jared Carter wrote that William "was convinced that it was the work of the Lord but he did not as yet feel prepared to obey." Jared counseled him to obey this "very day" (in Black, 61), and William complied. He was rebaptized, helped build the Kirtland Temple, and for his efforts was "promised a restoration of sight, if faithful" (Smith, 2:207). It is not known whether this blessing was realized.

BIBLIOGRAPHY

Black, Susan Easton. *Who's Who in the Doctrine and Covenants*. Salt Lake City: Deseret Book, 1997.

Cannon, Donald Q., and Lyndon W. Cook., eds. *Far West Record: Minutes of The Church of Jesus Christ of Latter-day Saints, 1830–1844*. Salt Lake City: Deseret Book, 1983.

Smith, Joseph. *History of The Church of Jesus Christ of Latter-day Saints*. Edited by B. H. Roberts. 7 vols. 2d ed. rev. Salt Lake City: The Church of Jesus Christ of Latter-day Saints, 1932–51.

Whitmer, John. *An Early Latter Day Saint History: The*

Book of John Whitmer. Edited by F. Mark McKiernan and Roger D. Launius. Independence, Mo.: Herald Publishing House, 1980.

KWF

Carthage, Illinois

The county seat of Hancock County, about twenty-three miles southeast of Nauvoo. Two sections in the Doctrine and Covenants refer to Carthage. In 1831 the Lord directed William Law to preach the gospel in Carthage (124:88); it is not known whether Law fulfilled this assignment. Carthage and Carthage jail are referred to in 135:1, 4, and 7 in connection with the martyrdom of Joseph and Hyrum Smith.

Carthage was a hotbed of anti-Mormon activity in the 1840s. By 1843, Mormon voters controlled the election of county and legislative officers. Supporters of defeated candidates felt disenfranchised. In September, they held a multicounty "Great Meeting of Anti-Mormonism" at the Carthage courthouse. Resolutions were passed, challenging the political influence of Joseph Smith and calling for his extradition to Missouri (Smith, 5:528; 6:4–8). In February 1844, a similar meeting in Carthage proposed that a day be set aside for fasting and prayer that Joseph Smith would be destroyed (Smith, 6:221–23).

Amid this persecution, Joseph Smith and his brother Hyrum were accused of riot, a charge that stemmed from the destruction of the press used to print the *Nauvoo Expositor,* a bitterly anti-Mormon newspaper. On 24 June 1844, the Smith brothers went to Carthage to answer the charge of riot. There the charge was changed to treason. For the Smiths, Carthage was a scene of broken promises, illegal arraignment, and incarceration. Joseph and Hyrum Smith were "shot in Carthage jail, on the 27th of June, 1844, about five o'clock P.M., by an armed mob" (135:1). In 1845 a jury in the Carthage courthouse acquitted members of that mob of the charge of murder.

The Church purchased the Carthage Jail in 1903 and subsequently built a visitors' center on the historic property. *See* map, p. 277.

See also Illinois period; Martyrdom of Joseph and Hyrum Smith.

BIBLIOGRAPHY

Smith, Joseph. *History of The Church of Jesus Christ of Latter-day Saints.* Edited by B. H. Roberts. 7 vols. 2d ed. rev. Salt Lake City: The Church of Jesus Christ of Latter-day Saints, 1932–51.

GML

Cast out/cut off

The terms *cast out* and *cut off* appear several times throughout the Doctrine and Covenants and have similar meanings. In every instance, *cast out* or *cut off* connotes a separation of some sort. The revelations address this separation in two contexts:

1. The Lord's servants have the power to cast out devils from individuals (35:9; 84:67; 124:98).

2. Individuals themselves are cast out or cut off as a consequence of their behavior, being separated from the presence of God (29:41), the Church (42:37; 50:8; 51:2; 56:8–10), Christ's covenant disciples (1:14; 41:5; 42:75; 133:63), or their inheritance under the laws of CONSECRATION (64:35; 85:11; cf. 101:1–6). These are the most serious consequences, although what a particular individual is cast out or cut off from may not always be spelled out (42:20–28; 45:44; 52:6; 56:3; 63:63; 101:90).

The Doctrine and Covenants identifies specific reasons for individuals being cast out or cut off: hypocrisy (50:8); disobedience and refusing to repent (56:3; 42:20–28); not giving "the heart and a willing mind" to the work of the Lord (64:34–35); losing one's "savor" after being called to be "the salt of the earth," "a light unto the world," and "the saviors of men" (101:39–41; 103:9–10); failing to watch for (prepare for) the second coming of the Savior (45:39–44); and refusing, on the part of local and federal government officials, to grant REDRESS petitions of the Saints for their losses from persecutors in Missouri (101:86–90).

Fortunately, Jesus Christ is merciful; he is mankind's ADVOCATE, pleading the cause of all those who repent (38:14; 45:3; 63:63; 101:1–3, 9; 110:4–5). Thus, the determining factor in being cast out or cut off is not imperfection itself but an unwillingness to repent. Only those who "love darkness rather than light" and "will not repent" will be cast out (10:20–22; 42:20–28; cf. 29:43–45).

See also Church discipline; Judgment(s); Repentance.

MOR

Celestial kingdom. *See* Kingdoms of glory and perdition, vision of.

Celestial kingdom, law of. *See* Law of the celestial kingdom.

Celestial kingdom, vision of

A grand vision given to Joseph Smith where, in the prophetic tradition of Isaiah and John the Revelator, he saw the throne of God in the celestial kingdom, "whereon was seated the Father and the Son" (137:3; Smith, *Writings,* 175; *History,* 2:380–81; cf. Isa. 6:1–8; Rev. 5:7). Received on 21 January 1836 in his office on the third floor of the Kirtland Temple, this remarkable vision increased Joseph Smith's understanding about those who would be saved in the celestial kingdom. In April general conference of 1976, the First Presidency and the Quorum of the Twelve, under the leadership of President Spencer W. Kimball, presented a portion of the record of the vision to the members of the Church for their approval. After the revelation was accepted as the will of the Lord, it was canonized and placed in the standard works of the Church, first in the Pearl of Great Price and soon thereafter in Doctrine and Covenants 137. *See* Historical context and overview of Doctrine and Covenants 137 (p. 858).

This vision was not the first time in his ministry that Joseph Smith saw the Father, the Son, and a throne (76:19–24, 92). In the 1836 vision, however, Joseph Smith saw not only the Father and the Son in heaven but also Adam, Abraham, his own parents, and his brother Alvin in the celestial kingdom. Joseph "marveled how it was" that Alvin, who had died before the restoration of the gospel, could be in the celestial kingdom since he "had not been baptized for the remission of sins" (137:6; cf. 76:51; John 3:5; 2 Ne. 31:17). Joseph learned through this vision of the celestial kingdom that all those "who would have received [the gospel] if they had been permitted to tarry" on earth to embrace it will be saved in the celestial kingdom because the Lord will judge people "according to their works, according to the desire of their hearts" (137:7, 9; Smith, *Writings,* 175). Additionally, he learned that all children who die before the age of accountability will be saved in the celestial kingdom (137:10; Smith, *Writings,* 176).

In a part of the record of the vision not included in the canonized version, Joseph saw the recently called Twelve Apostles—in particular, William E. McLellin and Brigham Young—preaching the gospel, and he saw them "in the celestial kingdom of God" (Smith, *Writings,* 176).

The vision received in the evening of 21 January 1836 was of the future (cf. Rev. 7, where John also saw the celestial kingdom in the future): Joseph's parents were alive (his father was in the room with him), and so were the newly called Twelve Apostles.

Undergirding the vision is the ever-present atoning sacrifice of Jesus Christ, without which no one can be saved (20:21–29; Mosiah 3:17). Several years elapsed before Joseph was told exactly "how" God would save those who die without gospel ordinances. On 15 August 1840, at the funeral of Seymour Brunson, the Prophet taught the doctrine of baptism for the dead, an ordinance that provided an opportunity to interpret the earlier vision of the celestial kingdom in a much broader context that included vicarious temple work for the dead (124:28–36). Further clarification regarding temple work came in 1842 (124:127–28).

See also Kingdoms of glory and perdition, vision of; Salvation for the dead.

BIBLIOGRAPHY

Smith, Joseph. *History of The Church of Jesus Christ of Latter-day Saints.* Edited by B. H. Roberts. 7 vols. 2d ed. rev. Salt Lake City: The Church of Jesus Christ of Latter-day Saints, 1932–51.

———. *Personal Writings of Joseph Smith.* Compiled and edited by Dean C. Jessee. Rev. ed. Salt Lake City: Deseret Book, 2002.

RNH

Center place. *See* Independence, Missouri.

Cephas. *See* Peter, the apostle.

Certificate(s). *See* License/certificate(s).

Chaff. *See* Appendix E.

Chains

In the Doctrine and Covenants are four references to chains, each with at least one of three connotations: chains of darkness (38:5), chains of hell (138:23; 123:8), and chains of death (138:18, 23).

Chains of darkness represent the continuous spiritual bondage experienced by the wicked who refuse to repent in mortality or in the spirit world. These rebellious spirits dwell in HELL awaiting the "resurrection of the unjust" and the Final Judgment, which will come at the end of the earth after the MILLENNIUM (38:5; 76:17, 84–85, 106; 88:100–101; cf. 2 Pet. 2:4). They are subject to both the chains of darkness and the chains of hell. Except the SONS OF PERDITION, all "these . . . shall not be redeemed from the devil until the last resurrection, until the Lord, even Christ the Lamb, shall have finished his work" (76:85).

The Prophet Joseph Smith used the phrase "chains . . . of hell," along with the terms "an iron yoke," "a strong band," "handcuffs," "shackles," and "fetters," in describing the evil influences of the devil that had brought such "grief, sorrow, and care" upon the early members of the Church and the whole world (123:7–8). The chains of hell are experienced to one degree or another by all who permit themselves to come under the power and influence of the devil. Individuals are freed from the chains of hell to the degree that they repent and accept Jesus Christ as their Redeemer and Deliverer. "And the saints rejoiced in their redemption, and bowed the knee and acknowledged the Son of God as their Redeemer and Deliverer from death and the chains of hell" (138:23; cf. 2 Ne. 9:45; Alma 12:9–11; 13:30).

The chains of DEATH are experienced by all who die and enter the spirit world. The postmortal spirits of both the righteous and the wicked are limited or restrained, for they no longer have the privileges of having a physical body. "Even the prophets . . . waited for their deliverance, for the dead had looked upon the long absence of their spirits from their bodies as a bondage"

(138:49–50; cf. 45:17). The ATONEMENT of Jesus Christ allows all who have died to be freed from the chains of death through the universal RESURRECTION (Alma 11:44; 1 Cor. 15:22; cf. D&C 138:17–18, 23). Though all mankind will be resurrected, the level of individuals' eternal reward depends upon their faithfulness.

See also Redeem, redemption; Repentance.

DKJ

Changed in the twinkling of an eye. *See* Death; Millennium, the.

Chariots. *See* Appendix E.

Chariton, Missouri

On 9 August 1831, Joseph Smith and ten other men left Independence, Missouri, in canoes to return to Ohio. On 12 August, after traveling approximately one hundred miles, the company reached McIlwaine's Bend (probably near present-day Miami, Saline County, Missouri). There the Prophet received Doctrine and Covenants 61, warning the men of possible dangers they would face if they continued to journey on the river. At this point Joseph Smith and six others chose to leave the river and continue their journey overland. The other four chose to continue their journey on the Missouri in canoes. On 13 August, the Prophet's company crossed the Missouri at a point near "old" Chariton, Missouri (62, headnote). The party was met that day by Hyrum Smith, David Whitmer, Harvey Whitlock, and John Murdock, who were en route to Jackson County. At that time Joseph Smith received in their behalf the revelation recorded in section 62.

In 1820, Chariton County was formed with "old" Chariton as the county seat. Because of continued flooding, however, in 1832 the county seat was moved to Keytesville. Eventually "old" Chariton was abandoned and no longer exists. *See* map, p. 414.

BIBLIOGRAPHY

Booth, Ezra. Letter. In Eber D. Howe, *Mormonism Unvailed*. Painesville, Ohio: E. D. Howe, 1834.

Cahoon, Reynolds. Journal. Historical Department Archives. The Church of Jesus Christ of Latter-day Saints.

Parkin, Max H. *Missouri*. Vol. 4 of *Sacred Places: A Comprehensive Guide to Early LDS Historical Sites*, edited by LaMar C. Berrett. Salt Lake City: Deseret Book, 2004.

Smith, Joseph. *History of The Church of Jesus Christ of Latter-day Saints*. Edited by B. H. Roberts. 7 vols. 2d ed. rev. Salt Lake City: The Church of Jesus Christ of Latter-day Saints, 1932–51.

ALB

Charity

The "pure love of Christ" (Moro. 7:47), the LOVE God has for his children (34:3; John 3:16) and the love his children are instructed to have toward him and toward one another. Saints are commanded, "Above all things, clothe yourselves with the bond of charity, as with a mantle, which is the bond of perfectness and peace" (88:125; cf. 1 Cor. 13:13). Those who are filled with this "bond of perfectness and peace" are not "unfruitful in the knowledge of the Lord" (107:30–31), increase in confidence "in the presence of God," and will have the "doctrine of the priesthood . . . distil upon [their] soul[s] as the dews from heaven" (121:45).

Charity is most often connected with FAITH and HOPE and is the result of having those qualities (4:5; 6:19; 12:8; 18:19; cf. Moro. 7:40–44). In a revelation instructing Joseph Knight how he could assist with the work, the Lord explained, "No one can assist in this work except he shall be humble and full of love, having faith, hope, and charity" (12:8). Indeed, without charity, God's children "can do nothing" (18:19).

Priesthood quorums are instructed that their decisions are to be made in charity (107:30). Individuals are instructed to strive to "let [their] bowels . . . be full of charity towards all men" (121:45).

CFO

Chasten, chastening

Scold, rebuke, censure, discipline, punish. *Chasten* and its variations appear in the Doctrine and Covenants in several contexts.

1. The Lord chastens those he loves to bring them to REPENTANCE. In his revealed preface to the book, the Lord declared that one purpose of the revelations was to expose the errors of the Saints, that "inasmuch as they sinned they might be chastened, that they might repent" (1:27). In censuring the Saints for delaying the building of the Kirtland Temple, the Lord said, "Verily, thus saith the Lord unto you whom I love, and whom I love I also chasten that their sins may be forgiven, for with the chastisement I prepare a way for their deliverance in all things out of temptation, and I have loved you—wherefore, ye must needs be chastened and stand rebuked before my face" (95:1–2).

2. The revelations identify an array of sins that bring the chastening hand of the Lord. W. W. Phelps and Sidney Gilbert were chastened for lack of unity as a missionary companionship (61:8). Ziba Peterson was chastened for trying to hide his sins rather than confessing them (58:60). William E. McLellin was chastened "for the murmurings of his heart" (75:6–8). Bishop Newel K. Whitney and all three members of the First Presidency were upbraided by the Lord for negligence in teaching and setting in order their families (93:40–50). Concerning those who were involved in the School of the Prophets in the winter and spring of 1833, the Lord said, "Contentions arose in the school of the prophets; which was very grievous unto me . . . therefore I sent them forth to be chastened" (95:10). The Lord's "disciples, in days of old . . . were afflicted and sorely chastened" because they "sought occasion against one another and forgave not one another in their hearts" (64:8). In late summer of 1833, prideful hearts, covetousness, and lack of obedience to "words of wisdom and eternal life" of the Saints in Kirtland brought this response from the Lord: "Verily I say unto you, that I, the Lord, will chasten them and will do whatsoever I list, if they do not repent and observe all things whatsoever I have said unto them" (98:19–21). And although the Saints were unlawfully driven out of Jackson County, Missouri, in the fall of 1833, they were themselves guilty of serious sins and shortcomings and needed to be chastened. "There were jarrings, and contentions, and envyings, and strifes, and lustful and covetous desires among them. . . . They were slow to hearken unto the voice of the Lord their God. . . . In the day of their peace they esteemed lightly my counsel; but, in the day of their trouble, of necessity they

feel after me" (101:6–8). Forbearingly, the Lord added, "Notwithstanding their sins, my bowels are filled with compassion towards them. I will not utterly cast them off; and in the day of wrath I will remember mercy" (v. 9).

3. Chastening is a necessary principle in the spiritual development of the Lord's people. In a revelation to Brigham Young concerning the Saints' move west from Winter Quarters, the Lord declared, "My people must be tried in all things, that they may be prepared to receive the glory that I have for them, even the glory of Zion; and he that will not bear chastisement is not worthy of my kingdom" (136:31). Speaking of the beleaguered Saints in Missouri, the Lord proclaimed, "They must needs be chastened and tried, even as Abraham, who was commanded to offer up his only son. For all those who will not endure chastening, but deny me, cannot be sanctified" (101:4–5).

4. Whether a private or public chastisement is appropriate depends on how widely an offense is known. A revelation designated "the law of the Church" (42, headnote) says, "If thy brother or sister offend many, he or she shall be chastened before many. . . . If any shall offend in secret, he or she shall be rebuked in secret," both instances providing opportunity for repentance, "that the church may not speak reproachfully of him or her" (42:90–92).

5. Wars, though self-inflicted, and natural calamities, serve to chasten mankind for their wickedness. *See* Disasters, calamities.

In a revelation to Joseph Smith foreshadowing the American Civil War and subsequent wars among all nations, the Lord proclaimed, "And thus, with the sword and by bloodshed the inhabitants of the earth shall mourn; and with famine, and plague, and earthquake, and the thunder of heaven, and the fierce and vivid lightning also, shall the inhabitants of the earth be made to feel the wrath, and indignation, and chastening hand of an Almighty God, until the consumption decreed hath made a full end of all nations" (87:6).

See also Affliction(s); Church discipline; Judgment(s).

AKG

Chastity

Sexual purity; abstinence from desires, imaginations, or actions contrary to the proper use of the power of procreation. The word *chastity* does not appear in the Doctrine and Covenants, but the principle is clearly evident. The revelations identify great promises of blessings for obedience and serious consequences for disobedience.

The power of procreation is a sacred trust. In the eternities, that power distinguishes GODS from angels, those who are exalted in the highest part of the celestial kingdom from those who are not. Those who are chaste and are faithful to eternal MARRIAGE covenants become gods and are blessed with "eternal lives," the "continuation of the seeds," eternal "increase" (131:1–4; 132:15–17, 19–25). More immediate rewards for those who have CHARITY toward others and "let virtue garnish [their] thoughts unceasingly" include spiritual confidence, the constant companionship of the HOLY GHOST, personal radiance that comes from obedience to righteousness and truth, and everlasting dominions flowing "unto [them] forever and ever" (121:45–46). Conversely, denial of the faith, loss of the Spirit of the Lord, and fear are the consequences resulting from lustful desires—from committing ADULTERY in one's heart. Moreover, sexual immorality may result in excommunication from the Church (42:23; 63:16–17; 88:121).

See also Fornication; Virtue.

LED

Cheerfulness

Optimism, pleasantness, joyfulness. In several revelations in the Doctrine and Covenants, the Lord encouraged members of the Church to "be of good cheer," even when they face times of difficulty, as did the elders returning to Kirtland from a missionary journey to Missouri, who experienced dangers on the river at McIlwaine's Bend. The Lord said, "Be of good cheer, little children; for I am in your midst, and I have not forsaken you" (61:36). He also reassured priesthood leaders who were called to preach the gospel: "Wherefore, be of good cheer, and do not fear, for I the Lord am with you, and will stand by you" (68:6; cf. 78:18; 112:4). The

Lord instructed the Saints that activities on the Sabbath day should be done with "cheerful hearts and countenances" and promised "the fulness of the earth" to those who keep the Sabbath as he intended (59:13–16).

The inspired words of the Prophet Joseph Smith, written after he had languished for nearly five months in LIBERTY JAIL, teach that cheerfulness is not dependent on comfortable circumstances. In a long letter giving doctrine and instruction to the beleaguered Saints being driven from Missouri, the Prophet offered encouraging words: "Therefore, dearly beloved brethren, let us cheerfully do all things that lie in our power; and then may we stand still, with the utmost assurance, to see the salvation of God, and for his arm to be revealed" (123:17; cf. 121–23; 3:289–300).

See also Joy.

BIBLIOGRAPHY

Smith, Joseph. History of The Church of Jesus Christ of Latter-day Saints. Edited by B. H. Roberts. 7 vols. 2d ed. rev. Salt Lake City: The Church of Jesus Christ of Latter-day Saints, 1932–51.

CDG

Children

The word children is used in four ways in the Doctrine and Covenants:

1. The young offspring of mortal parents (e.g., 29:46–47; 68:25–28, 31).

2. Latter-day descendants of ancient ancestors, such as the children of Israel (Jacob), Judah, and Ephraim (e.g., 61:25; 109:61–62, 64; 133:30, 32). The promises made to the fathers are planted in their hearts, so that the ordinances of the gospel can be made available to their ancestors (e.g., 2:2; 110:15; 128:17–18).

3. Followers or adherents to a cause or principle, such as the children of Zion, children of God, children of light, children of disobedience (e.g., 58:51; 84:56, 58; 106:5; 121:17). The Lord referred to early members of the Church as "little children" (e.g., 50:40–41; 78:17).

4. A synonym for mankind. The term "children of men" is used dozens of times (e.g., 11:22; 96:4–5).

The revelations have much to say about young children. One plain and precious doctrine that had been lost to the world concerns the status and ACCOUNTABILITY of little children. The Doctrine and Covenants clearly teaches that "little children are holy, being sanctified through the atonement of Jesus Christ" (74:7; cf. 29:46). Children who die before the "years of accountability" are "saved in the celestial kingdom of heaven" (137:10). SATAN is not given power to "tempt little children, until they begin to become accountable" before the Lord (29:47). The Lord has specified eight years as the age when children begin to become accountable and are to be baptized (20:71; 68:25, 27). President Harold B. Lee taught that Satan is not permitted to tempt young children "in order to give parents their golden opportunity to plant in the hearts of little children those vital things except for which, when that time of accountability comes, they may have waited too long" (122). President Lee warned that the danger is that "Satan gets in his licks by trying to make those of us who are entrusted with their care and their training to be negligent and careless and allow them to develop those little tendencies that will lead them away, and will [make them] unfit for the great responsibilities in meeting the contest with Satan, and fail to put on that armor by the time they come to the age of accountability" (122).

It is very clear in the revelations that Heavenly Father cares deeply about his children here on earth. Thus, he has commanded that parents bring up their children in "light and truth" (93:40). In 1833 the Lord chastened and reminded each member of the First Presidency and Bishop Newel K. Whitney of their duties regarding their children and families (93:41–44, 47–50). The Lord warned that when parents fail to teach their children light and truth, they allow the "wicked one" to have power over them and their children (93:39, 42). Children need to be taught the principles of faith, repentance, baptism, and reception of the gift of the Holy Ghost, as well as to pray and to "walk uprightly before the Lord" (68:25–29). The Lord is so earnest about parents teaching their children the principles and ordinances of the gospel from the time they are young that he warned the sin

Christ and Child; *painting by Carl Bloch. "Little children are redeemed from the foundation of the world through mine Only Begotten" (D&C 29:46).*

of failing to teach them, and perhaps even the sins of children who become wayward, may "be upon the heads of the parents" (68:25; cf. Jacob 3:10). The idleness and wickedness of parents can influence their children to embrace the sins of their parents (68:31).

The Doctrine and Covenants also lays the doctrinal foundation for the Church practice of blessing little children by priesthood authority (20:70). A further example of the Lord's concern for children is his instruction that "children have claim upon their parents for their maintenance until they are of age" (83:4).

In the millennial day, children of the righteous will "grow up without sin unto salvation" (45:58). They will live until they are "old," to the "age of a tree," or the millennial "age of man," which Isaiah says is "an hundred years old." Nevertheless, "they shall not sleep in the dust, but they shall be changed [resurrected] in the twinkling of an eye" (63:50–51; 101:30–31; JST Isa. 65:20).

See also Innocent.

BIBLIOGRAPHY

Lee, Harold B. *Harold B. Lee.* Teachings of Presidents of the Church series. Salt Lake City: The Church of Jesus Christ of Latter-day Saints, 2000.

CJW

Chosen

Adjective used to designate persons or a people called, elected, appointed, set apart, or ordained, even foreordained, to serve as God's covenant people to take the gospel to the entire world.

The Lord has chosen disciples to raise "the voice of warning . . . unto all people" (1:4; cf. 88:80–82), to declare the gospel "with the sound of rejoicing" (29:4; cf. 19:37). Joseph Smith was chosen to do the work of the Lord (3:9; 24:1). Other individuals were also "called and chosen," such as William W. Phelps (55:1), Oliver Cowdery (9:4), Sidney Rigdon (35:3–4, 20; 100:9–11), Edward Partridge (41:9), and Thomas B. Marsh (112:16). President Joseph F. Smith saw in the spirit world "the noble and great ones who were chosen in the beginning to be rulers in the Church of God. Even before they were born, they, with many others, received their first lessons in the world of spirits and were prepared to come forth in the due time of the Lord to labor in his vineyard for the salvation of the souls of men" (138:55–56).

The chosen people of the Lord are called to be the "salt of the earth and the savor of men" (101:39–40), to "arise and shine forth, that [their] light may be a standard for the nations" (115:5). The Lord revealed that the patriarchal priesthood "rightly belongs to the literal descendants of the chosen seed, to whom the promises were made" (107:39–40). God promised Seth through his father Adam "that his posterity should be the chosen of the Lord, and that they should be preserved unto the end of the earth" (107:42; cf. 86:8–9).

It is possible to be called but not be chosen. "There are many who have been ordained among you, whom I have called but few of them are chosen" (95:5). Although the words *called* and *chosen* are sometimes used together, there is a difference: "There are many called, but few are chosen" (121:34). Many are invited to participate in living and preaching the gospel and leading in the Church, but those who, in the end, are not chosen are those whose "hearts are set so much upon the things of this world, and aspire to the honors of men" and fail to learn to righteously handle the powers of heaven;

instead, they cover their sins, gratify their pride and vain ambition, and exercise unrighteous dominion, or compulsion, on others (121:35–37).

The Lord himself explained the difference between *called* and *chosen:* "There has been a day of calling, but the time has come for a day of choosing; and let those be chosen that are worthy." Their worthiness "shall be manifest unto my servant, by the voice of the Spirit." Those who are chosen "shall be sanctified; and inasmuch as they follow the counsel which they receive, they shall have power . . . to accomplish all things pertaining to Zion" (105:35–37). When the Lord commanded the Saints to build the Kirtland Temple, he promised them that there he did "design to endow those whom I have chosen with power from on high" (95:8).

See also Call, calling; Covenant people of the Lord; Elect, election.

DKO

Christ, light of. *See* Light of Christ.

Church discipline

Church disciplinary councils are convened as circumstances dictate to determine whether to revoke, retain, or restore privileges of an individual's Church membership. The councils exist at the ward and stake level and at the level of the First Presidency and the Quorum of Twelve Apostles, who have jurisdiction in all the world. The First Presidency is "the highest council of the church . . . [which renders] a final decision upon controversies in spiritual matters" (107:80). The First Presidency also serves as an appellate council to consider appeals of decisions rendered by any of the other councils (102:27, 33).

The only way a person can become a member of The Church of Jesus Christ of Latter-day Saints is through baptism by appropriate priesthood authority. This process establishes a covenant relationship between the Church member and the Lord. Conversely, the only way a person's Church membership can be terminated and the covenant revoked is through a Church disciplinary council or by a written request from a member to have his or her name removed from the records of the Church.

Purposes of Church discipline

Elder M. Russell Ballard taught that "repentance and reformation are the primary objectives of any Church disciplinary action. . . . The purpose [of Church discipline] is threefold: [1] to save the soul of the transgressor, [2] to protect the innocent, and [3] to safeguard the Church's purity, integrity, and good name" (12). Church discipline is a subject that is inextricably intertwined with REPENTANCE. The responsibility to bring about repentance when needed is upon both the Church member and the priesthood leaders in the Church. The objective of both is to attain and retain eligibility, through the process of repentance, for individual members to enjoy the fulness of blessings offered through the ATONEMENT of the Savior. Church discipline is not exercised to punish or cause suffering, although it may be a painful experience for the person who is disciplined. That pain can be helpful to the repentant person: often it is only through suffering that hearts are sufficiently broken to accomplish complete repentance. Determining whether, what, and how discipline should be imposed is often difficult. Priesthood leaders must be faithful in their duty to sit in righteous judgment when necessary: "Any member of the church of Christ transgressing, or being overtaken in a fault, shall be dealt with as the scriptures direct" (20:80; cf. Moro. 6:7–8).

Just as no two people are alike, so also no two cases requiring discipline are alike. Church priesthood leaders consider many factors in each instance. Among other considerations are the following: the severity of the sin, the frequency of sinful actions, the level of gospel understanding and responsibility of the sinner, whether temple covenants are involved, the effect upon others, the level of Church responsibility and influence of the individual being disciplined, whether information concerning the sin was discovered or confessed, and, most important of all, the degree of repentance manifested by the transgressor. With so many variables involved, variations in council decisions on seemingly similar cases are to be expected. Only those who participate in council action would be privy to the reasons for the differences; all such information is confidential.

Principles underlying Church discipline

Priesthood leaders understand that when members seriously dishonor and violate sacred covenants, the Spirit of the Lord withdraws, and the individuals may lose their desire and perhaps even their capacity to keep their covenants. If that occurs, it is a blessing to the members for their covenants to be removed from them to prevent the deepening of spiritual condemnation. Covenants might be placed in abeyance and privileges withheld while repentance processes are accomplished. Church discipline is, therefore, one of the ways the Lord blesses his people. It represents an act of compassion and reflects concern of priesthood leaders for the people and their spiritual well-being.

Decisions of disciplinary councils ought to be in accord with doctrinal principles and written Church policies and practices as contained in the scriptures and official Church handbooks. When an issue cannot be resolved by reference to previously received divine direction, an appeal is to be made directly to the Lord. "In case of difficulty respecting doctrine or principle, if there is not a sufficiency written to make the case clear to the minds of the council, the president may inquire and obtain the mind of the Lord by revelation" (102:23). The Lord had earlier told priesthood leaders concerning unrepentant transgressors: "And him that repenteth not of his sins, and confesseth them not, ye shall bring before the church, and do with him as the scripture saith unto you, *either by commandment or by revelation*. And this ye shall do that God may be glorified—not because ye forgive not, having not compassion, but that ye may be justified in the eyes of the law, that ye may not offend him who is your lawgiver" (64:12–13; emphasis added).

It should be emphasized that Church action does not forgive sin—only the Lord does that. But disciplinary action taken by Church authorities helps clear the way for the Lord's FORGIVENESS. Understanding this truth helps Church members appreciate the value and blessing of being disciplined. They realize such action is actually an act of love, not an act of retribution. Church authorities are responsible to render judgment relative to the privileges of membership that are to be extended to or withdrawn from Church members. Leaders are responsible to learn about and to act in their divinely mandated responsibilities to maintain the standards of the kingdom of God. They have the responsibility to defend the doctrines of the Lord's kingdom, to purge iniquity from the Church where needed, and to assist members of the Church toward becoming sanctified Saints. These are the objectives of Church discipline, the purposes of the repentance process, and the charge given to priesthood leadership. Leading individuals to understand and apply the principles of repentance sometimes includes the need to take disciplinary action, which is to be both directed and confirmed by the Lord.

See also Bishop(s); Common council of the Church; Historical context and overview of Doctrine and Covenants 102 (p. 807).

BIBLIOGRAPHY

Ballard, M. Russell. "A Chance to Start Over: Church Disciplinary Councils and the Restoration of Blessings." *Ensign* 20 (September 1990): 12–19.

Simpson, Robert L. *Church Courts* [pamphlet]. Salt Lake City: The Church of Jesus Christ of Latter-day Saints, 1972.

Tanner, N. Eldon. "Our Responsibility to the Transgressor." *Ensign* 4 (November 1974): 76–78.

———. "Thou Mayest Choose for Thyself." *Ensign* 3 (July 1973): 7–10.

CMC

Church of Enoch

The church made up of Enoch and his followers who were translated and taken into heaven (Moses 7:69). There is one reference to the church of Enoch in the Doctrine and Covenants, and that is in association with the CHURCH OF THE FIRSTBORN, whose members are sanctified and exalted in the highest heaven (76:67; cf. 76:50–70).

LED

Church of Jesus Christ of Latter-day Saints, The

Joseph Smith organized The Church of Jesus Christ of Latter-day Saints as specified by revelation, "by the will and commandments of God," on the precise date on which he was told

the Church should be organized: 6 April 1830 (20:1; Smith, 1:64). This revelation, now recorded in Doctrine and Covenants 20, became, in a sense, the constitutional foundation of the Church. It was later accepted as the "Articles and Covenants" of the Church (Cowan, 47). *See* Doctrine and Covenants, historical development of. The revelation in section 20 briefly reviewed the Lord's earlier dealings with Joseph Smith, noted the essential nature of the mission of Jesus Christ and the importance of believing on his name and then spelled out the duties of ELDERS, PRIESTS, TEACHERS, and DEACONS, which, at this time, were the only PRIESTHOOD offices in the Church. The revelation also instructed Church members in their duties, spelled out the manner of baptism and the prayer to be used in this ordinance, and revealed the specific wording of the prayers to be used in administering the sacrament of the Lord's Supper.

On 6 April 1830 about fifty believers, some of whom had already been baptized, met in the log home of Peter Whitmer Sr. in Fayette, New York. After an opening prayer, Joseph Smith asked the members of the group if they would accept him and Oliver Cowdery as their teachers. The vote in favor was unanimous. Joseph then ordained Oliver an elder of the Church, after which Oliver ordained Joseph to the same office. The two new leaders then administered the sacrament of the Lord's Supper by blessing the emblems of bread and wine and serving them to the group. Next they conferred the GIFT OF THE HOLY GHOST upon the new members by the

1 THE *a*rise of the *b*Church of Christ in these last days, being one thousand eight hundred and thirty years since the *c*coming of our Lord and Savior Jesus Christ in the flesh, it being regularly *d*organized and established agreeable to the *e*laws of our country, by the will and commandments of God, in the fourth month, and on the sixth day of the month which is called April—

Doctrine and Covenants 20:1.

LAYING ON OF HANDS and confirmed them members of the Church of Christ. It was a spiritually exhilarating day as everyone in the little congregation seemed filled with the Spirit; some prophesied, and "all praised the Lord, and rejoiced exceedingly" (Smith, 1:78).

It took time for the full name of the Church to evolve. Section 20 identifies the Church as the Church of Christ, and it was called either that or the Church of Jesus Christ until 1834. The use of the term *Saints,* reflecting what the early Christians called themselves, came gradually. The first time the word *Saints* was used in this sense in a revelation was on 20 July 1831 (57:7–10). On 3 May 1834, in a conference held in Kirtland, Ohio, the members accepted a resolution proclaiming that the Church would be known thereafter as The Church of the Latter-day Saints (Smith, 2:63). Finally, on 26 April 1838 a revelation designated the name as The Church of Jesus Christ of Latter-day Saints (115:4).

The establishment of the Church was foreshadowed by several of Joseph Smith's early revelations declaring that "a great and marvelous work is about to come forth unto the children of men" (6:1; 11:1; 12:1; 14:1), that "the field is white already to harvest," and that the believer should "thrust in his sickle with his might, and reap while the day lasts" (e.g., 4:4; 6:3; 11:3; 12:3; 14:3). In March 1829, a revelation making known the calling of the Three Witnesses also referred to "this the beginning of the rising up and the coming forth of my church out of the wilderness" (5:14). The future was heralded more specifically in April 1829, when the Lord said to Joseph Smith that "if this generation harden not their hearts, I will establish my church among them" (10:53). In May 1829 the Lord told Hyrum Smith not to go out preaching immediately but to "wait a little longer, until you shall have my word, my rock, my church, and my gospel" (11:16).

The restoration of the priesthood was essential to the organization and proper functioning of the Church. The first step came on 15 May 1829 in Harmony, Pennsylvania, while Joseph Smith and Oliver Cowdery were working on the translation of the Book of Mormon. Finding baptism mentioned, they retired to the woods to pray about this important ordinance, wondering, no doubt, who had the authority to perform it (JS–H 1:68). Suddenly they were visited by a glorious heavenly messenger, who announced himself as "John, the same that is called John the Baptist in the New Testament," who had baptized the Savior (JS–H 1:72). He laid his hands on their heads, saying, "Upon you my fellow servants, in the name of Messiah I confer the Priesthood of Aaron, which holds the keys of the ministering of angels, and of the gospel of repentance, and of baptism by immersion for the remission of sins; and this shall never be taken again from the earth, until the sons of Levi do offer again an offering unto the Lord in righteousness" (13:1). This was the Aaronic, or lesser, priesthood, which gave them the authority to baptize as well as to confer the same priesthood on others. He then instructed Joseph and Oliver to baptize each other and again ordain each other, which they did.

John the Baptist told Joseph and Oliver that he was acting under the direction of Peter, James, and John, who would restore the higher, or Melchizedek, priesthood. This, they learned later, would give them the authority to administer in all the spiritual affairs of the Church, including the laying on of hands for the gift of the Holy Ghost. Exactly when this happened is uncertain, but sometime later these three ancient apostles appeared to Joseph and Oliver and ordained them "apostles, and especial witnesses" of Christ (27:12). They were also told to ordain each other as elders in the Church of Jesus Christ, although they were to defer this action until they could assemble others who had been baptized and allow them to vote on whether they would accept these two as their spiritual teachers (Smith, 1:60–61).

4 For thus shall *a*my *b*church be called in the last days, even **The Church of Jesus Christ of Latter-day** *c***Saints.**

Doctrine and Covenants 115:4.

Members of the Church understood that what had been established was, in actuality, a restoration of Christ's ancient church and gospel, "the only true and living church upon the face of the whole earth, with which I, the Lord, am well pleased, speaking unto the church collectively and not individually" (1:30), with all its attendant authority and responsibility. Various revelations to Joseph Smith emphasized the awesome importance of the work they were engaged in, as well as the duties of those who belonged to the Church. Referring to the great apostasy from the primitive Church, the Lord said that because of the influence of Satan, the Church had been driven "into the wilderness" (86:3). Now, however, it was "coming forth . . . out of the wilderness—clear as the moon, and fair as the sun, and terrible as an army with banners" (5:14). The Prophet and those who worked with him were given the power to begin "to bring it forth out of obscurity and out of darkness" (1:30). The Saints were also reminded that anything done in the name of the Lord must be done by proper priesthood authority (20:58, 73; 42:11; 63:62; 68:8, 17–19; 84:21; 107:8–20, 79–80; 113:7–8). In addition, the revelations received by Joseph Smith were scripture, "to be my law to govern my church" (42:59).

Church members were told, further, that they must "observe to keep all the commandments and covenants of the church" (42:78). They were to "instruct and edify each other, that ye may know how to act and direct my church, how to act upon the points of my law and commandments" and then "bind yourselves to act in all holiness before me" (43:8–9). They were to "shine forth, that thy light may be a standard for the nations," and that, for them, the church would be "a defense, . . . a refuge from the storm, and from wrath when it shall be poured out without mixture upon the whole earth" (115:5–6). Further, they were commanded to keep records of the work (21:1; 47:1–4; 69:1–8; 85:1).

When the Church was organized in 1830, its ecclesiastical structure was necessarily small, for its numbers were small. It was clear, however, that the organization would soon expand,

for ten months earlier a revelation had anticipated the calling of the Quorum of the Twelve APOSTLES (18:26–29). The expansion occurred gradually over the next five years until the hierarchical structure was completed in 1835.

At first the ecclesiastical organization consisted of elders, priests, teachers, and deacons, whose duties were spelled out in the "Articles and Covenants" (20; 22). The leaders, Joseph Smith and Oliver Cowdery, were identified simply as the first and second elders (20:2–3). The office of high priest was added in 1831, which occasioned the addition of verses 65–67 to section 20 (Anderson, 114–15). The revelation recorded now in section 107 clarified the distinction between the Aaronic, or lesser, priesthood and the Melchizedek, or higher, priesthood.

Another office introduced in the Church was that of BISHOP. On 4 February 1831 Edward Partridge was called by revelation to be "ordained a bishop unto the church, to leave his merchandise and to spend all his time in the labors of the church" (41:9). His responsibility was to care for the poor and needy in Missouri and to manage the various goods that were accumulated by the Church under the law of consecration. The second bishop to be called was Newel K. Whitney, who had similar responsibilities in Ohio (72:5–8).

After the move to Illinois, Bishops Whitney and Partridge had similar duties with respect to the wards in Nauvoo. These WARDS, however, were not ecclesiastical units. They were political divisions within which the bishops had temporal responsibilities but not spiritual ones. Not until the Church was established in Utah did wards become ecclesiastical units and bishops receive the added responsibility of presiding over ecclesiastical affairs in their respective wards.

On 6 April 1847, after the Saints had left Nauvoo to journey west, Bishop Whitney was sustained as Presiding Bishop of the Church. He was responsible for the temporal affairs of the Church under the direction of the First Presidency and Quorum of the Twelve Apostles.

The first ecclesiastical unit to be formed was the STAKE, which is still the basic unit of Church administration. The first area to be designated as a "stake in Zion" was Kirtland, Ohio, in 1832, though it was not as fully organized as modern stakes. Most of the affairs of that stake were handled by a council of HIGH PRIESTS, but in 1834 the Kirtland HIGH COUNCIL, the first official high council in the Church, was organized (102:3). It consisted of twelve high priests, with Joseph Smith as president. The Kirtland Stake was presided over by a stake presidency, which was also the First Presidency. It functioned primarily as a Church judicial body. In July 1834 another stake was organized in Clay County, Missouri, this time presided over by a stake presidency separate from the First Presidency of the Church (Allen and Leonard, 89–90). This became the permanent pattern for the Church. It was not until 1877, however, that the function of the stake with respect to wards was regularized, as it is today, so that ward bishops were directly responsible to stake presidents (Hartley, 3–36).

On 25 January 1832 Joseph Smith was sustained as President of the High Priesthood and ordained as such by Sidney Rigdon. Not long after that Joseph Smith chose as counselors Jesse Gause and Sidney Rigdon. A year later, Frederick G. Williams replaced Jesse Gause, who had become disaffected from the Church, and the presidency then became known as the First Presidency of the Church (90:1–6). Williams's name replaced that of Jesse Gause in the text of the March 1832 revelation calling Gause as a counselor (81:1). That same revelation clarified that Joseph Smith held the keys of the kingdom (81:2). A revelation on priesthood given through Joseph Smith states that the members of the presidency of the Church form a quorum to be "upheld by the confidence, faith, and prayer of the church" (107:22). It also says that the president is to "preside over the whole church" and be a "seer, a revelator, a translator, and a prophet, having all the gifts of God which he bestows upon the head of the church" (107:91–92). Since then members of the First Presidency and the Quorum of the Twelve have been sustained as "prophets, seers, and revelators" to the Church.

In addition to having two counselors in the First Presidency, Joseph Smith named Oliver Cowdery as assistant president on 5 December 1834 (Smith, 2:176). After Oliver Cowdery's defection, Hyrum Smith was appointed to receive the "gifts of the priesthood, that once were put upon him that was my servant Oliver Cowdery." Hyrum became assistant president and was identified, along with Joseph, as a "prophet, and a seer, and a revelator unto my church" (124:94–95). Only Oliver Cowdery and Hyrum Smith in turn held this position as assistant president of the Church to fulfill the law of witnesses, necessary in laying the foundation of the last dispensation (Smith, *Doctrines*, 1:216–19).

Still another office in the early Church hierarchy was that of PATRIARCH to the Church, or presiding patriarch. On 6 December 1834 Joseph Smith Sr. was ordained patriarch to the Church (Jessee et al., 440). In this position he had the responsibility of giving patriarchal blessings to all Church members. He died in September 1840 and was succeeded in the office of patriarch by his son Hyrum Smith. A revelation given on 19 January 1841 clarified that the office of patriarch "was appointed unto him [Hyrum] by his father." Hyrum was ordained patriarch to the Church as well as assistant president on 24 January (124:91–94). The office of patriarch, or "evangelical ministers," was to be hereditary (107:39–40; Smith, 3:381), though occasionally an acting patriarch to the Church was appointed. Over the years adjustments were made in the responsibilities of the Church patriarch, and in 1979 the office of patriarch to the Church was retired; by that time there were enough patriarchs in the various stakes of the Church to make his services as a general Church officer no longer needed.

On 14 February 1835, in Kirtland, Ohio, the Quorum of the Twelve Apostles was organized at a special meeting called for that purpose. Members of the Quorum were selected by the Three Witnesses to the Book of Mormon (Smith, 2:186–87). *See* Apostles, the first Twelve of latter days.

At first the responsibility of the Twelve extended only to doing missionary work throughout the world and setting in order the affairs of the churches outside the established stakes of

Zion. Though they went about their responsibilities enthusiastically, several members of the first quorum eventually defected and had to be replaced. In 1840 and 1841 most of the members of the Quorum fulfilled an all-important mission to the British Isles, as they had been commanded to do by revelation (118). *See* Apostles, the Twelve, mission to Great Britain.

The experiences on the apostles' mission to Great Britain strengthened and unified them as a quorum. After the apostles returned, Joseph Smith expanded their authority to include overseeing the affairs of stakes and otherwise expanded their responsibilities. Also, anticipating that he would not be with them for long, the Prophet stepped up the pace of his instructions, preparing the Quorum of the Twelve to take over the leadership of the Church. Finally, in March 1844, just three months before his death, he conferred upon the Twelve all the priesthood KEYS and authority he held and told them that the responsibility of leading the Church now rested upon their shoulders. This charge was confirmed upon them by the laying on of hands by the Prophet and his brother Hyrum, the assistant Church president (Esplin, 301–41). The Twelve now had the authority and responsibility to "bear off the kingdom" (Woodruff, 546). This laid the foundation for the succession of the Twelve to Church leadership after the death of Joseph Smith in June 1844.

About two weeks after the Twelve were organized, Joseph Smith introduced the office of SEVENTY. Several men were chosen to fill this office, and they were presided over by seven presidents, who eventually came to be known as the First Council of the Seventy. The assignment of the seventy was to "preach the gospel, and to be especial witnesses unto the Gentiles and in all the world" (107:25). The revelation that defined their duties indicated they were to "form a quorum, equal in authority to that of the Twelve," in their respective stewardships (107:26), and to act under the direction of the Twelve in preaching and administering the gospel (107:34).

The First Council of the Seventy continued to be sustained as General Authorities of the Church. The number of quorums of seventy grew over the years, though a quorum specifically called the First Quorum of the Seventy did not continue. Eventually the many quorums of seventy came under the jurisdiction of stakes, but beginning 3 October 1975 President Spencer W. Kimball began reorganizing the seventy to bring the office more into line with what was originally spelled out in the Doctrine and Covenants. The First Quorum of the Seventy was reorganized, and its members were designated General Authorities.

The designation First Council of the Seventy was changed, and the seven presiding seventies were identified simply as the Presidency of the Seventy. The numerous seventies quorums scattered throughout the stakes of the Church were discontinued 4 October 1986. Since 1976 additional Quorums of the Seventy have been organized to help administer the Church worldwide.

In summary, by early 1835 the basic ecclesiastical units of the Church were in existence. The First Presidency presided over the whole Church. The Quorum of Twelve Apostles was a traveling body, called as special witnesses of Christ and authorized to set in order Church affairs anywhere outside the stakes. More authority, including the right of succession to the presidency of the Church, was added later. The seventy, sometimes called the "Seventy Apostles," were to assist the Twelve in carrying out their responsibilities. The Patriarch to the Church had the special calling of giving blessings, and the Presiding Bishopric had a variety of temporal responsibilities, including the care of the poor.

In addition, there were two stakes of Zion, each presided over by a stake presidency assisted by a high council of twelve high priests. The stake high council was primarily a judicial body, although it later assumed greater advisory and administrative functions. Bishops in each stake presided over the Aaronic, or lesser, priesthood and also had important economic responsibilities.

In years to come, the responsibilities of these hierarchal bodies would be augmented from time to time and new offices would be added as the Church's numbers grew. All these leaders, acting under the direction of the First Presidency of the Church, provided the means for keeping the worldwide Church unified, as envisioned in the New Testament: "And he gave some, apostles; and some, prophets; and some, evangelists [patriarchs]; and some, pastors [bishops] and teachers; for the perfecting of the saints, for the work of the ministry, for the edifying of the body of Christ: Till we all come in the unity of the faith, and of the knowledge of the Son of God, unto a perfect man, unto the measure of the stature of the fulness of Christ" (Eph. 4:11–13).

See also Apostasy, the great; Priesthood offices; Priesthood, restoration of priesthood and priesthood keys.

BIBLIOGRAPHY

Allen, James B., and Glen M. Leonard. *The Story of the Latter-day Saints.* 2d ed. Salt Lake City: Deseret Book, 1992.

Anderson, Richard Lloyd. "The Organization Revelations (D&C 20, 21, and 22)." In *The Doctrine and Covenants,* edited by Robert L. Millet and Kent P. Jackson. Vol. 1 of Studies in Scripture series. Salt Lake City: Deseret Book, 1989.

Cowan, Richard O. *Answers to Your Questions about the Doctrine and Covenants.* Salt Lake City: Deseret Book, 1996.

Esplin, Ronald K. "Joseph, Brigham and the Twelve: A Succession of Continuity." *BYU Studies* 21 (Summer 1981): 301–41.

Hartley, William G. "The Priesthood Reorganization of 1877: Brigham Young's Last Achievement." *BYU Studies* 20 (Fall 1979): 3–36.

Jessee, Dean C., Mark Ashurst-McGee, and Richard L. Jensen, eds. *Journals, Volume 1: 1832–1839.* Vol. 1 of the Journals series of *The Joseph Smith Papers,* edited by Dean C. Jessee, Ronald K. Esplin, and Richard Lyman Bushman. Salt Lake City: Church Historian's Press, 2008.

Porter, L. Aldin. "A History of the Latter-Day Seventy." *Ensign* 30 (August 2000): 14–20.

Smith, Joseph. *History of The Church of Jesus Christ of Latter-day Saints.* Edited by B. H. Roberts. 7 vols. 2d ed. rev. Salt Lake City: The Church of Jesus Christ of Latter-day Saints, 1932–51.

Smith, Joseph Fielding. *Doctrines of Salvation.* Compiled by Bruce R. McConkie. 3 vols. Salt Lake City: Bookcraft, 1954–56.

Tanner, N. Eldon. "The Sustaining of Church Officers." *Ensign* 9 (November 1979): 18–19.

Turley, Richard E., Jr. "The Calling of the Twelve Apostles and the Seventy in 1835." In *Joseph: Exploring the Life and Ministry of the Prophet,* edited by Susan Easton Black and Andrew C. Skinner. Salt Lake City: Deseret Book, 2005.

Woodruff, Wilford. "The Keys of the Kingdom." *Millennial Star* 51 (2 September 1889): 545–49.

JBA

Church of Jesus Christ of Latter-day Saints, The, organizational development of. *See* Church of Jesus Christ of Latter-day Saints, The.

Church of the devil. *See* Great and abominable church.

Church of the Firstborn

Identification for disciples of Jesus Christ who are heirs of exaltation in the celestial kingdom. As joint-heirs with Christ they share the rights of the firstborn, receiving all that the Father has (93:21; 84:37–38; Rom. 8:17). *See* Exalt, exaltation.

Children of God qualify for inclusion in this assemblage by receiving all the covenants and ordinances of exaltation and faithfully "keeping the commandments." Hence, they are "washed and cleansed from all their sins"; they "overcome by faith, and are sealed by the Holy Spirit of promise," having been "begotten" through Christ into the exalted family of God. "They are they into whose hands the Father has given all things." "They are gods . . . [and] shall dwell in the presence of God and his Christ forever and ever" (76:50–70; 93:21–22). Among members of the church of the Firstborn are no hidden agendas and no deceitful craftiness, for "they see as they are seen, and know as they are known, having received of his fulness and of his grace" (76:94; cf. 76:71, 102; 77:11; 78:21; 88:5; 107:18–19).

LED

Church, great and abominable. *See* Great and abominable church.

Church, only true and living. *See* Only true and living church.

Cincinnati, Ohio

A city located on the Ohio River in southwestern Ohio; one of the largest cities in western America by 1830. Cincinnati was known as the "Queen of the West" and the "Gateway to the South." The city's growth was stimulated by shipbuilding and the completion of the Erie Canal, the final phase of an internal water system linking the Hudson River to the Ohio River (Taylor, 32–46).

In August 1831, Joseph Smith, Sidney Rigdon, and Oliver Cowdery were instructed by the Lord to go to Cincinnati on their return from Missouri to Kirtland and to preach against the wickedness there (60:6–7; 61:30–31). No report is included about Cincinnati in the Prophet's account of their travels (Smith, 1:202–6). A year earlier, the four missionaries to the Lamanites had spent "several days" in Cincinnati "and preached to many of the people, but without much success" (Pratt, 51). In Cincinnati in the fall of 1831, W. W. Phelps purchased the press and type for *The Evening and the Morning Star,* a periodical that published many of the revelations received by Joseph Smith (Perkins and Cannon, 75–76). In the early 1830s, Lyman Wight preached and converted about a hundred people in Cincinnati. These converts became the nucleus of the first Church branch in the community (Jenson, 1:93). *See* map, p. 355.

BIBLIOGRAPHY

Jenson, Andrew. *Latter-day Saints' Biographical Encyclopedia.* 4 vols. Salt Lake City: The Andrew Jenson History Company, 1901–36. Reprint, Salt Lake City: Western Epics, 1971.

Perkins, Keith W., and Donald Q. Cannon. *Ohio and Illinois.* Vol. 3 of *Sacred Places: A Comprehensive Guide to Early LDS Historical Sites,* edited by LaMar C. Berrett. Salt Lake City: Deseret Book, 2002.

Pratt, Parley P. *Autobiography of Parley P. Pratt.* Edited by Parley P. Pratt Jr. Salt Lake City: Deseret Book, 1966.

Smith, Joseph. *History of The Church of Jesus Christ of Latter-day Saints.* Edited by B. H. Roberts. 7 vols. 2d ed. rev. Salt Lake City: The Church of Jesus Christ of Latter-day Saints, 1932–51.

Taylor, George Rogers. *The Transportation Revolution, 1815–1860.* New York: Rinehart & Company, 1951.

MVB

Circumcision

Circumcision is referred to four times in three verses of the same section in the Doctrine and Covenants (74:2–3, 6), all in reference to the practice among Jews during the days of the New Testament apostles. Circumcision was instituted in Old Testament times among the children of Israel as a token of the covenant God made with Abraham (Gen. 17:9–14). It was continued among the Israelites as part of the LAW OF MOSES to New Testament times. After Jesus Christ came to the earth as the "mediator of the new covenant" (Heb. 12:24; cf. Heb. 8:6; D&C 76:69), fulfilling the law of Moses, contention arose among Christians concerning the need for the continued practice of circumcision.

The Prophet Joseph Smith received a revelation, now recorded in section 74, concerning 1 Corinthians 7:14, which is quoted in its entirety in 74:1. The Lord acknowledged that the law of circumcision had proved to be a stumbling block to the early Christian Saints (cf. Acts 15:1–2, 5), in that Jewish fathers "who believed not the gospel of Jesus Christ" were desirous that their sons be circumcised according to the old law, despite the Christian beliefs of their spouses (74:2–4). In this revelation the Lord made it clear that little children are "holy, being sanctified through the atonement" (74:7; cf. 29:46; Moro. 8:8), and therefore not in need of circumcision. As one solution to the controversy, Paul wrote to the Corinthian Saints "not of the Lord, but of himself, that a believer should not be united to an unbeliever; except the law of Moses should be done away among them, that their children might remain without circumcision" (74:5–6).

See also Historical context and overview of Doctrine and Covenants 74 (p. 779).

TAW

City of the living God

A phrase that occurs once in the Doctrine and Covenants, signifying the eternal abode of those who inherit exaltation in the celestial kingdom. They are "they who are come . . . unto the city of the living God, the heavenly place, the holiest of all" (76:66; cf. 63:49; Heb. 11:10; 12:22).

RLM

City of Zion. *See* New Jerusalem.

Civil war. *See* War(s).

Clean, cleanliness, cleanse(d)

Free from personal sins, from the spiritual corruptions and impurities of the world, "the blood of this wicked generation" (88:75; cf. 88:85, 138). Being thus cleansed is required of those who receive the fulness of spiritual blessings. "No man is possessor of all things except he be purified and cleansed from all sin" (50:28; cf. 76:52). Hence, very early in the restoration of the gospel (in January and again in November 1831), the Lord commanded his servants: "Be ye clean that bear the vessels of the Lord" (38:42; 133:5; cf. 38:10). *See* Vessels of the Lord.

The Lord is pleased with honest strivings but ultimately requires complete cleansing. The Lord commended William E. McLellin for accepting the gospel, and told him, "You are clean, but not all; repent, therefore, of those things which are not pleasing in my sight" (66:3). No one was to participate in the School of the Prophets (1832–33) "save he is clean from the blood of this generation" (88:138) through covenants and ordinances (88:127–41). In March 1833 the Lord said, "I, the Lord, will contend with Zion, and plead with her strong ones, and chasten her until she overcomes and is clean before me" (90:36).

Becoming clean is made possible only through the Savior and his ATONEMENT by OBEDIENCE to the laws and ordinances of the GOSPEL and "by keeping the commandments" (76:51–52; A of F 3). To Joseph Smith and Sidney Rigdon the Lord revealed that Jesus Christ "came into the world . . . to be crucified for the world, and to bear the sins of the world, and to sanctify the world, and to cleanse it from all unrighteousness" (76:41). Jesus pleads with the Father as an advocate for the salvation of those who believe in him (45:1–5; 88:74–75), but of the wicked and unrepentant he declares, "My blood shall not cleanse them if they hear me not" (29:17).

The Lord has specified that the cleansing required must be extensive: one's hands, heart, feet, and garments must be clean (88:74; 112:33). Cleansing one's hands, garments, and heart signify overcoming personal sins through REPENTANCE and obedience. "The ordinance of the washing of feet" symbolizes becoming "clean from the blood of this generation" (88:138–41). That this ordinance was to be performed by the "presiding elder of the church" (88:140) in the School of the Prophets in 1832–33, as it had been performed by the Savior himself upon his apostles in the meridian of time (John 13:2–17), portrays a great lesson in humility and the importance of leaders' being servants to others. *See* Wash, washed, washing(s).

In the scriptures, cleansing one's feet and garments symbolizes shedding responsibility for the sins of others. This requires faithful service to the Lord in proclaiming the message of the gospel to the world, thus placing accountability upon the hearers for their own sins and absolving the messenger from responsibility for those sins (112:28, 33; 24:15; 60:15; 75:20; 84:92; 135:5; cf. 2 Ne. 9:44; Jacob 1:19; 2:2; Acts 20:25–27). *See* Shake off the dust of thy feet.

The possibility of becoming clean is not limited to mortals on the earth. In his vision of the redemption of the dead, President Joseph F. Smith saw that the gospel is preached in the postmortal spirit world, "even unto all who would repent of their sins and receive the gospel" (138:31). He also learned that "the dead who repent will be redeemed, through obedience to the ordinances of the house of God, and after they have paid the penalty of their transgressions, and are washed clean, shall receive a reward according to their works, for they are heirs of salvation" (138:58–59).

In revealing the law of the Church in February 1831, the Lord said, "And let all things be done in cleanliness before me" (42:41). The principle of cleanliness thus extends from the "inward vessel" to the "outer vessel" as well (Alma 60:23–24), including one's body, clothing, and personal possessions. President Spencer W. Kimball taught, "We look forward to the day when, in all of our communities, urban and rural, there would be a universal, continued movement to clean and repair and paint barns and sheds, build sidewalks, clean ditch banks, and make our properties a thing of beauty to behold" (378).

See also Forgiveness; Pure, purify.

BIBLIOGRAPHY

Kimball, Spencer W. *The Teachings of Spencer W. Kimball.* Edited by Edward L. Kimball. Salt Lake City: Bookcraft, 1982.

DKO

Cleave. *See* Appendix E.

Coe, Joseph

Birth: 12 November 1784, Cayuga County, New York

Death: 17 October 1854, Kirtland, Ohio

In June of 1831 the Lord called Joseph Coe, an early convert to the Church, to accompany Joseph Smith and other Church leaders to Missouri (55:6). He, along with six other elders, witnessed Sidney Rigdon dedicate the land of Missouri on 2 August. The next day Coe participated when Joseph Smith dedicated the temple site at Independence and laid "a stone at the northeast corner of the contemplated temple" (Whitmer, 80).

In Kirtland, Coe oversaw land acquisition and served on the high council. By June 1837, he had joined with John Boynton and others who disapproved of Joseph Smith's leadership; they started their own church, called the Church of Christ.

BIBLIOGRAPHY

Cahoon, Reynolds. Diaries, 1831–1832. Church History Library, The Church of Jesus Christ of Latter-day Saints, Salt Lake City, Utah.

Whitmer, John. *An Early Latter Day Saint History: The Book of John Whitmer.* Edited by F. Mark McKiernan and Roger D. Launius. Independence, Mo.: Herald Publishing House, 1980.

RC

Colesville, Broome County, New York

A township in northeastern Broome County, in the southeast corner of the state of New York. Now called Nineveh, Colesville was the home of Joseph Knight Sr., his son Newel Knight, and their families. The Knights, their extended family, and some of their neighbors and friends were among the first converts to the Church in 1830 and 1831. They formed the COLESVILLE BRANCH of about sixty-eight members, who moved as a group from New York to Ohio and then on to Missouri, remaining faithful to the restored gospel through trying times (54:7–10). Joseph Smith, who at the time (July 1828–August 1830) lived about thirty miles south of Colesville in Harmony, Pennsylvania, often went to Colesville to visit, preach, and baptize those who accepted the gospel. The first public miracle of this dispensation occurred in Colesville when Joseph Smith cast the devil out of Newel Knight. It was in Colesville that Emma Smith and several others were baptized in June 1830 in a dammed-up stream convenient to the Knight home (Smith, 1:81–88).

Colesville is mentioned four times in the Doctrine and Covenants. In July 1830 Joseph Smith was told to "go speedily unto the church which is in Colesville," with the promise that the members "shall support thee," for which support they would be blessed "both spiritually and temporally" (24:3).

Later in the same month, the Prophet was told that his time was to "be devoted to the studying of the scriptures, and to preaching, and to confirming the church at Colesville" (26:1). In December 1830 Joseph Smith was told to "go to the Ohio," but he was not to go "until ye have . . . strengthened up the church whithersoever it is found, and more especially in Colesville; for, behold, they pray unto me in much faith" (37:1–2). Lastly, Colesville was near the place where Peter, James, and John restored the Melchizedek Priesthood (128:20). *See* maps, pp. 447 and 710.

See also New York period.

BIBLIOGRAPHY

Jessee, Dean C. "Joseph Knight's Recollection of Early Mormon History." *BYU Studies* 17, no. 1 (Autumn 1976): 29–30.

Smith, Joseph. *History of The Church of Jesus Christ of Latter-day Saints.* Edited by B. H. Roberts. 7 vols. 2d ed. rev. Salt Lake City: The Church of Jesus Christ of Latter-day Saints, 1932–51.

LCP

Colesville branch

David Whitmer stated there were about twenty persons from Colesville, New York, at Fayette, New York, on the day of the Church organization, 6 April 1830. None had been baptized previously under the Aaronic Priesthood, nor were any from Colesville baptized that day. Later in April, Joseph Smith visited Joseph Knight's family in Colesville, finding them "willing to reason with me upon my religious views" (Smith, 1:81). Newel Knight afterwards called on Joseph at Fayette and was baptized by David Whitmer the last week of May. Returning to Colesville in June, Joseph Smith and others prepared several members of the Knight family for baptism, and they, with the Prophet's wife, Emma, were baptized by Oliver Cowdery in Knight's millstream on 28 June 1830. The Prophet was arrested that day and taken to South Bainbridge (now Afton) for trial. Joseph Knight hired legal counselors James Davidson and John Reid to defend him. Joseph was exonerated both in that trial and in a second held in Colesville. He later returned to Colesville, confirming those individuals who had been baptized but not confirmed because of his arrest (26:1; Smith, 1:108). *See* Confirm, confirmed, confirming.

Newel Knight was ordained a priest in September. Hyrum Smith was sent to preside at Colesville in October 1830. Responding to revelation calling for removal of all Saints to Ohio, Joseph Smith and Sidney Rigdon were to strengthen the membership, "especially in Colesville," before departing (37:2). They preached at Colesville and elsewhere. When the Prophet left for Kirtland in late January 1831, Joseph and Polly Knight and their daughter Elizabeth accompanied him in a Knight family sleigh. Newel Knight was called to preside over the Colesville branch when the Prophet asked Hyrum to return to Kirtland on 3 March 1831. The Colesville Branch, now numbering about sixty-eight souls, met at Ithaca to journey to Ohio. Leaving that village on 25 April 1831, they went by boat on Cayuga Lake, the Cayuga-Seneca Canal, the Erie Canal to Buffalo, and then on Lake Erie to Fairport Harbor, Ohio, arriving on 14 May 1831. They were directed to consecrated land on Leman Copley's farm, Thompson Township, but Copley broke his covenant, forcing the branch members to abandon the farm. By revelation they were instructed to "journey . . . unto the land of Missouri" (54:8).

Colesville Township, New York, now called Nineveh, New York; photograph by George Edward Anderson, 1907. Joseph Knight's farm was in Colesville.

Arriving at Independence on 25 July 1831, they were sent to occupy land in Kaw Township. Members of the branch were present for the consecration of the land of Zion by Sidney Rigdon on 2 August and the dedication of the temple site at Independence by the Prophet on 3 August.

See also New York period.

BIBLIOGRAPHY

Hartley, William G. *Stand by My Servant Joseph: The Story of the Joseph Knight Family and the Restoration.* Provo, Utah: Joseph Fielding Smith Institute for LDS History; Salt Lake City, Utah: Deseret Book, 2003.

Porter, Larry C. "The Colesville Branch in Kaw Township, Jackson County, Missouri, 1831–1833." In *Missouri,* edited by Arnold K. Garr and Clark V. Johnson, 281–311. Regional Studies in Latter-day Saint Church History series. Provo, Utah: Department of Church History and Doctrine, Brigham Young University, 1994.

———. "A Study of the Origins of The Church of Jesus Christ of Latter-day Saints in the States of New York and Pennsylvania, 1816–1831." Ph.D. dissertation, Brigham Young University, 1971.

Smith, Joseph. *History of The Church of Jesus Christ of Latter-day Saints.* Edited by B. H. Roberts. 7 vols. 2d ed. rev. Salt Lake City: The Church of Jesus Christ of Latter-day Saints, 1932–51.

LCP

Coltrin, Zebedee

Birth: 7 September 1804, Ovid, Seneca County, New York

Death: 21 July 1887, Spanish Fork, Utah County, Utah

On 8 January 1831, Solomon Hancock shared the gospel with Zebedee Coltrin. The following day Coltrin was baptized in a pond close to his father's home. In June of that same year Coltrin was called to serve a mission in Missouri with Levi W. Hancock (52:29). They "immediately started" on their journey (Hancock, 35).

The mission companions baptized many as they traveled from Ohio to Missouri. New members shared the message with others, and large crowds gathered to hear the missionaries preach. In Solon, Shelly County, Ohio, one convert "immediately went to all his neighbors and invited them to come and hear us," Hancock recorded. "We had a large congregation to address" (36). Upon stopping in Winchester, Indiana, they

Zebedee Coltrin, 1804–1887.

Courtesy Church History Library

introduced their message to a schoolmaster. "He was so well pleased with the message that he spread the news as fast as possible and called a meeting." After baptizing him, Coltrin and Hancock discovered that "nearly all the people wanted to hear us" (Hancock, 37–38). They held an additional meeting at the courthouse, which resulted in several other baptisms. Thus, they continued to labor in Winchester and baptized approximately one hundred people. A mob eventually sent a threatening letter telling them to leave. Nevertheless, Coltrin and Hancock remained in the area and continued to preach. They baptized seventeen individuals who had planned to mob them (Hancock, 38–39).

Coltrin "enjoyed the spiritual gifts of the gospel in a great degree" (Jenson, 1:190), including being blessed with glorious visions (Smith, *Papers,* 2:164, 171) and the gift of speaking in tongues (Smith, *History,* 1:323). He remained faithful all his life. In 1833 he attended the School of the Prophets in Kirtland; in 1834 he was a member of ZION'S CAMP; in 1835 he was ordained a seventy and served as a president in the First Quorum of the Seventy.

Coltrin settled in Nauvoo in 1839 and, after a brief stay back in Kirtland, returned to Nauvoo by 1842. He left Nauvoo with the Saints in 1846 and arrived in Salt Lake City in 1847. He was called to settle the Spanish Fork area. There he assisted in building projects and served on the city council. From May 1873 until his death fourteen years later, he served as a patriarch, giving more than a thousand blessings.

BIBLIOGRAPHY

Coltrin, Zebedee. Autobiographical Sketch, 1880. Church History Library, The Church of Jesus Christ of Latter-day Saints, Salt Lake City, Utah.

Hancock, Levi Ward. The Life of Levi W. Hancock, copied from his own journal by Clara E. H. Lloyd. L. Tom Perry Special Collections, Harold B. Lee Library, Brigham Young University, Provo, Utah.

Jenson, Andrew. Latter-day Saints' Biographical Encyclopedia. 4 vols. Salt Lake City: The Andrew Jenson History Company, 1901–36. Reprint, Salt Lake City: Western Epics, 1971.

Smith, Joseph. History of The Church of Jesus Christ of Latter-day Saints. Edited by B. H. Roberts. 7 vols. 2d ed. rev. Salt Lake City: The Church of Jesus Christ of Latter-day Saints, 1932–51.

———. The Papers of Joseph Smith. Edited by Dean C. Jessee. 2 vols. Salt Lake City: Deseret Book, 1989–92.

RC

Comforter. See Holy Ghost, the.

Commandment(s)

In general, God's commandments tell people "the way wherein they must walk, and the work that they must do" (Ex. 18:20). Commandments undergird the relationship between the Lord and his people. Together, the words *commandment, commandments, command,* and *commanded* appear hundreds of times in the Doctrine and Covenants. They are often given in the first-person voice of the Lord, as in "a commandment I give unto you" (27:3), "keep my commandments" (6:9), "I command you again" (124:55), or "I have commanded you" (93:40). In the Lord's revealed preface to the first publication of revelations in this dispensation, he calls the revelations "the book of my commandments" (1:6). These commandments may be divided into four main types: general and specific commandments to the Church, and general and specific commandments to individuals.

The first are commandments directed to the general organization of the Church. These commandments were given so that the faithful "might have power to lay the foundation of this church" (1:30). For example, the manner of baptism was given to the Church "*by way of commandment*" (20:37). The Lord commanded that membership records (20:84) and historical records be kept (21:1). Commandments were given regarding COMMON CONSENT and the conduct of Church meetings in general (26:2; 41:2; 46:2).

Second, the Lord gave commandments to the Church that were specific in time and place. For example, the Saints were commanded to gather to Ohio (37:3), to Missouri with instructions for the conduct of the affairs of the Church there (58; 63; 105), to Iowa, or to the Mountain West (125:1–4; 136). The Lord commanded the construction of a temple and other buildings in Kirtland (88:119–20; 94:1–4), Missouri (115:8), and Nauvoo (124:27–31). Detailed explanations of how these commands were to be carried out often accompanied these commandments. When the Lord commanded the Saints to build a boarding house in Nauvoo, for instance, he detailed the purpose for the house (124:23–24, 60–61) and how the house was to be financed (124:62–83, 119–22).

Third, many commandments define the behavior required of all individual members of the Church. These commandments prohibit such sins as murder, adultery, theft, robbery, dishonesty, pride, unfairness, unkindness, and idleness. Saints are commanded to observe the Sabbath day and to work on the other six days of the week (68:29–31), to fast and pray (68:33; 88:76), to love and thank the Lord in all things (59:5, 7, 15–16), to esteem one's brother as oneself (38:25), to support one's family (75:28) and teach one's children (68:25–28), to behave properly in all respects (88:123–25; 136:20–29), to teach one another the doctrines of the kingdom (88:77), to obey the laws of the land (58:21), to care for the poor and the needy (83:1–6), and to keep the "everlasting covenant that cannot be broken" (78:11).

Fourth, many commandments were given

as personal instructions to individuals or small groups. These revelations include callings to serve missions, assignments of particular stewardships, and individual calls to repentance. Oliver Cowdery, for example, was commanded to preach repentance (6:9), to trifle not with sacred things (6:12), and to "rely upon the things which are written" (18:3). The Lord commanded Joseph Smith "to repent and walk more uprightly before me" (5:21). Several times the Lord says in the revelations, "What I say unto one I say unto all" (93:49), thus extending the application of the principles in these specific commandments beyond the individuals to whom they were addressed. The commandments offer useful examples of the blessings that come from faithful adherence to principles of righteousness and of the consequences for disobedience.

Because Latter-day Saints see God as their Father and themselves as his children, the term *commandment* in the Doctrine and Covenants is understood to include precepts, principles, instruction, guidance, invitation, love, and gentle counsel. For example, in 59:4–13, the Saints are commanded to love the Lord with all their might, mind and strength, to serve him in the name of Jesus Christ, to love their neighbors, not to steal, not to commit adultery, not to kill "nor do anything like unto it," to thank God in all things, to offer a sacrifice of a broken heart and contrite spirit, to confess one's sins and to rest and worship with singleness of heart on the Sabbath day. The words "nor do anything like unto it" assure that Latter-day Saints understand God's commandments are broad principles that do not always contain specific details.

The pervasive breadth of the commandments in the Doctrine and Covenants is reflected in the wide variety of forms used to convey these injunctions and instructions. For example, some commandments are given as simple imperatives: "Thou shalt not" (42:18–21; cf. 88:69); as strong recommendations: "It is expedient in me that" (105:9, 13, 19, 33), or as exhortations: "Let all thy" (42:40). In several instances, commandments are accompanied by explanations of the intention behind the commandment and why the commandment should be kept. For example: "That thou mayest more fully keep thyself unspotted from the world" (59:9).

God's commandments and their underlying principles are as old as the human family and have been known in all ages. God speaks in every language and to each nation after the manner of their own language (1:24; cf. 2 Ne. 29:12). Latter-day Saints find evidence that God has revealed principles to such lawgivers as Hammurabi, Solon, Justinian, Confucius, and Muhammad. OBEDIENCE to true principles results in blessings from God, whereas disobedience results in unhappiness and in the natural loss of opportunities for growth and progress.

Commandments are also to be understood in the context of a voluntary bilateral covenant relationship between God and his people, freely chosen and entered into personally and individually. Covenant making implies personal worthiness, and keeping the commandments is thus required for baptism and for entrance into the temple. Diligently observing the laws and commandments of the gospel in fulfillment of one's covenants with God opens the way to receive of God's fulness and to be glorified in him (93:19–20).

Another main function of commandments is to supply the conditions of membership in the community of Zion itself. Members are not to commit murder, to steal, to lie, to commit adultery, or to speak evil of their neighbor; these are conditions of maintaining good standing in the Church. Those who refuse to repent are to be cast out—excommunicated or disfellowshipped (42:18–29).

When individuals agree to live by his commandments, God agrees to show unlimited mercy, to extend life, to protect, to nourish, and to heal. The revelations in the Doctrine and Covenants make it clear that "when we obtain any blessing from God, it is by obedience to that law upon which it is predicated" (130:21). Miraculously, by divine mercy and grace, finite obedience can be answered with infinite blessings. The Doctrine and Covenants sets forth the promise that when people choose to keep the commandments of God, they will ultimately receive "the good things of the earth" and "be crowned with blessings from above" (59:3–4; see also v. 16; 64:34).

When considering the commandments of the Lord, it is important to realize that the Lord does not command in all things. He expects his people to be "anxiously engaged" in good causes and to "do many things of their own free will," bringing "to pass much righteousness" without being commanded (58:27; see also vv. 26–30).

JWW

Commandments, law of carnal. *See* Law of carnal commandments.

Common consent

A fundamental principle of governance in the Church, in which members are given the opportunity to sustain or oppose proposals. A July 1830 revelation declared that "all things shall be done by common consent in the church" (26:2). Church leaders at every level make decisions and then present them to the members for their consent or dissent.

Sometime before the Church was organized on 6 April 1830, Joseph Smith and Oliver Cowdery received a revelation in the Whitmer home in Fayette, New York, in which they were commanded to implement the principle of common consent. Joseph's history says that "the word of the Lord came unto us . . . commanding us, that I should ordain Oliver Cowdery to be an Elder in the Church of Jesus Christ, and that he also should ordain me to the same office, and that after having been thus ordained, we should proceed to ordain others to the same office, according as it should be made known unto us, from time to time." The revelation instructed Joseph and Oliver to ordain each other at a sacrament meeting attended by those they had baptized in order to receive "their sanction." Once Joseph and Oliver had "been accepted by them as their teachers," they could proceed with the ordinations as commanded (Smith, 1:239). Thus the principle of common consent in the governance of the Church was restored and implemented from the beginning of its organization.

Joseph and Oliver called the believers together for the proposed meeting, held Tuesday, 6 April 1830, at the Whitmer home. The first thing they did after prayer was ask those present to consent to the earlier revelation that Joseph should serve as the Church's presiding elder, with Oliver Cowdery presiding under Joseph. Joseph's history says that "the brethren & Sisters having by unanimous vote, accepted us . . . I proceeded to lay my hands upon Oliver Cowdery—and ordained him an Elder of the Church of Jesus Christ of Latter Day Saints, after which he ordained me also to the office of an Elder of said Church" (1:241–42). By the process of revelation, consent of the Saints to abide by the revelation, followed by solemn ordinances, common consent procedures in the Church were set in order, as sections 21 and 26 command. When Hiram Page upset this order by claiming in September 1830 that through a "certain stone" he had received revelations "concerning the upbuilding of Zion and the order of the Church" and so forth (28, headnote), another revelation reiterated that "all things must be done in order, and by common consent in the church" (28:13). The issue was resolved at a conference, when "after considerable discussion, reasoning and investigation [Hiram] agreed to renounce the stone and its author, and the brethren unanimously agreed to renounce them also" (Smith, 1:263).

Subsequent revelations reaffirmed the principle of common consent. Sections 38 and 102 highlight the importance of the "voice of the church" in appointing leaders (38:34). Section 42, the law of the Church, declared that no one be sent to preach the gospel unless his authorized calling and ordination were "known to the church" (42:11). Section 104 directed the members of "the order," the United Firm, who held and administered property belonging to the Church, arrive at their decisions by common consent (104:71–72; 85). Section 124 assigned the Saints to meet in general conference to "approve" or "disapprove" the appointment of Church leaders named by the Lord in the revelation (124:144). These same procedures are enacted in the Church today.

Common consent preserves individual moral AGENCY. *Common* means all are to speak for themselves, to make their own choice. "Everyone is perfectly free. . . . There is no compulsion whatsoever in this voting," said President N. Eldon Tanner. *Consent* means to agree to what is proposed by someone else, "a yielding of the mind or will to that which is proposed," according to Webster's 1828 dictionary. Latter-day Saints do not vote in the Church as in popular elections, hoping for their will to rule. Rather, they exercise their agency to consent or dissent from what is proposed. "When you vote affirmatively," said President Tanner, "you make a solemn covenant with the Lord that you will sustain, that is, give your full loyalty and support, without equivocation or reservation, to the officer for whom you vote" (38). Those who register a vote in opposition to what is being proposed are not ignored. They are invited to meet with appropriate presiding officers to discuss their reasons for dissenting. Care is taken to consider any evidence of unworthiness that might disqualify a person from serving in a calling being proposed.

BIBLIOGRAPHY

Smith, Joseph. *The Papers of Joseph Smith.* Edited by Dean C. Jessee. 2 vols. Salt Lake City: Deseret Book, 1989–92.

Tanner, N. Eldon. "The Solemn Assembly." *Ensign* 4 (May 1974): 38–45.

Webster, Noah. *An American Dictionary of the English Language.* 1828.

SCH

Common council of the church

A disciplinary council "provided for in the church for the trial of a president in the Presidency of the High Priesthood of the Church [a member of the First Presidency], which is presided over by the bishop of the church [the Presiding Bishop], assisted by twelve high priests chosen for the occasion" (Smith, *History,* 7:268). Doctrine and Covenants 107:82–84 says: "And inasmuch as a President of the High Priesthood shall transgress, he shall be had in remembrance before the common council of the church, who shall be assisted by twelve counselors of the High Priesthood; and their decision upon his head shall be an end of controversy concerning him. Thus, none shall be exempted from the justice and the laws of God, that all things may be done in order and in solemnity before him, according to truth and righteousness."

The calling of the Presiding Bishop to be "a *common judge* among the inhabitants of Zion" (107:74; emphasis added) authorizes him to preside over the *common council of the Church.* Elder John A. Widtsoe explained: "The Presiding Bishop's Court consists of the Presiding Bishop with his two counselors, and twelve High Priests especially chosen for the purpose. It is a tribunal extraordinary, from which there is no appeal, to be convened if it should be necessary to try a member of the First Presidency" (212). In early Church history, such a council was "called into existence several times. The Prophet Joseph Smith was tried before this council on charges made against him by Sylvester Smith after the return of Zion's Camp. Oliver Cowdery, David Whitmer [presidents pro tem in Missouri] and Frederick G. Williams [a counselor in the First Presidency] were each tried by this tribunal" (Smith, *Church,* 3:55). *See* Presidents of thy Church.

Since those early days, there has not been cause to convene the common council of the Church.

See also Church discipline; Cast out/cut off; Historical context and overview of Doctrine and Covenants 102 (p. 807).

BIBLIOGRAPHY

Smith, Joseph. *History of The Church of Jesus Christ of Latter-day Saints.* Edited by B. H. Roberts. 7 vols. 2d ed. rev. Salt Lake City: The Church of Jesus Christ of Latter-day Saints, 1932–51.

Smith, Joseph Fielding. *Church History and Modern Revelation.* 4 vols. Salt Lake City: The Church of Jesus Christ of Latter-day Saints, 1946–49.

Widtsoe, John A. *Priesthood and Church Government.* Salt Lake City: Deseret Book, 1939.

CMC

Concatenation. *See* Appendix E.

Concubines

A junior wife under the principle of plural MARRIAGE as practiced in ancient times. Section 132 was given in response to Joseph Smith's desire to understand the "principle and doctrine of [the ancient patriarchs and kings] having many wives and concubines" (132:1–2). According to 132:37–38, many of God's chosen leaders in times past practiced this doctrine, receiving not only wives but also concubines, or women of lower social status, into a married state with them. This practice was approved of the Lord when sanctioned by his authorized servants, but it was not approved "in those things which they received not of [the Lord]." Anciently, concubines, while being able to claim married status, did not have the same social standing or rights as that of a recognized wife. The term *concubines* appears in section 132, but it was not used in this dispensation to describe the status of plural wives, perhaps because the disparity which the term designated in times past is not appropriate in the proper exercise of the principle, or because at that time, in the early part of the nineteenth century, the term was sometimes used synonymously with *mistress*.

See also Historical context and overview of Doctrine and Covenants 132 (p. 849).

BIBLIOGRAPHY

Webster, Noah. *An American Dictionary of the English Language.* 1828.

DLB

Condemnation. *See* Appendix E.

Conference(s). *See* Meet, meetings.

Confess. *See* Repentance.

Confirmation meetings. *See* Meet, meetings.

Confirm, confirmed, confirming

The word *confirm* and its various forms are used in the Doctrine and Covenants in several contexts:

1. The PRIESTHOOD ordinance of LAYING ON OF HANDS after baptism to confirm, or establish, that the baptized person is now a member of The Church of Jesus Christ of Latter-day Saints and to bestow the GIFT OF THE HOLY GHOST (20:41, 68; 33:15). Early in this dispensation, special meetings, called "confirmation meetings," were held in which any number of people who had been recently baptized received this priesthood ordinance (46:6).

2. Strengthening members of the Church. Webster's 1828 dictionary defines *confirmation*

as "the act of . . . establishing" as well as "making more certain or firm." In 20:43 the Lord sets forth the duties of the apostles, which include to "confirm the church by the laying on of the hands." In July 1830, the Lord commanded Joseph Smith, Oliver Cowdery, and John Whitmer to devote their time to "studying of the scriptures, and to preaching, and to confirming the church at Colesville" (26:1). Such an assignment is akin to that of the apostle Paul, who traveled to "Syria and Cilicia" for the purpose of "confirming the churches" (Acts 15:41). Another example of *confirm* to mean strengthening is found in a letter to the Saints from Joseph Smith in September 1842, wherein he recounted many of the revelatory experiences associated with the restoration of the priesthood and the gospel, indicating that all these experiences combine in "confirming our hope" (128:21).

3. Affirming or supporting the truth of a claim. For instance, confirming "by the ministering of angels" that the Book of Mormon is true (20:10).

4. Bestowing/establishing (84:18, 30, 42; 107:40; cf. 27:12). For example, "the Lord confirmed a priesthood also upon Aaron and his seed" (84:18); the patriarchal priesthood was "confirmed to be handed down from father to son" (107:40); and "the Father teacheth him of the [gospel] covenant which he has renewed and confirmed upon you . . . for the sake of the whole world" (84:48).

DQC

Congregations of the wicked. *See* Wicked, the/wickedness.

Conscience

A person's inward sense of right and wrong, independence of mind. A universal gift of "light" is given to "every man that cometh into the world" (84:46; c.f. Moro. 7:16–19). It enlightens his eyes and quickens his understanding (88:11). The source of that LIGHT is Jesus Christ (84:45; 88:6; 93:2). The "light of Christ" (88:7) is retained by obedience, relinquished by disobedience, and restored by repentance. "Regardless of whether this inner light, this knowledge of right and wrong, is called the

Light of Christ, moral sense, or conscience, it can direct us to moderate our actions—unless, that is, we subdue it or silence it" (Packer, 9).

Doctrine and Covenants 134 outlines "inherent and inalienable" (134:5) rights that must be protected by governments in order to secure peace. Among those rights is the "free exercise of conscience" (134:2). This declaration of belief proclaims that governments have the right to make and enforce laws, but in so doing they must never seek to "control conscience" (134:4) and ever hold "sacred the freedom of conscience" (134:5). Joseph Smith explained: "We deem it a just principle . . . that all men are created equal, and that all have the privilege of thinking for themselves upon all matters relative to conscience. Consequently, then, we are not disposed, had we the power, to deprive any one of exercising that free independence of mind which heaven has so graciously bestowed upon the human family" (2:6–7). Though himself deprived of the free exercise of conscience, Joseph declared shortly before his martyrdom: "I am going like a lamb to the slaughter; but I am calm as a summer's morning; I have a conscience void of offense towards God, and towards all men" (135:4).

See also Light of Christ.

BIBLIOGRAPHY

Packer, Boyd K. "The Light of Christ." *Ensign* 35 (April 2005): 8–14.

Smith, Joseph. *History of The Church of Jesus Christ of Latter-day Saints.* Edited by B. H. Roberts. 7 vols. 2d ed. rev. Salt Lake City: The Church of Jesus Christ of Latter-day Saints, 1932–51.

EPR

Consecration

Dedication of an individual's resources to God for sacred purposes. Beginning in February 1831, the Lord revealed "the laws of consecration," whereby the Saints of this dispensation were to make sacred covenants to provide means for the poor and needy and to build up the kingdom of God on earth (42:2, 30, 34–35; 105:5, 29). The underlying principle of consecration rests in recognizing that the Lord is the Creator and that all things are his; mankind are the Lord's stewards over the earth and its riches

(104:13–14). In commanding the Saints to consecrate their worldly wealth and honest efforts to his Church, the Lord gives them an opportunity to become more godlike in blessing others.

Although the principles of consecration are the same for all of God's covenant people in all ages, the implementation of the financial aspects of consecration may vary according to the times and circumstances of the Saints, as directed by living prophets. In 1838, the financial portion of the law of consecration was adjusted to include the law of tithing. Over time, tithes and offerings have become the main means of financing the Church, rather than the consecration of property as described in the revelations of the early 1830s. Nonetheless, the principles of consecration—providing for the poor and serving to build up the kingdom of God—are in operation in the Church today. Worthy Latter-day Saints in modern times, who make sacred covenants of consecration, can and do give of their surplus through the current system of tithes and offerings and unselfishly give of their time and energies to build up the kingdom of God.

Commandments regarding consecration are a prominent theme in the Doctrine and Covenants, including the fact that the law of consecration is to be implemented within the organization of the Church under the direction of priesthood leaders. At least twenty-four revelations give instructions regarding consecration and its attendant aspects of stewardship, the Lord's storehouse, the United Firm, and the law of tithing (D&C 38, 42, 44, 48, 51, 54, 56, 58, 70, 72, 78, 82–85, 92, 96–97, 104–6, 119–20, and 136).

Bishops' storehouse: providing for the poor and needy

The Lord's command to provide for the poor and needy in this dispensation connects latter-day efforts with those of past dispensations. In the Old Testament the children of Israel were commanded to give the fruits of the harvest from each seventh year "that the poor of thy people may eat" (Ex. 23:11). In addition, the Lord commanded them to leave the corners of their fields and not to return after a harvest to glean that which remained. Rather, they were to "leave them for the poor and stranger" (Lev. 19:10). In the New Testament there was a time when the Saints "had all things common . . . and distribution was made unto every man according as he had need" (Acts 4:32–35). In the Book of Mormon, Alma recorded that in his day "they did impart of their substance, every man according to that which he had, to the poor, and the needy, and the sick, and the afflicted" (Alma 1:27).

When the restored Church was less than a year old, the Lord gave his law to those who had joined the Church in the area of Kirtland, Ohio. Caring for the poor, according to the Lord's law, was to be accomplished by the combined consecrated efforts of all the Saints. He instructed that "inasmuch as ye impart of your substance unto the poor, ye will do it unto me; and they shall be laid before the bishop of my church" (42:31). Lands and goods were thus consecrated for the use of the Church, meaning that those who gave their substance did so with a covenant and a deed. This procedure provided the sacred context of consecration within the covenant and satisfied the laws of the land by using a legal deed. Consecrated properties were given to members, who acted as stewards for the Lord in caring for the property and providing for their own support. The Lord commanded that any surplus derived from the operation of these stewardships "shall be kept in my storehouse, to administer to the poor and the needy, as shall be appointed by the high council of the church, and the bishop and his council" (42:32–34).

The Lord called Edward Partridge as the first bishop in his Church to oversee the consecrations (41:9). In addition, the Lord explained that Bishop Partridge was to "appoint a storehouse unto this church" (51:13). He commanded Bishop Partridge to take up residence in Independence, Missouri, and serve as bishop there (58:24). The Lord then called Newel K. Whitney to be the bishop in Ohio "to keep the Lord's storehouse; to receive the funds of the church in this part of the vineyard . . . that this also may be consecrated to the good of the church, to the poor and needy" (72:8–12).

The Lord revealed that women who have lost their husbands and children who have lost their fathers "have claim upon the church, or in other words upon the Lord's storehouse . . . and the storehouse shall be kept by the consecrations of the church; and widows and orphans shall be provided for, as also the poor" (83:1–6).

United Order or United Firm, Literary Firm

In addition to providing for the poor and needy, the Lord instructed that consecrated properties and funds were also to be used "for the purpose of purchasing lands for the public benefit of the church, and building houses of worship, and building up of the New Jerusalem" (42:34–35). The Lord further revealed that the commandments and revelations, which he had given through the Prophet Joseph Smith, were to be published to the world using funds generated from consecrated properties within this law. He appointed five additional brethren to assist Joseph Smith in managing this endeavor: Martin Harris, Oliver Cowdery, John Whitmer, Sidney Rigdon, and William W. Phelps (70:1). The organization of stewards over the revelations and commandments was officially called the Literary Firm. Members of the Literary Firm were charged to consecrate their time and talents to publish the revelations and other Church literature. Funds needed for publication were to be provided from the Lord's storehouse. Likewise, any profits generated from the sale of these items, after the "necessities" and "wants" of the Firm were taken care of, were to be given to the storehouse (70:2–8).

In March 1832, the Lord commanded that Joseph Smith and other Church leaders organize a mercantile firm in which Church properties, such as the Newel K. Whitney store in Kirtland, Ohio, and the A. Sidney Gilbert store in Independence, Missouri, were to be consecrated as Church-owned commercial businesses. In addition, these two buildings were each to serve as a "storehouse for the poor" (78:3). Further, the Literary Firm, the mercantile businesses, and the Lord's storehouses were to be organized under one head as the United Firm (later edited in the revelations to be the "order" or "United Order"; 78:8; 82:20; 92:1; 104:1, 5, 10, 48). The Prophet Joseph Smith traveled from Ohio to Missouri to sit in council with members there and to organize the United Firm. Members of the United Firm were to "be bound together by a bond and covenant that [could not] be broken by transgression, except judgment [should] immediately follow, in [their] several stewardships—to manage the affairs of the poor, and all things pertaining to the bishopric both in the land of Zion and in the land of Kirtland" (82:11–12). Edward Partridge, Newel K. Whitney, and A. Sidney Gilbert were called to join with members of the Literary Firm in forming the United Firm (82:11). The Lord indicated that the initial organization of the United Firm was to prepare Church members to accomplish the Lord's commands to provide for the poor, "that through my providence, notwithstanding the tribulation which shall descend upon you, that the church may stand independent above all other creatures beneath the celestial world" (78:13–14).

Members of the First Presidency presided over the consecrated properties of the Church and directed the work of the bishopric in providing for the poor. When Frederick G. Williams was called as a counselor in the First Presidency, replacing Jesse Gause, the Lord instructed that Williams should be a member of the United Order (92:1–2), in accordance with the Lord's explanation that "this order [United Firm] I have appointed to be an everlasting order unto you, and unto your successors, inasmuch as you sin not" (82:20). Other individuals were also added to the group of leaders overseeing the United Firm. For example, after John Johnson sold his home and farm in Hiram, Ohio, he consecrated the proceeds to the Church. Subsequently, the Lord revealed that "it is expedient in me that he [John Johnson] should become a member of the order [United Firm], that he may assist in bringing forth my word unto the children of men" (96:8).

Treasury

The Lord commanded that two treasuries be established to "print my words, the fulness of my scriptures [Joseph Smith Translation of the Bible], the revelations which I have given unto you, and which I shall, hereafter, from time to time give unto you—for the purpose of building up my church and kingdom on the earth" (104:58–59). Funds from the sale of scriptures were to be placed in a "sacred treasury" "for the purpose of printing these sacred things [the scriptures]" (104:60–66). The Lord also commanded that "another treasury" be prepared, "and all moneys that you receive in your stewardships, by improving upon the properties which I have appointed unto you, in houses, or in lands, or in cattle, or in all things save it be the holy and sacred writings, which I have reserved unto myself for holy and sacred purposes, shall be cast into the treasury as fast as you receive moneys" (104:67–68). This second treasury provided for the expenses of Church buildings and programs, as well as being available to be used in various individual stewardships (104:69–77). Stewards of his work were "to be equal, or in other words . . . have equal claims on the properties, for the benefit of managing the concerns of [their] stewardships, every man according to his wants and his needs, inasmuch as his wants are just—and all this for the benefit of the church of the living God, that every man may improve upon his talent, that every man may gain other talents, yea, even an hundred fold, to be cast into the Lord's storehouse, to become the common property of the whole church—every man seeking the interest of his neighbor, and doing all things with an eye single to the glory of God" (82:17–19).

Consecration and stewardships of personal property

The covenant of consecration involved assigning by legal deed to the Church all of one's property and possessions and receiving, also by legal deed, a stewardship of land or a business to provide for one's needs (42:30–32; 51:4–6). The determination of what was to be consecrated was simple: it was everything one owned. The determination of appointing a stewardship required great care. No two families or individuals have the same needs or preferences. The Lord explained that the bishop and those working with him were to appoint stewardships based upon the principle of "every man equal according to his family, according to his circumstances and his wants and needs" (51:3). Thus, the bishop considered the number and ages of the family's children. Additionally, a farmer would receive farm land; a tanner, a tannery; a printer, a print shop; and a businessman, a mercantile establishment (57:8–12; 104:19–42). The Prophet Joseph Smith wrote to Bishop Edward Partridge

No 1.

Titus Billings

BE IT KNOWN, THAT I, Of Jackson county, and state of Missouri, having become a member of the church of Christ, organized according to law, and established by the revelations of the Lord, on the 6th day of April, 1830, do, of my own free will and accord, having first paid my just debts, grant and hereby give unto *Edward Partridge* of Jackson county, and state of Missouri, bishop of said church, the following described property, viz:— *Sundry articles of furniture valued fifty five dollars twenty seven cents, — also two beds, bedding and extra clothing valued seventy three dollars twenty five cents, — also farming utensils valued forty one dollars, — also one horse, two waggons two cows and two calves valued one hundred forty seven dollars*

in Jackson county Mo,

For the purpose of purchasing lands, and building up the New Jerusalem, even Zion, and for relieving the wants of the poor and needy. For which I the said *Titus Billings* do covenant and bind myself and my heirs forever, to release all my right and interest to the above described property, unto him the said *Edward Partridge* bishop of said church. And I the said *Edward Partridge* — bishop of said church, having received the above described property, of the said *Titus Billings* do bind myself, that I will cause the same to be expended for the above-mentioned purposes of the said *Titus Billings* to the satisfaction of said church; and in case I should be removed from the office of bishop of said church, by death or otherwise, I hereby bind myself and my heirs forever, to make over to my successor in office, for the benefit of said church, all of the above described property, which may then be in my possession.

In testimony whereof, WE have hereunto set our hands and seals this ———— day of ———— in the year of our Lord, one thousand eight hundred and thirty ————

IN PRESENCE OF ————

[SEAL]

[SEAL]

Consecration deed for Titus Billings, first page. Billings consecrates his possessions to Bishop Edward Partridge and the Church. "And behold, thou wilt remember the poor, and consecrate of thy properties for their support that which thou hast to impart unto them, with a covenant and a deed which cannot be broken" (D&C 42:30).

BE IT KNOWN, THAT I, *Edward Partridge*

Of Jackson county, and state of Missouri, bishop of the church of Christ, organized according to law, and established by the revelations of the Lord, on the 6th day of April, 1830, have leased, and by these presents do lease unto *Titus Billings* of Jackson county, and state of Missouri, a member of said church, the following described piece or parcel of land, being a part of section No. *three* township No. *forty one* range No. *thirty two* situated in Jackson county, and state of Missouri, and is bounded as follows, viz:— *beginning eighty rods E. from the S. W. corner of S.d Sec, thence N. one hundred and Sixty rods, thence E. twenty seven rods 25l. thence S. one hundred and sixty rods thence W. twenty seven rods 25l to the place of beginning containing twenty seven 8/2 acres be the same more or less subject to roads and highways.*

And also have loaned the following described property, viz:— *Sundry articles of furniture valued fifty five dollars twenty seven cents, — also two beds, bedding and clothing valued seventy three dollars twenty five cents, — also sundry farming utensils valued forty one dollars, — also one horse, two cows, two calves and two waggons valued one hundred and forty seven dollars.*

TO HAVE AND TO HOLD the above described property, by him the said *Titus Billing* to be used and occupied as to him shall seem meet and proper. And as a consideration for the use of the above described property, I the said *Titus Billings* do bind myself to pay the taxes, and also to pay yearly unto the said *Edward Partridge* bishop of said church, or his successor in office, for the benefit of said church, all that I shall make or accumulate more than is needful for the support and comfort of myself and family. And it is agreed by the parties, that this lease and loan shall be binding during the life of the said *Titus Billings* unless he transgress, and is not deemed worthy by the authority of the church, according to its laws, to belong to the church. And in that case I the said *Titus Billings* do acknowledge that I forfeit all claim to the above described leased and loaned property, and hereby bind myself to give back the leased, and also pay an equivalent for the loaned, for the benefit of said church, unto the said *Edward Partridge* bishop of said church, or his successor in office. And farther, in case of said *Titus Billings* or family's inability in consequence of infirmity or old age, to provide for themselves while members of this church, I the said *Edward Partridge* bishop of said church, do bind myself to administer to their necessities out of any funds in my hands appropriated for that purpose, not otherwise disposed of, to the satisfaction of the church. And further, in case of the death of the said *Titus Billings* his wife or widow, being at the time a member of said church, has claim upon the above described leased and loaned property, upon precisely the same conditions that her said husband had them, as above described; and the children of the said *Titus Billings* in case of the death of both their parents, also have claim upon the above described property, for their support, until they shall become of age, and no longer; subject to the same conditions yearly that their parents were: provided however, should the parents not be members of said church, and in possession of the above described property at the time of their deaths, the claim of the children as above described, is null and void.

In testimony whereof, WE have hereunto set our hands and seals this _____ day of _____ in the year of our Lord, one thousand eight hundred and thirty _____

IN PRESENCE OF _____

[SEAL.]

[SEAL.]

Consecration deed for Titus Billings, second page. Bishop Edward Partridge deeds a stewardship to Billings. "And let my servant Edward Partridge, when he shall appoint a man his portion, give unto him a writing that shall secure unto him his portion, that he shall hold it, even this right and this inheritance in the church, until he transgresses and is not accounted worthy by the voice of the church, according to the laws and covenants of the church, to belong to the church" (D&C 51:4).

that the bishop and the members consecrating property and receiving stewardships were to determine together their needs and just wants, indicating that "there must be a balance or equilibrium of power, between the Bishop and the people, and thus harmony and good will may be preserved among you." If no agreement could be reached between the bishop and the member, the case was to be turned over to a council of twelve high priests (Smith, 1:364–65).

The Lord instructed that if any individuals produced "more than is necessary for their support after this first consecration," the residue property or money was "to be consecrated unto the bishop" to be kept "in my storehouse, to administer to the poor and the needy" and for purchasing lands, building houses of worship, and "building up of the New Jerusalem" (42:33–35).

Consecration and Zion

In a revelation given in April 1832, the Lord declared, "Zion must increase in beauty, and in holiness; . . . yea, . . . Zion must arise and put on her beautiful garments" (82:14). The Lord also revealed that unity among the Saints, gained from living the law of consecration, is "the union required by the law of the celestial kingdom" upon which Zion must be built (105:3–5). This unity requires equality. The Lord commanded, "Let every man esteem his brother as himself" (38:25) and explained, "If ye are not equal in earthly things ye cannot be equal in obtaining heavenly things" (78:6). The goal for a latter-day Zion is to be like the "Zion of Enoch," which the Lord took "into [his] own bosom" (38:4) "because they were of one heart and one mind, and dwelt in righteousness; and there was no poor among them" (Moses 7:18).

Challenges to living the law of consecration

The antithesis of consecration—covetousness—contributed to challenges the early Saints faced in living "the laws of consecration" (105:29). When the Saints were persecuted and eventually driven from their properties in Jackson County, Missouri, the Lord informed them that it was due to their disobedience and "covetous desires among them; therefore by these things they polluted their inheritances" (101:1, 6; cf. 104:4). This inability of Church members to live the law of consecration led to the dissolution of the United Firm. The Lord instructed the Prophet Joseph Smith to reorganize the United Firm as two firms, each under its own name in Ohio and Missouri, respectively (104:47–48), and to divide the properties of the Firm into individual stewardships, still under the principles of consecration. Sidney Rigdon was appointed "the place where he now resides, and the lot of the tannery for his stewardship" (104:20), Martin Harris and John Johnson were given land (104:24–26, 34–38), Frederick G. Williams and Oliver Cowdery were assigned the printing office, Newel K. Whitney the mercantile establishment and the ashery (104:39–42), and the Prophet Joseph Smith the lots for the house of the Lord (104:43–46).

Tithing

In early revelations the term *tithing* referred to all offerings and contributions to Church funds (64:23–24; 85:3; 97:11–12; 119, headnote; 119:3–4). Attempts by the Saints to live the law of consecration did not provide sufficient funds to build the kingdom. Either the Saints simply did not have sufficient surplus funds to contribute to the Lord's storehouse, or they allowed covetousness to dictate that their surplus was needed for personal wants in the future. While in Far West, Missouri, Bishop Partridge met with his counselors to determine how to meet the expenses of the kingdom, including building a temple; they proposed a plan of assessing the Saints' property and goods for a payment of "two cents upon the dollar for what every man shall be worth when he renders his inventory to the Bishop" (Cannon and Cook, 129–30). When the Prophet Joseph Smith inquired of the Lord concerning this plan, the Lord revealed that the time had come for the Saints to establish the law of tithing, or "one-tenth of all their interest annually," as a "standing law unto them forever" after an initial consecration of "all their surplus property" (119:1–7).

The Lord also instructed that a council be organized for the disposition of the tithes, "composed of the First Presidency of my Church, and of the bishop and his council, and by my high council [the Quorum of the Twelve Apostles]" (120:1).

While addressing the high council in Montrose, Iowa, on 6 March 1840 the Prophet Joseph Smith acknowledged the need for suspending the financial system of consecration as it had been revealed at first. The minutes record that "the law of consecration could not be kept here, and that it was the will of the Lord that we should desist from trying to keep it; and if persisted in, it would produce a perfect defeat of its object, and that he assumed the whole responsibility of not keeping it until proposed by himself" (Smith, 4:93; cf. 105:34). The president of the Church is the only one authorized by God to declare if, when, and how the law of consecration of properties should be implemented.

The law of consecration today

In 1838 the law of tithing became the source of financing Church expenses. Since that time the Saints have been given additional opportunities to consecrate some of their resources for a variety of programs essential to the building up of the kingdom of God on the earth—fast offerings, temple construction, missionary work, Book of Mormon distribution, the perpetual education fund, humanitarian aid, and so forth—all under the designation, "offerings."

The law of consecration involves much more than dedicating property or money for the building up of the kingdom of God on the earth. In summarizing the law of consecration, Elder Bruce R. McConkie explained that "righteous saints in all ages have *consecrated* their time, talents, strength, properties, and monies to the establishment of the Lord's work and kingdom in their respective days. As circumstances have required, these saints—having set their hearts on righteousness and having actually put first in their lives the things of God's kingdom—have been and are called upon to serve on missions, colonize wilderness areas, build temples, go to the ends of the earth on the Lord's errand, magnify calls in the ministry, and contribute of their means in the great welfare and building projects of the Church" (157).

The Lord's consecrated lands

The Lord said that he had consecrated lands where the Saints could live and build houses to his name. For example, "I have consecrated the land of Kirtland in mine own due time for the benefit of the saints of the Most High, and for a stake to Zion" (82:13). In the summer of 1831 the Lord commanded many of the elders of the Church to journey to Missouri, "which is the land which I have appointed and consecrated for the gathering of the saints" (57:1; cf. 52:2). More specifically, the Lord identified Missouri as "the place for the city of Zion" (57:2), and Independence, Missouri, as the center place where a temple is to be built (57:3). The Lord referred to the site for the temple as "the consecrated spot as I have appointed" (84:31). Similarly, the Lord commanded, "Let the city, Far West, be a holy and consecrated land unto me; and it shall be called most holy, for the ground upon which thou standest is holy. Therefore, I command you to build a house unto me" (115:7–8). With reference to the choice of land for the building of the Lord's house in Nauvoo, he promised, "If ye labor with all your might, I will consecrate that spot that it shall be made holy" (124:44). Thus, it might be safely surmised that sites for all temples are consecrated to be holy places. Similarly, stakes are designated as holy places of refuge for the Saints (101:20–22; 115:5–6).

BIBLIOGRAPHY

Cannon, Donald Q., and Lyndon W. Cook, eds. *Far West Record: Minutes of The Church of Jesus Christ of Latter-day Saints, 1830–1844.* Salt Lake City: Deseret Book, 1983.

McConkie, Bruce R. *Mormon Doctrine.* 2d ed. Salt Lake City: Bookcraft, 1966.

Smith, Joseph. *History of The Church of Jesus Christ of Latter-day Saints.* Edited by B. H. Roberts. 7 vols. 2d ed. rev. Salt Lake City: The Church of Jesus Christ of Latter-day Saints, 1932–51.

CJO

Constitution

In 1833 the Latter-day Saints who had been driven from their homes in Jackson County, Missouri, were desperately seeking ways to recover their property. On 16 December 1833 Joseph Smith received the revelation now recorded in section 101, which gave them hope that the Constitution of the United States was for their protection, for the Lord himself had established it to protect all people in their rights:

"And again I say unto you, those who have been scattered by their enemies, it is my will that they should continue to importune for redress, and redemption, by the hands of those who are placed as rulers and are in authority over you— according to the laws and constitution of this people, which I have suffered to be established, and should be maintained for the rights and protection of all flesh, according to just and holy principles; that every man may act in doctrine and principle pertaining to futurity, according to the moral agency which I have given unto him, that every man may be accountable for his own sins in the day of judgment. Therefore, it is not right that any man should be in bondage one to another. And for this purpose have I established the Constitution of this land, by the hands of wise men whom I raised up unto this very purpose" (101:76–80).

Partly because of this declaration Latter-day Saints revere the Constitution as an inspired document. That reverence was reemphasized on 27 March 1836 at the dedication of the Kirtland Temple. The dedicatory prayer, given to the Prophet by revelation, included the following petition: "Have mercy, O Lord, upon all the nations of the earth; have mercy upon the rulers of our land; may those principles, which were so honorably and nobly defended, namely, the Constitution of our land, by our fathers, be established forever" (109:54).

Besides these two direct references in the Doctrine and Covenants to the Constitution of the United States, section 134, which is a declaration of beliefs regarding governments and laws in general, has constitutional implications. It affirms that God instituted governments for the benefit of man (134:1), that all men are bound to sustain the governments under which they live and refrain from rebelling against them (134:5), that governments are bound to enact laws for the protection of the free exercise of religion (134:7), and that religious influence should not be mingled with civil GOVERNMENT whereby one "religious society is fostered and another proscribed in its spiritual privileges, and the individual rights of its members, as citizens, denied" (134:9).

The Constitution was written at a time of crisis for the fledgling American nation. The thirteen states were loosely confederated under a weak congress that had no power to deal with important national concerns or even to protect itself in the event of invasion. America badly needed an effective central government, yet the states were each so jealous of their independence that they were reluctant to surrender any of their sovereignty. The delegates to the constitutional convention, "wise men" whom the Lord raised up to prepare a constitution for their new nation, were a remarkable group: public spirited, well educated, and politically experienced. Many had studied the writings of the great political philosophers, from the ancient Greeks to the age of Enlightenment. The inspiration that went into the Constitution was, in part, a long-range historical process, as the Founders drew upon the experience and knowledge of the past. President J. Reuben Clark Jr., a former member of the First Presidency and a learned authority on the Constitution, once observed that the founders depended on "the wisdom of the long generations that had gone before and which had been transmitted to them through tradition and the pages of history" (in Hancock, 1:318).

One of the first things the delegates learned was the value of compromise, and almost everything in the Constitution was the result of wise and inspired compromise between strongly conflicting views. In the end, no one thought that what had been created was perfect, but under the circumstances it was the best that could be produced. As Benjamin Franklin said: "When you assemble a number of men to have the advantage over their joint wisdom, you inevitably assemble with those men, all their prejudices, their passions, their errors of opinion, their local interests, and their selfish views. From such an assembly can a perfect production be expected? It therefore astonishes me, Sir, to find this system approaching so near to perfection as it does. . . . The opinions I have had of its errors, I sacrifice to the public good" (in Oaks, 70).

Amid all the compromises, the founders incorporated into the Constitution certain fundamentals that might be considered among its most inspired aspects. Elder Dallin H. Oaks has identified five such fundamentals:

1. The principle of separation of powers into

three branches of government, each with specific powers but also with certain checks and balances that it can exercise on the others, thus lessening the possibility of tyranny.

2. The addition of a written bill of rights which, among other things, protects the people in their freedom of speech, the press, religion, and, as worded in the Declaration of Independence, the right to "Life, Liberty, and the pursuit of Happiness."

3. The division of power, or sovereignty, between the national government and the governments of each of the states. This unique system, called federalism, had never been tried, but it had the effect of granting to the national government the powers it needed to govern and protect the nation as a whole while still allowing the states to retain their individual sovereignty.

4. Popular sovereignty, which recognized important principles expounded by John Locke a century earlier: The people are the true source of governmental power, a government exists only by the consent of the people it governs, and it is there primarily to serve the interests of the people. The Preamble reads, "We the People of the United States . . . do ordain and establish this Constitution." This principle is also seen in the fact that the people have frequent and regular opportunity to make changes by voting on who will govern them.

5. The rule of law and not of men, which, says Elder Oaks, "is the basis of liberty" (73).

The Prophet Joseph Smith often showed his reverence for the Constitution. He frequently decried the mobbing and destruction of property heaped upon the Saints as violations of their constitutional rights. In March 1838 his "Political Motto of the Church" began with the words "The Constitution of our country formed by the Fathers of liberty" (*History*, 3:9). A year later he called it "a glorious standard; it is founded in the wisdom of God. It is a heavenly banner" (*History*, 3:304).

The Constitution was not perfect, however. The framers themselves recognized that and even wrote into it a provision for amendment. Church leaders, too, have recognized its imperfections. Joseph Smith called for giving the president of the United States greater power to intervene within the states, a significant change relating to states' rights. Brigham Young once declared that "the framers of the Constitution were inspired from on high to do that work. But was that which was given to them perfect, not admitting of any addition whatever? No; for . . . the Almighty has never yet found a man in mortality that was capable, at the first intimation, at the first impulse, to receive anything in a state of entire perfection. They laid the foundation, and it was for after generations to rear the superstructure upon it. It is a progressive—a gradual work" (7:14).

The Constitution has been changed in numerous ways. Most common and most controversial are changes that have come through judicial interpretation. These include, for example, court decisions regarding issues dealing with personal privacy, religion in public schools, and desegregation. Other changes have come through direct amendment. The first ten amendments (the Bill of Rights) were adopted by the first United States Congress because even the founders recognized that certain human rights were not sufficiently protected by the original Constitution. Later amendments changed the way in which the president and vice president are elected, prohibited slavery, defined citizenship and the right to vote, authorized income taxes, changed the way members of the Senate were elected, and expanded suffrage to women and, later, to eighteen-year-olds.

Joseph Smith's chief constitutional concern was with how much authority the federal government had to intervene within a state that was not protecting the rights of its citizens. This concern was related to the Saints' unsuccessful efforts to get help from the federal government in connection with their loss of homes and property in Missouri. At first the Prophet believed that the Constitution allowed the federal government to intervene in Missouri; however the only specific authority either Congress or the president had at the time was to call the militia into service for the purpose of putting down insurrections and repelling invasion. The term *insurrection* meant rebellion against the government (federal or state), and *invasion* referred to the incursion of some outside military force. Sending federal forces to deal with anything else, such as "domestic violence" (which is the best description of what was happening in Missouri), had to be at the behest of the legislature or governor of the state.

Despite his disappointment in his quest for help from the federal government, Joseph Smith continued to proclaim himself "the greatest advocate of the Constitution of the United States there is on the earth." Its only fault, he said in 1843, was that it was "not broad enough to cover the whole ground," for it did not provide the means for protecting the rights of the people who were suffering religious persecution: "Its sentiments are good, but it provides no means of enforcing them. It has but this one fault" (*History*, 6:56–57).

When Joseph Smith ran for president of the United States in 1844, he made this issue part of his presidential platform. He called for a Constitutional amendment that would give the president "full power to send an army to suppress mobs," without having to wait for an invitation from a state governor or legislature (*Views*, 9). His concerns were met a generation later, after the Civil War, when the Fourteenth Amendment prohibited any state from depriving a person of life, liberty, or property without due process of law. This paved the way for federal intervention if the states failed in their responsibilities, just as Joseph Smith had wanted.

See also Historical context and overview of Doctrine and Covenants 101 (p. 806) and 134 (p. 852); Missouri period; Redress.

BIBLIOGRAPHY

Hancock, Ralph C. "Constitution of the United States of America." In *Encyclopedia of Mormonism*, edited by Daniel H. Ludlow et al. 4 vols. New York: Macmillan, 1992.

Oaks, Dallin H. "The Divinely Inspired Constitution." *Ensign* 22 (February 1992): 68–74.

Smith, Joseph, Jr. *General Smith's Views of the Powers and Policy of the Government of the United States.* Nauvoo, Ill.: John Taylor, 1844.

———. *History of The Church of Jesus Christ of Latter-day Saints.* Edited by B. H. Roberts. 7 vols. 2d ed. rev. Salt Lake City: The Church of Jesus Christ of Latter-day Saints, 1932–51.

Young, Brigham. *Journal of Discourses.* 26 vols. London: Latter-day Saints' Book Depot, 1854–86.

JBA

Consumption. *See* Appendix E.

Contend, contention(s)

The word *contend* in various forms is used in the Doctrine and Covenants both positively and pejoratively. In the positive sense, the Lord instructs Oliver Cowery and David Whitmer to "contend [to strive or fight] against no church, save it be the church of the devil" (18:9, 20). *Contend* is also used to mean to implore, to urge vigorously, to encourage, even to chasten. The Lord said, "I, the Lord, will contend with Zion, and plead with her strong ones, and chasten her until she overcomes and is clean before me" (90:36). Thomas B. Marsh, president of the Quorum of the Twelve, was told to "contend [preach] . . . morning by morning; and day after day" with a "warning voice" to "the inhabitants of the earth" (112:4–5). Oliver Granger was told to contend [to strive, assist, or to work] for the financial "redemption of the First Presidency" of the Church (117:13). In all of these instances, *contend* is used positively.

In the pejorative sense, several sections use *contention* or *contending* to mean disputing, quarreling, arguing, dissenting, or otherwise causing strife. For example, the Lord said that when contentions arose in the School of the Prophets, it was "very grievous" to him (95:10; cf. 3 Ne. 11:29); what those contentions were is not explained. Brigham Young told the Saints at Winter Quarters, "Cease to contend one with another; cease to speak evil one of another" (136:23). Earlier in this dispensation the Lord had revealed that an important purpose of the Book of Mormon was to "bring to light the true points of [his] doctrine," and "establish [his] gospel, that there may not be so much contention" (10:62–63; cf. 74:3; 2 Ne. 3:12). "Jarrings, and contentions" among the Saints was one of the reasons why the Lord "suffered," or allowed, them to be driven from Jackson County, Missouri, in 1833 (101:1–9). During the dark days of Joseph Smith's confinement in LIBERTY JAIL, the Lord reassured him that, unlike Job, "thy friends do not contend against thee" (121:10).

DRD

Continuation of the seeds. *See* Exalt, exaltation; Marriage.

Continuation of the lives. *See* Marriage.

Contrite. *See* Appendix E.

Converted. *See* Baptism of fire and the Holy Ghost.

Copley, Leman

Birth: ca. 1781, Litchfield County, Connecticut

Death: ca. 22 May 1862, Thompson, Geauga County, Ohio

Most of the recorded events involving Leman Copley and the Church occurred during the first six months of 1831, especially May and June. Copley was baptized in Ohio sometime before 1 February 1831, the time of Joseph Smith's arrival at Kirtland. Copley, who owned a large farm in Thompson Township, a day's journey from Kirtland, offered "houses & provisions" at Thompson to both Joseph Smith's and Sidney Rigdon's families (Jensen et al., 93). On 4 February the Prophet received a revelation (41) in which Copley's offer was declined in favor of accommodations closer to Kirtland.

Later in the same month, section 42, known as "the law," was received. It included the principles of CONSECRATION, and Copley generously covenanted under those principles to let members of the Church migrating from New York settle on his property at Thompson. The time this covenant was made is not recorded but it probably occurred early in March when serious discussions took place concerning the settlement of these people (48).

At the beginning of May, Copley, who had been a member of the United Society of Believers in Christ's Second Appearing (SHAKERS), "was anxious that some of the elders should go to his former brethren and preach the gospel" (Whitmer, 26). This Shaker community was located at North Union, Ohio, now known as Shaker Heights, a suburb of Cleveland. Copley, though "apparently honest-hearted," nevertheless retained the "idea that the Shakers were right in some particulars of their faith," and "in order to have more perfect understanding on the

subject," Joseph Smith inquired of the Lord and received the revelation now recorded in section 49 (Smith, 1:167).

The manuscript of this revelation is dated 7 May 1831 (Jensen et al., 133), the same date for the revelation found in the journal of Ashbell Kitchell, the leading elder of the Shaker community at North Union. *The Evening and the Morning Star* also reported this revelation as having been received in May 1831.

According to these sources, then, the revelation was received on Saturday, 7 May 1831. On the following Saturday, 14 May, Sidney Rigdon and Leman Copley traveled to North Union, arriving in the evening. During that week members of the Church were beginning to settle on Copley's property at Thompson. Parley P. Pratt joined the two men on Sunday morning, and the three of them presented their message to the Shakers at the end of their regular worship service. The outcome of the mission initiated by this revelation was briefly reported by John Whitmer: the assigned elders "went and proclaimed according to the revelation given to them, but the shakers hearkened not to their words, and received not the gospel at that time" (26).

During the encounter, Copley received a stinging rebuke from Ashbel Kitchell, who wrote: "I then turned to Leman who had been crying while the message [D&C 49] was reading, and said to him, you hypocrite, you knew better;—you knew where the living work of God was; but for the sake of indulgence, you could consent to deceive yourself and them, but you shall reap the fruit of your own doings, &c.—This struck him dead also, and dried up his tears" (Flake, 98).

Parley P. Pratt and Sidney Rigdon left North Union the same day, but Leman Copley stayed until Monday morning. Kitchell reported, "But Leman tarried all night and started for home in the morning. He had a large farm, and about 100 Mormons were living with him, on it. When he got home, he found the Mormons had rejected him, & could not own him for one of them, because he had deceived them with the idea of converting us. He felt very bad;—was not able to rest;—came back to us and begged for union. After some consultation we concluded to give him union, and help him through; and to accomplish this, I went home with him, and held a meeting in the dooryard, among the Mormons; but few of them attended" (Flake, 98).

About two weeks later Leman Copley attended the general conference of the Church held during the first week of June at the Morley farm on the outskirts of Kirtland. Manifestations of false spirits afflicted several men at the conference. Philo Dibble reported one incident of a person being possessed by these spirits: "Next thing I saw a man came flying through the window from outside. He was straight as a man's arm as he sailed into the room over two rows of seats filled with men, and fell on the floor between the seats and was pulled out by the brethren. He trembled all over like a leaf in the wind. He was soon apparently calm and natural. His name was Lem[a]n Copley. He weighed over two hundred pounds. This I saw with my own eyes and know it is all true, and bear testimony to it" (Dibble, 303; for other accounts of this incident, see Hancock, 33; Parkin, 63). Joseph Smith's rebuke of these spirits settled the minds of those at the conference that these manifestations were not of God.

During that same week, or at least by 10 June, Leman Copley broke the covenant he had made and ordered members of the Church off his property. He was the principal covenant breaker, although selfishness among the Colesville Saints may also have contributed to the situation. Copley's ambivalence between two churches appears to be a significant factor in the whole incident, but he stayed in Thompson, indicating that he had decided not to make a full commitment to the Shakers or return to live at North Union.

There is uncertainty about what happened next. There are accounts of missionaries staying at his home at Thompson in 1832, and apparently there were friendly relations between them. At some point, however, Copley was disfellowshipped or excommunicated. He appeared at the April 1834 trial of Philastus Hurlbut (or Hurlburt), who had threatened the life of the Prophet Joseph Smith. Leman Copley testified against Joseph. Two years later, 1 April 1836, Copley went to Joseph Smith, and the Prophet

reported that he confessed that he "bore a false testimony against me in that suit, but verily thought, at the time, that he was right, but on calling to mind all the circumstances connected with the things that happened at the time, he was convinced that he was wrong, and humbly confessed it, and asked my forgiveness, which was readily granted. He also wished to be received into the Church again, by baptism, and was received according to his desire. He gave me his confession in writing" (2:433).

Copley stayed in Ohio after most members of the Church migrated elsewhere. After the death of Joseph Smith, he joined the Church of Christ (Brewsterite). At a conference of the Brewsterites held at Springfield, Illinois, on 29 September 1849, he and several others were expelled from that church for dissension. He then joined Austin Cowles's Church of Christ. Copley is buried in a county cemetery in present-day Thompson Township.

See also Historical context and overview of Doctrine and Covenants 41 (p. 747) and 49 (p. 755).

BIBLIOGRAPHY

Dibble, Philo. "Recollections of the Prophet Joseph Smith." *Juvenile Instructor* 27 (1892): 303–4.

Flake, Lawrence R. "A Mormon Interview. Copied from Brother Ashbel Kitchell's Pocket Journal. (by E.D.B.)." *BYU Studies* 20, no. 1 (Fall 1979): 95–99.

Hancock, Levi W. The Life of Levi W. Hancock, copied from his own journal by Clara E. H. Lloyd. L. Tom Perry Special Collections, Harold B. Lee Library, Brigham Young University, Provo, Utah.

Jensen, Robin Scott, Robert J. Woodford, and Steven C. Harper, eds. *Manuscript Revelation Books.* Facsimile edition. First volume of the Revelations and Translations series of *The Joseph Smith Papers,* edited by Dean C. Jessee, Ronald K. Esplin, and Richard Lyman Bushman. Salt Lake City: Church Historian's Press, 2009.

Parkin, Max. *A Study of the Nature and Causes of External and Internal Conflict of the Mormons in Ohio between 1830 and 1838.* N.p.: Department of Seminaries and Institutes of Religion of The Church of Jesus Christ of Latter-day Saints, 1967.

Smith, Joseph. *History of The Church of Jesus Christ of Latter-day Saints.* Edited by B. H. Roberts. 7 vols. 2d ed. rev. Salt Lake City: The Church of Jesus Christ of Latter-day Saints, 1932–51.

Whitmer, John. "The Book of John Whitmer Kept by

Commandment," ca. 1835–46. Community of Christ Library-Archives, Independence, Missouri.

RJW

Cornerstone of Zion. *See* Nauvoo, Illinois.

Cornerstone. *See* Appendix E.

Corrill, John

Birth: 17 September 1794, near Barre, Worcester County, Massachusetts

Death: 26 September 1842, Adams County, Illinois

John Corrill came in contact with the Church when Oliver Cowdery, Parley P. Pratt, Peter Whitmer Jr., and Ziba Peterson preached in Harpersfield, Ashtabula County, Ohio, and stayed at his house. Skeptical at first, Corrill recorded "apprehending there might be some truth in them, I went to Kirtland to see for myself" (5–6). He was baptized in early 1831 after satisfying himself that "this religion [was] much nearer the religion of the Bible than any other I could find" (Corrill, 12). After being ordained an elder in Kirtland in January and a high priest in June, he was called at the June conference to be a counselor to Bishop Edward Partridge and moved to Missouri that year. Later he was called as a third bishop in Independence, Missouri. Edward Partridge was the first, and Isaac Morley the second (Smith, 1:363).

Corrill's name appears in section 50, where he was admonished, along with Joseph Wakefield, Parley P. Pratt, and other elders, to "go forth among the churches and strengthen them by the word of exhortation" and to "labor in the vineyard" (50:37–38). In section 52 he was commanded to journey "speedily" to Missouri with Lyman Wight (52:7).

Part of Corrill's legacy included being "keeper of the Lord's Store House" (Smith, 2:524) and maintaining the Church's general history, or the "record of names, of the disciples in this land, according to the church covenants" (JH, 24 January 1832). He kept the record faithfully until he became disillusioned with Joseph Smith and the Church. The Prophet wrote, "[Corrill] said he would not yield his judgment to anything proposed by the Church, or any individuals of the Church, or even the Great I Am, given

through the appointed organ, as revelation, but would always act upon his own judgment" (3:66). By 1838 Corrill had testified against the Prophet at a series of court hearings in Richmond, Missouri (MH, 13 November 1838; Smith, 3:208–10). He was excommunicated in 1839 at Far West and in that same year published a pamphlet against the Church entitled *A Brief History of the Church of Christ of Latter Day Saints, (Commonly Called Mormons).* He never returned to the fellowship of the Saints.

BIBLIOGRAPHY

Corrill, John. *A Brief History of the Church of Christ of Latter Day Saints, (Commonly Called Mormons;) Including an Account of Their Doctrine and Discipline; with the Reasons of the Author for Leaving the Church.* St. Louis, Mo.: John Corrill, 1839.

Journal History of the Church, 24 January 1832. Church History Library, The Church of Jesus Christ of Latter-day Saints, Salt Lake City, Utah.

Manuscript History of the Church, 13 November 1838. Church History Library, The Church of Jesus Christ of Latter-day Saints, Salt Lake City, Utah.

Smith, Joseph. *History of The Church of Jesus Christ of Latter-day Saints.* Edited by B. H. Roberts. 7 vols. 2d ed. rev. Salt Lake City: The Church of Jesus Christ of Latter-day Saints, 1932–51.

ZLL

Council Bluffs, Iowa

A community on the east side of the Missouri River, across from WINTER QUARTERS, NEBRASKA (136, headnote). The principal settlement of the Saints was known as Kanesville, named in recognition of Colonel Thomas L. Kane, who, though not a member of the Church, championed the cause of the Latter-day Saints for many years. In December 1853, after the Saints left the area, "non-LDS residents incorporated Kanesville and renamed it Council Bluffs" (Bennett, "Council," 1:326; Cannon, "Kane," 2:779–80). From 1846 to 1852, about twelve thousand Mormons camped or built homes "below the east bluffs of the Missouri River," awaiting word from Brigham Young concerning migrating west (Bennett, "Council,"1:325–26). Brigham Young assigned Orson Hyde, a member of the Quorum of the Twelve, to supervise ninety encampments in the greater Council Bluffs area and to organize the pioneer movement to the West. Elder

Hyde faced many difficulties, including inadequate food supplies, poor shelter, sickness, and large numbers of people. Elder Hyde organized Church branches and community projects and kept the Saints informed with articles (published in the *Frontier Guardian* newspaper) on trail conditions, pioneering supplies, and directives from Brigham Young.

The Council Bluffs area was the site of the recruitment of the Mormon Battalion in July 1846; 543 men were enlisted into the United States army for the campaign against Mexico. In the main settlement of Kanesville at a conference of the Church held on 27 December 1847, the reorganized First Presidency of the Church was sustained: Brigham Young as president, with Heber C. Kimball as first counselor and Willard Richards as second counselor. The conference was held two months after Brigham Young and several apostles returned to the Winter Quarters–Council Bluffs area from the Salt Lake Valley, where they had journeyed the previous spring and summer in the advance company of pioneers. Over the next weeks and months, Church leaders organized Latter-day Saints for the trek west, following instructions in section 136, a revelation received by Brigham Young on 14 January 1847. The Saints began leaving Winter Quarters in the spring of 1848, and by the summer of 1852 most of the faithful Latter-day Saints had left Council Bluffs and migrated west. *See* map, p. 857.

See also Historical context and overview of Doctrine and Covenants 136 (p. 856).

BIBLIOGRAPHY

Bennett, Richard E. "Council Bluffs (Kanesville)." In *Encyclopedia of Mormonism,* edited by Daniel H. Ludlow et al. 4 vols. New York: Macmillan, 1992.

———. *Mormons at the Missouri, 1846–1852: "And Should We Die . . ."* Norman: University of Oklahoma Press, 1987.

Cannon, Donald Q. "Kane, Thomas L." In *Encyclopedia of Mormonism,* edited by Daniel H. Ludlow et al. 4 vols. New York: Macmillan, 1992.

Holmes, Gail Geo. "A Prophet Who Followed, Fulfilled, and Magnified: Brigham Young in Iowa and Nebraska." In *Lion of the Lord: Essays on the Life and Service of Brigham Young,* edited by Susan Easton Black and Larry C. Porter. Salt Lake City: Deseret Book, 1995.

Tyler, Daniel. *A Concise History of the Mormon Battalion in the Mexican War, 1846–1848.* Glorieta, N.M.: Rio Grande Press, 1881. Reprint, 1969.

SEB

Council of the Eternal God. *See* Council(s); Premortal existence.

Council(s)

A group of persons appointed to perform a particular function: to preside, to administer, to deliberate and recommend action, to arbitrate. Various councils are referred to in the Doctrine and Covenants.

The CHURCH OF JESUS CHRIST OF LATTER-DAY SAINTS is governed at all levels by councils. As early as April 1830, the Lord instituted a system of councils when he declared, "Every president of the high priesthood (or presiding elder), bishop, high councilor, and high priest, is to be ordained by the direction of a high council or general conference" (20:67). Later, after organizing his storehouse according to the principles of CONSECRATION, the Lord stated that consecrated properties were to be distributed to the poor and needy "as shall be appointed by the high council of the church, and the bishop and his council" (42:34). In connection with "the disposal of certain lands, known as the French farm" (96, headnote), the Lord instructed, "Let it be divided into lots, according to wisdom, for the benefit of those who seek inheritances, as it shall be determined in council among you" (96:3). Presidents of priesthood quorums are instructed to "sit in council" with members of their quorums, "to teach them their duty" (107:85–89; cf. 78:9–10).

Councils promote wise decision making by drawing upon the collective strength, wisdom, points of view, and experience of all council members. They promote greater harmony in the implementation of those decisions because members know that their voice has been heard and their counsel considered. The various councils referred to in the Doctrine and Covenants include the following:

1. The "bishop and his council"—a bishop and his two counselors (42:34; cf. 120:1).

2. A "council of high priests"—the council to

whom the Word of Wisdom was revealed on 27 February 1833 (89:1).

3. The first high council of the Church, organized in Kirtland, Ohio, on 17 February 1834—"appointed by revelation for the purpose of settling important difficulties . . . which could not be settled by the church or the bishop's council to the satisfaction of the parties" (102:2). The revelation establishing this high council set the pattern for all future stake high councils.

4. The council of the United Order (United Firm)—an organization of a number of leaders of the Church who covenanted to do their co-operative business according to the principles of consecration (78; 82; 92; 104:53, 74–77).

5. The council of the Twelve Apostles—sometimes referred to as "a Traveling Presiding High Council" (107:33).

6. The "council of the church"—also designated as "the Presidency of the High Priesthood," the "First Presidency of the Church," the "council of the High Priesthood," the "highest council of the church of God, and a final decision upon controversies in spiritual matters" (107:78–80; 102:26).

7. The "common council of the church"—convened to consider charges against "a President of the High Priesthood," presided over by the Presiding Bishop, assisted by "twelve counselors of the High Priesthood" (107:82–84). *See* Common council of the church.

8. "A council, composed of the First Presidency . . . and of the bishop and his council [the Presiding Bishopric], and by my high council [the Twelve Apostles]" (120:1)—having the responsibility for "the disposition of the properties tithed" (120, headnote).

9. The "Council of the Eternal God of all other gods before this world was" (121:32; cf. vv. 25–32).

BLD

Counsel(s)

Instruction, direction, advice. In the Doctrine and Covenants the word *counsel* is used in several contexts:

1. Invitations to listen to the counsel of the Lord. The Lord said to Joseph Smith, "Listen to the counsel of him who has ordained you" (78:2; cf. 100:2).

2. Blessings for heeding the Lord's counsel and negative consequences for rejecting it. To the Saints who had been driven from Jackson County, Missouri, the Lord promised that even though they had "esteemed lightly [his] counsel" (101:8), if "they hearken from this very hour unto the counsel which I, the Lord their God, shall give unto them . . . they shall . . . begin to prevail against mine enemies from this very hour" (103:5–6). Those same Saints were instructed that "inasmuch as they follow the counsel which they receive, they shall have power after many days to accomplish all things pertaining to Zion" (105:37). Conversely, the consequences for rejecting his counsel would be serious. Through Brigham Young, the Lord warned the Saints, "If any man shall seek to build up himself, and seeketh not my counsel, he shall have no power, and his folly shall be made manifest" (136:19). Joseph Smith was chastened for his role in the loss of the 116 pages of the Book of Mormon translation with these words: "For although a man may have many revelations, and have power to do many mighty works, yet if he boasts in his own strength, and sets at naught the counsels of God, and follows after the dictates of his own will and carnal desires, he must fall and incur the vengeance of a just God upon him" (3:4). The Lord added, "Thou hast suffered the counsel of thy director to be trampled upon from the beginning" (3:15), likely referring to the beginning of the circumstances that led to the loss of the manuscript. The same revelation indicates that Martin Harris had "set at naught the counsels of God, and has broken the most sacred promises which were made before God, and has depended upon his own judgment and boasted in his own wisdom" (3:13). The consequence for Martin Harris was that the Lord withdrew his Spirit, which caused him to suffer greatly (19:16–20). Harris was commanded to repent and to preach the basic principles of the gospel and was warned that "misery" would follow if "thou wilt slight these counsels" (19:20–33; cf. 63:55–56; 58:50).

3. Supplanting God's counsel with man's

counsel. The Lord reproved the Saints "because [they sought] to counsel in [their] own ways," affirming "that man should not counsel his fellow man, neither trust in the arm of flesh" if that counsel is not in harmony with the counsel the Lord has given (1:19; 56:14; 124:84; cf. 58:20).

4. Specific instructions from the Lord. Michael received "the keys of salvation under the counsel and direction of the Holy One, who is without beginning of days or end of life" (78:16).

5. Admonition from the Lord not to counsel him. The Lord revealed that those who were baptized in a previous religion must be baptized again into his Church. He made it clear that with the "new and . . . everlasting covenant" being restored, "old covenants" are "done away." Those who desired to enter his Church were to "enter . . . in at the gate, as [he had] commanded, and seek not to counsel [their] God" (22:1–4).

6. The Lord's instructions to individuals to receive counsel from the Prophet Joseph Smith and other Church leaders. Lyman Sherman's sins were forgiven as he was commended for his OBEDIENCE in seeking counsel from the Prophet (108:1). Orson Hyde, Orson Pratt, William Law, Hyrum Smith, and Amos Davies were all told to follow the counsel of Joseph Smith (103:40; 124:88–89, 91–95, 111–12). Joseph was assured by the Lord that although "fools shall have thee in derision . . . the pure in heart, and the wise, and the noble, and the virtuous, shall seek counsel, and authority, and blessings constantly from under thy hand" (122:1–2). Others were told to receive counsel from the leaders of the Church who were designated by the Lord as "plants of renown, and as watchmen upon her [Zion's] walls" (124:61; cf. 69:4).

DKO

Counselors

Individuals appointed to assist the presiding officer of an organization. The Doctrine and Covenants speaks of counselors to bishops, presidents of priesthood quorums, stake presidents, the president of the Church, and presidents of companies organized to travel west from Winter Quarters (42:31; 90:19, 21; 107:72, 76, 79; 124:126, 136, 142; 136:3). "As an assistant," President Gordon B. Hinckley

explained, "the counselor is not the president. He does not assume responsibility and move out ahead of his president. In presidency meetings, each counselor is free to speak his mind on all issues that come before the presidency. However, it is the prerogative of the president to make the decision, and it is the duty of the counselors to back him in that decision. His decision then becomes their decision, regardless of their previous ideas" (49).

In the early days of the Church, the counselors to the bishop of the Church assisted the bishop in administering the temporal needs of the Saints. This included receiving consecrations into the bishop's storehouse, appointing stewardships, and providing for the poor (42:31–34; 51:1–15). These counselors spent their full time in service to the Church, and "their families [were] supported out of the property which [was] consecrated to the bishop" (42:71–72). In addition to these welfare responsibilities, the bishop and his counselors, sometimes referred to as "the bishop and his council" (42:34; 120:1), are to "judge [the] people . . . according to the laws of the kingdom which are given by the prophets of God" (58:18).

The most frequent use of the term *counselors* in the Doctrine and Covenants is to counselors in the "quorum of the Presidency of the Church" (107:22; cf. 112:20, 30; 117:13; 120:1; 124:91, 103, 125–26). Counselors were called to assist the Prophet Joseph Smith in the "Presidency of the High Priesthood" (81, headnote; 81:2), even before the formal organization of the First Presidency in 1833. In 90:6–9, counselors in the First Presidency were declared "equal" with the Prophet Joseph Smith "in holding the keys of this last kingdom," when acting under the direction of the president; those keys do not continue with them at the death of the president.

Another context of the use of the word *counselors* contained in the Doctrine and Covenants is found in a revelation to Thomas B. Marsh, president of the Quorum of the Twelve Apostles. President Marsh was told that the Lord had "made" the First Presidency "counselors . . . unto [him]" (112:20, 30), indicating that the Twelve act under the direction of the First Presidency.

The instruction given to Frederick G. Williams when he was called as a counselor to Joseph Smith could well define the role of all those called as counselors in any organization of the Church of Jesus Christ. The Lord told him to be "faithful in counsel . . . in prayer always, vocally and in thy heart . . . in thy ministry in proclaiming the gospel" (81:3). He was to "succor the weak, lift up the hands which hang down, and strengthen the feeble knees" (81:5). If faithful in these duties, the Lord promised him "immortality, and eternal life in the mansions which I have prepared in the house of my Father" (81:6).

See also President, presidency.

BIBLIOGRAPHY

Hinckley, Gordon B. "In . . . Counsellors There Is Safety." *Ensign* 11 (November 1990): 48–51.

BLT

Country, countries

National or geographic areas. In the Doctrine and Covenants, *country* and *countries* are used to refer to the United States as a whole (20:1); regions within the boundaries of the United States designated as "eastern" (e.g., 39:14; 79:1; 99:1; 103:29), "western" (45:64, 75:15), and "south" countries (75:8, 17), and the "whole region of country" in the vicinity of Jackson County, Missouri (58:52). Moreover, the text speaks of "far countries" outside the United States, where "great wars" were to be anticipated (38:29); the "north countries," into which the "great deep" will be "driven" and from which the lost tribes of Israel will return in the last days in connection with the second coming of the Lord (133:17–26); and countries of the world generally, of which the Lord instructs the Saints to gain a knowledge that they "may be prepared" when they are sent out to "testify and warn the people" with the message of the restored gospel (88:78–81; 93:53).

RCF

Covenant people of the Lord

Those who have come unto God by entering into a covenant relationship with him. These peoples have existed from the beginning of earth's history. As part of this covenant God has promised priesthood, salvation, eternal families, and a special relationship with the heavens. These covenants bind his people with the responsibility to love the gospel, live it, and share it. As his covenant people have lapsed into apostasy again and again through time, God has reestablished his covenant with later generations, for example, Adam (Moses 5:1–12; 6:62–68), Enoch (Moses 7:1–4, 12–14, 18–21), Melchizedek (JST Genesis 14), Abraham (Abr. 2:6–12), the children of Israel (Ex. 19:1–8; Deut. 7:6–15; 14:2; 26:18), the Nephites (1 Ne. 15:14; 3 Ne. 20:26), and the Saints in the meridian of time (Acts 3:25; Eph. 2:19–20; 4:11–16). The Lord Jesus Christ declared to young Joseph Smith in the spring of 1820 that "all religious denominations were believing in incorrect doctrines and that none of them was acknowledged of God as His Church and kingdom" (Smith, 27). The Doctrine and Covenants is a record of God's reestablishment of a covenant people in the latter days. It is a handbook of instructions which, if followed, the Lord says, "Ye may be my people and I will be your God" (42:9).

Names for the covenant people

The term "covenant people" appears only once in the Doctrine and Covenants (42:36), yet the concept saturates its pages. The most commonly used terms are "my people" (e.g., 3:16; 39:11; 84:119; 110:10; 136:31); "my church" (e.g., 10:67–69; 45:1, 6; 64:37; 133:4); "my saints" (e.g., 57:10; 61:17; 101:64; 105:15; 124:25); "my friends" (e.g., 84:63, 77; 88:117; 94:1; 98:1; 105:26); and "my disciples" (e.g., 1:4; 41:5; 45:32; 84:91; 103:28).

Other terms used to denote a covenant people include those who are "chosen" (1:4; 19:9; 29:4; 95:8; 105:35–36); the "elect" (25:3; 29:7; 33:6; 35:20; 84:34); the "sons of God" (11:30; 35:2; 45:8; 128:23); "little children" (50:41; 61:36; 78:17); "children of the kingdom" (41:6; 84:59); "mine Israel" or "the house of Israel" (39:11; 52:2; 101:12; 103:17; 109:65, 67); "the church of the Firstborn" (78:21; 93:22; 107:19); "the seed of Abraham" (84:34; 103:17); the "Latter-day Saints" (115:4; 121:33; 128:24; 136:2); "them that my Father hath given me" (50:42; 27:14; 84:63); and "the weak things of the earth" (1:19; 35:13; 124:1; 133:59).

Some terms used for those who are not his covenant people include Babylon (1:16; 64:24; 86:3; 133:5, 7, 14); "the world" (23:2; 27:14; 30:4; 42:65; 70:6; 95:13); those who have broken covenants (1:13–16; 104:4); those who are "called" but not "chosen" (95:5–6; 121:34–40); and "the nations" (45:49; 64:37; 84:96; 115:5; 133:14, 59).

How to become a covenant people

One must make and keep covenants. In the earlier sections of the Doctrine and Covenants the Lord repeatedly commanded his people to take his name upon them (18:21, 24; 20:37, 77), to repent, be baptized by water, and receive the Holy Ghost (19:31; 33:11; 39:6–10; 53:3; 68:25). As the Restoration unfolded, additional covenants were revealed. Among them were those of the PRIESTHOOD (13; 27:8, 12–13; 84:33–39; 110:11–15) and of the temple, including eternal MARRIAGE (124:37–41; 131:1–4; 132:4–25). After making covenants with God, Saints must strive to keep their covenants through OBEDIENCE; they must walk uprightly before him (18:31; 68:28; 90:24; 100:15; 109:1).

Additionally, the Lord establishes his covenant people by gathering them physically and spiritually. He said, "Ye are called to bring to pass the gathering of mine elect . . . that they shall be gathered in unto one place upon the face of this land" (29:7–8). He commanded that they "be gathered unto me a righteous people, without spot and blameless" (38:31). Covenant people are to be "gathered unto it [Zion] out of every nation under heaven" (45:69, 71) and "stand in holy places" (101:22). Their gathering is to be done "carefully," "as it shall be counseled by the elders of the church at the conferences, according to the knowledge which they receive from time to time" (58:56; 105:24). The gathering is for a "defense, and for a refuge from the storm, and from wrath when it shall be poured out without mixture upon the whole earth" (115:6). Two biblical analogies are used: "I will gather them as a hen gathereth her chickens under her wings" (10:65; cf. 29:2), and "I must gather together my people, according to the parable of the wheat and the tares" (101:65; cf. 86:1–10). *See* Gather, gathering.

Roles of a covenant people

The Lord has assigned his people roles in the world: laborers and missionaries (33:3; 39:17; 88:70, 74–81); his agents (64:29); "children of light," "a light to the world," "an ensign unto the people," and "a standard for the nations" (45:9; 64:42; 86:11; 103:9; 106:5; 115:5); the salt of the earth—the "savor" and "saviors" of men (86:11; 101:39–40; 103:9–10); and judges (64:37–38; 75:21; cf. 20:13).

Establishing a covenant people in the latter days has not been easy, yet the Lord encouragingly reminded his Saints that he is well pleased with them collectively (1:30) and that they have the keys of the kingdom (42:69; 65:2; 81:2; 90:2), "the kingdom" itself (45:1; 50:35; 64:4; 72:1; 84:76; 138:44), and "the mysteries of the kingdom" (42:65; 63:23; 84:19; 90:14).

That the Lord has a covenant people is a primary theme of several sections of the Doctrine and Covenants. Sections 38 and 115 are instructions on gathering to Ohio and Missouri. Section 42 is the law of the Lord for his people. Section 84 is a formula for establishing a covenant people in the latter days. This formula includes temples (84:1–5), the priesthood and its ordinances (89:6–42), the scriptures (84:43–60), missionary work (84:61–96), and the presence of the Savior, Jesus Christ (84:97–102). The Lord affirmed that the "power of godliness" is "manifest unto men in the flesh" only through the ordinances of the Melchizedek Priesthood (84:19–25) and that by obedience to the oath and covenant of the priesthood, entrusted to his covenant people, Saints can obtain "all that [the] Father hath" (84:33–42). In sections 98, 101, 103, and 105, the Lord explained why he allowed his covenant people to be expelled from Jackson County, Missouri. Section 86 interprets the parable of the wheat and the tares, indicating the important role of the priesthood, which was restored to the covenant people of the last dispensation. Section 133 instructed the covenant people to gather: to come out "from the midst of wickedness, which is spiritual Babylon" (v. 14), and "send forth the elders of my church unto the nations" (v. 8), inviting them to accept the gospel and gather with the Saints of God, thus preparing to meet the Savior at his second coming. A study of these sections yields a wealth of insight about covenant people.

President Gordon B. Hinckley affirmed the reality and role of covenant people of the Lord in these words: "All of God's children are of His family, but there is a special relationship between God and the children of His covenant. . . . We are a covenant people, and great are the obligations which go with that covenant" (inside front cover).

See also Abrahamic covenant; New and everlasting covenant.

BIBLIOGRAPHY

Hinckley, Gordon B. "A Covenant People." *Friend* 32 (January 2002).

Smith, Joseph, Jr. "The Wentworth Letter." *Ensign* 32 (July 2002): 27–32.

JS

Covenant(s). *See* Abrahamic covenant; Covenant people of the Lord; Jesus Christ, Mediator of the new covenant; New and everlasting covenant; Ordinance(s).

Covenant, heirs according to the. *See* Abrahamic covenant.

Covenant, new and everlasting. *See* New and everlasting covenant.

Covet

"To desire inordinately; to desire that which it is unlawful to obtain or possess" (Webster, s.v. "covet"; cf. 56:17). Jehovah's injunction "thou shalt not covet" (Ex. 20:17; Mosiah 13:24), delivered by the prophets Moses and Abinadi to ancient Israel, is proclaimed anew through latter-day prophets Joseph Smith and Brigham Young to modern Israel in Doctrine and Covenants 19:25–26; 98:20; 104:4, 52; 117:4; and 136:20. Specific prohibitions mentioned in the Doctrine and Covenants include generally "that which is thy brother's" (136:20) and specifically "thy neighbor's wife" (19:25) and "thine own property" (19:26). In 1831 Joseph Smith warned that "God had often sealed up the heavens because of covetousness in the Church" (Cannon and Cook, 23).

Man's tendency is to covet the trivial at the expense of the vital. Elder Neal A. Maxwell explained, "Stubborn selfishness leads otherwise good people to fight over herds, patches of sand, and strippings of milk. All this results from what the Lord calls coveting 'the drop,' while neglecting the 'more weighty matters' (D&C 117:8)" (15). William Marks and Newel K. Whitney, who had been instructed to "speedily" sell Kirtland properties and move to Missouri, delayed in doing so and were chastened by the Lord for such coveting. "Covetous desires" was one of the reasons the Saints were allowed to be driven from Jackson County, Missouri, in 1833 (101:1–8). In the midst of these Jackson County persecutions, some Saints in Kirtland broke "the covenant through covetousness," precipitating the dissolution of the United Order and the consequent "sore" curse of God (104:4; 98:19–20).

Among the "otherwise good people" who were admonished for covetousness in the Doctrine and Covenants was Martin Harris, who had agreed to pay $3,000 for the printing of the Book of Mormon but was reluctant to do so. To Martin Harris the Lord said, "Thou shalt not covet thine own property, but impart it freely to the printing of the Book of Mormon" (19:26, 34–35). Martin repented and did as the Lord commanded.

The Saints migrating westward were instructed to "covet not that which is thy brother's" (136:20; cf. 88:123).

BIBLIOGRAPHY

Cannon, Donald Q., and Lyndon W. Cook, eds. *Far West Record: Minutes of The Church of Jesus Christ of Latter-day Saints, 1830–1844.* Salt Lake City: Deseret Book, 1983.

Maxwell, Neal A. "Put Off the Natural Man, and Come Off Conqueror." *Ensign* 20 (November 1990): 14–16.

Webster, Noah. *An American Dictionary of the English Language.* 1828.

EPR

Covill, James (Covel, Covell)

Birth: 19 September 1770, Chatham, Barnstable, Massachusetts

Death: February 1850, New York City, New York

The lives of Joseph Smith and James Covel intersected briefly early in January 1831. Covel approached the Prophet and "covenanted with the Lord that he would obey any command that the Lord would give to him" through Joseph (39, headnote). After he received the revelation now recorded as section 39 and dated 5 January, "James Covill rejected the word of the Lord, and returned to his former principles and people" (40, headnote). The following day, 6 January, the Prophet received section 40 in response to Covel's rejection.

The compilers of the *History of the Church* misidentified James Covel as "James Covill" and as a "Baptist minister" (Smith, 1:143). The Book of Commandments identified him only as "James (C.,)"; the Doctrine and Covenants, as "James Covill"; and the 1981 edition of the Doctrine and Covenants, following the lead of the *History of the Church,* as "James Covill, who had been a Baptist minister for about forty years."

The index to the manuscript Book of Commandments and Revelations lists him as "James a Methodist Priest" (Jensen et al., 386–87). The writing of this index is contemporaneous with that of sections 39 and 40, making it a more reliable source than that of the *History of the Church,* written about eight years later. No James Covel (Covill, Covell) has been found in the records of Baptist congregations for that area of New York and time period; however, James Covel in the records of the Methodists fits the profile of the man briefly mentioned in Latter-day Saint records.

James Covel was the fourth of six known children of James Covel and Sarah Hall. His father was a Baptist minister and his mother a Methodist. He married Sarah Gould on 28 October 1795, and they had ten children.

James Covel became a Methodist itinerant minister in 1791, forty years before the two revelations in the Doctrine and Covenants were received. He also became a medical practitioner, and most records give him the title of Doctor, M.D., or Rev. Dr. His elder brother, Zenas, and his own two oldest sons, James and Samuel, were also Methodist itinerant ministers. In addition, his sons Samuel and John were medical practitioners, as was he.

On 13 February 1830, the Rochester Conference of the "Methodist Society" met in Ontario, Wayne County, New York. The minutes record: "In committee of the whole it resolved to adopt the Conventional Articles of the Associated Methodist Churches. Dr. James Covel was elected President and Orren Miller Secretary, and the body adopted the name of Genesee Conference" (Drinkhouse, 2:243–44).

Ontario is located in the northwest corner of Wayne County, with Lake Ontario forming its northern border. Ontario was less than six miles from Palmyra and about thirty-three miles from Fayette, New York. Hence, James Covel was in the area when the Book of Mormon was published and the Church was organized. He remained in the area longer than the Saints, who migrated to Ohio beginning in January 1831.

Unfortunately, no known record outside Latter-day Saint Church records links this man directly with Joseph Smith, but there is also no other Methodist minister of forty years' experience named James Covel in that area during that time period for whom there are surviving records. It is not clear from sections 39 and 40 that James Covel actually received baptism; Diedrich Willers Jr., however, reported that he did (Porter, 103). Willers may be correct, but given that his is the only record that a baptism took place, caution is needed in stating it as a fact.

James Covel, as a medical doctor, manufactured and marketed various remedies under his name. One, Covel's Rheumatic Pills, were still being sold in 1880, more than thirty years after his death.

See also Historical context and overview of Doctrine and Covenants 39 (p. 746) and 40 (p. 747).

BIBLIOGRAPHY

Bassett, Ancel H. *A Concise History of the Methodist Protestant Church.* Pittsburgh: Charles A. Scott, 1877.

Drinkhouse, Edward J. *History of Methodist Reform: Synoptical of General Methodism, 1703–1898.* 2 vols. Baltimore, Md.: Board of Publication of the Methodist Protestant Church, 1899.

Jensen, Robin Scott, Robert J. Woodford, and Steven C. Harper, eds. *Manuscript Revelation Books.* Facsimile edition. First volume of the Revelations and Translations series of *The Joseph Smith Papers,* edited by Dean C. Jessee, Ronald K. Esplin, and Richard

Lyman Bushman. Salt Lake City: Church Historian's Press, 2009.

Porter, Larry C. "A Study of the Origins of The Church of Jesus Christ of Latter-day Saints in the States of New York and Pennsylvania, 1816–1831." Ph.D. dissertation, Brigham Young University, 1971.

Smith, Joseph. *History of The Church of Jesus Christ of Latter-day Saints.* Edited by B. H. Roberts. 7 vols. 2d ed. rev. Salt Lake City: The Church of Jesus Christ of Latter-day Saints, 1932–51.

RJW

Cowdery, Oliver

Birth: 3 October 1806, Wells, Rutland County, Vermont

Death: 3 March 1850, Richmond, Ray County, Missouri

Oliver Cowdery, 1806–1850.

Courtesy Church History Library.

Oliver Cowdery received a good basic education, but his only known early occupation was clerking in a store (Anderson, "Reuben," 1). Later, after a term of teaching, he became the main scribe for the Book of Mormon and later an important Church leader, clerk, historian, and newspaper editor. With Joseph Smith he received visits from heavenly beings, including those who restored priesthood keys pertaining to the dispensation of the fulness of times.

Lucy Mack Smith's biography tells how schoolteacher Cowdery boarded at the Smith home and learned that the youthful prophet was in northern Pennsylvania, slowly translating the ancient record after the loss of the 1828 manuscript. Joseph Smith said, "[The] Lord appeared unto a young man by the name of Oliver Cowdry and shewed unto him the plates in a vision . . . therefore he was desirous to come and write for me" (Smith, 1:10). When the school term ended, Cowdery, with Samuel Smith, walked some 120 miles to meet the translator on 5 April 1829, and within days the two began steady labor to produce the English text (JS–H 1:66–67).

The first revelation to Cowdery commended him for his desires to serve God, called him to "stand by my servant Joseph," and reminded him of the feelings of peace he had received when praying about the Prophet's work (6:18, 22–23). Soon Cowdery sought to translate but failed, and the Lord's counsel to him is often used as a model for seeking revelation. Cowdery was told to "study it out in your mind," pray, and the Lord would confirm a correct decision by a burning within (9:8).

Restoring angels appeared to the translators. After praying concerning the Savior's commands on baptism, Joseph Smith and Oliver Cowdery beheld John the Baptist, who laid his hands upon their heads and conferred upon them the Aaronic Priesthood, with its authority to baptize (JS–H 1:68–71). Soon the two returned to western New York for safety from persecution, staying at the Whitmer farm in Fayette. There Oliver, Martin Harris, and David Whitmer asked to be the three who would be chosen to see the plates "by the power of God" (e.g., 2 Ne. 27:12–14). The answer came that they might see both the plates and other ancient objects if they exercised faith (17:1). Their joint testimony of this event prefaces the Book of Mormon, declaring that an angel showed them the plates and the voice of God proclaimed the translation correct.

A list of restoration messengers was printed in the 1835 edition of the Doctrine and Covenants, in which the Lord spoke of sending Peter, James, and John to Joseph Smith and Oliver Cowdery, "by whom I have ordained you and confirmed you to be apostles, and especial witnesses of my name" (27:12). Previously John the Baptist had told Joseph and Oliver that these apostles held keys of the higher priesthood, which must be restored before Church leaders could lay their hands on others to bestow the gift of the Holy Ghost (JS–H 1:70, 72). The next year Joseph and Oliver performed this ordinance at the organization of the Church (Smith, 1:242, 303), an event which shows that Peter, James, and John had conferred the keys of the higher priesthood before 6 April 1830.

Soon Cowdery was counseled to remember that only the presiding prophet can give God's commands to the Church (28:2–7). Cowdery was then called to lead the first mission to the Indian tribes just west of Missouri (32:1–5); on the way he and his companions baptized more than a hundred persons in the area of Kirtland, Ohio, who were seeking biblical religion. After the mission to the LAMANITES was completed and Oliver returned to Kirtland, he was commanded to return to Missouri with John Whitmer with the manuscript revelations (69:1–2). Cowdery and William W. Phelps were assigned to edit the revelations for the Book of Commandments (57:11–13; 70:1–5). After a mob destroyed the press and most of the printed but unbound revelations in 1833, Cowdery was called back to Kirtland. From 1833 to 1836 he was in the highest Church leadership councils and generally was the editor of Church publications. The apex of his life was standing beside Joseph Smith in beholding the Savior accept the Kirtland Temple and receiving priesthood KEYS from Moses, Elias, and Elijah (110:1–16).

Cowdery held latent presiding keys after ancient apostles ordained him (27:9–13), and in mid-1830 he signed ordination certificates as "Second Elder" of the Church (McConkie, Father, 84). But that office was superseded by developments in the First Presidency while Cowdery was fulfilling his assignment to preside in Missouri from 1832 to 1833. After he returned to Kirtland in 1833, the Prophet ordained him "Assistant President" of the Church.

In the detailed minutes of 5 December 1834, Oliver Cowdery is ranked first after Joseph Smith, but Sidney Rigdon and Frederick G. Williams are also called "assistant Presidents"

(Smith, 1:20–21; 2:36). After the crisis period of 1837–38, Cowdery was rejected by the high council in Missouri as one of the presidents of the Church there (Cannon and Cook, 136). In 1838 he forfeited his calling as assistant president of the whole Church when he was excommunicated for disloyalty and opposing the Prophet (Cannon and Cook, 162–69). Thus Oliver Cowdery's priesthood authority was terminated, and the keys he had held were transferred to Hyrum Smith, who received the "honor, and priesthood, and gifts of the priesthood, that once were put upon him that was my servant Oliver Cowdery" (124:95). By 1844, the keys of presidency were held by Joseph and Hyrum Smith and also passively by the Twelve Apostles, the body called by an 1829 revelation (18), ordained in 1835, and in Nauvoo placed over all programs in all places under First Presidency direction. The Presidency and the Twelve shared "the keys of the dispensation . . . sent down from heaven" (112:32). Elder Bruce R. McConkie explained that Oliver Cowdery received presiding authority as the required second witness of priesthood restoration, and Hyrum and Joseph Smith exercised these powers as "two joint Presidents" (55–56). After the martyrdom of Joseph and Hyrum Smith, the office of assistant president was discontinued, the law of witnesses having been fulfilled.

Cowdery spent a decade outside the Church, first studying law and then practicing in Ohio and Wisconsin. A prominent attorney trained in his office called him "an able lawyer and a great advocate" (Anderson, Investigating, 41). Cowdery would have returned to the Church earlier, hoping for an apology for extreme statements made about him after his excommunication. That apology never came, but in 1848 he who had once been warned to "beware of pride" (23:1) returned anyway, publicly declaring to the Church in Iowa that he personally knew that Joseph Smith had ancient plates and that both men were present when both priesthoods had been "conferred by the holy angels of God" (Anderson, "Reuben," 402). Weakened by a lung condition, Cowdery spent his last year near the parents and siblings of his wife, Elizabeth Whitmer Cowdery, in Richmond,

Missouri. He readily accepted a political mission for the Church in Washington, D.C., intending to migrate to the Salt Lake Valley afterward. Instead he passed away, expressing love for the Savior and insisting on the truth of the Book of Mormon and on the reality of priesthood restoration (Anderson, "Biography," 63; Faulring, 351).

See also Priesthood, restoration of priesthood and priesthood keys.

BIBLIOGRAPHY

Anderson, Richard Lloyd. "A Brief Biography of Oliver Cowdery." In *Oliver Cowdery: Essays from BYU Studies and FARMS*, edited by John W. Welch and Larry E. Morris, 1–10. Provo, Utah: Neal A. Maxwell Institute for Religious Scholarship, Brigham Young University, 2006.

———. *Investigating the Book of Mormon Witnesses*. Salt Lake City: Deseret Book, 1981.

———. "Reuben Miller: Recorder of Oliver Cowdery's Reaffirmations." In *Oliver Cowdery: Essays from BYU Studies and FARMS*, edited by John W. Welch and Larry E. Morris, 401–19. Provo, Utah: Neal A. Maxwell Institute for Religious Scholarship, Brigham Young University, 2006.

Cannon, Donald Q., and Lyndon W. Cook, eds. *Far West Record: Minutes of The Church of Jesus Christ of Latter-day Saints, 1830–1844*. Salt Lake City: Deseret Book, 1983.

Faulring, Scott H. "The Return of Oliver Cowdery." In *Oliver Cowdery: Essays from BYU Studies and FARMS*, edited by John W. Welch and Larry E. Morris, 321–62. Provo, Utah: Neal A. Maxwell Institute for Religious Scholarship, Brigham Young University, 2006.

McConkie, Bruce R. *Mormon Doctrine*. 2d ed. Salt Lake City: Bookcraft, 1966.

McConkie, Mark. *The Father of the Prophet*. Salt Lake City: Bookcraft, 1993.

Smith, Joseph. *The Papers of Joseph Smith*. Edited by Dean C. Jessee. 2 vols. Salt Lake City: Deseret Book, 1989–92.

Smith, Joseph Fielding. *Doctrines of Salvation*. Compiled by Bruce R. McConkie. 3 vols. Salt Lake City: Bookcraft, 1954–56.

RLA

Cowdery, Warren A.

Birth: 17 October 1788, Wells, Rutland County, Vermont

Death: 23 February 1851, Kirtland, Lake County, Ohio

Warren Cowdery was baptized into the Church in late 1831. His younger brother Oliver Cowdery was one of the three witnesses of the Book of Mormon plates and Joseph Smith's main scribe for the book's translation. Sometime prior to Warren's baptism, Oliver gave Warren the privilege of examining some of the proof sheets of the Book of Mormon.

In a revelation dated 25 November 1834, Warren was "appointed and ordained a presiding high priest over [the] church" in Freedom, New York (106:1). A well-situated physician and apothecary, he was admonished to "preach [the] everlasting gospel . . . not only in his own place, but in the adjoining counties; and [to] devote his whole time to this high and holy calling" (106:2–3). The Lord said that there was "joy in heaven" when "Warren bowed to my scepter, and separated himself from the crafts of men." Consequently, the Lord promised him mercy and grace and, if he was faithful, "a crown . . . in the mansions of [the] Father" (106:6–8). The Lord said he would "lift him up," "notwithstanding the vanity of his heart," "inasmuch as he will humble himself before me" (106:7).

Perhaps it was this vanity the Lord spoke of that led to the troubles Cowdery encountered not long after the 1834 revelation was given. In September 1835, "the Council of the Presidency of the Church" convened to consider a letter from Warren A. Cowdery "in connection with certain other reports, derogatory to the character and teaching of the Twelve." Concerning the matter, "from the testimony of several witnesses (the Twelve) it was proved before the Council that said complaints originated in the minds of persons who were darkened in consequence of covetousness, or some other cause, rather than the spirit of truth" (Smith, *History*, 2:283). In early 1836, after moving to Kirtland, Cowdery met with the Prophet and the Twelve to discuss the letter he wrote, and the matter was resolved (Smith, *History*, 2:374–75; *Writings*, 199n211).

In Kirtland Warren Cowdery acted as a scribe, assistant Church recorder, high councilor, printing office agent, and editor of the *Latter Day Saints' Messenger and Advocate*. Along with his brother Oliver, Warren separated from the Church in 1838 but, unlike Oliver, he did not return to it. He remained in Kirtland until his death in 1851.

BIBLIOGRAPHY

Smith, Joseph. *History of The Church of Jesus Christ of Latter-day Saints.* Edited by B. H. Roberts. 7 vols. 2d ed. rev. Salt Lake City: The Church of Jesus Christ of Latter-day Saints, 1932–51.

———. *Personal Writings of Joseph Smith.* Compiled and edited by Dean C. Jessee. Rev. ed. Salt Lake City: Deseret Book, 2002.

KWF

Creation, the. *See* Earth, the; Man, creation of.

Creeds. *See* Appendix E.

Cross, take up your. *See* Take up your cross.

Crown(s)

A symbol for rewards given to the obedient; used as a noun and as a verb throughout the Doctrine and Covenants. The rewards are referred to as "a crown of eternal life" (20:14), "a crown of righteousness" (25:15; 29:13), a crown of "joy and . . . rejoicing" (52:43), "a crown of immortality, and eternal life" (81:6), "a crown of glory" (104:7; cf. 109:76), and "crowns of eternal lives" (132:55). In at least two instances, *crown* expresses the idea of rule, judgment, and dominion in the celestial realm—the Lord promised the twelve apostles who were with him at Jerusalem that they will wear white robes and "crowns upon their heads" and judge the whole house of Israel who are righteous (29:12). To the faithful, the Lord promises a place in "the mansions of my Father" (59:2; 106:8) and that they will "come up unto the crown prepared for [them], and be made rulers over many kingdoms" (78:15; cf. 76:108).

The Lord promises to "crown the faithful with joy and with rejoicing" (52:43), "much glory" (58:4; cf. 88:107; 101:65; 133:32), "blessings from above, yea, and with commandments not a few, and with revelations in their time" (59:4). Faithful missionaries are promised that they will be "laden with many sheaves" and

Road leading to the Hill Cumorah; photograph by George Edward Anderson, 1907. "And again, what do we hear? Glad tidings from Cumorah! Moroni, an angel from heaven, declaring the fulfilment of the prophets—the book to be revealed" (D&C 128:20).

"crowned with honor, and glory, and immortality, and eternal life" (75:5; 79:3).

See also Eternal life.

RDD

Crucified him unto themselves. *See* Sons of perdition.

Cumbered. *See* Appendix E.

Cumorah

A glacial drumlin or hill located in upstate New York, where Joseph Smith was directed by the angel Moroni to go to retrieve the golden PLATES from which he translated the Book of Mormon (JS–H 1:42, 51). The word *Cumorah* is used once in the Doctrine and Covenants (128:20). Interestingly, this is the only known account in which Joseph Smith used the word.

The Doctrine and Covenants makes it clear that the events that occurred in connection with Cumorah were in fulfillment of the words of ancient prophets (128:20). According to David Whitmer, Cumorah is the title the angel Moroni used to describe the location of the place where the plates were hidden (Cook, 27). *See* map, p. 476.

See also Doctrine and Covenants, what it says about the Book of Mormon.

BIBLIOGRAPHY

Cook, Lyndon W., ed. *David Whitmer Interviews: A Restoration Witness.* Orem, Utah: Grandin Book, 1991.

CJW

Cup

A term used in the Doctrine and Covenants with both literal and figurative meanings. In 20:78 is a reference to the literal cup from which one drinks when partaking of the SACRAMENT of the Lord's Supper. All other references are figurative and are used in three contexts:

1. The terrible anguish and suffering attending the ATONEMENT. Of his atoning sacrifice in the Garden of Gethsemane, the Savior told Martin Harris that his suffering caused him "to tremble because of pain, and to bleed at every pore, and to suffer both body and spirit—and would that [he] might not drink the bitter cup, and shrink" (19:18).

2. Wickedness. BABYLON, "the great persecutor of the church, the apostate, the whore . . . maketh all nations to drink of her cup" (86:3), and when "the cup of their iniquity is full," the Lord's anger will be "poured out without measure" (101:11; cf. 103:3). Hence, the Lord admonishes those preparing for his second coming to "go ye out from . . . Babylon, from the midst of wickedness, which is spiritual Babylon" (133:14). *See* Wicked, the/wickedness.

3. The anger or indignation of the Lord at the wickedness of the world. Early in this dispensation, in September 1830, the Lord said, "And it shall come to pass, because of the wickedness of the world, that I will take vengeance upon the wicked, for they will not repent; for the cup of mine indignation is full; for behold, my blood shall not cleanse them if they hear me not" (29:17). Four months later he said, "Behold, the day has come, when the cup of the wrath of mine indignation is full" (43:26). The Lord's JUDGMENTS do not always come immediately. Often he permits people to suffer the natural consequences of their wickedness through such means as wars, in which "the wicked shall slay the wicked" (63:33), and through natural disasters (88:88–91).

FFJ

Curse, cursing

A punishment typically pronounced and meted out by God (24:4–6; 29:41; 41:1). At times and under certain circumstances, God's servants also have been given license to pronounce curses (24:15; 103:24–26; 124:91–93; 132:47–48), but the meting out of the actual punishment is left in God's hands to carry out in his "own due time" (24:16). Wicked men may futilely "curse God and die" (45:32) or be cursed by their own law (24:17).

People are cursed for such actions as rejecting those doing God's work (24:15–16), persecuting the faithful and their leaders (103:24–26; 121:13–16), or forgetting God (133:2). Those who have accepted the gospel are especially cursed if they cease listening to God (41:1), refuse to support righteous leaders (24:4–6), violate covenants (104:2–5; 124:47–48), or perform less than God's commandments or go beyond them in unrighteousness (124:119–20). Descendants of Israel who are under a curse for transgressions are promised that the curse will be removed as they return to faith (109:62–66; 113:9–10). The people of the earth, and the earth itself as a whole, will be cursed if the requisite restored priesthood power and keys are not used to perform saving ordinances in the temple "for the redemption of the dead, and the sealing of the children to their parents" (138:46–48; cf. 27:9; 98:16–17; 110:14–15; 128:17–18).

The punishment associated with a curse may be spiritual or temporal. Some who are cursed may, in mortality, suffer physical loss, pain, or destruction (104:5; 121:13–16). At the Judgment the cursed will suffer spiritually when God commands them, "Depart from me, ye cursed, into everlasting fire, prepared for the devil and his angels" (29:27–28).

Curses are generally placed upon individuals, but "the waters" and "the land" have also come under curses (61:14–17; cf. 38:17–18; Gen. 3:17).

TBB

Curtain(s)

The words *curtain* and *curtains* are each used once in the Doctrine and Covenants, each with a its own meaning. *Curtain* in 88:95 is the "curtain of heaven" that will be "unfolded, as a scroll is unfolded" at the second coming of the Lord, unveiling the face of the Lord, when "all flesh shall see [the Lord] together" (88:95; 101:23). Elder Orson Pratt explained: "School children, who are in the habit of seeing maps hung up on the wall, know that they have rollers upon which they are rolled up, and that to expose the face of the maps they are let down. So will the curtain of heaven be unrolled so that . . . the face of the Lord will be unveiled" (16:328). *See* Jesus Christ, second coming of.

The term *curtains* is used in 101:21. Section 101 was given at a time when the Saints who had gathered to ZION (Missouri) were enduring severe persecution (101, headnote). Through the Prophet Joseph Smith, the Lord affirmed that "Zion shall not be moved out of her place, notwithstanding her children are scattered" (101:17). "There is none other place appointed than that which I have appointed . . . for the work of the gathering of my saints—until the day cometh when there is found no more room for them; and then I have other places which I will appoint unto them, and they shall be called stakes, for the curtains or the strength of Zion" (101:20–21). As the Church grew, organizational units called STAKES were established, and these stakes were likened to curtains that added strength to Zion's tent (cf. Isa. 54:2). Curtains in this context are analogous to tents constructed by nomads in ancient times (Tomasino, 2:542). Handwoven sheets of goat's hair were sewn together and then stretched over poles or wooden frames. Cords were attached and anchored to stakes in the ground for stability. As the family grew, additional sheets or curtains were adjoined, the cords lengthened, and stronger stakes added (Walton et al., 634). This practice is reflective of Isaiah's prophecy concerning Zion in the last days (Isa. 54, headnote). Elder Bruce R. McConkie wrote: "In prophetic imagery, Zion is pictured as a great tent upheld by cords fastened securely to *stakes*. Thus Isaiah, envisioning the latter-day glory of Israel, gathered to her restored Zion, proclaimed: 'Enlarge the place of thy tent, and let them stretch forth the curtains of thine habitations: spare not, lengthen thy cords, and strengthen thy stakes . . . ' (Isa. 54:2–7)" (764).

The Lord's message is clear: "Zion must increase in beauty, and in holiness; her borders must be enlarged; her stakes must be strengthened; yea, verily I say unto you, Zion must arise and put on her beautiful garments" (82:14; cf. Isa. 49:18–23; Moro. 10:31).

BIBLIOGRAPHY

McConkie, Bruce R. *Mormon Doctrine.* 2d ed. Salt Lake City: Bookcraft, 1977.

Pratt, Orson. *Journal of Discourses.* 26 vols. London: Latter-day Saints' Book Depot, 1854–86.

Tomasino, Anthony. "Curtain," no. 3749. In *The New International Dictionary of Old Testament Theology and Exegesis.* Edited by Willem A. VanGemeren. 5 vols. Grand Rapids, Mich.: Zondervan, 1997.

Walton, John H., Victor H. Matthews, and Mark W. Chavalas. *The IVP Bible Background Commentary: Old*

Testament. Downers Grove, Ill.: InterVarsity Press, 2000.

EDS.

Cut off. *See* Cast out/cut off.

Cutler, Alpheus

Birth: 29 February 1784, Plainfield, Sullivan County, New Hampshire

Death: 10 August 1864, Manti, Mills County, Iowa

While listening to Elders David W. Patten and Reynolds Cahoon preach the gospel, Alpheus Cutler's sick daughter, Lois, avowed her belief in their message, received a blessing, and was instantly healed. This miracle convinced others to join the Church, among them Alpheus Cutler, who was baptized on 20 January 1833 and ordained an elder shortly thereafter. By 1834, he and his family had settled in Kirtland, where he helped build the temple, was ordained a high priest on 29 April 1836, and served on the high council. After moving to Missouri, Cutler suffered persecution and the loss of his belongings and land with the rest of the Saints. He fled Missouri and settled in Nauvoo in 1839. In April 1839 he returned to Far West with members of the Twelve to assist in laying the cornerstone of the temple at Far West, before the apostles left on their mission to England (118:4–5). In Nauvoo Cutler served on the temple committee and on the high council (124:131–32).

After the Prophet Joseph Smith's martyrdom, Cutler was chosen as one of the bodyguards to escort the bodies of the Prophet and his brother Hyrum from Carthage to Nauvoo (Smith, 7:134–35). He was appointed third company captain in the Saints' exodus from Nauvoo and selected the Cutler's Park campsite (Nebraska); however, he did not go west with the Saints. He eventually settled in Manti, Iowa, and formed "The True Church of Jesus Christ" (Cutlerites) in 1853 (Cook, 255). He declared himself to be Joseph Smith's successor until, near the end of his life, "he acknowledged his apostasy to his grandson, Abraham Kimball," and avowed "that Joseph Smith was a Prophet of God, and I know that Brigham Young is his legal successor" (in Black, 81).

BIBLIOGRAPHY

Black, Susan Easton. *Who's Who in the Doctrine and Covenants.* Salt Lake City: Deseret Book, 1997.

Cook, Lyndon W. *The Revelations of the Prophet Joseph Smith.* Salt Lake City: Deseret Book, 1985.

Smith, Joseph. *History of The Church of Jesus Christ of Latter-day Saints.* Edited by B. H. Roberts. 7 vols. 2d ed. rev. Salt Lake City: The Church of Jesus Christ of Latter-day Saints, 1932–51.

KWF

For, behold, the Lord your Redeemer suffered **death** in the flesh; wherefore he suffered the pain of all men, that all men might repent and come unto him. And he hath risen again from the dead, that he might bring all men unto him, on conditions of repentance. 18:11–12

Damnation, damned

Consequences for failure to obey divine law. The Doctrine and Covenants speaks of damnation in three contexts: degrees of mental and physical suffering in both body and spirit (19:15–18; 76:33, 104–6), including being "delivered over to the buffetings of Satan" (78:12; 82:21; 104:9–10; 132:26); SONS OF PERDITION who receive the second death (76:32, 37–38, 43; 132:27); and those denied exaltation, or eternal lives (131:2–4; 132:16–18), who will live "separately and singly, without exaltation, in their saved condition, to all eternity" (132:17).

Although the revelations make clear that some of the punishment for sin will one day come to an end (19:6–12; 76:84–85, 102–7), it also affirms that some of the limitations associated with damnation endure eternally. Damnation is a continuum of limitations and restrictions associated with degrees of glory (88:21–24). Those in the telestial kingdom are damned in that they cannot come "where God and Christ dwell . . . worlds without end" (76:112). Those in the terrestrial kingdom are damned in that they "receive of the presence of the Son, but not of the fulness of the Father" (76:77). Even those in the two lower "heavens or degrees" in the celestial kingdom are damned in that they do not have a "continuation of the seeds [lives]" (that is, eternal increase of posterity) (131:1–4; 132:19–25).

Damnation arises from failure to repent of disobedience, rejection, or slothfulness in keeping God's laws and commandments (42:59–60; 56:2–4; 58:29; 93:31–32; 132:6); persecution of the Saints (121:23); failure to believe and be baptized (68:9; 84:74; 112:29); rejection of Christ (49:5; 132:22–23); failure to marry by priesthood authority (131:2–3; 132:4, 15–18); and violation of covenants entered into by proper priesthood authority (132:6–7, 13, 21).

Damnation is avoided by those who do not have an opportunity to hear and obey gospel principles in mortality but later learn them in the spirit realm and accept vicarious ordinances performed in their behalf in temples (138:32–33, 58).

See also Buffetings of Satan; Hell; Punish, punished, punishment.

DEB

Daniel

Ancient Jewish prophet mentioned by name twice in the Doctrine and Covenants: 116:1, in connection with Adam and the future gathering at Adam-ondi-Ahman, and 138:44, being present in the spirit world assembly when the Savior visited there after his crucifixion and before his resurrection. A reference to Daniel's prophecy of the kingdom of God on earth in the latter days, likened to a stone cut out of the mountain without hands that eventually fills the whole earth (Dan. 2:34–45), occurs in 65:2 (cf. Dan. 2:34–45), though Daniel is not named specifically in that passage.

Daniel, being richly endowed with the gift of prophecy, revelation, and the interpretation of dreams, prophesied of the work of God on the earth in the last days, the restoration of the gospel, the Resurrection, and the day of judgment. His prophecies were frequently referred to and explained by the Prophet Joseph Smith (5:65, 341, 343), and the Prophet Joseph forthrightly declared that he, Joseph, was one of the instruments in setting up the very kingdom spoken of by Daniel (6:365).

Daniel particularly specifies that the kingdom of God set up on earth in the latter days will never be destroyed nor left to other people (138:44; Dan. 2:44–45).

Daniel labeled wicked conditions just preceding the Savior's second coming, including the destruction of Jerusalem, as the "abomination of desolation" (Matt. 24:15; JS–M 1:12; Dan. 9:27). In the Doctrine and Covenants the Lord identifies this wickedness as the "desolation of abomination" (84:117; 88:85).

See also Historical context and overview of Doctrine and Covenants 65 (p. 770); Desolation of abomination; Kingdom of God/kingdom of heaven.

BIBLIOGRAPHY

Smith, Joseph. *History of The Church of Jesus Christ of Latter-day Saints.* Edited by B. H. Roberts. 7 vols. 2d

ed. rev. Salt Lake City: The Church of Jesus Christ of Latter-day Saints, 1932–51.

RJM

Darkness

Dark is the opposite of LIGHT, just as SATAN is the antithesis of Christ. The Doctrine and Covenants speaks of darkness in several contexts.

1. A symbolic reference to Satan and his influence. The Lord said, "For all flesh is corrupted before me; and the powers of darkness prevail upon the earth, among the children of men" (38:11; cf. 38:5; 50:23–25; 82:5). Of those who stole the 116 pages of the Book of Mormon manuscript, the Lord said, "Their hearts are corrupt, and full of wickedness and abominations; and they love darkness rather than light, because their deeds are evil; therefore they will not ask of me. Satan stirreth them up, that he may lead their souls to destruction" (10:21–22; cf. 24:1). Joseph Smith wrote to the Saints, "We should waste and wear out our lives in bringing to light all the hidden things of darkness, wherein we know them" (123:13; cf. vv. 7–11).

2. Obscurity and ignorance. In the Lord's preface to the Doctrine and Covenants, he declared that Joseph Smith and others would have "power to lay the foundation of this church, and to bring it forth out of obscurity and out of darkness" (1:30; cf. 5:14). In the dedication of the Kirtland Temple, Joseph Smith prayed that "thy church may come forth out of the wilderness of darkness, and shine forth fair as the moon, clear as the sun, and terrible as an army with banners" (109:73; cf. 45:28; 123:12).

3. The result of sin and apostasy. To Thomas B. Marsh, president of the Quorum of the Twelve Apostles, the Lord said, "Darkness covereth the earth, and gross darkness the minds of the people, and all flesh has become corrupt before my face" (112:23; cf. 1:15–16). He said also, "The whole world lieth in sin, and groaneth under darkness and under the bondage of sin . . . because they come not unto me" (84:49–50). In a revelation chastising the Church for delaying the building of the Kirtland Temple, the Lord said, "They are walking in darkness at noon-day" (95:6; cf. 12). Describing the state of those in the spirit world awaiting

knowledge of the gospel, President Joseph F. Smith wrote, "Where these were, darkness reigned, but among the righteous there was peace" (138:22). Messengers were "clothed with power and authority, and commissioned . . . to go forth and carry the light of the gospel to them that were in darkness . . . and under the bondage of sin" (138:30–57). See Bondage.

4. A symbol for the abode of Satan and his followers. The wicked will be consigned to "outer darkness" (101:91; 133:73; cf. 77:8; 121:4), which implies that the realms of the adversary are devoid of any light. Christ is the light, or the beginning of all light (88:6–13), and everything that is the opposite of light—or which cannot comprehend light—finds its source in Satan (10:2, 58; 11:11; 14:9; 39:2; 45:7; 88:67; 109:73). See Outer darkness.

5. One of the SIGNS of the second coming of Christ. "Before the day of the Lord shall come, the sun shall be darkened" (45:42; cf. 29:14; 34:9). The cause of that darkness has not been made known. See Jesus Christ, second coming of.

ALG

Daughters

The Doctrine and Covenants speaks of daughters in two contexts:

1. Female descendants of mortal parents, such as "faithful daughters" of "our glorious Mother Eve," women "who had lived through the ages and worshiped the true and living God" (138:39), or latter-day "daughters of Zion" (124:11).

2. Female disciples of Christ who, through covenants, ordinances, and the atonement of Jesus Christ, are spiritually begotten unto God and Christ. The Lord spoke to Emma Smith, calling her "my daughter," and explained: "For verily I say unto you, all those who receive my gospel are sons and daughters in my kingdom" (25:1). This concept is explained by King Benjamin as recorded in the Book of Mormon: "And now, because of the covenant which ye have made ye shall be called the children of Christ, his sons, and his daughters; for behold, this day he hath spiritually begotten you; for ye say that your hearts are changed

through faith on his name; therefore, ye are born of him and have become his sons and his daughters" (Mosiah 5:7). This same doctrine is found in 76:24: "By him [the Only Begotten of the Father], and through him, and of him, the worlds are and were created, and the inhabitants thereof are begotten sons and daughters unto God."

See also Sons of God.

DKO

David

King of Israel, ca. 1000–961 B.C. David was selected by the Lord to rule over his people (1 Sam. 16–1 Kgs. 2). Successful as a military leader, David secured the Israelites in the Holy Land. After he committed adultery with Bathsheba and arranged the murder of Uriah (2 Sam. 11), his later years were characterized by tragedy and intrigue. The Bible is frank to report his failings, yet, curiously, it continues to extol him as the ideal ruler. Passages that do so were changed in the Joseph Smith Translation, reminding readers of David's sins (e.g., JST 1 Kgs. 11:4, 6).

In the Book of Mormon, the Lord calls the possession of "many wives and concubines" by David "abominable" (Jacob 2:24). In response to Joseph Smith's questions regarding the legitimacy of the plural marriages of David and others, the Lord revealed that biblical plural marriages were approved "save in those things which they received not of me" (132:38). As a result of his sins "in the case of Uriah and his wife," David has "fallen from his exaltation" (132:39).

See also Marriage.

KPJ

Davies, Amos

Birth: 20 September 1813, Hopkinton, Rockingham County, New Hampshire

Death: 22 March 1872, Big Mound, Hancock County, Illinois

Amos Davies was a postmaster and a merchant in Commerce (Nauvoo), Illinois. He employed a number of Church members in his business and outfitted Elder Moses Tracy for his mission. Davies was baptized in April 1840.

On 19 January 1841, he was instructed to "pay stock into the hands of those whom I have appointed to build a house for boarding, even the Nauvoo House" (124:111). He was also directed to "hearken unto the counsel of" Joseph Smith, to "prove himself faithful," and to "abase himself" (124:112–14). Soon afterward he was ordained an elder and made a first lieutenant in the Nauvoo Legion.

Davies was involved in a number of difficulties with the law, including convictions for selling liquor illegally and for "indecent and abusive language about" the Prophet Joseph Smith (Smith, 4:549; 5:198, 200). When the Saints went west, he remained in Nauvoo, where he operated a mercantile business through the 1840s. In 1850 he traveled to California to dig for gold. By 1853 he was in Michigan, and by 1858 he had moved back to Illinois.

BIBLIOGRAPHY

Smith, Joseph. *History of The Church of Jesus Christ of Latter-day Saints.* Edited by B. H. Roberts. 7 vols. 2d ed. rev. Salt Lake City: The Church of Jesus Christ of Latter-day Saints, 1932–51.

KWF

Day of the Lord. *See* Day(s).

Day of visitation. *See* Day(s).

Day(s)

The words *day* and *days* appear more than 250 times in the Doctrine and Covenants, with several meanings:

1. A period of time or era, as in "for this is a day of warning, and not a day of many words" (63:58); "my disciples, whom I have chosen in these last days" (1:4); and "this order [of the priesthood] was instituted in the days of Adam" (107:41). Section 101 speaks of the Millennium as "that day" when "Satan shall not have power to tempt any man" (v. 28). Similarly, the revelations speak of the distant past as the "days of old" (22:3; 64:8; 76:7; 133:53).

2. A twenty-four-hour period of time, as in "tarry not many days in this place" (66:6; cf. 87:4; 88:87; 101:62; 107:46).

3. The period in a twenty-four-hour day between sunrise and sunset, distinct from night, as

in "the angels are crying unto the Lord day and night" (86:5; cf. 133:40, 56).

4. An unspecified length of time denoting the seven periods of creation, as in "on the seventh day he finished his work" (77:12; cf. 95:7; Facsimile 2:1). The book of Abraham uses *time* instead of *day* in speaking of the seven periods of creation (Abr. 4:8, 13, 19, 23, 31).

5. A particular day, as in "holy day" or "Sabbath day" (59:9; 68:29); or a specific day of the week or month, as in "the third day" (20:23), and "the sixth day of the month which is called April" (20:1; 21:3; cf. 76:11; 118:5).

6. The present twenty-four-hour period, as in "which [priesthood] I now confirm upon you who are present this day" (84:42; cf. 102:1).

7. A person's lifetime, as in "thy days are known, and thy years shall not be numbered less" (122:9; cf. 5:33; 18:15; 24:8; 29:43); or an aged person, as in "ancient of days" (27:11; 116:1).

8. The time of the second coming of the Lord and his judgment, as in the "day of the Lord" (43:17, 20; 45:39; 49:24; 87:8; cf. 61:39; 63:53; 101:32), and the "day of visitation" (56:16; 124:8, 10).

DRD

Deacon(s)

An office in the Aaronic, or lesser, PRIESTHOOD (84:30). Each deacon is ordained to the office by the laying on of hands, "according to the gifts . . . of God" and according to the "power of the Holy Ghost, which is in the one who ordains him" (20:60). Deacons are "to warn, expound, exhort, and teach, and invite all to come unto Christ" (20:59). A deacon is also called to assist a TEACHER in his priesthood duties, having the responsibility to watch over the Church as standing ministers (20:57; 84:111). A deacon belongs to a quorum (group) of twelve deacons, with one of their number called to preside as president, "to sit in council with them, and to teach them their duty, edifying one another, as it is given according to the covenants" (107:60–63, 85). Although deacons do not have "authority to baptize, administer the sacrament, or lay on hands" (20:58), the practice of the Church is

that they pass the sacrament to members of the congregation.

HDG

Dead works

Religious rites, ordinances, or works that do not bring salvation; they are not authorized by the Lord, are not performed with proper authority, and consequently are not sealed by the Holy Spirit of promise (76:53; 132:7). The Doctrine and Covenants speaks specifically of baptisms as "dead works" if they are performed outside the authority of the restored Church of Jesus Christ. Some early converts to the Church felt that because they had been baptized in other denominations they did not need to be baptized again (22, headnote). In direct response to this issue, the Lord declared: "For it is because of your dead works that I have caused this last covenant and this church to be built up unto me, even as in days of old" (22:3; cf. Moro. 8:23).

BLT

Dead, salvation for the. *See* Salvation for the dead.

Death

The Doctrine and Covenants speaks of two kinds of death: temporal or natural death, which is the separation of the body and the spirit, and spiritual death, which is the separation of an individual from the presence and blessings of God. Both of these deaths were brought about on this earth by the fall of Adam and Eve (29:40–43), and both of these deaths can be overcome through the ATONEMENT of Jesus Christ. Overcoming temporal death, through RESURRECTION, is an unconditional gift to all mankind by virtue of the atonement of the Savior; however, bodies will be raised to different levels of glory (88:27–32; cf. 1 Cor. 15:22). Overcoming spiritual death is not unconditional; it, too, is made possible through the Atonement, but in addition it requires "obedience to the laws and ordinances of the Gospel" (A of F 3). Temporal death is overcome through the resurrection into bodies of telestial, terrestrial, or celestial glory. These varied levels of glory correspond to different levels of overcoming spiritual death. In explaining consequences of the Fall, the Lord said that Adam was "cast out from the Garden of Eden, from my presence . . . wherein he became spiritually dead, which is the first death, even that same death which is the last death, which is spiritual, which shall be pronounced upon the wicked when I shall say: Depart, ye cursed" (29:41). In this verse, both the "first death" and "last death" are designated as spiritual death. The first spiritual death, being separated from the immediate presence of God, first experienced by Adam and consequently by his descendants, will be overcome through the Resurrection. The last spiritual death, meaning the second death, however, is that death suffered by SONS OF PERDITION, "the only ones on whom the second death shall have any power" (76:37). "Wherefore, he saves all except them— they shall go away into everlasting punishment, which is endless punishment, which is eternal punishment, to reign with the devil and his angels in eternity" (76:44). These are they who "sinned unto death" (64:7; cf. 76:31–35; 132:27).

The Doctrine and Covenants contains several phrases concerning temporal death:

• "Appointed unto death." The Lord promises that the sick who have faith to be healed, and are not appointed unto death, shall be healed (42:48). Even faith and a priesthood blessing will not heal someone who, according to the Lord's timing, is appointed unto death.

• "Shall not taste of death." At least two meanings of this phrase are found in the revelations:

1. "Those that die in me [the Lord] shall not taste of death, for it shall be sweet unto them," while for those that die "not in me," death "is bitter" (42:46–47).

2. Some of the Lord's servants are given "power over death" and permitted to continue their ministry on the earth as translated beings, a condition between mortality and resurrection. When their ministry is completed, they will not "taste" or "endure the pains of death" but shall be "changed in the twinkling of an eye from mortality to immortality" (3 Ne. 28, headnote, v. 8). Those given this privilege include John the Revelator (7:1–8), Elijah (110:13), Moses

and Alma (Alma 45:18–19), the three Nephites (3 Ne. 28), and Enoch and his city (107:48–49; Moses 7:68–69). Similarly, there will not be death, as it is known on the earth, during the MILLENNIUM. "In that day an infant shall not die until he is old; and his life shall be as the age of a tree [or as 63:50 indicates, "the age of man"]; and when he dies he shall not sleep, that is to say in the earth, but shall be changed in the twinkling of an eye" (101:29–31; cf. 63:50–51). Concerning the age of death in the Millennium, Isaiah taught that "there shall be no more thence an infant of days, nor an old man that hath not filled his days: for the child shall die an hundred years old" (Isa. 65:20).

• "Bands of death" and "chains of death." These phrases refer to the feeling of being in "bondage" when the body and the spirit are separated at death. To his disciples, just before his crucifixion, the Lord said, "For as ye have looked upon the long absence of your spirits from your bodies to be a bondage, I will show unto you how the day of redemption shall come" (45:17). Those who were in the postmortal spirit world rejoiced when the Savior visited them between his death and resurrection "to declare their redemption from the bands of death . . . the spirit and the body to be united never again to be divided, that they might receive a fulness of joy" (138:16–18; cf. 93:33–34). See Bondage.

• "Whether in life or in death." Several times in the revelations the Lord declared that the righteous will be blessed and the wicked will be brought to judgment "whether in life or in death" (50:5–9; 58:2; 76:59). He also admonished the Saints to "pray always that you enter not into temptation, that you may abide the day of his coming, whether in life or in death" (61:39).

• "Abide in my covenant, even unto death." In August 1833, as the Saints were being driven from Jackson County, Missouri, the Lord revealed: "And whoso layeth down his life in my cause, for my name's sake, shall find it again, even life eternal. Therefore, be not afraid of your enemies, for I have decreed in my heart, saith the Lord, that I will prove you in all things, whether you will abide in my covenant, even unto death, that you may be found worthy. For if ye will not abide in my covenant ye are not worthy of me" (98:13–15).

• "Fear not even unto death." Four months after the revelation in section 98, the Lord comforted the same beleaguered Saints in Missouri: "All they who suffer persecution for my name, and endure in faith, though they are called to lay down their lives for my sake yet shall they partake of all this glory. Wherefore, fear not even unto death; for in this world your joy is not full, but in me your joy is full" (101:32–36).

• "Stronger than the cords of death." When explaining the proper exercise of priesthood authority, the Lord instructed that after reproving someone, an "increase of love" is to be shown to the person reproved, "lest he esteem thee to be his enemy; that he may know that thy faithfulness is stronger than the cords of death" (121:43–44). The cords of death are strong, but they are temporary and will be overcome in the resurrection. Love and faithfulness, on the other hand, will endure forever.

• "Fall by the shaft of death." Here the Lord warned that "that man, who was called of God and appointed, that putteth forth his hand to steady the ark of God, shall fall by the shaft of death, like as a tree that is smitten by the vivid shaft of lightning" (85:8). In this instance, the meaning of the phrase seems to be that the person referred to will be taken suddenly in death. See Historical context and overview of Doctrine and Covenants 85 (p. 789).

In addition to these phrases concerning temporal death, the revelations include references to the grand council held at Adam-ondi-Ahman three years before the death of Adam (107:53–56) and to the deaths of Joseph Smith (5:21–22; 135:1–6; 136:37–39) and the Savior (18:11; 45:1–5; 138:7–8).

Like birth, death is a necessary event in the plan of salvation (Moses 6:62), the "great plan of happiness" (Alma 42:8; cf. 2 Ne. 9:6). For the righteous death is sweet and not something to be feared (42:46; cf. Alma 27:28).

See also Fall of Adam and Eve, the; Life, purposes of.

RT

Death, second. See Death; Kingdoms of glory and perdition, vision of.

Death, spiritual. See Death.

Death, temporal. See Death.

Debt(s)

Something owed to another, usually money. The Doctrine and Covenants speaks of debts in at least ten revelations, with several contexts:

1. Avoiding debt. The Lord revealed to the Saints in Kirtland, "Behold, it is said in my laws, or forbidden, to get in debt to thine enemies" (64:27). He told the First Presidency in Far West that they were to build a temple there but they were not to "get in debt any more for the building of a house unto my name," perhaps a reminder of the crippling debt incurred by the Church in the building of the Kirtland Temple (115:7–13).

2. Paying debts. Martin Harris was told to "pay the debt thou hast contracted with the printer. Release thyself from bondage" (19:35). Harris had mortgaged part of his farm to guarantee payment for the printing of the Book of Mormon and ended up selling the land to meet the obligation. When the United Firm had more debts than assets and their holdings were divided into individual stewardships, the Lord said, "Behold it is my will that you shall pay all your debts" (104:78). When the Saints were moving from Kirtland to Far West, Missouri, they were instructed to "let the properties of Kirtland be turned out for debts" (117:5). Oliver Granger was assigned to be an agent for the Church in Kirtland to sell Church properties and "contend earnestly for the redemption of the [debts of the] First Presidency" (117:12–14). When Joseph Smith went into hiding in Nauvoo to avoid unlawful prosecution, he assured the Saints that he had "left his affairs with agents and clerks" who "[would] see that all [his] debts [were] canceled in due time" (127:1).

3. Care for the poor. The bishop in Zion in the 1830s, and the Presiding Bishop at any time, had the charge to use the resources of the Lord's storehouse to pay the debts of the Church and to meet the needs of the poor of the Church: "to discharge every debt; that the storehouse of

the Lord may not be brought into disrepute before the eyes of the people" (72:13–14; 90:23; 119:1).

4. Divine aid to pay debt. The Lord promised to help the early leaders of the Church with their debts. He assured the members of the United Order/Firm in 1834 that if they were diligent, humble, and prayerful, he would "soften the hearts of those to whom you are in debt, until I shall send means unto you for your deliverance" (104:79–86). And again, in 1836, he assured Joseph Smith, who had gone to Salem, Massachusetts, in hopes of acquiring "a large amount of money" owed to eastern lenders, "Concern not yourselves about your debts, for I will give you power to pay them" (111, headnote; 111:5).

DQC

Deception

Having prophesied to his disciples during his earthly ministry that in the last days even the "very elect" might be deceived "if it were possible" (Matt. 24:24; JS–M 1:22), the Lord in the Doctrine and Covenants clearly teaches about the reality of Satan's power to lead people astray. "There are many spirits which are false spirits," he revealed in May 1831, "which have gone forth in the earth, deceiving the world" (50:2; cf. 52:14). The Prophet Joseph Smith learned early that the purpose of this deception—which is often carried out through human agents (10:22, 24–25; cf. 123:12)—is two-fold: to "destroy the work of God" and to "destroy the souls of men" (10:23, 27). Warning the Saints that they are not exempt from Satan's efforts (50:3) and acknowledging that it is not always easy to "tell the wicked from the righteous" (10:37), the Lord provided his people with several keys for detecting this deception and avoiding it. One of the most fundamental is recognizing that "the keys of the mysteries, and the revelations which are sealed" belong only to the Lord's duly anointed prophet and that "no one shall be appointed to receive commandments and revelations in this church" except the prophet (28:2, 7). "This shall be a law unto you," the Lord told the Church, "that ye receive not the teachings of any that shall come before you as revelations or

commandments; and this I give unto you that you may not be deceived, that you may know they are not of me. For verily I say unto you, that he that is ordained of me shall come in at the gate and be ordained as I have told you before, to teach those revelations which you have received and shall receive through him whom I have appointed" (43:5–7; cf. 42:11). This key was given to the Saints for the express purpose of helping them avoid deception (43:6); it is a principle through which Church members can "know assuredly" the validity of any statement purporting to be a commandment of God or to represent the doctrine of the Church (43:3).

Latter-day Saints can also detect and avoid deception by taking "the Holy Spirit for their guide" (45:57). Such protection, however, must be sought. Only by following the Spirit "in all holiness of heart, walking uprightly before [the Lord], considering the end of your salvation, doing all things with prayer and thanksgiving" can one hope to avoid being "seduced by evil spirits, or doctrines of devils, or the commandments of men" (46:7; cf. 10:5). One challenge early in the Restoration was false gifts of the Spirit. "Beware lest ye are deceived," the Lord warned. "And that ye may not be deceived seek ye earnestly the best gifts, always remembering for what they are given" (46:8), indicating that the best way to detect a counterfeit is to compare it with the true gifts of the Spirit. "I would that ye should always remember, and always retain in your minds what those gifts are, that are given unto the church," he emphasized (46:10), and that "they are given for the benefit of those who love me and keep all my commandments, and him that seeketh so to do" rather than to those that "ask . . . for a sign that they may consume it upon their lusts" (46:9). To assist the Saints in their efforts to use the gifts of the Spirit to avoid deception, the Lord promised the Church that "unto such as God shall appoint and ordain to watch over the church . . . are to have it given unto them to discern all those gifts" and that "unto some it may be given to have all those gifts, that there may be a head, in order that every member may be profited thereby" (46:27, 29). See Spiritual gifts.

The Lord has provided the Church with a

"pattern in all things" whereby members can determine whether or not someone "whose spirit is contrite, whose language is meek and edifieth," really is praying or speaking under the influence of the HOLY GHOST (52:14–16). According to this "pattern," such a person "is of God if he obey mine ordinances . . . and shall bring forth fruits of praise and wisdom, according to the revelations and truths which I have given you" (52:16–18). The popularity of several deceivers in the Book of Mormon who used the "power of speech" to lead God's people astray (Jacob 7:4; cf. Mosiah 27:8; Alma 30:18; Hel. 2:4) underscores the importance of this pattern for members of the Church today.

Joseph Smith provided the Saints with "three grand keys" by which they can avoid being deceived by an evil spirit appearing "as an angel of light" (129:8–9). "When a messenger comes saying he has a message from God, offer him your hand and request him to shake hands with you," Joseph instructed the Church. "If he be an angel he will do so, and you will feel his hand. If he be the spirit of a just man made perfect . . . he will not move," while the "devil as an angel of light . . . will offer you his hand, and you will not feel anything" (129:4–8).

Knowing the scriptures is likewise a key to avoiding deception: "Whoso treasureth up my word, shall not be deceived" (JS–M 1:37; cf. D&C 42:12; 1 Ne. 15:24; Hel. 3:29; 2 Tim. 3:12–17).

See also Satan.

AHH

Degrees of glory. *See* Kingdoms of glory and perdition, vision of.

Deign. *See* Appendix E.

Deliverance

Freedom or liberation from negative conditions or consequences; also, to turn someone or something over to another. In the Doctrine and Covenants is recorded a host of undesirable situations and enemies from which specific individuals and the Saints in general could be delivered. To Oliver Cowdery the Lord said that the gift of revelation "shall deliver you out of the hands of your enemies" (8:4). To Joseph Smith

the Lord said, "Thou hast been delivered from all thine enemies, and thou hast been delivered from the powers of Satan and from darkness" (24:1). *See* Satan.

Peter Whitmer Jr. was counseled to pray for his and Oliver Cowdery's deliverance from all their AFFLICTIONS (30:6), and James Covill was informed, "The days of thy deliverance [from PRIDE and cares of the world] are come, if thou wilt hearken to my voice . . . and be baptized" (39:10). "The poor who are pure in heart, whose hearts are broken . . . shall see the kingdom of God coming in power and great glory unto their deliverance; for the fatness of the earth shall be theirs" (56:18). The Lord assured his people that upon their REPENTANCE and OBEDIENCE, "I prepare a way for their deliverance in all things out of temptation" (95:1). *See* Temptation(s).

They could be delivered from other temporal matters as well: "I shall send means unto you for your deliverance [from debt]" (104:80). *See* Debt(s).

The Saints pleaded before the Lord "for a full and complete deliverance" from the yoke of lying reports and slanders (109:32), and the Prophet prayed, "Deliver thy people from the calamity of the wicked" (109:46). Deliverance is conditioned on obedience. The Lord rebuked those who claimed God would deliver Zion without complying with his commands regarding ZION'S CAMP (105:8).

The vision of President Joseph F. Smith affirmed the eager anticipation of those in the postmortal spirit world awaiting the coming of the Savior "to declare their redemption from the bands of death," as "the day of their deliverance was at hand" (138:12–18). *See* Salvation for the dead.

Another aspect of deliverance spoken of in the revelations pertains to Church members. Those who break the law of the land are to be delivered (handed over, turned over) to the proper authorities (42:79, 84–86), and if they break the laws of the Church, they are to be delivered to the authorities of the Church for possible disciplinary action (42:87, 89–93). *See* Church discipline.

In early Church history, those who broke sacred covenants in connection with the United

Order were to be "delivered over to the buffetings of Satan" (78:12; 82:21; 104:9–10). Even more serious, those who sin grievously after being "sealed by the Holy Spirit of promise" unto eternal life are "delivered unto the buffetings of Satan unto the day of redemption" (132:26). *See* Buffetings of Satan.

Ultimately, deliverance from all sin, death, and hell is made possible only through the GRACE of GOD THE FATHER manifested through the ATONEMENT of his Beloved Son, JESUS CHRIST (34:1–3; 76:39, 41–42; 138:18–19, 57; cf. 2 Ne. 9:10–19; John 3:16).

DKO

Desire(s)

The longings or cravings of the heart, often at the deepest level, that drive one's interests, thoughts, words, and behavior. *Desire* and its variants occur more than sixty times in several contexts in the Doctrine and Covenants:

1. Desires determine outcomes. God honors his children's agency and allows outcomes to be largely determined by their desires in spiritual matters and in temporal concerns. Some examples of desire playing an important role in spiritual matters include one's desire to help build up the kingdom of God (4:3; 6:8, 20; 11:8, 17; 58:44; 63:57), giving priesthood blessings only to those who desire them (24:14), receiving a witness of the truth (5:1, 23; 6:22; 11:14, 21; 15:4–6), identifying those who are to be called as apostles (18:27–28, 37–38), deciding who should be baptized (20:37), and judging those who die without a knowledge of the gospel, "according to the desire of their hearts" (137:7–9). An example of the Lord's allowing for individual desires in temporal concerns is the Lord's instructions to the elders traveling to and from Kirtland and Missouri: "You may return to bear record, yea, even altogether, or two by two, as seemeth you good, it mattereth not unto me; only be faithful. . . . I, the Lord, am willing, if any among you desire to ride upon horses, or upon mules, or in chariots, he shall receive this blessing, if he receive it from the hand of the Lord, with a thankful heart in all things. These things remain with you to do

according to judgment and the directions of the Spirit" (62:5–8; cf. 99:7).

2. A spectrum of desires from very evil to "most holy" (95:16). Evil desires include the devil's desire "to sift [Lyman Wight] as chaff" (52:12) and "carnal," "lustful," and "covetous" desires the Saints were commanded to avoid (3:4; 88:121; 101:6; 117:4). Casual desires of those who are neither "cold nor hot" (Rev. 3:15) are illustrated by the Shakers, of whom the Lord said, "They desire to know the truth in part, but not all" (49:2) and by candidates for the terrestrial kingdom who receive a testimony of Jesus but are not valiant therein: "honorable men of the earth . . . blinded by the craftiness of men," hence, "they obtain not the crown over the kingdom of our God" (76:75–79; cf. Alma 29:4–8). "Good desires," defined as "a desire to lay up treasures for yourself in heaven" (6:27), are exemplified by many who wanted to know what the Lord would have them do to best serve in the fledgling kingdom, including Joseph Smith Sr. (4:1–7), Oliver Cowdery (6; 8; 9), and David, John, and Peter Whitmer (14; 15; 16). "Most holy desires" are associated with temple worship (95:16).

3. A plurality of worthy desires in a given circumstance. This principle is shown in the conversation between the Lord and the apostle Peter concerning John's desire to continue his mortal ministry until the Savior's return and Peter's desire to "speedily come unto" the Lord at death (7:1–8). Both desires were appropriate and were granted by the Lord.

4. Desired outcomes require obedience. To the Saints in Kirtland who were concerned about who should receive revelations for the Church, the Lord said, "If ye desire the glories of the kingdom, appoint ye my servant Joseph Smith, Jun., and uphold him before me by the prayer of faith" (43:12; cf. v. 13). And to the Colesville Saints who were frustrated in their efforts to settle on land in Thompson, Ohio, under the principles of consecration, the Lord said, "If your brethren desire to escape their enemies, let them repent of all their sins, and become truly humble before me and contrite" (54:3).

5. A reciprocal relationship between desires and behavior. The desires of the heart, what

things one truly loves, drive behavior, and behavior greatly affects one's desires. For example, those who stole the 116 pages of the Book of Mormon manuscript desired to expose Joseph Smith as a false prophet by altering the words of Joseph's original translation and comparing them with an anticipated second translation. Of them the Lord said, "They love darkness rather than light, *because* their deeds are evil" (10:21; emphasis added; cf. John 3:19). That being true, it seems reasonable to conclude that doing good deeds can lead to loving light rather than darkness.

PAA

Desolating sickness. *See* Scourge.

Desolation of abomination

Twice in the Doctrine and Covenants, in 84:117 and 88:85, the Lord refers to "the desolation of abomination" that will arise in the last days. The second of these references specifically equates this desolation to "the wrath of God . . . which awaits the wicked, both in this world and in the world to come." Both of these sections were received in Kirtland in the second half of 1832, and the context of each is missionary work, as the Lord directs the recipients of the revelation to go forth and warn of impending JUDGMENT. By clearly laying out this danger, missionaries could demonstrate the need of accepting the gospel of Jesus Christ in order to avoid God's wrath. While this message of warning is directed to the Gentiles, it is also intended "to prepare the saints for the hour of judgment which is to come" (88:84). This judgment, which begins with the second coming of Jesus Christ, will be fully realized at the final judgment after the MILLENNIUM (88:87–115). *See* Jesus Christ, second coming of.

The Doctrine and Covenants phrase "desolation of abomination" echoes and reverses the biblical expressions "abomination that maketh desolate" (Dan. 11:31; 12:11; cf. 9:27) and "abomination of desolation" (Matt. 24:15; Mark 13:14; JS–M 1:12, 32; cf. D&C 45:19–21). The expression in Daniel relates to an abominable thing or person that either produces "desolation" or, alternately, feelings of "[being]

appalled" (Wenham, 1:29). The consensus of biblical scholarship generally sees it as referring to the efforts of the Seleucid king Antiochus IV Epiphanes, who desecrated the temple in Jerusalem in 167 B.C. He established a pagan altar, a statue of Zeus, or both in the sacred precincts, this "abomination" rendering the temple area "desolate." First Maccabees 1:54 seems to support this application of Daniel's prophecy, noting that Antiochus had a "desolating sacrilege" erected upon the altar of burnt offerings (cf. 2 Maccabees 6:5; Josephus, *Antiquities* 12.5.4 [pages 129–31]). Jesus gave Daniel's prophecy at least two other applications: one before or at the time of the destruction of Jerusalem by the Romans in A.D. 70 and one prior to his glorious final coming, which would signal the "end of the world, or the destruction of the wicked" (JS–M 1:4, 12, 32; cf. McConkie and Ostler, 613). For Jesus' words, the Greek text of Matthew 24:15 and Mark 13:14 mirrors the Septuagint's translation of Daniel 12:11, using the expression *to bdleugma tēs erēmōseōs,* or "the abominable things that cause desolation."

Several candidates for the "abomination" (*to bdleugma*) present themselves for the historical fulfillment of Jesus' prophecy. These include the Roman military advancing on Jerusalem, emblems of pagan worship erected on the temple ruins, or even the blasphemy of Jewish zealots installing a false high priest shortly before the Romans took Jerusalem—the text of Mark 13:14 actually suggests an abomination *who,* not *which,* stands where he ought not (Wenham, 1:29–30; France, 522–25). In connection with the last possibility, Josephus records in some detail the violent acts of Jewish extremists against each other and their impious acts in the temple itself, suggesting that these, along with a false high priest officiating there, caused the Lord to abandon his house even before its capture (*Jewish Wars* 4.3.12, 4.6.3–7.1 [pages 214–19, 267–70]).

"Of desolation" in Greek (*tēs erēmōseōs*) can be either a descriptive genitive, describing what kind of abomination is meant, or, better, an objective genitive, that is, "the abomination that makes desolate," causing the temple site to be empty and preventing true worship there. This second possibility may, in fact, explain the reversal of the order of the terms in the Doctrine and Covenants, which reads in both instances "desolation of abomination," meaning "abomination's desolation," emphasizing the desolation of the spirit that occurs because of such abominations as idolatry, murder, and sexual sins.

Just as the first-century "abomination of desolation" drove the Spirit from the Jerusalem Temple and has prevented proper worship from taking place on its site since, so desecrating through sin the spiritual temple of the body of Christ (the Church of Jesus Christ) deprives men and women of the Spirit of the Lord and the opportunity for proper worship, making them unprepared for the Lord's return (Robinson and Garrett, 3:65–66). Thus, while this message seems particularly for the "Gentiles," or those outside the true Church, it may also apply to members individually whose activities drive the Spirit out of their own lives, leaving them unprepared for the judgment of God.

BIBLIOGRAPHY

France, R. T. *The Gospel of Mark: A Commentary on the Greek Text.* The New International Greek Testament Commentary. Grand Rapids, Mich.: Eerdmans, 2002.

Josephus. *Jewish Antiquities.* Translated by Ralph Marcus and Allen Wikgren. Cambridge, Mass.: Harvard University Press, 1963.

———. *The Jewish Wars.* Translated by H. St. J. Thackeray. Cambridge, Mass.: Harvard University Press, 1928.

McConkie, Joseph Fielding, and Craig J. Ostler. *Revelations of the Restoration: A Commentary on the Doctrine and Covenants and Other Modern Revelations.* Salt Lake City: Deseret Book, 2000.

Robinson, Stephen E., and H. Dean Garrett. *A Commentary on the Doctrine and Covenants.* 4 vols. Salt Lake City: Deseret Book, 2000–2005.

Wenham, David. "Abomination of Desolation." In *The Anchor Bible Dictionary,* edited by David Noel Freedman. 6 vols. New York: Doubleday, 1992.

EDH

Destroyed in the flesh

The declared punishment, in addition to being "delivered unto the buffetings of Satan unto the day of redemption," for those who have been sealed up unto eternal life and then commit serious sin (132:19–27). The specific phrase "destroyed in the flesh" is found just once in the scriptures (132:26), and the meaning of the phrase is not there clarified. It has been taught that if a people were living in a theocracy, where civil law and religious law are the same, it would mean something as serious as capital punishment, such as was the case in ancient times for certain serious violations of the commandments of the Lord (Smith, 2:96–97; cf. Lev. 20:2–5, 10–16; 24:16–17; Josh. 1:18; 2 Chron. 15:12–15; Matt. 26:65–66; John 10:22–42). What might the phrase mean in modern times? Several dictionary meanings of the word *destroy* include "pull or break down"; "ruin financially, professionally, or in reputation"; "defeat"; "to neutralize the effect of"; "to make useless"; and "to bring to naught" (*Oxford* and *New World*, s.v. "destroy"). Any or some or all of these meanings might apply "in the flesh," or in mortality, to those spoken of in 132:19–27. The Lord uses the words *destroy* and *destroyed* in other verses of section 132 in reference to individuals who violate revealed principles associated with eternal marriage (132:41, 52, 54, 63–64). The scriptures are abundantly clear that the demands of justice will be served in every case. They are also clear that through the atonement of Jesus Christ, even those persons who have sinned seriously, who are willing to repent and suffer necessary and appropriate punishments, have claim upon mercy and can be redeemed.

See also Buffetings of Satan.

BIBLIOGRAPHY

Readers Digest Oxford Complete Wordfinder. Pleasantville, N.Y.: Oxford University Press, 1996.

Smith, Joseph Fielding. *Doctrines of Salvation.* Compiled by Bruce R. McConkie. 3 vols. Salt Lake City: Bookcraft, 1954–56.

Webster, Noah. *An American Dictionary of the English Language.* 1828.

Webster's New World Dictionary. 3d college edition. New York: Simon & Schuster, 1988.

LED

Destroyer

A term employed three times in the Doctrine and Covenants, each with a distinct meaning:

1. The destroyer seen in vision by W. W. Phelps on his return trip from Missouri to Kirtland with the Prophet Joseph Smith and nine other elders in August 1831 (61, headnote). On the third day of their journey, the travelers experienced dangers on the Missouri River. After setting up camp at McIlwaine's Bend, the record states, "Brother Phelps, in open vision by daylight, saw the destroyer in his most horrible power, ride upon the face of the waters; others heard the noise, but saw not the vision" (Smith, 1:202–3). *See* Historical context and overview of Doctrine and Covenants 61 (p. 767).

2. The destroyer in the parable about a nobleman and his vineyard (101:54, 43–62), who apparently represents any enemy of the Lord intent on destroying the Lord's vineyard or kingdom. *See* Parable regarding a certain nobleman/vineyard.

3. The destroyer in 105:15, who represents an agent whom the Lord will send "forth to destroy and lay waste [the Lord's] enemies . . . not many years hence." Such an agent would be "the destroying angel," from whom the Lord promised protection to those who are obedient to the WORD OF WISDOM and who walk "in obedience to the commandments" (89:18–21). It seems clear that the cleansing of the earth, the destruction of the wicked, will come at the hands of many destroying ANGELS sent by the Lord (38:11–12; 63:54; 77:8; 86:5–7).

BIBLIOGRAPHY

Smith, Joseph. *History of The Church of Jesus Christ of Latter-day Saints.* Edited by B. H. Roberts. 7 vols. 2d ed. rev. Salt Lake City: The Church of Jesus Christ of Latter-day Saints, 1932–51.

LED

Destroying angel. *See* Angel(s).

Detroit, Michigan

City located on the Detroit River, which connects Lake Erie with Lake St. Clair. Hyrum Smith and John Murdock were commanded to take a missionary journey to Missouri, traveling and teaching by way of Detroit, Michigan, "saying none other things than that which the prophets and apostles have written [i.e., the scriptures], and that which is taught them

by the Comforter through the prayer of faith" (52:8–10). They preached as missionaries in the Detroit area in June 1831 and stayed at the home of Almira Mack, Hyrum's cousin.

BIBLIOGRAPHY

O'Driscoll, Jeffrey S. *Hyrum Smith: A Life of Integrity.* Salt Lake City: Deseret Book, 2003.

DQC

Devil. *See* Satan.

Devotions. *See* Appendix E.

Dews of Carmel

A biblical image used once in the Doctrine and Covenants as a metaphor describing how the "knowledge of God" will descend upon the ministers of the gospel in the latter days (128:19). Similarly, the Lord promises those who administer the priesthood properly that "the doctrine of the priesthood shall distil upon thy soul as the dews from heaven" (121:45).

The power of the metaphor lies in understanding the importance of dew in the biblical world, as well as the significance of Israel's Mount Carmel. Dew was of vital importance for agriculture in the ancient Holy Land during the half-year period with no rain. High humidity produces moisture during the dry season in the form of dew at night. In Hosea 14:5 the Lord says, "I will be as the dew unto Israel" (cf. Gen. 27:28; Deut. 32:2; 33:28; Zech. 8:12).

Mount Carmel is a mountain range in the northwest of the Holy Land and is mentioned several times in Old Testament writings as a symbol of richness and fruitfulness (cf. Isa. 33:9; 35:2; Jer. 50:19). Hebrew *kerem-El* (or the English *Carmel*) means "Garden of God." The significance of this metaphor in the Doctrine and Covenants is heightened by the fact that Mount Carmel averages 250 dew nights a year (Orni and Efrat, 147).

BIBLIOGRAPHY

Orni, Efraim, and Elisha Efrat. *Geography of Israel.* 3d rev. ed. Jerusalem: Israel Universities Press, 1976.

DKO

Diabolical. *See* Appendix E.

Die in me. *See* Death.

Died without law. *See* Kingdoms of glory and perdition, vision of.

Differences of administration. *See* Spiritual gifts.

Diligence. *See* Appendix E.

Director(s)

A term that may legitimately be applied to anyone or anything appointed to give direction or instruction. The term occurs in 3:15, where the Lord chastises Joseph Smith for having "suffered the counsel of thy director to be trampled upon from the beginning" and losing, as a result, the 116 pages of Book of Mormon manuscript. In this context, *director* appears to refer to the Lord himself, although it could also refer to the HOLY GHOST or the URIM AND THUMMIM, which Joseph had in his possession at the time. *See* Historical context and overview of Doctrine and Covenants 3 (p. 716).

Other entities that function in the role of a "director" in the revelations include the high council and "general conference" of the Church, which are to direct the ordination of priesthood officers (20:67); the scriptures, which give direction on how to deal with transgressors (20:80); the Spirit, which gives directions for teaching and conducting meetings (42:13; 46:2); the First Presidency, under whose direction those who hold the priesthood, including the Quorum of the Twelve Apostles, officiate (107:10, 33); and the Quorum of the Twelve Apostles themselves, who direct the activities of the Seventy (107:34). Doctrine and Covenants 17:1 also refers to the "miraculous directors which were given to Lehi while in the wilderness," called "Liahona" by the Nephites (Alma 37:38).

AHH

Disasters, calamities

Earthquakes, violent storms, floods, hurricanes, tornadoes, tsunamis, epidemics of disease, wars, and so forth. Generally, disasters are the result of natural laws that govern the physical universe. Sometimes they are caused by man—for instance, wars, the spread of communicable diseases, the pollution of the atmosphere, or floods brought on by the breaking up of man-made dams. At other times they are caused by God to chasten the world because of wickedness. The Doctrine and Covenants lists many disasters, most of them in connection with the events of the last days in preparation for the second coming of the Lord. *See* Jesus Christ, second coming of.

Such disasters, however caused, are used by the Lord as punishment for wickedness and as a call to repentance. In a revelation and "prophecy on war" (87, headnote), the Lord said, "And thus, with the sword and by bloodshed the inhabitants of the earth shall mourn; and with famine, and plague, and earthquake, and the thunder of heaven, and the fierce and vivid lightning also, shall the inhabitants of the earth be made to feel the wrath, and indignation, and chastening hand of an Almighty God, until the consumption decreed hath made a full end of all nations" (87:6; cf. 1:17; 45:50).

The disasters identified in the Doctrine and Covenants include the following:

• "Earthquakes . . . in divers places" (45:33; cf. 29:13; 43:18; 45:48; 49:23; 88:89; 133:22).

• "Devouring fire" and "vapors of smoke" (29:21; 45:41; 97:26).

• "Thunderings, and . . . lightnings, and . . . tempests, and . . . great hailstorms" (43:21–25; cf. 29:16; 87:6; 88:90; 109:30).

• "Waves of the sea heaving themselves beyond their bounds" (88:90).

• "Famines and pestilences of every kind," including "plagues" (43:25; 84:97; 97:26).

• Domestic and world wars (87:1–8).

• "An overflowing scourge; for a desolating sickness shall cover the land" (45:31; cf. 5:19; 29:18–20) and "shall not be stayed until the Lord come" (97:23).

• A culminating destruction of the wicked and the burning of the earth at the coming of the Lord (29:9; cf. 38:12; 86:7; 101:24–25, 66; 112:24).

Associated with these events and just preceding the Lord's second coming, there will be SIGNS in the heavens and in the earth. For example, "the sun shall be darkened, and the moon shall be turned into blood, and the stars shall fall from heaven, and there shall be greater signs in heaven above and in the earth beneath; and there shall be weeping and wailing among the hosts of men" (29:14–16; cf. 34:9; 45:42; 88:87; 133:49). Consequently, the Lord has told the Saints to gather and "to prepare their hearts . . . against the day when tribulation and desolation are sent forth upon the wicked" (29:8), and he has promised that "if ye are prepared ye shall not fear" (38:30).

DKO

Discern, discernment. *See* Spiritual gifts.

Disciple(s), discipleship. *See* Covenant people of the Lord.

Dispensation of the fulness of times. *See* Dispensation(s).

Dispensation(s)

A period of time in which the plan of salvation is given by direct revelation to a designated servant of the Lord (128:9). A dispensation, like the rising of the sun, represents a renewal of the light of heaven. The Prophet Joseph Smith stands at the head of the "dispensation of the fulness of times" (128:18). As implied by this name, this is the final dispensation of the GOSPEL in earth's history (112:31–32), and in it all that was had in any past dispensation is to be restored. Peter testified that "all [the Lord's] holy prophets since the world began" spoke of this final "restitution of all things" (Acts 3:20–21). Thus, every principle of salvation and every available key, power, and authority necessary to teach the gospel and then to bring those who have embraced it back into the presence of God are to be restored in this dispensation. Every prophet who stood at the head of a past dispensation appeared to the Prophet Joseph Smith and Oliver Cowdery and bestowed upon them all "their rights, their keys, their honors, their majesty and glory, and the power of their priesthood" (128:20–22; 110:11–16). *See* Key(s).

The first dispensation of the gospel was presided over by Adam. The gospel was revealed to him by holy angels, by the voice of God, and by the gift of the Holy Ghost (Moses 5:58–59). This revelation of the gospel included all principles and ordinances of salvation, including the fulness of temple blessings (Smith, *History*, 4:207–8, 211–12; *Joseph Smith*, 93). As the patriarch of the human race and as the first prophet, seer, and revelator, Adam holds "the keys of salvation under the counsel and direction of the Holy One" (78:16) for all dispensations, or as Joseph termed them, the "keys of the universe" (*History*, 3:387; 4:209). It is under Adam's direction that all subsequent dispensations have been administered (Smith, *History*, 4:207–8).

Enoch, who stood six generations removed from Adam and who received both the PRIESTHOOD and the fulness of its blessings under his hands, also received a dispensation, or special ministry, from heaven (107:41–49). Enoch was specially called of God to declare the gospel revealed to Adam, establish ZION, build a holy city, and prepare a people to be taken into heaven in a translated state (Moses 6:21–8:1). *See* Translated beings.

Noah also received a special dispensation to warn the world of the impending flood, teaching as his fathers had taught the doctrine of faith, repentance, baptism in the name of Jesus Christ, and the necessity of receiving the Holy Ghost (Moses 8:24). Noah had received the priesthood under the hands of his grandfather Methuselah, who had received it from Father Adam (107:50–52).

In a subsequent generation, the Lord chose Abraham to be the father of the covenant race and to preside over his dispensation. As a result of the covenant God made with Abraham, his posterity are to take the blessings of salvation to the nations of the earth, and like their father Abraham, are to receive the promises of eternal union in marriage and endless seed (110:12; 132:29–50; Abr. 2:9–11). These promises were a renewal of the patriarchal order of the priesthood instituted in the days of Adam and "rightly" belong to the "literal descendants of the chosen seed" (107:40–41).

The last of the Old Testament dispensations was that of Moses, who was called out of the wilderness to deliver the Israelites from their Egyptian bondage and prepare them for entrance into the land of promise.

John the Baptist signaled the end of Moses'

dispensation as he, with the ordinance of baptism, prepared the way for Jesus Christ. John introduced Jesus as an "Elias" who was "to restore all things" (JST John 1:20–28). So it was that the Savior came in what Nephi called "the fulness of his own time" (2 Ne. 11:7), or as Lehi expressed it, "the fulness of time" (2 Ne. 2:3, 26), for this was the time upon which the eyes of all the holy prophets were fixed (Jacob 4:4). Jesus Christ restored to the house of Israel the fulness of that gospel taken from their fathers at the time of Moses (84:19–27; JST Ex. 34:1). The keys of presidency of the Savior's dispensation were conferred upon Peter, James, and John on the MOUNT OF TRANSFIGURATION (*Joseph Smith*, 158; Ehat and Cook, 9). These three men conferred those keys upon the heads of Joseph Smith and Oliver Cowdery (27:12–13; 128:20; JS–H 1:72). Other keys were brought by Moses, Elias, and Elijah (110:10–15).

In addition to these dispensations, gospel dispensations were had among the Jaredites (Ether 1–15), the Nephites (1 Ne.–Moro.), and possibly the lost tribes of Israel (2 Ne. 29:12–13; 3 Ne. 17:4).

The Doctrine and Covenants stands as a record of God's dispensing gospel knowledge and authority in the final dispensation, "the dispensation of the fulness of times," including some things unique to it (128:18–21; 124:41). Joseph Smith had all the keys necessary to establish this dispensation, as the fulness of all past dispensations were conferred upon him. Thus, in this, the last of all gospel dispensations, all things are to be made ready for the return of the Lord and Savior Jesus Christ (128:20–24; Acts 3:19–21; Eph. 1:10).

See also Covenant people of the Lord.

BIBLIOGRAPHY

Ehat, Andrew F., and Lyndon W. Cook, comps. and eds. *The Words of Joseph Smith.* Provo, Utah: Religious Studies Center, Brigham Young University, 1980.

Smith, Joseph. *History of The Church of Jesus Christ of Latter-day Saints.* Edited by B. H. Roberts. 7 vols. 2d ed. rev. Salt Lake City: The Church of Jesus Christ of Latter-day Saints, 1932–51.

———. *Joseph Smith.* Teachings of Presidents of the Church series. Salt Lake City: The Church of Jesus Christ of Latter-day Saints, 2007.

JFM

Dissenters. *See* Apostasy, of early dissenters from restored Church.

Divers. *See* Appendix E.

Diversities of operations. *See* Spiritual gifts.

Divine investiture of authority

Having AUTHORITY to speak and act in behalf of God. The doctrinal principle of divine investiture of authority has been explained by latter-day prophets. In 1916, the First Presidency released a statement entitled "The Father and the Son: A Doctrinal Exposition by the First Presidency and the Twelve," which stated in part: "The Father placed His name upon the Son; and Jesus Christ spoke and ministered in and through the Father's name; and so far as power, authority and Godship are concerned His words and acts were and are those of the Father" (939). Elder Bruce R. McConkie further explained, "Since [Christ] is one with the Father in all of the attributes of perfection, and since he exercises the power and authority of the Father, it follows that everything he says or does is and would be exactly and precisely what the Father would say and do under the same circumstances" (130).

This doctrine explains how the identity of the voice in a given revelation appears to change from one verse to another. For example, in section 29, the revelation begins, "Listen to the voice of Jesus Christ, . . . your advocate with the Father" (29:1, 5), but later the same revelation speaks of having "faith on the name of *mine Only Begotten Son*" (29:42; emphasis added; cf. 49:5–6, 28). Clearly, Jesus Christ is speaking for the Father and as if he were the Father, in verse 42. Because the Father and the Son are "one," or in complete unity, Jesus speaks the same words the Father would speak, so his words are indeed the very words of the Father (20:28; 35:2; 50:43; 93:2–5; John 5:43; 3 Ne. 20:35; 28:10).

The 1916 First Presidency exposition discusses other examples of divine investiture, including angels speaking in the name of the Son. In the Prophet Joseph Smith's description of the reception of section 27, he stated that "he was met by a heavenly messenger" who began his delivery of the contents of the revelation by saying, "Listen to the voice of Jesus Christ, your Lord, your God, and your Redeemer" (27, headnote; 27:1). The angel, through the principle of divine investiture, was speaking as if he were Jesus Christ. Other scriptural examples of angels speaking as if they are the Son include John's Revelation (Rev. 1:1; 19:9–10; 22:8–14).

The Lord also invests mortals with authority to act and speak in his name—the voice of the Lord's servants becomes the voice of the Lord: "What I the Lord have spoken, I have spoken, and I excuse not myself; and though the heavens and the earth pass away, my word shall not pass away, but shall all be fulfilled, *whether by mine own voice or by the voice of my servants, it is the same*" (1:38; emphasis added; cf. 21:5; 36:2; 64:29; 128:8; 132:58–59).

BIBLIOGRAPHY

First Presidency. "The Father and the Son: A Doctrinal Exposition by the First Presidency and the Twelve." *Improvement Era* 19 (August 1916): 934–42.

McConkie, Bruce R. *Mormon Doctrine.* 2d ed. Salt Lake City: Bookcraft, 1966.

DKJ

Divorce

Dissolution of the marriage contract. The word *divorce* is not used in the Doctrine and Covenants, but the concept of spouses' separating is included in the phrases "having put away their companions" and "have left their companions," and instructions are given about dealing with such cases (42:74–77). Divorce is a civil action governed by civil statutes. The sealing of couples in a temple is a priesthood ordinance and, in some countries, also a civil ceremony. Divorce is obtained from civil authority; cancellation of sealing from Church authority. The revelations discuss the principles relating to MARRIAGE, plural marriage, ADULTERY, and sealings but does not address divorce explicitly (42:22–26, 80; 49:15; 131:1–4; 132:1–66).

The law of Moses allowed for "a bill of divorcement" or "a writing of divorcement" (Deut. 24:1–4; Matt. 5:31). In Jesus' day such actions were relatively informal, favoring the desires of the husband. Jesus explained a higher law: divorce and remarriage, except for "fornication," constituted adultery for either party (Matt. 5:32; 19:9; Mark 10:10–12). That strict standard is not enforced in the Church today, as "divorces are permitted in accordance with civil statutes, and the divorced persons are permitted by the Church to marry again without the stain of immorality which under a higher system would attend such a course" (McConkie, 1:547).

BIBLIOGRAPHY

McConkie, Bruce R. *Doctrinal New Testament Commentary.* 3 vols. Salt Lake City: Bookcraft, 1965–73.

DEB

Doctrine(s)

Eternal truths essential for salvation. "The doctrines will remain fixed, eternal; the organization, programs, and procedures will be altered as directed by Him whose church this is" (Packer, 15–16). The central doctrine in the GOSPEL is that Jesus is the Christ, the Redeemer, and that through his atonement "all mankind may be saved, by obedience to the laws and ordinances of the Gospel" (A of F 3). Doctrines are found in the scriptures, official declarations, statements of the First Presidency and the Quorum of the Twelve Apostles, and in official publications of the Church. The importance of understanding doctrine was emphasized in the Lord's words to Hyrum Smith: "Wait a little longer, until you shall have my word, my rock, my church, and my gospel, that you may know of a surety my doctrine" (11:16).

The word *doctrine* in the title "Doctrine and Covenants" alerts one to the fact that it contains many doctrines essential for salvation. In it, the Savior refers to "true points of my doctrine," which reduce contention and lead one to him (10:62–63). "This is my doctrine," he declared. "Whosoever repenteth and cometh unto me, the same is my church" (10:67).

Examples of clear, focused doctrine found in the revelations include faith, repentance, baptism, reception of the Holy Ghost (68:25); priesthood (121:45); ordinance work for the dead (128:9); and resurrection (138:19). The Explanatory Introduction to the Doctrine and Covenants states, "In the revelations the doctrines of the gospel are set forth with explanations about such fundamental matters as the nature of the Godhead, the origin of man, the reality of Satan, the purpose of mortality, the necessity for obedience, the need for repentance, the workings of the Holy Spirit, the ordinances and performances that pertain to salvation, the destiny of the earth, the future conditions of man after the resurrection and the judgment, the eternity of the marriage relationship, and the eternal nature of the family."

"The word of God is the doctrine taught by Jesus Christ and by His prophets. . . . He teaches doctrine to open our hearts to His love. And He teaches doctrine to open our eyes to see spiritual realities, invisible to any mind not illuminated by the Spirit of Truth. . . . Doctrine gains its power as the Holy Ghost confirms that it is true" (Eyring, 73–74). Individuals are commanded to "teach one another the doctrine of the kingdom," with the promise that God's "grace shall attend you, that you may be instructed more perfectly . . . in doctrine" (88:77–78). Individuals are to use agency to "act in doctrine" (101:78).

BIBLIOGRAPHY

Eyring, Henry B. "The Power of Teaching Doctrine." *Ensign* 29 (May 1999): 73–75.

Packer, Boyd K. "Revelation in a Changing World." *Ensign* 19 (November 1989): 14–16.

DJR

Doctrine and Covenants and the Joseph Smith Translation of the Bible

The Joseph Smith Translation is a revelatory translation of the Old and New Testaments by the Prophet Joseph Smith created from June 1830 to June 1844. Divine truth was received by the Prophet while he was translating restored doctrinal and historical information about the gospel of Jesus Christ that clarified the Bible while greatly adding to the theology, scripture, and practices of the Church. The Joseph Smith Translation is the strongest witness for Jesus Christ of any version of the Bible today. It is inseparably interwoven with several

important teachings of the Doctrine and Covenants. During the Church's formative period of 1830 to 1833, Joseph Smith's translating the Bible was an essential activity in the doctrinal progress of the Church in the dispensation of the fulness of times, repeatedly adding to the content, growth, and history of the Restoration. Translating was a learning experience for Joseph Smith, who gained knowledge he did not previously have (42:56; 45:60–61; 76:15–18).

The Church in 1830

In June 1830 there was limited understanding in the Church concerning doctrine, organization, and procedure compared with what is known today. There were but two standard works (the Bible and the Book of Mormon), few ordinances, little concept of the building of Zion, no complex priesthood organization, and no clear doctrine about degrees of glory, temple endowment, eternal marriage, exaltation, age of accountability for baptism, and many other sacred matters. These would begin to be revealed through the process of Joseph Smith translating the Bible, adding to existing doctrine and to the official literature of the Church in the Doctrine and Covenants and in the Pearl of Great Price, which later became canonized standard works.

Sources

The original handwritten manuscripts of the Joseph Smith Translation, the published editions of the Doctrine and Covenants, and the official *History of The Church of Jesus Christ of Latter-day Saints* (7 vols.) are primary sources for understanding the role of Joseph Smith's translation of the Bible in the establishment of doctrine in his day. The original manuscripts are of particular value because they contain not only the text of the translation but also many dates showing when the Prophet was translating specific passages. Various handwriting styles identify different scribes. The dates, the identity of the scribes, and the geographical location where the translation occurred (not discernible in the published JST) coincide with known travels and activities of the Prophet and his associates chronicled in the *History of the Church.*

The Doctrine and Covenants contains frequent mention of the Prophet translating the

Bible, usually referring to it as the "translation" or the "new translation" (124:89). Since the Book of Mormon had been published in March 1830 and the papyrus containing the book of Abraham would not be obtained until July 1835 (and not translated until months later), reference to the "translation" or to "translating" generally meant the translation of the Bible, as in 9:1–2n*a*; 35, headnote; 35:20; 37:1; 42:56; 45:60–61; 73:3–4; 76:15–18; 77, headnote; 90:13; 91:1–3; 93:53. The Lord's instruction in the revelations often dealt with regulatory matters, including appointment of scribes (25:6; 35:20); temporarily ceasing translation while attending to other business (37:1; 71, headnote); resuming translating (41:7; 42:56n*a*; 73:3–4); continuing the work until it was finished (73:4);

hastening (93:53); and printing the translation (94:10; 124:89).

The Prophet's almost daily entries in the *History of the Church* refer at least twenty-six times to the ongoing Bible translation, especially between June 1830 and July 1833 while the initial translation was in progress (Smith, 1:131–33, 170, 211, 215, 219, 238, 242, 245, 253, 255, 273, 295, 322, 324, 331, 341, 365, 368–69), during the editing phase, and while plans were made for printing the "new translation" (124:89; Smith, 4:137, 164, 187, 493; 6:164–65).

Acquaintance with the original manuscripts, the published Doctrine and Covenants, and the *History of the Church* is persuasive that the Lord commanded Joseph Smith to translate the Bible

Translation of the Bible; *painting by Liz Lemon Swindle. "And a commandment I give unto thee—that thou shalt write for him; and the scriptures shall be given, even as they are in mine own bosom, to the salvation of mine own elect"* (D&C 35:20).

beginning in 1830 and continued to inspire and instruct him regarding it until the Prophet's death in 1844.

Method of translation

The Joseph Smith Translation is not a translation in the conventional sense. The Prophet would read from a copy of the King James Version of the Bible and dictate to a scribe, who would write the corrections and additions on paper as they were revealed to the Prophet and spoken aloud by him. The HOLY GHOST was the active translator.

An initial draft was begun in June 1830 with a revelation about Moses that served as an orientation for Moses before he wrote Genesis. This revelation also served as an orientation for Joseph Smith as he prepared to translate Genesis. The Prophet began at Genesis 1 and continued to Genesis 24, at which time the Lord directed him to turn to the New Testament (45:60–61), which he began on 8 March 1831 and completed on 31 July 1832. Thereafter, the translation of the Old Testament was resumed and completed on 2 July 1833. The Prophet's record indicates that he and his scribes spent many days translating the Bible (Smith, 1:245, 253, 273, 295), which in company with other official duties brought "many glorious seasons of refreshing" (Smith, 1:322).

During the remaining eleven years of his life, the Prophet and his counselors in the First Presidency worked at further editing and preparing the manuscripts for printing. The complete work was not published during the Prophet's lifetime. His copy of the King James Version of the Bible and the Joseph Smith Translation manuscripts (some 446 pages) are now in the possession of the Community of Christ in Independence, Missouri.

Specific connections

A connection between the Doctrine and Covenants and the Joseph Smith Translation is that the Doctrine and Covenants contains divine directives pertaining to the production and proposed printing of the Joseph Smith Translation.

A second connection is specific ties of doctrine and phraseology. In fact, the Doctrine and Covenants and the Joseph Smith Translation

present near-identical information not available elsewhere. The relationship deepens when the dates in the translation manuscripts show that some concepts appear there earlier than in the Doctrine and Covenants, thus giving the translation primacy as a source document. Consider the following examples:

a. Joseph Smith Translation Genesis 1–3 (Moses 1–4) and Doctrine and Covenants 29:30–45 were both written in the summer and fall of 1830. The translation material began in June 1830 in Harmony, Pennsylvania, and continued through the summer and early fall. Section 29 was received in September 1830 in Fayette, New York. Both documents discuss the spiritual and temporal creations of the earth, the rebellion of Satan, and the fall of Adam: the translation, in detail; section 29, in fundamental cause-and-effect principles. Although sufficient information is not available to ascertain precisely how much of Genesis 1–3 was translated by September and therefore which portion came first in this instance, a pattern soon emerges that the translation sometimes precedes the Doctrine and Covenants.

b. Joseph Smith Translation Genesis 9:10–14, written between 1 February 1831 and 7 March 1831, affirms the sanctity of human and animal life, authorizes the eating of animal flesh by man, and warns against wasting animal life and flesh. In doing so, the translation goes considerably beyond the corresponding King James text. A similarly detailed statement occurs in Doctrine and Covenants 49:19–21, recorded 7 May 1831, a short time after the passage in the translation was written.

c. Joseph Smith Translation Genesis 17:11, received between 1 February 1831 and 7 March 1831, stipulates that children begin to become accountable unto God at eight years of age. This important fact does not appear in the Doctrine and Covenants, however, until 68:25–27, which is dated November 1831, seven to nine months after the translation entry.

A third connection occurs with the lengthy Joseph Smith Translation revelation about Enoch and his city, which was revealed while the King James Version of Genesis 5:18–25 was being translated with John Whitmer and Sidney

Rigdon as scribes. Nowhere does the King James text state that the patriarch Enoch built a city and therefore says nothing about Enoch's righteous city being taken off the earth. Not in any known version of the Bible is the patriarch Enoch credited with building a city. The King James passage consists of 109 words. The corresponding Joseph Smith Translation passage has 5,240 words, with emphasis on Enoch's knowledge of Christ and the founding of the city of Zion, populated by righteous people who had no poor among them and all of whom were taken up from the earth by the Lord (Moses 6:21–8:5). Until this revelation was received in December 1830, there is no mention of Enoch in any of the revelations or writings of Joseph Smith. It is therefore noteworthy that soon after this revelation was recorded in the Joseph Smith Translation, two items appear in the Doctrine and Covenants about Enoch, both referring to his city being taken off the earth: 38:4, given on 2 January 1831, and 45:11–12, given on 7 March 1831. Without the translation, these passages in the Doctrine and Covenants would have no reference points.

The ZION OF ENOCH, which was successful in every desirable way, particularly in having no poor, became the model for the latter-day Church; the next twenty or so revelations (37–59) explain the law of CONSECRATION of property, given to enable the Church to build a Zion in the last days patterned after Enoch's ancient city. Because no other version of the Bible contains the information, the Joseph Smith Translation became a necessary source introducing the concept of Enoch's Zion.

A fourth connection is when a revelation occurs as a result of the translation, yet the text is not included in the Joseph Smith Translation but is placed in the Doctrine and Covenants, such as section 76, about the degrees of glory; 77, about the book of Revelation; and 91, concerning the Apocrypha. The Joseph Smith Translation connection is explained in the headnotes to each of these sections, as provided by the Prophet in the *History of the Church* (Smith, 1:245–55, 331–32).

A fifth connection is the collateral information provided by the translation manuscripts, necessary to understand the context of various passages in the Doctrine and Covenants. For example, 35:20, dated December 1830, calling Sidney Rigdon to write for the Prophet, makes no categorical statement that the translation is involved. Nevertheless, the translation manuscript, under the date of December 1830, contains the beginning of Sidney Rigdon's handwriting with the revelation on Enoch. The date and context are also confirmed by the *History of the Church* (Smith, 1:132–33, 139). With these multiple points of identification, the statement of 35:20 is identified and becomes even more meaningful because it declares that "the scriptures shall be given, even as they are in [the Lord's] own bosom," which is an apt description of the purpose of the Joseph Smith Translation. Without the translation manuscripts and the *History of the Church,* the deeper significance of 35:20 and several other passages would be lost (cf. Matthews, *Plainer Translation,* 255–66; "Doctrinal Connection," 27–42).

To identify connections may not always be possible, but once the pattern is perceived, the door is opened wide to many possibilities, including doctrine, organization and duties of priesthood quorums, and the wealth of information in the Doctrine and Covenants about the ministries of the early patriarchs from Adam on down.

1830–1833, revelatory years

The years 1830 through 1833 were very productive in the development of the Doctrine and Covenants. It is rewarding to compare the formative years of the Joseph Smith Translation (June 1830–July 1833) with the large number of sections of the Doctrine and Covenants received during that time. The "Chronological Order of Contents" in the introductory pages of the Doctrine and Covenants is useful for this purpose. It is quickly discerned that most of the doctrinally rich revelations (including sections 1, 29, 43, 45, 70, 77, 84, 88, 93, and 133) were received during the years the Prophet Joseph Smith was translating the Bible. This correspondence is consequential rather than merely coincidental. Sections 107 and 132, although bearing later dates, can also be included in the list, because much of the doctrinal content of these sections was revealed in 1831, as explained in the headnotes to these sections (1981 ed.). The role of the Joseph Smith Translation must be acknowledged in this highly revelatory period. It seems that a principal purpose of the translation was to be the catalyst for revelation in the early Church. Both the Joseph Smith Translation and the Doctrine and Covenants are strong witnesses for the Lord Jesus Christ.

Study Aids in the 1981 Doctrine and Covenants

Sections in the Doctrine and Covenants whose headings mention the Joseph Smith Translation are 35, 64, 71, 73, 74, 76, 77, 86, and 91.

Footnotes that mention the Joseph Smith Translation in the Doctrine and Covenants are 9:2; 35:20; 37:1; 38:4; 41:7; 42:56; 45:12, 60; 49:21; 67:11–12; 73:3; 76:17; 84:14, 24; 93:1, 53; 94:10; 104:58; 107:2; 109:76; 124:89; 132:22.

BIBLIOGRAPHY

Faulring, Scott H., Kent P. Jackson, and Robert J. Matthews, eds. *Joseph Smith's New Translation of the Bible: Original Manuscripts.* Provo, Utah: Religious Studies Center, Brigham Young University, 2004.

Joseph Smith Translation (JST). In the Holy Bible, King James Version. Salt Lake City: The Church of Jesus Christ of Latter-day Saints, 1979.

Matthews, Robert J. "Doctrinal Connection with the Joseph Smith Translation." In *The Doctrine and Covenants: A Book of Answers.* The 25th Annual Sidney B. Sperry Symposium, edited by Leon R. Hartshorn, Dennis A. Wright, and Craig J. Ostler. Salt Lake City: Deseret Book, 1996.

———. *"A Plainer Translation": Joseph Smith's Translation of the Bible, a History and Commentary.* Provo, Utah: Brigham Young University Press, 1975.

Smith, Joseph. *History of The Church of Jesus Christ of Latter-day Saints.* Edited by B. H. Roberts. 7 vols. 2d ed. rev. Salt Lake City: The Church of Jesus Christ of Latter-day Saints, 1932–51.

RJM

Doctrine and Covenants, as capstone scripture

A capstone is the highest or finishing stone in a structure; symbolically, it represents a crowning accomplishment or achievement. Critical building blocks of the true Church of

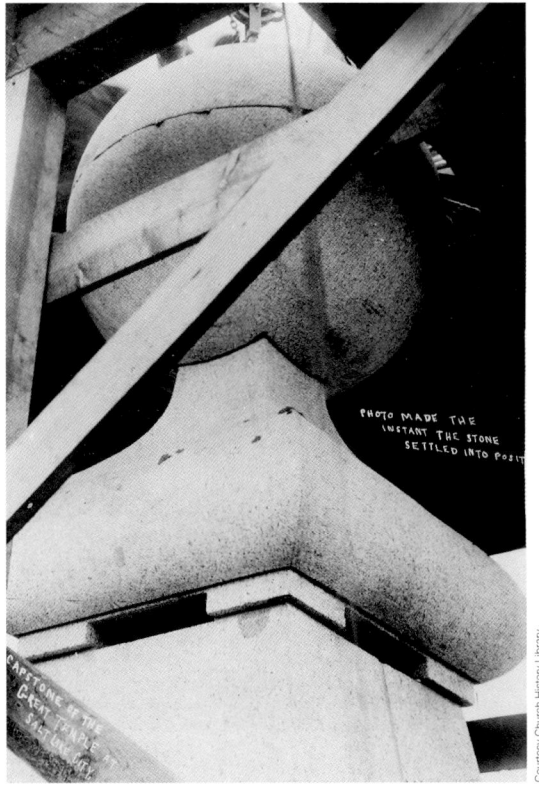

Photo made the instant the stone settled into posit[ion]

CAPSTONE OF THE GREAT TEMPLE SALT LAKE

Photograph taken 6 April 1892 at the moment the capstone of the Salt Lake Temple was put into place. The capstone is the granite ball on which the statue of the angel Moroni stands.

Jesus Christ include a foundation, a cornerstone, a keystone, and a capstone. The apostle Paul taught that the Church is "built upon the foundation of the apostles and prophets, Jesus Christ himself being the chief corner stone" (Eph. 2:20). The Prophet Joseph Smith said the Book of Mormon is the "keystone of our religion" (Book of Mormon Introduction), and President Ezra Taft Benson said that "the Doctrine and Covenants is the capstone, with continuing latter-day revelation" (83).

The Doctrine and Covenants is the capstone, or high point and crowning achievement of latter-day scripture, because of the doctrines and ordinances that are revealed throughout its pages. President Benson further taught that the "Doctrine and Covenants is the binding link between the Book of Mormon and the continuing work of the Restoration through the Prophet Joseph Smith and his successors. In the Doctrine and Covenants we learn of temple work, eternal families, the degrees of glory, Church organization, and many other great truths of the Restoration. . . . The Book of Mormon brings men to Christ. The Doctrine and Covenants brings men to Christ's kingdom, even The Church of Jesus Christ of Latter-day Saints, 'the only true and living church upon the face of the whole earth' [1:30]" (83).

As one studies the Doctrine and Covenants and the other scriptures, the blessings promised by President Benson will be received: "I promise you that as you more diligently study modern revelation on gospel subjects, your power to teach and preach will be magnified and you will so move the cause of Zion that added numbers will enter into the house of the Lord as well as the mission field" (85).

BIBLIOGRAPHY

Benson, Ezra Taft. "The Book of Mormon and the Doctrine and Covenants." *Ensign* 17 (May 1987): 83–85.

MSN

Doctrine and Covenants, as literature

Little has been written about the Doctrine and Covenants as literature, partly because there may be a concern that to speak of this unique volume of scripture as literature might imply that it is a creation of man rather than a book containing direct revelation from God. Nonetheless, to consider the Doctrine and Covenants as literature does not deny the role of divine inspiration in its creation; it is simply to recognize that literary elements, such as different literary genres, imagery, and figures of speech, in many of the sections of the book help to convey its divine message. Just as one can recognize the magnificent poetry of Isaiah, the flowing and elegant narrative of Luke, and the extensive symbolism of John in Revelation, so one can also appreciate the literary power of the Doctrine and Covenants without minimizing its status as sacred scripture.

As with the Bible and the Book of Mormon, not every passage in the Doctrine and Covenants would be considered literary. Throughout the book, however, are different genres that incorporate the experiential and artistic qualities that combine to create literature. The book includes visions, angelic annunciations, prophecies, prayers, epistles, parables, and poetry, with each genre often using such literary devices as simile, metaphor, personification, and imagery.

For example, in section 127 is an epistle with a textual range from businesslike prose to powerful, poetic imagery. The Prophet wrote, "I have left my affairs with agents and clerks who will transact all business in a prompt and proper manner, and will see that all my debts are canceled in due time, by turning out property, or otherwise, as the case may require, or as the circumstances may admit of" (127:1). But he also wrote, using images of light and darkness, as well as of time, "Inasmuch as they pursue me without a cause, and have not the least shadow or coloring of justice or right on their side in the getting up of their prosecutions against me; and inasmuch as their pretensions are all founded in falsehood of the blackest dye, I have thought it expedient and wisdom in me to leave the place for a short season" (127:1). In fact, one of the most beautiful phrases in the entire book is in this epistle when Joseph writes that "deep water is what I am wont to swim in" (127:2), a poignant metaphor for his life.

Parables are another literary form appearing in the text. Though most well-known parables come from the New Testament, there are also several in the Doctrine and Covenants: the parable of the twelve sons (38:26–27); the Lord's explanation of the parable of the wheat and the tares (86:1–7); the parable regarding the Lord's visits to kingdoms (88:51–61); the parable of the nobleman and the tower (101:43–62); and the parable of the woman and the unjust judge (101:81–91). The Lord also refers to New Testament parables including the parable of the fig tree (35:16) and the parable of the ten virgins (45:56–57). These parables serve as powerful means of helping readers to understand spiritual truths while reading about the world of common life. In the lengthy parable of the nobleman and the tower, for example, an account is given of a nobleman who sent his servants to plant twelve olive trees on his choice land, instructing them to build a tower for protection. The servants plant the trees, build a hedge around them, set watchmen, and even begin to build the tower, but they start to question the need for the tower and fail to complete it. As a result, the enemy comes during the night and breaks down the trees. The nobleman then tells one of his servants to gather other servants and redeem his land. Though this parable can be readily interpreted to refer to the experiences of the Saints in Jackson County, and the Lord himself identifies Joseph Smith as the servant in the parable (103:21), it is still a parable with multiple levels of application. The reader can learn from the parable, for instance, the importance of obeying the Lord and not questioning his judgment or the need for what he has commanded. One can also learn about the importance of being unified and about the Lord's willingness to forgive when one repents. *See* Parables in the Doctrine and Covenants.

A wide range of literary figures of speech is prevalent throughout the Doctrine and Covenants. Similes, for example, are frequently used: "clear as the moon, and fair as the sun, and terrible as an army with banners" (5:14); "as with the voice of a trump" (29:4); "blossom as the rose" (49:24); "like unto a judge sitting on a hill" (64:37); "his eyes were as a flame of fire; the hair of his head was white like the pure snow" (110:3); "as the dews from heaven" (121:45); "like wolves for the blood of the lamb" (122:6); "he is like a refiner's fire, and like fuller's soap" (128:24); "a globe like a sea of glass and fire" (130:7); the earth "will be made like unto crystal" (130:9); "'I am going like a lamb to the slaughter; but I am calm as a summer's morning'" (135:4); "like a woman that is taken in travail" (136:35); and "like unto circling flames of fire" (137:2).

Metaphors—one of the most poetic figures of speech—can also be frequently found in the text: "his sword is bathed in heaven, and it shall fall upon the inhabitants of the earth" (1:13); "made all nations drink of the wine of the wrath of her fornication" (35:11); "the veil of darkness shall soon be rent" (38:8); "those that die in me shall not taste of death, for it shall be sweet unto them; and they that die not in me, wo unto them, for their death is bitter" (42:46–47);

"your riches will canker your souls" (56:16); "receive a more exceeding and eternal weight of glory" (63:66); "the children of Zion" (84:56); "the sword of mine indignation" (101:10); "bowels also be full of charity towards all men, and to the household of faith, and let virtue garnish thy thoughts" (121:45); "a very large ship is benefited very much by a very small helm in the time of a storm" (123:16); and "clothe himself with charity" (124:116).

Such similes and metaphors build bridges from the commonplace and practical to the spiritual, helping one to better understand the latter because one is already familiar with the former. Everyone has tasted sweet food and bitter food, for example, so speaking of death as food that is sweet to those who die in the Lord and bitter to those who do not, provides an appreciation for how one's living this life can affect one's passing into the next.

Through the Prophet Joseph Smith, the Lord also personifies objects in communicating his message. For example, "the thunders shall utter their voices from the ends of the earth, speaking to the ears of all that live, saying—Repent, and prepare for the great day of the Lord" (43:21); "the whole world lieth in sin, and groaneth under darkness and under the bondage of sin" (84:49); "the lightnings . . . shall utter forth their voices" (43:22); the "earth rolls upon her wings, and the sun giveth his light by day, and the moon giveth her light by night, and the stars also give their light, as they roll upon their wings in their glory" (88:45); "the testimony of the voice of thunderings, and the voice of lightnings, and the voice of tempests, and the voice of the waves of the sea" (88:90); and "make hell itself shudder" (123:10). Personification helps bring to life the imagery, making it both more powerful and more memorable.

Archetypes—universal symbols that are enriched in their meaning as they are used throughout literature—are another example of poetic figures of speech often seen in the Doctrine and Covenants. A few references include such archetypes as rock (6:34; 10:69; 33:13), fire (29:12, 21, 28; 43:32–33; 63:17, 34, 54; 97:7, 26), water (5:16; 10:66; 133:29), veil (38:8; 67:10; 101:23; 110:1), and trump

(24:12; 29:4, 13, 26; 30:9; 42:6; 88:92, 94, 98–100, 102–6, 108–10). Further, *sword* can be found in the text as an archetype representing force and power, though it is used in different contexts. The sword can symbolize a number of things: God's judgment—"the anger of the Lord is kindled, and his sword is bathed in heaven, and it shall fall upon the inhabitants of the earth" (1:13); the word of God—"give heed unto my word, which is quick and powerful, sharper than a two-edged sword" (6:2; also see 11:2; 12:2; 14:2; 33:1); the Spirit—"the sword of my Spirit" (27:18); and acts of violence among people—"they will take up the sword, one against another" (45:33) and "with the sword and by bloodshed the inhabitants of the earth shall mourn" (87:6). Although the sword symbolizes different things, its archetypal significance as an image of power and force is consistent whether it represents the word of God or violent human acts.

It should be remembered that figures of speech used in the Doctrine and Covenants are not rare features of the text, occurring independently of one another and or randomly. Often the text in which they are placed is composed at the level of poetry, using artistic language with powerful imagery. Brigham Young University literature professor and writer Steven Walker calls section 128 "not only remarkable prose but sheer poetry" (103). In it the Prophet speaks metaphorically when he equates the restoration of the gospel with a voice: "Now, what do we hear in the gospel which we have received? A voice of gladness! A voice of mercy from heaven; and a voice of truth out of the earth; glad tidings for the dead; a voice of gladness for the living and the dead; glad tidings of great joy" (128:19). In the same section, he personifies nature: "Let the mountains shout for joy, and all ye valleys cry aloud; and all ye seas and dry lands tell the wonders of your Eternal King! And ye rivers, and brooks, and rills, flow down with gladness. Let the woods and all the trees of the field praise the Lord; and ye solid rocks weep for joy!" (128:23).

In section 121, the Lord uses the imagery of water extensively: telling Joseph Smith that his enemies' "prospects shall melt away as the hoar frost melteth before the burning rays of the rising sun" (v. 11); expressing the inevitability of his will coming to pass and the power of revelation from heaven by asking, "How long can rolling waters remain impure? What power shall stay the heavens? As well might man stretch forth his puny arm to stop the Missouri river in its decreed course, or to turn it up stream, as to hinder the Almighty from pouring down knowledge from heaven upon the heads of the Latter-day Saints" (v. 33); illustrating the gradual, peaceful way in which he sometimes teaches by promising that "the doctrine of the priesthood shall distil upon thy soul as the dews from heaven" (v. 45).

And though the Doctrine and Covenants is full of literary elements, these elements are not mere decoration. They do not simply make the text more interesting or appealing. Rather, they help to convey the Lord's message to his people with power and eloquence so that it can pierce their souls and help them become what he has in mind for them.

BIBLIOGRAPHY

Brugger, William H. "Section 76 as Literature in the Doctrine and Covenants." Master's thesis, Brigham Young University, 1993.

Swift, Charles. "The Literary Power of the Doctrine and Covenants." *Religious Educator* 10, no. 1 (2009): 21–31.

Walker, Steven C. "The Voice of the Prophet." *BYU Studies* 10, no. 1 (Autumn 1969): 95–106.

CS

Doctrine and Covenants, canonization of

The process by which texts are officially designated as scripture and become binding upon the Church is called canonization. By committing his revelations to writing, possibly as early as 1828, Joseph Smith started on a course to have them published and canonized. By November 1831, Joseph planned to publish most of the texts in the Book of Commandments and Revelations, a manuscript book into which John Whitmer and others hand-copied the texts of many of Joseph's revelations. That month Church leaders convened a conference in Hiram, Ohio, to plan the publication of these revelations. This gathering voted that the revelations should "be prized by this Conference to be worth to the Church the riches of the whole Earth" (Cannon and Cook, 32).

Printing in America had recently expanded, and a wide variety of religious and political groups were publishing newspapers and books, reaching wider audiences than ever before. Meanwhile, Latter-day Saint missionaries had been commanded to strictly apply the revelations in their ministry (cf. 32:4), but copies of the revelations could be handwritten only when the missionaries happened to be at Church headquarters or crossed paths with an elder who had a copy. Already a revelation had assigned the experienced editor William Phelps to be a printer for the Church (55:4). In the conference of 1 November 1831, Church leaders decided to print ten thousand copies of the revelations. That number was reduced to three thousand copies in April 1832 (Cannon and Cook, 26–27).

The Prophet dictated the texts that Whitmer copied into the Book of Commandments and Revelations, which Whitmer and Oliver Cowdery then took to Missouri (69:1–2). In Independence, Phelps and Cowdery began to publish the revelations. In July 1833, however, antagonistic citizens of Jackson County, Missouri, demanded that Phelps cease printing "the pretended revelations of Jo Smith" and destroyed the press and Phelps's home (*Telegraph,* 17 April 1835; 27 January 1837; Smith, 1:397–98). Some uncut signatures were preserved and later cut and bound. Thus, only a few copies of the Book of Commandments were preserved. Somehow the manuscript revelation book used as the source for the printing survived the violence and was returned to Kirtland, Ohio. There, in September 1834, shortly after Joseph returned from a journey to Missouri, the high council appointed him to head a committee to prepare the revelations for publication in an expanded form, along with seven theological lectures, as the Doctrine and Covenants. The printers relied not only on the Book of Commandments and Revelations but on a second manuscript repository of revelation texts called the Kirtland Revelation Book. Both manuscript copybooks of Joseph Smith's revelation texts were published in September 2009 by the Church Historian's Press as part of the Revelations and Translations Series of *The Joseph Smith Papers.*

Joseph Smith was away on business in Michigan in August 1835 when the other members of the committee appeared before a general Church assembly. This gathering of the Saints was the audience at which the committee appointed by the Kirtland high council reported on their stewardship over the publication; Church leaders sought the Saints' common consent to canonize the Doctrine and Covenants.

Oliver Cowdery held up the revelations and asked the brethren for their consent to publish them. William Phelps said "that he had examined it carefully, that it was well arranged and calculated to govern the Church in righteousness if followed would bring the members to see eye to eye. And further that he had received the testimony from God, that the Revelations and commandments contained therein are true, wherefore, he knew assuredly for himself having received witness from Heaven & not from men." John Smith followed with a similar expression of certainty, adding "that he was present when some of the revelations contained therein were given, and was satisfied they came from God"; others followed. Levi Jackman "arose and said that he had examined as many of the revelations contained in the book as were printed in Zion, & as firmly believes them as he does the Book of Mormon or the Bible and also the whole contents of the Book, he then called for the vote of the High Council from Zion, which they gave in favor of the Book and also of the committee." Newel Whitney rose and testified that he knew the revelations "were true, for God had testified to him by his holy Spirit, for many of them were given under his roof & in his presence, through President Joseph [Smith]" (KCMB, 103–5). Thus continued the process by which the revelations of Joseph Smith were endowed with canonical status. It culminated with a consensus "of all the members present, both male & female, & they gave a decided voice in favor of it & also of the committee. There being a very large portion of the church present" (KCMB, 106).

Many of the revelations of Joseph Smith were thus canonized by the process of their being divinely revealed to a prophet and then being accepted as such by the Saints. A similar process of selecting revelations and presenting them for sustaining by the Church has been continued as additional sections have been added to the Doctrine and Covenants.

See also Doctrine and Covenants, historical development of; Official Declaration 1; Official Declaration 2.

BIBLIOGRAPHY

Cannon, Donald Q., and Lyndon W. Cook, eds. *Far West Record: Minutes of The Church of Jesus Christ of Latter-day Saints, 1830–1844.* Salt Lake City: Deseret Book, 1983.

Kirtland Council Minute Book. Church History Library, The Church of Jesus Christ of Latter-day Saints, Salt Lake City, Utah.

Painesville [Ohio] Telegraph, 17 April 1835; 27 January 1837.

Smith, Joseph. *History of The Church of Jesus Christ of Latter-day Saints.* Edited by B. H. Roberts. 7 vols. 2d ed. rev. Salt Lake City: The Church of Jesus Christ of Latter-day Saints, 1932–51.

SCH

Doctrine and Covenants, explanatory introduction. *See* Doctrine and Covenants, historical development of.

Doctrine and Covenants, historical development of

The Doctrine and Covenants is primarily a collection of divine revelations and inspired writings received through the Prophet Joseph Smith and some of his successors as presidents of The Church of Jesus Christ of Latter-day Saints. There have been six principal editions published by the Church from the 1833 Book of Commandments to the 1981 edition of the Doctrine and Covenants.

1833 Book of Commandments—65 chapters

In the early years of The Church of Jesus Christ of Latter-day Saints, the Prophet Joseph Smith received many revelations. He may have written some of these in his own hand, but usually he dictated them to scribes who wrote them down. "In summer 1830 he [Joseph Smith] and

John Whitmer began to arrange and copy them" in a manuscript book labeled Commandments and Revelations. In late 1831 that book of revelations was taken to Independence, Missouri, by Oliver Cowdery and John Whitmer (69:1–8). There they and W. W. Phelps set the type to print the revelations as the Book of Commandments on the Church's printing press Phelps had set up in his home. "Church leaders in Missouri continued to update the [manuscript] volume when they received copies of revelations sent by mail or in person from Ohio" (Jensen et al., xxv) until it contained more than a hundred revelations. By the night of 20 July 1833, Phelps had set in type and printed sixty-five revelations (sixty-four complete and one incomplete; cf. chapter 65 in the Book of Commandments and section 64 in the 1981 edition) when the press was destroyed by a mob.

Before the Book of Commandments and Revelations began coming off the press in Independence, however, the publication of revelations received by the Prophet Joseph Smith had already begun with the publication of a revelation called the "Articles and Covenants of the Church of Christ" (originally published in *The Evening and the Morning Star,* June 1832; sections 20 and 22 in the 1981 edition). There is some debate regarding what constituted the Articles and Covenants. Although section 22 was printed along with section 20, some sources suggest that only section 20 was acknowledged as the Articles and Covenants (Robinson and Garrett, 1:126–28, 144–45). *See* Historical context and overview of Doctrine and Covenants 20 (p. 728) and 22 (p. 731).

At the first conference of the Church, held on 9 June 1830 in Fayette, New York, Joseph Smith read both revelations to the congregation, and they were "received by unanimous voice of the whole congregation" (Cannon and Cook, 1).

Copies were made and used by members and missionaries of the Church. One of those copies was given to E. D. Howe, the editor of the Painesville, Ohio, newspaper *The Telegraph.* He printed it on page 50, the first page of the 19 April 1831 issue of the paper, under the title "The Mormon Creed." In the introduction

A Book of Commandments for the Government of the Church of Christ. The forerunner to the Doctrine and Covenants, the Book of Commandments was printed in Independence, Missouri, in 1833. This copy belonged to Wilford Woodruff.

Howe noted that he had obtained the document "from the hand of Martin Harris."

That revelation was published as chapter 24 of the ill-fated Book of Commandments. The "Articles and Covenants" was the first of many chapters of the planned Book of Commandments that were printed in full or as excerpts in the first thirteen issues of *The Evening and the Morning Star* between June 1832 and June 1833 in Independence, Missouri. Phelps also printed it in June 1833 in the first issue of volume 2 of the newspaper.

Following is a list of the revelations printed in *The Evening and the Morning Star* before the press was destroyed. They are listed by the date of *The Evening and the Morning Star* issue and the chapter number in the Book of Commandments (BC) of each revelation. Although in the printed Book of Commandments the chapter numbers are in Roman numerals, they are given here in Arabic numerals for ease of reading. The corresponding section numbers of the revelations in the 1981 edition of the Doctrine and Covenants follow in brackets [ ]. Letters indicate instances where only a portion of the verse was printed in *The Evening and the Morning Star*. They correspond with the footnotes in the 1981 edition as places approximating where the printing concluded.

Doctrine and Covenants of the Church of the Latter Day Saints. The 1835 edition of the Doctrine and Covenants, the first to bear this title, was published in Kirtland, Ohio. The book added revelations to those previously printed in the Book of Commandments and also included the Lectures on Faith.

June 1832

Chapters 23 [22]; 24 [20]; 48 [45:1–71]; excerpts only 59 [58:55–56]; no BC chapter [72:24b–26]; no BC chapter [133:12–13a, 14–15a].

July 1832

Chapters 44 [42:11–72 (vv. 73–77 appeared in the *EMS* but were not printed in the BC]; 60 [59].

August 1832

Chapters 49 [46]; 53 [50].

September 1832

Chapter 29 [29]; no BC chapter [65].

October 1832

Chapters 47 [42:78–93]; 45 [43:15–35]; no BC chapter [68:1–15b, 22–35].

November 1832

Chapter 52 [49].

December 1832

Chapter 62 [61]; no BC chapter [72].

January 1833

Chapter 40 [38]; no BC chapter [83:1–2, 4–5].

February 1833

Chapter 64 [63:1–64]; no BC chapter [88:117–26].

March 1833

Chapter 1 [1]; no BC chapter [27:1–5b, 14–15c] [88:127–38 with editing].

April 1833

No chapters were printed in this issue.

May 1833

W. W. Phelps wrote in the introductory note: "Having given, in a previous number, the Preface to the book of Commandments now in

THEOLOGY.

LECTURE FIRST

ON THE DOCTRINE OF THE CHURCH OF THE

LATTER DAY SAINTS.

Of Faith.

SECTION I.

1 FAITH being the first principle in revealed religion, and the foundation of all righteousness, necessarily claims the first place in a course of lectures which are designed to unfold to the understanding the doctrine of Jesus Christ.

2 In presenting the subject of faith, we shall observe the following order:

3 First, Faith itself—what it is:

4 Secondly, The object on which it rests; and

5 Thirdly, The effects which flow from it.

6 Agreeably to this order we have first to show what faith is.

7 The author of the epistle to the Hebrews, in the eleventh chapter of that epistle, and first verse, gives the following definition of the word faith:

8 Now faith is the substance [assurance] of things hoped for, the evidence of things not seen.

9 From this we learn, that faith is the assurance which men have of the existence of things which they have not seen; and the principle of action in all intelligent beings.

10 If men were duly to consider themselves, and turn their thoughts and reflections to the operations of

A2

The Lectures on Faith. First included in the 1835 edition of the Doctrine and Covenants, the Lectures on Faith represented the "doctrine of the church."

PART SECOND.

COVENANTS AND COMMANDMENTS

OF THE LORD,

to his servants of the church of the

LATTER DAY SAINTS.

SECTION I.

1 Hearken, O ye people of my church, saith the voice of him who dwells on high, and whose eyes are upon all men; yea, verily I say, hearken ye people from afar, and ye that are upon the islands of the sea, listen together; for verily the voice of the Lord is unto all men, and there is none to escape, and there is no eye that shall not see, neither ear that shall not hear, neither heart that shall not be penetrated: and the rebellious shall be pierced with much sorrow, for their iniquities shall be spoken upon the house-tops, and their secret acts shall be revealed; and the voice of warning shall be unto all people, by the mouths of my disciples, whom I have chosen in these last days, and they shall go forth and none shall stay them, for I the Lord have commanded them.

2 Behold, this is mine authority, and the authority of my servants, and my preface unto the book of my commandments, which I have given them to publish unto you O inhabitants of the earth: wherefore fear and tremble, O ye people, for what I the Lord have decreed, in them, shall be fulfilled. And verily, I say unto you, that they who go forth, bearing these tidings unto the inhabitants of the earth, to them is power given to seal both on earth and in heaven, the unbelieving and rebellious; yea, verily, to seal them up unto the day when the wrath of God shall be poured out upon the wicked without measure: unto the day when the Lord shall come to recompense unto every man according to his work, and measure to every man according to the measure which he has measured to his fellow man.

3 Wherefore the voice of the Lord is unto the ends of the earth, that all that will hear may hear: prepare ye, prepare ye

The Covenants and Commandments of the Lord. "Part Second" of the 1835 edition of the Doctrine and Covenants contained the Lord's revelations, known as the "Covenants and Commandments of the Lord."

press, we give below, the close, or as it has been called, the Appendix." No BC chapter [133].

June 1833

The first issue of volume 2 starts with a reprint of "The Articles and Covenants of the Church of Christ."

Phelps had printed all but about twenty lines of chapter 65 for the Book of Commandments when in July a mob scattered the type, destroyed the press, dumped the printed sheets into the street for the horses to trample, tore down the home that housed the printing office, and tarred and feathered the printer. A few sets of printed sheets were recovered, but the project was ended. Somehow the manuscript copy of Commandments and Revelations, with the additional revelations copied in it, was not destroyed but was returned to Ohio. It became a supplement to a second manuscript book of revelations that had been started for use in Ohio shortly after the first book had been taken to Missouri. That book became known as the Kirtland Book of Revelations. These two manuscript books are designated Revelation Book 1 and Revelation Book 2 in *The Joseph Smith Papers*.

1835 Doctrine and Covenants—the Lectures on Faith and 103 sections (two sections inadvertently numbered LXVI)

Within fifty-three days after the press was destroyed in Independence, the Prophet Joseph Smith and other leaders of the Church met in Kirtland (11 September 1833) and resolved "that a press be established, and conducted under the firm name of F. G. Williams & Co." (Smith, 1:409). In a 10 October 1833 letter, Frederick G. Williams wrote to the Saints in Missouri that a council decided to "discontinue the building of the Temple during the winter, for want of materials" and to "set the hands immediately to erect a house for the printing office, which is to be thirty by thirty-eight feet on the ground; the first story to be occupied for the School of the Prophets this winter, and the upper story for the printing press. Oliver Cowdery started for New York on the first of October for the printing establishment, with eight hundred dollars. There will be as many hands employed upon the house as can work, and every exertion

made to get the printing into operation" (Smith, 1:418). The plan was to reprint *The Evening and the Morning Star* and to publish a new Church periodical called *The Latter Day Saints' Messenger and Advocate*. On 18 December 1833, Joseph Smith knelt in prayer with several Elders of the Church and "dedicated the printing press, and all that pertained thereunto, to God. . . . We then proceeded to take the first proof sheet of the reprinted *Star*, edited by Elder Oliver Cowdery" (Smith, 1:465).

With the reestablishment of the Church Printing Office in Kirtland, Ohio, the Prophet began to review and correct scribal and printing errors in the revelations that had been sent to Missouri and printed there for the Book of Commandments. He had also received more revelations that he needed to prepare for printing, most of which were recorded in the Kirtland Revelation Book. But not until the summer of 1835 could a new book of the revelations be printed. This time the volume was called the Doctrine and Covenants, reflecting its two principal parts: (1) the seven Lectures on Faith that had been given in the School of the Elders in the winter of 1834–35, representing the doctrine of the Church, and (2) the 103 revelations and articles representing the covenants and commandments. These 103 sections included the 65 revelations that had been printed for the Book of Commandments, with ten of the shorter revelations combined to make three sections, an additional 43 previously unpublished revelations the Prophet Joseph Smith had received, and two sections attributed to Oliver Cowdery: "Marriage" and "Governments and Laws in General." Also printed but not counted as a section were the minutes of the 17 August 1835 General Assembly of the Church, which contain "the written testimony of the Twelve . . . to the Book of the Lord's Commandments" (Smith 2:243–45).

1844 Nauvoo Edition—the Lectures on Faith and 111 sections

Before he and his brother Hyrum were murdered in Carthage, Illinois, on 27 June 1844, the Prophet Joseph Smith had been working on a new edition of the Doctrine and Covenants. He had prepared seven more revelations for inclusion in this new edition (103; 105; 112, 119; 124; 127; and 128 in the 1981 edition). John Taylor of the Quorum of the Twelve Apostles was the printer, and he added his tribute to the Prophet and Hyrum (135 in the 1981 edition), making 111 sections in the Nauvoo edition of the Doctrine and Covenants. This edition became the basis for all printings and translations of the Doctrine and Covenants until 1876.

1876 Salt Lake City Edition—the Lectures on Faith and 136 sections

President Brigham Young asked Elder Orson Pratt of the Quorum of the Twelve Apostles to prepare a new edition of the Doctrine and Covenants for publication in 1876. Besides changing the division of the verses in the revelations, Elder Pratt added 26 new sections and inserted them according to the date they had been received by the Prophet Joseph Smith. These added sections have the following numbers in the 1981 edition: 2; 13; 77; 85; 87; 108; 109; 110; 111; 113; 114; 115; 116; 117; 118; 120; 121; 122; 123; 125; 126; 129; 130; 131; 132; and 136. Section 132 replaced the earlier section on marriage thought to have been written by Oliver Cowdery; section 136 was received in Winter Quarters in January 1847 by President Brigham Young as he was directing the exodus of the Church west. The 1879 printing of the 1876 edition of the Doctrine and Covenants, done in England, was the first to include references in the margins, created under the leadership of Elder Orson Pratt (Woodford, 90). The 1908 and subsequent printings of this edition also contained the Manifesto by President Wilford Woodruff announcing that the Church had stopped the practice of plural marriage, renamed "Official Declaration 1" in the 1981 edition.

1921 Salt Lake City Edition—136 sections

Under assignment of President Heber J. Grant, six members of the Quorum of the Twelve Apostles prepared a new edition of the Doctrine and Covenants for publication in 1921. The most significant change in the 1921 edition was the omission of the Lectures on Faith, which had been a topic of discussion for some time "because they were not given or presented as revelations to the whole Church" ("Explanatory Introduction," first included in 1921 and revised in the 1981 edition of the Doctrine and Covenants). This is also the first edition to have the sections divided into two columns on each page.

1981 Salt Lake City Edition—138 sections

With the 1979 publication of the Latter-day Saint edition of the King James Version of the Bible, which included a revolutionary new footnoting system, a Topical Guide, a Bible Dictionary, and selections from the Prophet Joseph Smith's translation of the Bible, President Spencer W. Kimball asked the Scriptures Committee to prepare a new edition of the Book of Mormon, the Doctrine and Covenants, and the Pearl of Great Price. When the committee had completed its work, the following note was included in the Explanatory Introduction to the 1981 edition of the Doctrine and Covenants: "In the current edition of the Doctrine and Covenants three documents have been included for the first time. These are Sections 137 and 138, setting forth the fundamentals of salvation for the dead; and Official Declaration 2, announcing that all worthy male members of the Church may be ordained to the priesthood without regard for race or color.

"It is evident that some errors have been perpetuated in past editions, particularly in the historical portions of the section headings. Consequently this edition contains corrections of dates and place names and also a few other minor corrections when it seemed appropriate (such as discontinuing the unusual names beginning with section 78). [See Names, code.] These changes have been made so as to bring the material into conformity with the historical documents. Other special features of this latest edition include maps showing the major geographical locations in which the revelations were received, plus improvements in cross references, section headings, and subject-matter summaries, all of which are designed to help readers to understand and rejoice in the message of the Lord as given in the Doctrine and Covenants" ("Explanatory Introduction"). See Appendix B.

See also Doctrine and Covenants, canonization

of; Doctrine and Covenants, manuscripts of; Doctrine and Covenants, translations of.

BIBLIOGRAPHY

Cannon, Donald Q., and Lyndon W. Cook, eds. *Far West Record: Minutes of The Church of Jesus Christ of Latter-day Saints, 1830–1844.* Salt Lake City: Deseret Book, 1983.

Cook, Lyndon W. *The Revelations of the Prophet Joseph Smith.* Salt Lake City: Deseret Book, 1985.

Jensen, Robin Scott, Robert J. Woodford, and Steven C. Harper, eds. *Manuscript Revelation Books.* Facsimile edition. First volume of the Revelations and Translations series of The Joseph Smith Papers, edited by Dean C. Jessee, Ronald K. Esplin, and Richard Lyman Bushman. Salt Lake City: Church Historian's Press, 2009.

Robinson, Stephen E., and H. Dean Garrett. *A Commentary on the Doctrine and Covenants.* 4 vols. Salt Lake City: Deseret Book, 2000–2005.

Smith, Joseph. *History of The Church of Jesus Christ of Latter-day Saints.* Edited by B. H. Roberts. 7 vols. 2d ed. rev. Salt Lake City: The Church of Jesus Christ of Latter-day Saints, 1932–51.

The Evening and the Morning Star 1, nos. 1–12; 2, no. 13, June 1832–June 1833.

Woodford, Robert J. "The Historical Development of the Doctrine and Covenants." Ph.D. dissertation, Brigham Young University, 1974.

CDT

Doctrine and Covenants, manuscripts of

As with the Book of Mormon, there is a dictation manuscript, or original manuscript, for each revelation in the Doctrine and Covenants, and a publisher's manuscript used by those printing the revelations. Unlike the Book of Mormon, however, additional contemporaneous manuscripts of many of the revelations were written for various reasons.

Few of the original dictation copies of the revelations are known to still exist. Those include manuscripts for sections 121, 122, 123, 127, 128, and 136; with manuscripts for sections 5, 75, 93, and 100 as possible originals. Historical records are silent on the disposition of all the others. Perhaps they were discarded when published versions became available.

The two manuscript books used for publishing the Book of Commandments and the 1835 edition of the Doctrine and Covenants are in the Church History Library of The Church of Jesus Christ of Latter-day Saints. The first is commonly known as the "Book of Commandments and Revelations" and is mostly in the handwriting of John Whitmer. The second is the "Kirtland Revelation Book," mostly in the handwriting of Frederick G. Williams. The "Book of Commandments and Revelations" may have had its origin in the summer of 1830 when, the *History of the Church* records, Joseph Smith said, "I began to arrange and copy the revelations, which we had received from time to time; in which I was assisted by John Whitmer, who now resided with me" (1:104). Another possibility is that it was begun when John Whitmer was called by revelation on 8 March 1831 to "write and keep a regular history, and assist you, my servant Joseph, in transcribing all things which shall be given you" (47:1). Regardless, it is the manuscript book Oliver Cowdery and John Whitmer took to Missouri in November 1831 to print the Book of Commandments. The "Kirtland Revelation Book" was used to record revelations once the "Book of Commandments and Revelations" was taken to Missouri. Both of these manuscript books were used later to publish the 1835 edition of the Doctrine and Covenants. A few other documents may have also been used, but these, plus the manuscripts for the revelations in later editions of the Doctrine and Covenants, have not been positively identified, and many may not still exist.

Additional manuscripts of the revelations also existed before the revelations were published. Missionaries carried them in small vest pocket booklets. Other individuals, including A. Sidney Gilbert, kept a selection of the revelations that most affected their specific callings. Several diaries and journals include revelations given through Joseph Smith to their authors. Others, such as Doctrine and Covenants 76, were copied because of their doctrinal importance. Some were also printed in such early Church publications as *The Evening and the Morning Star.* Orson Pratt wrote: "We often had access to the manuscripts when boarding with the Prophet; and it was our delight to read them over and over again, before they were printed. And so highly were they esteemed by us, that we committed some to memory; and a few we copied for the purpose of reference in our absence on missions; and also to read them to the saints for their edification" ("Explanation," 228).

When one studies these early manuscripts it becomes immediately apparent that the revelations have gone through an editing process. Such alterations are of both theological and historical interest. Some members of the Church at that time felt Joseph Smith had no authorial role in the revelations, that he was merely God's mouthpiece. Some, however, noticed the linguistic "imperfections" of Joseph Smith's revelations, a point acknowledged in the preface to the first published collection of the revelations: "These commandments are of me, and were given unto my servants in their weakness, after the manner of their language" (1:24). Orson Pratt added: "Joseph, the Prophet, in selecting the revelations from the Manuscripts, and arranging them for publication, did not arrange them according to the order of the date in which they were given, neither did he think it necessary to publish them all in the Book of Doctrine and Covenants, but left them to be published more fully in his History. Hence, paragraphs taken from revelations of a later date, are, in a few instances, incorporated with those of an earlier date. Indeed, at the time of compilation, the Prophet was inspired in several instances to write additional sentences and paragraphs to the earlier revelations. In this manner the Lord did truly give 'line upon line, here a little and there a little,' the same as He did to a revelation that Jeremiah received, which, after being burned by the wicked king of Israel, the Lord revealed over again with great numbers of additional words. (See Jeremiah xxxvi. 32.)" ("Explanation," 260).

Near the end of his life, Joseph Smith affirmed, "I never told you I was perfect; but there is no error in the revelations which I have taught" (Smith, 6:366). Part of what kept the revelations free from "error" was that leading up to their publication in the Doctrine and Covenants (1835), Joseph Smith corrected them to keep pace with the emerging polity and doctrine of the Church. This process is particularly noticeable in such revelations as the Church's Articles and Covenants (20) and the "law" (42),

but there are scattered revisions in many of the revelations. In some cases, where it seemed to fit topically, Joseph Smith inserted additional information received in an earlier revelation. In other instances, he clarified meaning.

Spelling and grammatical errors were also corrected, and in later editions, English usage has also been updated. All the revelations in their current form have been canonized by the members of the Church in general conferences. The revelations in the 1835 edition were sustained as the word of the Lord in the conference of 17 August 1835 at Kirtland, Ohio. After twenty-six additional revelations were added in 1876, the whole compilation was again canonized in the October conference of 1880 in Salt Lake City. The Manifesto (OD 1) was canonized in the October conference of 1890. In the April conference of 1976 members of the Church voted to accept the resolution to include in the Pearl of Great Price Joseph Smith's vision of the celestial kingdom and Joseph F. Smith's vision of the redemption of the dead. These were transferred to the Doctrine and Covenants as sections 137 and 138 in the 1981 edition. Finally, the members of the Church canonized Official Declaration 2 (granting priesthood to all worthy male members) in the October conference of 1978.

The manuscripts used to publish the Book of Commandments and the 1835 edition of the Doctrine and Covenants are available for public scrutiny in *The Joseph Smith Papers* (Jensen et al.).

See also Doctrine and Covenants, canonization of; Doctrine and Covenants, historical development of; Doctrine and Covenants, translations of.

BIBLIOGRAPHY

Jensen, Robin Scott, Robert J. Woodford, and Steven C. Harper, eds. *Manuscript Revelation Books*. Facsimile edition. First volume of the Revelations and Translations series of *The Joseph Smith Papers*, edited by Dean C. Jessee, Ronald K. Esplin, and Richard Lyman Bushman. Salt Lake City: Church Historian's Press, 2009.

Pratt, Orson. "Explanation of Substituted Names in the Covenants." *The Seer* 2 (March 1854): 228.

———. "Priesthood." *Millennial Star* 19 (April 25, 1857): 257–60.

Smith, Joseph. *History of The Church of Jesus Christ of Latter-day Saints.* Edited by B. H. Roberts. 7 vols. 2d ed. rev. Salt Lake City: The Church of Jesus Christ of Latter-day Saints, 1932–51.

RJW

Doctrine and Covenants, printing and publication of.

See Doctrine and Covenants, historical development of.

Doctrine and Covenants, purposes of

The Doctrine and Covenants makes known the will of the Lord in the last days, particularly the eternal purposes and designs of God pertaining to the human family and to planet Earth. The revelations introduce and proclaim the word of the Lord, showing his divine order and objectives, which will be accomplished in the dispensation of the fulness of times. With utmost candor the Lord declared the message to be so important to every human soul that treating it lightly places one's eternal welfare in serious jeopardy.

The focus of the Doctrine and Covenants is on the last days, corrupt worldly conditions, and the plan of God through Jesus Christ to rescue as many as will believe and repent. Emphasis is also given to the future, both relatively immediate future events on earth and the extended future, such as life after death, the spirit world, resurrection, and the final destiny of man and the earth. The purposes of the Lord, stated and implied, are to inform mankind of these things that they might act with faith and make adequate preparation.

The voice of the Lord

The term *revelations* refers collectively to the various documents published as the Doctrine and Covenants, currently consisting of 138 numbered sections, mostly in chronological order according to when they were received, and two official declarations. Although mortal men were the instruments who penned the documents, the Lord JESUS CHRIST, through the HOLY GHOST, is the author, and it is his voice that is heard in the sacred pages.

Purposes stated in the Preface

The revealed Preface (1) contains the Lord's stated purposes for the revelations and why he commanded that they be published to the world. Prominent among the bold declaration about the wickedness of the world and the going astray of all mankind is this clear statement of purpose: "I the Lord, knowing the calamity which should come upon the inhabitants of the earth, called upon my servant Joseph Smith, Jun. . . . and gave him commandments . . . that [he and others] should proclaim these things unto the world; and all this that it might be fulfilled, which was written by the prophets" (1:17–18). Moreover, "that every man might speak in the name of God . . . that faith also might increase in the earth; that mine everlasting covenant might be established; [and] that the fulness of my gospel might be proclaimed . . . unto the ends of the world" (1:20–23). Further, if men "erred it might be made known," if they "sought wisdom they might be instructed," if they "sinned they might be chastened, that they might repent," and if humble "they might be made strong . . . and receive knowledge" (1:25–28).

A voice of warning

In clear and understandable language, the Lord declared that "the voice of warning shall be unto all people" (1:4). Later revelations repeatedly affirm that this is "a day of warning, and not a day of many words," and "every man [should] warn his neighbor" (63:58; 88:81; cf. 38:41; 63:37, 57; 84:114; 88:71; 89:4; 112:5). The revelations are "true" and should be searched; the decrees, prophecies, and promises that are in them "shall all be fulfilled"; "wherefore, fear and tremble, O ye people" (1:37, 7).

No apology

That there be no confusion as to the origin, authority, authenticity, and significance of the revelations, the Lord proclaimed: "Behold, this is mine authority, and the authority of my servants" (1:6). "I am God and have spoken it; these commandments are of me" (1:24). "I the Lord am willing to make these things known unto all flesh" (1:34). "What I the Lord have spoken, I have spoken, and I excuse not myself" (1:38). That is, the Lord offers no apology for his directness and the stern tone of these revelations.

It seems impossible that any serious reader of section 1 could fail to sense the strongly stated purposes of the revelations, the need for publication, and the worldwide scope and urgency of the warning.

To testify of Jesus Christ

Inspired scripture and the Holy Ghost testify of the person and the mission of Jesus Christ (e.g., 20:27; 42:17; 68:2–6; cf. John 5:39). The revelations in the Doctrine and Covenants are profoundly instructive concerning the MESSIAH—Jesus Christ—his personality, authority, and Godhood. For example, after revealing several pertinent matters about the nature of Jesus Christ (93:1–18), the Lord categorically explained: "I give unto you these sayings that you may understand and know how to worship, and know what you worship, that you may come unto the Father in my name" (93:19).

To leave without excuse

The word of the Lord "is quick and powerful, sharper than a two-edged sword" (11:2; 12:2; 14:2; 33:1). The revelations were given so that "all that will hear may hear" (1:11) and be saved and so that those who will not hear will be "left without excuse, and their sins [will be] upon their own heads" (88:82; 101:93). This warning applies to individuals, to groups, and even to whole nations (123:6; 124:3–8).

To prepare for future events

The revelations contain prophecies of earth-shaking events in the immediate future and also ultimate events that will come to every individual: death, a sojourn in the spirit world, resurrection of the body, and final judgment. Awareness of these coming events kindles a desire to be prepared (1:11–12). In fact, the necessity to prepare, with focus on the future, occurs at least forty-four times in the revelations.

Earth's origin, purpose, and destiny

At least two purposes of the EARTH are shown in the scriptures: the place for spirits to be born to receive physical bodies (Abr. 3:22–26), and the permanent home of the righteous after the resurrection. Latter-day revelation provides substantive information on these topics. For example, MARRIAGE and the bearing of children

are fundamental, "that the earth might answer the end of its creation; and that it might be filled with the measure of man, according to his creation before the world was made" (49:16–17). Ultimately, the earth will be "sanctified" and receive celestial glory, and celestial beings will "possess it forever and ever; for, for this intent was it made and created" (88:18–20, 26). The earth is God's "footstool" because he will again stand upon it (38:17). In its celestial condition it will be a Urim and Thummim and "will be Christ's" (130:8–9).

To introduce the final dispensation

The revelations introduce the scope and grandeur of "the dispensation of the fulness of times" (112:30–33; 128:18, 21), the culmination and focus and divine connection to all that has gone before, "proving to the world that the holy scriptures are true, and that God does inspire men and call them to his holy work in this age and generation, as well as in generations of old" (20:11).

In accomplishing its purposes, it is clear that the Doctrine and Covenants is not for the Church only but for the world, and it is necessary that it be published and authoritatively taught to all people as a voice of warning and as an invitation to come to Jesus Christ, its author.

RJM

Doctrine and Covenants, revealed appendix of. *See* Historical context and overview of Doctrine and Covenants 133 (p. 851).

Doctrine and Covenants, revealed preface of. *See* Historical context and overview of Doctrine and Covenants 1 (p. 712).

Doctrine and Covenants, testimony of the Twelve Apostles to the truth of

During a series of meetings 1–12 November 1831 regarding publication of the Book of Commandments, a discussion focused on a statement of testimony for the book. Joseph Smith sought divine guidance and received through revelation the testimony to which those attending the meeting were willing to attach their names.

This testimony, however, was not published

in the book. It may have been intended for inclusion in the back of the volume, as is the testimony of the witnesses to the Book of Mormon in the 1830 edition. Publication of the Book of Commandments was ended by the destruction of the press at Independence on 20 July 1833, so no supplementary information was included in the incomplete volumes bound by various individuals. This testimony is found in the *History of the Church* but without signatures (Smith, 1:226).

With slight adaptation, this same testimony was published in the back of the 1835 edition of the Doctrine and Covenants, witnessing the truth of the book by the Twelve Apostles, but no names were attached to it (1835 edition, 256). The names were included for the first time by Elder Brigham H. Roberts when the testimony was published in the *History of the Church* in 1902. He wrote, "In this testimony of the Twelve to the Book of Doctrine and Covenants, as published in the History of Joseph Smith in the *Millennial Star,* the names of the Apostles were not appended, but it is thought proper that they should be inserted here in the order in which they stood in the quorum" (Smith, 2:245n).

The 1921 edition of the Doctrine and Covenants was the first edition since the 1835 edition to include this testimony. It is found in the "Explanatory Introduction" with the names attached as found in the *History of the Church.* The "Explanatory Introduction" in at least English editions between 1921 and 1981 also included the original testimony of the witnesses to the Book of Commandments but with no names attached. The testimony of the Twelve Apostles was retained in the 1981 edition of the Doctrine and Covenants, but the testimony of the witnesses to the Book of Commandments was deleted.

See also Historical context and overview of Doctrine and Covenants 67 (p. 772).

BIBLIOGRAPHY

Doctrine and Covenants. 1835.

Smith, Joseph. *History of The Church of Jesus Christ of Latter-day Saints.* Edited by B. H. Roberts. 7 vols. 2d ed. rev. Salt Lake City: The Church of Jesus Christ of Latter-day Saints, 1932–51.

RJW

Doctrine and Covenants, translations of

As with translations of the Book of Mormon from English into other languages, early translations of the Doctrine and Covenants were made by converts to the Church who desired to share the gospel message with their fellow countrymen in their native language. The translations of the Book of Mormon preceded those of the Doctrine and Covenants in all languages except Welsh, and the Welsh translation of the Doctrine and Covenants (1851) was the first into any language other than English for that scripture. All the early translations were based on the 1844 Nauvoo edition of the Doctrine and Covenants or reprints of it made as early as 1845 in England. The Nauvoo edition contained the seven Lectures on Faith and 111 sections of revelations. After the 1876 English edition was published with 136 sections and with section 132 replacing the article on marriage traditionally attributed to Oliver Cowdery, it became the base edition for translation until the 1921 edition dropped the Lectures on Faith. The 1981 edition of the Doctrine and Covenants, containing 138 sections, Official Declaration 1, Excerpts from Three Addresses by President Wilford Woodruff regarding the Manifesto, and Official Declaration 2, is now the basis for translations.

As of August 2012, the Doctrine and Covenants has been translated from English into more than fifty languages. Most of these translations have been done since the Church created its Translation Division in 1965. Using both native-speaking converts and trained linguists to assist in the work, and with auxiliary substations around the world, that division supervises all of the translations of Church materials throughout the world.

As noted above, the first translation of the Doctrine and Covenants into a language other than English was into Welsh. It was done by John S. Davis (1822–82), a convert to the Church of three years. He replaced Elder Dan Jones, who as part of his missionary work

遭野蠻地射擊，身上各中四槍。

2 約翰ª·泰來和威拉·理查，十二使徒中的二位，是當時室內僅存的人；前者身中四槍，傷勢嚴重，但後來痊癒了；而後者，靠神的護佑逃過一劫，衣服上連個洞都沒有。

3 約瑟·斯密，主的ª先知和先見ᵇ，為世人的救恩所做的，除了耶穌之外，較任何曾在世上活過的人都多。在短短二十年裡，他靠神的恩賜和能力翻譯摩爾門經，使摩爾門經問世，並促成摩爾門經在兩大洲發行，將其中包含的圓滿ᶜ的永久福音傳到大地四方；他使這本由啟示和誠命結合而成的教義和聖約一書問世，並為了人類兒女的益處，使許多充滿智慧的其他文獻和教訓問世；聚集了數千後期聖徒，建立了一座大城，留下了不可磨滅的聲望和名譽。在神和他的人民眼中，他活得偉大，死得偉大；像古時候主大部分的受膏者那樣，他用自己的血ᵉ印證了他的使命和事工；他哥哥海侖ᵈ也一樣。他們活著不分開，死時也不分離！

4 約瑟在遇刺前兩三天，到卡太基去，將自己交給法律的虛妄要求時，說道：「我此去像一隻待宰的羔羊，但是我平靜得像夏日的早晨；我對神和對所有的人都有個無愧ª的良心。我將死得無辜，但是眾人談到我時會說——他被殘酷無情地謀殺了。」——當天早晨，海侖準備好要去的時候——應該說去被屠宰吧？是的，事實就是如此——他讀了摩爾門經以帖書第十二章結尾的以下這段經文，並將該頁摺了起來：

5 事情是這樣的，我祈求主賜恩典給外邦人，讓他們有仁愛。事情是這樣的，主對我說：如果他們沒有仁愛，對你是無關緊要的，你一向忠信：所以，你的衣服必被滌淨ª。因為你已看到自己的弱點，你必成為堅強，終必坐在我在父家裡預備的地方。我……現在要向外邦人告別，是的，也向我愛的弟兄們告別，等

2 a 南：泰來，約翰。
3 a 南：先知。
 b 南：先見。
 c 南：福音的復興。
 d 南：納府，伊利諾州（美國）。
 e 教約35:17;42:12；來9:16,17。
4 a 教約136:39。
5 a 賽53:7；教約88:74–75。

Chinese translation of Doctrine and Covenants 135.

SEZIONE 135

Martirio di Joseph Smith, il Profeta, e di suo fratello Hyrum Smith, il Patriarca, a Carthage, Illinois, il 27 giugno 1844 (History of the Church, 6:629–631). *Questo documento fu scritto dall'anziano John Taylor del Consiglio dei Dodici, che era stato testimone degli avvenimenti.*

1–2: Joseph e Hyrum Smith martirizzati nel carcere di Carthage; 3: viene proclamata la posizione di eminenza del Profeta; 4–7: il loro sangue innocente attesta la verità e la divinità dell'opera.

PER suggellare la testimonianza di questo libro e del Libro di Mormon, annunciamo il ᵃmartirio di ᵇJoseph Smith, il Profeta, e di Hyrum Smith, il Patriarca. Essi furono uccisi a fucilate nel carcere di ᶜCarthage il 27 giugno 1844, verso le cinque del pomeriggio, da una plebaglia armata, dipinta di nero, composta di centocinquanta o duecento persone. ᵈHyrum fu colpito per primo e cadde serenamente, esclamando: *Sono un uomo morto!* Joseph saltò dalla finestra e fu colpito a morte nel tentativo, esclamando: *O Signore, mio Dio!* Si sparò su di loro in modo brutale dopo che erano morti, ed entrambi ricevettero quattro pallottole.

2 ᵃJohn Taylor e Willard Richards, due dei Dodici, erano le sole persone nella stanza in quel momento; il primo fu ferito in modo selvaggio da quattro pallottole, ma da allora è guarito; il secondo, tramite la provvidenza di Dio, sfuggì senza neppure un foro nei vestiti.

3 Joseph Smith, il ᵃProfeta e ᵇVeggente del Signore, ha fatto di più, a parte solo Gesù, per la salvezza degli uomini in questo mondo di qualsiasi altro uomo che vi abbia mai vissuto. Nel breve spazio di vent'anni egli portò alla luce il Libro di Mormon, che tradusse per dono e potere di Dio, e per suo mezzo fu pubblicato in due continenti; mandò ai quattro canti della terra la ᶜpienezza del Vangelo che esso conteneva; portò alla luce le rivelazioni e i comandamenti che compongono questo libro di Dottrina e Alleanze, e molti altri saggi documenti e istruzioni per il beneficio dei figlioli degli uomini; radunò molte migliaia di Santi degli Ultimi Giorni, fondò una grande ᵈcittà e lasciò una fama e un nome che non possono essere uccisi. Visse da grande e morì da grande agli occhi di Dio e del suo popolo; e come la maggior parte degli unti del Signore nei tempi antichi, ha suggellato la sua missione e le sue opere col

---

135 1a DeA 5:22; 6:30.
   GS Martire, martirio.
  b GS Smith, Joseph jun.
  c GS Prigione di
    Carthage (USA).

  d GS Smith, Hyrum.
2a GS Taylor, John.
3a GS Profeta.
  b GS Veggente.
  c DeA 35:17; 42:12.

GS Restaurazione
  del Vangelo.
d GS Nauvoo (Illinois,
  USA).

Italian translation of Doctrine and Covenants 135.

in Wales had set up a print shop and started printing Church publications there. Davis was himself an experienced printer and had his own press. He continued printing Jones's Welsh Mormon periodical *Prohwyd y Jubili* (*Prophet of the Jubilee*), which had just been renamed *Udgorn Seion* (*Zion's Trumpet*). Davis published his translation of the Lectures on Faith, without the question-and-answer catechisms, in the January to May 1850 monthly issues of *Udgorn Seion*. In the May issue Davis advertised that he would bind the lectures in a separate booklet (Dennis, 108). He then translated and printed the Doctrine and Covenants in twenty sixteen-page signatures, which he sent to his subscribers with the *Udgorn Seion*. After the last signature went out with the 23 August 1851 issue, Davis bound all twenty signatures into a Doctrine and Covenants book in 1851 (Dennis, 142–43). In 1852 Davis translated and published the Book of Mormon in Welsh.

The second translation of the Doctrine and Covenants into a language other than English, this time without the Lectures on Faith, was into Danish by a Miss Mathiesen (Lambert, 2). That translation was checked and published in 1852 by Elder Erastus Snow of the Twelve Apostles. Not until the third Danish edition (1856) were the Lectures on Faith included (Lambert, 2).

The third language of translation was the 1876 publication of the Doctrine and Covenants in German. It had 110 sections, omitting the section on marriage, and was translated from English by Heinrich Eyring (Lambert, 3).

In 1887, 8 selected sections were translated into Spanish. The next year the Doctrine and Covenants was translated into Swedish by Janne Mattson Sjodahl (Lambert, 4).

In the early and mid 1900s, several more translations of all or parts of the Doctrine and Covenants were made: Dutch and 28 sections in French (Lambert, 7) in 1908; Hawaiian in 1914; Maori in 1919; selections from 41 sections in Norwegian in 1934; Czech in 1939; Armenian-West (Old) in 1941; and Portuguese in 1950. Thirteen translations of the Doctrine and Covenants (counting the selected sections in French, Norwegian, and Spanish) were created

in 115 years (1835–1950). The English Braille edition in six volumes was published in 1948.

Since 1951 the Doctrine and Covenants has been translated into many more languages and made accessible in print and on the Internet. Audio recordings of some translations have also been made available.

Appendix C contains a chronological listing of all the languages into which the Doctrine and Covenants has been translated, up to August 2012. It also notes the first time a translation became part of a triple combination of the scriptures (the Book of Mormon, Doctrine and Covenants, and Pearl of Great Price bound in one volume).

See also Doctrine and Covenants, historical development of.

BIBLIOGRAPHY

Dennis, Ronald D. *Welsh Mormon Writings from 1844 to 1862: A Historical Bibliography.* Provo, Utah: Religious Studies Center, Brigham Young University, 1988.

Lambert, A. C. "The Editions of the Doctrine and Covenants of The Church of Jesus Christ of Latter-day Saints in All Languages, 1833–1950." Mimeograph, 1950.

CDT

Doctrine and Covenants, what it says about itself

During a conference held at Hiram, Ohio, on 1 November 1831, Joseph Smith received a revelation that was designated to be the preface for what would become the Doctrine and Covenants. In this and other revelations contained in the book, the Lord revealed insights that help readers more fully understand the importance of this unique book of scripture.

> 24 Behold, I am God and have spoken it; these *commandments are of me*, and were given unto my servants in their weakness, after the manner of their *language, that they might come to understanding.

Doctrine and Covenants 1:24.

A compilation of revelations and inspired writings, the Doctrine and Covenants makes several references to its own publication, including instruction appointing individuals to publish it and how it should be funded (70:1–3; 72:21; 84:104; 104:58). This revelatory text is intended to "lay the foundation of this church, and to bring it forth out of obscurity and out of darkness" (1:30). As such, the Doctrine and Covenants is described as a "voice of warning" unto all people (1:4). It is to be a guide in conducting meetings, serving in the kingdom, and proclaiming the truth (20:45; 28:12; 75:4). More than a book of scripture just for members of the Church, the Doctrine and Covenants is directed to the "inhabitants of the earth," including the "unbelieving and rebellious" (1:1–2, 6, 8). The warning voice of the revelations is the Savior's voice. "Behold, I am God and have spoken it; these commandments [referring to the revelations in the Doctrine and Covenants] are of me" (1:24). While the revelations are of Christ, they are given "by the mouths" of his chosen disciples (1:4; cf. 135:3). Understanding this relationship of communication between the Savior, his authorized prophets, and the people at large is vital when dealing with the Doctrine and Covenants. "What I the Lord have spoken, I have spoken, and I excuse not myself," he declared authoritatively. And "whether by mine own voice or by the voice of my servants, it is the same" (1:38).

In 1831, some criticized the revelations and the language used therein. One member of this group attempted to create his own revelation and "imitate the language of Jesus Christ." His attempts failed, and he, along with others present at the conference, confessed that the revelations Joseph Smith received were indeed of God and profitable for all men (Smith, 1:226). On this occasion, the Lord stated: "And now I, the Lord, give unto you a testimony of the truth of these commandments which are lying before you. . . . For ye know that there is no unrighteousness in them, and that which is righteous cometh down from above, from the Father of lights" (67:4, 9).

The revelations in the Doctrine and Covenants warn all men to prepare "for that which is to come, for the Lord is nigh" (1:12) and will come "quickly to judgment" (99:5). The revelations are a testimony that the Lord's judgment will "recompense unto every man according to his work" (1:10). Fortunately, the Doctrine and Covenants not only warns people to prepare but guides their preparation so that they "might come to understanding" (1:24). Through these scriptures readers understand that they can be corrected when they err, be instructed as they seek wisdom, be chastened so that they might repent, and be humble so that they might become strong (1:25–28). Saints can prepare with confidence, being strengthened by the prophetic prayer that they "may be found worthy . . . to secure a fulfilment of the promises which thou hast made unto us, thy people, in the revelations given unto us" (109:11) and in knowing that "what I the Lord have decreed in them [revelations in the Doctrine and Covenants] shall be fulfilled" (1:7, 18).

"Search these commandments," the Savior said of the Doctrine and Covenants, "for they are true and faithful" (1:37). He further testified, "These words are given unto you, and they are pure before me; wherefore, beware how you hold them, for they are to be answered upon your souls in the day of judgment" (41:12). Therefore, those who "hearken" (1:1; 136:41) and "give heed unto [Christ's] word" (6:2) revealed in the Doctrine and Covenants can "receive knowledge from time to time" and be "blessed from on high"(1:28).

See also Doctrine and Covenants, as capstone scripture; Doctrine and Covenants, purposes of; Doctrine and Covenants, testimony of the Twelve Apostles to the truth of; Historical context and overview of Doctrine and Covenants 1 (p. 712).

BIBLIOGRAPHY

Smith, Joseph. *History of The Church of Jesus Christ of Latter-day Saints.* Edited by B. H. Roberts. 7 vols. 2d ed. rev. Salt Lake City: The Church of Jesus Christ of Latter-day Saints, 1932–51.

MOR

Doctrine and Covenants, what it says about the Bible

The Bible was instrumental in bringing young Joseph Smith to his knees in prayer in a grove of trees that would become known as the Sacred Grove. The promise found in the epistle of James concerning those who lacked wisdom led to the revelation known as the First Vision (JS-H 1:5–19). Thus, the Bible paved the way for all that was to come in bringing about the restoration of the Church of Jesus Christ, and it has a strong presence in the revelations found in the Doctrine and Covenants.

Though the Bible is referred to by name only twice in the Doctrine and Covenants (42:12; 138:6), references to it by the name "scriptures" or "holy scriptures" are more frequent (20:11, 35, 41, 69; 33:16; 74:7), especially as they relate to Joseph Smith's work in translating the Bible (35:20; 93:53; 94:10; 104:58). More than thirty Old Testament individuals are mentioned in the Doctrine and Covenants, including three women: Eve, Sarah, and Hagar (132:34, 65; 138:39). Seven New Testament individuals are named in the revelations: Peter, James, John the Beloved, Paul, John the Baptist, Nathanael, and Zacharias. The biblical persons mentioned most frequently in the Doctrine and Covenants are Abraham, Adam, Aaron, Moses, Melchizedek, and Enoch. In addition, the names of the following also appear: Abel, Cain, Cainan, Daniel, David, Elijah, Enos, Ezekiel, Gabriel, Isaac, Isaiah, Jacob, Jethro, Job, Joseph, Judah, Malachi, Methuselah, Michael, Noah, Seth, Shem, and Solomon. Others named in the Doctrine and Covenants who lived in Old Testament times, but are probably not the same persons as those listed in the priesthood line of authority given in section 84, include Caleb, Elihu, Esaias, Gad, and Jeremy (84:6–13).

The Doctrine and Covenants also refers to significant biblical events including the Creation (14:9; 20:18; 132:38); the fall of Adam and Eve (20:20; 29:40); the exodus from Egypt (8:3; 84:23–24; 89:21); the scattering and gathering of Israel (45:17, 24; 109:67; 110:11); and the atonement of Jesus Christ (76:69). It frequently speaks of such biblical places as Jerusalem (5:20; 29:12; 33:8; 45:18, 24; 77:15;

95:9; 109:62; 133:13, 21, 24; cf. 128:19) and Babylon (1:16; 35:11; 64:24; 86:3; 133:5, 7, 14), and interprets biblical passages (cf. 45; 74; 77; 86; 113; 132).

Additionally, the very language of the revelations in the Doctrine and Covenants is often that of the King James Version of the Bible. This may stem from nineteenth-century familiarity with the biblical text, both of Joseph Smith and of his associates, because the revelations are "after the manner of their language" (1:24) and come from the same revelatory source. Thus, the basic authenticity and historicity of the Bible, both the Old Testament and the New Testament, is confirmed by the Doctrine and Covenants, which provides inspired, latter-day, corroborating testimony concerning biblical events and the lives of a number of biblical personalities.

Speaking of the coming forth of the Book of Mormon, the Lord said, "Inasmuch as the knowledge of a Savior has come "unto the world, through the testimony of the Jews [the Bible], even so shall the knowledge of a Savior come unto my people—and to the Nephites, and the Jacobites, and the Josephites, and the Zoramites, through the testimony of their fathers [the Book of Mormon]" (3:16–17). The Doctrine and Covenants testifies that the Book of Mormon came not to destroy the Bible but to "build it up" (10:45–52). Thus, as Jesus said, "In the mouth of two or three witnesses shall every word be established" (6:28). The Doctrine and Covenants is among the "other books" Nephi saw in vision that would come forth in the last days to bear witness of the truth of the biblical record (1 Ne. 13:39–40).

The theology of the Doctrine and Covenants

12 And again, the ᵃelders, priests and teachers of this church shall ᵇteach the principles of my gospel, which are in the Bible and the ᶜBook of Mormon, in the which is the ᵈfulness of the ᵉgospel.

Doctrine and Covenants 42:12.

complements the fundamental truths found in the Bible. The Doctrine and Covenants is in harmony with the overarching spiritual themes of the Bible, which center in the redemption of Israel and salvation in and through Jesus Christ. The revelations build upon those themes and raise doctrinal understanding to the heights of exaltation. They speak of "things which have been kept hid from before the foundation of the world, things that pertain to the dispensation of the fulness of times" (124:38, 40–41; cf. 128:18). They clarify the meaning of priesthood authority, of salvation and exaltation, of kingdoms of glory, of temple ordinances for the living and the dead—endowments, sealings, eternal families, and godhood. The Doctrine and Covenants both affirms and expands upon the truths of the Bible.

See also Historical context and overview of Doctrine and Covenants 45 (p. 751), 74 (p. 779), 77 (p. 782), 86 (p. 790), 113 (p. 823), and 132 (p. 849); Isaiah quotations in the Doctrine and Covenants; Israel; John the Beloved/Revelator quotations in the Doctrine and Covenants; Paul quotations in the Doctrine and Covenants; Record of John.

RT

Doctrine and Covenants, what it says about the Book of Mormon

The Doctrine and Covenants contains valuable information concerning the Book of Mormon, its coming forth, its purpose and teachings, and its importance in the latter days. The Lord identified the Book of Mormon as the "stick of Ephraim" with Moroni holding the "keys" of that record (27:5). *See* Stick of Ephraim.

The Lord declared that the Book of Mormon is a "record of a fallen people," the Nephites, and that it contains the "fulness of the gospel of Jesus Christ" (20:9), which the ancient Nephite prophets and disciples "desired in their prayers should come forth unto this people" and which the Lord granted them because of their faith (10:46–50).

The coming forth

The Doctrine and Covenants affirms that God sent the Nephite prophet Moroni to Joseph

Smith to "reveal the Book of Mormon" (27:5; 128:20). Joseph was "called and chosen to write the Book of Mormon" (24:1), and it was by the mercy and power of God that he would have this "first gift," the "gift to translate the plates" upon which it was written (1:29; 5:4). He would be ordained to go forth and declare the Book of Mormon to the world; the Lord proclaimed, "This generation shall have my word through you" (5:6, 10).

Martin Harris, Joseph's scribe for the first part of the translation, lost 116 pages of the manuscript, which left both him and Joseph under condemnation for a time (3:4–10; 10:1–9). Because of this loss the Lord told Joseph not to retranslate that portion (known as the book of Lehi) but to translate the more relevant account from the plates of Nephi, which the Lord said would "throw greater views upon my gospel" (10:40–45). To ensure the book would be published in a timely manner, the Lord later commanded Martin Harris to "not covet [his] own property, but impart it freely to the printing of the Book of Mormon, which contains the truth and the word of God" (19:26).

For some time Joseph Smith was the only person who saw the PLATES, and this

> 54 And your *a*minds in times past have been *b*darkened because of *c*unbelief, and because you have treated *d*lightly the things you have received—
> 55 Which *a*vanity and unbelief have brought the whole church under condemnation.
> 56 And this condemnation resteth upon the children of *a*Zion, even all.
> 57 And they shall remain under this condemnation until they repent and remember the new *a*covenant, even the *b*Book of Mormon and the *c*former commandments which I have given them, not only to say, but to *d*do according to that which I have written—

Doctrine and Covenants 84:54–57.

responsibility weighed heavily upon him. The Lord assured Joseph that he would not allow him or this work to be destroyed (3:1–3; 17:4), and he would provide three witnesses to testify "by the power of God" that they had seen the plates and heard the voice of God declare that they are true (17:3; 5:12–15; 128:20). This testimony was to go forth with every copy of the Book of Mormon (5:11, 15).

Purposes of the Book of Mormon

The Book of Mormon was preserved according to the promises of the Lord so that his children might come to a knowledge of the Savior (3:16, 19–20). It is the way the Lord has chosen to "show unto this people that I had other sheep, and that they were a branch of the house of Jacob" (10:60; cf. John 10:16). Through the Book of Mormon "the Lamanites, and also all that had become Lamanites because of their dissensions" (10:48–49), "might come to the knowledge of their fathers . . . know the promises of the Lord . . . believe the gospel and rely upon the merits of Jesus Christ" in order to be saved (3:20).

The Lord's purpose in preserving the Book of Mormon was not to "destroy that which [the world has] received [the Bible], but to build it up" (10:52, 62; cf. 1 Ne. 13:40). The Lord indicated that the Book of Mormon has brought forth the "true points of my doctrine . . . that there may not be so much contention . . . concerning the points of my doctrine" (10:62–63). The coming forth of the Book of Mormon proves "to the world that the holy scriptures are true, and that God does inspire men and call them to his holy work in this age and generation, as well as in generations of old; thereby showing that he is the same God yesterday, today, and forever" (20:11–12).

Teachings of the Book of Mormon

The Lord explained that the Book of Mormon was given along with other scripture for our "instruction" (33:16). For this reason he told his servants to "teach the principles of my gospel, which are in the Bible and the Book of Mormon" (42:12).

The Lord affirmed that by the Book of Mormon and other scriptures "we know that there is a God in heaven, who is infinite and eternal . . . that he created man, male and female, after his own image," and he commanded them to love and serve him. One learns that by transgression of God's laws, men became sensual and devilish. Wherefore, God sent his Only Begotten Son to suffer temptations, be crucified, die, and be resurrected that he might ascend into heaven to sit down on the right hand of the Father and reign with him. All who believe, are baptized in his name, receive the gift of the Holy Ghost, and endure in faith to the end shall be saved (20:17–27). Furthermore, the Lord warned, "Beware of pride, lest ye become as the Nephites of old" (38:39).

The Importance of the Book of Mormon

In Doctrine and Covenants 84 the Lord indicated that the minds of members of the Church had been "darkened because of unbelief," having "treated lightly the things [they had] received"—"the Book of Mormon and the former commandments" which he had given them (84:54, 57). This neglect brought the "whole church under condemnation" (84:55–57). Concerning this charge, President Ezra Taft Benson taught:

"In section 84 of the Doctrine and Covenants, the Lord declares that the whole Church and all the children of Zion are under condemnation because of the way we have treated the Book of Mormon (verses 54–58). This condemnation has not been lifted, nor will it be until we repent. The Lord states that we must not only *say* but we must *do*. We have neither said enough nor have we done enough with this divine instrument—the key to conversion. As a result, as individuals, as families, and as the Church, we sometimes have felt the scourge and judgment God said would be 'poured out upon the children of Zion' because of our neglect of this book. . . . The Lord has inspired His servant to reemphasize the Book of Mormon to get the Church out from under condemnation—the scourge and judgment" (vii–viii; cf. 84:54–58). This message must be carried to the members of the Church throughout the world.

President John Taylor testified "that the Book of Mormon, and this book of Doctrine and Covenants . . . cost the best blood of the nineteenth century to bring them forth for the salvation of a ruined world" (135:6). Concerning the Book of Mormon, the Lord bore his own testimony: "As your Lord and your God liveth it is true" (17:6).

See also Book of Mormon, lost manuscript of (116 pages); Historical context and overview of Doctrine and Covenants 3 (p. 716), 5 (p. 717), 10 (p. 720), 17 (p. 725), and 20 (p. 728).

BIBLIOGRAPHY

Benson, Ezra Taft. *A Witness and a Warning: A Modern-day Prophet Testifies of the Book of Mormon.* Salt Lake City: Deseret Book, 1988.

CJW

Dodds, Asa

Birth: 1793, New York

Death: Unknown

Shortly after joining the Church, Asa Dodds accepted the assignment to preach the gospel with Orson Pratt. The two men were to travel from Ohio to Missouri. They served together until they reached Indiana. Pratt reported that Dodds stopped in Indiana while he continued on his journey (Pratt, 4). A short time later, during a conference held on 25 January 1832, at Amherst, Ohio, the Lord called several men to serve as missionaries. Asa Dodds was commanded to proclaim the gospel "unto the western countries" with Calves Wilson (75:15). Eight days after the receipt of the revelation, Dodds was ordained a high priest by Hyrum Smith. It is not known whether Dodds or Wilson fulfilled this mission. "Little is known of [Dodds's] whereabouts following [his] ordination. However, in 1850 he was residing in Farmington, Ohio, and working as a stonemason" (Black, 85).

BIBLIOGRAPHY

Black, Susan Easton. *Who's Who in the Doctrine & Covenants.* Salt Lake City: Deseret Book, 1997.

Pratt, Orson. *The Orson Pratt Journals.* Edited by Elden J. Watson. Salt Lake City: E. J. Watson, 1975.

RC

Dogs. *See* Appendix E.

Dominion. *See* Appendix E.

Dort, David

Birth: 6 January 1793, Surry, Cheshire County, New Hampshire

Death: 10 March 1841, Nauvoo, Hancock County, Illinois

Lucy Mack Smith traveled to Pontiac, Michigan, to visit her nephew David Dort. While there she "labored incessantly for the truth's sake, and succeeded in gaining the hearts of many, among whom were David Dort and his wife" (L. M. Smith, *History,* 216). Baptized in 1831, Dort responded to the Prophet's call for men to march with ZION'S CAMP in 1834. He moved his family to Kirtland in 1836 and served on the high council in 1837. In 1838 mob violence increased, and some prominent leaders began deserting and betraying the Church. Dort, however, remained faithful. He moved to Missouri, became a member of the Far West high council, and publicly reaffirmed his commitment to the Church and the Prophet Joseph Smith (Smith, *History,* 3:225). In January 1839 he signed a covenant along with more than two hundred other Saints to "assist one another, to the utmost of our abilities, in removing from this state [Missouri]" (Smith, *History,* 3:251–53). After Dort settled in Nauvoo, the Prophet called him to serve on the high council in January 1841 (124:131–32).

BIBLIOGRAPHY

Smith, Joseph. *History of The Church of Jesus Christ of Latter-day Saints.* Edited by B. H. Roberts. 7 vols. 2d ed. rev. Salt Lake City: The Church of Jesus Christ of Latter-day Saints, 1932–51.

Smith, Lucy Mack. *History of Joseph Smith by His Mother.* Edited by Preston Nibley. Salt Lake City: Bookcraft, 1958.

KWF

Dove, form of. *See* Form of a dove.

Dyed garments. *See* Jesus Christ, second coming of.

Behold, the time has fully come, which was spoken of by the mouth of Malachi—testifying that he [Elijah] should be sent, before the great and dreadful day of the Lord come—To turn the hearts of the fathers to the children, and the children to the fathers, lest the whole earth be smitten with a curse.

110:14–15

Eames, Ruggles

Birth: Unknown

Death: Unknown

In 1831 Ruggles Eames, a resident of Medina, Ohio, was baptized a member of the Church and ordained a priest. At the 25 January 1832 conference of the Church in Amherst, Ohio, Joseph Smith received a revelation appointing Eames to serve a mission with Stephen Burnett (75:35). Apparently, neither man responded to the Prophet's call. A few weeks later, Stephen Burnett was called to go with another man to preach the gospel (80:1–2). In 1832 Eames withdrew from the Church. His name appears on the United States Federal Census of 1840 as a resident of Van Buren County, Iowa, married, father of two children, and owner of three slaves. His whereabouts after 1840 and the circumstances of his death are unknown.

KWF

Earth, the

The planet prepared for spirit offspring of GOD THE FATHER to obtain physical bodies and to work out their eternal salvation. The revelations in the Doctrine and Covenants provide significant information concerning the organization of the earth, its purposes, and its ultimate destiny. The earth was organized over a period of six creative "days," or periods of indeterminate length (14:9; 77:10, 12; 93:9; cf. Abr. 4:5, 8, 13, 19, 23, 31) to provide a probationary place for mortal testing (Abr. 3:24–26). One of the divine purposes for the very existence of the earth is MARRIAGE and family—"that it might be filled with the measure of man, according to his creation before the world was made" (49:17). *See* Life, purposes of.

When Adam and Eve were placed in the Garden of Eden, both they and the earth were in a paradisiacal condition. After they partook of the fruit of the tree of knowledge of good and evil, they were expelled from the garden and from the literal presence of God. *See* Fall of Adam and Eve, the.

The earth too fell from its pristine glory to become a telestial world. The planet became what may be called "Mother Earth," a life-giving planet. Though devoid of its former glory, it retained its ability to provide for its inhabitants—man and beast—with that which was necessary to sustain life through earth's ordained telestial and terrestrial periods. The earth was organized to provide sustenance for the billions of male and female spirits destined to live their lives upon it "during the seven thousand years of its . . . temporal existence," perhaps counting from the fall of Adam and Eve to the end of the millennial reign of Christ (77:6–7, 12; Smith, 5:64). Concerning this period of time, the Lord said, "The earth is full, and there is enough and to spare; yea, I prepared all things, and have given unto the children of men to be agents unto themselves" (104:17). Mortals, therefore, are stewards over the resources of the earth and are accountable to God for how they use them (104:13–18). How they use those resources and how they work out their salvation upon the earth will affect their individual destinies for all eternity.

Being foreordained to become a celestial world, the earth abides the law of a celestial kingdom (88:17–19, 25–26). It therefore complies with the ordinances of baptism by water and by fire. Brigham Young remarked: "This earth . . . has been baptized with water [the flood in the time of Noah], will be baptized by fire and the Holy Ghost, and by-and-by will be prepared for the faithful to dwell upon" (8:83). The baptism by fire, or being "born again," will be in connection with the second coming of Jesus Christ. This rebirth of the earth follows the death of all things telestial, for when the Redeemer returns in glory, "every corruptible thing, both of man, or of the beasts of the field, or of the fowls of the heavens, or of the fish of the sea, that dwells upon all the face of the earth, shall be consumed; and also that of element shall melt with fervent heat; and all things shall become new, that my knowledge and glory may dwell upon all the earth" (101:24–25). When all things telestial have been removed, the earth will "be renewed and receive its paradisiacal glory" (A of F 10), a condition similar to the glory it had before the Fall. *See* Jesus Christ, second coming of.

In being renewed, earth's land masses will be restored to their original relationships: "And the land of Jerusalem and the land of Zion shall be turned back into their own place, and the earth shall be like as it was in the days before it was divided" in the days of Peleg (133:24; Gen. 10:25). The Son of God will reign over the earth for a thousand years, millennial conditions will prevail throughout the earth, and "Satan shall be bound" and "shall not have power to tempt any man" (45:55; 101:28; A of F 10). Alluding to his return to earth for his millennial reign, the Son of God described the earth as his "footstool" (38:17).

"When the thousand years are ended, and men again begin to deny their God," Satan will be "loosed" for a "little season" (29:22; 43:31; 88:111). When this season following the MILLENNIUM comes to an end, planet Earth will "die," or "pass away"; but it will be "quickened again," resurrected; "and there shall be a new heaven and a new earth," a celestial orb—the eternal home of those men and women who are worthy of celestial glory (29:23; 88:17–20, 25–26).

The statement in Revelation 4:6 concerning the glorified earth becoming as a "sea of glass" is confirmed in the Doctrine and Covenants (77:1). "This earth, in its sanctified and immortal state, will be made like unto crystal and will be a Urim and Thummim to the inhabitants who dwell thereon, whereby all things pertaining to an inferior kingdom, or all kingdoms of a lower order, will be manifest to those who dwell on it" (130:9).

In addition to clarifying the purpose, history, and destiny of the earth, the Doctrine and Covenants contains many qualifying phrases pertaining to the earth. For example:

• "Armies of the earth" (60:4), "nations of the earth" (43:23; 64:43), "inhabitants of the earth" (63:32; 87:6), "kindreds of the earth" (124:58), "honorable men of the earth" (76:75), "great ones of the earth" (109:55); these phrases all refer to people.

• "The end [singular] of the earth" (38:5; 43:31–32; 88:101), meaning that time at the end of the Millennium when the earth will be changed to a celestial sphere (88:17–20). This is not the same as the "end of the world," or the end of telestial wickedness, which will take

place when the Savior returns to the earth and establishes millennial conditions (see JS–M 1:4, 55; 13:39–41).

• "The ends [plural] of the earth" (1:11; 45:49; 105:29), "the four quarters of the earth" (33:6; 45:46; 77:8), "the four parts of the earth" (110:11), "the uttermost parts of the earth" (58:64), "the face of the earth" (5:33; 29:18; 63:33, 36) are phrases referring to the message of the gospel and the works of God being taken to every people and enveloping every corner of the globe.

• "The things of the earth" (30:2; cf. 25:10), or worldliness, as opposed to spiritual things.

• "The whole earth," its purposes, itself, and its inhabitants would be "smitten with a curse" and "utterly destroyed" or "utterly wasted" at the coming of the Lord if the gospel of Jesus Christ is not accepted and obeyed and temple ordinances are not performed for the living and the dead (1:30; 2:3; 5:19; 27:9; 98:17; 110:15; 128:17).

In fulfilling its destiny, Earth will join an endless procession of other worlds which have achieved the same glory, for as the Lord declared to Moses: "And as one earth shall pass away, and the heavens thereof even so shall another come; and there is no end to my works, neither to my words" (Moses 1:38; see also vv. 17–39; cf. D&C 76:24; 88:41–61; Moses 7:30).

BIBLIOGRAPHY

Smith, Joseph. *History of The Church of Jesus Christ of Latter-day Saints*. Edited by B. H. Roberts. 7 vols. 2d ed. rev. Salt Lake City: The Church of Jesus Christ of Latter-day Saints, 1932–51.

Young, Brigham. *Journal of Discourses*. 26 vols. London: Latter-day Saints' Book Depot, 1854–86.

RT

Eden, the Garden of

The first earthly dwelling place of Adam and Eve (Moses 3:8). Latter-day prophets have taught that the garden was located in Jackson County, Missouri, the center place of ZION, attributing that understanding to the Prophet Joseph Smith (Widtsoe, 394–97; Smith, 3:74; cf. Lee, 35; Benson, 587–88; McConkie, 303). In the Doctrine and Covenants, the only mention of the Garden of Eden by name is in 29:41,

Landscape of the Garden of Eden; painting by Grant Romney Clawson. Based on the Garden Room murals in the Los Angeles California Temple.

referring to Adam and Eve's being cast out of the garden. After leaving the garden, Adam and Eve dwelt at ADAM-ONDI-AHMAN (Woodruff, 71; 107:53–57; 117:8; cf. 116:1).

Though mentioned by name only once in the Doctrine and Covenants, the reality of people and events associated with the Garden of Eden is confirmed throughout the revelations. Adam is identified as Michael, "the father of all, the prince of all, the ancient of days" (27:11), who holds "the keys of salvation under the counsel and direction of the Holy One" (78:16). The reality of "our glorious Mother Eve" is affirmed (138:39), as is the reality of the devil and his role in the premortal realms, during the existence of the earth, and beyond (29:27–29, 36–37; 76:25–48). Modern revelation makes clear that Adam was given his AGENCY in the Garden of Eden and that by use of that agency, he brought about the Fall. When tempted of the devil, he transgressed the conditions of Eden and was cast out of the Garden and from God's presence (29:34–41). It seems clear that the singular use of "Adam" in these verses includes both Adam and Eve.

Evidently the whole earth will experience Eden-like conditions during the MILLENNIUM. Isaiah testified, "For the Lord shall comfort Zion: he will comfort all her waste places; and he will make her wilderness like Eden, and her desert like the garden of the Lord" (Isa. 51:3).

See also Fall of Adam and Eve, the.

BIBLIOGRAPHY

Benson, Ezra Taft. *The Teachings of Ezra Taft Benson*. Salt Lake City: Bookcraft, 1988.

Lee, Harold B. *The Teachings of Harold B. Lee*. Edited by Clyde J. Williams. Salt Lake City: Bookcraft, 1996.

McConkie, Bruce R. *Mormon Doctrine*. 2d ed. Salt Lake City: Bookcraft, 1977.

Smith, Joseph Fielding. *Doctrines of Salvation*. Compiled by Bruce R. McConkie. 3 vols. Salt Lake City: Bookcraft, 1954–56.

Widtsoe, John A. *Evidences and Reconciliations*. Arranged by G. Homer Durham. 3 vols in 1. Salt Lake City: Bookcraft, 1987.

Woodruff, Wilford. *Wilford Woodruff*. Teachings of Presidents of the Church series. Salt Lake City: The Church of Jesus Christ of Latter-day Saints, 2004.

MAG

Edify, edification

Intellectual and spiritual enlightenment communicated through the Holy Spirit. The word *edify* and its various forms are employed eleven times in the Doctrine and Covenants, but the associated principle of being enlightened by the Holy Spirit appears dozens of times.

When both teacher and hearer enjoy the power of the "Spirit of truth . . . both are edified and rejoice together. And that which doth not edify is not of God, and is darkness" (50:21–23). The Lord has revealed "a pattern in all things, that ye may not be deceived." Even if someone's speaking is impressive and seems to edify, the speaker is "of God" only "if he obey mine ordinances" (52:14–19). "All may be edified of all" when each person in a group is given "an equal privilege" to speak (88:122). Those in attendance are to "instruct and edify each other," that they may learn their duties and "know how to act and direct [the Lord's] church" (43:8–11; 107:85). All members are needed to labor in their respective callings and to contribute according to their talents, "that all may be edified together, that the system may be kept perfect" (84:110). "And let not the head say unto the feet it hath no need of the feet; for without the feet how shall the body be able to stand?" (84:109; cf. Eph. 4:11–16). The Lord promised Parley P. Pratt "a multiplicity of blessings, in expounding all scriptures and mysteries to the edification of the school [in Zion], and of the church in Zion" (97:1–5). Those who are strong are directed to edify those who are weak, that they may "become strong also" (84:106; cf. Rom. 15:1–2). Members of the School of the Prophets in Kirtland were instructed by revelation how to proceed in their meetings and were told to follow those instructions with "prayer and thanksgiving, as the Spirit shall give utterance in all your doings in the house of the Lord, in the school of the prophets, that it may become a sanctuary, a tabernacle of the Holy Spirit to your edification" (88:127–41). In a revelation to Brigham Young at Winter Quarters in January 1847 regarding the trek west, the Lord commanded the Saints to "let your words tend to edifying one another," a command that may well apply to all Saints in all circumstances (136:24).

CFO

Effectual. *See* Appendix E.

Egypt

The land of ancient Israel's captivity, located in northeastern Africa. The word *Egypt* appears once in the Doctrine and Covenants (136:22), the Lord himself declaring that he led ancient Israel out of Egypt and can also save latter-day Israel (136:22). The effect of ancient Egypt on scripture, sacred history, and the Doctrine and Covenants is far greater than a single entry might suggest.

Even without using the word *Egypt,* several passages in the revelations show latter-day parallels to events associated with ancient Egypt: Moses parting the Red Sea by the spirit of revelation (8:3); the destroying angel to pass over obedient Latter-day Saints as he passed over

ancient Israel (89:21); a latter-day prophet likened to Moses leading Israel out of bondage (103:15–20); and the Lord to soften the hearts of people in the last days as he did with Pharaoh (105:27; cf. Gen. 47:1–10).

Egypt has been conspicuous in the historical and cultural background of the work of the Lord for four thousand years, being visible in the Old and New Testaments, the Book of Mormon, and the books of Moses and Abraham in the Pearl of Great Price. Abraham, Jacob, Joseph, the twelve tribes, Moses, Aaron, and later Joseph, Mary, and the boy Jesus all had personal experiences in Egypt. The various Book of Mormon plates (1 Ne. 1:2; Morm. 9:32) and the plates of brass (Mosiah 1:4) were engraved in Egyptian. The first two of the Ten Commandments direct Israel away from the Egyptian religious practices of many gods and graven images (Ex. 20:3–5).

RJM

Elder(s)

An office in the Melchizedek Priesthood (107:7); an appropriate title in addressing those who hold any office in the Melchizedek Priesthood, whether elder, high priest, patriarch, seventy, or apostle. In that sense, "an apostle is an elder" (20:38) but with special keys and duties in the Church. The president of the Church is also designated as the "presiding elder of the church" (88:140; cf. 124:125). *See* Priesthood offices.

In the revelations, leaders of the Church are often identified as "the first elders of my church" (105:7, 13; 108:4), or simply, "the elders of the church" (20:16, 81; cf. 36:7; 42:89; 46:27; 52:1–2). In many instances "the elders of the church," or "the elders of my church," or just "elders," refer to all who hold the Melchizedek Priesthood (36:7; 41:2; 42:44; 44:1; 52:21; 64:1; 75:23; 115:3; 133:8; 138:57). On the day the Church was organized, Joseph Smith was sustained as the "first elder of this church," and Oliver Cowdery was sustained as the "second elder of this church" (20:2–3).

An elder is to be ordained "according to the gifts and callings of God unto him . . . by the power of the Holy Ghost, which is in the one who ordains him" (20:60). In some circumstances elders may serve as counselors to bishops (42:31, 71), although it is currently the general practice in the Church for counselors to bishops to be ordained high priests. An elder belongs to a QUORUM of ninety-six elders presided over by a president, who is to "sit in council with them, and to teach them according to the covenants" (107:60, 89). Elders are "to administer in spiritual things" and "have a right to officiate in all . . . offices of the church when there are no higher authorities present" (107:12). The duties of an elder include ordaining other elders and priests, teachers, and deacons; baptizing and confirming those who join the Church; administering the sacrament; watching over the Church; and taking the lead in meetings when a high priest is not present (107:11) and conducting those meetings "as they are led by the Holy Ghost, according to the commandments and revelations of God" (20:38–45). Elders are also to bless little children (20:70) and those who are sick (42:43–44).

MISSIONARY WORK is an important calling of elders. "All the faithful elders of [the] church" are instructed, "Go ye into all the world, preach[ing] the gospel to every creature" (68:7–9; cf. 42:12–14; 133:8–11). The Lord says to them: "Ye are not sent forth to be taught, but to teach the children of men the things which I have put into your hands by the power of my Spirit; and ye are to be taught from on high. Sanctify yourselves and ye shall be endowed with power, that ye may give even as I have spoken" (43:15–16).

Missionary service does not end with death. In his vision of the redemption of the dead, President Joseph F. Smith saw "that the faithful elders of this dispensation, when they depart from mortal life, continue their labors in the preaching of the gospel of repentance and redemption, through the sacrifice of the Only Begotten Son of God, among those who are in darkness and under the bondage of sin in the great world of the spirits of the dead" (138:57). See Salvation for the dead.

HDG

Elect, election

Those who "hear [the Lord's] voice and harden not their hearts" (29:7; cf. 84:33–34).

The Lord promised that he would gather his "elect from the four quarters of the earth" (33:6) and provide an inspired translation of the Bible "to the salvation of mine own elect" (35:20).

Emma Smith, wife of the Prophet Joseph Smith, is described as "an elect lady" (25:3). The Prophet explained, "*Elect* meant to be *Elected* to a *certain work* &c, & that the revelation was then fulfilled by Sister Emma's Election to the Presidency of the Soc[i]ety, she having previously been ordained to expound the Scriptures" (2:371). President Gordon B. Hinckley interpreted this same phrase in a broader sense: "Emma was called 'an elect lady.' That is, to use another line of scripture, she was a 'chosen vessel of the Lord.' (See Moro. 7:31.)" (91).

Election, a form of *elect,* is used twice in the Doctrine and Covenants. One use is in connection with Sidney Gilbert's "calling and election in the church" to be an agent to buy land for the Church (53:1, 4; 57:6). In this context the term "calling and election" simply means to be appointed to a position in the Church. The other use is in the phrase "election of grace": "The Lord hath redeemed his people, Israel, according to the election of grace, which was brought to pass by the faith and covenant of their fathers" (84:99). This *election* comes through covenants, obedience, and the GRACE of God.

See also Chosen; More sure word of prophecy.

BIBLIOGRAPHY

Hinckley, Gordon B. "'If Thou Art Faithful.'" *Ensign* 14 (November 1984): 89–92.

Smith, Joseph. *The Papers of Joseph Smith.* Edited by Dean C. Jessee. 2 vols. Salt Lake City: Deseret Book, 1989–92.

TRV

Elect lady. *See* Smith, Emma.

Election of grace. *See* Grace.

Element(s)

The words *element* and *elements* are found in three sections of the Doctrine and Covenants, with somewhat different applications:

1. In section 93 *elements* refers to the makeup of the physical body of man. Verses 33 and 34

teach that "man is spirit. The elements are eternal, and spirit and element, inseparably connected [in a resurrected state], receive a fulness of joy; and when separated, man cannot receive a fulness of joy." Verse 35 adds that the "elements," or physical bodies of mankind, are considered "the tabernacle of God, even temples," and that such "temples" are not to be "defiled."

2. Section 101 uses the word *element* to mean the physical matter of which the world is made—corruptible matter "of element" that will "melt with fervent heat; and all things shall become new" when the Savior returns to the earth in judgment and "all flesh shall see [him] together" (101:23–25).

3. Section 122 employs the term *elements* to mean all the negative environmental influences and powers that may be arrayed against Joseph Smith: "If the heavens gather blackness, and all the elements combine to hedge up the way." While Joseph was incarcerated in LIBERTY JAIL, the Lord enumerated over a dozen discomforting scenarios that the Prophet could face but promised "that all these things shall give thee experience, and shall be for thy good," and the Lord would stand by him "forever and ever" (122:4–9).

LED

Elias

A name-title used in the Doctrine and Covenants for at least four men who have had, or will yet have, important roles in bringing about the restoration of the fulness of the gospel of Jesus Christ in the latter days.

One Elias is Elijah, the Old Testament prophet, "who was with Moses on the Mount of Transfiguration" (138:45). He is listed as being among those who were visited by Jesus in the world of spirits following the crucifixion (138:36–51). Because Elijah was both a restorer and a preparer (Mal. 4:5–6; D&C 110:13–15), Joseph Smith taught that his name (in its Greek form, *Elias*) can be used to represent anyone who has the calling of a forerunner, gatherer, or restorer (Ehat and Cook, 327–28, 333–36); thus Elijah is probably the Elias mentioned in 76:100.

Another Elias, who received "the keys of

bringing to pass the restoration of all things spoken by the mouth of all the holy prophets since the world began, concerning the last days" (27:6), was identified by Joseph Smith as Noah (Ehat and Cook, 8, 13). This Elias was Gabriel, who visited Zacharias to tell him of the birth of his son, John the Baptist (27:6–7; cf. Luke 1:8–19).

In the Kirtland Temple, a restorer of KEYS called Elias appeared to Joseph Smith and Oliver Cowdery and "committed the dispensation of the gospel of Abraham, saying that in us and our seed all generations after us should be blessed" (110:12). The language points to ancient scriptural promises (e.g., Gen. 22:18; Abr. 2:9–11) and suggests that Elias restored keys pertaining to the covenant of Abraham and the joining of worthy women and men to create eternal family units. The identity of this messenger is not known.

The apostle John, who was both a restorer of priesthood and a facilitator of the gathering of Israel and restoring all things, is also called Elias (77:14; 7:1–6).

The role of the Elias in section 77, to whom is given the power to seal and gather Israel and to "restore all things" (v. 9), resembles the assignment given to the apostle John in the same section (v. 14). This Elias may be another prophet-angel or a composite of all the ministers of preparation and restoration (128:20–21), perhaps even Jesus Christ himself, of whom all Eliases are types (see JST John 1:21–22, 28).

BIBLIOGRAPHY

Ehat, Andrew F., and Lyndon W. Cook, comps. and eds. *The Words of Joseph Smith.* Provo, Utah: Religious Studies Center, Brigham Young University, 1980.

KPJ

Elihu

Melchizedek Priesthood bearer who lived between the time of Abraham (ca. 2000 B.C.) and the time of Moses (ca. 1260 B.C.). In a modern revelation Elihu was identified in Moses' priesthood lineage; he received the priesthood "under the hand of Jeremy" and ordained Caleb (84:8–9). The Old Testament refers to several men named Elihu (Job 32–37; 1 Sam. 1:1; 1 Chr.

12:20; 26:7); however, none fit the time frame of 84:8–9.

RJM

Elijah

Old Testament prophet from the ninth century B.C., whose name means "My God is Jehovah." Elijah preached repentance in Israel and was in conflict with the kingdom's ruling family and its paganized religion (1 Kgs. 17–2 Kgs. 2). He was translated (110:13). The Doctrine and Covenants confirms the New Testament account of his presence at the transfiguration of Jesus (138:45; cf. Matt. 17) and lists him among the ancient Saints who were "with Christ in his resurrection" (133:55; cf. Matt. 27:52–53). *See* Mount of Transfiguration; Transfiguration.

The Doctrine and Covenants confirms Malachi's prophecy that Elijah would return to the earth in the latter days and perform a ministry without which the earth would be wasted at Christ's coming (2:1–3; 35:4; 138:47–48; Mal. 4:5–6). Section 2 includes Moroni's quotation of Malachi's prophecy about Elijah in words that clarify those in the Bible: "He shall plant in the hearts of the children the promises made to the fathers, and the hearts of the children shall turn to their fathers" (2:2). Joseph Smith included the Malachi passage as it is in the King James translation in an 1842 letter to the Church, indicating, "I might have rendered a plainer translation to this, but it is sufficiently plain to suit my purpose as it stands" (128:17–18). In President Joseph F. Smith's vision of the redemption of the dead, the prophecy is mentioned with emphasis on how Elijah's coming foreshadows "the great work to be done in the temples of the Lord in the dispensation of the fulness of times, for the redemption of the dead, and the sealing of the children to their parents" (138:48).

Elijah holds "the keys of the power of turning the hearts of the fathers to the children, and the hearts of the children to the fathers" (27:9; cf. 2:2; 138:47). Joseph Smith taught that Elijah was the last of the prophets to hold that sealing power, which is necessary "to administer in all the ordinances of the priesthood and without the authority is given the ordinances could

not be administered in righteousness" (Ehat and Cook, 43). Hence, Elijah's coming in the latter days to restore the sealing KEYS was a necessary part of the restoration of all things (110:16). On 3 April 1836, Elijah appeared to Joseph Smith and Oliver Cowdery in the Kirtland Temple. The Prophet recorded, "Elijah the prophet, who was taken to heaven without tasting death, stood before us, and said: Behold, the time has fully come, which was spoken of by the mouth of Malachi—testifying that he [Elijah] should be sent, before the great and dreadful day of the Lord come—To turn the hearts of the fathers to the children, and the children to the fathers, lest the whole earth be smitten with a curse" (110:13–15).

When Jesus returns, again to "drink of the fruit of the vine" with his servants on the earth, Elijah will be among the participants (27:5–9).

See also Elias; Salvation for the dead; Seal, sealed.

BIBLIOGRAPHY

Ehat, Andrew F., and Lyndon W. Cook, comps. and eds. *The Words of Joseph Smith*. Provo, Utah: Religious Studies Center, Brigham Young University, 1980.

KPJ

Emblems. *See* Appendix E.

End of the world/end of the earth

According to the Prophet Joseph Smith and the Joseph Smith Translation of the Bible (JST), the *end of the world* refers to the destruction of the wicked at the time of Christ's second coming (JS–M 1:4, 55; JST Matt. 13:39–41; Smith, 2:271). *See* Jesus Christ, second coming of.

The Doctrine and Covenants indicates that *the end of the earth* will come at the end of the MILLENNIUM (42:31), when "the earth shall be consumed and pass away, and there shall be a new heaven and a new earth" (29:22–28), a glorified, celestialized, resurrected earth, "that bodies who are of the celestial kingdom may possess it forever and ever" (88:20; 38:5; 88:101–2; cf. 107:42).

Other verses in the revelations are not so clear in differentiating the *end of the world* and the *end of the earth* (e.g., 19:3; 132:49) and require careful examination of context to determine the possible meaning.

See also Earth, the; World(s), world's, worldliness.

BIBLIOGRAPHY

Smith, Joseph. *History of The Church of Jesus Christ of Latter-day Saints.* Edited by B. H. Roberts. 7 vols. 2d ed. rev. Salt Lake City: The Church of Jesus Christ of Latter-day Saints, 1932–51.

JWL

Endless punishment. *See* Punish, punished, punishment.

Endless torment. *See* Punish, punished, punishment.

Endow, endowed, endowment

To endow is to bestow a gift, authority, or power; an endowment is that gift, authority, or power. In a revelation recorded in 1843, *endowment* was associated with the bestowal of priesthood KEYS, authority, and power upon Joseph Smith as prophet, seer, and revelator (132:7, 45, 59). Among members of The Church of Jesus Christ of Latter-day Saints, *endow* and *endowment* generally denote the bestowal of power and blessings associated with TEMPLE ordinances and covenants. When considered in the historical context of Joseph Smith's time, these terms also carry a pentecostal connotation encompassing a wide range of spiritual experiences.

Early in 1831, the Lord commanded the Saints in New York to migrate to "the Ohio." There, he promised, they should be "endowed with power from on high" (38:32, 38; 39:15; 43:16). In 1833, the Lord chastened the Saints for delaying the building of the temple in Kirtland, Ohio, but promised that he would give them power to build it if they would keep his commandments. It was the Lord's "design" that the temple be the place where he would "endow those whom [he had] chosen with power from on high" (95:1–8, 11). In the aftermath of ZION'S CAMP, in June 1834, another revelation promised the eventual redemption of ZION and a "great endowment and blessing to be poured out" upon the elders of the Church in that yet-to-be-built temple, if they "are faithful and

continue in humility before me" (105:9–12, 18, 33).

In late March 1836, the house of the Lord in Kirtland was formally dedicated (109). In connection with that day of dedication, the Prophet recorded: "I met the quorums in the evening. . . . Brother George A. Smith arose and began to prophesy, when a noise was heard like the sound of a rushing mighty wind, which filled the Temple, and all the congregation simultaneously arose, being moved upon by an invisible power; many began to speak in tongues and prophesy; others saw glorious visions; and I beheld the Temple was filled with angels, which fact I declared to the congregation. The people of the neighborhood came running together (hearing an unusual sound within, and seeing a bright light like a pillar of fire resting upon the Temple), and were astonished at what was taking place. This continued until the meeting closed at eleven p.m." (Smith, 2:428). On 3 April 1836, the Lord accepted the Kirtland "house" and confirmed the "endowment with which my servants have been endowed" (110:7, 9). *See* Historical context and overview of Doctrine and Covenants 109 (p. 817); Kirtland Temple dedication.

The Doctrine and Covenants thus documents many promises of the Lord to endow his faithful followers with power from on high. To these promises, and their fulfillment, must be added the testimony of the Prophet Joseph Smith's personal history and the journals of Church members that are replete with accounts of pentecostal and covenantal experiences—endowments from on high bestowed upon the Saints during the early days of the restoration of the fulness of the gospel of Jesus Christ.

The endowment of spiritual manifestations discussed above is not the same as the ordinances of the *endowment* received by faithful Saints in holy temples throughout the world since the building of the Nauvoo Temple (124:39). That endowment, explained Brigham Young, is "to receive all those ordinances in the house of the Lord, which are necessary for you, after you have departed this life, to enable you to walk back to the presence of the Father, passing the angels who stand as sentinels, being enabled to give them the key words, the signs and tokens, pertaining to the holy Priesthood, and gain your eternal exaltation" (416). In April 1841, a reference to *endowment* was made in a lengthy revelation linking the term with the building of the Nauvoo Temple (124:39).

The word *endowment* also appears in Official Declaration 1 referring to the ENDOWMENT HOUSE in Salt Lake City. Before the Salt Lake Temple was completed, it was the location dedicated for the solemnizing of eternal marriages.

See also Wash, washed, washing(s).

BIBLIOGRAPHY

Smith, Joseph. *History of The Church of Jesus Christ of Latter-day Saints*. Edited by B. H. Roberts. 7 vols. 2d ed. rev. Salt Lake City: The Church of Jesus Christ of Latter-day Saints, 1932–51.

Young, Brigham. *Discourses of Brigham Young*. Selected by John A. Widtsoe. Salt Lake City: Deseret Book, 1978.

JFD

Endowment House

The primary temporary facility where Latter-day Saints received TEMPLE blessings before the completion of the Salt Lake Temple and other Utah temples in the closing decades of the nineteenth century. Temple blessings had been administered in such places as Brigham Young's office and the Council House, but these facilities needed to accommodate other functions as well. There was thus an immediate need for a separate facility where the Saints might receive their temple blessings. Construction of the Endowment House, as the structure soon came to be called, commenced during the summer of 1854. Located in the northwest corner of the temple block (where the visitors' center with the Christus statue is today), the Endowment House was a two-story adobe structure that measured 44 by 34 feet. Construction was relatively simple and so progressed rapidly. The building was completed by the spring of the following year and was dedicated 5 May 1855. Even though the Saints regarded this building as only a "temporary temple" (Holzapfel, 336), President Brigham Young named it "The House of the Lord." He promised that "the spirit of the Lord would be in it, for no one will be permitted

to go into it to pollute it" (Lund, 213). Over the years this prophetic statement was confirmed through repeated spiritual experiences within its walls. The dedicatory prayer was offered by Heber C. Kimball, who presided over the work in this holy house. The first endowments and sealings were performed that same day (JH, 5 May 1855).

The ground floor contained a series of four ordinance rooms, each one being a step higher than the one before, giving a sense of upward progress. The celestial room and a sealing room were on the second floor. In 1856, the year after the building opened, an addition provided a baptismal font, which was dedicated on 2 October. Here the Saints renewed their covenants through rebaptism, received their temple endowments, and performed baptisms for the dead.

For the next three decades, the Endowment House was an influence for good in the lives of Latter-day Saints. Thousands received their endowment, with between twenty-five and thirty receiving these blessings on a typical day. Outgoing missionaries received instructions from Church leaders and were set apart there. The Endowment House also provided the setting for as many as twenty-five hundred eternal marriages each year.

President Brigham Young specified that certain ordinances, including endowments for the dead and the sealing of children to parents, could not be performed in the Endowment House but must be done in temples (Cowan, 72–73). President Heber C. Kimball continued to have general supervision of this work until his death in 1868. Elder Wilford Woodruff was also heavily involved, spending from thirty to sixty days each year helping to administer sacred ordinances in the Endowment House.

By the late 1880s, the Salt Lake Temple was nearing completion and three other Utah temples were in service, so there was less need for the aging adobe Endowment House. Because unauthorized plural marriages were allegedly performed there, President Wilford Woodruff ordered that the Endowment House be "taken down without delay" (OD 1). Carried out in November of 1889, this destruction was a public gesture to demonstrate the Church's willingness to stop the practice of plural MARRIAGE.

See also Endow, endowed, endowment; Salvation for the dead; Seal, sealed.

BIBLIOGRAPHY

Cowan, Richard O. *Temples to Dot the Earth.* Springville, Utah: Cedar Fort, 1997.

Holzapfel, Richard Neitzel. "The Endowment House." In *Encyclopedia of Latter-day Saint History,* edited by Arnold K. Garr, Donald Q. Cannon, and Richard O. Cowan. Salt Lake City: Deseret Book, 2000.

Journal History of the Church, 1896–1923. Church History Library, The Church of Jesus Christ of Latter-day Saints, Salt Lake City, Utah.

Lund, A. William. "The Endowment House." *Improvement Era* 39, no. 4 (April 1936): 213.

Lundwall, N. B. *Temples of the Most High.* Salt Lake City: Bookcraft, 1947.

ROC

Endure, endure to the end

A word or phrase that means to persist in righteous thought, word, and deed throughout mortality and beyond, in spite of temptations and trials encountered along the way. The Doctrine and Covenants teaches that those who endure to the end will inherit ETERNAL LIFE and be saved or exalted in the kingdom of God (e.g., 14:7; 18:22; 53:7; 121:8, 29). The Lord promises that those who endure in faith shall "overcome the world" and receive "an inheritance upon the earth when the day of transfiguration shall come" (63:20, 47), either in the Millennium or in eternity (45:58; 88:26).

Those in ancient Israel who "hardened their hearts" were not able to "endure [God's] presence" in the wilderness. That principle would apply both in time and in eternity (84:24; cf. 76:53, 60, 62; 93:19; Jacob 1:7).

Courtesy Church History Library.

The Endowment House in Salt Lake City, about 1855. Located on the northwest corner of Temple Square, this structure was built and dedicated in 1855 to be used for temple ordinances while the Saints labored to complete the nearby Salt Lake Temple. The Endowment House was taken down in 1889, as mentioned in Official Declaration 1 by President Wilford Woodruff.

The Lord "requireth the heart and a willing mind," as well as OBEDIENCE, in order to qualify for his blessings (64:34–36). Indeed, those who will not endure the Lord's chastening or being tried "even as Abraham" cannot be sanctified (101:4–5). The Lord has promised those who "suffer persecution for my name, and endure in faith, though they are called to lay down their lives for my sake," shall receive great blessings "when the Lord shall come," including the revelation of "all things" (101:32–36).

The Prophet Joseph Smith taught that to be seated at the marriage feast described in Luke 22 was to have a place in the kingdom of heaven and "that those who keep the commandments of the Lord and walk in His statutes to the end, are the only individuals permitted to sit at this glorious feast" (2:19; cf. 58:6–11). See Marriage of the Lamb.

When defining his GOSPEL, the Savior included enduring to the end as one of the fundamental principles, along with faith, repentance, baptism, and reception of the Holy Ghost (3 Ne. 27:13–21). The Doctrine and Covenants affirms the importance of enduring with the following promise, "But blessed are they who are faithful and endure, whether in life or in death, for they shall inherit eternal life" (50:5). Enduring to the end in righteousness is thus an important doctrine in the gospel of Jesus Christ. See Righteous, the/righteousness.

BIBLIOGRAPHY

Smith, Joseph. *History of The Church of Jesus Christ of Latter-day Saints.* Edited by B. H. Roberts. 7 vols. 2d ed. rev. Salt Lake City: The Church of Jesus Christ of Latter-day Saints, 1932–51.

JPL

Enemy, enemies

In a broad sense, *enemy* means adversary. The Doctrine and Covenants identifies SATAN as "the enemy" of righteousness and "the great persecutor of the church" (86:3). Those who likewise seek to undermine or overthrow the works of God and who persecute those who strive to live in accordance with the gospel are known, generally, as enemies. In several passages, the Lord counsels the Saints how to live so that Satan, the "enemy to all righteousness" (Mosiah 4:14),

and his followers, both seen and unseen, will not have POWER over them: "Gird up your loins and be prepared. Behold, the kingdom is yours, and the enemy shall not overcome" (38:9). "Go thy way and do as I have told you, and fear not thine enemies; for they shall not have power to stop my work" (136:17). "Be diligent in keeping all my commandments, lest judgments come upon you, and your faith fail you, and your enemies triumph over you" (136:42). See Gird up your loins; Commandment(s); Faith; Fear; Judgment(s); Obedience.

In addition to defining *enemies* as the unrighteous and ungodly in general, the Doctrine and Covenants also uses the term in reference to specific adversaries of Church members and leaders. For example, in the revelation given to the Prophet Joseph Smith recorded in section 27, he is commanded not to "purchase wine neither strong drink of your enemies" (v. 3). The instruction to make "new among you" WINE that could be used for the sacrament was, perhaps, a response to those "enemies" who were seeking to poison and kill Joseph Smith (vv. 3–4). In this context, the term *enemy* probably referred to specific wicked and conspiring people, not just nonbelievers. In a similar vein, Joseph Smith and Sidney Rigdon were commanded to "confound your enemies; call upon them to meet you both in public and in private; and inasmuch as ye are faithful their shame shall be made manifest" (71:7). The specific enemies referred to in this revelation were Ezra Booth, Simonds Ryder, and other apostates, some of whom had written derogatory articles in local newspapers and held public meetings denouncing "Mormonism" and defaming the character of Joseph Smith. In accordance with this revelation, Joseph and Sidney preached in communities in Ohio, responding to the outrageous claims of their apostate enemies and "to mitigate public prejudice against the new Church" (Cook, 117). Other specific "enemies" referred to in the Doctrine and Covenants include those enemies "in the secret chambers" seeking the lives of the Saints in New York (38:28), those who conspired against Joseph Smith in his imprisonment in LIBERTY JAIL (122:4, 6–7), and those who sought to arrest and extradite him from Illinois to Missouri on trumped-up charges (127:1–2).

The most frequent use of the term *enemies* in the Doctrine and Covenants, however, is to refer to persecutors of Church members in Missouri. In June 1831 the Lord revealed to the Saints that "if ye are faithful ye shall assemble yourselves together to rejoice upon the land of Missouri, which is the land of your inheritance, which is now the land of your enemies" (52:42). Over the next several years, Latter-day Saints gathering in Missouri faced PERSECUTION, death, and expulsion from Jackson County and later from the state. Those involved in this persecution are referred to as enemies in several revelations (101, 103, 105). With the Missouri persecutions as the context, section 98 contains important instructions concerning how the Saints are to deal with their enemies. Although the revelation contains counsel concerning the appropriate response to one's enemies, including when it is justified to retaliate or go to war, the underlying message is of the necessity of patience (v. 25) and forgiveness (vv. 40–45). *See* Missouri period.

BIBLIOGRAPHY

Cook, Lyndon W. *The Revelations of the Prophet Joseph Smith.* Salt Lake City: Deseret Book, 1985.

BLT

Enjoined. *See* Appendix E.

Enmity. *See* Appendix E.

Enoch

An ancient patriarch, seventh generation from Adam, noted eleven times in the Doctrine and Covenants. In the Bible, only four verses treat him and his work (Gen. 5:21–24), although the existence of three ancient apocryphal texts bearing his name attests to his enduring legacy.

Through Joseph Smith, more about Enoch has come to light, now recorded in Moses 6–7 and in the Doctrine and Covenants. Scriptural sources record nothing about his birth. Twice he received priesthood blessings from Adam, the first at "twenty-five years . . . when he was ordained" and again when "he was sixty-five."

Furthermore, Enoch "saw the Lord, and he walked with him, and was before his face continually . . . three hundred and sixty-five years." Moreover, he was present in "the valley of Adam-ondi-Ahman," where, "three years previous to the death of Adam," he was a recipient of Adam's "last blessing." The proceedings of that occasion, including Adam's prophecy about "whatsoever should befall his posterity unto the latest generation," were "written in the book of Enoch" (107:48–49, 53, 56–57).

The second blessing of Enoch by Adam, when Enoch was sixty-five, may tie to Enoch's prophetic call, for after he turned sixty-five, "the Spirit of God descended . . . upon him," and "he heard a voice from heaven, saying: Enoch, my son, prophesy" (Moses 6:25–27). Although Enoch was reticent to accept the call (Moses 6:31), from that time on "he walked with [the Lord]" (107:49).

In time, Enoch built a city and drew in those obedient to the Lord. This city became known as "the City of Holiness, even ZION," a city that enjoyed both a divine protecting hand and the presence of the Lord himself. Later, the Lord took the inhabitants of the city "up into heaven" (Moses 7:16–21). This last act became a proof of the Lord's far-reaching powers, and in ancient times, "all holy men" sought the translated city (45:11–14).

So remarkable was the translation of Enoch's community that it stands as evidence of Jesus' advocating power for righteous souls: "As many as have believed in my name . . . by the virtue of the blood which I have spilt, have I pleaded before the Father for them" (38:4). Scripture contrasts the happy lot of Enoch and his fellow citizens with the fate of "the residue of the wicked" whom the Lord keeps "in chains of darkness until the judgment" (38:5; cf. Moses 7:28–39).

Enoch is listed among several religious leaders whom some claim to follow, though they "received not the gospel, neither the testimony of Jesus" (76:100–101). He is also among those through whom the priesthood was handed down from the days of Adam (84:6–17) and among many ancient prophets, apostles, and patriarchs who were supported in their afflictions and redeemed by the Lord (133:52–55).

Enoch's enormous influence is seen by the fact that in ancient times the higher priesthood was known as the "order of Enoch" and God's congregation was designated as the "church of Enoch . . . whose names are written in heaven" (76:57, 67–68). Enoch was translated when he was 430 years old (107:49).

See also Book of Enoch; Church of Enoch; Order of Enoch; Translated beings; Zion; Zion of Enoch.

BIBLIOGRAPHY

Draper, Richard D., S. Kent Brown, and Michael D. Rhodes. *The Pearl of Great Price: A Verse-by-Verse Commentary.* Salt Lake City: Deseret Book, 2005.

McConkie, Joseph Fielding, and Craig J. Ostler. *Revelations of the Restoration: A Commentary on the Doctrine and Covenants and Other Modern Revelations.* Salt Lake City: Deseret Book, 2000.

Nibley, Hugh. *Enoch the Prophet.* Salt Lake City: Deseret Book, 1986.

Robinson, Stephen E., and H. Dean Garrett. *A Commentary on the Doctrine and Covenants.* 4 vols. Salt Lake City: Deseret Book, 2000–2005.

SKB

Enoch, book of. *See* Book of Enoch.

Enoch, church of. *See* Church of Enoch.

Enoch, order of. *See* Order of Enoch.

Enoch, Zion of. *See* Zion of Enoch.

Enos

HIGH PRIEST, ordained PATRIARCH, and grandson of Adam, who ordained him at the age of 134 years and 4 months (107:44). Enos was "taught . . . in the ways of God" by his father, Seth; he "begat many sons and daughters" and died at age 905 (Moses 6:13–18). A revelation on PRIESTHOOD in the Doctrine and Covenants affirms that the patriarchal priesthood to which Enos was ordained was "instituted in the days of Adam, and came down by lineage . . . from Adam to Seth . . . [to] Enos" and so forth (107:39–52).

Enos was present with seven generations of patriarchs and the "residue of [Adam's] posterity who were righteous" at ADAM-ONDI-AHMAN three years before the death of Adam. In that gathering Adam bestowed his last blessing upon those

present. The Lord appeared, "and they rose up and blessed Adam, and called him Michael, the prince, the archangel" (107:53–54).

RJM

Ensign

A flag, banner, standard, or symbol raised up as a signal to gather. Figuratively, latter-day ZION is to be an ensign to which the faithful from every nation will gather (64:41–43). The Saints are to "lift up an ensign of peace" to all people, friends and enemies alike, "unto the ends of the earth" (105:38–40). The term is found frequently in the writings of Isaiah, where it can also be understood figuratively to refer to some aspect of the restoration of the gospel (Isa. 5:26; 11:10, 12; 18:3). Accordingly, concerning the identity of the "root of Jesse" mentioned in Isaiah 11:10, Joseph Smith proclaimed, "Thus saith the Lord, it is a descendant of Jesse, as well as of Joseph, unto whom rightly belongs the priesthood, and the keys of the kingdom, for an ensign, and for the gathering of my people in the last days" (113:5–6; cf. Isa. 11:12). *See* Isaiah quotations in the Doctrine and Covenants.

The term *standard* is sometimes used as a synonym for *ensign* (45:9; 98:34; 115:4–5).

See also Gather, gathering.

TBB

Ephraim

Second son of Joseph (Gen. 41:52), who, along with Manasseh, was adopted by Jacob (Israel) as his own child and upon whom he bestowed the birthright blessing (Gen. 48:19–20; cf. Deut. 33:17; 1 Chr. 5:1–2; Jer. 31:9). Thus the descendants of Ephraim became a tribe in Israel and exerted a leadership role in Old Testament times among the tribes, especially in the kingdom of Israel. Ephraim's descendants were largely scattered throughout the earth when Assyria destroyed the kingdom of Israel (ca. 722 B.C., 2 Kgs. 15:29; 17:6). The Doctrine and Covenants affirms that the tribe of Ephraim is once again to play a leadership role in the last days, especially in the gathering of Israel. Some of this will take place through the "rod" of Jesse, who will be a descendant of Joseph, specifically through Ephraim (113:3–4). *See* Isaiah quotations in the Doctrine and Covenants.

Ephraim's tribal leadership is also highlighted when the Lord speaks of the tribes of Israel, "they who are in the north countries" (133:26), bringing their rich treasures unto Ephraim. The returning tribes will be "crowned with glory" in Zion "by the hands of the servants of the Lord, even the children of Ephraim," and be filled with joy; "this is the blessing of the everlasting God upon the tribes of Israel, and the richer blessing upon the head of Ephraim and his fellows" (133:30–34).

In a revelation in Kirtland, Ohio, 11 September 1831, the Lord, speaking about obtaining an inheritance in Zion (Missouri), declared that "the rebellious shall be cut off out of the land." He then specified that "the rebellious are not of the blood of Ephraim" (64:35–36). This may mean that those who are literally of Ephraim will not rebel, but more likely it indicates that while Ephraimites will largely be true to the Lord, those who do rebel will be disowned from the prestigious tribe, which will need the most valiant of Israelites to fulfill all its responsibilities in the last days.

Ephraim is also mentioned in 27:5, where the Lord revealed that he "committed the keys of the record of the stick of Ephraim," the Book of Mormon, to Moroni.

See also Stick of Ephraim.

KMM

Ephraim, stick of. *See* Stick of Ephraim.

Equality

In the Doctrine and Covenants, the concept of equality is used in four contexts:

1. In the law of CONSECRATION. The Lord's law of consecration defines equality as having equal claim upon the resources of the bishop's storehouse, "according to his family, according to his circumstances and his wants and needs" (51:3), "inasmuch as his wants are just" (82:17). The Lord said, "In your temporal things you shall be equal, and this not grudgingly" (70:14). The Saints must be "equal in the bonds of heavenly things, yea, and earthly things also, for the obtaining of heavenly things. For if ye are not

equal in earthly things ye cannot be equal in obtaining heavenly things" (78:5–6). He also said, "Let every man . . . be alike among this people, and receive alike, that ye may be one" (51:9).

2. In teaching. "Appoint among yourselves a teacher, and let not all be spokesmen at once; but let one speak at a time and let all listen unto his sayings, that when all have spoken that all may be edified of all, and that every man may have an equal privilege" (88:122).

3. In priesthood leadership. Counselors in the First Presidency are "accounted as equal" with the prophet-president in holding the keys of the kingdom (90:6). The Quorum of the Twelve Apostles is "equal in authority and power" to that of the First Presidency (107:24). Also, the "high council in Zion" and "the standing high councils, at the stakes of Zion," formed quorums "equal in authority . . . to the quorum of the presidency, or to the traveling high council" (107:36–37). It is clear that there is a hierarchy of presiding authority among all these quorums (107:33–34, 65–68); however they are all equally authorized to preside over and manage the affairs of the Church in their respective stewardships, as directed by the president of the Church.

4. Among exalted beings. In celestial glory the Father makes those who dwell in his presence "equal in power, and in might, and in dominion" (76:95). The Saints, or holy ones, shall be "made equal with [the Lamb of God]" (88:107). They become joint-heirs with Christ, co-inheritors with him of all that the Father has (50:27; 76:55, 59; 84:38). *See* Exalt, exaltation.

DKO

Esaias

A Melchizedek Priesthood bearer who lived in Abraham's day "and was blessed of him" (84:13). He is uniquely noted as having received the priesthood "under the hand of God," (84:12); all the others listed in a recounting of their priesthood lineage from Adam to Moses were ordained by mortals (84:6–17). Esaias ordained a prophet named Gad (84:11). Nothing else is known of this Esaias. He is not to be confused with the Jewish prophet Isaiah, who lived about thirteen hundred years later and whose name, in Greek translation, is Esaias, as seen in Luke 3:4; 4:17; and Acts 8:28–30. The Esaias in 76:100 seems to refer to this early Esaias, because the same sentence also refers to Isaiah.

RJM

Escutcheon. *See* Appendix E.

Especial. *See* Witness, witnesses.

Essaying. *See* Appendix E.

Eternal damnation. *See* Punish, punished, punishment.

Eternal life

The greatest of all the gifts of God (14:7). Eternal life is more than immortality, or living forever, which results from overcoming physical death through resurrection (29:43). Rather, eternal life is to be "crowned with honor, and glory, *and* immortality" (75:5; emphasis added; cf. 128:23; 138:51). Eternal life is spoken of as a crown to symbolize the supremely exalted status of those who enter the highest degree of the celestial kingdom of God the Father and stand on his right hand (20:14; 66:12; 88:4–5; 131:1–4; 138:51). It is the same as exaltation or godhood, the kind of life the Heavenly Parents of all mankind enjoy, including a fulness of glory and "a continuation of the seeds forever and ever" (132:19). Therefore, those who obtain eternal life also obtain "eternal lives," meaning that in the resurrection they will have an eternal increase, a continuation of lives, or posterity, forever; they will possess "all power," even having "the angels . . . subject unto them" (132:19–20, 24). They will have "all things" placed in their hands by God the Eternal Father, which comprehends "his fulness" and "his glory" (76:55–56).

Thus, one of the preeminent requirements for gaining eternal life is participation in the eternal MARRIAGE covenant. Without this priesthood ordinance, even men and women who are worthy to inherit other parts of the celestial kingdom "cannot be enlarged, but remain separately and singly, without exaltation, in their saved condition, to all eternity; and from henceforth are not gods, but are angels of God forever and ever"

(132:17; cf. 131:1–4). The Prophet Joseph Smith clearly taught the relationship between eternal life and eternal marriage: "Except a man and his wife enter into an everlasting covenant and be married for eternity . . . by the power and authority of the Holy Priesthood, they will cease to increase when they die; that is, they will not have any children after the resurrection. But those who are married by the power and authority of the priesthood . . . will continue to increase and have children in the celestial glory" (5:391).

Dozens of references in the revelations identify other divine requirements for obtaining eternal life. The Lord promises this gift to those who receive the restored GOSPEL in faith and work righteousness (20:14; cf. 10:50; 59:23); remain firm and diligent in keeping the commandments (5:22; 30:8); "seek the face of the Lord always, that in patience ye may possess your souls" (101:38); and become sanctified through REPENTANCE (133:62).

Faithful missionaries, those who labor with their might, lift up their "voices as with the sound of a trump," and proclaim "the truth according to the revelations and commandments" which the Lord has given are promised eternal life (75:4). Concomitantly, those who lay down their lives for the name of Jesus Christ will be blessed with "life eternal" (98:13). The phrases "eternal life" and "life eternal" are the exact equivalent of each other. The Lord commands all persons "to give diligent heed to the words of eternal life," meaning the commandments and covenants he has given through his servants (84:43–44; 98:20; cf. 1:37–38; 21:4–5).

Because eternal life is a gift made possible through the ATONEMENT of JESUS CHRIST (45:8), it is essential that all individuals know by the power of the Holy Ghost "that Jesus Christ is the Son of God, and that he was crucified for the sins of the world," or "believe on" and "continue faithful" in the testimonies of those who know (46:13–14). The Lord has made clear, however, that knowing is not sufficient; one must endure in faithfulness to the end of one's life in order to inherit eternal life (50:5). *See* Endure, endure to the end.

Authorized servants of God, possessing

the KEYS of the Holy PRIESTHOOD, have power to seal up men and women (husbands and wives) to eternal life (132:7, 19–20; cf. 68:12). Individuals so sealed while still in mortality may receive "the more sure word of prophecy," which means they know "by revelation and the spirit of prophecy, through the power of the Holy Priesthood" that they will receive eternal life (131:5). *See* Seal, sealed.

See also Exalt, exaltation; More sure word of prophecy; Salvation.

BIBLIOGRAPHY

Smith, Joseph. *History of The Church of Jesus Christ of Latter-day Saints.* Edited by B. H. Roberts. 7 vols. 2d ed. rev. Salt Lake City: The Church of Jesus Christ of Latter-day Saints, 1932–51.

ACS

Eternal lives. *See* Marriage.

Eternal punishment. *See* Punish, punished, punishment.

Eternal round, one. *See* One eternal round.

Eternity

A term used in the Doctrine and Covenants with variant meanings and contexts:

1. The heavens. "Thus saith the Lord . . . the same which looked upon the wide expanse of eternity . . . before the world was made" (38:1, 12; cf. Moses 7:41). Section 88 teaches that God is "in the bosom of eternity" and "in the midst of all things"—the light, the life, the law, and the power by which all things exist and continue (88:5–13).

2. Immortality, or forever—having no end. God said that the righteous "shall be gathered unto me in time and in eternity," time being mortality and eternity being immortality (39:22; cf. 38:20; 72:3). The all-inclusive phrase "for time and for all eternity" (132:7, 18–19) represents an everlasting covenant made for this life and forever. "From eternity to eternity means from the spirit existence through the probation which we are in, and then back again to the eternal existence which will follow" (Smith, 1:12), or "from days of old, and for ages to come" (76:7). The Lord God, the Savior, is the same "from eternity to eternity" (76:4).

3. The "riches of eternity." The "riches of eternity" are frequently alluded to: "If ye seek the riches which it is the will of the Father to give unto you, ye shall be the richest of all people, for ye shall have the riches of eternity" (38:39; 67:2; 78:18). When the Father shares with the righteous all that he has (84:38; cf. 50:27; 76:55, 59), would that not be "the riches of eternity" and "the wonders of eternity" (38:39; 76:8), "immortality and eternal life" (Moses 1:39)? God, understandably, is displeased when his children "seek not earnestly the riches of eternity" (68:31). *See* Rich, riches.

4. The "solemnities of eternity." The Lord wants his followers to ponder things everlasting, things of an eternal nature: "Let the solemnities of eternity rest upon your minds" (43:34).

BIBLIOGRAPHY

Smith, Joseph Fielding. *Doctrines of Salvation.* Compiled by Bruce R. McConkie. 3 vols. Salt Lake City: Bookcraft, 1954–56.

DKO

Ether

The last Jaredite prophet and record keeper. Moroni's abridgment in the Book of Mormon of the Jaredite record is known as the book of Ether. The one reference to the book of Ether in the Doctrine and Covenants is in connection with the MARTYRDOM OF JOSEPH AND HYRUM SMITH. Before they left for Carthage Jail and ultimately their martyrdom, Hyrum Smith "turned down the leaf" containing Ether 12:36–38, perhaps reflecting his own feelings and bidding farewell (135:4–5).

DKO

Evangelical ministers. *See* Patriarch(s).

Eve

"The mother of all living . . . the first of all women," the mother of the human family on the earth, and the wife of Adam (Moses 4:26–27; Gen. 3:20). Mentioned once by name in the Doctrine and Covenants, she was, with Adam, among "the great and mighty ones," the spirits of the righteous, in attendance in the postmortal spirit world when the Savior visited as a spirit between his crucifixion and his resurrection (138:38–39).

Negative attitudes held by some in the world concerning Eve's role in the Fall are the result of an incomplete and shallow understanding of the plan of salvation and Eve's nobility and character. Only in latter-day revelation and the teachings of modern prophets is it made clear that Eve rightly shares eternal glory with Adam in the presence of God. Her comprehension of the necessity and eternal benefits of the Fall, and also the joy of redemption through the Only Begotten Son of God, is magnificently expressed in Moses 5:9–11.

Eve existed as an intelligent premortal spirit and was chosen by the Father because of her righteousness to be placed in the Garden of Eden with Adam. *See* Eden, the Garden of.

President Spencer W. Kimball taught that the story of Eve being formed from Adam's rib is figurative (71). In every particular she is a child of God (McConkie, 242).

Eve was a most beneficial and complementary companion to her husband, Adam, truly "an help meet [or appropriate] for him" (Moses 3:18, 20) to share responsibilities, happiness, difficulties, and work incident to mortality and family life. After the Fall, of necessity they ate bread by the sweat of their brow, as the Lord had commanded (Moses 5:1), and Eve shared in these labors with Adam (Moses 5:1). Their marriage relationship was designated by the Lord to be permanent, as they were married before they were mortal and subject to death and the Lord commanded that they should "remain" together (Moses 4:18; McConkie, 242).

See also Fall of Adam and Eve, the.

BIBLIOGRAPHY

Kimball, Spencer W. "The Blessings and Responsibilities of Womanhood." *Ensign* 6 (March 1976): 70–73.

McConkie, Bruce R. *Mormon Doctrine.* 2d ed. Salt Lake City: Bookcraft, 1966.

RJM

Everlasting covenant. *See* New and everlasting covenant.

Adam and Eve Teaching Their Children; *painting by Del Parson. In his vision of the redemption of the dead, President Joseph F. Smith saw "our glorious Mother Eve, with many of her faithful daughters who had lived through the ages and worshiped the true and living God" (D&C 138:39).*

Everlasting fire. *See* Fire.

Everlasting punishment. *See* Punish, punished, punishment.

Evil

The antithesis of GOOD; devil-inspired attitudes and behavior that make one guilty before God and lead to spiritual degeneration and unhappiness.

The Doctrine and Covenants identifies the devil as "that evil one" who "taketh away light and truth, through disobedience, from the children of men" (93:36–39) and who, through "evil design," tried to destroy belief in the translation of the Book of Mormon, stirring men "up to iniquity against that which is good . . . that he may lead their souls to destruction" and "destroy the work of God" (10:14, 20–23). The Lord said of those who, in this instance, were led by the devil: "They love darkness rather than light, *because* their deeds are evil" (10:21; emphasis added), indicating that doing evil can cause a love of darkness in mankind (cf. 29:43–45).

The revelations contain the general injunction to "forsake all evil and cleave unto all good" (98:11; cf. 124:116) and indicate that those guilty of a crime should be punished "according to their criminality and their tendency to evil among men" (134:8). The revelations also identify a number of evils that are to be avoided: evil speaking, specifically against one's neighbor (20:54; 42:27; 136:23); refusing to forgive one another "in their hearts" (64:8); unbelief and disobedience (76:17; 84:76); taking the Lord's name in vain (136:21; cf. 63:59–64); and adding to or taking from what the Lord has commanded (98:6–7, 10; 124:119–20; cf. 10:67–68; 93:20–25). In section 105, the Lord said of Saints in Missouri that they were "full of all manner of evil, and do not impart of their substance, as becometh saints, to the poor and afflicted among them" (105:3).

In section 27 the Lord instructed: "Take upon you my whole armor, that ye may be able to withstand the evil day." Here, "the evil day" likely refers to the evils and temptations of the world, "the fiery darts of the wicked" (27:15–18; cf. Eph. 6:11–17). *See* Armor of God.

In section 46 the Lord enumerated several sources of evil, including "evil spirits, or doctrines of devils, or the commandments of men; for some are of men, and others of devils." In order to protect the Saints from these seductive influences, the Lord instructed them that they were "commanded in all things to ask of God, who giveth liberally; and that which the Spirit testifies unto you even so I would that ye should do in all holiness of heart, walking uprightly before me, considering the end of your salvation, doing all things with prayer and thanksgiving" (46:7).

Eventually, evil brings unhappiness and misery (Morm. 2:13; cf. 3 Ne. 27:11; Alma 41:3–13), and should be avoided. Its presence, however, is evidence of the divine gift of AGENCY, a necessary part of the plan of salvation. The Lord revealed, "It must needs be that the devil should tempt the children of men, or they could not be agents unto themselves; for if they never should have bitter they could not know the sweet" (29:39; cf. 2 Ne. 2:11–13; Moses 6:47–57). *See* Fall of Adam and Eve, the.

Everyone experiences some level of evil in this world. That experience highlights the contrast between good and evil and exalts the feelings of joy the gospel of Jesus Christ brings (e.g., 11:13–14; 18:14–16; 42:61; 45:71; 133:33).

See also Satan.

LED

Evil spirits. *See* Historical context and overview of Doctrine and Covenants 50 (p. 756).

Exalt, exaltation

The word *exalt* and its various forms are used in several contexts in the Doctrine and Covenants:

1. To aggrandize or honor oneself. Speaking of Martin Harris, the Lord said, "He exalts himself and does not humble himself sufficiently before me" (5:24). In a revelation to Thomas B. Marsh, president of the Quorum of the Twelve Apostles, and to "all the Twelve," the Lord commanded, "Exalt not yourselves" (112:14–15). Sidney Rigdon was chastised because "he exalted himself in his heart, and received not counsel" (63:55). As a general principle, the

Lord revealed, "He that exalteth himself shall be abased, and he that abaseth himself shall be exalted" (101:42; cf. 112:3; 124:114). *See* Humble, humility.

2. To be made better, lifted up, advanced in one's condition or in the eyes of others. Speaking of the nations of the earth, the Lord promised the Saints, "I will visit and soften their hearts, many of them for your good, that ye may find grace in their eyes, that they may come to the light of truth, and the Gentiles to the exaltation or lifting up of Zion" (124:9). In the dedicatory prayer of the Kirtland Temple, Joseph Smith prayed for "all the presidents of [the] church, that thy right hand may exalt them, with all their families" (109:71). Thomas B. Marsh was told, "By thy word many high ones shall be brought low, and by thy word many low ones shall be exalted" (112:8). It is the Lord's purpose to provide for his Saints, but it is to be done in the Lord's "own way." That way is for the Saints to practice the principles of consecration, for the rich to share their abundance with the poor, "that the poor shall be exalted, in that the rich are made low" (104:13–18).

3. To be physically raised up to new geographical heights. In connection with the Savior's second coming, there will be great convulsions of the earth. The earth will "tremble and . . . reel to and fro as a drunken man." The valleys shall be "exalted," and the mountains "made low" (49:23; cf. 109:74).

4. To achieve the highest blessings bestowed upon God's children. In the premortal estate, spirit children were born of divine parents. These spirits are clothed with physical bodies of flesh and bones when they are born into mortality. The body and spirit are separated at death and inseparably reunited in the resurrection. Those who are sanctified in Christ through obedience to the laws and ordinances of the gospel will come forth in the morning of the first resurrection to their exaltation (76:50–70) and "receive a fulness of joy" (93:33–34; 138:17).

One's inheritance in the world to come will be determined by the laws that one obeys. Those who abide a celestial law will receive a celestial glory; likewise, those who abide either terrestrial or telestial law receive either terrestrial

or telestial glory (88:16–32). Entrance into the celestial kingdom is obtained through the ordinance of baptism (76:50–52). Within the celestial kingdom are "three heavens or degrees" of glory. One obtains the highest heaven in the celestial kingdom only in and through the ordinance of eternal MARRIAGE (131:1–4). Those married according to the celestial order are promised that through their faithfulness they may "inherit thrones, kingdoms, principalities, and powers, dominions, all heights and depths," and that they will enjoy a "continuation of the seeds" forever (132:19–24). That is, they "will continue to increase and have children in the celestial glory" (Smith, 5:391). "Wherefore . . . they are gods" (76:58; cf. 76:50–70), receiving the same blessings as Abraham, Isaac, and Jacob, who "have entered into their exaltation, according to the promises, and sit upon thrones, and are not angels but are gods" (132:37). Those who do not "enter into this order of the priesthood [meaning the new and everlasting covenant of marriage]" (131:1–4) will not be exalted in the life to come but will "remain separately and singly, without exaltation . . . to all eternity; and from henceforth are not gods, but are angels of God forever and ever" (132:17). Joseph Smith taught that by following the prescribed path, faithful Saints may obtain "the same power, the same glory and the same exaltation, until [they] arrive at the station of a god, and ascend the throne of eternal power, the same as those who have gone before" (6:306).

The Lord assured Joseph Smith of his exaltation with the words, "I am the Lord thy God, and will be with thee even unto the end of the world, and through all eternity; for verily I seal upon you your exaltation, and prepare a throne for you in the kingdom of my Father, with Abraham your father" (132:49; cf. 121:7–8). *See* More sure word of prophecy.

See also Eternal life; Gods; Kingdoms of glory and perdition, vision of; Salvation.

BIBLIOGRAPHY

Smith, Joseph. *History of The Church of Jesus Christ of Latter-day Saints.* Edited by B. H. Roberts. 7 vols. 2d ed. rev. Salt Lake City: The Church of Jesus Christ of Latter-day Saints, 1932–51.

JFM

Excommunication. *See* Church discipline.

Exhort. *See* Appendix E.

Exigency. *See* Appendix E.

Expedient, expediency

Necessary, useful, advantageous, or profitable, under specific circumstances. As used in the Doctrine and Covenants, expedient actions were a means to a desired end; they were necessary and desirable and often based on timing. Depending on timely obedience, opportunities can be taken or lost. For instance, at some points the work of translating was expedient, and at other times it was not (9:11; 37:1; 73:3–4). Of the many times *expedient* is used, most are associated with the words "in me," where the Lord explains that an act is advantageous or necessary for his purposes, as, for example, Sidney Rigdon acting as a spokesman (100:9), John Whitmer keeping a history (47:1), the Church making Kirtland a strong stake (96:1), elders receiving their endowment (105:33), and Church members going to Ohio (37:3).

In other passages, Latter-day Saints were told not to do something because the timing was not expedient, such as redeeming Zion (105:9, 13) and teaching certain people (42:57; 45:72; cf. 44:1–3; 71:1; 96:5). At other times some action or proposed activity had no particular bearing on proposed outcomes and therefore was evidently not expedient. In these circumstances, the Lord used such phrases as "as seemeth you good," and "it mattereth not unto me" (60:5; 62:5; cf. 80:3).

Jesus promised that "whatsoever ye ask the Father in my name it shall be given unto you, that is expedient for you; and if ye ask anything that is not expedient for you, it shall turn unto your condemnation" (88:64–65). In determining what is expedient in any and all circumstances, Jesus taught that one must "ask the Father in my name, in faith believing that you shall receive, and you shall have the Holy Ghost, which manifesteth all things which are expedient unto the children of men" (18:18).

MJW

Expound. *See* Appendix E.

Extortion. *See* Appendix E.

Eye single. *See* Eye(s).

Eye(s)

Terms with both literal and figurative meanings. Literally, the organ of sight. The Three Witnesses were assured that they would be able to testify to the reality of the plates of Mormon, the breastplate, the Urim and Thummim, the sword of Laban, and "the miraculous directors" (that is, the "Liahona"; Alma 37:38) because they would see these items "with [their] eyes" (17:1–3; cf. 45:37; 127:6; 128:2; 133:45). In trying to describe the glorious presence of Jesus Christ, the Prophet Joseph Smith testified that the Lord's "eyes were as a flame of fire" (110:3). The expression "see eye to eye" in 84:98, which parallels the usage of the phrase in Isaiah 52:8 in the King James Version (cf. Mosiah 15:29; 3 Ne. 16:18; 20:32), can be rendered from the Hebrew with the sense that people "will see it with their own eyes" (NIV Isa. 52:8). The righteous who "remain" after the scourging of the wicked will be eyewitnesses of the Lord's marvelous works concerning the redemption of Zion. They will be "filled with the knowledge of the Lord, and shall see eye to eye, and shall lift up their voice . . . together" (84:98) in singing the new song given in 84:99–102.

Figurative meanings for *eye* or *eyes* are found in the Doctrine and Covenants in several contexts:

1. An "eye single to the glory of God" (4:5; 82:19; cf. 27:2; 55:1; 59:1; 88:67), signifying a person's loyalty to the Lord and his or her willingness to follow the will of God in all things.

2. God's omniscience, his awareness of all people and all happenings, as in "the same which knoweth all things, for all things are present before mine eyes" (38:2; cf. 1:1; 62:2; 67:2; 121:2, 4).

3. A person's intent and desires, the focus of attention, symbolically revealed by the eyes, as in "they also seek not earnestly the riches of eternity, but their eyes are full of greediness" (68:31; cf. 56:17; 128:17).

4. Obtaining knowledge and understanding, as in "by the power of the Spirit our eyes were opened and our understandings were

enlightened, so as to see and understand the things of God" (76:12; cf. 76:19; 88:11; 110:1; 138:11, 29). In a revelatory question-and-answer session, recorded in section 77, the question is asked about the meaning of the eyes of the beasts seen by John the Beloved in the book of Revelation. The response is, "Their eyes are a representation of light and knowledge, that is, they are full of knowledge" (v. 4).

5. Being changed "in the twinkling of an eye," referring to righteous mortals in the Millennium who instead of experiencing death and subsequent burial are changed instantaneously from mortality to a resurrected state (43:32; 63:51; 101:31).

6. Perception of someone or how someone is viewed. The early Saints in Missouri were told by the Lord that if they would faithfully follow his instructions, Missourians not of their faith would see them in a positive light: "I will give unto you favor and grace in their eyes . . . in this way you may find favor in the eyes of the people" (105:25–26; cf. 45:72; 63:15; 90:23). John Taylor wrote that Joseph Smith "lived great, and he died great in the eyes of God and his people" (135:3).

7. In the view of, or in the judgment of, such as "in the eyes of the law" (64:13) or "it is meet in mine eyes that she should go" (90:30; cf. 121:16).

RGM

Ezekiel

An Old Testament prophet (ca. 590–572 B.C.) mentioned four times by name in scripture, twice in the Old Testament (Ezek. 1:3; 24:24) and twice in the Doctrine and Covenants (29:21; 138:43). The authenticity of his life and teachings is confirmed by the latter-day scriptures.

Things which "have not come to pass but surely must" were "spoken by the mouth of Ezekiel the prophet." For example, "there shall be a great hailstorm sent forth to destroy the crops of the earth," "the beasts of the forest and the fowls of the air shall devour" the wicked, and "the whore of all the earth, shall be cast down by devouring fire, . . . for abominations shall not reign" (29:14–21; cf. 43:25; 109:30; Ezek. 13:11, 13; 38:22; 39:17–20).

In his vision of the great and mighty ones in the world of spirits, President Joseph F. Smith saw "Ezekiel, who was shown in vision the great valley of dry bones, which were to be clothed upon with flesh, to come forth again in the resurrection of the dead, living souls" (138:43). Ezekiel's vision of the dry bones that were covered once again with sinews, flesh, and skin, and finally filled with their spirits and restored to the land of Israel, their inheritance, is recorded in Ezekiel 37:1–14.

DKO

Organize yourselves; prepare every needful thing; and establish a house, even a house of prayer, a house of fasting, a house of faith, a house of learning, a house of glory, a house of order; a house of God. 88:119

Faith

Faith is confidence and trust in someone or something that drive one's thoughts, feelings, and behavior. Faith unto salvation must be centered in GOD THE FATHER and his Son, JESUS CHRIST, and his atoning sacrifice (20:29). In the preface to the Doctrine and Covenants, the Lord revealed that a principal purpose of the revelations of the Restoration is "that faith also might increase in the earth" (1:21). The revelations recorded in the Doctrine and Covenants are rich in explaining and applying many facets of faith. In addition, the revelations evidence that God continues to manifest himself to mortals and to direct his Church in the latter days (20:11–12).

Faith is required to serve in God's kingdom

The work of the restoration of the fulness of the gospel required and continues to require faith. Referring to the translation of the Book of Mormon plates and the spirit of revelation, the Savior said to Oliver Cowdery, "Remember that without faith you can do nothing; therefore ask in faith" (8:10; cf. 18:19). He told both Joseph Smith Sr. and Joseph Knight Sr. that they must have faith to participate in the marvelous work he was about to bring forth on the earth (4:5–6, 12:8).

As evidenced by the testimony of the Three Witnesses, sacred experiences do not come unless there is faith. Martin Harris had asked to see the Book of Mormon plates as a witness to him. In essence, Harris said, "If you show me the plates, I will have faith." In response, the Lord told Martin Harris that to be one of the three special witnesses, he needed to "humble himself in mighty prayer and faith, in the sincerity of his heart, then will I grant unto him a view of the things which he desires to see" (5:24). When the Lord called Oliver Cowdery, David Whitmer, and Martin Harris to be three special witnesses of the Book of Mormon plates and other sacred items, he admonished them that "it is by your faith that you shall obtain a view of them, even by that faith which was had by the prophets of old" (17:2; Smith, 1:52–59).

Faith brings signs and other blessings

The Lord warned the Saints that "faith cometh not by signs, but signs follow those that believe" (63:9). Witnessing SIGNS cannot substitute for true faith and can lead to spiritual weakness and personal apostasy (63:12–13). On the other hand, the Lord promised that signs "shall follow them that believe," including power to "do many wonderful works" in the name of Jesus Christ: to "cast out devils," to "heal the sick," to "open the eyes of the blind," to "unstop the ears of the deaf" that "the tongue of the dumb shall speak," and that poison administered to them "shall not hurt them" (84:65–72). The Saints are commanded, however, not to "boast themselves of these things, neither speak them before the world" (84:73; cf. 105:24). The revelations of the Doctrine and Covenants refer to both the faith of those who have power to heal and those who have the faith to be healed (42:48–52; 46:19–20), explaining also how to serve those who "have not faith to be healed" (42:43).

"When faith comes it brings its train of attendants with it—apostles, prophets, evangelists, pastors, teachers, gifts, wisdom, knowledge, miracles, healings, tongues, interpretation of tongues, etc. All these appear when faith appears on the earth, and disappear when it disappears from the earth; for these are the effects of faith, and always have attended, and always will, attend it. For where faith is, there will the knowledge of God be also, with all things which pertain thereto—revelations, visions, and dreams, as well as every necessary thing, in order that the possessors of faith may be perfected, and obtain salvation; for God must change, otherwise faith will prevail with him. And he who possesses it will, through it, obtain all necessary knowledge and wisdom, until he shall know God, and the Lord Jesus Christ, whom he has sent—whom to know is eternal life" (*Lectures*, 83).

Learning by faith

Faith is also a component of education. The Lord commanded the Saints to "seek learning, even by study and also by faith" (88:118). Although all aspects of education can be enhanced by approaching learning through sincere study and the prayer of faith, this principle is especially true regarding gospel truths. Eternal truths may be searched out but never fully understood without faith. Faith can open the heavens to knowledge and understanding. President Harold B. Lee explained, "Let no one think that 'learning by faith' contemplates an easy or lazy way to gain knowledge and ripen it into wisdom. From heavenly instructions and added to which are the experiences of almost anyone who has sought diligently for heavenly guidance, one may readily understand that *learning by faith requires the bending of the whole soul through worthy living to become attuned to the Holy Spirit of the Lord,* the calling up from the depths of one's own mental searching, and the linking of our own efforts to receive the true witness of the Spirit" (10; emphasis added). Thus, learning by faith requires individuals to obey the truths of the gospel as part of their seeking knowledge.

Faith to endure

Faith includes facing life's challenges with confidence in the Lord's promise: "Search diligently, pray always, and be believing, and all things shall work together for your good, if ye walk uprightly and remember the covenant wherewith ye have covenanted one with another" (90:24; cf. 100:15). Some blessings of faith come only when we are united in prayer and effort with others (29:6). The Lord promised that the Holy Ghost and other blessings would come through "the prayer of faith" (42:14; 93:51; cf. 18:18; 35:9). And the shield of faith, as part of the "whole armor" of God, adds power to stand against "all the fiery darts of the wicked" (27:15–18).

The Kirtland Temple was to be a "house of faith" (88:119; cf. 109:16). The same is true of other latter-day temples and buildings of worship. Within their walls, faith is increased and strengthened by sacred ordinances, inspired talks, lessons, and counsel. The activities within dedicated buildings should focus on faith in Jesus Christ. If such is the case, those who enter their doors are nourished with the good word of God, fellowship, and recommitment to holy covenants.

Church members are to uphold the First Presidency by their "confidence, faith, and prayer" (107:22). The same principle is true for all who serve and lead in the Church. None can do so effectively without the sustaining faith and support of those they serve.

Those who receive the testimony of the restoration of the gospel "in faith, and work righteousness, shall receive a crown of eternal life" (20:14). In the vision of celestial glory, the Prophet Joseph Smith and Sidney Rigdon heard a heavenly voice bear record that those "who overcome by faith, and are sealed by the Holy Spirit of promise" will inherit that kingdom (76:53).

The first lecture in LECTURES ON FAITH teaches that faith is the "first principle in revealed religion, and the foundation of all righteousness." The third lecture explains "that three things are necessary in order that any rational and intelligent being may exercise faith in God unto life and salvation. First, the idea that he actually exists. Secondly, a *correct* idea of his character, perfections, and attributes. Thirdly, an actual knowledge that the course of life which he is pursuing is according to his will. For without an acquaintance with these three important facts, the faith of every rational being must be imperfect and unproductive; but with this understanding it can become perfect and fruitful, abounding in righteousness, unto the praise and glory of God the Father, and the Lord Jesus Christ" (*Lectures,* 38–39).

Faith and OBEDIENCE are inextricably connected. Faith inspires obedience (Heb. 11), and obedience is necessary to maintain faith, as the Lord instructed the Saints going west: "Be diligent in keeping all my commandments, lest . . . your faith fail you" (136:42).

See also Belief, believing; Hope.

BIBLIOGRAPHY

Lectures on Faith. Salt Lake City: Deseret Book, 1985.

Lee, Harold B. "The Iron Rod." *Ensign* 1 (June 1971): 5–10.

Smith, Joseph. *History of The Church of Jesus Christ of Latter-day Saints.* Edited by B. H. Roberts. 7 vols. 2d ed. rev. Salt Lake City: The Church of Jesus Christ of Latter-day Saints, 1932–51.

CJO

Fall of Adam and Eve, the

The result of Adam and Eve partaking of the fruit of the tree of knowledge of good and evil, the "forbidden fruit," in the Garden of Eden. Two revelations in the Doctrine and Covenants speak directly of the Fall: sections 29:34–50 and 93:38. Important truths concerning the Fall are revealed in these verses. First, it is affirmed that Adam and Eve were given their AGENCY in the matter of the Fall (29:35), and that when tempted of the devil, Adam "partook of the forbidden fruit and transgressed the commandment, wherein he became subject to the will of the devil" (29:40). Because of their transgression, Adam and Eve suffered a spiritual DEATH and were cast out of the Garden of Eden and from God's presence (29:41). Nevertheless, God ensured that Adam and Eve and their posterity should not die a temporal, or physical, death until they had the opportunity to hear the GOSPEL of "repentance and redemption, through faith" in JESUS CHRIST, which was the only way they could be redeemed from both temporal and spiritual death (29:42–45; cf. 2 Ne. 2:19–27; 9:6–27). "Little children" and "he that hath no understanding" are exempted from the same ACCOUNTABILITY required of others and "are redeemed from the foundation of the world" through the Savior's ATONEMENT (29:46–50).

Unique to the Doctrine and Covenants is the clear statement that "every spirit of man" is twice INNOCENT—once "in the beginning" (in the premortal life), and as a result of "God having redeemed man from the fall," they are innocent "again, in their infant state" (93:38) when born into mortality. Hence, though all mankind are born into a world of sin (Moses 6:55), they come to the earth personally free of sin. They are accountable and punished "for their own sins, and not for Adam's transgression" (A of F 2).

Growing out of these truths revealed about the Fall are questions that are not fully addressed in the Doctrine and Covenants; however, other latter-day scriptures and prophetic commentary provide helpful answers. Verses in the Book of Mormon (2 Ne. 2:22–25) and in the Pearl of Great Price (Moses 5:4–12) affirm clearly that the Fall was a necessary and positive step in God's plan of salvation. First, the

Adam and Eve Driven Out of Eden; *engraving by Paul Gustave Doré, 1865. "Wherefore, I, the Lord God, caused that he should be cast out from the Garden of Eden, from my presence, because of his transgression, wherein he became spiritually dead, which is the first death" (D&C 29:41).*

Fall opened the gates of mortality for the myriad of spirits waiting to come to the earth. The prophet Lehi explained that had Adam and Eve not partaken of the fruit of the tree of knowledge of good and evil, "they would have had no children"; indeed, said Lehi, "Adam fell that men might be" (2 Ne. 2:23–25). And when Eve learned of the full significance of the Fall, she "was glad, saying: Were it not for our transgression we never should have had seed" (Moses 5:11). Both Lehi and Eve declared that the Fall not only brought *mortal life* to mankind but made possible *eternal life* through the atonement of Jesus Christ (2 Ne. 2:26–29; Moses 5:11).

Why, then, was the fruit of the tree of knowledge of good and evil "forbidden"? Wherein did Adam and Eve transgress a commandment?

Moses 3:16–17 and explanations by latter-day prophets teach that the commandment regarding the tree of knowledge of good and evil can be viewed as a conditional commandment rather than as an absolute commandment; thus, the fruit of the tree was forbidden only if Adam and Eve wished to stay in the Garden of Eden. Eating the fruit transgressed, or violated, the Edenic conditions they enjoyed in the garden. The Lord instructed Adam that he could "freely eat" of every tree of the garden except the tree of knowledge of good and evil. Of that tree he could not eat "freely" because there was a consequence attached, which consequence was death. Adam was told, however, "Thou mayest choose for thyself, for it is given unto thee" (Moses 3:16–17).

Latter-day prophets explain that such a transgression was not a sin. Joseph Smith said, "Adam did not commit sin in eating the fruits, for God had decreed that he should eat and fall—but in compliance with the decree he should die" (Ehat and Cook, 63; spelling and punctuation modernized). President Joseph Fielding Smith taught: "Just why the Lord would say to Adam that he forbade him to partake of the fruit of that tree is not made clear in the Bible account, but in the original as it comes to us in the Book of Moses it is made definitely clear. It is that the Lord said to Adam that if he wished to remain as he was in the garden, then he was not to eat the fruit, but if he desired to eat it and partake of death he was at liberty to do so. So really it was not in the true sense a transgression of a divine commandment" (4:81; cf. Oaks, 72–75; Widtsoe, 192–95). But it was a transgression of the "limits of Eden" (Oaks, 73) and required that Adam and Eve be expelled from the garden, become mortal, and experience the challenges, travails, and opportunities of mortality in a fallen world. When the angel instructed Adam and Eve about the true significance of the Fall in the plan of salvation, they rejoiced and "blessed the name of God" (Moses 5:4–12).

Another question arises concerning the role of SATAN in the Fall. Why would Satan, who had rebelled against God (29:36–39) and declared war upon the Saints (76:25–29), tempt Adam to do the very thing that would further the work of God and give the spirit children of God the opportunity of mortal life, resurrection, and salvation? One answer is that Satan, not knowing "the mind of God" and wanting to "destroy the world" (Moses 4:6), having already been cast out of heaven into the earth (29:36–37; Rev. 12:9), would be eager for the spirits who had refused to follow him in the PREMORTAL EXISTENCE to come to earth, as mortals, so that he would have another opportunity to "deceive and to blind men, and to lead them captive at his will" (Moses 4:4). God uses the devil's fiendish designs for his own purposes—as an aid in mankind's exercise of agency (29:39).

Just as the fall of Adam and Eve was an intended and critical component in God's plan of salvation, so also was the atonement of Jesus Christ. The Atonement redeems all mankind from the Fall (unconditionally from temporal death, and conditionally from spiritual death) enabling all to choose ETERNAL LIFE "by obedience to the laws and ordinances of the Gospel" (A of F 3; cf. 20:17–26; Hel. 14:16–17). Adam and Eve are to be honored, even revered, for their transgression in Eden.

See also Eden, the Garden of.

BIBLIOGRAPHY

Ehat, Andrew F., and Lyndon W. Cook, comps. and eds. *The Words of Joseph Smith.* Provo, Utah: Religious Studies Center, Brigham Young University, 1980.

Oaks, Dallin H. "The Great Plan of Happiness." *Ensign* 23 (November 1993): 72–75.

Smith, Joseph Fielding. *Answers to Gospel Questions.* Compiled by Joseph Fielding Smith Jr. 5 vols. Salt Lake City: Deseret Book, 1957–66.

Widtsoe, John A. *Evidences and Reconciliations.* Arranged by G. Homer Durham. 3 vols. in 1. Salt Lake City: Bookcraft, 1960.

LED

False brethren. *See* Apostasy, of early dissenters from restored Church.

False spirits. *See* Historical context and overview of Doctrine and Covenants 50 (p. 756).

Family, families

A recurring theme in the Doctrine and Covenants is that families are to be nurtured, supported, provided for, and protected (20:47, 51; 23:6; 57:15; 58:25; 84:103; 90:19–21; 105:21; cf. 19:34–36). Families are to be wise in the use of their own resources and those of the Church. The Lord instructed the members of the First Presidency and "especially mine aged servant Joseph [Smith], Sen.": "Let your families be small . . . as pertaining to those who do not belong to your [biological] families; that those things that are provided for you, to bring to pass my work, be not taken from you and given to those that are not worthy—and thereby you be hindered in accomplishing those things which I have commanded you" (90:25–27).

Under the principles of CONSECRATION, stewardships and Church support were to be offered fairly, "every man equal according to his family . . . his circumstances . . . his wants and needs" (51:3; cf. 48:6). Help was available to needy families (42:30, 39; 52:40; 105:3) and also to the families of those called into Church or missionary service that took the breadwinner away from labors that otherwise would have provided for the family (42:71; 75:24–26, 28). Several times the Lord assured those who were concerned about their families in such cases that "they are in mine hands" and that he would "provide" for them (100:1; 118:3; cf. 31:5). Such provision at times came from the consecrations of others, as when the Church was moving west, when "the poor, the widows, the fatherless, and the families of those who have gone into the army" were to be sustained by those who had means to share (136:8; cf. 83:1–6).

In March 1833 at Kirtland, Church leaders, including all three members of the First Presidency and Bishop Newel K. Whitney, were chastened concerning their neglect of family matters. They were instructed to repent, pray diligently, and put their houses in order (93:41–50). Obedience to the Lord's commandments brings blessings to families (136:11). The Lord also revealed specific instructions to other Church leaders for the benefit of their families. William Law and Sidney Rigdon, counselors in the First Presidency, were told not to take their families from Nauvoo "unto the eastern lands," counsel both men disregarded, as they apostatized from the Church (124:82–83, 103–8).

Brigham Young, after numerous missions away from home, sometimes with his wife facing dire circumstances, was told, "It is no more required at your hand to leave your family as in times past, for your offering is acceptable to me" (126:1).

In the context of the Missouri persecutions, the Lord instructed the Latter-day Saints to "renounce war and proclaim peace" (98:16). However, he also justified them in protecting their families against repeated aggressions. If, after three appropriate warnings, an enemy continued to "smite" a man's family, he was justified in defending his loved ones as necessary. The Lord said, "Thine enemy is in thine hands; and if thou rewardest him according to his works thou art justified." But, if a person is even yet willing to "spare him," the Lord added, "thou shalt be rewarded for thy righteousness" (98:23–33).

In 1995 the First Presidency and Quorum of the Twelve Apostles issued "The Family: A Proclamation to the World," declaring that "marriage between a man and a woman is ordained of God and that the family is central to the Creator's plan for the eternal destiny of His children." The proclamation outlines the roles of husbands and wives and the principles upon which happiness in families may be obtained.

See also Children; Marriage.

BIBLIOGRAPHY

First Presidency and Council of the Twelve Apostles. "The Family: A Proclamation to the World." *Ensign*, November 1995, 102.

TDO

Far West, Missouri

Located in Mirable Township in Caldwell County, Missouri, Far West was a relatively short-lived Latter-day Saint community, existing from 1836 to 1839. Before this community was established, Jackson County had served as the main gathering place from 1831 to 1833. In mid to late 1833, violence erupted between the citizens of Jackson County and the Latter-day Saints, resulting in the Saints' expulsion from the county. At the time of their removal, most Church members relocated to the north in Clay County, where at first the citizens were considerably more open than Jackson County's old-time settlers had been to have the Latter-day Saints as neighbors. The citizens of Clay County did not expect the Saints to remain in the county permanently, however, and by the early summer of 1836 continued immigration into the region led to increased tensions and threats of renewed hostilities. On 29 June a committee of citizen leaders drafted a lengthy petition requesting that the Latter-day Saints relocate, promising assistance if they removed peaceably. To avoid conflict and for the sake of friendship with Clay County residents, Church leaders agreed to look elsewhere.

As early as 1834, Latter-day Saint families had begun moving north and east from Clay County into the more sparsely populated Ray County. Still later, in March 1836, Missouri Church leaders began searching out possible sites for permanent settlement in some of the less-inhabited regions of that county. After making extensive explorations, on 8 August 1836

William W. Phelps and John Whitmer, two members of the Missouri presidency acting as agents in behalf of the Church, purchased a one-mile-square plat (640 acres) near Shoal Creek as the main gathering place in Missouri. The site was subsequently named Far West.

As Latter-day Saints began moving into Far West and the surrounding region, Missourians thought the Mormon problem might be solved if a separate county were created exclusively for them. Alexander W. Doniphan, Clay County's representative to the state legislature and a sympathizer with the Saints, spearheaded the bill. Passage of the measure came on 29 December 1836. The new county was named Caldwell in honor of Matthew Caldwell of Kentucky, a friend, Indian scout, and soldier who had served with Alexander Doniphan's father, Joseph Doniphan.

Far West is significant to the Latter-day Saints for several reasons. From 1836 to 1839, Far West was the center of the religious and

Courtesy Church History Library.

Temple site at Far West, Missouri; photograph by George Edward Anderson, 1907. "Let the city, Far West, be a holy and consecrated land unto me; and it shall be called most holy, for the ground upon which thou standest is holy" (D&C 115:7).

political activities of the Latter-day Saints in northern Missouri. When Caldwell County was created in December 1836, Far West was designated as the county seat. From 1836 to 1839, Far West was the primary gathering place for the Latter-day Saints. Joseph Smith left Kirtland, Ohio, on 12 January 1838 and arrived at Far West on 14 March, where he took up permanent residence, thereby making Far West the Church's new headquarters. Plans were made, excavation begun, and a site dedicated for a temple in the town square. Seven revelations received by Joseph Smith at Far West between March and July 1839 have been canonized and included in the Doctrine and Covenants. See Historical context and overview of Doctrine and Covenants 113–15 (pp. 823–26) and 117–20 (pp. 828–31).

Church president Joseph F. Smith was born to Hyrum and Mary Fielding Smith at Far West on 13 November 1838. On 26 April 1839, members of the Quorum of the Twelve met at the temple site at Far West to mark their official departure for their mission to Great Britain.

The hostilities that broke out between the Missourians and the Latter-day Saints during the summer and fall of 1838 culminated in Missouri governor Lilburn W. Boggs issuing his extermination order. Joseph Smith and several other Church leaders were imprisoned, and the Latter-day Saints were expelled from the state. Many took refuge in Quincy, Adams County, Illinois, during the early winter months of 1839.

Caldwell County land records show that in April 1909 the Church reacquired a parcel of land at Far West that included the temple site. The property remained unimproved until the mid-1960s, when the first steps were undertaken to convert the property into an official Church historical site. This occurred in large part due to the work of Alvin R. Dyer, an assistant to the Quorum of the Twelve and later an additional counselor in the First Presidency. In 1968, under the direction of Church architect Emil B. Fetzer, the Far West temple site was landscaped to create a park-like visitors' area. Dedication services were held on 3 August 1968. Church leaders present included Joseph Fielding Smith, president of the Quorum of

the Twelve and an additional counselor in the First Presidency; Alvin R. Dyer; Harold B. Lee and Mark E. Petersen, members of the Quorum of the Twelve; James A. Cullimore, assistant to the Quorum of the Twelve; and Victor L. Brown, counselor in the Presiding Bishopric. President Dyer conducted the services and offered the dedicatory prayer. Approximately six hundred Latter-day Saints attended.

Since 1968, the Church has purchased additional land adjoining the temple site. See maps, pp. 414, 416, and 710.

See also Missouri period.

BIBLIOGRAPHY

Baugh, Alexander L. "The Mormon Temple Site at Far West, Caldwell County, Missouri." In The Missouri Mormon Experience, edited by Thomas M. Spencer. Columbia: University of Missouri Press, 2010, 75–99.

"'Center Stake of Zion.'" Church News, 10 August 1968, 6–7, 10.

History of Caldwell and Livingston Counties, Missouri. St. Louis: National Historical Company, 1886

Johnson, Clark V. "Let Far West Be Holy and Consecrated." In The Prophet Joseph: Essays on the Life and Mission of Joseph Smith, edited by Larry C. Porter and Susan Easton Black, 226–45. Salt Lake City: Deseret Book, 1988.

Laws of the State of Missouri, 1st Session, 9th General Assembly, 1836–1837. Jefferson City, Mo.: Jeffersonian Office, 1837.

Parkin, Max H. "Latter-day Saint Conflict in Clay County." In Missouri, edited by Arnold K. Garr and Clark V. Johnson, 254–58. Regional Studies in Latter-day Saint Church History series. Provo, Utah: Department of Church History and Doctrine, Brigham Young University, 1994.

ALB

Fasting

Fasting is the voluntary practice of denying oneself food and water or worldly pursuits as a sign of devotion, penitence, and commitment to the Lord. During the Savior's mortal ministry, Jesus referred to the principle and importance of fasting (Matt. 6:16–18; 17:21; cf. 4:1–2). In modern times the Lord instructed the Saints on three different occasions about the fast.

When the Prophet Joseph Smith organized the School of the Prophets in Kirtland, Ohio, in 1832, the Lord directed those involved to "continue in prayer and fasting from this time forth" (88:76). In the same revelation, the brethren were told to organize a "house of fasting" (88:119). A few months later the Lord declared that a solemn assembly should be called in which the members were to come with their "fastings and . . . mourning" (95:7). All three of these directives encouraged the early Saints to fast as a part of their spiritual preparation and temple worship.

An earlier revelation uses a different meaning of the term *fasting*. Speaking of Sabbath day worship, the Lord decreed that on this holy day "only let thy food be prepared with singleness of heart that thy fasting may be perfect" (59:13). This reference to fasting may have as much to do with refraining ("fasting") from worldliness on the Lord's day as it does with abstaining from food and water.

Fasting represents a measure of spiritual depth and renewal. Anciently, Isaiah described an effect of fasting when he wrote, "The Lord shall guide thee continually, and satisfy thy soul in drought" (Isa. 58:11). President Spencer W. Kimball referred to fasting as "a personal wellspring of power" (80). President Gordon B. Hinckley later observed that the "program of the fast day . . . is so simple and so beautiful that I cannot understand why people everywhere do not take it up" (85).

See also Prayer; Sabbath, the.

BIBLIOGRAPHY

Hinckley, Gordon B. "Let Us Move This Work Forward." *Ensign* 15 (November 1985): 83–85.

Kimball, Spencer W. "Becoming the Pure in Heart." *Ensign* 8 (May 1978): 79–81.

KJW

Father Whitmer. *See* Whitmer, Peter Sr.

Father, the. *See* God the Father.

Fayette, New York

A township in Seneca County, New York, named after American Revolutionary War hero the Marquis de La Fayette; Church headquarters during fall and winter 1830. Twenty sections in the Doctrine and Covenants were received in Fayette (14–18, 20–21, 28–40). There

Reconstructed log home at the Peter Whitmer Sr. farm in Fayette, New York. The Church was organized in the original log home on 6 April 1830.

the Lord revealed to Joseph Smith that "a great and marvelous work is about to come forth unto the children of men" (14:1). That work was advanced with the completion of the Book of Mormon translation at the home of Peter Whitmer Sr. in Fayette (14, headnote).

In June 1829 the Lord promised Oliver Cowdery, David Whitmer, and Martin Harris that they would be called to be the three special witnesses of the Book of Mormon plates spoken of in Ether 5:2–4 and 2 Nephi 27:12 (17:1–9). "Not many days after" that revelation was received, in "a piece of woods convenient to Mr. Whitmer's house," the three men were shown the Book of Mormon plates by the angel Moroni (Smith, 1:54; D&C 17, headnote; 128:20).

On 6 April 1830, the organizational meeting of the Church was held in the Whitmer home in Fayette (20; 21). Of that sacred event, Joseph said, "We dismissed with the pleasing knowledge that we were now individually members of, and acknowledged of God, 'The Church of Jesus Christ'" (1:79). The first three Church conferences were held in Fayette in June and September of 1830 and January 1831 (29–30; 38; Smith 1:84, 115, 140). In July 1830 Joseph Smith was promised by the Lord that the Saints in Fayette would "support" him and that they would be blessed "both spiritually and temporally" (24:3).

In Fayette the Lord revealed that "no one shall be appointed to receive commandments and revelations in this church excepting my servant Joseph Smith" (28:2; cf 43:1–7). This revelation came in response to Hiram Page's claim to be receiving revelations for the Church. The Lord also revealed that "ye are called to bring to pass the gathering of mine elect" (29:7), and missionaries were called to gather the Lord's children into his Church (31–36). While they spread the good news and gathered converts, Joseph Smith was engaged in the translation of the Bible (35, headnote).

The headquarters of the Church moved from Fayette, New York, to Kirtland, Ohio, early in 1831, in obedience to the revelation, "Ye shall go to the Ohio, and this because of the enemy and for your sakes" (37:1).

Joseph Smith recorded significant events of the Restoration. He wrote of "the voice of God in the chamber of old Father Whitmer, in Fayette" (128:21). This had reference to the revelation received by Joseph Smith and Oliver Cowdery when they earnestly prayed to the Lord for the promise of John the Baptist to be realized concerning their future reception of the Melchizedek Priesthood (Smith, 1:60–61).

Today a rebuilt farmhouse and a visitors' center–meetinghouse are located on the Whitmer property. *See* maps, pp. 447 and 710.

See also New York period.

BIBLIOGRAPHY

Porter, Larry, C. "A Study of the Origins of The Church of Jesus Christ of Latter-day Saints in the States of New York and Pennsylvania, 1816–1831." Ph.D. dissertation, Brigham Young University, 1971.

Smith, Joseph. *History of The Church of Jesus Christ of Latter-day Saints.* Edited by B. H. Roberts. 7 vols. 2d ed. rev. Salt Lake City: The Church of Jesus Christ of Latter-day Saints, 1932–51.

LCP

Fear

The word *fear* appears more than thirty times in the Doctrine and Covenants, with two different meanings:

1. Having respect, honor, and love for God that leads to willing obedience to his commandments. "For thus saith the Lord—I, the Lord, am merciful and gracious unto those who fear me, and delight to honor those who serve me in righteousness and in truth unto the end" (76:5; cf. 10:56). The message of the "servants of God" in the last days and the trumpeting angels announcing the final events of the second coming of the Lord is to be, "Fear God and give glory to him, for the hour of his judgment is come" (133:38; cf. 45:39; 88:104; 101:84). President Spencer W. Kimball taught what it means to fear God: "Above all, I hope you will teach them [the youth] faith in the living God and in his Only Begotten Son—not a superficial, intellectual kind of acceptance, but a deep spiritual inner feeling of dependence and closeness; not a fear composed of panic and terror, but a fear of the Lord composed mostly of intense love and admiration and awesome nearness in a relationship of parent and offspring—father and son—father and daughter" (73). *See* Faith.

2. Feelings of anxiety, apprehension, doubt, intimidation, even terror. The revelations speak of this kind of fear attending those who disregard God and his commandments; those who give too much heed to the philosophies, vagaries, and influence of men; and Saints who face enemies, persecution, worries, and hardships. In his revealed preface to the Doctrine and Covenants, the Lord warns the wicked to "fear and tremble" because all the judgments and destructions decreed in the revelations "shall be fulfilled" (1:7; cf. 1:1–39; 34:8; 133:42) and in another revelation affirms that "fear shall come upon every man" because of wickedness and war (63:6, 33). Once Zion is redeemed, "the nations of the earth shall tremble because of her, and shall fear because of her terrible ones" (64:43; cf. 45:74–75). In the final days of

warning before the second coming of the Lord, when the Lord bears his own testimony in the form of natural calamities, "all things shall be in commotion; and surely, men's hearts shall fail them; for fear shall come upon all people" (88:88–91). After revealing that there were adulterers and adulteresses among the Saints, the Lord warned, "He that looketh on a woman to lust after her, or if any shall commit adultery in their hearts, they shall not have the Spirit, but shall deny the faith and shall fear" (63:16).

Fear that comes from giving too much heed to the opinions of others is exemplified in the experience of James Covill, whose "fear of persecution and the cares of the world caused him to reject the word" (40:2; cf. 3:7). The Lord expressed displeasure with some of the missionaries on their way to Missouri, "for they will not open their mouths, but they hide the talent which I have given unto them, because of the fear of man" (60:2; cf. 124:7). David and Peter Whitmer and Jared Carter were all instructed not to be afraid in their missionary endeavors (30:1, 11; 79:4). Fear was given as the reason Oliver Cowdery was unable to translate (9:7–11) and certain elders of the Church were unable to receive promised blessings (67:3).

The Lord repeatedly counseled the Saints not to fear. He reassured them that "if ye are prepared ye shall not fear" (38:30). Even when the Saints were being severely persecuted in Missouri in the summer of 1833, the Lord said, "Verily I say unto you my friends, fear not, let your hearts be comforted . . . waiting patiently on the Lord, for your prayers . . . shall be granted" (98:1–2). Several times the Lord reminded the Saints that they need not fear because his kingdom was theirs and he would stand by them (10:55; 35:27; 38:15; 50:41; 68:6). Very early in the Restoration the Lord revealed to Joseph Smith and Oliver Cowdery this reassuring promise about the fledgling group of Saints: "Therefore, fear not, little flock; do good; let earth and hell combine against you, for if ye are built upon my rock, they cannot prevail" (6:33–35; cf. 25:9; 30:5; 124:87). During the horrors of his confinement in Liberty Jail, the Prophet Joseph Smith was told, "Fear not what man can do, for God shall be with you forever

and ever" (122:9; cf. 101:35–36). And in a revelation to Brigham Young to the Saints on their way to the Salt Lake Valley, the Lord said, "Fear not thine enemies; for they shall not have power to stop my work," and "they are in mine hands and I will do my pleasure with them" (136:17, 30).

BIBLIOGRAPHY

Kimball, Spencer W. *The Teachings of Spencer W. Kimball.* Edited by Edward L. Kimball. Salt Lake City: Bookcraft, 1982.

BLS

Feast of fat things. *See* Wine on the lees.

Feet, shake off the dust of thy. *See* Shake off the dust of thy feet.

Feet shod with the preparation of the gospel of peace. *See* Armor of God.

Feet, washing of. *See* Wash, washed, washing(s).

Feigned. *See* Appendix E.

Felicity. *See* Appendix E.

Fellowship. *See* Appendix E.

Fetters. *See* Appendix E.

Fiery darts of the adversary/of the wicked

Penetrating, devouring attractions or TEMPTATIONS, intended to draw people away from OBEDIENCE to the COMMANDMENTS of God. The two references to fiery darts in the Doctrine and Covenants attribute the source of fiery darts to the adversary and to the wicked:

1. The Lord chastened the Prophet Joseph Smith in connection with the loss of the 116 manuscript pages of the Book of Mormon translation, saying, "You should have been faithful; and [God] would have extended his arm and supported you against all the fiery darts of the adversary" (3:8; cf. 1 Ne. 15:24; Hel. 5:12).

2. In a reference to the teachings of the apostle Paul to the Ephesians (Eph. 6:16) concerning putting on the whole armor of God, the Lord encouraged his latter-day Saints to take "the shield of faith wherewith ye shall be

able to quench all the fiery darts of the wicked" (27:17). *See* Faith.

Qualifying for the support of heaven (3:8) and being able to "withstand the evil day" (27:15) requires avoiding attractive, tempting fiery darts, whether they come from the adversary or the wicked, who are inspired by the adversary.

See also Satan.

LED

Fire

A dualistic symbol, at times representing the good, the divine, and the celestial, and at other times symbolizing the evil, the demonic, and the punitive. The Prophet Joseph Smith spoke of the resurrection and eternal rewards and punishments: "Some shall rise to the everlasting burnings of God; for God dwells in everlasting burnings and some shall rise to the damnation of their own filthiness, which is as exquisite a torment as the lake of fire and brimstone" (6:317). "If the fire can scathe a green tree for the glory of God, how easy it will burn up the dry trees to purify the vineyard of corruption" (135:6).

The entrance to the celestial kingdom is revealed to be "like unto circling flames of fire" (137:2). The metaphorical language "like unto" indicates that the nature of God's abode is like unto God himself—glorious! Indeed, God, along with all exalted, celestial beings, radiates a light that has the brilliance of fire (5:19; 50:24; 130:7; 133:41). Similarly, John the Beloved is spoken of as a "flaming fire and a ministering angel" (7:6), emphasizing the GLORY with which God clothes his servants. Additionally, the Lord said that his twelve apostles will return with him at his second coming in a "pillar of fire" (29:12). Even the Savior's eyes are like "a flame of fire" (110:3), perhaps symbolizing his omniscience and penetrating power.

The sanctifying power of the HOLY GHOST is often spoken of as fire or the "baptism of fire" (20:41; cf. 19:31; 33:11; 39:6). *See* Baptism of fire and the Holy Ghost.

The Holy Ghost cleanses, purifies, and improves those who receive it. Similarly, at his second coming Jesus Christ will be "like a refiner's fire" and will "sit as a refiner and purifier of silver" (128:24). Not only will the living creations of God be sanctified but the earth too will be sanctified "so as by fire" (43:32).

The gift of tongues, because it is a gift of the Spirit, is spoken of as "cloven tongues as of fire" (109:36), thereby indicating the source of such gifts.

Although occasionally used in literal terms (45:41), fire is often a symbol for general wickedness or worldliness from which the Saints are commanded to flee (36:6). As a negative symbol, it illustrates God's punitive consequences for the wicked: "everlasting," "unquenchable," "eternal," or "devouring" fire (29:28; 43:33; 63:34, 54; 76:105; 97:26; 101:66). It should be understood that "endless" and "eternal" refer not to the length of the punishment but rather to its divine nature, because God is "endless" and "eternal" (19:4–13; Moses 7:35); actual punishment and suffering in the postmortal spirit world will have an end, except in the case of SONS OF PERDITION, those over "whom the second death" has power and who "go away into the lake of fire and brimstone, with the devil and his angels" (76:36–37; cf. 63:17). *See* Hell; Punish, punished, punishment.

Fire is also a sign of Christ's coming (45:41), and those who have embraced wickedness are frequently warned of the dangers that await them (45:50, 57; 76:44; 133:41). God's fiery destruction of the wicked at Christ's return blesses the righteous by removing all EVIL from the face of the earth (35:14). *See* Jesus Christ, second coming of.

In the end, the GREAT AND ABOMINABLE CHURCH—the epitome of all that opposes God, his words, and his work—will be "devour[ed]" by heaven-sent fire that both cleanses and consumes (29:21).

That same fire, however, will preserve and save the righteous (1 Ne. 22:17).

BIBLIOGRAPHY

Smith, Joseph. *History of The Church of Jesus Christ of Latter-day Saints.* Edited by B. H. Roberts. 7 vols. 2d ed. rev. Salt Lake City: The Church of Jesus Christ of Latter-day Saints, 1932–51.

ALG

First death. *See* Death.

First elder/second elder. *See* Church of Jesus Christ of Latter-day Saints, The; Priesthood.

First fruits

A term used once in the Doctrine and Covenants in reference to people in two contexts: the righteous dead who will be the first to be resurrected and caught up to meet Jesus Christ at his second coming, and the "saints that are upon the earth, who are alive," who have obtained a preeminent position in relationship to God and "a good hope of glory in him," because of their righteousness. These also "shall be quickened and be caught up to meet him" (88:96–98; Jacob 4:11; cf. James 1:18; Rev. 14:4).

Jesus Christ is the prototype for both, "being the first that should rise" (2 Ne. 2:8), "the first-born from the dead" (Col. 1:18), "the firstfruits of them that slept" (1 Cor. 15:20–23), as well as having a preeminent relationship with his Father because of the Atonement, "the firstfruits unto God, inasmuch as he shall make intercession for all the children of men" (2 Ne. 2:9).

In the Old Testament, *first fruits* referred to the first produce of the harvest, "corn, . . . wine, . . . oil, and the . . . fleece of thy sheep," indeed, "the firstfruits of all thine increase" (Deut. 18:4; Prov. 3:9; cf. Ex. 23:16; Lev. 23:10; Num. 18:12). As the first and best of the harvest, these products were given to the priest as an offering to God. In harmony with this concept, the term *first fruits* in the Doctrine and Covenants refers to the best of God's people, both living and dead. They are the righteous who have proven worthy to be offered to God as first fruits (88:96–98).

DLB

First preacher. *See* Cowdery, Oliver.

First Presidency. *See* Church of Jesus Christ of Latter-day Saints, The; Priesthood.

First resurrection. *See* Resurrection, the.

First Vision. *See* God, man seeing; New York period; Palmyra, New York; Smith, Joseph, Jr.

Firstborn, Church of the. *See* Church of the Firstborn.

Firstborn, Jesus Christ as. *See* Jesus Christ, as Firstborn.

Firstborn of Aaron. *See* Bishop(s).

Fishing River, Missouri

Fishing River, in Clay County, Missouri, is associated with the place where Joseph Smith received Doctrine and Covenants 105 (headnote), which is sometimes called "the Fishing River revelation." In actuality, the revelation was received not on Fishing River but at a location between Fishing River and a smaller tributary known in the 1830s as the Little Fishing River and today called the East Fork or East Branch of the Fishing River. The revelation likely received its unofficial name because Fishing River was the most prominent geographic feature in the area. *See* map, p. 414.

See also Zion's Camp.

ALB

Flesh

Term with several meanings:

1. The soft component of the bodies of men and animals. This is its meaning in Doctrine and Covenants 20:40, in which the flesh of Jesus Christ is that part of his body other than blood (cf. 29:18–19; 36:6; 89:12; 130:22; 138:17, 43). In reference to animals, the Lord said, "Wo be unto man that sheddeth blood or that wasteth flesh and hath no need (49:19–21).

2. Living creatures, especially humans. For example, in the Lord's preface to his revelations, he declared that he is "willing to make [his gospel] known unto all flesh" (1, headnote; 1:34; cf. 38:16; 61:6; 101:16; 133:60).

3. A mortal body or mortality (93:4; 76:74; 132:26; 138:20, 34; cf. 2 Ne. 10:24).

4. Resurrected bodies. Holy men of ancient times were promised that although they would not see "a day of righteousness" while they lived in mortality, they would see it "in their flesh" (45:12–14; cf. Job 19:25–27).

5. The carnal, sensual, and devilish aspects of fallen man (20:20; 36:6; cf. 1 Jn. 2:15–16).

See Carnal, sensual, and devilish; Fall of Adam and Eve, the.

The term *flesh* is employed in a variety of phrases. When used with arm, as in "arm of flesh," it refers to human strength and wisdom (1:19; cf. 2 Ne. 4:34); to "be one flesh" refers to the coming together of a man and woman in marriage and acting as one (49:16; cf. Moses 3:24); and "according to the flesh" describes the right of inheritance of a son from his father (86:8–9).

DRD

Folly. *See* Appendix E.

Forbidden fruit. *See* Fall of Adam and Eve, the.

Foreknowledge of God. *See* God, nature of; Foreordination.

Foreordination

The determination in premortality of certain events or assignments before they occur on earth and is based on God's omniscience and the righteous use of AGENCY. Like the Savior, individuals may be assigned particular missions based on their premortal obedience.

The Doctrine and Covenants speaks of two forms of foreordination. The first involves the foreknowledge of God regarding events of the plan of salvation. The Lord "looked upon the wide expanse of eternity, and all the seraphic hosts of heaven, before the world was made" (38:1). The earth was ordained "before the world was made" to be the residence for mankind and was prepared with "all things" necessary for their existence (49:17; 104:17). Similarly, before the atonement of Christ was accomplished, little children were saved "from the foundation of the world" (29:46). These and other events were foreordained parts of God's eternal plan.

The second form refers to God's acquaintance with each of his children and their assignment to specific tasks. "Noble and great ones" were "chosen in the beginning to be rulers in the Church of God" (138:55; cf. Abr. 3:22–23). After receiving lessons in the spirit world, they "were prepared to come forth in the due time of the Lord to labor in his vineyard for the salvation of the souls of men" (138:56). For example, Joseph Smith surmised that he was "ordained from before the foundation of the world" (127:2). Most important, the Doctrine and Covenants emphasizes that JESUS CHRIST was foreordained to fulfill his eternal calling. Christ "was in the beginning with the Father," foreordained as the "light and the Redeemer of the world" (93:21, 9).

See also Premortal existence.

SCE

Forgiveness

Withholding punishment; granting pardon. The Savior is a loving, forgiving God: "I, the Lord, forgive sins, and am merciful unto those who confess their sins with humble hearts" (61:2) and unto "those who confess their sins before me and ask forgiveness" (64:7). He assures his people that all who repent shall be forgiven (1:32; 68:24): "He who has repented of his sins, the same is forgiven, and I, the Lord, remember them no more" (58:42). The Lord gave numerous examples of individuals he had forgiven or will forgive, conditional upon their full REPENTANCE: Thomas B. Marsh (31:5; 112:3); Edward Partridge (36:1; 64:17); William E. McLellin (75:8); elders of the Church (29:3; 50:36; 62:3; 64:3; 84:61); Sidney Rigdon, Joseph Smith, and Oliver Cowdery (60:7); Vinson Knight (124:76); Isaac Galland (124:78); and Joseph Smith (132:50).

Sometimes the Lord has to remind sinners to seek forgiveness through repentance, and his reminders come in the form of correction, chastisement, and rebuke: "Whom I love I also chasten that their sins may be forgiven, for with the chastisement I prepare a way for their deliverance in all things out of temptation, and I have loved you—wherefore, ye must needs be chastened and stand rebuked before my face" (95:1–2).

Forgiveness is available from a loving God, even for sins as grievous as ADULTERY (42:25). There are three exceptions, however, for which forgiveness is not granted: Those who kill shall not be forgiven (42:18); one who commits blasphemy against the Holy Ghost (76:32–38;

132:27); and one who breaks the oath and covenant of the PRIESTHOOD "and altogether turneth therefrom" (84:39–41). *See* Murder, murderers; Sons of perdition.

Two passages give extended instruction about forgiving others:

1. Doctrine and Covenants 64:8–10 teaches that the Saints are to forgive others *in their hearts* (not merely with words but with deep, sincere feeling); if they do not, they are guilty of "greater sin": "I say unto you, that ye ought to forgive one another; for he that forgiveth not his brother his trespasses standeth condemned before the Lord; for there remaineth in him the greater sin. I, the Lord, will forgive whom I will forgive, but of you it is required to forgive all men." To this the Lord added: "Inasmuch as you have forgiven one another your trespasses, even so I, the Lord, forgive you" (82:1).

2. Doctrine and Covenants 98:39–48 details the Lord's law of forgiveness: the Saints are to repeatedly forgive their enemies, who, if they repent, shall also escape the Lord's vengeance.

See also Atonement, the; Grace; Jesus Christ; Justice; Mercy.

DKO

Form of a dove

In a revelation given to Joseph Smith in Kirtland, Ohio, in 1833, the Lord revealed a portion of the record of John the Baptist, in which John testified that at the baptism of the Savior, "the Holy Ghost descended upon him in the form of a dove" (93:15; cf. Matt. 3:16; Mark 1:10; Luke 3:22; 1 Ne. 11:27; 2 Ne. 31:8). The Prophet Joseph Smith explained that John the Baptist "had the privilege of beholding the Holy Ghost descend in the form of a dove, or rather in the *sign* of the dove, in witness of that administration. The sign of the dove was instituted before the creation of the world, a witness for the Holy Ghost, and the devil cannot come in the sign of a dove. The Holy Ghost is a personage, and is in the form of a personage. It does not confine itself to the *form* of the dove, but in *sign* of the dove. The Holy Ghost cannot be transformed into a dove; but the sign of a dove was given to John to signify the truth of the deed, as

the dove is an emblem or token of truth and innocence" (5:260–61).

See also Holy Ghost, the.

BIBLIOGRAPHY

Smith, Joseph. *History of The Church of Jesus Christ of Latter-day Saints.* Edited by B. H. Roberts. 7 vols. 2d ed. rev. Salt Lake City: The Church of Jesus Christ of Latter-day Saints, 1932–51.

FFJ

Fornication

Voluntary sexual relations between unmarried persons. In some scriptures, the meaning includes other forms of sexual immorality and lewdness (1 Cor. 5:1, 9–11; 2 Cor. 12:19–21) and, beyond that, in a figurative sense, to spiritual fornication—forsaking, or being unfaithful to, a covenant relationship with the true God, indulging in the worship of idols or worldliness (1:15–16; 2 Chr. 21:11; Rev. 19:2; cf. Jer. 3:1, 14, 20; Isa. 24:5).

There are four references in the Doctrine and Covenants to fornication. Three of them (35:11; 88:94, 105) speak of the judgments at the last day upon the wicked, those who have been "made . . . [to] drink of the wine of the wrath of her [Babylon's] fornication" and who suffer the inevitable consequences of indulging in wickedness, sexual or otherwise. The Lord instructed the Saints, "Go ye out from . . . Babylon, from the midst of wickedness, which is spiritual Babylon" (133:14). The fourth reference (42:74; cf. Matt. 5:32) is to those who have "put away their companions for the cause of fornication." This fornication may be ADULTERY or perhaps other forms of unfaithfulness including spiritual fornication, such as physical, mental, or emotional abuse, or even apostasy.

See also Virtue.

LED

Foster, James

Birth: 1 April 1786, Hillsboro, Hillsboro County, New Hampshire.

Death: 12 December 1846, Jacksonville, Morgan County, Illinois

James Foster was baptized by 1834 and participated in the 1834 march of ZION'S CAMP. While in the camp, he became so ill that the

Prophet Joseph Smith suggested he not go on, but Foster insisted on continuing, and Joseph prophesied a full recovery because of his faith (MH, addendum 6, n. 10; Smith, 2:90). In early 1838, having been called in Kirtland as one of the presidents of the Seventy (1837), Foster served in the leadership of the Kirtland Camp, which was formed to help the Saints travel from Kirtland, Ohio, to Missouri. Foster was instrumental in organizing the camp; he received a vision of about five hundred Saints "going up to Zion . . . moving in order" and "encamping in order by the way" (Smith, 3:88). Because of "rumors he had heard from the west," however, he later "proposed to disband and break up the camp." When his proposal was not accepted, he left the camp to visit his son-in-law in DeWitt, Missouri, where he lived until he was expelled from Missouri with the rest of the Saints in 1839 (Smith, 3:144–46).

In Nauvoo, Foster, along with Levi Hancock, Zera Pulsipher, Henry Herriman, Daniel Miles, Josiah Butterfield, and Joseph Young, was called "to preside over the quorum of seventies" (124:138). In April conference of 1841 he was tried for impropriety but after explaining his action, he was allowed to "continue his standing in the Church" (Smith, 4:342). He died later that year while living in Jacksonville, Illinois. At the October 1844 general conference of the Church, "President [Brigham] Young said, that the seventies [First Council] had dropped James Foster, and cut him off, and we need not take an action upon his case" (TS, 5:693; cf. Smith, 7:297).

BIBLIOGRAPHY

Manuscript History of the Church, Vol. 1, Addenda 1–16. Church History Library, The Church of Jesus Christ of Latter-day Saints, Salt Lake City, Utah.

Smith, Joseph. *History of The Church of Jesus Christ of Latter-day Saints*. Edited by B. H. Roberts. 7 vols. 2d ed. rev. Salt Lake City: The Church of Jesus Christ of Latter-day Saints, 1932–51.

Times and Seasons 5, no. 20 (1 November 1844): 693.

ZLL

Foster, Robert D.

Birth: 14 March 1811, Braunston, Northampton County, England

Death: Unknown

Robert D. Foster, a physician, came into the Church in the late 1830s and soon afterward traveled with the Prophet Joseph Smith and Sidney Rigdon to Washington, D.C., to seek redress for the wrongs suffered in Missouri. The Prophet asked Foster to keep a daily journal of their travels, but he failed to do so (Smith, *History*, 4:89). At one point Joseph Smith wrote that he and Foster had formed a "very intimate" acquaintance and that he was "quite anxious" to visit Foster because of it (Smith, *Writings*, 500). Over the next few years, Foster achieved distinction in Nauvoo for holding such positions as surgeon-general for the Nauvoo Legion, University of Nauvoo regent, and magistrate of Hancock County. While Foster enjoyed such prominence, he also struggled with his behavior as well as his relationship with Joseph Smith and other Church leaders. Foster was admonished in Doctrine and Covenants 124 to obey the Lord; "build a house for my servant Joseph," according to a previous contract; "repent of all his folly, and clothe himself with charity; and cease to do evil, and lay aside all his hard speeches" (124:115–16). Additionally, Foster was commanded to "pay stock" into the Nauvoo House and to "hearken unto the counsel of my servants Joseph, and Hyrum, and William Law." He was promised that if he adhered to these commandments, "it shall be well with him forever and ever" (124:117–18).

Foster reported that he invested in the Nauvoo House and contributed to building Joseph Smith a house (Smith, *History*, 5:287). In April 1844, however, Joseph Smith "preferred" charges "before the High Council against . . . Foster 'for unchristianlike conduct in general, for abusing my character privily, for throwing out slanderous insinuations against me, for conspiring against my peace and safety, for conspiring against my life, for conspiring against the peace of my family, and for lying.'" He was excommunicated 18 April 1844 (Smith, *History*, 6:333, 341). Foster ultimately joined William and Wilson Law and became a leader in the apostate church they formed. He was a cofounder of the *Nauvoo Expositor* and an accessory to the Prophet's martyrdom. Foster was eventually acquitted of murder charges and later expressed deep sorrow concerning Joseph's death. Foster admitted that he was "the most miserable wretch that the sun shines upon. If I could recall eighteen months of my life I would be willing to sacrifice everything I have upon earth. . . . I did love Joseph Smith more than any man that ever lived, if I had been present I would have stood between him and death." When Foster was asked, "Why did you do as you have done? You were accessory to his murder," he replied: "I know that, and I have not seen one moment's peace since that time. I know that Mormonism is true, and the thought of meeting (Joseph and Hyrum) at the bar of God is more awful to me than anything else" (Smith, *History*, 7:513). Under pressure from the citizens of Nauvoo, Foster left town. By 1850 he was practicing law in New York and later returned to Illinois, settling in Loda, Iroquois County.

BIBLIOGRAPHY

Smith, Joseph. *History of The Church of Jesus Christ of Latter-day Saints.* Edited by B. H. Roberts. 7 vols. 2d ed. rev. Salt Lake City: The Church of Jesus Christ of Latter-day Saints, 1932–51.

———. *Personal Writings of Joseph Smith.* Compiled and edited by Dean C. Jessee. Rev. ed. Salt Lake City: Deseret Book, 2002.

ZLL

Foundation(s)

The beginnings or undergirding base upon which buildings, institutions, or accomplishments are built and sustained. The word *foundation* has several different meanings in the Doctrine and Covenants:

1. The PREMORTAL EXISTENCE, before the creation of this world, when measures were taken to implement God's plan of salvation for his children. Such measures include redemption of mankind through the Atonement (29:46); revelation, including "things that pertain to the dispensation of the fulness of times" (124:41; 128:18; cf. 35:18); salvation for the dead (124:33; 128:5, 8, 18); foreordination of Joseph Smith (127:2; cf. Abr. 3:23; Jer. 1:4–5); and laws and blessings (132:5; 130:20–21). The phrases "foundation of the world" and "foundations of the world" appear numerous times in each of the standard works (e.g., 1 Ne. 10:18; 2 Sam. 22:16; Matt. 13:35; Moses 6:54).

2. The beginnings of the restoration of Christ's Church upon the earth, that is, revelation, the Book of Mormon, the restoration of priesthood and saving ordinances. The Doctrine and Covenants clearly teaches that Joseph Smith was called to "lay the foundation of this church . . . the only true and living church upon the face of the whole earth" (1:30). It was to be "the foundation of a great work" (64:33), "which foundation he did lay, and was faithful" (136:38). Doctrine and Covenants 138:53 notes that "Hyrum Smith, Brigham Young, John Taylor, Wilford Woodruff, and other choice spirits . . . were reserved to come forth in the fulness of times to take part in laying the foundations of the great latter-day work."

3. The settlement of specified lands, for example, Kirtland (94:1; cf. 48:6) and Zion (58:7; 119:2; 124:39, 118; cf. 78:15; 124:2).

4. The substructure of a building. Three actual building foundations are mentioned: two in Kirtland, Ohio—a house for the First Presidency (94:3–6) and a printing house (94:10–12)—and one in Missouri, the Far West temple site (115:7–11). The foundation of a tower is mentioned in the parable found in Doctrine and Covenants 101:44–64. *See* Parable regarding a certain nobleman/vineyard.

5. The creation of the EARTH. Doctrine and Covenants 45:1 confirms that Jesus Christ "laid the foundation of the earth" and "made the heavens and all the hosts thereof."

6. An organization (the United Firm/United Order) as a means of accomplishing the commandments of the Lord pertaining to the poor (78:1–14; cf. 104, headnote).

7. Missionary efforts. Missionary companionships going from Kirtland to Missouri were instructed to take different routes so as not to "journey in another's track" nor "build upon another's foundation" (52:33).

KLA

Free, freedom, freely

The words *free, freedom,* and *freely* are used in the Doctrine and Covenants with several meanings:

1. Without cost. The ancients of America "did leave a blessing upon this land in their prayers, that whosoever should believe in this gospel in this land might have eternal life; yea, that it might be free unto all of whatsoever nation, kindred, tongue, or people they may be" (10:50–51). The Saints on their way to the West were told to "be diligent in preserving what thou hast . . . ; for it is the free gift of the Lord thy God, and thou art his steward" (136:27).

2. Without compulsion or constraint in the exercise of AGENCY. The Lord taught, "It is not meet that I should command in all things; for he that is compelled in all things, the same is a slothful and not a wise servant; wherefore he receiveth no reward. Verily I say, men should be anxiously engaged in a good cause, and do many things of their own free will, and bring to pass much righteousness" (58:26–29; cf. 124:69). Section 134, a statement of "belief with regard to earthly governments and laws in general" (headnote), declares that in making laws, governments should preserve "the freedom of the soul," hold "sacred the freedom of conscience," and allow citizens the "free exercise of their religious belief," so long as such freedoms do not "infringe upon the rights and liberties of others" (vv. 4–5, 7).

3. Without confinement in slavery, prison, or sin. The early Saints were told, "Lift up your voices and spare not. Call upon the nations to repent, both old and young, both bond and free" (43:20; cf. 24:11). The Prophet Joseph Smith proclaimed that temple ordinances for the dead will "redeem them out of their prison; for the prisoners shall go free" (128:22; cf. 138:42). As for being in BONDAGE to sin, the Lord implored, "Abide ye in the liberty wherewith ye are made free; entangle not yourselves in sin, but let your hands be clean, until the Lord comes" (88:86).

4. Without subjection to kings and rulers other than Christ. The Lord has promised that "in time ye shall have no king nor ruler, for I will be your king and watch over you. Wherefore, hear my voice and follow me, and you shall be a free people, and ye shall have no laws but my laws when I come, for I am your lawgiver, and what can stay my hand?" (38:21–22; cf. 58:22; 98:8).

5. Without restraint; in abundance. Concerning the gathering of his people to the true gospel in the last days, the Lord said, "For, behold, I will gather them as a hen gathereth her chickens under her wings, if they will not harden their hearts; yea, if they will come, they may, and partake of the waters of life freely" (10:65–66). Martin Harris was commanded, "Thou shalt not covet thine own property, but impart it freely to the printing of the Book of Mormon, which contains the truth and the word of God" (19:26). He was obedient to that command and sold 150 acres of land to pay for the printing of the Book of Mormon. In the same revelation, he was told to "speak freely to all; yea, preach, exhort, declare the truth, even with a loud voice, with a sound of rejoicing" (19:37).

Freedom is also used in the Doctrine and Covenants as the name of a town in upstate New York where Warren Cowdery, Oliver Cowdery's older brother, was called to serve as the "presiding high priest" over the Church "in the land of Freedom and the regions round about" (106:1).

KLA

Freedom, New York

A township situated in the northeast corner of Cattaraugus County, New York. In 1834 Joseph Smith visited Freedom and recruited men for ZION'S CAMP. In November 1834, Warren A. Cowdery, brother of Oliver Cowdery, was appointed the presiding high priest of the Freedom branch (106:1–8; Porter, 248–49). On 22–25 May 1835, members of the Quorum of the Twelve Apostles held a conference in Freedom (Smith, 2:224–25). *See* map, p. 447.

BIBLIOGRAPHY

Porter, Larry C. *New York and Pennsylvania.* Vol. 2 of *Sacred Places: A Comprehensive Guide to Early LDS Historical Sites,* edited by LaMar C. Berrett. Salt Lake City: Deseret Book, 2000.

Smith, Joseph. *History of The Church of Jesus Christ of Latter-day Saints.* Edited by B. H. Roberts. 7 vols. 2d

ed. rev. Salt Lake City: The Church of Jesus Christ of Latter-day Saints, 1932–51.

LCP

French farm. *See* Historical context and overview of Doctrine and Covenants 96 (p. 802).

Friend(s)

Companions, associates, colleagues, or confidants. The words *friend, friends,* and *friendly* appear many times in the Doctrine and Covenants. The Prophet Joseph Smith declared his loyalty to the Saints as a "never deviating friend" (128:25), and while he was in LIBERTY JAIL, he was specifically told by the Lord that his friends were standing by him (121:9–10). In a "declaration of belief regarding governments and laws" (134, headnote), the Church declared its position concerning justification for defending family and friends from "unlawful assaults": "We believe that men should appeal to the civil law for redress of all wrongs and grievances, . . . but we believe that all men are justified in defending themselves, their friends, and property, and the government, from the unlawful assaults . . . of all persons in times of exigency, where immediate appeal cannot be made to the laws" (134:11).

The Savior referred to the Prophet and members of the First Presidency (93:45; 100:1), his apostles (84:63), and the Jewish people (45:52) as his friends. To those "called of God in the church unto the ministry," he said that it was "expedient that I give unto you this commandment, that ye become even as my friends in days when I was with them, traveling to preach the gospel in my power" (84:77–86).

The Savior gave specific commandments to those he calls friends: "Ye shall call upon me while I am near" (88:62); gather in solemn assemblies (88:117; 109:6); lay the "foundation of the city of the stake of Zion" (94:1); "fear not, . . . be comforted; . . . rejoice evermore, and in everything give thanks" (98:1); and obey specific instructions concerning the United Order (104:1). Joseph Knight was directed to pray among his friends (23:6). The Saints in Jackson County, Missouri, were to make friends with "the mammon of unrighteousness," perhaps meaning those outside the Church (82:22; cf.

105:23–26). The salutation used among members of the School of the Prophets included a profession of friendship and brotherhood "through the grace of God" (88:133).

Specific blessings are given to those the Savior identifies as his friends: he will uphold those called to serve him (93:51); they will be guided by the voice of his Spirit and inspired to "know how to act in the discharge of [their] duties concerning the salvation and redemption" of others (103:1; cf. 97:1); they will receive the Comforter, "even the Holy Spirit of promise" (88:3); and they will have an inheritance with Christ (93:45).

WJM

Fruit(s)

In the Doctrine and Covenants, the word *fruit* has both literal and metaphorical meanings. Literally, of course, fruit refers to the edible parts of some plants. For example, grapes, "the fruit of the vine" (27:5; 89:16), olives, "the fruit of my vineyard" (101:45, 101), the "forbidden fruit" in the Garden of Eden (29:40), as well as other plants (89:11, 16).

Metaphorically, *fruit* is used in several contexts: converts of missionary efforts, as in the promise of "joy in the fruit of your labors" (6:31; cf. 4:4; 6:3; 33:7–9); descendants, as in Abraham's seed, "the fruit of his loins" (132:30); righteousness or good works of believers, as in bringing forth "fruit meet for their Father's kingdom" (84:58; 97:7, 9; 101:100; 107:31); the righteous, living and dead, as in those at the Second Coming who are designated "Christ's, the first fruits" (88:96–98).

See also First fruits.

KLA

Fuller, Edson

Birth: 1809, New York
Death: Unknown

Edson Fuller was baptized in 1831 while living with his family and working as a carpenter in Chardon, Ohio. In early June 1831, at a conference of the Church held at Kirtland, Ohio, the Prophet designated fourteen sets of elders to travel to Missouri. These elders were not to "journey in another's track" (52:33) as they labored to spread the gospel message. Edson Fuller and Jacob Scott were among those directed to "go two by two" and "take their journey" to Missouri (52:10, 28). It appears that Fuller did not fulfill this mission, but between April and May 1831 he proselyted with Harvey Whitlock in the Amherst, Ohio, area. Several accounts mention Fuller's unusual actions when preaching. Levi Hancock reported that at times Fuller "would fall and turn black in the face." Josiah Jones described him as "lying on the floor" until he would "jump up and cling to a beam for a while and then drop like a log on the floor" (in Black, 93). A number of Church members manifested concern over Fuller's behavior and claimed he was possessed by false spirits. On 1 September 1831 he was, with others, "silenced from holding the office of Elders in this Church" and shortly thereafter was excommunicated from the Church (Cannon and Cook, 11, 261). In 1840 he lived in Chardon, Ohio, with his wife and three children and worked as a farmer; by 1850 they had moved to Grand Rapids, Michigan.

BIBLIOGRAPHY

Black, Susan Easton. *Who's Who in the Doctrine and Covenants.* Salt Lake City: Deseret Book, 1997.

Cannon, Donald Q., and Lyndon W. Cook, eds. *Far West Record: Minutes of The Church of Jesus Christ of Latter-day Saints, 1830–1844.* Salt Lake City: Deseret Book, 1983.

KWF

Fuller's soap

Soap, generally consisting of alkalis and fats, used to remove dirt and stains from cloth and clothes. In ancient Israel, a "fuller's field" was the area used to spread large quantities of cloth to dry and be sun-bleached (e.g., Isa. 7:3; 36:2). Fullers' work became symbolic of spiritual cleansing from sin (e.g., Jer. 2:22; 4:14).

The phrase "fullers' soap" (plural possessive) occurs in the Bible only in Malachi 3:2, a verse consisting of two synonymous couplets. The first rhetorically asks who will be able to endure the Lord's coming, meaning Jesus' second coming. The second couplet then describes the purifying power of the Lord's glory, "for he is like a refiner's fire, and like fullers' soap." Malachi

3:2, including the phrase "fuller's soap" (rendered as a singular possessive), is quoted in 3 Nephi 24:2, as part of the resurrected Lord's recitation of Malachi 3–4 (3 Ne. 24–25), and in Doctrine and Covenants 128:24. Toward the end of section 128, a letter to the Church on baptism for the dead and sealing keys, Joseph Smith encouraged the Saints to offer a book "containing the records of our dead" as an acceptable offering to the Lord (v. 24). In this context and because "the great day of the Lord is at hand" (v. 24; cf. Mal. 4:1), the Prophet quoted Malachi 3:2–3, reminding the Saints of the need to be prepared for the Lord's coming and its attendant purifying power (128:24).

See also Jesus Christ, second coming of; Malachi; Malachi quotations in the Doctrine and Covenants.

DMP

Fullmer, David

Birth: 7 July 1803, Chillisquaque, Northumberland County, Pennsylvania

Death: 21 October 1879, Salt Lake City, Salt Lake County, Utah

David Fullmer moved from Pennsylvania to Richmond County, Ohio, in 1835. He was baptized in September 1836 and ordained an elder in February 1837. He moved to Missouri in the fall of 1837, living first in Caldwell County and then at Adam-ondi-Ahman in Daviess County. In 1839 his family was driven from the state of Missouri with the rest of the Saints, and they settled in Nauvoo, Illinois. There he was ordained a high priest and served on the Nauvoo high council (124:132) and the Nauvoo city council. Fullmer received his endowment in the Nauvoo Temple in December 1845.

David Fullmer left Nauvoo with the Saints in 1846. On the way west, he presided over the branch of the Church in the temporary settlement of the Saints at Garden Grove, Iowa, before proceeding to the Salt Lake Valley in 1848.

Fullmer was active in Church and civic affairs in the West. He served as a counselor to Salt Lake Stake president Daniel Spencer from 1849 to 1866, including four years (1852–56) as acting president while Daniel Spencer was on a mission to England. In 1870 David Fullmer was ordained a patriarch.

His contributions to civil service included helping to draft a constitution for the provisional state of Deseret and serving in the territorial legislature, as treasurer of the University of Deseret, as treasurer pro tem of Salt Lake County, and as treasurer of Salt Lake City. Because of his prominence in Church and civic affairs, he was often asked to give public speeches on Temple Square. The *Deseret News* of 3 May 1857 reports him as saying, "I would not give my experience in the gospel for all the gold and riches of the world, for it is worth much more to me" (in Black, 95).

BIBLIOGRAPHY

Black, Susan Easton. *Who's Who in the Doctrine and Covenants.* Salt Lake City, Utah: Bookcraft, 1997.

LED

Fulness

Completeness, entire abundance, maximum available, all-encompassing. *Fulness* is used in the Doctrine and Covenants in many contexts and with varied frequency. There may be variations in the wording of the same concept in each of the following examples:

Fulness of the gospel
Fulness of the Father
Fulness of times
Fulness of his glory
Fulness of the earth
Fulness of my scriptures
Fulness of John's record
Fulness of truth
Fulness of joy
Fulness of the Holy Ghost
Fulness of the priesthood
Infinity of fulness

The phrase "infinity of fulness," perhaps meaning a limitless abundance or completeness of all the components, listed and unlisted, that make up the nature of God, is found in 109:77. In that verse Joseph Smith pleads with the Lord to "hear us in these our petitions, and answer us from heaven, thy holy habitation, where thou sittest enthroned, with glory, honor, power, majesty, might, dominion, truth, justice, judgment, mercy, and an infinity of fulness, from everlasting to everlasting." That same fulness that the Father enjoys is promised to all those who qualify for exaltation in the highest heavens (76:51–60) and are given "all that [the] Father hath" (84:38).

LED

Fulness of my gospel. *See* Gospel, the.

Fulness of the Father. *See* Fulness.

Fulness of times. *See* Dispensation(s).

And we know also, that sanctification through the **grace**
of our Lord and Savior Jesus
Christ is just and true, to all
those who love and serve God
with all their mights, minds,
and strength. But there is a
possibility that man may fall
from grace and depart from
the living God; therefore let
the church take heed and
pray always, lest they fall into
temptation. 20:31–33

Gabriel. *See* Noah.

Gad

Bearer of the Melchizedek Priesthood who lived between the time of Abraham (ca. 2000 B.C.) and Moses (ca. 1260 B.C.). In a modern revelation Gad was identified in Moses' priesthood lineage. Gad was ordained by Esaias, and he in turn ordained Jeremy (84:10–12). Nothing else is known of this Gad. Other men named Gad in the Old Testament are much later (cf. Gen. 30:10–11; 1 Sam. 22:5). The lost book of Gad the seer (1 Chr. 29:29) is the work of a prophet by that name in David's day (ca. 1000 B.C.; cf. 2 Sam. 24:11).

RJM

Galatia. *See* Asia.

Galland, Isaac

Birth: 15 May 1791, Somerset County, Pennsylvania

Death: 27 September 1858, Fort Madison, Lee County, Iowa

Before he was baptized and ordained an elder on 3 July 1839, Isaac Galland was involved in land transactions with the Church. On 26 February 1839, Galland, an agent for the New York Land Company, announced that twenty thousand acres of the "half-breed tract" (between the Des Moines and Mississippi rivers) was for sale to Mormons for two dollars per acre, to be paid in twenty annual payments without interest (Roberts, 2:5–6). On 25 March, Joseph advised, "The Church would do well to secure to themselves the contract of the land which is proposed to them by Mr. Isaac Galland" (3:298). A purchase price of nine hundred dollars paid annually for twenty years was agreed upon and the purchase made ("Letter," 276).

Galland was "the honored instrument the Lord used to prepare a home for us," Joseph said of the man responsible for the transaction (4:270). The Lord said more: "I, the Lord, love him for the work he hath done, and will forgive all his sins" (124:78). The Lord asked Galland to contribute funds toward the construction of a "boarding house" in Nauvoo and to take a journey with Hyrum Smith "to accomplish the work that my servant Joseph shall point out to

them" (124:56, 79). It is not known whether Galland contributed the requested funds, but it is known that at the request of Joseph, he journeyed with Hyrum to Pennsylvania to negotiate land purchases and exchanges in the name of the Church (Smith, 4:406). Unfortunately, Galland's negotiations proved more harmful than beneficial. On 18 January 1842, Joseph revoked the "power of attorney given to Dr. Isaac Galland to transact business for the Church," explaining embarrassment over land deals (Smith, 4:495).

Angered by Joseph's actions, on 2 February 1842, Galland left the Church. From 1842 to 1853 he lived in Keokuk, Iowa, where he was "a firm and zealous believer in Spiritualism, and was heard to say that Joe Smith was the dupe of his own impostures; that Smith was simply a so-called spiritual medium" (Madsen, 10). The last two years of his life were spent with friends in Fort Madison, Iowa.

BIBLIOGRAPHY

"Letter of Isaac Galland to Samuel B. Swasey, July 22, 1839," as cited in Lyndon W. Cook, "Isaac Galland—Mormon Benefactor." *BYU Studies* 19, no. 3 (Spring 1979): 261–84.

Madsen, John M. "Study of Dr. Isaac Galland." n.p., 18 August 1964. L. Tom Perry Special Collections, Harold B. Lee Library, Brigham Young University, Provo, Utah.

Roberts, B. H. *A Comprehensive History of The Church of Jesus Christ of Latter-day Saints, Century One.* 6 vols. Salt Lake City: The Church of Jesus Christ of Latter-day Saints, 1930. Reprint, Provo, Utah: Brigham Young University Press, 1965.

Smith, Joseph. *History of The Church of Jesus Christ of Latter-day Saints.* Edited by B. H. Roberts. 7 vols. 2d ed. rev. Salt Lake City: The Church of Jesus Christ of Latter-day Saints, 1932–51.

SEB

Garden of Eden. *See* Eden, the Garden of.

Garment(s)

A word synonymous with clothing. *Garment(s)* is used in the Doctrine and Covenants to describe both the actual clothing worn by an individual (42:40, 42; 122:6) and the spiritual state of an individual. Of the latter, the term is often associated with ridding oneself of unclean garments, which represent one's sinful nature

(36:6; 61:34; 88:85; 112:33; cf. 2 Nephi 9:14). The term also designates a level of personal righteousness leading to exaltation (36:6; 61:34; 88:85; 109:76; 112:33; cf. 29:13). The relationship between clothing and one's spiritual state or calling can be understood by recognizing that one function of clothing is to be a marker of identification within a social structure, providing an individual both meaning and place within that structure (Ex. 28, 39; 2 Chr. 18:9; 2 Sam. 13:18; D&C 20:6; 133:46, 48, 51; cf. 45:44; 65:5; 85:7). Thus the condition of the clothing symbolically represents the state of the wearer: unclean clothing is equated with sin, and clean clothing with righteousness. Associated with garments is the act of investiture, in which an individual is clothed to demonstrate worthiness of inclusion within the divine Zion society. In 109:76–80, the dedicatory prayer for the Kirtland Temple, the Prophet Joseph Smith pleads that the Saints "may be clothed upon with robes of righteousness, . . . and crowns of glory upon our heads. . . . And let these, thine anointed ones, be clothed with salvation." Similar language is used in the dedication of Solomon's temple and in Psalms: "Let thy priests, O Lord God, be clothed with salvation" (2 Chr. 6:41) and "let thy priests be clothed with righteousness" (Ps. 132:9). This plea will be fulfilled when the righteous dead come forth "to receive a crown of righteousness, and to be clothed upon, even as [Christ is], to be with [him], that we may be one" (29:13). The process culminates as the individual who has been invested now invests others. In 133:32, the lost of Israel shall be found and "crowned with glory, even in Zion, by the hands of the servants of the Lord." Thus, those invested with the garments of exaltation become like God with the power to invest others with the same transformation.

DLB

Garnish. *See* Appendix E.

Gate(s)

Term employed with several meanings. The Doctrine and Covenants refers to the *gate*, or entryway, into the kingdom of God as a "strait

gate" (*strait* meaning narrow or strict). The strait gate employed in 22:2, 4 is proper baptism into the restored Church (cf. 2 Ne. 31:17). *See* Strait, straight.

Those who are called of God to speak for him are to "come in at the gate" by authorized ordination (43:7). Those who receive exaltation must be married by proper priesthood authority and have that ordinance "sealed unto them by the Holy Spirit of promise," for "strait is the gate, and narrow the way that leadeth unto the exaltation and continuation of the lives" (132:19–22). Contrariwise, "broad is the gate, and wide the way that leadeth to the deaths; and many there are that go in threat, because they receive me not, neither do they abide in my law" (132:25). *See* Exalt, exaltation; Marriage.

In addition to the strait gate of commandments and ordinances, the Doctrine and Covenants refers to the literal gate to the celestial kingdom. The Prophet Joseph Smith beheld the celestial kingdom of God in vision and noted the grandeur of the entryway into that kingdom: "I saw the transcendent beauty of the gate through which the heirs of that kingdom will enter, which was like unto circling flames of fire" (137:1–2). In several revelations the Lord promises that the "gates of hell shall not prevail against" his Church or the faithful members of his Church, which is founded on revelation and the gospel of Jesus Christ (128:10; 18:5; 33:11–13). Moreover, hell's gates will not prevail against those who follow the prophet (21:4–6), those who keep the Lord's commandments (17:8; 98:22), and those who endure faithfully to the end (10:69). By metonymy (a figure of speech in which one term represents other attributes associated with it) the "gates" of HELL represent all the hellish efforts and powers trying to destroy individuals and the eternal work of God on the earth. In the dedicatory prayer of the Kirtland Temple, Joseph Smith petitioned the Lord that "no combination of wickedness shall have power to rise up and prevail over thy people upon whom thy name shall be put" in the holy temple (109:26).

DKO

Gather, gathering

Gathering can be considered in two contexts: a spiritual gathering out of "the midst of wickedness, which is spiritual Babylon," into the gospel, and a physical gathering into particular geographical areas. Both of these gatherings are included in the Lord's declarations: "Go ye out from Babylon. Be ye clean that bear the vessels of the Lord" (133:5, 14). "Ye are called to bring to pass the gathering of mine elect; for mine elect hear my voice and harden not their hearts; wherefore the decree hath gone forth from the Father that they shall be gathered in unto one place upon the face of this land, to prepare their hearts and be prepared in all things against the day when tribulation and desolation are sent forth upon the wicked" (29:7–8; cf. 33:6). "For, behold, I will gather them as a hen gathereth her chickens under her wings, if they will not harden their hearts; yea, if they will come, they may, and partake of the waters of life freely" (10:65–66). The KEYS of the gathering were delivered to Joseph Smith and Oliver Cowdery by Moses on 3 April 1836 in the Kirtland Temple (110:11).

The gathering of the Saints into designated geographical areas is an important focus in the Doctrine and Covenants. In December 1830, the Saints were directed to gather in Ohio (37:3). Seven months later, in July 1831, the Lord affirmed that he had "appointed and consecrated" Missouri "for the gathering of the saints" and indicated that Independence, Jackson County, was "the center place" (57:1–3). Still, he cautioned, the gathering should be done not "in haste" but in an orderly manner under the direction of Church leaders (58:56). The Saints began gathering to Independence, Missouri, in 1831, but were driven from their homes and property in 1833. After the Saints were forced out of Jackson County, the Lord instructed, by means of a parable (101:43–62), that gathering to the central place—that is, Jackson County, Missouri—was still to be pursued but "should wait for a little season" (105:9–19; cf. 124:49–51). The Saints then gathered at Far West, Missouri (115:7–8), then at Nauvoo in Illinois (124:55), and ultimately "to the West" (136:1). With all these different gathering places, the Lord has not forgotten the center place. He has promised, "Zion shall not be moved out of her place, notwithstanding her children are scattered. They that remain, and are pure in heart, shall return, and come to their inheritances, they and their children, with songs of everlasting joy, to build up the waste places of Zion" (101:17; vv. 17–23). See Zion, redemption of.

In the meantime, "other places" have been appointed by the Lord for Saints to gather worldwide, "and they shall be called stakes, for the curtains or the strength of Zion" (101:20–22).

In the early days of this dispensation, those who joined the Church in countries outside the United States of America were encouraged to leave their native lands and travel to Zion in America. Many thousands of Saints obeyed that counsel. About the middle of the twentieth century, however, Church leaders began instructing the Saints to remain in their homelands and build up stakes of Zion there. At the Mexico City area conference in 1972, Elder Bruce R. McConkie declared: "The place of gathering for the Mexican Saints is in Mexico; the place of gathering for the Guatemalan Saints is in Guatemala; the place of gathering for the Brazilian Saints is in Brazil; and so it goes throughout the length and breadth of the whole earth. Japan is for the Japanese; Korea is for the Koreans; Australia is for the Australians" (45). Gathering into stakes throughout the world helps the missionary cause and provides the faithful "a defense" and a "refuge from the storm, and from wrath when it shall be poured out without mixture upon the whole earth" (115:6).

Joseph Smith taught that "the main object [of gathering] was to build unto the Lord a house [or temple] whereby He could reveal unto His people the ordinances of His house and the glories of His kingdom, and teach the people the way of salvation" (5:423). In harmony with this principle, the Lord has inspired the leaders of the Church to build temples wherever there are sufficient numbers of members gathered in stakes around the world.

See also Israel.

BIBLIOGRAPHY

McConkie, Bruce R. In Mexico and Central America Area General Conference Report, Mexico City, August 25–27, 1972. Salt Lake City: The Church of Jesus Christ of Latter-day Saints, 1973.

Smith, Joseph. *History of The Church of Jesus Christ of Latter-day Saints*. Edited by B. H. Roberts. 7 vols. 2d ed. rev. Salt Lake City: The Church of Jesus Christ of Latter-day Saints, 1932–51.

ROC

Gause, Jesse

Birth: ca. 1784, East Marlborough, Chester County, Pennsylvania

Death: ca. September 1836

Jesse Gause was born about 1784 in Pennsylvania. He was an active Quaker until 1829, when he joined the United Society of Believers of Christ's Second Appearing (SHAKERS). By the fall of 1831 he had been introduced to the restored gospel and baptized. Gause was called in March 1832 to serve as a counselor to Joseph Smith, an action "regarded as a step toward the formal organization of the First Presidency" (81, headnote). To magnify his calling, Gause was admonished to "succor the weak, lift up the hands which hang down, and strengthen the feeble knees" (81:5). Gause later "failed to continue in a manner consistent with [his] appointment" (81, headnote), and the appointment was transferred to Frederick G. Williams, whose name now appears instead of Gause's in the text of the section: "Verily, verily, I say unto you my servant Frederick G. Williams: . . . hearken to the calling wherewith you are called, even to be a high priest in my church, and a counselor unto my servant Joseph Smith, Jun." (81:1).

There is evidence that Gause was one of the scribes for the Joseph Smith translation of the Bible (Jennings, 183–85). In April 1832 Gause traveled from Kirtland to Missouri with Joseph Smith and others, taking an active part in the numerous meetings held there. He returned to Kirtland by August of that year. Sometime early in that month, he stopped at North Union, Ohio, where he attempted to persuade his wife to reunite with him and to join the Church. She had stayed with the Quakers after his baptism. A letter written by Shaker elder Matthew Houston notes that "Jesse Gause from Hancock . . . was here [North Union, Ohio,] a few days since after his wife Minerva." According to the letter, "she utterly refused being his slave any longer [and] he had to go away without her. [Although] he [tried] what the law could do for him he was very much [e]nraged . . . at any rate she cut off Old Jesse [very] handsomely—& he felt it to his gizzard" (in Woodford, 364).

Jesse Gause was called on a mission with Zebedee Coltrin in August 1832. He and Coltrin began their mission but parted when Coltrin returned to Kirtland because of illness. At that point, Jesse Gause "walked right out of the history of the Church" (Woodford, 364). He was excommunicated on 3 December 1832.

"What happened to Jesse Gause? Although no death record has been found, he almost certainly died sometime between mid-August 1835, and mid-September 1836. He was definitely no longer in touch with the Mormons of Kirtland by December 3, 1832, or with his family by September 14, 1836, since, on that date, Jesse's two oldest children, seventeen-year-old Harriet Amelia and sixteen-year-old Hannah, petitioned the Orphans Court in Chester County, Pennsylvania, to appoint their uncle Jonathan Gause as their guardian" (Jennings, 215).

BIBLIOGRAPHY

Houston, Matthew, to Seth Y. Wells, 10 August 1832, North Union, Ohio, as cited in Robert J. Woodford, "Jesse Gause, Counselor to the Prophet." *BYU Studies* 15 (Spring 1975): 362–64.

Jennings, Erin B. "The Consequential Counselor: Restoring the Root(s) of Jesse Gause." *Journal of Mormon History* 34, no. 2 (Spring 2008): 182–227.

ZLL

Generation(s)

The Doctrine and Covenants speaks of generations in at least four contexts:

1. The latter days. Joseph Smith was told "this generation shall have my word through you" (5:10). Both Oliver Cowdery and Hyrum Smith were both promised, "If you desire, you shall be the means of doing much good in this generation" (6:8; 11:8, 22). These and references to other individuals in the early Church apply to the time in which the revelation was

given and by extension to all the latter days (e.g., 5:18; 20:11; 31:3; 35:12; 84:4–5, 31; 88:85, 138), what the Lord called "this unbelieving and stiffnecked generation" (5:8), "a crooked and perverse generation" (33:2; 34:6), an "untoward generation" (meaning crooked, unruly, rebellious; 36:6; cf. 109:41), a "wicked generation" (88:75), and "a generation of vipers" (121:23).

2. Life span from parents to children. The Lord will eventually avenge the Saints of their enemies to "the third and fourth generation, so long as they repent not, and hate me, saith the Lord" (124:50; cf. 98:28–30, 37, 46; 69:8; 103:26; 124:50).

3. People living at a specific time period. Jesus taught his disciples in his lifetime: "This generation of Jews shall not pass away until every desolation which I have told you concerning them shall come to pass" (45:21). He also told them concerning the generation in which the times of the Gentiles would be fulfilled in the last days that "there shall be men standing in that generation, that shall not pass until they shall see an overflowing scourge; for a desolating sickness shall cover the land" (45:31; cf. 5:19–20; 84:97; 97:23).

4. All time and eternity. The coming forth of the Book of Mormon evidences "that God does inspire men and call them to his holy work in this age and generation, as well as in generations of old" (20:11; cf. 84:18). In the prayer dedicating the Kirtland Temple, Joseph Smith asked the Lord for the Saints to "honorably hold a name and standing in this thy house, to all generations and for eternity" (109:24; cf. 110:12). John Whitmer was instructed to prepare a history, "which shall be for the good of the church, and for the rising generations that shall grow up on the land of Zion, to possess it from generation to generation, forever and ever" (69:8; cf. 70:8).

DKO

Gentile(s)

The word Gentile has several meanings that can be traced back etymologically to one original concept, the idea of a people or tribe. The English word Gentile comes from a Latin word

that means "tribe, clan, family, people, etc." In this sense Gentile is a good translation of the Hebrew goy/goyim in the Hebrew Old Testament and the Greek ethnos/ethnē in the Greek New Testament, both of which also mean "people." Probably influenced by the usage in the Vulgate, the King James Old Testament renders goy(im) as Gentiles in only 30 of the more than 550 times it occurs in the Hebrew Bible. In the other 520-plus verses where goy(im) occurs, it is translated nation(s) or heathen.

The central concept of Gentile as a people lies behind several uses of the word in the Doctrine and Covenants:

1. Gentile is often used to designate a person or people who are not Israelites, that is, blood descendants of Jacob, whose name was changed by the Lord to Israel (Gen. 32:28; McConkie, 310–11; Nyman, 286). This usage is exemplified in passages where Gentiles is used in contrast to members of the house of Israel, such as in 18:6: "It must needs be that the children of men are stirred up unto repentance, both the Gentiles and also the house of Israel." Other passages where this differentiation is made clear include 14:10; 86:11; 90:8. The following passages contrast Gentile(s) with Jews: 18:26; 20:9; 21:12; 90:9; 107:33–35, 97; 112:4; 113:10; 133:8. Verse 4 of section 57 contains a unique contrast: "Wherefore, it is wisdom that the land should be purchased by the saints, and also every tract lying westward, even unto the line running directly between Jew and Gentile." In this context, Jew means "Lamanites," members of the house of Israel, in contrast to cultural or political Gentiles, people living east of the western boundary of Missouri (see 19:27 for the LAMANITES being a remnant of the JEWS). This is the same sense in which Nephi, a descendant of Joseph, used the word Jew to describe himself: "I say Jew, because I mean them from whence I came" (2 Ne. 33:8).

2. Nations and peoples of the earth that nurture scattered ISRAEL. The Lord instructed Joseph Smith to write a proclamation to the "kings of the world" and to the leaders of "all the nations of the earth," inviting them to come with their gold and their silver "to the help of my people," that the Gentiles may come "to the exaltation

or lifting up of Zion" (124:2–11). Jacob, paraphrasing Isaiah 49:23, said, "The kings of the Gentiles shall be nursing fathers unto them, and their queens shall become nursing mothers; wherefore, the promises of the Lord are great unto the Gentiles" (2 Ne. 10:9).

3. Israelites who live in Gentile nations and have assumed the cultural heritage of the Gentiles among whom they live. Thus, in the dedicatory prayer of the Kirtland Temple, Latter-day Saints are "identified with the Gentiles" (109:60). That is, the Saints living in the United States of America, a Gentile nation, are thought of as being cultural Gentiles, yet they are among "the remnants of Israel in their scattered condition among the Gentiles" and are to "put on the authority of the priesthood," which they have "a right to by lineage" (113:8–10). This same usage occurs in 14:10, where the Lord says, "I must bring forth the fulness of my gospel from the Gentiles [converted Israelites of Gentile cultural heritage] unto the house of Israel [unconverted Israelites regardless of heritage]." Similarly, in 133:12, the revelation says, "Let them, therefore, who are among the Gentiles [and who are converted to the gospel message, leave the unconverted and] flee unto Zion [the converted people who are latter-day Israel]." The Book of Mormon title page uses *Gentile* to refer to Israelites of the latter days who are of Gentile cultural heritage when it states that the Book of Mormon will "come forth in due time by way of the Gentile." That is, the Book of Mormon will be brought forth by an Israelite whose Israelite background is masked by his Gentile cultural heritage. Joseph Smith's bloodline was from the house of Israel (2 Ne. 3:6–15), but his cultural and political heritage was Gentile.

4. The mission field, in which Latter-day Saint missionaries seek to find and teach scattered Israel and any non-Israelites who will respond to the message of the restored gospel of Jesus Christ. This is made clear in passages such as 133:8, "Send forth the elders of my church unto the nations which are afar off; unto the islands of the sea; send forth unto foreign lands; call upon all nations, first upon the Gentiles, and then upon the Jews." And 88:84 says, "Therefore, tarry ye, and labor diligently, that you may be perfected in your ministry to go forth among the Gentiles for the last time, as many as the mouth of the Lord shall name, to bind up the law and seal up the testimony, and to prepare the saints for the hour of judgment which is to come."

5. A uniquely Latter-day Saint usage to designate "any outside the Mormon community" (*Oxford English Dictionary*, s.v. "Gentile").

See also Times of the Gentiles.

BIBLIOGRAPHY

McConkie, Bruce R. *Mormon Doctrine.* 2d ed. Salt Lake City: Bookcraft, 1966.

Nyman, Monte S. "Gentile(s)." In *Book of Mormon Reference Companion*, edited by Dennis L. Largey et al., 286. Salt Lake City: Deseret Book, 2003.

PYH

Gentiles, times of the. *See* Times of the Gentiles.

Gift of Aaron

Doctrine and Covenants 8 refers to a spiritual gift Oliver Cowdery possessed as the gift of Aaron. This is likely a reference to a divining rod and the same gift referred to less specifically in section 6. The earliest manuscript of section 8 refers to Oliver's gift as "the gift of working with the ~~sprout~~ <rod> Behold it ~~hath~~ <has> told you things Behold there is no other power save God that can cause this ~~thing~~ <rod> ~~of Nature~~ to work in your hands for it is the work of God & therefore whatsoever ~~ye~~ <you> shall ask <me> to tell you by that means that will ~~he~~ <I> grant unto you that ~~ye~~ <you> shall know remember that without faith ~~ye~~ <you> can do nothing trifle not with these things do not ask for that which ~~ye~~ <you> ~~had not~~ ought <not> ask that ~~ye~~ <you> may know the mysteries of God" (Jensen et al., 16–17). The record of the revelation published in the 1833 Book of Commandments refers to Oliver's "gift of working with the rod," calling it "this rod of nature" (ch. 7, v. 3).

Evidence suggests that such RODS were used anciently and in early Latter-day Saint history (Woodford, 185–89). Moses and his brother, Aaron, both had rods. The Bible recounts a variety of miracles in which these rods played a role

(Ex. 7–8; Num. 17, 20; Heb. 9:4). How Oliver Cowdery obtained such a rod is unknown, but such means of REVELATION as Oliver's rod, Lehi's "miraculous directors," Joseph's URIM AND THUMMIM, and the stones of the brother of Jared are attested to both anciently and in the early years of the Restoration (Ether 3:21–25; D&C 17:1).

When sections 6 and 8 were given in 1829, such gifts were suspect. Skepticism of "means," as the scriptures call such gifts, was a result of the Enlightenment's hostility toward instruments through which "marvelous works" were performed (8:8–9; cf. Alma 37; 1 Ne. 16:26–29; Mosiah 8:13–18; D&C 10:1; JS–H 1:62). This may explain why the Church did not publish the explicit reference to Oliver's rod in the 1835 Doctrine and Covenants, instead referring more generally to the biblical "gift of Aaron" (8:6). The revelations encourage Oliver's righteous use of this gift. The Lord legitimizes, not criticizes, such gifts. Neither Joseph nor Oliver denied Oliver's gifts (cf. Moro. 10:8, 24). Oliver considered them sacred. As commanded, he did not trifle with the rod or make it known to unbelievers (6:12). Little is known about it in this skeptical generation, but it is clear that Joseph Smith forged a link with ancient times when rods and stones were associated with the priestly or prophetic office and considered a means of revelation (Bushman, 240–41).

BIBLIOGRAPHY

A Book of Commandments. [Independence, Mo.]: W. W. Phelps & Co., 1833.

Bushman, Richard Lyman. *Believing History: Latter-day Saint Essays*. Edited by Reid L. Neilson and Jed Woodworth. New York: Columbia University Press, 2004.

Jensen, Robin Scott, Robert J. Woodford, and Steven C. Harper, eds. *Manuscript Revelation Books*. Facsimile edition. First volume of the Revelations and Translations series of *The Joseph Smith Papers*, edited by Dean C. Jessee, Ronald K. Esplin, and Richard Lyman Bushman. Salt Lake City: Church Historian's Press, 2009.

Woodford, Robert J. "The Historical Development of the Doctrine and Covenants." Ph.D. dissertation, Brigham Young University, 1974.

SCH

Gift of the Holy Ghost

A sacred blessing, offered in the ordinance of confirmation, which entitles the worthy recipient to the companionship of the third member of the Godhead. After authorized baptism by immersion in water, individuals are confirmed new members of The Church of Jesus Christ of Latter-day Saints "by the laying on of hands" and, at the same time, are given the gift of the Holy Ghost (20:41, 43; 25:8; 33:15; 35:5–6; 36:2; 39:23; 49:14; 55:1, 3; 76:52; 84:64, 74). *See* Laying on of hands.

The revelations present this pairing of ordinances as *two baptisms,* the first by water and the second by "the laying on of hands for the baptism of fire and the Holy Ghost" (20:41; cf. 19:31; 33:11; 39:6). Joseph Smith explained the importance of both ordinances: "Baptism by water is but half a baptism, and is good for nothing without the other half—that is, the baptism of the Holy Ghost" (5:499). Those who receive these baptisms "with an eye single to [the Lord's] glory" have their sins remitted and are sanctified, or purified, by the Holy Spirit (55:1; 53:3; 2 Ne. 31:17). The reception of the HOLY GHOST thus inaugurates a process whereby faithful disciples are spiritually born again and cleansed of spiritual impurity (5:16; cf. Mosiah 27:25). *See* Born of me.

Importantly, the ordinance of the SACRAMENT both reinitiates this process and calls to mind the promised blessing of the companionship of the Holy Ghost. Sacramental prayers remind Saints that the renewal of baptismal covenants made with the Lord is coupled with the corresponding promise that "they may always have his Spirit to be with them" (20:77, 79). The language of the sacramental prayers also implies a critical distinction: all of God's children can receive spiritual communication or comfort through the Holy Ghost, but the "Spirit shall not always strive with man" (1:33). The "gift" offered in authorized ORDINANCES entails "always" having the Spirit as a constant companion, if one remains worthy (20:77, 79).

So central to God's plan is this spiritual companionship and its attendant sanctifying power that the revelations refer to FAITH, REPENTANCE, BAPTISM BY WATER, and the gift of the Holy Ghost as, simply, "my gospel" (39:6; 3 Ne. 27:13–21). *See* Gospel, the.

Martin Harris was commanded to refrain from preaching doctrinal "tenets" and, instead, to emphasize that same gospel core: "declare repentance and faith on the Savior, and remission of sins by baptism, and by fire, yea, even the Holy Ghost" (19:31). These identical fundamentals are taught to those in the spirit world who "died in their sins, without a knowledge of the truth" (138:31–33), and they should be taught by parents to "children in Zion" (68:25).

BIBLIOGRAPHY

Smith, Joseph. *History of The Church of Jesus Christ of Latter-day Saints.* Edited by B. H. Roberts. 7 vols. 2d ed. rev. Salt Lake City: The Church of Jesus Christ of Latter-day Saints, 1932–51.

JSF

Gifts of the Spirit. *See* Spiritual gifts.

Gilbert, Algernon Sidney

Birth: 28 December 1789, New Haven, New Haven County, Connecticut

Death: 29 June 1834, near Fishing River, Clay County, Missouri

In 1827 Algernon Sidney Gilbert and Newel K. Whitney entered a mercantile partnership and opened a small store in Kirtland, Ohio, under the name of N. K. Whitney and Company. While engaged in this business enterprise, both men accepted baptism in 1830 into The Church of Jesus Christ of Latter-day Saints. Gilbert lived only four years after his baptism. During these years the Lord recognized his talents and the unique contributions he made to the Church. In June 1831 Gilbert wanted to know his "work and appointment in the Church" (53, headnote). He was told by revelation to "forsake the world. Take upon you mine ordination, even that of an elder . . . be an agent unto this church [and] . . . take your journey with my servants" (53:2–5). Gilbert was ordained an elder and on 20 June 1831 left Kirtland in company with Joseph Smith and others on a journey to Independence, Missouri.

After arriving in Independence, Gilbert was told by the Lord through his prophet to "plant himself in this place [Independence], and

establish a store . . . and thus provide for my saints" (57:8, 10). He did as directed and established a mercantile store in Independence before returning to Kirtland with W. W. Phelps (61:7). He remained in Kirtland long enough to gather needed supplies for the new store before returning to "his business, and to his agency in the land of Zion" (64:18).

Once in Zion, Gilbert was named one of seven high priests "to manage the affairs of the poor, and all things pertaining to the bishopric both in the land of Zion and in the land of Kirtland" (82:12). While he was functioning in this capacity, a difficulty arose between him and Church leaders in Kirtland. It stemmed from a 10 December 1832 letter written by Gilbert. Unfortunately, the letter is not extant. Because of this letter, Orson Hyde and Hyrum Smith accused Gilbert and others of "low, dark, and blind insinuations" (Smith, 1:319). The Lord said, "I am not well pleased with my servant . . . Sidney Gilbert" (90:35).

Although severely rebuked, Gilbert retained his position in the Church. He followed the Lord's counsel in December 1833 to retain "my storehouse" in Independence, even though he had been forced by mobs to close the establishment (101:96). Gilbert died of cholera in 1834 and was buried with other members of ZION'S CAMP who also succumbed to the disease.

See also Gilbert and Whitney store in Kirtland, Ohio; Historical context and overview of Doctrine and Covenants 53 (p. 759).

BIBLIOGRAPHY

Bangerter, Geraldine Hamblin, and Susan Easton Black. *My Servant Algernon Sidney Gilbert: Provide for My Saints (D&C 57:10).* Salt Lake City: Rollins, Hamblin and Bangerter Families, 1989.

Smith, Joseph. *History of The Church of Jesus Christ of Latter-day Saints.* Edited by B. H. Roberts. 7 vols. 2d ed. rev. Salt Lake City: The Church of Jesus Christ of Latter-day Saints, 1932–51.

SEB

Gilbert and Whitney store in Kirtland, Ohio

After launching Kirtland's first store in a log cabin in 1823, Newel K. Whitney and his partner, Algernon Sidney Gilbert, established a store in 1827 under the name N. K. Whitney and Company (Bangerter and Black, v–vi, 10–11). Over the next few years, the store served as the local post office and became one of the best-stocked mercantile stores in northeastern Ohio. After Whitney joined the Church and was appointed to be the bishop in Kirtland, the store also served as a bishop's storehouse and the headquarters of the Church for approximately eighteen months, from the fall of 1832 until the early spring of 1834. Joseph and Emma Smith lived in accommodations on the second story of the building above the store. During this period, twenty-one revelations in the Doctrine and Covenants, sections 84 through 104, were received or recorded by Joseph Smith at or near his home above the store. It was here that the School of the Prophets met and the Saints were instructed to establish a "house of God," or temple (88:119), and where the revelation known as the Word of Wisdom was received (89). Conferences were held here, and

the Prophet worked on the inspired translation of the Bible (Smith, 1:322–24, 334–35). The store is mentioned specifically twice in the Doctrine and Covenants: Whitney and Gilbert are told in September 1831 not to sell the store "yet for a little season," even "until the residue of the church, which remaineth in this place [Kirtland], shall go up unto the land of Zion" (63:42; 64:26). Seven years later, although the store is not mentioned, Newel Whitney is told to leave Kirtland and "come up to the land of Adam-ondi-Ahman" (117:11).

The store was restored by The Church of Jesus Christ of Latter-day Saints in 1984 to be used as a visitors' center. In 1988 United States president Ronald Reagan presented the Church with the President's Historic Preservation Award for the restoration efforts (Perkins and Cannon, 11).

Joseph Smith's son Joseph III was born in the living quarters above the Gilbert and Whitney

The Gilbert and Whitney store in Kirtland, Ohio; photograph by Welden C. Andersen. In 1831 Sidney Gilbert was commanded to move to Independence, Missouri, and open a store there. Regarding the operation in Kirtland, the Lord further directed, "Let my servant Newel K. Whitney retain his store, or in other words, the store, yet for a little season" (D&C 63:42).

store in Kirtland on 6 November 1832. *See* map, p. 345.

See also Kirtland, Ohio; Ohio period.

BIBLIOGRAPHY

Bangerter, Geraldine Hamblin, and Susan Easton Black. *My Servant Algernon Sidney Gilbert: Provide for My Saints (D&C 57:10).* Salt Lake City: Rollins, Hamblin and Bangerter Families, 1989.

Perkins, Keith W., and Donald Q. Cannon. *Ohio and Illinois.* Vol. 3 of *Sacred Places: A Comprehensive Guide to Early LDS Historical Sites,* edited by LaMar C. Berrett. Salt Lake City: Deseret Book, 2002.

Smith, Joseph. *History of The Church of Jesus Christ of Latter-day Saints.* Edited by B. H. Roberts. 7 vols. 2d ed. rev. Salt Lake City: The Church of Jesus Christ of Latter-day Saints, 1932–51.

MVB

Gird up your loins

A biblical phrase referring to tucking up one's robe into a loin belt, thus freeing the legs for movement. The phrase is used both literally and metaphorically. Literal uses in actually girding up the loins in preparation for actions requiring movement are recorded in the Old Testament (e.g., Ex. 12:11; 1 Kgs. 18:46; 2 Kgs. 4:29; 9:1). Likewise, the Old Testament uses the phrase metaphorically to refer to getting ready for any physical, emotional, or spiritual labor (e.g., Prov. 31:17; Isa. 11:5).

The Doctrine and Covenants employs this phrase metaphorically. The Saints are commanded to ready themselves for the Second Coming (36:8) by being "watchful" and "sober" (61:38), purifying themselves (38:8–9), and wearing the whole ARMOR OF GOD to protect them from EVIL, "lest [they] be found among the wicked" (27:15; 43:19). Those ready are promised that the Second Coming "shall not overtake [them] as a thief" (106:5; cf. 75:22). *See* Jesus Christ, second coming of.

The Lord's servants are charged with readying themselves "for the work," which involves taking up the cross, following the Lord, and feeding his sheep (112:7, 14). But they are not left alone in this preparation, for the Lord will help them prepare: "I will gird up their loins, and they shall fight manfully for me" (35:13–14).

BIBLIOGRAPHY

Johnson, Bo. "Chaghar." In *Theological Dictionary of the Old Testament,* edited by G. Johannes Botterweck and Helmer Ringgren, 4:213–16. 15 vols. Grand Rapids, Mich.: Eerdmans, 1980.

King, Philip J., and Lawrence E. Stager. *Life in Biblical Israel.* Louisville, Ky.: Westminster John Knox Press, 2001.

BKS

Glory

The splendor, brightness, luster, brilliance, magnificence, intelligence, and honor that are centered in God and extended by grace and blessing to his faithful children. God the Eternal Father is a being of great glory—he possesses every divine attribute, characteristic, and quality in perfection. Jesus Christ, who is Jehovah, the firstborn spirit child of the Father, possesses the glory of the Only Begotten of the Father in the flesh. He received "a fulness of the glory of the Father" (93:11, 16). The everlasting gospel has been restored so that men and women might become partakers of that glory (133:57). "Blessed are you for receiving mine everlasting covenant," the Savior said in 1831, "even the fulness of my gospel, sent forth unto the children of men, that they might have life and be made partakers of the glories which are to be revealed in the last days" (66:2).

Moses was instructed that God's work and glory are to "bring to pass the immortality and eternal life of man" (Moses 1:39). Members of the household of faith who focus their efforts and concentrate their labors on God's transcendent purpose and who maintain "an eye single to the glory of God" begin to be filled with light. Through time and spiritual experience, they come to comprehend all things (4:5; 27:2; 55:1; 59:1; 88:67).

Of those who are instructed in the law of the Church and become sanctified through that understanding, the divine word attests that "glory shall be added to the kingdom which ye have received" (43:9–10). Mortality is not intended to be easy and is often filled with trauma, tragedy, and misfortune. Nevertheless, those who endure tribulation with optimism and faith in the Father's plan prepare themselves for the glory of God here and hereafter

(58:3–4; 136:31). Indeed, those who overcome by patience and faith shall receive "a more exceeding and eternal weight of glory" (63:66; cf. 76:56). Men and women prepare in this life for the life to come. Those who seek to abide by the law of Christ, the law of the celestial kingdom, receive a portion of that glory here in preparation for receiving a fulness of that glory in the resurrection (88:22–31), thereby enabling the faithful to enter into what the scriptures call the rest of God, "which rest is the fulness of his glory" (84:24). Such sanctified souls are then fit for the highest kingdom of glory (76:50–70, 92–96).

Zion is a community of the pure in heart (97:21), a holy commonwealth made up of people who seek the interest of their neighbor and do all things with an eye single to the glory of God (82:19). In a day yet future, the center place of Zion, the New Jerusalem, will be established in Independence, Missouri (57:2–3), and the glory of the Lord will rest upon that community (45:67; 64:41; 84:101; 88:119; 97:15). Before the Savior's second coming, his coming in glory (7:3; 45:16, 44), he will come and minister within the walls of that temple, which will be filled with the glory of God (84:5).

The revelations declare that "the glory of God is intelligence, or, in other words, light and truth" (93:36–37). That is far more than an invitation to acquire education and learning, although "it is impossible for a man to be saved in ignorance" (131:6). God's glory centers not alone in his having a fulness of truth but also in his being bathed in light, for light is spiritual power inherent in the perfect application of eternal truth. That glory reflects brilliance and splendor, sanctified affections, and perfected righteousness (88:4–13; cf. 50:24).

In the highest heaven, families will be united forever, friendships will be renewed and continued, and "that same sociality which exists among us here will exist among us there, only it will be coupled with eternal glory, which glory we do not now enjoy" (130:2).

RLM

Gnashing of teeth

The clenching or grinding of teeth in rage or anguish. The phrase occurs in six verses in the Doctrine and Covenants and refers to the suffering and anguish of the wicked as a result of the judgments of God. This phrase is usually paired with weeping and wailing (19:5; 133:73). Individuals identified in the revelations that qualify for such anguish include the following:

1. Those who choose to suffer rather than repent. They will be found on the Lord's "left hand" (19:4–5). See Repentance.

2. Those in the early days of the Church in Missouri who failed to abide the principles of consecration regarding inheritances. Their "names are not found written in the book of the law," and therefore, they "shall not find an inheritance among the saints of the Most High" (85:1–11).

3. Those "wicked, unfaithful, and unjust stewards," the government officials who turned a deaf ear to the persecutions of the Saints in Missouri. They will receive "their portion among hypocrites, and unbelievers" (101:85–91). See Wicked, the/wickedness.

4. Those who reject the Lord's servants and the testimony "revealed unto them." This evidently is referring to the solemn proclamation the Lord called Joseph Smith to make to "all the nations of the earth" (124:1–8).

5. Those enemies who hindered the Saints from building a temple in Jackson County, Missouri, in the early 1830s (124:49–51).

6. Those who are proud and "all that do wickedly." These are they who reject the Lord, whether in the past, present, or future, and who reject the Lord's servants when they are sent to them (133:63–74). See Pride.

In two instances "gnashing of teeth" is used in connection with the wicked being assigned to their fate, sometimes identified as outer darkness (101:91; 133:73), which darkness is inherent in the devil and his power (e.g., 24:1; 82:5). Inasmuch as there are many levels of disobedience, it is reasonable to believe that the severity and duration of God's punishment, which brings a gnashing of teeth, will vary accordingly. The Lord revealed that it is not intended "that there shall be no end to this torment" (19:6) and that all, except the SONS OF PERDITION, will be saved in one of three kingdoms of glory (76:43–44; cf. vv. 50–112), though some will suffer in "hell" and "shall not be redeemed from the devil until the last resurrection" (76:85, 106). *See* Kingdoms of glory and perdition, vision of.

See also Hell; Punish, punished, punishment.

JWL

God, council of the eternal. *See* Council(s).

God, foreknowledge of. *See* God, nature of.

Godhead, the. *See* God the Father; Jesus Christ; Holy Ghost, the.

God, kingdom of. *See* Kingdom of God/kingdom of heaven.

God, man seeing

The appearance of God the Eternal Father and the Lord Jesus Christ to Joseph Smith Jr. marked the beginning of the dispensation of the fulness of times. This supernal event serves as a pattern by which other incidences of man seeing God may be identified, understood, and applied.

The Prophet Joseph Smith and those with whom he labored in mortality saw the Father and/or the Son on several occasions (Baugh, 285): the First Vision, when the Father and the Son appeared to the Prophet Joseph (described in "Explanatory Introduction" to the Doctrine and Covenants and recorded in the Pearl of Great Price [JS–H 1:13–17]); Joseph Smith and Sidney Rigdon seeing the Son "on the right hand of the Father" (76:22–23); Joseph Smith and Oliver Cowdery seeing the Son in the Kirtland Temple (110:2–4); Joseph Smith seeing the Father and the Son in his vision of the celestial kingdom (138:18).

The Doctrine and Covenants also includes President Joseph F. Smith's vision of the redemption of the dead, wherein he records that "the Son of God appeared" (138:18) to the inhabitants of paradise. Other incidents include the promise of the appearance of Jesus Christ at his second coming (29:11; 34:6–7; 35:21; 130:1; 133:19).

The Doctrine and Covenants also describes several points of doctrine relevant to man seeing God: Man cannot see God without being "quickened by the Spirit of God" (67:11; cf. 84:21–22). "When the Savior shall appear we shall see . . . that he is a man like ourselves" (130:1). Seeing the Lord is promised to anyone who "forsaketh his sins and cometh unto me, and calleth on my name, and obeyeth my voice, and keepeth my commandments" (93:1). Seeing God is conditional and is experienced according to God's "own time, and in his own way, and according to his own will" (88:68).

BIBLIOGRAPHY

Baugh, Alexander L. "Parting the Veil: Joseph Smith's Seventy-six Documented Visionary Experiences." In *Opening the Heavens: Accounts of Divine Manifestations, 1820–1944,* edited by John W. Welch and E. B. Carlson. Provo, Utah: Brigham Young University Press, 2005.

DKJ

God, nature of

The Prophet Joseph Smith said, "It is the first principle of the gospel to know for a certainty the character of God" (6:305). The Doctrine and Covenants contains an abundance of information about the attributes of God. These attributes are the same whether one is speaking of GOD THE FATHER or his Only Begotten Son, JESUS CHRIST, for they are one, both possessing all attributes in perfection (93:3; 3 Ne. 12:48; cf. 20:28).

The overarching attribute of God is LOVE. Indeed, "God is love" (1 Jn. 4:16). The preeminent expression of that love is the ATONEMENT of Jesus Christ, "the great and wonderful love made manifest by the Father and the Son in the coming of the Redeemer into the world; that through his atonement, and by obedience to the principles of the gospel, mankind might be saved" (138:3–4; cf. 34:3; 45:3–5; 133:52–53). Although God's love is constant, his approval and blessings, on one hand, and his chastisements and JUDGMENTS, on the other, are conditioned on mankind's behavior. Even his chastisements are a manifestation of his love. He chastens his children "that their sins may be forgiven" (95:1–2) and that they may "learn

The Sacred Grove; photograph by George Edward Anderson, 1907. "I had actually seen a light, and in the midst of that light I saw two Personages, and they did in reality speak to me" (JS–H 1:25).

obedience, if it must needs be, by the things which they suffer" (105:5–6; cf. 101:1–9). Such chastening comes because God is also a God of JUSTICE (82:4; 84:102) and "cannot look upon sin with the least degree of allowance" (1:31); "justice and judgment are the penalty which is affixed unto [his] law" (82:4), from which none are "exempt" (10:28; cf. 88:40; 107:84; 127:3). God is also a God of MERCY (3:10; 70:18). Hence, though he cannot look upon sin with the least degree of allowance, "nevertheless, he that repents and does the commandments of the Lord shall be forgiven" (1:32; cf. 101:9). That promise of merciful FORGIVENESS is reiterated many times in the revelations in the Doctrine and Covenants. As a general principle, anyone who confesses and forsakes his sins and keeps the commandments is promised forgiveness (58:42–43; cf. 61:2; 84:61). More than a dozen times the Lord identifies individuals, promising mercy and forgiveness based on their REPENTANCE and OBEDIENCE (e.g., Emma Smith, 25:3; Thomas B. Marsh, 31:5; 112:1–3; Edward Partridge, 36:1; Joseph Smith, Sidney Rigdon, and Oliver Cowdery, 60:6–7; several elders returning to Kirtland from a mission to Missouri, 62:1–3; Isaac Morley and Edward Partridge, 64:16–17; Joseph Smith, 90:1–3 and 132:49–50; Lyman Sherman, 108:1; Joseph Smith and Oliver Cowdery, 110:5; and Vinson Knight and Isaac Galland, 124:74–76, 78). It is through his mercy that God not only forgives sins but manifests himself unto his people (110:7), those who are humble and meek (97:1–2). The Lord explained, "I, the Lord, am merciful and gracious unto those who fear me, and delight to honor those who serve me in righteousness and in truth unto the end" (76:5; cf. 46:15). Critical events have taken place because of his mercy: for example, the Atonement (29:1) and the translation of the Book of Mormon (1:29; cf. 128:19–21).

In addition to possessing the attributes of love, justice, and mercy, God is also patient. A number of times in the Doctrine and Covenants, the Lord speaks of his wrath being poured out upon the wicked (e.g., 1:9; 56:1; 63:6; 87:6), but that wrath is not unleashed upon the rebellious until "the cup of their iniquity is full"

(101:11; cf. 29:17; 43:26; Ether 2:9–10), their "days of probation are past," and their "destruction is made sure," as with the Nephites of old (Hel. 13:38). Even then, God's wrath is not unbridled fury but an expression of divine justice, measured "to every man according to the measure which he has measured to his fellow man" (1:10). Undoubtedly, the resulting destruction of souls will be accompanied by God's weeping, as in the days of Noah (Moses 7:24–40).

Critically important attributes of God are his omniscience and foreknowledge. He "knoweth all things, for all things are present before [his] eyes," including "all things . . . past, present, and future" (38:2; 130:7; cf. 2 Ne. 9:20; W of M 1:7; Alma 13:3; Moro. 7:22).

Knowing for a certainty the character of God brings with it an understanding of man's potential. "If men do not comprehend the character of God, they do not comprehend themselves," said Joseph Smith (6:303). The Doctrine and Covenants and latter-day prophets teach clearly that God is a glorified, resurrected, exalted man with a "body of flesh and bones as tangible as man's; the Son also" (130:22) and that it is possible for the faithful to become like him—to receive "all that [the] Father hath" (84:38) and to become GODS themselves (76:50–70; 132:19–25). In section 93 the Lord referred to the testimony of John the Baptist concerning him. John observed that the Savior received "not of the fulness ['of the glory of the Father'; v. 16] at first, but continued from grace to grace, until he received a fulness," that is, "all power, both in heaven and on earth" (vv. 13, 17). After quoting John, the Lord explained how his disciples can follow this pattern: "I give unto you these sayings that you may understand and know how to worship, and know what you worship, that you may come unto the Father in my name, and in due time receive of his fulness. For if you keep my commandments you shall receive of his fulness, and be glorified in me as I am in the Father; therefore, I say unto you, you shall receive grace for grace" (vv. 19–20).

The Prophet Joseph Smith taught: "God himself was once as we are now, and is an exalted man, and sits enthroned in yonder heavens! . . . He was once a man like us; yea . . . God himself, the Father of us all, dwelt on an earth, the same as Jesus Christ Himself did; . . . and you have got to learn how to be gods yourselves, and to be kings and priests to God, the same as all gods have done before you, namely, by going from one small degree to another, and from a small capacity to a great one; from grace to grace, from exaltation to exaltation, until you . . . sit in glory, as do those who sit enthroned in everlasting power" (6:305–6). Concerning that long learning process the Prophet explained: "When you climb up a ladder, you must begin at the bottom, and ascend step by step, until you arrive at the top; and so it is with the principles of the gospel—you must begin with the first, and go on until you learn all the principles of exaltation. But it will be a great while after you have passed through the veil before you will have learned them. It is not all to be comprehended in this world; it will be a great work to learn our salvation and exaltation even beyond the grave" (6:306–7).

Godhood is the achievement of divinity by uncreated intelligence (93:29; cf. 50:24) through obedience to eternal gospel law and by the grace and mercy of God the Father and his Beloved Son, Jesus Christ (Smith, 6:310–12).

Such an understanding of the nature and character of God and his relationship to mankind is the foundation of the theological edifice of The Church of Jesus Christ of Latter-day Saints, for upon it rests the doctrine of immortality of the human soul, spirit and body, which in turn is the basis for the divine reality of eternal MARRIAGE, eternal increase, and eternal family relationships—the exaltation of all mankind!

See also One eternal round.

BIBLIOGRAPHY

Smith, Joseph. *History of The Church of Jesus Christ of Latter-day Saints.* Edited by B. H. Roberts. 7 vols. 2d ed. rev. Salt Lake City: The Church of Jesus Christ of Latter-day Saints, 1932–51.

RT

God, same yesterday, today, and forever. *See* One eternal round.

God, sons of. *See* Sons of God.

Gods

Perfected beings who have all power and knowledge and have no end. Latter-day scripture confirms the glorious doctrine that the children of God have the potential to become as their Father and their Savior are. Lorenzo Snow expressed this elevated truth in a frequently quoted aphorism: "As man now is, God once was / As God now is, man may be" (Smith, 46). "Wherefore, as it is written, they are gods, even the sons of God" (76:58; cf. Ps. 82:1, 6; John 10:34). "These are they who are just men made perfect" (76:69); "all things are theirs" (76:59); and the Father "makes them equal in power, and in might, and in dominion" (76:95). They come forth to "receive a crown of righteousness, and to be clothed upon, even as I am, to be with me, that we may be one" (29:13).

The Lord describes in Doctrine and Covenants 121:28–32 "a time to come in the which nothing shall be withheld, whether there be one God or many gods, they shall be manifest"; "all thrones and dominions, principalities and powers, shall be revealed and set forth upon all who have endured valiantly for the gospel of Jesus Christ," "according to that which was ordained in the midst of the Council of the Eternal God of all other gods" (vv. 29, 32).

Revelation describes the eternal potential of God's children in remarkable detail and gives instruction for how to attain "the fulness of [his] glory" (132:6), "an exceeding, and an eternal weight of glory" (132:16). Those who do not enter into and abide by the new and everlasting covenant of MARRIAGE, the Lord warned, "remain separately and singly, without exaltation, in their saved condition, to all eternity; and from henceforth are not gods, but are angels of God forever and ever" (132:17).

On the other hand, "if a man marry a wife by my word, which is my law, and by the new and everlasting covenant, and it is sealed unto them by the Holy Spirit of promise, by him who is anointed, unto whom I have appointed this power and the keys of this priesthood; and it shall be said unto them—Ye shall come forth in the first resurrection; and if it be after the first resurrection, in the next resurrection; and shall inherit thrones, kingdoms, principalities, and powers, dominions, all heights and depths . . . ; and they shall pass by the angels, and the gods, which are set there, to their exaltation and glory in all things, as hath been sealed upon their heads, which glory shall be a fulness and a continuation of the seeds forever and ever. Then shall they be gods, because they have no end; therefore shall they be from everlasting to everlasting, because they continue; then shall they be above all, because all things are subject unto them. Then shall they be gods, because they have all power" (132:19–20).

The Doctrine and Covenants identifies some who have already risen to this exalted state: Abraham, Isaac, and Jacob, who "did none other things than that which they were commanded; and because they did none other things than that which they were commanded, they have entered into their exaltation, according to the promises, and sit upon thrones, and are not angels but are gods" (132:37).

See also Historical context and overview of Doctrine and Covenants 76 (p. 780) and 132 (p. 849); Exalt, exaltation; Kingdoms of glory and perdition, vision of.

BIBLIOGRAPHY

Smith, Eliza R. Snow. *Biography and Family Record of Lorenzo Snow.* Salt Lake City: Deseret News Company, Printers, 1884.

DKO

God's works cannot be frustrated

It is impossible for mortal man or for Lucifer to thwart the Lord's plans, purposes, and doings. This truth was taught by the Lord in connection with the loss of the 116 pages of Book of Mormon manuscript entrusted to Martin Harris in the early summer of 1828 (3; 10). Those who stole the manuscript intended to wait for Joseph Smith to translate the same material again, change their copy, and then claim Joseph was a false prophet. Centuries before, the Lord had frustrated such a plan by having Nephi keep two sets of plates, the large plates of Nephi and the small plates of Nephi, both covering the same early period of Nephite history. Mormon included his abridgment of the large plates as well as the full text of the small plates in the records he passed on to his son Moroni.

After adding his own record, Moroni deposited the plates in the Hill Cumorah and in 1827 delivered them to Joseph Smith.

Inasmuch as both sets of plates addressed parallel accounts of early Nephite history, Joseph Smith was instructed not to translate again the portion of the record from the large plates but to translate the small plates of Nephi, thus frustrating the plans of the enemies of Joseph Smith and still providing an account of Nephite history from the time Lehi left Jerusalem down to the reign of King Benjamin—the same period of time covered by the lost manuscript. Hence, the Lord said, "The works, and the designs, and the purposes of God cannot be frustrated, neither can they come to naught. . . . Remember, remember that it is not the work of God that is frustrated, but the work of men" (3:1, 3; cf. Morm. 8:21–22).

See also Book of Mormon, lost manuscript of (116 pages).

LED

God the Father

The Prophet Joseph Smith declared that "if men do not comprehend the character of God, they do not comprehend themselves" (6:303). The Doctrine and Covenants affirms that the Father "is the same God yesterday, today, and forever. . . . By these things we know that there is a God in heaven, who is infinite and eternal, from everlasting to everlasting the same unchangeable God, the framer of heaven and earth, . . . and that he created man, male and female, after his own image and in his own likeness" (20:12, 18).

The Father's glory, might, and dominion can be comprehended only "by the power of the Holy Spirit, which God bestows on those who love him, and purify themselves before him" (76:116). The Father understands his children's needs (84:83) and is "a discerner of the thoughts and intents of the heart" (33:1).

The Doctrine and Covenants confirms the relationship of mankind to the Father and declares these truths:

1. "The Father has a body of flesh and bones as tangible as man's" (130:22).

2. As spirit offspring, man was "in the beginning with the Father" (93:23).

3. The Savior received "a fulness of the glory of the Father" (93:16), and in due time others may "receive of [the Father's] fulness" (93:19).

4. Though presently separated from his glorified presence because of the Fall, "every one that hearkeneth to the voice of the Spirit cometh unto God, even the Father" (84:47).

5. The Father can manifest himself to those in mortality (130:3; cf. John 14:23).

"Kingdom of my Father"

In several places in the Doctrine and Covenants the Savior refers to the kingdom of his Father. Joseph Smith was told by the Lord, "I . . . prepare a throne for you in the kingdom of my Father" (132:49). Such is the promise for all the faithful: "eternal life in the mansions which I have prepared in the house of my Father" (81:6). The Savior provides an opportunity for mankind to "come unto the kingdom of [his] Father" (18:44). Joseph Smith and Sidney Rigdon saw in vision the Son on the right hand of the Father (76:23) and bore witness: "We saw the glory of the celestial, which excels in all things—where God, even the Father, reigns upon his throne forever and ever" (76:92). After the earth has "filled the measure of its creation, it shall be crowned with glory, even with the presence of God the Father" (88:19). Those who are faithful in obtaining the Melchizedek Priesthood and magnifying their calling are promised "all that [the] Father hath" (84:38). Those who bring souls unto God shall find "rest with them" and experience great joy with them "in the kingdom of [the] Father" (16:6; cf. 18:10–16).

See also God, man seeing; God, nature of; Gods; Jesus Christ.

BIBLIOGRAPHY

Smith, Joseph. *History of The Church of Jesus Christ of Latter-day Saints.* Edited by B. H. Roberts. 7 vols. 2d ed. rev. Salt Lake City: The Church of Jesus Christ of Latter-day Saints, 1932–51.

RCJ

Good

Beneficial, appropriate, suitable to a purpose, virtuous; ultimately Godlike; morally excellent.

The Doctrine and Covenants uses *good* to refer to things, attributes, and behaviors that are in harmony with the will and purposes of Jesus Christ and his Father, as directed by the Spirit, "which leadeth to do good—yea, to do justly, to walk humbly, to judge righteously" (11:12).

Things which are good

The Lord commended the faithful Saints who traveled to Missouri in 1831 to begin laying the foundations of Zion and promised them "for their reward the good things of the earth" (59:3–4). In the same revelation the Lord assured those who cheerfully honor the Sabbath day "the fulness of the earth . . . and the good things which come of the earth, whether for food or for raiment, or for houses, or for barns, or for orchards, or for gardens, or for vineyards" (59:16–17; cf. 64:34).

In a revelation known as the Word of Wisdom, the Lord designated "strong drink," "tobacco," and "hot drinks" as "not good for man." He listed "all wholesome herbs," "flesh also of beasts and of the fowls of the air," and "all grain" as "ordained for the use of man" (89:5–14).

The Prophet Joseph Smith and his counselors in the First Presidency were instructed to "study and learn, and become acquainted with all good books, and with languages, tongues, and people" (90:15). Because governments exist for the "good and safety of society," Latter-day Saints are expected to "step forward and use their ability in bringing offenders against good laws to punishment" (134:1, 8).

The term *good* is linked with things in life that one experiences, as in "all things shall work together for good to them that walk uprightly, and to the sanctification of the church" (100:15; cf. 90:24; 98:3; 111:11). After listing several serious challenges Joseph Smith had experienced or would yet experience, the Lord said, "Know thou, my son, that all these things shall give thee experience, and shall be for thy good" (122:7).

Attributes which are good

Several times in the revelations the Lord directed the Saints to "be of good cheer" (78:18). The elders returning to Kirtland from a mission to Missouri in the summer of 1831 and who had suffered a canoe accident on the river at McIlwaine's Bend were reassured with these words: "Be of good cheer, little children; for I am in your midst, and I have not forsaken you" (61, headnote, v. 36; cf. 68:6; 112:4).

Certain desires are noted as good in the revelations (11:27). Oliver Cowdery was told, "If you have good desires—a desire to lay up treasures for yourself in heaven—then shall you assist in bringing to light, with your gift, those parts of my scriptures which have been hidden because of iniquity" (6:27; cf. 7:4–5, 8).

Behavior which is good or which brings about good

The Lord declared, "For behold, it is not meet that I should command in all things; . . . men should be anxiously engaged in a good cause, and do many things of their own free will, and bring to pass much righteousness. . . . And inasmuch as men do good they shall in nowise lose their reward" (58:26–28). He encouraged Joseph Smith and Oliver Cowdery, as well as his "little flock," to "do good" and promised "good for [their] reward," even if "earth and hell" were to combine against them (6:33–34).

Several revelations directed individuals to actions that would be for the good of the Saints or the Church. The Lord promised members of the Church that if they would "give heed" to the words of the Prophet, he would "cause the heavens to shake for [their] good" (21:4–6; cf. 35:24). Sidney Gilbert was instructed to establish a store in Missouri "for the good of the saints" (57:8; cf. 55:4). John Whitmer, as Church historian, was to be engaged in "preaching and expounding, writing, copying, selecting, and obtaining all things which shall be for the good of the church" (69:8). Other revelations promise that obedience to the Lord's direction will bring good results (35:24; 51:17; 82:14–16; 96:5; 124:7–10; cf. 33:4; 35:12; 82:6).

The Savior is the epitome of that which is good, and he is the ultimate source of all good things (Moro. 7:22). He is "the good shepherd, and the stone of Israel," and those who build "upon this rock [him] shall never fall" (50:44; cf. Hel. 5:12).

One's perception of what is good, or appropriate, for a particular situation is often referred to in the revelations as the basis for decision making, with the phrase "as seemeth me [the Lord] good" (40:3; 42:16; 52:6; 56:4); "as seemeth him [or them or you] good" (41:8; 48:3; 58:38; 60:5; 61:35; 62:5; 64:28). In several situations, the Lord gives permission for others to make decisions based on what they deem to be "good," indicating that "it mattereth not unto [him]" (60:5; 61:22; 63:40; cf. 27:2; 80:3).

See also Evil.

LED

Gospel of Abraham. *See* Abrahamic covenant.

Gospel, letter of the. *See* Letter of the gospel.

Gospel, the

The "glad tidings" (76:40), even "glad tidings of great joy" (79:1), that JESUS CHRIST "came into the world . . . to be crucified for the world, and to bear the sins of the world, and to sanctify the world, and to cleanse it from all unrighteousness; that through him all might be saved whom the Father had put into his power and made by him" (76:41–42). These glad tidings, or the gospel, include "the doctrine of the resurrection and the redemption of mankind from the fall, and from individual sins on conditions of repentance" (138:19). In one revelation the gospel is designated as "the gospel of peace," its author being the "Prince of Peace" (27:16; Isa. 9:6).

The Doctrine and Covenants often speaks of "the everlasting gospel" (e.g., 36:5; 77:8–9, 11; 79:1; 88:103; 109:29, 65; 133:36; 138:25), which, in its broadest sense, consists of "all of the laws, principles, doctrines, rites, ordinances, acts, powers, authorities, and keys necessary to save and exalt men in the highest heaven hereafter" (McConkie, 331). Jesus identified the first principles and ordinances of the gospel when he proclaimed: "And this is my gospel—repentance and baptism by water, and then cometh the baptism of fire and the Holy Ghost" (39:6; 66:2; cf. 3 Ne. 27:13–21; A of F 4). The Doctrine and Covenants contains a comprehensive elucidation of those laws, doctrines, principles, ordinances, and keys that constitute the gospel of

Jesus Christ. *See* Baptism by water; Faith; Gift of the Holy Ghost; Repentance.

The revelations explain how the gospel is administered by PRIESTHOOD authority. The higher, or Melchizedek, priesthood oversees the whole of the gospel plan, including all of the doctrines and ordinances of exaltation, the preaching of the gospel in all the world, conferring the gift of the Holy Ghost, and ultimately obtaining a knowledge of God (20:38–45; 84:19; 107:8–10, 23–35, 38). The lesser, or Aaronic, priesthood administers the PREPARATORY GOSPEL, consisting of the outward principles and ordinances, including repentance, baptism, the letter of the gospel, and the ministering of angels (13; 84:27–28; 107:20). *See* Letter of the gospel.

Because the gospel is intended for all people, both the living and the dead, the Lord repeatedly emphasized in many sections of the Doctrine and Covenants the command to preach the gospel everywhere to everyone (e.g., 35:15; 36:5; 68:8; 73:1; 81:3). In these last days, God has sent forth angels possessing the everlasting gospel to commit to every nation, kindred, tongue, and people (77:8–9; 133:36–37). At some point, one hundred and forty-four thousand high priests from "every nation, kindred, tongue, and people" are to be ordained to administer "the everlasting gospel" and "to bring as many as will come to the church of the Firstborn" (77:11). *See* Church of the Firstborn.

The Doctrine and Covenants affirms that the gospel existed in ancient times. In section 66 the Lord equated "the fulness of my gospel" with "mine everlasting covenant" (66:2)—the same gospel that enabled Abraham, Isaac, and Jacob to become exalted (132:37). The Prophet Joseph Smith taught that "the gospel has always been the same; the ordinances to fulfill its requirements, the same; and the officers to officiate, the same; and the *signs* and *fruits* resulting from the promises, the same" (*TS,* 904; spelling modernized). Thus, "the new and everlasting covenant" (132:6–7), the Lord's everlasting covenant, revealed anew to Joseph Smith, is had again on earth in the DISPENSATION of the fulness of times. *See* New and everlasting covenant.

Certain KEYS pertaining to the covenant God made with Abraham, called "the gospel of Abraham," were restored to the earth in 1836 by an ancient prophet named Elias (110:12).

Jesus and the apostles taught the everlasting gospel in the meridian dispensation, but many Jews rejected the gospel because they gave heed to the traditions of their fathers (74:2, 4).

The Doctrine and Covenants confirms the New Testament teaching that Jesus Christ took his gospel to the spirit world during his post-mortal ministry (1 Pet. 3:18–19; 4:6). Section 138 describes how the gospel was preached to the spirits in prison—the Savior organized the righteous spirits and commissioned them to go forth and "carry the light of the gospel to them that were in darkness, even to all the spirits of men" (138:30–37). The faithful elders of this dispensation, after they die, "continue their labors in the preaching of the gospel . . . among those who are in darkness . . . in the great world of the spirits of the dead" (138:57), and "the dead who repent will be redeemed, through obedience to the ordinances of the house of God, and after they have paid the penalty of their transgressions, and are washed clean, shall receive a reward according to their works, for they are heirs of salvation" (138:58). *See* Salvation for the dead.

The Doctrine and Covenants also stands as a witness of the divinity of the Book of Mormon, declaring that it contains "the fulness of the gospel" (20:9; 42:12; 135:3), meaning that the Book of Mormon teaches clearly the glad tidings of the ATONEMENT and what individuals must do to lay hold on the everlasting effects of that redemptive act. Further, the Doctrine and Covenants testifies of the divinity of the work of the Prophet Joseph Smith in bringing the gospel to all people (135:3; cf. 18:4–5, 17).

BIBLIOGRAPHY

McConkie, Bruce R. *Mormon Doctrine.* 2d ed. Salt Lake City: Bookcraft, 1966.

Times and Seasons 3 (1 September 1842): 904.

ACS

Gould, John

Birth: 11 May 1808, Ontario, Canada

Death: 9 May 1851, Cooley's Mill, Pottawattamie County, Iowa

In 1831, Pastor John Gould and members of

his Free Will Baptist congregation left Spafford, New York, and traveled to Kirtland, Ohio, having been converted to the message of the restored gospel. By the fall of 1833, Joseph Smith had sent Orson Hyde and Gould from Ohio to Missouri with instructions for the Saints there. In reflecting on this assignment, Hyde recalled the exhausting nature of their journey "through a sickly fever and ague country." He also noted the fears they faced when surrounded by mobs "who threatened to wring our heads off from our shoulders" (Hyde, 790). On 12 October 1833 the Lord gave a message of comfort to Joseph Smith and Sidney Rigdon concerning Hyde and Gould: "Thy brethren, my servants Orson Hyde and John Gould, are in my hands; and inasmuch as they keep my commandments they shall be saved" (100:14). They returned safely to Kirtland on 25 November 1833. Gould assisted the Prophet Joseph and others in recruiting volunteers for ZION'S CAMP.

On 6 April 1837 Gould was sustained as one of the seven presidents of the Seventy. In September of that year he was released from the Seventy and later (1844) ordained a high priest. Gould joined the Saints in Nauvoo, where he received his endowment in the Nauvoo Temple in February 1846. He went west with the Saints to the Salt Lake Valley in 1847 but returned that same year to Cooley's Mill, Iowa, where he died shortly before his forty-third birthday.

BIBLIOGRAPHY

Black, Susan Easton. *Who's Who in the Doctrine and Covenants.* Salt Lake City: Deseret Book, 1997.

Cook, Lyndon W. *The Revelations of the Prophet Joseph Smith.* Salt Lake City: Deseret Book, 1985.

Hyde, Orson. "Autobiographical History of Orson Hyde." *Millennial Star* 26, no. 47 (1864): 742–44, 760–61, 774–76, 790–92.

Jessee, Dean C., ed. *The Papers of Joseph Smith.* 2 vols. Salt Lake City: Deseret Book, 1989–92.

RC

Government

The Doctrine and Covenants records a variety of ways the word *government* is used. In addition to references to civil governments, others refer to the priesthood as a form of Church government (102:8; 124:143). The Doctrine

and Covenants highlights the United States government as having divine origins. It records that the Lord raised up "wise men" to establish the CONSTITUTION, which serves as a model form of government (101:80). God approves of laws that are based upon "constitutional" standards and support the principles "of freedom in maintaining rights and privileges" that belong "to all mankind" (98:5).

The Doctrine and Covenants encourages the Saints to befriend those laws that are constitutional; laws that are "established, and should be maintained for the rights and protection of all flesh, according to just and holy principles" (98:6; 101:77). "All men are bound to sustain and uphold the respective governments in which they reside, while protected in their inherent and inalienable rights by the laws of such governments; and that sedition and rebellion are unbecoming every citizen thus protected" (134:5; cf. v. 3). Latter-day Saints are also expected to seek for honest and wise leaders to serve in government and to uphold them in their positions (98:10; cf. 134:5–6). In the dedicatory prayer of the Kirtland Temple, the Prophet Joseph Smith petitioned the Lord to "have mercy upon the rulers of our land" (109:54).

The Doctrine and Covenants states the purposes and limitations of civil government, which "were instituted of God for the benefit of man" to make and administer laws "for the good and safety of society" (134:1). They should not encroach on religious freedoms (134:4). The Doctrine and Covenants identifies important principles concerning civil governments:

1. "No government can exist in peace, except such laws are framed and held inviolate as will secure to each individual the free exercise of conscience, the right and control of property, and the protection of life" (134:2).

2. Civil governments are specifically charged to allow citizens "the free exercise of their religious belief," and they do not have a right to "proscribe them in their opinions, so long as . . . such religious opinions do not justify sedition nor conspiracy" (134:7).

3. Governments should not allow favoritism of religious sects "whereby one religious society

is fostered" and another limited in "its spiritual privileges" (134:9).

The Doctrine and Covenants affirms that governments should enact laws to punish criminals appropriately, and "for the public peace and tranquility all men should step forward and use their ability in bringing offenders against good laws to punishment" (134:8). After the Saints were driven from Missouri, the Lord directed that they appeal to all levels of government for justice and redress (101:76–77, 86–88), promising that governmental leaders who failed to discharge their duties will be held accountable by God (101:89–90; cf. 134:1).

The Doctrine and Covenants records "the broken faith of the State [of Illinois] as pledged by the governor" in failing to protect the Prophet Joseph and Hyrum Smith from the "conspiracy of traitors and wicked men" (135:7).

See also Historical context and overview of Doctrine and Covenants 134.

REL

Grace

An attribute of Deity, possessed by him in perfection (66:12; 93:12–13); unearned divine assistance, unmerited divine favor, and divine enabling strength and power (LDS Bible Dictionary, s.v. "grace"). God's grace includes his condescension, his tender and patient mercies, the bestowal of his Spirit and spiritual gifts, and the added measure of strength beyond one's own to face the challenges of this life and accomplish what would otherwise be impossible.

To receive grace is to receive a gift that cannot be bartered for, purchased, or earned. Beyond mankind's best efforts, grace is needed to receive the blessings of heaven, including the resurrection and redemption from hell, and "the greatest of all the gifts of God," which is "salvation," or "eternal life" (6:13; 14:7). To receive that greatest gift, disciples of JESUS CHRIST must manifest gratitude and love for the Lord through loyal discipleship. The ATONEMENT is a finished work, and the Master's grace is sufficient for all (17:8; 18:31; cf. 2 Cor. 12:9; Ether 12:27).

Although JUSTIFICATION (acquittal from sin; exoneration; pronouncement of innocence) and sanctification (the process of being cleansed and purified; *see* Sanctify, sanctification) are true and vital parts of the GOSPEL plan and come to mankind through the grace of God, individuals must remain spiritually vigilant, because one can "fall from grace" (20:30–34). Through willful sin one can separate oneself from the Spirit of God and the peace that comes from faithful adherence to God's commandments. On the other hand, mankind can progress, as did the Savior, "from grace to grace," advancing from one level of spirituality to a higher level, receiving "grace for grace"; that is, receiving blessings added to blessings in return for obedience and service to God and fellow beings (93:12–13). Jesus, "the prototype or standard of salvation" (*Lectures*, 76), received "grace for grace . . . until he received a fulness" (93:12–13). The more he freely gave of himself in obedience to the Father, the more the Father shed forth his grace upon him. All true followers of the Savior can receive the same fulness by keeping the commandments and striving to be like him in the way they interact with others to bless their lives, the emulation of Jesus Christ being the highest form of worship. The Lord said, "I give unto you these sayings that you may understand and know how to worship, and know what you worship, that you may come unto the Father in my name, and in due time receive of his fulness. For if you keep my commandments you shall receive of his fulness, and be glorified in me as I am in the Father; therefore, I say unto you, you shall receive grace for grace" (93:19–20; cf. 50:40).

The phrase "election of grace" (84:99) refers to the premortal existence and the manner in which God's chosen people come to earth. Those who developed the talent for spirituality in the first estate, who zealously and nobly stood in defense of the Father's plan of salvation, the great plan of happiness, come to this earth through a designated channel as descendants of Abraham, Isaac, and Jacob, as members of the house of Israel. Having exercised exceedingly great faith in that first estate, they were prepared to serve a redemptive function in mortality (86:8–10; 138:53–56; cf. Alma 13:3). When it came time for the earth to be populated, God determined through his infinite foreknowledge when and where the children of Israel would be born (cf. Deut. 32:8–9), for they would be a crucial means whereby all the people of the planet would be blessed (124:58; Abr. 2:8–11). Theirs would be a leavening influence throughout the world. Thus, God performs a gracious and kindly act, one planned from before the foundations of the world, in behalf of all his children. When the end of the world comes, when the Savior returns in glory to cleanse the earth of wickedness, when the great millennial era dawns, a new song will be sung by the faithful: "The Lord hath brought again Zion; / The Lord hath redeemed his people, Israel, / According to the election of grace, / Which was brought to pass by the faith / And covenant of their fathers" (84:99).

Those who become members of the CHURCH OF THE FIRSTBORN—who become joint heirs with Christ to "all that [the] Father hath" (84:33–39; Rom. 8:14–18) and who, by grace, are entitled to inherit the riches of eternity as though they themselves were the firstborn—enter the highest degree of the celestial kingdom and receive "of his fulness and of his grace" (76:94).

See also Mercy.

BIBLIOGRAPHY

Lectures on Faith. Salt Lake City: Deseret Book, 1985.

RLM

Grace for grace. *See* Grace.

Grace to grace. *See* Grace.

Granger, Oliver

Birth: 7 February 1794, Phelps, Ontario County, New York

Death: 25 August 1841, Kirtland, Lake County, Ohio

In 1833 at Sodus, New York, Oliver Granger, a noted businessman, was baptized and ordained an elder by Brigham and Joseph Young. He subsequently gathered with the Saints to Kirtland, Ohio. There he served faithfully as a missionary, temple laborer, and high councilor before fleeing from religious persecution in Ohio to Far West, Missouri, in June 1838 (Cook, 230).

In July 1838, the Lord through the Prophet Joseph Smith instructed Granger to "contend earnestly for the redemption of the First Presidency" as the Church's financial agent in Ohio, because the Prophet had been accused of "running away" to Missouri and "cheating [his] creditors" back in Kirtland (117:13; Smith, 3:164). In a letter of recommendation, the First Presidency described Granger as "a man of the most strict integrity and moral virtue" (Smith, 3:350).

Over the next several years Granger successfully represented the financial interests of the Church in Ohio and Iowa. Two men who were not Latter-day Saints later affirmed: "We . . . firmly believe that the course which he has pursued in settling the claims, accounts, etc., against the former citizens of Kirtland township, has done much credit to himself, and all others that committed to him the care of adjusting their business with this community, which also furnishes evidence that there was no intention on their part of defrauding their creditors" (Smith, 3:165). Horace Kingsbury wrote of Granger's management of the Church's financial affairs that his work was "truly praiseworthy, and has entitled him to my highest esteem, and ever grateful recollection" (3:174).

Granger died on 25 August 1841 at Kirtland while serving as the First Presidency's representative. "A vast concourse" of mostly non-Mormon Ohioans attended his funeral, a tribute to his sterling reputation (Smith, 4:409). Though "his sacrifice [would] be more sacred . . . than his increase," the Lord promised that Granger's "name shall be had in sacred remembrance from generation to generation, forever and ever" for his work on behalf of the Church (117:12–13).

BIBLIOGRAPHY

Cook, Lyndon W. *The Revelations of the Prophet Joseph Smith.* Salt Lake City: Deseret Book, 1985.

Smith, Joseph. *History of The Church of Jesus Christ of Latter-day Saints.* Edited by B. H. Roberts. 7 vols. 2d ed. rev. Salt Lake City: The Church of Jesus Christ of Latter-day Saints, 1932–51.

RLN

Gratitude. *See* Thankfulness, thanksgiving.

Great and abominable church

The combined forces of evil that war against the Lord's people in any period of time. Two references in the Doctrine and Covenants name the great and abominable church, both in connection with the destruction of wickedness at the end of the world. *See* End of the earth/end of the world.

In section 29, the Lord revealed that in the LAST DAYS, great devastations would come upon the world. In the process of destroying wickedness, "the great and abominable church, which is the whore of all the earth, shall be cast down by devouring fire, according as it is spoken by the mouth of Ezekiel the prophet, who spoke of these things" (29:21). The prophecy from Ezekiel is probably Ezekiel 38–39, which foretells in dramatic apocalyptic symbols the ultimate destruction of the forces of evil. In section 88, the Lord speaks of "that great church, the mother of abominations, that made all nations drink of the wine of the wrath of her fornication, that persecuteth the saints of God." That evil force will be destroyed: "Behold, she is the tares of the earth; she is bound in bundles; her bands are made strong, no man can loose them; therefore, she is ready to be burned" (88:94). These passages give context to Nephi's vision in 1 Nephi 14. Nephi saw the latter days, in which the forces of good, called the "church of the Lamb" of God, are engaged in mortal conflict with the forces of evil, called, among other things, the "great and abominable church." The Saints are armed "with the power of God in great glory," but God's wrath is poured out on the great and abominable church (1 Ne. 14:14–17).

See also Babylon.

BIBLIOGRAPHY

Jackson, Kent P. *From Apostasy to Restoration.* Salt Lake City: Deseret Book, 1996.

Robinson, Stephen E. "Early Christianity and 1 Nephi 13–14." In *The Book of Mormon: First Nephi: The Doctrinal Foundation,* edited by Monte S. Nyman and Charles D. Tate Jr., 177–91. Provo, Utah: Religious Studies Center, Brigham Young University, 1988.

KPJ

Great and dreadful day of the Lord

The "day of the Lord" designates a time of divine judgment, a day of reckoning, usually connected with Jesus' second coming (43:17, 20–22; cf. Joel 2:1, 11, 31; 2 Pet. 3:10). The phrase "great and dreadful day of the Lord" occurs five times in the Doctrine and Covenants, always in connection with Malachi's prophecy: "I will send you Elijah the prophet before the coming of the great and dreadful day of the Lord: and he shall turn the heart of the fathers to the children, and the heart of the children to their fathers, lest I come and smite the earth with a curse" (Mal. 4:5–6). In Doctrine and Covenants 2:1 Moroni conveyed to Joseph Smith a revised version of Malachi's words (cf. JS–H 1:38); 110:14–16 emphasizes the fulfillment of Malachi's prophecy, indicating it "is near, even at the doors"; 128:17–18 quotes Malachi 4:5–6 and relates it to baptism for the dead. Doctrine and Covenants 138:46 indicates "Malachi, the prophet who testified of the coming of Elijah" was one of the righteous dead in the spirit world awaiting the coming of the Savior to that world "to declare their redemption from the bands of death" (138:16).

The Hebrew phrase translated "the great and dreadful day of the Lord" in the King James Version occurs in Malachi 4:5 (and also in Joel 2:31, where KJV has "the great and the terrible day"). In Hebrew, "great and dreadful" emphasizes one significant aspect of the "day of the Lord"—that it will be very dreadful. It does not mean this "day" will be "great," or wonderful, for some people and "dreadful for others." Similar expressions in scripture include "great and terrible wilderness" (Deut. 1:19); "great and abominable church" (1 Nephi 13:6); and "great and marvelous work" (D&C 6:1).

See also Jesus Christ, second coming of; Judgment(s).

BIBLIOGRAPHY

Pike, Dana M. "'The Great and Dreadful Day of the Lord': The Anatomy of an Expression." *BYU Studies* 41, no. 2 (2002): 149–60.

DMP

Great and marvelous work

A phrase often used to refer to the restoration of the GOSPEL and the Church through the Prophet Joseph Smith in the latter days. The phrase "great and marvelous work" is used four times in the Doctrine and Covenants (6:1; 11:1; 12:1; 14:1). The entire phrase reads: "a great and marvelous work is about to come forth unto" (6:1; 14:1) or "among" (11:1; 12:1) "the children of men." This phrase introduced revelations calling Oliver Cowdery, Hyrum Smith, Joseph Knight Sr., and David Whitmer to the work of the ministry.

President Joseph Fielding Smith defined the phrase and connected it to Isaiah's messianic prophecy that the Lord would "do a marvellous work among this people, even a marvellous work and a wonder" (Isa. 29:14). Moreover, President Smith taught that "this marvelous work is the restoration of the Church and the Gospel with all the power and authority, keys and blessings which pertain to this great work for the salvation of the children of men" (1:35).

The Book of Mormon contains a nearly identical phrase referring to the latter-day restoration: "For the time cometh, saith the Lamb of God, that I will work a great and a marvelous work among the children of men" (1 Ne. 14:7; cf. 1 Ne. 22:8; 2 Ne. 25:17; 3 Ne. 21:9). Thus, the Doctrine and Covenants, the Bible, and the Book of Mormon all use a similar phrase to depict the prophesied restoration of the gospel of Jesus Christ.

Variations of this phrase occur three other times in the Doctrine and Covenants. One reference promises Oliver Cowdery, "Thou shalt know mysteries which are great and marvelous" (6:11), and two references describe the attributes of God and his works: "Great is his wisdom, marvelous are his ways" (76:2) and "Great and marvelous are the works of the Lord" (76:114). This phraseology is consistent with Book of Mormon variations of the phrase, which always refer to the works of the Lord and his servants (e.g., 1 Ne. 1:14; 2 Ne. 1:10; Jacob 4:8; Ether 4:15) or the words of the Lord and his servants (e.g., 3 Ne. 3:16; 17:16–17; 19:34; Ether 11:20; 12:5).

See also Church of Jesus Christ of Latter-day Saints, The.

BIBLIOGRAPHY

Smith, Joseph Fielding. *Church History and Modern Revelation.* 2 vols. Salt Lake City: Deseret Book, 1953.

MAG

Greatest of all the gifts of God

ETERNAL LIFE, or the "gift of salvation" awarded to the righteous who "hold out faithful to the end" (6:13; 14:7). Nephi equates the "greatest of all the gifts of God" with partaking of the fruit of the tree of life, which fruit was "most sweet, above all" and "desirable above all" (1 Ne. 8:11; 15:36).

KJW

Griffin, Selah J.

Birth: 17 March 1799 (?), Redding, Fairfield County, Connecticut

Death: Unknown

In 1827 Selah Griffin was the supervisor of highways and practiced his trade as a blacksmith in Morgan, Ohio, before moving to Kirtland. Sometime before June 1831 he was baptized, and in early June 1831 he was ordained an elder. He was called by revelation to serve a mission with Newel Knight: "And let my servants Newel Knight and Selah J. Griffin both be ordained, and also take their journey" (52:32). When Newel Knight was instructed to remain with the Colesville Saints traveling to Missouri, the command was revoked, and Selah was reassigned to journey with Thomas B. Marsh "speedily to the land of Missouri" (56:5–6). At an August 1831 conference in Jackson County, Missouri, Bishop Edward Partridge asked Griffin to settle in Jackson County, which he did; however, mob violence forced him to abandon his property, tools, and business in November 1833. Griffin wrote: "In November they Strip us of guns and Drive us a crost the river in to Clay County the lose of property . . . in the hol amounted was Seven hundred And Seventy five dollars is My los Buy the mob" (Johnson, 454).

After being ordained a seventy in 1836, Griffin settled in Caldwell County, Missouri, only to be driven out in the winter of 1838–39 after Governor Boggs signed the extermination order. Griffin filed an affidavit with the state of Missouri seeking redress for his losses but was never reimbursed. He moved to Knox, Illinois, and did not go with the Saints when they migrated west.

BIBLIOGRAPHY

Johnson, Clark V., ed. *Mormon Redress Petitions: Documents of the 1833–38 Missouri Conflict.* Provo, Utah: Religious Studies Center, Brigham Young University, 1992.

KWF

Grover, Thomas

Birth: 22 July 1807, Whitehall, Washington County, New York

Death: 20 February 1886, Farmington, Davis County, Utah

After hearing Joseph Smith preach, Thomas Grover was baptized by Warren A. Cowdery in September in 1834. Grover subsequently sold his New York farm for five hundred dollars and moved to Kirtland, Ohio. Upon meeting the Prophet, Grover willingly consecrated his money, which was used to purchase building materials for the Kirtland Temple (Porter, 1). Grover continued to be generous in his contributions to the Church throughout his life.

In January 1836, Grover was set apart to serve on the Kirtland high council by Joseph and Hyrum Smith and Sidney Rigdon. Shortly after receiving this appointment, he moved to Far West, where he served in the same capacity (Porter, 7). Expelled from Missouri in 1839, he relocated in Nauvoo, where he was a member of the high council (124:131–32). Grover also served in the Nauvoo Legion, as a bodyguard of Joseph Smith, and as a missionary to the southern states, Michigan, and Canada.

Grover was one of the first to leave Nauvoo for the West in February 1846. At the request of Brigham Young, Grover served on high councils in Salt Lake and Farmington (Porter, 7). In civic affairs, he was probate judge of Davis County and a member of the Utah legislature.

BIBLIOGRAPHY

Porter Family Histories. Church History Library, The Church of Jesus Christ of Latter-day Saints, Salt Lake City, Utah.

RC

Guile. *See* Appendix E.

For behold the field is white already to harvest; and lo, he that thrusteth in his sickle with his might, the same layeth up in store that he perisheth not, but bringeth salvation to his soul; and faith, hope, charity and love, with an eye single to the glory of God, qualify him for the work. 4:4–5

Hagar

An Egyptian handmaid of Sarah who became Abraham's second wife and by whom he had his first son, Ishmael (Gen. 16:1–16; 21:9–21; 25:12). "God commanded Abraham, and Sarah gave Hagar to Abraham to wife. And why did she do it? Because this was the law; and from Hagar sprang many people. This, therefore, was fulfilling, among other things, the promises" (132:34). In modern revelation the Lord said, "Sarah . . . administered unto Abraham according to the law when I commanded Abraham to take Hagar to wife" (132:65).

DKO

Hancock, Levi W.

Birth: 7 April 1803, Springfield, Hampden County, Massachusetts

Death: 10 June 1882, Washington, Washington County, Utah

Levi W. Hancock was baptized in Kirtland, Ohio, on 16 November 1830, by Parley P. Pratt. He was one of the converts garnered by the Lamanite missionaries on their way through Kirtland to western Missouri (Hancock, 32). Hancock wrote of Elder Pratt: "Oh, how I loved that man who baptised me. The first time I saw him he looked like an angel to me" (36). Soon after his baptism, Hancock was ordained an elder by Oliver Cowdery.

Levi Hancock was among a large number of brethren called to travel to Missouri in the summer of 1831 to help lay the foundations of Zion, doing missionary work along the way (52:1–2, 10, 29; 58:6–7). He was part of the missionary group commended by the Lord for their faithful labors as they approached the land of Zion (62:1–4).

In 1834 Hancock was a member of ZION'S CAMP. In February 1835 he was called as a president of the First Quorum of the Seventy and served faithfully in this position until his death forty-seven years later. He moved with his family to Missouri in 1836, where he was appointed to the Clay County high council and later to the Far West high council. In the spring of 1839 the Hancocks were driven from the state of Missouri with the rest of the Saints. After moving to Nauvoo, Hancock served as a police

Levi W. Hancock, 1803–1882.

Courtesy Church History Library.

officer and a member of the Nauvoo Legion. He received his endowment in the Nauvoo Temple in December 1845.

Hancock went west with the Saints in 1846. He was the only general authority in the Mormon Battalion, and he served as the chaplain and spiritual leader to the company. Of that experience Andrew Jenson wrote, "His wise counsel and exemplary course did much to mould the character of the soldiers" (1:189). After his discharge from the Battalion in California in 1847, Hancock traveled eastward to meet his family who were still on the trail from Winter Quarters to the Salt Lake Valley. When they arrived in the valley he took up his trade of carpentry and built a home for his family. He resided in Salt Lake City for a time, before moving to Payson, Manti, and back to Salt Lake City between 1850 and 1863. About 1866 Hancock moved south again to help establish a number of communities—Harrisburg, Leeds, and Washington. He was ordained a patriarch in 1872.

Levi Hancock was an unassuming servant of the Lord, more effective in his influence than he was aware. Heber C. Kimball said of him: "Brother Hancock thought that he was not so talented as some of his brethren but I say he is and moreso . . . [his] talents were not the gift of speaking as with a tongue . . . but it was experience and the gift of God" (Hovey, 24). His love of Joseph Smith and loyalty to him was unbounded. In the Prophet's last speech to the Nauvoo Legion just before his martyrdom, he placed his hand on the head of Levi Hancock and said, "This day the Lord has shown to me that which he has never shown me before that I have thousands of friends that never pretended friendship while others have sought to crawl into my bosom on account of my good feelings towards them and . . . seek my life" (Pace, 4–5).

BIBLIOGRAPHY

Hancock, Levi W. The Life of Levi Hancock. Typescript. L. Tom Perry Special Collections, Harold B. Lee Library, Brigham Young University, Provo, Utah.

Hovey, Joseph Grafton. "Autobiography of Joseph Grafton Hovey, 1812–1847." Typescript. L. Tom Perry Special Collections, Harold B. Lee Library, Brigham Young University, Provo, Utah.

Jenson, Andrew. Latter-day Saints' Biographical Encyclopedia. 4 vols. Salt Lake City: The Andrew Jenson History Company, 1901–36. Reprint, Salt Lake City: Western Epics, 1971.

Pace, William Bryan. Autobiography of William Bryan Pace. Typescript. L. Tom Perry Special Collections, Harold B. Lee Library, Brigham Young University, Provo, Utah.

KWP

Hancock, Solomon

Birth: August 1793, Springfield, Hampden County, Massachusetts

Death: 2 December 1847, near Council Bluffs, Pottawattamie County, Iowa

Solomon Hancock was baptized a member of the Church by December 1830 and ordained an elder by June 1831. On 7 June 1831, he and Simeon Carter were called to "take their journey" to Missouri and to "preach by the way" (52:27). While traveling through Indiana and Illinois and into Missouri, they shared the gospel with numerous individuals, baptizing more than seventy people. According to his son Charles, Solomon Hancock wrote of that mission, "We went to Jackson County and filled

our mission preaching and baptizing when the door was opened." The land of Zion, Hancock further recalled, "was very rich and productive abounding in much wild fruit and honey and game made it appear lovely and desirable for settlers." Under the counsel of Joseph Smith, "the spirit of gathering was encouraged. And we began to preach for the Saints to gather to Jackson County Missouri the land of Zion to learn more of the ways of the Lord." After fulfilling their responsibilities in Missouri, the two men returned to Ohio, "preaching by the way as the spirit of the Lord held us and arrived at home late in the fall" (Hancock, 32).

Solomon Hancock moved to Jackson County, Missouri, in 1832 and later settled in Clay County, where he served on the high council. While living in Missouri, he traveled to Kirtland and participated in the temple dedication in 1836. During the persecutions in Missouri, he and his brothers protected and fed six hundred men, women, and children who had been driven from their homes. Exiled from Missouri in 1839, he relocated to Illinois, first in Adams County and then in Hancock County, where he presided over the Yelrome branch of the Church (the Morley settlement) near Lima. With increasing persecution, including the burning of homes in the Morley settlement, Hancock moved to Nauvoo. He left Nauvoo in 1846, starting west with the Saints, but died in 1847 near Council Bluffs, Iowa.

BIBLIOGRAPHY

Hancock, Charles. Autobiography. Church History Library, The Church of Jesus Christ of Latter-day Saints, Salt Lake City, Utah.

RC

Hand(s)

A part of the physical body used symbolically in the scriptures in what might be called anatomy imagery. The words hand and hands are used in the Doctrine and Covenants dozens of times with several meanings or contexts, as illustrated in the following examples:

1. The literal body part at the end of the arm. "I will lay my hand upon you by the hand of my servant Sidney Rigdon" (36:2; cf. 6:37; 8:8; 20:41; 68:27; 129:5, 8).

2. Direction, or position of favor or disfavor. "God doth not walk in crooked paths, neither doth he turn to the right hand nor to the left, neither doth he vary from that which he hath said" (3:2). "We beheld the glory of the Son, on the right hand of the Father" (76:20; cf. 19:5; 29:12, 27; 133:56).

3. The controlling or protecting POWER of God. Joseph Smith and Sidney Rigdon, while on a mission, were assured, "Your families are well; they are in mine hands" (100:1). And to the concerned Saints driven from their homes and land in Jackson County, Missouri, the Lord said, "Let your hearts be comforted concerning Zion; for all flesh is in mine hands" (101:16; cf. 38:22; 63:25; 67:2; 97:19; 112:15; 121:12).

4. An agent of discipline; judgments from God. "The people in Ohio call upon me in much faith, thinking I will stay my hand in judgment upon the nations, but I cannot deny my word. . . . Inasmuch as they do repent and receive the fulness of my gospel, and become sanctified, I will stay mine hand in judgment" (39:16–18). In a revelation referred to as a "prophecy on war" (87, headnote), the Lord said, "With the sword and by bloodshed . . . and with famine, and plague, and earthquake . . . shall the inhabitants of the earth be made to feel the wrath, and indignation, and chastening hand of an Almighty God, until the consumption decreed hath made a full end of all nations" (87:6; cf. 19:10; 121:2, 4).

5. An idiom meaning close or near. "The kingdom of heaven is at hand" (33:10), and "the time is soon at hand that I shall come in a cloud with power and great glory" (34:7; cf. 39:21; 43:17; 45:37; 63:53; 128:24; 138:15).

6. An expression of stewardship or responsibility. "It is required of the Lord, at the hand of every steward, to render an account of his stewardship, both in time and in eternity" (72:3). Oliver Cowdery and David Whitmer were told by the Lord, "By your hands I will work a marvelous work among the children of men" (18:37–44; cf. 31:5–7). Under the principles of consecration, the "money" and "meat" belonging to the bishop's storehouse were to "be kept in the hands of the bishop" (51:13). The Lord revealed that he established the Constitution of the United States "by the hands of wise men" whom he "raised up unto this very purpose" (101:80).

7. An expression meaning in the custody, keeping, or care of. The Lord told Oliver Cowdery that the gift of the "spirit of revelation" would "deliver [him] out of the hands of [his] enemies" (8:3–4; 10:5; 101:71).

8. As a symbol for spiritual cleanliness. To the "first laborers in this last kingdom," the Lord commanded, "Organize yourselves, and prepare yourselves, and sanctify yourselves; yea, purify your hearts, and cleanse your hands and your feet before me, that I may make you clean . . . from the blood of this wicked generation; . . . let your hands be clean, until the Lord comes" (88:74–86).

9. An attribution of human characteristics (personification): "holy hands" (60:7), "chastening hand" (87:6), "fostering hand" (109:69), "friendly hands" (121:9), "damning hand" (123:7), and "iron hand" (123:9).

DKO

Hands, laying on of. *See* Laying on of hands.

Hands, lifting up holy. *See* Lifting up holy hands.

Happiness. *See* Joy.

Hardheartedness. *See* Heart(s).

Harmony, Pennsylvania

Harmony Township (now Oakland) was part of the town of Willingborough, Luzerne County, Pennsylvania, until it became a separate township in 1809. The next year, Susquehanna County was divided from Luzerne County and Harmony Township was organized as part of the new county. It bears the name given to the area by those who settled there in 1789. The village of Harmony, which no longer exists, was situated two miles south of the Pennsylvania–New York state line on the Oquago turnpike and east bank of the Susquehanna River. In 1790 or 1791, Isaac and Elizabeth Hale, Emma Smith's parents, located in what was Willingborough Township, Luzerne County. Their homestead was not in the village of Harmony but rather

Courtesy Church History Library.

Home of Joseph and Emma Smith, Harmony, Pennsylvania; photograph by George Edward Anderson, 1907. The center section was the home of Joseph and Emma Smith while Joseph worked on translating the Book of Mormon. The taller, two-story structures on either side are subsequent additions.

in the Great Bend of the Susquehanna, where the river runs in an east-west course, and on the north bank.

Joseph Smith arrived in Harmony in early November 1825, hired by Josiah Stowell to dig for a purported Spanish silver mine. While boarding at the Hale home, Joseph met Isaac and Elizabeth's daughter Emma. The couple married at South Bainbridge, Chenango County, New York, on 18 January 1827. Joseph and Emma then moved to the Smith family's frame home in Manchester, Ontario County, New York. There Joseph farmed with his father and on 22 September received the gold plates from the angel Moroni at the Hill Cumorah. Because of mob pressure, Joseph and Emma moved to Harmony in December 1827. There Joseph purchased thirteen and one-half acres from Isaac Hale, and Joseph and Emma occupied a small,

two-story frame home. With the aid of a scribe, Martin Harris, Joseph translated 116 pages of manuscript (12 April through 14 June 1828); these pages were lost by Martin during a visit to Palmyra, New York. With the aid of a new scribe, Oliver Cowdery, Joseph was able to continue the translation. During this process the Prophet and Oliver received the Aaronic and Melchizedek priesthoods from heavenly messengers along the banks of the Susquehanna. First came John the Baptist, 15 May 1829, and then Peter, James, and John, May or June 1829 (13:1; 27:12; 128:20). The Prophet's little frame home became a house of revelation throughout Joseph and Emma's intermittent tenure in Harmony from July 1828 to August 1830. Joseph received fifteen revelations recorded in the Doctrine and Covenants during this period (3–13; 24–27). *See* Historical context and overview of Doctrine and Covenants 3–13 (pp. 716–24) and 24–27 (pp. 732–36).

Joseph and Emma maintained their home in Harmony until the translation of the Book of Mormon was nearly completed. Interference from the local mob again forced them to vacate their home and take up residence at the Whitmer farm in Fayette, New York, by 1 June 1829. There the translation was completed and arrangements made for the publication of the Book of Mormon in Palmyra. Joseph returned to Harmony in October 1829 to await the completion of the printing. When the book came off the press in March 1830, he was at the Grandin Press, and on 6 April 1830 he organized the Church at Fayette. Joseph and Emma returned to their Harmony home until conditions again became untenable and required them to move once more to the Whitmer farm by early September 1830. They never returned to live in Harmony again. Their farm and home were sold to Joseph McKune Jr. for three hundred dollars on 8 June 1833. When Oakland Township was divided from Harmony Township in December 1853, the former Isaac Hale and Joseph Smith properties were within Oakland's boundaries. *See* maps, pp. 447 and 710.

BIBLIOGRAPHY

Blackman, Emily C. *History of Susquehanna County, Pennsylvania.* Philadelphia: Claxton, Remsen & Haffelfinger, 1873.

Gordon, Thomas F. *A Gazetteer of the State of Pennsylvania.* Philadelphia: T. Belknap, 1832.

Porter, Larry C. "A Study of the Origins of The Church of Jesus Christ of Latter-day Saints in the States of New York and Pennsylvania, 1816–1831." Ph.D. dissertation, Brigham Young University, 1971.

LCP

Harris, Emer

Birth: 29 May 1781, Cambridge, Washington County, New York

Death: 28 November 1869, Logan, Cache County, Utah

Emer Harris, brother of Martin Harris, was baptized by Hyrum Smith on 10 February 1831. Shortly thereafter, he joined the Saints in Kirtland, Ohio. On 25 January 1832, the Lord called Emer and Simeon Carter to be "united in the ministry" as missionary companions (75:30). The two men began their mission together, but Emer eventually joined with his brother Martin, while Simeon went with Jared Carter. Emer later recalled that Martin had been with him most of the time since he left Kirtland and that eighty-two individuals had been baptized and many more had believed what they taught. In a similar vein, *The Evening and the Morning Star* reported that "brothers Martin and Emer Harris have baptized one hundred persons at Chenango point, New-York, within a few weeks" (70). Additionally, in Springville, Susquehanna County, Pennsylvania, the brothers organized a branch with seventy members. After returning from his mission in midsummer of 1833, Emer, having purchased a farm, labored both on his land and on the Kirtland Temple as a carpenter.

Emer moved his family from Kirtland to Far West, Missouri, in the fall of 1838, and in December of that year they were expelled with the Saints. They moved to Illinois, first to Quincy and then to Commerce, where Emer worked as a carpenter on the Nauvoo Temple. By 1852 he had migrated to Utah and shortly after his arrival there was ordained a patriarch.

BIBLIOGRAPHY

Harris, Emer. Notebook, 1817–1846. Church History Library. The Church of Jesus Christ of Latter-day Saints, Salt Lake City, Utah.

The Evening and the Morning Star 1 (February 1833): 70.

Tuckett, Madge Harris, and Belle Harris Wilson. *The Martin Harris Story with Biographies of Emer Harris and Dennison Lott Harris.* Provo, Utah: Vintage Books, 1983.

RC

Harris, George W.

Birth: 1 April 1780, Lanesboro, Berkshire County, Massachusetts

Death: 1857, Council Bluffs, Pottawattamie County, Iowa

George W. Harris was baptized in the fall of 1834 by Orson Pratt in Terre Haute, Indiana. He is named once in the Doctrine and Covenants, in 124:132, where he is listed as a member of the Nauvoo high council in 1841. For several years before that time and for many years afterward, George Harris was prominent in Church and political affairs. He served as a member of high councils in Far West, Missouri; Nauvoo, Illinois; and Council Bluffs, Iowa. In March 1838 he hosted Joseph Smith when the Prophet arrived in Far West from Kirtland. Joseph Smith recorded, "We were immediately received under the hospitable roof of Brother George W. Harris, who treated us with all possible kindness" (3:9). Brother Harris joined other Saints in petitioning for REDRESS from persecutions in Missouri, documenting personal losses of nearly ten thousand dollars, none of which was recovered. He served as an alderman and president pro tem of the city council in Nauvoo and affixed his signature to the document that declared the *Nauvoo Expositor* a public nuisance. The destruction of that press and consequent charges against Joseph Smith led to the martyrdom of Joseph and Hyrum Smith. When the main body of the Saints left Nauvoo for the West in February 1846, Harris was appointed commissary of the first encampment. At Council Bluffs, where the Saints camped for the winter of 1846–47, he served as bishop and then as a high councilor; however, he rejected the counsel of Church leaders to gather to Salt Lake City and remained in Council Bluffs.

BIBLIOGRAPHY

Smith, Joseph. *History of The Church of Jesus Christ of Latter-day Saints.* Edited by B. H. Roberts. 7 vols. 2d ed. rev. Salt Lake City: The Church of Jesus Christ of Latter-day Saints, 1932–51.

RC

Harris, Martin

Birth: 18 May 1783, Easton, Albany County, New York

Death: 10 July 1875, Clarkston, Cache County, Utah

Martin Harris was baptized 6 April 1830 by Oliver Cowdery. No one contributed more financial support in the infancy of the Church than Martin Harris, and few received such severe chastisements or varied callings from God. In July 1828, the Lord, through the Prophet Joseph Smith, called Harris a "wicked man" for his careless disregard of the sacred. He had relied "upon his own judgment" instead of turning to

Martin Harris, 1783–1875; photograph by Savage and Ottinger.

God and in so doing lost the 116-page manuscript of the Book of Mormon (3:12–13).

Wanting relief from this condemnation, in March 1829 Harris asked Joseph to speak to God in his behalf. As he did so, Joseph received a revelation that gave hope to Harris. Joseph told him of three witnesses who would see the gold plates (5:15; 17:2). At the Whitmer home in Fayette, New York, Joseph added, "It is the will of God that you should look upon the plates, in company with Oliver Cowdery and David Whitmer" (Smith, *Biographical,* 164). Harris went into the woods near the Whitmer farmhouse with the designated others "to obtain, by fervent and humble prayer, the fulfilment of the promises given" of viewing the plates. Their initial attempt to see the plates was unsuccessful. Harris withdrew from the others, believing "his presence was the cause of [their] not obtaining" a view of the plates (Smith, *Church,* 1:54). Joseph, Oliver Cowdery, and David Whitmer did receive an angelic manifestation and were shown the plates. Later, "the same vision was opened" to Joseph and Martin. "'Tis enough; 'tis enough; mine eyes have beheld," said Harris of the vision (Smith, *Church,* 1:55).

Even though he was severely chastened for losing the Book of Mormon manuscript (19:13–20), Harris was still confident of the prophetic calling of Joseph Smith. On 25 August 1829 Harris agreed to secure the cost of publishing the Book of Mormon and guaranteed printer E. B. Grandin of Palmyra, New York, a payment of three thousand dollars. Grandin accepted the guarantee and began to print the Book of Mormon, until he learned that Harris was wavering on their agreement. At that time, the Lord admonished Harris to "not covet thine own property, but impart it freely to the printing of the Book of Mormon" (19:26). He forewarned Harris that "misery thou shalt receive if thou wilt slight these counsels, yea, even the destruction of thyself and property" (19:33). Then, in no uncertain terms, the Lord said, "Pay the debt thou hast contracted with the printer. Release thyself from bondage" (19:35). Harris satisfied the debt on 7 April 1831 by selling part of his farm.

Not until the debt was satisfied was Harris mentioned again in a revelation. On 7 June 1831 the Lord instructed him to travel to Missouri to attend a Church conference (52:24). Harris obeyed, and on 19 June, in company with Joseph and other Church leaders, he began a journey to Missouri. After he reached Independence, Missouri, he was called by God to give funds to build up Zion: "It is wisdom in me that my servant Martin Harris should be an example unto the church, in laying his moneys before the bishop of the church" (58:35). Harris gave the requested money to the bishop.

A few months later, on 12 November 1831, Harris was called with several others as "stewards over the revelations and commandments" (70:1–5). He was to help manage, print, and distribute revelations so "that the revelations may be published, and go forth unto the ends of the earth" (72:20–21). The Lord warned that "an account of this stewardship" would be required "in the day of judgment" (70:4). Harris was also called as a member of the United Firm,

an organization that generated revenue for the operations of the Church. As a member, he was expected to give personal funds for "the affairs of the poor, and all things pertaining to the bishopric both in the land of Zion and in the land of Kirtland" (82:12).

In addition to these assignments, on 17 February 1834 Harris was selected to be a member of the Kirtland high council, the first such council in the Church (102:34). Then, again, on 23 April 1834, the Lord told Harris to "devote his moneys for the proclaiming of my words, according as my servant Joseph Smith, Jun., shall direct" (104:24–26). That is the last mention of Harris in the Doctrine and Covenants, though he did travel from Kirtland, Ohio, to Missouri with ZION'S CAMP in the summer of 1834. As one of the Three Witnesses of the Book of Mormon he helped select the members of the first Quorum of the Twelve Apostles in this dispensation (Smith, *Church,* 2:186–87). Harris stayed in Kirtland instead of moving with the Saints to Missouri in 1837. In September 1837 he withdrew from the Church. For the next thirty-two years he associated with dissident religious groups in Kirtland. In 1870 he reunited with The Church of Jesus Christ of Latter-day Saints in the Salt Lake Valley. From 1870 to 1875 he resided in Cache County, Utah, taking every opportunity to bear witness of the truthfulness of the Book of Mormon and the restoration of the gospel.

BIBLIOGRAPHY

Smith, Joseph. *History of The Church of Jesus Christ of Latter-day Saints.* Edited by B. H. Roberts. 7 vols. 2d ed. rev. Salt Lake City: The Church of Jesus Christ of Latter-day Saints, 1932–51.

Smith, Lucy Mack. *Biographical Sketches of Joseph Smith the Prophet and His Progenitors for Many Generations.* London: S. W. Richards, 1853. Reprint, London: William Bowden, 1969.

———. *History of Joseph Smith by His Mother.* Edited by Preston Nibley. Salt Lake City: Bookcraft, 1958.

Tuckett, Madge Harris, and Belle Harris Wilson. *The Martin Harris Story with Biographies of Emer Harris and Dennison Lott Harris.* Provo, Utah: Vintage Books, 1983.

SEB

Harvest

The season or process of gathering in crops or fruits from the field (agriculture), from the vine (viticulture), and from the garden (horticulture). Figuratively, in the PARABLE OF THE WHEAT AND THE TARES (86:1–7; Matt. 13:24–30, 36–43), *harvest* refers to the end of the world when the righteous are separated from the wicked. From the time the Savior first spoke the parable to the time of his second coming, the Lord's servants are commissioned to gather the wheat from the tares in preparation for the harvest.

In ancient and modern scripture the world is compared to a field (Matt. 13:38; D&C 86:2), which is declared as "white [ripe] already to harvest." The Lord of the harvest encourages all his laborers to thrust in their sickles with their might and reap the fruits (converts) while the day lasts, and treasure up their own salvation (4:4; 6:3; 11:3; 12:3; 14:3; 33:3, 7). Wheat and tares grow together until the harvest is fully ripe, and then the wheat will be gathered out, the tares bundled, and the field burned (86:4–7; 101:64–66). *See* Parable of the wheat and the tares.

The Lord specifically warns the selfish rich and others who refuse to hearken to his voice about "the harvest [being] ended, and [their] souls not saved" (45:2; 56:16).

DKO

Haws, Peter

Birth: 17 February 1795, Young Township, Leeds County, Ontario, Canada

Death: 1862, California

After being baptized in Canada, Peter Haws moved to Kirtland, Ohio. By 1839 he had served a brief mission in Illinois with Erastus Snow. When he moved to Nauvoo, he "brought considerable property. . . . By the counsel of the Presidency, [Haws] . . . converted his funds to feeding the poor, bringing in meat and flour, &c." (Smith, 6:440). He also owned a steam-operated sawmill and was appointed a member of the Nauvoo Agricultural and Manufacturing Association (1841–45). In 1841, the Prophet Joseph Smith instructed Haws and three others by revelation to build the Nauvoo House, "a house for boarding, . . . that the weary traveler may find health and safety while he shall contemplate the word of the Lord" (124:23). Haws fully embraced this calling. In 1843 the Prophet "went to the Temple, and found a large assembly, and Brother Haws preaching about the Nauvoo House" (Smith, 5:283). That same year Haws solicited "twenty-five hands to go with him to the Pine country, to get lumber for the Nauvoo House" (Smith, 5:369). Haws also gathered donations while on a mission to fund construction of the Nauvoo House and the temple (Black, 129). Between 1840 and 1844 he served as an alternate on the Nauvoo high council and in 1844 became a member of the Council of Fifty. In 1845 he was appointed captain of the eighth company for the move west. He went to Council Bluffs, Iowa, in 1846. In 1848 he visited Lyman Wight's apostate settlement in Texas. Upon returning to Iowa, he publicly criticized the Twelve, claiming the "Council of Fifty held powers superior to those of Twelve Apostles" (Cook, 261). He was excommunicated from the Church in early 1849 and by 1854 had moved near the Humboldt River in Nevada.

BIBLIOGRAPHY

Black, Susan Easton. *Who's Who in the Doctrine and Covenants.* Salt Lake City: Deseret Book, 1997.

Cook, Lyndon W. *The Revelations of the Prophet Joseph Smith.* Salt Lake City: Deseret Book, 1985.

Smith, Joseph. *History of The Church of Jesus Christ of Latter-day Saints.* Edited by B. H. Roberts. 7 vols. 2d ed. rev. Salt Lake City: The Church of Jesus Christ of Latter-day Saints, 1932–51.

KWF

Healing the sick. *See* Priesthood.

Hearken. *See* Appendix E.

Heart(s)

The symbolic center of spiritual, emotional, psychological, and physical attributes. In the Doctrine and Covenants the heart symbolizes the core inner being from which the characteristics of the SOUL and the intent of the will are manifest to God (6:16). The metaphor of the heart is used throughout the scriptures to encompass man's relationship to God. The LAW OF MOSES is summarized in this statement: "Thou shalt love the Lord thy God with all thine heart, and with all thy soul, and with all thy might" (Deut. 6:4–6). Jesus used similar words when questioned concerning the greatest command-ment (Matt. 22:36–37; Mark 12:28–30; cf. D&C 4:2; 59:5). In the Doctrine and Covenants the heart metaphorically represents what the Lord requires (64:22, 34) and is the conduit be-tween human beings and God (1:2).

The first principles of the GOSPEL of Jesus Christ are defined in terms of the heart: An honest heart is necessary for faith (11:10), hav-ing a broken heart and a contrite spirit is the condition required for repentance and baptism (20:37), and knowledge and comfort shall be given to those who invite the Holy Ghost to dwell in their hearts (8:1–2; 84:88; 88:3). Only the Lord is able to discern the "thoughts and the intents" of the heart (6:16). Individuals are invited to pray (19:28; 81:3), ponder (88:62, 71), and treasure the words of the Lord in their hearts (6:20). Favorable characteristics of the heart include sincerity (5:24), openness (23:2–3), lowliness (32:1), singleness (36:7), holiness (46:7), softness (109:56), and integrity (124:15, 20). Admonishment is given to prepare with "full purpose of heart" to preach (18:27–28), bear testimony (58:5–6), and be obedient (132:3). The heart is the indicator of joy found in such phrases as "lift up thy heart and rejoice" (25:13) and "cheerful hearts and countenances" (59:15).

Turning away from the Lord is described as hardening the heart (82:21), resulting in unbe-lief (20:15), which will be prevalent in the last days when many will "turn their hearts from me because of the precepts of men" (45:29, 33). Other sins of the heart include doubt (58:29), adultery (63:16), lack of forgiveness (64:8), seeking evil (64:16), murmuring (75:7), and being proud (98:20). The influence of SATAN to "harden the hearts of the people . . . that they will not believe my words" is apparent in the in-cident of the lost 116 manuscript pages (10:10–32). Satan also seeks to "turn their hearts away from the truth" (78:10), and he will reign in the hearts of the enemies of the Church in the last days (86:3).

The restoration of the gospel and the appear-ance of Elijah in the Kirtland Temple to "turn the hearts of the fathers to the children, and the children to the fathers" (110:15; cf. 2:2) focused the Saints on temple and genealogical work. Assurance has been given that all who die without a knowledge of the gospel but "who would have received it with all their hearts" will be heirs of the celestial kingdom, as the Lord will "judge all men according to . . . the desire of their hearts" (137:8–9). The crowning achievement of the Lord's people will be the es-tablishment of Zion: "for this is Zion—THE PURE IN HEART" (97:21), where the house of the Lord will be built and "all the pure in heart that shall come into it shall see God" (97:16).

See also Broken heart and contrite spirit; Desire(s).

JHS

Heathen nations

Nations or peoples, sometimes called pa-gan or GENTILE, some of whom worship idols or other false gods and are ignorant of the true God of Israel or do not believe in him (Ps. 135:15–18). The Lord speaks of the heathen nations three times in the Doctrine and Covenants:

1. They are to be redeemed during the MILLENNIUM. "And then shall the heathen na-tions be redeemed, and they that knew no law shall have part in the first resurrection; and it shall be tolerable for them" (45:54). The level of that redemption will depend upon the level of their acceptance and obedience to the laws and ordinances of the gospel of Jesus Christ. The "first resurrection," at the beginning of the Millennium, will include celestial and terrestrial people. *See* Kingdoms of glory and perdition, vi-sion of.

2. Inasmuch as they "knew no law" (45:54), God's judgment will be less rigorous for them than for those who knowingly reject the servants of the Lord (75:18–22).

3. They are spoken of as being akin to "the house of Joseph" (90:10). Inasmuch as they are identified with Joseph, it is apparent that literal descendants of Joseph, not a sprinkling but a considerable number, are among the heathen nations as part of the worldwide scat-tering of Israel (Lev. 26:33; Deut. 28:64; Jer. 9:16; Ezek. 36:19–20; 1 Ne. 22:3–5; 2 Ne.

10:22). Therefore, they are part of the gathering (Jer. 31:10; Ezek. 36:24), to be brought about by their accepting the gospel of Jesus Christ preached among them by representatives of The Church of Jesus Christ of Latter-day Saints (90:9–11).

RJM

Heaven(s)

There are at least three contexts in which the term *heaven* is used in the Doctrine and Covenants.

The place where God dwells and the future home of the valiant

Heaven is the residence of the Godhead and their base of operations for the entire universe. Joseph Smith taught, "There are two kinds of beings in heaven, namely: Angels, who are resurrected personages, having bodies of flesh and bones" and "the spirits of just men made perfect, they who are not [yet] resurrected" (129:1, 3). The Son of God "received all power, both in heaven and on earth" (93:17), and he "now reigneth in the heavens" (49:6). "In the celestial glory there are three heavens or degrees" (131:1).

To those who hearken to his servants, the Lord promises he will "cause the heavens to shake for [their] good" (21:6; 35:24). Power is given to righteous priesthood holders to seal on earth and in heaven (1:8; 132:46); in other words, what is recorded and bound on earth shall be recorded and bound in heaven (124:93; 127:7; 128:8, 10). The "power and authority" of the Melchizedek Priesthood is to hold the keys of "the mysteries of the kingdom of heaven, [and] to have the heavens opened" (107:18–19; cf. 84:42; 112:32). "The rights of the priesthood are inseparably connected with the powers of heaven" (121:36). The Father and the Son came from heaven and spoke to Joseph Smith in the Sacred Grove (1:17). Priesthood was confirmed upon the Lord's servants "by [his] own voice out of the heavens" (84:42).

The expanse or atmosphere around the earth

Speaking of God's creations, "their courses are fixed, even the courses of the heavens and the earth, which comprehend the earth and all the planets" (88:43). The Lord declared, "The heavens and the earth are in mine hands" (67:2). The Saints will be instructed "of things both in heaven and in the earth" (88:79). "The doctrine of the priesthood," the Lord said, "shall distil upon thy soul as the dews from heaven" (121:45). *See* Earth, the.

At his second coming, the Lord will "clothe the heavens with blackness" (133:69) and will cause the heavens to shake (43:18; 45:48; 49:23; 84:118) and stars to fall from heaven, in addition to other signs in heaven (29:14; 45:42). "Angels shall fly through the midst of heaven, . . . and immediately there shall appear a great sign in heaven, and all people shall see it together" (88:92–93; cf. 133:17, 36). The Savior will come in his "glory in the clouds of heaven" (45:16). "There shall be silence in heaven . . . ; and immediately after shall the curtain of heaven be unfolded, as a scroll is unfolded after it is rolled up, and the face of the Lord shall be unveiled" (88:95). *See* Curtain(s).

Living Saints "shall be quickened and be caught up to meet him," and Saints who have died "shall come forth, . . . and they also shall be caught up to meet him in the midst of the pillar of heaven" (88:96–97). Heaven and earth shall pass away (that is, die, be changed), and "a new heaven and a new earth" will follow (29:23; 45:22; 56:11). *See* Pillar of heaven.

A figure of speech

Metaphorically, the heavens are said to have "wept" at the fall of Lucifer in the premortal existence (76:25–27) and to have "smiled" upon the earth as "truth is established in her bowels; / And she is clothed with the glory of her God" (84:101).

See also Kingdom of God/kingdom of heaven.

DKO

Heaven, curtain of. *See* Curtain(s).

Heaven, war in. *See* War in heaven.

Heed. *See* Appendix E.

Heel

In Doctrine and Covenants 121:16, the idiom "lift up the heel" is used to describe the actions of the wicked: "Cursed are all those that shall lift up the heel against mine anointed." This idiom also appears in John 13:18: "He that eateth bread with me hath lifted up his heel against me." The passage in John is, in turn, parallel to Psalm 41:9: "Yea, mine own familiar friend, in whom I trusted, which did eat of my bread, hath lifted up his heel against me." The exact meaning of the idiom is unclear, though it is possible that it refers to revealing the sole of one's foot to another, still seen as an act of contempt in some cultures today (Whitacre, 333). In the biblical examples cited, this act is performed by a close friend or ally and therefore represents a betrayal. It is possible that the use of the idiom in section 121 refers to the role that friends-turned-betrayers played in the imprisonment of Joseph Smith in Liberty Jail and the general persecution of the Saints during the autumn and winter of 1838–39. *Heel* is also found in 124:99, where William Law is conditionally promised that he would be "led in paths where the poisonous serpent cannot lay hold upon his heel," most likely an allusion to Genesis 3:15 and the serpent's ability to "bruise his [Christ's] heel" (cf. Moses 4:21; Genesis 49:17).

BIBLIOGRAPHY

Whitacre, Rodney A. John. In *IVP New Testament Commentary,* edited by Grant R. Osborne, D. Stuart Briscoe, and Haddon Robinson. Downers Grove, Ill.: InterVarsity Press, 1999.

DLB

Heirs according to the covenant. *See* Abrahamic covenant; Priesthood.

Hell

The rage, the power to lead captive, and the opposition of SATAN (10:26; 122:1, 7; 123:7–8); a place and state of mind where those who do not repent in mortality suffer to meet the demands of JUSTICE and prepare for the final JUDGMENT and RESURRECTION (76:84–85, 105–6; cf. Mosiah 3:24–27). Perhaps drawing on both meanings of the word, again and again in the Doctrine and Covenants the Lord promises the obedient that the GATES of hell will not prevail against them (10:69; 17:8; 18:5; 21:6; 33:13; 98:22; cf. 6:34; 128:10).

One significant contribution of the Doctrine and Covenants concerning hell is that it is not a place of everlasting torment (19:6–12), except for SONS OF PERDITION (29:36–38; 76:31–37, 43–48; 88:24, 102). Although suffering in hell will be "sore" indeed (19:15–20), all except the sons of perdition will be brought out and placed in a kingdom of glory, depending upon their level of obedience to the laws of those kingdoms (88:21–24). Speaking of those who will inherit the telestial kingdom, the Lord says they will be "cast down to hell and suffer the wrath of Almighty God, until the fulness of times" (76:106). They "shall not be redeemed from the devil until the last resurrection, until the Lord, even Christ the Lamb, shall have finished his work" (76:85). It is clear that the suffering will end, and even those who inherit the lowest of the three kingdoms of glory will be "servants of the Most High" (76:112), all made possible through the ATONEMENT of Jesus Christ. Such a doctrine stands in stark contrast to the belief held by some that hell is a bottomless pit, an inferno of eternal suffering and misery for all but the most righteous in mortality.

See also Judgment(s); Kingdoms of glory and perdition, vision of; Outer darkness; Punish, punished, punishment; Wicked, the/wickedness.

ALG

Herb. *See* Appendix E.

Heritage. *See* Appendix E.

Herriman (or Harriman), Henry

Birth: 9 June 1804, Bradford, Essex County, Massachusetts

Death: 17 May 1891, Huntington, Emery County, Utah

At his death in 1891 Henry Herriman had served faithfully as a general authority of the Church for more than fifty-three years. His decision to be baptized on 29 August 1832 led to a "parting of the ways" between Henry and his twin brother, Hiram, and other family members (Harrington, 1). Herriman moved to Kirtland, Ohio, in 1833. In 1834 he marched with ZION'S CAMP, feeling "constrained to perform this mission by the Spirit of God to expose my life for the welfare and salvation of the Saints" (Harriman, 4).

Herriman was ordained a seventy in March 1835 and set apart as one of the seven presidents of the Seventy in early 1838. In a revelation to Joseph Smith in 1841, the Lord listed Herriman with six other men as having been called "to preside over the quorum of seventies . . . to bear record of [the Lord's] name in all the world, wherever . . . mine apostles, shall send them" (124:138–39). He helped organize the Kirtland Camp, a group of five hundred Saints who moved from Kirtland to Missouri in 1838. He was briefly "made a prisoner by an armed force" in Missouri (Herriman, 8) and was one of the few Saints who were permitted "to pass and re-pass in and through the county of Daviess during the winter, to-wit [1838]," after Governor Boggs issued the infamous extermination order (Smith, 3:210). Herriman was expelled from Missouri with the rest of the Saints and settled in Nauvoo in 1839. He served a mission to the eastern states with Thomas Butterfield in 1842, and in 1844 he went on another brief mission to Cape Cod, where he learned of the martyrdom of the Prophet Joseph Smith. In 1845, he was elected lieutenant colonel of the Nauvoo Legion.

In 1848, Herriman helped lead the Saints west as captain of the first hundred in Heber C. Kimball's company (Smith, 7:626). Herriman participated in the construction of a fort in the Salt Lake Valley, which was named after him. He led a company of handcart missionaries from Salt Lake City to the east. He then traveled to Great Britain and served there between 1857 and 1858. Upon learning of the march of Johnston's army to Utah, he returned to help defend the Saints. Called by Brigham Young to settle in southern Utah, Herriman established himself in Dixie and remained there until his death.

BIBLIOGRAPHY

Harriman, Henry H. "A Short History of Henry H. Harriman." Typescript. Church History Library, The Church of Jesus Christ of Latter-day Saints, Salt Lake City, Utah.

Harrington, Alta. "Life History of Henry Harriman, Pioneer, 1848." N.p.

Smith, Joseph. *History of The Church of Jesus Christ of Latter-day Saints.* Edited by B. H. Roberts. 7 vols. 2d ed. rev. Salt Lake City: The Church of Jesus Christ of Latter-day Saints, 1932–51.

KWF

Hicks, John A.

Birth: 1810, New York

Death: Unknown

John A. Hicks joined the Church in Upper Canada and then moved to Nauvoo. On 19 January 1841 he was listed as one with the responsibility to preside over the elders quorum (124:137). Determined to meet the needs of those he served, he wrote an epistle "TO THE ELDERS SCATTERED ABROAD," anxious to determine "how many are on the Lord's side, how many there are laboring in the vineyard . . . [for] it is necessary that every one should render an account of his stewardship" (TS, 340). A month after Hicks's epistle was printed, objections to him were raised regarding his continuing as a member of the elders quorum presidency. He was excommunicated on 5 October 1841 (Smith, 4:341, 428). Hicks is later mentioned as a member of the apostate mob at Carthage and is reported to have said "that it was determined to shed the blood of Joseph Smith by not only himself, but by the Laws, Higbees, Fosters, Joseph H. Jackson, and many others, whether he was cleared by the law or not" (Smith, 6:560).

BIBLIOGRAPHY

Smith, Joseph. *History of The Church of Jesus Christ of Latter-day Saints.* Edited by B. H. Roberts. 7 vols. 2d ed. rev. Salt Lake City: The Church of Jesus Christ of Latter-day Saints, 1932–51.

Times and Seasons 2, no. 9 (1 March 1841): 340.

RC

Hiding place, the Lord's

An allusion to the Lord's longsuffering attitude and delayed retribution toward those who persecuted the Saints and drove them from their lands.

When Joseph Smith sought direction concerning the Saints who had been driven from their homes and lands in Jackson County, Missouri, in the fall of 1833, the Lord instructed the Saints to "importune at the feet of the judge; . . . the governor; and . . . the president." He then promised that if none of these government officials heeded their cries for REDRESS, "then will the Lord arise and come forth out of his hiding place, and in his fury vex the nation" (101:86–89). After the march of ZION'S CAMP, the Lord again reminded the Saints, "I do not require at their hands to fight the battles of Zion; for, as I said in a former commandment, even so will I fulfil—I will fight your battles. Behold, the destroyer I have sent forth to destroy and lay waste mine enemies; and not many years hence they shall not be left to pollute mine heritage, and to blaspheme my name upon the lands which I have consecrated for the gathering together of my saints" (105:14–15).

The Saints did importune, but no relief was forthcoming. In fact, persecutions continued, and they were driven farther north in Missouri. Three years later, in the dedicatory prayer of the Kirtland Temple, Joseph Smith reminded the Lord of the earlier promise and made an earnest plea for the Lord to "make bare thine arm" and to let his "anger be kindled" and his "indignation fall upon" the persecutors if they did not repent, "that they may be wasted away, both root and branch, from under heaven" (109:47–53). Three more years passed, and PERSECUTION continued and intensified. The extermination order issued by Governor Boggs in 1838 resulted in the expulsion of the Saints from Missouri and the confinement of the Prophet Joseph Smith and other leaders in LIBERTY JAIL.

It had been six years since the Lord promised to come out of his hiding place to punish the enemies of the Saints. After nearly five long months in Liberty Jail and with the Saints in desperate straits struggling to survive in western Illinois, Joseph pleaded to understand: "O God, where art thou? And where is the pavilion that covereth thy hiding place? How long shall thy hand be stayed . . . ? Yea, O Lord, how long shall they suffer these wrongs . . . before thine heart shall be softened toward them, and thy bowels be moved with compassion toward them? . . . let thy hiding place no longer be covered. . . . Let thine anger be kindled against our enemies; and, in the fury of thine heart, with thy sword avenge us of our wrongs" (121:1–5). Rather than avenging the Saints by destroying their

enemies at that time, the Lord called for Joseph to be at peace and patiently endure the persecutions. He reminded the Prophet of the suffering of Job (121:9–10) and the Savior (122:8), telling him, "Thine adversity and thine afflictions shall be but a small moment" (121:7) and "all these things shall give thee experience, and shall be for thy good" (122:7). He also assured Joseph, "I have in reserve a swift judgment in the season thereof" for "those that shall lift up the heel against mine anointed" (121:16, 24).

But the season for judgment was not yet. The Saints were instructed to make a careful record of the names of the persecutors, damages to both character and property, and libelous publications—a record to be published for governments and the whole world to see. Joseph Smith told the Saints that compiling such a record was "enjoined on us by our Heavenly Father, before we can fully and completely claim that promise which shall call him forth from his hiding place" (123:1–11). Exactly when the promise was to be fulfilled would be determined, not according to the Saints' timetable of painful, anxious waiting, but "in the season thereof" (121:24), in the Lord's "own due time" (24:16; 71:10).

See also Historical context and overview of Doctrine and Covenants 101 (p. 806); Missouri period; Parable of the woman and the unjust judge.

LED

Higbee, Elias

Birth: 23 October 1795, Galloway, Gloucester County, New Jersey

Death: 8 June 1843, Nauvoo, Hancock County, Illinois

From his baptism in 1832 until his unexpected death in 1843, Elias Higbee was at the center of Church events, devoted to the Prophet Joseph Smith and the gospel of Jesus Christ. The Prophet Joseph Smith wrote: "His loss will be universally lamented, not only by his family, but by a large circle of brethren who have long witnessed his integrity and uprightness, as well as a life of devotedness to the cause of truth" (5:421).

After his conversion to the Church in Cincinnati, Ohio, Elias Higbee moved with his family to Missouri in 1833 to join the Saints. In Clay County, Missouri, he served as a clerk, historian, recorder, and high councilor in the Church. Higbee was elected judge of Caldwell County and appointed to the Far West high council in 1837. His ordering the militia to protect the Saints in that county triggered the Battle of Crooked River.

The Doctrine and Covenants contains one reference to Elias Higbee. In 1838 he asked Joseph Smith specific questions about Isaiah 52:1–2. In his response the Prophet spoke of latter-day servants who hold priesthood power "to bring again Zion, and the redemption of Israel" (113:7–10). *See* Historical context and overview of Doctrine and Covenants 113 (p. 823).

In November 1839 Higbee and Joseph Smith met with United States president Martin Van Buren and presented the Church's case concerning the wrongs suffered by the Saints in Missouri. When informed "that the decision [was] against [them]," Higbee stated: "I feel a conscience void of offense towards God and man in this matter; that I have discharged my duty here; . . . we have made our last appeal to all earthly tribunals; that we should now put our whole trust in the God of Abraham, Isaac, and Jacob" (Smith, 4:88). Higbee returned to Nauvoo in May 1840 and later that year served on the temple committee. He received his endowment before he died of cholera in 1843.

BIBLIOGRAPHY

Smith, Joseph. *History of The Church of Jesus Christ of Latter-day Saints.* Edited by B. H. Roberts. 7 vols. 2d ed. rev. Salt Lake City: The Church of Jesus Christ of Latter-day Saints, 1932–51.

KWF

High council

A council to arbitrate and adjudicate Church decisions, especially disciplinary decisions. Before the 1834 organization of a standing stake high council, Joseph Smith convened such councils ad hoc, according to the law of the Church revealed in February 1831 (42). On 17 February 1834, Joseph told an assembly of twenty-four priesthood brethren that he "would show the order of councils in ancient days . . .

as shown to him by vision." He explained that "Jerusalem was the seat of the church council in ancient days." He taught that "the apostle, Peter, was the president of the council and held the keys of the Kingdom of God on the earth, was appointed to this office by the voice of the Savior and acknowledged in it by the voice of the church. He had two men appointed as counsellors with him, and in case Peter was absent, his counsellors could transact business . . . alone" (KCMB, 29–30). Joseph explained that Church councils operated on principles of jurisprudence different from those of secular courts: "It was not the order of heaven in ancient councils to plead for and against the guilty as in our judicial courts (so called) but that every counsellor when he arose to speak, should speak precisely according to evidence and according to the teaching of the Spirit of the Lord" (KCMB, 30).

Based on this pattern, Joseph created the Church's first stake presidency and high council. While continuing as head of the Church, Joseph Smith and his counselors, Sidney Rigdon and Frederick G. Williams, also served as the presidency of this new standing high council of the Church's first stake, in Kirtland, Ohio. Twelve high priests—Joseph Smith's father, his uncle John Smith, Joseph Coe, John Johnson, Martin Harris, John S. Carter, Jared Carter, Oliver Cowdery, Samuel H. Smith, Orson Hyde, Sylvester Smith, and Luke Johnson—were chosen as high councilors and unanimously sustained by the brethren present. The "counsellors were then asked whether they accepted their appointments, and whether they would act in that office according to the law of Heaven: to which they all answered, that they accepted their several appointments, and would fill their offices according to the grace of God bestowed upon them" (KCMB, 32).

Clerks kept minutes of Joseph's teachings on how the council should be organized. They recorded that "many questions have been asked during the time of the organization of this council and doubtless some errors have been committed, it was, therefore, voted by all present that Bro Joseph should make all necessary corrections by the Spirit of inspiration hereafter"

(KCMB, 31). Joseph began that job the next day, and the following day, 19 February, a larger gathering of priesthood holders and other Church members met to review and consent to the new "constitution of the high council of the church of Christ" (KCMB, 36). The minutes Joseph refined were subsequently canonized in the Doctrine and Covenants and appear as section 102.

Then, at the 19 February meeting, Joseph laid his hands on the heads of his two councilors and blessed them with "wisdom to magnify their office, and power over all the power of the adversary" (KCMB, 36–37). He then laid his hands on the heads of the twelve men called as high councilors and set them apart. He blessed them with "wisdom and power to counsel in righteousness upon all subjects that might be laid before them [as members of the Church high council]" (KCMB, 37; 102:3). "He also prayed that they might be delivered from those evils to which they were most exposed and that their lives might be prolonged on the earth" (KCMB, 37). Then, in the name of Jesus Christ, Joseph gave them a charge to "do their duty in righteousness and in the fear of God" (KCMB, 37). They signified their acceptance of Joseph's charge by raising their right hands. Joseph pronounced the council organized "according to the ancient order, and also according to the mind of the Lord" (KCMB, 37).

The organization of the high council contributed significantly toward establishing a stake of Zion in Kirtland, an ecclesiastical jurisdiction based on imagery from Isaiah 33:20 and 54:2 and applied to the restored Church in earlier revelations (96:1; 94:1). Moreover, these minutes provided for other standing high councils to be established as well as temporary councils to be organized beyond Zion and her stakes.

The Church's first high council went to work immediately with a disciplinary case. As specified in the minutes, the councilors drew numbers 1 through 12, with even-numbered councilors responsible to prevent insult and injustice against the accused person and the odd-numbered councilors responsible to ensure the interests of the Church. Ezra Thayer charged Curtis Hodges, an elder, with preaching too loudly and unclearly and asserting that he was justified in doing so when corrected. Elder Hodges said he was not guilty. Witnesses confirmed "that bro. Hodges was guilty of hollowing [hollering] so loud that he, in a measure, lost his voice" (KCMB, 38). Oliver Cowdery, who had drawn number 1, summarized the Church's case against Hodges. Joseph Coe, who had drawn number 2, summarized the case from Hodges's perspective "but could say but few words" (KCMB, 38). Thayer restated his accusations and Hodges restated his pleas. In other words, the case was conducted exactly as section 102 specified, including the ruling of Joseph Smith, president of the council. He announced "that the charges in the declaration had been fairly sustained by good witnesses, also, that bro. H. [Hodges] ought to have confessed when rebuked by bro Thayer, also that if he had the Spirit of the Lord at the meetings where he hollowed, he must have abused it, and grieved it away. All the council agreed with the decision." Brother Hodges then confessed his error, acknowledging that he could now see it, and would repent (KCMB, 39).

Though unusual, this high council hearing was straightforward and followed the instructions set forth in section 102. These same procedures continue to guide the standing high councils of the Church today, of which there is one in each stake of Zion.

See also Church discipline; Historical context and overview of Doctrine and Covenants 102 (p. 807); Standing councils/ministers/presidents; Traveling high council/bishops/elders/high priests/ministers/presiding high council.

BIBLIOGRAPHY

Kirtland Council Minute Book. Church History Library, The Church of Jesus Christ of Latter-day Saints, Salt Lake City, Utah.

SCH

High-minded. *See* Appendix E.

High priest(s)

An office in the Melchizedek Priesthood. The Doctrine and Covenants reveals that this "higher, or Melchizedek Priesthood," is named such "because Melchizedek was such a great high priest" (107:1–5, 18). DEACON, TEACHER, PRIEST, and ELDER are offices in the PRIESTHOOD revealed in April 1830. The office of BISHOP was added to the Aaronic Priesthood the following February and that of high priest to the Melchizedek Priesthood in June 1831. At a conference held on 3 June 1831, twenty-three men were ordained high priests. Scripturally, the office of high priest is found in the Bible and the Book of Mormon, but Alma 13 specifically enumerates the qualifications for the office as well as the need for it. In summary, those ordained as high priests are men who have exhibited "exceeding faith and good works" in the premortal life and here on earth. They are to "teach [God's] commandments unto the children of men," so that the people "might look forward on the Son of God . . . for a remission of their sins, that they might enter into the rest of the Lord" (Alma 13:3, 6, 16).

The commitment of the newly ordained high priests in this dispensation was immediately tested. Three days after their ordination, Joseph Smith received a revelation in which the Lord declared that the next conference of the Church would be "held in Missouri, upon the land which I will consecrate unto my people" (52:2). He then announced the names of thirty-two men who were to travel to Missouri for the conference, most of them to do missionary work along the way. Twenty-one of the twenty-three high priests were among those named in the revelation (Cannon and Cook, 7; D&C 52).

John Whitmer, who had recently been called to keep the history of the Church (D&C 47), and Joseph Smith Sr., who had been called the previous month to manage the farm owned by Frederick G. Williams (Jensen et al., 142–43), were not required to make the journey.

In the months following the restoration of the office of high priest, the Lord revealed the authority and the duties of those ordained to it. They were to be the leaders of the Church "to whom the kingdom and power have been given" (72:1). They could officiate in any of the "lesser offices" of the priesthood (68:19; cf. 107:10, 17, 71), including the office of bishop (68:14–15), and had authority to ordain others to the priesthood (20:66). In the beginning, they were expected to "travel" as missionaries (84:111) and preside in the areas where there was no designated leader, but as the Church grew, their assignment was changed to "standing" ministers, with the option to travel "if they choose" (124:133–35). In this regard, Frederick G. Williams was called "to be a high priest in my church, and a counselor unto my servant Joseph Smith, Jun." (81:1); Warren A. Cowdery was "appointed and ordained a presiding high priest over my church, in the land of Freedom [New York] and the regions round about" (106:1); and the president of the Church was designated as "the Presiding High Priest over the High Priesthood of the Church" (107:64–67).

Under Joseph Smith's direction, some high priests were called to serve on councils to help govern and regulate the Church. They functioned with the faith that "God always bears testimony by his presence in counsel to his Elders when they assemble themselves in perfect faith and humble themselves before the Lord and their wills being swallowed up in the will of God" (Cannon and Cook, 19–20). Some served on high councils that were organized "for the purpose of settling important difficulties which might arise in the church, which could not be settled by the church or the bishop's council to the satisfaction of the parties" (102:2). Other councils were temporary and assembled to discuss a single issue, such as the one in which the decision was made to print the revelations (Cannon and Cook, 26–32).

Available records do not indicate when the high priests were first organized as a QUORUM, but there is evidence that there was a quorum by 1836 (Smith, 4:69–70). There was still only one quorum in Nauvoo (124:133–36), but over time, as the Church expanded, high priests quorums were aligned within stakes. Today, bishops, most bishop's counselors, stake presidencies, members of high councils, patriarchs, temple presidents and their counselors, sealers, mission presidencies, and all General Authorities are high priests. Once a man is released from any of these positions, he remains a high priest and is a member of the quorum within the stake in which he lives, with the stake presidency serving as the presidency of the quorum.

BIBLIOGRAPHY

Cannon, Donald Q., and Lyndon W. Cook, eds. *Far West Record: Minutes of The Church of Jesus Christ of Latter-day Saints, 1840–1844.* Salt Lake City: Deseret Book, 1983.

Jensen, Robin Scott, Robert J. Woodford, and Steven C. Harper, eds. *Manuscript Revelation Books.* Facsimile edition. First volume of the Revelations and Translations series of *The Joseph Smith Papers,* edited by Dean C. Jessee, Ronald K. Esplin, and Richard Lyman Bushman. Salt Lake City: Church Historian's Press, 2009.

Smith, Joseph Fielding. *Church History and Modern Revelation.* 4 vols. Salt Lake City: The Church of Jesus Christ of Latter-day Saints, 1946–49.

RJW

High Priesthood. *See* Priesthood.

Highway cast up in the midst of the great deep. *See* Israel.

Hiram, Ohio

A township in northern Portage County, Ohio, about thirty miles southeast of Kirtland. From 12 September 1831 to March 1832, John Johnson's farmhouse in Hiram was the residence of Joseph Smith and his family and the headquarters of the Church (Backman, 82–83). In Hiram, Joseph received eighteen revelations recorded in the Doctrine and Covenants (1, 65–71, 73–74, 76–81, 99, 133). The journal of William E. McLellin, for whom the revelation recorded in section 66 was given, indicates that it was received in Hiram, Ohio (McLellin, 45–46, 246–48). The *History of the Church* (1:235) and the Far West Record (31–33) indicate that section 70 was received in Hiram.

Some of the important principles received in these revelations include the following: "from thence shall the gospel roll forth unto the ends of the earth" (65:2), "he that believeth and is baptized shall be saved" (68:9), and "the Lord requires of every man" an accounting of his stewardship (70:9). While translating the Bible at the Johnson farmhouse, Joseph Smith and Sidney Rigdon saw God the Father and Jesus Christ and received a glorious vision of future kingdoms (76). The Lord revealed that a history of the Church should be written (69:3), a storehouse for the poor should be established (78:3), and the organization of the First Presidency should be formalized (81, headnote). On 1 November 1831, the Lord directed the publishing of revelations received by Joseph (67, headnote). The preface (1) and appendix (133) of the proposed publication, the Book of Commandments, were also revealed to Joseph at the Johnson farmhouse (Backman, 90–93).

On 24 March 1832, Joseph Smith and Sidney Rigdon were tarred and feathered by a mob and left for dead. Both survived the ordeal, however, and left Hiram to live in Kirtland. While on a visit to Missouri shortly after the tar-and-feathering incident, Joseph wrote to his wife, Emma, "God is my friend: in him I shall find comfort. I have given my life into his hands. . . . I Count not my life dear to me, only to do his will" (*Writings,* 264–65; punctuation modernized).

The Johnsons' farmhouse has been restored and a visitors' center–meetinghouse was built on the property (Perkins and Cannon, 51–54). The buildings were dedicated by President Gordon B. Hinckley in October 2001 (Stahle, 3–4). *See* maps, pp. 461 and 710.

See also Ohio period.

BIBLIOGRAPHY

Backman, Milton V., Jr. *The Heavens Resound: A History of the Latter-day Saints in Ohio, 1830–1838.* Salt Lake City: Deseret Book, 1983.

Black, Susan Easton. "Hiram, Ohio: Tribulation." In *The Prophet Joseph: Essays on the Life and Mission of Joseph Smith,* edited by Larry C. Porter and Susan Easton Black. Salt Lake City: Deseret Book, 1988.

Cannon, Donald Q., and Lyndon W. Cook, eds. *Far West Record: Minutes of The Church of Jesus Christ of Latter-day Saints, 1830–1844.* Salt Lake City: Deseret Book, 1983.

Perkins, Keith W., and Donald Q. Cannon. *Ohio and Illinois.* Vol. 3 of *Sacred Places: A Comprehensive Guide to Early LDS Historical Sites,* edited by LaMar C. Berrett. Salt Lake City: Deseret Book, 2002.

Smith, Joseph. *History of The Church of Jesus Christ of Latter-day Saints.* Edited by B. H. Roberts. 7 vols. 2d ed. rev. Salt Lake City: The Church of Jesus Christ of Latter-day Saints, 1932–51.

———. *Personal Writings of Joseph Smith.* Compiled and edited by Dean C. Jessee. Rev. ed. Salt Lake City: Deseret Book, 2002.

Stahle, Shaun D. "John Johnson home will have place in history." *Church News,* 3 November 2001, 3–4.

MVB

Hoar frost. *See* Appendix E.

Holy city

The designation "holy city" appears in the revelations for four sacred locations:

1. The premillennial city of New Jerusalem in Zion, Jackson County, Missouri. Joseph Smith prayed that from "all the ends of the earth" the servants of the Lord "may gather out the righteous to build a holy city to thy name" (109:57–58; cf. 57:1–3; Moses 7:62; Ether 13:8).

2. The millennial city of the New Jerusalem in Zion. At the beginning of the Millennium, "the holy city, new Jerusalem," shall come down from heaven to meet the New Jerusalem on this earth (Moses 7:62). "The graves of the saints shall be opened; and they shall come forth and stand on the right hand of the Lamb, when he shall stand upon Mount Zion, and upon the holy city, the New Jerusalem" (133:56).

3. The heavenly holy city where the resurrected righteous receive their eternal inheritance. "Blessed are the dead that die in the Lord, from henceforth, when the Lord shall come, and old things shall pass away, and all things become new, they shall rise from the dead and shall not die after, and shall receive an inheritance before the Lord, in the holy city" (63:49).

4. The city of Far West, in northern Missouri, where a foundation was laid for a future temple. "Let the city, Far West, be a holy and consecrated land unto me; and it shall be called most holy, for the ground upon which thou standest is holy" (115:7).

DKO

Holy Ghost, in the form of a dove. *See* Form of a dove.

Holy Ghost, the

The third member of the Godhead. Referred to by various titles—"Holy Spirit," "Spirit of God," "the Spirit"—the Holy Ghost occupies a prominent place in the revelations of the Restoration. Though ancient and modern scripture is replete with references to the Holy Ghost,

Latter-day Saints have perhaps their most comprehensive description of his nature and mission in the Doctrine and Covenants.

Nature

Because the Holy Ghost, like others in the Godhead, is a god, his influence and powers both surpass human understanding and extend well beyond his person (e.g., 35:19; 42:17). The Father, Son, and Holy Ghost enjoy such unity, in fact, in both their perfection and purpose that they are denominated "one God" in the revelations (20:28). That oneness notwithstanding, the revelations show that each member of the Godhead is a separate divine person. In a significant departure from traditional Christian theologies, the Doctrine and Covenants maintains that the Holy Ghost, rather than constituting the mind of God or his omnipresent essence filling creation, is instead a discrete "personage of Spirit," coterminous with neither the Father nor the Son (130:22). Though the revelations affirm the embodiment of the latter two, they are silent on the question of the Holy Ghost's past or future habitation of a "body of flesh and bones" (130:22). It is appropriate in light of Church doctrine to use the pronouns *he, his,* or *him* when speaking of the Holy Ghost, though the revelations routinely employ *it* and *its.* Because the Holy Ghost facilitates the acquisition of divine knowledge or power, the text sometimes refers, metaphorically, to his dwelling in, descending upon, filling, being poured out upon, or even sitting or resting upon individuals—or, conversely, to one's being "in the Spirit" (130:22–23; 8:2; 84:27, 88; 19:38; 93:15; 27:18; 107:56; 138:11; 76:11, 28, 80, 113, 115).

The Holy Ghost should not be confused with other elements in the revelations described with similar language. The Holy Ghost, for instance, is separate from (but in some ways related to) the "light" or "Spirit" of Christ, which, like the Holy Ghost, serves as a conduit of divine enlightenment, but which, unlike the Holy Ghost, proceeds "forth from the presence of God to fill the immensity of space" (88:12; cf. 84:45–46). The Holy Ghost ministers through the Light of Christ. Similarly, both Jesus Christ and the Holy Ghost are referred to in scripture as "Comforter" and the "Spirit of truth" (6:15; 50:17–21; 88:3–4; 93:9, 11, 26; John 14:16–26).

Mission

The Holy Ghost, with the Father and the Son, seeks the "immortality and eternal life of man" (Moses 1:39). In God's wisdom, however, the Holy Ghost plays unique parts in the drama of human salvation.

The Holy Ghost is a revelator. Along with heavenly messages brought by ministering angels and God himself, revelations come by the "power of the Holy Ghost" (20:35; cf. 90:11, 14). *See* Revelation.

Indeed, the Doctrine and Covenants regularly refers to the Spirit as God's "voice" (18:35, 47; 52:1; 75:1; 88:66; 97:1). Importantly, revelations from the Holy Ghost pertain to both "heart" and "mind"; his influence can be felt as a "burn[ing] within" and experienced as mental enlightenment (6:15; 8:2; 9:8; 11:13; 76:10–12). *See* Heart(s); Mind.

God's servants should "speak as they are moved upon by the Holy Ghost," with the promise that when they "preach . . . by the Spirit," not only will their inspired words constitute "scripture" but the Holy Ghost will confirm their truth to faithful hearers (68:3–4; 50:14–21; cf. 14:8; 18:32; 25:7; 28:1, 4; 34:10; 43:15; 99:2; 100:8). Church leaders are to conduct Church meetings and ordain others to priesthood offices "as they are led by the Holy Ghost" (20:45, 60; 46:2). Spiritual gifts are "given by the Holy Ghost" (46:7, 11–27). The Holy Ghost enables Saints to pray inspired prayers so that their petitions might accord with "the will of God" (46:30; 50:30). All spiritual things are seen or understood "by the power of the Holy Spirit," but of the "knowledge" imparted by the Holy Ghost, testimony "of the Father and of the Son" is paramount (76:116; 121:26; 20:26–27; 42:17). Faithful Saints know "by the Holy Ghost . . . that Jesus Christ is the Son of God, and that he was crucified for the sins of the world" (46:13; cf. 21:9).

The Holy Ghost is a purifier. Sanctification, the process whereby spiritual impurity is exchanged for holiness, is made possible "through the grace of our Lord and Savior Jesus Christ" and is realized in the reception of the Holy Ghost, both in the ordinance of confirmation and thereafter through the Holy Ghost's continued refashioning of the faithful (20:31) through their repentance. As flame refines impure metal, so the Saints are "sanctified by the Spirit" (84:33). *See* Sanctify, sanctification.

The Holy Ghost is a comforter. Through the Holy Ghost, God "speak[s] peace" to human hearts and minds (6:23). Those willing to take "the Holy Spirit for their guide" are taught by "the Comforter . . . the peaceable things of the kingdom" (45:57; 36:2). When Saints "walk in the meekness of [the Lord's] Spirit" they are promised "peace" in Christ (19:23). Similarly, the Holy Ghost fills the "soul with joy" (11:13). Gospel teaching, when accompanied by the Holy Ghost, results in understanding, rejoicing, and edification for both teacher and hearer (50:22). Latter-day Saint temples, because "the Spirit shall give utterance in all your doings in the house of the Lord," become "a tabernacle of the Holy Spirit to your edification" (88:137). It is in temples, in fact, that God makes available to his children the "fulness of the Holy Ghost" (109:15).

The Holy Ghost is a sealer. For earthly acts to be of "efficacy, virtue, or force in and after the resurrection," they must be "entered into and sealed by the Holy Spirit of promise"—the Holy Ghost acting as an agent of divine ratification (132:7). *See* Seal, sealed.

Though the ratifying seal of the Holy Ghost applies to "all [gospel] covenants, contracts, bonds, obligations, oaths, vows," etc. (132:7), the revelations highlight this aspect of the Holy Ghost's mission with regard to eternal marriage (132:19–24) and the "promise . . . of eternal life" in particular (88:3–4). A husband and wife married according to God's authority and sealed by the Holy Spirit of promise, if faithful thereafter, attain to "exaltation and glory in all things" (132:19). Those who "overcome by faith" and who are "just and true" can, in this life, receive "the more sure word of prophecy," which means knowing that they are "sealed up unto eternal life, by revelation and the spirit of prophecy, through the power of the Holy Priesthood" (76:53; 131:5–6; 124:124). *See* More sure word of prophecy.

Not surprisingly, the revelations place "blasphemy against the Holy Ghost" as chief among the most serious sins (132:27; cf. 76:35, Alma 39:5–6). *See* Blasphemy against the Holy Ghost.

See also Gift of the Holy Ghost; God the Father; Laying on of hands.

JSF

Holy men that ye know not of

In Doctrine and Covenants 49:8 the Lord calls upon all men to repent, "for all are under sin, except those which I have reserved unto myself, holy men that ye know not of." Who might such men be? President Joseph Fielding Smith explained: "'Holy men that ye know not of,' who were without sin, and reserved unto the Lord, are translated persons such as John the Revelator and the Three Nephites, who do not belong to this generation and yet are in the flesh in the earth performing a special ministry until the coming of Jesus Christ" (1:192).

See also Translated beings.

BIBLIOGRAPHY

Smith, Joseph Fielding. *Church History and Modern Revelation.* 4 vols. Salt Lake City: The Church of Jesus Christ of Latter-day Saints, 1946–49.

LED

Holy places

In preparation for the Savior's return, the Lord commanded his Saints to "stand in holy places" (45:32; cf. 87:8). The temple of the Lord is a holy place (109:12–13; 117:16; 124:39). Another is where the "gathering together" of the Saints occurs (101:22, 64). The Lord designated that "gathering together" on "the land of Zion, and . . . her stakes . . . is for a defense, and for a refuge from the storm, and from wrath" (115:6). Stakes provide a strong defense and refuge when members strive to live the gospel in their homes and meet in chapels to be instructed, perform ordinances, and make covenants. President James E. Faust declared, "As we recall the commandment to stand in holy places, we should remember that beyond the temple, the most sacred and holy places . . . should be our own dwelling places" ("Message," 5). He also taught, "Our chapels are dedicated . . . as holy places" ("Standing," 68).

The Lord has designated several locations as holy cities or holy places. *See* Holy city.

Commenting on the meaning of the phrase "stand in the holy place," recorded in Joseph Smith–Matthew 1:12–13 (cf. 45:32), one Latter-day Saint observed, "*Standing* apparently means here *to take one's stand.* By standing with holy feet on whatever ground, one stands in a holy place. Holy feet sanctify polluted ground just as polluted feet pollute holy ground. Standing steadfast, *saints* sanctify the places where they live" (Meservy, 210).

BIBLIOGRAPHY

Faust, James E. "First Presidency Message: 'Who Shall Ascend into the Hill of the Lord?'" *Ensign* 31 (August 2001): 2–5.

———. "Standing in Holy Places." *Ensign* 35 (May 2005): 62–68.

Meservy, Keith H. "Jesus and Josephus Told of The Destruction of Jerusalem." In *The New Testament and the Latter-day Saints.* Orem, Utah: Randall Book, 1987.

KRA

Holy Priesthood after the Order of the Son of God, the. *See* Priesthood; Historical context and overview of Doctrine and Covenants 107 (p. 815).

Holy Spirit of promise. *See* Holy Ghost, the.

Honest, honestly

Just, truthful, sincere, and characterized by integrity. The word *honest* is used five times in the Doctrine and Covenants, the first three of which appear as modifiers of the word *heart* and as part of conditional clauses upon which specific blessings are predicated. The Lord promised Oliver Cowdery knowledge if he asked "in faith, with an honest heart" (8:1). Similarly, Hyrum Smith was promised a gift (revelation) if he desired of the Lord in faith with an honest heart (11:10). The Lord revealed that some members of the school in the land of Zion needed to be chastened, in contrast to those whose "hearts are honest, and are broken, and their spirits contrite" (97:3–8). The other instances of the word occur in the Lord's instructions to the Saints to seek and sustain "honest" elected officials (98:10) and in the declaration in section 135 that the INNOCENT BLOOD of Joseph and Hyrum Smith "will touch the hearts of honest men among all nations" (135:7). The single use of the adverb *honestly* appears in the Lord's instructions to Bishop Edward Partridge, where it modifies the verb *deal*. In implementing the law of CONSECRATION, Bishop Partridge was to admonish the Saints to "deal honestly" with each other (51:9).

See also Hypocrisy, hypocrites; Truth.

RCF

Honorable men of the earth. *See* Kingdoms of glory and perdition, vision of.

Hope

The Doctrine and Covenants uses *hope* in two contexts: (1) a generic wishing for or desiring of a particular outcome, not generally related to the gospel of Jesus Christ, and (2) a gospel-centered hope—a longing for the things of righteousness, and a confidence and optimism regarding the future, born of faith in Jesus Christ.

The one use of *hope* in the generic sense is in connection with those who opposed the Restoration and accused Joseph Smith of transgression. Of them the Lord said, "Their hope shall be blasted, and their prospects shall melt away as the hoar frost melteth before the burning rays of the rising sun" (121:11, 14).

In a gospel sense, the Doctrine and Covenants employs *hope* in three dimensions:

First, the earliest and most frequent references to hope are in concert with the other two classic Christian virtues, FAITH and CHARITY. These three are required of all who desire to serve God (4:5) and to "assist in this work," the "great and marvelous work" of the Restoration (12:1, 8). Oliver Cowdery was counseled by the Lord to exercise "patience, faith, hope and charity" in his relationship with Joseph Smith (6:19). Also, Cowdery and David Whitmer, two of the Three Witnesses, were reminded that "if you have not faith, hope, and charity, you can do nothing" (18:19).

Second, *hope* describes the expectation of obtaining a glorious RESURRECTION. President Joseph F. Smith saw in vision those who had "departed the mortal life, firm in the hope of a glorious resurrection, through the grace of God the Father and his Only Begotten Son, Jesus Christ" (138:14). The Lord counseled that the Saints should "live together in love, insomuch that thou shalt weep for the loss of them that die, and more especially for those that have not hope of a glorious resurrection" (42:45).

Third, *hope* describes the happy expectation of SALVATION for all mankind through the restoration of the fulness of the gospel—the ministration of "divers angels, from Michael or Adam down to the present time, all declaring their . . . keys . . . and the power of their priesthood" (128:21), establishing "a whole and complete and perfect union, and welding together of dispensations, and keys, and powers, and glories" (128:18), making available to all, living or dead, the message of the gospel and the ordinances of salvation (cf. 128:15–23). The Prophet Joseph Smith rejoiced in these great blessings, as "giving us consolation . . . , confirming our hope" (128:21).

The Book of Mormon makes clear that one cannot be saved in the kingdom of God without having this gospel-centered hope, which hope comes of faith and leads to charity (cf. Ether 12:4–9; Moro. 7:39–48; 10:20–22).

PAA

Hosanna. *See* Appendix E.

Hot drinks. *See* Word of Wisdom.

Humble, humility

Unpretentious, teachable; modesty, meekness, mildness. An attribute of JESUS CHRIST that his true disciples seek to develop. In a revelation for Joseph Knight, even before the Church was organized, the Savior declared, "No one can assist in this work except he shall be humble and full of love, having faith, hope, and charity" (12:8). The Spirit leads one to walk humbly (11:12); "my Spirit is sent forth into the world to enlighten the humble and contrite" (136:33). The Lord commanded his followers to declare and publish glad tidings among every people, "and thou shalt do it with all humility" (19:29–30). Bishop Newel K. Whitney was instructed to "travel . . . about and among all the churches, searching after the poor to administer to their wants by humbling the rich and the proud" (84:112). Doctrine and Covenants 20:37 teaches that humility is the first requirement for one to be worthy of baptism and membership in God's kingdom. The rest of the requirements wonderfully define what real humility is: "desire to be baptized, and come forth with broken hearts and contrite spirits, and witness before the church that they have truly repented of all their sins, and are willing to take upon them the name of Jesus Christ, having a determination to serve him to the end, and truly manifest by their works that they have received of the Spirit."

The Savior warned Martin Harris in the strongest terms to confess and repent of his sins, "lest I humble you with my almighty power" (19:20). All mankind has a choice: humble yourselves, or be humbled (49:10). Great benefits come to those who do humble themselves, as the Lord promised Thomas B. Marsh: "Be thou humble; and the Lord thy God shall lead thee by the hand, and give thee answer to thy prayers" (112:10). Those who truly humble themselves will be gathered by the Redeemer under his tender and protective care (29:2)—they will "escape their enemies" (54:3); their sins will be forgiven (61:2); they will "learn wisdom" (136:32); and they will escape the burdens of debt (104:78–82). The Saints who were driven from Jackson County, Missouri, in 1833 were promised "a great endowment and blessing . . . , inasmuch as they are faithful and continue in humility before me" (105:12). The humble shall be "made strong, and blessed from on high, and receive knowledge from time to time" (1:28). Not only are the "blessings of the kingdom" given to the humble (61:37) but, the Lord declared, "It is your privilege, and a promise I give unto you . . . , that inasmuch as you strip yourselves from jealousies and fears, and humble yourselves before me, for ye are not sufficiently humble, the veil shall be rent and you shall see me and know that I am—not with the carnal neither natural mind, but with the spiritual" (67:10).

See also Pride.

DKO

Humphrey, Solomon

Birth: 23 September 1775, Canton, Hartford County, Connecticut

Death: September 1834, Clay County, Missouri

Solomon Humphrey, a Baptist exhorter and a resident of Stockholm, New York, was "baptized, presumably by JS [Joseph Smith], when he visited JS at Palmyra, Wayne Co., New York, in fall 1830" (Jessee et al., 1:415).

Humphrey migrated to Kirtland, Ohio. Shortly after arriving, he and Joseph Wakefield were called to serve a mission "into the eastern lands" and "labor with their families, declaring none other things than the prophets and apostles, that which they have seen and heard and most assuredly believe" (52:35–36). The missionaries returned to western New York and baptized several family members as well as John Smith and George A. Smith, uncle and cousin, respectively, to Joseph Smith.

Humphrey served other missions later. He also worked on the Kirtland Temple, attended the School of the Prophets, and was a member of ZION'S CAMP. After Zion's Camp was disbanded, Humphrey elected to remain in Missouri. There, with several other elders and high priests, he volunteered to be one of those to go and preach "the gospel of peace" (Cannon and Cook, 92).

BIBLIOGRAPHY

Cannon, Donald Q., and Lyndon W. Cook, eds. *Far West Record: Minutes of The Church of Jesus Christ of Latter-day Saints, 1830–1844.* Salt Lake City: Deseret Book, 1983.

Jessee, Dean C., Mark Ashurst-McGee, and Richard L. Jensen, eds. *Journals, Volume 1: 1832–1839.* Vol. 1 of the Journals series of *The Joseph Smith Papers,* edited by Dean C. Jessee, Ronald K. Esplin, and Richard Lyman Bushman. Salt Lake City: Church Historian's Press, 2008.

"Obituary." *Latter Day Saints' Messenger and Advocate* 1, no. 11 (August 1835): 176.

RC

Huntington, William, Sr.

Birth: 28 March 1784, New Grantham, Cheshire County, New Hampshire

Death: 19 August 1846, Mount Pisgah, Harrison County, Iowa

William Huntington Sr. embraced Presbyterianism after attending a series of religious revivals in Watertown, New York. By 1832 he had begun to search for another religion. He first heard of Mormonism and the Book of Mormon in the winter of 1832–33; he believed the Book of Mormon and began preaching it to others. He was baptized a member of the Church in 1835. In August 1836, Huntington sold his farm and moved his family to Kirtland, Ohio, then to Missouri, and then to Illinois. While residing in Nauvoo, he served on the high council (124:131–32). He worked as a stonemason on the Nauvoo Temple and left Nauvoo for the West on 9 February 1846. In May of that year he was assigned to preside over the Saints in Mount Pisgah and died there in August.

BIBLIOGRAPHY

Bradley, Martha Sonntag, and Mary Brown Firmage Woodward. *4 Zina's: A Study of Mothers and Daughters on the Mormon Frontier.* Salt Lake City: Signature Books, 2000.

Young, Zina D. H. Collection, Letters (1806–35). Zina Baker Huntington and William Huntington to Dorcas Baker and Oliver Baker. Church History Library, The Church of Jesus Christ of Latter-day Saints, Salt Lake City, Utah.

RC

Hyde, Orson

Birth: 8 January 1805, Oxford, New Haven County, Connecticut

Death: 28 November 1878, Spring City, Sanpete County, Utah

Orson Hyde was orphaned at a young age. He moved to Kirtland, Ohio, in 1819 and became caught up in the religious fervor of the area. He was a Campbellite pastor when he first met Mormon missionaries (Hyde, 742, 744). Initially resistant to Mormonism, he was baptized by his former Campbellite mentor, Sidney Rigdon, in the Chagrin River on 30 October 1831 (Hyde, 760–61).

Soon after his conversion, he was called on the first of thirteen missions "to proclaim the everlasting gospel, by the Spirit of the living God, from people to people, and from land to land, in the congregations of the wicked, in their synagogues" (68:1, 6–8).

On 25 January 1832 Hyde was called along

Orson Hyde, 1805–1878.

with Samuel H. Smith to "take their journey into the eastern countries, and proclaim the things which I have commanded them; and inasmuch as they are faithful, lo, I will be with them even unto the end" (75:13). Less than two years later, when he and John Gould were absent from their families for several days while delivering instructions to the oppressed Saints of Missouri, the Prophet Joseph Smith became concerned for their safety but was divinely assured: "My servants Orson Hyde and John Gould, are in my hands; and inasmuch as they keep my commandments they shall be saved. Therefore, let your hearts be comforted" (100, headnote, vv. 14–15).

Orson Hyde's call to the Kirtland high council and as a clerk is recorded on 17 February 1834 (102:3). Just one week later he was called to serve another mission "with my servant Orson Pratt, whithersoever my servant Joseph Smith, Jun., shall counsel them" (103:40). Nearly a year later, on 15 February 1835, Orson Hyde was called to the Quorum of the Twelve

Apostles. A few years later, Elder Hyde is listed among the Twelve Apostles in a Nauvoo revelation subsequent to the Quorum being reorganized at the death of David W. Patten and the apostasy of Thomas Marsh (124:129).

A study of Orson Hyde's life reveals the highs and lows of those involved in early Church history. In 1837 Elder Hyde served a mission to England, resulting in the baptism of fifteen hundred souls. By October 1838 he had stumbled into apostasy, signing an affidavit highly critical of the Prophet Joseph Smith and other leaders of the Church (Smith, 3:165–67). He repented and went on to do much good in the service of the Lord (Hyde, 792). On 24 October 1841, Elder Hyde, from atop the Mount of Olives, fulfilled a prophecy of Joseph Smith by dedicating JERUSALEM for the return of the JEWS and the building of the temple (Smith, 4:xxxi–xxxiii, 456–59).

Years later his brief estrangement in 1838 affected his seniority in the Quorum of the Twelve. In 1875 President Brigham Young changed the seniority of some members of the Quorum of the Twelve, which reflected their periods of apostasy. The reordering placed John Taylor ahead of both Orson Pratt and Orson Hyde, so Orson Hyde was released as the president of the Quorum, and John Taylor took his place (Taylor, 191–92). Elder Hyde served as a member of the Twelve until his death at the age of seventy-three.

See also Apostles, the first Twelve of latter days; Apostles, the Twelve, mission to Great Britain.

BIBLIOGRAPHY

Hyde, Orson. "History of Orson Hyde." *Latter-day Saints' Millennial Star* 26 (1864): 742–44, 760–61, 774–76, 790–92.

Smith, Joseph. *History of The Church of Jesus Christ of Latter-day Saints.* Edited by B. H. Roberts. 7 vols. 2d ed. rev. Salt Lake City: The Church of Jesus Christ of Latter-day Saints, 1932–51.

Taylor, John. *The Gospel Kingdom.* Selected by G. Homer Durham. Salt Lake City: Bookcraft, 1944.

TRV

Hymnbook. *See* Smith, Emma.

Hypocrisy, hypocrites

Hypocrites are those who pretend to be something they are not or pretend not to be something they are, as, for example, those who hide their testimonies "because of the fear of man" (60:2–3.) In the religious sense, hypocrites are people who profess to have virtues or beliefs that they do not practice. They feign loyalty to the Church, but often their hearts are centered on the world (cf. 41:5; 112:23–26; Matt. 23:1–33).

In 1831 the Lord revealed that there were hypocrites among the Saints—those who were under the influence of false spirits, and who had "deceived some, which [had] given the adversary power." Those who were deceived "shall be reclaimed; but the hypocrites shall be detected and shall be cut off, either in life or in death" (50:6–8). The Lord had warned the Saints about being deceived and told them to avoid spiritual deceptions by seeking truth through the Spirit and through the Prophet (28:1–2; 43:6–7; 45:57; 50:10–35; 52:14–19; cf. 64:37–39). *See* Deception.

Although the word *hypocrisy* is not used in reference to those who stole the 116 pages of Book of Mormon translation in order to change the words and thus claim Joseph Smith was a false prophet, the principle is clearly evident when the Lord said of them, "Wo be unto him that lieth to deceive because he supposeth that another lieth to deceive, for such are not exempt from the justice of God" (10:28; cf. vv. 8–33). The Lord warned the members of the United Order that if they did not consider that all the properties of the order really belonged to the Lord, they would be "found hypocrites" (104:55).

Hypocrites often undermine religion. President Spencer W. Kimball stated: "There are those who receive the benefits of the Church while not only failing to make any contributions to it but actually being destructive of it and its standards. Those hypocritical unbelievers use their powers to destroy rather than to build up" (112).

The Lord condemns hypocritical priesthood leaders who seek to "cover [their] sins" or "gratify [their] pride" and "vain ambition" through "unrighteous dominion." He declared that righteous priesthood leaders govern "by kindness, and pure knowledge, . . . without hypocrisy, and without guile" (121:34–43).

Ultimately, unrepentant hypocrites will be among the wicked who experience "weeping, and wailing, and gnashing of teeth" (101:90–91; 124:8).

See also Honest, honestly.

BIBLIOGRAPHY

Kimball, Spencer W. *The Teachings of Spencer W. Kimball.* Edited by Edward L. Kimball. Salt Lake City: Bookcraft, 1982.

BLS

And again, verily I say unto you, I command you again to build a house to my name, even in this place, that you may prove yourselves unto me that ye are faithful in all things whatsoever I command you, that I may bless you, and crown you with honor, **immortality**, and eternal life.

124:55

I Am. *See* Jehovah.

Idle, idleness

Idleness is akin to laziness, slothfulness, and indolence. Idleness, both temporal and spiritual, is condemned by the Lord. In the "law to govern my church" (42:59), the Lord declared, "Thou shalt not be idle; for he that is idle shall not eat the bread nor wear the garments of the laborer" (42:42). Idleness is antithetical to the charge given by God to Adam after the Fall: "Cursed shall be the ground *for thy sake;* in sorrow shalt thou eat of it all the days of thy life. . . . By the sweat of thy face shalt thou eat bread, until thou shalt return unto the ground—for thou shalt surely die" (Moses 4:23, 25; emphasis added). Being diligent and productive, and not idle or lazy, is essential for temporal survival and success. In this way, the Lord's warning that the idle "shall not eat the bread nor wear the garments of the laborer" is literal. This was particularly true under the law of CONSECRATION. To receive a stewardship whereby each would receive "according to his circumstances and his wants and needs" (51:3), each was expected to avoid idleness and contribute according to his capacity.

The Lord also decried idleness in spiritual matters. To become sanctified and more Christlike in nature, the Saints were admonished to "cast away your idle thoughts and your excess of laughter" (88:69) and "cease to be idle; cease to be unclean; cease to find fault one with another; cease to sleep longer than is needful" (88:124). The Lord admonished, those called to proclaim the gospel and build up the kingdom of God on earth, "Thou shalt not idle away thy time, neither shalt thou bury thy talent that it may not be known" (60:13) "but labor with [thy] might" (75:3). Spiritual idleness stunts spiritual growth and slows the work of the Lord. To combat the natural tendency to be spiritually and temporally indolent, the Lord commanded that one "be anxiously engaged in a good cause, and do many things of [one's] own free will, and bring to pass much righteousness" (58:27).

BLT

Idolatry. *See* Appendix E.

Idumea

Figurative expression for the world (that is, the wickedness of the world)—"the Lord . . . shall come down in judgment upon Idumea, or the world" (1:36).

The word *Idumea* is the Greek form of the Hebrew *Edom* and refers both to the descendants of Esau and to the land they controlled. The land was located southeast of the Salt Sea (the Dead Sea) and south of the land of Moab. Although they were blood relatives, the Israelites and the Edomites deeply disliked and often fought each other.

See also Babylon; Judgment(s); World(s), world's, worldliness.

LED

Illinois period

The Illinois period of Church history bvegan with the expulsion of the Saints from Missouri during the winter of 1838–39 and continued until their removal from western Illinois early in 1846. During these seven years, the Saints saw important developments in practical, religious, and doctrinal matters. The history of the period is rooted in the revelations and experiences of the past and nourished with additional revealed truths. While in Nauvoo, Joseph Smith published a basic statement of beliefs (Articles of Faith) and then unfolded a broader view of God's plan for his children. The Prophet expanded the meaning of the gathering, introduced doctrines and related temple ordinances necessary for exaltation, and shared the sealing KEYS to ensure a smooth transition of leadership. Ten sections of the Doctrine and Covenants were received during the Illinois period (124–32; 135).

Latter-day Saints carried with them to Nauvoo fresh memories of challenging experiences with neighbors and government leaders in Ohio and Missouri. Because of growing Mormon populations, other settlers in western Missouri felt threatened by revelations promising the Saints "an inheritance in the land of Zion" (64:30). The story of the Saints in Missouri differed from the biblical story of the Israelites, who drove their enemies out of the promised land (Num. 33:50–56; Deut. 4:35–38). Instead, while noting that the Church in Jackson County had enemies, the revelations warned against bloodshed. The Lord told the Saints to purchase properties in Missouri (Zion) through their consecrations (57:4–5; 58:50–55; 63:24–31).

In 1835 an assembly in Kirtland defined Church views on government and laws, hoping to prevent misinterpretations of doctrines and practices that promoted gathered communities of faith. Additionally, the document defended the right of people who suffered personal abuse or loss of property to "appeal to the civil law for redress" (134:11). The Saints who fled from Jackson County and those expelled from northern Missouri after several bloody attacks and battles suffered serious losses. Yet pleas to Missouri courts and legislators for protection, recognition of their civil and religious rights, and REDRESS for lost property fell on deaf ears.

For five years after the founding of Nauvoo in 1839, impoverished Church members continued to seek relief from the federal government.

Western Illinois and Eastern Iowa, 1839–1846.

Consistent with the Lord's counsel to the Jackson County exiles (101:76–95), Joseph Smith's instructions from LIBERTY JAIL in March 1839 invited the Saints to report their losses to a committee for presentation in the nation's capital (123). The Prophet led the first delegation to Washington, D.C., in November 1839 to deliver a petition and nearly five hundred individual claims. Interviews with President Martin Van Buren, Senator John C. Calhoun, and the Illinois congressional delegation yielded some sympathy but no action. Four months later the Senate Judiciary Committee rejected the petition. A second delegation in 1842 placed another copy of the request and two hundred new claims before the House of Representatives. Congressional committees again refused to endorse the redress bill. A final appeal in early 1844 consisted of a petition fifty feet long and signed by nearly thirty-five hundred Nauvoo residents. Both Congress and President John Tyler rejected claims totaling nearly $2.4 million. Church leaders next turned to written petitions to state governors and grass-roots appeals to citizens of the states. When these, too, failed, other options emerged.

One of these was Joseph Smith's candidacy for the presidency of the United States in the 1844 election. Lieutenant General Joseph Smith stood for office as a private citizen on a Union ticket inviting support from Americans of all political persuasions. He promised to use his influence "for the protection of injured innocence . . . in maintaining the laws & Constitution of the United States . . . for the general good of mankind" (Ehat and Cook, 320). Revelations from the Ohio years had celebrated the nation's Constitution as a divinely sanctioned base for religious and civil freedoms (98:4–7; 101:76–80; 134:1). The Lord affirmed the need to obey civil law and sustain governments (42:79, 85–87; 58:21–22; 109:54). He cautioned that only good and wise men would protect constitutional freedoms, for "when the wicked rule the people mourn" (98:8–10). State and federal officials had failed in their obligations, the Saints concluded, thus jeopardizing the integrity of the government. It was time for Latter-day Saints to step forward and save a threatened constitution.

The Prophet's death ended the short-lived campaign. Two years later the Church abandoned Illinois for a new place of refuge in the valleys of the Rocky Mountains. There the Saints expected to enjoy the rights denied them elsewhere.

The 1835 Kirtland statement on government suggested another option for righting the wrongs of Missouri—self-defense when warranted. After the Saints' expulsion from Jackson County, Joseph Smith organized ZION'S CAMP to reclaim property the Saints had purchased from the federal government and lost through subterfuge and force (103:11–20, 29–40). The expected assistance of Missouri governor Dunklin failed to materialize, but the Lord placed the mission's failure in part on the Saints themselves and postponed efforts to redeem Zion (101:1–2; 103:1–4; 105:1–9).

During the Nauvoo years, self-defense was provided under state charter by the Nauvoo Legion. Twice militiamen rescued Joseph Smith when he was arrested on warrants accusing him of complicity in an attempted assassination of Missouri governor Lilburn Boggs. During the tense last weeks of June 1844, Joseph Smith acquiesced to Illinois governor Thomas Ford's decision to disarm the Nauvoo Legion to lessen the fears of non-Mormon citizens. The concept of a government-sanctioned militia to protect Mormon lives and property continued in Utah Territory, where the territorial militia was fondly called the Nauvoo Legion.

While appeals for redress were underway in the early 1840s, the rapid growth of Church membership created new challenges. The revealed concept of gathering out of wicked Babylon into a righteous land of Zion had become a central belief for the Church (Isa. 11:12; 2 Ne. 29:14; D&C 33:6; 45:66–71; 57:1–2, 14–15; 110:11). The Lord confirmed the practice of gathering after the Saints were forced to leave Jackson County (101:63–75). After the expulsion from northern Missouri in the winter of 1838–39, some members questioned the wisdom of concentrating themselves in large groups. From Liberty Jail, the Prophet counseled the Saints to find temporary gathering places until the Lord opened other doors. Before long, Joseph Smith followed the expelled

Saints into western Illinois, where in 1841 he organized STAKES in Nauvoo and across the Mississippi River in Iowa Territory (124–25). With Nauvoo as the cornerstone stake, Joseph organized seven other Illinois stakes and sanctioned the Kirtland Stake as well. Then, in May 1841, the First Presidency disorganized five of the new units to encourage a cluster of communities closer to Nauvoo, where manpower and tithes were needed to build the TEMPLE.

The second mission of the Twelve to the British Isles began in 1839 (118). Under Brigham Young's leadership, the apostles strengthened the Church there and published the Book of Mormon. Beginning in 1840, emigration through Liverpool helped boost the population of Nauvoo. President Young (126) and others of the Twelve returned to Illinois in 1841 to help settle migrating British converts, manage the sale of Church properties in Nauvoo, and oversee the collection of tithes to support construction of the temple.

At the April conference of 1844, the Prophet identified all of North and South America as the land of Zion. He prophesied that the continents would be filled with stakes, beginning with large cities in the United States. This anticipated expansion was temporarily halted after the Prophet's death, however, inasmuch as all efforts focused on completing the Nauvoo Temple and providing temple endowments for those who would build up new stakes. Quietly the Twelve continued plans for relocating in the West. When mobs began burning Mormon properties in rural Hancock County in September 1845, the Twelve agreed to move all Church members out of Illinois the following spring.

It was the temple that kept the Church in Nauvoo after Joseph Smith's death and that defined the central purpose of the Church. At the October 1840 conference in Nauvoo, the Saints sustained Joseph Smith's proposal to build a house of the Lord. The Prophet then expounded on baptism for the dead, a topic he had briefly addressed at Seymour Brunson's funeral two months earlier, in August. These two discourses explained the ordinance that was needed by the worthy dead to become "heirs of the celestial kingdom of God" (137:7–8). The Prophet and others commented often on the Lord's power to save people in all times and places. The restoration of the PRIESTHOOD, Joseph Smith wrote, created not just a "welding link . . . between the fathers and the children . . . [but] a whole and complete and perfect union, and welding together of dispensations . . . from the days of Adam even to the present time" (128:18).

Within weeks of this funeral sermon in August 1840, the Saints began performing baptisms for their deceased relatives in the Mississippi River. In January 1841 the Lord emphasized that except in times of poverty these and other proxy ordinances should be performed in a temple (124:29–42). Baptisms outside the house of the Lord ceased in October 1841 and began again a month later in a temporary wooden font in the unfinished Nauvoo Temple. In September 1842, Joseph Smith set forth procedures for performing and recording proxy baptisms. He said a witness must record the ordinances so that they "may be recorded in heaven . . . [and] bound in heaven." These records would be archived in the temple to bless future generations and as evidence for the final judgment (127:7–8; 128).

Other ordinances were also performed outside the temple in temporary, dedicated spaces. Joseph and Hyrum Smith gave washings, anointings, and endowments to a few selected men on 4–5 May 1842 in the upper room of Joseph's Red Brick Store. Women received these ordinances the following year, and some of the endowed couples were sealed and received additional ordinances. The Prophet introduced the endowment and sealing to preserve the knowledge and keys after his death. When pressure increased to force the Saints from Illinois, Brigham Young dedicated ordinance rooms in the third level of the temple in December 1845 for endowments and sealings. By 8 February, more than fifty-five hundred Saints had received their endowment and more than one thousand couples had been sealed. With the temple still unfinished, President Young offered the building to the Lord as a monument to Joseph Smith before he left Nauvoo. A formal dedication of the more nearly finished building took place privately on 30 April and publicly on 1 May 1846.

In July 1843 Joseph Smith dictated a revelation concerning the new and everlasting covenant, including the eternity of the MARRIAGE covenant and plurality of wives (132). He had shared aspects of this revelation privately in Kirtland and had sealed a few couples in Nauvoo the previous September. Only a marriage performed with proper priesthood authority, the Prophet had taught, would endure beyond the grave.

Rumors of plural marriage created problems within and without the Church in Nauvoo. Internal opponents rejected all of the doctrines centered on the temple and its ordinances, including the Prophet's teachings defining the nature of God and of mankind's eternal potential (129; 130; 131). They declared Joseph Smith a fallen prophet and organized the Reformed Mormon Church. In a public challenge, they launched the *Nauvoo Expositor* to expose temple doctrines and practices. Behind the scenes, they plotted with political opponents in western Illinois to kill Joseph Smith. The Prophet's political opponents began challenging Latter-day Saints' voting strength in Hancock County in 1843, when their own candidates failed to win election. When the *Expositor* appeared, Nauvoo's city council declared it a public nuisance and the mayor, Joseph Smith, ordered the city marshal to destroy the paper and press. This action led to arrest warrants against city officials, a journey to Carthage to answer charges, and the ultimate death of the Prophet and his brother Hyrum on 27 June 1844. The Church survived the loss of these leaders, contrary to the expectations of their killers. Rather than hurt the Lord's work, John Taylor wrote, "their *innocent blood* on the banner of liberty, and on the *magna charta* of the United States, is an ambassador for the religion of Jesus Christ, that will touch the hearts of honest men among all nations" (135:7). *See* Martyrdom of Joseph and Hyrum Smith.

Throughout his life's ministry, Joseph Smith clearly understood his prophetic calling to lay the foundations of the restored Church of Jesus Christ for the last dispensation. The Prophet knew he would face opposition. As persecution from without and perfidy from within increased, he hastened to prepare others to succeed him. Early revelations had defined relationships among presiding offices and the patterns for ensuring a continuity of revelatory and priesthood authority. As the organization matured and circumstances changed, the specifics of succession changed. Initially, Joseph's successor was to have been the second elder, or assistant president, Oliver Cowdery (20:2–3; 21:1–5, 10–12; 28:1–7; 35:17–20; 43:2–7). Later, two counselors shared the keys (81:1–2; 90:1–4; 107:22, 91–92). After high councils were created in Kirtland (102) and Missouri, a second succession channel existed through the president of the council in Zion, "if he [Joseph Smith] should now be taken away" (Cannon and Cook, 71; cf. 70–73, 151). This role shifted to the traveling high council, or Council of the Twelve, when they were called a year later. A revelation in 1835 clarified the functions and relationships of priesthood councils (107:9–10, 23–24, 33, 36–37, 63–67, 91–92). Joseph Smith reinstated the office of assistant president in 1841 (124:91–95, 123–28) and told the Saints in Nauvoo of his brother Hyrum's new role. From that time forward both Hyrum Smith, as assistant president, and Brigham Young, as president of the Quorum of the Twelve, held the latent presiding authority. In time, both of these prophets, seers, and revelators received the temple ordinances and the sealing keys of the priesthood.

Because Hyrum Smith died with his brother at Carthage, the Twelve stepped forward to lead with the senior apostle at the head. A Nauvoo conference in August sustained the Twelve and their quorum president, Brigham Young, as presiding authorities for the whole Church. The Twelve pushed forward the Prophet's temple project. Then, after the Saints received their promised blessings, President Young led the Church to a safer place of refuge. By revelation, he defined an organization and spiritual standards for the western migration (136). A vision identified for him a specific site for a new headquarters in the Great Salt Lake Valley.

A quarter century after Joseph Smith's first vision, the way to salvation he so earnestly sought in 1820 was firmly planted in the restored Church of Jesus Christ. By the end of the Illinois period, the revelations found in the Doctrine and Covenants—together with their associated ordinances and practices—gave Church members new understandings of the consecrated life, covenant marriages, and mankind's eternal potential. With the foundation of the last dispensation in place, the Church was prepared to move forward in its mission to prepare a people to receive the millennial Christ.

See also Gather, gathering; Historical context and overview of Doctrine and Covenants 124–32 (pp. 837–51) and 135 (p. 854); Nauvoo, Illinois.

BIBLIOGRAPHY

Cannon, Donald Q., and Lyndon W. Cook, eds. *Far West Record: Minutes of The Church of Jesus Christ of Latter-day Saints, 1830–1844.* Salt Lake City: Deseret Book, 1983.

Ehat, Andrew F., and Lyndon W. Cook, comps. and eds. *The Words of Joseph Smith.* Provo, Utah: Religious Studies Center, Brigham Young University, 1980.

Hartley, William G. "Nauvoo Stake, Priesthood Quorums, and the Church's First Wards." *BYU Studies* 32 (Winter–Spring 1992): 57–80.

Johnson, Clark V., ed. *Mormon Redress Petitions: Documents of the 1833–1838 Missouri Conflict.* Provo, Utah: Religious Studies Center, Brigham Young University, 1992.

Leonard, Glen M. *Nauvoo: A Place of Peace, a People of Promise.* Salt Lake City: Deseret Book; Provo, Utah: Brigham Young University Press, 2002.

Porter, Larry C., and Milton V. Backman Jr. "Doctrine and the Temple in Nauvoo." *BYU Studies* 32 (Winter–Spring 1992): 41–57.

GML

Image

A likeness, copy, counterpart, or symbol of an original form. Man is made in the image and likeness of God, who "created man, male and female, after his own image and in his own likeness, created he them" (20:18; cf. Gen. 1:26–27; Mosiah 7:27; Ether 3:15–16; Abr. 4:26–27). The Doctrine and Covenants affirms that Seth "was in the express image of his father, Adam," insomuch that he "could be distinguished from him only by his age" (138:40; 107:43). When the Savior appears, "We shall see that he is a man like ourselves" (130:1); that he is in the image and likeness of God, who "has a body of flesh and bones as tangible as man's; the Son also" (130:22). In every dispensation God has condemned the making and worshiping of "any graven image" (Ex. 20:4–5, 23; cf. Mosiah 13:12; 3 Ne. 21:17).

In restoring his Church in this dispensation, the Lord decried the apostasy and idolatry of a wicked world in which "every man walketh in his own way, and after the image of his own god, whose image is in the likeness of the world, and whose substance is that of an idol, which waxeth old and shall perish in Babylon . . . which shall fall" (1:16). *See* Babylon.

RHC

Immanuel. *See* King Immanuel.

Immortality

Living forever in a resurrected state; the inseparable uniting of body and spirit.

Immortality is a free gift to all mankind: "For as in Adam all die, even so in Christ shall all be made alive" (1 Cor. 15:22). "They shall rise from the dead and shall not die after" (D&C 63:49; cf. Alma 11:45; 12:18). The EARTH itself will attain a "sanctified, immortal, and eternal state" (77:1). "Notwithstanding it shall die, it shall be quickened again" (88:25–26). Beasts also, "in their destined order or sphere of creation," will experience "the enjoyment of their eternal felicity" (77:3). At the end of the MILLENNIUM, "there shall be a new heaven and a new earth. For all old things shall pass away, and all things shall become new, even the heaven and the earth, . . . and beasts, the fowls of the air, and the fishes of the sea" (29:23–24). Evidently, "all things which were created" and became mortal because of the Fall (2 Ne. 2:22–26) will receive immortality by virtue of the ATONEMENT. President Joseph Fielding Smith taught, "Every creature on the earth, whether it be man, *animal, fish, fowl,* or *other creature,* that the Lord has created, is *redeemed from death* on the *same terms* that man is redeemed. These creatures are not responsible for death coming into the world any more than we were, and since they have been created by the Father, they are entitled to their *redemption and eternal duration*" (*Doctrines*, 2:281). *See* Death; Fall of Adam and Eve, the.

There is a distinction between immortality and ETERNAL LIFE, which are both made possible through the atonement of Jesus Christ. God told Moses, "For behold, this is my work and my glory—to bring to pass the immortality *and* eternal life of man" (Moses 1:39; emphasis added). Immortality is living forever; eternal life is a life like God's, living forever in an exalted state in the highest heaven in the celestial kingdom, having achieved the station of a god by full obedience to the laws and ordinances of the gospel of Jesus Christ. *See* Gods.

Such full obedience, once the body and the spirit are inseparably joined in the RESURRECTION, brings a fulness of JOY (93:33–34; Alma 40:21–26). The Lord has said, "Then shall they be gods, because they have all power, and the angels are subject unto them." They are granted "exaltation and continuation of the lives," or "eternal lives" (132:19–24; cf. 76:50–70). The Prophet Joseph Smith taught that means they "will continue to increase and have children in the celestial glory" (*History*, 5:391). The distinction between immortality and eternal life appears several times in the Doctrine and Covenants, where the Lord promises the faithful they will be "raised in immortality unto eternal life" (29:43) or crowned with both "immortality, and eternal life" (75:5; 81:6; 124:55; 128:12, 23; 138:51).

BIBLIOGRAPHY

Smith, Joseph. *History of The Church of Jesus Christ of Latter-day Saints*. Edited by B. H. Roberts. 7 vols. 2d ed. rev. Salt Lake City: The Church of Jesus Christ of Latter-day Saints, 1932–51.

Smith, Joseph Fielding. *Doctrines of Salvation*. Compiled by Bruce R. McConkie. 3 vols. Salt Lake City: Bookcraft, 1954–56.

LGO

Immutable. *See* Appendix E.

Impositions. *See* Appendix E.

Inalienable. *See* Appendix E.

Inculcate. *See* Appendix E.

Independence, Missouri

Independence, Missouri, began as a frontier outpost and trailhead for those traveling the Santa Fe Trail in the 1820s. After the establishment of Jackson County by the Missouri legislature in 1826, Independence was selected as the county seat.

The first Latter-day Saints to visit Independence were the missionaries called by revelation to inaugurate the preaching of the gospel to the LAMANITES in Indian Territory—Oliver Cowdery, Parley P. Pratt, Peter Whitmer Jr., and Ziba Peterson (30:5–8; 32:1–5). Frederick G. Williams joined the original four after his conversion in Kirtland in November 1830. The missionaries to the Lamanites arrived in Independence on 13 January 1831, having journeyed more than a thousand miles from Fayette, New York, in three months' time. Soon after their arrival, Cowdery, Pratt, and Williams crossed the United States border into Indian Territory, where they preached for a short time to the Delaware tribe. Meanwhile, to provide financial support, Whitmer and Peterson set up a tailor shop situated above a mercantile store operated by Lilburn W. Boggs.

During the summer of 1831, Joseph Smith and more than two dozen high priests and elders from Ohio traveled to Independence, Missouri. As instructed by revelation, they went to western Missouri to determine firsthand the location of ZION and the temple and to hold a conference (52:1–5). On 20 July 1831, within just a few days after his arrival in Jackson County, Joseph Smith received a revelation indicating that Independence was the "center place" of Zion and that the location of the temple would be on property "lying westward, upon a lot which is not far from the courthouse" of the community (57:1–3). Accordingly, on 2 August 1831, Church leaders and members assembled on the property of Joshua Lewis, a Church member living in Kaw Township, about eight miles west of Independence, where Sidney Rigdon dedicated the land of Zion (Smith, *History*, 1:196–97).

The following day, 3 August, Joseph Smith and several others assembled on a small rise about a half mile west of the center of Independence. There the Prophet dedicated the site for the temple of the NEW JERUSALEM (Smith, *History*, 1:199). Reflecting on this event in 1835, Joseph Smith wrote: "Having received, by an heavenly vision, a commandment, in June . . . to take my journey to the western boundaries of the State of Missouri, and there designate the very spot, which was to be the central spot, for the commencement of the gathering together of those who embrace the fulness of the everlasting gospel [see 52:1–5]—I accordingly undertook the journey with certain ones of my brethren, and, after a long and tedious journey, suffering many privations and hardships, I arrived in Jackson county Missouri; and, after viewing the country, seeking diligently at the hand of God, he manifested himself unto me, and designated to me and others, the very spot upon which he designed to commence the work of the gathering, and the upbuilding of an holy city, which should be called Zion" ("Elders," 179). On 4 August, the day following the dedication of the temple site, a conference was held, once again on Joshua Lewis's property (Smith, *History*, 1:199). On 9 August, in company with ten elders, Joseph Smith began the return journey to Ohio.

Between 1831 and 1833, several hundred members of the Church settled in Jackson County, where they established five branches on some two thousand acres of land purchased by the Church. Four branches of the Church were organized in Kaw Township west of Independence—Prairie, Whitmer, Colesville, and Blue River—and were exclusively Mormon settlements. Members of the Independence branch, however, lived among the "Gentile" citizens of the community. Land records show the Church purchased nearly 180 acres in the Independence area, most of it west of town. Perhaps the most significant purchase was made by Bishop Edward Partridge on 19 December 1831, when he purchased from Jones H. Flournoy just over sixty-three acres that included the site dedicated by Joseph Smith for the temple in Zion four months before.

Independence also served as headquarters of the Church for the members living in the county. The Missouri bishopric, composed of Edward Partridge (bishop), Isaac Morley (counselor), and John Corrill (counselor), presided over most matters of Church business and policy. In addition, William W. Phelps supervised the printing of *The Evening and the Morning Star* and Book of Commandments in Independence, and A. Sidney Gilbert operated the bishop's storehouse there. Members of the Independence branch included William E. McLellin, Titus Billings, Chapman Duncan, Hiram Rathbun, Vienna Jacques, Charles Allen, Edmund Durfee, James H. Rollins, and for a time, Oliver Cowdery. These and nearly two hundred other Saints living in or near Independence were among the twelve hundred Saints expelled from the county in late 1833.

Doctrine and Covenants 82 and 83 were received by the Prophet Joseph Smith while on a visit to Independence in April 1832. Five months later while back in Kirtland, Joseph Smith received section 84, in which the Lord revealed that a temple was to be built in Independence in that generation (84:1–5, 31–32). *See* Historical context and overview of Doctrine and Covenants 82 (p. 786), 83 (p. 786), and 84 (p. 787).

The Saints were prevented from building that temple by their enemies, and the Lord released them from that obligation at that time (124:49–51). The Lord, however, has made clear that Zion "shall not be moved out of her place" (101:16–20). That means that the city of the New Jerusalem and a temple will yet be built in the Independence area. The Lord will appear in the city of the New Jerusalem in Independence as part of his second coming (133:56; cf. 42:9, 35, 62, 67).

In early 1904, The Church of Jesus Christ of Latter-day Saints purchased nearly twenty-six acres in Independence that included part of the sixty-three acres originally purchased by Edward Partridge in 1831. Three buildings are situated on the property today: the Missouri Independence Mission office (the building also houses other regional Church offices), the Independence Missouri Stake Center, and the Independence Visitors' Center. The city also serves as the headquarters of several Restorationist churches, the most prominent being the Community of Christ (formerly the

Reorganized Church of Jesus Christ of Latter Day Saints). *See* maps, pp. 355, 414, 708, and 710.

See also Gather, gathering; Jackson County, Missouri; Missouri period; Zion, redemption of.

BIBLIOGRAPHY

Smith, Joseph. *History of The Church of Jesus Christ of Latter-day Saints.* Edited by B. H. Roberts. 7 vols. 2d ed. rev. Salt Lake City: The Church of Jesus Christ of Latter-day Saints, 1932–51.

———. "To the Elders of the Church of Latter Day Saints." *Latter Day Saints' Messenger and Advocate* 1, no. 12 (September 1835): 179.

ALB

Inheritance

Something granted to another by a benefactor; something offered to those who, by association and diligence, qualify for a promised reward. The Doctrine and Covenants contains dozens of references to inheritance in several contexts.

The promise of eternal life in the kingdom of God

"Blessed are they who are faithful and endure, whether in life or in death, for they shall inherit eternal life" (50:5; cf. 51:19). Other references to this same promise include the following: "be faithful, keep my commandments, and ye shall inherit the kingdom of heaven" (6:37; cf. 10:55); "he who is faithful and wise in time is accounted worthy to inherit the mansions prepared for him of my Father" (72:4); "he that is a faithful and wise steward shall inherit all things" (78:22); to his "friends" the Lord promises "an inheritance with me" (93:45); and to the righteous dead "an inheritance before the Lord, in the holy city" (63:49). Those who enter into an eternal MARRIAGE by proper authority and keep their covenants "shall inherit thrones, kingdoms, principalities, and powers, dominions, all heights and depths . . . and they shall pass by the angels, and the gods, which are set there, to their exaltation and glory in all things" (132:19–24). *See* Eternal life.

The promise of inheriting the earth

All who qualify for entrance into any part of the celestial kingdom (131:1–4) will inherit the EARTH as an eternal abode: "The earth abideth the law of a celestial kingdom, . . . wherefore, it shall be sanctified; yea, notwithstanding it shall die, it shall be quickened again . . . and the righteous shall inherit it" (88:25–26). The Lord specifies that it is the "meek" (88:17), "the poor who are pure in heart" (56:18–20), those "with an eye single to [his] glory" (59:1–2), and "he that endureth in faith and doeth [his] will" (63:20–21) who shall inherit the earth in eternity.

In eternity and also during the MILLENNIUM, the earth will be given to the righteous for an inheritance. "For they that are wise and have received the truth, and have taken the Holy Spirit for their guide . . . shall abide the day [the destructions at the second coming of the Lord]. . . . And the earth shall be given unto them for an inheritance; and they shall multiply and wax strong, and their children shall grow up without sin unto salvation" (45:56–58; cf. 101:101).

The promise of inheritances in the land of Zion

In the Doctrine and Covenants, most references to inheritance pertain to inheritances of land and stewardships in Church callings in Kirtland and in ZION, according to the laws of CONSECRATION. For instance, the revelations designated certain properties to be given to members of the Kirtland Temple building committee (94:13–14). When the holdings of the United Order were divided among individual members, the Lord specified which properties were to be given to whom as stewardships (104:24–45).

The revelations designate Missouri as "the land of promise, and the place for the city of Zion," with "Independence [as] the center place" (57:1–3). The Saints were told it was to be "the land of your inheritance" (52:5, 42; 55:5; cf. 45:65; 48:4), an "everlasting inheritance" (57:5). Individual inheritances in Zion were to be established under the laws of consecration (51:1–10; 58:36; 63:29–48; 64:20–30; 70:17). Inheritances were given to those "appointed to administer spiritual things" for they are "worthy of [their] hire, even as those who are appointed to a stewardship to administer in temporal things," and were to receive food, raiment, houses, and lands for "an inheritance" (70:12–16). Those whose names were not written "in the book of remembrance," or "the book of the law," were not to receive an inheritance among the Saints (85:3, 9–11).

The early Saints were unable to establish Zion in the land of their inheritance, partly because of their own transgressions (101:1–8), but they were promised that "Zion shall not be moved out of her place" (101:17) and "shall be redeemed, although she is chastened for a little season" (100:13; 103:11–14). See Zion, redemption of.

DKO

Innocent

Guiltless, without fault. One can be considered innocent in a number of contexts:

1. Through having kept God's law (such as JESUS CHRIST).

2. Through not yet being accountable for sin (such as little CHILDREN).

3. Through receiving a remission of sins through the ATONEMENT.

4. Through being obedient to the laws of the land (134:6; 109:49).

One who is innocent is uncondemned (104:7), just, or right before God (Rom. 5:9). The Doctrine and Covenants teaches that "every spirit of man was innocent in the beginning; and God having redeemed man from the fall, men became again, in their infant state, innocent before God" (93:38). See Fall of Adam and Eve, the.

Because some spirits in the PREMORTAL EXISTENCE exercised "exceeding faith and good works" (Alma 13:3), whereas others chose to defy the Father and his plan of salvation, it is evident that there was a gradation of faithfulness there.

Through the infinite and eternal work of "the Lamb slain from the foundation of the world" (Rev. 13:8; Moses 7:47; cf. 1 Pet. 1:19–20), the ATONEMENT of Jesus Christ, all spirits are declared innocent as they enter mortality (93:38). Further, because of the Atonement, that innocence continues until one arrives at the age and state of ACCOUNTABILITY. Hence, little children do not need baptism (29:46–50; 74:7; cf. 20:71; Moro. 8:5–16).

Jesus calls his disciples to become as little children—to be "submissive, meek, humble, patient, full of love," and willing to submit to God (Matt. 18:3; Mosiah 3:19; 3 Ne. 11:37–38). He also calls upon his Saints to be as little children in the sense that little children are innocent, decreed pure and clean and just by our Redeemer.

See also Innocent blood.

RLM

Innocent blood

Although little children are considered INNOCENT by virtue of the Atonement (29:46–47; 74:7), the innocent blood spoken of in Doctrine and Covenants 132:7 is the precious blood of Christ, one whose life required neither pardon nor redemption. To shed innocent blood is to "assent unto" Christ's death, "after ye have received [the] new and everlasting covenant" (132:27), to be of such an evil disposition that one seeks to crucify the Son of God afresh (Heb. 6:6; Smith, 6:314–15). These are they who "deny the truth and defy [Christ's] power—. . . having denied the Holy Spirit after having received it, and having denied the Only Begotten Son of the Father, having crucified him unto themselves and put him to an open shame." These are SONS OF PERDITION, "the only ones on whom the second death shall have any power" (76:31–35, 37).

In another context, *innocent blood* refers to the blood of Joseph and Hyrum Smith, who, although innocent of the charges against them, were brutally murdered in Carthage, Illinois.

BIBLIOGRAPHY

Smith, Joseph. *History of The Church of Jesus Christ of Latter-day Saints.* Edited by B. H. Roberts. 7 vols. 2d ed. rev. Salt Lake City: The Church of Jesus Christ of Latter-day Saints, 1932–51.

RLM

Integrity. *See* Appendix E.

Intelligence

Intelligence is used in the Doctrine and Covenants with two meanings:

1. "The light *of* truth," which "was not

created or made, neither indeed can be" (93:29–30; emphasis added) and which is that part of man which has always existed. President Joseph Fielding Smith cautioned: "Some of our writers have endeavored to explain what an intelligence is, but to do so is futile, for we have never been given any insight into this matter beyond what the Lord has fragmentarily revealed. We know, however, that there is something called intelligence which always existed. It is the real eternal part of man, which was not created or made. This intelligence combined with the spirit constitutes a spiritual identity or individual" (11).

2. "Light *and* truth," an attribute of God and man—TRUTH enlightened by REVELATION, declared to be "the glory of God" (93:36, cf. 93:24–28; emphasis added). Elder John A. Widtsoe taught: "Among the many great truths revealed to the Prophet Joseph Smith, none is more beloved by the Church than 'The Glory of God is intelligence.' The word intelligence, as used in common speech, means readiness in learning, quickness of mind. Its higher Gospel meaning is more profound. The intelligent man is he who seeks knowledge and uses it in accordance with the plan of the Lord for human good. This is implied in the revelation from which the quotation is made, for the full sentence reads, 'The glory of God is intelligence, or in other words, light and truth.' When men follow the light their knowledge will always be well used. Intelligence, then, becomes but another name for wisdom" (50). *See* Wisdom, wise.

The acquisition of truth is important, but to be designated as intelligence, the truth must be illuminated by LIGHT—revelation from heaven. Gaining such intelligence, truth *and* light, serves as a catalyst for the acquisition of more intelligence, with the promise that the "light groweth brighter and brighter until the perfect day" (50:24). "Whatever principle of intelligence we attain unto in this life, it will rise with us in the resurrection. And if a person gains more knowledge and intelligence in this life through his diligence and obedience than another, he will have so much the advantage in the world to come" (130:18–19).

BIBLIOGRAPHY

Smith, Joseph Fielding. *The Progress of Man.* Salt Lake City: Deseret Book, 1964.

Widtsoe, John A. Conference Report, April 1938.

CWB

Interpolations. *See* Appendix E.

Inviolate. *See* Appendix E.

Iowa

A territory in the United States in 1841 that became a state in 1846. Iowa is mentioned once in the Doctrine and Covenants: "What is the will of the Lord concerning the saints in the Territory of Iowa?" (125:1). The Lord answered, instructing the Saints to gather to places he would designate through the Prophet Joseph Smith. Specifically they were to "build up a city" and name it Zarahemla (125:3). Complying with the Lord's will, Latter-day Saints established the settlements of Zarahemla, Ambrosia, and Nashville (Hartley and Anderson, 12–18). These settlements were abandoned in 1846 when the Saints left Nauvoo and moved west. In 1841 William Law was instructed to proclaim the "everlasting gospel" unto the inhabitants of Burlington and Madison, Iowa. It is not known to what extent he fulfilled that assignment (124:88). *See* map, p. 857.

See also Historical context and overview of Doctrine and Covenants 125 (p. 840).

BIBLIOGRAPHY

Hartley, William G., and A. Gary Anderson. *Iowa and Nebraska.* Vol. 5 of *Sacred Places: A Comprehensive Guide to Early LDS Historical Sites,* edited by LaMar C. Berrett. Salt Lake City: Deseret Book, 2006.

DQC

Isaac

Son of Abraham and father of Jacob (Israel). Isaac is usually mentioned in connection with his father, Abraham, and his son Jacob (e.g., 136:21). He is one "by whom the promises remain," pertaining to the ABRAHAMIC COVENANT (27:10), who will be "in the presence of the Lamb" in the hereafter (133:55).

Abraham was commanded to offer up Isaac (132:36, 50). The law governing the response of the righteous to ill-treatment by an enemy (98:23–48) was given to Isaac and all other ancient prophets and apostles (98:32). Isaac, like Abraham and Jacob, obeyed the law of plural marriage and is now exalted as a god (132:1, 37). Isaac was seen by President Joseph F. Smith in the spirit world (138:41).

DKO

Isaiah

Prophet of the kingdom of Judah who prophesied between ca. 740 and 690 B.C. (Isa. 1:1; 6:1). Messianic prophecies are abundant in Isaiah's writings, as well as warnings, instructions, and prophecies to and about the covenant people and their neighboring nations. His prophecies and language appear frequently in the Doctrine and Covenants. Section 113 contains answers to specific questions about the meaning of some of Isaiah's prophecies (vv. 1–10). Isaiah is also mentioned by name in 76:100 and 138:42. His poetry-laden writings are often quoted by other prophets. Christ specifically identified Isaiah's writings as deserving of special study (3 Ne. 23:1–3).

See also Isaiah quotations in the Doctrine and Covenants.

TBB

Isaiah quotations in the Doctrine and Covenants

Isaiah is the Old Testament prophet quoted most often in the Book of Mormon and, arguably, in the Doctrine and Covenants as well. Nearly two-thirds (86 of 138) of the revelations recorded in the Doctrine and Covenants share characteristic language, phrases, or terms recorded in Isaiah. While some of the shared language in the Doctrine and Covenants occurs as extended passages taken from Isaiah's writings, the preponderance of the shared language is in short phrases and terminology. Only 113:1–10, which comments on the identity of individuals and the meaning of phrases in Isaiah 11 and 52, and 138:42, which speaks of the Redeemer's work as described in Isaiah 61:1, identify Isaiah as the originator of the language. In every other instance the Doctrine and Covenants incorporates the Isaianic language without referring to

the book of Isaiah itself. Rather, the phrases from Isaiah are used in a manner that suggests the speaker is so familiar with the language that he uses it as his own. A sample of the shared Isaianic language is found in the accompanying table.

This use of Isaianic language in the Doctrine and Covenants is impressive both for its quantity and also its breadth. The revelations share terms and phrases from about 80 percent of the chapters of Isaiah (54 of 66 chapters), yet nearly 90 percent (147 of 171) of the shared terms and phrases are used three times or fewer in the entire Doctrine and Covenants text. Thus, while the Doctrine and Covenants draws both broadly and abundantly from the words of Isaiah, no particular term or phrase is used too repetitively or enjoys special attention.

This broad and prevalent occurrence of Isaianic language in the latter-day revelations suggests that either the Prophet Joseph Smith was extraordinarily familiar with Isaiah's writings and accordingly borrowed terminology from them extensively as he communicated the revelations he received from God, or the shared language finds its way into the Doctrine and Covenants because the Lord chose to use King James Translation Isaianic language to communicate, inspire, and reveal truths to the Prophet. Likely both factors contributed to the phenomenon.

Students of the book of Isaiah typically recognize that the first thirty-five chapters (Isa. 1–35) focus primarily on themes of warning, chastisement, and judgment, followed by four historical chapters that chronicle events that transpired during King Hezekiah's reign (Isa. 36–39). The last twenty-seven chapters (Isa. 40–66) focus more on God's ability and plans to restore and redeem his people. Not surprisingly, then, more than half the occurrences of Isaianic language in the prophecies of the Restoration that constitute the Doctrine and Covenants come from the last twenty-seven chapters of Isaiah rather than the first thirty-nine.

One paradigm for analyzing Isaiah's writings divides them into three categories: warnings of apostasy and sin, admonitions and counsel to repent, and prophecies of future events.

QUOTES, PHRASES, AND LANGUAGE	DOCTRINE & COVENANTS	ISAIAH
Broken mine everlasting covenant	1:15	24:5
Babylon the great, which shall fall	1:16	21:9
Marvelous work is about to come forth	4:1; 6:1; 11:1; 12:1; 14:1; 18:44	29:14
Helmet of salvation	27:18	59:17
Not fearing what man can do	30:11	51:7
All nations shall tremble	34:8	64:2
Mine arm is not shortened	35:8	50:2; 59:1
For I am your lawgiver	38:22	33:22
Go ye out. . . . Be ye clean that bear the vessels of the Lord	38:42; 133:5	52:11
To be a light to the world . . . Gentiles	45:9; 86:11	42:6
My strong reasoning	45:10; 71:8	41:21
Overflowing scourge	45:31	28:15
Your souls shall live	45:46	55:3
Scorner shall be consumed	45:50	29:20
And for the valleys to be exalted, and for the mountains to be made low, and for the rough places to become smooth—and all this when the angel shall sound his trumpet	49:23	40:4
Blossom as the rose	49:24	35:1
Behold, I will go before you and be your rearward	49:27	52:12
And now come, saith the Lord, by the Spirit, unto the elders of his church, and let us reason	50:10	1:18
A feast of fat things . . . of wine on the lees well refined	58:8	25:6
The willing and obedient shall eat the good of the land of Zion in these last days	64:34	1:19
Prepare ye the way of the Lord, make his paths straight	65:1; 133:17	40:3
And push many people to Zion with songs of everlasting joy upon their heads	66:11; 101:18; 109:39; 133:33	35:10
No weapon that is formed against you shall prosper	71:9; 109:25	54:17
For the Lord is God, and beside him there is no Savior	76:1	43:11
Wisdom of the wise shall perish, and the understanding of the prudent shall come to naught	76:9	29:14
Eye has not seen, nor ear heard, nor yet entered	76:10	64:4

QUOTES, PHRASES, AND LANGUAGE	DOCTRINE & COVENANTS	ISAIAH
Their worm dieth not, and the fire is not quenched	76:44	66:24
Trodden the wine-press alone	76:107; 88:106; 133:50–52	63:3
Lift up the hands which hang down, and strengthen the feeble knees	81:5	35:3
Put on her beautiful garments	82:14	52:1
The voice of one crying in the wilderness	88:66	40:3
Bind up the law and seal up the testimony	88:84; 109:46; 133:72	8:16
Every knee shall bow, and every tongue shall confess	88:104	45:23
And shall run and not be weary, and shall walk and not faint	89:20	40:31
My strange act	95:4; 101:95	28:21
Line upon line, precept upon precept	98:12; 128:21	28:10
All flesh shall see me together	101:23	40:5
In that day an infant shall not die until he is old; and his life shall be as the age of a tree	101:30	65:22
Darkness covereth the earth, and gross darkness the minds of the people	112:23	60:2
A refuge from the storm	115:6	25:4
Solitary places to bud	117:7	35:1
For they are as grass, and all their glory as the flower thereof which soon falleth	124:7	40:6–7
In the day of visitation	124:8	10:3
Bear him up as on eagles' wings	124:18, 99	40:31
The box-tree, and the fir-tree, and the pine-tree, together with all the precious trees of the earth	124:26	41:19; 60:13
How beautiful upon the mountains are the feet of those that bring glad tidings of good things, and that say unto Zion: Behold, thy God reigneth!	128:19	52:7
For he shall make bare his holy arm in the eyes of all the nations, and all the ends of the earth shall see the salvation of their God	133:3	52:10
An highway shall be cast up	133:27	11:16
And in the barren deserts there shall come forth pools of living water; and the parched ground shall no longer be a thirsty land	133:29	35:7
O that thou wouldst rend the heavens, that thou wouldst come down, that the mountains might flow down at thy presence.	133:40	64:1

QUOTES, PHRASES, AND LANGUAGE	DOCTRINE & COVENANTS	ISAIAH
For since the beginning of the world have not men heard nor perceived by the ear, neither hath any eye seen, O God, besides thee, how great things thou has prepared for him that waiteth for thee	133:45	64:4
Who is this that cometh . . . ? . . . wine-vat . . . loving kindness . . . days of old	133:46–53	63:1–9
When I called again there was none of you to answer; yet my arm was not shortened at all that I could not redeem, neither my power to deliver	133:67	50:2
And this shall ye have of my hand—ye shall lie down in sorrow	133:70	50:11
I am going like a lamb to the slaughter	135:4	53:7

First, though warnings are abundant in the Doctrine and Covenants, the revelations do not draw upon Isaiah for language of warning, except for a few instances in which Isaianic terms are used to describe the apostate world into which the gospel was restored (e.g., 1:15–16; 112:23; cf. Isa. 24:5; 60:2).

Second, Isaiah's language of admonition and counsel appears somewhat more frequently in the Doctrine and Covenants. For example, individuals and groups are variously counseled and admonished to "be ye clean that bear the vessels of the Lord" (38:42; 133:5; cf. Isa. 52:11), to seek the Lord "early" and to "call upon" him while he is "near" (88:62, 83; cf. Isa. 55:6; 26:9), and to "bind up" and "seal" the law and their testimonies as they proclaim the word of God (88:84; 109:38; cf. Isa. 8:16).

Third, and in contrast to the occasional occurrence of Isaianic language of warnings and admonitions, Isaiah's prophetic language pervades the Doctrine and Covenants. Often prophetic phrases from Isaiah are used to describe the latter-day restoration that has occurred and is occurring. For example, the "marvelous work" of the Restoration has begun causing the "wisdom of the wise" to "perish" (e.g., 4:1; 6:1; 11:1; 12:1; 14:1; 18:44; 76:9; cf. Isa. 29:14). The latter-day "voice . . . in the wilderness" (88:66; 128:20) has cried out, "Prepare ye the way of the Lord" (65:1; 133:17; cf. Isa. 40:3) as the "light" of the gospel is sought out by the "Gentiles" (45:9, 28; 86:11; cf. Isa. 42:6; 60:3). Truth is being revealed "line upon line, precept upon precept" (98:12; 128:21; cf. Isa. 28:10) as

God performs his "strange act" (101:95; cf. Isa. 28:21). The desert has begun to "blossom as the rose" (49:24; cf. Isa. 35:1) as Zion prepares to "arise and put on her beautiful garments" (82:14; cf. Isa. 52:1).

Isaiah's prophetic language foretelling the second coming of Christ is also common in the Doctrine and Covenants. For example, at the advent of the millennial Messiah, the "nations" will "tremble" at his presence (34:8; cf. Isa. 64:2), "the scorner shall be consumed" and those that "watched for iniquity" will be destroyed (45:50; cf. Isa. 29:20). When he appears, the "valleys" will "be exalted," "the mountains" will "be made low" (49:23; 109:74; cf. Isa. 40:4), and an "overflowing scourge" shall cover the land (45:31; Isa. 28:15). Jesus will appear, proclaiming that he had "trodden the wine-press alone" (76:107; 88:106; cf. Isa. 63:3). "All flesh shall see" him "together" (101:23; cf. Isa. 40:5) and "every knee shall bow, and every tongue shall confess" that he is the Christ (88:104; cf. Isa. 45:23) as he becomes their "lawgiver" (38:22; cf. Isa. 33:22). Eventually, the righteous shall dwell in Zion, having "songs of everlasting joy upon their heads" (66:11; 101:18; 133:33; cf. Isa. 35:10).

See also Doctrine and Covenants, what it says about the Bible; Historical context and overview of Doctrine and Covenants 113 (p. 823).

TBB

Ishmaelites

Descendants of Ishmael and his family who about 600 B.C. followed Lehi and his family out of Jerusalem to the Western Hemisphere. The one reference to the Ishmaelites in the Doctrine and Covenants is in connection with the assurance that through the Book of Mormon record, the Ishmaelites, along with descendants of Lehi, might come to know the Savior—know of his promises, believe his gospel, rely upon his merits, and be glorified and saved (3:16–20).

DKO

Israel

The gospel provides two broad, related definitions of the word *Israel:* an ancient nation, descended from Abraham, Isaac, and Jacob, whose history is recounted in the Old Testament; and the COVENANT PEOPLE OF THE LORD of any lineage (Rom. 9:6–7; Gal. 3:26–29; Abr. 2:9–10). The Doctrine and Covenants uses the word in a variety of contexts.

Old Testament names of God

In a revelation, the Lord identified himself in biblical language as the "Mighty One of Israel" (36:1). This title appears only in Isaiah in the Old Testament (Isa. 1:24; 30:29) and once in Nephi's writings, in which he was commenting on Isaiah (1 Ne. 22:12). To his modern Church, the Lord called himself the "stone of Israel" (50:44), a title found elsewhere only in Genesis 49:24. Joseph Smith addressed God as the "Lord God of Israel" at the beginning of the dedicatory prayer of the Kirtland Temple (109:1). This title is found more than a hundred times in the Old Testament and once in the New Testament. Each of these names ties the modern Church to the Lord's ancient people and shows that the latter-day work continues God's work from the past.

Israel in the Bible

The Doctrine and Covenants teaches important doctrinal and historical concepts concerning the ancient people of Israel—information so essential that one cannot understand the Old Testament fully without it (for example, 84:18–27). Moses taught the Israelites in the wilderness to prepare them to see the face of God. But they rebelled and proved themselves unworthy, forfeiting blessings they otherwise would have had as the Lord's Saints. As a result, the Lord took the Melchizedek PRIESTHOOD from them (84:25). The consequences of this action were profound because the Melchizedek Priesthood "administereth the gospel and holdeth the key of the mysteries of the kingdom, even the key of the knowledge of God." In its ordinances, "the power of godliness is manifest," and without those ordinances and without the higher priesthood, "the power of godliness is not manifest unto men in the flesh" (84:19–21). "In his wrath," the Lord left Israel with the Aaronic Priesthood instead, which was held only by the tribe of Levi, its KEYS descending through the family of Aaron to John the Baptist (84:18, 26–27). These passages help with understanding the history of the ancient Israelites after Moses' time, for they were deprived not only of Melchizedek Priesthood but also of the gospel knowledge that would have accompanied it had they been faithful. These passages also help with understanding why the Book of Mormon—the record of another branch of Israel that enjoyed the blessings of the Melchizedek Priesthood and the gospel in its fulness—is quite different from the Old Testament.

Several passages in the Doctrine and Covenants evoke images of ancient Israel in the days of Moses to teach members of the modern-day Church about God's relationship to them. "I am he who led the children of Israel out of the land of Egypt," the Lord said, "and my arm is stretched out in the last days, to save my people Israel" (136:22; cf. 103:17–18; 105:26). The spirit "by which Moses brought the children of Israel through the Red Sea on dry ground" is the same spirit of revelation experienced among Latter-day Saints (8:3). Early Church members were to travel as the ancient Israelites had (61:25). The Lord would raise up a man to guide them as his ancient people were led by Moses (103:16), the "great law-giver of Israel" (138:41). And "the destroying angel shall pass by them, as the children of Israel, and not slay them" (89:21).

The Latter-day Saints

In many passages in the Doctrine and Covenants, the Lord refers to the Latter-day Saints as Israel, often with biblical language and allusions to biblical themes. Doing so identifies the

Lord's people in modern times as being part of his work that has spanned all generations, and it reminds Church members today that the same covenant blessings promised to the ancient patriarchs will be theirs as well if they live worthily.

The Church and its people are Israel (42:39; 109:70). Its bishops are judges in Israel (58:17; 107:72, 76). Its army is the army of Israel (105:26, 30), just as its traveling camp is the Camp of Israel (136:1). "Israel shall be saved," the Lord said (38:33). Indeed, "Israel shall be saved in mine own due time; and by the keys which I have given shall they be led, and no more be confounded at all" (35:25). One passage identifies only the righteous as Israel: "And in that day all who are found upon the watchtower, or in other words, all mine Israel, shall be saved" (101:12). "For ye are the children of Israel, and of the seed of Abraham. . . . And as your fathers were led at the first, even so shall the redemption of Zion be" (103:17–18).

Israel in the last days

Most references to Israel in the Doctrine and Covenants are in contexts that foretell events of the last days. None of the passages, including those that concern the gathering, refer to a modern country by that name or to the geographical area of the Holy Land. They refer instead to Israel as a people. In virtually every case, the passages refer to the entire house of Israel without differentiating among Jews, descendants of Lehi, or others of the covenant family. Through the Restoration, descendants of Judah and Lehi learn who they are in God's plan (Book of Mormon, title page). Regarding others of the house of Israel, "Whether this lineage is of blood or adoption does not matter" (Widtsoe, 322). Some of the prophecies include references to the GENTILES, best defined in the scriptures as the "nations" or the "peoples" and usually referring to those who are not descendants of Abraham, Isaac, and Jacob. In combination, Israel and the Gentiles include all the people of the earth (18:6). Through the Gentiles the fulness of the gospel will be taken to the house of Israel (14:10).

The Doctrine and Covenants confirms Jesus' New Testament statement that the Twelve will be the judges of the house of Israel (Matt. 19:28; Luke 22:30). They will "judge the whole house of Israel, even as many as have loved me and kept my commandments, and none else" (29:12). Key to understanding an apocalyptic scripture in the book of Revelation (Rev. 7:4), the revelations clarify that 144,000 high priests (12,000 from each tribe of Israel) will be called upon to seal others to ETERNAL LIFE and bring them into the CHURCH OF THE FIRSTBORN (77:11). Because the passage identifies these men as "they who are ordained out of every nation, kindred, tongue, and people"—a phrase that sometimes means "all people" but often refers specifically to the Gentiles—this expression reminds one of the universality of the gospel and the availability of its highest blessings to all of God's children.

The gathering of Israel

The prophecies of the gathering and restoration of Israel presuppose the historical fact of the scattering. The Lord and his prophets told the ancient Israelites that if they violated the covenant of worthiness by which they inhabited their promised land, they would be driven from it and scattered among the nations (Deut. 4:25–27). Accordingly, thousands from the kingdom of Israel, or the northern ten tribes, were deported by the Assyrians and relocated elsewhere; their descendants were scattered throughout the world. These descendants are called "lost" because, to use Nephi's words, they are "lost from the knowledge of those who are at Jerusalem" (1 Ne. 22:4). Over a century later, during the lifetime of Nephi, thousands from the kingdom of Judah were deported by the Babylonians or fled out of the Holy Land. Their descendants, the Jews, have for the most part retained their religious tradition and cultural identity, unlike their scattered counterparts of the northern ten tribes.

For these and all others, the gathering is dependent on joining the Lord's people by covenant. All must "come to a knowledge of the truth," "believe in the Messiah" (109:67), and embrace the restored GOSPEL. That is accomplished through faith in Jesus Christ, repentance, baptism, and reception of the Holy Ghost. As individuals are baptized, they take upon themselves the name of Christ and become members of the covenant family of Israel, regardless of their genealogical origin (Gal. 3:27–29; 2 Ne. 30:2; 3 Ne. 16:13; Abr. 2:10).

God's latter-day work with respect to the people of Israel will be all-encompassing, and it will be in fulfillment of promises he made to their fathers (84:99). He will recover them (39:11) and gather them (77:9, 14; 137:6) from all parts of the earth to which they were dispersed (110:11). As they were scattered throughout the world, so will they be gathered from throughout the world (3 Ne. 20:13; 21:26–29). Ephraim, the birthright tribe, is being gathered first and has been called to take the lead in this work (133:30–34). Modern scripture teaches that the focus of the gathering is more spiritual than geographical: The scattered remnants will "return to the Lord from whence they have fallen" (113:10) and gather to Christ and his Church in their various homelands. In this gathering, they will be saved (86:11; 90:8), restored (45:17), and redeemed (84:99; 109:67; 113:8). None of this process is independent of The Church of Jesus Christ of Latter-day Saints because the restoration of Israel is under the direction of "those whom God should call in the last days, who should hold the power of priesthood" to bring to pass this work—"to bring again Zion, and the redemption of Israel" (113:8). The keys for it were given by Moses to Joseph Smith in 1836, "the keys of the gathering of Israel from the four parts of the earth, and the leading of the ten tribes from the land of the north" (110:11).

Many Latter-day Saints are so close to the ongoing gathering of Israel and the return of its lost remnants that they often do not see that it is happening already nor how remarkable it is. It is now, and will continue to be, so miraculous that it is described in the scriptures with profound symbols. The Doctrine and Covenants expresses it using images from the Old Testament: "And they who are in the north countries"—the lands to which they were scattered—"shall come in remembrance before the Lord" (133:26; cf. Jer. 23:8; 31:8). Just as when God brought their ancestors out of Egypt on a divinely prepared path, "an highway shall be cast up in the midst of the great deep" for their latter-day return (133:27). This prophecy draws language from Isaiah: "And there shall be an highway for the remnant of his people, which shall be left, from Assyria; like as it was to Israel in the day that he came up out of the land of Egypt" (Isa. 11:16). Indeed, the latter-day gathering will eventually eclipse even the deliverance of Israel out of Egypt: "They shall no more say, The Lord liveth, which brought up the children of Israel out of the land of Egypt; but, The Lord liveth, which brought up and which led the seed of the house of Israel out of the north country, and from all countries whither I had driven them" (Jer. 23:7–8).

See also Gather, gathering.

BIBLIOGRAPHY

Jackson, Kent P. *Lost Tribes and Last Days: What Modern Revelation Tells Us about the Old Testament.* Salt Lake City: Deseret Book, 2005.

Widtsoe, John A. *Evidences and Reconciliations.* Arranged by G. Homer Durham. 3 vols in 1. Salt Lake City, Utah: Bookcraft, 1960.

KPJ

Israel, camp of. *See* Camp of Israel, camp of the Lord.

Israel, house of. *See* Israel.

Israel, lost tribes, return of. *See* Israel.

Israel, scattering and gathering of. *See* Israel.

And if it so be that you should labor all your days in crying repentance unto this people, and bring, save it be one soul unto me, how great shall be your **joy** with him in the kingdom of my Father! And now, if your joy will be great with one soul that you have brought unto me into the kingdom of my Father, how great will be your joy if you should bring many souls unto me! 18:15–16

Jackson County, Missouri

Created by the Missouri legislature on 15 December 1826 with Independence as the county seat; named in honor of United States president Andrew Jackson. At that time the county extended from the Missouri River on the north to the Little Osage River on the south, a distance of approximately seventy-five miles. In 1835, the county was reduced to the size it is today, which is one-third its original size.

Situated on the western boundary of Missouri, Jackson County at the time of its incorporation was also on the western boundary of the United States. Many of the region's first settlers were drawn there by the economic opportunities associated with the Santa Fe Trail, which originated in Independence. The first Latter-day Saints in Jackson County were Oliver Cowdery, Peter Whitmer Jr., Parley P. Pratt, Ziba Peterson, and Frederick G. Williams, who arrived in January 1831 to preach to the Indian tribes just over the border in present-day Kansas. *See* Lamanites.

Although they did not succeed in their efforts with the Indians, the missionaries did succeed in establishing a small branch of the Church in Jackson County. In July 1831, Joseph Smith and several leading elders, obedient to the Lord's instructions (52:1–5), journeyed to Jackson County. Four revelations were received during that visit. Two of them (recorded in sections 57–58) provided understanding of the region, designating Independence as the "center place" of the city of ZION, identifying a temple site, and instructing Church members to purchase property in the region. The other two revealed principles relating to the Sabbath (59) and gave instructions regarding the brethren's return to Kirtland (60). During the next two years, branches of the Church were established, one in Independence (Blue River Township), and four others—Prairie, Whitmer, Colesville, and Blue River (in Kaw Township)—with property ownership totaling more than twenty-one hundred acres.

Within two years, the Saints numbered approximately twelve hundred, almost a third of the county's estimated population of thirty-three hundred. By late 1833, religious, political, economic, and social differences between the newcomers and the previous settlers culminated in hostilities between the two groups. The Saints were expelled from the county, most of them finding refuge in Clay County to the north.

The Saints sought REDRESS through the courts and by petitioning government officials, but little action was taken. In 1834, some two hundred Mormon volunteers, known as ZION'S CAMP, journeyed from Ohio to Missouri to join with Missouri state militia to help the displaced Church members reclaim their land, but Missouri governor Daniel Dunklin refused to intervene. Nonetheless, from 1834 to 1838, the Saints in Missouri continued to hope that they would soon be able to return to Jackson County and there build the city of Zion and a temple. But the hostilities that took place against the Saints in Jackson County in 1833 were repeated in northern Missouri in 1838, resulting in a regional war against the Mormons and in their forced removal from the state by order of Missouri governor Lilburn W. Boggs. After establishing a new place of gathering at Nauvoo, Illinois, Joseph Smith received a revelation rescinding for a time the commandment to establish Zion and build a temple in Jackson County (124:49–51); however, the Lord made clear that Zion has not been "moved out of her place" (101:17–21; cf. 90:37; 105:1–41), that Jackson County, Missouri, with Independence as the center place, remains the location where the NEW JERUSALEM will be established. At a future day and time before the second coming of Christ, revelation will be given to latter-day prophets directing the establishment of Zion, where "Christ will reign personally upon the earth" (A of F 10). *See* map, p. 414.

See also Independence, Missouri; Missouri period.

BIBLIOGRAPHY

History of Jackson County, Missouri, Containing a History of the County, Its Cities, Towns, Etc., Biographical Sketches of Its Citizens, Jackson County in the Late War, General and Local Statistics, Portraits of Early Settlers and Prominent Men, History of Missouri, Maps of Clinton County, Etc., Etc. Kansas City: Union Historical Company, Birdsall, Williams, & Co., 1881.

ALB

Jacob

Name changed to Israel; father of twelve sons, whose descendants are known as the twelve tribes of Israel. Together with his grandfather and father, Abraham and Isaac, Jacob is one "by whom the promises remain" pertaining to the Abrahamic covenant (27:10; cf. 133:55; 136:21; 138:41) and who will be "in the presence of the Lamb" in the hereafter (133:55). The Doctrine and Covenants identifies the Lamanites as children of Jacob (10:59–62; 109:61–62, 65), and therefore heirs of those same promises, and declares that one day they "shall blossom as the rose" (49:24). The Doctrine and Covenants also identifies covenant people of the Lord who are to "gather out the righteous to build a holy city to [Jehovah's] name" (109:54–58).

The law governing the response of the righteous to ill-treatment by an enemy (98:23–38) was given to Jacob and all other ancient prophets and apostles. Jacob, like Abraham and Isaac, obeyed the law of plural marriage and is now exalted as a god (132:1, 37). Jacob was seen by President Joseph F. Smith in his vision of the spirit world (138:41).

DKO

Jacobites

Descendants of Lehi's son Jacob who followed their progenitor as faithful friends of Nephi's descendants (Jacob 1:13; 4 Ne. 1:36–37; Morm. 1:8). The one reference to the Jacobites in the Doctrine and Covenants is in connection with the assurance that they, along with other Lehites and Ishmaelites, through the Book of Mormon record might come to know the Savior—know of his promises, believe his gospel, rely upon his merits, and be glorified and saved (3:16–20).

DKO

Jacques, Vienna

Birth: 10 June 1787, Beverly, Essex County, Massachusetts

Death: 7 February 1884, Salt Lake City, Salt Lake County, Utah

In 1833, Bostonian Vienna Jacques (or Jaques), who was baptized into the Church the previous year, journeyed to Kirtland, taking with

Vienna Jacques, 1787–1884.

her fourteen hundred dollars. On 8 March 1833, Joseph Smith asked Jacques to consecrate her money to the Church. Obediently she gave all that she had. For her consecration, the Lord said, "It is my will that my handmaid Vienna Jaques should receive money to bear her expenses, and go up unto the land of Zion . . . and receive an inheritance from the hand of the bishop; that she may settle down in peace" (90:28–31). The money she needed was given to her, and in the summer of 1833 Jacques went to Zion. Unfortunately, persecution drove her from her inheritance there to northern Missouri. "I was aware when you left Kirtland that the Lord would chasten you," Joseph Smith wrote on 4 September 1833. He advised, "Live in strict obedience to the commandments of God" (1:408).

Before leaving Missouri, Vienna married Daniel Shearer, with whom she moved to Nauvoo. Joseph Smith III "remembered her as 'a frequent visitor to our home'" (in Black, 146). By the time she left Nauvoo for Salt Lake City in 1846 her marriage had ended, and she drove her own wagon across the plains. She was given a lot in Salt Lake City where she lived alone until her death. At her passing, the *Woman's Exponent* reported, "She was true to her covenants and esteemed the restoration of the Gospel as a priceless treasure" ("In Memoriam," 152).

BIBLIOGRAPHY

"In Memoriam—Vienna Jaques." *Woman's Exponent* 12 (1 March 1884): 152.

Smith, Joseph. *History of The Church of Jesus Christ of Latter-day Saints.* Edited by B. H. Roberts. 7 vols. 2d ed. rev. Salt Lake City: The Church of Jesus Christ of Latter-day Saints, 1932–51.

SEB

James

Apostle and member of the presidency of the Church of Jesus Christ in the first century A.D. There are three references to James in the Doctrine and Covenants. One reference is in connection with the Lord's promise that he would make Peter "to minister" for James and John, and that those three would be given "the keys of this ministry" (7:7). Joseph Smith, in rejoicing over events of the Restoration, wrote of the appearance of Peter, James, and John "in the wilderness between Harmony, Susquehanna county, and Colesville, Broome county, on the Susquehanna river, declaring themselves as possessing the keys of the kingdom, and of the dispensation of the fulness of times" (128:20). The Lord affirmed that Peter, James, and John conferred those keys on Joseph Smith and Oliver Cowdery (27:12–13).

DKO

James, George

Birth: 1797, Massachusetts

Death: November 1864, Brownhelm, Lorain County, Ohio

George Fitch James was baptized by 1831 and, as recorded in Doctrine and Covenants 52:38, was to be ordained a priest. For a short time he was faithful, but he subsequently struggled with his Church duties and was accused of failing to "take up his cross and magnify his calling . . . in going out to proclaim the gospel." James confessed his failure, asked for forgiveness, and was given the Prophet's "hand of fellowship" (MH, 4 April 1834; Smith, 2:47).

In November 1834 Joseph Smith wrote to James, notifying him that because of complaints against him, his priesthood authority was suspended until matters were resolved (MH, 10 November 1834; Smith, 2:170). By 1836 James had returned to fellowship and was anointed in the Kirtland Temple 26 March 1836 (*Kirtland,* 13). He did not move to Missouri or Illinois with the Saints but remained in Ohio.

BIBLIOGRAPHY

Kirtland Elders' Quorum Record, 1836–1841. Edited by Lyndon W. Cook and Milton V. Backman Jr. Provo, Utah: Grandin, 1985.

Manuscript History of the Church, 4 April 1834. Church History Library, The Church of Jesus Christ of Latter-day Saints, Salt Lake City, Utah.

Smith, Joseph. *History of The Church of Jesus Christ of Latter-day Saints.* Edited by B. H. Roberts. 7 vols. 2d ed. rev. Salt Lake City: The Church of Jesus Christ of Latter-day Saints, 1932–51.

ZLL

Jared

HIGH PRIEST and ordained PATRIARCH who lived between the time of Adam and Noah (Gen. 5:1–20; Moses 6:10–22). At age 162 Jared became the father of Enoch, whom he taught "in all the ways of God" (Moses 6:21). Jared was one of a number of "preachers of righteousness" who "spake and prophesied," and taught faith and repentance "unto the children of men" in his day. He died at age 962 (Moses 6:20–24).

The Doctrine and Covenants, in a revelation on PRIESTHOOD, adds important details about Jared. He was ordained (and blessed) by Adam in the patriarchal order of the priesthood when Jared was 200 years old (107:47). Jared was present with seven generations of patriarchs and the "residue of [Adam's] posterity who were righteous" at ADAM-ONDI-AHMAN, three years before the death of Adam. In that gathering Adam bestowed his last blessing upon those present. The Lord appeared, "and they rose up and blessed Adam, and called him Michael, the prince, the archangel" (107:53–54). The Jared of 107:20–24 is not to be confused with the Jared of the Book of Mormon (Ether 1:32–33), who lived many generations later.

RJM

Jared, brother of

The spiritual leader of the Jaredites, who journeyed to the New World "from the great tower, at the time the Lord confounded the language of the people." He was "a large and mighty man, and a man highly favored of the Lord" (Ether 1:33–34; cf. Gen. 11:1–9; Omni 1:22; Mosiah 28:17; Ether 1:1–43).

The brother of Jared is listed once in the Doctrine and Covenants, in connection with the promise of the Lord to the Three Witnesses of the Book of Mormon that they would "have a view of the plates, and also of the breastplate, the sword of Laban, the Urim and Thummim, which were given to the brother of Jared upon the mount, when he talked with the Lord face to face, and the miraculous directors which were given to Lehi while in the wilderness" (D&C 17:1). *See* Witness, witnesses; Urim and Thummim.

The name of the brother of Jared is not revealed in the Book of Mormon or the Doctrine and Covenants; however, the Prophet Joseph Smith said his name was Mahonri Moriancumer, a name he learned through revelation as he blessed the son of Reynolds Cahoon. *See* Cahoon, Reynolds.

See also Historical context and overview of Doctrine and Covenants 17 (p. 725).

LED

Jehovah

One of the traditional titles for the God of Israel. This title occurs six times in the Doctrine and Covenants (109:34, 42, 56, 68; 110:3; 128:9). It appears four times in the King James Version of the Bible, where it represents a traditional Christian transliteration of the Hebrew title for God, *yhwh* (Ex. 6:3; Ps. 83:18; Isa. 12:2; 26:4). *Jehovah* does not occur in the King James New Testament, but it does occur in two verses in the Book of Mormon (2 Ne. 22:2; Moro. 10:34) and in two verses in the book of Abraham (Abr. 1:16; 2:8).

A variation of the title "Jehovah" is "I AM," another King James Bible version of a Hebrew title for the God of Israel. It occurs in the Doctrine and Covenants three times (29:1; 38:1; 39:1) and in Exodus 3:14 and John 8:58, where the God of Israel, Jesus Christ, refers to himself as "I AM." The difference between the King James translation "I AM" and "Jehovah" is that the former appears to be a Hebrew first-person verbal form that means "I am" or "I Exist," whereas "Jehovah" appears to be a third-person verbal form that means either "He is/exists" or "He causes to be/exist."

Latter-day Saints today clearly associate the title "Jehovah" with JESUS CHRIST, the Son of God. In a 1916 doctrinal exposition by the First Presidency and the Twelve, Jesus is called "Jehovah," while GOD THE FATHER is designated "by the exalted name-title 'Elohim.'" Although they are two separate beings, the Father and the Son share many of the same titles, including the title "Father." As the First Presidency and the Twelve explained in 1916, Christ, as the Creator, is the Father of this earth; he is the Father of those who accept him as the Redeemer and take his name upon themselves (Mosiah 5:7); and he is considered as Father because he is invested with the divine authority of God the Father and has thus spoken and "ministered in and through the Father's name" ("Father," 13–18). *See* Divine investiture of authority.

The Old Testament, probably because many plain and precious parts have been removed (1 Ne. 13:20–29), makes no distinction between God the Father and his Son, Jesus Christ. Therefore all the titles for Deity in the Old Testament refer simply to the God of Israel. Thus, the Hebrew titles for "Jehovah," and "Elohim," whether used singly or together, as in "Jehovah Elohim," are translated as "LORD God" in the King James Bible. In line with this precedent, throughout much of the nineteenth century Latter-day Saint writings did not use "Jehovah" exclusively as a title for Christ. Perhaps in that same tradition, when the Prophet Joseph Smith addressed Deity in Doctrine and Covenants 109, the dedicatory prayer of the Kirtland Temple in 1836, he used titles that Latter-day Saints today might use for either God the Father or for Jesus Christ. Thus, in section 109, "Jehovah" is addressed in a way that today one might expect to refer to God the Father (109:34, 42, 56). Other examples in 109 of possible shared titles include "Lord God of Israel" (109:1); "Lord"

(109:4, and many times thereafter), a title that most often refers to the Son but can be used for the Father; "Most High" (109:9, 19), probably used for both the Father and the Son, though the Old Testament uses it almost exclusively for Jehovah; "Holy Father" (109:10, 14, 22, 24, 29, 47), most likely referring to God the Father but could also refer to Christ as "the very Eternal Father" (Mosiah 16:15; Alma 11:38–39); "Mighty God of Jacob" (109:68; cf. 1 Ne. 21:26; 2 Ne. 6:18), a title used in the Old Testament for Jehovah (Gen. 49:24; Ps. 132:2, 5); and "Lord God Almighty" (109:77), which could refer to either the Father or the Son.

This interchangeability of titles should not be misconstrued to mean that the prophets of the Restoration did not understand the correct concept of the Godhead. On the contrary, in this same section, three verses refer clearly to God the Father and Christ the Son as separate beings: "And now we ask thee, Holy Father, in the name of Jesus Christ, the Son of thy bosom" (109:4); "turn away thy wrath [O Lord] when thou lookest upon the face of thine Anointed" (109:53); and "singing Hosanna to God and the Lamb" (109:79).

In their commentary on section 109, Robinson and Garrett asked the question and suggested an answer: "So, does the Prophet address the Father or the Son in Doctrine and Covenants 109? The answer is yes. The prayer is directed formally to the Father in the name of the Son (v. 4) according to commandment [14:8; 2 Ne. 32:9], but it also acknowledges the divinity of the Son and his direct role in restoring the fulness of his gospel and guiding the destiny of his Church." Further, they wrote, "There is nothing incorrect in Joseph addressing God the Son and referring to his activities and commandments in a prayer directed overall to God the Father" (4:43).

Because an accurate pronunciation of the Hebrew *yhwh* has no theological significance for Latter-day Saints and because "Jehovah" appears in the Doctrine and Covenants, the Book of Mormon, and the book of Abraham, Latter-day Saints use the common pronunciation "Jehovah."

BIBLIOGRAPHY

First Presidency. "The Father and the Son: A Doctrinal Exposition by The First Presidency and the Quorum of the Twelve Apostles." *Improvement Era,* August, 1916, 934–42. Reprint, *Ensign* 32 (April 2002): 13–18.

Robinson, Stephen E., and H. Dean Garrett. *A Commentary on the Doctrine and Covenants.* 4 vols. Salt Lake City: Deseret Book, 2000–2005.

PYH

Jeremy

A bearer of the Melchizedek Priesthood who lived sometime between the days of Abraham and the days of Moses (ca. 2000 B.C.–1260 B.C.). In a modern revelation Jeremy was identified in Moses' PRIESTHOOD lineage (84:6–16). Jeremy was ordained by Gad and ordained Elihu. Nothing more is known of him. He is not to be confused with the Jeremy of Matthew 2:17, whose name is a Greek form of *Jeremiah,* the name of the Jewish prophet who lived ca. 600 B.C. The Jeremy of Matthew 27:9 is not clearly identifiable, although some scholars suggest he is the same as the Jeremiah of ca. 600 B.C., even though the prophecy about the thirty pieces of silver is not found in currently extant writings of that Jeremiah (Ogden and Skinner, 630). A version of the prophecy of thirty pieces of silver is found in Zechariah (11:12–13), who lived and prophesied ca. 520 B.C., eighty years after the Jeremiah of ca. 600 B.C.

BIBLIOGRAPHY

Ogden, D. Kelly, and Andrew C. Skinner. *The Four Gospels.* Verse by Verse series. Salt Lake City: Deseret Book, 2006.

RJM

Jerusalem

Chief city of the Jews in the land of Israel, where the most important events in the history of the world transpired—the ATONEMENT and RESURRECTION of JESUS CHRIST. Specific references teach that Jerusalem is a type of things to come. Just as the Savior clearly foretold the destruction of ancient Jerusalem, so he foretells the desolating scourges, consumption, and destruction that will overtake the whole earth before and during his second coming (5:20). As part of a restoration of what he taught his apostles on the MOUNT OF OLIVES about the SIGNS of the LAST DAYS and of his coming in glory (Matt. 24:3–46; Luke 21:7–36; JS–M 1:4–55; cf. 95:9), the Savior gave details about the dramatic fall of Jerusalem and its temple in the first century A.D. (D&C 45:18–24). The magnificent temple that Herod reconstructed a few decades before Jesus' ministry would be leveled (Galbraith et al., 185), and the Jews of Jerusalem would experience every prophesied desolation (45:21) and be scattered among all nations (45:24). *See* Jesus Christ, second coming of.

Other references to Jerusalem speak of its imminent rebuilding and its glorious future. Answering Joseph Smith's questions about John's Revelation, the Lord explained that two witnesses, or prophets, would be "raised up to the Jewish nation in the last days, at the time of the restoration, and to prophesy to the Jews after they are gathered and have built the city of Jerusalem in the land of their fathers" (77:15). This dramatic pronouncement clearly forecasts as early as 1832 that a Jewish nation would be reestablished in their ancient homeland and that the city of Jerusalem would be built up again by gathering Jews.

During the dedicatory prayer for the Kirtland Temple, the Prophet Joseph Smith pleaded with the Lord to "have mercy upon the children of Jacob, that Jerusalem, from this hour [1836], may begin to be redeemed" (109:62).

The NEW JERUSALEM and Old Jerusalem will become places of refuge and places for sacred temple ordinances (124:36). Jews were commanded to flee to Jerusalem and to "the mountains of the Lord's house" (133:13). *See* Mountains of the Lord's house.

The Lord will speak again from Jerusalem, and his voice will be heard worldwide (45:49; 133:21). Separated continents will be gathered back into one land mass, and the land of Zion and the land of Jerusalem will be "turned back into their own place" in the physical position the two Jerusalems enjoyed before the earth was divided (133:23–24; Galbraith et al., 7, 548–49).

Jerusalem awaits a glorious era of reinstatement, restoration, and redemption, living on to become a millennial city of God and later a celestialized, eternal city of God.

See also Desolation of abomination; Mount Zion.

BIBLIOGRAPHY

Galbraith, David B., D. Kelly Ogden, and Andrew C. Skinner. *Jerusalem, the Eternal City.* Salt Lake City: Deseret Book, 1996.

DKO

Jesse, rod of. *See* Historical context and overview of Doctrine and Covenants 113 (p. 823).

Jesse, root of. *See* Historical context and overview of Doctrine and Covenants 113 (p. 823).

Jesus Christ

Second member of the Godhead and the only name given of the Father by which salvation can be administered to the human family (18:3). Jesus Christ is the most significant person who ever has been born or who ever will be born on this earth, and with the Father, he is man's greatest benefactor. His atoning sacrifice and bodily resurrection far exceed in value all earthly events and are God's specific remedy for mankind's greatest need: redemption from DEATH of the body and from the awful consequences of sin.

Jesus' atonement comprehends the earth and all life upon the face of the earth. The benefits of the ATONEMENT are as broad as the fall of Adam. *See* Fall of Adam and Eve, the.

Words are inadequate to describe Jesus' majesty, magnificence, and benevolence. His ministry pertaining to earth and the human family began before the foundations of the earth were laid and will never end. He is both God and Son of God. He was God, with the Father, ages before he was born on earth, during which time he was known as JEHOVAH, Holy One of Israel, and promised MESSIAH. He was God while on earth in mortal flesh accomplishing the infinite atonement and RESURRECTION. He is God now, in heaven at the right hand of the Father. As God he will return to earth and reign forevermore.

Sources of information

True scripture testifies of Jesus Christ: his divine Sonship, infinite atonement, bodily resurrection, and whatever about him is expedient for man to know. The Bible and Book of Mormon represent the work of Jesus Christ in past dispensations; the Doctrine and Covenants contains revelations from the same Jesus Christ pertaining to the establishment of the DISPENSATION of the fulness of times in the latter days. The "fulness of times" is a "welding together of dispensations . . . from the days of Adam even to the present time," and additional things never before revealed (128:18; 27:13) will be given as the premortal purposes of God pertaining to earth and mankind will be brought to fulfillment.

Living links to the past

The revelations given by Jesus Christ focus on building the present dispensation, which requires the endorsement of doctrinal and historical aspects of the earlier dispensations (20:11, 21; 33:16; 42:12) by declaring certain ancient events to be true, thus establishing an overall doctrinal framework: Jesus created the EARTH so spirits can obtain physical bodies; it also becomes man's celestial home (14:9; 49:16–17; 88:17–20, 25–26; Abr. 3:22–24; 1 Ne. 17:36); the fall of Adam and Eve, which introduced sin and death, was a necessary reality (20:20; 29:39–44); and Jesus Christ's atonement and resurrection are historical events, made necessary by the Fall (20:21–24; 138:18–19). Doctrinal sameness in all the dispensations certifies to only one plan of redemption instituted in the PREMORTAL EXISTENCE and only one Redeemer (132:8–12). This plan was revealed by angels under the direction of Jesus Christ in every past dispensation and is now restored to the earth by the personal ministry of the leaders of all former dispensations (now resurrected beings) visiting Joseph Smith to teach and ordain him; they were sent by the same Jesus Christ, making every dispensation Jesus' particular handiwork (27:8–12; 112:31–33; 128:21). In latter-day revelation Jesus has sent living links from all past dispensations to form the dispensation of the fulness of times, showing himself as God of them all.

Authority of the revelations

Jesus Christ declares definitively that he is the author of the revelations in the Doctrine and Covenants and that the messages therein are true (1:6, 33–37; 5:20). They are spoken "unto all men, and there is none to escape; and there is no eye that shall not see, neither ear that shall not hear, neither heart that shall not be penetrated" (1:2). "I, Jesus Christ, . . . have spoken it. . . . For it is my voice which speaketh them unto you; for they are given by my Spirit unto you . . . ; wherefore, you can testify that you have heard my voice, and know my words" (18:33–36; 2 Ne. 32:3). The revelations were given to "my servants in their weakness, after the manner of their language" (1:24; 67:5), who are commanded to publish them "unto the ends of the earth" (1:11; cf. vv. 6–11).

A testament of Jesus Christ

The Doctrine and Covenants contains thousands of words spoken by Jesus Christ about himself and his eternal ministry, often in first-person singular, proclaiming in plain terms who he is, what man needs to know about him, what he has done for man's redemption, what he requires man to do himself, and future events coming upon earth that will ultimately affect all mankind. The words, always informative, offer encouragement, hope, and direction, commanding repentance, commitment, and faith. Mankind's need for the influence of the HOLY GHOST is oft-repeated. Some words are sharp reproofs and warnings, coupled with promises of FORGIVENESS and JOY following REPENTANCE.

Knowledge about Jesus Christ comes by learning his words and feeling the witness of the Spirit. In addition to receiving doctrinal expositions, warnings of impending world-shaking calamities, the glories of the great MILLENNIUM and building ZION and the NEW JERUSALEM, one also feels Jesus' concern for everyone's individual happiness, physical health, family joy, education, personal safety, and such things as are to be experienced now, before eternal SALVATION is received.

Necessity of knowledge

"It is impossible" to be saved in ignorance (131:6), and ETERNAL LIFE comes only by knowing God and Jesus Christ (132:24). Jesus has given the revelations so that one may understand "how to worship" and "know what [to]

Abide with Me; *painting by Liz Lemon Swindle. "Verily, I say unto my servant Joseph Smith, Jun., or in other words, I will call you friends, for you are my friends, and ye shall have an inheritance with me" (D&C 93:45).*

worship" and "come unto the Father in [his] name" (93:19; cf. 130:18–21).

Two particularly rewarding explanations, one about the Lord himself, the other about his creations, are here noted. First, the definition that "endless punishment" means the type of punishment, rather than its duration, is a "mystery of godliness" (19:4–12); second, the cycle of existence from "spiritual" to "temporal" to "spiritual" applies to "all things whatsoever" that Jesus has created (29:30–45), from original creation through the fallen condition and then on to redemption. This eternal framework is key to understanding the plan of redemption, the history and future of the earth, and one's own destiny.

Preeminence of Jesus

Most of the revelations contain statements of Jesus' Godhood, attesting to his absolute authority to speak, to command, to promise, and to revoke.

Before the foundation of the world

Jesus was with the Father in the beginning (93:21) and is the Great I Am who "looked upon the wide expanse of eternity" before he "laid the foundation of the earth" (38:1–4; 45:1). He was foreordained to be the Creator and the Redeemer even "before" the earth existed (1 Pet. 1:20), and thus is said to be "slain from the foundation of the world" (Rev. 13:8; Moses 7:47). Although his sacrifice of his life was not made until the meridian of time, it was unalterably anchored in the plan. "At the first organization in heaven we were all present and saw the Savior chosen and appointed, and the plan of salvation made and we sanctioned it" (Ehat and Cook, 60; cf. Smith, 4:597). The inseparable association between Jesus, the human family, and the earth is of very ancient date. Lucifer's rebellion against the Father and the Son occurred, war developed, Lucifer (the devil) and his followers were cast down to earth, and the long war against God has been raging on earth ever since (29:36–38; 76:25–38; Moses 4:1–4; Rev. 12:7–10). An awareness that God's children witnessed these premortal events enables them to correctly perceive the purpose and importance of mortal life.

Jesus' Godhood

In addition to being Creator and Redeemer, Jesus is the Firstborn of the Father's spirit children (93:21), the Only Begotten of the Father (20:21) in the mortal flesh; and the first to rise in the RESURRECTION (Acts 26:23; Rev. 1:5), "that in all things he might have the preeminence" (Col. 1:13–19).

Jesus is Jehovah (110:3), the God of Israel (10:57; 11:29), the Son of the living God (14:9), who was crucified for the sins of the world (35:2) and rose the third day (20:23). He is man's ADVOCATE with the Father (45:1–4; 110:4) and Judge of all mankind (76:68; 19:3). His authority is evident when he refers to the revelations as "my commandments" (1:6, 24; cf. 6:2; 11:2) and identifies himself as "God, the greatest of all" (19:16, 18), having "almighty power" (19:14, 20; 20:24). Jesus speaks from the standpoint that he dwells in an "infinity of fulness" (109:77).

Jesus was sent to earth by the Father (132:23–25) and is "a light which cannot be hid in darkness" (14:9). He alone is the Savior (76:1). His wisdom is great, his ways are marvelous, "and the extent of his doings none can find out." His purposes never fail; he is "merciful and gracious" and "delight[s] to honor those who serve [him]" (76:2–5). He "knoweth all things, for all things are present before [his] eyes" (38:2). His works and designs cannot be frustrated (3:1); he does not vary from what he has said (3:2); his "eyes are upon all men" (1:1); he takes whom he will in death and preserves whom he will in life (63:2–5; 42:45–48). He commands and revokes as seemeth him good (56:4–6; 58:32). He rules "in the heavens above, and among the armies of the earth" (60:4; 117:6). His word is "quick and powerful,

sharper than a two-edged sword," which divides asunder "both joints and marrow," "soul and spirit"; therefore, men ought to give heed to his word (6:2; 33:1). Jesus will return to earth to recompense the faithful (133:52–53), but the wicked will be "utterly destroyed by the brightness of [his] coming" (5:19).

Heir of the Father

As the firstborn spirit child of the Father and the Only Begotten in the flesh, Jesus is the heir to all that the Father has (Heb. 1:2). He has received "a fulness of the glory of the Father" and "all power, both in heaven and on earth" (93:4–20).

The faithful become "heirs of God, and joint-heirs with Christ" (Rom. 8:17). Although the term *joint-heirs* does not occur in the Doctrine and Covenants, the principle is taught in connection with "the church of the Firstborn." All members of this "church" inherit the same rights and privileges as though they were firstborn, and they are "partakers of the glory of the same" (93:21–22) that Jesus has, even "all that [the] Father hath" (84:38). They are "gods," "priests and kings" (76:54–69), and "shall inherit thrones, kingdoms . . . all heights and depths" (132:19–20). Said Jesus, "Except ye abide my law ye cannot attain to this glory" (132:21–24).

Jesus and the Father

The loving relationship between the Father and the Son, so evident in many passages of scripture (19:24; John 8:29; 10:17; 3 Ne. 11:7; 11:11) is formulated in a most interesting manner in the Doctrine and Covenants. Jesus said: "I . . . accomplished . . . the will of him *whose I am,* even the Father" (19:2; emphasis added). Similar passages, speaking of the righteous, read: "All [things] are theirs and they are Christ's, and *Christ is God's*" (76:59; emphasis added; cf. 1 Cor. 3:23). "These shall dwell in the presence of God *and his Christ* forever" (76:62; emphasis added). These passages illustrate the divine Sonship of Jesus, his perfect allegiance to his Father, and the righteous as being "begotten sons and daughters unto God" (76:24).

Effect of the Fall upon mankind, necessitating the Atonement

Mortal, finite man is universally held captive by two kinds of death inherited from the fall of Adam (Moses 6:55; Mosiah 3:16). These are "temporal death," meaning death of the physical body, and "spiritual" death, meaning to be shut out from the presence of God because of sin (29:40–47; Moses 5:4).

The Fall is so powerful that without divine intercession every mortal body, at death, would return to the earth, never to rise again, and every person's spirit would become a miserable devil, subject to Satan forever, without hope or means of escape (2 Ne. 9:6–9). The Fall makes Christ's atonement necessary (Morm. 9:12). Only Jesus Christ could free mankind from the grasp of death and sin. He alone was sent by the Father to make the sacrificial payment to satisfy JUSTICE (19:24; 49:5; 3 Ne. 27:13–14; Alma 42:12–15), and even he was able to do so only because, first, it was given him by the Father (Hel. 5:11; Morm. 7:5–6) to "have life in himself" (John 5:26) with supremacy over death (John 10:17–18), which he received as the Only Begotten of the Father in the flesh (1 Ne. 11:18, 21); and second, he was without sin because of his complete obedience to the Father's will (20:22). His atonement was not the finite sacrifice of a human being but the infinite sacrifice of a God (Alma 34:9–11). These unique attributes can be called the "merits of Jesus Christ" (3:20; 2 Ne. 31:19; Moro. 6:4; 7:27–28). The Fall had captured mankind, but Jesus rescued mankind (Eph. 4:8; 2 Ne. 33:6). Man's dependency on Jesus Christ is one not of convenience but of necessity. If Jesus had not accomplished the Atonement, nothing anyone could do for himself would ever make up for the loss.

The blood of the Atonement

That the shedding of Jesus' blood was necessary in the atoning process is affirmed by Jesus' own words: "by the virtue of the blood which I have spilt" (38:4); "Father, . . . behold the blood of thy Son which was shed" (45:4), "who wrought out this perfect atonement through the shedding of his own blood" (76:69). The choice of words is descriptive: *virtue* denotes strength and integrity; *wrought out* denotes completeness,

accomplished with thoroughness, expending tremendous effort, far beyond the ordinary. All these qualities are implicit in the phrase "perfect atonement." The most telling description of both pain and bloodshed are Jesus' words: "Which suffering caused myself, even God, the greatest of all, to tremble because of pain, and to bleed at every pore, and to suffer both body and spirit—and would that I might not drink the bitter cup, and shrink" (19:18). Jesus was willing to complete the sacrifice at Gethsemane (Matt. 26:36–39), which was beyond mortal comprehension or ability (Mosiah 3:7), because of his love for the world (34:3).

Worth of souls

Every soul, living, departed, or yet to be born, is of great worth unto God, and Jesus' infinite atonement will reach every one (18:10–13). At "the last great day of judgment," Jesus will judge all mankind by their deeds (19:3). Because most people have not heard the GOSPEL while on earth, they will not have obeyed the requirements for salvation. While Joseph Smith pondered this situation, Jesus revealed to him that all who die without a knowledge of the gospel "who would have received it with all their hearts, shall be heirs" of the celestial kingdom of God (137:7–9). The question arises concerning how that is to be accomplished. To waive all requirements would rob justice. The Lord in premortal councils made ample provision for those who would not hear the gospel in mortality to be taught in the postmortal spirit world (138:32–35; 1 Pet. 3:18–20; 4:6), with necessary ordinances performed vicariously in earthly temples (124:37–44; 128:11–17; 138:53–59). *See* Salvation for the dead.

Washed clean

Jesus Christ's solemn message is that by great effort he has overcome the world and man's work is to believe in him, repent (18:41–43; 20:29), be born again, be washed clean by baptism of water and of the Holy Ghost (5:16; 76:52; 138:59), be virtuous, pure in heart and mind (88:74; 112:28; 121:45), being justified and sanctified by GRACE (20:30–32), and endure to the end, keeping all the commandments, or they cannot be saved (14:7; 53:7; 56:2). "The

Lord cannot look upon sin with the least degree of allowance," but allowance is made for everyone who repents (1:31–32).

Resurrection of the body

In the revelations in the Doctrine and Covenants, Jesus confirms the doctrine of resurrection taught in the other standard works (29:13; 63:49, 52; 76:1–119; 133:56) and specifies at least three items not obvious in the other sources: Postmortal spirits look upon the long separation from their bodies as a bondage (45:17; 138:50); resurrection is essential for a fulness of joy (93:33–34; 138:17); and such translated beings as Enoch, Moses, and Elijah were resurrected with Christ (133:54–55).

Scope of the Atonement

The Atonement is as comprehensive as the Fall, touching the whole earth and everything upon the earth, renewing everything lost by the Fall (101:23–26; A of F 10; 2 Ne. 2:22–26), and is also extended to other inhabited worlds (76:24; cf. 88:46–61). Jesus descended below all things that he might rise above all things (88:6; 122:8).

All things in the name of Jesus

All things having to do with salvation "must be done in the name of Christ" (46:31; Moses 5:8). Specific items include prayers (18:18, 21; 24:5), baptism (18:22, 41; 20:37; 49:13), partaking of the sacramental emblems (20:77, 79), worship (18:40; 20:29), and meeting together (20:55, 61; cf. 6:32; 42:1). This unvarying principle is a commandment: "Thou shalt love the Lord thy God . . . ; and in the name of Jesus Christ thou shalt serve him" (59:5; 20:29); "No man shall come unto the Father but by me or by my word" (132:12). The only way to do this is by joining his true Church by baptism and obeying the commandments (18:21–22, 41–42; 20:37; 23:7).

"Jesus Christ is the name which is given of the Father, and there is none other name given whereby man can be saved; wherefore, all men must take upon them [this] name . . . wherefore, if they know not the name . . . , they cannot have place in the kingdom of my Father" (18:23–25). This fundamental law is illustrated by the requirement that the true Church must

carry the name of Christ (115:4; 3 Ne. 27:5–8) and that the priesthood is "after the order of the Only Begotten Son" (76:57; 107:1–4; Alma 13:1, 2, 7). Perhaps no item is so oft-repeated in latter-day scripture as the commandment to take upon oneself the name of Jesus Christ.

Names and descriptive titles of Jesus Christ

The Doctrine and Covenants contains at least seventy-seven descriptive names and titles referring to Jesus Christ. Most of these are in first-person singular because they are terms used by Jesus to identify himself and to authenticate the revelations. As is typical of names and titles, the words describe Jesus' Godhood, character, and redeeming mission, emphasizing that which is essential. Nearly all of the names are also found in the other standard works, but sometimes they appear in the Doctrine and Covenants in combinations that constitute a new term and form a simple sentence.

NAMES AND TITLES	REFERENCE
Advocate	29:5
Almighty	84:96
Almighty God	OD 1
Alpha and Omega	19:1
Alphus and Omegus	95:17
Beginning and the End	38:1
Beloved Son	93:15
Bridegroom	33:17–18
Creator of the first day	95:7
Creator of worlds	38:3; 76:24; 93:9–10
Christ	38:4
Christ the Lamb	76:85
Christ the Lord	19:1
Deliverer from death	138:23
Endless	19:10
Eternal King	128:23
Firstborn	93:21
First and the last	110:4
God	19:16–18
God of Abraham, Isaac, and Jacob	136:21

NAMES AND TITLES	REFERENCE
God Almighty	OD 1
God of Enoch	45:11
God of Heaven	OD 1
God of Israel	109:1
Good Shepherd	50:44
Great I Am	38:1
Holy One	78:16
Holy One of Zion	78:15
Israel's God	127:3
Jehovah	110:3
Jesus	21:9
Jesus that was crucified	45:52
Jesus Christ	35:2
Judge	76:68
King	38:21
King Immanuel	128:22
Lamb	76:85
Lamb of God	88:106
Life of men	93:9
Life of the world	10:70
Light of men	93:9
Light of the world	10:70
Light and the Redeemer	93:9
Light which cannot be hid	14:9
Light which shineth in darkness	6:21
Living God	50:1
Lord	5:2
Lord God	20:16
Lord God Almighty	109:77
Lord of Hosts	1:33
Lord of Sabaoth	95:7
Lord Jesus Christ	21:1
Lord of the whole earth	55:1
Maker	30:2
Mediator	76:69
Messenger of salvation	93:8
Messiah	13:1

NAMES AND TITLES	REFERENCE
Mighty God of Jacob	109:68
Mighty One of Israel	36:1
Most High	109:9
Only Begotten Son	20:21
Only Begotten Son of God	138:57
Redeemer	8:1
Redeemer of the world	93:9
Savior	19:41; 76:1
Savior of the world	43:34
Son	76:73
Son Ahman	78:20
Son of God	10:57
Son of the living God	55:2
Son of Man	58:65
Son of thy bosom	109:4
Spirit of truth	93:9, 26
Stem of Jesse	113:1–2
Stone of Israel	50:44
True light	88:50
Word	93:8

Some of the foregoing names are used repeatedly: *Lord, God,* and *Christ* are used hundreds of times.

Items about Jesus Christ uniquely identified or clarified in the Doctrine and Covenants

The Doctrine and Covenants contains statements about Jesus that either the other standard works do not have or that are sufficiently vague in that they cannot be understood without further revelation. Consider, for example, the following:

1. Four names describing Jesus, not given elsewhere or clarified: "Stone of Israel" (50:44); "Son Ahman" (78:20); "Lord of Sabaoth, which is by interpretation, the creator of the first day" (95:7); and the meaning of the "Stem of Jesse" (113:1–2).

2. "I am . . . a light which cannot be hid in darkness" (14:9), a strong addition to the more familiar "light of the world" (10:70).

3. The "light of Christ" fills "the immensity of space" and is in the sun, moon, stars, and earth (88:7–13).

4. The "law of Christ" is the celestial law (88:20–21).

5. The PRIESTHOOD was originally called "*the Holy Priesthood, after the Order of the Son of God*" (107:2–4; cf. 76:57; Alma 13:1, 2, 7, 16).

6. Jesus appeared personally to Adam and blessed him at a sacred gathering of his family at ADAM-ONDI-AHMAN (107:53–55).

7. Between the time of his death and his resurrection, Jesus organized the righteous spirits in the spirit world to preach to the spirits in prison; he did not personally minister to those imprisoned spirits (138:1–37; a clarification of 1 Peter 3:18–20 and D&C 76:73).

8. Jesus' atonement applies directly to the earth, which shall die, be quickened (29:22–24; 88:25–26; Isa. 51:6), and become a celestial world fit for celestial beings, even "the presence of God the Father" (88:17–20).

9. Jesus' atonement applies to men, beasts, fowls, fish, and "creeping things," all of which will be redeemed and have joy (29:23–25; 77:2–3).

10. Jesus is the Savior of many inhabited worlds in addition to this earth (76:24; 88:42–63).

11. Jesus will not come in the form of a woman nor as a man traveling on the earth (49:22).

12. Jesus "shall be red in his apparel" at his second coming (133:48). This description is in Isaiah 63:1–8, but is so unclear that Bible commentators view it symbolically and not as a specific event.

13. Jesus will return to earth and partake of the sacramental emblems with the righteous of all dispensations (27:4–14), a sacred occasion briefly alluded to in Matthew 26:29; Mark 14:25; Luke 22:18.

14. Jesus progressed from "grace to grace" and "grace for grace" until he received all truth. Man must progress the same way (93:12–20, 26, an expansion of John 1:16–17).

Prophecies and promises

Jesus declared that his "prophecies and promises . . . shall all be fulfilled" (1:37). Some

will be dramatic and full of noise: considerable movement of the land and the seas (43:25; 45:33; 87:6; 88:89; 133:22–24), destructive activity of the weather (29:16), and shifting of the starry heavens (29:14; 84:118; 133:49) accompanied by thunder, fierce lightning, war, pestilence, plague, famine (43:21–25; 45:31; 87:6), blood, fire, vapor, smoke (45:41), and the "trump of God" sounding long and loud, making ears to "tingle" (43:18–22). The "whole earth shall be in commotion," and "men's hearts shall fail them" with fear (45:26; 88:91). The Lord Jesus will return in great glory; all flesh shall see him, and every corruptible thing shall be consumed and "melt with fervent heat" (101:23–25).

The quiet promises

In contrast to the outwardly dramatic events, other promises are quietly fulfilled independent of visual observation but causing dramatic inward changes. These promises of Jesus are often so subtly stated that without a serious search they almost go unnoticed. In a way they are the most immediate while being the quietest, because they apply to man's need for daily spiritual nourishment. For instance, the Holy Ghost will lead one to do good, to walk humbly, "enlighten [the] mind," "fill [the] soul with joy" (11:12–13), and teach "the peaceable things of the kingdom" (39:6; 42:61). The Lord promises to lead the faithful by the hand and answer their prayers (112:10). "Search diligently, pray always, and be believing, and all things shall work together for your good" (90:24).

Physical strength and "treasures of knowledge, even hidden treasures," are promised for obedience to the "Word of Wisdom" and the other commandments (89:1, 18–21). Jesus promises to be the advocate of those who believe on his name and to plead their cause before the Father (45:4–5; 62:1). Jesus' "great and last promise" (88:75) to those who prepare themselves is to "unveil his face unto" them "in his own time, and in his own way, and according to his own will" (67:10; 93:1; 88:68–69, 75).

Although these and many other promises were originally spoken to other individuals, all who desire to live righteously can apply many of them to themselves and obtain the blessing by faith (for example, 11:27; 93:49).

Jesus' wide range of instruction

Jesus gave directions concerning real estate purchases (57:4–6); the size of buildings, including the number of levels and rooms (94:2–6; 124:145); a printing enterprise (55:4; 57:11; 94:10–12); temples (88:119; 109:1–4; 110:7–10); a hotel (124:22–24); dry goods stores (57:8–9; 63:42; 104:39); schoolbooks (55:4; 88:118; 90:15); curriculum (55:4); schools (55:4; 88:127–138; 97:3); hymnbooks (25:11, 12); a tannery (104:20); horses, mules, chariots, and canals (62:7; 61:22–24); living quarters (41:7–8; 104:24, 34); other daily necessities, such as proper food and drink (89:1–21); aesthetic matters, such as the fragrance and beauty of flowers (59:18–20); and being of "good cheer" (61:36; 68:6; 78:18; cf. 59:15). The Lord mentioned modern geographic locations such as South Carolina; Great Britain; Independence, Missouri; Cincinnati; New York; Albany; and Boston (87:1–3; 57:3; 60:6; 84:114).

Jesus and the dispensation of the fulness of times

Two themes dominate the words of Jesus in the Doctrine and Covenants: the prevailing wickedness of the world and Jesus' message of salvation. The revelations are a formal "voice of warning . . . unto all people" (1:4; 38:41; 63:37–38), addressing an unbelieving world "ripening in iniquity" (5:8; 18:6; 29:9–11). The world does not seek the righteousness of God, but "every man walketh in his own way" (1:14–16). "Gross darkness" covers "the minds of the people, and all flesh has become corrupt" (112:23), and "peace shall be taken from the earth" (1:35). Mankind is not preparing as they should for the second coming of the Lord.

"Knowing the calamity that should come upon the . . . earth," Jesus Christ called upon Joseph Smith and through him brought forth the Book of Mormon, restored the true gospel and the priesthood, and established "the only true and living church upon the face of the whole earth" (1:17–33).

Conclusion

The revelations of Jesus Christ in the Doctrine and Covenants portray the nature of God, of man, and of the earth, and detail the purposes of the living God, linking every dispensation to the dispensation of the fulness of times and every true prophet to the Lord Jesus Christ. Jesus' own words offer a comprehensive understanding of his eternal ministry among the living and the dead on earth and in heaven. This is Jesus bearing testimony of the great latter-day restoration through the instrumentality of the Prophet Joseph Smith.

See also God the Father; Jesus Christ, as Firstborn; Jesus Christ, Mediator of the new covenant; Jesus Christ, merits of; Jesus Christ, sons and daughters of; Jesus Christ, second coming of; Light of Christ; Mercy.

BIBLIOGRAPHY

Ehat, Andrew F., and Lyndon W. Cook, comps. and eds. *The Words of Joseph Smith.* Provo, Utah: Religious Studies Center, Brigham Young University, 1980.

Smith, Joseph. *History of The Church of Jesus Christ of Latter-day Saints.* Edited by B. H. Roberts. 7 vols. 2d ed. rev. Salt Lake City: The Church of Jesus Christ of Latter-day Saints, 1932–51.

RJM

Jesus Christ, as Father and Son. *See* Divine investiture of authority.

Jesus Christ, as Firstborn

In the scriptures *Firstborn* applies to Jesus in four contexts, three of them referring to his preeminence and one referring to his Church:

1. Firstborn of the Father's spirit children. Thus Jesus said, "I was in the beginning with the Father, and am the Firstborn" (93:21; cf. Rom. 8:29; Col. 1:15; Heb. 1:6).

2. Firstborn of Mary into mortality (Matt. 1:25).

3. Firstborn from the dead (Acts 26:23; 1 Cor. 15:20, 23; Col. 1:18; Rev. 1:5; 2 Ne. 2:8).

4. Most references in the Doctrine and Covenants to *Firstborn* are to the "church of the Firstborn" (76:54, 67, 71, 94, 102; 77:11; 78:21; 88:5; 93:21–22; 107:19). *See* Church of the Firstborn.

Scriptural emphasis on *firstborn* signifies primogeniture, the right of the eldest son to inherit his father's possessions. Faithful believers, through covenants and ordinances of the gospel, receive blessings as though they were firstborn; hence, Jesus said: "All those who are begotten through me are partakers of the glory of the same [i.e., glory of the Firstborn], and are the church of the Firstborn" (93:22; cf. Mosiah 5:7; Gal. 3:27–29; Rev. 14:4). They become joint-heirs with Christ of all that the Father has (84:37–38; Rom. 8:17).

Selection of the firstlings (that open the womb; Ex. 13:2, 12) for animal sacrifice was symbolic of Christ's firstborn status (Moses 5:7; Ex. 12:5; 1 Cor. 5:7; 2 Ne. 11:4).

See also Jesus Christ; Jesus Christ, sons and daughters of.

RJM

Jesus Christ, Creator. *See* Jesus Christ

Jesus Christ, Mediator of the new covenant

The Savior's role as ADVOCATE for the redemption of mankind through the fulness of the GOSPEL. To mediate is to place oneself between parties who are at variance so as to effect their reconciliation. Mankind is estranged from God through the Fall (20:20; 29:40–42; Mosiah 3:19). The "covenant" is "the fulness of [the] gospel" (66:2). Only through Jesus Christ's righteousness (his merits) (2 Ne. 2:3, 8; Hel. 14:13; Moro. 6:4), his divine Sonship and appointment from the Father (19:2, 24; 31:13; 76:13; 93:2–5; Hel. 5:9, 11), his atoning blood (Alma 34:9–11), and the fulness of the gospel covenant can he be the Mediator to make possible a reconciliation of man with God. JESUS CHRIST "wrought out this perfect atonement through the shedding of his own blood" (76:69). Jesus' ATONEMENT provides salvation from physical death through resurrection and from spiritual death through forgiveness of sin. By conquering death and sin, the Savior overcame the effects of the Fall. The role of mankind in the reconciliation process is to accept the work of the Mediator, Jesus Christ, by coming unto him through the principles and ordinances of the gospel—faith, repentance, baptism, reception of the Holy Ghost, and

endurance to the end (76:40–41, 50–53; 2 Ne. 31:17–21; 3 Ne. 11:32–36; 27:13–21; Moro. 10:30–32; Rom. 5:2; 1 Tim. 2:5–6; A of F 3, 4).

Why it is called the new covenant

The gospel of Jesus Christ is called the "covenant" (39:11), "everlasting covenant" (45:9; 66:2), "new covenant" (76:69; 107:19), and "new and an everlasting covenant" (22:1; 132:6–7). The fulness of the gospel covenant was on earth from Adam to Moses, and Jesus was the Mediator and Savior from the beginning. The law of Moses was "added because of transgressions" (Gal. 3:19; cf. JST Gal. 3:19–20). After the LAW OF MOSES was fulfilled by Jesus Christ and the fulness of the gospel was proclaimed by the New Testament Church, the gospel covenant was sometimes spoken of as the "new" covenant to distinguish it from the law of Moses, or the "old" covenant. This is the perception given in Doctrine and Covenants 22 and in the book of Hebrews 8–12, especially 8:13.

The fulness of the gospel of Jesus Christ, the everlasting covenant, is the same in every dispensation, but if it is lost through apostasy, the restoration can be called a "new and an everlasting covenant" because it is new to the new DISPENSATION.

Testament and *covenant* are often interchangeable (cf. Heb. 9:15–18, 20; JST Heb. 9:15–18, 20); thus, the "New Testament" is the record of the "new covenant" in that day, as are the Doctrine and Covenants and Book of Mormon (84:57) in this day.

See also Atonement, the; New and everlasting covenant.

RJM

Jesus Christ, merits of

The attributes, perfections, and atoning work of the Savior JESUS CHRIST, upon which all must rely to be saved and exalted (3:19–20; cf. 2 Ne. 2:8). Because of the Fall, all are subject to hunger, thirst, fatigue, decay, and physical DEATH. Further, lost and fallen mortals inevitably leave the strait and narrow path and become guilty of sin, resulting in various levels of spiritual death, or separation from God's influence. Mankind simply cannot save themselves from these conditions (cf. Alma 22:14). Being justified, sanctified, and ultimately saved and exalted come only through the "grace of our Lord and Savior Jesus Christ," as individuals are obedient "to the laws and ordinances of the Gospel" and strive to "love and serve God with all their mights, minds, and strength" (20:29–31; A of F 3; cf. 25:15–16; 2 Ne. 10:24; 25:23; Moro. 10:32–33). Jesus Christ gained the right to share his merits with mankind, becoming their ADVO-CATE before the Father, because he "wrought out this perfect atonement through the shedding of his own blood" (76:69; 34:1–3; 45:1–5; 110:4; Moro. 7:27–28). True disciples of Jesus Christ learn to trust in his good works—his matchless life, his timeless teachings, his perfections, and his sufferings and death in their behalf. In short, individuals are saved by his merits, by power well beyond their own.

See also Atonement, the; Fall of Adam and Eve, the; Grace; Justification; Mercy; Salvation; Sanctify, sanctification.

RLM

Jesus Christ, second coming of

The Lord's anticipated return to the earth. The Doctrine and Covenants contains significant information about the second coming of JESUS CHRIST. These revelations include the Lord's own witness of his return, indications of its imminence, where the Lord will appear, SIGNS that will precede his coming, preparations that are to be made in anticipation of the event, and details concerning what will happen in conjunction with his appearance.

The Lord's witness of his return

Of reassuring significance is the Lord's own testimony of his return in glory. To elders assembled for the second conference of the Church, he promised, "For I will reveal myself from heaven with power and great glory, with all the hosts thereof" (29:11). In other verses he reiterated that such an event "surely shall come" (39:21).

The time is nigh at hand

There has been and continues to be much speculation about when the Second Coming will occur. The Savior said that he would come "as a thief in the night" (106:4; 1 Thes. 5:2) and in "an hour you think not" (51:20; 124:10). Not even the angels in heaven know the exact time of his coming, and they will not know until he comes (49:7). Although the precise day and time are not given, the revelations emphasize that the time is "nigh at hand" (43:17; 29:9), "even at the doors" (110:16). Indeed, the promise "I come quickly" is scattered throughout the Doctrine and Covenants (e.g., 33:18; 35:27; 41:4; 51:20; 88:126).

Where the Lord will appear

When he comes in glory, the Lord will appear in the heavens and subsequently stand on the MOUNT OF OLIVES, which will "cleave in twain" (45:48; Zech. 14:4). His appearance on the Mount of Olives will bring an end to the Battle of Armageddon and set the stage for one of the more poignant and ironic moments in the history of the world: "And then shall the Jews look upon me and say: What are these wounds in thine hands and in thy feet? Then shall they know that I am the Lord; for I will say unto them: These wounds are the wounds with which I was wounded in the house of my friends. I am he who was lifted up. I am Jesus that was crucified. I am the Son of God. And then shall they weep because of their iniquities; then shall they lament because they persecuted their king" (45:51–53; Zech. 12:10; 13:6; Rev. 1:7).

Certain passages indicate that the Second Coming actually encompasses several appearances of the Savior in addition to his return in glory. He will "set his foot" upon the Mount of Olives in Jerusalem (45:48; Zech. 14:4); he will appear on MOUNT ZION with 144,000 of the faithful (133:18; cf. vv. 20, 56); he will come suddenly to his temple in the latter days (36:8; 42:36; 133:2); and he will appear at ADAM-ONDI-AHMAN at a gathering of righteous priesthood leaders (Dan. 7:13–14; D&C 116).

Signs of the Second Coming

Although the exact time of the Second Coming will not be revealed, the Lord has said, "And he that believeth shall be blest with signs . . . : And unto you it shall be given to know the signs of the times, and the signs of the coming of the Son of Man" (68:10–11).

Employing the image of a fig tree whose new shoots and tender leaves announce the approach of summer, the Lord revealed in numerous passages signs that will indicate that his coming is near at hand. "And it shall come to pass that he that feareth me shall be looking forth for the great day of the Lord to come, even for the signs of the coming of the Son of Man" (45:39).

The following signs that the Savior's second coming is approaching are spoken of in the Doctrine and Covenants (not necessarily in chronological order):

A "desolating sickness" and an "overflowing scourge" shall "pass over by night and by day, and the report thereof shall vex all people." This scourge shall not be lifted until the Lord comes (45:31; 97:23).

There will be cataclysmic events and natural disasters of tremendous magnitude. "And they shall behold blood, and fire, and vapors of smoke" (45:41).

"The sun shall be darkened, and the moon shall be turned into blood, and the stars shall fall from heaven, and there shall be greater signs in heaven above and in the earth beneath" which shall cause "weeping and wailing" among men (29:14–15; 34:9).

There shall be "wars and rumors of wars, and the whole earth shall be in commotion, and men's hearts shall fail them" (45:26).

"There shall be earthquakes also in divers places, and many desolations; yet men will harden their hearts against me, and they will take up the sword, one against another, and they will kill one another" (45:33).

There will be "a great hailstorm sent forth to destroy the crops of the earth" (29:16). The Lord will "send forth flies upon the face of the earth, which shall take hold of the inhabitants thereof, and shall eat their flesh, and shall cause maggots to come in upon them" (29:18). "Their flesh shall fall from off their bones; and their eyes from their sockets" and "the beasts of the forest and the fowls of the air shall devour them" (29:19–20).

The "love of men shall wax cold, and iniquity shall abound" (45:27), and "among the wicked, men shall lift up their voices and curse God and die" (45:32).

Even with all of the calamities and horrors that are prophesied to take place, the Lord reassured his disciples and counseled them, "Be not troubled, for, when all these things shall come to pass, ye may know that the promises which have been made unto you shall be fulfilled" (45:35).

Preparations for the Second Coming

A recurring theme concerning the Second Coming is the importance of preparation. The revelations contain passages discussing preparation by the Church, or kingdom of God, while others are directed toward personal preparation.

The first section of the Doctrine and Covenants, often referred to as the Lord's preface, contains the pronouncement: "Wherefore the voice of the Lord is unto the ends of the earth . . . : Prepare ye, prepare ye for that which is to come, for the Lord is nigh" (1:11–12). One of the main responsibilities of the Church in helping prepare the world for the second coming of Jesus Christ is to fulfill the Lord's command that "the gospel must be preached unto every creature" (58:64). The Saints are "called to prune my vineyard with a mighty pruning, yea, even for the last time" (24:19); "for the last time call upon the inhabitants of the earth" (43:28), for it is "the eleventh hour, and the last time that I shall call laborers into my vineyard" (33:3). The Lord said, "Send forth the elders of my church unto the nations which are afar off; unto the islands of the sea; send forth unto foreign lands; call upon all nations. . . . Yea, let the cry go forth among all people: Awake and arise and go forth to meet the Bridegroom. . . . Prepare yourselves for the great day of the Lord" (133:8, 10). The Lord's servants are to "go forth baptizing with water" and invite all to repent and prepare themselves for the great day of the Lord (39:19–21; 42:7).

Another important preparatory work expected of the Saints individually and collectively before the Second Coming is the work done in the temples for the living and for the dead. Elijah's prophesied return (2:1; cf. Mal. 4:5–6) to restore the necessary KEYS for this work and to "plant in the hearts of the children the promises made to the fathers" (2:1–2; 138:47; 110:13–16) foreshadowed "the great work to be done in the temples of the Lord" during this final dispensation "for the redemption of the dead, and the sealing of the children to their parents, lest the whole earth be smitten with a curse and utterly wasted at his coming" (138:48; 2:1–3). *See* Salvation for the dead.

Specific admonitions of personal preparation for the Second Coming include the following:

"Be faithful, praying always, having your lamps trimmed and burning, and oil with you, that you may be ready at the coming of the Bridegroom" (33:17). This counsel has reference to the PARABLE OF THE TEN VIRGINS (Matt. 25:1–13), in which only half the virgins were wise and had sufficient oil to meet the BRIDEGROOM at his coming. "When I shall come in my glory, shall the parable be fulfilled which I spake concerning the ten virgins" (45:56).

"Gird up your loins and be watchful and be sober. . . . Pray always that you enter not into temptation, that you may abide the day of his coming, whether in life or in death" (61:38–39). The Lord's Saints are told, "Entangle not yourselves in sin, but let your hands be clean, until the Lord comes" (88:86), for "he that is not purified shall not abide the day. Wherefore, gird up your loins and be prepared" (38:8–9). "Wherefore, prepare ye, prepare ye, O my people; sanctify yourselves; gather ye together, . . . go ye out from Babylon" (133:4–5, 14).

Those whose faithfulness includes the payment of tithes are promised that they "shall not be burned at his coming" (64:23).

An overarching principle of preparation for disciples of the Lord is to "stand in holy places" and "not be moved" (45:32; 87:8; 101:22). Commenting on these HOLY PLACES, President Ezra Taft Benson said, "Holy men and women stand in holy places, and these holy places consist of our temples, our chapels, our homes, and the stakes of Zion, which are, as the Lord declares, 'for a defense, and for a refuge from the storm, and from wrath when it shall be poured out without mixture upon the whole earth'" (115; cf. D&C 115:6).

Details of what will happen when the Lord appears in glory

The "great and dreadful day" (2:1; 110:16) of the Lord's appearance in glory will follow the testimony of the servants of the Lord and the testimony "of the voice of thunderings, and the voice of lightnings, and the voice of tempests, and the voice of the waves of the sea heaving themselves beyond their bounds" (88:88–90). *See* Great and dreadful day of the Lord.

The Lord's arrival in glory will be a time of rejoicing for the righteous who have looked forward to his coming. Parley P. Pratt expressed the expectant plea of the faithful Saints of God in the hymn "Come, O Thou King of Kings":

> *Come, O thou King of Kings!*
> *We've waited long for thee,*
> *With healing in thy wings,*
> *To set thy people free.*

To the wicked, however, the Lord's appearance "shall be terrible unto them, that fear may seize upon them, and they shall stand afar off and tremble. And all nations shall be afraid because of the terror of the Lord, and the power of his might" (45:74–75).

The Second Coming is to be a day of recompense (1:10; 56:19) and a day of JUDGMENT (1:36). "My reward is with me," said the Lord (54:10; 56:19). "Therefore, I must gather together my people, according to the PARABLE OF THE WHEAT AND THE TARES, that the wheat may be secured in the garners to possess eternal life, and be crowned with celestial glory, when I shall come in the kingdom of my Father to reward every man according as his work shall be; while the tares shall be bound in bundles, and their bands made strong, that they may be burned with unquenchable fire" (101:65–66; 38:12; Matt. 13:24–30, 36–40).

"And calamity shall cover the mocker, and the scorner shall be consumed; and they that have watched for iniquity shall be hewn down and cast into the fire" (45:50).

The time of the Second Coming will be a time of great commotion physically and emotionally for the earth's inhabitants. "All nations shall tremble" (34:8). "Wherefore, be not deceived, but continue in steadfastness, looking forth for the heavens to be shaken, and the earth to tremble and to reel to and fro as a drunken man, and for the valleys to be exalted, and for the mountains to be made low, and for the rough places to become smooth" (49:23; 109:74).

Associated with the coming of the Lord is a powerful manifestation of intense heat, brightness, and glory. "And so great shall be the glory of his presence that the sun shall hide his face in shame, and the moon shall withhold its light, and the stars shall be hurled from their places" (133:49).

The wicked and every corruptible thing shall be consumed (101:24). "For the hour is nigh and the day soon at hand when the earth is ripe; and all the proud and they that do wickedly shall be as stubble; and I will burn them up, saith the Lord of Hosts, that wickedness shall not be upon the earth" (29:9; 133:64).

Section 88 outlines a series of events heralded by blasts of angelic trumpets. "And immediately there shall appear a great sign in heaven, and all people shall see it together" (88:93), and the angel will announce that the GREAT AND ABOMINABLE CHURCH is ready to be burned. Then shall this angel sound his TRUMP "both long and loud, and all nations shall hear it" (88:94).

At that time there shall be silence in heaven for the space of half an hour, and then "the curtain of heaven be unfolded, as a scroll is unfolded . . . and the face of the Lord shall be unveiled" (88:95). The inhabitants of the earth shall then see him as he is—a glorified, exalted man (130:1). See Curtain(s).

Fulfilling prophecies recorded in the Doctrine and Covenants as well as in the Old and New Testaments, the Lord will be "red in his apparel" when he comes in glory (133:48; Isa. 63:1–3; Rev. 19:13). It shall be asked, "Who is this that cometh down from God in heaven with dyed garments . . . traveling in the greatness of his strength?" (133:46). These "dyed garments" are symbolic of the Savior's having "trodden the wine-press alone, even the wine-press of the fierceness of the wrath of Almighty God" (88:106). The Savior himself shall be heard to say, "I have trodden the wine-press alone, and have brought judgment upon all people; and

none were with me; and I have trampled them in my fury, and I did tread upon them in mine anger, and their blood have I sprinkled upon my garments, and stained all my raiment" (133:50–51).

When he comes "in a cloud with power and great glory" (34:7), the Twelve which were with him at Jerusalem will stand at his right hand "in a pillar of fire" (29:12), and the "saints that are upon the earth, who are alive, shall be quickened and be caught up to meet him" (88:96). "And they who have slept in their graves shall come forth, for their graves shall be opened; and they also shall be caught up to meet him in the midst of the pillar of heaven" (88:97; 133:56). See Pillar of heaven.

The Doctrine and Covenants indicates that those who will accompany the Savior will be the heirs of celestial glory (76:63).

Another trump shall sound, and "then cometh the redemption of those who are Christ's at his coming; who have received their part in that prison which is prepared for them, that they might receive the gospel, and be judged according to men in the flesh" (88:99).

The third trump shall sound, and "then come the spirits of men who are to be judged, and are found under condemnation" (88:100; 43:18). Then the fourth trump shall sound and an angel announce, "There are found among those who are to remain" those who "shall remain filthy still" (88:102).

The fifth trump shall sound, "for every ear shall hear it, and every knee shall bow, and every tongue shall confess . . . : Fear God, and give glory to him who sitteth upon the throne" (88:104).

And the sixth trump shall sound and the angel announce, "She is fallen who made all nations drink of the wine of the wrath of her fornication" (88:105; 1:16; 29:21).

A seventh and final trump shall sound, and the angel shall say, "It is finished! The Lamb of God hath overcome and trodden the wine-press alone, even the wine-press of the fierceness of the wrath of Almighty God" (88:106). See Winepress.

When he comes, "his voice shall be heard among all people" (133:21). He shall command the islands to become one land, and the earth "shall be like as it was in the days before it was divided" (133:24). He shall "reveal all things" (101:32) and usher in the MILLENNIUM. "And the Lord, even the Savior, shall stand in the midst of his people, and shall reign over all flesh" (133:25).

See also Marriage of the Lamb; Resurrection, the.

BIBLIOGRAPHY

Benson, Ezra Taft. *Come unto Christ.* Salt Lake City: Deseret Book, 1983.

Pratt, Parley P. "Come, O Thou King of Kings." *Hymns of The Church of Jesus Christ of Latter-day Saints,* no. 59. Salt Lake City: The Church of Jesus Christ of Latter-day Saints, 1985.

RLH

Jesus Christ, sons and daughters of

Individuals who accept JESUS CHRIST through the GOSPEL covenant (25:1; cf. Mosiah 5:7) by receiving "the testimony of Jesus, and [believing] on his name" (76:51), "repentance and baptism by water, and then . . . the baptism of fire and the Holy Ghost" (39:6). This new relationship between humankind and the Savior is possible only because "he gave his own life" (34:3) and "was crucified for the sins of the world" (35:2).

In the Doctrine and Covenants the Lord called Emma Hale Smith "my daughter" (25:1) and referred to Oliver Cowdery (9:1), Orson Pratt (34:3), and Joseph Smith as "my son" (121:7). Those who become children of Christ experience a new perspective by which they learn to bring their desires into conformity with his will; they see themselves as his, being "willing to take upon them the name of Jesus Christ, having a determination to serve him to the end," and to "always remember him" (20:37, 77). God's greatest blessings are reserved for the sons and daughters of Jesus Christ. Because of the Savior's atoning sacrifice, he gives his children power to become "begotten sons and daughters unto God" (76:24; cf. 34:3; 11:28–30), that is, to be one with Christ as Christ is "one in the Father" (35:2). *See* Atonement, the.

The children of Christ receive his authorized servants, his Father, and his Father's kingdom (84:35–38). Through his GRACE, the Savior promises his children who continue in willing OBEDIENCE to his COMMANDMENTS that they may receive "truth and light, until [they are] glorified in truth and [know] all things" (93:28; cf. 50:24). They may eventually "receive of his fulness" and become "partakers of [his] glory" and members of the "church of the Firstborn" (93:20–22), "into whose hands the Father has given all things" (76:55, 58–59).

See also Born of me; Church of the Firstborn; Eternal life.

CFO

Jethro

High priest of Midian and Moses' father-in-law; a man of spiritual stature and wisdom. Jethro received the Melchizedek Priesthood from Caleb and ordained Moses to that same priesthood (JST Ex. 18:1; 84:6–7). He taught Moses administrative principles (Ex. 18:13–26). The Doctrine and Covenants gives the source of Moses' priesthood (84:6–7), which the Bible does not do. Jethro, because he was a descendant of Abraham through Abraham's son Midian, was not of the house of Israel (Jacob).

RJM

Jew(s)

Derived from the Hebrew word *yehudi*, the word *Jew* originally denoted someone of the tribe or house of Judah. The Prophet Joseph Smith referred to the descendants of Judah in the dedicatory prayer of the Kirtland Temple when he prayed that "the children of Judah may begin to return to the lands which thou didst give to Abraham, their father" (109:64).

The word *Jew* or *Jews* is often used to identify a much larger group than those who are strictly of the tribe of Judah. The Doctrine and Covenants applies the name to persons living in ancient ISRAEL who accepted Jehovah as God and tried to live according to his laws. After the northern kingdom of Israel fell and the ten tribes therein were scattered, the tribe of Judah sought to preserve the law and the prophets. Subsequently, the name *Jew* came to be used to designate any survivor of the house of Israel, particularly those who settled in the land of

Israel after the Babylonian captivity and who occupied the land at the birth of Christ. Examples of this usage include 3:16; 45:21; 74:2; and 84:28, where we learn that John the Baptist "was ordained by the angel of God at the time he was eight days old unto this power, to overthrow the kingdom of the Jews, and to make straight the way of the Lord."

In a related sense, both the Book of Mormon and the Doctrine and Covenants refer to the children of Lehi as descendants, or remnants, of the Jews (19:27). Nephi, for example, writes, "Then shall the remnant of our seed know concerning us, how that we came out from Jerusalem, and that they are descendants of the Jews" (2 Ne. 30:4). President Joseph Fielding Smith noted, "Not only in the Book of Mormon are the descendants of Lehi called Jews, but also in the Doctrine and Covenants. In section 19, this is found: 'Which is my word to the Gentile, that soon it may go to the Jew, of whom the Lamanites are a remnant, that they may believe the gospel, and look not for a Messiah to come who has already come.' Again, in giving instruction to the elders who had journeyed from Kirtland to Missouri, the Lord revealed the place for the building of the temple and gave instruction for the purchase of land 'lying westward, even unto the line running directly between Jew and Gentile.' This line westward was the dividing line between the whites and Indians" (*Doctrines*, 3:264; D&C 57:4). In this context the word *Jews* in 98:17 may well refer to the LAMANITES, or Native Americans, settled along the western border of Missouri. Clearly the Lord had concern for this remnant of the Jews and for turning their hearts to the prophets and the hearts of the prophets to them.

The Doctrine and Covenants also uses the name *Jew* or *Jews* for the descendants of the ancient Jews who survived the dissolution of the Jewish state after the destruction in A.D. 70. This sense of the term includes those in modern times who claim such descent, as well as those who have been accepted into the group through marriage or conversion to Judaism. This group also includes those who are citizens of the modern state of Israel as well as those living elsewhere (45:51; 77:15). It is in this sense of the term that the restored gospel will be taken "first unto the Gentiles and then unto the Jews" (107:33–35, 97; cf. 18:26; 21:12; 90:9; 112:4; 133:8).

BIBLIOGRAPHY

Smith, Joseph Fielding. *Answers to Gospel Questions.* Compiled by Joseph Fielding Smith Jr. 5 vols. Salt Lake City: Deseret Book, 1957–66.

———. *Doctrines of Salvation.* Compiled by Bruce R. McConkie. 3 vols. Salt Lake City: Bookcraft, 1954–56.

TRV

Jewels

Treasured possessions. Speaking concerning his faithful covenant people, the Lord said to the prophet Malachi: "And they shall be mine . . . in that day when I make up my jewels" (Mal. 3:17; cf. Ex. 19:5). Twice in the Doctrine and Covenants reference is made to "my jewels" in this same sense. In reproving some elders who lacked the courage to "open their mouths," thereby "[hiding] the talent" the Lord had given them (knowledge and testimony of the restored gospel) "because of the fear of man," the Lord warned that if they were "not more faithful," they would lose what had been given them. He added, "For I, the Lord, rule in the heavens above, and among the armies of the earth; and in the day when I shall make up my jewels, all men shall know what it is that bespeaketh the power of God" (60:2–4).

The second reference to jewels concerns those who had been driven out of Jackson County, Missouri, in 1833. The Lord chastised the Saints for their unrighteousness, identifying several specific transgressions that contributed to their being driven from their homes. He promised, however, "Yet I will own them, and they shall be mine in that day when I shall come to make up my jewels. . . . Notwithstanding their sins, my bowels are filled with compassion towards them. I will not utterly cast them off; and in the day of wrath I will remember mercy" (101:1–9). That promise is secure for those who "remain, and are pure in heart," and "bring forth fruit and works meet for [the Lord's] kingdom" (101:18, 100).

RCF

Job

A righteous man of Old Testament times noted for patience and faith in God while suffering much affliction, including loss of family, possessions, and health and his friends charging him with transgression (Job 1–42). In a revelation to Joseph Smith, suffering in LIBERTY JAIL, the Lord reminded Joseph that he was not yet as Job in that his friends did not charge him with transgression (121:9–10). Scripture does not define when Job lived, and many commentators even doubt his existence; however, the entry in the Doctrine and Covenants is compelling that Job is real and his record essentially true. Perhaps Job's greatest utterance is his testimony of a future bodily resurrection because of the Redeemer (Job 19:25–27).

RJM

John, record of. *See* Record of John.

John the Baptist

Jesus said, "Among those that are born of women there is not a greater prophet than John the Baptist" (Luke 7:28; cf. *Joseph Smith*, 79–87). Joseph Smith explained that John's exclusive privileges of preparing the way for the Savior's earthly ministry, baptizing Jesus and seeing the dove as a prearranged sign that Jesus was indeed the Son of God, and being the sole legal administrator "in the affairs of the kingdom" in his day, "holding the keys of power" and wresting "the keys, the kingdom, the power, the glory from the Jews," are primary evidences of John's greatness (*History*, 5:260–61).

The many references to John the Baptist in the Doctrine and Covenants (13, headnote; 27:7–8; 35:4; 84:27–28; 93:6–18, 26; 133:55) and the teachings of the Prophet Joseph Smith bring his ministry into sharper focus and meaning than is conveyed by the New Testament alone. On 15 May 1829, John personally ordained Joseph Smith and Oliver Cowdery and gave them the KEYS of the Aaronic PRIESTHOOD (13:1; 27:7–8; cf. JS–H 1:68–72).

It was John's privilege to restore the Aaronic Priesthood because he was the legal heir, the rightful representative by lineage, by mortal ministry, and foreordination to introduce the ancient order of the Aaronic Priesthood into the DISPENSATION of the fulness of times.

Foreordination

John was foreordained in the Grand Council in heaven to be the prophet to prepare the way for JESUS CHRIST, to "overthrow the kingdom of the Jews" in the meridian dispensation, and to restore the Aaronic Priesthood in the dispensation of the fulness of times (27:7–8; 35:4; 84:27–28; *Joseph Smith*, 81–82). His earthly ministry was foretold by Isaiah (Isa. 40:3), Lehi (1 Ne. 10:7–10), Nephi (1 Ne. 11:27; 2 Ne. 31:4), and Malachi (Mal. 3:1; Matt. 11:10).

Announcement by Gabriel

John's forthcoming birth and ministry were announced to his father, Zacharias, by the angel Gabriel (ELIAS, or Noah), the same being who would subsequently announce to Mary the forthcoming birth of Jesus (27:7; Luke 1:5–19, 26–33). The extraordinary stature of the messenger signifies the extraordinary nature of the message. Gabriel, whom Joseph Smith identified as Noah, "stands next in authority to Adam in the Priesthood" (*History*, 3:386). John's birth was widely publicized and "noised abroad" (Luke 1:65) because of Zacharias's prominence and the miraculous events associated with the birth (Luke 1:5–25; 57–64). The people wondered, "What manner of child shall this be!" (Luke 1:66), and "all men mused . . . whether he were the Christ" (Luke 3:15).

Credentials

To fulfill the particular responsibilities of John's ministry, certain details were observed. To hold the keys and to function in the Aaronic Priesthood, it was necessary that he be of Aaron's lineage (107:13–16, 20; 84:27–28; Luke 1:5–13; Ex. 40:12–15). He was "filled with the Holy Ghost from his mother's womb," ordained (set apart) to his unique ministry by an angel when he was eight days old, and baptized in his childhood (84:27–28). He went forth "in the spirit and power of Elias" (Luke 1:17; cf. D&C 27:7). His priesthood ordination probably came at about age thirty, consistent with the ancient requirement (Num. 4:3). John held the keys of the Aaronic Priesthood (Smith, *Joseph Smith*, 82–85) and did in his ministry what the

LAW OF MOSES was designed to do: bring people to Christ (Gal. 3:24).

Three-fold ministry

John's ministry consisted of preaching, baptizing, and prophesying that the MESSIAH was *soon* to come (Matt. 3:1–17), testifying that the Messiah *had come* and was the person called Jesus (John 1:15–34), and directing the people to leave him and follow the Messiah (John 3:25–36). John was imprisoned, and Jesus sent angels to minister to him (JST Matt. 4:11). Beheaded by the order of Herod Antipas (Mark 6:19–29), John was "with Christ in his resurrection" (133:55).

Doctrinal teachings

Doctrine and Covenants 93:6–18, as well as the Joseph Smith Translation (JST Luke 3:4–11), ascribes a much wider range of doctrine to John's teachings than is found in other sources. John "bore record of the fulness of [Jesus'] glory" (93:6). He saw that Jesus "received not of the fulness at the first, but received grace for grace . . . until he received a fulness" (93:12–14). John saw that Christ "was in the beginning, before the world was," and that "the worlds were made by him" (93:7–10). He saw the Holy Ghost descend upon Jesus and heard God's voice at Jesus' baptism (93:15). He also saw that Jesus received a "fulness of the glory of the Father" (93:16–17). In that same revelation the Prophet Joseph Smith was promised that if he was faithful, he would "receive the fulness of the record of John," which was "hereafter to be revealed" (93:6, 18).

See also Elias; Historical context and overview of Doctrine and Covenants 13 (p. 723); Priesthood, restoration of priesthood and priesthood keys; Record of John.

BIBLIOGRAPHY

Matthews, Robert J. *A Burning Light: The Life and Ministry of John the Baptist.* Orem, Utah: Granite, 2000.

Smith, Joseph. *History of The Church of Jesus Christ of Latter-day Saints.* Edited by B. H. Roberts. 7 vols. 2d ed. rev. Salt Lake City: The Church of Jesus Christ of Latter-day Saints, 1932–51.

———. *Joseph Smith.* Teachings of Presidents of the Church series. Salt Lake City: The Church of Jesus Christ of Latter-day Saints, 2007.

RJM

John the Beloved/Revelator

John, the brother of James and disciple of the Lord, was also known as the Beloved (7:1; 3 Ne. 28:6) and the Revelator (77:2; 128:6). After the Lord's resurrection, John requested that his temporal death be postponed until the Second Coming. His request, however, is only hinted at in the New Testament (John 21:20–23). The Doctrine and Covenants makes it clear that the reason for John's request was his desire to continue his work of bringing souls to the Lord. In response to this loving and self-sacrificing request, the Lord not only granted John his desire but spelled out more precisely what He wanted him to do. His task would be that of an angel to "minister for those who shall be heirs of salvation who dwell on the earth" and to "prophesy before nations, kindreds, tongues and people" (7:1–6).

The Doctrine and Covenants also reveals John's postmortal assignment. He, with his fellow apostles, "shall stand at my right hand at the day of my coming in a pillar of fire, being clothed with robes of righteousness, with crowns upon their heads, in glory even as I am, to judge the whole house of Israel, even as many as have loved me and kept my commandments, and none else" (29:12).

In the meantime, John's writings would prove important to the faithful. The Lord declared that prophecies "spoken by mine apostles must be fulfilled; for as they spoke so shall it come to pass" (29:10). Specifically, in referring to a prophecy made by John (Rev. 8:10–11), the Lord stated that "there are many dangers upon the waters . . . ; for I, the Lord, have decreed in mine anger many destructions upon the waters; yea, and especially upon *these* waters" (that is, the river upon which the brethren would return to Kirtland, Ohio, from their mission to Missouri; 61:4–5; emphasis added). "Behold, I, the Lord, in the beginning blessed the waters; but in the last days, by the mouth of my servant John, I cursed the waters" (61:14). *See* Historical context and overview of Doctrine and Covenants 61 (p. 767); Water(s).

This was not the only revelation in which the Lord validated John's writings. Indeed, section 77 contains brief interpretations of some images John saw in vision on the Isle of Patmos and which he recorded in the book of Revelation. The Lord also referred to John 14:16 in 88:3, where he explained the term "another Comforter."

The last reference to John in the Doctrine and Covenants was made by Joseph Smith in his letter to the Saints concerning baptism for the dead. He noted that John was well aware of the work for the dead and had this principle in mind when he recorded that the dead, both "small and great" (Rev. 20:12), would be "judged out of those things . . . written in the books, according to their works." "Those things" included the records of ordinances performed for them in the temple (128:6–7). *See* Salvation for the dead.

The John referred to in 93:6–18 is John the Baptist, but his words greatly influenced the writings of his disciple, John the Beloved (cf. John 1:1–34). *See* Record of John.

See also Historical context and overview of Doctrine and Covenants 77 (p. 782); John the Beloved/Revelator quotations in the Doctrine and Covenants.

RDD

John the Beloved/Revelator quotations in the Doctrine and Covenants

Several times the Doctrine and Covenants explicitly quotes or refers to the writings of John, one of the Lord's chief apostles. Taken together, the references show that John's testimony acted as a catalyst in restoring important doctrines. For instance, Christians had long debated whether or not John had been translated. The first reference in the Doctrine and Covenants to John's writings settles that issue in the affirmative (7:1–8). While Joseph Smith and Sidney Rigdon were considering the implications of John 5:29, the Lord opened to them the vision dealing with the three degrees of glory (76:15–19). The Prophet's work while translating the book of Revelation caused him to go to the Lord with questions concerning some of the images John saw. The answers to these questions are now found in Doctrine and Covenants 77, an important key to understanding parts of John's work.

Additionally, the Doctrine and Covenants clarifies or amplifies some of John's writings. For example, concerning the Lord's promise in John 14:16–17, 26 that he would give the disciples "another Comforter," the revelations show that the gift included God's promise of eternal life (88:3–4). Also, this modern scripture makes it clear that the books referred to in Revelation 20:12, out of which the dead are judged, consist of two sets: the records kept here on earth and the record kept in heaven (128:6–7).

In addition to adding to or clarifying doctrinal understanding, the Doctrine and Covenants declares that modern revelation does not add to or diminish in any way John's book of prophecy or the Bible itself but instead sets the pattern that hereafter all "the revelations of God . . . shall come . . . by the gift and power of the Holy Ghost, the voice of God, or the ministering of angels" (20:35). It also affirms John's prophecy that God will curse the WATERS in the last days that none will be safe upon them "but he that is upright in heart" (Rev. 8:8–9; 11:6; D&C 61:14–16).

Further similarities to John's writings are seen in 88:92–116, where angels, trumps, and great destructions all reflect in content and tone Revelation 8–9, 14. A comparison between the two texts shows, however, that in spite of the same imagery and time frame, they are quite independent of each other.

The Doctrine and Covenants is laced with numerous phrases from the Bible, more than six hundred of which follow exactly or closely parallel those used by John. The imagery used to describe the Savior in section 110 follows that found in Revelation 1:14–16; the Lord's reference to himself as "Alpha and Omega," found numerous times in the Doctrine and Covenants (for example, 19:1; 38:1; 45:7; 61:1; 63:60; 75:1; 84:120; 132:66), is exclusive to John in the New Testament; Rev. 1:8, 11; 21:6; 22:13); only John refers to the second death (Rev. 21:8), a reference to which is found in 63:17; and John's statement that the gospel will be preached to every nation, kindred, tongue, and people (Rev. 14:6) is employed six times in the Doctrine and Covenants (7:3; 42:58; 77:8; 88:103; 112:1; 133:37).

Further, John states that the Lord is as a light

that shines in darkness, but "the darkness comprehended it not" (John 1:5). Those words are used exactly or paraphrased at least seven times in the Doctrine and Covenants (6:21; 10:58; 11:11; 34:2; 39:2; 45:7; 88:49). The idea that Jesus came to his own and they rejected him (John 1:11) is found six times (6:21; 10:57; 11:29; 39:3; 45:8; 133:66). The phrase "the fields . . . are white already to harvest" (John 4:35) appears seven times (4:4; 6:3; 11:3; 12:3; 14:3; 33:3, 7). Finally, John is the only New Testament writer to refer to the Holy Ghost as the "Comforter" (John 14:26; cf. 21:9; 31:11; 39:6; 47:4; 52:9; 79:2; 88:3–4; 124:97).

RDD

Johnson, Aaron

Birth: 22 June 1806, Haddam, Middlesex County, Connecticut

Death: 10 May 1877, Springville, Utah County, Utah

Aaron Johnson was baptized on 16 April 1836 and within a year moved to Kirtland. At Joseph Smith's advice, he purchased a land for his "inheritance" (Johnson, 4–5). He relocated to Far West, Missouri, in 1838, and then to Nauvoo, Illinois, in 1839. In Far West he was ordained a seventy and served on the high council, and in Nauvoo he served as justice of the peace (MH, 17 December 1843; Smith, 6:117) and as a member of the Nauvoo Legion and city council.

Johnson is referred to in the Doctrine and Covenants in connection with his calling to the Nauvoo high council, which was restructured in January 1841. He was called to replace Seymour Brunson, who had died five months before. The Lord said, "Seymour Brunson I have taken unto myself; . . . verily I say unto you, let my servant Aaron Johnson be ordained unto this calling in his stead" (124:132).

After the martyrdom of the Prophet Joseph Smith, Johnson left Nauvoo, selling his land for only $150. This was the same land he had purchased for more than $4,000. In 1846 he went west, temporarily staying at Garden Grove, Iowa, where he served as bishop. In 1850 he traveled across the plains and ultimately helped settle Springville, Utah. Over the next twenty-seven years Johnson served in various civil and Church capacities: chief justice of Utah County; member of the Utah legislature; member of political, public, and educational committees; the first bishop in Springville; and patriarch.

BIBLIOGRAPHY

Johnson, Alan P. *Aaron Johnson, Faithful Steward: A Documentary History*. Salt Lake City: Publishers Press, 1991.

Manuscript History of the Church, 17 December 1843. L. Tom Perry Special Collections, Harold B. Lee Library, Brigham Young University, Provo, Utah.

Smith, Joseph. *History of The Church of Jesus Christ of Latter-day Saints*. Edited by B. H. Roberts. 7 vols. 2d ed. rev. Salt Lake City: The Church of Jesus Christ of Latter-day Saints, 1932–51.

ZLL

Johnson, John

Birth: 11 April 1778, Chesterfield, Cheshire County, New Hampshire

Death: 30 July 1843, Kirtland, Lake County, Ohio

John "Father" Johnson went to Kirtland to investigate the restored gospel shortly after Joseph Smith moved to Ohio from New York. Johnson's wife, Elsa, had been suffering from chronic rheumatism "so that she could not raise her hand to her head for about two years." After Joseph Smith blessed her and "she was healed immediately," John's son Luke recalled, "My father was satisfied in regard to the truth of 'Mormonism,' and was baptized by Joseph Smith, jun. . . . and furnished him and his family a home" (834). While living on the Johnson farm between 1831 and 1832, Joseph worked on his translation of the Bible and received several revelations now found in the Doctrine and Covenants, including section 76, the vision of the degrees of glory. *See* Kingdoms of glory and perdition, vision of.

John Johnson's name appears in three sections of the Doctrine and Covenants. In 96:6–9, Johnson was called as a member of the United Order and was promised eternal life as long as he kept the commandments. The Lord indicated that Johnson was a descendant of Joseph of old and "a partaker of the blessings of the promise made" to Joseph's fathers. *See* Abrahamic covenant.

Johnson was ordained a high priest by June

1833. In 102:3, he was called to the high council in Kirtland, Ohio, where he served from 1834 to 1837.

Finally, in 104:24, as the United Order was being dissolved and its properties redistributed to the Order's former members as individual stewardships, Johnson was told that the land which he had "obtained in exchange for his former inheritance" was to be given to Martin Harris. Moreover, he, Johnson, was to "have the house in which he lives, . . . save the ground which [had] been reserved for the building of [the Lord's] houses," and he was instructed to "sell the lots that are laid off for the building up of the city of [the] saints" (104:34, 36).

Ultimately Johnson, struggling with financial difficulties and the failed Kirtland Safety Society, became disaffected from the Church and its leaders. In 1837 his membership on the high council was "objected to" (Smith, 2:510). He "withdrew from [the] Church by 1838" (Cook, 199).

John Johnson was the father of Luke and Lyman Johnson, both of whom were members of the first Quorum of the Twelve Apostles.

BIBLIOGRAPHY

Cook, Lyndon W. *The Revelations of the Prophet Joseph Smith.* Salt Lake City: Deseret Book, 1985.

Johnson, Luke. "History of Luke Johnson." *The Latter-day Saints' Millennial Star* 26 (31 December 1864): 834–36; 27 (7 January 1865): 5–7.

Smith, Joseph. *History of The Church of Jesus Christ of Latter-day Saints.* Edited by B. H. Roberts. 7 vols. 2d ed. rev. Salt Lake City: The Church of Jesus Christ of Latter-day Saints, 1932–51.

ZLL

Johnson, Luke S.

Birth: 3 November 1807, Pomfret, Windsor County, Vermont

Death: 9 December 1861, Salt Lake City, Salt Lake County, Utah

Luke Johnson was baptized by Joseph Smith on 10 May 1831, having witnessed the conversion of his parents, John and Elsa, and the miraculous recovery of his mother's chronic rheumatism following a blessing from the Prophet.

John Johnson's farm in Hiram, Ohio; photograph by Welden C. Andersen.

Courtesy Church History Library

Luke S. Johnson, 1807–1861.

Not long afterward, he served a mission in South Ohio, where he helped organize the Chippewa Branch. He also accompanied Sidney Rigdon on a mission to New Portage, Ohio, where they baptized "about fifty or sixty," and Pittsburgh, where they preached the gospel to Rigdon's relatives. Luke Johnson baptized Rigdon's mother and oldest brother and "also several others in that neighborhood, and we organized a Branch" (835).

In November 1831, Luke Johnson, along with his brother-in-law Orson Hyde, his brother Lyman Johnson, and William E. McLellin requested "that the mind of the Lord be made known" concerning them (68, headnote). In the revelation that followed, they were told that they should "speak as . . . moved upon by the Holy Ghost" and "preach the gospel to every creature, acting in the authority which I have given you, baptizing in the name of the Father, and of the Son, and of the Holy Ghost." They were to "be of good cheer, and . . . not fear" (68:3, 8, 6). The Lord would stand by them, and they would bear record that Jesus Christ is the Son of God.

Johnson's name also appears in 102:3, in which he was called to the Kirtland high council, and in 75:8–9 in connection with a mission to "the south countries." After his first companion, William E. McLellin, left the mission early, Johnson was joined by Seymour Brunson, with whom he "baptized over one hundred persons" and organized a branch of the Church in Lawrence County, Ohio, and in Cabal County, Virginia (Johnson, 835).

In February 1835 Johnson was appointed to the Quorum of the Twelve Apostles. In this capacity he served missions to the eastern states, New York, and Upper Canada. By 1837, however, he became caught up in financial matters and allowed his mind to become "darkened" as he left to "pursue [his] own course." In his personal history he acknowledged that because of this pursuit, he had "lost the Spirit of God, and neglected [his] duty" (5–6). He joined with other dissenters in "denouncing the Church" (Black, 156), and he was excommunicated at Far West, Missouri, in December 1837.

Johnson repented of his disaffection and returned to the Church in 1846 because, as he said, "My heart is with this people. I want to be associated with the saints; go with them into the wilderness and continue with them to the end" (in Black, 156). He arrived in Salt Lake in July 1847, settled in Tooele County, and "was ordained a bishop to preside over that settlement." At Johnson's death in 1861, Brigham Young observed, "Since his return to the church he has lived up to the truth to the best of his ability" (Roberts, 5:143).

See also Apostles, the first Twelve of latter days.

BIBLIOGRAPHY

Black, Susan Easton. *Who's Who in the Doctrine and Covenants.* Salt Lake City: Deseret Book, 1997.

Johnson, Luke. "History of Luke Johnson." *The Latter-day Saints' Millennial Star* 26 (1864): 834–36; 27 (1865): 5–7.

Roberts, B. H. *A Comprehensive History of The Church of Jesus Christ of Latter-day Saints, Century One.* 6 vols. Salt Lake City: The Church of Jesus Christ of Latter-day Saints, 1930. Reprint, Provo, Utah: Brigham Young University Press, 1965.

ZLL

Johnson, Lyman E.

Birth: 24 October 1811, Pomfret, Windsor County, Vermont

Death: 20 December 1856, near Prairie du Chien, Crawford County, Wisconsin

In February 1831 Lyman Johnson was baptized by Sidney Rigdon. Nine months later, the Lord, through the Prophet Joseph Smith, granted the request of Johnson and three others who desired to know "the mind of the Lord" concerning them (68, headnote). The revelation instructed them and "all the faithful elders of [the] church" that "whatsoever they shall speak when moved upon by the Holy Ghost shall be scripture, shall be the will of the Lord, shall be the mind of the Lord, shall be the word of the Lord, shall be the voice of the Lord, and the power of God unto salvation. . . . Wherefore, be of good cheer, and do not fear, for I the Lord am with you, and will stand by you; and ye shall bear record of me, even Jesus Christ, that I am the Son of the living God. . . . Go ye into all the world, preach the gospel to every creature, acting in the authority which I have given you" (68:7, 4, 6–8). In January of 1832 Johnson was

Lyman E. Johnson, 1811–1856.

Courtesy Church History Library

called by revelation to serve a mission to the east with Orson Pratt (75:14). This companionship enjoyed much success, baptizing "more than one hundred converts" (Cook, 111). He attended the School of the Prophets and was a member of ZION'S CAMP. On 14 February 1835, at age twenty-three, he was the first man called as an apostle in this dispensation, though he was the most junior member of the Quorum of the Twelve Apostles because they were ordered by age when the Quorum was first organized.

Johnson "claimed to have lost $6,000" in the Kirtland Safety Society banking failure in 1837. He blamed the Prophet Joseph Smith and consequently was disfellowshipped (Cook, 111). The next year, on 13 April 1838, he was excommunicated for charges including "bringing distress to the inocent," assaulting Phineas Young, failing to attend Church meetings, "not observing his prayers," failing to observe the Word of Wisdom, and "seeking to injure the character of Joseph Smith jr" (Cannon and Cook, 171–76).

Johnson moved to Iowa, where he practiced law in Davenport and in Keokuk. At age forty-five he drowned in the Mississippi River when his sleigh broke through the ice near Prairie du Chien, Wisconsin. In June 1877 Brigham Young stated that Lyman said "at one of our Quorum meetings" after he had apostatized, "Brethren—I will call you brethren—I will tell you the truth. If I could believe 'Mormonism'— it is no matter whether it is true or not—but if I could believe 'Mormonism' as I did when I traveled with you and preached, if I possessed the world I would give it. I would give anything, I would suffer my right hand to be cut off, if I could believe it again. Then I was full of joy and gladness. My dreams were pleasant. When I awoke in the morning my spirit was cheerful. I was happy by day and by night, full of peace and joy and thanksgiving. But now it is darkness, pain, sorrow, misery in the extreme. I have never since seen a happy moment" (19:41).

See also Apostles, the first Twelve of latter days.

BIBLIOGRAPHY

Cannon, Donald Q., and Lyndon W. Cook, eds. *Far West Record: Minutes of The Church of Jesus Christ of*

Latter-day Saints, 1830–1844. Salt Lake City: Deseret Book, 1983.

Cook, Lyndon W. *The Revelations of the Prophet Joseph Smith.* Salt Lake City: Deseret Book, 1985.

Prairie du Chien (Wisconsin) Courier, 22 December 1859.

Smith, Joseph. *History of The Church of Jesus Christ of Latter-day Saints.* Edited by B. H. Roberts. 7 vols. 2d ed. rev. Salt Lake City: The Church of Jesus Christ of Latter-day Saints, 1932–51.

Young, Brigham. *Journal of Discourses.* 26 vols. London: Latter-day Saints' Book Depot, 1854–86.

KWF

Josephites

Descendants of Lehi's son Joseph who followed their progenitor in being faithful friends of Nephi's descendants (Jacob 1:13; 4 Ne. 1:36–37; Morm. 1:8). The one reference to the Josephites in the Doctrine and Covenants is in connection with the assurance that they along with other Lehites and Ishmaelites, through the Book of Mormon record might come to know the Savior—know of his promises, believe his gospel, rely upon his merits, and be glorified and saved (3:16–20).

DKO

Joseph of Egypt

A favored son of Jacob (Israel). Due to his status with his father and prophecies of his own leadership, Joseph was sold by his jealous brothers into slavery in Egypt. Despite facing severe trials, he rose to great power, second only in position to Pharaoh. His political status, obedience, and prophetic ability allowed him to save the Egyptians and many of his fellow Hebrews from famine, including his estranged family (Gen. 37; 39–46).

In the context of persecutions of Latter-day Saints in Missouri, the Lord declared his law concerning justification for entering armed conflict (98) wherein he revealed that he gave this same law to Joseph and his fathers, Jacob, Isaac, and Abraham (98:32). Additionally, the Lord included Joseph as one of the fathers "by whom the promises remain" (27:10) and revealed that Joseph, with others, will "drink of the fruit of the vine" with him at some future time on the earth (27:5–14). *See* Abrahamic covenant.

The Doctrine and Covenants contains significant promises to Joseph's descendants. In a revelation on the meaning of several passages in Isaiah, the Lord identified both the "rod out of the stem of Jesse" and the "root of Jesse" (Isa. 11:1–4, 10–12) as a descendant of Jesse and Joseph, a "servant in the hands of Christ . . . , on whom there is laid much power" and "unto whom rightly belongs the priesthood, and the keys of the kingdom, for an ensign, and for the gathering of my people in the last days" (113:4–6; cf. 86:8–9; 96:7; 107:40). Latter-day Saints identify the "rod" and the "root" as the Prophet Joseph Smith.

Modern revelation includes the promise of a day when "the arm of the Lord shall be revealed in power in convincing . . . the house of Joseph," who are scattered among the heathen nations, "of the gospel of their salvation" (90:10).

KMM

Joseph Smith Translation of the Bible. *See* Doctrine and Covenants and the Joseph Smith Translation of the Bible.

Joy

State of happiness, felicity; emotion experienced by achieving success in truly worthwhile endeavors. The Lord commands his followers, "Lift up your hearts and rejoice" (27:15; cf. 25:13). How does joy come? "My Spirit . . . shall fill your soul with joy" (11:13), and you can feel "joy in the fruit of your labors" (6:31), especially in bringing other souls to the Savior (18:15–16). Faithful laborers will see joy in the face of the Master (88:52). God feels joy as he watches returning prodigals: "How great is his joy in the soul that repenteth" (18:13). The righteous are gathered out of all nations and help "push" others to ZION; they help build up Zion, while singing "songs of everlasting joy" (45:71; 66:11; 101:18; 133:33). Receiving REVELATION, KNOWLEDGE, and understanding of the MYSTERIES of the KINGDOM and peaceable things all bring joy (42:61, 65). To the Saints going to the West, the Lord said, "If thou art sorrowful, call on the Lord thy God with supplication, that your souls may be joyful" (136:29). Proper FASTING also brings joy (59:13). Although joy is available in this world, there is greater joy in the world to come: "In this world your joy is not full, but in me your joy is full" (101:36). "A faithful, a just, and a wise steward shall enter into the joy of his Lord, and shall inherit eternal life" (51:19). *See* Eternal life.

In the NEW JERUSALEM, the Lord will "crown the faithful with joy and with rejoicing" (52:43). The spirit body and the physical body, inseparably connected through the RESURRECTION, never again to be divided, may receive a fulness of joy (93:33–34; 138:17).

President Joseph F. Smith saw the spirits of the just in the world of spirits, "filled with joy and gladness, and [they] were rejoicing together because the day of their deliverance ['from the bands of death'] was at hand" (138:15–16).

DKO

Judah

The fourth son of Jacob, through Leah (Gen. 29:32–35). There are three references to Judah in the Doctrine and Covenants. The first is in the dedicatory prayer of the Kirtland Temple, in which the Prophet Joseph Smith petitioned God that "the children of Judah may begin to return to the lands which thou didst give to Abraham, their father" (109:64). The phrase "children of Judah" means the JEWS, the descendants of Judah.

The other two references to Judah appear in section 133 in connection with the second coming of the Lord. In preparation for the Savior's return, the revelation says, "Let them who be of Judah flee unto Jerusalem, unto the mountains of the Lord's house" (133:13). *See* Mountains of the Lord's house.

When Christ comes, the righteous of Judah, "after their pain, shall be sanctified in holiness before the Lord, to dwell in his presence day and night, forever" (133:35). These blessings, of course, are for those of Judah who accept Jesus Christ and keep his commandments (29:12).

TRV

Judge in Israel. *See* Bishop(s).

Judgment(s)

Valuation or assessment; determination of merit or guilt; rewards or punishments. The Doctrine and Covenants speaks of two kinds of judgments—the judgments of men and the judgments of God.

Judgments of men

The revelations warn men against unrighteous judgment because, as the Lord taught Joseph Smith, "You cannot always judge the righteous, or . . . you cannot always tell the wicked from the righteous" (10:37). When the early Saints suffered injustices and persecution at the hands of their enemies, they had a natural tendency to seek revenge. Yet the Lord reminded them: "Leave judgment alone with me, for it is mine and I will repay" (82:23). Further, as the Saints contemplated being reestablished in Jackson County, Missouri, the Lord commanded them to "talk not of judgments," meaning condemnations that would come upon the wicked, "neither boast of faith nor of mighty works" that could provoke the enemies of the Church (105:24).

There are times, however, when righteous judgment is required, and the Doctrine and Covenants speaks of those conditions as well. For example, a bishop must be "a judge in Israel, to do the business of the church, to sit in judgment upon transgressors upon testimony as it shall be laid before him according to the laws, by the assistance of his counselors" (107:72–78). Reminding bishops of their dependence upon him, the Lord said, "Let no man think he is ruler; but let God rule him that judgeth" (58:20). It is through the inspiration of the HOLY GHOST that judgments by authorized priesthood leaders are to be made (121:34–46). *See* Church discipline.

At other times judgments must be made with common sense, the best available knowledge, and through counseling with others. For example, the Lord said to early missionaries that "it mattereth not unto me . . . whether they go by water or by land; let this be as it is made known unto them according to their judgments hereafter" (61:22; cf. 60:5; 62:8). In the revelation known as the Word of Wisdom the Lord directed that tobacco "is not good for man" but could be used for sick and bruised livestock "with judgment and skill" (89:8). The statement on the role of government, found in section 134, explains that "all governments have a right to enact such laws as in their own judgments are best calculated to secure the public interest" (134:5).

Judgments of God

The Doctrine and Covenants refers to the judgments of God in at least three different contexts:

1. The calamities and consequences that accompany the second coming of Jesus Christ. The revelations provide a "voice of warning" (1:4) to all people concerning the judgments of God that will be poured out upon a wicked world: "Prepare ye, prepare ye for that which is to come, for the Lord is nigh; and the anger of the Lord is kindled, and his sword is bathed in heaven, and it shall fall upon the inhabitants of the earth" (1:12–13). Moreover, the "unbelieving and rebellious"—those who knowingly reject the fulness of the gospel—will know "the wrath of God [that will] be poured out upon the wicked without measure . . . when the Lord shall come to recompense unto every man according to his work, and measure to every man according to the measure which he has measured to his fellow man" (1:8–10). Through faith in Christ, repentance from sin, and obedience to the principles and ordinances of the GOSPEL, one is gathered to the Church. Though the devil "shall have power over his own dominion

. . . the Lord shall have power over his saints, and shall reign in their midst, and shall come down in judgment upon Idumea, or the world" (1:35–36). Other passages likewise testify of the necessity of worthiness in order to be prepared to abide the coming of the Lord (e.g., 43:22–29; 88:84, 92; 133:3–5, 14–15, 19). Further, the Lord directs his servants to "reprove the world of all their unrighteous deeds, and to teach them of a judgment which is to come" (84:87), saying, "Fear God and give glory to him, for the hour of his judgment is come" (133:37–45; cf. 43:15–29; 109:38). *See* Jesus Christ, second coming of.

The hardships of the last days—the prophesied SIGNS preceding the Savior's second coming, such as wars, earthquakes, famines, pestilences, and so forth (29:14–21; 45:31–42; 63:32–33; 88:87–91)—will cause many Saints to suffer, for these judgments of God affect both the righteous and wicked. "Concerning the coming of the Son of Man," the Prophet Joseph Smith taught, "it is a false idea that the Saints will escape all the judgments, whilst the wicked suffer; for all flesh is subject to suffer, and 'the righteous shall hardly escape;' still many of the Saints will escape, for the just shall live by faith; yet many of the righteous shall fall a prey to disease, to pestilence, etc., by reason of the weakness of the flesh, and yet be saved in the Kingdom of God. So that it is an unhallowed principle to say that such and such have transgressed because they have been preyed upon by

The Last Judgment; *mural by John Scott. Mural in the Washington D.C. Temple. "And the righteous shall be gathered on my right hand unto eternal life; and the wicked on my left hand will I be ashamed to own before the Father"* (D&C 29:27).

disease or death, for all flesh is subject to death; and the Savior has said, 'Judge not, lest ye be judged'" (4:11).

2. The consequences individuals suffer in mortality because of sin. The Saints are not exempt from the judgments, sorrows, and hardships that come about as a consequence of their own wrong deeds: "For instead of blessings, ye, by your own works, bring cursings, wrath, indignation, and judgments upon your own heads, by your follies, and by all your abominations, which you practise before me, saith the Lord" (124:48). For example, the sins of Martin Harris brought a withdrawal of the Lord's Spirit (19:20); the contention, envy, strife, lust, and coveting of early Saints "polluted their inheritances" (101:6); the setting "at naught the counsels of God" by Joseph Smith brought a loss of "privileges for a season" (3:13–14; cf. 10:2; 93:42–50). In many cases, God's judgments are conditional and can be averted if the individuals repent and faithfully follow the Lord (39:16–19; 82:2; 84:54–59; 136:42).

3. The Final Judgment, in which all mankind must stand *before the judgment-seat of Christ*" (135:5). Although there are many intermediate judgments of man by God—including at the time of DEATH and again at RESURRECTION—the ultimate judgment is the Final Judgment, which will occur at the end of the MILLENNIUM. "But behold, the residue of the wicked have I kept in chains of darkness until the judgment of the great day, which shall come at the end of the earth" (38:5). "And this shall be the sound of his trump, saying to all people, both in heaven and in earth, and that are under the earth—for every ear shall hear it, and every knee shall bow, and every tongue shall confess, while they hear the sound of the trump, saying: Fear God, and give glory to him who sitteth upon the throne, forever and ever; for the hour of his judgment is come" (88:104). It is at this judgment that "the rebellious shall be pierced with much sorrow; for their iniquities shall be spoken upon the housetops, and their secret acts shall be revealed" (1:3) and the deceivers and hypocrites will be exposed, "for, thus saith the Lord, I will bring them to judgment" (50:6). At this judgment "every man may be accountable for his own sins" (101:78), books will be opened "to convince all of their ungodly deeds which they have committed against [the Lord]" (99:5), and an accounting of stewardships, both temporal and spiritual, will be required (70:4; 104:11–18). The revelations in the Doctrine and Covenants bear testimony of the ultimate triumph of good over evil and of God over SATAN at the last Judgment. "For the days come," the Lord declared, "that I will send forth judgment unto victory" (52:11; cf. 19:1–3). For the wicked, this judgment will be a "day of vengeance" (133:51), while "the righteous shall be gathered on [the Lord's] right hand unto eternal life" (29:27).

See also God, nature of; Justice; Mercy; Punish, punished, punishment.

BIBLIOGRAPHY

Smith, Joseph. *History of The Church of Jesus Christ of Latter-day Saints.* Edited by B. H. Roberts. 7 vols. 2d ed. rev. Salt Lake City: The Church of Jesus Christ of Latter-day Saints, 1932–51.

BLT

Justice

The divine law of cause and effect. It is expressed in the Lord's dictum, "Whatsoever ye sow, that shall ye also reap; therefore, if ye sow good ye shall also reap good for your reward" (6:33). Justice is the law of the harvest. It assures a moral balance in the universe. Therefore, while justice may be viewed negatively by the disobedient, it should be viewed positively by the obedient.

"Justice and judgment" are intrinsic aspects of divine law (82:4), for justice, like MERCY, is an eternal, constant principle with God (88:40). Indeed, being one of the divine principles of governance with which he is "enthroned," justice is an eternal, unchanging dimension of the moral nature of the Creator himself (109:77). Indeed, he is described as being "full of" justice (84:102). The justice found on earth, therefore, has its origin in the justice of heaven, which, in turn, is an extension of the innate justice of God. Consequently, human justice is truly just only to the degree to which it reflects its divine origin; hence the importance of the counsel to seek civil officers who "will administer the law in equity and justice" (134:3).

Because the standard for human justice is a reflection of divine justice, religious liberty becomes an inherent right, not merely a political privilege (134:7). The Prophet Joseph Smith clearly understood that truth. His statement concerning his enemies in Missouri and Illinois reflects that understanding: "They . . . have not the least shadow or coloring of justice or right on their side in the getting up of their prosecutions against me" (127:1). The Lord warned other enemies of Joseph's—specifically, those who had altered the 116 pages of Book of Mormon manuscript because they felt the situation required it—that they were "not exempt from the justice of God" (10:28).

Although the principle of mercy should never be ignored, neither can justice be robbed (Alma 42:25). This truth applies to all members of the Church as well. No member of the Church, regardless of his position, is above the law, for "none shall be exempted from the justice and the laws of God" (107:84). When cases are being adjudicated before a high council court, "every man is to speak according to equity and justice" (102:16). The same principle was to be sought by the Saints from the civil courts of the land (105:25).

In the final analysis, only SATAN and his minions will suffer the full weight of divine justice. There will be no mitigating influence of mercy extended to them, for they sought to be a law unto themselves to "abide in sin." Therefore, they "cannot be sanctified by law, neither by mercy, justice, nor judgment. Therefore, they must remain filthy still" (88:35; cf. 29:44).

For the rest of the Father's children, however, his justice, tempered by his mercy through the ATONEMENT of his Son JESUS CHRIST (19:16–19), will ensure that all shall find their rightful place in the kingdom of God. In doing so, all will attain that glory which they are prepared to receive. Mercy will claim its own, and so will justice (88:40; cf. Alma 42:22–24).

See also God, nature of.

RT

Justification

The word *justification* is used twice in the Doctrine and Covenants (20:30; 98:38) and,

with associated words *justify* and *just,* has two different meanings or usages. First, to justify is to defend something as true, right, or correct. It is to support something as lawful and good. Such support or justification can come from man, as in supporting just laws, or it can come from God, who supports his Saints in defending themselves against unjust laws and actions (98:5–6, 38; 134:7). In a closely related context, the scriptures often use the word *just* to describe something that is fair, proper, correct, upright, or righteous. For example, Hyrum Smith was commanded to "do *justly,* to walk humbly, [and] to judge righteously" (11:12; emphasis added). Similarly, under the law of consecration, the Saints were appointed "according to [their] wants and needs, inasmuch as [their] wants are just" (82:17), and that "whoso is found a faithful, a *just,* and a wise steward shall enter into the joy of his Lord, and shall inherit eternal life" (51:19; emphasis added).

The second context for the term *justification* as used in the revelations is to be declared blameless, without guilt, and in good standing before the Lord. The Articles and Covenants of the Church, recorded in section 20, declare that "we know that justification through the grace of our Lord and Savior Jesus Christ is just and true" (20:30). Through the ATONEMENT of the Lord, one becomes *justified,* or pronounced innocent through abiding by the principles and ordinances of the GOSPEL and any specific law or commandment given by the Lord (for example, 132:5–7). Other terms used in the revelations related to the doctrine of justification in one's life include "remission of sins" (84:64; cf. 20:37; 55:1–2), "blameless" (4:2), "clean" (88:74; 138:59), "forgiven" (1:32; 58:42; cf. 64:7), "guiltless" (58:30), and "just men made perfect through Jesus the mediator" (76:69). Viewing justification in the context of the Atonement, the just are "they who received the testimony of Jesus, and believed on his name and were baptized after the manner of his burial, . . . that by keeping the commandments they might be washed and cleansed from all their sins, and receive the Holy Spirit." These Saints "overcome by faith, and are sealed by the Holy Spirit of promise, which the Father sheds forth upon all those who are just and true" (76:51–53; cf. 132:6–8).

See also Just men made perfect; Sanctify, sanctification.

BLT

Just men made perfect

Persons who are faithful in the testimony of Jesus, have lived the celestial law, and are cleansed of sin. They are "just men made perfect through Jesus the mediator of the new covenant, who wrought out this perfect atonement through the shedding of his own blood" (76:69). The scriptures speak of such righteous, trustworthy individuals as Noah (Moses 8:27); Mary's husband, Joseph (Matt. 1:19); Lot (2 Pet. 2:7); King Benjamin (Mosiah 2:4); and Jacob (Enos 1:1) as just men. Even these "just men," however, must be "made perfect" through JESUS CHRIST. To be made perfect, just men and women must believe on the name of Jesus, be baptized, keep the commandments, and receive "the Holy Spirit by the laying on of the hands" (76:52). They must "overcome by faith, and [be] sealed by the Holy Spirit of promise, which the Father sheds forth upon all those who are just and true" (76:53; cf. 138:12; Moro. 10:32–33). They are among the sanctified, "those who love and serve God with all their mights, minds, and strength" (20:30–31). They will "come forth in the resurrection of the just," are given "all things," and "shall dwell in the presence of God and his Christ forever and ever" (76:59–65). The spirits of just men made perfect, who reside in the postmortal spirit world awaiting the resurrection, may be assigned to minister to mortals on the earth. The Prophet Joseph Smith was given the KEYS by which a person can discern whether a messenger is a resurrected being, the spirit of a just man made perfect, or the devil pretending to be of God (129:1–9).

See also Atonement, the; Justification; Perfect, perfection.

LGO

The **keys** of the kingdom of God are committed unto man on the earth, and from thence shall the gospel roll forth unto the ends of the earth, as the stone which is cut out of the mountain without hands shall roll forth, until it has filled the whole earth. 65:2

Key(s)

A term used as a symbol to denote the means by which something is revealed, discovered, or made manifest; also denotes the AUTHORITY by which the PRIESTHOOD is governed. The revelations in the Doctrine and Covenants deal with both the key(s) of knowledge and the key(s) of administration. The key(s) of knowledge are associated with the GIFT OF THE HOLY GHOST and participating in the rites or ORDINANCES of the GOSPEL. Holding such keys is the privilege of every faithful member of the Church. The key(s) of administration, however, are associated with those holding presiding positions in the organization of the Church, including the leadership of priesthood QUORUMS. These keys come with a particular calling and are surrendered when one is released from that calling. To hold such keys one must be properly called, sustained, ordained, and set apart (20:65; 42:11).

The key of knowledge

As the prophet standing at the head of this DISPENSATION, Joseph Smith held "the keys of the mysteries of the kingdom," meaning the ability to unlock the truths essential to salvation that can be known only by REVELATION, or those doctrines revealed only through participation in the ordinances of the gospel (64:5; 28:1–2; 35:18; 84:19). This authority also rests with his successors (81:2; cf. 128:11).

In some measure the key of the "mysteries" or the "key of the knowledge of God" (84:19) is intended to rest with every faithful member of the Church. All within the Church are privileged to know the truthfulness of the gospel by the revelation of the Spirit. There is no salvation without personal revelation or without what has come to be called a personal testimony (131:6). As used in holy writ, the word *mystery* or the expression "mysteries of the kingdom" has reference to those things that can be known only by personal revelation. Speaking to "those who serve me in righteousness and in truth," the Lord said, "To them will I reveal all mysteries, yea, all the hidden mysteries of my kingdom from days of old, and for ages to come, will I make known unto them the good pleasure of my will concerning all things pertaining to my kingdom. Yea, even the wonders of eternity

shall they know, and things to come will I show them, even the things of many generations" (76:5–8).

As first used in the Doctrine and Covenants, the word *keys* denotes special spiritual gifts promised by the Lord to Oliver Cowdery. He is promised two gifts or keys, the first being a knowledge of the mysteries of the kingdom (6:10–11) and the second being the gift of translating ancient records, which gift he was invited to hold even as Joseph Smith held it (6:25–28). In both instances the promised blessing centered on the spirit of revelation. The plan of salvation is for all men, and thus all men are entitled to possess the "keys of the mysteries of the kingdom" (64:5). They cannot be saved independent of such knowledge, for it "is impossible for a man to be saved in ignorance" (131:6). Yet, the Lord's house is a house of order, and it is equally true that there is no salvation independent of the Church and kingdom of God. So it is that the keys of the knowledge of God, in their fulness, flow only through the channels of the priesthood to faithful members of the Church. Nevertheless, the "Spirit of Jesus Christ," or "light of Christ," is given to "every man that cometh into the world" and will lead those who hearken to it to the fulness of the gospel (84:45–48; Moro. 7:16–19; cf. 93:2, 31–32; JST John 1:1–9). *See* Light of Christ.

Salvation requires revelation, revelation requires the HOLY GHOST, and the promise of the companionship of the Holy Ghost comes by the LAYING ON OF HANDS by those holding the priesthood. Citizenship in the Church and kingdom of God grants spiritual freedom and independence of knowledge to each of its citizens.

Those holding the gift of the Holy Ghost have power to unlock the heavens and receive revelation that is immediate to their circumstances and personal to their needs. In like manner, it is the right of members of the Church to entertain angels. Indeed, so great was the anticipation of the Saints in Nauvoo to do so that Joseph Smith gave them "three grand keys" by which the correct nature of ministering angels and spirits could be discerned (129). In the ordinances of the Melchizedek Priesthood, the Saints are also promised that they can be endowed with "the power of godliness" (84:19–21) Thus, as Joseph prepared the Saints to enter the temple, he "spoke of delivering the keys of the Priesthood to the Church, and said that the faithful members of the Relief Society should receive them in connection with their husbands, that the Saints whose integrity has been tried and proved faithful, might know how to ask the Lord and receive an answer" (*History,* 4:604). Joseph Smith also spoke of the "grand Key-words of the Holy Priesthood" (Facsimile 2, Fig. 3), explaining that they were known to all who held the priesthood from the days of Adam, including Seth, Noah, Melchizedek, and Abraham. All gospel ordinances testify of Christ, doing so by the spirit of revelation. Keywords constitute knowledge by revelation that is intended to unlock the gates of heaven to those who are prepared to enter and would of necessity need to be given to all who were intended to enter therein (130:9–11). President Brigham Young explained: "Your endowment is, to receive all those ordinances in the house of the Lord, which are necessary for you, after you have departed this life, to enable you to walk back to the presence of the Father, passing the angels who stand as sentinels, being enabled to give them the key words, the signs and tokens, pertaining to the holy Priesthood, and gain your eternal exaltation" (416).

"What is a key?" asked President Joseph F. Smith. "It is," he responded, "the right or privilege which belongs to and comes with the Priesthood, to have communication with God. . . . It is the right to enjoy the blessing of communication with the heavens, and the privilege and authority to administer in the ordinances of the gospel of Jesus Christ, to preach the gospel of repentance, and of baptism by immersion for the remission of sins. That is a key. You who hold the Priesthood have the key or the authority, the right, the power or privilege to preach the gospel of Jesus Christ, which is the gospel of repentance and of baptism by immersion for the remission of sins" (142).

In true religion the key of knowledge is always associated with the spirit of revelation and is not the exclusive province of any but rather the privilege of all. Such knowledge stands independent of office or position, bound by neither gender nor age. During his mortal ministry Jesus Christ accused the scribes and doctors of the law of having taken away the "key of knowledge," meaning the fulness of the scriptures: "Ye enter not in yourselves into the kingdom; and those who were entering in, ye hindered" (Luke 11:52; JST Luke 11:53).

The keys of administration

The Church and kingdom of God is governed by priesthood, and the priesthood in turn is governed by those holding the "keys of the kingdom" (65:2; 90:2–3, 6; 97:14) or, in the language of revelation, "the right of presidency" (107:8), which includes the "keys of the church" (42:69), and the "keys of the holy priesthood" (124:34, 123). During his mortal ministry, Jesus Christ conferred the "keys of the kingdom" upon the Twelve whom he had called (Matt. 18, headnote; v. 18). He chose Peter to stand at their head, who with James and John constituted the First Presidency. "Unto you three," the Lord said, "I will give this power and the keys of this ministry until I come" (7:1–7; cf. Matt. 16:19; Smith, *History,* 3:386). Peter, James, and John in turn conferred this same authority upon the heads of Joseph Smith and Oliver Cowdery in the spring of 1829 (JS–H 1:72; D&C 27:12–13; 128:20).

Confirming Joseph Smith's appointment, the Lord said, "For I have conferred upon you the keys and power of the priesthood, wherein I restore all things, and make known unto you all things in due time" (132:45). The Lord continued with words of explanation and instruction: "And verily, verily, I say unto you, that whatsoever you seal on earth shall be sealed in heaven; and whatsoever you bind on earth, in my name and by my word, saith the Lord, it shall be eternally bound in the heavens; and whosesoever sins you remit on earth shall be remitted eternally in the heavens; and whosesoever sins you retain on earth shall be retained in heaven. And again, verily I say, whomsoever you bless I will bless, and whomsoever you curse I will curse, saith the Lord; for I, the Lord, am thy God" (132:46–47).

In March 1832 and again in March 1833, the Lord directed that the First Presidency be organized (81:1–7; 90:1–6), with the Quorum of the Twelve being appointed in February 1835 (107). These constitute the leading quorums of the Church. When the Quorum of the First Presidency is dissolved at the death of the president, the Quorum of the Twelve automatically becomes the leading quorum of the Church. Thus, it is the responsibility of the Twelve to reorganize the First Presidency. Although each member of these two quorums has all the keys of the kingdom conferred upon him at the time of his ordination, he may use them only under the direction of the "President of the High Priesthood" (107:65–66), or president of the Church's leading quorum (132:7; McConkie, 412–13). "For unto you, the Twelve, and those, the First Presidency," the Lord said, "who are appointed with you to be your counselors and your leaders, is the power of this priesthood given, for the last days and for the last time, in the which is the dispensation of the fulness of times. Which power you hold, in connection with all those who have received a dispensation at any time from the beginning of the creation; for verily I say unto you, the keys of the dispensation, which ye have received, have come down from the fathers, and last of all, being sent down from heaven unto you" (112:30–32).

Every office and calling within the Church functions under the direction of those holding the necessary keys or presidency. No one calls oneself to an office or position in the Church. All who hold positions must be properly called, sustained, and set apart to their particular position. All who serve in a ward do so under the direction of their ward bishop. The scope of their calling is limited to the boundaries of their ward. The bishop functions under the direction of a stake president, who in turn functions under the direction of the general officers of the Church. All who serve do so under the direction of those holding the necessary presidency or keys. In like manner, all ordinances and rites must be performed with the approval and under the direction of those same keys to be of "efficacy, virtue, or force" either in this life or the life to come (132:7). Thus, keys discipline and direct the use of priesthood, ensuring that the Lord's house will always be a house of order.

In connection with the keys of administration,

several references in the Doctrine and Covenants identify individuals or divisions of the priesthood given keys to oversee certain functions or bring about important events:

1. Joseph Smith and Oliver Cowdery were given keys to "bring to light" records confirming the truth of the gospel (6:25–28).

2. The Aaronic Priesthood possesses the "keys of the ministering of angels" (13:1; 84:26).

3. Moroni holds the "keys of the record of the stick of Ephraim," the Book of Mormon (27:5).

4. Elias, also known as Gabriel, holds with others "the keys of . . . the restoration of all things" (27:6; cf. 77:9, 14; JST John 1:20–28).

5. Adam had "given unto him the keys of salvation under the counsel and direction of the Holy One" (78:16).

6. Counselors in the First Presidency, Sidney Rigdon and Frederick G. Williams, were to be equal to Joseph Smith in holding the "keys of this last kingdom" and the "keys of the school of the prophets" (90:6–7) and to exercise them only under his direction.

7. The Melchizedek Priesthood holds "the keys of all the spiritual blessings of the church" (107:18).

8. Moses committed to Joseph Smith the "keys of the gathering of Israel," ELIAS the "gospel of Abraham," and Elijah the power to "turn the hearts of the fathers to the children, and the children to the fathers, lest the whole earth be smitten with a curse" (110:11–15). The Prophet explained that the "office and work of Elijah . . . is one of the greatest and most important subjects that God has revealed. He should send Elijah to seal the children to the fathers, and the fathers to the children. . . . We want the power of Elijah to seal those who dwell on earth to those who dwell in heaven. This is the power of Elijah and the keys of the kingdom of Jehovah" (*History*, 6:251–52). With the coming of these three ancient prophets, the Lord declared, "Therefore, the keys of this dispensation are committed into your hands" (110:16; cf. 112:32; 128:18).

9. To Thomas B. Marsh, president of the Quorum of the Twelve Apostles, the Lord said,

"Thou art the man whom I have chosen to hold the keys of my kingdom, as pertaining to the Twelve, abroad among all nations" (112:16).

10. Hyrum Smith, taking the place of his father, Joseph Smith Sr., as patriarch to the Church, was called to hold the "keys" of the priesthood pertaining to the "sealing blessings" of the Church (124:123–24).

11. The Quorum of the Twelve Apostles holds the "keys to open up the authority of [the Lord's] kingdom upon the four corners of the earth" (124:128; cf. 107:35).

12. Michael, Gabriel, Raphael, and "divers angels, from Michael or Adam down to the present time," all declared to Joseph Smith "their dispensation, their rights, their keys, their honors, their majesty and glory, and the power of their priesthood" (128:21).

13. Joseph Smith, as president of the Church, was given the "keys of this priesthood," meaning the "new and everlasting covenant," including eternal MARRIAGE (132:4–19; cf. 66:2).

See also Priesthood, restoration of priesthood and priesthood keys.

BIBLIOGRAPHY

McConkie, Bruce R. *Mormon Doctrine.* 2d ed. Salt Lake City, Utah: Bookcraft, 1966.

Smith, Joseph. *History of The Church of Jesus Christ of Latter-day Saints.* Edited by B. H. Roberts. 7 vols. 2d ed. rev. Salt Lake City: The Church of Jesus Christ of Latter-day Saints, 1932–51.

Smith, Joseph F. *Gospel Doctrine.* Salt Lake City: Deseret Book, 1986.

Young, Brigham. *Discourses of Brigham Young.* Selected by John A. Widtsoe. Salt Lake City: Deseret Book, 1978.

JFM

Kick against the pricks

A phrase found in the Doctrine and Covenants describing one who has rejected "the principles of righteousness" in the exercise of the priesthood, who has thus grieved the Spirit and lost the power of the priesthood: "He is left unto himself, to kick against the pricks [or goads], to persecute the saints, and to fight against God" (121:36–38). This phrase reflects Acts 9:5, in which the Lord addressed the recalcitrant Saul on the road to Damascus: "I am Jesus whom thou persecutest: it is hard for thee to kick against the pricks" (cf. 26:14).

In antiquity, animals used for drawing wagons or plows were guided by a driver, who walked behind them and used a goad—a pointed stick sometimes tipped with metal (Judg. 3:31; 1 Sam. 13:21)—to direct the animal by pricking it. In Ecclesiastes this image is used in a positive metaphor: "The words of the wise are as goads" (Eccl. 12:11).

To "kick against the pricks" was a common Greek proverb that expressed the futility of resisting divine influence in one's conduct. The phrase is not usually found in Jewish writings; in the New Testament it is found only in Acts, which is attributed to Luke, a Gentile.

See also Broken heart and contrite spirit; Priesthood, proper exercise of.

DRS

Kimball, Heber C.

Birth: 14 June 1801, Sheldon, Franklin County, Vermont

Death: 22 June 1868, Salt Lake City, Salt Lake County, Utah

After his baptism in 1832, Heber Chase Kimball and his family moved to Kirtland, Ohio. On 14 February 1835 he was called to the Quorum of the Twelve Apostles. His name appears in the "Testimony of the Twelve Apostles to the Truth of the Book of Doctrine and Covenants" (D&C, Explanatory Introduction) in which the Twelve affirm that the commandments contained in the Doctrine and Covenants were "given by inspiration of God, and are profitable for all men and are verily true." *See* Doctrine and Covenants, testimony of the Twelve Apostles to the truth of.

On 4 June 1837 Joseph Smith said, "Brother Heber, the Spirit of the Lord has whispered to me: 'Let my servant Heber go to England and proclaim my Gospel, and open the door of salvation to that nation.'" Elder Kimball "felt a determination to go at all hazards" (Whitney, 104). He and others journeyed from Ohio to New York and then sailed aboard the *Garrick* to Liverpool. "When we were within six or seven feet of the pier, I leaped on shore . . . and for the first time in my life I stood on British ground, among

Heber C. Kimball, 1801–1868.

strangers. . . . I put my trust in God, believing that He would assist me in publishing the truth, give me utterance, and be a present help in time of need" (Whitney, 119). He enjoyed much success in sharing the gospel in England.

In 1838 Elder Kimball moved from Kirtland to Far West, Missouri, and later, because of persecution against the Saints, left for Illinois, eventually settling in Nauvoo. With the Quorum of the Twelve he served another mission to Great Britain between 1839 and 1841. On 19 January 1841, a revelation to the Prophet Joseph Smith at Nauvoo named Heber C. Kimball as a member of the Twelve, which quorum holds "the keys to open up the authority of my kingdom upon the four corners of the earth" (124:128).

Heber C. Kimball journeyed west with Brigham Young and the Camp of Israel, arriving in the Salt Lake Valley in July 1847. On 27 December 1847, having returned to Council Bluffs, Iowa, he was sustained as first counselor to Brigham Young in the presidency of the Church. Five years before, Hyrum Smith had given him a blessing promising that "you shall be blessed with a fulness and shall be not one whit behind the chiefest; as an apostle you

shall stand in the presence of God to judge the people; and as a prophet you shall attain to the honor of the three" (Smith, 464).

Heber C. Kimball died at age sixty-seven as a result of a carriage accident about a month before in which he was thrown violently to the ground.

See also Apostles, the first Twelve of latter days; Apostles, the Twelve, mission to Great Britain.

BIBLIOGRAPHY

Smith, Joseph Fielding. *Essentials in Church History*. Salt Lake City: Deseret News Press, 1953.

Whitney, Orson F. *Life of Heber C. Kimball*. 3d. ed. Salt Lake City: Bookcraft, 1967.

SEB

Kimball, Spencer W.

Birth: 28 March 1895, Salt Lake City, Salt Lake County, Utah

Death: 5 November 1985, Salt Lake City, Salt Lake County, Utah

In Thatcher, Arizona, as young Spencer Woolley Kimball was growing to manhood, his father remarked, "I have dedicated him to the Lord and to His service. He will become a mighty man in the Church." At age eight he was baptized, at twelve ordained a deacon, and at fourteen taught his first Sunday School class. By fifteen he "took down the family Bible, climbed the stairs to his attic room . . . and began at Genesis." He read nightly for about a year "until he could shut the book with great pride, finished" (56–57, 196).

President Kimball served a mission in the central states. When the Mount Graham Stake in Arizona was formed, he was selected as president. To visit all the wards in his stake, he had to travel 1,750 miles. On 8 July 1943 President J. Reuben Clark telephoned Spencer Kimball and said, "The brethren have just chosen you to fill one of the vacancies in the Quorum." Brother Kimball's response was, "I am so weak and small and limited and incapable. Of course, there could be only one answer to any call from the Brethren" (189). Ordained an apostle by President Heber J. Grant, President Kimball was tireless in his efforts to serve in the Quorum of the Twelve Apostles, even though he suffered greatly from physical ailments. His many illnesses led President Harold B. Lee to remark, "Spencer lives from blessing to blessing" (401).

On 30 December 1973 Spencer W. Kimball was sustained as president of The Church of Jesus Christ of Latter-day Saints. Under his leadership, the First Quorum of the Seventy was reorganized and additional scriptures were included first in the Pearl of Great Price and later in the Doctrine and Covenants (137; 138). In 1979 the Latter-day Saint edition of the King James Version of the Bible, with extensive footnotes, cross-references, a Topical Guide, and a Bible Dictionary, was published. A similarly annotated English edition of the Book of Mormon, Doctrine and Covenants, and Pearl of Great Price followed in 1981. Missionary work moved forward at an unprecedented rate, and temples began to dot the earth. But President Kimball's announcement that all worthy male Church members could hold the priesthood may be the most remarkable development in the progress of the Church.

"After extended meditation and prayer in the sacred rooms of the holy temple," Spencer W. Kimball and the members of the Twelve who were with him received a revelation in early June 1978 "extending priesthood and temple blessings to all worthy male members of the Church." On 30 September 1978, at the 184th semiannual general conference of the Church, N. Eldon Tanner, a counselor in the First Presidency, read and then called for a sustaining vote on what became known as Official Declaration 2. The vote was "*unanimous in the affirmative*" (OD 2).

Official Declaration 2 is an 8 June 1978 letter written by the First Presidency: "To all general and local priesthood officers of The Church of Jesus Christ of Latter-day Saints throughout the world." In the letter, the First Presidency wrote of witnessing "the expansion of the work of the Lord over the earth" and expressed gratitude that "people of many nations have responded to the message of the restored gospel." The Presidency revealed that the Lord had heard their prayers and by revelation confirmed that "the long-promised day has come when every faithful, worthy man in the Church may receive the holy priesthood, with power to exercise its divine authority, and enjoy with his loved ones

every blessing that flows therefrom, including the blessings of the temple."

See also Official Declaration 2.

BIBLIOGRAPHY

Kimball, Edward L., and Andrew E. Kimball Jr. *Spencer W. Kimball*. Salt Lake City: Bookcraft, 1977.

SEB

Kingdom(s)

Realm, domain, or organization over which someone has sovereignty or control. The word *kingdom* is used in several contexts in the Doctrine and Covenants, most of which refer to some dimension of the kingdom of God. Other designations include the "kingdom of the devil," the "kingdoms of this world," and the "kingdom of the Jews."

The "kingdom of God" refers generally to all of God's works and also to more limited dimensions of his work, such as the celestial, terrestrial, and telestial kingdoms (88:22–24; cf. 76:50–112), and the kingdom of heaven and the kingdom of God on the earth—the restored Church of Jesus Christ (e.g., 42:69; 65:2, 6; 90:16; 103:35; 105:32; 109:72; 115:19).

The Doctrine and Covenants makes clear that not only the Father but Jesus Christ is mankind's God (38:1; 62:1; 66:13; 95:17) and that the Father and the Son reign over the kingdom of God on earth and in heaven (50:27; 76:28, 68; 105:32), as well as many other kingdoms in the heavens: "There are many kingdoms; for there is no space in the which there is no kingdom; and there is no kingdom in which there is no space, either a greater or a lesser kingdom. And unto every kingdom is given a law; and unto every law there are certain bounds also and conditions" (88:37–38, 46–47; cf. Moses 1:32–35).

The following chart gives examples of uses of the word *kingdom* in the Doctrine and Covenants.

DESIGNATION	REFERENCES
My kingdom	7:4; 27:13; 63:23; 112:16; 124:128
His kingdom	65:5; 76:114; 131:4

DESIGNATION	REFERENCES
The kingdom	29:5; 41:6; 50:35; 71:1; 82:24; 109:72
Kingdom of glory	88:24
Kingdom of God	6:3; 20:29; 56:18; 65:2, 5–6; 138:44
Kingdom of heaven	6:37; 39:19; 65:6; 106:3; 128:10; 137:10
My Father's kingdom	27:4; 84:38, 74
Their Father's kingdom	84:58
Kingdom of my Father	15:6; 18:15; 101:65; 132:49
Kingdom of the devil	10:56
Kingdom of the Jews	84:28
Kingdoms of the/this world	84:82; 103:7–8; 105:32
Kingdom of our God	76:28, 79; 105:32
General use	78:15; 88:36–37; 93:53; 128:23; 130:9–10; 132:19

See also Kingdom of God/kingdom of heaven; Kingdoms of glory and perdition, vision of.

LED

Kingdom of God/kingdom of heaven

Because of such references as Doctrine and Covenants 25:1—"all those who receive my gospel are sons and daughters in my kingdom"—members of The Church of Jesus Christ of Latter-day Saints often refer to the Church as the kingdom of God upon the earth. This interpretation is substantiated by section 65, which records that "the keys of the kingdom of God are committed unto man on the earth" (v. 2). Verses 5 and 6 of that section instruct members to "call upon the Lord, that his kingdom may go forth upon the earth, that the inhabitants thereof may receive it, and be prepared for the days to come, in the which the Son of Man shall come down in heaven, clothed in the brightness of his glory, to meet the kingdom of God which is set up on the earth. Wherefore, may the kingdom of God go forth, that the kingdom of heaven may come."

Just as the phrase "kingdom of God" is used to refer to the Church on the earth (e.g., 65:2, 5, 6; 97:14; 138:44), so it also refers interchangeably to the kingdom of heaven, where the

faithful shall rest (e.g., 6:3, 13; 12:3; 20:29). The coming of God's kingdom in great glory from heaven is spoken of in 56:18; and 137:1, 7 speak of the celestial kingdom, where the blessed reside.

The name "kingdom of heaven" is used in context with the reward that the faithful will inherit (6:37; 10:55; 58:2); the warning of the need to repent because the kingdom of heaven is coming to earth (33:10; 39:19; 42:7; cf. 65:6); the gift of the *"keys of the kingdom of heaven"* to the apostle Peter (128:10); the truth that little "children who die before they arrive at the years of accountability are saved in the celestial kingdom of heaven" (137:10); the admonition to seek "diligently the kingdom of heaven" (106:3); and the blessing associated with the Melchizedek Priesthood of having "the privilege of receiving the mysteries of the kingdom of heaven" (107:18–19).

See also Kingdom(s); Kingdoms of glory and perdition, vision of.

MSN

Kingdom of the devil. *See* Satan.

Kingdoms of glory and perdition, vision of

A vision witnessed by the Prophet Joseph Smith and Sidney Rigdon on 16 February 1832. *See* Historical context and overview of Doctrine and Covenants 76 (p. 780).

The revelation may be organized under the following headings:
• The Lord's delight in honoring the faithful (76:1–10)
• Vision of the Father and the Son (76:11–24)
• Vision of Lucifer's rebellion in the premortal life (76:25–29)
• Vision of the suffering of those who become the sons of perdition in mortality (76:30–39, 43–49)
• Vision of the celestial kingdom (76:50–70, 92–96)
• Vision of the terrestrial kingdom (76:71–80, 97)
• Vision of the telestial kingdom (76:81–89, 98–112)

KINGDOMS OF GLORY AND PERDITION

- Some comparisons regarding the kingdoms of glory (76:62, 70–71, 76–77, 82, 86–88, 91, 97, 101)
  - Conclusion (76:113–19)

The Lord's delight in honoring the faithful

After declaring that "his purposes fail not, neither are there any who can stay his hand" (76:3), the Lord promises great blessings to those who "serve [him] in righteousness and in truth unto the end" (76:5). Those promises include not only eternal glory in the hereafter but abundant revelations here on earth—hidden mysteries, his will pertaining to his kingdom, the wonders of eternity, knowing of things to come, wisdom, understanding to reach to heaven, the secrets of his will, "even those things which eye has not seen, nor ear heard, nor yet entered into the heart of man" (76:10).

Vision of the Father and the Son

Early in the vision Joseph and Sidney were privileged to see the Father and the Son and "holy angels, and them who are sanctified before his throne, worshiping God, and the Lamb" (76:21). They heard "the voice bearing record" that Jesus is "the Only Begotten of the Father," that he is the creator of worlds, and that he is the Savior of the inhabitants of those worlds. Speaking of Christ, the voice bore record that it is "by him, and through him, and of him" that the inhabitants of those worlds are "begotten sons and daughters *unto* God" (76:20–24; emphasis added). It is true that all mankind are sons and daughters *of* God in the sense that their spirits were "begotten and born of heavenly parents, and reared to maturity in the eternal mansions of the Father" (First Presidency, 77). But to be "begotten sons and daughters *unto* God" requires another dimension. All must be "born again," "born of God," "born of the Spirit," "changed from their carnal and fallen state, to a state of righteousness, being redeemed of God, becoming his sons and daughters," or "they can in nowise inherit the kingdom of God" (Mosiah 27:24–26; cf. Mosiah 5:7). That spiritual rebirth is made possible "by," "through," and "of" Christ. In his poetic version of the vision, in connection with verse 24, Joseph Smith wrote:

Whose inhabitants, too, from the first to the
  last,
Are sav'd by the very same Saviour of ours;
And, of course, are begotten God's daughters
  and sons,
By the very same truths, and the very same
  pow'rs. ("Vision," 83)

Joseph and Sidney not only saw the Savior but "conversed" with him "in the heavenly vision" (76:14). Neither the content of the conversation nor the method of communication is explained in the revelation. The statement "this is the testimony, last of all, which we give of him" (76:22) means not that theirs will be the last testimony ever to be given but that their testimony is the last, or latest, of many that had been given to that time.

Lucifer's rebellion in the premortal world

Lucifer means "shining one or light-bringer." Before he rebelled and became SATAN (Moses 4:4), the devil was known as "Lucifer, a son of the morning," and was "an angel of God who was in authority in the presence of God" (76:25–26). "A son of the morning" could refer to the light he once possessed in the premortal world; it may also indicate that he was among the early-born spirits there or that he was one of "the noble and great ones" (Abr. 3:22) as a premortal spirit before his rebellion. Not content with whatever status and authority he had, Lucifer envied JESUS CHRIST, who was the "Firstborn" (93:21) and "Chosen from the beginning" (Moses 4:2) to be the Savior of the world. Lucifer wanted desperately to be the Savior, but on his own terms, which included stripping mankind of AGENCY as well as taking to himself the power and place of God the Father (Moses 4:1–4). Those terms were neither acceptable nor possible in God's eternal plan of salvation. Denied his goal, Lucifer rebelled against God, "and also a third part of the hosts of heaven turned he away from [God] because of their agency; and they were thrust down [into the earth], and thus came the devil and his angels" (29:36–37; Rev. 12:7–10). After his rebellion, Lucifer was known as "Perdition," "Satan," and "that old serpent." He "maketh war with the saints of God, and encompasseth them round about" (76:29). His goal is "to deceive and to blind men, and to lead them captive at his will, even as many as [will] not hearken unto [God's] voice" (76:26–29; Moses 4:4). He has dedicated his total effort to making all men "miserable like unto himself" (2 Ne. 2:18, 27). *See* Premortal existence; War in heaven.

The suffering of those who qualify in mortality to become sons of perdition

The voice of the Lord spoke the words now recorded in 76:40–42 while Joseph Smith and Sidney Rigdon watched in vision. They learned that individuals do not become SONS OF PERDITION because of lack of knowledge or through deception. Having received the Holy Spirit, having known and experienced the power of God, they, like those who followed Lucifer in his rebellion in premortal life "because of their agency" (29:36), have "suffered themselves through the power of the devil to be overcome, and to deny the truth and defy [God's] power" (76:31). They deny Christ himself, "having crucified him unto themselves and put him to an open shame" (76:35). Putting Christ to an open shame includes deliberate, defiant, flagrant, public violation of the truths and principles exemplified and taught by the Savior. "They cannot be redeemed from their spiritual fall, because they repent not; for they love darkness rather than light" (29:44–45). Nothing can be done to save them. "That which breaketh a law, and abideth not by law, but seeketh to become a law unto itself, and willeth to abide in sin, and altogether abideth in sin, cannot be sanctified by law, neither by mercy, justice, nor judgment. Therefore, they must remain filthy still" (88:35). It would have been better for them never to have been born (76:32), never to have left the premortal world where they shared goodness, light, and truth with heavenly parents and siblings. Instead, they become "vessels of wrath, doomed to suffer the wrath of God, with the devil and his angels in eternity" (76:33).

Sons of perdition are the only ones who suffer the second DEATH, a spiritual death, "an everlasting death as to things pertaining unto righteousness" (Alma 12:32; cf. 76:37). Those who qualify in mortality to become sons of perdition will be resurrected, as all mortals will be, but sons of perdition will not be redeemed from HELL into a kingdom of any glory (76:38–39, 44; 88:32; 1 Cor. 15:22; Alma 11:41; 12:15–18). They are the only ones who will not be "saved" (76:42–44). Although the word *saved* is often used to mean exaltation, it is also used to refer to all those who are redeemed from hell, including those who go to the telestial kingdom (76:88). The context in which the word *saved* is used is important in determining which meaning is intended. Sons of perdition "shall go away into everlasting punishment, which is endless punishment, which is eternal punishment . . . where their worm dieth not, and the fire is not quenched" (76:44). *See* Punish, punished, punishment.

As to the final disposition of sons of perdition, the revelation says, "The end thereof, neither the place thereof, nor their torment, no man knows." Though the Lord shows their suffering by vision to "many," the vision is "straightway" shut up again, so that the end, width, height, depth, and misery thereof is known only by those "who are made partakers thereof," those "who are ordained unto this condemnation" (76:45–48). *Ordained* in this instance simply means "consigned." Given these statements by the Lord, speculation concerning the final destiny of sons of perdition seems an unproductive enterprise.

Celestial kingdom

It should be noted that section 76, when speaking of the celestial kingdom, refers only to the highest degree of that kingdom. Doctrine and Covenants 131:1 teaches that "in the celestial glory there are three heavens or degrees." To obtain the highest degree requires obedience to "the new and everlasting covenant of marriage." Without that covenant, persons may enter into one of the two lower degrees of the celestial kingdom, "but that is the end of [their] kingdom; [they] cannot have an increase"; they cannot be exalted; they cannot become GODS (131:2–4; 132:15–26). Section 76 says of those who are celestial: "They shall overcome all things"; "they are gods, . . . wherefore, all things are theirs" (76:58–60). Ultimately made equal in "power, and in might, and in dominion," they "see as they are seen, and know as they are known, having received of [God's] fulness and of his grace" (76:94–95). Such individuals have no guile, no hidden agendas, no privately held views of one another; rather, they are open, honest, and enjoy godlike relationships. They are members of the "church of Enoch, and of the Firstborn," having acquired the "power of godliness" through the ordinances of the holy priesthood "after the order of Melchizedek, which was after the order of Enoch, which was after the order of the Only Begotten Son" (84:19–21; 76:54–57, 67). They qualify to come forth in the resurrection of the just, the "first fruits" of the resurrection, and to come with Christ "in the clouds of heaven" when he returns "to reign on the earth over his people" (88:98; 76:63–65). They come to Mount Zion, "unto the city of the living God, the heavenly place, the holiest of all" (76:66).

To qualify for celestial blessings they must receive both the testimony of Jesus and the GOSPEL. The testimony of Jesus comes as a spiritual witness from the Holy Ghost to those who seek with honest hearts (1 Cor. 12:3; James 1:5; Moses 1:24; 5:9; Moro. 10:4–5). To receive the gospel means to believe, or have faith, in Jesus Christ; to repent; to receive the gift of the Holy Ghost; and to overcome all obstacles by faithful, sustained obedience to the commandments 39:5–6; 3 Ne. 11:32–40; 27:13–22). Those who meet these requirements are "cleansed from all their sins" and are "sealed by the Holy Spirit of promise" (76:51–53). They are "just men made perfect"; they do not make themselves perfect. Though they have learned to live in harmony with the laws of God (that is, they have become "just") they must be absolved from former sins and mistakes to be considered perfect. And it is by the GRACE of God, through the ATONEMENT of Jesus Christ, that those former sins are remitted and just souls are thus made perfect (76:69).

Evidently, being made perfect, being justified according to eternal laws of heaven, does not mean everyone will immediately and simultaneously have conferred on them a fulness of "all things"—"power," "might," and "dominion" (76:58–60, 95; 132:20). Celestial beings who are resurrected or "quickened by a *portion* of the celestial glory shall then receive

of the same, even a fulness" (88:29; emphasis added). President Joseph Fielding Smith said, "To be 'made equal in power, and in might, and in dominion,' does not mean that all shall advance with equal rapidity to perfection, but that the means are given to them as sons of God by which they may obtain this fulness" (*Modern*, 58). The Prophet Joseph Smith taught the same principle: "When you climb up a ladder, you must begin at the bottom, and ascend step by step, until you arrive at the top; and so it is with the principles of the gospel—you must begin with the first, and go on until you learn all the principles of exaltation. But it will be a great while after you have passed through the veil before you will have learned them. It is not all to be comprehended in this world; it will be a great work to learn our salvation and exaltation even beyond the grave" (*History*, 6:306–7).

Terrestrial kingdom

Doctrine and Covenants 76:71–80 identifies those who receive the terrestrial glory as the following:

• Those "who died without law" (72)

• "Spirits of men kept in prison, whom the Son visited, and preached the gospel unto them, that they might be judged according to men in the flesh; who received not the testimony of Jesus in the flesh, but afterwards received it" (73–74)

• "Honorable men of the earth, who were blinded by the craftiness of men" (75)

• "They who are not valiant in the testimony of Jesus" (79)

The characteristics identified in these categories are neither absolutely definitive nor comprehensive. For instance, not all those who died without the law, meaning the gospel, will go to the terrestrial kingdom. Some will receive the gospel in the postmortal spirit world and qualify for the celestial kingdom (137:7–9; 138:30–37, 58–59). Others who died without law, who are unrepentant liars, sorcerers, and adulterers, will go to the telestial kingdom (76:103). These verses do not address the issue of those who die having been taught the gospel and who have even professed belief in it but who still earn only a terrestrial reward because they did not live the gospel beyond a terrestrial level of righteousness—they may have received gospel ordinances and been among the "honorable men of the earth" (76:75) but did not meet the requirement of "keeping the commandments" according to the "law of a celestial kingdom" (76:52–53; 88:21–22). In this regard, there is nothing in these verses to say that those who attain the terrestrial kingdom "received," that is, obeyed, the gospel either in mortality or in the postmortal spirit world. The revelation says they received a testimony of Jesus, yet a clear distinction is made in section 76 between "the testimony of Jesus" and "the gospel"—the gospel being the truths and ordinances that would qualify them for the celestial kingdom (76:82, 101). It appears that those individuals described in verses 73 and 74 received a testimony of Jesus in the postmortal spirit world but were not valiant in that testimony (76:79) sufficient to accept the fulness of the gospel there. The same terrestrial reward, evidently, awaits those who received a testimony of Jesus during mortality and who are "honorable men of the earth" (76:75) but whose testimony of Jesus likewise did not motivate them to accept and obey the fulness of the gospel (138:30–37, 57–58).

Although all the information that might be desired is not included in 76:71–80, enough is revealed to present a general profile of terrestrial personalities—honorable souls who have a testimony of Jesus but who do not choose to receive the fulness of the gospel.

Telestial kingdom

Just as those who love and obey the truth with all their hearts and receive celestial rewards and those who are honorable men who receive a testimony of Jesus but are not valiant enough in that testimony to receive the gospel are given terrestrial rewards, so those who choose to live wickedly, rejecting both Christ and the gospel thus consign themselves to telestial rewards. As the glory of the sun and moon vastly outshines the glory of the stars, so the glory of the celestial and terrestrial kingdoms vastly outshines the glory of the telestial kingdom. But the telestial kingdom is, nonetheless, a kingdom of some glory, unlike the darkness of perdition, which is not a kingdom of any glory (88:24). All telestial inhabitants will not be of the same glory. Paul

taught, "For one star differeth from another star in glory. So also is the resurrection of the dead" (1 Cor. 15:41–42).

Those who will be in the telestial kingdom are the following:

- "They who received not the gospel of Christ, neither the testimony of Jesus" (82)
- "They who deny not the Holy Spirit" (83)
- They who "say they are some of one and some of another"—some of Paul, or Apollos, or Cephas, or Christ, or John, or Moses, or Elias, or Esaias, or Isaiah, or Enoch; "but received not the gospel, neither the testimony of Jesus, neither the prophets, neither the everlasting covenant" (99–101)
- "They who are liars, and sorcerers, and adulterers, and whoremongers, and whosoever loves and makes a lie" (103; Rev. 22:15 adds murderers)

Although inhabitants of the telestial kingdom may claim allegiance to Christ or to one or another of his authorized servants, they do not receive a true witness of Jesus Christ as the Redeemer and Savior of mankind. In a sense, each of them "walketh in his own way, and after the image of his own god, whose image is in the likeness of the world" (1:16). That "world" includes the sins listed in verse 103. As wicked as they are, however, they "deny not the Holy Spirit" (76:83). To deny the Holy Spirit "after having received it" is to become a son of perdition. Those who are consigned to the telestial kingdom do not qualify as sons of perdition. They have never known and been made partakers of the power of God through the power of the Holy Ghost sufficiently to deny it and rebel against it, and thus become sons of perdition. They cannot deny that which they have never received (76:31–36).

The vision makes clear that those in the telestial kingdom are "heirs of salvation" (76:88); that they "shall be servants of the Most High" (76:112); that, although they cannot go where God and Christ dwell, they will receive "of the Holy Spirit" (76:86); and that the glory of the telestial kingdom "surpasses all understanding" (76:89). A period of suffering in hell will be required to qualify unrepentant liars, sorcerers, adulterers, whoremongers, and those who not only lie but who revel in it for citizenship in the telestial kingdom. "These are they who are thrust down to hell" (76:84). Their spirits are called up, judged unworthy of RESURRECTION at the beginning of the MILLENNIUM, and then "cast down to hell," to suffer personally for their sins—sins Christ would have paid for had they repented (88:100; 76:106; 19:15–18). They are not "redeemed from the devil until the last resurrection," at the end of the Millennium (76:85; 88:101). Their suffering will entail a humbling, cleansing process. They will be brought to "bow the knee" and "confess to him who sits upon the throne" that "he is God" and "his judgments are just" (76:110; Mosiah 16:1; 27:31). Their obeisance and confession, and their suffering, made efficacious by virtue of the atonement of Jesus Christ, will satisfy the demands of JUSTICE and cleanse them. No longer liars, sorcerers, whoremongers, and so forth and having complied with "the law of a telestial kingdom" (88:24), they shall be brought out of hell, resurrected, and placed in the telestial kingdom. Of them Charles W. Penrose, later to become an apostle and counselor in the First Presidency, wrote in 1897: "Those who were cast down to the depths for their sins, who rejected the gospel of Jesus, who persecuted the saints, who reveled in iniquity, who committed all manner of transgressions except the unpardonable crime, will also come forth in the Lord's time, through the blood of the Lamb and the ministry of His disciples and their own repentance and willing acceptance of divine law, and enter into the various degrees of glory and power and progress and light, according to their different capacities and adaptabilities. They cannot go up into the society of the Father nor receive of the presence of the Son, but will have ministrations of messengers from the terrestrial world, and have joy beyond all expectations and the conception of uninspired mortal minds. They will all bow the knee to Christ and serve God the Father, and have an eternity of usefulness and happiness in harmony with the higher powers. They receive the telestial glory" (74–75). Joseph and Sidney saw that "the inhabitants of the telestial world . . . were as innumerable as the stars in the firmament of heaven, or as the sand upon the seashore" (76:109).

Some comparisons of the kingdoms of glory

• The difference in the glory of the kingdoms is likened to the difference in glory of the sun, or celestial; the moon, or terrestrial; and the stars, or telestial (76:70–71, 91–92, 96–98).

• Those in the celestial kingdom will "dwell in the presence of God and his Christ forever and ever" (76:62); those in the terrestrial kingdom will receive of "the presence of the Son," and of "the Holy Spirit," "but not of the fulness of the Father" "through the ministration of the celestial" (76:76–77, 86–87); those in the telestial kingdom will receive "of the Holy Spirit through the ministration of the terrestrial," "the administering of angels . . . who are appointed to be ministering spirits for them" (76:86, 88).

• A clear distinction is made in section 76 between "the testimony of Jesus" and "the gospel" (vv. 82, 101). Those in the celestial kingdom are those who received both the testimony of Jesus and the gospel (76:51–52); those in the terrestrial kingdom received the testimony of Jesus but were not valiant in that testimony or in receiving the gospel (76:73–74, 79); those in the telestial kingdom "received not the gospel of Christ, neither the testimony of Jesus" (76:82, 101).

Conclusion

The vision throws a flood of light on mankind's eternal possibilities. Rather than one heaven and one hell where all are either "saved" or "damned" to the same degree, this revelation affirms that there are eternal rewards commensurate with every level of obedience or disobedience. People attain to different kingdoms of glory because God grants "unto men according to their desire" (2 Ne. 28:30; Alma 12:9–11; 29:4–8). All will end up where they truly DESIRE to be, their desire being illustrated by their willingness or unwillingness to "receive" the spiritual gifts and opportunities offered to them by a loving Heavenly Father and the Savior Jesus Christ. "For what doth it profit a man if a gift is bestowed upon him, and he receive not the gift? Behold, he rejoices not in that which is given unto him, neither rejoices in him who is the giver of the gift" (88:33). The desire of one's HEART is manifested in decisions made each moment, each day. The accumulated effect of decisions made in the premortal life, mortality, and the postmortal spirit world will bear unmistakable witness of what one desires and what level of eternal law one is willing and able to abide (64:34; 88:21–24). If, along the way, one's temporary behavior, for whatever reason, does not match the innermost desires of one's heart, provision is made in the plan of salvation for REPENTANCE and perhaps suffering to bring behavior and eternal rewards into line with the heart. And the sooner it is done, the less painful the process is (1:31–33; 19:15–20; 58:42–43; 138:30–37, 57–59; Alma 34:30–41). Although Mormon's testimony of being happy or miserable with whom one dwells in eternity speaks only of the extremes—that is, dwelling with either God or the thoroughly wicked—the principle applies at many different levels. In the final analysis, it seems that in the "merciful plan of the great Creator" (2 Ne. 9:6), each one will rise or sink through the exercise of one's own moral agency to the level of one's comfort zone.

See also Appendix A, "The Vision"; Kingdom(s); Kingdom of God/kingdom of heaven.

BIBLIOGRAPHY

First Presidency. "The Origin of Man." *Improvement Era* 13 (November 1909): 75–81; or *Ensign* 31 (February 2002): 26–30.

Penrose, Charles W. *Mormon Doctrine.* Salt Lake City: Geo. Q. Cannon and Sons Company, 1897.

Smith, Joseph. *History of The Church of Jesus Christ of Latter-day Saints.* Edited by B. H. Roberts. 7 vols. 2d ed. rev. Salt Lake City: The Church of Jesus Christ of Latter-day Saints, 1932–51.

———. "The Vision." *Times and Seasons* 4, no. 6 (1 February 1843): 83.

Smith, Joseph Fielding. *Church History and Modern Revelation.* Second Series. Salt Lake City: Deseret News Press, 1948.

LED

King Immanuel

A name-title of JESUS CHRIST. *Immanuel* means "God with us." This name-title, therefore, joins the Lord's regal authority to his ever-present association with his children, both living and dead. It appears once in the Doctrine and Covenants, where Joseph Smith exults in the restoration of the gospel and the redemption of mankind: "Brethren, shall we not go on in so great a cause? Go forward and not backward. Courage, brethren; and on, on to the victory! Let your hearts rejoice, and be exceedingly glad. Let the earth break forth into singing. Let the dead speak forth anthems of eternal praise to the King Immanuel, who hath ordained, before the world was, that which would enable us to redeem them out of their prison; for the prisoners shall go free" (128:22).

RDD

Kirtland, Ohio

Headquarters of the Church and home of the Prophet Joseph Smith, 1831 to 1837. Kirtland, Ohio, was a place of revelations and visions and of organizational and doctrinal development of the Church from 1831 to 1837. It was the center of missionary work and the place where Latter-day Saints built their first TEMPLE. In that temple members experienced the greatest pentecostal season (great spiritual outpourings, as on the day of Pentecost; Acts 2:1–18) in the history of the Church. It was also a place from which, after a period of apostasy and persecution, members left their homes and temple and moved westward in search of religious freedom.

The community was named after Judge Turhand Kirtland, a land agent of the Connecticut Land Company who surveyed and then began selling property in Connecticut's Western Reserve. This area was in the northwest corner of what is now Ohio, which had been reserved by Connecticut to give as compensation to its military veterans when other lands in the Northwest Territory were ceded to the federal government in 1786. Fourteen years later, Connecticut ceded the Western Reserve to the federal government, and it was incorporated into the Northwest Territory.

One of the earliest settlers of this wilderness was Christopher Crary, who arrived there in 1811. The population of Kirtland in 1830 was 1,000 persons, being about the same as Cleveland, and like Cleveland, it had doubled since 1820 (Backman, 23, 33–35, 38–39, 140; Prusha, 1–6, 9–16, 29–30). Although Kirtland

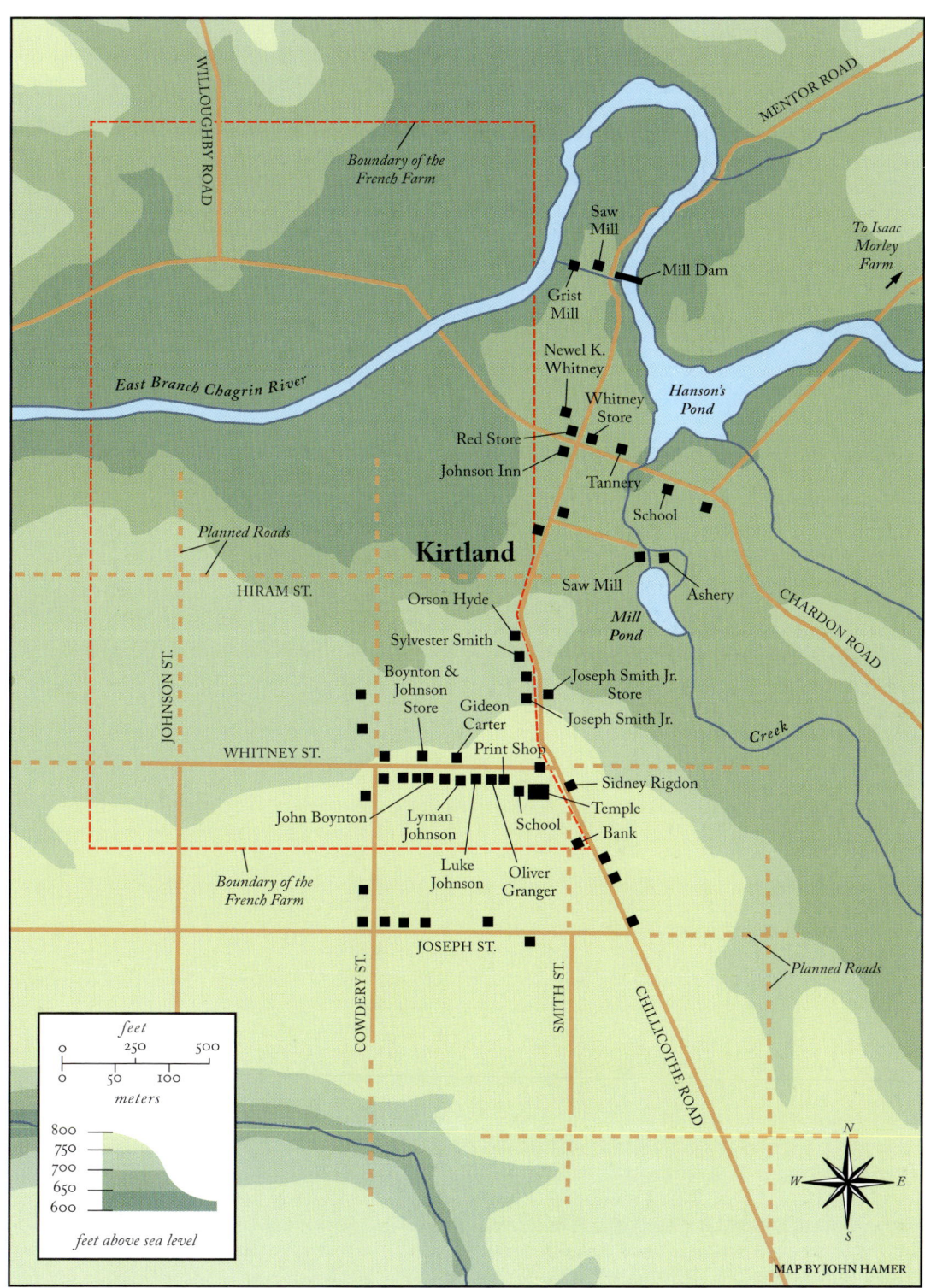

Kirtland, Ohio, in the 1830s.

Map labels:

WILLOUGHBY ROAD

MENTOR ROAD

Boundary of the French Farm

Saw Mill

Mill Dam

To Isaac Morley Farm

Grist Mill

East Branch Chagrin River

Newel K. Whitney

Hanson's Pond

Whitney Store

Red Store

Johnson Inn

Tannery

School

Kirtland

Planned Roads

HIRAM ST.

Saw Mill

Ashery

Orson Hyde

Mill Pond

CHARDON ROAD

Sylvester Smith

JOHNSON ST.

Boynton & Johnson Store

Joseph Smith Jr. Store

Gideon Carter

Joseph Smith Jr.

WHITNEY ST.

Print Shop

Creek

John Boynton

Lyman Johnson

Sidney Rigdon

School

Temple

Bank

Luke Johnson

Oliver Granger

Boundary of the French Farm

COWDERY ST.

JOSEPH ST.

SMITH ST.

CHILLICOTHE ROAD

Planned Roads

feet
0   250   500
0   50   100
meters

800
750
700
650
600

feet above sea level

N
W   E
S

MAP BY JOHN HAMER

345

continued for many decades as primarily an agricultural community, the first store and post office were established there in 1827 under the direction of A. Sidney Gilbert and Newel K. Whitney, and mills and factories were in operation there by 1830. See Gilbert and Whitney store in Kirtland, Ohio.

Six months after the Church was organized, missionaries to the LAMANITES introduced the gospel in Kirtland and other parts of the Western Reserve, and within one month there were approximately the same number of members in Kirtland and vicinity as there were in New York State. Shortly after Joseph Smith learned of the conversions in Ohio, he was instructed by the Lord to move to that state (37:3).

Except for one year when he was living in John Johnson's home in nearby Hiram, Ohio, Kirtland was home of the Prophet from February 1831 to January 1838. He received forty-six revelations in Kirtland that are included in the Doctrine and Covenants (Chronological Order of Contents). This total represents a greater number than was recorded in any other community (Anderson, 93–102; Olson, 329). The Kirtland revelations include information regarding laws of the Church (42), the prophecy on war (87), the School of the Prophets (88), the Word of Wisdom (89), and priesthood quorums and keys (107, 110).

The basic pattern of Church government was also unfolded in Kirtland with the organization of the first group of high priests and the calling of the first bishops and counselors, the first patriarch, and the first First Presidency. The first stake and high council were also organized in Kirtland, with the First Presidency serving as the stake presidency. And in 1835 the first Quorum of Twelve Apostles and the first quorums of seventy were organized in this community (Anderson, 145–52; Backman, 237–55).

A significant activity in Kirtland between 1833 and 1836 was the building of the Kirtland Temple. This was a tremendous community project directed by the First Presidency in harmony with visions and revelations they received. During this construction, Church membership increased rapidly from 150 in 1833 to about 1,300 in 1836 (Backman, 140). The temple still stands. It is owned by the Community of Christ (formerly the Reorganized Church of Jesus Christ of Latter Day Saints).

Some of the great visions of this dispensation occurred near the Morley farm in 1831, in the Newel K. Whitney store in 1833, and in the Kirtland Temple in 1836. During these visions Joseph Smith and other witnesses saw the Father, the Son, Adam, Abraham, Moses, Elias, and Elijah. Men and women testified that in addition to seeing heavenly beings, they experienced an unusual outpouring of the Spirit, including the spiritual gifts of prophesying, speaking in tongues, interpretation of tongues, and healings (Anderson, 107–13, 169–91; Backman, 240, 266–67, 284–308).

The greatest pentecostal experience in the history of the Restoration was followed by a period of apostasy and persecution. Before the end of the summer in 1838, most Latter-day Saints had fled Kirtland, moving west to Missouri.

Today, the most prominent building in the community is the Kirtland Temple, which stands near the brow of a hill overlooking a restored historic village of the 1830s. In Historic Kirtland, which was dedicated in May 2003, are various restored or rebuilt sites, including the Newel K. Whitney store, the Whitney home, a schoolhouse, the Johnson Inn, an ASHERY, a water-powered sawmill, and an auditorium that is outwardly a two-story representation of an old grist mill (Perkins and Cannon, 8–19).

See also Kirtland Temple dedication; maps, pp. 355, 461, and 710; Ohio period.

BIBLIOGRAPHY

Anderson, Karl Ricks. Joseph Smith's Kirtland: Eyewitness Accounts. Salt Lake City: Deseret Book, 1989.

Backman, Milton V., Jr. The Heavens Resound: A History of the Latter-day Saints in Ohio, 1830–1838. Salt Lake City: Deseret Book, 1983.

Olson, Earl E. "The Chronology of Ohio Revelations." BYU Studies 11, no. 3 (1971): 329–49.

Perkins, Keith W., and Donald Q. Cannon. Ohio and Illinois. Vol. 3 of Sacred Places: A Comprehensive Guide to Early LDS Historical Sites, edited by LaMar C. Berrett. Salt Lake City: Deseret Book, 2002.

Prusha, Anne B. A History of Kirtland, Ohio. Mentor, Ohio: Lakeland Community College Press, 1982.

MVB

Kirtland Temple. *See* Kirtland Temple dedication; Temple(s).

Kirtland Temple dedication

The service dedicating the Kirtland Temple, the first TEMPLE built in the DISPENSATION of the fulness of times. Eliza R. Snow recalled that "no mortal language can describe the heavenly manifestations" of that occasion. The congregation, she added, felt a "sweet spirit of love and union" (Morgan, 58, 62). Another participant, Benjamin Brown, wrote that during this dedication he had a glorious, never-to-be-forgotten experience and compared the outpouring of the Spirit on that occasion with events that took place on the day of Pentecost (10–11; Acts 2). *See* Pentecost, day of.

On Sunday, 27 March 1836, approximately three years after Latter-day Saints began building the Kirtland Temple, a large crowd gathered early in the morning in front of the building. During those three years, Church membership in Kirtland had increased from about 150 to about 1,300 (Backman, 140), and in addition many visitors were there. Between 7:00 A.M. and 8:00 A.M. Church leaders entered the building, and Joseph Smith dedicated the pulpits on the main floor of the temple.

At 8:00 A.M. the front doors were opened, and shortly thereafter the main floor was filled with eight hundred to one thousand participants. Church leaders sat in pulpits and choir members sat in the four choir lofts in the corners of the room. After all seats were occupied, Joseph Smith ordered the front doors closed. Recognizing that many were disappointed because they could not attend the dedicatory service, Joseph Smith instructed others to hold a meeting in the schoolhouse located west of the temple. He later scheduled a second dedicatory service, held the following Thursday, 31 March (Smith, *History,* 2:410–11, 433; *MA,* 274; Backman, 294–96).

The dedicatory service began at 9:00 A.M. Sidney Rigdon, who conducted the meeting, began by reading Psalms 96 and 24. He also spoke for two and a half hours, using as his main text Matthew 8:18–20. He declared that because the Kirtland Temple had been built by divine revelation, it was different from all other contemporary buildings. He also talked about the trials of the Savior during his life. A major theme of this powerful discourse was that in this modern day of science and intelligence, our Redeemer might say, "The foxes have holes, and the birds of the air have nests; but the Son of man hath not where to lay his head" (Matt. 8:20). After Sidney Rigdon's sermon, which caused many in the congregation to shed tears, he called upon all the quorums of the Church to acknowledge Joseph Smith as prophet and seer and to support him with their prayers. All quorums complied by standing as groups (Smith, *History,* 2:411–16; *MA,* 276).

After a twenty-minute midday intermission, the solemn assembly continued. Joseph Smith delivered a short address and then read the dedicatory prayer (109). Following the prayer, the congregation and the choir, located in the four corners of the building, sang with extraordinary fervor "The Spirit of God," one of five hymns written by W. W. Phelps sung during this meeting.

The sacrament of the Lord's Supper was then administered to the congregation, after which Church leaders, including Joseph Smith, Oliver Cowdery, and Sidney Rigdon, bore their testimonies. "Elder B. [Brigham] Young, one of the Twelve, gave a short address in tongues; Elder D. [David] W. Patten interpreted and gave a short exhortation in tongues himself" (*MA,* 281). Joseph Smith, Frederick G. Williams, David Whitmer, Truman Angell, and Heber C. Kimball testified that during this meeting they saw an angel or angels (Smith, *Writings,* 212–13; *History,* 2:416–18, 420, 426–28; Backman, 298–300).

The congregation "sealed the proceedings of the day" with the Hosanna Shout "by shouting hosanna, hosanna, hosanna to God and the Lamb, three times, sealing it each time with amen, amen, and amen" (Smith, *History,* 2:427–28; *Writings,* 213). The service concluded about 4:00 P.M. (*MA,* 281).

"For the benefit of those who could not get into the house on the preceding Sabbath," a second dedicatory service was held on Thursday, 31 March. The "services of the day were commenced, prosecuted and terminated in the same manner as at the former dedication, and the Spirit of God rested upon the congregation, and great solemnity prevailed" (Smith, *History*, 2:433).

See also Historical context and overview of Doctrine and Covenants 109 (p. 817); Ohio period.

BIBLIOGRAPHY

Backman, Milton V., Jr. *The Heavens Resound: A History of the Latter-day Saints in Ohio, 1830–1838.* Salt Lake City: Deseret Book, 1983.

Brown, Benjamin. *Testimonies for the Truth.* Liverpool, England, 1853.

Latter-day Saints' Messenger and Advocate 2, no. 6 (March 1836): 281.

Morgan, Nicholas G., comp. *Eliza R. Snow, an Immortal: Selected Writings.* Salt Lake City: Nicholas G. Morgan Sr. Foundation, 1957.

Smith, Joseph. *History of The Church of Jesus Christ of Latter-day Saints.* Edited by B. H. Roberts. 7 vols. 2d ed. rev. Salt Lake City: The Church of Jesus Christ of Latter-day Saints, 1932–51.

———. *Personal Writings of Joseph Smith.* Compiled and edited by Dean C. Jessee. Rev. ed. Salt Lake City: Deseret Book, 2002.

MVB

Knight, Joseph, Sr.

Birth: 3 November 1772, Oakham, Worcester County, Massachusetts

Death: 2 February 1847, Iowa Territory

While farming and milling in Colesville, Broome County, New York, in 1827, Joseph Knight Sr. employed and lodged Joseph Smith Jr. as a hired hand. Knight and some family members believed Joseph Smith's account about visitations from the angel Moroni. Knight assisted Joseph Smith to court Emma Hale, whom Joseph had met while he was lodging at the Hale home earlier in Harmony, Pennsylvania. Knight also provided him and Oliver Cowdery food and paper during the Book of Mormon translation efforts in 1829. In May 1829 Knight asked Joseph Smith to inquire of the Lord how he should assist the Lord's work. Section 12 came in response, instructing Knight to "keep my commandments, and seek to bring forth and establish the cause of Zion" (12:6). He was told that if he asked he would receive and that

Joseph Knight Sr., 1772–1847.

Courtesy Church History Library

those who desire to reap the prepared harvest are called to the work.

In April 1830, as a result of earnest desires by Knight and four other men, Joseph Smith inquired of the Lord and received section 23. Verses 6–7 manifested to Knight that he must take up his cross and "pray vocally before the world as well as in secret, and in [his] family, and among [his] friends, and in all places" (23:6). Knight's duty also was to "unite with the true church" and exhort continually, in order to receive "the reward of the laborer" (23:7).

Joseph Knight and his wife, Polly Peck Knight, their seven children, and members of their extended families were baptized during 1830 and became the COLESVILLE BRANCH, numbering about sixty members (who were the subjects of several revelations). Knight arranged for lawyer friends to defend Joseph Smith during court hearings in 1830. With the Colesville Branch, Knight moved early in 1831 to Thompson, Geauga County, Ohio, and then to Kaw Township, Jackson County, Missouri, by late July 1831. Polly died soon after the family arrived in Missouri.

Joseph Knight moved to Clay County,

Missouri, in 1833, where he married Phebe Crosby Peck, widow of Benjamin Peck, a brother of Polly Peck Knight. Joseph Knight moved to Caldwell County, Missouri, in 1837 and to Nauvoo, Illinois, by 1840. He was ordained a high priest in Nauvoo. In August 1842, Joseph Smith wrote about the "faithful few" who had helped lay the foundation of the Church and stood by him in every hour of peril, specifically his "beloved brother" Father Knight, who had been "faithful and true" for the previous fifteen years (5:124). Joseph Knight left Nauvoo during the exodus and died at Mt. Pisgah (now Union County), Iowa Territory.

BIBLIOGRAPHY

Hartley, William G. *Stand by My Servant Joseph: The Story of the Joseph Knight Family and the Restoration.* Provo, Utah: Joseph Fielding Smith Institute for Latter-day Saint History; Salt Lake City: Deseret Book, 2003.

Smith, Joseph. *History of the Church of Jesus Christ of Latter-day Saints.* Edited by B. H. Roberts. 7 vols. 2d ed. rev. Salt Lake City: The Church of Jesus Christ of Latter-day Saints, 1932–51.

WGH

Knight, Newel

Birth: 13 September 1800, Marborough, Windham County, Vermont

Death: 11 January 1847, in wilderness (now Niobrara, Nebraska)

While Joseph Smith Jr. worked in 1827 for Newel Knight's parents, Joseph and Polly Peck Knight, in Colesville, New York, he told Newel Knight about the visits from Moroni, and Newel believed him. In spring 1830, Joseph Smith performed the first miracle in the Church by casting a devil out of Newel Knight. Soon thereafter Knight was baptized by David Whitmer. Knight and his wife, Sally Colburn Knight, were among approximately sixty Knight relatives baptized in 1830 who became the COLESVILLE BRANCH. Late that year Knight became president of the Colesville Branch. Early in 1831, in response to a commandment (38:32), he led the branch to Ohio, where revelation (51) directed that they settle in Thompson, Ohio. There they attempted to live the law of CONSECRATION as outlined in section 42.

During June 1831, Joseph Smith received three revelations relating to Newel Knight's

callings and to his branch's problems involving land ownership. At a Church conference held during the first week in June near Kirtland, the first ordinations to the office of HIGH PRIEST took place (Smith, 1:175–79). Knight was one of the elders in attendance. At the close of the conference, on 7 June, a revelation (52) directed that certain men be paired to go forth preaching, and specifically that Knight, already an elder, be ordained (52:32), which may mean he was to be ordained a high priest, and take his journey with Selah Griffin.

Meanwhile, Church members at Thompson, most of them members of the Colesville Branch, were divided on questions regarding the consecration of properties. Knight and other branch members asked Joseph Smith how to proceed. He inquired of the Lord and received a revelation that gave directions for the Church at Thompson (54). It instructed Knight to "stand fast in the office whereunto I have appointed you." Because the covenant of consecration had been broken, the Saints at Thompson were told to "flee the land," journey to Missouri, select leaders, and in Missouri "seek ye a living like unto men" rather than consecrating, until directed otherwise (54:2, 7, 9).

Because that group insisted that Knight continue to be their leader (Hartley, 119), a revelation on 15 June (56) revoked his missionary call. It assigned Thomas Marsh to replace him as Griffin's companion, and instructed Knight to lead the Saints at Thompson, Ohio, to Missouri.

Knight moved with those Saints to Kaw Township in Jackson County, Missouri, by late July 1831. After they were forced from Jackson County late in 1833, Knight settled in Clay County. When a stake was created there in 1834, he became a member of its high council. His wife, Sally, died in 1834, after which Knight, by assignment, returned to Kirtland to help build the temple. While he was there, Joseph Smith performed the marriage of Newel Knight to Lydia Goldthwaite Bailey. Knight attended the temple dedications and then returned to Missouri. In 1837 he moved to Caldwell County, where he was a miller and millwright. He served on the Far West stake high council. Early in 1839, forced from Missouri, he relocated to Nauvoo, where he built and operated mills. On 19 January 1841, a revelation (124:131–32) lists him as a member of the Nauvoo high council.

In April 1846, during the Saints' exodus from Nauvoo, Brigham Young assigned Knight and his family to a company that, unable to reach the Rocky Mountains that season, wintered among Ponca Indians on the Niobrara River in northern Nebraska. There Knight was a member of the high council until his death in January 1847.

See also Historical context and overview of Doctrine and Covenants 54 (p. 759).

BIBLIOGRAPHY

Hartley, William G. *Stand by My Servant Joseph: The Joseph Knight Family and the Restoration.* Provo, Utah: Joseph Fielding Smith Institute for Latter-day Saint History; Salt Lake City: Deseret Book, 2003.

Knight, Newel. Journals and Autobiography. Church History Library, The Church of Jesus Christ of Latter-day Saints, Salt Lake City, Utah.

———. "Newel Knight's Journal." In *Scraps of Biography: Tenth Book of the Faith-Promoting Series.* Salt Lake City: Juvenile Instructor Office, 1883. Reprinted in *Classic Experiences and Adventures.* Salt Lake City: Bookcraft, 1969.

Smith, Joseph. *History of The Church of Jesus Christ of Latter-day Saints.* Edited by B. H. Roberts. 7 vols. 2d ed. rev. Salt Lake City: The Church of Jesus Christ of Latter-day Saints, 1932–51.

WGH

Knight, Vinson

Birth: 14 March 1804, Norwich, Hampshire County, Massachusetts

Death: 31 July 1842, Nauvoo, Hancock County, Illinois

One evening in 1834, Vinson Knight was resting on a buffalo robe in his home in Perrysburg, New York, when two men knocked at the door and introduced themselves as Parley P. Pratt and Joseph Smith. The Knights had no interest in their message, but because of the late hour, they invited the men to stay. The conversation begun by the two visitors intrigued the family and led to their baptism in the spring of 1834. By 1835 Vinson Knight and his family had moved to Kirtland, Ohio.

In 1836, Knight became a counselor to Bishop Newel K. Whitney and later, after relocating to Missouri, he served as bishop pro tem in Adam-ondi-Ahman. After leaving Missouri in 1839, Knight was designated a Church agent to purchase land in Illinois and Iowa. In that same year he was called to serve as bishop of the lower ward in Commerce. In an 1841 revelation, the Lord commanded him to "put stock into" the Nauvoo House and with Samuel H. Smith and Shadrach Roundy "to preside over the bishopric" in Nauvoo (124:74, 141). He was instructed to "lift up his voice long and loud . . . to plead the cause of the poor and the needy." Faithfulness would bring the Lord's acceptance of his offering. His family was to "rejoice and turn away their hearts from affliction," for the Lord had "chosen him and anointed him," and would forgive him of his sins—he was to be "honored in the midst of his house" (124:75–76). Faithful to the end of his life, Knight served as a member of the Nauvoo city council and a regent of the University of Nauvoo. He died in Nauvoo of typhoid fever at age thirty-eight.

BIBLIOGRAPHY

Biographies of Vinson Knight and Abigail Meade McBride and copies of letters obtained from a descendant of Rispah Lee Knight. Church History Library, The Church of Jesus Christ of Latter-day Saints, Salt Lake City, Utah.

RC

Knowledge

That which can be learned through revelation, study, or experience. The Lord stated, "And truth is knowledge of things as they are, and as they were, and as they are to come" (93:24). The pursuit of knowledge is essential for salvation, for the Lord has declared, "It is impossible for a man to be saved in ignorance" (131:6; cf. 50:40).

How to gain spiritual knowledge

Joseph Smith was promised by the Lord that through the HOLY GHOST he would receive knowledge "that has not been revealed since the world was until now" (121:26). Several verses in the Doctrine and Covenants identify personal traits and actions that are essential to receiving knowledge from the Lord. For example, humility (1:28), prayer, faith, an honest heart (8:1;

cf. 10:52; 42:61); and diligence and obedience (130:19). The Lord promised those who obey the WORD OF WISDOM "great treasures of knowledge, even hidden treasures" (89:19). Those who preach the gospel are assured, "As the dews of Carmel, so shall the knowledge of God descend upon them" (128:19). *See* Dews of Carmel.

Knowledge and the priesthood

The Melchizedek Priesthood holds "the key of the mysteries of the kingdom, even the key of the knowledge of God" (84:19). *See* Keys.

The "sealing and binding power" that makes sacred ordinances efficacious in the heavens is inherent in the "keys of the kingdom, which consist in the key of knowledge" (128:14). For the prophet and president of the Church, who holds and exercises every key of the Melchizedek Priesthood, "there is no difficulty in obtaining a knowledge of facts in relation to the salvation of the children of men, both as well for the dead as for the living" (128:11). Any power or influence of the priesthood should be exercised, along with other virtues, by "pure knowledge" (121:41–42), meaning unadulterated, or perhaps revealed, knowledge.

The Lord stated that the Quorum of the Twelve Apostles and the Seventy are to seek unanimity in making their decisions with, among other virtues, knowledge (107:30). As a blessing for their diligence in acting according to the Christlike attributes identified in verse 30, quorum members "shall not be unfruitful in the knowledge of the Lord" (107:31).

Knowledge and accountability

The revelations refer to knowledge in connection with ACCOUNTABILITY. For example, those who have knowledge of the scriptures will be judged according to that which is written in them (20:13). The Lord also said, "And, again, I say unto you, that whoso having knowledge, have I not commanded to repent?" (29:49).

The importance of both spiritual and temporal knowledge

The Doctrine and Covenants bears witness of the importance of restoring a knowledge of the covenants the Lord made with ancient peoples, so that their descendants, such as the LAMANITES, "might come to the knowledge of their fathers, and that they might know the promises of the Lord, and that they may believe the gospel and rely upon the merits of Jesus Christ, . . . that through their repentance they might be saved" (3:16–20).

In addition to spiritual knowledge, the Lord commanded the Saints to seek knowledge "in all things that pertain unto the kingdom of God, that are expedient for you to understand," including secular knowledge (88:78–79). The purpose of having such knowledge is so that they can be "prepared in all things" when they are sent out to "warn the people" of impending judgments (88:80–91; cf. 4:6). Joseph Smith and other members of the First Presidency were similarly instructed: "It is my will that you should . . . obtain a knowledge of history, and of countries, and of kingdoms, of laws of God and man, and all this for the salvation of Zion" (93:53). In addition, the Saints were told to gather "up a knowledge of all the facts" concerning the persecutions and sufferings they had endured at the hands of their Missouri persecutors to present to government officials for redress (123:1–6).

The revelation explaining the gifts of the Spirit affirms that "the word of knowledge" is a spiritual gift, given so "that all may be taught to be wise and to have knowledge" (46:18). The Lord reminds all that knowledge gained in this life provides advantages in the world to come (130:18–19).

See also Learning.

DJG

My son Orson, hearken and hear and behold what I, the Lord God, shall say unto you, even Jesus Christ your Redeemer; the **light** and the life of the world, a light which shineth in darkness and the darkness comprehendeth it not; who so loved the world that he gave his own life, that as many as would believe might become the sons of God. Wherefore you are my son. 34:1–3

Laban

Custodian of the "record of the Jews . . . engraven upon plates of brass" (1 Ne. 3:3) in Jerusalem at the time of the prophets Jeremiah and Lehi. It is this record that Lehi sent his sons back to Jerusalem to obtain before proceeding to the promised land (1 Ne. 3:1–7; 4:1–38; 5:14). In the Doctrine and Covenants, Laban is mentioned once, in connection with his SWORD, with which Nephi killed him (1 Ne. 4:7–18; 2 Ne. 5:14) and which Oliver Cowdery, David Whitmer, and Martin Harris were promised, by their faith, to be able to see, along with the plates, the breastplate, the Urim and Thummim, and "the miraculous directors," the Liahona (17:1–2; cf. Jacob 1:10; W of M 1:13; Mosiah 1:16).

DKO

Laden. *See* Appendix E.

Lake of fire and brimstone. *See* Fire.

Lamanite mission. *See* Historical context and overview of Doctrine and Covenants 32 (p. 740); Lamanites.

Lamanites

The name *Lamanite* derives from the name of a group of Book of Mormon people who followed Laman and Lemuel, the two eldest sons of Lehi, in a rebellion against their younger brother Nephi (2 Ne. 5:1–25). The name distinguished this group from those who remained loyal to Nephi and who became known as Nephites (Jacob 1:13–14). The distinctions between these two groups became blurred as the years passed, as some Lamanites converted to the Nephites and some Nephites dissented to the Lamanites (Alma 23:8–18; 3 Ne. 2:14–16; Alma 47:36). For about two hundred years after the resurrected Savior's ministry among them, the Nephites and Lamanites became a united people, and there were no "Lamanites, nor any manner of -ites" among them (4 Ne. 1:17). When the name *Lamanite* again appears in the record, it is adopted by a group who rebelled against the Church of Christ (4 Ne. 1:20) and who were, apparently, descendants of all who had been part of the earlier Book of Mormon history.

The Doctrine and Covenants seems to confirm this amalgamation in its listing of the descendants of Lehi who would be brought to a true knowledge of the Savior through the testimony of the Book of Mormon, identifying them as Nephites, Jacobites, Josephites, Zoramites, Lamanites, Lemuelites, and Ishmaelites and then seemingly grouping all of them under the term *Lamanites* (3:16–20). These groups are among the ancestors of the American Indians. The Lord also refers to the Lamanites as a remnant of the JEWS (19:27; 57:4; cf. 2 Ne. 30:3–5). This may, in part, acknowledge the genealogical effect of the uniting of the people of Zarahemla with the Nephites about 200 B.C. (Omni 1:14–19). The people of Zarahemla had journeyed to the Americas with Mulek, a son of Zedekiah, king of the Jews (Hel. 6:10).

The name *Lamanite*, when applied to latter-day descendants of the Book of Mormon people, appears to include all who have survived to modern times and who have remained in the Americas. Specifically indicated are those among the tribes of the American Indians (30:5–6; 54:8).

Lamanites to blossom as a rose

The Lord promised Book of Mormon prophets and disciples of Jesus Christ that the time would come when the gospel would be taken to their descendants in the latter days by way of the Book of Mormon (10:46–48; Enos 1:13–18). The Lord affirmed in modern times that the promise would be fulfilled (3:16–20) when the Lamanites, who had become a "fallen" people (20:9; 109:65–67), would respond to the gospel message and would blossom as a rose (49:24).

Mission to the Lamanites

In September 1830 the Lord directed that a mission be undertaken to the Lamanites. Oliver Cowdery was appointed by revelation to lead this mission (28:8–9, 14). Peter Whitmer Jr., Parley P. Pratt, and Ziba Peterson were later assigned to accompany Oliver (30:5–6; 32:1–3). This became one of the first official missions undertaken by the Church. The first Native Americans encountered by these missionaries were an encampment of the Catteraugus tribe near Buffalo, New York. Copies of the Book of Mormon were left with tribal members who could read. Moving westward, the missionaries stopped at Kirtland, Ohio, where Parley P. Pratt had formerly been associated with a group known as the Disciples of Christ, or Campbellites. Sidney Rigdon, who lived at nearby Mentor, was the leader of this group. The missionaries taught and baptized Rigdon and a number of his congregation. One of these converts, Frederick G. Williams, accompanied the missionaries as they continued their journey westward.

The missionaries spent several days among the Wyandot tribe in Sandusky, Ohio, before traveling on to Independence, Missouri. They visited briefly with the Shawnees and then crossed the Kansas River to the Delaware Reservation. The Delaware chief and many of the tribe became greatly interested in the missionaries' message. This stirred up the envy of the Indian agents and some sectarian missionaries,

and the Latter-day Saint missionaries were required to leave the reservation because they were not officially licensed to preach there. Thus ended the first mission to the Lamanites. Although the missionaries recorded no baptisms among the Lamanites, they had "preached the gospel in its fulness, and distributed the record of their forefathers among three tribes, viz: the Catteraugus Indians, near Buffalo, N.Y., the Wyandots of Ohio, and the Delawares west of Missouri." Leaving Indian country, they "came over the line, and commenced laboring in Jackson County, Missouri, among the whites." Elder Parley P. Pratt recorded that there they "were well received, and listened to by many; and some were baptized and added to the Church" (39–44).

Remnant to vex Gentiles

In a revelation given to Joseph Smith 25 December 1832, the Lord revealed that conflicts

Mission to the Lamanites, 1830–1831.

and difficulties were to come upon the United States and other nations. In this revelation reference is made to "remnants who are left of the land," who will marshal themselves and vex the Gentiles "with a sore vexation" (87:5). While this reference to "remnants" does not specifically mention Lamanites, it is possible that they could be included in this category. Although the Doctrine and Covenants does not explain the nature of this "sore vexation," the significance of this revelation may be clarified somewhat if considered in conjunction with the following Book of Mormon references: 3 Nephi 16:10–16; 20:13–22; 21:11–24; and Mormon 5:20–24. Perhaps current and future relationships between the "Gentiles" and the "remnants" of the seed of Lehi (1 Ne. 13:34; D&C 109:65) in the Americas will make plain the fulfillment of this prophecy.

See also Borders of the Lamanites; Doctrine and Covenants, what it says about the Book of Mormon.

BIBLIOGRAPHY

Pratt, Parley P. *Autobiography of Parley P. Pratt.* Edited by Parley P. Pratt Jr. Salt Lake City: Deseret Book, 1985.

DLL

Lamb, marriage of the. *See* Marriage of the Lamb.

Lamech

Ordained PATRIARCH, son of Methuselah and father of Noah (Moses 8:5–9); he begat sons and daughters and died at age 777 (Moses 8:10–11). Lamech is the first of the early patriarchs listed in 107:39–52 to be ordained in the patriarchal order of the Melchizedek PRIESTHOOD by someone other than Adam; he was ordained at age 32 by Seth (107:51). A revelation on priesthood in the Doctrine and Covenants affirms that the patriarchal order to which Lamech was ordained was "instituted in the days of Adam, and came down by lineage" (107:39–52).

For some reason not explained in scripture, Lamech is not mentioned as being present at the family gathering at ADAM-ONDI-AHMAN (107:53–57), although genealogical lists indicate he was living at the time. The Lamech of 107:51 is not to be confused with the unrighteous Lamech of Genesis 4 and Moses 5.

RJM

Land of the living

People on the earth as opposed to those who are dead. The phrase "land of the living" occurs in Job 28:13 and Psalms 27:13 and 116:9. The Lord used this phrase when calling Frederick G. Williams to serve as a high priest and counselor to Joseph Smith in the First Presidency (81:3). Frederick was promised that he would be blessed inasmuch as he was faithful in his "ministry in proclaiming the gospel in the land of the living, and among thy brethren." The differentiation between "land of the living" and those "among thy brethren" seems to indicate that the "land of the living" in this instance refers to those who have yet to receive the gospel.

RJM

Last day(s)

"Last day" refers to the final judgment day, and "last days" refers to the last dispensation, the final time period before the second coming of the Lord.

Last day

Examples of references to the last day include the following: Saints are called to serve God with all their heart, might, mind, and strength in order to "stand blameless before God at the last day" (4:2; 5:35; 9:14; 17:8). All men who desire salvation must take upon them the name of Christ, "for in that name shall they be called at the last day" (18:23–24). Satan and his works will be destroyed "at the end of the world, and the last great day of judgment" (19:3), and telestial candidates will not be resurrected until that "great and last day" (88:102; cf. 76:81–85, 98–107).

Last days

Examples of references to the last days are the following: Prophets have spoken of terrible things the Lord will pour out on the wicked in the last days (109:45; cf. 29:14–21; 45:26–27, 31–33, 40–42; 88:87–91). Thus, disciples are chosen to raise "the voice of warning" unto all people. The Church has been established in "these last days" to facilitate taking that warning voice to the world (20:1; 1:1–39; 53:1; cf. 84:2). The name of the Savior's Church in the last days is "The Church of Jesus Christ of Latter-day Saints" (115:4). The Lord is bringing forth his word, the fulness of the gospel, and the glories of his kingdom in "the last days" (39:11; 66:2; 86:4; 128:17). Prophets in all ages have prophesied of the restoration of all things in "the last days" (27:6; 109:23). Priesthood and priesthood keys have been restored in "the last days and for the last time" (112:30–32), and righteous men hold the power of the priesthood for the gathering of God's people in "the last days" (113:6, 8). God's "arm is stretched out in the last days" to save the covenant people of Israel (136:22). Joseph Smith, as the Prophet and the president of the Church, was given the keys of sealing power in "the last days" (132:7). The Lord's agents will provide for the Saints, and the Church will sit like a judge "to judge the nations" in "these last days" (64:30, 37).

The Doctrine and Covenants testifies of other important events and principles that will be evidenced in the last days: God has cursed the waters but blessed the land (61:14, 17); "the willing and obedient shall eat the good of the land of Zion" (64:34); two prophets will be raised up to the Jewish nation (77:15; cf. Rev. 11:1–14); and the desolation of abomination will come again, this time upon the world, as it came upon the Jews in the first century A.D. (84:117; JS–M 1:12, 32). In 1833 the Lord revealed the Word of Wisdom, "showing forth the order and will of God in the temporal salvation of all saints in the last days . . . in consequence of evils and designs which do and will exist in the hearts of conspiring men in the last days" (89:2–4).

All are invited to come "and partake of the waters of life freely," with great promises to those who choose to do so (10:66–70). All are reminded that "this is a day of warning, and not a day of many words. For I, the Lord, am not to be mocked in the last days" (63:58).

See also Jesus Christ, second coming of.

DKO

Laughter

Spontaneous sounds expressing mirth, joy, amusement, scorn, ridicule, embarrassment, and so forth. The word *laughter* appears in the Doctrine and Covenants in three contexts, with three different modifiers ("much" laughter, "excessive" laughter, "all" laughter).

1. In connection with the SABBATH day. *Laughter* appears in a revelation identifying appropriate attitudes and activities for the Sabbath day. The Saints were commanded to keep the Lord's day holy through resting from their labors, going "to the house of prayer," offering up their sacraments, vows, and oblations, preparing their food "with singleness of heart," and fasting and prayer. The Lord promised, "Inasmuch as ye do these things with thanksgiving, with cheerful hearts and countenances, *not with much laughter,* for this is sin, . . . the fulness of the earth is yours" (59:9–16; emphasis added).

2. In reference to ongoing, day-to-day strivings toward sanctification. In December 1832, the Saints were commanded to "sanctify yourselves that your minds become single to God." They were invited to draw near unto God and seek him diligently, with the promise that he would draw near unto them, and even that they might see him, "in his own time, and in his own way, and according to his own will." To qualify for "the great and last promise" of seeing the Lord, the Saints were told to "cast away [their] idle thoughts and [their] *excess of laughter* far from [them]" (88:63, 68–69; emphasis added). *See* Sanctify, sanctification.

3. In regard to TEMPLE worship. The Lord commanded the Saints to "establish a house, even a house of prayer, a house of fasting, a house of faith, a house of learning, a house of glory, a house of order, a house of God," that their "incomings [and] . . . outgoings . . . [and] all [their] salutations may be in the name of the Lord." In connection with that command, he said, "Therefore, cease from all your light speeches, from *all laughter,* from all your lustful desires, from all your pride and light-mindedness" (88:119–21; emphasis added).

These instructions about laughter are a reminder that "the things of God are of deep import; and time, and experience, and careful and ponderous and solemn thoughts can only find them out" (Smith, 3:295). Nevertheless, although *excessive* laughter is to be avoided at all times, *much* laughter is not in keeping with Sabbath worship, and *all* laughter is inappropriate in sacred temple worship, the Saints are not to be gloomy, dispirited, or sad. On the contrary, "there is . . . a time to weep, and a time to laugh" (Eccl. 3:1, 4). Although laughter in connection with Sabbath worship should be controlled, the revelation says the Saints are to observe the Sabbath "with cheerful hearts and countenances" (59:15). In the midst of persecution and unlawful imprisonment, the Prophet Joseph Smith wrote, "Let us cheerfully do all things that lie in our power; and then may we stand still, with the utmost assurance, to see the salvation of God, and for his arm to be revealed" (123:17). Moreover, the Prophet taught, "Happiness is the object and design of our existence; and will be the end thereof, if we pursue the path that leads to it; and this path is virtue, uprightness, faithfulness, holiness, and keeping all the commandments of God" (5:134–35). In a revelation to Brigham Young at Winter Quarters the Lord said, "If thou art merry, praise the Lord with singing, with music, with dancing, and with a prayer of praise and thanksgiving. If thou art sorrowful, call on the Lord thy God with supplication, that your souls may be joyful" (136:28–29).

Cheerfulness, including appropriate laughter, is acceptable to the Lord. Inappropriate laughter is wrong and will be met with righteous judgment. When the Lord returns to the earth and confronts "the nations of the earth" who have rejected and scorned and mocked the Lord and the gospel message, "they that have laughed shall see their folly" and "shall be consumed" (45:49–50).

BIBLIOGRAPHY

Smith, Joseph. *History of The Church of Jesus Christ of Latter-day Saints.* Edited by B. H. Roberts. 7 vols. 2d ed. rev. Salt Lake City: The Church of Jesus Christ of Latter-day Saints, 1932–51.

NHW

Law, William

Birth: 8 September 1809, Tyrone County, Ireland

Death: 12 January 1892, Shullsburg, LaFayette County, Wisconsin

In 1836 William Law abandoned his Presbyterian leanings for the restored gospel, in spite of his father's opposition. "My father is much opposed to [Mormonism] from evil reports &c. which he has heard," he wrote (in Cook, 8). In November 1839 Law moved from Canada to Nauvoo to gather with the Latter-day Saints. With his brother Wilson as a partner, Law operated a steam mill and opened a general store in Nauvoo. In 1840 he promised Joseph Smith a hundred dollars to defray Joseph's traveling expenses to Washington, D.C. (Smith, 4:51).

In 1841, William Law was advised to buy stock in the Nauvoo House (124:82) and to remain in Illinois and "not take his family unto the eastern lands, even unto Kirtland" (124:83, 87). He was to "go and proclaim [the] everlasting gospel with a loud voice" to the inhabitants of Warsaw and Carthage, Illinois, and to those residing in Burlington and Madison, Iowa (124:88). The Lord admonished him to "hearken to the counsel" of Joseph Smith and to "support the cause of the poor, and publish the new translation of my holy word unto the inhabitants of the earth" (124:89). Law was called to be a counselor to Joseph Smith in the First Presidency and to assist Joseph "in making a solemn proclamation unto the kings of the earth" (124:91, 107). Calling upon the Lord would bring him blessings; being humble and without guile would bring the Spirit to teach him truth. Like Jesus' ancient disciples, signs would follow him; miracles would attend his ministry, even to raising the dead if he were directed to do so. For these divine blessings, Law was to praise God (124:82–83, 87–91, 97–101, 107, 126). For his diligence in these matters, he was promised a "multiplicity of blessings, that he shall not be forsaken, nor his seed be found begging bread" (124:90).

From 1842 to 1843 Law faithfully fulfilled his calling in the presidency by defending the Prophet's character against the anti-Mormon pronouncements of John C. Bennett. His loyalty faltered in the winter of 1843, however. On 18 April 1844 he was excommunicated. On 7 June 1844 the first and only edition of the anti-Mormon newspaper *The Nauvoo Expositor* was published, with Law as an owner and proprietor.

NAUVOO EXPOSITOR.

—THE TRUTH, THE WHOLE TRUTH, AND NOTHING BUT THE TRUTH.—

VOL. I.]   NAUVOO, ILLINOIS, FRIDAY, JUNE 7, 1844.   [NO. 1.

Nauvoo Expositor. *The newspaper published by William Law in Nauvoo, Illinois, on 7 June 1844, which inflamed public sentiment against Joseph Smith and led to his martyrdom.*

The printing of the newspaper and the destruction of the *Expositor* press led to the arrest, imprisonment, and murder of Joseph and Hyrum Smith. On 29 September 1844 Law was charged with contributing to their deaths; he was acquitted the following day.

After leaving Nauvoo, Law moved to Rock Island County, then to Daviess County, Illinois, and then to Shullsburg, Wisconsin. He supported himself as a physician and surgeon. In 1887 Law said, "The great mistake of my life was my having anything to do with Mormonism" (in Cook, 104–6).

See also Apostasy, of early dissenters from restored Church.

BIBLIOGRAPHY

Law, William, to Wilheim Wyl, January 20, 1887, in *The Daily Tribune* (Shullsburg, Wisconsin), July 3, 1887, as cited in Lyndon W. Cook, *William Law: Biographical Essay, Nauvoo Diary, Correspondence, Interview.* Orem, Utah: Grandin Book, 1994.

Perkins, Keith W., and Donald Q. Cannon. *Ohio and Illinois.* Vol. 3 of *Sacred Places: A Comprehensive Guide to Early LDS Historical Sites,* edited by LaMar C. Berrett. Salt Lake City: Deseret Book, 2002.

Smith, Joseph. *History of The Church of Jesus Christ of Latter-day Saints.* Edited by B. H. Roberts. 7 vols. 2d ed. rev. Salt Lake City: The Church of Jesus Christ of Latter-day Saints, 1932–51.

SEB

Law(s)

All things are governed by law. The power of God—the Light of Christ—is the "law by which all things are governed" (88:13). Likewise, "every kingdom is given a law; and unto every law there are certain bounds also and conditions" (88:38). Generally, the Doctrine and Covenants speaks of two kinds of laws: the laws of God and the laws of man. God's laws are divine and spiritual—COMMANDMENTS, ORDINANCES, principles, and practices that are given to guide and govern his children in their eternal progression. Conversely, the laws of man are temporal and temporary, being changed and adapted to the circumstances and culture of mortals. God's laws are always good and beneficial for man, because God is good and loves all his children. Man's laws, however, may not always promote goodness and righteousness. Therefore, the Lord reveals in the Doctrine and Covenants his will concerning the role of both divine law and human law and man's relationship to each. "Obtain a knowledge," the Lord commanded in 1833, "of laws of God and man" (93:53).

Laws of man

Latter-day Saints believe that "governments were instituted of God for the benefit of man; and that he holds men accountable for their acts in relation to them, both in making laws and administering them, for the good and safety of society" (134:1). Just as God will hold governments and leaders accountable for the laws they enact, he will hold men accountable for their actions in relationship to such laws. Latter-day Saints believe in "obeying, honoring, and sustaining the law" (A of F 12). Early in the history of the Church, the Lord revealed to the Prophet Joseph Smith: "Let no man break the laws of the land. . . . Wherefore, be subject to the powers that be, until he reigns whose right it is to reign, and subdues all enemies under his feet" (58:21–22). Amidst the persecutions of the Latter-day Saints in Missouri—when the constitutional rights of Church members were being violated both by individuals and by the GOVERNMENT—the Lord reiterated that the Church should observe and support the constitutional law of the land (98:6), which, the Lord himself declared, "I have suffered to be established, and should be maintained for the rights and protection of all flesh, according to just and holy principles" (101:77).

Two years later, the Church in a formal declaration of belief regarding the role of governments and laws declared that "all men are bound to sustain and uphold the respective governments in which they reside, while protected in their inherent and inalienable rights by the laws of such governments; and that sedition and rebellion are unbecoming every citizen thus protected, and should be punished accordingly; and that all governments have a right to enact such laws as in their own judgments are best calculated to secure the public interest; at the same time, however, holding sacred the freedom of conscience" (134:5). That same declaration likewise urged the Saints to "appeal to the civil law for redress of all wrongs and grievances" while yet recognizing the need to defend one's self, family, friends, and property "in times of exigency, where immediate appeal cannot be made to the laws, and relief afforded" (134:11; cf. 105:25). These revelations and statements clearly show that obedience to the just laws of man is a spiritual expectation similar to obedience to God's laws. "And as pertaining to law of man, whatsoever is more or less than this, cometh of evil. I, the Lord God, make you free, therefore ye are free indeed; and the law also maketh you free" (98:7–8).

Laws of God

Joseph Smith understood and clearly articulated the primacy of God's laws. "The Almighty God has taught me the principle of law," the Prophet declared (5:471). From these revelations, he learned that man's laws are not "on a parallel with the law of heaven; because we do not consider that it is formed in the same wisdom and propriety; neither do we consider that it is sufficient in itself to bestow anything on man in comparison with the law of heaven" (Dahl and Cannon, 388). The Doctrine and Covenants refers to God's laws as the governing principles of his kingdoms both in heaven and on earth. The ordinances, teachings, and practices of the Church are referred to by the Lord in scripture as "the law of my church" (43:9). Section 42, which outlines many of the Lord's commandments to the Saints and gives directions concerning Church practices, was described as "the Laws of the Church of Christ" (Jensen et al., 95). "Thou shalt take the things which thou hast received, which have been given unto thee in my scriptures for a law, to be my law to govern my church," the Lord declared (42:59). These laws—commandments, principles, ordinances, and practices—were given by the Lord for the preservation and salvation, both temporal and spiritual, individual and institutional, of God's earthly kingdom. "Ye shall observe the laws which ye have received and be faithful. And ye shall hereafter receive church covenants, such as shall be sufficient to establish you, both here and in the New Jerusalem" (42:66–67). Numerous passages of scripture refer to CONSECRATION and stewardship as God's law (42:30–37, 53–55, 70–73; 51; 54).

Laws concerning conduct becoming Latter-day Saints and how to deal with transgressors of those laws were likewise revealed (42:88–93; 102). Tithing became a "standing law" (119:4) unto the Church. Celestial MARRIAGE—a new and everlasting covenant of marriage—was referred to by the Lord as "my law" (132:12), "and the conditions thereof . . . were instituted from before the foundation of the world" (132:5). In short, the GOSPEL of Jesus Christ, the commandments of the Lord, and Church practices are referred to as the laws of God and are given for the purpose of blessing God's children in mortality and saving them in eternity. These laws are also referred to in the revelations as "the law of Christ" (88:21), "the law of the celestial kingdom" (105:4–5), "the law of my Holy Priesthood" (132:28), and "the laws of consecration" (105:29). See Law of the celestial kingdom.

The glory to which one is resurrected by virtue of the redemptive power of Christ's atonement is also governed by eternal law. "And unto every kingdom is given a law; and unto every law there are certain bounds also and conditions" (88:38). Those who are resurrected to and inherit celestial glory are those who are "sanctified from all unrighteousness" by the "law of Christ" (88:17–21). Those who inherit terrestrial glory are those who do not "abide the law of a celestial kingdom" (88:22) and those "who cannot abide the law of a terrestrial kingdom cannot abide a terrestrial glory. And [those] who cannot abide the law of a telestial kingdom cannot abide a telestial glory; therefore [they are] not meet for a kingdom of glory. Therefore [they] must abide a kingdom which is not a kingdom of glory" (88:23–24). See Kingdoms of glory and perdition, vision of; Resurrection, the.

Whether on earth or in heaven, law is inextricably linked to ACCOUNTABILITY and consequence. OBEDIENCE to law yields blessings, and disobedience subjects one to consequences for violation of law, whether it be God's laws or man's. "There is a law, irrevocably decreed in heaven before the foundations of this world, upon which all blessings are predicated—and when we obtain any blessing from God, it is by obedience to that law upon which it is predicated" (130:20–21).

The Doctrine and Covenants teaches that man is subject to law—both the laws of man and the laws of God. Obedience to law is expected of disciples (41:5). "If the law of man is binding upon man when acknowledged," the Prophet Joseph Smith declared, "how much more must the law of heaven be! And as much as the law of heaven is more perfect than the law of man, so much greater must be the reward if obeyed. The law of man promises safety in temporal life; but the law of God promises that life which is eternal, even an inheritance at God's own right hand, secure from all the powers of the wicked one" (Dahl and Cannon, 388–89).

See also Constitution.

BIBLIOGRAPHY

Dahl, Larry E., and Donald Q. Cannon, eds. *Encyclopedia of Joseph Smith's Teachings*. Salt Lake City: Deseret Book, 2000.

Jensen, Robin Scott, Robert J. Woodford, and Steven C. Harper, eds. *Manuscript Revelation Books*. Facsimile edition. First volume of the Revelations and Translations series of *The Joseph Smith Papers*, edited by Dean C. Jessee, Ronald K. Esplin, and Richard Lyman Bushman. Salt Lake City: Church Historian's Press, 2009.

Smith, Joseph. *History of The Church of Jesus Christ of Latter-day Saints*. Edited by B. H. Roberts. 7 vols. 2d ed. rev. Salt Lake City: The Church of Jesus Christ of Latter-day Saints, 1932–51.

BLT

Law and the prophets

A term for the Old Testament, used commonly in New Testament times (John 1:45; Acts 24:14). In Jesus' day, the Old Testament was viewed as a collection of books in three categories (Luke 24:44): the Law (Genesis through Deuteronomy), the Prophets (historical and prophetic books), and the Writings (literary books). But "the law and the prophets" was used popularly to represent the Old Testament in general. In the Book of Mormon, Jesus taught his disciples, "Keep my commandments. And this is the law and the prophets, for they truly testified of me" (3 Ne. 15:10) and "all things whatsoever ye would that men should do to you, do ye even so to them, for this is the law and the prophets" (3 Ne. 14:12).

In the Doctrine and Covenants, the phrase appears only once, in a passage about offending God by failing to acknowledge his hand in all things: "Behold, this is according to the law and the prophets" (59:21–22). The language suggests that the phrase here means according to the scriptures or consistent with the scriptures.

KPJ

Lawful heirs according to the flesh

The literal seed of Abraham who have claim, as descendants of the ancient patriarch, to all the blessings of the PRIESTHOOD and the restored gospel. In the Doctrine and Covenants the Lord tells Joseph Smith that he is of Abraham's seed and an heir to the promises made to Abraham (132:30–31) and that Joseph and the Lord's "servants," to whom section 86 is addressed, are "lawful heirs" of the priesthood, "according to the flesh," and are to be "a savior unto my people Israel" (86:1, 9–11; 113:4–8; Abr. 2:9–11). The Lord has also made it clear that a claim to the rights and powers of the priesthood can only be realized through individual righteousness (121:34–46). The Book of Mormon declares its purpose to make the gospel covenant known to the "remnant of the house of Israel," the descendants of Abraham through his grandson Jacob (Israel), that they may lay claim to their promised blessings (Title page; 1 Ne. 15:12–14; 3 Ne. 16:4–5, 11–12). Consistently since the Church was restored, missionaries with Book of Mormon in hand have been sent out to help fulfill this divine commission (35:25; 38:33; 39:11; 84:2; 110:11). By commandment, these missionaries also proclaim the gospel to "all nations, kindreds, tongues and people" (42:58) of every lineage that they too may enjoy all the blessings of the ABRAHAMIC COVENANT. Though not the literal seed of Abraham and therefore not lawful heirs according to the flesh, all who accept the fulness of the gospel are "accounted" as the seed of Abraham and are, by adoption, "heirs according to the covenant" (52:2; Abr. 2:10; Gal. 3:27).

JFM

Law of carnal commandments

A system of rituals and ordinances that were part of the LAW OF MOSES, revealed as a schoolmaster to help the children of Israel understand and accept the GOSPEL of Jesus Christ (Gal. 3:24; 2 Ne 25:30; Mosiah 13:28–31; Alma 25:15–16; 4 Ne 1:12). This teaching was necessary because they had rejected a fulness of the gospel (84:23–27). The single Doctrine and Covenants reference to the law of carnal commandments (84:27) refers to the Mosaic "'performances and ordinances' such as dietary restrictions, purification rituals, and additional offerings" practiced by the Israelites prior to the coming of Christ. These practices were "all intended to reinforce self-control and create greater self-discipline (obedience) in the lives of the children of Israel so they could reclaim the higher promises, principles, and priesthood that had been enjoyed by their forebears" (Holland, 147).

The Aaronic PRIESTHOOD bestowed on the Prophet Joseph Smith in 1829 (13:1) restored the preparatory gospel revealed to Moses, including the KEYS to the ministry of angels, repentance, and the ordinance of baptism for the remission of sin (84:26–27; 107:20). Because the law of carnal commandments was fulfilled with the completion of Christ's mortal ministry (74:3; 3 Ne. 12:46; 15:1–6), that part of the Mosaic law is not practiced as part of the preparatory gospel, or Aaronic Priesthood, in the Church today.

See also Letter of the gospel.

BIBLIOGRAPHY

Holland, Jeffrey R. *Christ and the New Covenant: The Messianic Message of the Book of Mormon.* Salt Lake City: Deseret Book, 1997.

DAW

Law of circumcision. *See* Circumcision.

Law of consecration. *See* Consecration.

Law of Moses

The lower law, administered by the Levitical or Aaronic PRIESTHOOD, given to Moses for the children of Israel on MOUNT SINAI after they had rejected the higher law and the invitation to sanctify themselves and enter into God's

presence (84:19–26; Ex. 20:19; Deut. 5:23–27). The law of Moses pointed to JESUS CHRIST (2 Ne. 11:4; 25:24, 30; Jacob 4:5; Alma 25:15–16) as it regulated the administration of the temple and the lives of the Israelites. Christ clarified that he had come to fulfill the law and to provide a higher law, one written in the heart (3 Ne. 15:2–10; 2 Cor. 3; Heb. 8). Although the law of Moses was God's commandment, it could not provide salvation (Mosiah 3:14–15; 13:27–28; 16:13–15).

In the Doctrine and Covenants, direct references to the law of Moses also emphasize its fulfillment in Christ and its own insufficiency to save. In section 22 "law of Moses" is used as a parallel to "dead works" to describe baptism without priesthood authority (v. 2), emphasizing that ordinances performed under the fulness of the Restoration replace baptisms previously received, just as Christ's gospel replaced the law of Moses. The Lord declared that "it is because of your dead works that I have caused this last covenant and this church to be built up" (v. 3). The revelation recorded in section 74 uses "law of Moses" in this New Testament context to explain 1 Corinthians 7:14, which concerns the potential problem of a Christian having a Jewish spouse who insists their children be subject to the law of Moses, "which law was fulfilled" (74:3). The revelation indicates that it was the apostle Paul's view that a believer should not be married to an unbeliever "except the law of Moses should be done away among them" (74:5).

See also Circumcision; Dead works; Historical context and overview of Doctrine and Covenants 22 (p. 731) and 74 (p. 779); Law of carnal commandments.

BIBLIOGRAPHY

Robinson, Stephen E., and H. Dean Garrett. *A Commentary on the Doctrine and Covenants.* 4 vols. Salt Lake City: Deseret Book, 2000–2005.

JCL

Law of Sarah. *See* Marriage.

Law of the celestial kingdom

The principles, laws, and ordinances that a person must obey and keep to qualify for an inheritance in God's highest heaven. The phrase "law of the [a] celestial kingdom" appears three times in the Doctrine and Covenants. In section 88, the Lord explains, "For he who is not able to abide the law of a celestial kingdom cannot abide a celestial glory" (88:22). In section 105, the Lord speaks of the redemption of Zion, including the need for the Saints to be "chastened until they learn obedience, if it must needs be, by the things which they suffer." He makes it clear that the Saints at that time were "not united according to the union required by the law of the celestial kingdom" and that "Zion cannot be built up unless it is by the principles of the law of the celestial kingdom; otherwise I cannot receive her unto myself" (105:4–5; sections 101 and 103 enumerate specific transgressions the Saints were guilty of and what must be done before Zion could be redeemed). *See* Zion, redemption of.

Although the phrase "law of the celestial kingdom" appears just three times in the Doctrine and Covenants, the principles, laws, and ordinances inherent in that law are everywhere apparent in the revelations. In setting forth the law of the harvest (Gal. 6:7–8), also known as the law of restoration (Alma 41), the scriptures firmly decree that one may not ignore or set at naught things of righteousness in this life and expect to enjoy the beauty and glory of the highest heaven hereafter. "This life is the time for men to prepare to meet God" (Alma 34:32), a time to put off the natural man and put on Christ, to deny oneself of all ungodliness and worldly lusts (JST Matt. 16:26), to cultivate the gifts of the Spirit, and begin to acquire Christlike attributes. While one may not be able to fully attain moral perfection or live the celestial law completely in this life, one can strive diligently to keep the commandments of God and acquire holiness line upon line, precept upon precept. A fulness of the glory of the celestial kingdom will not come until after the resurrection (88:27–29), but a foretaste, a portion, of that glory can be felt through the power of the HOLY GHOST by those who earnestly strive to keep the "law of the celestial kingdom."

See also Historical context and overview of Doctrine and Covenants 101 (p. 806), 103 (p. 808), and 105 (p. 812); Kingdoms of glory and perdition, vision of.

RLM

Laying on of hands

The placing of hands on the head of a person by a PRIESTHOOD holder to bestow or confer priesthood, blessings, callings, and gifts from God. This prescribed method of administering in the priesthood is used in three contexts:

1. Bestowal of the HOLY GHOST. The most frequent references in the Doctrine and Covenants to the practice of the laying on of hands is in connection with the ORDINANCE of confirming a person a member of the Church, after baptism, for the reception of "the gift of the Holy Ghost" (49:14; 39:23; 68:25, 27; cf. 35:6; 53:3; 55:1; 76:52; Acts 8:15–19), also called "the baptism of fire and the Holy Ghost" (20:41; cf. 33:11; 39:6). *See* Gift of the Holy Ghost; Baptism of fire and the Holy Ghost.

In performing this ordinance, priesthood holders are acting on behalf of the Lord, as if the Lord were administering the ordinance. To Edward Partridge the Lord said: *"I will lay my hand upon you by the hand of my servant Sidney Rigdon, and you shall receive* my Spirit, the Holy Ghost, even the Comforter, which shall teach you the peaceable things of the kingdom" (36:2; emphasis added). To Ezra Thayer and Northrop Sweet, when he called them as missionaries, the Lord promised, "And whoso having faith *you shall confirm* in my church, by the laying on of the hands, and *I will bestow* the gift of the Holy Ghost" (33:15; emphasis added).

The laying on of hands for the gift of the Holy Ghost is available to all, not just to those who have the opportunity to receive the ordinance themselves while in mortality. In President Joseph F. Smith's vision of the redemption of the dead, he saw that this ordinance was taught to the spirits in the postmortal spirit world along with "all other principles of the gospel that were necessary for them to know in order to qualify themselves that they might be judged according to men in the flesh, but live according to God in the spirit" (138:33–34; cf. 1 Pet. 4:6). The ordinances of baptism and the laying on of hands for the gift of the Holy Ghost are performed vicariously for them by mortals in modern temples. *See* Salvation for the dead.

2. Conferral of the priesthood and ordination to offices therein. Oliver Cowdery was "called of God . . . to be the second elder of this church, and ordained under [Joseph Smith's] hand" (20:3; cf. 21:11). William W. Phelps was instructed that if he would be baptized "with an eye single" to the glory of the Lord, he would be forgiven of his sins, receive the Holy Spirit, and be "ordained by the hand of my servant Joseph Smith, Jun., to be an elder unto this church" (55:1–3). In section 84 the Melchizedek Priesthood line of authority is traced from Moses back to Adam, each man receiving the priesthood "under the hand" of another (84:6–16). Also, the patriarchal line of authority from Adam to Noah is recounted in section 107, each man being "ordained" "by" or "under the hand" of a previous patriarch (107:46–52).

3. Bestowal of blessings. "Every member of the church of Christ having children is to bring them unto the elders before the church, who are to lay their hands upon them in the name of Jesus Christ, and bless them in his name" (20:70). Moreover, the Lord revealed, "the elders of the church, two or more, shall be called" to administer to the sick "and shall pray for and lay their hands upon them in my name; and if they die they shall die unto me, and if they live they shall live unto me" (42:43–44; cf. 24:13; 35:9; 66:9; 84:68; Mark 16:18).

All of "the administering of ordinances and blessings upon the church, by the laying on of the hands" is to be done under the presiding authority of the president of the Church, the "Presiding High Priest over the High Priesthood of the Church" (107:64–67).

MSN

Learning

Obtaining KNOWLEDGE and understanding through study, experience, and REVELATION. One of the express purposes of the Doctrine and Covenants is to instruct God's servants as they "sought wisdom" that they "might come to understanding" (1:24–28). Indeed, the revelations are given to the Saints for their "profit and learning" (46:1); they give some detail concerning what to learn and how to learn, as well as identifying a place where significant learning can take place.

What to learn

In a revelation on priesthood, the Lord said, "Wherefore, now let every man learn his duty, and to act in the office in which he is appointed, in all diligence" (107:99–100). He warned that those who exercise the priesthood unrighteously have yet to learn "that the rights of the priesthood are inseparably connected with the powers of heaven" and that serious consequences follow such unrighteous behavior (121:34–38). On the other hand, the Lord has asked his Saints to "learn that he who doeth the works of righteousness shall receive his reward, even peace in this world, and eternal life in the world to come" (59:23; cf. 136:32–33).

Additionally, the Lord instructed that one must learn of him (19:23; 32:1); learn parables (35:16); learn that only those who endure to the end are saved (53:7); learn of his will (58:1; 105:1); "learn to impart one to another as the gospel requires" (88:123; cf. 105:3); "learn wisdom" (97:1; 136:32); and "learn obedience" (105:6).

How to learn

The Lord has repeatedly commanded his people to gain greater understanding through learning from the scriptures as well as from other good books. He counseled Hyrum Smith to "study [his] word," both that which had been and that which would yet be revealed (11:22), for "the Book of Mormon and the holy scriptures [were] given . . . for [our] instruction" (33:16). The Lord instructed that books should be selected, written, and printed "for schools in this church, that little children also may receive instruction before me as is pleasing unto me" (55:4). Furthermore, the Prophet Joseph Smith was instructed to "study and learn, and become acquainted with all good books, and with languages, tongues, and people" (90:15; cf. 88:78–80; 93:53).

In addition to intellectual study, one must learn "also by faith" (88:118) and by "humbling himself and calling upon the Lord his God" (136:32). Explaining how one learns by faith,

President Harold B. Lee taught, "Let no one think that 'learning by faith' contemplates an easy or lazy way to gain knowledge and ripen it into wisdom. . . . Learning by faith requires the bending of the whole soul through worthy living to become attuned to the Holy Spirit of the Lord, the calling up from the depths of one's own mental searching, and the linking of our own efforts to receive the true witness of the Spirit" (92–93).

Where to learn

The TEMPLE was to be established as "a house of prayer, a house of fasting, a house of faith, a house of learning, a house of glory, a house of order, a house of God" (88:119; cf. 109:7–8). The School of the Prophets was to be organized therein to instruct "all the officers of the church, . . . those who are called to the ministry in the church," for "their instruction in all things that are expedient for them" (88:127; see also vv. 128–41).

See also School(s); Wisdom, wise.

BIBLIOGRAPHY

Lee, Harold B. *The Teachings of Harold B. Lee*. Edited by Clyde J. Williams. Salt Lake City: Bookcraft, 1996.

DJG

Lectures on Faith

Seven lectures on the theology, or FAITH, of The Church of Jesus Christ of Latter-day Saints given in the School of the Elders in Kirtland, Ohio, early in the winter of 1834–35. The Lectures on Faith constituted the first part, or the doctrine, of the Doctrine and Covenants from 1835 until 1921. "Although profitable for doctrine and instruction, these lectures have been omitted from the Doctrine and Covenants since the 1921 edition because they were not given or presented as revelations to the whole Church" (D&C, Explanatory Introduction). The Lectures on Faith grew out of the need the Prophet Joseph Smith had noted for a "school for the Elders, wherein they might be more perfectly instructed in the great things of God, during the coming winter" (2:169). After noting on 1 December 1834 that "no month ever found me more busily engaged than November" (2:170), Joseph said: "Our school for the Elders was now well attended, and with the lectures on theology, which were regularly delivered, absorbed for the time being everything else of a temporal nature. The classes, being mostly Elders gave the most studious attention to the all-important object of qualifying themselves as messengers of Jesus Christ, to be ready to do His will in carrying glad tidings to all that would open their eyes, ears and hearts" (2:175–76). The lectures contained sets of catechisms (a series of questions and answers) that were added to the first five lectures to help the elders gain understanding. He noted that the elders were pleased to have the help the catechisms provided.

Lecture 1 discusses what faith is and notes that it is the assurance "of things hoped for, the evidence of things not seen" (Heb. 11:1). It is the principal power of action in all intelligent human beings. This lecture has 13 sets of questions and answers.

Lecture 2 discusses how to obtain faith in God from the testimony of Father Adam, who knew him, was taught by him, walked and talked with him, and taught his children about him. God is the object of one's faith. Lecture 2 has 148 items in its catechism.

Lectures 3 and 4 identify and discuss the need to gain the "correct" knowledge of the "character, perfections, and attributes" (*Lectures*, 38) that make God the supreme Deity: knowledge, faith or power, justice, judgment, mercy, and truth. Lecture 3 has 24 questions and answers; Lecture 4 has 11.

Lecture 5 discusses the nature of the Godhead and the relationships that exist within it—God the Father; his Son, Jesus Christ; and the Holy Ghost. Lecture 5 has 18 questions and answers.

Lecture 6 discusses how one must be willing to sacrifice all earthly things to be able to know that the path he is pursuing on earth accords with the will of God. It also notes "that a religion that does not require the sacrifice of all things never has power sufficient to produce the faith necessary unto life and salvation" (*Lectures*, 69).

Lecture 7 discusses how the effects of faith give perspective and power to make one more like God and his Son and eventually be saved in their presence. Hence, faith is the power to perfection.

See also Doctrine and Covenants, historical development of.

BIBLIOGRAPHY

Dahl, Larry E., and Charles D. Tate Jr. *The Lectures on Faith: In Historical Perspective.* Provo, Utah: Religious Studies Center, Brigham Young University, 1990.

Lectures on Faith. Salt Lake City: Deseret Book Company, 1985.

Smith, Joseph. *History of The Church of Jesus Christ of Latter-day Saints.* Edited by B. H. Roberts. 7 vols. 2d ed. rev. Salt Lake City: The Church of Jesus Christ of Latter-day Saints, 1932–51.

CDT

Lee, Ann

Birth: 29 February 1736, Manchester, Lancashire, England

Death: 8 September 1784, Watervliet, Schenectady County, New York

At age thirty-four, Ann Lee became the leader of the United Society of Believers in Christ's Second Appearing, also known as the SHAKERS, a name first used to ridicule the society's mode of religious worship. Her proclaimed vision of Adam and Eve in a sexual act in the Garden of Eden was the cornerstone of the society's beliefs (Campion, 24). Although a mother of four, after the vision Lee became celibate and "took up her cross against the carnal gratifications of the flesh." She pronounced herself the "Female Christ"—Ann the Word. She proclaimed, "I feel the blood of Christ running through my soul and body!" (Campion, 25, 35).

Persecution followed Ann Lee's pronouncements. She and a few of her followers fled England for America in 1774. They settled in a wilderness area near Albany, New York. Although they were sequestered from most American settlers, more persecution followed. Lee was imprisoned and later kidnapped. After these incidents, "Mother [Lee] sat in a chair almost all day and sang in unknown tongues the whole time," reported her followers (Campion, 140). Her teachings and the societies she established continued after her death. A stronghold of Shakerism was established in North Union, Ohio (now Shaker Heights, a suburb of Cleveland). In 1831 Joseph Smith received a revelation refuting some of the teachings of Ann

Lee (49), who is mentioned in the headnote to section 49.

See also Historical context and overview of Doctrine and Covenants 49 (p. 755).

BIBLIOGRAPHY

Campion, Nardi Reeder. *Mother Ann Lee, Morning Star of the Shakers.* Hanover & London: University Press of New England, 1990.

Evans, Frederick William. *Shakers: Compendium of the Origin, History, Principles, Rules and Regulations, Government, and Doctrines of the United Society of Believers in Christ's Second Appearing: With Biographies of Ann Lee. . . .* New York: D. Appleton and Company, 1859.

SEB

Lehi

A Book of Mormon prophet (ca. 600 B.C.), father of Laman, Lemuel, Sam, Nephi, Jacob, Joseph, and unnamed daughters. Lehi wrote his teachings and prophecies in the book of Lehi, which was translated by Joseph Smith and lost by Martin Harris (headnotes to 3; 10). Reference is made in the Doctrine and Covenants to the "miraculous directors [the Liahona] which were given to Lehi while in the wilderness" (17:1; cf. 1 Ne. 16:10, 16; 18:12; 2 Ne. 5:12; Mosiah 1:16; Alma 37:38).

DKO

Lemuelites

Descendants of Lehi's son Lemuel, who followed his father out of Jerusalem ca. 600 B.C. to the western hemisphere. The Doctrine and Covenants affirms the promises of the Lord that the Lemuelites, along with other descendants of Lehi, through the Book of Mormon record might come to know the Savior and his promises, believe his gospel, rely upon his merits, and be glorified and saved (3:16–20; cf. Enos 1:13–18).

DKO

Lesser priesthood. *See* Priesthood.

Letter of the gospel

A description of one dimension of Aaronic PRIESTHOOD responsibility: "to administer in outward ordinances, the letter of the gospel . . . agreeable to the covenants and commandments" (107:20). The term appears once in the Doctrine and Covenants and seems to refer to the ordinances and performances prescribed in the scriptures for those holding the Aaronic Priesthood, such as "the baptism of repentance." The term likely draws on the letter-spirit dichotomy found in the New Testament (e.g., Rom. 2:28–29; 2 Cor. 3:3–18). The Melchizedek Priesthood holds the "keys of all the spiritual blessings of the church" (107:18), which can be understood as the more internal, or spiritual, ordinances of confirmation and of the temple, as contrasted with the more external (letter) ordinances designated as duties for Aaronic Priesthood holders, such as the performance of baptism by water and the administration of the sacrament (20:46–59).

JCL

Levi. *See* Sons of Levi.

Levi, sons of. *See* Sons of Levi.

Levitical Priesthood. *See* Priesthood.

Liberty, Clay County, Missouri

The community of Liberty, Clay County, Missouri, figured prominently in the early history of the Church. It was first settled in 1820 and designated in 1822 by the Missouri legislature as the Clay County seat.

After the expulsion of the Latter-day Saints from Jackson County in late 1833, most Church members sought refuge in Clay County. Most of them did not settle in Liberty but instead established more than a dozen small settlements, many of which were located within a few miles of the town. During the three years the Mormons lived in Clay County (1833–36), they went to Liberty to work, purchase and sell commodities, and socialize.

For much of the time during the years 1833 to 1836, the other citizens of Liberty and Clay County were more open, tolerant, and friendly toward the Mormons than the citizens of Jackson County had been. This was perhaps primarily because the county was more politically mixed (Whigs and Democrats), and fewer citizens were of the "frontier" element. A number of prominent individuals in Liberty and the surrounding area befriended the Mormons,

including Alexander W. Doniphan, David R. Atchison, Peter H. Burnett, William T. Wood, Michael Arthur, Shubael Allen, John Thornton, Joel T. Turnham, and Amos Rees (Reese).

After the 31 October 1838 arrest of Joseph Smith and several other Church leaders and their November arraignment before circuit court judge Austin A. King in Richmond, Missouri, Joseph Smith, Sidney Rigdon, Hyrum Smith, Lyman Wight, Caleb Baldwin, and Alexander MacRae were incarcerated in Liberty Jail beginning 1 December 1838. Although Sidney Rigdon was released early in 1839, the remaining prisoners remained confined until 6 April. Portions of a twenty-nine-page letter dictated by Joseph Smith from LIBERTY JAIL on 20 March 1839 became sections 121, 122, and 123 of the Doctrine and Covenants. *See* maps, pp. 414 and 708.

BIBLIOGRAPHY

Parkin, Max H. "A History of the Latter-day Saints in Clay County, Missouri, from 1833 to 1837." Ph.D. dissertation, Brigham Young University, 1976.

Smith, Joseph. *Personal Writings of Joseph Smith.* Compiled and edited by Dean C. Jessee. Rev. ed. Salt Lake City: Deseret Book, 2002.

ALB

Liberty Jail

On 31 October 1838, Joseph Smith was taken into custody at Far West, Missouri, by state militia authorities for alleged unlawful acts stemming from the "Mormon War," armed conflicts between Mormons and Missourians. After periods of incarceration in Independence and Richmond, Missouri, Joseph Smith, Sidney Rigdon, Hyrum Smith, Lyman Wight, Alexander McRae, and Caleb Baldwin were ordered by Judge Austin A. King to be taken to Liberty Jail to await trial on the charge of treason. Their imprisonment in Liberty Jail lasted about four months, from 1 December 1838 to 6 April 1839; in a hearing held 25 January 1839, the charge against Sidney Rigdon was dropped, resulting in his release. Fear of mob action threatened against him if he left the jail prompted Rigdon to return to Liberty Jail and await an opportune time to escape. With the help of the jailor and the sheriff, that escape was made possible in February 1839 (Smith, *History*, 3:264).

Liberty Jail was constructed in the early 1830s and was a formidable structure. In 1888, assistant Church historian Andrew Jenson visited the site and made a detailed description of what remained of the jail: "The whole structure is a double building, the inner being built of hewn oak logs about a foot square and the outside of rock. . . . The rock walls are two feet thick, and in building them a space of about one foot was left between the rock and timber, which space was filled up with loose rock. Thus . . . the prison walls are virtually four feet thick. . . . The outside dimensions of the building are: 22½ feet long, 22 feet wide and 12 feet high to the square. The door is on the east end, facing the street, and is 5½ feet high and 2½ feet wide, and opens to what was the upper apartment." Jenson also

described the interior of the jail: "We found the space inside to measure about 14½ feet from east to west, and 14 feet from north to south. From the basement floor to the ceiling we should judge it to be about 14 feet, two feet of which is under ground." Jenson also noted that the height of the lower room—the cell or dungeon area—measured six and one-half feet, while the height of the upper room measured about seven feet from the floor to the ceiling (163).

During his incarceration in Liberty Jail, Joseph Smith corresponded with Church leaders, family, and friends. Eight of his letters written from Liberty Jail have survived. In the 1870s, while preparing a new edition of the Doctrine and Covenants, Orson Pratt excerpted several passages from the Prophet's 20 March 1839 letter to form sections 121, 122, and 123 of the Doctrine and Covenants. *See* Historical context

The jail in Liberty, Missouri; photograph ca. 1878. A double-walled structure of stone and wood divided into two levels and measuring roughly fourteen feet square on the inside. Joseph Smith and five of his companions were confined here during the winter of 1838–1839.

and overview of Doctrine and Covenants 121 (p. 831), 122 (p. 833), and 123 (p. 836).

Besides the six Latter-day Saints who were incarcerated in Liberty Jail during the winter of 1838–39, one other later spent time there— Orrin Porter Rockwell. In March 1843, Rockwell was arrested and charged with the attempted assassination of former Missouri governor Lilburn W. Boggs. He was held in Independence for most of his nine-month confinement; on two occasions, however, he was transferred to Liberty Jail and was incarcerated there at the time of his release on 11 December 1843.

Liberty Jail remained in use as a jail until around the mid-1850s, after which it was used as an ice house and subsequently fell into disrepair. In 1900, Homer R. Stephens purchased the property, and in 1903 he constructed a home on the site, using some of the original stones in the construction of basement walls and floor. In 1939 the LDS Church purchased the home and property, and ten years later missionary couples were assigned to live in the home to provide information to visitors.

Primarily through the efforts of Alvin R. Dyer, at one time president of the Central States Mission and later a counselor in the First Presidency, an LDS visitors' center was constructed and dedicated in 1963. The central feature of the center is the reconstruction of a full-size cutaway replica of the 1830s jail. The reconstructed jail includes the stones from the original structure that had been incorporated into the basement of the Stephens home.

Today, the reconstructed jail reminds visitors of the sacrifice and commitment to the restored gospel made by the Prophet Joseph Smith and his fellow prisoners.

BIBLIOGRAPHY

Dyer, Alvin R. "Bureau of Information Erected on the Site of the Liberty Jail at Liberty, Missouri." *Missouri Historical Review* 57 (1963): 379–88.

———. *The Refiner's Fire: Historical Highlights of Missouri.* Salt Lake City: Deseret Book, 1976.

Jenson, Andrew. *Autobiography of Andrew Jenson.* Salt Lake City: Deseret News Press, 1938.

McLaws, Monte B. "The Attempted Assassination of Missouri's Ex-Governor, Lilburn W. Boggs." *Missouri Historical Review* 60 (October 1965): 50–62.

Smith, Joseph. *Personal Writings of Joseph Smith.* Compiled and edited by Dean C. Jessee. Rev. ed. Salt Lake City: Deseret Book, 2002.

ALB

License/certificate(s)

Credential providing evidence of authority, commission, or privileges. *License* appears in two contexts in the Doctrine and Covenants:

1. Those ordained to various offices of the priesthood were given a license authorizing them to perform the duties of their calling (20:63–64).

2. Sidney Gilbert was instructed by the Lord to move to Jackson County, Missouri, and "establish a store" in order to obtain resources "to buy lands for the good of the saints." Gilbert was also to "obtain a license" enabling him to "send goods also unto the people . . . and thus provide for [the] saints, that [the] gospel may be preached unto those who sit in darkness" (57:6–10).

Certificate(s) appears also in two contexts:

1. Members of the Church moving to a new area "may take a letter certifying that they are regular members and in good standing, which certificate may be signed by any elder or priest" who is "personally acquainted" with the members (20:84). Similarly, members going to reside in Zion (Missouri) were to take to the bishop in Zion "a certificate from three elders of the church, or a certificate from the bishop," indicating they were worthy to receive "an inheritance, and to be received as a wise steward" under the principles of CONSECRATION (72:17–18, 25).

2. Proper records were to be kept of baptisms for the dead, and certificates were to be sent to Church headquarters affirming that such baptisms were attended by witnesses who saw with their eyes and heard with their ears, and that the record was true (128:3–5).

RCF

Life, purposes of

The Prophet Joseph Smith taught that "happiness is the object and design of our existence" (*History*, 5:134), and the Book of Mormon prophet Lehi affirmed, "Men are, that they might have joy" (2 Ne. 2:25). The revelations in the Doctrine and Covenants contain at least five purposes of mortality that are critically important to the realization of happiness and joy:

To obtain a body of flesh and bones

A fulness of happiness, or joy, can be achieved only when the body of flesh and bones and the spirit of man are "inseparably connected" (93:33–34). Though all of the reasons why a body of flesh and bones is important may not as yet be revealed, it is clear that spirits, both righteous and wicked, long for such bodies (45:17; 138:14–15, 18, 50). The fact that wicked spirits desire bodies of flesh and bone is also illustrated in scripture (cf. Matt. 8:28–32) and explained by Joseph Smith: "We came to this earth that we might have a body and present it pure before God in the celestial kingdom. The great principle of happiness consists in having a body. The devil has no body, and herein is his punishment. He is pleased when he can obtain the tabernacle of man, and when cast out by the Savior he asked to go into the herd of swine, showing that he would prefer a swine's body to having none. All beings who have bodies have power over those who have not" (*Joseph Smith*, 211).

To gain needed experience

The Lord answered Joseph Smith's own soul-cry of forsakenness while in LIBERTY JAIL with the words: "Know thou, my son, that all these things shall give thee experience, and shall be for thy good. The Son of Man hath descended below them all. Art thou greater than he?" (122:7–8). Explaining why it was necessary to "wait for a little season for the redemption of Zion," the Lord indicated that the elders needed to "be prepared, and . . . be taught more perfectly, and have experience, and know more perfectly concerning their duty" (105:9–10). This knowledge and experience comes through living through the day-to-day and year-to-year challenges of mortality.

Elder Orson F. Whitney said: "No pain that we suffer, no trial that we experience is wasted. It ministers to our education, to the development of such qualities as patience, faith, fortitude and humility. All that we suffer and all that we endure, especially when we endure it patiently, builds up our characters, purifies our hearts, expands our souls, and makes us more tender and charitable, more worthy to be called the children of God . . . and it is through sorrow and suffering, toil and tribulation, that we gain the education that we come here to acquire and which will make us more like our Father and Mother in heaven" (Kimball, 98–99).

To be tested

The Savior announced in premortal councils concerning the spirits designated to live upon this planet, "There is space there, and we will take of these materials, and we will make an earth whereon these may dwell; and we will prove them herewith, to see if they will do all things whatsoever the Lord their God shall command them" (Abr. 3:24–25; cf. Mosiah 3:19). The Doctrine and Covenants affirms in unmistakable terms that such testing is both essential and provided for on the earth. The Lord revealed that he would "give unto the faithful line upon line, precept upon precept; and I will try you and prove you herewith . . . even unto death" (98:12–15). Of the Saints who were driven out of Jackson County, Missouri, in 1833, the Lord declared, "They must needs be chastened and tried, even as Abraham" (101:4–5). He further explained, "My people must be tried in all things, that they may be prepared to receive the glory that I have for them" (136:31). Each of these instances contains the principle that those who cannot endure testing and chastening cannot be sanctified and are not worthy of the Savior or his kingdom.

To make covenants and administer gospel ordinances for the living and the dead

The Lord referred to his GOSPEL as an "everlasting covenant" (1:22). *See* New and everlasting covenant.

Individuals receive the Savior and his gospel by making covenants with him through ordinances (39:5–6). The restoration of the gospel included covenants that are made through ordinances, such as baptism, the sacrament (20:72–79), washings and anointings, endowments, and the new and everlasting covenant of MARRIAGE (124:37–39; 131:2; 132:7, 19). Covenants are made available and their attendant ordinances are administered for both the living and the dead. Joseph Smith explained the prophecy of

Malachi concerning Elijah's coming to turn the heart of the fathers to the children and the heart of the children to the fathers, lest the earth be smitten "with a curse" or be "utterly wasted" at the Savior's coming (Mal. 4:5–6; D&C 2:3; 128:17). The Prophet said, "It is necessary in the ushering in of the dispensation of the fulness of times . . . that a whole and complete and perfect union, and welding together of dispensations, and keys, and powers, and glories should take place, and be revealed from the days of Adam even to the present time" (128:18). Joseph declared that the salvation of the dead is "necessary and essential to our salvation" (128:15) and that the salvation of both the living and the dead must be secured by priesthood authority, which has power to bind on earth and in heaven (128:9).

By the authority of that priesthood, families are sealed together for eternity in the temples of the Lord, and generations of families are sealed to one another, eventually completing the "welding together of dispensations" from the days of Adam (128:18) to the end of time. The role of temples in accomplishing that grand design was "instituted from before the foundation of the world" (124:33; cf. vv. 27–42, 55; 97:10–17), and promises were made that all would have opportunity for the saving ordinances of the gospel to be performed for them in temples (138:50–54). Those living in the dispensation of the fulness of times have a weighty responsibility for seeing that those promises are realized. The Prophet Joseph Smith taught: "The greatest responsibility in this world that God has laid upon us is to seek after our dead. . . . For it is necessary that the sealing power should be in our hands to seal our children and our dead for the fulness of the dispensation of times—a dispensation to meet the promises made by Jesus Christ before the foundation of the world for the salvation of man" (*History*, 6:313). "Those Saints who neglect it in behalf of their deceased relatives, do it at the peril of their own salvation" (Smith, *History*, 4:426). *See* Salvation for the dead.

To become like Heavenly Father and the Savior

All these purposes serve the grand, overall purpose of preparing in mortality to become like God—to become one with the Father and the Son and learn all the attributes of godliness. Being children of heavenly parents, all humankind have the potential to become like their heavenly parents and to pursue with them their work and glory: the "continuation of the seeds forever and ever" (132:19) and helping their own posterity to achieve immortality and eternal lives (132:24). *See* God, nature of; Gods; Perfect, perfection.

The Lord has made the purposes of mortal life clear and has provided the means by which his children may accomplish them.

BIBLIOGRAPHY

Kimball, Spencer W. *Faith Precedes the Miracle*. Salt Lake City: Deseret Book, 1972.

Maxwell, Neal A. "Willing to Submit." *Ensign* 15 (May 1985): 70–73.

Smith, Joseph. *History of The Church of Jesus Christ of Latter-day Saints*. Edited by B. H. Roberts. 7 vols. 2d ed. rev. Salt Lake City: The Church of Jesus Christ of Latter-day Saints, 1932–51.

———. *Joseph Smith*. Teachings of Presidents of the Church series. Salt Lake City: The Church of Jesus Christ of Latter-day Saints, 2007.

LED

Lifted up at the last day

To be raised up in the RESURRECTION of the just to SALVATION in the kingdom of God. The phrase "lifted up at the last day" is used five times in the Doctrine and Covenants, always including what is required to attain that blessing. To Joseph Smith the Lord said, "And if thou art faithful in keeping my commandments, thou shalt be lifted up at the last day" (5:35). To Oliver Cowdery the Lord promised, "Stand fast in the work wherewith I have called you, and a hair of your head shall not be lost, and you shall be lifted up at the last day" (9:14). To the Three Witnesses of the Book of Mormon the Lord promised that if they obeyed the instructions they were given concerning their witness of seeing the gold plates "the gates of hell [would] not prevail against [them]; for my grace is sufficient for you, and you shall be lifted up at the last day" (17:5–8). To the elders of the Church gathered for a conference in Kirtland, in June 1831, the Lord used a variation of the phrase when he said, "I, the Lord, . . . will crown the faithful with joy and with rejoicing . . . , and I will lift them up at the last day" (52:43–44). Six months later at a conference in Amherst, Ohio, where missionary companionships and other assignments were given, the Lord twice included the promise that the "faithful shall overcome all things, and shall be lifted up at the last day" (75:16, 22).

Book of Mormon use of the phrase is parallel to that in the Doctrine and Covenants both in meaning and in requirements to achieve the promised blessing. Alma associates being lifted up at the last day with entering into the rest of the Lord (Alma 13:29; cf. 1 Ne. 13:37; Mosiah 23:22; Alma 36:3; 3 Ne. 27:14–22; Morm. 2:19). The exact phrase is not employed in the Bible, but in the New Testament John seems to be referring to the same principle when he quotes Jesus, saying, "Every one which seeth the Son, and believeth on him, may have everlasting life; and I will raise him up in the resurrection of the just at the last day" (JST John 6:40).

RJM

Lifting up holy hands

The act of raising the hands accompanying PRAYER (Neh. 8:6; Ps. 63:4; 134:2; 141:2), an oath or covenant (Gen. 14:22; Ps. 119:48; Rev. 10:5–6), or the giving of a blessing to someone (Luke 24:50; cf. 1 Ne. 21:22). The phrase appears once in the Doctrine and Covenants, in the Lord's instructions to Sidney Rigdon, Joseph Smith, and Oliver Cowdery to "take their journey for Cincinnati" and there to "lift up their voice and declare my word with loud voices, without wrath or doubting, lifting up holy hands upon them" (60:6–7). These three brethren were on their way home to the Kirtland area from Missouri, where they had gone in obedience to revelation to hold a conference and begin to establish Zion (52:1–5; 57:1–5; 58:1–14). Thus it appears they were to preach the gospel and bless and pray over the inhabitants of Cincinnati,

"lifting up holy hands" in so doing. No record of their missionary efforts there is extant.

DLB

Light

The meaning of the word *light* is discussed in several contexts in the Doctrine and Covenants:

1. A reference to the POWER of God.

This power, or light, "proceedeth forth from the presence of God to fill the immensity of space," by which he creates, governs all creation, gives life, gives physical light, and enlightens minds (88:5–13). This power is identified as "the light of truth," "the light of Christ," "the Spirit of Jesus Christ," and "the Spirit of truth." *See* Light of Christ; Spirit of truth.

Section 88 lists five functions of the power of God's light:

• The power of creation—of the sun, moon, stars, and the earth (vv. 7–10; cf. 29:31–32).

• The power or "law by which all things are governed" (vv. 13, 40–42).

• The power "which giveth life to all things" (v. 13). Each order of life receives light according to its particular purpose and capacity—the world of plants ordered by photosynthesis, the world of insects, birds, and animals operating by instinct, and the world of mankind functioning with reason (45:1; 77:4; 93:9).

• The power that gives physical light, which "enlighteneth your eyes" (v. 11); the light of the sun, moon, and stars (vv. 7–9), which give light to the earth and to each other (vv. 43–45). This light is the light the sun and moon will refuse to give as one of the signs of the second coming of the Savior (v. 87; cf. 133:49).

• The power that "quickeneth your understandings" (v. 11). This function of the "Spirit of Jesus Christ" is given to "every man that cometh into the world," with the promise that all who hearken to it will be enlightened and taught "of the covenant" which the Lord "confirmed" upon Joseph Smith, which covenant is the fulness of the restored gospel (84:45–48; cf. 66:2). It is the light that will grow "brighter and brighter" in those who keep God's commandments "until the perfect day," when "he is glorified in truth and knoweth all things" (50:24; 93:28: cf. 88:40). The Lord has promised that "if your eye be single to my glory, your whole bodies shall be filled with light, and there shall be no darkness in you; and that body which is filled with light comprehendeth all things" (88:67). But with that promise of ever-increasing light there comes a warning—the light of understanding can be lost. The Lord explained that anyone who sins and "repents not, from him shall be taken even the light which he has received; for my Spirit shall not always strive with man" (1:33; cf. 82:3–4; 93:39).

2. A reference to Christ himself.

In the Doctrine and Covenants the Lord refers to himself many times as "the life and light of the world," meaning he is the source of life and light in all its functions (10:70; 11:28; 12:9; 39:2; 45:7; cf. 34:2; 50:27; 93:9).

3. A reference to the example expected of God's covenant people.

Speaking of the early Saints who had been driven from their homes in Jackson County, Missouri, in 1833, the Lord said, "They were set to be a light unto the world, and to be the saviors of men; and inasmuch as they are not the saviors of men, they are as salt that has lost its savor, and is thenceforth good for nothing but to be cast out and trodden under foot of men" (103:9–10; cf. 106:8; 101:39–40; 115:5; 124:6).

4. A reference to the Restoration.

In telling his early apostles in A.D. 33 about the restoration of the gospel that would come in the last days, the Savior said, "And when the times of the Gentiles is come in, a light shall break forth among them that sit in darkness, and it shall be the fulness of my gospel; but they receive it not; for they perceive not the light, and they turn their hearts from me because of the precepts of men" (45:28–29; cf. 45:9). President Joseph F. Smith, in the vision of the redemption of the dead, saw the Lord choose messengers in the postmortal spirit world and send them "forth and carry the light of the gospel to them that were in darkness" (138:30).

5. A modifier lending meaning to several phrases.

"Light *of* truth"—referring to "intelligence, or the light of truth," which "was not created or made, neither indeed can be." It is that eternal, uncreated part of man, which was "in the beginning with God" (93:29; emphasis added). *See* Intelligence.

"Light *and* truth" (different from light *of* truth)—attributes of God and man that encompass not only TRUTH as "knowledge of things as they are, and as they were, and as they are to come" but also truth as enlightened by light from heaven, or revelation, so that it "forsake[s] that evil one" and is properly understood and applied (93:24–25, 36–37).

"Father of lights"—concerning Him who gave the revelations to the Prophet Joseph Smith that were soon to be published. The Lord assured the elders gathered at a special conference in Hiram, Ohio, in 1831, "Ye know that there is no unrighteousness in them, and that which is righteous cometh down from above, from the Father of lights," clearly a reference to God (67:9).

"Children of light"—perhaps referring to those who have taken upon themselves the light and understanding of the gospel, or, perhaps, to those who, through gospel covenants and ordinances, have been "spiritually begotten" of Christ and are therefore "called the children of Christ," who is the light of the world (106:5; Mosiah 5:7).

"Angel of light"—referring to the devil's appearing to someone, pretending to be an angel from God, in an attempt to deceive. Such was the case reported by Joseph Smith in identifying those who had come to him in restoring the gospel: "The voice of Michael on the banks of the Susquehanna, detecting the devil when he appeared as an angel of light" (128:20; cf. 129:4–9; Alma 30:52–53; 2 Ne. 9:9). The Prophet gave no further explanation of this event.

"Light speeches" and "light-mindedness"—used in connection with instructions concerning conduct in the temple, where solemnity, dignity, and reverence are to be maintained. Perhaps the terms refer to conversations with little substance, importance, or depth, inappropriate for a particular setting or occasion, or to speaking superficially, making light of sacred things (88:121; cf. 124:38–40; 63:59–64).

"Esteemed lightly my counsel"—referring to the attitude of some of the Saints in 1833 that brought on persecutions from their neighbors in Missouri. In chastening the Saints regarding a number of other sins, the Lord added, "In the day of their peace they esteemed lightly my counsel; but, in the day of their trouble, of necessity they feel after me" (101:8). *Lightly,* with a connotation of weight rather than illumination in this instance, seems to mean not taking seriously the counsel of the Lord or considering it as not very important. The Lord said a similar attitude, called "vanity and unbelief," "brought the whole church under condemnation . . . [for treating] lightly the things you have received . . . and they shall remain under this condemnation until they repent and remember . . . the Book of Mormon and the former commandments which I have given them, not only to say, but to do according to that which I have written" (84:54–57; cf. 128:15).

BGS

Light-minded. *See* Appendix E.

Light of Christ

The "power of God," which "proceedeth forth from the presence of God to fill the immensity of space." The light of Christ is the power by which God creates and "the law by which all things are governed." It is the ultimate source of "life to all things." That "light" also has an important revelatory function that "quickeneth" one's understanding. The Lord has not revealed just how he creates and governs his creations, or how he gives life and LIGHT to the world through this "power of God" identified as "the light of Christ" (88:5–13), nor has he explained the relationship of this power to the power of the PRIESTHOOD. Several latter-day prophets, however, have taught that it is by the priesthood that God creates and governs in the universe (e.g., Young, 130; Taylor, 129–30; Faust, 36–37; McConkie, 33). Though little has been revealed about the other functions of the light of Christ, the Lord has revealed much about the revelatory aspect of that power.

The term "light of Christ" is found once in the Doctrine and Covenants, in 88:7. The only other uses of the term in scripture are found in Moroni 7:18–19 and Alma 28:14. Moroni equates the light of Christ with the "Spirit of Christ," the revelatory agency "sent forth by the power and gift of Christ" that is "given to every man, that he may know good from evil" (Moro. 7:14–19). In Doctrine and Covenants 84:45–48, the source of the light that is given to "every man that cometh into the world" is called "the Spirit of Jesus Christ," and the promise is given that any who hearken to that light will be enlightened and brought to the fulness of the gospel. Doctrine and Covenants 93:2 affirms that Christ himself is "the true light that lighteth every man that cometh into the world" (cf. John 1:9).

From these examples we see that different terms are used to refer to the same revelatory power given to every man. In like manner, various terms are used in reference to different dimensions and various measures of that "power of God," "the light of Christ" which enlightens minds and proceeds forth from God's presence to "fill the immensity of space" (88:7, 11–13). For instance, the terms used in scripture to refer to the source of spiritual gifts include the "Spirit of God" (46:11, 17; Moro. 10:8–9), the "Holy Ghost" (46:13–16; 1 Cor. 12:3), "the Spirit" (46:16; 1 Cor. 12:4–11), and "the Spirit of Christ" (Moro. 10:17). Other phrases used in the revelations to refer to this same revelatory power include "my Holy Spirit" (99:2); "the Spirit of truth" (50:17, 19, 21); "the Spirit of the living God" (61:28); "the Comforter" (35:19); and "the light of truth" (88:6). Several of these terms state or imply the involvement of the HOLY GHOST.

What, then, is the relationship between the light of Christ and the Holy Ghost? President Joseph F. Smith explained: "The Holy Ghost as a personage of Spirit can no more be omnipresent in person than can the Father or the Son, but by his intelligence, his knowledge, his power and influence, over and through the laws of nature, he is and can be omnipresent throughout all the works of God. It is not the Holy Ghost who in person lighteth every man who is born into the world, but it is the light of Christ, the Spirit of Truth, which proceeds from the source of intelligence, which permeates all nature, which lighteth every man and fills the immensity of space. You may call it the Spirit of God, you may call it the influence of God's intelligence, you may call it the substance of his power, no matter what it is called, it is the spirit of intelligence that permeates the universe and gives to the spirits of men understanding, just as Job has said (Job 32:8; Doc. and Cov. 88:3–13.)" (61).

President Joseph Fielding Smith wrote: "This man here, another one over there, and a man over in England, are confirmed members of the Church. The question arises, 'How can the Holy Ghost be with them all at the same time?' He does not have to be, but the power of the Holy Ghost is such that it can be manifest in every place at the same moment of time. . . . Thus when it becomes necessary to speak to us, he is able to do so by acting through the other Spirit, that is, through the Light of Christ. . . . The person of the Holy Ghost can work through the Spirit of Christ that permeates everything, or he can work by personal contacts" (1:40, 54).

Addressing the various dimensions and measures of the light of Christ, President Marion G. Romney taught: "There are three phases of the light of Christ that I want to mention. The first one is the light which enlighteneth every man that cometh into the world; the second phase is the gift of the Holy Ghost; and the third is the more sure word of prophecy" (43). Although it is a common practice to use the term "light of Christ" when referring to just the first phase of that power, the light that enlighteneth everyone who comes into the world, it seems clear that the revelatory function of the light of Christ is inherent in all levels of spiritual communications and is used by the Holy Ghost to do his work.

See also Gift of the Holy Ghost; Revelation.

BIBLIOGRAPHY

Faust, James E. "Keeping Covenants and Honoring the Priesthood." *Ensign* 23 (November 1993): 36–37.

McConkie, Bruce R. "The Doctrine of the Priesthood." *Ensign* 12 (May 1982): 32–33.

Romney, Marion G. "The Light of Christ." *Ensign* 7 (May 1977): 43–45.

Smith, Joseph F. *Gospel Doctrine.* Salt Lake City: Deseret Book, 1986.

Smith, Joseph Fielding. *Doctrines of Salvation.* Compiled by Bruce R. McConkie. 3 vols. Salt Lake City: Bookcraft, 1954–56.

Taylor, John. *The Gospel Kingdom.* Selected by G. Homer Durham. Salt Lake City: Bookcraft, 1944.

Young, Brigham. *Discourses of Brigham Young.* Selected by John A. Widtsoe. Salt Lake City: Deseret Book, 1978.

LED

Light of truth

A term with at least three different connotations:

1. Doctrine and Covenants 88:6–13 identifies the light of truth as the power by which Christ is "in all and through all things" and equates it with the "light of Christ," "which light proceedeth forth from the presence of God to fill the immensity of space," the power by which God creates, governs his creations, gives life and LIGHT, and enlightens minds.

2. In 124:9, the Lord promises to soften the hearts of many "that they may come to the light of truth," evidently meaning they will come to the truths of the gospel of Jesus Christ, or to Christ himself.

3. In 93:29, the light of truth is used to mean "intelligence," something that "was not created or made, neither indeed can be," the self-existing, eternal part of man that "was also in the beginning with God."

Among the four volumes of scripture that constitute the standard works of the Church, the term "light of truth" is found only in the Doctrine and Covenants.

See also Intelligence; Light of Christ; Spirit of truth; Truth.

LED

Line running directly between Jew and Gentile

Phrase appearing in Doctrine and Covenants 57:4, in which the Saints are instructed to purchase land in Jackson County, Missouri, in the region west of the community of Independence (that is, the "Gentiles") to the edge of the county, which bordered on Indian territory. *See* Gentile(s).

The term *Jews* is an idiomatic expression illustrating the belief held by the Saints that the Native American Indians were descendants of the LAMANITES in the Book of Mormon, whose forefathers had come from the land of Jerusalem, or the land of the JEWS. This is why the Native American Indians are called "Jews" (2 Ne. 30:4; 33:8).

See also Borders of the Lamanites.

ALB

Literal descendant of Aaron. *See* Bishop(s).

Literary Firm. *See* Consecration.

Little season. *See* Millennium, the.

Loins, gird up your. *See* Gird up your loins.

Lord, acceptable year of the. *See* Acceptable day of the Lord/acceptable year of the Lord.

Lord, arm of the. *See* Arm of the Lord.

Lord, great and dreadful day of the. *See* Great and dreadful day of the Lord.

Lord, supper of the. *See* Marriage of the Lamb.

Lord, vessels of the. *See* Vessels of the Lord.

Lost tribes of Israel. *See* Israel.

Love

Strong affection, fondness, and devotion toward someone or something. *Love* is employed in the Doctrine and Covenants in several contexts.

The love of the Father and the Son for all mankind

President Joseph F. Smith, in recording his vision of the redemption of the dead, bore witness of "the great and wonderful love made manifest by the Father and the Son in the coming of the Redeemer into the world," to perform "the great atoning sacrifice" (138:2–3). The apostle John wrote that "God so loved the world, that he gave his only begotten Son" (John 3:16). And Jesus, speaking of himself, said that it was because of his love for the world "that he gave his own life, that as many as would believe might become the sons of God" (34:3; cf. 133:53). The love of the Father and the Son for all the children of men is the same. That love is expressed not only to groups but to individuals. To Oliver Cowdery, Christ promised, "Be faithful and diligent in keeping the commandments of God, and I will encircle thee in the arms of my love" (6:20). Concerning Hyrum Smith the Lord declared, "I, the Lord, love him because of the integrity of his heart, and because he loveth that which is right before me" (124:15). In a revelation chastening the early Saints for delaying the building of the Kirtland Temple, the Lord instructed, "Verily, thus saith the Lord unto you whom I love, and whom I love I also chasten that their sins may be forgiven, for with the chastisement I prepare a way for their deliverance in all things out of temptation, and I have loved you" (95:1).

The love of mankind for the Father and the Son

In the beginning, God "created man, male and female, after his own image . . . and gave unto them commandments that they should love and serve him, the only living and true God, and that he should be the only being whom they should worship" (20:18–19). To the Saints gathering in Zion in 1831 the Lord commanded, "Thou shalt love the Lord thy God with all thy heart, with all thy might, mind, and strength; and in the name of Jesus Christ thou shalt serve him" (59:5).

The measure of that love is the degree to which one keeps the commandments. To both ancient and modern disciples the Savior said, "If ye love me, keep my commandments" (124:87; John 14:15, 21). Great promises are given to "all those who love and serve God with all their mights, minds, and strength"—even "sanctification" (20:31), "the mysteries of his kingdom . . . by the power of the Holy Spirit" (76:114–18), and the many other SPIRITUAL GIFTS given by the HOLY GHOST (46:8–26). Conversely, the Lord revealed, "If you keep not my commandments, the love of the Father shall not continue with you, therefore you shall walk in darkness" (95:12). Given the abiding love of the Father for his children, even his disobedient children, this verse could mean that the disobedient person will not feel the same love toward the Father as he once did, rather than that the Father's love for that person will not continue. It may also mean that the Father's blessings will not continue, as the Father withdraws the Spirit from the disobedient soul, leaving him to walk in darkness.

The love of mankind for each other

As a corollary to the commandment to love God with all one's heart, might, mind, and strength, God directed, "Thou shalt love thy neighbor as thyself" (59:5–6). As part of "the law" revealed to the Church in February 1831, the Lord instructed the Saints, "Thou shalt live together in love, insomuch that thou shalt weep for the loss of them that die, and more especially for those that have not hope of a glorious resurrection" (42:45). In the same revelation, the Lord commanded husbands, "Thou shalt love thy wife with all thy heart, and shalt cleave unto her and none else" (42:22). When organizing the School of the Prophets, the Lord instructed, "See that ye love one another; cease to be covetous; learn to impart one to another as the gospel requires" (88:123). Love for one another is not just for brothers and sisters in the gospel but for all mankind, as Thomas B. Marsh, the president of the Quorum of the Twelve, learned from the Lord: "I know thy heart, and have heard thy prayers concerning thy brethren [of the Twelve]. Be not partial towards them in love above many others, but let thy love be for them as for thyself; and let thy love abound unto all men" (112:11).

Love as a qualification for service in the Lord's kingdom

In calling Joseph Smith Sr. to service in the restored kingdom of God, the Lord instructed, "Faith, hope, charity and love, with an eye single to the glory of God, qualify him for the work" (4:1–7). Joseph Knight was reminded, "No one can assist in this work except he shall be humble and full of love, having faith, hope, and charity, being temperate in all things" (12:8). Instructions concerning proper priesthood administration make it clear that "no power or influence can or ought to be maintained by virtue of the priesthood, only by persuasion, by long-suffering, by gentleness and meekness, and by love unfeigned" (121:41). Also, although someone may need to be reproved, as when a priesthood leader is "moved upon by the Holy Ghost," that priesthood leader is to show forth "afterwards an increase of love toward him whom [he has] reproved, lest he esteem [him] to be his enemy" (121:43).

Love can be lost and misdirected

Speaking to his disciples in Jerusalem concerning the signs of the times preceding his second coming, the Lord revealed, "And the love of men shall wax cold, and iniquity shall abound" (45:27; cf. JS–M 1:10, 30; Matt. 24:12). What causes love to wax cold, or leads mankind to love darkness rather than light? Of those who stole the 116 pages of Book of Mormon translation, the Lord said, "They love darkness rather than light, because their deeds are evil; therefore they will not ask of me. Satan stirreth them up, that he may lead their souls to destruction" (10:21–22; cf. 29:45; Moses 5:13; John 3:18–21).

See also Charity.

DKO

Lowliness of heart. *See* Humble, humility.

Lucifer. *See* Satan.

Lust

Carnal urges, sensual appetites, usually in reference to sexual desire but extended to include desires for self-indulgent gratification of other bodily or worldly cravings. The Doctrine and Covenants contains verses employing both these connotations. In regard to sexual lust, the revelations warn that "he that looketh on a woman to lust after her . . . shall not have the Spirit, but shall deny the faith and shall fear" (63:16). Further, "if he repents not he shall be cast out" (42:23). The broader connotation seems to be used when the Lord instructed the Saints to "cease . . . from all your lustful desires," as well as other sins, in connection with the command to build the Kirtland Temple (88:119–21) and when he explained that "lustful and covetous desires" were among the reasons why the Lord "suffered" the enemies of the Church to expel the Saints from Jackson County, Missouri, in 1833 (101:1–6). The broader meaning is also appropriate in relation to those who seek signs "that they may consume it upon their lusts," that is, they seek signs for their own gratification rather than for the glory of God (46:9).

See also Adultery; Carnal, sensual, and devilish; Fornication.

LED

Lyman, Amasa

Birth: 30 March 1813, Lyman, Grafton County, New Hampshire

Death: 4 February 1877, Fillmore, Millard County, Utah

Amasa Mason Lyman was about two years old when his father abandoned the family. After his mother's remarriage, Lyman lived with his grandfather and then with his uncle. During these traumatic times, Lyman said he became "thoughtful on the subject of religion, and found peace with God" ("History," 472). When he heard the gospel of Jesus Christ preached, he embraced it and was baptized on 27 April 1832. Because of the ill feeling his conversion caused in his uncle's family, Lyman left New Hampshire on a seven-hundred-mile journey to join the Saints in Ohio. At Hiram, Ohio, he stayed with the John Johnson family for a period and met the Prophet Joseph Smith. The Prophet called him on a mission, and on 23 August 1832 ordained him an elder. Lyman labored with Zerubbabel Snow in southern Ohio and Cabell County, Virginia, and later in 1833 with William F. Cahoon in the east (Jenson, 96–97). "He held 150 meetings and saw about one hundred souls added to the Church" (Jenson, 98).

In 1834, soon after returning to Kirtland, he marched with Zion's Camp, an experience he characterized as "afford[ing] us ample opportunity to evince our faith by offering our lives for the truth" (Lyman, *Amasa*, 43). He married shortly after his return and continued his missionary efforts both in the east and in Ohio before relocating to Far West, Missouri, in 1837.

When the Saints were expelled from Missouri in 1839 and after being released from jail in Richmond, Missouri, Lyman settled in Commerce (later Nauvoo), Illinois, and was listed as a counselor in the high priests quorum (124:136). On 20 August 1842, at age twenty-nine, Lyman was ordained an apostle by Brigham Young. He was called as a counselor to the First Presidency early in 1843. When the Prophet Joseph Smith was martyred, Lyman supported the Twelve Apostles as holding the keys of the kingdom: "I do not rise to electioneer. . . . I have been at the back of Joseph Smith,

Amasa M. Lyman, 1813–1877.

Courtesy Church History Library

and will be at the back of the Twelve forever" (Smith, 7:236–37). Later he was chosen to "organize a company" with George A. Smith to emigrate west (136:14). In April 1863, Lyman was appointed to settle in Fillmore, Millard County, Utah. In his later years, he professed strange doctrines concerning the Savior and the Atonement and was excommunicated from the Church on 12 May 1870. His blessings were restored posthumously.

BIBLIOGRAPHY

Jenson, Andrew. *Latter-day Saint Biographical Encyclopedia.* 4 vols. Salt Lake City: Andrew Jenson History Co., 1901–36. Reprint, Salt Lake City: Western Epics, 1971.

Lyman, Albert R. *Amasa Mason Lyman, Trailblazer and Pioneer from the Atlantic to the Pacific.* Edited by Melvin A. Lyman. Delta, Utah: Melvin A. Lyman, 1957.

Lyman, Amasa. "Amasa Lyman's History." *Millennial Star* 27 (1865): 472–73.

Smith, Joseph. *History of The Church of Jesus Christ of Latter-day Saints.* Edited by B. H. Roberts. 7 vols. 2d ed. rev. Salt Lake City: The Church of Jesus Christ of Latter-day Saints, 1932–51.

KWF

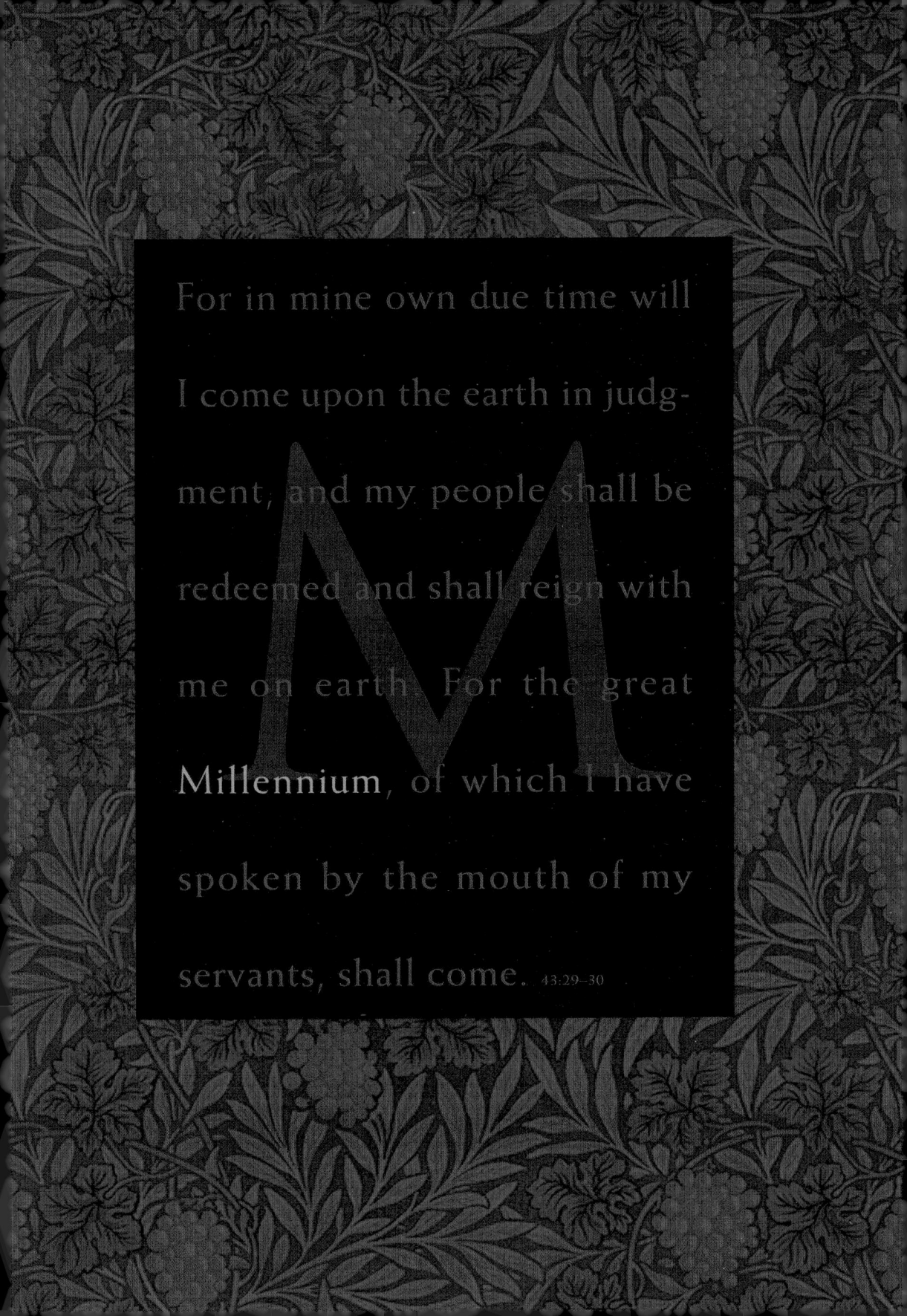

For in mine own due time will I come upon the earth in judgment, and my people shall be redeemed and shall reign with me on earth. For the great **Millennium**, of which I have spoken by the mouth of my servants, shall come. 43:29–30

Madison, Iowa

Likely Fort Madison, Iowa, the oldest U.S. military garrison on the upper Mississippi. Referred to once in the Doctrine and Covenants (124:88), Madison, Iowa, is located on the west side of the Mississippi River about ten miles north of Nauvoo (Brown et al., Map 28). William Law was commanded to "proclaim my everlasting gospel . . . unto the inhabitants of Warsaw . . . Carthage . . . Burlington, and . . . Madison" (124:88). It is not known whether Law fulfilled that mission. *See* map, p. 277.

BIBLIOGRAPHY

Brown, S. Kent, Donald Q. Cannon, and Richard H. Jackson, eds. *Historical Atlas of Mormonism.* New York: Simon and Schuster, 1994.

DQC

Magna Charta

A charter of liberties and political rights obtained from King John of England in 1215. The memorial to the martyrs Joseph and Hyrum Smith penned by John Taylor found in 135:7 contains the term "magna charta": "They were innocent of any crime, as they had often been proved before, and were only confined in jail by the conspiracy of traitors and wicked men; and their *innocent blood* on the floor of Carthage jail is a broad seal affixed to 'Mormonism' that cannot be rejected by any court on earth . . . ; and their *innocent blood* on the banner of liberty, and on the *magna charta* of the United States, is an ambassador for the religion of Jesus Christ" (emphasis added). Here, "magna charta" refers to the United States CONSTITUTION. The Lord, and therefore, The Church of Jesus Christ of Latter-day Saints, considers the United States Constitution to be an inspired document (98:5–6; 101:77–80; 109:54). Modern prophets have spoken about the Constitution and its divine origins (Cannon, 46, 120, 133).

See also Historical context and overview of Doctrine and Covenants 135 (p. 854); Martyrdom of Joseph and Hyrum Smith.

BIBLIOGRAPHY

Cannon, Donald Q. *Latter-day Prophets and the United States Constitution.* Provo, Utah: Religious Studies Center, Brigham Young University, 1991.

DQC

Magnify. *See* Appendix E.

Mahalaleel

HIGH PRIEST and ordained PATRIARCH in the time of Adam; lived 895 years (Moses 6:20). Mahalaleel was the son of Cainan and the father of Jared (Gen. 5:12–17; Moses 6:19–20). A modern revelation on PRIESTHOOD adds important details about Mahalaleel. At age "four hundred ninety-six years and seven days," he was ordained in the patriarchal order of the priesthood and blessed by Adam (107:39–52). Mahalaleel was present with seven generations of patriarchs and the "residue of [Adam's] posterity who were righteous" at ADAM-ONDI-AHMAN three years before the death of Adam. In that gathering Adam bestowed his last blessing upon those present. The Lord appeared, "and they rose up and blessed Adam, and called him Michael, the prince, the archangel" (107:53–54).

RJM

Make his paths straight. *See* Strait, straight.

Malachi

One of the latest of the Old Testament prophets, dated linguistically to about 500 B.C. His name, meaning "My Messenger," is probably drawn from Malachi 3:1. His ministry was in Jerusalem after the return of the Jews from the Exile. Chapters 1 and 2 of Malachi contain the Lord's complaints primarily against the priests at the temple. Chapters 3 and 4 are mostly a collection of short prophecies, generally pertaining to the last days. His most oft-quoted words among Latter-day Saints are his admonitions concerning tithing (Mal. 3:8–12) and "turn[ing] the heart of the fathers to the children, and the heart of the children to their fathers" (128:17). Quotations from Malachi in the Doctrine and Covenants have a clear latter-day focus. Joseph Smith said that Malachi "had his eye fixed on the restoration of the priesthood" and "the glories to be revealed in the last days" (128:17). *See* Malachi quotations in the Doctrine and Covenants.

KPJ

Malachi quotations in the Doctrine and Covenants

Important prophecies concerning latter-day events from the writings of the Old Testament prophet Malachi (Mal. 3–4). Jesus quoted extensively from Malachi's writings when he visited the children of Lehi (3 Ne. 24–25), and Moroni quoted from them to Joseph Smith (JS–H 1:36–39). In the Doctrine and Covenants, Malachi's words are quoted and discussed, and phrases from his prophecies are used in a variety of contexts.

Using language from Malachi 3:1 that might be applied to many people, the Lord told Sidney Rigdon that he had been sent forth "to prepare the way before me" (35:4). Early converts and Church leaders were sent forth to preach and administer saving ordinances, "preparing the way before my face for the time of my coming" (39:20; 84:107; 124:139). The restored gospel itself is "a messenger before my face to prepare the way before me" (45:9), and the entire effort of the latter-day Church is "preparing of the way before the time of his coming" (77:12).

Malachi foretold that the Lord would "suddenly come to his temple" (Mal. 3:1), and in the Doctrine and Covenants, Jesus identified himself as the one who would come (36:8; 133:2). In response to Malachi's question, "Who may abide the day of his coming?" (Mal. 3:2), the Savior answered in the Doctrine and Covenants: those who would hear his voice, be purified, and overcome temptation (35:21; 38:8; 61:39). Using the same words found in Malachi 3:17, the Lord said concerning the faithful, "Yet I will own them, and they shall be mine in that day when I shall come to make up my jewels" (101:3; 60:4). See Jewels.

In an 1842 letter to the Saints, Joseph Smith quoted Malachi 3:2–3, changing only the words "who may abide" and "who shall stand" to "who *can* abide" and "who *can* stand." To Malachi's words he added these: "Let us, therefore, as a church and a people, and as Latter-day Saints, offer unto the Lord an offering in righteousness" (128:24; emphasis added), drawing words from Malachi 3:3. When restoring the Aaronic Priesthood, John the Baptist promised that it would "never be taken again from the earth, until the sons of Levi do offer again an offering unto the Lord in righteousness" (13:1), again echoing Malachi 3:3. As for the Latter-day Saints, they are to "offer a sacrifice unto the Lord thy God in righteousness, even that of a broken heart and a contrite spirit" (59:8, 11).

Malachi 4:1 from the King James Version is quoted in its entirety in Doctrine and Covenants 133:64. In two other revelations, however, the phrase, "the day that cometh shall burn them up," is changed to "*I* will burn them up" (29:9; 64:24; emphasis added; cf. JS–H 1:37).

The prophecy of Malachi perhaps most recognized in the Doctrine and Covenants is that of the coming of Elijah (Mal. 4:5–6). To Elijah, the Lord "committed the keys of the power of turning the hearts of the fathers to the children, and the hearts of the children to the fathers, that the whole earth may not be smitten with a curse" (27:9; cf. 98:16–17). Moroni quoted the prophecy to Joseph Smith with important variations from the King James translation (cf. Mal. 4:5–6; D&C 2). Two important differences are "I will reveal unto you the Priesthood, by the hand of Elijah the prophet" in place of "I will send you Elijah the prophet" and "he shall plant in the hearts of the children the promises made to the fathers" in place of "he shall turn the heart of the fathers to the children." In Joseph Smith's 1842 letter to the Saints, he quoted Malachi's prophecy of Elijah and explained that the welding link necessary to assure that the earth would not be destroyed at Christ's coming is provided by temple ordinances for the dead (128:18). In his preserved sermons and writings, Joseph Smith commented more on Malachi's prophecy of Elijah than on any other biblical passage (69–74). President Joseph F. Smith referred to the prophecy when discussing Elijah and "the great work to be done in the temples of the Lord" (138:48; cf. 138:46–48). See Salvation for the dead.

The fulfillment of Malachi's prophecy of the coming of Elijah is recorded in the Doctrine and Covenants. On 3 April 1836, Elijah appeared in the Kirtland Temple to Joseph Smith and Oliver Cowdery, saying: "Behold, the time has fully come, which was spoken of by the mouth of Malachi—testifying that he [Elijah] should be sent, before the great and dreadful day of the Lord come—to turn the hearts of the fathers to the children, and the children to the fathers, lest the whole earth be smitten with a curse—therefore, the keys of this dispensation are committed into your hands; and by this ye may know that the great and dreadful day of the Lord is near, even at the doors" (110:13–16). *See* Historical context and overview of Doctrine and Covenants 110 (p. 819).

BIBLIOGRAPHY

Smith, Joseph. *Joseph Smith's Commentary on the Bible.* Comp. Kent P. Jackson. Salt Lake City: Deseret Book, 1994.

KPJ

Mammon of unrighteousness

This phrase occurs once in the Doctrine and Covenants, when the Lord gave the Saints in Missouri the same commandment he had given his disciples in the New Testament: "This is wisdom, make unto yourselves friends with the mammon of unrighteousness, and they will not destroy you" (82:22; cf. Luke 16:9).

The English word *mammon* in the New Testament is a transliteration of the Aramaic *mamona,* which means "wealth" or "profit." In the Sermon on the Mount, Jesus said, "Ye cannot serve God and mammon" (Matt. 6:24; 3 Ne. 13:24). Mammon came to be personified as the god of riches. Jesus commanded his disciples anciently to follow the example of the unjust steward, who made friends by forgiving debts, to make "friends of the mammon of unrighteousness; that, when ye fail, they may receive you into everlasting habitations" (Luke 16:9). While the meaning of unrighteous mammon may be money gained by deceit, the point is that one can use money to make friends, which may ultimately render earthly and eternal benefits.

Likewise in the Doctrine and Covenants, making "friends with the mammon of unrighteousness" is a figurative expression for the Saints in Missouri to make friends with their enemies and to leave judgment to the Lord (82:22–23). In regard to this passage, President Joseph Fielding Smith said: "It is not intended that in making friends of the 'mammon of unrighteousness' [Luke 16:9] that the brethren

were to partake with them in their sins; to receive them to their bosoms, intermarry with them and otherwise come down to their level. They were to so live that peace with their enemies might be assured. They were to treat them kindly, be friendly with them as far as correct and virtuous principles would permit. . . . If they could allay prejudice and show a willingness to trade with [them] and show a kindly spirit, it might help to turn them away from their bitterness" (1:323).

Another application of making friends with the "mammon of unrighteousness," in the context of 82:22, may be to make friends of riches themselves, that is, use them properly, that "they will not destroy you."

BIBLIOGRAPHY

Smith, Joseph Fielding. *Church History and Modern Revelation.* 2 vols. Salt Lake City: Deseret Book, 1953.

DRS

Man, creation of

The Doctrine and Covenants makes clear that the creation of man began long before the events in the Garden of Eden. Man was created spiritually before the world was (49:17; cf. Moses 3:5), and even before that spiritual creation, man existed as INTELLIGENCE. "Man was also in the beginning with God. Intelligence, or the light of truth, was not created or made, neither indeed can be" (93:29). Therefore, mankind was not "created" in the traditional sense of *ex nihilo,* or out of nothing, since "intelligence" exists coeternally with God (Smith, 6:310–11). A Heavenly Father and a Heavenly Mother clothed intelligence in a spirit body and thus each became a spirit child of God (First Presidency).

The Doctrine and Covenants confirms the biblical reality of the earthly creation. Adam was created by God (29:34) and was the "first man" (84:16; cf. Moses 3:7). "On the seventh day he [God] finished his work, and sanctified it, and also formed man out of the dust of the earth" (77:12). Adam and Eve were created in a state of innocence and became "subject" to Satan's will only through transgression (29:40). Moreover, "every spirit of man was innocent in the beginning; and God having redeemed man from the fall, men became again, in their infant state, innocent before God" (93:38). *See* Innocent.

The Doctrine and Covenants teaches the eternal necessity of "man" being created male and female, with man and woman coming together as husband and wife to produce children. Were it not so, the earth would not "answer the end of its creation . . . that it might be filled with the measure of man, according to his creation before the world was made" (49:16–17).

BIBLIOGRAPHY

First Presidency and Council of the Twelve Apostles. *The Family: A Proclamation to the World.* Salt Lake City: The Church of Jesus Christ of Latter-day Saints, 1995.

Smith, Joseph. *History of The Church of Jesus Christ of Latter-day Saints.* Edited by B. H. Roberts. 7 vols. 2d ed. rev. Salt Lake City: The Church of Jesus Christ of Latter-day Saints, 1932–51.

MAG

Man, natural. *See* Natural man.

Man, potential to become like God. *See* Exalt, exaltation; God, nature of; Gods.

Manchester, New York

The center of Manchester Township is ten miles north of Canandaigua, the county seat of Ontario County. What became Manchester Township was the easternmost part of Farmington Township. On 31 March 1821 it was divided from Farmington Township, forming Burt Township, and on 16 April 1822 Burt was renamed Manchester. Manchester village is seven miles northeast of Canandaigua. When Joseph Smith Sr. and Alvin Smith contracted with an agent in Canandaigua for their 99.5-acre farm (ca. 1820) the land was still in Farmington Township. The Smiths at that time built and occupied a log house in Palmyra Township, under an arrangement with Samuel Jennings, who owned the land. They would cross the township line to work their land in Farmington (later Manchester, 1822). In early spring 1820 Joseph Smith sought the Lord in prayer on that woodland farm to ask "which of all the sects was right." The Father and the Son appeared to him and in response to his inquiry "answered that [he] must join none of them" (JS–H 1:18–19).

Three years later, the angel Moroni appeared to Joseph in the garret of the log home in Palmyra Township on 21–22 September 1823. An excerpt from Moroni's discourse with Joseph at that time was later mistakenly recorded as having taken place in the Manchester frame home (2, headnote). The Smiths lived in the log home in Palmyra Township until 1825, when they moved into the new Manchester (formerly Farmington) home begun by Alvin Smith in 1822.

On 25 October 1825 Joseph Smith was visited by Josiah Stowell of Chenango County, New York, and asked to assist in Stowell's search for a purported Spanish silver mine in Harmony, Susquehanna County, Pennsylvania. There Joseph met Emma Hale and later married her at South Bainbridge, New York, 18 January 1827. The newlyweds moved to the Manchester frame home and farmed with Father Smith. Joseph received the gold plates from Moroni at the Hill Cumorah on 22 September 1827. Unable to begin the translation because of strenuous efforts by the local mob to steal the plates, Joseph and Emma moved to Harmony. Oliver Cowdery, a schoolteacher, boarded at the Smith's Manchester home during the school year, approximately October 1828 to March 1829. He traveled to Pennsylvania in April 1829, where he became a scribe to Joseph.

Father and Mother Smith had lost ownership of the Manchester farm as early as 20 December 1825 due to complications attending their failure to make payments on the farm. They had been allowed by Lemuel Durfee Sr., the new owner, to remain as renters until spring of 1829, when they were required to vacate it. They moved back to their old Palmyra log home, which was now occupied by Hyrum Smith. Although identified as "Manchester" revelations, Doctrine and Covenants 19 (March 1830), 22 (16 April 1830), and 23 (April 1830) were actually received by the Prophet in the Palmyra log home and not the Manchester frame home. *See* maps, pp. 447 and 476.

See also New York period; Palmyra, New York.

BIBLIOGRAPHY

Enders, Donald L. "The Joseph Smith, Sr., Family: Farmers of the Genesee." In *Joseph Smith The Prophet, The Man,* edited by Susan Easton Black and Charles D. Tate Jr. Provo, Utah: Religious Studies Center, Brigham Young University, 1993.

Gordon, Thomas F. *Gazetteer of the State of New York.* Philadelphia: T. K. and P. G. Collins, Printers, 1836.

Hedges, Andrew H. "'All My Endeavors to Preserve Them': Protecting the Plates in Palmyra, 22 September–December 1827." In *Journal of Book of Mormon Studies.* Vol. 8, 1999, edited by S. Kent Brown and others. Provo, Utah: Foundation for Ancient Research and Mormon Studies, Brigham Young University.

Jensen, Robin Scott, Robert J. Woodford, and Steven C. Harper, eds. *Manuscript Revelation Books.* Facsimile edition. First volume of the Revelations and Translations series of *The Joseph Smith Papers,* edited by Dean C. Jessee, Ronald K. Esplin, and Richard Lyman Bushman. Salt Lake City: Church Historian's Press, 2009.

Porter, Larry C. "A Study of the Origins of the Church of Jesus Christ of Latter-day Saints in the States of New York and Pennsylvania, 1816–1831." Ph.D. dissertation, Brigham Young University, 1971.

Smith, Joseph. *History of The Church of Jesus Christ of Latter-day Saints.* Edited by B. H. Roberts. 7 vols. 2d ed. rev. Salt Lake City: The Church of Jesus Christ of Latter-day Saints, 1932–51.

Spafford, Horatio Gates. *A Gazetteer of the State of New-York.* Albany: B. D. Packard, 1824.

LCP

Manifesto, the. *See* Official Declaration 1.

Mantle. *See* Appendix E.

NO.5.

The Smith family's frame home in Manchester, New York; photograph by George Edward Anderson, 1907. The line between Palmrya Township and Manchester Township ran through the Smiths' property during their time in the area. Their early log home was on the Palmyra side; this later home was on the Manchester side.

Courtesy Church History Library

Many are called, but few are chosen. *See* Chosen.

Marks, William

Birth: 15 November 1792, Rutland, Rutland County, Vermont

Death: 22 May 1872, Plano, Kendall County, Illinois

William Marks was baptized and ordained a priest in New York in the 1830s. After his ordination, he moved his family to Kirtland and opened a book and stationery store. In May 1837 the office of the *Messenger and Advocate* was transferred to him. On 3 September 1837 he was called to serve on the Kirtland high council (*History*, 3:721). In a revelation given to Joseph Smith on 8 July 1838, William Marks and Newel K. Whitney were commanded to settle their business in Kirtland and move to Missouri: "Let them awake, and arise, and come forth, and not tarry, for I, the Lord, command it" (117:2). If they tarried in fulfilling this command, they were told, "it shall not be well with them" (117:3). Marks was further admonished to "be faithful over a few things, and he shall be a ruler over many" and to "preside in the midst of my people in the city of Far West" (117:10). Marks left Kirtland but not before the Saints were driven from Missouri. He joined the Saints in Commerce (later Nauvoo) and served as stake president there. On 19 January 1841, by revelation, Marks was told to ordain Isaac Galland to "accomplish the work" appointed him by Joseph Smith (124:79). He was also told to buy stock in the Nauvoo House "as seemeth him good, for himself and his generation, from generation to generation" (124:80).

Unfortunately, Marks's faith faltered. Joseph Smith, noting Marks's failings and those of William Law, said, "What can be the matter with these men? Is it that the wicked flee when no man pursueth, that hit pigeons always flutter, that drowning men catch at straws, or that Presidents Law and Marks are absolutely traitors to the Church[?]" (6:170). On 7 October 1844 Marks was rejected as the Nauvoo stake president. After the rejection, he identified himself with different spurious organizations successively, led by Sidney Rigdon, James Strang,

Charles B. Thompson, and John E. Page. In 1859 he affiliated with the Reorganized Church of Jesus Christ of Latter Day Saints (RLDS). He was one of three men who in 1860 ordained Joseph Smith III as president of the RLDS church (now Community of Christ). In March 1863 he was named first counselor to President Joseph Smith III.

BIBLIOGRAPHY

The History of the Reorganized Church of Jesus Christ of Latter Day Saints. 8 vols. Independence, Mo.: Herald House, 1967–76.

Smith, Joseph. *History of The Church of Jesus Christ of Latter-day Saints.* Edited by B. H. Roberts. 7 vols. 2d ed. rev. Salt Lake City: The Church of Jesus Christ of Latter-day Saints, 1932–51.

SEB

Marriage

The legal union of a man and a woman as husband and wife. The revelations in the Doctrine and Covenants establish marriage as an institution ordained by God (49:15) and an ordinance of the holy PRIESTHOOD (132:19; A of F 3) necessary for exaltation in the celestial kingdom (131:1–4; 132:19–24). These points are made more clearly here than in any other book of scripture. These revelations also provide counsel and direction regarding duties and responsibilities in married life.

Examples of teachings related to marriage

In a revelation directed to Emma Smith, the Lord admonished her in her duties as a wife, explaining "the office of thy calling shall be for a comfort unto my servant . . . thy husband, in his afflictions, with consoling words, in the spirit of meekness" (25:5). That admonition apparently has general application to all wives, as the last verse says, "Verily, verily, I say unto you, that this is my voice unto all" (25:16). That husbands are to have that same concern for their wives is made clear in a revelation "embracing the law of the Church," which says, "Thou shalt love thy wife with all thy heart, and shalt cleave unto her and none else" (42, headnote; 42:22). Thomas B. Marsh, who would soon be called as the president of the Quorum of the Twelve Apostles, was told to "govern your house in meekness" (31:9; cf. 121:34–46).

All three members of the First Presidency and Bishop Newel K. Whitney were chastened by the Lord concerning their neglect of family duties (93:41–50). Section 74 explains the meaning of 1 Corinthians 7:14 and Paul's counsel relative to marriages between Church members and those who are not members. Section 83 contains the law of the Church for the support of women and children by husbands and fathers and for the care of widows and orphans (vv. 1–6). And surely the promise that in the life to come the "same sociality which exists among us here will exist among us there, only it will be coupled with eternal glory," applies to marriage relationships (130:2).

In a revelation concerning a colony of SHAKERS near Kirtland who viewed celibacy as the highest order of a spiritual life, the Lord taught important truths about marriage.

1. "Whoso forbiddeth to marry is not ordained of God, for marriage is ordained of God unto man" (49:15). Proper marriage, ordained of God, is of vital importance in a modern world that largely considers marriage a man-made institution that evolved with civilization.

2. Marriage is "lawful" before God, and couples "shall be one flesh" (49:16). This metaphor suggests an intended unity of a husband and wife and affirms the lawfulness of sexual union.

3. Procreation within marriage is lawful and expected, "that the earth might answer the end [purpose] of its creation; and that it might be filled with the measure of man, according to his creation before the world was made" (49:16–17; cf. 1 Ne. 17:36). Marriage and procreation are the Lord's established means by which spirit children leave the premortal life, are clothed with a physical body, and experience a necessary mortal probation. Thus, a husband and wife become partners with God in fulfilling "the Creator's plan for the eternal destiny of His children"—his and their divine purposes (First Presidency; Moses 1:38–39).

In mid-May 1843 Joseph Smith traveled from Nauvoo to Ramus, Illinois, to visit family and close friends. His inspired teachings on that occasion were later canonized and appear as Doctrine and Covenants 131. See Historical context and overview of Doctrine and Covenants 131 (p. 847).

The Prophet taught that for anyone to attain exaltation, the highest heaven in the celestial kingdom, "a man must enter into . . . [the new and everlasting covenant of marriage]; and if he does not, he cannot obtain it. He may enter into the other, but that is the end of his kingdom; he cannot have an increase" (131:1–4; brackets in original). This revelation, along with section 132, makes it clear that marriage is an ordinance of the GOSPEL that must be obeyed, consistent with the teachings of Article of Faith 3. Explaining what the word *increase* means, Joseph Smith said, "Except a man and his wife enter into an everlasting covenant and be married for eternity . . . by the power and authority of the Holy Priesthood, they will cease to increase when they die; that is, they will not have any children after the resurrection. But those who are married by the power and authority of the priesthood . . . will continue to increase and have children in the celestial glory" (*History*, 5:391).

The most extensive revelation in the scriptures concerning marriage is section 132. Recorded in 1843, the revelation contains information revealed to Joseph Smith as early as 1831, probably in connection with his work on the inspired translation of the Bible, as well as information relating to the time in 1843 when the revelation was recorded in Nauvoo. Early in the revelation a distinction is made between "*a*" new and everlasting covenant (v. 4), and "*the*" new and everlasting covenant (v. 6). "*The* new and everlasting covenant" is "the fulness of [the] gospel" (66:2; 133:57), the overarching umbrella that comprehends all the principles and ordinances of the gospel, which the Lord said "was instituted for the fulness of my glory" (132:6; cf. Smith, *Doctrines*, 1:153–58). Thus, marriage is "a" new and everlasting covenant, a subset of "the" new and everlasting covenant.

The conditions of *the* new and everlasting covenant are carefully given in 132:6–14. Verse 7 explains that all gospel covenants, including marriage, must meet four conditions to be acceptable to God and to be of "efficacy . . . [and] force in and after the resurrection from the dead": They must be sealed by the Holy Spirit of promise, performed by proper authority, entered into for time and eternity, and authorized by revelation and commandment through God's anointed prophet. Another important point is made in verses 8–13. The Lord's house is a house of order, and what is done therein must be according to his law. Verse 12 says, "I give unto you this commandment—that no man shall come unto the Father but by me or by my word, which is my law, saith the Lord."

The Lord spoke of civil marriage in verses 15–17; addressed a marriage performed for time and eternity but without proper authority in verse 18; and described an acceptable eternal marriage and its blessings in verses 19–28. Finally, the Lord gave instructions regarding plural marriage (vv. 29–49, 58–66).

Civil unions of a man and a woman

Persons whose marriages are contracted by civil or religious agencies are lawful before the Lord for time but do not meet the conditions of the new and everlasting covenant and hence are not binding beyond the grave. The Lord declared that because they did not abide his law, "they cannot be enlarged, but remain separately and singly, without exaltation, in their saved condition, to all eternity; and from henceforth are not gods, but are angels of God forever and ever" (132:17). That is true even if the couples covenant between themselves that their marriage is "for time and for all eternity" but do not meet the other requirements of the Lord's law (v. 18).

Eternal marriage of a man and a woman

Those whose marriage will endure "for time and for all eternity" meet the requirements and are promised that "they shall pass by the angels, and the gods, which are set there, to their exaltation and glory in all things, . . . which glory shall be a fulness and a continuation of the seeds forever and ever. Then shall they be gods, . . . because they have all power, and the angels are subject unto them. . . . For strait is the gate, and narrow the way that leadeth unto the exaltation and continuation of the lives, and . . . broad is the gate, and wide the way that leadeth to the deaths; and many there are that go in thereat,

because they receive me not, neither do they abide in my law" (132:18–25). "Continuation of the seeds" (v. 19), "continuation of the lives" (v. 22), and "eternal lives" (v. 24) all point to the promise of power to beget and bear children in the world to come, helping to fulfill the promise God made with Abraham and to those who become the seed of Abraham through gospel covenants that their children would be as "innumerable as the stars; or, if ye were to count the sand upon the seashore ye could not number them" (vv. 30–31; cf. Abr. 2:9–11; Gen. 13:14–16; 15:5; Gal. 3:27–29). Those who do not obey the new and everlasting covenant of marriage remain "separately and singly, without exaltation" (v. 17). The "deaths" spoken of in 132:25 refer to the everlasting loss such persons experience as a result of their inability to perpetuate the "seeds" forever (vv. 17–25). In the words of Malachi 4:1, they have "neither root nor branch," having not been sealed to ancestry (root) nor possessing the power to have eternal posterity (branch).

Plural marriage

An article on marriage written by Oliver Cowdery was included in the Doctrine and Covenants from 1835 until 1876. That article stated, "We believe, that one man should have one wife; and one woman, but one husband, except in case of death, when either is at liberty to marry again" (1835 edition, sect. CI, para. 4). In the 1876 edition of the Doctrine and Covenants, the revelation that had introduced the principle of plural marriage became section 132, replacing the earlier article on marriage. Elder Orson Pratt observed, "Like the Church of God in all former ages, we receive no new ordinances, neither old ordinances, only by new revelation." He continued, "We would not dare presume to enter into this or that form of marriage, pertaining to plural matrimony, by any former revelation; it has been by new revelation that these things have been done" (26).

The portion of section 132 concerning plural marriage was revealed as early as 1831 in answer to Joseph Smith's asking to "know and understand" wherein the Lord justified Abraham and others in earlier times in "having many wives and concubines" (v. 1). The Lord explained that

Abraham and others were not under condemnation for having plural wives because they had been obedient to the Lord's law (vv. 29–36). Many persons after Abraham practiced plural marriage righteously, but some, according to the revelation, including David and Solomon, abused the principle by taking wives not authorized by the Lord (vv. 37–39).

A related passage is found in the Book of Mormon. Through the prophet Lehi, the Lord commanded the Nephites to have only one wife, and Lehi's son Jacob rebuked the Nephites for excusing themselves "in committing whoredoms, because of the things which were written concerning David, and Solomon." Jacob also reinforced the need for the Lord's direction in practicing plural marriage when he wrote, "For if I will, saith the Lord of Hosts, raise up seed unto me, I will command my people; otherwise they shall hearken unto these things," that is, having one wife (Jacob 2:23–35). Inherent in these examples is the principle that plural marriage is to be practiced only when God commands it by revelation to his authorized servants.

This revelation concluded with a discussion of what is designated in verse 65 as "the law of Sarah." Basically, that law is that a first wife, once she is taught the law, is to agree to a second wife, as did Sarah, when Abraham was commanded to take her handmaid, Hagar, to wife. If she refuses, the revelation says her husband is "exempt from the law of Sarah" and can receive whomever the Lord "will give unto him," presumably without her permission (vv. 64–65). Perhaps anticipating that what was said in those verses might leave one with questions, the Lord promised to reveal more hereafter "pertaining to this law" (v. 66).

Just as revelation was required to restore the practice of plural marriage in this dispensation, so also was revelation required for the practice to cease. President Wilford Woodruff received that revelation, which led him to issue the Manifesto in 1890, calling for the discontinuance of the practice. See Official Declaration 1.

Reasons the Lord commanded the practice of plural marriage

Section 132 contains the following statements, which provide some answers to the question of why the early restored Church practiced plural marriage.

1. "By this law is the continuation of the works of my Father, wherein he glorifieth himself" (v. 31); "God is thus glorified and exalted in the salvation and exaltation of all His children" (Smith, *History,* 6:306).

2. Joseph Smith was told: "Go ye, therefore, and do the works of Abraham; enter ye into my law . . . for I have conferred upon you the keys and power of the priesthood, wherein I restore all things" (vv. 32–45).

3. "To fulfil the promise which was given by my Father before the foundation of the world, and for their exaltation in the eternal worlds, that they may bear the souls of men; for herein is the work of my Father continued" (vv. 58–63).

See also Historical context and overview of Doctrine and Covenants 132 (p. 849).

BIBLIOGRAPHY

Bachman, Danel W. "The Eternity of the Marriage Relationship." In *Riches of Eternity,* edited by John K. Challis and John G. Scott. Salt Lake City: Aspen Books, 1993.

Doctrine and Covenants. 1835. Church Historical Library, The Church of Jesus Christ of Latter-day Saints, Salt Lake City, Utah.

First Presidency and Council of the Twelve Apostles. *The Family: A Proclamation to the World.* Salt Lake City: The Church of Jesus Christ of Latter-day Saints, 1995.

Pratt, Orson. Conference Report, April 1880, 25–27.

Smith, Joseph. *History of The Church of Jesus Christ of Latter-day Saints.* Edited by B. H. Roberts. 7 vols. 2d ed. rev. Salt Lake City: The Church of Jesus Christ of Latter-day Saints, 1932–51.

Smith, Joseph Fielding. *Doctrines of Salvation.* Compiled by Bruce R. McConkie. 3 vols. Salt Lake City: Bookcraft, 1954–56.

DWB

Marriage of the Lamb

An event associated with the second coming of Jesus Christ. The marriage of the Lamb (58:11) represents the uniting of the Savior, symbolically referred to as the BRIDEGROOM (33:17; 65:3; 88:92; 133:10, 19), with his BRIDE, meaning the Church and its righteous members. This event includes what is referred to in the Doctrine and Covenants as the "supper of the house of the Lord" (58:9), "the supper of the Lord" (58:11), and "the supper of the Lamb" (65:3).

This marriage and supper are patterned after customs among the Israelites. Following the marriage ceremony, the couple "were crowned with garlands, and a marriage deed was signed. After the prescribed washing of hands and benediction, the marriage supper was held" (LDS Bible Dictionary, s.v. "marriage").

According to the Doctrine and Covenants, the invitation to the Lamb's marriage and subsequent supper is to be extended to all. "First, [shall] the rich and the learned, the wise and the noble," and "then shall the poor, the lame, and the blind, and the deaf, come in unto the marriage of the Lamb, and partake of the supper of the Lord" (58:10–11).

This invitation is reminiscent of the parable of the marriage of the king's son found in the New Testament (Matt. 22:1–14). In it the Savior taught that those who had first been invited to the marriage feast by the King "made light of it, and went their ways" (Matt. 22:5). The king then had his servants go into the highways and invite to the marriage "as many as ye shall find" (Matt. 22:9).

Although the invitation is extended to all, only the faithful will be admitted to the supper. Joseph Smith taught, "Those who are found faithful to the Lord . . . will be found worthy to inherit a seat at the marriage-supper" (Smith, 2:19). In preparation for this great event, the "keys of the kingdom of God are committed unto man on the earth" (65:2). Possessing the necessary KEYS, the Lord's servants are charged to go forth and "prepare . . . the supper of the Lamb, make ready for the Bridegroom" (65:3) and prepare for the day when "the Son of Man shall come down . . . to meet the kingdom of God which is set up on the earth" (65:5). As in the PARABLE OF THE TEN VIRGINS in the New Testament, those who "are wise and have received the truth, and have taken the Holy Spirit for their guide, and have not been deceived" shall be prepared for the marriage of the Lamb and "abide the day" (45:56–57; 63:54).

See also Jesus Christ, second coming of.

BIBLIOGRAPHY

Smith, Joseph. *History of The Church of Jesus Christ of Latter-day Saints.* Edited by B. H. Roberts. 7 vols. 2d ed. rev. Salt Lake City: The Church of Jesus Christ of Latter-day Saints, 1932–51.

RLH

Marsh, Thomas B.

Birth: 1 November 1799, Acton, Middlesex County, Massachusetts

Death: January 1866, Ogden, Weber County, Utah

Thomas B. Marsh was baptized on 3 September 1830 by David Whitmer. A few days later he was ordained an elder and told by revelation that he was blessed "because of [his] faith in my work" (31:1). He was further told to "lift up your heart and rejoice, for the hour of your mission is come" (31:3), and that he was to "be a physician unto the church" (31:10).

On 6 June 1831, he was called by revelation to travel to Missouri with Ezra Thayre and to preach the gospel "by the way" (52:22). Thayre was unable to leave on the mission when Marsh was ready to travel. Joseph Smith received a revelation instructing Marsh to journey with Selah Griffin instead: "Wherefore, I revoke the commandment which was given unto my servants Thomas B. Marsh and Ezra Thayre, and give a new commandment unto my servant Thomas, that he shall take up his journey speedily to the land of Missouri, and my servant Selah J. Griffin shall also go with him" (56:5). Marsh and his companion left Kirtland in June 1831. On 25 January 1832 he was called by revelation to fulfill the appointed mission with Ezra Thayre (75:31). He and Thayre preached the gospel in New York.

In 1835 Thomas B. Marsh was called to the Quorum of the Twelve Apostles. One of the first official acts of the Quorum was to testify to the truthfulness of the Doctrine and Covenants ("Explanatory Introduction"). *See* Doctrine and Covenants, testimony of the Twelve Apostles to the truth of.

On 23 July 1837, in a revelation directed to Marsh as president of the Quorum of the Twelve Apostles, the Lord said, "There have been some few things in thine heart and with thee with which I, the Lord, was not well pleased" (112:2). He was admonished to be "humble; and the Lord thy God shall lead thee by the hand, and give thee answer to thy prayers" (112:10). On 8 July 1838 Marsh was told, again by revelation, to "remain for a season in the land of Zion, to publish my word" (118:2).

In August 1838 the oft-quoted "cream strippings" incident occurred. Marsh's wife, Elizabeth, and George W. Harris's wife, Lucinda, decided to make cheese, and, as George A. Smith explained, "Mrs. Marsh, wishing to make some extra good cheese, saved a pint of strippings from each cow and sent Mrs. Harris the milk without the strippings" (3:283). From small beginnings the issue of strippings escalated to Church trials and an appeal to the First Presidency. Marsh did not sustain the decision of the Prophet, nor did he endure well the persecutions heaped upon members of the Church in Missouri at that time. According to Joseph Smith, "[Marsh] made affidavit . . . to all the vilest slanders, aspersions, lies and calumnies towards [Joseph Smith] and the Church" (*History*, 3:167). Marsh was excommunicated on 17 March 1839, and for the next eighteen years, he remained outside the Church. In the summer of 1857, after being rebaptized, he journeyed with the Walker Company to the Salt Lake Valley, arriving on 4 September 1857. The next day he visited Brigham Young. "He came into my office and wished to know whether I could be reconciled to him, and whether there could be a reconciliation between himself and the Church of the living God," recalled President Young (5:206).

Thomas B. Marsh was baptized on 16 July 1857. On his birthday, 1 November 1862, he was endowed in the ENDOWMENT HOUSE. He died impoverished and an invalid at age sixty-six.

See also Apostles, the first Twelve of latter days; Historical context and overview of Doctrine and Covenants 112 (p. 822).

BIBLIOGRAPHY

Smith, George A. *Journal of Discourses*. 26 vols. London: Latter-day Saints' Book Depot, 1854–86.

Smith, Joseph. *History of The Church of Jesus Christ of Latter-day Saints*. Edited by B. H. Roberts. 7 vols. 2d ed. rev. Salt Lake City: The Church of Jesus Christ of Latter-day Saints, 1932–51.

Young, Brigham. *Journal of Discourses*. 26 vols. London: Latter-day Saints' Book Depot, 1854–86.

SEB

Martyrdom of Joseph and Hyrum Smith

From his first youthful utterance in the Palmyra woods to his last prayer at Carthage, Joseph Smith sought to do the will of God. His search, combined with committed obedience, enabled sacred truths from dispensations past to be revealed. Revelations, translations, covenants, and eternal truths were his life's labor. Joseph's devotion to God "left a fame and name that cannot be slain" (135:3). Yet persecution was also the lot of Joseph and his brother Hyrum. Ridicule, arrest warrants, and evil speaking against them were their common foes. Doctrines held sacred by the brothers (for example, temple ordinances and the nature of God) were distorted in an attempt to disprove their claims of divine revelation and to arouse public sentiment against them. Despite heavenly protection throughout their ordeals, in June of 1844 Joseph was filled with premonitions of his impending death: "All the enemies upon the face of the earth may roar and exert all their power to bring about my death, but they can accomplish nothing, unless some who are among us and enjoy our society, have been with us in our councils, participated in our confidence . . . join with our enemies, turn our virtues into faults, and, by falsehood and deceit, stir up their wrath and indignation against us, and bring their united vengeance upon our heads" (6:152).

Joseph's premonitions became reality when William and Wilson Law, Chauncey and Francis Higbee, Robert and Charles Foster, and others sought his destruction. Their evil plans ignited public sentiment as they divulged their intent in the *Nauvoo Expositor*. The first and only issue of that newspaper branded Joseph as a base seducer, liar, and murderer and called for the

THE TWO MARTYRS,

Joseph & Hyrum Smith

Murdered at Carthage, Ill. June 27th 1844.

The Two Martyrs, Joseph and Hyrum Smith; *engraving by an unknown nineteenth-century artist.* "Henceforward their names will be classed among the martyrs of religion; and the reader in every nation will be reminded that the Book of Mormon, and this book of Doctrine and Covenants of the church, cost the best blood of the nineteenth century to bring them forth for the salvation of a ruined world. . . . They lived for glory; they died for glory; and glory is their eternal reward. From age to age shall their names go down to posterity as gems for the sanctified"* (D&C 135:6).

repeal of the Nauvoo Charter. Swift action by the Nauvoo city council led to the *Expositor* being declared a public nuisance. After the press and type were destroyed, the publishers fled to the county seat of Carthage and there charged Joseph and Hyrum with riot and the destruction of their property.

Events surrounding the *Expositor* incident fueled the prejudice and hatred festering in Carthage and such nearby towns as Warsaw. Thomas Sharp, editor of the *Warsaw Signal*, wrote: "War and extermination is inevitable! Citizens, Arise, One and All!!! Can you stand by and suffer such Infernal Devils! to rob men of their property and rights, without avenging them? We have no time to comment: every man will make his own. *Let it be made with powder and ball!!!*" (Roberts, 2:236).

Joseph and Hyrum Smith were arrested twice on the charge of riot and discharged. The legal process, however, did not pacify their enemies in Carthage or Warsaw. Governor Thomas Ford

yielded to public outcries and demanded that the Smith brothers appear in a Carthage courtroom. Joseph and Hyrum attempted to escape another courtroom scene, but their attempt was abated when friends entreated them to give themselves up to the law in Carthage. Of their entreaties Joseph said, "If my life is of no value to my friends it is of none to myself" (6:549).

Early in the morning of 24 June 1844 the Smith brothers left Nauvoo for Carthage. As Joseph turned to gaze upon Nauvoo for the final time, he said, "This is the loveliest place and the best people under the heavens; little do they know the trials that await them" (6:554).

For Joseph and Hyrum, Carthage was a scene of broken promises, conspiracy oaths, illegal arraignment, and incarceration. Accusations of riot were turned to treason; secrets once whispered were now shouted. Throngs unabashedly declared that the Smith brothers would not leave Carthage alive. Joseph wrote to his wife Emma: "I am very much resigned to my lot,

Mob at Carthage Jail; *painting by William Maughan. "To seal the testimony of this book and the Book of Mormon, we announce the martyrdom of Joseph Smith the Prophet, and Hyrum Smith the Patriarch. They were shot in Carthage jail, on the 27th of June, 1844, about five o'clock p.m., by an armed mob—painted black—of from 150 to 200 persons"* (D&C 135:1).

knowing I am justified and have done the best that could be done. Give my love to the children and all my friends. . . . May God bless you all" (Roberts, 2:268–69).

Mobbers gathered around the jail where Joseph and Hyrum were confined sang, "Where now is the Prophet Joseph?" concluding with "Safe in Carthage jail!" Everyone knew that the Smith brothers were not safe, however, for even the governor, though not in boisterous song, had joined the chorus of conspirators, mobs, and military in abetting the deaths of Joseph and Hyrum (Roberts, 2:281).

On the afternoon of 27 June 1844, while Joseph and Hyrum were conversing with two members of the Twelve—John Taylor and Willard Richards—in a bedroom on the second floor of the jail, "an armed mob—painted black—of from 150 to 200 persons" surrounded the jail (135:1). Despite early attempts to protect themselves against mob violence, the four men were no match for the number and brutality of the assassins.

Hyrum was the first to fall. One ball pierced the upper panel of the bedroom door and struck him in the face just left of the nose. He fell back crying, "*I am a dead man!*" (135:1). Bending over the body of his lifeless brother, Joseph sobbed, "Oh dear, brother Hyrum!" (Smith, 6:618). John Taylor was the second victim of the murderous mob; four balls pierced his body. Joseph was next. He "leaped from the window, and was shot dead in the attempt, exclaiming: *O Lord my God!*" (135:1). John Taylor survived the attack and Willard Richards miraculously "escaped, without even a hole in his robe" (135:2).

Of the deaths of Joseph and Hyrum Smith, John Taylor wrote, "Henceforward their names will be classed among the martyrs of religion; and the reader in every nation will be reminded that the Book of Mormon, and this book of Doctrine and Covenants of the church, cost the best blood of the nineteenth century to bring them forth for the salvation of a ruined world" (135:6).

See also Carthage, Illinois; Historical context and overview of Doctrine and Covenants 135 (p. 854); Illinois period; Magna Charta.

BIBLIOGRAPHY

Roberts, B. H. *A Comprehensive History of The Church of Jesus Christ of Latter-day Saints, Century One.* 6 vols. Salt Lake City: The Church of Jesus Christ of Latter-day Saints, 1930. Reprint, Provo, Utah: Brigham Young University Press, 1965.

Smith, Joseph. *History of The Church of Jesus Christ of Latter-day Saints.* Edited by B. H. Roberts. 7 vols. 2d ed. rev. Salt Lake City: The Church of Jesus Christ of Latter-day Saints, 1932–51.

SEB

Marvelous work. *See* Great and marvelous work.

Matthew

One of the original apostles called by Jesus and writer of the book of Matthew in the New Testament. Matthew is named once in the Doctrine and Covenants, where the Prophet Joseph Smith quotes Matthew 16:18–19, affirming that the Lord gave to Peter "the keys of the kingdom of heaven," including the power to seal on earth and in heaven, and to receive revelation "in relation to the salvation of the children of men, both as well for the dead as for the living" (128:9–11).

Before his call, Matthew was also known as Levi. He was a publican, a tax collector who seems to have been working not for Rome but rather for Herod Antipas, in whose tetrarchy he was operating (LDS Bible Dictionary, s.v. "Matthew"). His "receipt of custom" was located in or near the Galilean city of Capernaum, where he collected import duties on goods going between the tetrarchies of Antipas and his half-brother Philip (Matt. 10:1–4; Mark 2:14; Luke 5:27). Matthew's writings evidence a thorough knowledge of the Old Testament, and they appear to be directed toward convincing the JEWS that Jesus was indeed the MESSIAH, a fulfillment of the prophecies of the ancient prophets (e.g., Matt. 1:22–23; 2:17–18, 23; 4:13–14; 8:16–17). Little is known of his later life; tradition suggests he died as a martyr.

LED

McLellin, William E.

Birth: 18 January 1806, Smith County, Tennessee

Courtesy Church History Library

William E. McLellin, 1806–1883.

Death: 24 April 1883, Independence, Jackson County, Missouri

While teaching school in Illinois, William McLellin met Latter-day Saint missionaries bound for Missouri in the summer of 1831. He listened to them and prayed for discernment. His "searches and researches" led him to "acknowledge the truth and Validity of the book of Mormon and also that I had found the people of the Lord—The Living Church of Christ." McLellin wrote that he was "immersed according to the commandments of Jesus Christ . . . and was confirmed by the watter's edge" (31–34). McLellin, whose wife had recently died, joined the missionaries on their trek to Missouri and back to Ohio. At a conference in Amherst, Ohio, he met Joseph Smith and returned with him to Hiram, Ohio. There, on 29 October 1831, McLellin served as scribe while Joseph dictated the revelation now recorded as section 66. McLellin wrote in his journal: "This revelation give great joy to my heart because some important questions were answered which had dwelt upon my mind with anxiety" (46).

McLellin played a role in the November 1831 conference at Hiram. Accepting the Lord's challenge to imitate a revelation (67), he "endeavored to write a commandment like unto one of the least of the Lord's, but failed" (MH, 162).

When he obeyed the commands in the revelation to him (66), promised blessings were forthcoming, as when the Lord told him to "lay your hands upon the sick, and they shall recover" (66:9). He did so, as in the following case: "Sunday eve Mrs Smith was taken very sick where I was and I prayed for her and laid my hands upon her and she was restored to health" (McLellin, 66).

But McLellin disobeyed several commandments in the revelation to him, including disregarding the law of CONSECRATION, for which the Lord rebuked him. A Church council in Ohio excommunicated him in 1832 and made his reinstatement conditional on "filling his mission to the South countries according to the commandment of Jesus Christ" given in 75:8 (Smith, 270). After being reinstated he served that mission beginning in January 1833, "determined to keep all the commandments of God" (McLellin, 89). He was one of the original members of the first latter-day Quorum of Twelve Apostles from its inception in 1835 until his apostasy in 1838. In his role as an apostle, he and the other members of the Quorum sought from Joseph a "great revelation" to guide the apostles in their missionary labors, resulting in the composite revelation recorded in section 107 (KCMB, 198).

The October 1831 revelation said that McLellin should repent and obtain eternal life (66:3, 12). But McLellin was inconsistent; his determination wavered. On 11 May 1838, he testified before a bishop's council in Far West, Missouri, that he had been critical of Joseph Smith and that he had quit "praying and keeping the commandments of God, and went his own way, and indulged himself in his lustfull desires" (Scriptory Book, 40). He was subsequently excommunicated and spent the next four decades struggling to reconcile his undeniably divine testimony with his antagonism toward Joseph Smith.

See also Apostasy, of early dissenters from restored Church; Apostles, the first Twelve of latter days; Historical context and overview of Doctrine and Covenants 66 (p. 771).

BIBLIOGRAPHY

Kirtland Council Minute Book. Church Historical Library, The Church of Jesus Christ of Latter-day Saints, Salt Lake City, Utah.

Manuscript History of the Church, Book A–1. Church Historical Library, The Church of Jesus Christ of Latter-day Saints, Salt Lake City, Utah.

McLellin, William E. *The Journals of William E. McLellin, 1831–1836.* Edited by Jan Shipps and John W. Welch. Urbana: University of Illinois Press; Provo, Utah: BYU Studies, 1994.

The Scriptory Book of Joseph Smith Jr. Church Historical Library, The Church of Jesus Christ of Latter-day Saints, Salt Lake City, Utah.

Smith, Joseph. *Personal Writings of Joseph Smith.* Compiled and edited by Dean C. Jessee. Rev. ed. Salt Lake City: Deseret Book, 2002.

SCH

McIlwaine's Bend, Missouri River

In August 1831, Joseph Smith and ten other elders traveled in canoes on the Missouri River toward St. Louis on their return journey to Ohio from Independence, Missouri. The Prophet's history records, "Nothing very important occurred till the third day, when many of the dangers so common upon the western waters, manifested themselves; and after we had encamped upon the bank of the river, at McIlwaine's Bend, Brother Phelps, in open vision by daylight, saw the destroyer in his most horrible power, ride upon the face of the waters; others heard the noise, but saw not the vision" (1:202–3). The next morning the Prophet received the revelation concerning danger in traveling on water in the latter days (61).

McIlwaine's Bend must have been the name local residents used because it is not found on contemporary maps. Nature and man have changed the course of the river somewhat over the years, and the site of McIlwaine's Bend is difficult to determine today. Calculations based on journal accounts place it approximately "five miles west of the town of Miami, Saline County," Missouri (Parkin, 139–40). Trusting these calculations, cartographers have placed the site as it is represented on Map 5 in the back

of the 1981 edition of the Doctrine and Covenants. *See* map, p. 414.

See also Historical context and overview of Doctrine and Covenants 61 (p. 767); Water(s).

BIBLIOGRAPHY

Parkin, Max H. *Missouri.* Vol. 4 of *Sacred Places: A Comprehensive Guide to Early LDS Historical Sites,* edited by LaMar C. Berrett. Salt Lake City: Deseret Book, 2004.

Smith, Joseph. *History of The Church of Jesus Christ of Latter-day Saints.* Edited by B. H. Roberts. 7 vols. 2d ed. rev. Salt Lake City: The Church of Jesus Christ of Latter-day Saints, 1932–51.

RJW

Measure of man

A phrase appearing once in the Doctrine and Covenants, referring to the spirits in the premortal world appointed to live upon this earth. The revelation says, "Marriage is ordained of God unto man. Wherefore, it is lawful that he should have one wife, and they twain shall be one flesh, and all this that the earth might answer the end of its creation; and that it might be filled with the *measure of man,* according to his creation before the world was made" (49:15–17; cf. Moses 3:5; emphasis added). Elder James E. Talmage wrote: "The population of the earth is fixed according to the number of spirits appointed to take tabernacles of flesh upon this planet; when these have all come forth in the order and time appointed, then, and not till then, shall the end come" (194). And President Joseph F. Smith taught, "These spirits have been coming to this earth to take upon them tabernacles . . . from the morn of creation until now, and will continue until the winding up scene, until the spirits who were destined to come to this world shall have come and accomplished their mission in the flesh" (94).

See also Man, creation of.

BIBLIOGRAPHY

Smith, Joseph F. *Gospel Doctrine.* Salt Lake City: Deseret Book, 1989.

Talmage, James E. *Articles of Faith.* Salt Lake City: The Church of Jesus Christ of Latter-day Saints, 1961.

RCF

Measure. *See* Appendix E.

Meat. *See* Word of Wisdom.

Mediator. *See* Jesus Christ, Mediator of the new covenant.

Meek, meekness

Mildness of temper; gentleness; not easily provoked or irritated; forbearing; teachable; modest. Many times in the Doctrine and Covenants the Lord instructs both individuals and members generally to be meek in their attitudes and in their preaching of the gospel.

A troubled Martin Harris was counseled to find peace by walking in meekness (19:23, 41). Emma Smith was called to "comfort" her husband "with consoling words, in the spirit of meekness," and to "continue in the spirit of meekness" (25:5, 14). Thomas B. Marsh was instructed to govern his house in meekness (31:9), and Parley P. Pratt was counseled to maintain a spirit of meekness in his mission to the Lamanites (32:1). The Lord promised that the "poor and the meek" would have the gospel preached unto them and that they would eventually inherit the earth (35:15; 88:17; cf. 84:106; 97:2; 109:72). Additionally, the Lord instructed that members of the Church should share the gospel "in mildness and in meekness" (38:41; cf. 63:57; 100:7; 118:3), a pattern apparently not followed by many of the Saints in Missouri, which disobedience caused antagonism (101:1–8). Joseph Smith was instructed to send a "solemn proclamation" to "all the kings of the world, to the four corners thereof," inviting all to come and help build up Zion; that proclamation was to be written in "the spirit of meekness and by the power of the Holy Ghost" (124:2–4).

In warning the Saints against false teachers, the Lord said that even if someone speaks with meek and edifying language, that person is of God only "if he obey mine ordinances . . . according to the revelations and truths which I have given" (52:16–17). W. W. Phelps was warned to repent, "for he seeketh to excel, and he is not sufficiently meek before me" (58:40–41). An anguishing Joseph Smith wrote of the principle of meekness while being detained in Liberty Jail, declaring, "No power or influence can or ought to be maintained by virtue of the priesthood, only by persuasion, by long-suffering, *by gentleness and meekness,* and by love unfeigned" (121:41; emphasis added). The revelations in the Doctrine and Covenants affirm the truth taught by Elder Neal A. Maxwell that "a true community of Saints . . . [has] a high ratio of those who are meek, being low demanders and high performers" (98).

See also Humble, humility.

BIBLIOGRAPHY

Maxwell, Neal A. *If Thou Endure It Well.* Salt Lake City: Bookcraft, 1996.

GP

Meet, meetings

The words *meet* and *meetings* have one or more meanings as used in the Doctrine and Covenants:

1. Proper, fit, worthy of, or suited to a particular circumstance. One of the most familiar passages in the scriptures using the word in this manner is found in Genesis 2:18. Speaking of the creation of Eve, God said, "I will make him [Adam] an help meet for him." In the Doctrine and Covenants, the term is used many times in the context of the propriety, or lack of it, of a given course of action. "For behold, it is not meet that I should command in all things" (58:26). In the revelation giving the "Word of Wisdom," the Lord said that drinking strong drinks "is not good, neither meet in the sight of your Father" (89:5). In other historical contexts, the Lord instructed the Saints on the necessity of their bringing "forth fruit and works meet for my kingdom" (101:100; cf. 84:58).

2. Church meetings. The Lord commanded that the Church "meet in conference once in three months, or from time to time as said conferences shall direct or appoint" (20:61). In addition to these general conferences, other meetings were to be held to instruct and uplift members of the Church, including sacrament meetings, missionary, and priesthood meetings (44:1–4; 62:4; 107:85–89). In the early days of the Church "confirmation meetings" (46:6) were held in which those who had been recently baptized were confirmed members of the Church. Today, confirmations are conducted at a regular sacrament meeting or at a baptismal

service. The various public meetings held by the Church, both in early Church history and today, are in fulfillment of the Lord's command: "See that the church meet together often" (20:55, 61, 75). The Lord declared: "Ye are commanded never to cast any one out from your public meetings, which are held before the world" (46:3). While public meetings are open and no one should be denied admission, the Lord stated that the sacrament of the Lord's Supper could be withheld from members of the Church who are deemed unworthy by the presiding officer, whose right it is as a judge in Israel to determine worthiness to partake of the sacrament (46:4). Closely related to that responsibility is the charge given by the Lord to "conduct all meetings as they are directed and guided by the Holy Spirit" (46:2) and ensure that meetings are spiritually edifying and "according to the commandments and revelations of God" (20:45).

3. To come face to face with. Joseph Smith and Sidney Rigdon were instructed, "Confound your enemies; call upon them to meet you both in public and in private; and inasmuch as ye are faithful their shame shall be made manifest" (71:7). As Joseph and Hyrum Smith were leaving for Carthage, Hyrum "turned down the leaf" of a page in the Book of Mormon that speaks of meeting one's accusers "before the judgment-seat of Christ" (135:4–5; Ether 12:36–38). The most frequent use of *meet* in this sense has to do with both the living and the dead being prepared to meet the Savior at his second coming (45:45; 88:92, 96–97; 109:75; 133:10, 19, 44).

4. Satisfying a necessary requirement. The Doctrine and Covenants uses *meet* in this sense once: "Priesthood leaders are instructed to follow the policy of carefully interviewing all candidates for ordination" to the priesthood "to insure that they meet the established standards for worthiness" (OD 2).

BLT

Melchizedek

Ancient king and PRIESTHOOD leader, contemporary with Abraham. His name, "My (Divine) King Is Righteousness," praises God. The Bible tells little about Melchizedek, but much can be learned about him from Alma 13, Joseph Smith's translation of Genesis 14, the Doctrine and Covenants, and Joseph Smith's sermons.

Melchizedek led his people to repent and create a covenant community (Alma 13:17–18). He was a "priest of the most high God" (Gen. 14:18). He administered the sacrament to Abraham, blessed him, and received tithes from him. "Abraham received the priesthood from Melchizedek, who received it through the lineage of his fathers, even till Noah" (84:14; cf. Ehat and Cook, 244–46). Melchizedek was ordained a high priest after the order of the Son of God, having power to perform great miracles and "to stand in the presence of God; to do all things according to his will, according to his command." "And men having this faith, coming up unto this order of God, were translated and taken up into heaven." Melchizedek was "a priest of this order," and he and his people were translated (JST Gen. 14:25–40). *See* Translated beings.

Before Melchizedek's day, the higher priesthood was called "*the Holy Priesthood, after the Order of the Son of God.* But out of respect or reverence to the name of the Supreme Being, to avoid the too frequent repetition of his name, they, the church, in ancient days, called that priesthood after Melchizedek, or the Melchizedek Priesthood" (107:3–4). The Book of Mormon prophet Alma testified, "there were many before him, and also there were many afterwards, but none were greater" (Alma 13:19).

BIBLIOGRAPHY

Ehat, Andrew F., and Lyndon W. Cook, comps. and eds. *The Words of Joseph Smith.* Provo, Utah: Religious Studies Center, Brigham Young University, 1980.

KPJ

Melchizedek Priesthood. *See* Priesthood.

Memorial. *See* Appendix E.

Mercy

The gracious kindness and compassion of God expressed in his many beneficent acts in behalf of mankind throughout the ages. Far and away the most significant and universal example of divine mercy to take place on this earth is that of "Jesus Christ, your Redeemer, the Great

I AM, whose arm of mercy hath atoned for your sins" (29:1).

Expressions of mercy are among the many diverse ways the Lord has appealed to mankind (43:25). The Book of Mormon was translated "through the mercy of God" (1:29). Those who are faithful to their covenants "shall obtain mercy" (54:6), for God is "full of mercy" (84:102). He mercifully responds to the meek (97:2), to the merciful (88:40), to those who confess their sins (61:2), and to those who FEAR him (76:5). He is merciful to people even in their weaknesses, sins, and vanity (38:14; 50:16; 64:3–4; 97:6; 101:9; 106:7), "suiting his mercies according to the conditions of the children of men" (46:15). He assures all mankind that those who receive his servants "as a little child, receiveth my kingdom; and blessed are they, for they shall obtain mercy" (99:3).

At the last judgment, all those who have repented of their sins and acknowledged JESUS CHRIST as their Savior and Redeemer (heirs of the three degrees of glory) will be found as joint-heirs with Christ on God's right hand—the hand of mercy—while those who fail to do so (the sons of perdition) "cannot be sanctified by law, neither by mercy" (88:35), and will be found on God's left hand—"exposed to the whole law of the demands of justice" (Alma 34:16; D&C 19:5; 29:27). See Justice.

The dedicatory prayer for the Kirtland Temple (109) contains several pleas for mercy. It begins with an expression of gratitude for the mercy of God toward the faithful Saints (v. 1). This is followed by a plea for the merciful FOR-GIVENESS of their transgressions (v. 34). The Prophet Joseph even prayed for mercy for the "wicked mob, who have driven thy people, that they may cease to spoil, that they may repent of their sins if repentance is to be found" (v. 50). Mercy was sought for all nations and for the political leaders in America (v. 54). The prayer also includes a plea from Joseph for the Lord to have mercy upon his family (vv. 69–70).

When the Lord subsequently appeared to Joseph Smith and Oliver Cowdery in the Kirtland Temple, he told them, "I will manifest myself to my people in mercy in this house" (110:7). In reviewing the events surrounding the coming forth of the gospel in this, the dispensation of the fulness of times, the Prophet Joseph wrote: "Now, what do we hear in the gospel which we have received? A voice of gladness! A voice of mercy from heaven" (128:19).

See also Atonement, the; Grace; Repentance.

RT

Meridian of time

A phrase used twice in the Doctrine and Covenants to refer to the time of the Savior's earthly ministry (20:26; 39:3). One meaning of the word *meridian* is noon, or midday, the time at which the sun reaches its highest point. Another meaning also has to do with "the highest point; as the meridian of life; the meridian of power or of glory" (Webster, s.v. "meridian"). Surely the time of greatest glory thus far on this earth was the coming of Jesus Christ to perform his earthly mission, appropriately designated in the revelations as the "meridian of time." Both references in the Doctrine and Covenants to the meridian of time testify that earlier prophetic promises of his coming to the earth have been realized, that he *came in the meridian of time* (20:26; emphasis added).

Between the receipt of sections 20 and 39, April 1830 and January 1831, the Lord revealed the book of Moses to Joseph Smith. The book of Moses includes the only other scriptural uses of "meridian of time," all four instances prophesying that Jesus Christ "shall come in the meridian of time" (Moses 5:57; 6:57, 62; cf. 7:46).

BIBLIOGRAPHY

Webster, Noah. *An American Dictionary of the English Language.* 1828.

DKO

Merits of Jesus Christ. *See* Jesus Christ, merits of.

Messiah

Used three times in the Doctrine and Covenants, the English word *Messiah* arises from *Messias,* the Greek transliteration of the Hebrew *māšîach,* "anointed." The Greek term meaning "anointed" is *christos,* the root of the word *Christ.* Both forms, *Messias* and *Christ,* are used in John 1:41 and 4:25; *Messiah* is not used elsewhere in the New Testament. While *Messiah* and *Christ* are thus interchangeable terms, both the Book of Mormon and the Doctrine and Covenants at times use these titles for the Only Begotten of the Father in different senses, apparently to nuance aspects of his mission. When the use of these English terms varies, the explanation may be found in the context or associations intended for the passages in which they appear.

In the surviving Old Testament, *māšîach* is most commonly used for the anointed king of Israel or Judah, although it also appears for anointed priests and once, in the case of Elisha, for an anointed prophet (1 Kgs. 19:16). In the intertestamental period, Old Testament prophecies and royal psalms came to be seen as looking forward to an ideal Davidic king, who, extant evidence suggests, came to be viewed as "*the* Messiah," a future royal or priestly figure who would deliver Israel (de Jonge, 779–86; Jule, 889–90; Pike, 536). Thus without Restoration insight, the Old Testament as it now stands does not explicitly refer to "the Messiah" (the apparent references in Daniel 9:25–26 are less clear in Hebrew and Greek than they seem in the KJV).

Evidence from the Book of Mormon, however, confirms that even before the destruction of Jerusalem in 586 B.C., such prophets as Lehi looked forward to the coming of "the Messiah" (e.g., 1 Ne. 1:19; 10:4–17; 12:18; 15:13; 2 Ne. 2:6). Lehi and his son Nephi being from a Jewish background, often refer to the promised Savior as "Messiah"; the title "Christ" was revealed to Lehi's son Jacob (2 Ne. 10:3, the first occurrence of the term in the Book of Mormon). Significantly, that use of *Christ* follows Jacob's reflections on the prophecies of Isaiah and after a revelation from an angel that increased his understanding of the personal applications of the Atonement. Likewise, the words of Isaiah and the angel later led Nephi to use the title "Jesus Christ" (2 Ne. 25:19). Whether Nephite prophets actually used a different word to distinguish between *Messiah* and *Christ* is impossible to know, but *Christ* is the regularly preferred form in the Book of Mormon from Jacob's revelation in 2 Nephi 10 onwards (Pike, 537).

The change in English terminology may indicate a shift from an "Old Testament" expectation of the Messiah to a more "New Testament" understanding of the mission of JESUS CHRIST.

Coming from a Christian background, Joseph Smith and other early Saints were more familiar with the Greek-based title "Christ." Not surprisingly, this is the word most commonly used in the latter-day revelations to refer to Jesus as God's anointed; however, each time the Doctrine and Covenants refers to Jesus as "Messiah," there seems to be a purposeful design by the Lord to summon associations with Old Testament Israel. The first occurrence is in 13:1, in which the resurrected John the Baptist confers the Aaronic Priesthood upon Joseph Smith and Oliver Cowdery "in the name of Messiah." The fact that the Aaronic Priesthood originated in the Mosaic system, that the sons of Levi are prominent in the Old Testament and mentioned specifically in this context in Malachi 3:1–4 (McConkie and Ostler, 119), and that Joseph Smith identified John the Baptist as the only legal administrator of the Aaronic Priesthood at that time (84:27; Smith, *History,* 5:261; *Joseph Smith,* 84–85) all combine to help explain why *Messiah* is used in this passage. In 19:27 the context pertains to the Jews' receiving the Book of Mormon "that they may believe the gospel, and look not for a Messiah to come who has already come." Likewise, in the dedicatory prayer of the Kirtland Temple, Joseph Smith ended the section that dealt with the children of Jacob, the house of David, and the remnants of Israel with the plea that they would "believe in the Messiah" (109:61–67).

BIBLIOGRAPHY

de Jonge, Marinus. "Messiah." In *The Anchor Bible Dictionary,* edited by David Noel Freedman, 4:777–88. 6 vols. New York: Doubleday, 1992.

Jule, Donald. "Messiah." In *Eerdmans Dictionary of the Bible,* edited by David Noel Freedman, 889–90. Grand Rapids, Mich.: Eerdmans, 2000.

McConkie, Joseph Fielding, and Craig J. Ostler. *Revelations of the Restoration: A Commentary on the Doctrine and Covenants and Other Modern Revelations.* Salt Lake City: Deseret Book, 2000.

Pike, Dana M. "Messiah." In *Book of Mormon Reference Companion,* edited by Dennis L. Largey et al., 536–37. Salt Lake City: Deseret Book, 2003.

Smith, Joseph. *History of The Church of Jesus Christ of Latter-day Saints.* Edited by B. H. Roberts. 7 vols. 2d ed. rev. Salt Lake City: The Church of Jesus Christ of Latter-day Saints, 1932–51.

———. *Joseph Smith.* Teachings of Presidents of the Church series. Salt Lake City: The Church of Jesus Christ of Latter-day Saints, 2007.

EDH

Mete. *See* Appendix E.

Methuselah

Ancient high priest and ordained patriarch, son of Enoch and grandfather of Noah. Methuselah was not translated with Enoch's city so as to provide a righteous lineage for Noah on the earth (Moses 8:2–3) and perhaps to be a witness of Noah's ministry. Methuselah was present at the family gathering at ADAM-ONDI-AHMAN where the Savior appeared and where Adam blessed his righteous posterity (107:53–56).

Methuselah was ordained a patriarch at age 100 by Adam, and he in turn ordained Noah when Noah was just 10 years of age (107:50, 52). These details establish an unbroken patriarchal priesthood line from Adam to Noah, of which the biblical record says nothing.

Methuselah was a righteous man and prophesied of Noah's ministry, as had Enoch (Moses 8:2–3). He apparently also had knowledge of astronomy, including Kolob (Smith, 269, 470–71).

Although Methuselah is credited in the Bible with living longer than any other human—969 years (Gen. 5:27), the manuscript of Joseph Smith's Translation of the Bible indicates that both Adam and Methuselah lived to be nearly 1,000 years old (Jackson and Swift, 1–11).

Latter-day revelation adds much knowledge about Methuselah even as it shows there is much more that is not known.

BIBLIOGRAPHY

Jackson, Kent P., and Charles Swift. "The Ages of the Patriarchs in the Joseph Smith Translation." In *A Witness for the Restoration,* edited by Kent P. Jackson and Andrew C. Skinner. Provo, Utah: Religious Studies Center, Brigham Young University, 2007.

Smith, Joseph Fielding. *Man: His Origin and Destiny.* Salt Lake City: Deseret Book, 1965.

RJM

Michael. *See* Adam.

Might. *See* Appendix E.

Miles, Daniel

Birth: 23 July 1772, Sanbornton, Belknap County, New Hampshire

Death: 12 October 1845, Hancock County, Illinois

Daniel Sanborn Miles was baptized in April 1832 and had gathered with the Saints in Kirtland by 1836. By March 1838, he had moved to Far West, Missouri, and when the Saints were expelled from Missouri, he moved to Illinois.

Miles's name appears in Doctrine and Covenants 124. Part of this revelation, dated 19 January 1841, included a call for the members of the Church to "approve" or "disapprove" of local and general officers of the Church (124:144). Miles was listed as one of seven "to preside over the quorum of seventies; which quorum is instituted for traveling elders to bear record of [the Lord's] name in all the world" (124:138–39).

Miles had been called to the First Quorum of the Seventy in 1837 and had contributed to and signed a resolution "drawn up and approved by the quorum of Seventies and their Presidents" and published in the *Messenger and Advocate.* Among other issues, the resolution discussed the Word of Wisdom as a revelation from God (*MA*, 510–11).

Miles died at age seventy-three in October 1845 before the Saints moved west. Joseph Young, one of the presidents of the Seventy, characterized Daniel Miles as "a man of good faith, constant in his attendance at the meetings of the council, until the time of his death, which occurred at quite an advanced stage of his life" (Jenson, 1:192).

BIBLIOGRAPHY

Jenson, Andrew. *Latter-day Saints' Biographical Encyclopedia.* 4 vols. Salt Lake City: The Andrew Jenson History Company, 1901–36. Reprint, Salt Lake City: Western Epics, 1971.

Latter-day Saints' Messenger and Advocate 3, no. 32 (May 1837): 510–11.

ZLL

Millennium, the

A thousand-year period of righteousness on the EARTH. The DISPENSATION of the fulness of times will lead into the millennial era. Many of the revelations given in this last dispensation, are to prepare the Saints for that future time. The Millennium will be ushered in by the appearances of the Savior that compose his second coming and attendant events. The Savior "will reveal [himself] from heaven with power and great glory, with all the hosts thereof, and dwell in righteousness with men on earth a thousand years, and the wicked shall not stand" (29:11). There is a space of time between the opening of the seventh seal and the coming of the Savior wherein those things spoken of in Revelation 9 will take place (77:13; cf. 77:6–7; Rev. 5).

The revelations in the Doctrine and Covenants emphasize that the dawning of the Millennium is near, "even at the doors" (110:16), and that the Saints must be ready for the time when Jesus Christ will return to the earth to reign (29:10–11; 38:8; 43:28–30; 64:23; 104:59).

The Savior will reign during the Millennium

One distinction that separates the Millennium from any previous time period is that "Christ will reign personally upon the earth" (A of F 10). The Lord explained, "In time ye shall have no king nor ruler, for I will be your king and watch over you . . . , and you shall be a free people, and ye shall have no laws but my laws when I come, for I am your lawgiver" (38:21–22; cf. 58:22). In a later revelation he said: "In mine own due time will I come upon the earth in judgment, and my people shall be redeemed and shall reign with me on earth. For the great Millennium, of which I have spoken by the mouth of my servants, shall come" (43:29–30). The Prophet Joseph Smith clarified that "Christ and the resurrected Saints will reign over the earth during the thousand years. They will not probably dwell upon the earth, but will visit it when they please, or when it is necessary to govern it" (5:212).

The two centers of millennial government will be the Old JERUSALEM in Israel and the NEW JERUSALEM in Missouri (133:21; Isa. 2:2–4; Micah 4:1–3, 7; Moses 7:62–64). When Christ comes to reign, all man-made governments will end, for "the consumption decreed"—that is, wars, famine, plagues, earthquakes, thunder, and lightning—shall make "a full end of all nations" (87:6). In contrast, the kingdom of God (the Church on earth) will have gone forth to fill the earth, prepared to meet and join with the kingdom of heaven (65:2–6).

Physical changes on the earth and life upon it

In the Millennium "the earth will be renewed and receive its paradisiacal glory" (A of F 10). "When the earth shall be transfigured" (63:20–21), "every corruptible thing, both of man, or of the beasts of the field, or of the fowls of the heavens, or the fish of the sea, that dwells upon all the face of the earth, shall be consumed" (101:24). All forms of life, both plant and animal, that survive that cleansing will be able to abide the paradisiacal glory that will prevail during the Millennium. That glory, it appears, will be similar to the glory enjoyed in the Garden of Eden before the Fall (Isa. 51:3). In that state, "the enmity of man, and the enmity of beasts, yea, the enmity of all flesh, shall cease" (101:26). Isaiah foresaw that in that day "the wolf also shall dwell with the lamb, and the leopard shall lie down with the kid; and the calf and the young lion and the fatling together; and a little child shall lead them. And the cow and the bear shall feed; their young ones shall lie down together: and the lion shall eat straw like the ox" (Isa. 11:6–7).

The whole face of the earth will be changed. When the Lord appears in glory, ushering in the Millennium, "that of element shall melt with fervent heat; and all things shall become new" (101:25). The Lord will "break down the mountains, and the valleys shall not be found. He shall command the great deep, and it shall be driven back into the north countries, and the islands shall become one land; and the land of Jerusalem and the land of Zion shall be turned back into their own place, and the earth shall be like as it was in the days before it was divided" (133:22–24). "In the barren deserts there shall come forth pools of living water; and the parched ground shall no longer be a thirsty land" (133:29). Such conditions can "make solitary places to bud and to blossom, and to bring forth in abundance" (117:7).

The earth will be filled with knowledge

Speaking of the increased knowledge that will be available during the Millennium, a revelation declared, "Yea, verily I say unto you, in that day when the Lord shall come, he shall reveal all things—things which have passed, and hidden things which no man knew, things of the earth, by which it was made, and the purpose and the end thereof—things most precious, things that are above, and things that are beneath, things that are in the earth, and upon the earth, and in heaven" (101:32–34). A remarkable promise is given that "in that day whatsoever any man shall ask, it shall be given unto him" (101:27). At the beginning of the Millennium, all living souls will be made aware of the "secret acts of men, and the thoughts and intents of their hearts, and the mighty works of God" in ages past (88:109). It may very well be the time when the sealed portion of the Book of Mormon will be made available—that which contains "a revelation from God, from the beginning of the world to the ending thereof" (2 Ne. 27:7–11; cf. Ether 3:25, 27; 4:4–7).

Transfiguration of people, death, and resurrection

At the time of the Savior's second coming, "the saints that are upon the earth, who are alive, shall be quickened and be caught up to meet him" (88:96). They will return to the earth and continue to live on the earth until they "die" at the "age of man" (63:50). But DEATH in the Millennium is simply a change from paradisiacal mortality to a resurrected state "in the twinkling of an eye," as two revelations explain: "Children shall grow up until they become old; old men shall die; but they shall not sleep in the dust, but they shall be changed in the twinkling of an eye" (63:50–51); "in that day an infant shall not die until he is old; and his life shall be as the age of a tree [according to Isaiah, that is one hundred years old, Isa. 65:20]; and when he dies he shall not sleep, that is to say in

the earth, but shall be changed in the twinkling of an eye, and shall be caught up, and his rest shall be glorious" (101:30–31). Hence the scriptural affirmation, "And there shall be no sorrow because there is no death" in the Millennium (101:29).

The family unit will continue during the Millennium. It will be a glorious time to raise children. The righteous, those who "are wise and have received the truth, and have taken the Holy Spirit for their guide . . . shall abide the day. And the earth shall be given unto them for an inheritance; and they shall multiply and wax strong, and their children shall grow up without sin unto salvation. For the Lord shall be in their midst, and his glory shall be upon them, and he will be their king and their lawgiver" (45:57–59). Families "shall build houses, and inhabit them; and they shall plant vineyards, and eat the fruit of them. They shall not build, and another inhabit; they shall not plant, and another eat: for as the days of a tree are the days of my people, and mine elect shall long enjoy the work of their hands" (Isa. 65:21–24).

Satan will be bound for a thousand years and then loosed for a "little season"

Another prominent aspect of the millennial era is that "Satan shall be bound" (43:31; cf. 84:100) and "shall not have power to tempt any man" (101:28). The Lord explained further that "he shall have no place in the hearts of the children of men" (45:55). It seems, then, that both the power of God and the righteousness of the people will nullify the power of SATAN to tempt anyone (cf. 1 Ne. 22:15–17, 26; 2 Ne. 30:18). That check on Satan's power will last for a thousand years. "When the thousand years are ended, and men again begin to deny their God," however, Satan will be loosed, and God will "spare the earth but for a little season" (29:22; 88:110–11).

During that little season, Satan will gather his armies for a final struggle against God and Christ. Michael, the archangel, will gather his armies, the hosts of heaven, and the final battle of the war that began in premortality (Rev. 12:7–11) will take place. In the Doctrine and Covenants that final battle is called "the battle of the great God." Satan will lose that battle, "and the devil and his armies shall be cast away into their own place, that they shall not have power over the saints any more at all" (88:110–14). The devil and his angels "shall go away into everlasting punishment" (76:44). The rest of mankind shall inherit kingdoms of glory according to their faithfulness (88:20–25).

At that point, the end of the millennial earth "shall come, and the heaven and the earth shall be consumed and pass away, and there shall be a new heaven and a new earth" (29:23).

See also Jesus Christ, second coming of; Judgment(s); Resurrection, the.

BIBLIOGRAPHY

McConkie, Bruce R. *The Millennial Messiah: The Second Coming of the Son of Man.* Salt Lake City: Deseret Book Company, 1982.

Smith, Joseph. *History of The Church of Jesus Christ of Latter-day Saints.* Edited by B. H. Roberts. 7 vols. 2d ed. rev. Salt Lake City: The Church of Jesus Christ of Latter-day Saints, 1932–51.

CJO

Miller, George

Birth: 25 November 1794, near Stanardville, Orange County, Virginia

Death: 1856, Marengo, McHenry County, Illinois

In the 1830s George Miller, who owned a substantial home and farmed three hundred acres, was a respected member of the Presbyterian church in Macomb Township, Illinois. There he first heard of the restored gospel, and though he dismissed it, in 1839 he supplied Mormon refugees from Missouri with much-needed grain. He later met Joseph Smith, who had just been allowed to escape from custody in Missouri, and he invited the Prophet to preach to a gathering of people; the Prophet agreed. Miller wrote of the experience, "I had no remaining doubts left in regard to the truth of the prophet" (24–25). His experience with the Prophet, as well as receiving a miraculous healing blessing, were catalysts leading to his baptism on 10 August 1839. Immediate persecution followed. His "cattle were shot . . . fences laid down, and the flocks and herds of the prairies turned on [his] grain fields." Vexed "by petty lawsuits," Miller was forced to pay judgments

George Miller, 1794–1856.

and was denied money owed him (Miller, 26). In January 1841, he was called by revelation to assist in building the Nauvoo House and appointed to the office of bishop (124:20–23). In the same revelation, the Lord said, "George Miller is without guile; he may be trusted because of the integrity of his heart; and for the love which he has to my testimony I, the Lord, love him. . . . Let no man despise my servant George, for he shall honor me" (124:20–21).

Miller applied himself diligently to his calling. He also served as a regent of the University of Nauvoo and as a colonel and brigadier general in the Nauvoo Legion. He completed several missions, was appointed to act as trustee-in-trust for the Church, and was elected to the Nauvoo city council. He was devoted to the Prophet Joseph Smith, who identified him as one of a "faithful band" of those who "love the God that I serve; they love the truths that I promulge; they love those virtuous, and those holy doctrines that I cherish in my bosom with the warmest feelings of my heart; and with that zeal which cannot be denied" (*Papers*, 2:416). Miller was one of the first six men who received the temple endowment in this dispensation, 4 May

1842, in the upper story of Joseph Smith's Red Brick Store (Smith, *History,* 5:1–2).

After Joseph's death, Miller followed the leadership of Brigham Young until the Saints were at Winter Quarters, Nebraska. There, Miller and Young differed regarding the route the Saints should take to go west. In March 1847, he resigned his Church membership, and on 8 November 1847, the Twelve withdrew fellowship from him (Smith, *History,* 7:618). He united with the apostate sect established by Lyman Wight in Texas but became disaffected from them and joined the Strangites in Michigan. Miller died in 1856 in Marengo, Illinois.

BIBLIOGRAPHY

Miller, George. "Journal of History." Compiled by H. H. Smith, n. p., n. d. Church History Library, The Church of Jesus Christ of Latter-day Saints, Salt Lake City, Utah.

Smith, Joseph. *History of The Church of Jesus Christ of Latter-day Saints.* Edited by B. H. Roberts. 7 vols. 2d ed. rev. Salt Lake City: The Church of Jesus Christ of Latter-day Saints, 1932–51.

———. *The Papers of Joseph Smith.* Edited by Dean C. Jessee. 2 vols. Salt Lake City: Deseret Book, 1989–92.

KWF

Millstone. *See* Appendix E.

Mind

That eternal element of the spirit at the seat or center of one's conscious mental capacities and intellectual processes; "intelligence, or the light of truth, was not created or made, neither indeed can be" (93:29). The Father, Son, and Holy Ghost communicate with individual souls by speaking to the mind (or intellect) and symbolically through the HEART (or feelings). Mortals may "inquire and obtain the mind of the Lord by revelation" (102:23) about spiritual and temporal matters. Using the capacities of the mind is prerequisite to receiving REVELATION or spiritual confirmation through the Holy Spirit: The Lord told Oliver Cowdery regarding the gift of translation that "you must study it out in your mind" before asking if it be right (9:8). In another revelation the Lord told Oliver, "I will tell you in your mind and in your heart, by the Holy

Ghost." Such enlightenment requires faith, an honest heart, and belief that one will receive (8:1–2). If these steps are not followed, one's mind may become "darkened" (10:2; 84:54, 80). God will sometimes blind wicked "minds, that they may not understand his marvelous workings" (121:12; cf. 112:23).

The Lord told an assembly of elders in Kirtland, Ohio, to "treasure up in [their] minds continually the words of life," whereupon "my Spirit shall be in your hearts" (84:85, 88), and, as he told Oliver Cowdery, "enlighten thy mind" and "speak peace to your mind" (6:15, 23). The "carnal" or "natural mind" of man, like the natural mortal body, cannot "abide the presence of God," except it be "quickened by the Spirit of God" (67:10–13; cf. Moses 1:11).

The Lord "requireth the heart and a willing mind" (64:34), or the total commitment and complete devotion of his mortal sons and daughters, who are admonished to love him, serve him, and keep his commandments with all their souls, or "with all your heart, might, mind and strength" (4:2; 20:31; 33:7; 59:5; 98:47). The apostle James called to repentance those "double minded" and "unstable" persons who are torn between serving God's purposes and their own (James 1:8; 4:8). The "mind" and "will" (generally interchangeable terms) of the Lord represent the Lord's views, wishes, aims, desires, and purposes; thus, when the servants of the Lord "speak when moved upon by the Holy Ghost," their words "shall be the will of the Lord, [and] shall be the mind of the Lord" (68:4). In commanding the Saints to build the Kirtland Temple, the Lord said: "It is my will that you should build a house. . . . Now here is . . . the mind of the Lord" (95:11, 13). If it is right, one may "obtain the mind of the Lord by revelation" (102:23). Such revelation usually comes to humble, righteous individuals or groups who come before the Lord in unity, "with one heart and with one mind" (45:65), striving to sanctify themselves that their "minds become single to God." Those whose "eye" and "minds" are "single to God" are promised they will see the Lord "in his own time, and in his own way, and according to his own will" (88:67–68). Knowing "the mind and will of the

Lord" (133:61; cf. 95:13) is having "the mind of Christ" (1 Cor. 2:16), which is to "think what [Christ] thinks, know what he knows, say what he would say, and do what he would do in every situation—all by revelation from the Spirit" (McConkie, 2:322). Such knowledge of "the mind of Christ" is knowing God and Jesus Christ, or having "life eternal" (John 17:3).

BIBLIOGRAPHY

McConkie, Bruce R. *Doctrinal New Testament Commentary.* 3 vols. Salt Lake City: Bookcraft, 1965–73.

RHC

Minister, ministering. *See* Appendix E.

Ministering of angels. *See* Angel(s).

Ministering spirits

ANGELS who "are appointed to minister for" those in the telestial kingdom after the final judgment and resurrection. It seems clear that these angels are resurrected beings (76:88; cf. 129:1) and that the additional designation, "ministering spirits," simply means persons assigned to be "ministering servants" (132:16; 136:37) or "ministering angel[s]" (7:6; cf. 20:10), in some aspect of God's service. The telestial inhabitants to whom they minister are those "who receive not of [God's] fulness in the eternal world, but of the Holy Spirit through the ministration of the terrestrial" (76:86).

TBB

Ministers, standing. *See* Standing councils/ministers/presidents.

Miracles

Any supernatural occurrence wrought by the power of God, beyond mortal man's ability to perform. Miracles conform to a higher law rather than the natural law of the present mortal world.

The Fall of Adam rendered all mankind in desperate need of redemption from sin and death, but it also made man unable to redeem himself. The purpose of the GOSPEL of Jesus Christ is to rescue man by changing him from his fallen natural condition to a condition of salvation. Hence, intercession through the power and work of God is absolutely necessary.

Because such a change takes place outside the laws that govern mortality, it appears miraculous to mankind (88:34–42; cf. Hel. 12:7–20).

Thus, unless a person has been influenced by, wrought upon, and changed by the miraculous power of God through the ATONEMENT of Christ and the revelatory and cleansing effect of the HOLY GHOST, he or she is not saved (76:50–54, 69). This necessary change can come only by the power of God and will be needed as long as there is one person on earth to be saved (Moro. 7:35–38).

Miracles, SIGNS, and wonders are performed by God and Jesus Christ, by authorized servants, and by those who believe in God and his power. When miracles are done in meekness and under the inspiration of the Holy Ghost, they will build FAITH and bring salvation to the participants. Those who seek signs (miracles) will see signs "but not unto salvation" (63:7). Miracles (signs) "come by faith, not by the will of men" (63:10–11). Because faith in Christ is neither engendered nor maintained by miracles alone (63:9), the Lord cautions the Saints against "boast[ing] themselves of these things" and speaking them "before the world" (84:73; cf. 24:13–14, 138:26). Numerous types of miracles follow those who believe and seek the Lord's help through PRAYER, but "not for a sign that they may consume it upon their lusts" (46:9; 35:8–9; 45:8; 63:9). Such signs are manifested by the Holy Ghost (46:10–33).

Miracles further God's work on earth but not all miracles are essential for individual salvation; however, such miracles as forgiveness of sins, sanctification by the Holy Ghost, personal revelation, a Spirit-borne testimony that Jesus is the Christ, participation in ordinances and covenants performed by divine priesthood authority, and becoming spiritually born again, are necessary for every person.

See also Spiritual gifts.

RJM

Missionary work

Teaching the GOSPEL to everyone. The resurrected Lord commanded immediately before his ascension that the gospel be preached to all the world (Matt. 28:19–20; Mark 16:15–16).

In the latter days he has used almost the same language in outlining missionary responsibilities: "Go ye into all the world, preach the gospel to every creature, acting in the authority which I have given you, baptizing in the name of the Father, and of the Son, and of the Holy Ghost. And he that believeth and is baptized shall be saved, and he that believeth not shall be damned. And he that believeth shall be blest with signs following, even as it is written" (68:8–10).

Joseph Smith emphasized the responsibility laid upon Church members: "After all that has been said, the greatest and most important duty is to preach the Gospel" (2:478).

The revelations in the Doctrine and Covenants provide important insights on many aspects of missionary work. Following are questions and answers from modern revelation concerning carrying the gospel message to the world.

Who should go?

The Lord identified his designated missionary force in these words: "And now this calling and commandment give I unto you concerning all men—that as many as shall come before my servants Sidney Rigdon and Joseph Smith, Jun., embracing this calling and commandment, shall be ordained and sent forth to preach the everlasting gospel among the nations" (36:4–5; cf. 63:37; 88:81). See Abrahamic covenant.

Recent prophets have reiterated the same call. For example, President Spencer W. Kimball said, "I have been asked, 'Should every young man who is a member of the Church fill a mission?' And I respond with the answer the Lord has given: Yes, every worthy man should fill a mission. The Lord expects it of him. And if he is not now worthy to fill a mission, then he should start at once to qualify himself" (29).

What qualifications has the Lord outlined in scripture for his missionaries?

"And faith, hope, charity and love, with an eye single to the glory of God, qualify him for the work. Remember faith, virtue, knowledge, temperance, patience, brotherly kindness, godliness, charity, humility, diligence" (4:5–6).

What are the standards for those who want to be considered as missionaries?

"And go ye out from among the wicked. . . . Be ye clean that bear the vessels of the Lord" (38:42; cf. 133:5).

What of individuals whose circumstances prevent them from serving full-time missions?

There are circumstances which can preclude some from full-time missionary service. The Lord said, "And again, verily I say unto you, that every man who is obliged to provide for his own family, let him provide, and he shall in nowise lose his crown; and let him labor in the church" (75:28).

In today's world where various conditions preclude full-time service, the Church has provided alternative methods of serving the Lord. Temple missions, Church Educational System assistance missions, Deseret Industries missions, family history missions, and bishops' storehouse missions are just a few. No one with a desire to serve need be excluded.

In what manner are missionaries to go forth?

"See that ye serve him with all your heart, might, mind and strength, that ye may stand blameless before God at the last day" (4:2). To fulfill the requirement of having the testimony given by the mouth of two or more witnesses (2 Cor. 13:1), to protect against false accusers, and to enable mutual encouragement and obedience, the Lord instructed, "And ye shall go forth in the power of my Spirit, preaching my gospel, two by two, in my name, lifting up your voices as with the sound of a trump, declaring my word like unto angels of God" (42:6).

Who oversees the preaching of the gospel and opening new areas to proselyting efforts?

Although each area of the world is covered by a designated mission and presided over by an assigned mission president, the ultimate responsibility is laid upon the First Presidency and the Quorum of the Twelve Apostles. "Verily I say unto you, my servant Thomas [then president of the Quorum of the Twelve Apostles], thou art the man whom I have chosen to hold the keys of my kingdom, as pertaining to the Twelve, abroad among all nations—that thou mayest be my servant to unlock the door of the kingdom in all places where my servant Joseph, and my servant Sidney, and my servant Hyrum [the First Presidency], cannot come; for on them have I laid the burden of all the churches for a little season. Wherefore, whithersoever they shall send you, go ye, and I will be with you; and in whatsoever place ye shall proclaim my name an effectual door shall be opened unto you, that they may receive my word" (112:16–19).

What are missionaries to teach?

"And again, the elders, priests and teachers of this church shall teach the principles of my gospel, which are in the Bible and the Book of Mormon, in the which is the fulness of the gospel" (42:12). "And let them journey from thence preaching the word by the way, saying none other things than that which the prophets and apostles have written, and that which is taught them by the Comforter through the prayer of faith" (52:9). "Behold, I send you out to reprove the world of all their unrighteous deeds, and to teach them of a judgment which is to come" (84:87).

Consistency worldwide in what is being taught is essential if the Church is to comply with Paul's injunction that there must be "one Lord, one faith, one baptism" (Eph. 4:5). Latitude as to the teaching style, the sequence of concepts taught, and the timing of the teachings is left to the individual pairs of missionaries "as they shall be directed by the Spirit" (42:13).

How are missionaries to teach?

The Lord instructed, "And let your preaching be the warning voice, every man to his neighbor, in mildness and in meekness" (38:41). Missionaries are to teach by the power of the Holy Ghost. Orson Hyde, for example, "was called by his ordination to proclaim the everlasting gospel, by the Spirit of the living God, from people to people, and from land to land, in the congregations of the wicked, in their synagogues, reasoning with and expounding all scriptures unto them" (68:1). When honest inquirers are taught under the direction of the Spirit, three elements are always there: they understand the message, both the missionaries and the investigator are edified, and all of them rejoice together as the Spirit bears witness to the

truth of what they are discussing (50:17–22). The restored gospel is reasonable (50:10–12), unchanging (20:12; 35:1), able to be learned by study as well as by faith (88:118), and can be revealed to each sincere investigator by inquiring of the Lord (42:61).

Why send the young and unlearned to teach such a precious gospel?

One modern miracle is how and why the Church sends out unschooled young men and women to preach the gospel. The Lord said, "That the fulness of my gospel might be proclaimed by the weak and the simple unto the ends of the world, and before kings and rulers" (1:23), "wherefore, I call upon the weak things of the world, those who are unlearned and despised, to thresh the nations by the power of my Spirit; and their arm shall be my arm, and I will be their shield and their buckler; and I will gird up their loins, and they shall fight manfully for me; and their enemies shall be under their feet; and I will let fall the sword in their behalf, and by the fire of mine indignation will I preserve them" (35:13–14).

What is the Lord's curriculum for preparing his missionaries, and why are they to learn it?

The Lord requires that missionaries not go totally unprepared nor remain ignorant. He said: "And I give unto you a commandment that you shall teach one another the doctrine of the kingdom. Teach ye diligently and my grace shall attend you, that you may be instructed more perfectly in theory, in principle, in doctrine, in the law of the gospel, in all things that pertain unto the kingdom of God, that are expedient for you to understand; of things both in heaven and in the earth, and under the earth; things which have been, things which are, things which must shortly come to pass; things which are at home, things which are abroad; the wars and the perplexities of the nations, and the judgments which are on the land; and a knowledge also of countries and of kingdoms—that ye may be prepared in all things when I shall send you again to magnify the calling whereunto I have called you, and the mission with which I have commissioned you. Behold, I sent you out to testify and warn the people, and it becometh every man who hath been warned to warn his neighbor. Therefore, they are left without excuse, and their sins are upon their own heads" (88:77–82).

Although it would take a lifetime to master even a few of those disciplines, the Lord expects his servants to be conversant in many areas of interest to the peoples of the world who will be attracted not only to the clean, wholesome look of the missionaries but also to the depth of their interest and knowledge of the world in which they live.

What help is promised to faithful missionaries?

It would appear to the casual observer that such a professionally untrained missionary force would be destined to immediate failure. And that would be the case were it not for these scriptural promises: "Neither take ye thought beforehand what ye shall say; but treasure up in your minds continually the words of life, and it shall be given you in the very hour that portion that shall be meted unto every man" (84:85, cf. 100:5–8). "And whoso receiveth you, there I will be also, for I will go before your face. I will be on your right hand and on your left, and my Spirit shall be in your hearts, and mine angels round about you, to bear you up" (84:88).

What protection is promised to missionaries in a world hostile to the Lord's messengers?

Considering the conditions in which many young missionaries serve, it is a miracle that more of them are not injured or killed. And yet there are promises made to faithful missionaries that enable them to have fewer accidents and deaths and accidents per capita than do their counterparts who stay at home (Oaks, 9). "And any man that shall go and preach this gospel of the kingdom, and fail not to continue faithful in all things, shall not be weary in mind, neither darkened, neither in body, limb, nor joint; and a hair of his head shall not fall to the ground unnoticed. And they shall not go hungry, neither athirst" (84:80). "Verily, thus saith the Lord unto you—there is no weapon that is formed against you shall prosper" (71:9).

What is the Lord's purpose in having the gospel preached to all the world?

Often the question is asked why Latter-day Saint missionaries are sent to Christian nations as well as other nations. The Lord did not limit the command to take his gospel to all the world to those who had never heard a part of his gospel before. There seems to be a dual reason for preaching the gospel: that all mankind might be partakers of the blessings which the Lord has in store for his faithful children, and that those who will heed can avoid many of the calamities foretold in the latter days (e.g., 43:25–26; 45:26–33; 63:32–37; 88:84–94). "And for this cause, that men might be made partakers of the glories which were to be revealed, the Lord sent forth the fulness of his gospel, his everlasting covenant, reasoning in plainness and simplicity—To prepare the weak for those things which are coming on the earth, and for the Lord's errand in the day when the weak shall confound the wise, and the little one become a strong nation, and two shall put their tens of thousands to flight" (133:57–58).

What consequences come from rejecting the Lord's messengers and their message?

From the very beginning of the Doctrine and Covenants to the very end, the Lord has warned of the calamities that inescapably follow rejection of the warning voice: "After your testimony cometh wrath and indignation upon the people. For after your testimony cometh the testimony of earthquakes, that shall cause groanings in the midst of her, and men shall fall upon the ground and shall not be able to stand. And also cometh the testimony of the voice of thunderings, and the voice of lightnings, and the voice of tempests, and the voice of the waves of the sea heaving themselves beyond their bounds. And all things shall be in commotion; and surely, men's hearts shall fail them; for fear shall come upon all people" (88:88–91).

Is a mission worth the sacrifices one must make to serve?

In a day when so much emphasis is put on the reward for effort expended, the Lord puts priorities in proper eternal perspective. The Lord declared: "For many times you have desired of me to know that which would be of the most worth unto you. Behold, blessed are you for this thing, and for speaking my words which I have given you according to my commandments. And now, behold, I say unto you, that the thing which will be of the most worth unto you will be to declare repentance unto this people, that you may bring souls unto me, that you may rest with them in the kingdom of my Father" (15:4–6; 16:4–6).

What are some of the immediate rewards for engaging in missionary work?

The Lord described immediate benefits of doing missionary work: "Lift up your heart and rejoice, for the hour of your mission is come; and your tongue shall be loosed, and you shall declare glad tidings of great joy unto this generation. You shall declare the things which have been revealed to my servant, Joseph Smith, Jun. You shall begin to preach from this time forth, yea, to reap in the field which is white already to be burned. Therefore, thrust in your sickle with all your soul, and your sins are forgiven you, and you shall be laden with sheaves upon your back, for the laborer is worthy of his hire. Wherefore, your family shall live" (31:3–5).

What is the ultimate reward and good that comes from missionary service?

Participating in the salvation and exaltation of spirit brothers and sisters is part of one's eternal reward. The Lord urges his Saints to "remember the worth of souls is great in the sight of God. . . . Wherefore, you are called to cry repentance unto this people. And if it so be that you should labor all your days in crying repentance unto this people, and bring, save it be one soul unto me, how great shall be your joy with him in the kingdom of my Father! And now, if your joy will be great with one soul that you have brought unto me into the kingdom of my Father, how great will be your joy if you should bring many souls unto me!" (18:10, 14–16).

See also Apostasy, the Great; Great and marvelous work.

BIBLIOGRAPHY

Hinckley, Gordon B. "Some Thoughts on Temples, Retention of Converts, and Missionary Service." *Ensign* 27 (November 1997): 49–52.

Kimball, Spencer W. *President Kimball Speaks Out.* Salt Lake City: Deseret Book, 1981.

Oaks, Dallin H. "Miracles." *Ensign* 31 (June 2001): 6–17.

Smith, Joseph. *History of The Church of Jesus Christ of Latter-day Saints.* Edited by B. H. Roberts. 7 vols. 2d ed. rev. Salt Lake City: The Church of Jesus Christ of Latter-day Saints, 1932–51.

RLB

Missouri period

The Missouri period of early Latter-day Saint history spanned approximately eight years (1831–39) and is divided by historians into three shorter periods: the Jackson County period (1831–33), the Clay County period (1833–36), and the northern Missouri period (1836–39).

Jackson County, January 1831 to November 1833

In September 1830, less than six months after the organization of the Church, Joseph Smith received revelatory instructions appointing Oliver Cowdery, Peter Whitmer Jr., Parley P. Pratt, and Ziba Peterson to travel from New York to the western frontier border of the United States to preach the gospel to the LAMANITES in the newly created Indian Territory west of Missouri (28:8; 30:5; 32:1–5). Simultaneous to the calling of these missionaries, the Prophet began to receive revelatory understanding concerning the establishment of ZION, or the NEW JERUSALEM. "No man knoweth where the city Zion shall be built," the revelation declared, "but . . . I say unto you that it shall be on the borders by the Lamanites" (28:9). At the time, the Prophet's understanding of the Zion established by Enoch first began to be made known to him (Moses 5). By December 1830, however, he likely realized that the Zion spoken of in the revelations to Moses (see Moses 6–7) entailed establishing an actual society or community of true believers who were "of one heart and one mind, and dwelt in righteousness" (Moses 7:18). From these and other revelations that Joseph Smith received, it became clear to the Prophet that the Saints were to eventually assemble and establish a permanent settlement in the western region of Missouri.

Of One Heart, Emma on the Ice; *painting by Liz Lemon Swindle. After her husband's arrest in Far West, Missouri, Emma Smith was forced to flee with the couple's four young children, crossing the frozen Mississippi River into Illinois in the winter of 1838–1839. Joseph later summarized his feelings for Emma:* "How glorious were my feelings when I met that faithful and friendly band. . . . With what unspeakable delight, and what transports of joy swelled my bosom, when I took by the hand, on that night, my beloved Emma—she that was my wife, even the wife of my youth, and the choice of my heart. Many were the reverberations of my mind when I contemplated for a moment the many scenes we had been called to pass through, the fatigues and the toils, the sorrows and sufferings, and the joys and consolations, from time to time, which had strewed our paths and crowned our board. Oh what a commingling of thought filled my mind for the moment, again she is here, even in the seventh trouble—undaunted, firm, and unwavering—unchangeable, affectionate Emma!" *(History of the Church, 5:107).*

Leaving in mid-October from Fayette, New York, the four elders called to preach to the Lamanites traveled to northeastern Ohio, where they taught the restored gospel to Sidney Rigdon, a former Baptist and Campbellite minister, and many of his followers. In a few weeks' time the missionaries baptized approximately 130 converts. Among these converts was Frederick G. Williams, who joined with the elders as they left Ohio to continue their trek west. After a very arduous journey during the middle of winter, the five missionaries arrived in Independence, Missouri, in mid-January 1831, marking the beginning of the Latter-day Saints' presence in Jackson County.

The mission to the Lamanite tribes living just over the western Missouri border, however, was short-lived. Unbeknownst to the elders, they needed permission from government authorities to preach to the tribes. Having failed to obtain that permission, they were forced to return to Jackson County, where they decided that Parley P. Pratt should return to report their activities to Joseph Smith. The other missionaries remained in Missouri. When Elder Pratt arrived in Kirtland in March 1831, Joseph Smith had moved there, and the call had been issued for the New York Saints to follow him to Kirtland (37). By mid-May 1831, the Colesville, Fayette, and Manchester branches had relocated from New York to Ohio.

At the conclusion of the first Church conference held in Ohio, 3–6 June 1831, Joseph Smith received a revelation directing that he, Sidney Rigdon, and more than two dozen pairs of missionaries travel to Missouri (52:3). The revelation further indicated that upon their arrival the location of Zion would be revealed (52:5). Pursuant to these instructions, the Prophet left Kirtland in mid-June and arrived in western Missouri a month later. On 20 July he received the landmark revelation. "This is the land of promise, and the place for the city of Zion," the revelation declared. "Behold, the place which is now called Independence is the center place; and a spot for the temple is lying westward, upon a lot which is not far from the courthouse" (57:2–3). On 2 August, Sidney Rigdon dedicated the land of Zion for the Latter-day Saints.

The following day, 3 August, the Prophet led a group of Church members to a grassy knoll on the outskirts west of Independence and there designated and dedicated the spot for the great latter-day temple in the New Jerusalem. The Doctrine and Covenants includes six revelations received by Joseph Smith during his two-month's journey to and from western Missouri (see sections 57–62).

With their newly acquired understanding of the location of Zion, Church members were called and appointed under the direction of Joseph Smith and Bishops Edward Partridge and Newel K. Whitney to journey to Jackson County and take up residence (63:41; see also 54:8–9; 57:15). In addition, members relocating to Missouri were expected to consecrate property and money so that lands in Jackson County could be purchased (42:34–35; 57:4–8; 58:51; 63:25–31; 72:15–17, 24–26). Yet, not everyone was expected to gather to Zion, and even the Prophet continued to live in Kirtland, which remained the headquarters of the Church. The establishment of two Church centers, one in Missouri and one in Ohio, created difficulties in establishing ecclesiastical stability in both areas. Constant two-way communication was necessary to ensure proper implementation of Church policies and operations. For example, in April 1832, Joseph Smith and a small company traveled to Missouri to meet with local Church leaders to establish the United Firm, clarify matters associated with CONSECRATION, and settle personal differences that had arisen (82; 83). By mid-1833 approximately twelve hundred Latter-day Saints had taken up residence in Jackson County (more than one-third of the county's estimated population of thirty-three hundred) and had established five branches of the Church. A sixth settlement, known as the Cincinnati branch, was short-lived and did not become an established Latter-day Saint community.

But the growing Mormon presence, in addition to the cultural, social, political, and economic differences between the Saints and other Jackson County residents, generated misunderstandings between the two groups. On 20 July 1833, several community leaders confronted Church leaders in Independence and demanded

Northwestern Missouri, 1831–1839.

that the Saints leave the county, pledging that if they complied, they would not be harmed or molested and would be given sufficient time to dispose of their property and businesses without a loss. When the Saints rebuffed those demands, a mob ransacked the printing offices of the Church-operated *The Evening and the Morning Star,* which also served as the home of William W. Phelps, the Church printer. The press and type were thrown into the street, printed materials were destroyed, and the building all but demolished. The nearby Church-owned store was spared a similar fate when A. Sidney Gilbert agreed to cease operations. Bishop Edward Partridge and Charles Allen were publicly tarred and feathered at the county courthouse. With little hope of recourse, three days later Church leaders signed a memorandum promising that half the Church members would leave the county by January 1834 and the other half by April 1834. After this agreement was reached, much of the agitation ceased.

Peace did not prevail for long, however. In late October 1833, the Saints received a letter from Church leaders in Ohio instructing those who signed the memorandum to leave as promised, but others were to "not sell any of their inheritances, nor move out of the county" (Smith, 1:417). When the Saints publicly declared that they intended to remain and would defend their lands and homes if necessary, the earlier settlers were incensed, seeing this as a breach of the Saints' promise to leave the county, and they stepped up activities to bring about their removal (Roberts, 1:342). Beginning the last day of October and continuing through the first week of November, Church members at the Whitmer, Prairie, Colesville, and Blue River settlements and those living in Independence were harassed, threatened, and attacked, resulting in the deaths of one member of the Church and two Missourians. Church leaders acceded to the demands of the local authorities and agreed to leave immediately. By 8 November, nearly every Latter-day Saint had left the county.

Clay County, November 1833 to August 1836

Following their expulsion from Jackson County, several families relocated in neighboring counties (Van Buren, Lafayette, and a few others), but most sought refuge northward across the Missouri River in Clay County. There they found the citizens to be more welcoming than Jackson County's old-time settlers had been, and many of the Saints were offered temporary lodging and employment. Meanwhile, Church leaders petitioned Missouri governor Daniel Dunklin and United States president Andrew Jackson, outlining their grievances against the Jackson County residents (101:86–88). They also employed the services of Alexander W. Doniphan, a young attorney in Liberty, Missouri, to assist them in seeking RE-DRESS. With a promise from Governor Dunklin of state assistance in restoring the Saints to their lands, Joseph Smith received a revelation in February 1834 calling for the organization of ZION'S CAMP (103). In June 1834, the company, more than two hundred strong, arrived in Missouri to assist the governor in restoring the Saints to their property. By this time, however, Dunklin had changed his mind and refused to intervene. Without government support, the reinstatement of the Saints displaced from Jackson County was virtually impossible; Joseph Smith received a revelation disbanding Zion's Camp and informing the Saints that the redemption of Zion's "center place" (57:3) was yet future (105:19, 31–32). *See* Zion, redemption of.

Believing that the redemption would be soon coming, most of the Latter-day Saints who had relocated in Clay County remained, where they eventually established more than a dozen small scattered settlements, most of which were south of Liberty, the county seat. To provide ecclesiastical leadership, at the conclusion of Zion's Camp Joseph Smith organized the Missouri presidency, consisting of a presidency (David Whitmer, William W. Phelps, and John Whitmer), and a twelve-member high council. Latter-day Saint emigration to the region also continued, though not as extensively as during the Jackson County period. By 1836, approximately fifteen hundred Latter-day Saints lived in Clay County, their numbers causing local residents to once again be concerned about their increasing presence, which led community activists to once again propose their removal. This time, however, rather than resorting to physical violence (although there was some), Clay County's other citizens opted to allow the Latter-day Saints to search out new lands for settlement and relocate peacefully.

Northern Missouri, August 1836 to February 1839

In March 1836, Missouri Church leaders began searching out possible sites for permanent settlement in sparsely populated areas of unincorporated northern Ray County. During the next several months, after making extensive explorations, Church leaders purchased property in the area of Shoal and Goose creeks, including a one-mile square plat (640 acres) in Mirable Township purchased on 8 August 1836. Latter-day Saints began moving to Far West and the surrounding region in significant numbers. With the increased population, in December 1836 Alexander W. Doniphan, Clay County's representative in the state legislature and a man sympathetic to the Latter-day Saints, sponsored a bill to create a county exclusively for the Saints. The bill also proposed the formation of

a second "gentile" county, situated to the north of Caldwell County, named Daviess County. On 29 December 1836, the Missouri legislature passed the bill creating the two counties.

Far West became the largest community in Caldwell County, and smaller Latter-day Saint settlements were established on or near Shoal, Log, Bush, Mill, Panther, Mud, and Plum creeks and Crooked River. Most of the settlements were named after the principal founders and included the following: Allred (William, William M., and Wiley Allred); Curtis (Jeremiah Curtis); Carter (Simeon and Orlando Carter); Durfey (James and Perry Durfey); Free (Absalom and Joseph Free); Lyon, also called Salem (Aaron C. Lyon); Myers (Jacob Myers); Plumb (Merlin Plumb); Stevens (Roswell Stevens); and Hawn/Haun's Mill (Jacob Hawn/Haun). These sites were all abandoned when the Saints were expelled from the state in 1839.

Although Daviess County was not intended for Latter-day Saint settlement, a number of communities were established by Latter-day Saints in 1838: ADAM-ONDI-AHMAN (Diahman

Exodus Routes from Missouri to Illinois, 1838–1839.

for short), the largest settlement; Marrowbone (also called Ambrosia); Honeycreek; Lickfork; and Grindstone Fork. On 19 May 1838, while visiting Lyman Wight at Adam-ondi-Ahman, Joseph Smith received the only revelation received at that locale currently canonized in the Doctrine and Covenants (116). To better serve Church members in Daviess County, the Adam-ondi-Ahman stake was organized on 28 June 1838, with John Smith as president and Reynolds Cahoon and Lyman Wight as counselors. Vinson Knight was appointed bishop pro tem. A temple site at Adam-ondi-Ahman was also dedicated. After the surrender to Missouri authorities in November 1838, Latter-day Saints living in Daviess County were forced to leave the county, and most temporarily relocated in Caldwell County before making their way out of the state in early 1839.

Joseph Smith visited Far West for the first time in late October and early November 1837. His visit lasted only a few days before he returned to Kirtland, Ohio. In January 1838, however, he left Kirtland to permanently relocate to Missouri. He arrived at Far West on 14 March 1838, thus making Far West the new headquarters of the Church. The Doctrine and Covenants includes seven revelations (113–15; 117–20) received by Joseph Smith at Far West during this time.

From August through November 1838, several civil disturbances broke out between the Missourians and the Latter-day Saints living in northern Missouri. The entire contest, known as the Mormon War, was perpetuated primarily by religious intolerance on the part of a significant number of the earlier settlers residing in the northern counties; however, there was also some culpability on the part of the Saints. The most tragic scenes associated with the hostilities included a skirmish between Caldwell County and Ray County militia at Crooked River, which resulted in the deaths of four men—one Missourian and three members of the Caldwell contingent, including Elder David W. Patten of the Quorum of the Twelve. The most lamentable scene was the attack against the Saints at Hawn/Haun's Mill in eastern Caldwell County on 30 October, where seventeen Latter-day Saint men and boys were killed and another fourteen wounded in an attack on an almost defenseless community. The Mormon War came to an end in late October and early November when Missouri governor Lilburn W. Boggs issued the Extermination Order calling for the removal of Latter-day Saints from the state and called out twenty-five hundred state militia to march on Far West. Recognizing the hopelessness of the situation, Church leaders capitulated to the governor's demands.

After the Church's surrender, several leaders were taken into state custody by Missouri militia officers. From 12 to 29 November 1838 a preliminary hearing was held in Richmond in the 5th Judicial Circuit Court of Judge Austin A. King. At the conclusion of the hearing, King ordered Joseph and Hyrum Smith, Sidney Rigdon, Caleb Baldwin, Alexander McRae, and Lyman Wight bound over to the jail in Liberty, Missouri, to stand trial the following spring on the charge of treason against the state. During this incarceration, the Prophet dictated a letter, extracts of which became sections 121 to 123.

In addition to those incarcerated in LIBERTY JAIL, Parley P. Pratt of the Quorum of the Twelve, Norman Shearer, Darwin Chase, Luman Gibbs, and Morris Phelps were ordered to remain in the jail in Richmond, Missouri, to stand trial on the charge of murder for the death of Moses Rowland, who died from wounds he received in the Battle of Crooked River. In April 1839 Shearer and Chase were released; Pratt, Phelps, Gibbs, and King Follett (who had been jailed later on a separate charge) were ordered to be taken to Boone County Jail in Columbia, Missouri, to await their hearing.

While these Church leaders languished in prison, Brigham Young, president of the Quorum of the Twelve, supervised the removal of Church members from Missouri. Adams County, Illinois, became the temporary gathering place for the Latter-day Saint exiles. During the winter of 1839 (most left in February), hundreds of homeless families made their way across northern Missouri to the Mississippi River, crossing over to Quincy, where the citizens opened their hearts to the suffering

Latter-day Saints, providing them with homes, food, and temporary employment.

Final hearings for the Latter-day Saint prisoners held in Liberty and Columbia jails were never held. In January 1839, the court ordered that Sidney Rigdon be released from Liberty Jail. The remaining prisoners—Joseph Smith, Hyrum Smith, Caleb Baldwin, Alexander McRae, and Lyman Wight—remained confined until the first week in April, when they were transported to Gallatin in Daviess County for their hearing. Shortly after their arrival in Gallatin, however, Judge Thomas Burch ordered a change of venue and decreed that the trial be moved to Columbia. On the evening of 16 April, while en route to Boone County, William Morgan, the Daviess County sheriff, released the prisoners. On 22 April the Prophet and his companions arrived in Quincy amid great rejoicing by their family and friends.

The prisoners in Columbia Jail—Parley P. Pratt, Luman Gibbs, Morris Phelps, and King Follett—remained confined for several more months, with no prospect that their case would ever come to trial. On 4 July 1839, Independence Day, the prisoners broke out of jail. Pratt and Phelps succeeded in making their escape, but Follett was recaptured in the attempt and remained imprisoned until October 1839, when he was finally acquitted. The last prisoner, Gibbs, who by this time had apostatized, was eventually released.

See also Illinois period; New York period; Ohio period.

BIBLIOGRAPHY

Baugh, Alexander L. *A Call to Arms: The 1838 Mormon Defense of Northern Missouri.* Provo, Utah: Joseph Fielding Smith Institute for Latter-day Saint History and BYU Studies, 2000.

———. "From High Hopes to Despair: The Missouri Period, 1831–39." *Ensign* 31 (July 2001): 44–55.

Gentry, Leland H. *A History of the Latter-day Saints in Northern Missouri from 1836 to 1839.* Provo, Utah: Joseph Fielding Smith Institute for Latter-day Saint History and BYU Studies, 2000.

Jennings, Warren Abner. "Zion Is Fled: The Expulsion of the Mormons from Jackson County, Missouri." Ph.D. dissertation, University of Florida, 1962.

Parkin, Max H. "A History of the Latter-day Saints in Clay County, Missouri, from 1833 to 1837." Ph.D. dissertation, Brigham Young University, 1976.

Roberts, B. H. *A Comprehensive History of The Church of Jesus Christ of Latter-day Saints, Century One.* 6 vols. Salt Lake City: The Church of Jesus Christ of Latter-day Saints, 1930. Reprint, Provo, Utah: Brigham Young University Press, 1965.

Smith, Joseph. *History of The Church of Jesus Christ of Latter-day Saints.* Edited by B. H. Roberts. 7 vols. 2d ed. rev. Salt Lake City: The Church of Jesus Christ of Latter-day Saints, 1932–51.

ALB

Missouri River

The headwaters of the Missouri River originate in Montana and meander through North and South Dakota, Iowa, Nebraska, Kansas, and Missouri before reaching the Mississippi River just north of St. Louis, Missouri.

The Missouri River was used by Latter-day Saints as a principal means of travel for many years. The first group of Saints to travel on the Missouri River was the Colesville branch, a group of approximately seventy Church members who journeyed from Thompson, Ohio, to Jackson County, Missouri, in June and July 1831. In August 1831, Joseph Smith and a small company of men traveled east from Independence on the Missouri River in canoes before being instructed in a revelation given at MCILWAINE'S BEND (between Carroll and Saline counties) to take their journey on land (61, headnote).

During the first decade after the Church was organized, some Latter-day Saints traveled to and from the eastern and western parts of the state of Missouri on the Missouri River. Throughout the pioneer period (1846–69), thousands of Saints made their way to the West by traveling on the Missouri River.

In March 1839, with Joseph Smith and other leaders in jail and the Saints being driven from the state of Missouri, the Prophet wrote: "As well might man stretch forth his puny arm to stop the Missouri river in its decreed course, or to turn it up stream, as to hinder the Almighty from pouring down knowledge from heaven upon the heads of the Latter-day Saints" (121:33). *See* map, p. 414.

ALB

Mocked. *See* Appendix E.

More or less

Adding to or taking away from what the Lord has revealed. Five times in the Doctrine and Covenants, in different contexts, the Lord affirms the importance of not taking away or adding to what he has revealed.

1. Declaring that "whosoever repenteth and cometh unto me, the same is my church," the Lord said, "Whosoever declareth more or less than this, the same is not of me, but is against me; therefore he is not of my church" (10:67–68).

2. Defining truth as "knowledge of things as they are, and as they were, and as they are to come," the Lord said, "And whatsoever is more or less than this is the spirit of that wicked one who was a liar from the beginning" (93:24–25).

3. Justifying members of the Church "in befriending that law which is the constitutional law of the land," the revelation continues, "and as pertaining to the law of man, whatsoever is more or less than this, cometh of evil" (98:6–7).

4. Telling the Saints to seek "diligently" for, and uphold "honest," "wise," and "good" persons in government, the Lord cautioned, "otherwise whatsoever is less than these cometh of evil" (98:9–10).

5. Affirming that no one was eligible to buy stock in the Nauvoo House "unless he shall be a believer in the Book of Mormon, and the revelations," the Lord declared, "For that which is more or less than this cometh of evil, and shall be attended with cursings and not blessings" (124:119–20).

The same principle is taught in the Old Testament (Deut. 4:2), the New Testament (Rev. 22:18–19), and the Book of Mormon (3 Ne. 11:39–40). Clearly, the Lord has commanded, "Ye shall not add unto the word which I command you, neither shall ye diminish ought from it, that ye may keep the commandments of the Lord your God which I command you" (Deut. 4:2). This does not mean that the Lord himself will not add to or adjust what he has previously revealed. He will reveal that which is expedient (18:18; 88:78–79, 127) for a given time and circumstance and will "give unto the faithful line upon line, precept upon precept" (98:12; 128:21) according to their willingness to receive his word (Alma 12:10–11), even to a fulness of truth and light (93:26–29). In the dispensation of the fulness of times, "things which have been kept hid from before the foundation of the world" will be revealed (124:41; 128:18). Through living prophets, the Lord will provide continuing revelation "adapted to the circumstances in which the children of the kingdom are placed" (Smith, 5:135).

BIBLIOGRAPHY

Smith, Joseph. *History of The Church of Jesus Christ of Latter-day Saints.* Edited by B. H. Roberts. 7 vols. 2d ed. rev. Salt Lake City: The Church of Jesus Christ of Latter-day Saints, 1932–51.

LED

More sure word of prophecy

"A man's knowing that he is sealed up unto eternal life, by revelation and the spirit of prophecy, through the power of the Holy Priesthood" (131:5; cf. 2 Pet. 1:19); knowing that one's calling and election is made sure. Hosts of spirit children of God in the premortal life, on the basis of their commitment to righteousness there, elected to be in the family of Christ (a member of the Church), with the promise that if they were faithful in mortality, their election would be made sure. They are called and elected when they accept the gospel in mortality and are baptized into the kingdom of God. Nonetheless, such calling and election, whenever received, must be "made sure" by obedience to all the ordinances and covenants of the gospel (Smith, *History,* 4:358–60). President Joseph Fielding Smith taught that "those who press forward in righteousness, living by every word of revealed truth, have power to make their calling and election sure. They receive the more sure word of prophecy and know by revelation and the authority of the priesthood that they are sealed up unto eternal life. They are sealed up against all manner of sin and blasphemy except the blasphemy against the Holy Ghost and the shedding of innocent blood. But the mere fact of being married for time and eternity in the temple, *standing alone,* does not give them this guarantee. Blessings pronounced upon couples in connection with celestial marriage are con-ditioned upon the subsequent faithfulness of the participating parties" (*Doctrines*, 2:46). *See* Innocent blood.

Having one's calling and election made sure, receiving the more sure word of prophecy, and being sealed up unto ETERNAL LIFE against "all manner of blasphemies" does not ensure exalta-tion without consequences for subsequent sin-ning. The Lord has made it clear that those thus sealed, who later sin seriously, "shall come forth in the first resurrection, and enter into their ex-altation; *but they shall be destroyed in the flesh, and shall be delivered unto the buffetings of Satan unto the day of redemption*" (132:19–27; empha-sis added). *See* Buffetings of Satan.

The fulness of the power and authority of the Melchizedek Priesthood, essential to seal-ing persons up to eternal life, was restored to Joseph Smith and Oliver Cowdery in the Kirtland Temple on 3 April 1836 by Elijah the prophet (110:13–16; Smith, *History*, 6:251–53; cf. 149–51, 298–99, 305). Those priesthood keys are now held by the living prophets, seers, and revelators in The Church of Jesus Christ of Latter-day Saints. *See* Seal, sealed.

If there is a distinction between the term "the more sure word of prophecy" and the related terms "having one's calling and election made sure" and being "sealed up unto eternal life," it is that with the more sure word of prophecy, a person is told while still in mortality, "by reve-lation and the spirit of prophecy, through the power of the Holy Priesthood" (131:5), that he has been sealed up unto eternal life. Myriads of others who are not so informed make their calling and election sure by a lifetime of consis-tent faithfulness to their gospel covenants. Such consecrated Saints can receive the quiet, reas-suring, sustaining power of the HOLY GHOST that their lives are in harmony with the purposes of God, that he approves of their offerings, that his promises are unfailing, and that with continued faithfulness they will indeed receive the greatest of all the gifts of God—eternal life (6:13; 14:7).

Doctrine and Covenants 131:6, given by the Prophet Joseph Smith in context with verse 5 (knowing that one is "sealed up unto eternal life") contains an interesting thought concerning one's being consciously aware of one's spiritual status before God. It reads, "It is impossible for a man to be saved in ignorance." Usually this statement is used to support the idea that much gospel knowledge is needed for one to be saved. That is true, but there may also be an additional meaning of that statement. Could verse 6 mean it is impossible to be saved in ignorance of the fact that one is being saved? President David O. McKay taught the importance of being aware of the development of spirituality and of feeling it developing within one's soul: "Spirituality, our true aim, is the consciousness of victory over self, and of communion with the Infinite. Spirituality impels one to conquer difficulties and acquire more and more strength. To feel one's faculties unfolding, and truth expanding in the soul, is one of life's sublimest experi-ences" (72). Such consciousness and feeling can be experienced whether one receives the more sure word of prophecy or, more informally, the whisperings of the Holy Ghost that the prom-ised blessing of having one's calling and elec-tion made sure will someday be realized, if not in this life, then in the next. The Prophet Joseph Smith taught that such assurances are "an an-chor to the soul, sure and steadfast" (*History*, 5:388–89), which he would understand by his own experience, having been told by the Lord, "I seal upon you your exaltation, and prepare a throne for you in the kingdom of my Father, with Abraham your father" (132:49).

See also Historical context and overview of Doctrine and Covenants 131 (p. 847).

BIBLIOGRAPHY

McKay, David O. *Man May Know for Himself.* Salt Lake City: Deseret Book, 1967.

Smith, Joseph. *History of The Church of Jesus Christ of Latter-day Saints.* Edited by B. H. Roberts. 7 vols. 2d ed. rev. Salt Lake City: The Church of Jesus Christ of Latter-day Saints, 1932–51.

Smith, Joseph Fielding. *Doctrines of Salvation.* Com-piled by Bruce R. McConkie. 3 vols. Salt Lake City: Bookcraft, 1954–56.

LED

Morley, Isaac

Birth: 11 March 1786, Montague, Hampshire County, Massachusetts

Death: 24 June 1865, Fairview, Sanpete County, Utah

Isaac Morley is mentioned in two sections of the Doctrine and Covenants (52:23; 64:15–16, 20). "Father Morley," as he was affectionately called, was a faithful member and leader in the Church from the time of his baptism to the end of his life.

He was baptized by Parley P. Pratt in Kirtland, Ohio, 15 November 1830, and ordained an elder shortly thereafter. On 3 June 1831, at a conference of the Church held at the Morley farm near Kirtland, Morley was ordained a high priest and appointed as first counselor to Bishop Edward Partridge (Cannon and Cook, 7). Just four days later, he was called to serve a mission to Missouri as a companion to Ezra Booth (52:23). This companionship was chastened by the Lord because "they sought evil in their hearts. . . . They condemned for evil that thing in which there was no evil." One was forgiven; the other was not. "Behold, I, the Lord, was angry with him who was my servant Ezra Booth, and also my servant Isaac Morley . . . ; nevertheless I have forgiven my servant Isaac Morley" (64:15–16). In that same revelation, Father Morley was instructed to sell his Kirtland farm and give the proceeds to the Church, which he did (64:20). He moved to Missouri in 1831, first to Jackson County and then, to avoid persecution, north to Clay County, and then farther north to Far West, in Caldwell County. Morley served as a counselor to Bishop Partridge in Missouri from 1831 to 1838. He was called from Missouri to serve a mission with Bishop Partridge to the eastern states in 1835. Following Morley's fifteen-month mission to Massachusetts, Joseph Smith recorded, "Attended [elders] school. Isaac Morley came in from the east" (2:301). Two days later the Prophet wrote: "The word of the Lord came unto me, saying—Behold, I am well pleased with my servant Isaac Morley, and my servant Edward Partridge, because of the integrity of their hearts in laboring in my vineyard, for the salvation of the souls of men. Verily I say unto you, their sins are forgiven them; therefore say unto them, in my name, that it is my will that they should tarry for a little season, and attend the school, and also the solemn assembly, for a wise purpose in me" (2:302–3). Morley did remain in Kirtland for a time and participated in the dedication of the Kirtland Temple, during which he sat to the right of Bishop Partridge in the Aaronic Priesthood pulpits. After glorious temple experiences, Morley returned to Missouri and was ordained a patriarch 4 November 1837 by Joseph Smith, Sidney Rigdon, and Hyrum Smith.

The Morleys left Missouri with the rest of the Saints in 1838 and settled in Illinois, establishing a community named Yelrome (*Morley* spelled backwards, with an *e* added at the end), twenty-five miles south of Nauvoo. He served as president of the Lima stake in that area until the stake was discontinued in 1843, when many of the Saints moved to Nauvoo for protection from mob violence. Morley did not leave Yelrome for Nauvoo until two years later, in the fall of 1845, after mobs burned his grain, his cooper shop, and his home.

Morley left Nauvoo in 1846, and, after a stay in Winter Quarters for a time, arrived in the Salt Lake Valley in 1848. In 1849 he led a group of fifty families south to settle near Manti, Utah. He represented the area as a member of the state legislature from 1851 to 1855. Later, at the suggestion of Brigham Young, he returned to Salt Lake City. For the last ten years of his life, Father Morley's assignments to give patriarchal blessings included traveling to Canada and California and giving hundreds of blessings. His health and energy ebbing, he visited a daughter in Fairview, Utah, where he died at the age of seventy-nine.

See also Morley, Isaac, farm.

BIBLIOGRAPHY

Cannon, Donald Q., and Lyndon W. Cook, eds. *Far West Record: Minutes of The Church of Jesus Christ of Latter-day Saints, 1830–1844.* Salt Lake City: Deseret Book, 1983.

Smith, Joseph. *History of The Church of Jesus Christ of Latter-day Saints.* Edited by B. H. Roberts. 7 vols. 2d ed. rev. Salt Lake City: The Church of Jesus Christ of Latter-day Saints, 1932–51.

RHM

Isaac Morley's farm near Kirtland, Ohio; photograph by Welden C. Andersen. In 1831 the Lord declared, "And again, I say unto you, that my servant Isaac Morley may not be tempted above that which he is able to bear, and counsel wrongfully to your hurt, I gave commandment that his farm should be sold" (D&C 64:20).

Morley, Isaac, farm

In 1812 Isaac and Lucy Morley homesteaded on their 130-acre farm one mile northeast of the Newel K. Whitney store in Kirtland, Ohio. In the late 1820s they joined Sidney Rigdon's Reformed Baptist congregation and soon formed a society on their farm with about five other families, holding all things common (cf. Acts 2:44). They called their organization "the 'Family' or the 'Big Family'" (Backman, 15, 36). This group joined the Church in the fall of 1830 when Parley P. Pratt's party of missionaries, on their way from New York to the western borders of Missouri to preach to the Lamanites (32:1–5), brought them the Book of Mormon and the message of the Restoration (Backman, 8).

Four months later Joseph Smith arrived in Kirtland and after staying with the Newel K. Whitney family for a few weeks, lived on the Morley farm for nearly seven months, February to September 1831. During the time the Prophet was with the Whitneys and on the Morley farm, he received many revelations (41–64; 57–62 were received while he was on a mission to Missouri). In September 1831, as Joseph Smith was preparing to move from Morley's farm to John Johnson's farm in Hiram, Ohio, he received a revelation in which Isaac Morley was commanded to sell his farm and move to Missouri. Morley sold fifty acres and moved to Missouri. The remaining eighty acres, managed by the United Firm (a holding and management organization for Church assets), continued to be a principal destination for Saints gathering to the Kirtland area in the early 1830s (Backman, 69–73). *See* map, p. 345.

See also Ohio period.

BIBLIOGRAPHY

Backman, Milton V., Jr. *The Heavens Resound: A History of the Latter-day Saints in Ohio, 1830–1838.* Salt Lake City: Deseret Book, 1983.

GML

Mormon

Nephite record-keeper and abridger of the PLATES who shaped the structure and content of the Book of Mormon. Although Mormon is not mentioned by name in the Doctrine and Covenants except in the headnote to section 10, the theft of the 116 manuscript pages in June 1828 (3; 10) brought one dimension of Mormon's inspired editorial work into sharp focus. His decision to put the small plates of Nephi with the remainder of his record "for a wise purpose . . . , according to the workings of the Spirit of the Lord" which was in him, provided a supplementary record, even though Mormon did not know at the time why the Lord wanted it done (W of M 1:3–7).

The stolen 116 pages of manuscript were a translation of Mormon's abridgment of the book of Lehi. The loss was compensated by the translation of the small plates of Nephi, consisting of the books of 1 and 2 Nephi, Jacob, Enos, Jarom, and Omni. In directing the Prophet Joseph Smith on how to handle the loss, the Lord indicated that the doctrinal and prophetic content of the small plates of Nephi did "throw greater views upon [the] gospel" than what was contained in the stolen manuscript (10:44–45).

See also Book of Mormon, lost manuscript of (116 pages); Doctrine and Covenants, what it says about the Book of Mormon.

RJM

Mormon redress petitions. *See* Redress.

Moroni

New World prophet (ca. A.D. 421), son of Mormon, and last writer on the Book of Mormon PLATES. In the latter days, the resurrected Moroni appeared to the Prophet Joseph Smith and instructed him each year from 1823 to 1827 in preparation for receiving the gold plates (JS–H 1:29–59). In 1830 in Harmony, Pennsylvania, Jesus Christ indicated that he had committed to Moroni "the keys of the record of the stick of Ephraim" (27:5). The Lord further prophesied on that occasion that one day he would "drink of the fruit of the vine" with Joseph Smith, Moroni, and other prophets (27:5–14). In an epistle written by Joseph Smith

in Nauvoo, Illinois, in 1842, the Prophet testified that Moroni fulfilled prophecy by revealing the Book of Mormon (128:20). In 1918 in Salt Lake City, Utah, the Lord testified through President Joseph F. Smith that Moroni had quoted the prophet Malachi to Joseph Smith and had taught Joseph that Elijah would return before the coming of the great and dreadful day of the Lord (138:46; JS–H 1:36–38).

See also Doctrine and Covenants, what it says about the Book of Mormon.

FFJ

Moses

The Doctrine and Covenants attests the exemplary role of Moses as a prophet (133:63) and "the great law-giver of Israel" (138:41). The Lord identified Moses as one who enjoyed the "spirit of revelation" (8:2) as guided by the Holy Ghost. Moses, a righteous man who held the PRIESTHOOD and exercised it under the direction of God, thereby delivered the children of Israel from Egyptian bondage, divided the Red Sea, and led the Israelites through on "dry ground" (8:3). Moses held the Melchizedek Priesthood, which he obtained from "his father-in-law, Jethro"; the priesthood lineage of Moses from Jethro back to Adam is given in 84:6–16. The significance of Moses' ministry is emphasized by the fact that all faithful priesthood holders "become the sons of Moses and of Aaron . . . and the elect of God" (84:33–34) in the same sense that all faithful believers in the gospel who are baptized are counted as Abraham's seed (Abr. 2:10; Gal. 3:27–29). Moses is further honored as one of the "great and mighty ones who were assembled in [the] vast congregation of the righteous" awaiting the advent of the Savior into the postmortal spirit world following his crucifixion (138:38–41). He is also listed with Enoch and Noah and the prophets who were before them as among those who were loved of the Savior, sustained in their afflictions, and redeemed (133:52–54). Even some who "received not the gospel, neither the testimony of Jesus" claim to be followers of Moses (76:100–101).

During his earthly ministry Moses "sought diligently to sanctify his people that they might behold the face of God" (84:23). Because of the wickedness of the people, however, Moses was removed "out of their midst, and the Holy Priesthood also" (84:25).

The Doctrine and Covenants repeatedly compares the roles of Moses and Joseph Smith. Joseph Smith was raised up to lead the people "like as Moses led the children of Israel" (103:16, 21). Modern Israel is commanded to look to Joseph Smith and, by extension, the living prophet, as the one appointed to receive commandments and revelations for the Church, "even as Moses" (28:2). As "President of the office of the High Priesthood," the prophet is to "preside over the whole church, and to be like unto Moses" (107:91). The command given to Joseph Smith to build a temple so sacred ordinances could be performed is explained by citing the example of Moses and the tabernacle: "He should build a tabernacle . . . that those ordinances might be revealed which had been hid from before the world was" (124:38). Moses is listed in 132:1, 38 as one among several of the Lord's servants who, in their day, were authorized by the Lord to marry plural wives.

The Doctrine and Covenants also affirms Moses' postmortal ministry. He appeared as a translated being "on the Mount of Transfiguration," conferring priesthood KEYS upon Peter, James, and John (138:45; Smith, 2:109–11). See Mount of Transfiguration.

With Elijah and John the Baptist, Moses was "with Christ in his resurrection" (133:55). As a resurrected being, Moses appeared on 3 April 1836 in the Kirtland Temple and committed "the keys of the gathering of Israel from the four parts of the earth, and the leading of the ten tribes from the land of the north" upon Joseph Smith and Oliver Cowdery (110:11).

See also Law of Moses; Sons of Moses and of Aaron.

BIBLIOGRAPHY

Smith, Joseph Fielding. *Doctrines of Salvation.* Compiled by Bruce R. McConkie. 3 vols. Salt Lake City: Bookcraft, 1954–56.

REL

Moses and of Aaron, sons of. *See* Sons of Moses and of Aaron.

Mote. *See* Appendix E.

Mother of abominations. *See* Great and abominable church.

Mount of Olives

Located just east of the city of JERUSALEM. The Mount of Olives, or Olivet, is mentioned once by name in the Doctrine and Covenants, in a prediction of the "coming of the Bridegroom" (Jesus), which says that "he shall stand upon the mount of Olivet" (133:19–20). But the mount is also obviously referred to in the Lord's recounting of the signs of the times there: "And then shall the Lord set his foot upon this mount, and it shall cleave in twain" (45:48, cf. 45:16–55; Zech. 14:4). The atoning suffering of which the Savior speaks in 19:16–19 commenced in Gethsemane, a garden of olive trees on the western slope of the Mount of Olives.

The Mount of Olives is a chain of four prominent hills, connected by high saddles, running north and south about two thousand meters, or about a mile and a quarter. Each hill features a spectacular view of Jerusalem to the west. The mount's name was derived in biblical times from the many olive gardens (olive tree orchards) on its slopes. The white limestone of the mountain chain was too soft for building stone, so few buildings were erected anciently on the mount. Numerous tombs and graves were cut into the soft limestone all along the chain, so that large parts of the mountain were set apart as cemeteries, some of which are still in use. The deep Kidron Valley (the "brook Cedron" of John 18:1 is a generally dry creek bed with water flowing through it only in the rainy season) runs north and south between the Mount of Olives and Jerusalem's Temple Mount and "city of David" (2 Sam. 5:7–9). The southernmost hill of the Mount of Olives chain was known as the "mount of corruption," where high places had been built for worshipping false gods in Old Testament times (1 Kgs. 11:7; 2 Kgs. 23:13). The northernmost hill of the chain is Mount Scopus. The BYU Jerusalem Center for Near Eastern Studies is on the saddle just south of Scopus. The two central hills, connected by a high saddle, were the main body of the Mount of Olives and the site of most biblical

The Transfiguration; *painting by W. H. Margetson. "He that endureth in faith and doeth my will, the same shall overcome, and shall receive an inheritance upon the earth when the day of transfiguration shall come; when the earth shall be transfigured, even according to the pattern which was shown unto mine apostles upon the mount" (D&C 63:20–21).*

references. David ascended the mount when fleeing Absalom's revolt (2 Sam. 15:30). When Jesus was in Jerusalem, he often spent nights on the Mount of Olives (Luke 21:37; John 8:1), probably at the village of Bethany, which is on the mountain's lower east slope (John 12:1). Jesus went over the mountain to enter Jerusalem in triumph just days before his crucifixion (Matt. 21:1–11; Mark 11:1–11; Luke 19:29–40). He went to the mountain to speak his prophecies concerning the destruction of ancient Jerusalem and latter-day signs of the times (Matt. 24:3–51; Mark 13:3–37; D&C 45:16–55; JS–M 1:4–55). After his resurrection, Jesus took his disciples to the Mount of Olives, where he ascended into heaven as they watched (Luke 24:50–52; Acts 1:9–12).

JRC

Mount of Transfiguration

Place identified with the TRANSFIGURATION of Jesus, Peter, James, and John (Matt. 17:1–13; Mark 9:2–10; Luke 9:28–36) when Moses and Elias (Elijah) appeared as translated beings and "the Savior, Moses, and Elias, gave the keys to Peter, James, and John" (Smith, *History*, 3:387). The Doctrine and Covenants provides just one passage specifically mentioning the Mount of Transfiguration, from which two important details not recorded in other scripture can be gleaned: Peter, James, and John saw the earth in its transfigured form; and the Lord has not seen fit to reveal the complete account of what took place upon the mount (63:20–21). Moses and Elijah later appeared to Joseph Smith and Oliver Cowdery on 3 April 1836 in the Kirtland Temple, again conferring priesthood KEYS as was done on the Mount of Transfiguration (110:11–16; cf. 138:45).

Multiple sources provide additional detail regarding the Mount of Transfiguration. This includes those present hearing the voice of the Father (Matt. 17:5; cf. 2 Pet. 1:17–18); Peter, James, and John's witnessing the majesty of Jesus (Luke 9:29; cf. John 1:14; Smith, 1:283); and the apostles learning that Moses and Elijah spoke to Jesus about his impending death and resurrection (JST Luke 9:31), presumably in anticipation and preparation for the ordeal of his upcoming atonement. Joseph Smith also revealed that John the Baptist was present (JST Mark 9:3). He may have acted in the capacity of a witness and transitional figure, having prepared the way for the coming of Christ and being the last legal administrator of the Aaronic Priesthood before Jesus' coming (McConkie, 1:404; Smith, *History*, 5:257–58; 5:261; *Joseph Smith*, 84–85). These events prefigure similar happenings that took place shortly after the dedication of the Kirtland Temple (cf. section 110). No authoritative source identifies the precise location where the transfiguration took place, although Mount Hermon and Mount Tabor have been proposed (Ogden and Skinner, 337).

See also Doctrine and Covenants, historical context and overview of sections 63 and 110.

BIBLIOGRAPHY

McConkie, Bruce R. *Doctrinal New Testament Commentary.* 3 vols. Salt Lake City: Bookcraft, 1965–73.

Ogden, D. Kelly, and Andrew C. Skinner. *The Four Gospels.* Verse by Verse series. Salt Lake City: Deseret Book, 2006.

Smith, Joseph. *History of The Church of Jesus Christ of Latter-day Saints.* Edited by B. H. Roberts. 7 vols. 2d ed. rev. Salt Lake City: The Church of Jesus Christ of Latter-day Saints, 1932–51.

———. *Joseph Smith.* Teachings of Presidents of the Church series. Salt Lake City: The Church of Jesus Christ of Latter-day Saints, 2007.

DMW

Mount Sinai

A mountain located somewhere in the Sinai Peninsula, east of Egypt. Mount Sinai is also called Mount Horeb in some Old Testament passages (Ex. 3:1, Mal. 4:4). After fleeing from Egypt, the ancient Israelites followed Moses to the base of Mount Sinai, where they encamped for nearly a year (Num. 1:1) and constructed the tabernacle (Ex. 25–27). Here Moses received first the higher Melchizedek PRIESTHOOD law and then the preparatory Aaronic Priesthood law of Moses, which he gave to the Israelites (Ex. 19:1–34:2; JST Ex. 34:1–2; D&C 84:23–27).

Doctrine and Covenants 29:13 mentions Mount Sinai in a prophecy regarding the resurrection of the righteous: "For a trump shall sound both long and loud, even as upon Mount Sinai, and all the earth shall quake, and they shall come forth—yea, even the dead which died in me, to receive a crown of righteousness." *See* Trump(s).

The reference in 29:13 seems to be to the trumpet blown at Mount Sinai that called Israel to the mountain to receive the word of God (Ex. 19:13, 19). The actual location of the scriptural Mount Sinai is not known. A mountain known as Jebel Musa, which is Arabic for "the mountain of Moses," is located among the granite peaks of the southern Sinai Peninsula. It has been identified since Byzantine times (ca. fourth century A.D.) as the site where Moses received revelation and where Israel camped. It rises 7,500 feet above sea level and is visited by numerous tourists and pilgrims who regard it as the biblical Mount Sinai. A sixth century A.D. Byzantine fortress-monastery is at the base of the mountain. It is known as Saint Catherine's Monastery and is operated by Greek Orthodox monks.

JRC

Mount Zion

Term used in the Doctrine and Covenants in a number of contexts:

1. The city of the NEW JERUSALEM with a temple there. Section 84 speaks of "the gathering of his saints to stand upon Mount Zion, which shall be the city of New Jerusalem" (84:2; cf. A of F 10). The same section says that "the sons of Moses and of Aaron shall be filled with the glory of the Lord, upon Mount Zion in the Lord's house" (84:32). *See* Sons of Moses and of Aaron.

2. A heavenly Mount Zion. Section 76, speaking of those resurrected to exaltation in the celestial kingdom, teaches that "these are they who are come unto Mount Zion, and unto the city of the living God, the heavenly place, the holiest of all" (v. 66; cf. vv. 50–70).

3. A mount upon which Christ will stand in connection with his second coming. Section 133 states that "the Lamb . . . shall stand upon Mount Zion, and upon the holy city, the New Jerusalem" (133:56; cf. v. 18). These verses may apply to the Lord's return to earth in both the context of a latter-day Jerusalem in the land of Israel and the New Jerusalem on the American continent. *See* Jesus Christ, second coming of.

4. An extended interpretation, beyond a specific time and geography (as explained concerning the biblical Mount Zion below), to include the church and kingdom of God, with members of The Church of Jesus Christ of Latter-day Saints acting as "saviours . . . on mount Zion" through works performed in modern TEMPLES on behalf of the dead (Obad. 1:21).

Taken together, these four contexts present Mount Zion as a place of holiness for both the righteous among the Latter-day Saints in mortality and the righteous resurrected in the presence of God. For the Saints in mortality Mount Zion seems to include the temples of the Lord and the community of Latter-day Saints in the STAKES of ZION, eventually culminating in the city of the New Jerusalem in Jackson County, Missouri.

The concepts of Mount Zion in the Doctrine and Covenants are in harmony with the biblical understandings of the role and location of Mount Zion but go beyond them. In the Bible, Mount Zion is generally identified with the city of JERUSALEM, in the land of Israel. In the writings of Isaiah, Mount Zion seems to refer specifically to Jerusalem's ancient Temple Mount (Isa. 8:18, 18:7), also known as Mount Moriah (e.g., 2 Chr. 3:1), but by extension seems to include the whole of ancient Jerusalem (Isa. 4:5, 29:7–8). Even in the case of these Isaiah passages, however, an understanding of Mount Zion that expands beyond the time and geography of ancient biblical Jerusalem and its Temple Mount seems consistent with the view that Isaiah spoke not only of people and things in his own time and land but also of people and things in other parts of the world and at other times (2 Ne. 6:4, 3 Ne. 23:2). In this regard, passages in Isaiah that refer to Mount Zion may therefore be legitimately applied to the contexts of such passages in the Doctrine and Covenants (including 76:66; 84:2, 32; 133:18, 56), and conversely, the spirit of passages in the Doctrine and Covenants about Mount Zion may be applied to teachings found in the Bible.

Since Crusader times (twelfth century A.D.), the name Mount Zion has also been used for the southwest hill of Jerusalem's old city, on both sides of Zion's Gate. But this identification has no basis in ancient history or the biblical record and should not be allowed to confuse the scriptural understanding of Mount Zion.

JRC

Mountains of the Lord's house

A phrase employed once in the Doctrine and Covenants, in which the Lord instructs the Jews to return to JERUSALEM in the last days to prepare for the second coming of the Savior: "And let them who be of Judah flee unto Jerusalem, unto the mountains of the Lord's house" (133:13). The "mountains of the Lord's house" refers to the location of the temple that once stood in old Jerusalem and will again be built there (124:36). In the same revelation the Lord commands his Saints and "them . . . who are among the Gentiles" to "flee unto Zion," to sanctify themselves. "All people," Saints, Gentiles, and Jews, are commanded to "awake and arise and go forth to meet the Bridegroom" and prepare "for the great day of the Lord." They are told, "Go ye out from among the nations, even from Babylon, from the midst of wickedness, which is spiritual Babylon" (133:4–14).

A similar phrase, "mountain [singular] of the Lord's house" is found in both Isaiah and Micah, referring to a time "in the last days" when "the mountain of the Lord's house shall be established in the top of the mountains, and shall be exalted above the hills; and all nations shall flow unto it" (Isa. 2:2–3; cf. Micah 4:1–2). Commenting on this scripture at the dedication of the newly built Conference Center in Salt Lake City, President Gordon B. Hinckley said: "I believe that prophecy applies to the historic and wonderful Salt Lake Temple. But I believe also that it is related to this magnificent hall. For it is from this pulpit that the law of God shall go forth, together with the word and testimony of the Lord" (69). By extension, perhaps, the prophecy could apply in some degree not only to buildings in Salt Lake City but also to buildings in many locations throughout the world where Latter-day Saints gather in sacred temples, striving to sanctify themselves in preparation for the Savior's return to the earth.

See also Jesus Christ, second coming of.

BIBLIOGRAPHY

Hinckley, Gordon B. "This Great Millennial Year." *Ensign* 30 (November 2000): 67–71.

JRC

Municipal(s). *See* Appendix E.

Murder, murderers

The shedding of INNOCENT BLOOD of another human being (132:19, 26) with malice aforethought; those who commit murder. One of the Ten Commandments is "thou shalt not kill" (Ex. 20:13; cf. D&C 59:6), which is a translation of the Hebrew verb meaning not to murder. In the "law" of the Lord revealed in Doctrine and Covenants 42, the Lord warned, "And he that kills [murders] shall not have forgiveness in this world, nor in the world to come" (42:18). The Lord further stipulated that "if any persons among you shall kill they shall be delivered up and dealt with according to the laws of the land; for remember that he hath no forgiveness; and it shall be proved according to the laws of the land" (42:79). Condemnation is placed on

those who murder God's chosen people: "Wo unto all those that discomfort my people, and drive, and murder, and testify against them, saith the Lord of Hosts; [they] shall not escape the damnation of hell" (121:23). The Prophet Joseph Smith explained that murderers "cannot have forgiveness. David sought repentance at the hand of God carefully with tears, for the murder of Uriah; but he could only get it through hell: he got a promise that his soul should not be left in hell" (6:253). "Such characters [murderers]," the Prophet said on another occasion, "cannot be forgiven, until they have paid the last farthing" (4:359). When viewed together, these statements seem to indicate that although Christ's ATONEMENT does not afford FORGIVENESS for the sin of murder, it does make it possible for murderers to satisfy the demands of JUSTICE through their own suffering, paying the "last farthing."

Another sense of *murder*, which likewise has no forgiveness in this world nor in the world to come, is "the blasphemy against the Holy Ghost, . . . in that ye commit murder wherein ye shed innocent blood, and assent unto my death" (132:27). That after receiving the "NEW AND EVERLASTING COVENANT" and achieving a perfect knowledge of Christ, whoever disobeys and denies that sacred covenant and knowledge in effect assents to the Savior's death and, in a sense, participates in the shedding of innocent blood—his blood. They "crucify to themselves the Son of God afresh, and put him to an open shame" (Heb. 6:6). *See* Sons of perdition.

BIBLIOGRAPHY

Smith, Joseph. *History of The Church of Jesus Christ of Latter-day Saints.* Edited by B. H. Roberts. 7 vols. 2d ed. rev. Salt Lake City: The Church of Jesus Christ of Latter-day Saints, 1932–51.

DKO

Murdock, John

Birth: 15 July 1792, Kortwright, Delaware County, New York

Death: 23 December 1871, Beaver County, Utah.

John Murdock spent years seeking for the gospel of Jesus Christ before learning of the Restoration and joining the Church in the

John Murdock, 1792–1871.

fall of 1830. He wrote that "the spirit of the Lord rested on me" when he read the Book of Mormon, "witnessing to me of the truth." John's wife, Julia Clapp Murdock, "was filled with the spirit as [he] read" to her. They were baptized and confirmed, and he was ordained an elder. "It was truly a time of the outpouring of the spirit," he wrote. "I know the spirit rested on me as it never did before" (7–8).

Julia Murdock died just hours after giving birth to twins in April 1831, leaving her husband to care for their five children. He made the selfless decision to accept an invitation from Joseph Smith to let him and Emma, whose twins had just died at birth, adopt John's newborn twins. Then through revelation Murdock was called to preach and travel to Missouri in the summer of 1831 (52:8–9). He balanced his priesthood responsibilities to nurture his children and preach the gospel the best he could. He left his other children in the care of relatives and fellow Saints and endured a long, sickly, but successful mission to Missouri. When he returned to Kirtland in June 1832, he found his

children well except for little Joseph, who had died of measles after suffering exposure when the Prophet was dragged from his home and tarred and feathered in March 1832 (Murdock, 12).

Murdock regained his health and continued to nurture his children and serve in the Church in Ohio until August 1832, when through another revelation the Lord called him back to the mission field (99:1). In that revelation the Lord sent him to the east "to proclaim mine everlasting gospel unto the inhabitants thereof, in the midst of persecution and wickedness," to give his hearers the opportunity to either receive or reject the Lord (99:1–4). The revelation showed the Lord's knowledge of the Murdock family's situation and told him how to provide for his motherless children and perform his mission. Meanwhile, Murdock was given a choice to inherit Zion in a few years or continue his missionary labors for the rest of his life (99:7–8). He wrote that having received the instruction in section 99, "I immediately commenced to arrange my business and provide for my children and send them up to the Bishop in Zion," Edward Partridge; John then set out to preach the gospel. Some received him as section 99 foretold; others, including his in-laws, rejected his message. When Murdock "met with a Dr. Matthews, a very wicked man" who rejected his offering, he and his companion obeyed the Lord's instructions: "We bore testimony according to the commandment and the Lord helped us in tending to the ordinance" of cleansing their feet (99:4; Murdock, 12). *See* Shake off the dust of thy feet; Wash, washed, washing(s).

John Murdock's life was filled with service to the Lord. He was a volunteer in ZION'S CAMP and a member of the high council in both Clay County and Far West, Missouri. After moving to Nauvoo, he served as a bishop and later in a stake presidency in nearby Lima. He went west with the Saints to the Salt Lake Valley—his two eldest sons served in the Mormon Battalion—and in Utah he again served on a high council and as a bishop. John Murdock was one of the first missionaries to Australia, and after his return to Utah, he was ordained a patriarch and served as a stake president.

After the death of his first wife, Julia, in 1831, Murdock married Amoranda Turner in 1836; she died in 1837. The following year he married Electa Allen, with whom he had three children. Electa died in 1845. Murdock married Sarah Zufelt in 1846. Shortly afterward the family left Nauvoo for the West.

BIBLIOGRAPHY

Murdock, John. "An Abridged Record of the Life of John Murdock, Taken from His Journal by Himself." Typescript. L. Tom Perry Special Collections, Harold B. Lee Library, Brigham Young University, Provo, Utah.

SCH

Murmur. *See* Appendix E.

Music. *See* Songs, singing.

Mysteries

Truths about God, his kingdom, and his dealings with man that are received and understood only through revelation by the power of the HOLY GHOST. The Lord, as evidenced in all the standard works of the Church, has promised to reveal the "mysteries of God" to those who ask in PRAYER, and exercise FAITH, diligence, and OBEDIENCE to the COMMANDMENTS of God (e.g., 8:11; 42:61, 65; 63:23; 1 Ne. 10:19; Alma 12:9–11; Ps. 25:14; Matt. 11:25). "For thus saith the Lord—I, the Lord, am merciful and gracious unto those who fear me, and delight to honor those who serve me in righteousness and in truth unto the end. Great shall be their reward and eternal shall be their glory. And to them will I reveal all mysteries, yea, all the hidden mysteries of my kingdom from days of old, and for ages to come, will I make known unto them the good pleasure of my will concerning all things pertaining to my kingdom. Yea, even the wonders of eternity shall they know, and things to come will I show them, even the things of many generations. And their wisdom shall be great, and their understanding reach to heaven; and before them the wisdom of the wise shall perish, and the understanding of the prudent shall come to naught. For by my Spirit will I enlighten them, and by my power will I make known unto them the secrets of my will—yea, even those things which eye has not seen, nor ear heard, nor yet entered into the heart of man" (76:5–10; cf. 76:114–17).

In addition to the general knowledge of what the mysteries of God are and how they can be understood, the revelations in the Doctrine and Covenants link a knowledge of the mysteries of God to the restoration of the gospel in the last days—the restoration of priesthood and priesthood keys, the true Church with living prophets and apostles, temple covenants and ordinances, and modern scripture. For example, Joseph Smith and Oliver Cowdery were commanded by the Lord as they translated the Book of Mormon to "ask that you may know the mysteries of God, and that you may translate and receive knowledge from all those ancient records which have been hid up" (8:11). The Book of Mormon restored many plain and precious truths to the world and was certainly part of the fulfillment of the promise that "the mysteries of God shall be unfolded unto you" (6:7; 10:60–68; cf. 11:7).

Anciently, it was declared that "surely the Lord God will do nothing, but he revealeth his secret unto his servants the prophets" (Amos 3:7). The role of PROPHETS, both ancient and modern, is to reveal God's will and unfold his mysteries to those prepared to receive them (Alma 12:9–10). Modern revelation confirms that role and witnesses of the mysteries of God being revealed through the Lord's anointed prophets. The "keys of the mystery of those things which have been sealed, even things which were from the foundation of the world" are held by the prophet-president of the Church (35:18; cf. 28:7; 64:5; 90:14).

With the restoration of the Melchizedek PRIESTHOOD came "the key of the mysteries of the kingdom, even the key of the knowledge of God" (84:19)—"to have the privilege of receiving the mysteries of the kingdom of heaven, to have the heavens opened unto them, to commune with the general assembly and church of the Firstborn, and to enjoy the communion and presence of God the Father, and Jesus the mediator of the new covenant" (107:19). *See* Church of the Firstborn; Key(s).

The ultimate "mystery of God" is knowing the Father and the Son, which is ETERNAL LIFE (John 17:3). This knowledge of God and the accompanying "power of godliness" is obtained only through the Melchizedek Priesthood and receiving the ORDINANCES pertaining to it, specifically the ordinances of the temple (84:19–20; cf. 97:10–16; 124:27–28, 34, 39–41).

To some, spiritual things may seem mysterious, inexplicable, or even foolish. Yet to those who seek the "mysteries of God" on his terms and in his prescribed manner, those truths that are obscure to the "natural man" (1 Cor. 2:14) and hidden from the wicked and worldly will be manifest plainly. Recipients of these "mysteries" testify that the works of the Lord are indeed marvelous and the "mysteries of his kingdom . . . surpass all understanding in glory, and in might, and in dominion" (76:114).

BLT

And we know that all men must repent and believe on the **name** of Jesus Christ, and worship the Father in his name, and endure in faith on his name to the end, or they cannot be saved in the king-dom of God. 20:29

Name of the Church. *See* Church of Jesus Christ of Latter-day Saints, The.

Name written on their foreheads. *See* Name(s); Seal, sealed.

Name(s)

A designation or title that identifies a person or persons. Having a name is of temporal and eternal significance. Children in The Church of Jesus Christ of Latter-day Saints are to be brought "unto the elders before the church, who are to lay their hands upon them in the name of Jesus Christ, and bless them in his name" (20:70). With that blessing, the children are given a name by which they are to be known in mortality. The names of members of the Church are kept in "the general church record of names" and updated, names of new members are added, and the names of those who "have been expelled from the church [are] blotted out" (20:82–83; cf. 85:3–5). Those who come into the Church through baptismal covenants also take upon themselves the name of Christ and renew those covenants each week by partaking of the sacrament (20:37, 75–79). "Behold, Jesus Christ is the name which is given of the Father, and there is none other name given whereby man can be saved; wherefore, all men must take upon them the name which is given of the Father, for in that name shall they be called at the last day" (18:23–24; cf. 109:4). Not only members of the Church but also the Church itself bears the name of Jesus Christ (115:3–4; 127:12; 128:21; 136:2; cf. 20:1; 21:11).

Having taken the name of Christ, the Saints are instructed to do many things "in [his] name." The Lord instructed that "all things must be done in the name of Christ, whatsoever you do in the Spirit" (46:31). In the dedicatory prayer of the Kirtland Temple, the Prophet Joseph Smith prayed that through the influence of temple worship all the "incomings," "outgoings," and "salutations may be in the name of the Lord" (109:16–19). The Saints are to assemble (42:1–3), pray unto the Father (50:31; 88:64; 109:4), and worship the Father (18:40; 20:29; 59:5) in the name of Christ. The Lord brought about the restoration of the gospel "that every man might speak in the name of God the

Lord" (1:20). Oliver Cowdery was to be involved in "bearing [the Lord's] name before the world," and the Twelve Apostles and the Seventy are designated "special witnesses of the name of Christ in all the world" (24:10; 107:23–25; cf. 27:12; 112:4, 12).

All must be careful how the name of the Lord is used. The Lord said, "Wherefore, let all men beware how they take my name in their lips—for behold, verily I say, that many there be who are under this condemnation, who use the name of the Lord, and use it in vain, having not authority" (63:6–62; cf. 136:21). He also warned that "the heaviest of all cursings" will come to those who "have professed my name" but "hear me not" (41:1; cf. verse 5; 50:4–7; 112:26).

Ordinances of salvation are to be performed in the name of Jesus Christ, for example, baptism (18:29, 41; 20:25; 84:74) and conferring priesthood (13:1). This also applies to all ordinances that are to remain in force in the hereafter (132:7–14). The Saints are promised that in the name of Jesus Christ "they shall do many wonderful works": "cast out devils; . . . heal the sick; . . . open the eyes of the blind, and unstop the ears of the deaf," cause the dumb to speak, and be protected from the serpent's poison (84:66–72). Temples are to be built "in the name of the Lord": Kirtland, Ohio (97:15; 109:2; 110:6–7); Far West, Missouri (115:10–14); Nauvoo, Illinois (124:22).

Some other uses of *name* in the Doctrine and Covenants include the following:

1. The Saints were to gather up "the names of all persons that have had a hand in their oppressions" in Missouri, publish them "to all the world," and "present them to the heads of government" in seeking REDRESS for their losses (123:3, 6; cf. 101:81–99).

2. Joseph Smith was told that "the ends of the earth shall enquire after thy name, and fools shall have thee in derision, and hell shall rage against thee; while the pure in heart, and the wise, and the noble, and the virtuous, shall seek counsel, and authority, and blessings constantly from under thy hand" (122:1–2). This prophecy is reminiscent of Moroni's prophecy that Joseph's name "should be had for good and

evil among all nations, kindreds, and tongues" (JS–H 1:33).

3. The Father's name shall be written on the foreheads of 144,000 servants of the Lord standing with him on MOUNT ZION in connection with his second coming (133:18–19; cf. 77:9–11). Concerning this gathering, Joseph Smith taught, "The servants of God are sealed in their foreheads, which signifies sealing the blessing upon their heads, meaning the everlasting covenant, thereby making their calling and election sure" (5:530).

4. The names of Saints, faithful to the principles of CONSECRATION, are to be recorded in the "book of the law of God," while the names of those who are not faithful "shall not be found" (85:1–11).

5. The names of those who are to inherit the celestial kingdom "are written in heaven" (76:68) and "recorded in the book of the names of the sanctified" (88:2).

6. All who enter the celestial kingdom in the hereafter will receive a "white stone . . . whereon is a new name written, which no man knoweth save he that receiveth it. The new name is the key word," but its function is not defined in the revelation (130:10–11).

BIBLIOGRAPHY

Smith, Joseph. *History of The Church of Jesus Christ of Latter-day Saints.* Edited by B. H. Roberts. 7 vols. 2d ed. rev. Salt Lake City: The Church of Jesus Christ of Latter-day Saints, 1932–51.

DKO

Names, code

Twenty-four code names, or pseudonyms (false names), were used to disguise the names of individuals, places, and assignments in five revelations published in the 1835 Doctrine and Covenants (78; 82; 92; 96; 103) and in two additional revelations added to the 1844 edition (104; 105). The pseudonyms were not original to the revelations. The early manuscripts verify, as Orson Pratt later wrote, that the actual names were originally given and then pseudonyms were inserted before printing (Whittaker, 4).

Joseph Smith received these revelations between March 1832 and June 1834, but none of them were published in the 1833 Book of Commandments. All seven revelations are concerned with the United Firm, called the United Order in published versions of these revelations, which is the group of men who held and managed the Church's assets until 1834. *See* Consecration.

In section 78 the Lord announced the need for the organization of this "order" (78:4) and called for Joseph Smith, Sidney Rigdon, and Newel K. Whitney to travel to Missouri to meet with Church leaders there who would join them in the firm. Section 78 thus began the process of merging the Church's expensive printing operation with Whitney's profitable store and related properties. This merger is veiled somewhat in published versions of section 78. Where verse 3 speaks generally of "an organization of my people," manuscript versions speak more specifically of "an organization of the literary and mercantile establishments of my church" (Harper, 277–79). The Church had enemies who were also, sometimes, creditors. Joseph and his brethren kept the issues behind section 78 as confidential as possible to avoid giving the Church's enemies information they could use to cripple it financially or otherwise undermine the building of Zion. Thus, beginning with section 78, revelations that deal with purchasing land for Zion or otherwise managing the Church's properties use pseudonyms when speaking of specific Church leaders and the properties or tasks over which they were stewards (Whittaker, 3). Inserted in the earliest known manuscript of section 78, for example, are the names *Ahashdah* for Bishop Newel K. Whitney, *Gazelam* or *Enoch* for Joseph Smith, and *Pelagoram* for Sidney Rigdon (Jensen et al., 267).

Section 82 joined Church leaders in Kirtland, Ohio, with Church leaders in Independence, Missouri, to form the United Firm, or Order. The revelation names the men who belonged to the United Firm. When it was first published in 1835, however, section 82 used pseudonyms rather than the men's actual names. Similarly, pseudonyms were used in other revelations that added new members to the Firm (92; 96) or discussed Zion (103; 105) or gave directions to members of the firm regarding the properties or tasks over which they were stewards (104).

Later, when the need for confidentiality had passed, Elder Orson Pratt acted under the direction of President Brigham Young to publish the actual names and the reasons for using the pseudonyms. As part of his work on the 1876 edition of the Doctrine and Covenants, Elder Pratt inserted in parentheses after the pseudonyms all the original names he could remember. By the 1921 edition most of the remaining identities had been discovered, and the practice of inserting them in parentheses continued. In the 1981 edition, however, the pseudonyms were removed from the text, with four exceptions in section 82.

Research by David Whittaker published in 1983 drew on Orson Pratt's memory and a previously unknown manuscript written by William Phelps about 1863 in which he identified the actual names associated with the pseudonyms and offered meanings for the mysterious words. The Phelps document made it possible to replace the remaining four pseudonyms in section 82 with the real names: Edward Partridge for *Alam,* Algernon Sidney Gilbert for *Mahalaleel,* John Whitmer as *Horah,* and Phelps himself as *Shalemanasseh* (Whittaker, 5).

By interpreting the pseudonyms, Phelps's document implies that they belong to an actual language. Some, *Enoch* and *Gazelem,* for example, are in the Bible or the Book of Mormon. Some sound Hebraic, and it may be that Joseph's study of Hebrew influenced the selection of these names. Their origin remains uncertain, however. No known records reveal their source.

BIBLIOGRAPHY

Harper, Steven C. *Making Sense of the Doctrine and Covenants.* Salt Lake City: Deseret Book, 2008.

Jensen, Robin Scott, Robert J. Woodford, and Steven C. Harper, eds. *Manuscript Revelation Books.* Facsimile edition. First volume of the Revelations and Translations series of *The Joseph Smith Papers,* edited by Dean C. Jessee, Ronald K. Esplin, and Richard Lyman Bushman. Salt Lake City: Church Historian's Press, 2009.

Whittaker, David J. "Substituted Names in the Published Revelations of Joseph Smith." *BYU Studies* 23, no. 1 (1983): 1–9.

SCH

Nashville, Iowa

A Latter-day Saint village across the Mississippi River from Nauvoo and south of Montrose, Iowa. On 24 June 1839, Bishop Vinson Knight bought the undeveloped Nashville site from Isaac Galland, and Latter-day Saints moved onto the property. Elias Smith presided over ninety members of the Nashville Branch, one of nine branches in the Zarahemla Stake (Cannon, 33). On 30 August 1840, Joseph and Hyrum Smith preached to a large assembly in Nashville about eternal judgment and the eternal duration of matter (Smith, 4:182). In 1841 the Lord encouraged further settlement of Nashville and other gathering places in Iowa (125:3–4). The Twelve Apostles endorsed the greater settlement of Iowa in a September 1841 epistle: "An Epistle of the twelve, to the saints scattered abroad among the nations." Nashville was abandoned when the Latter-day Saints moved west ("Epistle," 2:520–21). *See* map, p. 277.

BIBLIOGRAPHY

Cannon, Donald Q. "Mormon Satellite Settlements in Hancock County, Illinois, and Lee County, Iowa." In *The Iowa Mormon Trail: Legacy of Faith and Courage,* edited by Susan Easton Black and William G. Hartley. Orem, Utah: Helix Publishing, 1997.

"An Epistle of the Twelve, to the Saints scattered abroad among the Nations." *Times and Seasons* 2, no. 21 (1 September 1841): 520–21.

Smith, Joseph. *History of The Church of Jesus Christ of Latter-day Saints.* Edited by B. H. Roberts. 7 vols. 2d ed. rev. Salt Lake City: The Church of Jesus Christ of Latter-day Saints, 1932–51.

GML

Nathan

Servant of the Lord holding priesthood keys whereby he gave King David multiple wives and concubines (132:39). Although Nathan had several other notable contacts with David (2 Sam. 7; 12; 1 Kgs. 1), none of these are mentioned in the Doctrine and Covenants.

RJM

Nathanael of old

One of the first disciples of the Savior. Upon seeing Nathanael, the Savior declared, "Behold an Israelite indeed, in whom is no guile!" (John 1:47). When Nathanael testified, "Rabbi, thou art the Son of God; thou art the King of Israel" (John 1:49), the Savior promised Nathanael that he would "see heaven open, and the angels of God ascending and descending upon the Son of man" (John 1:50–51).

In a revelation to Joseph Smith in 1831, the Lord commanded that Edward Partridge be ordained the first bishop of the latter-day Church (41:9) and said of Partridge, "His heart is pure before me, for he is like unto Nathanael of old, in whom there is no guile" (41:9–11).

FFJ

Natural man

Every human being born into mortality. Each person, through mortal birth biologically inherits the consequences of the Fall of Adam, including spiritual and physical (temporal) death. But because of the atonement of Christ, each one can be spiritually reborn, becoming alive in Christ by obedience to the gospel (5:16; Mosiah 3:19; 5:7; A of F 3). Many scriptures deal with the concept of the "natural man" and teach that the GOSPEL of Christ is the only remedy (e.g., 1 Cor. 2:11–14; Mosiah 3:19; Alma 26:20–21; Moses 1:11–14; D&C 29:42–44; 49:5; 68:9). In the scriptures the term *flesh* often refers to the mortal, natural man (e.g., 1:19; 38:11; 67:11; 112:23; 2 Ne. 2:5; 4:34; Moses 3:7). *See* Flesh.

The natural man, "sensual and devilish" (20:20; cf. Alma 42:10), having spiritual limitations, cannot know the things of God, "because they are spiritually discerned" (1 Cor. 2:14; 76:116). Obedience to gospel laws and ordinances makes it possible to see beyond the veil and behold the face of Christ (93:1), "not with the carnal neither natural mind, but with the spiritual" (67:10). "Neither can any natural man abide the presence of God, neither after the carnal mind" (67:12). Although the natural man is temporarily limited in spiritual knowledge and enjoyment, the natural condition of mortality, including enduring "bitter" experiences, is necessary in the onward progress from premortal spirit to resurrected exaltation (29:39; 123:7; cf. 2 Ne. 2:22–24). Perhaps nowhere else in scripture does the Lord summarize more beautifully and succinctly than in 29:31–45 the cycle from SPIRITUAL to TEMPORAL, "which is the beginning

of my work," and from temporal to spiritual, "which is the last of my work."

See also Carnal, sensual, and devilish; Fall of Adam and Eve, the.

BIBLIOGRAPHY

McConkie, Bruce R. *A New Witness for the Articles of Faith.* Salt Lake City: Deseret Book, 1985.

RJM

Nature of God. *See* God, nature of.

Naught. *See* Appendix E.

Nauvoo, Illinois

Headquarters of the Church from 1839 to 1846. The city of Nauvoo, Illinois, is "situated on the east bank of the Mississippi river, at the head of the Des Moines Rapids, in Hancock county, bounded on the east by an extensive prairie of surpassing beauty, and on the north, west, and south, by the Mississippi." "The name . . . is of Hebrew origin, and signifies a beautiful situation, or place, carrying with it, also, the idea of rest; and is truly descriptive of the most delightful location" (Smith, 4:268; Ps. 48:2). In a revelation to the Prophet Joseph Smith, the Lord designated the stake and city of Nauvoo as "a cornerstone of Zion" (124:2).

Ten sections in the Doctrine and Covenants were received or recorded during the Nauvoo era: eight at Nauvoo (124–29; 132; 135) and two at Ramus (130–31), a small community about thirty miles east of Nauvoo. Sections 124 through 126 are revelations to Joseph Smith in 1841. Section 124 instructs the Prophet to make a proclamation to "all the nations of the earth," "to all the kings of the world," and to United States government officials, declaring that the time has come to "favor" Zion and invites them to help in her establishment (124:1–11). Several attempts were made to produce the proclamation over the next three years, but the task was not complete before Joseph Smith's death. In 1845, however, under the direction of the Quorum of the Twelve, such a proclamation, written by Parley P. Pratt, was published in New York and England (Cook, 243). *See* Solemn proclamation.

Also in section 124, the Lord calls for the

building of the Nauvoo Temple (vv. 27–55) and the Nauvoo House, a hotel, "a resting-place for the weary traveler, that he may contemplate the glory of Zion" (v. 60). The Nauvoo House was begun, but due to the pressures of building the temple, it was not completed by the time the Saints left Nauvoo in 1846. Additionally, in section 124 the Lord identifies individuals who are to be sustained in the First Presidency, the Quorum of the Twelve Apostles, the patriarch to the Church, the seventies, the bishopric, and the priesthood quorums of high priests, elders, priests, teachers, and deacons (vv. 123–45).

Section 125 has to do with the settlements of the Saints in Iowa, across the river from Nauvoo, and section 126 is a revelation for Brigham Young.

Sections 127 and 128 are letters written to the Saints in September 1842 while the Prophet was in hiding to avoid extradition to Missouri to face trumped-up charges in connection with the attempted assassination of Governor Lilburn W. Boggs. These two sections deal with important matters in connection with baptisms for the dead—proper procedures, the necessity of eye and ear witnesses, and proper recording.

Section 129 reveals "three grand keys by which the correct nature of ministering angels and spirits may be distinguished" (headnote). Sections 130 and 131 contain doctrine taught by the Prophet Joseph Smith when he visited the Saints in Ramus, Illinois, in April and May 1843.

Section 132 is a revelation outlining a "new and everlasting covenant" of eternal MARRIAGE between "a man" and "a wife" (132:18–28), as well as the principle of plural marriage as revealed to Abraham and other ancient patriarchs and prophets (132:29–66). Parts of this revelation were received by Joseph Smith as early as 1831, but the revelation as it appears as section 132 was recorded in Nauvoo in July 1843 (headnote).

Section 135, the last section in the revelations identified with Nauvoo, was written by Elder John Taylor, an eyewitness of the MARTYRDOM OF JOSEPH AND HYRUM SMITH. It is a testament to the divine mission of Joseph and

Joseph Smith and Nauvoo Temple; *painting by Valoy Eaton. The Prophet and his associates bidding farewell to Nauvoo. "When Joseph went to Carthage to deliver himself up to the pretended requirements of the law, two or three days previous to his assassination, he said: "I am going like a lamb to the slaughter; but I am calm as a summer's morning; I have a conscience void of offense towards God, and towards all men. I SHALL DIE INNOCENT, AND IT SHALL YET BE SAID OF ME—HE WAS MURDERED IN COLD BLOOD" (D&C 135:4).*

Hyrum and to the ultimate accountability of those who killed them.

In addition to the revelations during the Nauvoo years, Joseph Smith shared gems of revealed knowledge in frequent, scripture-based sermons (Ehat and Cook, xv–xxi). He also played a key role in Nauvoo's founding and development. Temporal events in Nauvoo were the backdrop against which this dispensation's first prophet, seer, and revelator completed his mission.

In the winter of 1838–39, fleeing a state-ordered extermination order in Missouri, Latter-day Saints crossed the icy Mississippi River to Illinois. There, they created a refuge for thousands to flock to in coming years: Nauvoo, the city beautiful. They built shops, businesses, and hundreds of homes, and on the nearby prairie

they cleared twenty thousand acres of farmland. They established a chartered city; ran newspapers *Times and Seasons* and the *Wasp,* which became the *Nauvoo Neighbor;* organized a city militia, the Nauvoo Legion; and established the University of Nauvoo. From libraries to grist mills, from the music hall to the arsenal, Nauvoo was a haven of industry, culture, and civilization (Leonard, *Nauvoo,* 146–61). Yet, the Saints were obliged to abandon Nauvoo and follow their leader, Brigham Young, into the wilderness. Their removal from Nauvoo began on 4 February 1846 and continued through mid-September, when the battle of Nauvoo forced the final few hundred Saints across the Mississippi River into Iowa.

The Saints who relocated to the valleys of the Rocky Mountains did not forget the City of

Courtesy Church History Library

Main Street in Nauvoo, Illinois; photograph by George Edward Anderson, 1907. The Mississippi River can be seen in the distance. On the left is the Nauvoo House, begun by the Saints in 1841. Commanding the construction of the building, the Lord declared, "And let the name of that house be called Nauvoo House; and let it be a delightful habitation for man, and a resting-place for the weary traveler, that he may contemplate the glory of Zion, and the glory of this, the corner-stone thereof" (D&C 124:60). The Nauvoo House was not completed as designed. After Emma Smith married Lewis Bidamon in December 1847, they converted the unfinished structure into their residence, known as the Riverside Mansion, which they occupied in the 1870s.

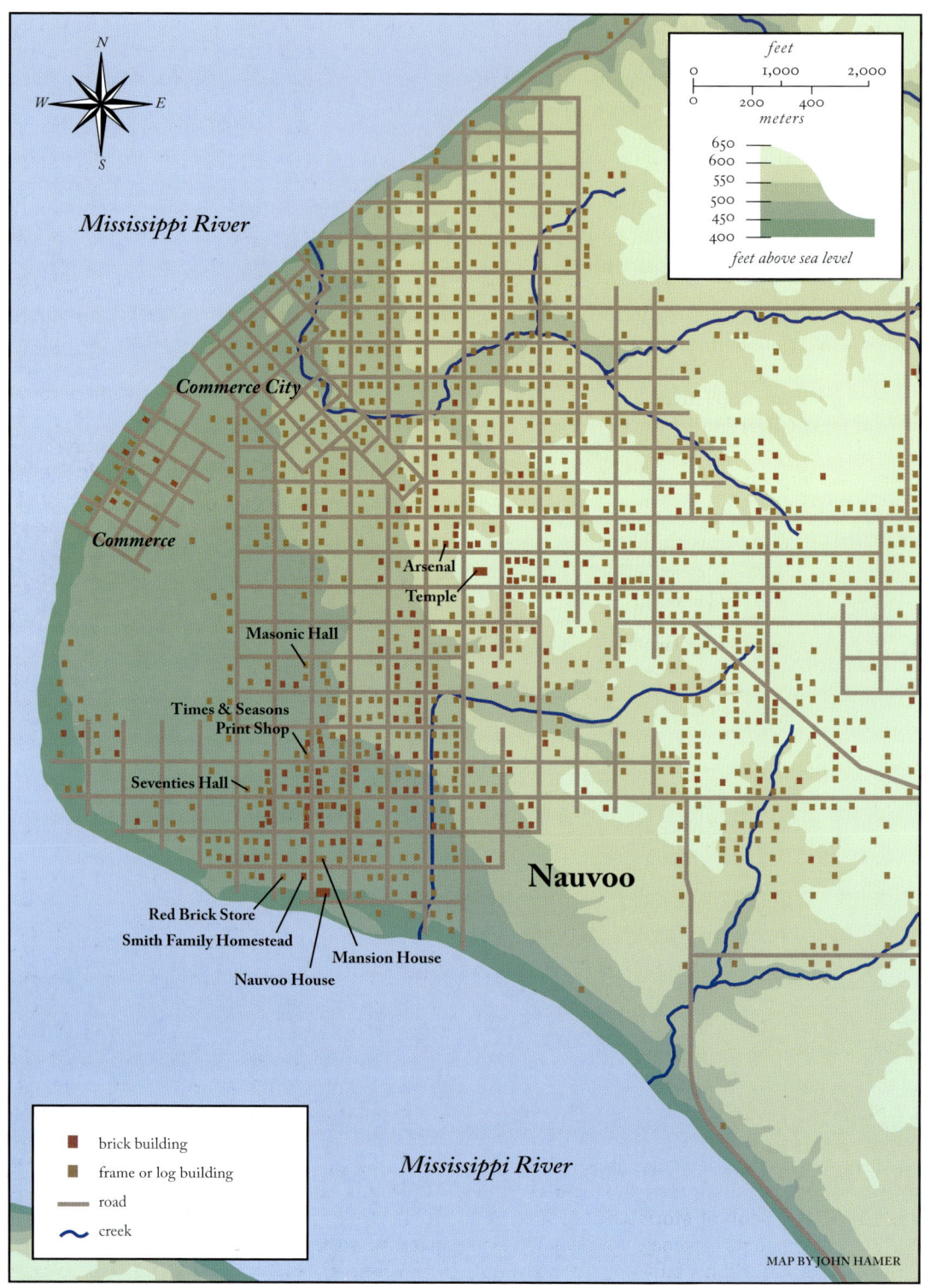

feet

0   1,000   2,000

0   200   400

meters

650
600
550
500
450
400

feet above sea level

Mississippi River

Commerce City

Commerce

Arsenal
Temple

Masonic Hall

Times & Seasons
Print Shop

Seventies Hall

Nauvoo

Red Brick Store
Smith Family Homestead
Mansion House
Nauvoo House

■ brick building
■ frame or log building
— road
〜 creek

Mississippi River

MAP BY JOHN HAMER

Nauvoo, Illinois, in the 1840s.

Joseph. In their new western gathering place, these former residents, known as the "Old Nauvooers," spoke often about their experiences. The city they left, soon a town of some eleven hundred residents, continued to attract visitors. Among them were Latter-day Saint missionaries passing through, journalists looking for a story, and former residents. When tourism became a national pastime after World War II, celebrants of Nauvoo's historic past restored buildings, put up monuments, and retold stories of sacrifice and faith. The reconstruction of the Nauvoo Temple in 2000 to 2002, not as a historic shrine but as a functioning temple, refocused attention on Nauvoo's original purpose as a spiritual heartland for Latter-day Saints (124:2).

See also Illinois period.

BIBLIOGRAPHY

Cook, Lyndon W. *The Revelations of the Prophet Joseph Smith*. Salt Lake City: Deseret Book, 1985.

Ehat, Andrew F., and Lyndon W. Cook, comps. and eds. *The Words of Joseph Smith*. Provo, Utah: Religious Studies Center, Brigham Young University, 1980.

Leonard, Glen M. *Nauvoo: A Place of Peace, a People of Promise*. Salt Lake City: Deseret Book; Provo, Utah: Brigham Young University Press, 2002.

———. "Remembering Nauvoo: Historiographical Considerations." *Journal of Mormon History* 16 (1990): 25–39.

Smith, Joseph. *History of The Church of Jesus Christ of Latter-day Saints*. Edited by B. H. Roberts. 7 vols. 2d ed. rev. Salt Lake City: The Church of Jesus Christ of Latter-day Saints, 1932–51.

GML

Nauvoo House. *See* Nauvoo, Illinois.

Nauvoo Temple. *See* Temple(s).

Nefarious. *See* Appendix E.

Nephi

Son of Lehi, a prophet who traveled with his family from Jerusalem to the New World around 600 B.C. Nephi, who was a major contributor to the Book of Mormon, is referred to in the Doctrine and Covenants mainly in connection with his and his father's record written on the PLATES of Nephi and the loss of the 116

manuscript pages of that record (10:38–45). *See* Book of Mormon, lost manuscript of (116 pages).

Twice, however, Nephi is referred to personally in the revelations. In Fayette, New York, in October 1830, the Lord commanded early Latter-day Saint missionaries Ezra Thayre and Northrop Sweet to boldly preach the gospel so that they might "become even as Nephi of old, who journeyed from Jerusalem in the wilderness" (33:8). Later, when the Latter-day Saints were suffering intense persecution in Missouri in 1833, the Lord counseled them concerning defending their families by referring to the experience of Nephi. The Saints were encouraged to patiently endure threats from their enemies three times (98:23–27), whereupon they should explicitly warn the offenders to cease their threats (98:28). If the guilty parties continued to threaten their families, the Saints were counseled to patiently endure more if possible (98:30), but if lives were endangered, they were also justified in defending themselves and their families (98:29, 31). The Lord revealed to the Saints: "This is the law I gave unto my servant Nephi" as well as to other ancient prophets and apostles (98:32).

See also Doctrine and Covenants, what it says about the Book of Mormon.

FFJ

Nephites

Descendants of Nephi, a son of Lehi. After Lehi's family left Jerusalem and traveled to the New World, Lehi's descendants separated into two principal groups called the Nephites and the LAMANITES—named after Lehi's sons Nephi and Laman. In the Book of Mormon, the terms *Nephites* and *Lamanites* eventually came to refer to those who followed God and those who did not, respectively, rather than to merely biological descendants of Nephi and Laman (Jacob 1:13–14; Alma 3:11; 4 Ne. 1:36–38). In July 1828, after chastising Joseph Smith for losing 116 pages of translation, the Lord reminded the Prophet that notwithstanding that unfortunate event, the knowledge of Jesus Christ would still come forth "to the Nephites" and others of Lehi's descendants "through the testimony of their fathers" (3:17), meaning the Book of Mormon. In that same revelation, Joseph was reminded that the Lord allowed the Lamanites "to destroy their brethren the Nephites, because of their iniquities and their abominations" (3:18). At a Church conference in Hiram, Ohio, in November 1831, the Lord testified that after Joseph Smith "received the record of the Nephites," he was given "power to translate through the mercy of God, by the power of God, the Book of Mormon" (1:29). Earlier that same year in a conference of the Church in Fayette, New York, the Lord warned the Saints about seeking for riches: "Beware of pride, lest ye become as the Nephites of old" (38:39; cf. 2 Ne. 26:10; Jacob 1:16; 2:12–14; Moro. 8:27). In October 1918, President Joseph F. Smith received a revelation in which he learned that after the Savior's crucifixion, the soon-to-be resurrected "Redeemer spent his time during his sojourn in the world of spirits, instructing and preparing the faithful spirits of the prophets who had testified of him in the flesh" in order "that they might carry the message of redemption unto all the dead" (138:36–37). Among those who received this instruction from the postmortal Savior were "the prophets who dwelt among the Nephites and testified of the coming of the Son of God" (138:49).

See also Doctrine and Covenants, what it says about the Book of Mormon.

FFJ

New and everlasting covenant

The fulness of the GOSPEL of Jesus Christ restored through the Prophet Joseph Smith (66:2); the covenant of salvation which the God of heaven extends to his children who choose the path of faithfulness and obedience by which they may return to his presence. That covenant is designated as "everlasting" because its principles remain unchanged from generation to generation and from dispensation to dispensation. And yet, to emphasize that the covenant has been restored anew in this last dispensation, it has been denominated the "new and everlasting covenant." It embraces "all covenants, contracts, bonds, obligations, oaths, vows, performances, connections, associations, or

expectations" which will be of "efficacy, virtue, or force in and after the resurrection from the dead" (132:6–7). Thus, baptism or any other restored ordinance may be referred to as "a" new and everlasting covenant, whereas the composite of all covenants necessary for salvation constitute "the" new and everlasting covenant, "even that which was from the beginning" (49:9; cf. 22:1; 131:1–4; 133:57). All gospel ordinances involve covenants and bear witness of Jesus Christ. To reject the covenants and the ordinances of the gospel is to reject Christ and suffer damnation (112:29; cf. 49:5). Covenants are as eternal as the gospel itself.

In modern revelation the Lord has said, "I have sent mine everlasting covenant [the fulness of the gospel] into the world, to be a light to the world, and to be a standard for my people, and for the Gentiles to seek to it, and to be a messenger before my face to prepare the way before me" (45:9).

JFM

New heaven and a new earth. *See* Millennium, the.

New Jerusalem

A sacred city and the central gathering place for the Saints of God in the latter days (42:9, 35–36). The New Jerusalem, "the city of Zion," will be located in Independence, Jackson County, Missouri (57:1–3).

As early as 1831 the Lord instructed the Saints to go to Missouri and begin laying the foundation for the building up of ZION. Joseph Smith, other Church leaders, and several missionaries traveled to Missouri as directed (52:2). During the brief time they were there, the Lord revealed that Independence was "the center place," and "the place for the city of Zion" (57:1–3; 58:6–7; cf. 28:9; 42:9, 35, 62; 48:5). More than twelve hundred Latter-day Saints soon moved to Jackson County, Missouri, but were not welcomed by the citizens already living there. In 1833 they were driven by their enemies from Independence and forced to settle elsewhere. The Lord revealed that this expulsion was partly because of their own transgressions—"jarrings, and contentions, and envyings, and strifes, and lustful and covetous desires among them" (101:6). Consequently, the settlement of the center place in Jackson County was to be postponed for a season (100:13; 103:4; 105:9; 136:18). The Lord said, however, that "Zion shall not be moved out of her place" and assured the Saints that the "pure in heart" would eventually return to build up the promised Zion. In the interim, the places of gathering would be in the stakes of Zion throughout the world (101:16–22).

When established, the New Jerusalem will be "a city of refuge, a place of safety for the saints of the Most High God." As the second coming of the Savior approaches, wickedness and persecution will increase until the only safe place to dwell will be in Zion and her stakes (45:66–71; 115:6). The risen Lord explained to Book of Mormon peoples that this New Jerusalem would be set up in the last days (3 Ne. 21:22–23). "And the powers of heaven shall be in the midst of this people; yea, even I will be in the midst of you" (3 Ne. 20:22).

In the millennial day there will be two world headquarters—one in Old Jerusalem and one in New Jerusalem. The New Jerusalem in heaven—the general assembly of the Church of the Firstborn—will join with the New Jerusalem on earth (JST Gen. 9:23; Moses 7:62–64; cf. 133:56), and a "paradisiacal glory" will be established on earth once more (A of F 10). In fulfillment of Isaiah's prophecy, the law will go forth from Zion and the word of the Lord from Jerusalem (Isa. 2:3).

See also Zion, redemption of.

RLM

New song. *See* Songs, singing.

New translation. *See* Doctrine and Covenants and the Joseph Smith Translation of the Bible.

New York City. *See* Albany, Boston, and New York City.

New York period

After a succession of moves to various locations in Vermont and New Hampshire, the Joseph Smith Sr. family experienced the devastating "year without a summer," which was "Eighteen Hundred and Froze to Death," or the year 1816, while they were tenant farmers at Norwich, Vermont. Climatic conditions attributed to an 1815 volcanic eruption of Mount Tambora on the island of Sumbawa in the Dutch East Indies (Indonesia) put an immense amount of fine dust into the atmosphere that circulated around the globe with varied effects. In Vermont it created killing frosts and snows that wasted farm crops for an entire growing season.

Toward the end of 1816, Father Smith joined a steady flow of discouraged migrants from Vermont seeking a more hospitable geographic location. He found conditions favorable to their needs in Palmyra, New York, and sent for his family to follow him. Lucy and the children arrived by 1 January 1817. Sometime during 1818 or 1819, they built a log home on the property of Samuel Jennings south of the village of Palmyra, near the Stafford Road in Palmyra Township. The exact location of their log structure was fixed by highway surveyors on 13 June 1820. From this home Joseph Smith Sr. and Alvin Smith contracted for 99.5 acres of farmland in adjoining Farmington (later Manchester) Township, Ontario County.

The history of The Church of Jesus Christ of Latter-day Saints had its beginnings with the family of Joseph Smith Sr. and Lucy Mack Smith in western New York, 1816 to 1831. Numerous religious denominations were represented in the vicinity of Palmyra. The most predominant were the Presbyterians, Baptists, Methodists, and Quakers. A revivalistic surge in the region prompted young Joseph Smith Jr., who was concerned for the welfare of his immortal soul, to seek answers in prayer. Following the biblical admonition, "If any of you lack wisdom, let him ask of God" (James 1:5), he called upon the Lord in the seclusion of a wooded grove near the family log home in the early spring of 1820. He testified that both the Father and the Son appeared to him, and in answer to his inquiry as to which church he should join, he was instructed that he must join none of them. This defining revelation, known as the First Vision, is considered to be the premier moment in the restoration of the gospel. Joseph Smith learned from the outset of these formative years to depend on varied forms of continuing revelation for divine guidance in reestablishing the Lord's Church and kingdom on earth.

Instructed by his heavenly visitors in the grove that the fulness of the gospel would yet be revealed to him, Joseph awaited further confirmation. Three and one-half years elapsed before a series of visitations commenced in fulfillment of this promise. While making supplication to the Lord for guidance on the evening of 21 September 1823, Joseph was visited by an angelic figure in the garret of the Palmyra log home. The messenger, identifying himself as Moroni, explained to him the existence of a record containing an account of the ancient inhabitants of this continent. The record, written on gold plates and hidden in a nearby hill, told of the appearance of the resurrected Savior to his people in the western hemisphere and contained the fulness of the gospel that was given to them by the Lord. During the night Joseph was instructed by the angel in three visits and a fourth appearance the following morning. On

Sacred Grove; *painting by Greg Olsen. "In accordance with this, my determination to ask of God, I retired to the woods to make the attempt. It was on the morning of a beautiful, clear day, early in the spring of eighteen hundred and twenty. . . . I kneeled down and began to offer up the desires of my heart to God. . . . I saw a pillar of light exactly over my head, above the brightness of the sun, which descended gradually until it fell upon me. . . . When the light rested upon me I saw two Personages, whose brightness and glory defy all description, standing above me in the air. One of them spake unto me, calling me by name and said, pointing to the other—This is My Beloved Son. Hear Him!" (JS–H 1:14–17).*

22 September, Joseph was directed to the place on the hill where the record was hidden. He found the stone box containing the record and also the URIM AND THUMMIM, to be used as interpreters in translating the plates. The angel also allowed him to see in open vision SATAN and his hosts so that he might not be deceived about the literal existence of that opposition. Moroni forbade Joseph's taking the plates at that time but directed him to begin a series of four annual visits to the hill, during which he would receive further instruction. These visits were to take place on 22 September of each year. Joseph faithfully met that charge, and on 22 September 1827 the plates were delivered into his possession to be translated.

During the four years while Joseph was instructed and prepared to receive the plates, he grew in other ways that also prepared him for the task ahead. The death of his eldest brother, Alvin, on 19 November 1823 was a highly sobering and mournful loss for the entire family. The economic situation of the Smith family was adversely affected by Alvin's death. He had been indispensable in making the annual payments on the farm contract held by a Canandaigua land agent.

Alvin, who was a carpenter, had directed the construction of a frame home on the Manchester property, beginning in 1822. The hiring of another carpenter, Russell Stoddard, to assist in completing the home created an additional complication when Stoddard attempted to wrest ownership of the home and farm from the Smiths. His untimely demands for payment of services, plus the Smiths' inability to raise the funds to meet the regular payment on the contract for the property, caused the loss of their Manchester farm in December 1825. Lemuel Durfee, the new owner, allowed the Smiths to stay on as renters until the spring of 1829, when they were obliged to leave the frame home and move back to their old log home in Palmyra Township. *See* Manchester, New York; Palmyra, New York.

While those events were yet future, in October 1825 Joseph and his father were hired by Josiah Stowell to assist him in digging for Spanish treasure rumored to have been buried in Harmony, Pennsylvania. The Smiths were pleased at the prospect of earning money to help make their contracted payment. The search for hidden wealth proved futile, but in the process Joseph met the daughter of Isaac Hale at his Susquehanna County home where Stowell's work crew boarded. After leaving Harmony Joseph courted her during his continued employment by Josiah Stowell and then by Joseph Knight Sr., who lived further up the Susquehanna River in Chenango and Broome counties in New York. Joseph Smith and Emma Hale were married at South Bainbridge (now Afton), Chenango County, New York, on 18 January 1827.

The newlyweds immediately went to live with Father and Mother Smith in the frame home in Manchester, and Joseph farmed with his family that season. He was thus in position to receive the gold plates from Moroni at the Hill Cumorah on 22 September 1827. Once it was known that he had been to the hill and had received the plates, every imaginable stratagem was employed by designing persons to take them from him. His attempts at translation were frequently disrupted or prevented altogether by those enemies. The Hale family was contacted in Harmony, Pennsylvania, and Alva Hale, Emma's brother, arrived in Manchester, New York, in December 1827 with a horse and wagon to take the couple and the golden plates to a more secure place.

After a brief stay with the Hales, Joseph and Emma Smith acquired from Isaac Hale the use of thirteen acres and moved a small, two-story frame home onto the property. There the translation of the gold plates began. Joseph identified certain characters from the plates and through the Urim and Thummim obtained definitions of those characters; Emma acted as his scribe. Martin Harris, a friend and wealthy supporter, journeyed from Palmyra to Harmony in February 1828 and, with the idea of assessing the authenticity of the characters by learned linguists, took the transcript to eastern cities for examination. At Albany, New York, Luther Bradish, a New York assemblyman from Franklin County, was contacted, and in New York City, Professors Charles Anthon and Samuel Lapham Mitchill were among those known to have been shown the transcript. Martin Harris came away from that experience with a certainty of the validity of the undertaking. The Prophet stated that prophecy was fulfilled during the course of this eastern venture when he gave an interpretation of Isaiah 29 and its relation to Harris's visit with "one that is learned" (Isa. 29:11).

Reporting back to the Prophet at Harmony, Martin Harris next leased out his acreage and joined Joseph in Harmony to act as his scribe, which he did from 12 April 1828 to 14 June 1828. At that time Harris, much besieged by his wife, Lucy, and others, requested permission to take the 116-page manuscript they had produced to show his household at Palmyra in an attempt to quiet their concerns. After a series of pleadings with the Lord through Joseph, Harris was put under covenant to show them only to his wife and four other family members, and he was reluctantly allowed to take the writings home. Harris broke his word and showed them not only to those designated but also to others.

When Harris failed to return at the appointed time, Joseph himself traveled to Manchester and asked him to report with the manuscript. A highly dejected Harris finally appeared at the Smith frame home with the disconcerting news that the 116 pages had been stolen from him and irretrievably lost. Suspicion centered on Lucy Harris as the person primarily responsible for the theft. Joseph was divested of the plates and the Urim and Thummim for a time, and Harris was permanently discontinued as scribe. The Prophet received a revelation in which both he and Martin Harris were chastised for their roles in the loss and he was warned not to attempt to retranslate the lost manuscript, as the text had been altered by the enemy in order to "destroy him, and also the work" (10:19; cf. sections 3; 10). See Book of Mormon, lost manuscript of (116 pages).

The plates and the Urim and Thummim were returned to Joseph, reportedly on 22 September 1828. Although Emma Smith and Samuel H. Smith gave some assistance, Joseph did not acquire a permanent scribe until April 1829. Oliver Cowdery, a teacher in the Stafford Road School of the Manchester district, boarded

in the frame home of Joseph Smith Sr. While there he learned of the Prophet and the work of translation. At the end of his 1828–29 contract year, Cowdery went with Samuel H. Smith to see Joseph in Harmony. The pair stopped at the Peter Whitmer Sr. farm in Fayette, New York, and Cowdery visited with his friend David Whitmer, who was later to become an important link in the completion of the translation. At Harmony, Cowdery received an additional confirmation that the work was of divine origin, and he began his duties as scribe on 7 April 1829 (6:15–17, 22–24; Smith, *History,* 1:32–35).

In the midst of their work, a question encountered in the translation process concerning baptism and the authority to baptize took Joseph and Cowdery to a wooded area near the banks of the Susquehanna on 15 May 1829. Their prayers were answered by a heavenly messenger, John the Baptist, who instructed them and conferred upon them the Aaronic Priesthood (13). Joseph Smith and Oliver Cowdery were directed to baptize and then to ordain each other to that priesthood. John the Baptist told them that he had been sent by the ancient apostles Peter, James, and John, who held the keys to the Melchizedek Priesthood, to initiate their receiving these ordinances. He said further that the Melchizedek Priesthood "would in due time be conferred" upon them (JS–H 1:72). Although an exact date was not given by the Prophet, the conferral of the Melchizedek Priesthood and the apostleship to Joseph and Oliver occurred sometime in May or June 1829 "in the wilderness between Harmony . . . and Colesville . . . on the Susquehanna river" (128:20). *See* Priesthood, restoration of priesthood and priesthood keys.

Before the work of translation could be completed in Harmony, the translator, his scribe, and the safety of the plates were again imperiled by severe local opposition. At the instigation of the Prophet, Oliver Cowdery wrote to his friend David Whitmer in Seneca County, New York, for assistance. Whitmer went to Harmony and moved them to a place of respite at the Peter Whitmer Sr. farm in Fayette, where they were situated "in the beginning of the month of June" 1829 (Smith, *History,* 1:48). In that month the translation was finished and a copyright secured on 11 June through Richard R. Lansing, clerk of the New York Northern District Court, who resided at Utica. The Three Witnesses—Oliver Cowdery, David Whitmer, and Martin Harris— were visited by Moroni on the Whitmer farm and shown the gold plates and other artifacts (17; Smith, *History,* 1:53–55). An additional eight witnesses viewed the plates at Joseph's hands in the woods near the Smith log home in Palmyra Township soon afterwards (Smith, *History,* 1:57–58).

In June 1829 the Prophet applied to Egbert B. Grandin, editor of the *Wayne Sentinel,* printer, and owner of the Palmyra Book Store, to publish the Book of Mormon. At first he refused on religious grounds, thinking the volume to be a fraud, but he was finally convinced by friends and family that it was a legitimate business opportunity. The contract called for five thousand copies to be produced for $3,000. Martin Harris stood as security for the project by a mortgage agreement with Grandin on 25 August 1829. Printing began that August, and the first copies were made available for public sale in Grandin's Palmyra Book Store on 26 March 1830. Because of a sectarian boycott of the book that limited sales, Martin Harris sold 151 acres of his farm to retire the mortgage.

When Joseph Smith and Oliver Cowdery first moved from Harmony and established themselves at Fayette in June 1829, they went into the Whitmer log home alone to petition the Lord for guidance on how to proceed with structuring the emerging Church. The Prophet stated that "the word of the Lord came unto us," and they were given a rather detailed outline for organization (*History,* 1:60–61). Action on the

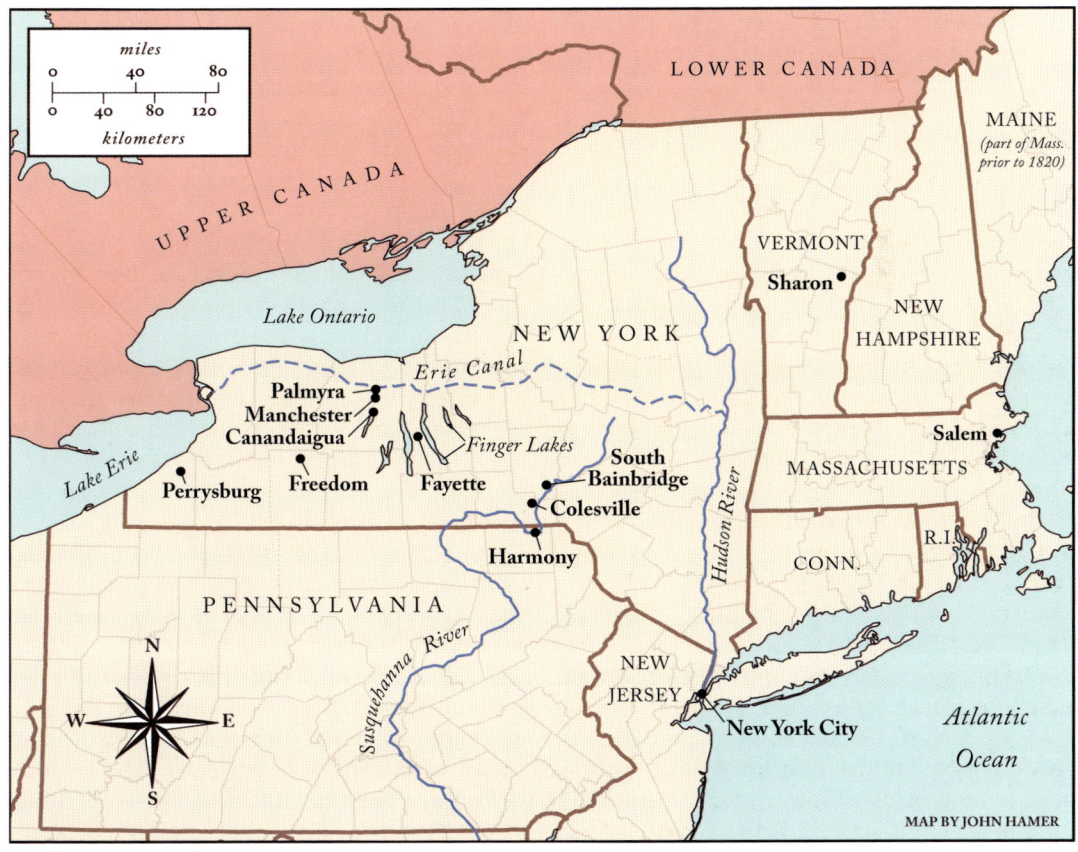

Northeastern United States.

matter, however, was deferred until they were given the precise day for that momentous event to take place and arrangements could be made for the brethren to assemble to give the needed sanction to Joseph Smith and Oliver Cowdery to act as their religious leaders. By prophecy and revelation, the desired date was later given—6 April 1830. On that date interested persons and nearly sixty adherents of the newly restored faith gathered at the Whitmers' home, where six appointed organizers established the Church of Christ "agreeable to the laws of our country, by the will and commandments of God" (20:1). Sustained to lead the organization, Joseph was ordained as first elder and Oliver as second. Those who had been previously baptized were confirmed members of the Church and given the gift of the Holy Ghost. Others were ordained to priesthood offices. Joseph received the titles of seer, translator, and prophet (21:1).

Although there had been some effective proselyting before the organization of the Church, an extended effort was now launched, using copies of the newly published Book of Mormon, and numbers were added to the faith. Branches of the Church were formed at Fayette, Seneca County, and Colesville, Broome County, and a branch was headquartered in Palmyra, which also included Saints from Manchester, as they united to form a congregation from Wayne and Ontario counties. The Prophet was particularly involved in the conversion of people who were connected to Joseph Knight Sr. in Colesville Township. In the process the Prophet stirred the ire of the sectarian community and was charged with being a "disorderly person." He was arrested, tried, and acquitted in two trials, one held at South Bainbridge, Chenango County, and the other at Colesville, Broome County, June–July 1830.

Joseph and Emma Smith now resided at their homestead in Harmony, Pennsylvania. By commandment, quarterly conferences had been called for at the organization of the Church on 6 April 1830 (20:61–62). Each of three conferences in New York was eventually held at the Fayette farm of the Whitmers, on 9 June and 26 September 1830 and 2 January 1831. At the time of the 26 September 1830 conference, a unique prophecy was fulfilled. The Lord had informed his prophets both ancient and modern that a knowledge of the Savior and the gospel as contained in the Book of Mormon would go to the posterity of the LAMANITES (3:16–20; 10:46–50; Enos 1:13–18). Under the leadership of Oliver Cowdery, three other missionaries, Peter Whitmer Jr., Parley P. Pratt, and Ziba Peterson, were called in September and October 1830 to undertake a lengthy journey to the Indians west of the Missouri state line in Unorganized Indian Territory (28; 30; 32). Leaving Fayette in mid-October 1830, they made contact en route with the Seneca near Buffalo, the Wyandot in Ohio, and finally the Shawnee and Delaware in Indian Territory, but with minimal results and no known Native American converts. They had, however, gleaned some 130 proselytes from the white population while passing through the Kirtland-Mentor area (October–November 1830) on their way to Missouri. These converts were primarily from among Sidney Rigdon's Reformed Baptist congregations. Other converts were soon added through their labors in Jackson and Lafayette counties, Missouri, after the missionaries were prohibited by government officials from continued proselyting in Unorganized Indian Territory.

The ramifications of the mission to the Lamanites brought sweeping changes among the New York and Ohio congregations. Sidney Rigdon and Edward Partridge traveled from Ohio to talk with the Prophet in Seneca County, New York, in early December 1830. The approximate time of their arrival is identified by a revelation the Prophet received that pertained to himself and Sidney Rigdon. That revelation was recorded in Doctrine and Covenants 35 and is dated 7 December 1830. Rigdon and Partridge took with them the welcome news that the 130 Ohio converts from October to November 1830 now numbered several hundred.

A request from the visitors for additional guidance resulted in revelatory direction being given to Edward Partridge (36) dated 9 December 1830. Edward Partridge immediately applied for baptism. The Prophet is reported to have baptized him in the Seneca River on 11 December.

These events were soon followed by an astounding call from the Lord for all New York Saints to gather in Ohio (37:1–4). The revelation was received at Canandaigua, New York, on 30 December 1830. As the Saints assembled for what would prove to be their last New York conference at the Whitmer farm on 2 January 1831, they desired further confirmation of the commanded move. The word of prophecy and an expanded explanation were received through the Prophet: "Wherefore, for this cause I gave unto you the commandment that ye should go to the Ohio; and there I will give unto you my law; and there you shall be endowed with power from on high" (38:32).

Joseph and Emma Smith did not delay their departure. They left Fayette with Joseph Knight and certain others by sleigh soon after 24 January 1831 and arrived in Kirtland on 4 February. There the Prophet made plans for the arrival of the New York Saints who were to follow in the spring. Members of the three New York branches felt their needs were best served by traveling by boat to Ohio. The Colesville branch was the first organized unit to set out for Kirtland in the spring of 1831. Some sixty-eight Saints, who had waited for the seasonal opening of the waterways, met at Ithaca, New York, by 23 April and on 25 April traveled by steamboat the length of Cayuga Lake to its northern outlet. There they boarded a canal boat that took them through the Cayuga-Seneca Canal to the Erie Canal and on to the harbor at Buffalo, New York. There they waited for the ice to break up on Lake Erie. In Buffalo they were soon joined by about eighty Saints from Fayette, who used the Cayuga-Seneca Canal from Seneca County to the Erie Canal and then west to Buffalo. Some fifty Saints from Palmyra also used the Erie Canal to Buffalo. Each branch made its transportation arrangements on a steamboat or sailing vessel from Buffalo Harbor via Lake Erie to Fairport Harbor in Ohio and then overland to Kirtland. The first to sail from Buffalo were Lucy Mack Smith and the Fayette Branch on the steamboat *Niagara* under Captain Blake on 8 May 1831. By the later part of May 1831, more than two hundred members from the three

branches had moved from New York to Ohio in obedience to the Lord's command.

During the New York period, Joseph Smith received revelations now recorded in Doctrine and Covenants 2 through 40, including the revelations received in Pennsylvania.

See also Illinois period; Missouri period; Ohio period.

BIBLIOGRAPHY

Backman, Milton V., Jr. *Eyewitness Accounts of the Restoration.* Orem, Utah: Grandin Book, 1983.

———. *Joseph Smith's First Vision.* Salt Lake City: Bookcraft, 1980.

Bennett, Richard E. "'Read This I Pray Thee': Martin Harris and the Three Wise Men of the East." *Journal of Mormon History* 36, no. 1 (Winter 2010): 178–216.

Bushman, Richard Lyman. *Joseph Smith: Rough Stone Rolling.* New York: Alfred A. Knopf, 2005.

Jensen, Robin Scott, Robert J. Woodford, and Steven C. Harper, eds. *Manuscript Revelation Books.* Facsimile edition. First volume of the Revelations and Translations series of *The Joseph Smith Papers,* edited by Dean C. Jessee, Ronald K. Esplin, and Richard Lyman Bushman. Salt Lake City: Church Historian's Press, 2009.

Porter, Larry C. "The Restoration of the Aaronic and Melchizedek Priesthoods." *Ensign* 26 (December 1996): 30–47.

———. "A Study of the Origins of the Church of Jesus Christ of Latter-day Saints in the States of New York and Pennsylvania, 1816–1831." Ph.D. dissertation, Brigham Young University, 1971,

Smith, Joseph. *History of The Church of Jesus Christ of Latter-day Saints.* Edited by B. H. Roberts. 2d ed. rev. 7 vols. Salt Lake City: The Church of Jesus Christ of Latter-day Saints, 1932–51.

Smith, Lucy Mack. Autobiography and notes, ca. 1850. Vault MSS 230, Handwritten autobiography and miscellaneous notes, L. Tom Perry Special Collections, Brigham Young University, Provo, Utah.

Smith, Lucy [Mack]. *Biographical Sketches of Joseph Smith, the Prophet and His Progenitors for Many Generations.* London and Liverpool: Published for Orson Pratt by S. W. Richards, 1853.

Staker, Mark Lyman. *Hearken, O Ye People: The Historical Setting of Joseph Smith's Ohio Revelations.* Salt Lake City: Greg Kofford Books, 2009.

LCP

Nicolaitane band

Elements of Christian congregations in Ephesus and Pergamum. In Doctrine and

Covenants 117:11 the Lord uses an expression reminiscent of the Nicolaitans of the book of Revelation (Rev. 2:6, 15). Some early Christian sources associated the Nicolaitans with Nicolas, the proselyte of Antioch, who was one of seven men chosen to assist the apostles in temporal affairs. Nicolas accused the group (the Nicolaitans) of libertine or lawless behavior (Acts 6:5). The postapostolic evidence of Irenaeus, Hippolytus, and Clement of Alexandria may not be completely reliable, and biblical scholars differ regarding how closely the Nicolaitans should be associated with other apostate groups mentioned in Revelation, namely those who "hold the doctrine of Balaam" in Pergamum (Rev. 2:14) and those who followed the false prophetess Jezebel in Thyatira (Rev. 2:20; Hemer, 87–94; Robinson and Garrett, 4:126). Nevertheless, a general pattern of apostasy influenced by worldliness—probably social pressures in connection with idol worship and sexual license—seem to have been factors troubling Christians in the Roman province of Asia in the first century.

This background helps to explain the Lord's referring to the Kirtland apostates in 1838 as "the Nicolaitane band" (117:11). By this time the collapse of the Kirtland Safety Society in 1837 had led to a widespread revolt against the authority of Joseph Smith because of the financial losses suffered by many speculators. While faithful members of the Church subsequently left Kirtland for Missouri, Bishop Newel K. Whitney chose to remain behind to settle his affairs and try to sell his property. This concern for worldly matters led him to associate with some of the apostates and inclined him toward the same concerns that had led others to leave the Church. The Lord admonished him to "be ashamed of the Nicolaitane band and of all their secret abominations, and of all his littleness of soul" (117:11).

The Lord's reference to the latter-day Nicolaitans as a "band" suggests that the Kirtland apostates, who had ostensibly left the Church because of financial concerns but had actively conspired against the Prophet's life (Smith, 3:1–3) were akin to another band of conspirators, Gadianton's band in the Book of Mormon (e.g., Hel. 2:4–6, 8, 10–11; 6:18; 11:2; Rhodes, 282–83).

BIBLIOGRAPHY

Beale, G. K. *The Book of Revelation: A Commentary on the Greek Text.* The New International Greek Testament Commentary. Grand Rapids, Mich.: Eerdmans, 1999.

Cargal, Timothy B. "Nicolaitans." In *Eerdmans Dictionary of the Bible,* edited by David Noel Freedman, 963–64. Grand Rapids, Mich.: Eerdmans, 2000.

Hemer, Colin J. *The Letters to the Seven Churches of Asia in Their Local Setting.* Sheffield, England: Sheffield Academic Press, 1986. Reprint, Grand Rapids, Mich.: Eerdmans, 2001.

McConkie, Joseph Fielding, and Craig J. Ostler. *Revelations of the Restoration: A Commentary on the Doctrine and Covenants and Other Modern Revelations.* Salt Lake City: Deseret Book, 2000.

Rhodes, Michael D. "Gadianton Robbers." In *Book of Mormon Reference Companion,* edited by Dennis L. Largey et al., 282–83. Salt Lake City: Deseret Book, 2003.

Robinson, Stephen E., and H. Dean Garrett. *A Commentary on the Doctrine and Covenants.* 4 vols. Salt Lake City: Deseret Book, 2000–2005.

Smith, Joseph. *History of The Church of Jesus Christ of Latter-day Saints.* Edited by B. H. Roberts. 7 vols. 2d ed. rev. Salt Lake City: The Church of Jesus Christ of Latter-day Saints, 1932–51.

Watson, Duane F. "Nicolaitans." In *The Anchor Bible Dictionary,* edited by David Noel Freedman, 4:1106–7. 6 vols. New York: Doubleday, 1992.

EDH

Noah

An ordained PATRIARCH who preserved human and animal life, PRIESTHOOD, and a testimony of the gospel through the Great Flood. Latter-day revelation confirms the biblical account of Noah and contributes significant information not elsewhere available about his unique ministry.

Noah was ordained to the priesthood at ten years of age by his grandfather Methuselah, who had been ordained by Adam (107:50–52). This same priesthood was continued through Noah to Melchizedek, who later ordained Abraham (84:14–15). Thus priesthood authority, personal reminiscence, a written record of the earliest patriarchs (Abr. 1:31), and a knowledge of the gospel were all handed down in an unbroken line from Adam to Abraham, Noah being the historical link before and after the Flood.

Noah was a child of promise. His great-grandfather Enoch, his grandfather Methuselah, and his father, Lamech, prophesied of his unique ministry to be a "comfort" to them in saving his family through the Flood, preserving the promise of continual posterity that had been made to them (Moses 7:42–45, 52, 60; 8:2–10).

Noah declared the GOSPEL of Jesus Christ in plainness (Moses 8:19–24; 2 Pet. 2:5). When his life was threatened by unbelievers, he was protected by the power of God (Moses 8:18–26). Noah is the angel Gabriel and "stands next in authority to Adam in the Priesthood" (Smith, 3:386). He is one of several individuals called Elias in the Doctrine and Covenants, in which role he appeared to Zacharias to tell him of the forthcoming birth of John the Baptist, and holds the "keys of bringing to pass the restoration of all things . . . concerning the last days" (27:6–7; Luke 1:5–20). As Gabriel, Noah is listed among those who visited Joseph Smith, "declaring their dispensation, their rights, their keys . . . , and the power of their priesthood," bringing about the Restoration (128:21–22); he is also among the many ancient prophets, apostles, and patriarchs who were supported in their afflictions and redeemed by the Lord (133:52–55). *See* Priesthood, restoration of priesthood and priesthood keys.

Noah was among those gladly welcoming the Savior when he visited the postmortal spirit world between his crucifixion and resurrection (138:12–16, 41). His name appears in the scripture that President Joseph F. Smith was pondering when he received the vision of the redemption of the dead, published as Doctrine and Covenants 138 (vv. 9, 28).

Noah was "perfect in his generation" (Moses 8:27; Gen. 6:9). He obeyed every commandment given him of God and fulfilled the purpose of his ministry. Undoubtedly, he was a "just m[a]n made perfect through Jesus the mediator of the new covenant" (76:69).

BIBLIOGRAPHY

Smith, Joseph. *History of The Church of Jesus Christ of Latter-day Saints.* Edited by B. H. Roberts. 7 vols. 2d ed. rev. Salt Lake City: The Church of Jesus Christ of Latter-day Saints, 1932–51.

RJM

Nobleman. *See* Parable regarding a certain nobleman/vineyard.

No respecter of persons

A phrase indicating that the Lord acts justly and without prejudice in his dealings with his children. The phrase appears twice in the Doctrine and Covenants:

1. In the revealed preface to the revelations, the Lord assured the Saints, "I am no respecter of persons." He desires that "all flesh," everyone on earth, come to a knowledge of the gospel and the "true and living church" (1:6; 30–35).

2. In section 38 the Lord proclaimed, "All flesh is mine, and I am no respecter of persons" (v. 16). He then employed a parable of a man and his twelve sons to teach that arbitrary treatment of others is not just. The Lord's standard is that "every man esteem his brother as himself, and practise virtue and holiness before [him]" (38:24–27). *See* Parable regarding a father and sons.

RCF

Nowise. See Appendix E.

High priests after the **order** of the Melchizedek Priesthood have a right to officiate in their own standing, under the direction of the presidency, in administering spiritual things, and also in the office of an elder, priest (of the Levitical order), teacher, deacon, and member. 107:10

Oath(s). *See* Appendix E.

Obedience

A fundamental principle of the GOSPEL of Jesus Christ. The first word in the Doctrine and Covenants is *hearken,* which means more than merely listening. It implies hearing the word of God and obeying. Obedience to God is "the first law of heaven" and as such is repeatedly referenced in the revelations (Smith, 16:248). Section 130 teaches that "when we obtain any blessing from God, it is by obedience to that law upon which it is predicated" (v. 21). The blessings of obedience have both immediate and eternal results—both temporal and spiritual rewards.

Temporally, obedience to the laws of God, specifically the WORD OF WISDOM, brings "health in [the] navel and marrow to [the] bones" (89:18). And in a different context, the Lord promised that "the willing and obedient shall eat the good of the land of Zion in these last days" (64:34).

Spiritually, obedience qualifies one to receive guidance and direction from the Holy Ghost— "wisdom and great treasures of knowledge, even hidden treasures" (89:19; cf. 93:1). Knowledge and intelligence gained through diligence and obedience not only bless one in this life but also yield "advantage in the world to come" (130:19). Furthermore, Saints are "accepted of [God]" if they "obey [his] ordinances" (52:15–16). Through the ATONEMENT of Jesus Christ and "by obedience to the principles of the gospel, mankind [can] be saved" (138:4) and ultimately receive "eternal life, which gift is the greatest of all the gifts of God" (14:7). *See* Eternal life.

On the other hand, disobedience offends God and results in the forfeiture of promised blessings: "I command and men obey not," the Lord declared. "I revoke and they receive not the blessing" (58:32). ZION, in particular, will not be established until God's people "learn obedience" (105:2–6). Disobedience yields condemnations, curses, chastening (e.g., 41:1; 56:3; 59:21; 101:6–8) and the loss of the Spirit: "And that wicked one cometh and taketh away light and truth, through disobedience" (93:39). *See* Curse, cursing.

In contrast, obedience assures God's approbation and blessings: "I, the Lord, am bound when ye do what I say; but when ye do not what I say, ye have no promise" (82:10).

See also Commandment(s); Righteous, the/righteousness; Wicked, the/wickedness.

BIBLIOGRAPHY

Smith, Joseph F. *Journal of Discourses.* 26 vols. London: Latter-day Saints' Book Depot, 1854–86.

BLT

Oblations. *See* Appendix E.

Obviate. *See* Appendix E.

Offend, offenses

To violate or transgress a moral or divine law, to cause hurt feelings or resentment, to vex or injure. Scripturally, one can offend God or one's fellowman. "In nothing doth man offend God, or against none is his wrath kindled, save those who confess not his hand in all things, and obey not his commandments" (59:21). Those who, after committing serious sins, refuse to repent and seek FORGIVENESS must be delivered to Church disciplinary councils "that ye may not offend him who is your lawgiver" (64:13). *See* Church discipline.

In the final verses of the "law of the Church" (42, headnote), laws are included that govern the confession of sins: If persons offend, they should reconcile privately (42:88; cf. Matt. 18:15); if individuals offend and do not confess, the matter goes before a leaders' meeting, or disciplinary council (42:89); those who offend many shall be chastened before many (42:90); those who offend openly "shall be rebuked openly, that [they] may be ashamed" (42:91; cf. 1 Tim. 5:20: "rebuke before all, that others also may fear"). On the other hand, those who offend secretly shall be rebuked secretly and have opportunity to secretly confess to those offended and to God (42:92). In the Church today practices concerning public and private chastening are governed by policies set forth by the First Presidency of the Church.

For those who offend in breaking the covenant of CONSECRATION, it would have been better to be drowned in the depths of the sea

(54:5). Those who offend God's "little ones" shall be severed from the ordinances of his house (121:19). Offenders against good laws should be brought to punishment, according to the nature of the offense, and "by the laws of that government in which the offense [was] committed" (134:8).

See also Repentance.

DKO

Official Declaration 1

The announcement of the revelation that the contracting of plural marriages was to cease. The principal difference between the first 138 sections of the Doctrine and Covenants and the two official declarations at the end of the Doctrine and Covenants is that the two official declarations are not records of revelations but public notices based on REVELATION.

Official Declaration 1 is an example of continuing revelation. It is not known fully why and when the Lord commanded the Prophet Joseph Smith to introduce the practice of plural MARRIAGE, but Doctrine and Covenants 132 and Jacob 2:30 suggest that the purpose for restoring the ancient practice of plural marriage was "to multiply and replenish the earth, according to my commandment, and to fulfil the promise which was given by my Father before the foundation of the world, . . . that they may bear the souls of men; for herein is the work of my Father continued, that he may be glorified" (132:63). Although it is not known exactly when section 132 was revealed to the Prophet Joseph Smith, the heading states that the "doctrines and principles involved in this revelation" had been known to him "since 1831." It may have been as early as the mid-1830s that the Prophet Joseph Smith was commanded to enter into plural marriage, after the keys of "the gospel of Abraham" and the sealing authority were restored (110:12). Joseph Smith and several others received plural wives in Nauvoo before the practice was generally made known. In 1852 the revelation was first publicly announced. Ten years later the United States government passed legislation aimed at stopping the practice, but the law was not strongly enforced until about 1882, when the Edmunds

Act was passed, which strengthened the earlier law. The Edmunds-Tucker Act of 1887 made plural marriage a serious offense. It not only punished those convicted of plural marriage but limited the Saints' participation in the political process and disincorporated the Church as a legal institution. The Saints, during these years, continued the practice, feeling the laws prohibiting polygamy were unconstitutional. When the Supreme Court of the United States declared in 1879 that the Edmunds Act of 1862 was constitutional, the Court thus upheld the antipolygamy legislation, putting the members of the Church in a very difficult situation and leaving them with no further legal appeal.

The Lord had already given revelations that endorsed the Constitution of the United States and directed the Saints to be obedient to the constitutional laws of the land (98:5–6; 101:77–80); however, the Lord also had told the members of the Church in 1841, "When I give a commandment to any of the sons of men to do a work unto my name, and those sons of men go with all their might and with all they have to perform that work, and cease not their diligence, and their enemies come upon them and hinder them from performing that work, behold, it behooveth me to require that work no more at the hands of those sons of men, but to accept of their offerings" (124:49). Both of those scriptures apply to the circumstances of the Latter-day Saints in the last half of the nineteenth century, and revelation was required for a resolution.

Over the history of the world, the Lord has given direction that was later changed by him. That is why continuing revelation is the lifeblood of the Church. Without constant revelation the Church would cease to be the Lord's Church. The Prophet Joseph Smith taught "that which is wrong under one circumstance, may be, and often is, right under another. God said, 'Thou shalt not kill;' at another time He said 'Thou shalt utterly destroy.' This is the principle on which the government of heaven is conducted—by revelation adapted to the circumstances in which the children of the kingdom are placed. Whatever God requires is right, no matter what it is, although we may not see

IS ENDORSED.

The People Accept the Manifesto!

THE VOTE UNANIMOUS

President Cannon Gives the Reasons For Its Issuance.

PRESIDENT WOODRUFF SPEAKS.

He Is Thankful the Saints Have Sustained Him in His Action in Issuing It.

Sunday saw a big increase in the attendance at the tabernacle, and the demand for admission was so great that had there been ten times the usual room, it would have all been filled. The one big feature of the conference, of course, was the presentation of the official manifesto, in regard to polygamy, and which is as follows:

OFFICIAL DECLARATION.

To whom it may concern:

Press dispatches having been sent for political purposes, from Salt Lake City, which have been widely published, to the effect that the Utah Commission, in their recent report to the secretary of the Interior, allege that plural marriages are still being solemnized and that forty or more such marriages have been contracted in Utah since last June or during the past year; also that in public discourses the leaders of the church have taught, encouraged

at the head of the church would ever be permitted to lead the people astray. God would not permit it. Were he (the speaker) to attempt to direct the people wrong, he would be removed. President Woodruff said he had but a few years to live on the earth, and he would not knowingly do anything that would deprive him of the privilege of meeting in the hereafter the good men who had gone before.

The first speaker on Sunday morning was

President George Q. Cannon.

We are living in peculiar times. The work of God was being assailed in various directions. However, this was no new thing. It had been the lot of the Saints from the beginning to contend with difficulties and overcome obstacles. They had had to pass through scenes which had tested their faith, integrity and fidelity. The elders who had been faithful in preaching the gospel, had not neglected to tell the people whom they baptized the character of the difficulties which they would have to encounter when they espoused the cause of God. They were warned to expect the same fate which attended the ancient disciples of Jesus Christ, how their names would be cast out as evil.

Many things in this church had come in contact with the traditions and preconceived ideas of men. There were many things to-day which perhaps conflicted with the previous views of Latter-day Saints. There was scarcely a thinking man or woman in the church of Christ who had not indulged in reflections concerning the future of this work, and some of those views had been rudely upset by subsequent events. God was the author of this work, and He would conduct it to suit His purposes and not those of man.

Let them think of how many doctrines had been taught that were new to the world which God had revealed in our day. How would they understand these unless the spirit of God bore testimony to them? Who on the earth believed them? They were not sanctioned by tradition, they were not upheld by the common belief of men. They were new to this generation, and yet, though they shook the prejudices of mankind and perhaps startled the Latter-day Saints, when they sought of God for a testimony concerning them, He never failed to give unto them His Holy Spirit which gave the assurance that they were of God and not of man. And so it will be to the end. The presidency of this church have to walk just as the rai[n]s walk; they have to depend upon the revelations of God as they come to them. They had their faith tested as the Saints have and so with the Apostles. All that they could do was to seek the mind and will of God.

He would lose all hope for humanity but for the Latter-day Saints. It filled him with horror when he saw the course which men and women were taking outside of this church, and witnessed the fate which was coming upon the people of this and other nations, and felt thankful to our Heavenly Father that he had established a church whose standard of purity was unequaled, and in which all impurity was denounced and dealt with. Virtue among the people was at a low standard outside of this church. The Latter-day Saint who indulged in

Announcing the Manifesto. From the Salt Lake Herald, *7 October 1890.*

the reason thereof till long after the events transpire" (*History*, 5:135).

In the beginning the Lord commanded that animal sacrifice, pointing to the atonement of Jesus Christ, be part of the gospel (Moses 5:4–8). With the ultimate sacrifice of Christ, however, the sacrifice of animals was done away and replaced by the sacrifice of a broken heart and a contrite spirit (3 Ne. 9:19–20).

In the April 2012 general conference of the Church, Elder D. Todd Christofferson spoke of

how revelation comes to the Church to change policy and procedures. He cited as examples Acts 10 concerning taking the gospel to the gentiles and Acts 15 regarding the requirement of circumcision. This same principle of revelation applies in the case of Official Declaration 1.

On 26 September 1890, after much prayer and meditation, President Wilford Woodruff, moved upon for the temporal salvation of the Church, announced that his "advice to the Latter-day Saints is to refrain from contracting any marriage forbidden by the law of the land" (OD 1). In general conference on 6 October 1890 President Lorenzo Snow, after the Manifesto had been read to the assembled Saints, moved that this "declaration concerning plural marriages [be accepted] as authoritative and binding" upon the Church. A sustaining vote was then taken and it was unanimous (OD 1).

Although the sustaining vote was unanimous, discussion continued about stopping the practice. On several occasions President Woodruff explained why the Manifesto was issued. "Excerpts from Three Addresses by President Wilford Woodruff Regarding the Manifesto" appear in the Doctrine and Covenants. In those accounts President Woodruff assured the Saints: "The Lord will never permit me or any other man who stands as President of this Church to lead you astray. . . . If I were to attempt that, the Lord would remove me out of my place" (Excerpt 1); "The God of heaven commanded me to do what I did do. . . . I went before the Lord, and I wrote what the Lord told me to write" (Excerpt 2); "The Son of God felt disposed to have that thing presented to the Church and to the world for purposes in his own mind" (Excerpt 3).

Some members of the Church, however, continued the practice. In 1904 Joseph F. Smith reaffirmed the Manifesto with this statement: "I hereby announce that all [plural] marriages are prohibited, and if any officer or member of the Church shall assume to solemnize or enter into any such marriage he will be deemed in transgression against the Church and will be liable to be dealt with according to the rules and regulations thereof, and excommunicated therefrom" (*Gospel*, 280).

The position of the Church today is very plain. President Gordon B. Hinckley stated: "If any of our members are found to be practicing plural marriage, they are excommunicated, the most serious penalty the Church can impose. Not only are those so involved in direct violation of the civil law, they are in violation of the law of this Church. . . . More than a century ago God clearly revealed unto His prophet Wilford Woodruff that the practice of plural marriage should be discontinued, which means that it is now against the law of God. Even in countries where civil or religious law allows polygamy, the Church teaches that marriage must be monogamous and does not accept into its membership those practicing plural marriage" (71–72).

Official Declaration 1 has been published as part of the Doctrine and Covenants since 1908.

See also Historical context and overview of Doctrine and Covenants 132 (p. 849).

BIBLIOGRAPHY

Deseret Evening News. (11 October 1890): 2.

Hinckley, Gordon B. "What Are People Asking about Us?" *Ensign* 28 (November 1998): 70–72.

Smith, Joseph. *History of The Church of Jesus Christ of Latter-day Saints.* Edited by B. H. Roberts. 7 vols. 2d

Courtesy Church History Library

Wilford Woodruff, 1807–1898. Regarding the revelation that led to the Manifesto, President Woodruff taught in the October 1890 general conference: "The Lord will never permit me or any other man who stands as President of this Church to lead you astray. It is not in the programme. It is not in the mind of God. If I were to attempt that, the Lord would remove me out of my place, and so He will any other man who attempts to lead the children of men astray from the oracles of God and from their duty" (News, 2).

ed. rev. Salt Lake City: The Church of Jesus Christ of Latter-day Saints, 1932–51.

Smith, Joseph F. *Gospel Doctrine.* Salt Lake City: Deseret Book, 1986.

KWP

Official Declaration 2

The announcement of the revelation extending priesthood and temple blessings to all worthy males and thus "all of the privileges and blessings which the gospel affords" to "every worthy member of the Church . . . without regard for race or color."

President N. Eldon Tanner, first counselor in the First Presidency, presented the declaration at the general conference of the Church on 30 September 1978 after explaining that it had been approved unanimously by the First Presidency, the Quorum of the Twelve Apostles, and all other general authorities of the Church. The constituent assembly gathered at the conference also sustained the declaration unanimously. Official Declaration 2 was sent in a letter from the First Presidency dated 8 June 1978 to all general and local priesthood officers of the Church.

It is clear that leaders of the Church had anticipated that a change would someday come with respect to the priesthood restriction, but they waited for the needed revelation. Over a considerable period of time before June 1978, President Kimball had asked his counselors and the Twelve to research carefully the scriptures and statements of earlier brethren in an exhaustive study of all that had been recorded concerning the matter. It had been a focus of discussions in their weekly temple meetings and in private conversations (Tate, 279; Dew, 456–57; McConkie, 127). In addition, President Kimball spent much time alone in the temple, pleading with the Lord for guidance. He recalled: "Day after day I went alone and with great solemnity and seriousness in the upper rooms of the temple, and there I offered my soul and offered my efforts to go forward with the program. I wanted to do what he wanted. I talked about it to him and said, 'Lord, I want only what is right'" (*Teachings,* 451). In a fireside address 25 February 1979, President Kimball testified, "I want you to know, as a special witness of the Savior, how close I have felt to him and to our Heavenly Father as I have made numerous visits to the upper rooms in the temple, going on some days several times by myself. The Lord made it very clear to me what was to be done" ("Savior," 36).

On Thursday, 1 June 1978, the general authorities held their regular monthly fast and testimony meeting in the Salt Lake Temple. After that meeting, President Kimball excused all the General Authorities except his counselors and the ten members of the Quorum of the Twelve who were present that day. Elder Mark E. Petersen was in South America and Elder Delbert L. Stapley was in the hospital. President Kimball then opened another meeting, the focus of which was the issue of the priesthood restriction. The following observations of some of those present describe what happened in that meeting:

Elder David B. Haight: "Humbly then the prophet asked each of us to express his feelings regarding the matter, and we did so. As each responded, we witnessed an outpouring of the Spirit which bonded our souls together in perfect unity—a glorious experience. . . . President Kimball then suggested that we have our prayer at the altar. . . . The prophet of God pour[ed] out his heart, pleading eloquently for the Lord to make his mind and will known to his servant, Spencer W. Kimball. The prophet pleaded that he would be given the necessary direction which could expand the Church throughout the world by offering the fullness of the everlasting gospel to all men, based solely upon their personal worthiness without reference to race or color" (Tate, 279–80).

Elder Bruce R. McConkie: "It was during this prayer that the revelation came. The Spirit of the Lord rested mightily upon us all; we felt something akin to what happened on the day of Pentecost and at the dedication of the Kirtland Temple. From the midst of eternity, the voice of God, conveyed by the power of the Spirit, spoke to his prophet. . . . And we all heard the same voice, received the same message, and became personal witnesses that the word received was the mind and will and voice of the Lord. . . . On this occasion, because of the importuning and the faith, and because the hour and the time had arrived, the Lord in his providences poured out the Holy Ghost upon the First Presidency and the

Twelve in a miraculous and marvelous manner, beyond anything that any then present had ever experienced" ("Revelation," 128, 133–4).

President Gordon B. Hinckley: "There was a hallowed and sanctified atmosphere in the room. For me, it felt as if a conduit opened between the heavenly throne and the kneeling, pleading prophet of God who was joined by his Brethren. . . . Every man in that circle, by the power of the Holy Ghost, knew the same thing. It was a quiet and sublime occasion. There was not the sound 'as of a rushing mighty wind,' there were not 'cloven tongues like as of fire' (Acts 2:2–3) as there had been on the Day of Pentecost. But there was a Pentecostal spirit, for

© Intellectual Reserve, Inc.

The First Presidency who announced Official Declaration 2: (left to right) *first counselor N. Eldon Tanner, president Spencer W. Kimball, and second counselor Marion G. Romney; photograph by Eldon K. Linschoten. "He has heard our prayers, and by revelation has confirmed that the long-promised day has come when every faithful, worthy man in the Church may receive the holy priesthood, with power to exercise its divine authority, and enjoy with his loved ones every blessing that flows therefrom, including the blessings of the temple. Accordingly, all worthy male members of the Church may be ordained to the priesthood without regard for race or color" (OD 2).*

the Holy Ghost was there. . . . We left that meeting subdued and reverent and joyful. Not one of us who was present on that occasion was ever quite the same after that. Nor has the Church been quite the same. . . . There was perfect unity among us in our experience and in our understanding" (70).

Elder David B. Haight: "President Kimball arose from the altar. (We surrounded it according to seniority, I being number twelve.) For some unknown reason, he turned to his right, and I was the first member of the circle he encountered. He put his arms around me, and as I embraced him I felt the beating of his heart and the intense emotion that filled him. He then continued around the circle, embracing each of the Brethren. No one spoke. Overcome with emotion, we simply shook hands and quietly went to our dressing rooms" (Tate, 280).

A week after the revelation was received, a special temple meeting was called in which the First Presidency and the Twelve met with all the available general authorities of the Church. They were instructed by President Kimball regarding the revelation and Official Declaration 2, which they sustained unanimously. The announcement was then made to the world and a letter, dated 8 June 1978, was sent to all general and local authorities of the Church, authorizing the ordination of worthy male members of the Church to the priesthood "without regard for race or color."

Significance of the revelation

In a ten-stake fireside in Kansas City, Missouri, on 2 September 1978, President Spencer W. Kimball stated: "Until recently there was one group of people that had not been permitted to have the priesthood. But since June ninth of this year every boy that has ever been born is eligible for the priesthood if he will qualify. It matters not as to his color or his race. . . . One of the Brethren said yesterday that now has come one of the greatest changes and blessings that has ever been known" (*Teachings*, 451). Ten years later President Hinckley wrote, "We have cause to rejoice and to praise the God of our salvation that we have seen this glorious day." "Tremendous, eternal consequences for millions over the earth are flowing from that manifestation" (70). Elder

McConkie added his assessment: "It was a revelation of such tremendous significance and import; one that would reverse the whole direction of the Church, procedurally and administratively; one that would affect the living and the dead; one that would affect the total relationship that we have with the world; one, I say, of such significance that the Lord wanted independent witnesses who could bear record that the thing had happened. . . . This affects our missionary work and all of our preaching to the world. . . . This affects what is going on in the spirit world" ("Revelation," 134–5).

The revelation of 1978 opened the way for The Church of Jesus Christ of Latter-day Saints to fulfill the Lord's command given two thousand years ago for his apostles to preach the gospel to "every creature" in "all nations" in "all the world" (Matt. 28:19; Mark 16:15; Luke 24:47).

Speculation about the reasons for such delayed opportunities serve no useful purpose. The reasons for earlier restrictions "are known to God," and "He has not yet made [them] fully known to man" (First Presidency).

BIBLIOGRAPHY

Dew, Sheri L. *Ezra Taft Benson: A Biography.* Salt Lake City: Deseret Book, 1987.

First Presidency of The Church of Jesus Christ of Latter-day Saints. 1969.

Hinckley, Gordon B. "Priesthood Restoration." *Ensign* 18 (October 1988): 69–72.

Kimball, Spencer W. "The Savior: The Center of Our Lives." New Era 10 (April 1980): 33–36.

———. *The Teachings of Spencer W. Kimball.* Edited by Edward L. Kimball. Salt Lake City: Bookcraft, 1982.

McConkie, Bruce R. "The New Revelation." In *Priesthood.* Salt Lake City: Deseret Book, 1986.

Tate, Lucile C. *David B. Haight: The Life Story of a Disciple.* Salt Lake City: Bookcraft, 1987.

EDL

Ohio period

The period in Church history from 1831 to 1838. For more than seven and a half years, from October 1830 to the summer of 1838, northeastern Ohio was a gathering place for Latter-day Saints. This era was characterized by missionary expansion, Church growth, the first TEMPLE, and an unusual pentecostal season. It was a period of remarkable visions and other spiritual manifestations, revelations of doctrinal and organizational developments, and the publication of many important works. The last phase of the Ohio period was marred by persecution, apostasy, and expulsion.

Ohio became the seventeenth state in the union in 1803, the same year the nation doubled in size with the Louisiana Purchase. Ohio had been part of the old Northwest Territory, land that was north of the Ohio River and east of the Mississippi. After the French and Indian War of 1763, France relinquished the area to England, and twenty years later England surrendered the land to the United States. The Northwest Ordinance of 1787 provided that eventually the area would be divided into states, specified that there was to be no slavery, and guaranteed religious freedom. Two of the states carved out of the Northwest Territory were Ohio and Illinois, states where the Latter-day Saints established headquarters.

The rapid growth of the Church and the gathering of Latter-day Saints in northeastern Ohio paralleled significant changes in the young republic. The population of the United States was almost doubling every twenty years, and while there was great growth in eastern urban areas, there was also rapid expansion westward, especially between Ohio and Missouri. The transportation revolution of roads, canals, and railroads greatly accelerated the western expansion. Much rich land was also available on convenient terms in what was then western America. This was also a period of a great religious revival. The Second Great Awakening reached a new peak during the 1830s and 1840s as large numbers of people united with different religious communities, thereby creating a fertile field for missionaries.

The principal Latter-day Saint gathering place in Ohio was in an area in the northeastern part of the state known as the Western Reserve. After initial surveys in about 1800, settlers, primarily from New England and New York, began moving into the Reserve. By 1830 Ohio was one of the fastest growing states in the nation (Backman, 21–32).

In October 1830, four missionaries to the LAMANITES introduced the gospel to settlers in

Kirtland and vicinity. In one month they converted about 130 individuals, including Sidney Rigdon, Frederick G. Williams, Newel K. Whitney, Isaac Morley, John Murdock, Titus Billings, and Lyman Wight. Before the missionaries left Kirtland, they called leaders to serve and organized branches and congregations with meetings held in homes of the new converts. By the end of 1830 there were as many members in northeastern Ohio as in the state of New York.

After Joseph Smith learned from Sidney Rigdon and Edward Partridge about the numbers of converts in the Western Reserve, he received a revelation instructing him and other Saints to move to Ohio (38:31–32). Ohio thus became the first gathering place for the

Latter-day Saints. Joseph Smith arrived in Kirtland on 1 February 1831, and within five months about two hundred New York Saints moved to the Western Reserve region of Ohio. In the summer of 1831 Joseph Smith traveled to western Missouri and identified Independence, Jackson County, as ZION, the central gathering place for Church members. Subsequently, most New York Saints and early converts from Ohio moved to western Missouri, creating two gathering places for the Church—Ohio and Missouri.

Kirtland, Ohio, remained the headquarters of the Church and the home of Joseph Smith, except for one year, from September 1831 to September 1832, when Joseph lived in Hiram, Ohio. By 1832, within a journey of one or two

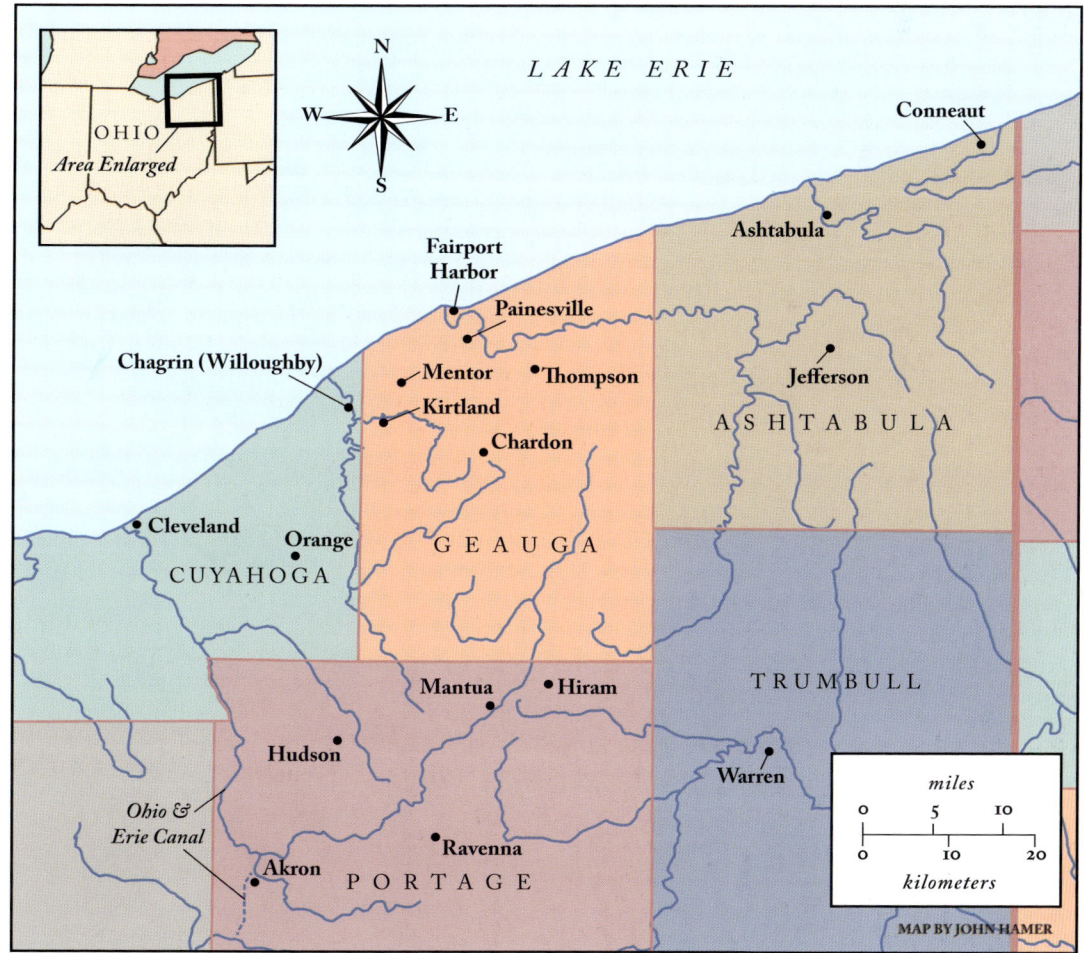

Northern Ohio, 1830–1838.

days from Kirtland in almost any direction, members could provide lodging and preaching opportunities for elders. There were Church branches northeast of Kirtland at Thompson (Madison) and Rome; southeast at Hiram, Nelson, and Shalersville; and southwest at Mayfield, Orange, Warrensville, and Amherst (south of Cleveland). About forty-two miles southwest of Kirtland another branch was located at New Portage (now Barberton), near Akron. New Portage was the site of at least seven conferences attended by Joseph Smith (Backman, 47–48; Perkins and Cannon, 38–76).

Every year before the exodus from Ohio, Joseph Smith traveled to other communities, where he instructed Latter-day Saints and recorded revelations, twelve of which are in the Doctrine and Covenants. Among these journeys were five to western Missouri, four to Michigan, several to Canada and New York City, and others to Albany, New York, and Boston and Salem, Massachusetts. Joseph averaged about two thousand miles of travel outside Ohio every year (Backman, 113–15).

Before 1838, Kirtland was the principal center from which missionary activity occurred as hundreds of new converts left their homes to preach the gospel in the United States, Canada, and the British Isles. During this time, all nineteenth-century presidents of the Church— Brigham Young, John Taylor, Wilford Woodruff, and Lorenzo Snow—joined the Church and gathered to Kirtland. The first three presidents of the Relief Society (in Nauvoo and Utah)— Emma Smith, Eliza R. Snow, and Zina D. Huntington—lived in Kirtland at the time of the TEMPLE dedication, and Elizabeth Ann Whitney, a counselor to the first two general Relief Society presidents, was one of the earliest converts in Kirtland.

The rapid growth of the Church continued in Ohio during most of the 1830s and accelerated during the building of the Kirtland Temple. From mid-1833 to mid-1836, the population of Latter-day Saints in Kirtland increased from about 150 to 1,300, while the non-Mormon population remained about 1,200 (Backman, 140).

Joseph Smith received thirty-nine revelations now recorded in the Doctrine and Covenants in New York and Pennsylvania before February 1831, and the number of revelations increased significantly in Ohio. Between February 1831 and July 1837 Joseph received sixty-four revelations in Ohio, including forty-five in Kirtland (more than in any other place), seventeen in Hiram, and one each in Thompson and Amherst. Almost half of the revelations recorded in the Doctrine and Covenants were received in Ohio.

After he received a commandment to translate the Bible, Joseph Smith was actively involved in that project from June 1830 to the summer of 1833 and beyond. During that time, while praying, contemplating, and seeking answers, he received and dictated revelations relating to many significant doctrines. Revelations received in Ohio that relate to the Prophet's work on the Bible include sections 45, 73, 76, and 86. During this time he received numerous revelations, some of which grew out of the translation process and others independent of that endeavor. In Ohio he received revelations pertaining to the publication, preface, and appendix to the Book of Commandments (1; 133), the basic laws of the Church (42), education and, specifically, the organization of the School of the Prophets (88), the Word of Wisdom (89), and the building and purpose of the Kirtland Temple (88, 94, 95). He also received a remarkable prophecy on war (87).

Many additional revelations came as a result of questions about the expansion of Church government. Between 1831 and 1836 the basic pattern of Church government was established, including the offices of bishop, high priest, First Presidency, and high council and the calling of the Quorum of the Twelve Apostles and the first quorums of seventies (Anderson, 93–105; Backman, 237–56).

In 1834 Joseph Smith received a revelation regarding the organization of ZION'S CAMP (103:15–40). On 1 May, one group of volunteers left Kirtland and traveled south to New Portage, where the main group was organized under the direction of Joseph Smith. Nine participants in Zion's Camp were called to serve in the original Quorum of the Twelve Apostles and all of the first Quorum of the Seventy including the seven presidents, participated in that historic march to Missouri (Backman, 199).

In January 1834, five months after the Latter-day Saint press in Independence, Missouri, was destroyed, Kirtland became the center for Church publications. During the mob violence in Missouri in July 1833, most copies of the Book of Commandments (which included eighteen revelations received in Ohio) were destroyed, creating a need for another publication of Joseph Smith's revelations. In 1835 Latter-day Saints published in Kirtland the first edition of the Doctrine and Covenants, which contained Joseph Smith's revelations, thirty-eight of which had been received in Ohio, and the LECTURES ON FAITH, a series of lectures to the School of the Elders in Kirtland, Ohio, in the winter of 1834–35. Latter-day Saints also published issues of *The Evening and the Morning Star,* the first hymnal, a second edition of the Book of Mormon (1837), and a new periodical, *The Latter-day Saints' Messenger and Advocate* (October 1834–September 1837) in Kirtland. The *Messenger and Advocate* included doctrinal discourses, missionary reports, Oliver Cowdery's early history of the Church, and other information for the benefit of the Saints.

Throughout the Ohio period, not only did Joseph Smith receive by revelation answers to his inquiries but he and others gained knowledge and faith through an outpouring of spiritual gifts. The Prophet and others saw in vision the Father, the Son, and many other heavenly beings, and during the great pentecostal season that took place before, during, and after the dedication of the Kirtland Temple, Latter-day Saints were blessed with gifts of prophecy, tongues, interpretation of tongues, and healings (Anderson, 107–13; Backman, 287–306).

Although the first half of 1836 was a period of unusual spiritual feasts in Kirtland, peace was soon replaced with controversy, apostasy, and persecution. The last revelation received in Ohio and an account preserved in the Doctrine and Covenants was recorded in July 1837 (112); the next-to-last had been received in April 1836 (110) (Olson, 329–49; Smith, 217–19). Conflicts interrupted the spirit of inquiry and possibly the recording and preserving of history. Because of increased persecution, most of the approximately two thousand Latter-day Saints in the Kirtland vicinity moved west in 1838.

Several reasons and forces explain the apostasy and persecution in the Church headquarters in Kirtland. Violence sometimes occurred in the new nation when old settlers believed that their traditional lifestyle was being threatened. Persecution of Latter-day Saints in various forms had occurred from the beginning of their settlement in Ohio. The mob actions to tar and feather Joseph Smith and Sidney Rigdon in Hiram in 1832 was one of many manifestations of early intolerance. Vexatious lawsuits and threats of attack characterized this decade (Backman, 97–100, 155, 321–23, 331–33). Meanwhile, after the building and dedication of the temple, the spirit of sacrifice among some Latter-day Saints was replaced by an emphasis on self-improvement and selfishness. In 1837 Latter-day Saints became a majority in the Kirtland Township, and although no members of that faith had been elected to any major office in the community before 1837, they or their friends won every significant office within one year. In 1838, during the exodus of Latter-day Saints from Ohio, active members of the Church did not run for office. These political factors combined with economic factors. The Panic of 1837 created an atmosphere of economic irritation and played a role in the collapse of the Kirtland Safety Society, a bank in Kirtland established by members of the Church. Joseph Smith, who had recommended the establishment of this bank, became a scapegoat for the bank failure and was blamed for the problems of the Saints. Criticism of him and his supporters intensified; pressures from critics outside the Church united with pressures from dissidents within. During the apostasy that followed, one-third of the Church leaders were excommunicated, and possibly 10 to 12 percent of the members turned against the Prophet. *See* Apostasy, of early dissenters from restored Church.

Brigham Young, one of those who remained faithful, was among the first to leave Kirtland in December 1837. In January 1838 Joseph

Smith fled for his life, joining faithful Saints in Missouri. Some contemporaries speculated that if Joseph Smith had not left Kirtland, he would have been killed in Ohio rather than in Illinois (Backman, 310–29, 335–52). The last large group of Saints to leave Kirtland for Missouri was known as the Kirtland Camp. In July 1838 this group of approximately five hundred men, women, and children left Kirtland under the direction of the seventies, traveling west to Missouri in a long train of wagons.

After their expulsion from Missouri later that year or early in 1839, many Latter-day Saints who had lived in Kirtland and other Ohio communities migrated to Illinois and built new homes near the banks of the Mississippi in what became Nauvoo, the city beautiful (Backman, 352–66). *See* map, p. 345.

See also Illinois period; Kirtland Temple dedication; Missouri period; New York period.

BIBLIOGRAPHY

Anderson, Karl Ricks. *Joseph Smith's Kirtland: Eyewitness Accounts.* Salt Lake City: Deseret Book, 1989.

Backman, Milton V., Jr. *The Heavens Resound: A History of the Latter-day Saints in Ohio, 1830–1838.* Salt Lake City: Deseret Book, 1983.

Olson, Earl E. "The Chronology of Ohio Revelations." *BYU Studies* 11, no. 3 (1971): 329–49.

Perkins, Keith W., and Donald Q. Cannon. *Ohio and Illinois.*Vol. 3 of *Sacred Places: A Comprehensive Guide to Early LDS Historical Sites,* edited by LaMar C. Berrett. Salt Lake City: Deseret Book, 2002.

Smith, Joseph. *Personal Writings of Joseph Smith.* Compiled and edited by Dean C. Jessee. Rev. ed. Salt Lake City: Deseret Book, 2002.

MVB

Olaha Shinehah, plains of

Identified in 117:8 as the "land where Adam dwelt." It is apparently part of, or in the vicinity of, ADAM-ONDI-AHMAN, in the northern area of the state of Missouri in the United States of America. The name "Olaha Shinehah, may be, and in all probability is, from the language of Adam. We may without great controversy believe that this is the name which Adam gave to this place, at least we may venture this as a probable guess. Shinehah, according to the Book of Abraham, is the name given to the sun (Abraham 3:13). . . . Elder Janne M. Sjodahl

commenting on the name, Olaha Shinehah, has said: 'Shinehah means sun, and Olaha is possibly, a variant of the word Olea, which is "the moon." (Abraham 3:13.) If so the plains of Olaha Shinehah would be the Plains of the Moon and the Sun, so called, perhaps because of astronomical observations there made'" (Smith, *Church,* 3:125).

Abraham states that the early patriarchs from Adam on down had knowledge of "the planets, and of the stars" (Abr. 1:31; 3:1–17). An entry in the Egyptian grammar and alphabet states that the patriarchs sought out this information by the Urim and Thummim (Smith, "Grammar," 24).

BIBLIOGRAPHY

Smith, Hyrum M., and Janne M. Sjodahl. *The Doctrine and Covenants . . . with Historical and Exegetical Notes.* Salt Lake City: Deseret News Press, 1941.

Smith, Joseph, trans. "Grammar and Alphabet of the Egyptian Language," abt. 1836. Photocopy and typescript of original in Church History Library, The Church of Jesus Christ of Latter-day Saints, Salt Lake City, Utah.

Smith, Joseph Fielding. *Church History and Modern Revelation.* 4 vols. Salt Lake City: The Church of Jesus Christ of Latter-day Saints, 1946–49.

RJM

Olive leaf. *See* Historical context and overview of Doctrine and Covenants 88 (p. 792).

Olivet, mount of. *See* Mount of Olives.

Omaha Nation

An American Indian tribe in the eastern part of Nebraska Territory on whose land the Saints established a temporary settlement (1846–48) called Winter Quarters (Coates, 275–300). It was here that Brigham Young received a revelation in January 1847 about organizing pioneer companies for the westward trek to the Salt Lake Valley (136, headnote). Latter-day Saints who did not go west with the advance company, who reached the Salt Lake Valley in 1847, moved from Winter Quarters east across the Missouri River to COUNCIL BLUFFS, IOWA.

See also Winter Quarters, Nebraska.

BIBLIOGRAPHY

Coates, Lawrence G. "Cultural Conflict: Mormons and Indians in Nebraska." *BYU Studies* 24 (Summer 1984): 275–300.

DQC

One eternal round

A phrase affirming God's righteous constancy in all his works—past, present, and future.

Twice in the Doctrine and Covenants God's "course" is defined as "one eternal round" (3:2; 35:1). One technical meaning of *course* is a point on a compass used to chart a direction or a path to be followed. In response to the loss of the 116 pages of the Book of Mormon translation, the Lord declared to the Prophet Joseph Smith in the summer of 1828 that God's "works, . . . designs, and . . . purposes . . . cannot be frustrated, neither can they come to naught. For God doth not walk in crooked paths, neither doth he turn to the right hand nor to the left, neither doth he vary from that which he hath said, therefore his paths are straight, and his course is one eternal round" (3:1–2; cf. Alma 7:20; 37:12).

Not only is God's course undeviating but it is also constant through all time, as the Lord declared in a revelation for the benefit of Sidney Rigdon in 1830: "Listen to the voice of the Lord your God, even Alpha and Omega, the beginning and the end, whose course is one eternal round, the same today as yesterday, and forever" (35:1; cf. 1 Ne. 10:19).

A *round* is an event in a series of similar events, as in, for example, a round of golf. God's straight, undeviating course and sameness throughout eternal linear time (past, present, and future) is one eternal round in that it involves treading the same path again and again from "eternity to eternity" (76:4).

See also God, nature of.

JST

One hundred and forty-four thousand. *See* Historical context and overview of Doctrine and Covenants 77 (p. 782); Seal, sealed.

One mighty and strong. *See* Historical context and overview of Doctrine and Covenants 85 (p. 789).

Only Begotten of the Father. *See* Jesus Christ.

Only true and living church

The only Church possessing the fulness of the gospel of Jesus Christ and the authority from God to officiate in the ordinances of salvation, with Christ at its head, directing it by divine revelation. In the revealed preface to the Book of Commandments, the first canonized collection of revelations received by Joseph Smith, the Lord said that the Restored Church was "the only true and living church upon the face of the whole earth, with which I, the Lord, am well pleased, speaking unto the church collectively and not individually" (1:30).

Elder Neal A. Maxwell wrote that the word *only* in this description suggests "the exclusive ecclesiastical, authority-bearing agent for our Father in heaven in this dispensation." As to the word *true*, "The Church is not . . . conceptually compromised by having been made up from doctrinal debris left over from another age. . . . It is based upon the *fullness* of the gospel of him whose *name* it bears." As to the word *living*, "The Church is neither dead nor dying, nor is it even wounded" but rather is "alive, aware, and functioning. It is not a museum that houses a fossilized faith; rather, it is a kinetic kingdom characterized by living faith in living disciples" (45–46).

The phrase "only true and living church" does not mean that men and women of other Christian faiths are not genuine followers of Christ or that all the doctrines in traditional Christianity are false. "Have the Presbyterians any truth?" Joseph Smith asked. "Yes. Have the Baptists, Methodists, &c., any truth? Yes. . . . We should gather all the good and true principles in the world and treasure them up, or we shall not come out true 'Mormons'" (5:517; cf. 5:498–99). Elder Orson F. Whitney observed in 1928: "Perhaps the Lord needs such men on the outside of His Church to help it along. . . . They are among its auxiliaries, and can do more good for the cause where the Lord has placed them, than anywhere else. . . . God is using more than one people for the accomplishment of His great and marvelous work" (59).

See also Church of Jesus Christ of Latter-day Saint, The; Great and marvelous work.

BIBLIOGRAPHY

Maxwell, Neal A. *Things As They Really Are.* Salt Lake City: Deseret Book, 1978.

Smith, Joseph. *History of The Church of Jesus Christ of Latter-day Saints.* Edited by B. H. Roberts. 7 vols. 2d ed. rev. Salt Lake City: The Church of Jesus Christ of Latter-day Saints, 1932–51.

Whitney, Orson F. Cited by Ezra Taft Benson, "Civic Standards for the Faithful Saints," *Ensign* 2 (July 1972): 59–61.

RLM

Oracle(s)

In the scriptures, the words *oracle* and *oracles* are used with three meanings:

1. The revelations of the Lord (90:4–5; 124:39, 126).

2. Those who receive revelation (the "living oracles"). In Official Declaration 1, Excerpts by President Wilford Woodruff, paragraph 1, the word *oracles* is probably a reference to revelators. That is clearly the case in 1 Peter 4:11, and it is in this way that the word is often used in the Church today (e.g., Ballard, 59; Faust, 2).

3. Holy places in which revelation is received. In Old Testament usage, the term *oracle* referred to "the most holy place" in Solomon's temple (e.g., 1 Kgs. 6:16; 8:6). Therefore, "in a general sense, any sacred place where oracles are received is called an *oracle*. A temple is an oracle in this sense" (McConkie, 547).

BIBLIOGRAPHY

Ballard, M. Russell. "When Shall These Things Be?" *Ensign* 26 (December 1996): 56–61.

Faust, James E. "First Presidency Message: Continuing Revelation." *Ensign* 26 (August 1996): 2–7.

McConkie, Bruce R. *Mormon Doctrine.* 2d ed. Salt Lake City: Bookcraft, 1979.

TLG

Orange, Ohio

A township in Cuyahoga County, located about fifteen miles southwest of Kirtland. On 29 October 1831, having returned to Hiram, Ohio, from a conference in Orange, Joseph Smith "inquired of the Lord" in behalf of William E. McLellin and received a revelation (66, headnote). McLellin's journal reports the revelation was received in Hiram, Ohio, on 29 October (McLellin, 44–46).

In 1831, the Orange-Warrensville Branch became one of the largest branches in the Church (Murdock, 9). On 25–26 October 1831, an important conference was held at the Serenus (also spelled Sirenes) Burnett home in Orange. At the conference, several brethren were ordained to priesthood offices, and many of them expressed a willingness to consecrate their all to the Lord. In addition, the Three Witnesses and several of the Eight Witnesses of the Book of Mormon bore testimony of the restored gospel (Smith, 1:219–20; Cannon and Cook, 19–26). Orange was also the birthplace of James A. Garfield, president of the United States. *See* map, p. 461.

BIBLIOGRAPHY

Cannon, Donald Q., and Lyndon W. Cook, eds. *Far West Record: Minutes of The Church of Jesus Christ of Latter-day Saints, 1830–1844.* Salt Lake City: Deseret Book, 1983.

Johnson, Luke. "History of Luke Johnson." *The Latter-day Saints' Millennial Star* 26 (1864): 835.

McLellin, William. Journals of William McLellin. Church History Library, The Church of Jesus Christ of Latter-day Saints, Salt Lake City, Utah.

Murdock, John. Journal. Typescript. L. Tom Perry Special Collections, Harold B. Lee Library, Brigham Young University, Provo, Utah.

Smith, Joseph. *History of The Church of Jesus Christ of Latter-day Saints.* Edited by B. H. Roberts. 2d ed. rev. 7 vols. Salt Lake City: The Church of Jesus Christ of Latter-day Saints, 1932–51.

MVB

Ordain, ordained, ordination(s)

Appoint, assign, commission, or authorize by divine AUTHORITY; confer by the LAYING ON OF HANDS. In the Doctrine and Covenants, the word *ordain* and its variations are used with several meanings:

1. To confer PRIESTHOOD, priesthood office, priesthood KEYS, or Church position by the laying on of hands. Priesthood ordinations in the Restored Church began with John the Baptist conferring the Aaronic Priesthood upon Joseph Smith and Oliver Cowdery (13:1; 27:8), followed by their receiving the Melchizedek Priesthood from Peter, James, and John (27:12). Then

came the keys of the kingdom and the keys of the DISPENSATION of the fulness of times (128:20; cf. 112:30–32). By the authority of this priesthood and its keys, men were ordained to the various offices of the priesthood as Church organization grew to include deacons, teachers, priests, bishops, elders, high priests, patriarchs, seventies, and apostles. Church positions of bishoprics, stake presidencies, and the First Presidency were ordained as they were needed.

There are dozens of references to such ordinations, and instructions concerning proper procedure. For example, the Lord said, "Every elder, priest, teacher, or deacon is to be ordained according to the gifts and callings of God unto him; and he is to be ordained by the power of the Holy Ghost, which is in the one who ordains him" (20:60). Moreover, "no person is to be ordained to any office in this church, where there is a regularly organized branch of the same, without the vote of that church" (20:65). The Lord also declared, "It shall not be given to any one to go forth to preach my gospel, or to build up my church, except he be ordained by some one who has authority, and it is known to the church that he has authority and has been regularly ordained by the heads of the church" (42:11).

There is a hierarchy of priesthood authority and presiding responsibility in the Church. "The Melchizedek Priesthood holds the right of presidency, and has power and authority over all the offices in the church in all ages of the world, to administer in spiritual things" (107:8; cf. 107:10, 21–27, 33–38, 58–68, 91–92). More than ordination to the priesthood or to an office is required to merit the Lord's blessings. Those who hold the priesthood and are found "magnifying their calling" are promised great blessings, whereas those who shirk their responsibilities will suffer severe penalties (84:33–44; 95:5–6, 12; 107:99–100).

2. To set someone apart to a specific calling by the laying on of hands. Emma Smith was told, "And thou shalt be ordained under his [Joseph Smith's] hand to expound scriptures, and to exhort the church, according as it shall be given thee by my Spirit" (25:7). *Ordain,* in this instance, is equivalent to the current practice of *setting apart* auxiliary leaders, teachers,

and so forth to callings in the Church in which authority is given to administer organizations without conferring priesthood or priesthood office.

3. To appoint, approve, establish, decide upon. Joseph Smith and Sidney Rigdon saw "things which were from the beginning before the world was, which were ordained of the Father" (76:11–13). Again, many references in the revelations use *ordain* in this sense. For example, certain foods are "ordained for the use of man" (89:10–14; cf. 49:18–19), and guidelines are given to help the Saints avoid being deceived by "things which are not ordained of [God]" (50:35; cf. 43:1–7). Those who forbid to marry and those who forbid to eat meat are "not ordained of God" (49:15, 18). No one understands the ultimate fate of the SONS OF PERDITION "except those who are ordained unto this condemnation" (76:48). Some things were "ordained in the midst of the Council of the Eternal God of all other gods before this world was" to come forth at the end of time (121:32). Joseph Smith explained that vicarious baptism for one's ancestors is "only to answer the will of God, by conforming to the ordinance and preparation that the Lord ordained and prepared before the foundation of the world, for the salvation of the dead" (128:5, 22). *See* Salvation for the dead.

DKO

Order

There are three main uses of the term *order* in the Doctrine and Covenants:

1. God's kingdom, both in heaven and on earth, is one of order, meaning that it is perfectly organized and orderly. All things are to be done in righteousness, appropriateness, and timeliness (20:68). Because God's house is one of order, he has commanded that the Church, the temples, and the homes of the Saints be established and maintained after this pattern of order (88:119; 90:15–16, 18; 93:40–50).

2. The PRIESTHOOD is called "*the Holy Priesthood, after the Order of the Son of God*" (107:3; cf. 124:123; Alma 13:9, 14–16). In this context, *order* means a group of individuals who are joined together by a common characteristic, status, or honor. It also implies a

grouping by rank or achievement. In the vision of the three degrees of glory, those obtaining a celestial reward are described as "priests and kings, who have received of his fulness, and of his glory; and are priests of the Most High, after the order of Melchizedek, which was after the order of Enoch, which was after the order of the Only Begotten Son" (76:56–57). Both the Melchizedek and Aaronic, or Levitical, priesthoods are referred to in the revelations as orders (84:18; 107:9–10, 40–41).

3. The United Order is described by the Lord as "an organization of my people, in regulating and establishing the affairs of the storehouse for the poor of my people, both in this place [Kirtland] and in the land of Zion [Missouri]— for a permanent and everlasting establishment and order unto my church, to advance the cause, which ye have espoused, to the salvation of man, and to the glory of your Father who is in heaven" (78:3–4). *See* Consecration.

The name "United Order" is a code name and appears in the text in place of the organization's actual name, the "United Firm" (78; 104, headnote). *See* Names, code.

Specific counsel and stipulations regarding participation in this United Order are given in several revelations (92:1; 104:1, 21, 47–48, 53; cf. 78; 82).

See also Order of Enoch.

BLT

Order of Enoch

The expression "order of Enoch" appears once in scripture: "priests of the Most High, after the order of Melchizedek, which was after the order of Enoch, which was after the order of the Only Begotten Son" (76:57). Before the days of Mechizedek "it was called *the Holy Priesthood, after the Order of the Son of God*" (107:1–4; cf. 124:123). It is known today as the Melchizedek PRIESTHOOD, the "higher" priesthood, "the holiest order of God," which holds "the keys of all the spiritual blessings of the church" (84:18; 107:18), "the key of the mysteries of the kingdom, even the key of the knowledge of God" (84:19). *See* Key(s).

This priesthood was held by Adam and was

handed down through the generations to Moses (84:6–16).

See also Order.

SKB

Ordinance(s)

From the verb *ordain,* meaning to set in order, arrange, or prepare. The noun *ordinance* means a decree given by an AUTHORITY and can thus refer to a particular rite or observance established by one in authority. The common usage of this term within the Church today is in reference to the rites practiced under the authority of the PRIESTHOOD; however, *ordinance* can also mean a rule, an edict, a decree, or a precept. Among the earliest uses in the Doctrine and Covenants, the term has the meaning of a precept that one must "obey" (52:15–16; 53:6; 64:5). But the term also refers to rituals enacted by priesthood authority (21:10–11; 84:20–21; 88:139–40; 107:14, 20, 67). The term is used several times in section 124, referring both to rituals (baptism for the dead, vv. 30, 33, 38) and to precepts ("the ordinance of my holy house," v. 39; establishing a president over a quorum of high priests, v. 134), with two uses that may reflect either emphasis (vv. 40, 46). Likewise, in section 128, both precept (keeping a record, vv. 4–5) and ritual (general work for the dead, vv. 8, 12) are present. In 138:54 the term is used to describe the rituals of the temple.

Many other references are not as clear because the surrounding context does not provide enough information. For example, in 1:15 the reader is told that some have "strayed from mine ordinances, and have broken mine everlasting covenant." The term refers either to precepts established in the GOSPEL or to restored rites necessary for SALVATION. Similarly, in 77:14, it is unclear whether the term refers to the decree given to John the Revelator concerning his specific mission or to the ritual associated with reception of that mission. In 121:19, those who became traitors to the Saints will be "severed from the ordinances of mine house," probably referring to loss of blessings associated with temple ordinances but possibly also to the loss of blessings resulting from being cut off from the precepts of God's kingdom. In 136:4, the term probably means the precepts of God, but again, not enough information is given to make this certain. It appears that by the late 1800s the meaning of the term *ordinance* in public discourse seems to focus on rites, as all four references in Official Declaration 1 use the term to designate ritual practice.

Because the ordinances of the GOSPEL are also associated with covenants made between members of the Church and God, the full power of the ordinances is experienced only through both accepting the ordinance and obeying the precepts of the covenants entered into (130:20–21; 52:15–16).

See also Baptism by water; Endow, endowed, endowment; Gift of the Holy Ghost; Ordain, ordained, ordination(s); Wash, washed, washing(s).

DLB

Outer darkness

The state in eternity of those who reject the Lord's word. In 1831 the Lord warned that those who "obeyed not my voice when I called to you out of the heavens; . . . [and] believed not my servants, and when they were sent unto you ye received them not . . . shall go away into outer darkness, where there is weeping, and wailing, and gnashing of teeth" (133:71–73). In describing the Saints' suffering at the hands of mobs in Missouri, the Lord promised that if the nation did not address the cries of the children of Zion, then he would "vex the nation . . . [and] cut off those wicked, unfaithful, and unjust stewards, and appoint them their portion among hypocrites, and unbelievers; even in outer darkness, where there is weeping, and wailing, and gnashing of teeth" (101:89–91).

The term "outer darkness" is found four other times in the standard works, three times in Matthew, in which at least two references (Matt. 8:12; 22:13) describe the location of those who are cast out of a feast. In Matthew 8, the children of the kingdom, who apparently have demonstrated insufficient faith, are cast out into outer darkness, where there is weeping, wailing, and gnashing of teeth, instead of sitting down with Abraham, Isaac, and Jacob. In Matthew 22, the unprepared wedding guest is cast out into outer darkness. Because of the feasts in both references, some have described outer darkness not as a state of absolute dark but as one that is contrasted with the light and happiness within the house.

Two additional references use the term "outer darkness" to refer to those who are cast out. In Matthew 25, the unprofitable servant is cast out of his master's household after the master's return (Matt. 25:30). In the Book of Mormon, the wicked are cast out, they who "chose evil works rather than good; therefore the spirit of the devil did enter into them, and take possession of their house—and these shall be cast out into outer darkness" (Alma 40:13). In all six references, being cast into outer darkness is associated with imagery of a house or dwelling place; more specifically, the individual, through his own choices, is to be cut off from the community of God and cast out from his dwelling.

When considering all the scriptures that deal with those consigned to outer darkness, it is clear that their suffering is temporary (19:5–12; 63:16–17; 76:85, 102–6), except for the SONS OF PERDITION (76:31–39), of whom the Lord said, "The end thereof, neither the place thereof, nor their torment, no man knows" (76:45–48; cf. 43:33).

See also Hell; Punish, punished, punishment; Satan.

DLB

Outward ordinances. *See* Priesthood; Letter of the gospel.

And this greater priesthood administereth the gospel and holdeth the key of the mysteries of the kingdom, even the key of the knowledge of God. Therefore, in the ordinances thereof, the power of godliness is manifest. And without the ordinances thereof, and the authority of the priesthood, the power of godliness is not manifest unto men in the flesh. 84:19–21

Packard, Noah

Birth: 7 May 1796, Plainfield, Hampshire County, Massachusetts

Death: 17 February 1860, Springville, Utah County, Utah

Noah Packard joined the Church in June 1832, having received his testimony of the Book of Mormon after reading it twice. He wrote that "the Lord poured out His spirit upon me and the scriptures were opened to [my] understanding, and [I was] convinced that the Book of Mormon was a true record . . . containing the fullness of the gospel of Jesus Christ which was to come forth at the time of the restitution of the house of Israel" (2). Packard later served several missions, during which he found himself boldly proclaiming the gospel with great success. He recorded, "As I was young in the ministry, I had desired a good smart elder to go with me to the east; but . . . was left alone; but what was lacking in a smart companion, the Lord made up by pouring out His spirit upon me." Thus, he was able to "confound any that came . . . to oppose Mormonism or the gospel" (3).

In fall 1835 Packard moved to Kirtland, Ohio, after selling his farm for twenty-two hundred dollars, of which he lent one thousand dollars to the Church to help with the construction of the Kirtland Temple and "donated four hundred dollars to discharge the debts which had been contracted to build the House [Kirtland House]" (Packard, 3; Smith, 2:281). During this time he was ordained a high priest and called to the Kirtland high council. He left Kirtland for Missouri in the fall of 1838 but spent the winter in Wellsville, Ohio, before moving to Quincy, Illinois, in the spring of 1839.

In 1840 Packard moved to Nauvoo, where he served as a counselor to Don Carlos Smith in the presidency "over a quorum of high priests" (124:133, 136). He served in that calling until Smith's death later that year and then was called to serve in that same capacity with George Miller as president, "until the Church left Nauvoo for Salt Lake Valley" (Packard, 3–4).

Later Packard served more missions, again finding significant success. He wrote that by 1845 he had traveled "15,000 miles, preached 480 times, and baptized 53 into the Church." He

also noted that his service was "mostly performed on foot with a valise on my back and always . . . without a cent of money in my pockets" (4).

In 1850 Packard arrived in Utah and ultimately settled in Springville. Though he faced trials throughout his life, such as the death of his son Orren, who was tragically "run over with a loaded wagon" (Packard, 5), and "unjustifiable attacks and false charges" against him stemming from a disagreement he had with other Church members in Springville over the construction of the tabernacle there (Black, 206–7), Packard remained faithful until his death. One historian wrote that "he died as he had lived firm and unshaken in the gospel of Christ" (Jenson, 2:685).

BIBLIOGRAPHY

Black, Susan Easton. *Who's Who in the Doctrine and Covenants*. Salt Lake City: Deseret Book, 1997.

Jenson, Andrew. *Latter-day Saints' Biographical Encyclopedia*. 4 vols. Salt Lake City: The Andrew Jenson History Company, 1901–36. Reprint, Salt Lake City: Western Epics, 1971.

Packard, Noah. "A Synopsis of the Life and Travels of Noah Packard." Typescript. L. Tom Perry Special Collections, Harold B. Lee Library, Brigham Young University, Provo, Utah.

Smith, Joseph. *History of The Church of Jesus Christ of Latter-day Saints*. Edited by B. H. Roberts. 7 vols. 2d ed. rev. Salt Lake City: The Church of Jesus Christ of Latter-day Saints, 1932–51.

ZLL

Page, Hiram

Birth: 1800, Westminster, Windham County, Vermont

Death: 12 August 1852, near Excelsior Springs, Ray County, Missouri

Hiram Page learned about the coming forth of the Book of Mormon from the Peter Whitmer Sr. family. He was privileged to be one of the Eight Witnesses shown the plates by the Prophet Joseph Smith. He was baptized on 11 April 1830, just five days after the Church was organized.

Before the conference of 26 September 1830, Page found a stone which he believed possessed qualities that enabled him to be a revelator. In the summer of 1830, Page took up his stone to discover the location of the city of Zion (28:9). The Lord directed that Oliver Cowdery tell Page the devil had deceived him about the revelatory properties of the stone (28:11–12). Demonstrating loyalty and faith toward Church leaders, Page "broke [the stone] to powder and burnt the writings" (Harris, 273).

Upon leaving New York in 1831, Page settled in Thompson, Ohio, before journeying to Independence, Missouri. During the persecutions that befell the Saints in Independence in 1833, Page was viciously whipped; he carried the scars from this incident for the rest of his life (Smith, *History*, 4:394–95).

Page became one of the founders of Far West, Missouri. He was a faithful member of the Church until the spring of 1838, when his three brothers-in-law, Oliver Cowdery, David Whitmer, and John Whitmer, were excommunicated. Influenced by them, Page lost confidence in Joseph Smith and withdrew from the Church; however, there is no indication in the historical records that he was disciplined or excommunicated.

Page settled on a farm in Excelsior Springs, Missouri, where he remained the rest of his life. He never denied his testimony of seeing the gold plates as one of the Eight Witnesses of the Book of Mormon. In 1847, when William E. McLellin wrote to him, asking if he had retained his faith in the Book of Mormon, Page responded with a stirring testimony: "It would be doing injustice to myself, and to the work of God of the last days, to say that I could know a thing to be true in 1830, and know that same thing to be false in 1847. To say my mind was so treacherous that I had forgotten what I saw. . . . And to say that those holy Angels who came and showed themselves to me as I was walking through the field, to confirm me in the work of the Lord of the last days—three of whom came to me afterwards and sang an hymn in their own pure language; yea, it would be treating the God of heaven with contempt, to deny these testimonies, with too many others to mention here" (63).

See also Historical context and overview of Doctrine and Covenants 28 (p. 736).

BIBLIOGRAPHY

Harris, Emer. Statement, 6 April 1856. Utah Stake General Minutes, 1855–56, LR 9629, series 11, vol.

10. Church Historical Library, The Church of Jesus Christ of Latter-day Saints, Salt Lake City, Utah.

Page, Hiram. Letter to William E. McCllelin, Ray Co., Missouri, 30 May 1847. *Ensign of Liberty of the Church of Christ* 1, no. 4 (January 1848): 49–64]

Smith, Joseph. *History of The Church of Jesus Christ of Latter-day Saints.* Edited by B. H. Roberts. 7 vols. 2d ed. rev. Salt Lake City: The Church of Jesus Christ of Latter-day Saints, 1932–51.

Smith, Joseph F. "Comments of the Day." *Contributor* 8, no. 4 (February 1887): 157–60.

BGS

Page, John E.

Birth: 25 February 1799, Trenton Township, Oneida County, New York

Death: 14 October 1867, Sycamore, DeKalb County, Illinois

John Edward Page was baptized by Emer Harris, brother of Martin Harris, in 1833 (Page, 103). He moved to Kirtland in 1835, and in 1836 and 1837 he served two missions to Canada. Of these missions he testified that he was "sustained by the power of God" and was able to baptize "upwards of six hundred persons" while he "travelled more than five thousand miles, principally on foot and under the most extreme poverty" (Page, 103). In 1838 he led Canadian Saints to Missouri, joining the Kirtland Camp en route.

Page's name appears in Doctrine and Covenants 118 and 124. In 118, which was received on 8 July 1838, Page was called with John Taylor, Wilford Woodruff, and Willard Richards to "fill the places" of former apostles John F. Boynton, William E. McLellin, Lyman Johnson, and Luke Johnson, all of whom had been excommunicated in Kirtland for apostasy (118:6; cf. JH, 10 December 1837; 11 May 1838; Smith, 2:528; 3:20, 31–32). Page was ordained an apostle at Far West on 19 December 1838 "under the hands of Elders B. Young and H. C. Kimball" (Page, 103).

In a revelation received in 1841, Page is listed among the "Twelve [who] hold the keys to open up the authority of [the Lord's] kingdom upon the four corners of the earth" (124:128–29). In 1838 he lost his wife and two children "as martyrs" in the persecution of the Saints in Missouri (Page, 103). He did not go on a mission to

John E. Page, 1799–1867; painting by Kenneth Corbett.

England with other members of the Twelve in 1839. In 1840 he was appointed to travel with Orson Hyde to Jerusalem; he got as far as the eastern states and stopped there to preach.

On 26 June 1846, two years after the death of the Prophet Joseph Smith, Page was excommunicated from the Church. He supported James J. Strang as Joseph Smith's successor and became a leader in Strang's group. Three years later he left the Strangites for James C. Brewster's offshoot and then joined the Hedrickites in 1862, with whom he worked to secure the Independence temple site. He died in DeKalb County, Illinois, at age sixty-eight.

BIBLIOGRAPHY

Journal History of the Church, 10 December 1837; 11 May 1838. Church History Library, The Church of Jesus Christ of Latter-day Saints, Salt Lake City, Utah.

Page, John. "History of John E. Page." *The Latter-day Saints' Millennial Star* 27 (February 18, 1865): 103.

Smith, Joseph. *History of The Church of Jesus Christ of Latter-day Saints.* Edited by B. H. Roberts. 7 vols. 2d ed. rev. Salt Lake City: The Church of Jesus Christ of Latter-day Saints, 1932–51.

ZLL

Palms in our hands

A sign of reverence and praise offered to one's king. In 1836, during the prayer dedicating the Kirtland Temple, Joseph Smith pleaded with the Lord to remember the members of the Church who had suffered and sacrificed so much to build the temple (109:5, 72). Using imagery that parallels the New Testament book of Revelation, the Prophet Joseph anticipated that day when the Latter-day Saints would triumph over their enemies and worship the Lord "clothed upon with robes of righteousness, with *palms in our hands,* and crowns of glory upon our heads, and reap eternal joy for all our sufferings" (109:73–76; emphasis added; cf. Rev. 7:9–10).

The palm tree was very common in ancient Israel. Palm branches were used for the celebrations of the Feast of Tabernacles (Lev. 23:40; Neh. 8:14–15), and beautiful carvings of palm trees decorated the temple of Solomon (1 Kgs. 6:29, 32). As ancient Israelites spread clothes across the path of a new king in conjunction with his coronation (2 Kgs. 9:13), so when Jesus Christ—Israel's true king—triumphantly entered Jerusalem riding on a donkey the Sunday before his crucifixion and resurrection, followers paid homage by taking "branches of palm trees" (John 12:13), lining his path with the branches and with clothes (Matt. 21:8; Mark 11:8) and crying out "Hosanna: Blessed is the King of Israel" (John 12:13; cf. Matt. 21:9; Mark 11:9–10). This event is commemorated every year as Palm Sunday, one week before Easter.

FFJ

Palmyra, New York

When established on 27 January 1789, Palmyra Township was part of Ontario County (county seat at Canandaigua), which included the six million acres of the Phelps and Gorham Purchase. On 11 April 1823, when Wayne County was created from Ontario and Seneca counties, the township of Palmyra became part of Wayne County, with Lyons as the county seat; Macedon Township was divided from Palmyra Township that same year.

Joseph Smith Sr. arrived in the village of Palmyra in 1816 from Norwich, Vermont, to find a suitable location for his family; he then

© Intellectual Reserve, Inc.

The Sacred Grove, where Joseph Smith received the First Vision, in which he beheld God the Father and his Son, Jesus Christ.

sent for them to join him. Lucy Mack Smith and the children made the journey in the winter of 1816–17, arriving in January 1817. They relocated two miles south of the village in Palmyra Township on Stafford Road, about 1818–20, during which period they constructed a log home on the property of Samuel Jennings. The exact location of their log house was fixed by two highway commissioners from the village of Palmyra on 13 June 1820 as they took a reading with the Old Town Compass while standing on "the south line of Township No 12 2d range of townships in the town of Palmyra three rods fourteen links southeast of Joseph Smith's dwelling house" (Porter, 17). The log home was in Palmyra Township, approximately fifty-two feet north of the Palmyra-Farmington (later Palmyra-Manchester, 1822) town line.

From this home Joseph Smith Jr. went into the woods to pray. There he experienced the First Vision, in which the Father and Son appeared, instructing him not to join any of the existing denominations. In about 1822 the Smiths began to build a frame home just over the line in Manchester Township but continued to live in the Palmyra log home during the construction.

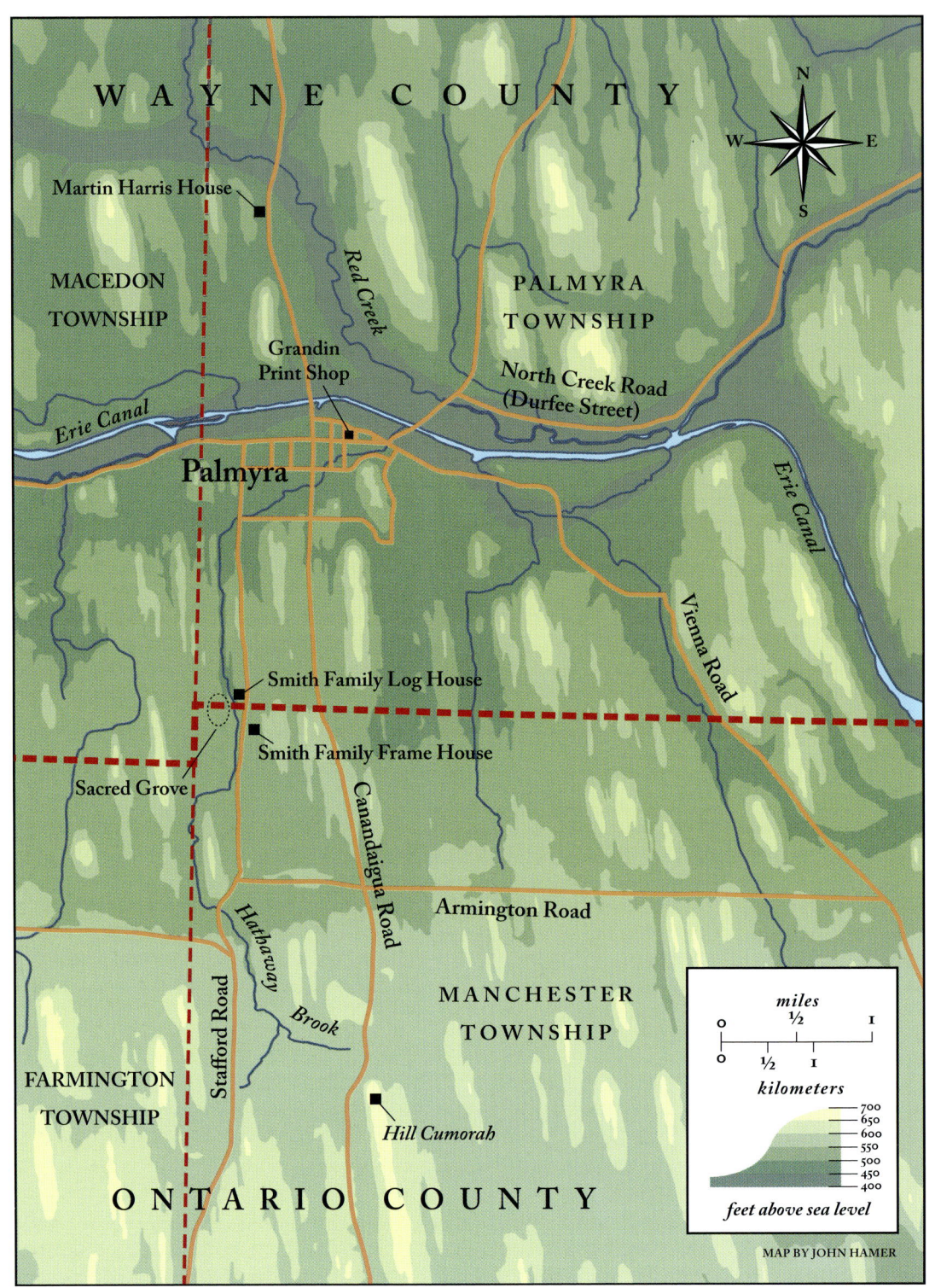

WAYNE COUNTY

Martin Harris House

MACEDON
TOWNSHIP

Red Creek

PALMYRA
TOWNSHIP

Grandin
Print Shop

North Creek Road
(Durfee Street)

Erie Canal

Palmyra

Erie Canal

Vienna Road

Smith Family Log House

Smith Family Frame House

Sacred Grove

Canandaigua Road

Armington Road

Hathaway

Brook

MANCHESTER
TOWNSHIP

Stafford Road

FARMINGTON
TOWNSHIP

Hill Cumorah

ONTARIO COUNTY

miles
0   ½   1

0   ½   1
kilometers

700
650
600
550
500
450
400
feet above sea level

MAP BY JOHN HAMER

Palmyra and Manchester, New York, in the 1820s.

The angel Moroni visited Joseph in the garret of the log house, 21–22 September 1823. Section 2 is an extract from Moroni's words to Joseph on that occasion. Although the words of Moroni in section 2 are commonly thought to have been given in the Manchester frame home, they were actually spoken in the Smiths' Palmyra log house. The Manchester frame home was not occupied by the family until 1825.

Alvin Smith died in the log home on 19 November 1823. Hyrum Smith and Jerusha Barden occupied that same home after their marriage on 2 November 1826, and two daughters were born there. After the Smiths lost title to their farm and the Lemuel Durfee family bought it, Joseph Sr. and Lucy remained in the Manchester frame home for a short time until the spring of 1829, when they moved back to the Palmyra log home and lived with Hyrum. From that log home the Eight Witnesses went into the woods and viewed the gold plates. From there Joseph went to arrange for the printing of the Book of Mormon by Egbert B. Grandin. There Oliver Cowdery copied much, if not all, of the printer's copy of the Book of Mormon from the original manuscript. The manuscript pages of the translated Book of Mormon were then carried to Grandin's Printing Shop in Palmyra village by Oliver Cowdery and Hyrum Smith.

When the Book of Mormon was released for sale at the Grandin Book Store in March 1830, the Prophet and Joseph Knight Sr. journeyed from Harmony, Pennsylvania, to be present. On their way to the Palmyra log home they encountered Martin Harris on the road, concerned over a prospective dearth of sales of the book and making a strong request for a revelation on the matter. He was invited to spend the night with them. Martin was the recipient of that revelation, now recorded in Doctrine and Covenants 19, which was given through the Prophet at the log house in Palmyra Township. Section 19 has previously been identified as having been given in Manchester, but the Smiths had not lived in the Manchester frame home since the spring of 1829. Their log home became the focal point of the Palmyra-Manchester branch after the organization of the Church at Fayette on 6 April 1830. Section 22, revealed on 16 April 1830, and section 23, received in April 1830, were both given to the Prophet in the Palmyra log home rather than at Manchester. The Joseph Smith Sr. family left their Palmyra home in October or November 1830, moving to Seneca County on the Cayuga-Seneca Canal in Seneca Falls Township east of Waterloo. The Hyrum Smith family moved to Colesville, Broome County, New York, where Hyrum presided over the branch. Martin Harris and some fifty members of the Palmyra-Manchester branch left Palmyra for Kirtland, Ohio, on the Erie Canal sometime during the last two weeks of May 1831. *See* maps, pp. 447 and 710.

See also Manchester, New York; New York period.

BIBLIOGRAPHY

Enders, Donald L. "The Joseph Smith, Sr., Family: Farmers of the Genesee." In *Joseph Smith: The Prophet, The Man,* edited by Susan Easton Black and Charles D. Tate, Jr. Provo, Utah: Religious Studies Center, Brigham Young University, 1993.

Gordon, Thomas F. *Gazetteer of the State of New York.* Philadelphia: T. K. and P. G. Collins, 1836.

Jensen, Robin Scott, Robert J. Woodford, and Steven C. Harper, eds. *Manuscript Revelation Books.* Facsimile edition. First volume of the Revelations and Translations series of *The Joseph Smith Papers,* edited by Dean C. Jessee, Ronald K. Esplin, and Richard Lyman Bushman. Salt Lake City: Church Historian's Press, 2009.

Jessee, Dean C. "Joseph Knight's Recollection of Early Mormon History." *BYU Studies* 17, no. 1 (Autumn 1976): 29–30.

Porter, Larry C. "A Study of the Origins of the Church of Jesus Christ of Latter-day Saints in the States of New York and Pennsylvania, 1816–1831." Ph.D. dissertation, Brigham Young University, 1971.

Smith, Lucy Mack. Autobiography and notes, ca. 1850. Vault MSS 230, Handwritten autobiography and miscellaneous notes, L. Tom Perry Special Collections, Brigham Young University.

LCP

Parable(s). *See* Parables in the Doctrine and Covenants.

Parable of the fig tree(s)

A short parable symbolizing the nearness of Christ's second coming and the warning to watch for the signs of that event. The Doctrine and Covenants refers twice to the parable of the fig tree, originally given as part of the Savior's discourse on the MOUNT OF OLIVES, which was recorded in the New Testament (Matt. 24:32–33; Mark 13:28–29; JS-M 1:38–39; Luke 21:29–31) and revealed anew to Joseph Smith.

1. "Ye look and behold the fig trees, and ye see them with your eyes, and ye say when they begin to shoot forth, and their leaves are yet tender, that summer is now nigh at hand; even so it shall be in that day when they shall see all these things, then shall they know that the hour [of the coming of the Son of Man] is nigh" (45:37–38). The fig tree loses its leaves in the winter, and its branches show signs of budding in late winter or early spring, a visual reminder that the warm season (summer) is near. Before the Savior's coming, the elect will recognize the litany of events described in 45:22–36—the gathering of Israel, wars and rumors of wars, the love of men waxing cold, earthquakes and many desolations—and shall "know that he is near, even at the doors" (JS-M 1:39; cf. D&C 45:38). In the midst of these upheavals the disciples are promised, "Be not troubled, for, when all these things shall come to pass, ye may know that the promises which have been made unto you shall be fulfilled" (45:35).

2. Section 35 reveals that the "poor and the meek shall have the gospel preached unto them, and they shall be looking forth for the time of [Christ's] coming, for it is nigh at hand—and they shall learn the parable of the fig tree, for even now already summer is nigh" (35:15–16). Thus, the coming of the fulness of the GOSPEL through Joseph Smith, preached to the poor and the meek (35:17), is here understood to be an important sign that the Second Coming is near, and an integral factor in the interpretation of the parable of the fig tree.

The parable in Joseph Smith–Matthew teaches, "But of that day, and hour, no one knoweth; no, not the angels of God in heaven, but my Father only" (JS-M 1:40). The Prophet Joseph clarified this verse when he taught: "Did Christ speak this as a general principle throughout all generations? Oh no, he spoke in the present tense—no man that was then living upon the footstool of God knew the day or the hour. But he did not say that there was no man throughout all generations that

should not know the day or the hour. No, for this would be in flat contradiction with other scripture, for the prophet says that God will do nothing but what he will reveal unto his servants the prophets. Consequently, if it is not made known to the prophets it will not come to pass" (Ehat and Cook, 180–81; spelling and punctuation modernized).

See also Jesus Christ, second coming of.

BIBLIOGRAPHY

Ehat, Andrew F., and Lyndon W. Cook, comps. and eds. *The Words of Joseph Smith*. Orem, Utah: Grandin Book, 1994.

GS

Parable of the ten virgins

A parable describing the mixed readiness of members of the Church at the second coming of Jesus Christ. The parable of the ten virgins is found in Matthew's record of the Savior's discourse on the Mount of Olives (Matt. 25:1–13); the Doctrine and Covenants refers to it three times (33:17; 45:56–59; 63:53–54) and adds understanding to its interpretation. In Matthew's account, ten virgins (members of the Church) await the coming of the BRIDEGROOM (Christ). When the bridegroom is delayed, five of the virgins exhaust the supply of oil for their lamps and have to go out to buy more. They are away when the bridegroom comes and admits to the wedding the five wise virgins who had sufficient oil. The remaining five, when they return, are refused entrance.

In the Doctrine and Covenants, the Savior teaches that this parable will be fulfilled when "Satan shall be bound, that he shall have no place in the hearts of the children of men. And at that day, when I shall come in my glory, shall the parable be fulfilled which I spake concerning the ten virgins" (45:55–56; cf. JST Matt. 25:1). Until the coming of the Son of Man, however, "there will be foolish virgins among the wise; and at that hour cometh an entire separation of the righteous and the wicked; and in that day will I send mine angels to pluck out the wicked and cast them into unquenchable fire" (63:53–54).

The wise virgins "have received the truth, and have taken the Holy Spirit for their guide, and have not been deceived." As a result, "they shall

Five of Them Were Wise; *painting by Walter Rane. "And at that day, when I shall come in my glory, shall the parable be fulfilled which I spake concerning the ten virgins. For they that are wise and have received the truth, and have taken the Holy Spirit for their guide, and have not been deceived—verily I say unto you, they shall not be hewn down and cast into the fire, but shall abide the day" (D&C 45:56–57).*

not be hewn down and cast into the fire, but shall abide the day" (45:57). The rewards for being wise virgins are described: "The earth shall be given unto them for an inheritance; and they shall multiply and wax strong, and their children shall grow up without sin unto salvation. For the Lord shall be in their midst, and his glory shall be upon them, and he will be their king and their lawgiver" (45:58–59). Therefore the Saints are admonished to "be faithful, praying always, having your lamps trimmed and burning, and oil with you, that you may be ready at the coming of the Bridegroom" (33:17).

See also Bride; Jesus Christ, second coming of; Parable of the fig tree(s).

GS

Parable of the wheat and the tares

An allegory of Jesus from the New Testament (Matt. 13:24–30, 36–43). After a farmer has sown good wheat in his field, an enemy sows the seeds of weeds (tares). When both kinds of plants begin to sprout, the farmer decides they should grow together until the harvest, lest the wheat plants be pulled up and destroyed along with the weeds. "In the time of harvest I will say to the reapers, Gather ye together first the tares, and bind them in bundles to burn them: but gather the wheat into my barn" (Matt. 13:30). When the disciples asked Jesus for an explanation, he said: "The good seed are the children of the kingdom; but the tares are the children of the wicked one; . . . the harvest is the end of the world; and the reapers are the angels." At the end of the world, "all things that offend" and they who "do iniquity" will be gathered out and destroyed (Matt. 13:38–39, 41). Consistent with the revelations in the Doctrine and Covenants, Joseph Smith's translation of the Bible reverses the order of the gathering. First the wheat will be gathered to the safety of the barn, and then the tares will be bound in bundles to be burned (JST Matt. 13:30).

Section 86 places the parable in the context of the ancient apostasy: "The field was the world, and the apostles were the sowers of the seed." After the apostles' time, Satan "soweth the tares; wherefore, the tares choke the wheat and drive the church into the wilderness." But in the last days, "even now while the Lord is

Enemy Sowing Tares; *painting by James Tissot, ca. 1885. "And after they have fallen asleep the great persecutor of the church, the apostate, the whore, even Babylon, that maketh all nations to drink of her cup, in whose hearts the enemy, even Satan, sitteth to reign—behold he soweth the tares; wherefore, the tares choke the wheat and drive the church into the wilderness" (D&C 86:3).*

beginning to bring forth the word . . . the blade is springing up and is yet tender" (86:2–4). The Lord instructs his angels, who are awaiting his command "to gather the tares that they may be burned" (38:12): "Pluck not up the tares while the blade is yet tender (for verily your faith is weak), lest you destroy the wheat also. Therefore, let the wheat and the tares grow together until the harvest is fully ripe." Then the final harvest will begin: "Ye shall first gather out the wheat from among the tares, and after the gathering of the wheat, behold and lo, the tares are bound in bundles, and the field remaineth to be burned" (86:6–7).

Section 88 speaks of the destruction of wickedness at the end of the world. After the testimony of the Lord's servants, the earth will experience the "testimony of earthquakes," "the testimony of the voice of thunderings, . . . lightnings, . . . tempests, and the voice of the waves of the sea heaving themselves beyond their bounds" prior to the Lord's coming (88:89–90). The great and abominable church will be destroyed: "Behold, she is the tares of the earth; she is bound in bundles; her bands are made strong, no man can loose them; therefore, she is ready to be burned" (88:94).

In another revelation, the Lord applied the parable to the gathering that was then already underway: "I must gather together my people, according to the parable of the wheat and the tares, that the wheat may be secured in the garners to possess eternal life, and be crowned with celestial glory . . . while the tares shall be bound in bundles, and their bands made strong, that they may be burned with unquenchable fire" (101:65–66).

See also Apostasy, the great; Historical context and overview of Doctrine and Covenants 86 (p. 790).

KPJ

Parable of the woman and the unjust judge

A modern application (recorded in 101:81–92) of a parable given by the Lord anciently (recorded in Luke 18:1–8). In Doctrine and Covenants 101:81 the Master posed a question, as he often did in New Testament times: "Now, unto what shall I liken the children of Zion?" And he answered: "I will liken them unto the parable of the woman and the unjust judge." Then he explained the purpose of the parable: "For men ought always to pray and not to faint" ("not to faint" means not to give up, not to despair). The parable teaches the importance of perseverance and persistence in prayer.

In the parable a woman petitioned a judge to be avenged of her adversary. After ignoring her for a time, the judge finally acquiesced to help her because of her continual petitions (vv. 82–84).

The Lord likened the parable to the children of Zion, the Saints in Missouri (vv. 85–89). A key verb in the parable is *importune*, which means "to request with urgency; to press with solicitation; to urge with frequent or unceasing application" (Webster, s.v. "importune"). The Saints were to importune for REDRESS of wrongs committed against them in their expulsion from their homes and properties in Jackson County. Specifically, they were to importune unwearyingly at the feet of the judge, then the governor, and then the president. If the president of the United States failed to right the wrongs, then the Lord would "in his fury vex the nation" (v. 89). The prophesied consequences of those political leaders ignoring the injustices and sufferings of the Saints are dire: The Lord, "in his hot displeasure, and in his fierce anger, in his time, will cut off those wicked, unfaithful, and unjust stewards, and appoint them their portion among hypocrites, and unbelievers; even in outer darkness" (vv. 90–91).

The Saints were encouraged to redouble their prayers, importuning the Lord that he soften the hearts of their enemies so that he could be merciful and refrain from inflicting those dreadful consequences upon them (v. 92).

See also Historical context and overview of Doctrine and Covenants 101 (p. 806); Hiding place, the Lord's.

BIBLIOGRAPHY

Webster, Noah. *An American Dictionary of the English Language.* 1828.

DKO

Parable regarding a certain nobleman/vineyard

A parable (recorded in 101:43–62) given to teach the Lord's will "concerning the redemption of Zion" (v. 43). In the parable, a certain nobleman (the Lord) had a choice spot of land in his vineyard (Zion, Jackson County, Missouri), and he instructed his servants (the Saints in Zion) to plant twelve olive trees (the settlements where the Saints lived in Zion) (v. 44).

The Saints in Zion were to set watchmen (Church leaders) round about them and build a tower (a temple) to overlook or keep watch over the land, to be a "watchman upon the tower" to keep the trees from being broken down when the enemy shall come to spoil (a clear foreshadowing of what lay ahead) (v. 45). The watchman "would have seen the enemy while he was yet afar off" (v. 54), but building the temple at that time was made impossible by persecution (124:40–50).

The servants (the Saints) obeyed at first, established their communities and worked to protect them, accepted their watchmen-leaders, and began to build a temple—at least, they revered the site of the temple and had meetings there but were negligent in erecting the temple itself (v. 46).

The Saints' rationalizing, questioning, negligence, divisiveness, and disobedience (vv. 6–8) for more than two years after the dedication of the temple site gave their adversaries the advantage, and they proceeded to "break down" the Saints' settlements and expel them from the lands of their inheritance (vv. 47–51).

The Lord of the vineyard chastened his servants for their neglect, disobedience, and irresponsibility for attempting to establish Zion without the temple and for putting their resources into less important enterprises (vv. 52–54).

The Lord commissioned his servant, Joseph Smith, to gather up the "strength of mine house," young men and middle-aged warriors, and journey to the choice spot of his vineyard and redeem it by force of arms (vv. 55–58). This effort, known as ZION'S CAMP, is explained further in sections 103 and 105. Even then, in 1833, there was potential to "redeem Zion, and establish her waste places, no more to be thrown down, were the churches, who call

themselves after my name, willing to hearken to my voice" (101:75).

The servant (Joseph Smith) inquired of the Lord concerning the redemption of Zion: "When shall these things be?" The divine answer was vague: "When I will." The Prophet and others eventually understood that there would be a long time between Zion's Camp and Zion's redemption: "After many days" all things would be fulfilled (vv. 59–62; cf. 105:37). In fact, the Lord had spoken in an earlier revelation in Zion, Jackson County: "The time has not yet come, for many years, for them to receive their inheritance in this land" (58:44).

See also Historical context and overview of Doctrine and Covenants 101 (p. 806); Hiding place, the Lord's; Parable of the woman and the unjust judge; Zion, redemption of.

DKO

Parable regarding a father and sons

A story or allegory describing equity, justice, and UNITY between a father and his twelve sons. Throughout his mortal ministry, Christ often used parables to teach important principles to his disciples. In this dispensation, parables were again used in the revelations recorded in the Doctrine and Covenants. The first parable is found in 38:26–27 and tells of a man with twelve sons. All of the sons honor and serve their father obediently, and the father is "no respecter of them" (38:26). The question is then asked if the father could still claim to be just were he to give preferential treatment to one or another of his sons. As the parable makes clear, the father, if he were just, would reward each son equally. The parable follows an exhortation for "every man [to] esteem his brother as himself" (38:25). It concludes with the divine injunction to be one, with the warning from the Lord that if Church members are not one, then they "are not mine" (38:27). The parable emphasizes the role of oneness expected among members of the Church as it underscores God's just nature in treating all fairly. The revelation recorded in this section was given at a conference where the Saints were discussing the recent command to "assemble together at the Ohio" (37:3). They were to be unified in their effort to move, assisting each other equitably (38:35). The Saints were further promised that if they moved to Ohio, the Lord would give them his "law," including the law of CONSECRATION (42:30–42). This parable foreshadows the commandment to "be equal" (70:14). The Lord instructed his Saints to "be alike among this people, and receive alike, that ye may be one, even as I have commanded you" (51:9).

DLB

Parable regarding the Lord's visits to kingdoms

A parable attesting to the breadth and reach of our Lord's creative and redemptive labors (88:51–61). Acting under the direction of GOD THE FATHER, JEHOVAH created worlds without number, and his infinite ATONEMENT is as broad as his creation. The Atonement is infinite in the sense that Christ redeems all that he creates (76:22–24; Moses 1:27–35; 7:30; Heb. 1:2; Nelson, 167).

Jesus Christ will visit and allow the inhabitants of the populated worlds to receive "the light of the countenance of their lord, every man in his hour, and in his time, and in his season . . . every man in his own order . . . that his lord might be glorified in him, and he in his lord, that they all might be glorified" (88:58–60).

Elder Orson Pratt explained that during earth's MILLENNIUM, the inhabitants of Zion "will be made glad by the countenance of their Lord for a thousand years, during which the earth will rest. Then what? He withdraws. What for? To fulfill other purposes, for he has other worlds or creations and other sons and daughters, perhaps just as good as those dwelling on this planet, and they, as well as we, will be visited. . . . Thus he will go, in the time and in the season thereof, from kingdom to kingdom or from world to world, causing the pure in heart, the Zion that is taken from these creations [see Moses 7:31], to rejoice in his presence" (17:331–32).

BIBLIOGRAPHY

Nelson, Russell M. *Perfection Pending*. Salt Lake City: Deseret Book, 1998.

Pratt, Orson. *Journal of Discourses*. 26 vols. London: Latter-day Saints' Book Depot, 1854–86.

RLM

Parables in the Doctrine and Covenants

Two of the seven parables in the Doctrine and Covenants are unique to that book of

PARABLES IN THE DOCTRINE AND COVENANTS

PARABLE	D&C REFERENCES	NT REFERENCES	NOTES
Fig tree	45:36–38	Matt. 24:32–33 Mark 13:28–29 Luke 21:29–31	Essentially the same as the NT.
Ten virgins	45:56–57 33:17 63:53–54	Matt. 25:1–13	D&C does not repeat parable but refers to it and gives interpretive information.
Wheat and tares	86:1–7 101:64–66	Matt. 13:24–30, 36–43	D&C assumes knowledge of the parable. Includes portions and gives interpretive information.
Woman and the unjust judge	101:81–92	Luke 18:1–8	Parable retold with application to the Saints' experience in 1833.
Certain nobleman/vineyard	101:43–62 103:21–28	Matt. 21:33–46 Mark 12:1–12 Luke 20:9–18	Similar but with application to the Saints' experience in the early 1830s.
Father and sons	38:26–27	None	Unique to D&C.
Lord's visits to kingdoms	88:51–61	None	Unique to D&C.

scripture; the other five are the same as, or similar to, parables in the New Testament but with specific application to the Saints' circumstances in the 1830s. The accompanying chart identifies each parable by name, cites the Doctrine and Covenants references and the New Testament references where applicable, and notes briefly similarities and differences between the accounts of the parables. For details about each parable, see the separate articles under the names of the parables.

LED

Paradise of God. *See* Spirit world, postmortal.

Parenting. *See* Children; Family, families.

Partridge, Edward

Birth: 27 August 1793, Pittsfield, Berkshire County, Massachusetts

Death: 27 May 1840, Nauvoo, Hancock County, Illinois

Edward Partridge, proprietor of a hat shop in Painesville, Ohio, first learned of the Book of Mormon in the fall of 1830. Wanting to know more, he journeyed to New York with Sidney Rigdon to meet the Prophet Joseph Smith in December 1830. Partridge believed the gospel message and after being baptized by Joseph, he asked the Prophet to seek the Lord's will concerning him. The answer he received was, "You are blessed, and your sins are forgiven you, and you are called to preach my gospel as with the voice of a trump" (36:1).

Partridge was called in Kirtland to be the first bishop of the Church, "and this because his heart is pure before me, for he is like unto Nathanael of old, in whom there is no guile" (41:11). Many of the later references to Edward Partridge in the revelations are related to his duties as a presiding bishop of the Church (42:10; 51; 57:7; 58:14, 24, 62; 60:10; 82:11). Of his calling, he wrote, "I sometimes feel my station is above what I can perform to the acceptance of my Heavenly Father" (6–7).

In 1831 Partridge was called to travel to Missouri with Joseph Smith and others (52:24). He settled in Jackson County that same year and continued to serve as bishop. In July 1833 he recorded that he was "daubed with tar from head to foot, and then had a quantity of feathers put upon me; and all this because I would not agree to leave the county, and my home where I had lived two years." He bore the "abuse with so much resignation and meekness, that it appeared to astound the multitude, who permitted me to retire in silence, many looking very solemn, their sympathies having been touched" (Smith, 1:391).

Partridge also labored as a missionary in Missouri, Illinois, Indiana, and Ohio. He eventually settled in Far West, where soldiers "took logs from a hovel" he had built for his cows and burned them (Partridge, 57). He was taken prisoner in Far West and then moved to the jail in Richmond, where Joseph Smith and other Church leaders awaited trial. Of his incarceration Partridge wrote, "The vilest of the vile did guard us and treat us like dogs; yet we bore our oppressions without murmuring" (52–53). He was released on 18 November 1838. On 25 March 1839 the Prophet wrote from LIBERTY JAIL to the Saints "and to Bishop Partridge in

Edward Partridge, 1793–1840; engraving by H. B. Hall and Sons.

particular" the stirring words contained in sections 121, 122, and 123.

Partridge wrote to Joseph on 13 June 1839 of his afflictions: "I have not at this time two dollars in the world, one dollar and forty-four cents is all. I owe for my rent, and for making clothes for some of the poor. . . . What is best for me to do, I hardly know" (Smith, 3:376). The Prophet's response is not known.

In Nauvoo, Partridge served as bishop of the upper ward; unfortunately, his service was brief. While building a home outside of town and attempting to move furniture, he collapsed from exhaustion; he died in May 1840 at age forty-six. In January 1841 the Lord revealed to Joseph Smith that he had received Bishop Partridge "unto myself" (124:19).

BIBLIOGRAPHY

Partridge, Edward Jr. "Biography and Family Genealogy," 1878. Church History Library, The Church of Jesus Christ of Latter-day Saints, Salt Lake City, Utah.

Smith, Joseph. History of The Church of Jesus Christ of Latter-day Saints. Edited by B. H. Roberts. 7 vols. 2d ed. rev. Salt Lake City: The Church of Jesus Christ of Latter-day Saints, 1932–51.

SEB

Patience

Enduring without murmuring; not easily provoked; calmly diligent; persevering and constant. In many of his calls to labor in his kingdom, the Lord invited his servants to work patiently in their ministries. For example, Joseph Smith Sr. was counseled to cultivate patience along with "faith, virtue, knowledge, temperance . . . brotherly kindness, godliness, charity, humility, [and] diligence" (4:6). Oliver Cowdery was directed to be patient in his role as scribe while working with Joseph Smith (6:19; 9:3). Hyrum Smith was instructed that he should patiently wait for the publication of the Book of Mormon before going forth to preach the gospel (11:19); the newly organized Church was instructed to patiently receive Joseph's revelations (21:5). Joseph Smith (24:8), Thomas B. Marsh (31:9), William E. McLellin (66:9), Newel Knight (54:10), and the Missouri Saints (98:2, 23–26) were all counseled to be patient in their afflictions. Lyman Sherman (108:4), and

William Law (124:88) were counseled to be patient in their ministries. The Lord reminded the Nauvoo Saints to be patient in all the works he had appointed unto them, so that they might not lose their reward (124:4). The Lord enjoined the Saints to "seek the face of the Lord always, that in patience ye may possess your souls" (101:38), and "continue in patience until ye are perfected" (67:13). The Lord commanded the Twelve Apostles and the Seventy to make all their decisions "in all righteousness . . . and long suffering . . . and . . . *patience*" (107:30; emphasis added).

In the Book of Mormon, patience is often combined with the injunction to be long-suffering and characterizes a quality of the Savior's suffering (1 Ne. 19:9; cf. Mosiah 4:6; Alma 9:11).

Elder Neal A. Maxwell noted that patience is "clearly not fatalistic, shoulder-shrugging resignation"; rather, it is "a willingness, in a sense, to watch the unfolding purposes of God with a sense of wonder and awe—rather than pacing up and down within the cell of our circumstance" (28–30).

BIBLIOGRAPHY

Maxwell, Neal A. "Patience." Ensign 10 (October 1980): 28–31.

GP

Patriarch(s)

A term meaning "father." There are two main types of patriarchs in The Church of Jesus Christ of Latter-day Saints: those who are fathers of families, or natural patriarchs, and those who are ordained to the office of patriarch in the Melchizedek PRIESTHOOD, who serve as stake patriarchs. In the scriptures, the ancient prophets and fathers of nations, such as Adam, Noah, and Abraham, are also referred to as patriarchs (Abr. 1:31).

Joseph Smith stated, "An Evangelist is a Patriarch. . . . Wherever the Church of Christ is established in the earth, there should be a Patriarch for the benefit of the posterity of the Saints" (3:381). In earlier dispensations, the kingdom of God was administered through the patriarchal order of the priesthood. "The order of this priesthood was confirmed to be handed down from father to son" and "was instituted in the days of Adam, and came down by lineage." The line of authority in that patriarchal priesthood, from Adam through ten generations to Noah, is given in 107:40–52. From the days of Noah and the Flood to the meridian of time, the kingdom of God was directed by prophets specially called of God. During the Savior's ministry and since the Restoration, the administration of God's kingdom on the earth has been by an ecclesiastical or priesthood order, presided over by a First Presidency, a Quorum of the Twelve Apostles, Seventies, and others, including patriarchs. The requisite priesthood, lines of authority, keys, and duties of all these offices are carefully outlined in the Doctrine and Covenants.

When the Church was much smaller, the Twelve were given the responsibility "to ordain evangelical ministers, as they shall be designated unto them by revelation" (107:39). Today, stake presidents recommend Melchizedek Priesthood holders in their respective stakes to hold the office of patriarch, and after a recommendation is approved by the Twelve (107:39), the stake president is authorized to perform the ordination.

The primary duty of stake patriarchs is to give patriarchal blessings to worthy Church members. In these blessings, the patriarch declares the lineage of the member as pertaining to the house of Israel. As well, "the patriarch, looking into the future, enumerates the blessings and promises, some special, others general, to which the person . . . is entitled" (Widtsoe, 322). Blessings so promised are conditioned upon the member's faithfulness.

Throughout much of this dispensation, in addition to stake patriarchs, there was a patriarch to the Church who was sustained as a general authority. The first such patriarch was Joseph Smith Sr., who was followed by his son Hyrum (124:91–92, 124; 135:1). This office was held primarily by members of the Smith family until 1979, when the office of patriarch to the Church was discontinued "because of the large increase in the number of stake patriarchs and the availability of patriarchal services throughout the world" ("Report," 1).

BIBLIOGRAPHY

"Report of the 149th Semiannual General Conference of The Church of Jesus Christ of Latter-day Saints." *Ensign* 9 (November 1979): 1.

Smith, Joseph. *History of The Church of Jesus Christ of Latter-day Saints.* Edited by B. H. Roberts. 7 vols. 2d ed. rev. Salt Lake City: The Church of Jesus Christ of Latter-day Saints, 1932–51.

Widtsoe, John A. *Evidences and Reconciliations.* Arranged by G. Homer Durham. 3 vols. Salt Lake City: Bookcraft, 1960.

BRM

Patriarchal blessings. *See* Patriarch(s).

Patten, David W.

Birth: 14 November 1799, Theresa, near Indian River Falls, New York

Death: 25 October 1838, Battle of Crooked River, Missouri

David W. Patten learned of the Restoration from his brother John and traveled from Michigan to Indiana to see him and learn more. On the day he heard his first sermon about the Restoration, Patten bore testimony of the message and accepted an invitation for baptism. He was baptized 15 June 1832 by his brother. Thereafter he served a series of missions before moving to Kirtland, Ohio, and then to Clay County, Missouri. Patten was blessed with many gifts of the Spirit—he spoke in tongues, prophesied, saw visions, cast out evil spirits, and enjoyed the gift of healing to a remarkable degree in terms of frequency and success.

While serving a mission in Paris, Tennessee, Patten denounced his detractors "in the most unmeasured terms" and prophesied, "Before you die some of you will see the streets . . . run with the blood of its own citizens" (Wilson, 50). The prophecy was fulfilled when General John Morgan viciously attacked Kentucky and Tennessee in his well-documented raids during the Civil War.

Elder Patten was ordained an apostle on February 15, 1835, and three years later he was appointed to the presidency pro tem of the Church in Missouri. While in that quorum, he withstood mobs and identified the sins of individuals who reviled and opposed his ministerial efforts. Once he threw a man bodily out of the house he was preaching in. As rumors spread, a report of the incident indicated that "Patten had cast out one devil, soul and body" (Jenson, 1:77).

Elder Patten later asked the Prophet Joseph if he could die as a martyr. "The Prophet, greatly moved, expressed extreme sorrow, 'for' . . . 'when a man of your faith asks the Lord for anything, he generally gets it'" (Wilson, 53). In April 1838 Patten was directed by revelation to "settle up all his business as soon as he possibly can, and make a disposition of his merchandise, that he may perform a mission" the following spring (114:1). Six months later, three Latter-day Saints were kidnapped by Missourians. At daybreak on 25 October, "Captain Fear Not," as Patten was known, led a charge, routed the Missourians, and freed the prisoners in the Battle of Crooked River. Several were wounded in the attack, including Patten. While being transported to the nearby community of Far West, he asked to be left to die. Nevertheless, he was carried within a mile of Far West to the home of Stephen Winchester. Patten said to his wife, "Whatever you do else, O do not deny the faith" (Wilson, 69). She heeded his charge and died in Nauvoo "a saint . . . having died *in* the Lord" ("Obituary," 325). Patten said to Church leaders, "I feel that I have kept the faith, I have finished my course" (Wilson, 69). He died that evening. At his funeral, Patten was eulogized by the Prophet Joseph Smith as "a man that has done just as he said he would—he has laid down his life for his friends" (3:175).

In 1841 the Lord declared of Patten: "[He] is with me at this time" and "I have taken [him] unto myself . . . his priesthood no man taketh from him" (124:19, 130). Patten's colleagues in the Twelve held him in high esteem. Heber C. Kimball named a son David Patten Kimball, and Brigham Young approved the naming of an Arizona settlement St. David in honor of Elder Patten.

BIBLIOGRAPHY

Jenson, Andrew. *Latter-day Saints' Biographical Encyclopedia*. 4 vols. Salt Lake City: Western Epics, 1971.

Crooked River, Missouri; photograph by George Edward Anderson, 1907. Apostle David W. Patten was killed here, along with three others, in a skirmish with a mob in October 1838.

"Obituary." *Times and Seasons* 2, no. 3 (15 February 1841): 324–26.

Smith, Joseph. *History of The Church of Jesus Christ of Latter-day Saints.* Edited by B. H. Roberts. 7 vols. 2d ed. rev. Salt Lake City: The Church of Jesus Christ of Latter-day Saints, 1932–51.

Wilson, Lycurgus A. *The Life of David W. Patten.* Salt Lake City: Deseret News Press, 1900.

DFB

Paul

Apostle, missionary, and author of several New Testament epistles. Paul is mentioned in the Doctrine and Covenants in the context of specific commentary on his teachings as well as on his exemplary faithfulness. The six references to him by name all fall into one of these two categories. Numerous other references to his teachings occur as the Lord clarified and shed light on them to the Prophet Joseph Smith. Notable are two instances in which Paul's ministry and sufferings are referred to. The Lord taught Oliver Cowdery and David Whitmer that their calling was the same as Paul's was anciently (18:9). Later, in an epistle to the Saints in Nauvoo, Joseph felt that he could glory in tribulation as Paul had (127:2). Paul is also referred to specifically in regards to his teachings on the relationship between heavenly and earthly likenesses, divisions among those who follow various religious leaders, and salvation for the dead (76:96–99; 128:13–16). There is a large number of references to Paul's teachings in which the apostle's name is not mentioned; the few references that do use his name draw primarily upon his great example of faith in Jesus Christ. Paul faced trials similar to those faced by the early Saints and therefore provides an important biblical example of missionary work in a day of persecution and trial.

See also Paul quotations in the Doctrine and Covenants.

TAW

Paul quotations in the Doctrine and Covenants

A careful reading of the Doctrine and Covenants reveals that many of the phrases and principles in the revelations mirror the writings of Paul. At times the Pauline language appears in inspired writings of the Prophet Joseph Smith (e.g. 137:1; cf. Acts 7:56); at other times the Lord's revealed wording incorporates language common to Paul's writings (e.g. 17:8; cf. 2 Cor. 12:9). Joseph Smith's frequent use of the language of the Pauline epistles in the revelations and in his own epistles preserved in the Doctrine and Covenants indicates that he was intimately familiar with Paul's writings. He drew on them to express some of his innermost feelings, offer doctrinal clarifications, and convey the revelations he had received from the Lord. He relied more heavily on the epistles to the Roman and Corinthian Saints than he did on any of the other writings in the second half of the New Testament (Acts to Revelation), although he also used the book of Revelation extensively.

The accompanying chart contains the most concrete examples of Paul's language that appear in the Doctrine and Covenants using the New Testament language and order. There are other echoes elsewhere in the revelations, but in these examples, even if the text does not match exactly, the wording and concepts from Paul's epistles are unmistakable.

Besides the paraphrases and echoes of Paul's language, a significant number of direct quotations from his letters appear in the Doctrine and Covenants. Some of them are introduced as such, and others are simply quoted without specific identification of their source. These quotations of Paul's writings, unlike those listed previously, are tied more closely to their original Pauline source. In these the original text of Paul's epistle shapes the contours of the discussion in the Doctrine and Covenants. These mainly appear in contexts where the Prophet was seeking further clarification on the writings of Paul, possibly during his own study of the epistles, because most of these references do not correspond to the time he was directly working on the Pauline epistles in his new translation of the Bible. Others may represent the Lord using Pauline teachings as he reveals truth:

• Doctrine and Covenants 27:15–18 reflects Ephesians 6:13–18 with changes that do not appear in the Joseph Smith Translation.

• Doctrine and Covenants 46:11–25 offers

- "Power of God unto salvation" (Rom. 1:16/D&C 68:4)
- "All things work together for good" (Rom. 8:28/D&C 90:24; 98:3; 100:15; 105:40)
- "Vessels of wrath" (Rom. 9:22/D&C 76:33)
- "Patient in tribulation" (Rom. 12:12/D&C 24:8; 31:9; 66:9)
- "Subject unto the higher powers" (Rom. 13:1/D&C 58:22)
- "Fulness of the blessing of the gospel" (Rom. 15:29; cf. D&C 1:23)
- "The weak things of the world" (1 Cor. 1:27/D&C 1:19; 35:13; 124:1; 133:58–59)
- "I have fed you with milk, and not with meat" (1 Cor. 3:2; Heb. 5:12–14/D&C 19:22)
- "Hidden things of darkness" (1 Cor. 4:5/D&C 123:13)
- "Tempted above that ye are able" (1 Cor. 10:13/D&C 64:20)
- "Manifestation of the Spirit" (1 Cor. 12:7/D&C 5:16)
- "Bond or free" (1 Cor. 12:13; Gal. 3:28; Eph. 6:8; Col. 3:11/D&C 24:11; 43:20)
- "Covet earnestly the best gifts" (1 Cor. 12:31/D&C 46:8)
- "For one star differeth from another star in glory" (1 Cor. 15:41/D&C 76:81, 98)
- "A great door and effectual is opened unto me" (1 Cor. 16:9/D&C 100:3; 112:19; 118:3)
- "Not lawful for a man to utter" (2 Cor. 12:4/D&C 76:115)
- "My grace is sufficient for thee" (2 Cor. 12:9/D&C 17:8; 18:31)
- "Fulness of times" (Eph. 1:10/D&C 27:13; 76:106; 112:30; 121:31; 124:41; 128:18, 20; 138:48, 53)
- "Sealed with that holy Spirit of promise" (Eph. 1:13/D&C 76:53; 124:124; 132:7, 18–19, 26)
- "Sealed unto the day of redemption" (Eph. 4:30/D&C 124:124; 132:26)
- "Whole armour" (Eph. 6:11, 13/D&C 27:15)
- "Your feet shod with the preparation of the gospel of peace" (Eph. 6:15/D&C 27:16; cf. 112:7)
- "Fiery darts of the wicked" (Eph. 6:16/D&C 3:8; 27:17)
- "Thrones, or dominions, or principalities, or powers" (Col. 1:16/D&C 121:29; 132:13, 19)
- "With the trump of God . . . shall be caught up together with them in the clouds" (1 Thes. 4:16–17/D&C 88:96–98; 109:75)
- "As a thief in the night" (1 Thes. 5:2/D&C 45:19; 106:4)
- "Giving heed to seducing spirits, and doctrines of devils" (1 Tim. 4:1/D&C 46:7)
- "Crown of righteousness" (2 Tim. 4:8/D&C 25:15; 29:13)
- "The general assembly and church of the firstborn" (Heb. 12:23/D&C 76:54, 67, 71, 94, 102; 77:11; 78:21; 88:5; 93:22; 107:19)

commentary and clarification of Paul's list of the gifts of the Spirit in 1 Corinthians 12:4–11. In both passages, the same order is followed in listing the gifts; the Doctrine and Covenants expands and refines Paul's descriptions of the gifts (cf. Moro. 10:8–19).

• Doctrine and Covenants 74:1 quotes 1 Corinthians 7:14. Doctrine and Covenants 74:2–7 offers commentary on Paul's original meaning.

• Doctrine and Covenants 76:71, 78, 81, and 96–98 quote from and offer an inspired expansion of 1 Corinthians 15:40–42.

• Doctrine and Covenants 76:99–101 references 1 Corinthians 1:12 and 3:22, clarifying meaning.

• Doctrine and Covenants 88 is replete with Pauline wording and imagery found in 1 Corinthians 15. Specifically, the key phrases are the "celestial" (88:2, 4, 18, 20, 22, 25, 28–29/1 Cor. 15:40), and the "terrestrial" (88:21, 23, 30/1 Cor. 15:40) kingdoms.

• Doctrine and Covenants 121:28 comments upon 1 Corinthians 8:5 and declares that in time the full meaning of that verse will be revealed.

• Doctrine and Covenants 127:2 draws upon Paul's expression in Romans 5:3 about glorying in tribulation.

• Doctrine and Covenants 128:13–14 quotes 1 Corinthians 15:46–48 word for word as it appears in the King James Version of the Bible (though the wording of v. 46 had been previously changed in the Joseph Smith Translation) and then offers inspired commentary.

• Doctrine and Covenants 128:15 quotes Hebrews 11:40, using wording that is slightly different from that of both the King James Version and the Joseph Smith Translation.

• Doctrine and Covenants 128:16–18 quotes 1 Corinthians 15:29 exactly as it appears in the King James Version of the Bible and then offers inspired commentary.

• Doctrine and Covenants 137:1 draws directly upon 2 Corinthians 12:3 ("whether in the body, or out of the body, I cannot tell") as the Prophet Joseph Smith described a vision in which he saw his deceased brother Alvin.

Clearly Joseph Smith was familiar with the language of Paul. Furthermore, both Paul and Joseph Smith received revelation from the Holy Ghost and taught truths of the gospel, often in a common language.

See also Doctrine and Covenants, what it says about the Bible.

TAW

Pavilion. *See* Appendix E.

Peace

Condition of calm, restful quiet, or tranquility. Two kinds of peace are mentioned: freedom from civil disturbance and freedom from spiritual disturbance. Of civil peace, early Church leaders wrote that governments need laws securing rights in order to "exist in peace" (134:2) and that for the public peace all citizens should help bring offenders of good laws to punishment (134:8). Latter-day Saints should "renounce war and proclaim peace" (98:16); "lift a standard of peace" (98:34); "lift up an ensign of peace, and make a proclamation of peace" (105:39); and "sue for peace" (meaning pursue peace; 105:38).

Multiple sources discuss spiritual peace. Although all men are warned that "the day speedily cometh . . . when peace shall be taken from the earth" (1:35), generally the message of the Savior and the prophets is "the gospel of peace" (27:16), or in other words, the good news or glad tidings of peace. *See* Gospel, the.

CHARITY creates a "bond of perfectness and peace" (88:125). The HOLY GHOST teaches the "peaceable things of the kingdom" (36:2), and those "peaceable things" bring JOY and life eternal (42:61). Workers of righteousness receive the reward of "peace in this world, and eternal life in the world to come" (59:23). When making decisions of what to do, what to say, and where to go, one may have the right conclusion "signalized" to one by "the peace and power" of God's Spirit (111:8). The Lord said to Oliver Cowdery, "Did I not speak peace to your mind concerning the matter?" (6:23), and to Joseph Smith, "My son, peace be unto thy soul" (121:7); a calm assurance that all was in God's hands. God is full of peace (84:102), so his disciples may also be full of peace; "you shall have peace in me" (19:23), for he is the source, being the Prince of Peace. It is possible to "[sleep] in peace" (45:46), that is, to continue on after death with the promise of the Lord's perfect redemption. The righteous in the spirit world live in peace (138:22). The NEW JERUSALEM is called "a land of peace" (45:66), as was Melchizedek's city: *Salem* or *shalem* means "Peace."

The idiomatic expression "hold your peace" (10:37; 11:22) means to cease to speak about; to patiently wait to proceed.

See also Rest.

DKO

Pearls cast before swine

A biblical phrase, repeated in the Doctrine and Covenants, referring to giving "the things which belong to the children of the kingdom," especially the truths of God's law, "to them that are not worthy" (41:5–6). On 4 February 1831, the Prophet Joseph Smith received a revelation promising "ye shall receive my law, that ye may know how to govern my church and have all things right before me" (41:3). Of this promised revelation, the Lord declared, "He that receiveth my law and doeth it, the same is my disciple; and he that saith he receiveth it and doeth it not, the same is not my disciple" (41:5). Drawing upon the language of the Sermon on the Mount (cf. Matt. 7:6), he compared delivering the law to those who were unworthy as giving it "to dogs, or the pearls to be cast before swine" (41:6). In the biblical account, those designated as "dogs" and "swine" remain unclear, although the text points to a division between believers and unbelievers (LDS Bible Dictionary, s.v. "dog" and "swine"). Joseph Smith's translation of the Bible compares the "pearls" in Matthew 7:6 to "the mysteries of the kingdom" (JST Matt. 7:10).

In the revelation recorded as section 41, the Lord offered subtle commentary upon the biblical passage and a clarification of it. He taught that those who receive his law but will not do it are not his disciples and are to be "cast out from among you; for it is not meet that the things which belong to the children of the kingdom should be given to them that are not worthy" (41:5–6). This expanded context may include other members of the kingdom who are not "worthy" rather than limiting the application to members and nonmembers.

TAW

Pentecost, day of

One of the three major Israelite feasts prescribed in the LAW OF MOSES, in addition to Passover and Tabernacles (cf. Ex. 23:14–17). Also called Shavuot (Hebrew, "weeks"), Pentecost (Greek, "fiftieth") took place seven weeks, or fifty days, after Passover, in celebration of the grain harvest (cf. Lev. 23:15–16; Deut. 16:16). In ancient Israel, Pentecost festivities included making various sacrifices of animals and grain offerings and observing the day as a holy day, abstaining from "servile work" (Lev. 23:21; cf. vv. 15–20). After the Savior's resurrection, he promised his disciples that they soon would be endowed "with power from on high" (Luke 24:49; Acts 1:1–5). After the Savior's resurrection and ascension, the disciples gathered in Jerusalem for Pentecost, where they received powerful manifestations of the Holy Spirit, including the sound of "a rushing mighty wind," the appearance of "cloven tongues like as of fire," and the ability "to speak with other tongues" (Acts 2:1–4).

One passage in the Doctrine and Covenants refers to the day of Pentecost. In the dedicatory prayer of the Kirtland Temple (1836), the Prophet Joseph Smith asked the Lord to endow his "ministers . . . with power from on high . . . as upon those on the day of Pentecost" (109:35–36). Years earlier, in December 1830 and January 1831 (37–38) the Lord had commanded the Saints to move from New York to Ohio and to build a temple, promising to endow them "with power from on high," and instructing them "to tarry, even as mine apostles at Jerusalem," awaiting the promise to be fulfilled (38:32; 95:8–9; cf. Acts 1:4). For several weeks before, during, and after the dedication of the Kirtland Temple, these Pentecostal promises were fulfilled in marvelous and dramatic fashion (Backman, 284–309; Harper, 327–71).

See also Kirtland Temple dedication.

BIBLIOGRAPHY

Backman, Milton V., Jr. *The Heavens Resound: A History of the Latter-day Saints in Ohio, 1830–1838.* Salt Lake City: Deseret Book, 1983.

Harper, Steven C. "'A Pentecost and Endowment Indeed': Six Eyewitness Accounts of the Kirtland Temple Experience." In *Opening the Heavens: Accounts of Divine Manifestations, 1820–1844,* edited by John W. Welch. Salt Lake City: Deseret Book, 2005.

FFJ

Perdition. *See* Satan.

Perfect, just men made. *See* Just men made perfect.

Perfect, perfection

Without flaw, correct in every detail, complete, ideal, unerring; in a spiritual context, sanctified, made whole, fully justified. The principle of perfection appears dozens of times in the Doctrine and Covenants in references to the Savior and his work, to the promise of eventual perfection of the Saints, and to the process of achieving perfection.

The Savior and his work

Perfection of God's children, exaltation in the celestial kingdom of God, is made possible only "through Jesus the mediator of the new covenant, who wrought out this *perfect atonement* through the shedding of his own blood" (76:69; emphasis added). At the end of the Millennium, "when Christ shall have subdued all enemies under his feet, and shall have *perfected his work* . . . he shall deliver up the kingdom, and present it unto the Father, spotless, saying: I have overcome and have trodden the wine-press alone, even the wine-press of the fierceness of the wrath of Almighty God. Then shall he be crowned with the crown of his glory, to sit on the throne of his power . . . forever and ever" (76:106–8; emphasis added).

The Savior's work for the salvation of mankind will not be done until "a whole and complete and *perfect* union, and welding together of dispensations, and keys, and powers, and glories should take place, and be revealed from the days of Adam even to the present time" and beyond, until every soul who lived on this earth and who desires salvation has had the

saving ORDINANCES performed for him (128:18; emphasis added). President Brigham Young taught: "When shall we receive our inheritances so that we can say they are our own? When the Savior has completed the work, when the faithful Saints have preached the Gospel to the last of the spirits who have lived here and who are designed to come to this earth; when the thousand years of rest shall come and thousands and thousands of Temples shall be built, and the servants and handmaids of the Lord shall have entered therein and officiated for themselves, and for their dead friends back to the days of Adam; when the last of the spirits in prison who will receive the Gospel has received it . . . then and not till then, will the Saints receive their everlasting inheritances" (17:117).

Perfection of the Saints

Teachings in the revelations confirm that mankind can be "made" perfect. For example, in writing about baptism for the dead, Joseph Smith taught, "Their salvation is necessary and essential to our salvation, as Paul says concerning the fathers—that they without us cannot *be made perfect*—neither can we without our dead *be made perfect*" (128:15, 18; emphasis added). The Lord counseled the early Saints to "continue in patience until ye are *perfected*" (67:13; emphasis added). In January 1841, the Lord revealed that he provided the officers of the Church, from the First Presidency to the deacons quorums, "for the work of the ministry and the *perfecting* of my saints" (124:123–44; emphasis added). In explaining the requirements to enter the various kingdoms of glory, the Lord made clear that those who enter the celestial kingdom must abide the celestial law, saying, "That which is governed by law is also preserved by law and *perfected* and sanctified by the same" (88:34; emphasis added).

Working toward perfection

The Lord gave the Saints much instruction concerning how they were to keep their ministry, Church practices, instruction, and personal lives progressing toward perfection. For example, through temple worship and participation in the School of the Prophets, they could be "*perfected* in their ministry for the salvation of Zion, and of the nations of Israel, and of the Gentiles, as many as will believe" (90:7–8; cf. 88:84; 97:13–14; emphasis added). In order for the Church to function properly, "that the system may be kept *perfect*," the Lord commanded, "Let every man stand in his own office, and labor in his own calling; and let not the head say unto the feet it hath no need of the feet; for without the feet how shall the body . . . stand? . . . The body hath need of every member, that all may be edified together" (84:109–10; emphasis added). Effective teaching and learning are critical in striving toward perfection. The Lord commanded, "Teach ye diligently and my grace shall attend you, that you may be instructed *more perfectly* in theory, in principle, in doctrine, in the law of the gospel, in all things that pertain unto the kingdom of God, that are expedient for you to understand; . . . that ye may be prepared . . . when I shall send you . . . out to testify and warn the people" (88:78–83; emphasis added). After the Saints were expelled from Jackson County, Missouri, in 1833, the Lord revealed that the redemption of Zion would have to "wait for a little season," that the Saints "may be prepared, and that my people may be taught *more perfectly*, and have experience, and know *more perfectly* concerning their duty, and the things which I require at their hands" (105:9–10; emphasis added). The term *more perfectly* suggests a continuum toward ultimate perfection. That principle is illustrated in the Lord's promise: "That which is of God is light; and he that receiveth light, and continueth in God, receiveth more light; and that light groweth brighter and brighter until the *perfect* day" (50:24; emphasis added).

Perfection in one's personal life is achieved only through the ATONEMENT of JESUS CHRIST which makes just men perfect (76:69). Through the GRACE and MERCY of God, the children of God can grow up to become like their Father in Heaven; they can become perfect as he is perfect (Matt. 5:48). Perfection is both a journey and a destination for those who qualify for exaltation in the celestial kingdom. Though there are practices the Saints can perfect in this life (59:13–14), the Prophet Joseph Smith taught that "it will be a great work to learn our salvation and exaltation even beyond the grave" (6:307). The Lord's promises are sure. Through the Father's merciful plan of salvation, made operational through the sacrifice of his Only Begotten Son Jesus Christ, OBEDIENCE to the laws and ordinances of the GOSPEL enable ETERNAL LIFE and perfection. All who "come unto Christ" can be "perfected in him" (Moro. 10:32–33; cf. 107:43).

See also Gods; Just men made perfect; Life, purposes of.

BIBLIOGRAPHY

Smith, Joseph. *History of The Church of Jesus Christ of Latter-day Saints.* Edited by B. H. Roberts. 7 vols. 2d ed. rev. Salt Lake City: The Church of Jesus Christ of Latter-day Saints, 1932–51.

Young, Brigham. *Journal of Discourses.* 26 vols. London: Latter-day Saints' Book Depot, 1854–86.

LED

Perrysburg, New York

Location where Doctrine and Covenants 100 was received. During October 1833, Joseph Smith and Sidney Rigdon went on a missionary journey "to the east, and to Canada." While the Prophet and Sidney were staying at the home of Freeman Nickerson in the Perrysburg area, the Lord revealed section 100 in response to Joseph's and Sidney's concern about their families back in Kirtland (100, headnote; Smith, 1:416–22).

Perrysburg Township, Cattaraugus County, was taken from Olean and Ischua townships on 13 April 1814. It is twenty miles northwest of the village of Ellicottville, the county seat. Between 1829 and 1831 Freeman Nickerson's family acquired some 573 acres in Perrysburg Township, which included most of what became the community of South Dayton. A branch of the Church was organized in the Nickerson home in 1833. Today the village of South Dayton is in Dayton Township, which was divided from Perrysburg on 7 February 1835. *See* map, p. 447.

BIBLIOGRAPHY

Adams, William, ed. *Historical Gazetteer and Biographical Memorial of Cattaraugus County, N. Y.* Syracuse: Lyman, Horton & Co., Limited, 1893.

Gordon, Thomas F. *Gazetteer of the State of New York.* Philadelphia: T. K. and P. G. Collins, Printers, 1836.

Smith, Joseph. *History of The Church of Jesus Christ of Latter-day Saints.* Edited by B. H. Roberts. 7 vols. 2d ed. rev. Salt Lake City: The Church of Jesus Christ of Latter-day Saints, 1932–51.

South Dayton [NY] News, August 16, 1906.

LCP

Persecution(s)

Trial, opposition, or suffering, especially because of one's commitment to the gospel. "It always has been when a man was sent of God with the priesthood and he began to preach the fullness of the gospel," declared the Prophet Joseph Smith, "that he was thrust out by his friends, who are ready to butcher him if he teach things which they imagine to be wrong; and Jesus was crucified upon this principle" (5:425). The scriptures are replete with examples of righteous men and women who were persecuted because of their religious beliefs and their efforts in proclaiming the gospel. "Blessed are they which are persecuted for righteousness' sake," Jesus taught in the Sermon on the Mount. "Blessed are ye, when men shall revile you, and persecute you, and shall say all manner of evil against you falsely, for my sake. Rejoice, and be exceeding glad: for great is your reward in heaven: for so persecuted they the prophets which were before you" (Matt. 5:10–12). Likewise, suffering persecution due to religious belief is a prominent feature of the historical landscape of The Church of Jesus Christ of Latter-day Saints, and several revelations in the Doctrine and Covenants deal directly with such persecution.

The headnote to section 98 declares that this revelation "came in consequence of the persecution upon the Saints in Missouri." In section 99 the Lord directed John Murdock to go to the eastern states "to proclaim mine everlasting gospel unto the inhabitants thereof, in the midst of persecution and wickedness" (v. 1). Section 101 addressed the serious persecution members of the Church were experiencing in Missouri. In that revelation, the Lord declared: "And all they who suffer persecution for my name, and endure in faith, though they are called to lay down their lives for my sake yet shall they partake of all this glory. Wherefore, fear not even

unto death; for in this world your joy is not full, but in me your joy is full. Therefore, care not for the body, neither the life of the body; but care for the soul, and for the life of the soul" (vv. 35–37). Although the Lord reserves special rewards for those who faithfully endure persecution, even unto death, persecution is not desirable in and of itself, nor should disciples actively seek after it. The blessings and glory promised do not come just because one is persecuted but rather in consequence of faithful endurance and unwavering righteousness. Although followers of Christ do not seek persecution, they should not fear it. As indicated in the example of James Covill, "fear of persecution" can prevent complete consecration to the kingdom of God (40:2).

Although Joseph Smith understood persecution would be a lifetime companion, he pleaded with the Lord at the dedication of the Kirtland Temple to be mindful of his own plight and to give him strength to faithfully endure. In that dedicatory prayer, he also prayed that God would likewise strengthen the suffering and persecuted Saints and "confound, and astonish, and . . . bring to shame" those who persecute the Church (109:24–34, 46–53, 68). Persecution and opposition adversely affected work on the Nauvoo Temple. While hiding from his "oppressors" (127:3), the Prophet wrote an epistle to the Church and declared: "And again, verily thus saith the Lord: Let the work of my temple, and all the works which I have appointed unto you, be continued on and not cease; and let your diligence, and your perseverance, and patience, and your works be redoubled, and you shall in nowise lose your reward, saith the Lord of Hosts. And if they persecute you, so persecuted they the prophets and righteous men that were before you. For all this there is a reward in heaven" (127:4). *See* Historical context and overview of Doctrine and Covenants 127 (p. 842).

Persecution, however persistent and however painful, will never destroy the work of God, and it need not destroy one's faith and devotion. Joseph Smith declared: "If a man stands and opposes the world of sin, he may expect to have all wicked and corrupt spirits arrayed against him.

But it will be but a little season, and all these afflictions will be turned away from us, inasmuch as we are faithful, and are not overcome by these evils. By seeing the blessings of the endowment rolling on, and the kingdom increasing and spreading from sea to sea, we shall rejoice that we were not overcome by these foolish things" (5:141).

See also Affliction(s); Historical context and overview of Doctrine and Covenants 123 (p. 836); Martyrdom of Joseph and Hyrum Smith; Missouri period; Trial, tried, try.

BIBLIOGRAPHY

Smith, Joseph. *History of The Church of Jesus Christ of Latter-day Saints.* Edited by B. H. Roberts. 7 vols. 2d ed. rev. Salt Lake City: The Church of Jesus Christ of Latter-day Saints, 1932–51.

BLT

Persons, no respecter of. *See* No respecter of persons.

Persuasions of men

Arguments or influence of mortals as compared to the counsels of God.

Martin Harris was a financial benefactor and friend of Joseph Smith and also twenty years older than Joseph. Thus, when Martin pleaded with twenty-two-year-old Joseph to allow him to show the 116 pages of Book of Mormon translation to his skeptical wife, it must have been difficult for Joseph to deny his friend's petition, despite initial refusals from the Lord. Allowing Joseph to experience a painful lesson, the Lord gave permission upon the third request but with strict instructions regarding the care of the manuscript (Smith, 1:21). Martin Harris did not follow the instructions, and the manuscript was lost. The Lord chastised Joseph for heeding "the persuasions of men. For, behold, you should not have feared man more than God" (3:6–7). In section 5 Joseph was again commanded "to yield to the persuasions of men no more" and to "be firm in keeping the commandments" (5:21–22). Joseph's painful experience undoubtedly taught him that he could not be true to God unless he was able to resist pressure from foes and friends alike. *See* Book of Mormon, lost manuscript of (116 pages).

Similarly the Lord reproved David Whitmer for failing to give "heed unto my Spirit, and to those who were set over you, but have been persuaded by those whom I have not commanded" (30:1–2).

BIBLIOGRAPHY

Smith, Joseph. *History of The Church of Jesus Christ of Latter-day Saints.* Edited by B. H. Roberts. 7 vols. 2d ed. rev. Salt Lake City: The Church of Jesus Christ of Latter-day Saints, 1932–51.

RIE

Perverse. *See* Appendix E.

Peter

Chief apostle of Jesus Christ in the New Testament, and in company with James and John restored the Melchizedek Priesthood and its keys to Joseph Smith and Oliver Cowdery. Peter is mentioned six times in the Doctrine and Covenants and many times in Joseph Smith's teachings. Most references to Peter in latter-day revelation are related to priesthood, both to his own calling and to his role in the restoration of priesthood and its keys.

John the Baptist told Joseph and Oliver that Peter, James, and John held the keys of the Melchizedek Priesthood, which would be conferred upon them (JS–H 1:72). Doctrine and Covenants 27:12 affirms that Joseph and Oliver had been ordained apostles and "especial witnesses" by Peter, James, and John.

In an epistle to the Church (6 September 1842), Joseph Smith quoted Jesus' promise to give Peter the keys of the kingdom (128:10) and also that Peter, James, and John declared to him (Joseph) that they possessed the "keys of the kingdom, and of the dispensation of the fulness of times!" (128:20). The Prophet explained: "The Savior, Moses, and Elias, gave the keys to Peter, James, and John, on the mount. . . . How have we come at the Priesthood in the last days? It came down, in regular succession. Peter, James, and John had it given to them and they gave it to others" (3:387).

Doctrine and Covenants 49:11–14 affirms Peter's teachings of faith in Christ, repentance, baptism in water, and the laying on of hands for the Holy Ghost (cf. Acts 2:37–38);

7:1–8 recounts a conversation between Jesus, John, and Peter, adding details not preserved in the biblical account (cf. John 21:20–25); and 138:5–10 recites Peter's teachings of Jesus' ministry in the postmortal spirit world (1 Pet. 3:18–20; 4:6), which eventually led to the revelation recorded in section 138.

See also Priesthood, restoration of priesthood and priesthood keys.

BIBLIOGRAPHY

Smith, Joseph. *History of The Church of Jesus Christ of Latter-day Saints.* Edited by B. H. Roberts. 7 vols. 2d ed. rev. Salt Lake City: The Church of Jesus Christ of Latter-day Saints, 1932–51.

RJM

Peterson, Ziba

Birth: Unknown

Death: 1849, Placerville, Eldorado County, California

Ziba Peterson, baptized into the Church on 18 April 1830, is mentioned in Doctrine and Covenants 32 and 58. In section 32, Peterson was commanded to join Parley P. Pratt, Oliver Cowdery, and Peter Whitmer Jr. on a mission "into the wilderness among the Lamanites" (32:1–3). They were promised that the Lord would "go with them and be in their midst" and that "nothing [would] prevail against them" (32:3). This mission led Peterson and his companions to the Catteraugus tribe in New York, where they were "kindly received,"and then to the Wyandots in Sandusky, Ohio (JH, 8). Notably, this mission also resulted in the conversion of Pastor Sidney Rigdon and much of his congregation, which had spread across several counties in northeastern Ohio, including Kirtland (JH, 7). Rigdon accepted a copy of the Book of Mormon from the missionaries and within two weeks declared that he was ready for baptism (Smith, 1:124–25).

In section 58, the record of a revelation given on 1 August 1831, Peterson was chastened "for all his sins; for he confesseth them not, and he thinketh to hide them" (v. 60). Three days later he confessed his transgression, "which was satisfactory to the Church as approved by unanimous vote" (Cannon and Cook, 9). He left the Church in May 1833 and was excommunicated 25 June 1833.

In 1848 Peterson moved his family to a mining town in California called "Dry Diggins," later known as Hangtown and still later as Placerville. He passed away a short time after moving there.

BIBLIOGRAPHY

Cannon, Donald Q., and Lyndon W. Cook, eds. *Far West Record: Minutes of The Church of Jesus Christ of Latter-day Saints, 1830–1844.* Salt Lake City: Deseret Book, 1983.

Journal History of the Church, October 1830. Church History Library, The Church of Jesus Christ of Latter-day Saints, Salt Lake City, Utah.

Smith, Joseph. *History of The Church of Jesus Christ of Latter-day Saints.* Edited by B. H. Roberts. 7 vols. 2d ed. rev. Salt Lake City: The Church of Jesus Christ of Latter-day Saints, 1932–51.

ZLL

Pharaoh. *See* Egypt.

Phelps, William W.

Birth: 17 February 1792, Hanover, Morris County, New Jersey

Death: 7 March 1872, Salt Lake City, Salt Lake County, Utah

William W. and his wife, Stella (Sally) Waterman Phelps, were looking for a church like the one established by Jesus in the New Testament. When they had been married five years, Phelps purchased a Book of Mormon from Parley P. Pratt on 9 April 1830. That night William and Sally stayed up comparing the Book of Mormon to the Holy Bible, and by daybreak William declared, "I am going to join that church; I am convinced that it is true" (Bowen, 23).

As a newspaper editor in New York state, Phelps started the *Western Currier* at Homer, edited the *Lake Light* in Turnansburg, and in the 1820s the *Ontario Phoenix.* To keep the editor "from joining the Mormons," two Presbyterians had him arrested. Within six months Phelps left his printing establishment and moved to Kirtland, Ohio, where he wrote, "Now, notwithstanding my body was not baptized into this church till Thursday the [16th] of June, 1831, yet my heart was there from the time I became acquainted with the book of Mormon . . . and

Courtesy Church History Library

William W. Phelps, 1792–1872.

when I for the first time, held a conversation with our beloved brother Joseph" (*MA*, 96).

After being baptized and being ordained an elder, he was called to preach the gospel, promised the "power to give the Holy Spirit," and called to assist Oliver Cowdery in writing "books for schools in this church" (55:1–4; Smith, 1:184–85).

Phelps went to Missouri with Joseph Smith and Sidney Rigdon, where it was revealed to the Prophet that Phelps should "be planted in this place, and be established as a printer unto the church" (57:11). Phelps was promised an inheritance in the land of Zion but was warned about his desire to excel and his lack of meekness (58:40–41). On their way home from Missouri to Kirtland, Phelps "in daylight vision, saw the destroyer riding in power on the face of the waters" (61, headnote). *See* Historical context and overview of Doctrine and Covenants 61 (p. 767); Waters.

Obedient to the Lord's instructions, he moved to Jackson County, Missouri (57:11–12),

where he published the Church newspaper, *The Evening and the Morning Star*. In 1832 he received a letter from the Prophet, an excerpt of which is contained in section 85. As one of several men appointed by the Lord "to be stewards over the revelations and commandments" (70:1–5), Phelps obtained from Oliver Cowdery and John Whitmer manuscript copies of the revelations to be published (67, headnote) and began printing the Book of Commandments. On 20 July 1833, his printing press was destroyed by a mob. *See* Doctrine and Covenants, historical development of; Missouri period.

David Whitmer served as president of the Church in Missouri from 1834 to 1838; W. W. Phelps and John Whitmer were his counselors. All three were rejected at Far West in February 1838 because of questionable financial dealings, and they were subsequently excommunicated (Smith, 3:3–8, 19). Phelps was received back into fellowship in early 1841; he wrote the Prophet Joseph a letter of apology and confession. When the Saints at Quincy resolved unanimously to receive Brother Phelps back into fellowship, Joseph wrote, "I shall be happy once again to give you the right hand of fellowship, and rejoice over the returning prodigal," concluding his letter with the couplet: "Come on, dear brother, since the war is past, / For friends at first, are friends again at last" (4:162–64). Phelps moved to Nauvoo, where he assisted in the publication of two Church newspapers, the *Times and Seasons* and *The Nauvoo Neighbor*. He also served as a clerk and scribe to Joseph Smith. W. W. Phelps was invited to speak at Joseph Smith's funeral (Smith, 7:134).

Phelps left Nauvoo with the Saints in 1846 and resided in Winter Quarters for a time before journeying to the Salt Lake Valley by 1849. He was a faithful pioneer, member of the legislative assembly of the Territory of Utah, chief engineer and surveyor general of the Great Salt Lake Valley, speaker of the state house of representatives, and member of the board of regents for the University of Deseret. In his later years, Phelps served as an ordinance worker in the ENDOWMENT HOUSE on Temple Square.

Phelps is probably best known for composing many Latter-day Saint hymns, including twenty-nine of the ninety hymns Emma Smith selected for the 1835 hymnal. His hymn "The Spirit of God" was sung at the KIRTLAND TEMPLE DEDICATION. For many years the Tabernacle Choir has opened their weekly broadcast with Phelps's hymn "Gently Raise the Sacred Strain." He died at age eighty and was buried in Salt Lake City.

BIBLIOGRAPHY

Bowen, Walter Dean. "The Versatile W. W. Phelps—Mormon Writer, Educator, Pioneer." Master's thesis, Brigham Young University, August 1958.

Latter-day Saints' Messenger and Advocate 1, no. 7 (April 1835): 96.

Smith, Joseph. *History of The Church of Jesus Christ of Latter-day Saints.* Edited by B. H. Roberts. 7 vols. 2d ed. rev. Salt Lake City: The Church of Jesus Christ of Latter-day Saints, 1932–51.

RHM

Pillar of fire. *See* Fire.

Pillar of heaven

That which upholds, supports, or sustains heaven, perhaps referring to either the eternal laws and principles, or to persons abiding those laws and principles, or both, that make heaven what it is. The scriptures also use the word *pillar* in association with different qualifiers, all signifying, as does the phrase "pillar of heaven," miraculous conduits through which the power, glory, and presence of God are manifested and where a conjoining of heaven and earth occurs: "pillar of fire" (29:12; 1 Ne. 1:6; Hel. 5:24, 43), "pillar of light" (JS–H 1:16), and "pillar of a cloud" (Ex. 13:21; cf. D&C 34:7; 45:45; 76:102; 84:5; 109:75; JS–H 1:68).

"Pillar of heaven" (singular) occurs just once in all scripture, and that is in the Doctrine and Covenants, wherein the Lord promises that at his second coming the righteous on the earth and in their graves "shall be caught up to meet him in the midst of the pillar of heaven" (88:96–97). These souls are designated as "Christ's, the first fruits" (88:98). Such are members of "the church of the Firstborn" (76:54, 67; 78:21), and are caught up to "dwell in the presence of God and his Christ forever and ever" (76:62), thereby uniting heaven and earth. To dwell in the "midst of" the Father and the Son and other

saved and sanctified persons, all in perfect harmony according to celestial principles, could well be considered as dwelling in the "midst of the pillar of heaven" (88:97).

"Pillars of heaven" (plural) appears twice in scripture (Job 26:11; Abr., facsimile 1, item 11) and could refer to multiple persons, laws, or principles that uphold, sustain, and support heaven.

GBW

Pit

Term used in the Doctrine and Covenants as a symbol for that which hinders or prevents the progress of others. In the prayer dedicating the Kirtland Temple, the Prophet Joseph Smith petitioned the Lord concerning protection for the Latter-day Saints, asking "that he who diggeth a pit for them shall fall into the same himself" (109:25). The principle that those who dig pits for others will eventually fall into those pits themselves is taught in many other scriptures. (e.g., 121:13; Ps. 57:6; Prov. 26:27; Eccl. 10:8; 1 Ne. 14:3; 22:14).

During Joseph Smith's terrible experiences as a prisoner in LIBERTY JAIL, the Lord told the Prophet, "If thou shouldst be cast into the pit, or into the hands of murderers, and the sentence of death passed upon thee . . . know thou, my son, that all these things shall give thee experience, and shall be for thy good" (122:7). In this instance, *pit* could represent Liberty Jail itself as well as the persecutions heaped upon the Prophet Joseph Smith.

FFJ

Plagues. *See* Scourge.

Plants of renown. *See* Watchman, watchmen.

Plates

The Doctrine and Covenants refers to three different sets of ancient metal plates: the gold plates, the small plates of Nephi, and the large plates of Nephi (see "A Brief Explanation about the Book of Mormon," in the introductory pages of the Book of Mormon). In July 1828, after Joseph Smith translated from the gold plates 116 pages of manuscript and Martin Harris lost them through negligence, the Lord declared that the gold plates had been preserved to fulfill the divine promise that Lehi's descendants would receive knowledge of Jesus Christ through the Book of Mormon (3:16–19). After Joseph Smith received permission to resume translation, the Lord told him that the lost 116 pages contained "an abridgment of the account of Nephi" (10:44), which had been inscribed onto the gold plates from "the [large] plates of Nephi" (10:38). The Lord reminded Joseph Smith that the account on the lost manuscript stated that "a more particular account was given of these things upon the [small] plates of Nephi" (10:39), which record Mormon included with his abridgment of the large plates. Instead of having Joseph retranslate the abridgment of the large plates of Nephi, the Lord commanded the prophet to "translate the engravings which are on the [small] plates of Nephi" (10:41). Concerning the difference between the version of events on the large plates and that on the small plates, the Lord stated, "There are many things engraven upon the [small] plates of Nephi which do throw greater views upon my gospel" (10:45; 1 Ne. 6:3–6). After he resumed translating, the Prophet received a revelation in March 1829 concerning Martin Harris's desire to have a witness that he was indeed in possession of the gold plates (5:1). In that revelation, the Lord testified that Joseph currently had "a gift to translate the plates" (5:4) and no other gift would be granted to him until he finished translating. A few months later, in June 1829, Joseph Smith received another revelation assuring Oliver Cowdery, David Whitmer, and Martin Harris that if they had faith in the Lord, they would be permitted to "have a view of the plates" (17:1). The Three Witnesses were also commanded to testify concerning the existence of the plates and the truthfulness of Joseph's translation of them (17:2–6).

See also Book of Mormon, lost manuscript of (116 pages); Doctrine and Covenants, what it says about the Book of Mormon.

FFJ

Plural marriage. *See* Marriage.

Pollute, pollution

To corrupt, defile, or destroy the purity or sanctity of something. In the Doctrine and Covenants the Lord uses the word *pollute* or its various forms in ten verses (84:59; 88:134; 101:6, 97; 103:14; 105:15; 109:20; 110:8; 124:24, 46) and in several contexts. Zion, or "my holy land," is not to be polluted, neither by the disobedience of the Saints (84:59; cf. 101:6; 103:13–14) nor by the Lord's enemies (105:14–15) without serious consequences. In the prayer dedicating the Kirtland Temple, Joseph Smith prayed that "no unclean thing shall be permitted to come into thy house to pollute it" (109:20), and the Lord promised that he would appear to and speak unto his servants with his "own voice" if the Saints keep his commandments and do "not pollute this holy house" (110:8; cf. 128–36). Beyond the temple in Nauvoo, the Lord added the Nauvoo House (124:24) as well as "mine holy grounds, and mine holy ordinances, and charters, and my holy words" (124:46) to the list of things that were not to be polluted by disobedience. The specific disobedience the Lord referred to in the last instance was failing to hearken to his voice or the voice of his servants.

The instructions that Sidney Gilbert was not to sell the Lord's "storehouse" to the Lord's "enemies" and that the Saints were to retain "claim" on their properties in Jackson County, Missouri, make it clear that whatever the Lord has "appointed" is not to be polluted by enemies of the kingdom "by the consent of those who call themselves after [the Lord's] name" (101:96–99).

LED

Polygamy. *See* Marriage.

Ponder, pondering

To weigh a matter thoughtfully and contemplate its significance; to reflect, to wonder. In a revelation called the "'olive leaf' . . . plucked from the Tree of Paradise" (88, headnote), the Lord gave a commandment to ponder and pray about his revealed word: "I leave these sayings with you to *ponder* in your hearts, with this commandment which I give unto you, that ye shall *call upon me* while I am near" (88:62; emphasis added; cf. 30:3). The Doctrine and Covenants contains several references to disciples who pondered God's word, called upon him for enlightenment, and received momentous revelations. *See* Revelation.

The restoration of the fulness of the gospel began with the First Vision, which came as a result of Joseph Smith's reflecting "again and again" on the promise found in James 1:5 that God gives wisdom to those who ask of him in faith (JS–H 1:12 cf. JS–H 1:11; 28–54; D&C 20:5–6). Reflecting on the significance of baptism they found mentioned while translating the Book of Mormon, Joseph Smith and Oliver Cowdery inquired of the Lord, which led to the coming of John the Baptist and the restoration of the Aaronic Priesthood (13:1; JS–H 1:68–69). The extraordinary vision described in section 76 came as Joseph and Sidney Rigdon "meditated" on the things they were translating in the Gospel of John (76:19). *See* Historical context and overview of Doctrine and Covenants 76 (p. 780).

Just as young Joseph Smith's first vision followed "serious reflection" (JS–H 1:8), so were section 138 and Official Declaration 2 prompted by the pondering of seasoned prophets. President Spencer W. Kimball's revelation concerning the priesthood being given to "every faithful, worthy man in the Church . . . without regard for race or color" came to him "after extended meditation and prayer" (OD 2). *See* Official Declaration 2.

Similarly, seventy-nine-year-old President Joseph F. Smith "sat in [his] room pondering over the scriptures; and reflecting upon the great atoning sacrifice that was made by the Son of God, for the redemption of the world" (138:1–2). His mind was turned to passages in the "writings of the apostle Peter" (138:5), specifically to 1 Peter 3:18–20, and 4:6. As he "pondered over these things which are written" (138:11), he received a vision pertaining to the salvation of the dead, now described in section 138. *See* Historical context and overview of Doctrine and Covenants 138 (p. 859); Salvation for the dead.

RIE

Pontus. *See* Asia.

Poor, the

Individuals with insufficient money or possessions. Although other scriptures refer to those who are poor in spirit (Matt. 5:3 // 3 Ne. 12:3), the Doctrine and Covenants refers to those who are poor in temporal matters. The Lord, his Church, and his true disciples have at all times reached out in kindness and charity to the temporally poor and less fortunate. The Lord commanded his Saints in this dispensation, as he has in all dispensations, to "look to the poor and the needy, and administer to their relief that they shall not suffer" (38:35: cf. 42:34, 37; 44:6; 72:12; 84:105; 109:55; 124:75), reminding them that "he that doeth not these things, the same is not my disciple" (52:40). Bishops are not to wait for the poor to come to them for assistance but are to be "searching after the poor to administer to their wants" (84:112; 124:21).

There are always those who are poor among mankind (Matt. 26:11), and the Lord has a special interest in their welfare. He has promised that the poor whose hearts are pure and whose spirits are contrite "shall see the kingdom of God coming in power and great glory unto their deliverance; for the fatness of the earth shall be theirs. For behold, the Lord shall come, and his recompense shall be with him, and he shall reward every man, and the poor shall rejoice; and their generations shall inherit the earth from generation to generation, forever and ever" (56:18–20; cf. 35:15; 88:17).

Ideally, the Lord's way of looking after the poor is through the law of CONSECRATION. Known as the "law of the church," the principles of consecration were revealed beginning early in 1831 (42:30–42, 53–55, 70–73; cf. 51:3–5, 9; 78:3–14; 82:11–12, 17–20; 83:1–6; 104:13–18). The Saints were commanded: "Thou wilt remember the poor, and consecrate of thy properties for their support that which thou hast to impart unto them, with a covenant and a deed which cannot be broken. And inasmuch as ye impart of your substance unto the poor, ye will do it unto me" (42:30–31, 34, 39; cf. Matt. 25:31–46). In this way, "the poor shall be exalted, in that the rich are made low" (104:16).

The principles of consecration teach that all things belong to the Lord and are given to mankind as stewardships. The widow's mite and the wealthy person's plenty are equally sacred when offered freely, with full purpose of heart (Mark 12:42–44). Those who truly consecrate their property will be blessed (124:75–76, 89–90); those who withhold it will be condemned: "If any man shall take of the abundance which I have made, and impart not his portion, according to the law of my gospel, unto the poor and the needy, he shall, with the wicked, lift up his eyes in hell, being in torment" (104:18; cf. 56:16; 105:2–6).

It is not only the selfish rich who are reproved by the Lord, however. To the lazy, covetous poor, the Lord says, "Wo unto you poor men, whose hearts are not broken, whose spirits are not contrite, and whose bellies are not satisfied, and whose hands are not stayed from laying hold upon other men's goods, whose eyes are full of greediness, and who will not labor with your own hands" (56:17).

If the Saints were to embrace fully the principles of consecration, the Church would be like the ancient city of Zion, and there would be "no poor among them" (Moses 7:18). Because of early failures to obey the financial aspects of this divine law, the Lord no longer required it of the Saints (Smith, *History,* 4:93). To meet the financial needs of the Church, the Lord then commanded obedience to the ancient law of tithing (119, 120). Under his inspiration, another ancient practice (Isa. 58:6–7) specifically designed to assist the poor was restored in the latter-day Church—fasting and fast offerings (Young, 12:115). Church members abstain from two consecutive meals once a month and contribute the value of those meals as an offering to help the needy (Smith, "Observance," 148). Through fast offering funds, along with other welfare enterprises, the Church has extensive involvement in humanitarian efforts across the world, providing food, clothing, medical and other supplies, and training to help the poor and less fortunate.

In the prayer dedicating the Kirtland Temple, the Prophet Joseph Smith petitioned the Lord that the poor, as well as the "kings" and "great ones of the earth," would have their hearts "softened" and "that their prejudices may give way before the truth," a requirement for anyone, rich or poor, who desires the blessings of heaven (109:55–56, 72). The Lord promised that a future "feast of fat things" will be prepared for the poor. They will "come in unto the marriage of the Lamb and partake of the supper of the Lord" when Christ comes again (58:8, 11, 47).

See also Charity; Rich, riches.

BIBLIOGRAPHY

Smith, Joseph. *History of The Church of Jesus Christ of Latter-day Saints.* Edited by B. H. Roberts. 7 vols. 2d ed. rev. Salt Lake City: The Church of Jesus Christ of Latter-day Saints, 1932–51.

Smith, Joseph F. "Observance of Fast Day." *Improvement Era* 6 (December 1902): 146–49.

Young, Brigham. *Journal of Discourses.* 26 vols. London: Latter-day Saints' Book Depot, 1854–86.

LDN

Power

A noun used frequently throughout the revelations in the Doctrine and Covenants. Some uses of the word *power* denote the ability to act or to act upon, affect, or influence. Other nuances signify control or authority, dominion, rule, government, or command. In most instances, the term is used generically. Depending on the context, it can refer to God's power (1:36), or power used by SATAN (1:35), an individual (1:29), or a group (1:8, 30). The revelations also uses the word *power* as a noun that describes a specific endowment from God enabling those who possess it to regain God's presence and to become like him, including possessing all power (76:92–95; 132:20). This endowment includes power over death and over sin, including power over forces that sever relationships between individuals and God, wives and husbands, and children and parents. This endowment of power comes through the ATONEMENT of the Lord JESUS CHRIST.

Power of God

The largest number of uses of the term *power* refer to God's omnipotent abilities: "the power of God" (8:7), "the power of Jesus Christ" (11:10) and "the power of the Holy Ghost" (124:4). Beginning in section 1, the Lord testified that he would have power over his Saints (1:36). He exercises his power throughout the universe—power that gives life and takes it away (63:2–5; 88:7–10). He declared that "in me there is all power"; he is omnipotent (100:1; cf. 15:2; 16:2; 19:14; 20:24; 61:1; 84:28; 93:17).

Some passages suggest that God, though omnipotent, allows others to have power, including his children (58:27–28) and Satan (76:31), to accomplish his purposes but that he retains and ultimately exercises sovereign power (19:3; 63:59; 93:17, 42; 121:33; 136:17).

Satan's power

The revelations declare that Satan has power but that it is clearly subordinate to God's power. Satan has power over his limited dominion (1:35), but he coveted God's greater power (29:36). In his lust for God's power and his resulting rebellion, Satan persuaded "a third part of the hosts of heaven" to turn away from God (29:36). These spirit children of God could turn away because God had endowed them with AGENCY, which the Doctrine and Covenants associates closely with power (58:28). If Satan did not have the power to tempt, to provide choice, there would be no agency (29:39). Because God empowered man with agency to act independent of His will, individuals may choose to give to Satan their power, or agency (50:7; 76:31; 93:30–39, 42, 49). As Joseph Smith taught, "The devil has no power over us only as we permit him; the moment we revolt at anything which comes from God the Devil takes power" (Ehat and Cook, 59–60). Nonetheless, Satan's power to tempt is limited to those who are accountable, "for power is not given unto Satan to tempt little children, until they begin to become accountable before [the Lord]" (29:47). Thankfully, during the MILLENNIUM "Satan shall not have power to tempt any man"; he "shall be bound, that he shall have no place in the hearts of the children of men" (101:28; 45:55). At the end of the Millennium, after "the battle of the great God . . . the devil and his armies shall be cast away into their own place, that they shall not have power over the saints any more at all" (88:111–14). The wicked will then be dismissed from the Savior's presence because "they have no power" either (29:29).

Sharing or delegating God's power

As Satan saps power "through disobedience" (93:39), so the Lord bestows it on those who receive his words in righteousness (71:6). The revelations declare this kind of power-sharing many times. For example, they testify that the Lord delegated to his servants power to seal and to lay the foundation of the Church and bring it out of obscurity (1:8, 30), and he gave Joseph Smith power to translate the Book of Mormon (1:29; 3:12). Many instances are mentioned about the sharing or delegation of God's power with specific individuals or groups, as in section 7, wherein the early Christian apostle John requested of the Lord power over death so he could bring souls to him (7:2, 7); the Lord's declaring that the three witnesses to the Book of Mormon would see the plates by his power (17:3, 5, 7); and the Lord's telling John Murdock that he would have power to declare the gospel (99:2).

Priesthood power

Power and PRIESTHOOD are closely associated in the revelations. The relationship is explained in section 84, which testifies that the ORDINANCES of the Melchizedek Priesthood manifest the power of godliness, without which man cannot regain God's presence (vv. 19–23). Other associations of power with priesthood offices and ordinances are concentrated in sections 107, 128, 131, and 132.

Endowment of power

The instances of the word *power* that describe an endowment that enables its possessor to conquer all the effects of the Fall—including sin, death, and separation from God—are concentrated in sections that explain this endowment (29); that prophesy of this endowment (38); that describe the heirs of this endowment (76); that explain the relationships between priesthood, its ordinances, and this endowment of power (84); that describe the relationships between obedience to God's laws, resurrection, and this endowment of power (88); that emphasize the temple context of being endowed with power (109); and that set forth the terms and conditions of exaltation, the eventual state of those who possess and exercise this power

(132). Section 29 explains that without an endowment of this type of power, fallen mortals cannot regain God's presence (v. 29). Section 38 indicates that if the early Saints would migrate to Ohio, the Lord would endow them with power there (v. 32). Section 76 refers to those who obtain the full endowment of God's power—they dwell in God's presence and constitute the "church of the Firstborn"; and God "makes them equal in power, and in might, and in dominion" (vv. 94–95). Section 84 includes an important, detailed description of how the power of godliness, without which we cannot regain God's presence, is manifest in the temple ordinances of the Melchizedek Priesthood (vv. 19–23). Those who are faithful to the "oath and covenant which belongeth to the priesthood" receive all that the Father has (vv. 33–44). Section 88 further describes God's power in the universe (vv. 7–13) and associates man's sharing of it with obedience to God's laws (vv. 21–40). *See* Light of Christ.

In section 109, the dedicatory prayer of the house of the Lord in Kirtland, Ohio, God's power is acknowledged (vv. 77, 79), and it is prayed that the Saints may feel God's power and leave the temple armed with it (v. 22), that the ordinances performed in the temple would manifest "power from on high" (v. 35), and that the wicked will be powerless to prevail over the Saints (vv. 26, 33). Ultimately, section 132 describes the law that governs how covenants associated with priesthood ordinances enable couples to "come forth in the first resurrection . . . and . . . inherit thrones, kingdoms, principalities, and powers" (v. 19). "Then shall they be gods, because they have all power" (v. 20).

Use and abuse of power

The revelations describe appropriate and inappropriate uses of power, as in the declaration in section 121 that priesthood power neither can nor ought to be exercised unrighteously (vv. 34–46). The Doctrine and Covenants forbids the use of power except in righteousness. The revelations take the gospel view that mankind is already fallen and corrupt and that those who choose to make and keep gospel covenants can receive an endowment of God's power by degrees, sufficient to regain his presence and,

indeed, to become like him (132:20–21). Such divine power is desirable, but it cannot be controlled or handled without righteousness (121:36). It distills upon the virtuous and charitable but evaporates when abused (121:37–46). Individuals who, like Satan and his hosts and the many mentioned in section 121, use the limited power they have for selfish, covetous, compulsory purposes, corrupt the power God has given them (121:34–41). The Doctrine and Covenants testifies that God has absolute power, and it explains how he uses it to empower his covenant-keeping children with the "power of godliness" (84:20; 132:20–21).

BIBLIOGRAPHY

Ehat, Andrew F., and Lyndon W. Cook, comps. and eds. *The Words of Joseph Smith.* Provo, Utah: Religious Studies Center, Brigham Young University, 1980.

SCH

Pratt, Orson

Birth: 19 September 1811, Hartford, Washington County, New York

Death: 3 October 1881, Salt Lake City, Salt Lake County, Utah

Orson Pratt was baptized on his nineteenth

Orson Pratt, 1811–1881; portrait by Charles Carter.

birthday by his brother Parley and was soon called to preach the gospel in Missouri (34; 52:26). After he returned to Kirtland, Ohio, from this mission, Pratt became the first man in this dispensation to serve as an elders quorum president. He then served another mission (75:14), during which, he recorded, he "traveled on foot near 4,000 miles, attended 207 meetings . . . baptized 104 persons and organized several new branches of the church" (in England, 31).

After returning to Kirtland, Pratt worked on the limestone foundation of the temple before joining ZION'S CAMP (103:40). On 26 April 1835, at age twenty-three, he was ordained an apostle (Smith, 2:187; cf. 124:128–29). During his service as one of the Twelve Apostles, Pratt earned a "Certificate of Proficiency" in Hebrew and taught English grammar. His teaching career was interrupted when religious persecution drove Latter-day Saints from Ohio to Missouri and from there to Illinois. In Illinois, he taught at the University of Nauvoo. Elder Pratt served a mission to Great Britain with others of the Twelve from 1839 to 1841.

Unfortunately, after his return to Nauvoo, his faith wavered, and he was excommunicated on 20 August 1842. A few months later, on 20 January 1843, Pratt was rebaptized by Joseph Smith and "received the Priesthood and the same power and authority as in former days" (in England, 85).

After the martyrdom of Joseph and Hyrum Smith, Pratt sustained Brigham Young and the Twelve, himself included, as the leaders of the Church and traveled with them to the Great Basin (136:13). He and Erastus Snow were the first to enter the Salt Lake Valley, and after traversing Emigration Canyon, Pratt dedicated the valley. He returned to Iowa and from there in 1848 journeyed to England to preside over the Church in the British Isles. There, his literary contributions included the booklet *The Kingdom of God* and the pamphlet *New Jerusalem, or the Spirit of Modern Prophecy.* He also served as editor of the *Millennial Star.*

Upon returning to the States, Pratt presided over the territorial legislature of Utah and served as a regent of the University of Deseret and as

the historian and general Church recorder. In 1875 when President Young reorganized the Twelve according to when those who had earlier left the Quorum were reinstated, Elder Pratt, who had been ranked second, was ranked fifth, and John Taylor became the senior apostle. In 1878 Pratt traveled to England to electrotype the Book of Mormon and Doctrine and Covenants, which he also arranged in verses with footnotes and references. He returned home to Utah in September 1879.

Orson Pratt, the last surviving faithful member of the original Quorum of the Twelve Apostles, died on 3 October 1881. At his request, his tombstone was inscribed: "My body sleeps for a moment, but my testimony lives and shall endure forever" (Whitney, 68).

See also Historical context and overview of Doctrine and Covenants 34 (p. 742); Apostles, the first Twelve of latter days; Apostles, the Twelve, mission to Great Britain.

BIBLIOGRAPHY

England, Breck. *The Life and Thought of Orson Pratt.* Salt Lake City: University of Utah Press, 1985.

Smith, Joseph. *History of The Church of Jesus Christ of Latter-day Saints.* Edited by B. H. Roberts. 7 vols. 2d ed. rev. Salt Lake City: The Church of Jesus Christ of Latter-day Saints, 1932–51.

Whitney, Orson F. Conference Report, October 1911, 68.

SEB

Pratt, Parley P.

Birth: 12 April 1807, Burlington, Otsego County, New York

Death: 13 May 1857, near Van Buren, Van Buren County, Arkansas

While preaching his Christian faith in western New York, Parley P. Pratt visited an aged Baptist deacon who told him of a new book. The next day he read the book—the Book of Mormon. Pratt wrote: "I read all day; eating was a burden, I had no desire for food; sleep was a burden when the night came, for I preferred reading to sleep. . . . I esteemed the Book, or the information contained in it, more than all the riches of the world" (2, 20, 22).

Pratt was baptized on 1 September 1830 by Oliver Cowdery and ordained an elder shortly

Courtesy Church History Library

Parley P. Pratt, 1807–1857.

thereafter. He immediately began to preach and converted his brother Orson Pratt (34, head-note). After his call to be a missionary to the Lamanites (32:1–2), he journeyed to Buffalo and from there to Ohio, and on to Independence, Missouri. Pratt was then called to preach to the SHAKERS in North Union, Ohio (49:1), to strengthen Church members in Ohio (50:37), and again to preach in Missouri (52:26). In August 1833 Pratt was called to "preside over the school in the land of Zion" and promised "a multiplicity of blessings, in expounding all scriptures and mysteries to the edification of the school, and of the church in Zion" (97:4–5). He became a recruiting officer for ZION'S CAMP in February 1834 (103:30).

On 21 February 1835 Pratt was ordained an apostle (Smith, 2:187; cf. 124:129). After his ordination, he served missions successively in Pennsylvania, New England, Canada, and New York. These missions, along with his missionary labors previous to his call as an apostle, yielded

a great harvest of souls that subsequently provided much leadership to the Church.

Of particular interest is Elder Pratt's mission to Canada and his fulfillment of prophecy there. In early 1836, Heber C. Kimball had given Pratt a blessing in which he was promised: "Thou shalt go . . . to the city of Toronto, . . . and there thou shalt find a people prepared for the fulness of the gospel, . . . and from the things growing out of this mission, shall the fulness of the gospel spread into England, and cause a great work to be done in that land" (Pratt, 110). Among those Pratt taught in Canada were John Taylor (third president of the Church) and Mary Fielding (mother of the sixth president of the Church). The converts he taught in Canada also provided necessary contacts in England, along with some of the first missionaries, to fulfill Kimball's prophecy there.

During his mission to New York, Pratt wrote *A Voice of Warning,* perhaps the most influential missionary tract aside from the Book of Mormon. First published in 1837, by the end of the century it was reprinted in more than thirty English editions and in seven additional languages (Givens and Grow, 119).

Pratt left New York to settle in Missouri in April, 1838. Tensions had escalated there, and in November, he was arrested and imprisoned in Independence, Richmond, and Columbia jails before escaping eight months later to freedom in Illinois.

Pratt served a mission to Great Britain with other members of the Twelve from 1839 to 1841 and then served as president of the British Mission from 1841 to 1842. While there he was founding editor and publisher of the *Millennial Star.* With Brigham Young, he oversaw the publishing of a British edition of the Book of Mormon and a hymnal emphasizing themes of the Restoration, thus setting the standard for LDS hymnbooks that would follow. Pratt's "The Morning Breaks, the Shadows Flee," originally published in the *Star,* opened the hymnal that included fifty of his hymns. He eventually became "the most prolific Mormon writer of his age, as editor, pamphleteer, essayist, historian, hymnist, and theologian" (Givens and Grow, 114).

Pratt's missionary and publishing labors did not end with his return to Nauvoo. He was on a mission to the eastern states when he was "constrained by the Spirit to start prematurely for home" (Pratt, 292). While en route, he learned of the deaths of Joseph and Hyrum Smith. Under the leadership of Brigham Young, Pratt continued his missionary work in the United States and the Pacific Islands and became the first LDS missionary to South America.

Shortly before leaving on another mission, on 7 September 1856 he wrote in his journal, "I preached my farewell discourse in the Tabernacle, in which I bore testimony to the Book of Mormon and of the calling of Joseph Smith, and of his Presidency and Apostleship" (400). Taking leave of family and friends, he journeyed to New York City, Philadelphia, and other areas. Near Van Buren, Arkansas, fifty-year-old Parley P. Pratt was murdered by an anti-Mormon antagonist. An observer recalled his dying words: "'I die,' said he, 'a firm believer in the Gospel of Jesus Christ as revealed through the Prophet Joseph Smith, and I wish you to carry this my dying testimony. I know that the Gospel is true and that Joseph Smith was a prophet of the Living God' and then added, 'I am dying a martyr to the faith'" (Givens and Grow, 383).

See also Apostles, the first Twelve of latter days; Apostles, the Twelve, mission to Great Britain.

BIBLIOGRAPHY

Givens, Terryl L., and Matthew J. Grow. *Parley P. Pratt: The Apostle Paul of Mormonism.* New York: Oxford University Press, 2011.

Pratt, Parley P. *Autobiography of Parley P. Pratt.* Edited by Parley P. Pratt Jr. Salt Lake City: Deseret Book, 1985.

Smith, Joseph. *History of The Church of Jesus Christ of Latter-day Saints.* Edited by B. H. Roberts. 7 vols. 2d ed. rev. Salt Lake City: The Church of Jesus Christ of Latter-day Saints, 1932–51.

SEB

Prayer

The act through which mortals communicate with God. Many action verbs are used in reference to prayer: *ask, petition, call upon, inquire, plead, supplicate, entreat, cry out, pour out, seek,* *search, implore,* and *importune.* Numerous revelations in the Doctrine and Covenants were received because Joseph Smith desired to know something, and he prayed to the Lord for an answer. For example, "as a consequence of the early brethren using tobacco in their meetings, the Prophet was led to ponder upon the matter; consequently, he inquired of the Lord concerning it. [The] revelation, known as the Word of Wisdom, was the result" (89, headnote; cf. 130:12–15). "The importance of prayer is emphasized by the fact that the most oft-repeated command given by God to men is to pray" (Romney, 48–49). The Savior counseled his followers to "pray always" (10:5; cf. 84:61), to pray "continually" (2 Ne. 9:52), and to pray "without ceasing" (3 Ne. 19:24, 30). Parents are obligated to teach their CHILDREN to pray (68:28). The instruction for the inhabitants of Zion was, "he that observeth not his prayers before the Lord let him be had in remembrance before the judge of my people" (68:33). Section 6 contains a number of admonitions that urged Oliver Cowdery to pray: "If you will ask of me you shall receive" (v. 5); "If thou wilt inquire, thou shalt know" (v. 11); "As often as thou hast inquired thou hast received" (v. 14); "Look unto me in every thought; doubt not, fear not" (v. 36).

In revelations directed to specific individuals, prayer is included, often with other elements, as a behavior that brings blessings: understanding the revelations (32:4); receiving the Spirit (19:38; cf. 42:14); avoiding temptation (20:33; 31:12; 61:39); avoiding becoming "faint" or weak and giving up (75:11; 88:126; 101:81); preventing Satan from having "power in you, and remov[ing] you out of your place" (93:49; cf. 10:5); and having "all things work together for your good, if ye walk uprightly" (90:24; cf. 81:3–6). The Lord has said that "every soul who forsaketh his sins and cometh unto me, and calleth on my name, and obeyeth my voice, and keepeth my commandments, shall see my face and know that I am" (93:1). Praying always will help one to be ready for the coming of the BRIDEGROOM (33:17; cf. 61:39).

Disciples are to pray to the Father in Christ's name (14:8), praying vocally and in the heart, publicly as well as privately (19:28; 23:6; 81:3).

When one asks in the Spirit, one asks "according to the will of God" (46:30). Prayer and FASTING are linked together (88:76). Saints should pray for the sick (42:44) and pray to avoid being "seduced by evil spirits, or doctrines of devils, or the commandments of men" (46:7). Prayers take place in the meetinghouse, which is a "house of prayer" (59:9), and in the temple, which is also a "house of prayer" (88:119; 109:8).

The Lord frequently referred to the "prayer of faith" (28:13; 41:3; 42:14; 93:51–52; 104:80), meaning that one prays "in faith believing" that answers will come according to the Lord's will (14:8). Answers to prayers do come if one is humble: "Be thou humble; and the Lord thy God shall lead thee by the hand, and give thee answer to thy prayers" (112:10). The Lord promised to "gather his people even as a hen gathereth her chickens under her wings, even as many as will hearken to my voice and humble themselves before me, and call upon me in mighty prayer" (29:2; cf. 5:24). He also promised answers to those who "ask in faith, being united in prayer" (29:6).

The Lord commanded his disciples to preach what is learned from the Comforter through the prayer of faith (52:9). "All victory and glory is brought to pass unto you through your diligence, faithfulness, and prayers of faith" (103:36). On their way to the Salt Lake Valley, the Saints were instructed, "If thou art merry, praise the Lord with singing, with music, with dancing, and with a prayer of praise and thanksgiving" (136:28).

On one occasion the Saints in Missouri were told that because they were slow to hearken to the voice of the Lord, he was slow to hearken to their prayers (101:7); however, hearkening to his voice guarantees blessings (130:20–21). A person who prays and is contrite is accepted of God (52:15). Oliver Cowdery cried unto God in his heart to receive a witness of the truth, and God answered by giving him peace of mind (6:22–24). The Doctrine and Covenants is a testament that indeed the Lord hears and answers prayers (88:2; 90:1; 98:2).

BIBLIOGRAPHY

Romney, Marion G. "Prayer and Revelation." *Ensign* 8 (May 1978): 48–50.

DKO

Prayer of faith. *See* Prayer.

Preach, preaching

To impart knowledge, instruct, or teach. "And this gospel of the kingdom shall be preached in all the world for a witness unto all nations" (Matt. 24:14), Jesus declared, and gave the charge to his disciples. Likewise, in this dispensation the Lord declared, "And if they desire to take upon them my name with full purpose of heart, they are called to go into all the world to preach my gospel unto every creature" (18:28; 1:4–5). The Prophet Joseph Smith taught, "The greatest and most important duty is to preach the Gospel" (2:478; cf. D&C 15; 16). The Doctrine and Covenants provides important insights concerning the conditions under which this duty should be carried out, specifics as to what is to be preached, and how this charge is to be fulfilled.

Although one may talk of one's religious beliefs and teach them to others, and though all members of the Church are under covenantal obligation to bear witness of the truths of the gospel, the scriptures generally and the Doctrine and Covenants specifically teach that preaching the gospel is different. The phrase "preach the gospel" implies being called to a specific assignment and being authorized to teach the principles of the restored gospel and administer the ordinances of salvation. In a revelation directed to Hyrum Smith, the Lord stated that "you need not suppose that you are called to preach until you are called" (11:15; cf. 23:4). In the revelation known as "the law of the Church" (42, headnote), the Savior declared, "Again I say unto you, that it shall not be given to any one to go forth to preach my gospel, or to build up my church, except he be ordained by some one who has authority, and it is known to the church that he has authority and has been regularly ordained by the heads of the church" (42:11). Numerous passages show that a call to preach the gospel must come by the direction of the authorized priesthood leaders of the Church (18:26–29; 19:36–37; 20:38–60; 36:5; 42:6; 49:1; 50:13–14, 17; 52:1–44; 53:3; 58:46–47, 63–64; 60:8, 13; 73:1–4; 84:76–77, 86; 107:25, 38; 138:30–32, 57). Some are called to preach by specific assignment whereas others are authorized to do so by virtue of the office they hold, but all "must be called of God, by prophecy, and by the laying on of hands by those who are in authority, to preach the Gospel and administer in the ordinances thereof" (A of F 5).

Concerning what is to be preached by these authorized servants, the revelations include the following:

• "The everlasting gospel, the doctrine of the resurrection and the redemption of mankind from the fall, and from individual sins on conditions of repentance" (138:19). *See* Fall of Adam and Eve, the; Gospel, the; Repentance; Resurrection, the.

• "Faith and repentance and remission of sins, according to [the Lord's] word, and the reception of the Holy Spirit by the laying on of hands" (53:3). *See* Faith; Gift of the Holy Ghost; Laying on of hands.

• "Repentance and remission of sins by way of baptism in the name of Jesus Christ, the Son of the living God" (55:2). *See* Baptism by water.

• "The things which have been revealed to [the Lord's] servant, Joseph Smith, Jun." (31:4).

• "The principles of [the] gospel, which are in the Bible and the Book of Mormon, in the which is the fulness of the gospel" (42:12).

• "None other things than that which the prophets and apostles have written, and that which is taught them by the Comforter through the prayer of faith" (52:9).

• "The fulness of [the] gospel . . . sent forth in these last days, the covenant . . . sent forth to recover [the Lord's] people, which are of the house of Israel" (39:11). *See* Israel.

Concerning how authorized servants are to fulfill their charge, the revelations include:

• Going "forth in the power of [the Lord's] Spirit, preaching [the] gospel, two by two, in [the Lord's] name, lifting up your voices as with the sound of a trump, declaring [the Lord's] word like unto angels of God" (42:6).

• Preaching "by the way, and bear[ing] testimony of the truth in all places, and call[ing] upon the rich, the high and the low, and the poor to repent" (58:47). *See* Testify.

• "Preach[ing] the word of truth by the Comforter, in the Spirit of truth" (50:17). *See* Historical context and overview of Doctrine and Covenants 50 (p. 756); Holy Ghost, the; Spirit of truth; Truth.

• Preaching that is a "warning voice, every man to his neighbor, in mildness and in meekness" (38:41; 100:7). *See* Meek, meekness.

• "Open[ing] your mouths in proclaiming [the Lord's] gospel, the things of the kingdom, expounding the mysteries thereof out of the scriptures, according to that portion of Spirit and power which shall be given unto you," according to the Lord's will (71:1).

• "Lifting up your voices as with the sound of a trump, proclaiming the truth according to the revelations and commandments," which the Lord has given (75:4). *See* Trump(s).

Numerous promises of blessings and assistance in the work, as well as eternal rewards for faithful preaching of the gospel were also pronounced (24:12; 38:33; 75:4–5; 84:80, 85; 100:7–8; 112:19). The Lord has placed a sacred responsibility upon the Church to preach the gospel to every nation, kindred, tongue, and people (90:11). He has taught Latter-day Saints how to do that and provided the means whereby it can be accomplished. The great challenge is, as the Prophet Joseph Smith declared, to "remember that your business is to preach the Gospel in all humility and meekness, and warn sinners to repent and come to Christ. Avoid contentions and vain disputes with men of corrupt minds, who do not desire to know the truth. . . . If you do your duty, it will be just as well with you, as though all men embraced the Gospel" (1:468).

See also Missionary work.

BIBLIOGRAPHY

Smith, Joseph. *History of The Church of Jesus Christ of Latter-day Saints*. Edited by B. H. Roberts. 7 vols. 2d ed. rev. Salt Lake City: The Church of Jesus Christ of Latter-day Saints, 1932–51.

BLT

Premortal existence

That period of time when all mankind lived with God as spirit beings, before being born on this earth as mortal beings with bodies of flesh and bone. "All human beings—male and female—are created in the image of God. Each is a beloved spirit son or daughter of heavenly parents. . . . In the premortal realm, spirit sons and daughters knew and worshipped God as their Eternal Father and accepted His plan by which His children could obtain a physical body and gain earthly experience to progress toward perfection and ultimately realize their divine destiny as heirs of eternal life" ("Family").

Several passages in the Doctrine and Covenants refer specifically to the premortal phase of man's eternal existence and address four general subjects: the spiritual creation; the form and substance of spirit beings; agency; and the council and war in heaven.

The spiritual creation

Concerning the premortal existence of man, the Lord declared, "Man was also in the beginning with God. Intelligence, or the light of truth, was not created or made, neither indeed can be" (93:29). President Joseph Fielding Smith wrote: "Some of our writers have endeavored to explain what an intelligence is, but to do so is futile, for we have never been given any insight into this matter beyond what the Lord has fragmentarily revealed. We know, however, that there is something called intelligence which always existed. It is the real eternal part of man, which was not created or made. This intelligence combined with the spirit constitutes a spiritual identity or individual" (*Progress*, 11). Concerning the creation of spirits, the First Presidency in 1909 explained, "The doctrine of the pre-existence,—revealed so plainly, particularly in latter days, pours a wonderful flood of light upon the otherwise mysterious problem of man's origin. It shows that man, as a spirit, was begotten and born of heavenly parents, and reared to maturity in the eternal mansions of the Father, prior to coming upon the earth in a temporal body to undergo an experience in mortality" ("Origin," 80).

JESUS CHRIST, in his divine premortal role and under the authority of his Father, directed the creation of all things spiritual and temporal. He declared: "I, the Lord God, created all things, of which I have spoken, spiritually, before they were naturally upon the face of the earth. . . . And I . . . had created all the children of men; and not yet a man to till the ground; for in heaven created I them; and there was not yet flesh upon the earth" (Moses 3:5; cf. D&C 38:1–3; 29:31–32; 76:24; John 1:1–3). All the spirits, thus created, were to come to EARTH as mortals. In addressing the proper role of MARRIAGE, the Lord stated that "marriage is ordained of God unto man . . . that the earth might answer the end of its creation; and that it might be filled with the measure of man, according to his creation before the world was made" (49:15–17). Thus, Elder James E. Talmage concluded, "The population of the earth is fixed according to the number of spirits appointed to take tabernacles of flesh upon this planet; when these have all come forth in the order and time appointed, then, and not till then, shall the end come" (194).

The form and substance of spirit beings

Spirits are in the form of man—"that which is spiritual being in the likeness of that which is temporal; . . . the spirit of man in the likeness of his person" (77:2). Nephi was privileged to see the Spirit of the Lord (that is, the Holy Ghost) and wrote, "I spake unto him as a man speaketh; for I beheld that he was in the form of a man; yet nevertheless, I knew that it was the Spirit of the Lord" (1 Ne. 11:11). The brother of Jared testified that he saw the spirit body of Jesus Christ; the Lord explained, "Behold, this body, which ye now behold, is the body of my spirit; and man have I created after the body of my spirit; and even as I appear unto thee to be in the spirit will I appear unto my people in the flesh" (Ether 3:16).

Spirit bodies consist of spirit matter. The Prophet Joseph Smith declared: "There is no such thing as immaterial matter. All spirit is matter, but it is more fine or pure, and can only be discerned by purer eyes; we cannot see it; but when our bodies are purified we shall see that it is all matter" (131:7–8).

Agency

Faithfulness in the premortal existence through the exercise of AGENCY is taught in the scriptures and the teachings of modern prophets. In his vision of the redemption of the dead, President Joseph F. Smith saw that many leaders of the Church in this dispensation were "among the noble and great ones who were chosen in the beginning to be rulers in the Church of God. Even before they were born, they, with many others, received their first lessons in the world of spirits and were prepared to come forth in the due time of the Lord to labor in his vineyard for the salvation of the souls of men" (138:55–56). These "noble and great ones" were foreordained to their earthly callings by virtue of their premortal faithfulness (see Abr. 3:22–23; Jer. 1:5; Alma 13:1–6). *See* Foreordination.

Additional evidence of the operation of agency in the premortal existence is in section 93. Verse 38 affirms that "every spirit of man was innocent in the beginning; and God having redeemed man from the fall, men became again, in their infant state, innocent before God." The fact that God's spirit children were "innocent in the beginning" and became innocent "again" when born into their mortal infant state indicates that choices were made between these two periods causing that innocence to diminish to one degree or another. *See* Innocent.

President Joseph Fielding Smith explained, "The spirits of men were not equal. They may have had an equal start, and we know they were all innocent in the beginning; but the right of free agency which was given to them enabled some to outstrip others, and thus, through the eons of immortal existence, to become more intelligent, more faithful, for they were free to act for themselves, to think for themselves, to receive the truth or rebel against it" (*Doctrines*, 1:59). The Prophet Joseph Smith explained that spirits in the premortal life exercised their agency in sustaining the plan of salvation with Jesus Christ as the Savior: "At the first organization in heaven we were all present and saw the Savior chosen and appointed and the plan of salvation made, and we sanctioned it" (*Joseph Smith*, 209). Implicit in these statements is an understanding that the spirits were taught the ways of God and were given agency to act upon the principles taught, and to develop aptitudes, talents and interests. Elder Bruce R. McConkie taught, "When we pass from preexistence to mortality, we bring with us the traits and talents there developed" (1:25). That is the same principle taught in the revelations about going from mortality to the postmortal spirit world. "Whatever principle of intelligence we attain unto in this life, it will rise with us in the resurrection. And if a person gains more knowledge and intelligence in this life through his diligence and obedience than another, he will have so much the advantage in the world to come" (130:18–19).

The council and the war in heaven

The revelations teach that "before this world was," in the "Council of the Eternal God" the plan of salvation was "ordained" (121:26–32). In that premortal council, all the spirits who were to come to this earth were given the opportunity to embrace the plan of salvation outlined by the Father, with Jesus Christ as the chosen Savior. One spirit, however, whom the Doctrine and Covenants identifies as "an angel of God, who was in authority in the presence of God," known as "Lucifer, a son of the morning . . . rebelled against God, and sought to take the kingdom of our God and his Christ" (76:25–28). He drew "a third part of the hosts of heaven" after him, and the resulting conflict surrounding that rebellion is called the "war in heaven." He and his followers were "thrust down" to the earth, "and thus came the devil and his angels" (29:36–37; Rev. 12:7–11; cf. Moses 4:1–4; Abr. 3:22–28). The devil's rebellion against God continues on the earth as "he [and his outcast spirit followers] maketh war with the saints of God, and encompasseth them round about" (76:29).

See also Spirit world, postmortal; War in heaven.

BIBLIOGRAPHY

First Presidency. "The Origin of Man." *Improvement Era* 13 (November 1909): 75–81; or *Ensign* (February 2002): 26–30.

First Presidency and Council of the Twelve Apostles. *The Family: A Proclamation to the World.* Salt Lake City: The Church of Jesus Christ of Latter-day Saints, 1995.

McConkie, Bruce R. *The Mortal Messiah: From Bethlehem to Calvary*. 4 vols. Salt Lake City: Deseret Book, 1979–81.

Smith, Joseph. *Joseph Smith*. Teachings of Presidents of the Church series. Salt Lake City: The Church of Jesus Christ of Latter-day Saints, 2007.

Smith, Joseph Fielding. *Doctrines of Salvation*. Compiled by Bruce R. McConkie. 3 vols. Salt Lake City: Bookcraft, 1954–56.

———. *The Progress of Man*. Salt Lake City: Genealogical Society of Utah, 1952.

Talmage, James E. *Articles of Faith*. Salt Lake City: The Church of Jesus Christ of Latter-day Saints, 1961.

BLT

Preparatory gospel

A term used once in the Doctrine and Covenants and defined as "the gospel of repentance and of baptism, and the remission of sins, and the law of carnal commandments," the keys of which are vested in the Aaronic PRIESTHOOD (84:26–27; cf. 13:1). Section 84 focuses on the limited spiritual power that the children of Israel were left with after they "hardened their hearts" and the Lord "took Moses . . . and the Holy [or Melchizedek] Priesthood" "out of their midst" (84:24–26; cf. JST Ex. 34:1–2). The preparatory nature of the Aaronic Priesthood is indicated in 84:27–28; obedience to this limited gospel was intended to prepare ancient Israel to receive the fulness of the GOSPEL when Christ came. Herein is a connection to the book of Hebrews, which emphasizes the contrast between the Melchizedek Priesthood of Christ with ordinances that have the power to save and the limits of the LAW OF MOSES (Heb. 7:11–28; cf. D&C 84:19–22), the law of Moses being a "schoolmaster to bring us unto Christ," or "until Christ" (Gal. 3:24–29; JST Gal. 3:24). These scriptures affirm both the important role of the Aaronic Priesthood as well as its inadequacy to provide the ordinances needed for complete sanctification and entrance into the presence of God.

JCL

President, presidency

Terms referring to presiding officers of the Church, priesthood QUORUMS, or other units within the Church, and in one instance, the president of the United States. Those who preside in the Church or in the PRIESTHOOD hold KEYS to direct the labors of others and to oversee the work of the Church or priesthood functions.

The president of the Church is referred to as the "President of the High Priesthood of the Church," and is "to preside over the whole church . . . yea, to be a seer, a revelator, a translator, and a prophet, having all the gifts of God which he bestows upon the head of the church" (107:65, 91–92). The president of the Church and his two counselors "form a quorum of the Presidency of the Church" (107:22; cf. 112:20, 30; 124:125), holding "the keys of the kingdom, which belong always unto the Presidency of the High Priesthood" (81:2). These keys are also held by members of the Quorum of the Twelve Apostles (112:30–32).

A president and two counselors form a presidency of each of the DEACONS, TEACHERS, PRIESTS, ELDERS, and HIGH PRIESTS quorums. The duty of these presidents is to "preside over" members of their quorums, "to sit in council with them, and to teach them their duty, edifying one another . . . according to the covenants" (107:85–89; 124:133–37, 142). A unique feature of a priests quorum is that, although the revelations call for "priests to preside over those who are of the office of a priest" (107:61; 124:142), the BISHOP is designated as "the president over the Priesthood of Aaron" and "is to preside over forty-eight priests, and sit in council with them, to teach them the duties of their office" (107:87–88). He acts in this calling as a high priest, appointed to his office by the First Presidency (68:19). Currently in the Church, bishops call one or two assistants from the priests quorum to help in administering the business of the quorum.

One unit of the early Church with a president was the School of the Prophets. Purposes and procedures for the school and the role of the president are outlined in 88:127–41. *See* School(s).

Another reference to "presidents" is in connection with the presiding officers of the Church in Missouri, at a time when the First Presidency of the Church was located in Kirtland, Ohio, and a presidency pro tem was appointed to preside over the affairs of the Church in Missouri, under the direction of the First Presidency in Kirtland. Thus, in the dedicatory prayer of the Kirtland Temple, Joseph Smith prayed, "Remember, O Lord, the presidents, even all the presidents of thy church" (109:71). *See* Presidents of thy Church.

The reference to the president of the United States is found in section 101, where the Saints were told to petition all levels of government, including the president of the nation, for REDRESS from their losses in Missouri at the hands of their enemies. The Lord promised, "If the president heed them not, then will the Lord arise and come forth out of his hiding place, and in his fury vex the nation" (101:86–95). *See* Hiding place, the Lord's.

LED

Presidents of thy Church

In the dedicatory prayer of the Kirtland Temple the Prophet Joseph Smith prayed, "Remember, O Lord, the presidents, even all the presidents of thy church" (109:71). At this time "all the presidents of [the Lord's] church" included the three members of the First Presidency of the Church located in Kirtland, Ohio, plus the three members of the presidency of the Church in Far West, Missouri (Zion).

In June 1834, Joseph Smith ordained "David Whitmer, as president in Zion, in my absence; and John Whitmer and William W. Phelps, as assistant presidents or counselors," to preside over the affairs of the Church in Zion under the direction of the First Presidency of the Church headquartered in Kirtland (Smith, 2:122–26). In the early part of 1838 all three members of this presidency were accused of transgression— among other things, selling their land in Zion contrary to the policies of the Church and revelations of the Lord. They were rejected by the high council and Saints in Zion, and excommunicated (Smith, 3:18–20; Cannon and Cook, 137–40, 149). By that time the headquarters of the Church and the First Presidency had moved from Kirtland to Missouri, so there was no need to appoint another presidency in Zion.

BIBLIOGRAPHY

Cannon, Donald Q., and Lyndon W. Cook, eds. *Far West Record: Minutes of The Church of Jesus Christ of Latter-day Saints, 1830–1844.* Salt Lake City: Deseret Book, 1983.

Smith, Joseph. *History of The Church of Jesus Christ of Latter-day Saints.* Edited by B. H. Roberts. 7 vols. 2d ed. rev. Salt Lake City: The Church of Jesus Christ of Latter-day Saints, 1932–51.

LED

Prevail. *See* Appendix E.

Pride

Haughtiness, arrogance, a sense of superiority in one's own ability or position, a gateway for sin, and a root cause of separation from God. The Doctrine and Covenants links pride, "selfishness" (56:8), apparel, riches, and "highmindedness" (42:40; 84:112; 90:17) with "covetousness," failure to repent, and other "detestable things" (98:19–20). The revelations contain specific warnings to individuals against pride. Emma Smith was told, "Continue in the spirit of meekness, and beware of pride" (25:14). Oliver Cowdery was cautioned, "Beware of pride, lest thou shouldst enter into temptation" (23:1). This warning was evidently forgotten later on, in 1838, when Oliver became prideful, rejected counsel from the leadership of the Church, was excommunicated, and did not return to the Church for ten years. "Pride and the cares of the world" kept James Covill, a Protestant minister, from accepting the fulness of the gospel (39:9; 40:1–3). In the context of temple worship, the Lord commanded all the Saints to, among other things, "cease . . . from all your pride and lightmindedness" (88:121). Priesthood holders are warned that if they seek "to cover [their] sins, or to gratify [their] pride, [their] vain ambition, or to exercise control or dominion or compulsion upon the souls of the children of men, in any degree of unrighteousness, behold, the heavens withdraw themselves; the Spirit of the Lord is grieved; and when it is withdrawn, Amen to the priesthood or the authority of that man" (121:37; cf. vv. 34–46).

Pride was central to the loss of the 116 manuscript pages of the Book of Mormon translation, for which the Lord chastised Martin Harris. Although the word *pride* is not used in these verses, Martin Harris's behavior clearly bespeaks an attitude of pride. The revelations say that Martin "exalts himself" (5:24), "has set at naught the counsels of God, and has broken the most sacred promises which were made before God, and has depended upon his own judgment and boasted in his own wisdom" (3:13).

The Doctrine and Covenants identifies pride as the cause of the Nephites' downfall (38:39) and reiterates several times Malachi's warning (Mal. 4:1) that in the last days "all the proud and they that do wickedly shall be as stubble; and I will burn them up, saith the Lord of Hosts" (29:9; 64:24; 133:64).

The revelations also confirm that the corrective for pride is not groveling self-criticism but humility. After chastening Martin Harris for his pride, the Lord assured him that he would be restored to favor with the Lord, "if he will bow down before me, and humble himself in mighty prayer and faith, in the sincerity of his heart" (5:24). To Warren Cowdery, Oliver's older brother and presiding high priest over the Church in Freedom, New York, the Lord said, "Blessed is my servant Warren, for I will have mercy on him; and, notwithstanding the vanity of his heart, I will lift him up inasmuch as he will humble himself before me" (106:7).

Clearly, to assist in the work of the Lord requires humility and "an eye single to the glory of God," the very antithesis of pride, which is the extolling of oneself (4:5).

See also Humble, humility.

NEL

Priest(s)

Term used in the Doctrine and Covenants in three contexts:

1. Aaronic priests in ancient Israel. Speaking of members of the Church in this dispensation who will not receive an inheritance among the Saints in Zion because their names are not "written in the book of the law," the revelation states, "it shall be done unto them as unto the children of the priest, as will be found recorded in the second chapter and sixty-first and second verses of Ezra" (85:11–12).

2. Men who receive the highest glory in the celestial kingdom, and are designated "priests and kings, who have received of his [God's] fulness, and of his [God's] glory" (76:56).

3. Those who are ordained to the office of priest in the Aaronic PRIESTHOOD in this dispensation. This is the most common use of *priest* in the revelations. The duties of a priest include taking "the lead of meetings when there is no elder present" (20:49); "visit[ing] the house of each member, and exhort[ing] them to pray vocally and in secret and attend to all family duties" (20:47, 51); "ordain[ing] other priests, teachers, and deacons" (20:48); and to "preach, teach, expound, exhort, and baptize, and administer the sacrament" (20:46, 76). "In all these duties the priest is to assist the elder if occasion requires" (20:52).

Like those ordained to other PRIESTHOOD OFFICES, a priest is to be "ordained according to the gifts and callings of God unto him . . . by the power of the Holy Ghost, which is in the one who ordains him" (20:60). A priest belongs to a quorum of forty-eight priests, presided over by a bishop acting in his office as president of the Aaronic Priesthood (107:87–88).

Early in this dispensation, priests were authorized to sign letters certifying that members with whom they were acquainted were in good standing in the Church, when those members moved to a new area of the Church (20:84). Also, in order to keep Church membership records updated, teachers and priests from the various branches were sent to "conferences held by the elders of the church" to report who had joined the Church and who had been "expelled" (20:81–83).

HDG

Priestcrafts. *See* Appendix E.

Priesthood

The power and authority to act in the name of God. References to the priesthood, its offices and functions, are found throughout the Doctrine and Covenants, especially in sections 20, 84, and 107. *See* Historical context and overview of Doctrine and Covenants 20 (p. 728), 84 (p. 787), and 107 (p. 815).

Priesthood authority is required in the performance of all gospel ORDINANCES and directs the teaching of the GOSPEL. It can only be conferred upon a man "by the laying on of hands by those who are in authority" and "by the power of the Holy Ghost, which is in the one who ordains him" (A of F 5; 20:60). Priesthood does not and cannot exist where there is no revelation. Explaining the necessity of the restoration of priesthood in the dispensation of the fulness of times, Oliver Cowdery observed that "it was as easy to be seen that amid the great strife and noise concerning religion, none had authority from God to administer the ordinances of the Gospel. For the question might be asked, have men authority to administer in the name of Christ, who deny revelations, when His testimony is no less than the spirit of prophecy, and His religion based, built, and sustained by immediate revelations, in all ages of the world when He has had a people on earth?" (JS–H 1:71n; "Letter," 15).

Two priesthoods

"There are, in the church, two priesthoods, namely, the Melchizedek and Aaronic, including the Levitical Priesthood." A distinction may be made between the Aaronic Priesthood and the Levitical Priesthood in that all worthy members of the tribe of Levi could function in certain duties in the "Levitical," while only Aaron and his descendants held the right to preside in that priesthood.

"Why the first is called the Melchizedek Priesthood is because Melchizedek was such a great high priest. Before his day it was called *the Holy Priesthood, after the Order of the Son of God.* But out of respect or reverence to the name of the Supreme Being, to avoid the too frequent repetition of his name, they, the church, in ancient days, called that priesthood after Melchizedek, or the Melchizedek Priesthood" (107:1–4).

After the days of Melchizedek, who was contemporary with Abraham, the children of Israel found themselves in bondage in Egypt. They were liberated by Moses, to whom the Lord had committed the fulness of the gospel. At Sinai, Moses sought to sanctify his people and to bring them into the presence of God. They refused this blessing, and God, in his wrath, took Moses and the Holy Priesthood from them. In its stead he gave them a lesser law and a lesser priesthood (84:19–26; JST Ex. 33:20; 34:1–2). While

they were in Egypt, the destroying angel spared the firstborn son of each family in Israel, and it became the obligation of the firstborn male in each Israelite family to attend to the duties of the lesser priesthood. Later, however, the Lord chose to have these priestly responsibilities rest solely upon the tribe of Levi. The presidency of this priesthood rested with Aaron and the firstborn of his sons through the generations to John the Baptist (Num. 3:1–13; D&C 84:27–28).

Restoration and functions of the Aaronic Priesthood

While laboring on the translation of the Book of Mormon, Joseph Smith and Oliver Cowdery became aware of the importance of the ordinance of baptism for the remission of sins. Desiring to know how they might receive this same blessing, Joseph and Oliver retired to a secluded spot along the banks of the Susquehanna River, where an angel from heaven appeared to them. He introduced himself as John, the same who was known in New Testament times as John the Baptist. John laid his hands upon their heads and conferred upon them the same priesthood by which he had baptized the Savior. His was the priesthood of Aaron, sometimes called the Levitical Priesthood. Having thus given both Joseph and Oliver the priesthood and its KEYS, he directed them to baptize each other. After their baptisms, John the Baptist then had these two men reordain each other to the priesthood (JS–H 1:71; D&C 13:1). This reordination emphasized the order that must exist in the Lord's house; that is, baptism is to precede the reception of the priesthood. John then explained that he was acting under the direction of Peter, James, and John, who held the keys of the Melchizedek Priesthood. That priesthood, John said, would soon be restored to them (JS–H 1:72).

"The power and authority of the lesser, or Aaronic Priesthood, is to hold the keys of the ministering of angels, and to administer in outward ordinances, the letter of the gospel, the baptism of repentance for the remission of sins, agreeable to the covenants and commandments" (107:20). It does not, however, have the POWER and authority to administer the ordinances of full salvation, as does the Melchizedek

Priesthood, and is "made without an oath," while "the Priesthood of Melchizedek is by an oath and covenant" (Smith, 5:555). Thus, all the authority the Lord gave to the tribe of Levi was held by John the Baptist and conferred by him upon Joseph Smith and Oliver Cowdery on 15 May 1829 (13:1; Mal. 3:1–4; Smith, 5:256–57).

All the offices of the Aaronic Priesthood (DEACON, TEACHER, PRIEST, and BISHOP) had been restored by 1831 (20:38–48; 41:9). Although the office of bishop is listed as an office in the Aaronic Priesthood, bishops in the Church today serve in both Aaronic Priesthood and Melchizedek Priesthood functions. In addition to holding the keys of the Aaronic Priesthood, and "administering all temporal things" (107:68) the bishop also holds the office of HIGH PRIEST in the Melchizedek Priesthood, and, as the presiding high priest oversees all priesthood and ward affairs (68:19).

Restoration and functions of the Melchizedek Priesthood

Within weeks of the coming of John the Baptist, Peter, James, and John appeared to Joseph Smith and Oliver Cowdery and bestowed the higher or Melchizedek Priesthood upon them. In addition to the priesthood, they conferred the "keys of the kingdom, and of the dispensation of the fulness of times" (128:20; cf. 27:12–13). With the priesthood and its keys restored, Joseph and Oliver could then proceed with the organization of the Church.

As the Church grew in numbers and strength, the various offices and QUORUMS of the priesthood were restored line upon line. Joseph and Oliver were sustained to preside as the first and second elders of the Church when it was organized 6 April 1830 (20:2–3). The first high priests were called and ordained at a conference held 3–6 June 1831 (Cannon and Cook, 7). In some instances the revelations refer to the office of high priest as the "high priesthood" (84:29; 107:65). The office of high priest is described as "the greatest of all" (107:64), as it is the duty of high priests to preside. On 25 January 1832, Joseph Smith was sustained as the "President of the High Priesthood" (107:65; Smith, 1:243). The First Presidency, a presidency of three high priests who would preside over the whole Church, was completed by 18 March 1833 (Smith, 1:334; cf. D&C 81:1–2; 90:6–8). The Prophet's father, Joseph Smith Sr., became the first patriarch in the Restoration on 18 December 1833. The members of the first Quorum of Twelve Apostles were called 14 February 1835 and ordained shortly thereafter; two weeks later, 28 February 1835, members of a quorum of seventies were called (Smith, 2:187, 203).

The priesthood exists independent of the Church, but the Church cannot exist independent of the priesthood. Section 84 teaches that the "priesthood continueth in the church of God in all generations, and is without beginning of days or end of years" (v. 17), affirming that the Church existed in all generations. Church organization and function are governed by the priesthood, and no one can hold an office in the priesthood without the sustaining vote of the Church (20:65; 26:2).

A primary function of the Melchizedek Priesthood is to administer the gospel (84:19). It is by the authority of this priesthood that messengers clothed with power and authority are sent forth to carry the light of the gospel to every nation, kindred, tongue, and people. While a priest may go forth and declare the gospel of repentance and baptism, as did John the Baptist, the Aaronic Priesthood does not have the power to confer the GIFT OF THE HOLY GHOST (20:46–52; JS–H 1:70). The bestowal of the gift of the Holy Ghost, the right to the constant companionship of the HOLY GHOST, comes only from the Melchizedek Priesthood. This priesthood directs all ordinances that are performed in the temple. It is also under the direction of the Melchizedek Priesthood that the gospel is taught in the spirit world. Thus, all who died without the opportunity to accept the gospel in this life will have that opportunity to accept or reject it in the spirit world before final judgment. Also, all those who die, with or without a knowledge of the gospel, will be taught in the spirit world, and will be able to improve their spiritual status (138:30–37, 57–58).

The Melchizedek Priesthood "is the channel through which all knowledge, doctrine, the plan of salvation, and every important matter is revealed from heaven" (Smith, 4:207). This priesthood holds the "key of the mysteries of the kingdom, even the key of the knowledge of God" (84:19), and the power to enter into God's presence (84:20–26). Only through this priesthood can Saints receive the knowledge whereby they might "pass by the angels, and the gods, which are set there, to their exaltation and glory in all things" (132:19).

"The power and authority of the higher, or Melchizedek Priesthood, is to hold the keys of all the spiritual blessings of the church—to have the privilege of receiving the mysteries of the kingdom of heaven, to have the heavens opened unto them, to commune with the general assembly and church of the Firstborn, and to enjoy the communion and presence of God the Father, and Jesus the mediator of the new covenant" (107:18–19). Only in the oath and covenant of the holy priesthood is the promise of exaltation found. The oath associated with the Melchizedek Priesthood represents the promise of the Father that those who keep the covenant they make in receiving the Melchizedek Priesthood will receive all that God has, a promise so profound and so far beyond human comprehension that to dramatize its truthfulness the Father attests to it by way of an oath, "which he cannot break, neither can it be moved" (84:40). The language of the oath and covenant are as follows:

"For whoso is faithful unto the obtaining these two priesthoods of which I have spoken, and the magnifying their calling, are sanctified by the Spirit unto the renewing of their bodies. They become the sons of Moses and of Aaron and the seed of Abraham, and the church and kingdom, and the elect of God. And also all they who receive this priesthood receive me, saith the Lord; for he that receiveth my servants receiveth me; and he that receiveth me receiveth my Father; and he that receiveth my Father receiveth my Father's kingdom; therefore all that my Father hath shall be given unto him. And this is according to the oath and covenant which belongeth to the priesthood" (84:33–44). Thus, those who receive the two priesthoods (Aaronic and Melchizedek) and magnify their calling become rightful heirs to all the power and

authority given to Moses and Aaron, and they also become heirs to all priesthood blessings promised to Abraham and his seed (Abr. 2:9–11). They will, through their faithful service, be "sanctified by the Spirit unto the renewing of their bodies" (84:33). As both body and spirit are made clean, they are able to put off the natural man and enjoy the company of angels and a state of purity that will enable them to enter into the presence of God. Of them the Lord has said, "They who dwell in his presence are the church of the Firstborn; and they see as they are seen, and know as they are known, having received of his fulness and of his grace; and he makes them equal in power, and in might, and in dominion" (76:94–95). *See* Church of the Firstborn.

It is by the authority of the priesthood that ordinances of blessing and ordinances of salvation are given. Ordinances of blessing include the blessing of the sick (42:43–52); the naming and blessing of young children (20:70); and patriarchal blessings given by ordained PATRIARCHS (107:18, 42: cf. verses 39–56), which declare by revelation tribal lineage in the house of Israel and give counsel, direction, and prophecy. Ordinances of salvation include baptism (20:72–74); the temple endowment (124:37–40; 110:9; 138:57–58); and eternal MARRIAGE (131:1–4; 132:19–25).

The patriarchal order of the priesthood

The Prophet Joseph Smith taught that "there are three grand orders of priesthood"—patriarchal, Aaronic, and Melchizedek orders (5:554–55). He also taught that "all priesthood is Melchizedeck; but there are different portions or degrees of it" (Ehat and Cook, 59); and that the "Melchisedek Priesthood . . . is the grand head, and holds the highest authority which pertains to the Priesthood" (4:207). Thus, the Melchizedek Priesthood comprehends and presides over all orders of the priesthood and functions under the direction of the "keys of the kingdom, which belong always unto the Presidency of the High Priesthood" (81:2). In all dispensations the Church has been presided over by a presidency of three high priests (107:8–10, 21–22, 29; 112:30–32).

Joseph Smith explained about the patriarchal order of the priesthood: "Go to and finish the temple, and God will fill it with power, and you will then receive more knowledge concerning this priesthood" (5:554–55). Through the sacred temple ordinance of eternal marriage, a faithful priesthood holder receives the privilege to preside as a father, or patriarch, in the most important unit in all eternity—a family. "In the celestial glory there are three heavens or degrees; and in order to obtain the highest, a man must enter into this order of the priesthood [meaning the new and everlasting covenant of marriage]; and if he does not, he cannot obtain it" (131:1–3). If they are faithful to their marriage covenants, a husband and wife "shall pass by the angels, and the gods, which are set there, to their exaltation" where there "shall be a fulness and a continuation of the seeds forever and ever . . . and continuation of the lives," even "eternal lives" (132:19–24), the power to have children in the eternities. This renews the promise made by God to Abraham that in this holy order he and Sarah might have seed as countless as the sands of the sea or the stars of the heavens (132:30). Thus, the fulness of salvation is found only in the sacred union of a man and woman in a marriage that is eternal. It is through this covenant that women share equally with their husbands the promises and blessings associated with the oath and covenant of the priesthood.

On 19 January 1841 the Lord told Joseph Smith that the "fulness of the priesthood" had not yet been restored to the earth because there was not a suitable place in which such blessings could be bestowed (124:28). To that end a temple was built in Nauvoo in which the fulness of all gospel blessings could be given to faithful Saints. Thereafter Joseph Smith observed, "If a man gets a fullness of the priesthood of God, he has to get it in the same way that Jesus Christ obtained it, and that was by keeping all the commandments and obeying all the ordinances of the house of the Lord" (5:424). The Prophet also declared that "the rights of the priesthood are inseparably connected with the powers of heaven, and that the powers of heaven cannot be controlled nor handled only upon the principles of righteousness" (121:36). It is by the principles of righteousness that a rightful patriarch, one who has entered into the new and everlasting covenant of marriage, is to preside in the family.

Who may hold the priesthood and its offices

God promised Abraham that his seed would be the rightful heirs to the priesthood. "In their hands," he said, "they shall bear this ministry and Priesthood unto all nations" through the "literal seed" of Abraham were to come those who would take the blessings "of the Gospel, which are the blessings of salvation, even of life eternal" to all other peoples (Abr. 2:9–11). Speaking to the early elders who laid the foundation of this dispensation, a revelation states: "Therefore, thus saith the Lord unto you, with whom the priesthood hath continued through the lineage of your fathers—for ye are lawful heirs, according to the flesh, and have been hid from the world with Christ in God—therefore your life and the priesthood have remained, and must needs remain through you and your lineage until the restoration of all things spoken by the mouths of all the holy prophets since the world began" (86:8–10). That restoration was continuing, and in September 1842, in connection with instructions about performing and recording baptisms for the dead, the Lord said, "I am about to restore many things to the earth, pertaining to the priesthood" (127:8).

Those who are not natural or rightful heirs of Abraham by birth become such through gospel covenants—they are "accounted" as the literal seed of Abraham and heirs of all the promises made to Abraham and his seed (Abr. 2:9–11; D&C 84:33–34; Gal. 3:26–29). The priesthood is the same, the ordinances are the same, and the promises are the same for all the seed of Abraham, whether by birth or through gospel covenants, in any age of the world.

All worthy male members of the Church are entitled to hold the priesthood. Worthiness is always a prerequisite to holding priesthood and performing any function in the name of the Lord. To receive the priesthood or be ordained to any of its offices also requires the sustaining vote of the Church (20:65). In the case of local offices, those affected must give their consent. In the case of the general offices of the Church, the whole Church must be called upon for a sustaining vote, which is called for at annual general conferences of the Church. As to ordination to office within the priesthood, the current pattern is for young men to receive the Aaronic Priesthood and be ordained to the office of a deacon at twelve years of age. At age fourteen a young man may be ordained a teacher; at sixteen years of age he may be ordained a priest. When eighteen years of age, a young man may receive the Melchizedek Priesthood and be ordained to the office of elder. Ordination to the office of high priest comes when a man is called to a position requiring that he be a high priest or when by virtue of age it is fitting that he join a high priests quorum because, generally, high priests are older men. The office of SEVENTY is reserved for men who serve as area authorities or general officers of the Church. To serve as a bishop, patriarch, seventy, or APOSTLE, a man must also hold the office of high priest.

See also Church of Jesus Christ of Latter-day Saints, The; Letter of the law; Ordain, ordained, ordination(s); Priesthood offices; Priesthood, proper exercise of; Priesthood, restoration of priesthood and priesthood keys; Priests of the Most High; Sons of Levi; Sons of Moses and of Aaron.

BIBLIOGRAPHY

Cannon, Donald Q., and Lyndon W. Cook, eds. *Far West Record: Minutes of The Church of Jesus Christ of Latter-day Saints, 1830–1844.* Salt Lake City: Deseret Book, 1983.

Ehat, Andrew F., and Lyndon W. Cook, comps. and eds. *The Words of Joseph Smith.* Provo, Utah: Religious Studies Center, Brigham Young University, 1980.

"Letter from Oliver Cowdery to W. W. Phelps," 7 September 1834. *Messenger and Advocate* 1, no. 1 (October 1834): 13–16.

Smith, Joseph. *History of The Church of Jesus Christ of Latter-day Saints.* Edited by B. H. Roberts. 7 vols. 2d ed. rev. Salt Lake City: The Church of Jesus Christ of Latter-day Saints, 1932–51.

JFM

Priesthood offices

There are nine offices in the PRIESTHOOD—four in the Aaronic Priesthood and five in the Melchizedek Priesthood. The four offices in the Aaronic Priesthood are DEACON, TEACHER, PRIEST, and BISHOP. The five offices in the Melchizedek Priesthood are ELDER, HIGH PRIEST, PATRIARCH,

SEVENTY, and APOSTLE. The office of bishop is an Aaronic Priesthood office and the bishop serves as president of the Aaronic Priesthood in a given ward (107:87–88), and he is also a high priest, the presiding high priest, who presides in a ward over all priesthood holders, both Aaronic and Melchizedek (68:15, 19; 107:16–17, 69–71, 76).

See also Historical context and overview of Doctrine and Covenants 20 (p. 728), 68 (p. 774), 84 (p. 787), and 107 (p. 815).

LED

Priesthood, Aaronic. *See* Priesthood.

Priesthood blessings. *See* Laying on of hands; Priesthood.

Priesthood, Levitical. *See* Priesthood.

Priesthood, Melchizedek. *See* Priesthood.

Priesthood, oath and covenant of. *See* Priesthood.

Priesthood, patriarchal. *See* Priesthood.

Priesthood, proper exercise of

Righteous administration of the functions of the PRIESTHOOD. The Doctrine and Covenants provides valuable information concerning the divine nature of priesthood, both in the heavens and on earth, the organization and function of priesthood quorums, and the responsibilities of the respective offices. The revelations give clear and specific teachings regarding the proper and improper use of priesthood—how its AUTHORITY is to be exercised. In writing from LIBERTY JAIL in March 1839, the Prophet Joseph Smith declared that "the rights of the priesthood are inseparably connected with the powers of heaven, and that the powers of heaven cannot be controlled nor handled only upon the principles of righteousness" (121:36). Righteousness is necessary to the proper use of priesthood. President Boyd K. Packer has reminded priesthood holders that "your authority comes through your ordination; your power comes through obedience and worthiness" (32). Section 121 gives specific examples, both negative and positive, of what it means to "handle" the priesthood.

Unrighteous exercise of priesthood

Examples given by the Lord of unworthy or improper use of priesthood include attempting to "cover our sins, or to gratify our pride, our vain ambition, or to exercise control or dominion or compulsion upon the souls of the children of men, in any degree of unrighteousness" (121:37). *See* Pride.

A man seeks to "cover [his] sins" when his public, priesthood life does not comport with his personal, private life—pretending to be more righteous and worthy than he is, hypocritically failing to maintain the standards of the gospel that priesthood leaders teach and expect others to live. Covering sins also involves rationalization, minimizing the seriousness of sin, and procrastination of repentance. Serving in priesthood capacities "to gratify our pride, [or] our vain ambition" (121:37) would be service for ulterior motives rather than with "an eye single to the glory of God" (4:5). This may be manifest in many ways, including holding and functioning within the priesthood to further a man's own interests as a status symbol or for the recognition and praise of men rather than for service to God's children. Vain ambition is always self-centered and selfish. To exercise unrighteous dominion is to attempt to compel or intimidate others by virtue of priesthood position or authority. The Lord condemns such unrighteousness, whether it be in the context of Church service or leadership in the home.

Righteous exercise of priesthood

In contrast to unrighteous exercise of priesthood, worthy priesthood bearers use "persuasion . . . long-suffering . . . gentleness . . . meekness . . . love unfeigned [unpretended] . . . kindness, and pure knowledge, which shall greatly enlarge the soul without hypocrisy, and without guile—reproving betimes with sharpness, when moved upon by the Holy Ghost; and then showing forth afterwards an increase of love toward him whom thou hast reproved, lest he esteem thee to be his enemy; that he may know that thy faithfulness is stronger than the cords of death" (121:41–44). In addition to the

instructions concerning righteous use of priesthood found in section 121, the Lord enjoins priesthood holders to have "charity towards all men, and to the household of faith," and to let virtue "garnish [their] thoughts unceasingly," promising that their confidence would "wax strong in the presence of God," that the Holy Ghost would be their "constant companion," and that their "scepter" would be "an unchanging scepter of righteousness and truth" (121:45–46). A scepter ordinarily means a staff borne by a sovereign as an emblem of authority. In this instance, it probably refers to one's priesthood.

Those who receive the Melchizedek Priesthood do so with an "oath and covenant" to magnify their calling and "live by every word that proceedeth forth from the mouth of God." Of those who do so, the Lord has said, "All that my Father hath shall be given unto him" (84:33–44). "All that my Father hath" includes "thrones, kingdoms, principalities, and powers, dominions, all heights and depths" (132:19), and a glorious resurrection unto eternal life, "the greatest of all the gifts of God" (6:13; 14:7).

BIBLIOGRAPHY

Packer, Boyd, K. "The Aaronic Priesthood" *Ensign* 11 (November 1981): 30–33.

BLT

Priesthood, restoration of priesthood and priesthood keys

Priesthood KEYS and authority were restored to the earth in this dispensation on several different occasions over a period of years. The process began in Harmony, Pennsylvania, where Joseph Smith and Oliver Cowdery were living while they translated the Book of Mormon plates. On 15 May 1829, according to Joseph's record, the two men retired to the woods along the banks of the Susquehanna River "to pray and inquire of the Lord respecting baptism for the remission of sins, that we found mentioned in the translation of the plates" (JS–H 1:68). In answer to their prayer, John the Baptist, a resurrected being, appeared to Joseph and Oliver, laid his hands on their heads, and conferred upon them the Aaronic Priesthood, "which holds the keys of the ministering of angels, and of the

Restoration of the Melchizedek Priesthood; *painting by Walter Rane. "And also with Peter, and James, and John, whom I have sent unto you, by whom I have ordained you and confirmed you to be apostles, and especial witnesses of my name, and bear the keys of your ministry and of the same things which I revealed unto them" (D&C 27:12).*

gospel of repentance, and of baptism by immersion for the remission of sins" (13:1). Following John the Baptist's instructions, Joseph then baptized Oliver and Oliver baptized Joseph—in that order—after which Joseph ordained Oliver to the Aaronic Priesthood and Oliver ordained Joseph—again, in that order, "for so we were commanded" (JS–H 1:71). After their baptism, Joseph reported, both men "were filled with the Holy Ghost" and prophesied of things to come (JS–H 1:73).

Among other things, Joseph recorded, John the Baptist taught that he was acting "under the direction of Peter, James and John, who held the keys of the Priesthood of Melchizedek, which Priesthood . . . would in due time be conferred on us" (JS–H 1:72). Precisely when and where this conferral eventually took place is unknown, but it is clear that Peter, James, and John were the ones who restored it to Joseph and Oliver (27:12). Quite possibly it took place at the same time Peter, James, and John were heard "declaring themselves as possessing the keys of the kingdom" somewhere "in the wilderness . . . on the Susquehanna river" between Harmony, Pennsylvania, and Colesville, New York (128:20). If so, it would have happened within two weeks or so of the appearance of John the

Baptist on 15 May 1829, because Joseph and Oliver moved from that area to Fayette, New York, in early June 1829 (Smith, *Papers,* 1:293).

Whatever the circumstances accompanying its restoration, Joseph and Oliver were told that they could not exercise the Melchizedek Priesthood until "such times, as it should be practicable to have our brethren, who had been and who should be baptized, assembled together . . . and have them decide by vote whether they were willing to accept us as spiritual teachers, or not" (Smith, *Papers,* 1:299). This vote took place at the organizational meeting of the Church in Fayette, New York, on 6 April 1830, after which Joseph and Oliver ordained each other to the office of elder and then laid their hands "on each individual member of the Church present that they might receive the gift of the Holy Ghost, and be confirmed members of the Church of Christ" (Smith, *Papers,* 1:303).

Joseph received numerous instructions about the functions and offices of the PRIESTHOOD over the course of the next several years, but no additional keys were restored until after the Kirtland Temple had been dedicated. On 3 April 1836, one week after the dedication, Joseph and Oliver "retired to the pulpit" of the temple after a meeting in which the Prophet had assisted in administering the sacrament to the assembled Saints (110, headnote). Hidden from the view of anyone in the temple by a heavy canvas curtain that could be lowered from the ceiling, Joseph and Oliver bowed themselves "in solemn and silent prayer" (110, headnote), after which the Savior appeared to them and formally accepted the Kirtland Temple. Then three ancient prophets appeared in succession, each of whom restored additional priesthood keys to the two men. First to appear was Moses, who "committed unto us," Joseph recorded, "the keys of the gathering of Israel from the four parts of the earth, and the leading of the ten tribes from the land of the north" (110:11). Elias appeared next and restored "the dispensation of the gospel of Abraham" (110:12), after which Elijah appeared "to turn the hearts of the fathers to the children, and the children to the fathers" (110:15)—a clear reference to the keys and authority he restored that were necessary to seal husbands,

wives, and children together as families for eternity (138:47–48) and to approve or seal the validity of "every ordinance and blessing of the gospel" (Smith, *Doctrines,* 2:94). *See* Seal, sealed.

The keys restored by Moses, Elias, and Elijah in connection with those Joseph and Oliver had earlier received from John the Baptist and Peter, James, and John constitute the "keys of this dispensation" (110:16). In addition to these messengers, Joseph Smith reported the coming of Michael, Gabriel, Raphael, "and of divers angels, from Michael or Adam down to the present time, all declaring their dispensation, their rights, their keys, their honors, their majesty and glory, and the power of their priesthood; giving line upon line, precept upon precept; here a little, and there a little" (128:21).

BIBLIOGRAPHY

Smith, Joseph. *The Papers of Joseph Smith.* Edited by Dean C. Jessee. 2 vols. Salt Lake City: Deseret Book, 1989–92.

Smith, Joseph Fielding. *Doctrines of Salvation.* Compiled by Bruce R. McConkie. 3 vols. Salt Lake City: Bookcraft, 1954–56.

AHH

Priests of the Most High

Melchizedek PRIESTHOOD holders who are exalted in the celestial kingdom. "They are they who are priests and kings, who have received of his fulness, and of his glory; and are priests of the Most High, after the order of Melchizedek, which was after the order of Enoch, which was after the order of the Only Begotten Son. Wherefore, as it is written, they are gods, even the sons of God" (76:56–58).

The only mention of this designation outside the Doctrine and Covenants refers to Melchizedek (Gen. 14:18; Heb. 7:1), who was "approved" of by God and ordained a high priest after the order of Enoch, eventually receiving the titles Prince of Peace, King of Heaven, and King of Peace (JST Gen. 14:25–40).

DLB

Prince of all. *See* Adam.

Prince of this world. *See* Satan.

Principalities. *See* Appendix E.

Printing office/schoolhouse

A significant but little-known structure built in Kirtland, Ohio. The printing office/schoolhouse was a two-story building, thirty by thirty-eight feet, built adjacent to the temple site. For three years, beginning in November 1834, this building served several important functions. The first floor housed the offices of the First Presidency, was the location of the School of the Elders and Hebrew school, and accommodated various other offices and meetings, including Sunday worship services. The second story housed the printing press of the Church. The first edition of the Doctrine and Covenants in 1835, the second edition of the Book of Mormon, and the first Church hymnbook were published there, as were the Church newspapers—*The Evening and the Morning Star* (continued after the destruction of the press in Independence), the *Messenger and Advocate,* the *Northern Times* (for one year) and two editions of the *Elders' Journal.*

The genesis of this important structure was a revelation recorded in section 94 in which the Lord called for the construction of two buildings: "a house for the presidency, for the work of the presidency, in obtaining revelations; and for the work of the ministry of the presidency, in all things pertaining to the church and kingdom" (94:3), and a house "for the work of the printing of the translation of my scriptures, and all things whatsoever I shall command you" (94:10). Each building was to have two stories and measure fifty-five by sixty-five feet (94:4–5, 11). In the end, neither of these buildings was built as specified. The financial pressures of building the Kirtland Temple and the very limited resources of the Saints necessitated a compromise: one building to serve both as offices for the First Presidency and as a printing establishment.

Moving ahead with plans to establish a printing press, on 11 September 1833 Frederick G. Williams, Sidney Rigdon, Newel K. Whitney, Joseph Smith, and Oliver Cowdery resolved that a printing office be established under the name of F. G. Williams & Co. (Smith, 1:409). One month later, 10 October 1833, in a "council meeting" of Church leaders in Kirtland under the direction of President Frederick G. Williams (Joseph Smith and Sidney Rigdon were away on a mission), it was "agreed that we should set the hands immediately to erect a house for the printing office, which is to be thirty by thirty-eight feet on the ground; the first story to be occupied for the School of the Prophets this winter, and the upper story for the printing press" (Smith, 1:418). The building was completed in November 1834 and indeed filled the various functions for which it was built.

Before the completion of the planned building, "a temporary printing office was established in the John Johnson inn" (Anderson, 123). It must have been this operation for which the Prophet prayed 6 December 1833. Under that date Joseph Smith's history reads, "Being prepared to commence our labors in the printing business, I ask God in the name of Jesus, to establish it for ever, and cause that His word may speedily go forth to the nations of the earth, to the accomplishing of His great work in bringing about the restoration of the house of Israel" (1:451). Twelve days later, 18 December 1833, this interim printing office was formally dedicated when a group of "elders assembled in the printing office, and bowed down before the Lord" and Joseph Smith "dedicated the printing press, and all that pertained thereunto, to God" (Smith, 1:465).

When the building to house the printing office was finished, the "lower story of [the] building was set apart" for use by "the school for the Elders, wherein they might be more perfectly instructed in the great things of God, during the coming winter" (Smith, 2:169). That "coming winter" was 1834–35 when the Lectures on Faith were delivered and studied and a Hebrew school was instituted. Also during that winter the press began operating in the upper level of the building to meet the publishing needs of the Church.

For the next three years the printing office/schoolhouse served those important purposes. It is interesting to note that even before the Kirtland Temple was dedicated, some preliminary initiatory ordinances were conducted in the building. Under the date of 21 January 1836 the Prophet's history records, "About three o'clock,

P. M., I dismissed the school, and the Presidency retired to the attic story of the printing office, where we attended the ordinance of washing our bodies in pure water. We also perfumed our bodies and our heads, in the name of the Lord" (2:379).

These glorious days for this sacred structure ended when the spirit of apostasy affected some of the Saints, which resulted in the apostates claiming ownership of the printing office. It was sold and eventually "attached to satisfy an unjust judgment of the county court" (Anderson, 125). On 16 January 1838 the printing office was destroyed by fire with its contents of seven hundred or eight hundred partly finished copies of the Book of Mormon. Thus came to an end this significant structure in the history of the Church.

See also Doctrine and Covenants, historical development of; Ohio period; School(s).

BIBLIOGRAPHY

Anderson, Karl Ricks. *Joseph Smith's Kirtland: Eyewitness Accounts.* Salt Lake City: Deseret Book, 1989.

Smith, Joseph. *History of The Church of Jesus Christ of Latter-day Saints.* Edited by B. H. Roberts. 7 vols. 2 ed. rev. Salt Lake City: The Church of Jesus Christ of Latter-day Saints, 1932–51.

KWP

Proclamation. *See* Solemn proclamation.

Promulgate. *See* Appendix E.

Prophecy, more sure word of. *See* More sure word of prophecy.

Prophecy, spirit of. *See* Revelation.

Prophet(s)

One who has authority to speak for God; in a general sense, anyone who has a testimony of JESUS CHRIST. When asked if he were a prophet, Joseph Smith answered, "Yes, and every other man who has the testimony of Jesus. For the testimony of Jesus is the spirit of prophecy.—[Rev. 19:10]" (3:28). On another occasion the Prophet said, "No man is a minister of Jesus Christ without being a Prophet. No man can be a minister of Jesus Christ except he has the testimony of Jesus; and this is the spirit of prophecy" (3:389). The Doctrine and Covenants uses the word *prophet* in a more limited sense, pointing to those called and ordained to speak officially for God to the world and to the Church, govern the kingdom of God on earth, and oversee the administration of saving ordinances for all mankind.

Joseph Smith was designated by the Lord as the prophet of the Restored Church, the only one "appointed to receive commandments and revelations in this church" (28:1–7; cf. 21:1; 43:1–7; 107:91–92; 127:12; 135:3). The living prophet, the president of the Church, is the only person authorized to exercise all the KEYS of the kingdom, keys given to the apostle Peter by the Lord and subsequently conferred upon Joseph Smith by Peter, James, and John (Matt. 16:18–19; D&C 27:12–13). The members of the First Presidency and the Quorum of the Twelve Apostles also hold the keys of the kingdom, but latently, and they all must act under the direction of the prophet (7:1–7; 81:1–2; 112:30–32; 124:125). Along with the prophet, other members of the First Presidency and the Twelve are designated as "Prophets, Seers, Revelators, and special witnesses to all the nations of the earth" (Smith, 2:417). It has been the practice of the Church, since the beginning of the dispensation of the fulness of times, that at the death of the president of the Church, the First Presidency is dissolved and the senior member of the Quorum of the Twelve Apostles is ordained, set apart, and sustained as the new president of the Church. He is then authorized to exercise all the keys of the kingdom, as other prophets have done before him.

Concerning the teachings of the Prophet Joseph Smith and his successors as president of the Church, the Lord has said, "Thou shalt give heed unto all his words and commandments which he shall give unto you as he receiveth them, walking in all holiness before me; for his word ye shall receive, as if from mine own mouth, in all patience and faith" (21:4–5). The obedient are promised that the gates of hell will not prevail against them, the powers of darkness will be dispersed from before them, and the heavens will shake for their good (21:6). The disobedient have no such promise (124:45–46).

Missionaries and teachers in the Church are commanded to teach "none other things than that which the prophets and apostles have written, and that which is taught them by the Comforter through the prayer of faith" (52:9; cf. 42:11–14).

At the beginning of 1833, at the direction of the Lord, a "school of the prophets" was organized in Kirtland, for the "instruction in all things that are expedient" for "all the officers of the church . . . those who are called to the ministry in the church." Principles and procedures to govern the school were outlined, and the school was established (88:127–41). In April 1833 the school was ended. Evidently, troubles had surfaced in the School of the Prophets, for in June 1833, the Lord revealed, "Contentions arose in the school of the prophets; which was very grievous unto me, saith your Lord; therefore I sent them forth to be chastened" (95:10).

The Doctrine and Covenants contains dozens of references to the general category of "prophets of old," whose writings constitute "the law and the prophets" (17:2; 59:22), indicating the authenticity of their words and affirming the fulfillment of their prophecies (e.g., 42:39; 66:2; 86:10; 138:21, 32, 36–48). In addition, many ancient prophets are named in the revelations and some of their roles and contributions documented, including Adam, Enoch, Noah, Melchizedek, Abraham, Elias, Moses, Elijah, Isaiah, Ezekiel, Daniel, and Malachi. A host of others are named in revelations that detail priesthood lineage from Adam to succeeding generations (84:6–16; 107:39–52). Some Book of Mormon prophets are also named, including the brother of Jared, Lehi, Nephi, and Moroni.

The revelations also contain information about future prophets. Section 133 speaks of those "who are in the north countries," whose prophets will hear the voice of the Lord, and "no longer stay themselves." They will come to Zion, bringing with them their "rich treasures," and "fall down and be crowned with glory, even in Zion, by the hands of the servants of the Lord, even the children of Ephraim" (133:26–34). Two other future prophets are mentioned in section 77. To the question "What is to be understood by the two witnesses, in the eleventh chapter of Revelation," the revelation answers, "They are two prophets that are to be raised up to the Jewish nation in the last days, at the time of the restoration, and to prophesy to the Jews after they are gathered and have built the city of Jerusalem in the land of their fathers" (77:15; cf. Rev. 11:1–15).

The overarching message of the Doctrine and Covenants concerning prophets is that the Saints can have complete confidence in their teachings. President Wilford Woodruff stated: "The Lord will never permit me or any other man who stands as President of this Church to lead you astray. It is not in the programme" ("Excerpts from Three Addresses by President Wilford Woodruff Regarding the Manifesto"). The Lord has promised again and again that his prophets speak for him and he will see that their testimonies are upheld and their prophecies fulfilled (1:37–38).

BIBLIOGRAPHY

Smith, Joseph. *History of The Church of Jesus Christ of Latter-day Saints*. Edited by B. H. Roberts. 7 vols. 2d ed. rev. Salt Lake City: The Church of Jesus Christ of Latter-day Saints, 1932–51.

HDG

Prophets, school of the. *See* School(s).

Propria persona

Latin term meaning "in one's own role or person." Joseph Smith, describing the importance of properly recording vicarious baptisms, noted in 128:8 that the dead would be judged by those ordinances that were performed "in their own *propria persona*, or by the means of their own agents." The Latin word *propria* is an adjective denoting one's perpetual or absolute property, and *persona* is a noun that originally meant the kind of mask used by an actor or the character played by the actor. By extension, *persona* came to mean the role one plays in life and eventually to mean the person himself (*Oxford*, s.v. "proprius" and "persona").

Roman usage also applied *persona* to the person involved in a court case, and it is in this sense that the expression came into modern legal usage, where "in propria persona" indicates that one is representing oneself in court rather than being represented by a lawyer or some other agent (Ballentine, s.v. "in propria persona"). This legal usage seems to have influenced Joseph Smith, because his use of the term in section 128 conveys the binding, legal sense of ordinances performed by agents, which can be as binding as if the subject had received them in person.

BIBLIOGRAPHY

Ballentine, James A. *Ballentine's Law Dictionary*. Edited by William S. Anderson. 3d ed. San Francisco: Bancroft-Whitney, 1969.

Oxford Latin Dictionary. Edited by P. G. W. Glare. Oxford: Clarendon Press, 2002.

EDH

Proscribe. *See* Appendix E.

Prudent. *See* Appendix E.

Prune my vineyard. *See* Vineyard.

Pulsipher, Zera

Birth: 24 June 1789, Rockington, Windham County, Vermont

Death: 1 January 1872, Hebron, Washington County, Utah

Zera Pulsipher was a Baptist minister when he first learned of the Church in the fall of 1831 as he and a "crowded congregation" were introduced to the Book of Mormon by Jared Carter (Pulsipher, 5–6). A few days later, Pulsipher received a vision in which he saw angels holding the Book of Mormon, indicating to him that the book was "the great revelation of the last days" (6). After his conversion and baptism, he had great desires to preach the gospel. In doing so he was privileged to baptize a future president of the Church, Wilford Woodruff. Later, he assisted in building the Kirtland Temple, and between the fall of 1837 and January 1838 he was instrumental in establishing a branch of twenty-nine members in Canada (Pulsipher, 6–7).

Pulsipher's name appears in 124:138 as a president of the quorum of seventies. He was ordained on 6 March 1838. He began his service by helping the Saints flee persecution in Kirtland and, later, by traveling to secure Adam-ondi-Ahman (Diahman, Daviess County, Missouri) at Joseph Smith's request. Regarding Adam-ondi-Ahman, Pulsipher wrote, "We . . . found a few brethren there surrounded by numerous mobs. . . . We stayed about a month, being

Zera Pulsipher, 1789–1872, and Mary Ann Brown Pulsipher, 1799–1886.

continually annoyed by mobs and thieves . . . yet all the while we expected to stay there and by faith and works retained our places" (11–12). Eventually, persecution forced Pulsipher from Missouri to Illinois. In Nauvoo he continued his service as one of the presidents of the seventies, and he received his endowment in the Nauvoo Temple in December 1845. He traveled west with the Saints, arriving in the Salt Lake Valley in the late 1840s, where he experienced harsh winters, the 1851 cricket infestation, the arrival of a hostile United States army, and "much labor" in the Church (Pulsipher, 23–25).

Pulsipher served in the presidency of the seventies until 1862, when he was dropped from the presidency and disciplined because he had "transcended the bounds of the Priesthood in the ordinance of sealing." It is not clear exactly what disciplinary action was taken, however, and in April 1862 the First Presidency authorized his rebaptism and ordination to the office of high priest. "Subsequently he was ordained a Patriarch" (Jenson, 1:194), in which office he served faithfully in southern Utah until his death in January 1872. Of "Dixie" (southwestern Utah) Pulsipher wrote, "I found it to be a very healthy section, and I enjoyed myself very well, considering the obscurity of the place" (26).

BIBLIOGRAPHY

Jenson, Andrew. *Latter-day Saint Biographical Encyclopedia.* 4 vols. Salt Lake City: Andrew Jenson History Company, 1901–36. Reprint, Salt Lake City: Western Epics, 1971.

Pulsipher, Zera. "History of Zera Pulsipher as Written by Himself." L. Tom Perry Special Collections, Harold B. Lee Library, Brigham Young University, Provo, Utah.

ZLL

Punish, punished, punishment

To inflict penalties, sorrow, pain, or anguish, or to withdraw privileges or opportunities as a consequence for disobedience. The words *punish, punished,* or *punishment* are found in three sections of the Doctrine and Covenants. Sections 19 and 76 describe both the nature of divine punishment and candidates for it, employing the adjectives *endless* (19:10, 12; 76:44), *eternal* (19:11; 76:44), and *everlasting*

(76:44). Section 134 declares the Church's position on civil punishment (134:6, 8, 10).

In section 19 the Lord explicitly unfolded what he termed the "mystery" of divine punishment. Apparently speaking of the punishment of souls that will eventually be redeemed and saved in a degree of glory, the Lord explains that the "endless" or "eternal" nature of their punishment is qualitative rather than quantitative. "It is not written that there shall be no end to this torment, but it is written *endless torment.* Again, it is written *eternal damnation;* wherefore it is more express than other scriptures, that it might work upon the hearts of the children of men, altogether for my name's glory. . . . For, behold, I am endless, and the punishment which is given from my hand is endless punishment, for Endless is my name. Wherefore—Eternal punishment is God's punishment. Endless punishment is God's punishment" (19:6–12).

In these instances, *eternal* and *endless* are used as nouns, not describing the duration of the punishment but identifying God as the one executing the punishment. The words *eternal* and *endless* can also be read as adjectives describing the effects of the punishment rather than its duration. For example, the atonement of Jesus Christ is accurately described as infinite and eternal (Alma 34:14), although it took place at one point in time. Its effects are well described by those adjectives. Moreover, the use of the word *eternal* in the phrase *eternal life* is used as an adjective describing the quality of one's everlasting life (132:19–24).

JUSTICE and punishment for sin are forever present in all the works of God, but mercifully, by virtue of the ATONEMENT of Jesus Christ, justice can be satisfied for individuals through REPENTANCE and suffering, and their punishment comes to an end. By these principles everyone who has lived, now lives, or will yet live on the earth will be saved in one of the kingdoms of glory, except SONS OF PERDITION (76:43–44; 88:21–24). *See* Kingdoms of glory and perdition, vision of.

In section 76, concerning the punishment of the sons of perdition, the Lord revealed: "They shall go away into everlasting punishment, which is endless punishment, which is eternal punishment, to reign with the devil and his angels in eternity. . . . Wherefore, the end, the width, the height, the depth, and misery thereof, they understand not, neither any man except those who are ordained unto this condemnation" (vv. 44–48). Because none but those who receive this punishment know its dimensions, it is not clear whether the words *endless* and *eternal* have precisely the same meaning in the description in section 76 of sons of perdition as the same words have in the description in section 19 of heirs of salvation. The added words "everlasting" and "their worm dieth not, and the fire is not quenched," may be intended to mean endless in duration (76:44).

Section 134 declares the Church's principles relative to punishment for crime, namely that governments should protect the innocent and punish those guilty of breaking good laws (134:6, 8), that punishment should be proportional to the offense (134:8), and that churches can justly excommunicate members but not take property, jeopardize life or limb, or otherwise inflict physical punishment (134:10).

Many verses in the revelations describe the consequences of disobedience, which clearly fit into the context of punishment but in which the word *punish* or its various forms are not used, for example, the withdrawal of the Spirit (1:31–33), so-called natural disasters (88:87–90), God's refusing to answer prayers (101:7–8), the loss of gifts (3:1–10; 9:11), darkness of mind regarding spiritual things (84:54–58; 95:6, 10–12), and denial of FORGIVENESS, the right to the priesthood, temple ordinances, and salvation (29:17; 121:16–22; 132:17).

See also Judgment(s); Mercy.

JFM

Pure, purify

Unmixed, uncontaminated, uncorrupted, faultless. *Pure* and its related forms appear dozens of times in the Doctrine and Covenants, in both figurative and literal contexts.

The Lord speaks of having a "pure people" (43:14; 100:16; cf. 88:74), who have pure garments (109:76). A pure people are those who have been "cleansed from all their sins" through FAITH on the Lord JESUS CHRIST and OBEDIENCE

to the principles of his GOSPEL (76:50–70). The Lord has promised that the "elect . . . will hear my voice, and shall see me . . . and shall abide the day of my coming; for they shall be purified, even as I am pure" (35:20–21), while "he that is not purified shall not abide the day" (38:8). Nevertheless, persons who are pure do not have to wait for that future time to receive great blessings. They are promised that by the power of the HOLY GHOST they will be able to see and understand the "mysteries of his kingdom," those things "which God bestows on those who love him, and purify themselves before him" (76:114–16; cf. 136:11, 37). In a revelation given to direct the Saints in discerning false spirits, the Lord said: "No man is possessor of all things except he be purified and cleansed from all sin. And if ye are purified and cleansed from all sin, ye shall ask whatsoever you will in the name of Jesus and it shall be done" (50:26–29; cf. 46:30; 88:64; Enos 1:15; Hel. 10:5; 3 Ne. 18:20).

There are at least a dozen references in the revelations to "pure in heart" or "purify your hearts." Perhaps this identification of the heart with purity has more to do with one's honest intent, longing for, and commitment to attain, rather than the current realization of complete personal purity. In this context the Lord describes Zion as "THE PURE IN HEART" (97:21), and it will be the pure in heart who will one day return to "build up the waste places of Zion" (101:18). In commanding the Saints to build the Kirtland Temple, the Lord promised, "My presence shall be there, for I will come into it, and all the pure in heart that shall come into it shall see God" (97:16). The promise of seeing God with one's own eyes may be realized for some in mortality but will undoubtedly be fulfilled for all the elect at some future time (cf. 35:21; 38:8; 45:44; 50:45; 88:68; 93:1). The word *see* also means to discern, understand, and come to know. In that sense, all who qualify in righteousness may go into the house of the Lord and see God, even now. Future rewards await the poor who are pure in heart (56:18–20), salvation is promised to "all those . . . who have been pure in heart, and have been slain in the land of Missouri" (124:54), and the future pure in heart will be the beneficiaries of the early Saints' gathering the details concerning their persecutions in Missouri (123:1–16).

In the revelations the Lord linked purity of heart with qualifications for service. He said that the call of Edward Partridge to be a "bishop unto the church" was "because his heart is pure before me, for he is like unto Nathanael of old, in whom there is no guile" (41:9–11; cf. 124:15). To Thomas B. Marsh and the Twelve and others sent by them to preach the gospel, the Lord commanded, "Purify your hearts before me; then go ye into all the world, and preach my gospel unto every creature who has not received it" (112:28, 16, 21).

In the Prophet Joseph Smith's prayer dedicating the Kirtland Temple, the phrases "our garments may be pure" and "we may be clothed upon with robes of righteousness" are idiomatic expressions asking that at the last day the Saints will be prepared to meet the Savior and "reap eternal joy for all our sufferings" (109:76).

Furthermore, the revelations speak of "pure water" (84:92), "pure wine" (89:5–6), "pure gold" (110:2), "pure snow" (110:3), "pure knowledge" (121:42), pure matter (131:7), a "pure eye" (121:1–2), "a pure stream" (97:8–9), purified bodies (131:8), and the purity of the Lord's words (41:12). In his rebuke of the murderers of Joseph and Hyrum Smith, Elder John Taylor wrote, "If the fire can scathe a green tree for the glory of God, how easy it will burn up the dry trees to purify the vineyard of corruption" (135:6).

DKO

Purposes of life. *See* Life, purposes of.

And again, I say unto you, I give unto you John A. Hicks, Samuel Williams, and Jesse Baker, which priesthood is to preside over the quorum of elders, which quorum is instituted for standing ministers; nevertheless they may travel, yet they are ordained to be standing ministers to my church, saith the Lord. 124:137

Quickened. *See* Appendix E.

Quorum(s)

A term that refers to a group of people having a specific assignment or to a body of those who hold a specific PRIESTHOOD office. The word *quorum* first appears in the Doctrine and Covenants in a revelation concerning PRIESTHOOD that Joseph Smith received on 28 March 1835. He joined that revelation with one he had received on 11 November 1831 to form section 107. That combined record of two revelations, first published in the 1835 Doctrine and Covenants, was titled "On Priesthood."

Instructions in the 1831 part of the section (vv. 59–100) specify how the Church's various ministerial offices were to be organized into their own respective bodies (later referred to as "quorums") with one of their number designated as president: a president each for the ELDERS, PRIESTS, TEACHERS, and DEACONS, and a president over the high priesthood. Membership numbers are set for each grouping of priesthood offices: the deacons' president presides over twelve deacons, the teachers' president over twenty-four teachers, the president of priests over forty-eight priests, and the elders' president over ninety-six elders. In the 28 March 1835 revelation (vv. 1–58), those instructions were expanded to say that the president of the priests needs to be a BISHOP and that those called to the newly established general level office of SEVENTY were to have seventy members per group, with a seven-man presidency. This 1835 revelation employs for the first time the term *quorum* with regards to the presiding bodies: the three presiding high priests of the Melchizedek Priesthood form a "quorum of the Presidency of the Church," the Twelve APOSTLES "form a quorum," as do the Seventy (vv. 22–26). Likewise, a stake HIGH COUNCIL "form[s] a quorum" (v. 36).

In practice the term *quorum* became applied to each body of priesthood offices (Minutebook, Dec. 1834–Dec. 1845). Though the maximum size of the different ministerial groups under each president is set forth in section 107, the only full Aaronic Priesthood quorum identified in Church records before 1847 was the teachers quorum at Far West, Missouri, which in May 1838 had twenty-four members (Minutebook, 25 May 1838).

In section 124, dated 19 January 1841, instructions call for men to be appointed to organize themselves as "the quorum of the Nauvoo House" and select a president "for the purpose" of building the Nauvoo House (vv. 119, 62). That revelation refers to Joseph Smith, Sidney Rigdon, and William Law as constituting "a quorum and First Presidency" (v. 126). It names three men to preside over "a quorum of high priests" in Nauvoo (vv. 133–36) and men to preside over "the quorum of elders" (v. 137), the "quorum of seventies" (v. 138), and a presidency each for the priests, teachers, and deacons (v. 142).

See also Historical context and overview of Doctrine and Covenants 107 (p. 815).

BIBLIOGRAPHY

Far West, Kirtland, and Nauvoo Teachers Quorum Minutebook. Church History Library, The Church of Jesus Christ of Latter-day Saints, Salt Lake City, Utah.

Hartley, William G. *My Fellow Servants: Essays on the History of the Priesthood.* Provo, Utah: BYU Studies, 2010.

WGH

All these had departed the mortal life, firm in the hope of a glorious **resurrection**, through the grace of God the Father and his Only Begotten Son, Jesus Christ. I beheld that they were filled with joy and gladness, and were rejoicing together because the day of their deliverance was at hand. 138:14–15

Railing. *See* Appendix E.

Ramus, Illinois

A Latter-day Saint settlement located twenty miles east of Nauvoo. The name *Ramus* means "branch." It was later named Macedonia and is now known as Webster. In the spring of 1843, Joseph Smith taught several important doctrines in public sermons and in speaking to small groups as he visited the Saints in Ramus. Excerpts from his teachings are recorded in Doctrine and Covenants 130 and 131. These excerpts include truths about angels and where they reside, the timing of the second coming of the Lord, the importance of gaining knowledge and intelligence in this life, the nature of the Godhead, the necessity of eternal marriage to gain exaltation, the more sure word of prophecy, and the nature of spirit matter.

In February 1840, Joel Hills Johnson organized a branch of fifty Church members in Ramus. A few months later, on 15 July 1840, the Ramus Stake was organized with Joel Johnson as president. It quickly grew to include five hundred members. On 4 December 1841, the stake organization was discontinued and a branch was organized in its stead, with John Lawson appointed presiding elder of the branch. Reasons for the discontinuation of the stake included disputes among stake leaders "over the procedures for collecting payment for lots" owned by the Church and sold to individual members, as well as the indictment of several Church members in the area for larceny. The guilty members were excommunicated and titles to the property owned by the Church at Ramus were transferred to Joseph Smith in Nauvoo (Rugh, 159–60; Smith, 4:453–54, 462–63, 467–68).

By April 1846, Latter-day Saints had left the settlement and journeyed west with the Saints from Nauvoo. Catherine Salisbury, Joseph Smith's sister, is buried in the Webster Cemetery. A plaque installed along the main street, commemorating the Latter-day Saint settlement in Ramus (Macedonia), indicates that the Community Church building in town is built on or near the foundation of the first Mormon chapel in Illinois. *See* map, p. 277.

BIBLIOGRAPHY

Rugh, Susan Sessions. "Conflict in the Countryside: The Mormon Settlement at Macedonia, Illinois." *BYU Studies* 32, no. 1 (Winter and Spring 1999): 149–74.

Smith, Joseph. *History of The Church of Jesus Christ of Latter-day Saints.* Edited by B. H. Roberts. 7 vols. 2d ed. rev. Salt Lake City: The Church of Jesus Christ of Latter-day Saints, 1932–51.

GML

Raphael

One of the great ones mentioned in 128:21 who in company with Michael (Adam) and Gabriel (Noah) conferred priesthood keys upon Joseph Smith to establish the dispensation of the fulness of times. Who he was as a mortal prophet is not known, but the passage suggests he was head of a dispensation.

The name *Raphael* occurs once in the Doctrine and Covenants and not at all in the Book of Mormon, the Pearl of Great Price, or the King James Version of the Bible. The apocryphal book of Tobias (Tobit) 12:15 identifies Raphael as one of the seven angels who stand before God. Raphael is prominent in noncanonical Jewish legend (Ginzberg, 7:399).

BIBLIOGRAPHY

Ginzberg, Louis, trans. *Legends of the Jews.* 7 vols. Philadelphia: Jewish Publication Society of America, 1966.

RJM

Rascality. *See* Appendix E.

Rearward. *See* Appendix E.

Reason, reasoning

Reason and its various forms are used in the Doctrine and Covenants as both nouns and verbs.

(1) As a noun, *reason* has to do with the cause, justification, or explanation for an action. Joseph Smith was told that the *reason* he had lost translating privileges for a time was because of his complicity in the loss of the 116 pages of the Book of Mormon manuscript through Martin Harris's breaking "sacred promises . . . depend[ing] upon his own judgment and boast[ing] in his own wisdom" (3:5–15). In November 1831, at a special conference

which was called to consider publishing revelations that had been received by the Prophet Joseph Smith to that time, the Lord explained to the elders gathered that the *reason* they had not received "the blessing which was offered" them was because of "fears in [their] hearts" (67:3). Just what that promised blessing was is not identified at that point in the revelation, but verses 10 and 11 may contain a clue; the elders may have expected to see the Savior. This lost blessing, however, was still possible with the requisite repentance and humility (67:10–13).

(2) As a verb, *reason* means to discuss, debate, explain in a logical manner. The Lord revealed that he had sent his "everlasting covenant into the world, to be a light to the world, and to be a standard for my people, and for the Gentiles to seek to it. . . . Wherefore, come ye unto it, and with him that cometh I will *reason* as with men in days of old, and I will show unto you my strong *reasoning*" (45:9–10; emphasis added). In an attempt to help the elders of the Church understand the importance of teaching by the Spirit and not by "some other way," the Lord invited, "And now come, saith the Lord, by the Spirit . . . and let us *reason* together, that ye may understand; let us *reason* even as a man *reasoneth* one with another face to face" (50:10–11; emphasis added; cf. verses 12–25).

Leman Copley, Sidney Rigdon and Parley P. Pratt were called to preach the restored gospel to the SHAKERS, a religious community in the Kirtland area to which Leman had formerly belonged. "My servant Leman shall be ordained unto this work, that he may *reason* with them, not according to that which he has received of them, but according to that which shall be taught him by you my servants" (49:4; emphasis added; cf. 66:7–8). Those servants were Sidney Rigdon and Parley P. Pratt (49:3). Orson Hyde was called "to proclaim the everlasting gospel, by the Spirit of the living God, from people to people, and from land to land, in the congregations of the wicked, in their synagogues, *reasoning* with and expounding all scriptures unto them" (68:1; emphasis added).

In December 1831, as a result of the publication of several newspaper articles written by an apostate, Ezra Booth, which had stirred up "unfriendly feelings" against Joseph Smith and the Church, the Prophet and Sidney Rigdon were instructed to lay aside their work on the inspired translation of the Bible for a season and proclaim the gospel (71, headnote), "expounding the mysteries thereof out of the scriptures, according to that portion of Spirit and power which shall be given unto you." Their mission was to "confound your enemies; call upon them to meet you both in public and in private; and inasmuch as ye are faithful their shame shall be made manifest. Wherefore, let them bring forth their strong *reasons* against the Lord" (71:1, 7–8; emphasis added).

DKO

Rebel, rebellious

To oppose, renounce, refuse allegiance to, or fight against a person, organization, or government in authority. The word *rebel* and its various forms are found in at least six contexts:

1. Rebellion against the Lord and his servants. In his revealed preface to the published revelations, the Lord warned that, in the end, "the rebellious shall be pierced with much sorrow; for their iniquities shall be spoken upon the housetops, and their secret acts shall be revealed," and that the Lord's servants would have power given to them "to seal both on earth and in heaven, the unbelieving and rebellious" (1:3, 8). In later revelations the Lord said, "Mine anger is kindled against the rebellious, and they shall know mine arm and mine indignation, in the day of visitation and of wrath upon the nations" (56:1, 4; cf. 63:2, 6).

The Lord revealed that "the rebellious are not of the blood of Ephraim," and "shall be cut off out of the land of Zion, and shall be sent away, and shall not inherit the land" (64:35–36). The Lord identified specific people and situations where rebellion was evident: changes in missionary assignments were made because of the "stiffneckedness of my people which are in Thompson [Ohio], and their rebellions" in connection with the settlement of the Colesville, New York, branch on lands under the principles of consecration (56:1–6); some of the "brethren in Zion" were chastised for their "rebellion" against Joseph Smith (84:76); and the Twelve were cautioned, "Exalt not yourselves; rebel not against my servant Joseph; for verily I say unto you, I am with him, and my hand shall be over him; and the keys which I have given unto him, and also to youward, shall not be taken from him till I come" (112:15).

2. Lucifer's rebellion against God in the premortal world and continued warfare against the Saints on earth. In explaining the origin of "the devil and his angels," the Lord said the devil "rebelled against me, saying, Give me thine honor, which is my power; and also a third part of the hosts of heaven turned he away from me because of their agency; and they were thrust down, and thus came the devil and his angels" (29:36–37; cf. Moses 4:1–4; Rev. 12:7–11). In the remarkable vision of the glories, Joseph Smith and Sidney Rigdon "beheld Satan, that old serpent, even the devil, who rebelled against God, and sought to take the kingdom of our God and his Christ—Wherefore, he maketh war with the saints of God, and encompasseth them round about" (76:28–29). See Premortal existence; Satan; War in heaven.

3. Prophecy about the rebellion of South Carolina in context with the American Civil War. On Christmas Day, 1832, the Prophet Joseph Smith received a revelation which stated: "Verily, thus saith the Lord concerning the wars that will shortly come to pass, beginning at the rebellion of South Carolina, which will eventually terminate in the death and misery of many souls" (87:1).

4. The rebellious in the postmortal spirit world when the Savior visited there after his death. In his vision of the redemption of the dead, President Joseph F. Smith saw that when Jesus went to the postmortal spirit world during the time between his death and resurrection, "unto the wicked he did not go, and among the ungodly and the unrepentant who had defiled themselves while in the flesh, his voice was not raised; neither did the rebellious who rejected the testimonies and the warnings of the ancient prophets behold his presence, nor look upon his face" (138:20–21). But even the rebellious were not forgotten by the Savior. President Smith learned that "our Redeemer spent his time

during his sojourn in the world of spirits, instructing and preparing the faithful spirits of the prophets who had testified of him in the flesh; that they might carry the message of redemption unto all the dead, unto whom he could not go personally, because of their rebellion and transgression" (138:36–37). See Salvation for the dead.

5. Rebellion against GOVERNMENT. In section 134, "a declaration of belief regarding governments and laws in general" (headnote), it is made clear that "sedition and rebellion are unbecoming every citizen" while they are being protected in their "inherent and inalienable rights" (v. 5).

6. Prayer for the "remnants of Jacob" to stop their rebellions. In the dedicatory prayer of the Kirtland Temple, Joseph Smith petitioned the Lord that he would cause "the remnants of Jacob, who have been cursed and smitten because of their transgression, be converted from their wild and savage condition to the fulness of the everlasting gospel; that they may lay down their weapons of bloodshed, and cease their rebellions" (109:65–66).

DKO

Recompense. *See* Appendix E.

Reconciliation. *See* Appendix E.

Record of John

A testimony of Jesus' divine Sonship, written by John the Baptist, that contributes to the understanding of the early chapters of the Gospel by John the Beloved. The entire record is not currently available, but a portion was revealed through the Prophet Joseph Smith in May 1833, with a promise that the fulness will yet be revealed (93:6–18).

Possible confusion of identity

Inasmuch as two righteous men named John, both closely associated with the Lord Jesus, are spoken of in John's Gospel, confusion arises as to whose record is being referred to in 93:18. Those who have understood that the reference is to a record written by John the Baptist include President John Taylor (55, 59), Elder Orson Pratt (16:58), Brigham Young University professor Sidney B. Sperry (472–75), and Elder Bruce R. McConkie (*Commentary,* 1:70–71; *Mortal,* 1:426–28). Other authors from various Christian backgrounds have noted strong relationships between John the Baptist and John the Beloved but ascribed only spoken testimony to the Baptist, whereas the Beloved is known to have left a written record (Matthews, 82–83).

Help from the Joseph Smith Translation

That Doctrine and Covenants 93:6–18 is speaking of John the Baptist's personal record is supported by JST Matthew 3:45–46 (cf. KJV Matthew 3:15–16), which the Prophet Joseph dictated in March and April 1831, more than two years before receiving section 93 (JST New Testament Manuscript 1). The Joseph Smith Translation prompts a conclusion that both passages refer to John the Baptist because the Prophet was responsible for both passages, the Matthew account is definitely speaking of the Baptist, and the two passages contain verbal and doctrinal similarities that emphasize that John the Baptist was eye and ear witness to the dove and the Father's voice. It appears that John the Revelator in writing his Gospel (John 1) was quoting a written record of John the Baptist.

BIBLIOGRAPHY

JST New Testament Manuscript 1, page 6. Dictated sometime between 8 March 1831 and 7 April 1831, according to the dates on the original JST manuscript.

Matthews, Robert J. *A Burning Light: The Life and Ministry of John the Baptist.* Orem, Utah: Granite, 2000.

Maxwell, Neal A. *Not My Will, but Thine.* Salt Lake City: Bookcraft, 1988.

McConkie, Bruce R. *Doctrinal New Testament Commentary.* 3 vols. Salt Lake City: Bookcraft, 1965–73.

———. *The Mortal Messiah: From Bethlehem to Calvary.* 4 vols. Salt Lake City: Deseret Book, 1979–81.

Pratt, Orson. *Journal of Discourses.* 26 vols. London: Latter-day Saints' Book Depot, 1854–86.

Sperry, Sidney B. *Doctrine and Covenants Compendium.* Salt Lake City: Bookcraft, 1960.

Taylor, John. *The Mediation and Atonement of Our Lord and Savior Jesus Christ.* Salt Lake City: Deseret News, 1882.

RJM

Record(s)

Revelations in the Doctrine and Covenants speak of ancient records, particularly those associated with the Book of Mormon (e.g., 1:29; 10:42; 27:5). The Lord attested that they were preserved to fulfill promises made to the ancient inhabitants of the Americas and to testify of the Savior and his gospel (3:16–20; 8:1, 11; 20:9). Therefore, Joseph Smith received careful instructions for handling and translating these records. The Lord also mentioned other records that would someday come forth (9:2).

The revelations frequently speak of "bearing record" in the same sense that one might bear TESTIMONY (58:6–7; cf. 5:1). Such testifying of truth includes, for example, witnessing of Christ (68:6; 112:4; 118:4), the fulness of the gospel (76:14; 58:63), the Book of Mormon (128:20), and the vision of the redemption of the dead (138:60). The Father bears record of those worthy of being sealed up "unto eternal life" (68:12), and the Holy Ghost bears record of the Father and the Son (20:27; 42:17).

The first commandment given at the meeting on 6 April 1830, when the Church was organized, was "there shall be a record kept among you" (21:1). At the Church's first conference held 9 June 1830, Oliver Cowdery was "appointed to keep the Church record and Conference minutes until the next conference" (Cannon and Cook, 2–5).

A revelation given 3 March 1831 instructed that John Whitmer should "write and keep a regular history" because Oliver Cowdery had been "appointed to another office." The Lord promised, "It shall be given him, inasmuch as he is faithful, by the Comforter, to write these things" (47:1, 3–4). A later revelation directed him to collect and write materials "which shall be for the good of the church, and for the rising generations" (69:8).

The importance of record-keeping is evidenced by including in the Doctrine and Covenants the minutes of a meeting held at Kirtland on 17 February 1834. Now included in section 102, these minutes record the organization of the first high council.

In a pair of letters written to the Saints at Nauvoo in September 1842, the Prophet

Joseph Smith stressed the importance of keeping accurate records. He directed that whenever ordinances were performed, a recorder should be present to assure and bear witness that the ordinances were carried out correctly (127:6; 128:2–3). A general recorder would then compile these individual records for the whole Church (128:4–5). These records would be taken into account at the final judgment (128:6–7; cf. Rev. 20:12). The Prophet insisted that a record must be made on earth in order for it to be recorded or bound in heaven (127:7; 128:7–9, 14). Earlier revelations had stipulated that the names of the wicked would be blotted out from the records on earth (20:83; 85:4–5, 12; cf. Ezra 2:61–62). Thus, the Prophet concluded his letters with an exhortation to present these records "in order" and "worthy of all acceptation" (127:9; 128:24).

"After a series of intervening clerks, historians, and recorders," Willard Richards was appointed Church Historian in 1842 and Church Recorder in 1843. For the next 129 years, the position of Church Historian and Recorder was held by a member of the First Presidency or Quorum of the Twelve. In 1972, the Church Historian's Office was renamed the Historical Department, under a General Authority managing director (Turley, 493). The title "Church Historian/Recorder" was revived in 2005 when Elder Marlin K. Jensen, a member of the First Quorum of the Seventy, was sustained to that position (Monson, 23).

Church leaders have also stressed the importance of Latter-day Saints compiling personal and family histories. President Spencer W. Kimball counseled that Church members should start a record and "begin today and write in it your goings and your comings, your deeper thoughts, your achievements, and your failures, your associations and your triumphs, your impressions and your testimonies" (Kimball, 61). He testified that this record would be a blessing to family members who would later read it.

BIBLIOGRAPHY

Cannon, Donald Q., and Lyndon W. Cook, eds. *Far West Record: Minutes of The Church of Jesus Christ of Latter-day Saints, 1830–1844.* Salt Lake City: Deseret Book, 1983.

Kimball, Spencer W. "President Kimball Speaks Out on Personal Journals." *Ensign* (December 1980): 60–61.

Monson, Thomas S. "The Sustaining of Church Officers." *Ensign* 35 (May 2005): 23–24.

Turley, Richard E., Jr. "Historian, Church." In *Encyclopedia of Latter-day Saint History,* edited by Arnold K. Garr, Donald Q. Cannon, and Richard O. Cowan. Salt Lake City: Deseret Book, 2000.

ROC

Red apparel. *See* Jesus Christ, second coming of.

Red Sea

Body of water separating the Arabian Peninsula and northeast Africa. Latter-day revelation confirms two events from the ancient Near East: "Moses brought the children of Israel through the Red Sea on dry ground" (8:3), and "the miraculous directors [Liahona] . . . were given to Lehi while in the wilderness, on the borders of the Red Sea" (17:1).

DKO

Redeem, redemption

Reclaim, repurchase, make, or cover payment; save. The Father sent his Only Begotten Son into the world to redeem his other children from the Fall and from their carnal state (49:5; cf. 84:99, 100; 88:17; 93:38). *See* Fall of Adam and Eve, the.

The ATONEMENT of JESUS CHRIST enables redemption from physical DEATH through the resurrection (88:14, 16), and from spiritual death through FORGIVENESS of sin. Being redeemed from sin comes "through faith on the name of [the] Only Begotten Son" (29:42), and people "cannot be redeemed from their spiritual fall" if they fail to repent (29:44). These principles, along with the saving ordinances of the GOSPEL, enable redemption for the living, as well as for the dead (128:22; 138:58).

In association with his second coming and the MILLENNIUM, the Lord said, "My people shall be redeemed and shall reign with me on earth" (43:29). "Then shall the heathen nations [non-Jews, those outside the covenant] be redeemed" (45:54). *See* Jesus Christ, second coming of.

Regarding the Judgment, "Little children are

redeemed from the foundation of the world" through the Atonement (29:46). *See* Children.

Through the sealing blessings of the Holy Spirit of Promise, the righteous can be "sealed up unto the day of redemption," notwithstanding temptations that come (124:124). *See* Seal, sealed.

Unrepentant sinners and covenant breakers, however, "shall be delivered over to the buffetings of Satan until the day of redemption" (78:12; 82:21; 104:9; 132:26), that day being the day when their suffering ends and they are redeemed or saved in a kingdom of glory. *See* Buffetings of Satan.

Terrestrial and telestial souls will be redeemed and receive what they have earned (88:99; 76:82, 85; cf. 138:36–37). Those assigned to telestial glory "are they who shall not be redeemed from the devil until the last resurrection" (76:85), and SONS OF PERDITION are "the only ones who shall not be redeemed" at all (76:38). *See* Kingdoms of glory and perdition, vision of.

In another context, the term *redemption* and its variant forms are used in the revelations when speaking of reclaiming the lands the Saints lost in Missouri when they were driven out of the state by their persecutors. The Lord promised that ultimately, after a little season of chastening, "Zion shall be redeemed" (100:13; 101:75; 103:13, 15; 105:2, 9, 34; 136:18). *See* Zion, redemption of.

DKO

Redemption of Zion. *See* Zion, redemption of.

Redound. *See* Appendix E.

Redress

To remedy, set right, compensate. Formal petitions to state and federal government officials from members of The Church of Jesus Christ of Latter-day Saints sought redress, or reparations, for losses due to the PERSECUTIONS suffered in Missouri from 1833 to 1839. Beginning 31 October 1833 and continuing through the first week of November, some twelve hundred Mormons were expelled from Jackson County, Missouri, by order of militia authorities and other local officials. At the time of their expulsion, most Church members sought refuge across the Missouri River in Clay County, situated to the north. Meanwhile, Orson Hyde and John Gould journeyed from Missouri to Ohio to inform Joseph Smith of the forced expulsion and the conditions of the Missouri Saints.

In a revelation received by the Prophet Joseph Smith on 16 December, instructions were given regarding the course of action to be taken by Missouri Church leaders, directing them to use the legal system in seeking redress. "Let them importune at the feet of the judge," the revelation stated. "And if he heed them not, let them importune at the feet of the governor; and if the governor heed them not, let them importune at the feet of the president" (101:86–88). With the assistance of four attorneys in Liberty—Alexander W. Doniphan, David R. Atchison, Amos Rees, and William T. Wood—efforts were made to rectify and resolve the situation. In late February 1834, a hearing was scheduled in Independence to consider the "Mormon problem," but the case was quickly dismissed. Having failed on the local level, Church leaders looked primarily to Missouri governor Daniel Dunklin for support but with only limited success. Dunklin subsequently agreed to intercede using state militia to assist the Latter-day Saints in restoring them to their Jackson County property on the condition that the Mormons provide a peacekeeping force to maintain order after being reinstated. This was the impetus behind the call-up and march of ZION'S CAMP; however, in June, after Zion's Camp arrived in Missouri, Dunklin chose not to call out the state militia and recommended the Mormons continue to seek redress through the civil courts.

On 10 April 1834, fourteen leading Missouri elders drafted a letter to U.S. president Andrew Jackson giving a general description of their sufferings. They requested he use his influence to either persuade the Congress to call out the militia in their behalf or give Governor Dunklin the power to intervene. The president's response to the request came through the office of U.S. Secretary of War Lewis Cass in a letter dated 2 May 1834. Cass informed the Latter-day Saint leaders that the president could not "call out a military force to aid in the execution of the state laws, until the proper requisition is made upon him by the constituted authorities" (Smith, 1:493), meaning Governor Dunklin.

A similar effort for redress came in 1839 following the expulsion of the Latter-day Saints from Missouri. In a letter dictated by Joseph Smith from Liberty Jail on 20 March 1839 (now canonized as Doctrine and Covenants 123), the Prophet instructed the Saints, most of whom had temporarily relocated in Adams County, Illinois, to draft legal affidavits detailing the suffering, persecution, and hardships they experienced in Missouri. His intent in issuing this request was to submit the petitions to the federal government in hopes of securing some redress (123:1–6). The Saints responded to the Prophet's request by preparing more than 770 statements. In late October 1839, Joseph Smith traveled to Washington D.C., where he spent several weeks meeting with a number of important officials, including U.S. president Martin Van Buren, leaders of the Senate, and other national officers. Although no official government action was taken in behalf of the Saints, Joseph Smith succeeded in bringing to the attention of many government leaders the nature and causes of the Missouri persecutions.

See also Constitution; Historical context and overview of Doctrine and Covenants 101 (p. 806) and 123 (p. 836); Missouri period; Parable of the woman and the unjust judge.

BIBLIOGRAPHY

Johnson, Clark V. "Government Responses to Mormon Appeals." In *Regional Studies in Latter-day Saint Church History: Illinois,* edited by H. Dean Garrett. Provo, Utah: Department of Church History and Doctrine, Brigham Young University, 1995, 183–204.

————. *Mormon Redress Petitions: Documents of the 1833–1838 Missouri Conflict.* Provo, Utah: Religious Studies Center, Brigham Young University, 1992.

"Reply of the General Government to the Petition of the Saints." In Joseph Smith, *History of The Church of Jesus Christ of Latter-day Saints.* Edited by B. H. Roberts. 7 vols. 2d ed. rev. Salt Lake City: The Church of Jesus Christ of Latter-day Saints, 1932–51.

ALB

Refuge

A safe haven, a shelter, a sanctuary of peace and serenity. Refuge is found wherever the covenant people of the Lord are gathered. That place becomes a holy community—"Zion, and . . . her stakes," places of peace, fortifications against evil, "for a defense, and for a refuge from the storm, and from wrath when it shall be poured out without mixture upon the whole earth" (115:6; cf. 124:36, 109; Isa. 4:5–6). As the Church gains sufficient strength throughout the world, STAKES are organized. The stakes of ZION, designated by the Lord as "curtains or the strength of Zion," are gathering places for the Saints (101:21) in preparation for the redemption of Zion, the establishment of the city of the NEW JERUSALEM, and the second coming of the Savior (45:66; A of F 1:10). "For the day of my visitation cometh speedily, in an hour when ye think not of; and where shall be the safety of my people, and refuge for those who shall be left of them?" (124:10). The answer is the Lord's everlasting covenant which he has sent into the world "to be a light to the world, and to be a standard for [his] people, and for the Gentiles to seek to it" (45:9). *See* New and everlasting covenant.

LDN

Remember

To bring to mind; to think of again and again. Remembering is an integral part of the covenantal relationship between man and God, encompassing awareness of things past, present, and future. Memory influences behavior and is essential to correct knowledge of one's identity.

Ancient Israelites were commanded to "remember the Lord thy God," his commandments and covenants (Deut. 8:2, 11, 18). From the time of Christ Saints have been instructed to remember the ATONEMENT as the manifestation of God's love for them (Luke 22:19–20; D&C 20:77, 79). As outward symbols of remembrance, the Lord commanded the Israelites to "make them fringes in the borders of their garments throughout their generations . . . that ye may look upon it, and remember all the commandments of the Lord, and do them . . . and be holy unto your God" (Num. 15:37–41).

Latter-day Saints today wear clothing to remind them of their sacred covenants and partake of the SACRAMENT each week in remembrance of the Atonement (20:77, 79; Asay, 18–23).

In the Doctrine and Covenants all are enjoined to remember the words of the Lord and his covenants (10:70; 84:57; 89:18; 90:24). The Saints are instructed to remember what the gifts of the Spirit are (46:10–29); to "remember the worth of souls is great," and share the knowledge of the gospel of Jesus Christ with others (18:1–16); and to "remember the poor, and consecrate of [their] properties for their support" (42:30; 52:40). In several revelations individuals are instructed to remember the commandments and promises given to them specifically (3:5; 6:10; 8:5; 33:14), and particular individuals are remembered by the Lord for their goodness (117:12; 124:78, 96). In the dedicatory prayer of the Kirtland Temple the Lord is petitioned to remember "the kings . . . and the great ones of the earth, and all people, and the churches, all the poor, the needy, and afflicted ones of the earth" (109:55), the Saints in their afflictions (109:47, 72), Joseph Smith and his family (109:68–70), and many others.

In a revelation directed to Joseph Smith Sr., the Lord instructs those that embark in the service of God to "remember faith, virtue, knowledge, temperance, patience, brotherly kindness, godliness, charity, humility, diligence" (4:1–7; cf. 12:8). The Saints are also counseled to remember to speak of the Lord and sacred things "with care, and by constraint of the Spirit" (63:59–64). In connection with the loss of the 116 manuscript pages of Book of Mormon translation the Lord taught Joseph Smith: "Remember, remember that it is not the work of God that is frustrated, but the work of men" (3:3).

Formal remembrance is noted in terms of partaking of the tokens of the sacrament (20:77, 79), Sabbath observance (59:12), temple ordinances (124:39), keeping accurate records of ordinances (127:9; cf. 128:9), and in attending to prayers (68:33; cf. 88:131).

The Lord does not forget nor forsake his covenant people. The lost tribes of Israel "shall come in remembrance before the Lord . . . and be crowned with glory, even in Zion" (133:26–32). Speaking of the Saints who were driven from Jackson County, Missouri, in 1833, partly "in consequence of their transgressions," the Lord said, "Notwithstanding their sins, my bowels are filled with compassion towards them. I will not utterly cast them off; and in the day of wrath I will remember mercy" (101:2, 9). Though chastising Joseph Smith for having "gone on in the persuasions of men," the Lord reassured the Prophet with these words: "But remember, God is merciful . . . repent . . . and thou art still chosen, and art again called to the work" (3:6, 10). Of those who truly repent the Lord says, "I, the Lord, remember [their sins] no more" (58:42).

The Lord invited the early Saints to "remember the great and last promise" and enjoined them to "sanctify yourselves that your minds become single to God, and the days will come that you shall see him; for he will unveil his face unto you, and it shall be in his own time, and in his own way, and according to his own will" (88:67–69).

BIBLIOGRAPHY

Asay, Carlos E. "The Temple Garment: 'An Outward Expression of an Inward Commitment.'" *Ensign* 27 (August 1997): 18–23.

JHS

Remnant(s)

A remaining part of an original whole. In the Doctrine and Covenants are four references to *remnant* and five additional references to *remnants*. These references identify four groups of people:

1. LAMANITES, who are a remnant of the JEWS, or of Jacob, the father of JUDAH or the Jews (19:27; 52:2; 109:65; cf. 2 Ne. 33:8).

2. Jews themselves, including some people from other tribes of ISRAEL who lived among them at the time of Jesus' earthly ministry, who were "scattered among all nations" at the prophesied destruction of Jerusalem (beginning about A.D. 70), and who will be gathered again after "the times of the Gentiles be fulfilled" (45:24–25, 43).

3. The descendants of all the tribes of Israel "in their scattered condition among the

Gentiles," which scattering began in 722 B.C., when the kingdom of Israel was taken into captivity by the Assyrians, and continued with the captivity of the kingdom of Judah by the Babylonians in 586 B.C. These remnants too will eventually "return to the Lord," and be gathered (113:10; 133:26–33; cf. Isa. 11:10–16).

4. "The remnants who are left of the land," after the American Civil War and other wars poured out "upon all nations," who will "vex the Gentiles with a sore vexation" (87:1–5).

DFB

Rend. *See* Appendix E.

Renewing of their bodies. *See* Priesthood.

Repentance

The process by which disciples of Christ remove sin from their lives and receive FORGIVENESS through the ATONEMENT of JESUS CHRIST. The Greek verb meaning "to repent" is *metanoi,* meaning to change one's mind, to reconsider. The Hebrew verb meaning "to repent" is *lashuv,* meaning to return, to come back (to God). God rejoices in the soul that comes back to him (18:13). As the Lord told John and Peter Whitmer, "The thing which will be of the most worth unto you will be to declare repentance . . . that you may bring souls unto me" (15:6; 16:6; cf. 18:10, 15–16). Missionaries and all Latter-day Saints are to "cry repentance" to all people (18:14; 33:10; 34:6; 58:47).

The commandment to repent

God commands all people to "repent and be baptized" (18:41–42; 33:11; 39:6; 49:13; 20:37). "I command all men everywhere to repent" (18:9; 133:16); "say nothing but repentance unto this generation" (6:9; 11:9); and "preach naught but repentance" (19:21). There are other doctrines that must be taught, but true repentance encompasses these doctrines. Parents are warned that they have the responsibility to teach their children to "understand the doctrine of repentance" (68:25).

Godly sorrow and suffering are necessary

There is a scriptural pattern for repentance. It begins with recognition that sin has occurred, and continues with remorse and contrition, with a "godly sorrow" that "worketh repentance to salvation" (2 Cor. 7:10). "Inasmuch as they sinned they might be chastened, that they might repent" (1:27; cf. 98:21). Chastening can purify and motivate one to complete the succeeding steps of repentance. President Ezra Taft Benson said: "Sometimes we regard all too lightly the principle of repentance, thinking that it only means confession, that it only means feeling sorry for ourselves. But it is more than that. It is a deep, burning, and heartfelt sorrow for sin that will drive us to our knees in humility and tears—a deep, heartfelt sorrow for sin that produces a reformation of life" (196).

Confession and forsaking are necessary

A desire to remove the stain and pain of sin is a sign of true repentance. The Lord said, "By this ye may know if a man repenteth of his sins—behold, he will confess them and forsake them" (58:43). "Wherefore, I command you again to . . . confess your sins, lest you suffer these punishments" (19:20). President Spencer W. Kimball taught: "No one can ever be forgiven of any transgression until there is repentance, and one has not repented until he has bared his soul and admitted his intentions and weaknesses without excuses or rationalizations. He must admit to himself that he has grievously sinned. When he has confessed to himself without the slightest minimizing of the offense, or rationalizing its seriousness, or soft-pedaling its gravity, and admits it is as *big* as it really *is,* then he is ready to begin his repentance" (10).

The Lord gives this comforting assurance: "I, the Lord, forgive sins, and am merciful unto those who confess their sins with humble hearts" (61:2); "I, the Lord, forgive sins unto those who confess their sins before me and ask forgiveness" (64:7).

To forsake means to give up, abandon, cease to do. It is mandatory, as quickly as possible, to expel sin and the propensity to sin from one's life. Forsaking sin also means burying it away in the past and leaving it there, not bringing it up any more. With sincere repentance, one is converted to the Lord and born again, by virtue of the Atonement and by the power of the HOLY GHOST, becoming a new person (5:16; Mosiah 27:25; Rom. 6:3–7). *See* Born of me.

Forgiveness for oneself and forgiving others

God assures the penitent soul: "he that repents and does the commandments of the Lord shall be forgiven" (1:32); "he who has repented of his sins, the same is forgiven, and I, the Lord, remember them no more" (58:42). Thus repentance brings forgiveness. Along with the blessing of being forgiven, however, is an obligation to forgive others. "Wherefore, I say unto you, that ye ought to forgive one another; for he that forgiveth not his brother his trespasses standeth condemned before the Lord; for there remaineth in him the greater sin. I, the Lord, will forgive whom I will forgive, but of you it is required to forgive all men" (64:9–10).

Consequences of choosing not to repent

The Doctrine and Covenants is explicit about the awful consequences facing those who refuse to repent: "every man must repent or suffer" (19:4, 15–18). Such persons "cannot be redeemed from their spiritual fall, because they repent not" (29:44). "My blood," the Lord said, "shall not cleanse them" (29:17); and he will pour out desolating scourges, consumptions, and destructions on them (5:19). "He that repents not, from him shall be taken even the light which he has received" (1:33), and he will be "cast out" (42:28), "cut off" (63:63), and "deliver[ed] . . . over unto the buffetings of Satan" (104:10). *See* Buffetings of Satan; Cast out/cut off.

Blessings for repenting

The Lord promises: "Inasmuch as they do repent and receive the fulness of my gospel, and become sanctified, I will stay mine hand in judgment" (39:18)—that is, the Lord's hand that inevitably comes down in retribution, and in JUSTICE, to inflict the consequences of disobedience and rebellion will be held back. The penitent can "escape their enemies" (54:3), especially the greatest enemies, death and hell. Those who have sinned can repent and be forgiven (50:39). In addition, they can help other people to repent and be forgiven, which brings JOY (18:13–16). The ultimate blessing is that "unto him that repenteth and sanctifieth himself before the Lord shall be given eternal life" (133:62).

The GOSPEL of Jesus Christ is occasionally referred to as the gospel of repentance (13:1; 84:27; 138:57). The word *gospel* means "good news"; therefore, it is the good news of repentance. Repentance is sometimes looked upon as a punishment, as a distasteful, negative thing. It does involve some pain, of course, but genuine repentance is a blessing—a happy, positive thing. And it is an ongoing process—a repentant member of the Church can renew the covenants and promises of the Lord made at baptism by worthily partaking of the SACRAMENT and be cleansed of sin.

For those who are not yet members of the Church, the naturally desired result of repentance is the simple, beautiful ordinance of baptism. But that brief act of total immersion in water never has, and never will, take away anyone's sins. It is not the baptismal water that cleanses sin; it is the Spirit-attended faith and repentance that precede the baptism that remove the stain and the pain—faith in the Savior and his atoning sacrifice and the genuine repentance to fulfill the disciple's part of making the Atonement work for him or her personally. The baptisms of water and of fire (the Holy Ghost) are the climax of the process that washes away and burns out all that is unclean and undesirable. Therefore, the phrase "baptism of repentance" (107:20; cf. 35:5) appropriately indicates that baptism is a fulfillment, or a concluding act, of all prior efforts to repent and return to God. Then, looking to the future, the newly baptized person remains on the path of repentance by keeping the covenants made at baptism. *See* Baptism by water; Gift of the Holy Ghost.

See also Church discipline; Mercy.

BIBLIOGRAPHY

Benson, Ezra Taft. *God, Family, Country: Our Three Great Loyalties.* Salt Lake City: Deseret Book, 1974.

Kimball, Spencer W. *Love versus Lust.* Brigham Young University Speeches of the Year. Provo, Utah: 5 January 1965.

DKO

Reproachfully. *See* Appendix E.

Reproving betimes with sharpness. *See* Priesthood, proper exercise of.

Rest

The word *rest* is used in the Doctrine and Covenants in at least four contexts:

1. As the common designation for that which remains, the remainder, as in "the rest of mine elders whom I have chosen" (108:4), or in "the rest of the dead . . . [who] live not again until the thousand years are ended" (88:101).

2. As a verb meaning to come down upon, to place upon, as in the Lord's conditional promise to James Covill that if he were faithful, the Lord's power "shall rest upon thee" (39:11–12). Or as he instructed the elders of the Church in preparation for their work, "Let the solemnities of eternity rest upon your minds" (43:34). And he promised the Kirtland Saints that if their temple "be not defiled, my glory shall rest upon it" (97:15).

3. As a period of relief or cessation of activity in order to refresh oneself. When the Lord reiterated the significance of the Sabbath, he reminded the Saints, "For verily this is a day appointed unto you to rest from your labors" (59:9–10). In a similar sense, the Nauvoo House is to be "a resting-place for the weary traveler, that he may contemplate the glory of Zion" (124:60). Moreover, the Lord promised the beleaguered Zion's camp, "Behold, I will give unto you favor and grace . . . that you may rest in peace and safety" (105:25).

4. As a gift of spiritual peace, tranquility, and joy. This unique rest of the Lord can come to the righteous (a) in mortal life; (b) in the spirit world; and, ultimately, (c) in the kingdom of heaven.

Regarding spiritual "rest" in this mortal world, President Joseph F. Smith explained, "The rest here referred to is not physical rest, for there is no such thing as physical rest in the Church of Jesus Christ. [This gift is] the spiritual rest and peace which are born from a settled conviction of the truth in the minds of men" (126). As the Lord told Lyman Sherman, "Your sins are forgiven you, because you have obeyed my voice in coming up hither this morning to receive counsel of him whom I have appointed. Therefore, let your soul be at rest concerning your spiritual standing" (108:1–2).

Referring to the spiritual "rest" in the postmortal spirit world, the Lord told several elders in Nauvoo, "If they live here let them live unto me; and if they die let them die unto me; for they shall rest from all their labors here, and shall continue their works [in paradise]" (124:86). And he promised the faithful Saints in Jackson County that "those that die shall rest from all their labors, and their works shall follow them" (59:2).

The highest and most glorious "rest" is spiritual rest in the kingdom of heaven. Such rest comes incrementally as one prepares for and finally enters into the presence of the Lord. This is the "rest" "ordained in the midst of the Council of the Eternal God of all other gods before this world was, that should be reserved unto the finishing and the end thereof, when every man shall enter into [the Lord's] eternal presence and into his immortal rest" (121:32). This is the "rest" which Moses "plainly taught to the children of Israel in the wilderness, and sought diligently to sanctify his people that they might behold the face of God; but they hardened their hearts and could not endure his presence; therefore, the Lord in his wrath . . . swore that they should not enter into his rest while in the wilderness, which rest is the fulness of his glory" (84:23–24). To receive rest in the presence of the Lord is the final goal, but that goal entails a process of cleansing and redemption through obedience and through the ordinances of the gospel. Accordingly, in Enoch's vision, Earth herself cries out, "When shall I rest, and be cleansed from the filthiness which is gone forth out of me? When will my Creator sanctify me, that I may rest?" (Moses 7:48). This gift of divine rest with its concomitant powers and blessings is given as the faithful come, step by step, line upon line, to know, accept, and live by all the laws and ordinances pertaining to the fulness of the gospel. Such is the direction and process pointed out by the Savior as he speaks of judgment, repentance, and atonement, for "it is meet unto you to know [these things] even as mine apostles . . . that you may enter into my rest" (19:8–9).

BIBLIOGRAPHY

Smith, Joseph F. *Gospel Doctrine*. Salt Lake City: Deseret Book, 1986.

NEL

Restoration of all things. *See* Elias.

Resurrection of the just. *See* Resurrection, the.

Resurrection of the unjust. *See* Resurrection, the.

Resurrection, the

The rising of the body from the grave after DEATH to be joined permanently with the spirit (63:49; 93:33–34; 138:43; cf. Alma 11:45). It is the process by which the body becomes immortal (29:13, 43) and is the perfection of the redemption of the soul (45:46; 88:16). The Doctrine and Covenants bears testimony to the resurrection of Jesus and of all humankind and contributes greatly to the knowledge of this subject, adding vital information in several areas and confirming the message of other scriptures.

The Doctrine and Covenants joins with the other scriptures in teaching that the resurrection is brought about by the ATONEMENT of Christ (88:14), "who wrought out this perfect atonement through the shedding of his own blood" (76:69). It is made possible "through the grace of God the Father and his Only Begotten Son, Jesus Christ" (138:14), "through the triumph and the glory of the Lamb, who was slain" (76:39). All will be resurrected, both the righteous and the unrighteous. "Before the earth shall pass away, Michael, mine archangel, shall sound his trump, and then shall all the dead awake, for their graves shall be opened, and they shall come forth—yea, even all" (29:26; cf. 43:18).

Jesus and the early Saints

Substantiating the testimony of the New Testament and the Book of Mormon, the Doctrine and Covenants teaches that JESUS CHRIST has "risen again from the dead" (18:12) and that Saints from the time of the Old Testament and the Book of Mormon were resurrected at Jesus' resurrection. Those "who had been faithful in the testimony of Jesus while they lived in mortality; and who had offered sacrifice in the similitude of the great sacrifice of the Son of God, and had suffered tribulation in their Redeemer's name" had all "departed the mortal life, firm in the hope of a glorious resurrection." After his crucifixion, Jesus "preached to them the everlasting gospel, the doctrine of the resurrection and the redemption of mankind from the fall" (138:12–14, 19). They were blessed by him "to come forth, after his resurrection from the dead, to enter into his Father's kingdom, there to be crowned with immortality and eternal life" (138:51), and thus they were, along with ancient prophets and patriarchs, "with Christ in his resurrection" (133:55). These verses reveal in plainness doctrines that are only hinted at in the Bible, including the truth that the Christian gospel was known and lived before the time of Jesus, that Jesus visited departed souls in the spirit world, and that faithful departed Christians who lived before Christ's mortal ministry were resurrected with him (e.g., Matt. 27:52–53; John 8:56; 1 Pet. 3:18–19; 4:6). *See* Salvation for the dead.

The resurrection of the just

The Doctrine and Covenants uses two sets of terms (just/unjust and first/last) to delineate the quality and order of the resurrection. The "resurrection of the just" (76:17) is the resurrection of those who will inherit the celestial kingdom (76:50–70). The phrase "first resurrection" pertains to sequence. It begins with Jesus' resurrection and continues into the MILLENNIUM with the resurrection of heirs of the celestial and terrestrial kingdoms. Heirs of the terrestrial kingdom, those "who have received their part in that prison which is prepared for them, that they might receive the gospel, and be judged according to men in the flesh" (88:99), will come forth in the Millennium but after the resurrection of those who qualify for the celestial kingdom (88:98–99). Similarly, "they that knew no law shall have part in the first resurrection; and it shall be tolerable for them" (45:54). The first resurrection thus includes the resurrection of those who are the "honorable men of the earth" (76:75) but who chose not to embrace the fulness of the gospel and its covenants.

The "last resurrection" comes at the end of the Millennium and will include those who will go to the telestial kingdom and SONS OF PERDITION (76:85; 88:32, 100–102).

Although all will rise again, one's faithfulness to the principles and ordinances of the GOSPEL will determine the nature of one's resurrection. "As many as would believe" shall be "raised in immortality unto eternal life" (29:43). A glorious resurrection will come to those who "received the testimony of Jesus, and believed on his name and were baptized after the manner of his burial . . . and receive the Holy Spirit by the laying on of the hands" and are "just and true" (76:51–53). "The righteous shall be gathered on my right hand unto eternal life" (29:27). "They who have done good" will come forth "in the resurrection of the just" (76:17). Those who are "just" in this life will be "made perfect" through JESUS CHRIST; "these are they whose bodies are celestial" (76:69–70). Those who marry for eternity and whose MARRIAGE is sealed by the Holy Spirit of promise "shall come forth in the first resurrection" (132:19).

At Jesus' second coming, the faithful dead will be resurrected and lifted up to meet him in the air. "When the trump shall sound for the dead," they will be "caught up in the cloud" to join him (109:75). "They who have slept in their graves shall come forth, for their graves shall be opened; and they also shall be caught up to meet him in the midst of the pillar of heaven— they are Christ's, the first fruits" (88:97–98). He will bring them with him when he comes "in the clouds of heaven to reign on the earth over his people" (76:63). "Behold, I will come," Jesus revealed to Joseph Smith, "and they shall see me in the clouds of heaven, clothed with power and great glory; with all the holy angels. . . . And the saints that have slept shall come forth to meet me in the cloud." The magnitude of this blessing will be such that Jesus can say, "If ye have slept in peace blessed are you; for as you now behold me and know that I am, even so shall ye come unto me and your souls shall live" (45:44–46).

The faithful, in the "resurrection of the just" (76:17), will be blessed immeasurably for all eternity. "The dead which died in me," Jesus said, will "receive a crown of righteousness" and "be clothed upon, even as I am, to be with me, that we may be one" (29:13). They will be "raised in immortality unto eternal life" (29:43). They will "arise and live" (43:18) and will "receive an inheritance before the Lord, in the holy city" (63:49). They will be "the church of the Firstborn" into whose hands the Father will give "all things." They will be "priests and kings" and will receive of the Father's fulness and of his glory. They will be "priests of the Most High, after the order of Melchizedek, which was after the order of Enoch, which was after the order of the Only Begotten Son," "wherefore . . . they are gods, even the sons of God." See Gods.

All things will be theirs, "whether life or death, or things present, or things to come, all are theirs and they are Christ's, and Christ is God's." They will "overcome all things" and will "dwell in the presence of God and his Christ forever and ever." They will "have part in the first resurrection . . . the resurrection of the just." They will dwell on "Mount Zion . . . the city of the living God, the heavenly place, the holiest of all" among "an innumerable company of angels . . . the general assembly and church of Enoch, and of the Firstborn." Their names will be "written in heaven," and their bodies will be "celestial," with a glory like "that of the sun, even the glory of God, the highest of all" (76:54–60, 62, 64–68, 70).

The faithful will rise with a "spiritual body" (88:27), meaning a body that will no longer be subject to death and corruption and will house both intelligence and soul in a perfect, eternal, union of matter and spirit (Alma 11:45). Those who in earth life obtained through righteousness and grace the characteristics of "a celestial spirit" will receive their earthly bodies again but "quickened by a portion of the celestial glory." They "shall then receive of the same, even a fulness" (88:28–29), and inherit "thrones, kingdoms, principalities, and powers, dominions" (132:19). They will "stand on the right hand of the Lamb, when he shall stand upon Mount Zion, and upon the holy city, the New Jerusalem" (133:56), "crowned with immortality and eternal life" (138:51). Indeed, it will be "a glorious resurrection" (138:14).

The resurrection of the unjust

The unjust will also be resurrected but will not share the glory that the faithful will receive, nor will they be resurrected at the same time. "The trump of God shall sound both long and loud, and shall say to the sleeping nations: Ye saints arise and live; ye sinners stay and sleep until I shall call again" (43:18). The Doctrine and Covenants gives more information about the resurrection of the righteous than of the unrighteous, but something of their future is made known. A fundamental principle is that all will receive a resurrection commensurate with the spiritual qualities they obtained in mortality: "Your glory shall be that glory by which your bodies are quickened." Those who in this life are "quickened by a portion of the celestial glory shall then receive of the same, even a fulness. And they who are quickened by a portion of the terrestrial glory shall then receive of the same, even a fulness. And also they who are quickened by a portion of the telestial glory shall then receive of the same, even a fulness. And they who remain [those consigned to perdition] shall also be quickened; nevertheless, they shall return again to their own place, to enjoy that which they are willing to receive, because they were not willing to enjoy that which they might have received" (88:29–32). Thus, in the resurrection of the unjust (76:17), all will rise again in the body but with the degree of glory that reflects their level of obedience or with no glory at all.

One profound message of the Restoration is that hell—spirit prison—is redemptive and not merely punitive. It is a place of moral rehabilitation intended to mold and tutor through suffering, repentance, and awareness of guilt not only those who did not embrace the gospel in this life but also even the wicked among God's children. It is a place of preparation for their resurrection to a degree of glory (see 76:39–44). After the resurrection of the just, those who on earth did not live worthily will be resurrected in due course once they are spiritually prepared in the world of spirits. But all who will not inherit the celestial kingdom will be "damned" in the sense that they will be cut off from celestial blessings (49:5).

The resurrection will continue throughout the Millennium. Those who "die" in the Millennium "shall not sleep in the dust, but they shall be changed in the twinkling of an eye" to resurrected, immortal beings (63:51; cf. 43:32; 101:31).

Those who will come forth in the last resurrection, at the end of the Millennium, to inherit the telestial kingdom, will be "the spirits of men who are to be judged, and are found under condemnation . . . these are the rest of the dead; and they live not again until the thousand years are ended, neither again, until the end of the earth" (88:100–101). Of them the Lord said, "And they that believe not" shall be raised to "eternal damnation; for they cannot be redeemed from their spiritual fall, because they repent not" (29:44). Similarly, "the unbelieving, and all liars, and whosoever loveth and maketh a lie, and the whoremonger, and the sorcerer, shall have their part in that lake which burneth with fire and brimstone, which is the second death. . . . They shall not have part in the first resurrection" (63:17–18) and "shall not be redeemed from the devil until the last resurrection" (76:85). Yet, they too will be redeemed from hell, eventually, and inherit a degree of glory, the telestial kingdom.

Recognizing that not all of God's JUDGMENTS are given unto men (29:30; cf. 43:33), the Doctrine and Covenants speaks of others, who, unwilling to repent or acknowledge the grace and sovereignty of God, will "remain until that great and last day, even the end, [and] shall remain filthy still" (88:102). The Lord said that these individuals, called the sons of perdition, will be subject to the second death and will not be redeemed (76:37–38). These are they concerning whom he said: "I [will] be ashamed to own [them] before the Father; wherefore I will say unto them—Depart from me, ye cursed, into everlasting fire, prepared for the devil and his angels" (29:27–28). They will be resurrected but will not inherit any degree of glory (88:24, 32).

See also Kingdoms of glory and perdition, vision of.

KPJ

Revelation

The process by which God communicates his will to man. "We believe also in the principle of direct revelation from God to man," President Joseph F. Smith declared. "The gospel cannot be administered, nor the Church of God continue to exist, without it. Christ is the head of his Church and not man, and the connection can only be maintained upon the principle of direct and continuous revelation" (104). Revelation is evidence of God's perfect love and his ever-present concern for the well-being of all of his children. The Bible states that "surely the Lord God will do nothing, but he revealeth his secret unto his servants the prophets" (Amos 3:7). Latter-day Saints witness to the world that God and Jesus Christ, being the "same . . . yesterday, today, and forever" (20:11–12), continue to reveal their mind and will to men on earth today, that the heavens are indeed open and that God, "knowing the calamity which should come upon the inhabitants of the earth, called upon [his] servant Joseph Smith, Jun., and spake unto him from heaven, and gave him commandments; and also gave commandments to others, that they should proclaim these things unto the world; and all this that it might be fulfilled, which was written by the prophets" (1:17–18).

Revelation is given to bless and strengthen individuals, families, congregations, nations, and indeed, the entire world. Concerning the world's need for continuing revelation, the Prophet Joseph Smith taught: "We are differently situated from any other people that ever existed upon this earth; consequently those former revelations cannot be suited to our conditions; they were given to other people, who were before us; but in the last days, God was to call a remnant, in which was to be deliverance, as well as in Jerusalem and Zion. Now if God should give no more revelations, where will we find Zion and this remnant?" (*History*, 2:52).

The Doctrine and Covenants is a collection of many of these revelations. The book itself illustrates the different ways in which revelation may come to man. In addition, the Doctrine and Covenants distinguishes between prophetic revelation—those communications from God to his children through his authorized mouthpiece, the prophet-leader of the Church, and personal revelation—those messages from God to individuals that come as answers to their prayers and as spiritual guidance given according to their own unique needs and circumstances.

Types of revelations contained in the Doctrine and Covenants

God uses different means, according to his will and purposes, to reveal truths to man.

There are at least five major types of revelations contained in the Doctrine and Covenants:

1. Personal visitations. The most important revelation in this dispensation was the visitation of the Father and the Son to the young boy, Joseph Smith, in 1820 (JS—H 1:1–20). Several sections in the Doctrine and Covenants record similar personal visitations of heavenly messengers and their accompanying messages. For example, section 2 gives an account of the visitation of the angel Moroni to Joseph Smith in 1823; section 13 gives an account of the restoration of the Aaronic Priesthood which occurred when John the Baptist appeared to, instructed, and ordained Joseph Smith and Oliver Cowdery on 15 May 1829; and section 110 gives an account of the personal visitation of the Lord Jesus Christ and the ancient prophets Moses, Elias, and Elijah to Joseph Smith and Oliver Cowdery in the Kirtland Temple on 3 April 1836.

2. Visions. Some revelations contained in the Doctrine and Covenants could be characterized as visions, whereby mortal man's "spiritual eyes" were opened and he viewed something that conveyed God's message to his mind, heart, and soul. Section 76 is the record of Joseph Smith's and Sidney Rigdon's series of visions, including the vision of the three degrees of glory. Sections 137 and 138 are likewise accounts of visions and the accompanying divine messages given to Joseph Smith in 1836 and to Joseph F. Smith in 1918, respectively.

3. URIM AND THUMMIM. The term means "lights and perfections" in Hebrew. In biblical times, stones in the breastplate of the high priest were apparently used at times for receiving revelation from God (Ex. 28:30, Lev. 8:8; Num. 27:21; Deut. 33:8; 1 Sam. 28:6). Joseph Smith obtained the Urim and Thummim at the time

he received the gold plates that contained the record that would become the Book of Mormon (JS–H 1:52, 59). The Book of Mormon refers to them as "interpreters" (Mosiah 8:13; 28:11–16). Not only did Joseph Smith use the Urim and Thummim in the translation of the Book of Mormon but before returning this divine instrument to the angel Moroni at the completion of the translation, he also used it as means to receive revelation from God. Several sections of the Doctrine and Covenants were received in this manner (3; 6; 7; 11; 14–17).

4. Voice of God. Though all revelation can be rightly described as the "voice of God," some revelations are delivered by an audible voice. For example, "the voice" bore record to Joseph Smith and Sidney Rigdon that Jesus Christ is the "Only Begotten of the Father" and the creator and savior of many worlds (76:23–24). The "voice of Jehovah" was heard by Joseph Smith and Oliver Cowdery, testifying of his own mission, and accepting the Kirtland Temple (110:3–7). Section 128 speaks of many voices of those who came to restore the gospel in the dispensation of the fulness of times—Peter, James, and John; God; Michael; Gabriel; Raphael; and of diverse angels, "from Michael or Adam down to the present time, all declaring their dispensation, their rights, their keys, their honors, their majesty and glory, and the power of their priesthood" (128:20–22). In addition, a voice from heaven in 1832 informed Joseph Smith of the beginnings of the United States Civil War, and the timing of the second coming of the Savior (130:12–15).

5. Inspiration. The most common means whereby the Lord communicates to man, both to the prophet and to other individuals, is through inspiration, or "the spirit of revelation," as the Doctrine and Covenants calls it. Ideas, thoughts, feelings, and actual words are communicated to the mind and heart "by the Holy Ghost" (8:2–3; cf. 11:13–14; Enos 1:10). Joseph Smith taught, "When you feel pure intelligence flowing into you, it may give you sudden strokes of ideas, so that by noticing it, you may find it fulfilled the same day or soon; (i.e.) those things that were presented unto your minds by the Spirit of God, will come to pass; and thus by learning the Spirit of God and understanding it, you may grow into the principle of revelation, until you become perfect in Christ Jesus" (History, 3:381).

Revelation to the Church through the Lord's authorized prophet

The Doctrine and Covenants teaches of revelation for the Church and the world. In it, the Lord declared that only the president of The Church of Jesus Christ of Latter-day Saints is "appointed" of the Lord to "receive commandments and revelations from my hand" and "none else shall be appointed unto this gift except it be through him" (43:2–5; cf. 28:1–7). Of this principle, President J. Reuben Clark Jr. taught: "Only the President of the Church, the Presiding High Priest, is sustained as Prophet, Seer, and Revelator for the Church, and he alone has the right to receive revelations for the Church, either new or amendatory, or to give authoritative interpretations of scriptures that shall be binding on the Church, or change in any way the existing doctrines of the Church. He is God's sole mouthpiece on earth for the Church of Jesus Christ of Latter-day Saints, the only true Church. He alone may declare the mind and will of God to his people. No officer of any other church in the world has this high right and lofty prerogative. So when any other person, irrespective of who he is, undertakes to do any of these things, you may know he is not 'moved upon by the Holy Ghost,' in so speaking, unless he has special authorization from the President of the Church" (10).

These principles concerning revelation establish order in the Church and are given by the Lord "that you may not be deceived" (43:6). "There is order in the kingdom of God," President Joseph Fielding Smith wrote. "There could not be order if every man was privileged to give commandments and claim the right to direct by revelation the members of the Church.

"This law is given for our government for all time. It is the one who holds the keys and who stands as the Presiding High Priest and President of the Church, who is the spokesman of the Lord for the members of the Church. Individual members may receive the inspiration and revelation for their own guidance, but not for the Church. Moreover, no member of the Church will profess to receive a revelation for his own guidance that is contradictory of any revelation coming from the President of the Church" (*Church History,* 1:172).

Personal revelation

The Doctrine and Covenants, along with the other standard works, teaches that all of God's children can have access to spiritual guidance in their lives. This is the promise of personal revelation. "I will impart unto you of my Spirit," the Lord declared to Hyrum Smith, "which shall enlighten your mind, which shall fill your soul with joy; and then shall ye know, or by this shall you know, all things whatsoever you desire of me, which are pertaining unto things of righteousness, in faith believing in me that you shall receive" (11:13–14). This revelation can come as a "still small voice, which whispereth through and pierceth all things" (85:6). In a revelation through Joseph Smith to Oliver Cowdery, the Lord explained an important principle of revelation. This particular instruction came in connection with Oliver's attempt to translate the Book of Mormon plates but can be applied to other circumstances where revelation is sought: "Behold, you have not understood; you have supposed that I would give it unto you, when you took no thought save it was to ask me. But, behold, I say unto you, that you must study it out in your mind; then you must ask me if it be right, and if it is right I will cause that your bosom shall burn within you; therefore, you shall feel that it is right" (9:7–8).

Of this passage of scripture Elder Dallin H. Oaks of the Quorum of the Twelve Apostles said: "Surely, the word 'burning' in this scripture signifies a feeling of comfort and serenity. That is the witness many receive. That is the way revelation works. . . . 'The language of peace, as spoken by the Lord, embraces a sense of quiet confidence, comfort, and warmth. It is gentle and calm, amiable and sweet; it is temperate and kind; it is orderly and identified by happiness, joy, and feelings of love' (Joseph Fielding McConkie and Robert L. Millet, *The Holy Ghost* [1989], 14)" (13).

Furthermore, it is important to understand that such feelings should be accompanied by an enlightened MIND. The Lord told Oliver Cowdery in an earlier revelation: "Yea, behold, I will tell you in your mind and in your heart, by the Holy Ghost, which shall come upon you and which shall dwell in your heart" (8:2).

Numerous passages in the Doctrine and Covenants testify of God's promise to give personal revelation to individuals according to their FAITH and needs (8:11; 11:7; 19:38; 20:35; 31:11; 34:10; 42:61; 75:27; 76:10; 79:2; 82:4; 84:46, 85; 88:63–67; 100:5–8; 121:26). Every baptized and confirmed member of the Church had the GIFT OF THE HOLY GHOST bestowed on them, which gives one the right, under certain qualifying conditions, to receive personal revelation. "No man can receive the Holy Ghost without receiving revelations," the Prophet Joseph Smith taught. "The Holy Ghost is a revelator" (*History,* 6:58). "Would God that all the Lord's people were prophets," Moses exclaimed, "and that the Lord would put his spirit upon them!" (Num. 11:29). Moses desired that all of his people would be blessed with personal revelation and the guiding influence of the Spirit. Herein lies the difference between personal revelation and revelation to the Lord's chosen prophet for the whole Church. President Harold B. Lee taught: "In a sense, the word *prophet* might apply to all faithful Church members. I do not mean that we have the right to receive revelations as to how this church might be run, or that members may have revelations as to how or who should be named in a stake or ward organization. But I do say that the bishop in his place, the mission president in his place, the stake president in his place, the quorum president, the auxiliary leader, the seminary teacher, the institute teacher, a father and mother in the home, a young person in his or her quest for a proper companion in marriage—each of us has the right to revelation. . . . In other words, anyone who enjoys the gift by which he may have God revealed has the spirit of prophecy, the power of revelation, and, in a sense, is a prophet within the sphere of responsibility and authority given to him" (154–55).

Spiritual preparation to receive revelation

Revelation, whether to the prophet-president of the Church or to an individual, is always given in accordance with divine law and requires spiritual preparation on the part of the recipient. As Oliver Cowdery learned, revelation cannot be had merely for the asking and studying (9:7–9). Several passages in the Doctrine and Covenants teach of the spiritual requirements for revelation. These include desiring with righteous intent (6:8, 20); a "prayer of faith" (42:14); OBEDIENCE to the commandments of God (63:23); meditating/pondering (76:19; 88:62; 138:11; cf. 1 Ne. 11:1); renewing covenants through worthily partaking of the SACRAMENT (20:77, 79); and patiently trusting in the Lord's will and timetable (67:13; 88:68; 98:12). See Trust.

Revelation is a living fountain of truth. Whatever the means of communication, God's promise of revelation—revelation to the prophet for the Church and the world, or personal revelation to help with unique challenges—is that "if thou shalt ask, thou shalt receive . . . knowledge upon knowledge, that thou mayest know the mysteries and peaceable things—that which bringeth joy, that which bringeth life eternal" (42:61).

See also Holy Ghost, the; Ponder, pondering; Prayer.

BIBLIOGRAPHY

Clark, J. Reuben Jr. "When Are Church Leaders' Words Entitled to Claim of Scripture?" *Church News,* 31 July 1954.

Lee, Harold B. *Stand Ye in Holy Places.* Salt Lake City: Deseret Book, 1974.

Oaks, Dallin H. "Teaching and Learning by the Spirit." *Ensign* 27 (March 1997): 6–14.

Smith, Joseph. *History of The Church of Jesus Christ of Latter-day Saints.* Edited by B. H. Roberts. 7 vols. 2d ed. rev. Salt Lake City: The Church of Jesus Christ of Latter-day Saints, 1932–51.

Smith, Joseph F. *Gospel Doctrine.* Salt Lake City: Deseret Book, 1986.

Smith, Joseph Fielding. *Church History and Modern Revelation.* 2 vols. Salt Lake City: Deseret Book, 1953.

BLT

Revelation of St. John. *See* John the Beloved/Revelator quotations in the Doctrine and Covenants.

Revelation, spirit of. *See* Revelation.

Revelator

One "who receives revelation from the Lord and conveys the revealed truth to another" (McConkie, 651). The word *revelator* is used in two contexts in the Doctrine and Covenants. First, the apostle John, author of the biblical book of Revelation, is referred to as "the Revelator, John" (77:2) and as "John the Revelator" (128:6). The other context refers to the presiding officers of the Church through whom truth is revealed for Church members and the world. For example, the Lord affirmed that Joseph Smith's role as revelator would enable Sidney Rigdon to "know the certainty of all things pertaining to the things of my kingdom on the earth" (100:11; cf. 5:10). As president of the high priesthood and "presiding elder over all [the Lord's] church" (124:125), Joseph Smith was to be a revelator, as well as a translator, SEER, and PROPHET (107:91–92). Hyrum Smith, as the assistant president and the patriarch of the Church, was also appointed as a prophet, seer, and revelator to the Church (124:91–95).

In The Church of Jesus Christ of Latter-day Saints, the president of the Church as well as members of the First Presidency and Quorum of the Twelve Apostles are sustained and revered as prophets, seers, and revelators ("Sustaining," 4).

BIBLIOGRAPHY

McConkie, Bruce R. *Mormon Doctrine.* 2d ed. Salt Lake City: Bookcraft, 1966.

"The Sustaining of Church Officers." *Ensign* 38 (May 2008): 4–7.

HDG

Revile. *See* Appendix E.

Rich, Charles C.

Birth: 21 August 1809, Campbell County, Kentucky

Death: 17 November 1883, Paris, Bear Lake County, Idaho

As a young man, Charles C. Rich showed little interest in religion until he was introduced to the Book of Mormon. "I studied carefully, anxiously, and prayerfully, that I might know if it were the Church of Jesus Christ. . . . The spirit would then whisper, you have not been baptized, you have not obeyed the Gospel;

but when I had complied with the law, then I . . . obtained a perfect knowledge of the truth, and could then bear a testimony of it to all the world" (Rich, 19:250).

Charles C. Rich was baptized on 1 April 1832. He marched with ZION'S CAMP in 1834 and upon his return to Kirtland was ordained a high priest on 12 April 1836. He was promised in his patriarchal blessing that the devil would not have power over him and that he would help to gather thousands to Zion.

Rich's devotion led to his appointments to positions of trust and authority in the Church. He served as president of the high priests quorum in Far West in 1837, defended the Saints against mobocracy, and fought in the Battle of Crooked River, assuming command after David W. Patten was wounded. After he was driven out of Missouri at great personal loss, he settled in Nauvoo, and was chosen by the Lord as one of twelve men to be on the "high council, for the corner-stone of Zion" (124:131). He also served in the stake presidency and as a political missionary to promote the Prophet's candidacy for president of the United States.

Active in community affairs, Rich served on the Nauvoo city council and in the Nauvoo Legion; first as a captain, and then as a brigadier general. When the Saints emigrated west, he was appointed to lead a company to the Salt Lake Valley (Smith, 7:481–82).

On 3 October 1847 he was chosen as a counselor in the Salt Lake Stake presidency, and in February 1849 he was called to the Council of the Twelve Apostles. Rich served for thirty-four years in that position. In 1851, Rich led a company of Saints to settle San Bernardino, California, and for seven weeks of the trek he suffered from the "bloody flux" and lost fifty-five pounds; nevertheless, he persisted in fulfilling his assignment, and returned to Salt Lake in 1857.

He served in the Utah territorial legislature (1858–60) and presided over the European mission (1860–62). Upon his return from Europe, he settled in the Bear Lake area. Rich was "honored and beloved by all who knew him. He was stricken with paralysis Oct. 24, 1880. . . . During all these three years of affliction he

Courtesy Church History Library.

Charles C. Rich, 1809–1883.

was never heard to complain or in any manner evince anything but a spirit of the utmost contentment and resignation" (Jenson, 1:103). He died in November 1883 at age seventy-four.

BIBLIOGRAPHY

Black, Susan Easton. *Who's Who in the Doctrine and Covenants*. Salt Lake City: Deseret Book, 1997.

Jenson, Andrew. *Latter-day Saint Biographical Encyclopedia*. 4 vols. Salt Lake City: Andrew Jenson History Co., 1901–1936. Reprint, Salt Lake City: Western Epics, 1971.

Rich, Charles C. *Journal of Discourses*. 26 vols. London: Latter-day Saints' Book Depot, 1854–86.

Smith, Joseph. *History of The Church of Jesus Christ of Latter-day Saints*. Edited by B. H. Roberts. 7 vols. 2d ed. rev. Salt Lake City: The Church of Jesus Christ of Latter-day Saints, 1932–51.

KWF

Rich, riches

Abundance, both temporal and spiritual. The riches of heaven and earth are God's to bestow upon his children; nevertheless, the most important riches he commands his children to seek are "the riches of eternity" (38:39; 67:2). The Lord cautions against seeking earthly riches because they can lead to pride (38:39; 56:16; cf. Jacob 2:12–19; 3 Ne. 6:15). The riches of the earth, however valuable, have a finite worth and belong only to this world. To gain salvation and exaltation, one must endure faithfully to the end, regardless of earthly riches (6:13). In 1836, Joseph Smith traveled to Salem, Massachusetts, expecting to pay Church debts with a reported hidden treasure. Instead, the Lord blessed him with a treasure of converts (111; Smith, 2:464–66).

The Lord declared that he made the earth rich, and has promised "the fulness of the earth" to those who keep the Sabbath day as he directs (59:16), and "a land of promise, a land flowing with milk and honey," as an inheritance he desires to give to his covenant people for time and all eternity (38:16–20).

In tutoring Joseph Smith and Oliver Cowdery, the Lord admonished them to "seek not for riches but for wisdom," and promised that "the mysteries of God shall be unfolded unto you, and then shall you be made rich. Behold, he that hath eternal life is rich" (6:7).

In conjunction with the move to Ohio, the Church was commanded to appoint individuals to take care of the poor and needy (38:32–35). The Lord's plan is to "consecrate of the riches of those who embrace my gospel among the Gentiles unto the poor of my people who are of the house of Israel" (42:30, 39).

The Lord instructed his Saints to gather their riches "with one heart and with one mind" and purchase their inheritance in the land of Zion (45:65; 51:1–6). They were unable to establish Zion at that time because as the Lord explained, "They . . . seek not earnestly the riches of eternity, but their eyes are full of greediness. These things ought not to be, and must be done away from among them" (68:31–32). Redeeming Zion is predicated upon obeying "the principles of the law of the celestial kingdom" (105:5), which include qualifying for the riches of eternity by sharing the riches of the earth (78:5–6).

BIBLIOGRAPHY

Smith, Joseph. *History of The Church of Jesus Christ of Latter-day Saints.* Edited by B. H. Roberts. 7 vols. 2d ed. Rev. Salt Lake City: The Church of Jesus Christ of Latter-day Saints, 1932–51.

RAB

Richards, Willard

Birth: 24 June 1804, Hopkinton, Middlesex, Massachusetts

Death: 11 March 1854, Salt Lake City, Salt Lake County, Utah

After reading the Book of Mormon, Dr. Willard Richards moved from Massachusetts to Kirtland, Ohio, in 1836 to investigate the Church. After a year and a half of investigating the restored gospel, thirty-two-year-old Richards was baptized by his cousin Brigham Young on the last day of December 1836. In June 1837 Richards was called to preach the gospel in the British Isles. It was in England that he met Jennetta Richards; they were married in 1838. On 1 April 1838 he was named first counselor to Joseph Fielding, president of the British Mission. In 1840, when members of the Twelve arrived in England, Richards learned of his apostolic call to fill a vacancy in the Quorum of the Twelve (118:6; cf. 124:129). He was ordained

Willard Richards, 1804–1854.

Courtesy Church History Library

on 14 April 1840 in England, the only apostle ordained outside the United States.

In April 1841, after serving for three years in the British Mission, Elder Richards returned to the United States, settling first in Warsaw, Illinois, and then in Nauvoo staying first with Brigham Young and then with the Prophet Joseph Smith. His move to the Prophet's residence was to facilitate the rapidly escalating clerical and literary work of the Church. Elder Richards served as a private secretary to Joseph Smith, Church recorder, clerk, and historian. In Nauvoo he also served on the city council and as clerk of the municipal court. In November 1841 Joseph wrote, "I have been searching all my life to find a man after my own heart whom I could trust with my business in all things, and I have found him.—Doctor Willard Richards is the man" (JH).

A year before the martyrdom Joseph prophesied that "the time would come that the balls would fly around [Willard] like hail, and he should see his friends fall on the right and on the left, but that there should not be a hole in his garment" (6:619). On 27 June 1844 at Carthage Jail the prophetic statement was fulfilled. Elder Richards was with the Prophet in Carthage Jail when he was martyred (135:2). Elder Richards's account, "Two Minutes in Jail," included in *History of the Church* (6:619–21), details the murders of Joseph and Hyrum Smith.

After the Prophet's death, the same loyalty Elder Richards had given to Joseph Smith was willingly extended to Brigham Young. He wrote, revised, and preserved Church historical records under President Young's direction. He was selected as the second counselor in the First Presidency of the Church organized 5 December 1847 and sustained by the members of the Church on 27 December 1847. He faithfully fulfilled this calling until his death from dropsy at age forty-nine.

BIBLIOGRAPHY

Journal History, 21 November 1841. Church History Library, The Church of Jesus Christ of Latter-day Saints, Salt Lake City, Utah.

Smith, Joseph. *History of The Church of Jesus Christ of Latter-day Saints*. Edited by B. H. Roberts. 7 vols. 2d

ed. rev. Salt Lake City: The Church of Jesus Christ of Latter-day Saints, 1932–51.

SEB

Riches of eternity. *See* Eternity; Rich, riches.

Rigdon, Sidney

Birth: 19 February 1793, St. Clair Township, Allegheny County, Pennsylvania

Death: 14 July 1876, Friendship, Allegany County, New York

The son of William Rigdon and Nancy Gallagher, Sidney Rigdon was the only counselor in the First Presidency who served during the entire administration of the Prophet. Before his baptism by Oliver Cowdery in November 1830, he had been a tanner, a farmer, and a minister. Best known as a powerful preacher, he had joined the United Baptists in 1817, and preached in the vicinity of Warren, Trumbull County, Ohio, from 1819 to 1821. During that time, he married Phebe Brook, 12 June 1820, at Warren. He later served as the minister of First Baptist Church of Pittsburgh (1821–24) but joined the Reformed Baptist (later Disciples of Christ or Campbellite) movement and became one of their influential preachers. He was living in Mentor, Geauga County, Ohio when the four missionaries to the Lamanites—Oliver Cowdery, Peter Whitmer Jr., Parley P. Pratt, and Ziba Peterson—passed through the area in the fall of 1830. Parley P. Pratt, who had been a member of Rigdon's congregation, introduced him to the Book of Mormon and the Restoration. After careful examination of their claims and the book, he was baptized, confirmed, and ordained an elder.

Sidney Rigdon immediately traveled to New York with Edward Partridge to meet Joseph Smith. Within days of his arrival, the Lord gave a revelation to the Prophet giving extensive counsel to Sidney and calling him to serve as a scribe for Joseph, to "tarry with him," and to "forsake him not" (35:22). From that point on, Sidney Rigdon had a leading role in Church affairs until the death of Joseph Smith. As a scribe, he wrote some of the revelations received by the Prophet but was most heavily involved as the scribe for the new translation of the Bible. Rigdon fulfilled the commandment to "tarry with him" as he served as one of his counselors in the Presidency of the Church (1832–44). In obedience to the counsel "forsake him not," he was with the Prophet during some of the most difficult events in his life. He suffered with Joseph Smith from the tarring and feathering at Hiram, Ohio, in March 1832, and he was incarcerated with him in the jail at Liberty, Missouri, from December 1838 to 25 February 1839 (Smith, 3:215, 264). Although his release had been ordered in January due to his ill health, Rigdon did not leave the jail until February for fear of reprisal.

Sidney Rigdon is mentioned frequently in the revelations; most of the time to act in concert with the Prophet Joseph Smith. Some revelations have him listed as receiving the revelation conjointly with the Prophet (40; 44; 71; 73; 76; 100). Several revelations guided him in his callings: first as a member of the Literary Firm (70:1), then as a member of the United Firm (78:9; 82:11; 104:20–22), and as a counselor in the Presidency of the Church (90:6;

102:3; 124:126). His official duties often required him to travel as directed by the Lord (37; 52:3; 42:4; 53:5; 55:5; 58:58; 60:6; 61:23; 78:9; 93:51; 100; 103:38; 111) and to preach the gospel (49; 61:30–31; 71; 103:29; 115:1–6). He was also given instruction concerning his family and temporal affairs (41:8; 63:65; 90:21; 93:44; 104:20) and to perform ordinances (36:2).

Sidney Rigdon was ordained to the office of high priest by Lyman Wight at the conference of June 1831 and was assigned to travel with the Prophet to Missouri to hold the next conference of the Church (52:1–3). The Lord directed Rigdon that while he was in Missouri, he should "consecrate and dedicate this land, and the spot for the temple, unto the Lord" (58:57). This was accomplished on 2 August 1831. In addition, the Prophet Joseph Smith dedicated the temple site in Independence the next day (Smith, 1:196–99). He also instructed him to "write a description of the land of Zion, and a statement of the will of God, as it shall be made known by the Spirit unto him; and an epistle and subscription, to be presented unto all the churches to obtain moneys, to be put into the hands of the bishop, of himself or the agent, as seemeth him good or as he shall direct, to purchase lands for an inheritance for the children of God" (58:50–51). His first attempt to write this description was rejected by the Lord (63:55–56), and so he rewrote it. This later version was read to various congregations of the Church by Oliver Cowdery and Newel K. Whitney and, through their efforts, money was raised for the gathering of the Saints.

Undoubtedly, one of the most important events in the life of Sidney Rigdon occurred on 16 February 1832. On that date, he and the Prophet were working on the new translation of the Bible in the book of John. While they were meditating about the message of John 5:29, a series of visions was opened to them which is recorded in Doctrine and Covenants 76. As part of that experience, they wrote: "We beheld the glory of the Son, on the right hand of the Father, and received of his fulness; and saw the holy angels, and them who are sanctified before his throne, worshiping God, and the Lamb, who

Sidney Rigdon, 1793–1876.

worship him forever and ever. And now, after the many testimonies which have been given of him, this is the testimony, last of all, which we give of him: That he lives! For we saw him, even on the right hand of God; and we heard the voice bearing record that he is the Only Begotten of the Father—that by him, and through him, and of him, the worlds are and were created, and the inhabitants thereof are begotten sons and daughters unto God" (76:20–24).

The Lord counseled in a November 1831 revelation, "that one be appointed of the High Priesthood to preside over the priesthood, and he shall be called President of the High Priesthood of the Church" (107:65). Joseph Smith was sustained in that position by the members of the Church at a conference in Amherst, Ohio, the following January (75, headnote) and he was ordained by Sidney Rigdon at the same time (England and Warner, 3:1128). Later, in March, he chose Jesse Gause and Sidney Rigdon to be, respectively, his first and second counselors in the presidency of the Church (KRB, 10–11). After Gause's apostasy, later that year, the presidency was reorganized in March 1833, with Frederick G. Williams replacing Jesse Gause; Sidney Rigdon became first counselor and Frederick G. Williams the second counselor. The presidency also became known as the First Presidency of the Church at that time (90, headnote).

The Lord gave Sidney Rigdon an additional responsibility in October 1833 to be a "spokesman unto my servant Joseph" (100:9). Rigdon would later use this calling as evidence that he was the legal successor to the Prophet.

During the Nauvoo period Sidney Rigdon was active in civic affairs, though perhaps less so in Church government. He traveled with Joseph Smith to Washington, D.C., to present to the federal government the grievances of Church members for their losses in Missouri. Rigdon was elected to the Nauvoo city council, and he served as city attorney and postmaster. He was also a member of the Nauvoo Masonic Lodge. He was, however, often ill during this period, and his influence as a Church leader began to diminish. Although he never publicly opposed plural marriage, he did not endorse

it. Also, Joseph Smith had for some time suspected Rigdon of being in league with John C. Bennett and of "deception and wickedness" in connection with his duties as postmaster, and the Prophet wrote to him on 27 March 1843 of his suspicions (5:312–13). Though these claims were never fully substantiated and Rigdon was sustained as a counselor to the Prophet at the conference of the Church the following month, Joseph rejected Rigdon as his counselor at the October conference; however, through the efforts of Hyrum Smith, he was retained (Smith, 6:49). Joseph reluctantly accepted Sidney Rigdon as his running mate when he ran for the Presidency of the United States in 1844. Rigdon moved to Pittsburgh ostensibly as part of the campaign and was living there when he learned of the Prophet's death. He quickly returned to Nauvoo and claimed the right to lead the Church as the Prophet's first counselor and as his spokesman. On the day before his death, Joseph Smith had said, "Poor Rigdon, I am glad he is gone to Pittsburg out of the way; were he to preside he would lead the Church to destruction in less than five years" (6:592–93).

Sidney Rigdon introduced his claim to leadership before the Saints in Nauvoo, and Brigham Young presented the claim of the Twelve. The Saints voted to sustain Brigham Young and the Twelve Apostles as leaders of the Church (Smith, 7:240–41), rejecting Rigdon's claims. Though Rigdon said he would sustain the action of the Saints, he rejected the Twelve and was excommunicated 8 September 1844 (Smith, 7:268–69). He moved back to Pittsburgh and attempted to lead a schismatic church, but it did not long survive. He later moved to Friendship, Allegany County, New York, where he died in 1876.

BIBLIOGRAPHY

England, Lynn, and W. Keith Warner. "President of the Church." In *Encyclopedia of Mormonism,* edited by Daniel H. Ludlow et al. 4 vols. New York: Macmillan, 1992.

Kirtland Revelation Book. Church History Library, The Church of Jesus Christ of Latter-day Saints, Salt Lake City, Utah.

Smith, Joseph. *History of The Church of Jesus Christ of Latter-day Saints.* Edited by B. H. Roberts. 7 vols. 2d

ed. rev. Salt Lake City: The Church of Jesus Christ of Latter-day Saints, 1932–51.

RJW

Riggs, Burr

Birth: 17 April 1811, New Haven, New Haven County, Connecticut

Death: 8 June 1860, Quincy, Adams County, Illinois

In 1831 Burr Riggs was baptized and ordained a high priest. By age twenty-one, he was called to be a missionary companion to Major Ashley to "take their journey . . . into the south country" (75:17). He was apparently of a contrary nature, for recorded at his excommunication trial of 1833 was "failing to magnify his calling as High Priest, and had been guilty of neglect of duty, of abusing the Elders, and of treating their admonitions with contempt" (Smith, 1:327). Riggs was reinstated and participated in ZION'S CAMP in 1834. During the march "the brethren" discovered "the skeleton of a man, almost entire, and between his ribs the stone point of a Lamanitish arrow." The Prophet identified the skeleton as that of Zelph, "a large, thick-set man, and a man of God." "Elder Burr Riggs retained the arrow" (Smith, 2:79).

Riggs returned to Kirtland and was ordained a seventy in 1835. By 1836 he had moved with his wife and family to Far West, Missouri, where he purchased two hundred acres. Unfortunately, by 1839, Riggs was again excommunicated and this time numbered among the apostates. He never returned to Church fellowship. In 1840, Riggs started practicing medicine with members of his family, including his father-in-law, Frederick G. Williams. After Williams died in 1842, Riggs continued to practice with his brother-in-law until 1847. Burr Riggs died in Illinois at age forty-nine.

BIBLIOGRAPHY

Smith, Joseph. *History of The Church of Jesus Christ of Latter-day Saints.* Edited by B. H. Roberts. 7 vols. 2d ed. rev. Salt Lake City: The Church of Jesus Christ of Latter-day Saints, 1932–51.

FGW

Righteous, the/righteousness

The "holy in heart"; virtue brought about by "conformity of heart and life to the divine law" (Webster, s.v. "righteous," "righteousness"). A "righteous person is one who makes and keeps gospel covenants" (Faust, 52). The Lord delights to honor the righteous and grants them great and eternal rewards (76:5–7; cf. 59:23).

As wickedness increases throughout the earth, the work of the Lord is to "raise up unto [himself] a pure people, that will serve [him] in righteousness" (100:16). The GOSPEL message is extended to the world by the Lord's servants to "warn the righteous to save themselves from the corruption of the world" (134:12; cf. 133:4, 7, 14), for the wicked "seek not the Lord to establish his righteousness" (1:16). Eventually there will be "an entire separation of the righteous and the wicked" (63:54).

To protect themselves from evil, the Saints are to put on the ARMOR OF GOD, part of which is "the breastplate of righteousness" (27:16–18). The breastplate is placed over the heart. President Harold B. Lee taught that the heart is "the center or the seat of the spiritual or the conscience or the conduct of men" and must be protected by righteousness (168). Such righteousness includes faithfully performing priesthood duties (13:1; 121:36; 107:30; 128:24) and offering the sacrifice unto God of a "broken heart and a contrite spirit" (59:8, 11). Additionally, the Saints are to be "engaged in a good cause," and "bring to pass much righteousness" (58:27). By acquiring CHARITY and purity of thought, they will be blessed with the constant companionship of the HOLY GHOST; and their scepter will become "an unchanging scepter of righteousness" (121:45–46). As a result they will be empowered by their righteousness. The Prophet Joseph Smith was promised that because of his righteousness God would stand by him "forever and ever" (122:4). But the Lord warned that he will "cut off" all who are overcome by the world and "do that which is not in truth and righteousness" (50:8–9).

As it is not always easy to "tell the wicked from the righteous" (10:37), the Lord gave two keys of discernment: (1) those who come not unto Christ and are not acquainted with his voice are not of God (84:50–53); and (2) through the Lord's "strange act"—i.e., that which he does or has his people do—"men may discern between the righteous and the wicked" (101:95). *See* Strange act.

Those who listen to the Lord's warning voice proclaimed by his servants and "work righteousness" (20:14) will "be gathered unto [the Lord] a righteous people, without spot and blameless" (38:31). Initially this gathering is to Zion and her stakes (45:71; 109:39, 58).

As the righteous are gathered before the Second Coming, the judgments of God will be poured out upon the earth until the Lord's work is completed, "which shall be cut short in righteousness" (84:97; cf. 52:11; 109:59). This phrase, in the same language as Romans 9:27–28 (where Paul paraphrases the Greek version of the Hebrew text of Isaiah 10:22), suggests that the Lord, upon his second coming, will righteously make "short work" of (i.e., quickly destroy) wickedness. *See* Jesus Christ, second coming of.

Upon death the righteous are gathered into spirit paradise, many of whom are "appointed messengers" to preach the gospel to those in "darkness" (138:22, 30). During the MILLENNIUM, the righteous will dwell in a state of righteousness with the Lord (29:11). Those born during the Millennium who "[live] in righteousness" will eventually be resurrected to dwell eternally with Christ (43:32). *See* Resurrection, the.

Finally, the righteous will gather on the right hand of God (29:27) where they shall "be clothed upon with robes of righteousness" (109:76) and receive crowns of righteousness (25:15; 29:13) and ETERNAL LIFE (20:14; 59:23). Then the sanctified EARTH will be given them to "inherit it" (88:26).

See also Wicked, the/wickedness.

BIBLIOGRAPHY

Faust, James E. "The Key of the Knowledge of God." *Ensign* 34 (November 2004): 52–55.

Lee, Harold B. *The Teachings of Harold B. Lee.* Edited by Clyde J. Williams. Salt Lake City: Bookcraft, 1996.

Webster, Noah. *An American Dictionary of the English Language.* 1828.

BKS

Rights of the Priesthood. *See* Priesthood, proper exercise of.

Rills. *See* Appendix E.

Rock(s), stone(s)

Terms used in the Doctrine and Covenants with several distinct meanings:

1. JESUS CHRIST. In one revelation the Savior refers to himself as a stone and rock: "I am . . . the stone of Israel. He that buildeth upon this rock shall never fall" (50:44; cf. Hel. 5:12).

2. REVELATION. Section 128 quotes the words of Jesus to Peter, "Upon this rock I will build my church" (128:10; cf. Matt. 16:18–19). Joseph Smith explained that the "rock" of Matthew 16 was "revelation" (5:258).

3. The GOSPEL. The Lord admonished Hyrum Smith to "build upon my rock, which is my gospel" (11:24; cf. 1 Ne. 13:36; 3 Ne. 27:13–21).

The term appears in the Doctrine and Covenants several times without being specifically defined but in association with the Lord's "word," "church," and "gospel" (11:16; 18:4–5). Building upon the rock offers protection against the powers, influences, and temptations of "earth and hell" (6:34; 10:69; cf. Hel. 5:12; 3 Ne. 11:39–40; 14:24–27).

4. ETERNAL LIFE. The context of 10:69 offers a unique interpretation of the term. The Lord promises that he will establish upon his rock Church members who endure to the end. The promise to those who endure to the end in righteousness is eternal life (14:7; 18:22; 3 Ne. 15:9). The gates of hell cannot prevail against those whose salvation has been secured.

5. Literal rocks or stones. Hiram Page possessed a stone through which he received false revelations (28:11–12). Those who attain the celestial kingdom will be given a "white stone" that will function as a URIM AND THUMMIM for them (130:10–11).

6. Metaphorical rocks or stones. The growth of the latter-day restored kingdom of God is represented as a stone cut out of a mountain

without hands rolling forth to fill the whole earth (65:2; cf. Dan. 2:30–45). Section 128 contains the image of the rocks of the earth "weep[ing] for joy" because of the restoration of the gospel and its power to offer eternal life to both the living and the dead (128:23). The Lord refers to the stake in Nauvoo as "a cornerstone" or "the cornerstone" of Zion (124:2, 23, 60, 131). Doctrine and Covenants 133:26 contains an intriguing symbolic reference to rocks in connection with the return of the lost tribes of Israel: "And they who are in the north countries shall come in remembrance before the Lord; and their prophets shall hear his voice, and shall no longer stay themselves; and they shall smite the rocks, and the ice shall flow down at their presence." Perhaps the interpretation of this passage must await the fulfillment of the prophesied events (e.g., 2 Ne. 25:7).

BIBLIOGRAPHY

Smith, Joseph. *History of The Church of Jesus Christ of Latter-day Saints*. Edited by B. H. Roberts. 7 vols. 2d ed. rev. Salt Lake City: The Church of Jesus Christ of Latter-day Saints, 1932–51.

ALG

Rod of Jesse.

See Historical context and overview of Doctrine and Covenants 113 (p. 823).

Rod(s)

The word *rod* appears twice in the Doctrine and Covenants:

1. In the question about the identification of "the rod spoken of in the first verse of the 11th chapter of Isaiah" (113:3). *See* Historical context and overview of Doctrine and Covenants 113 (p. 823).

2. In the phrase "rod of my mouth," wherein Martin Harris is commanded by the Lord to "repent, lest I smite you by the rod of my mouth" (19:15). Rod in this sense seems to mean an "instrument of punishment or correction; chastisement" (Webster, s.v. "rod").

Other scriptures use the same phrase and other phrases to convey the truth that God will smite the wicked of the earth with the words that come out of his mouth. Nephi quoted Isaiah, saying, "he shall smite the earth with the rod of his mouth, and with the breath of his lips shall he slay the wicked" (2 Ne. 21:4; cf. 7:8). John, in his vision of the King of kings, saw that "out of his mouth goeth a sharp sword, that with it he should smite the nations" (Rev. 19:15–16). The Lord repeatedly revealed through Joseph Smith that the word of God is "quick and powerful, sharper than a two-edged sword" (6:2; 11:2; 12:2; 14:2; 33:1), on the one hand exposing and punishing evil, and on the other hand leading the righteous to salvation (Hel. 3:29–30).

The word *rods* is employed only once in the Doctrine and Covenants, as a unit of measurement (1 rod equals 16½ feet), identifying the "forty rods long and twelve wide" dimensions of the temple lot in Kirtland (104:43).

Although publications of the revelations after the Book of Commandments (1835 and following) do not use the word *rod* in the text of what is now known as section 8, the Book of Commandments uses the phrase "gift of working with the rod" rather than "gift of Aaron" in verse 6, and "rod of nature" rather than "gift of Aaron" in verse 7. That these phrases may have alluded to an actual rod of some kind is suggested by the words "you shall hold it in your hands" in verse 8. Whatever the gift, Oliver Cowdery was promised that with it he would "do marvelous works" and receive answers to his prayers (8:8–9). There is no historical accounting of how Oliver may have used such a rod. There is substantial historical evidence that some of the early leaders of the Church, specifically Orson Hyde, Brigham Young, and Heber C. Kimball, possessed rods given to them by Joseph Smith, and used them as aids to REVELATION (Anderson, 521–32). Neither Joseph Smith nor Oliver Cowdery recorded why the phrases using the word *rod* were changed to "gift of Aaron." It may have been to shift the focus of the revelation from a physical object to its central message—the gift of receiving revelation and the power to translate ancient records through faith (8:6–11). *See* Gift of Aaron.

BIBLIOGRAPHY

Anderson, Richard L. "The Mature Joseph Smith and Treasure Seeking." *BYU Studies*. Provo, Utah: Brigham Young University Press, Fall 1984.

Roundy, Shadrach

Birth: 1 January 1789, Rockingham, Windham County, Vermont

Death: 4 July 1872, Salt Lake City, Salt Lake County, Utah

Shadrach Roundy, who joined the Church in 1831, was recognized by Joseph Smith as a kind man who once brought "a quarter of beef" to him, and about whom the Prophet wrote, "May all the blessings named above be poured upon [his head]" (MH; Smith, 2:327). This unselfishness characterized Roundy's life. After mob persecution intensified in Far West, he "made arrangements for his 'available property, to be disposed of by . . . providing means for the removing from this State of the poor and destitute'" (in Black, 255). He also served as Joseph Smith's bodyguard and in various Church capacities throughout his life.

Roundy's name appears in an 1841 revelation where he was listed as a counselor in "the bishopric" in Nauvoo (124:141). He labored faithfully, and was once pointed out by the Prophet as among some who would go a "great distance" to "the valleys of [the] mountains" and "do a great work in that land" (5:86). Roundy did indeed travel to the Salt Lake Valley. "He was one of three men to plow the first furrow," and there continued to magnify his service in the Church. He crossed the plains five times helping others make the trek west; he served as the bishop of the Salt Lake Sixteenth Ward and was later ordained a patriarch (Black, 255–56). He passed away in 1872, at the age of eighty-three, after overexerting himself while working in his garden.

BIBLIOGRAPHY

Black, Susan Easton. *Who's Who in the Doctrine and Covenants.* Salt Lake City: Deseret Book, 1997.

Deseret Evening News, 5 July 1872, Microfilm, Utah Valley Regional Family History Library, Provo, Utah.

Manuscript History of the Church, 9 December 1835. L. Tom Perry Special Collections, Harold B. Lee Library, Brigham Young University, Provo, Utah.

Smith, Joseph. *History of The Church of Jesus Christ of Latter-day Saints.* Edited by B. H. Roberts. 7 vols. 2d ed. rev. Salt Lake City: The Church of Jesus Christ of Latter-day Saints, 1932–51.

ZLL

Ryder, Symonds

Birth: 20 November 1792, Hartford, Windsor County, Vermont

Death: 1 August 1870, Hiram, Portage County, Ohio

At age twenty-one, Symonds Ryder traveled from Vermont to Hiram, Ohio, and purchased 116 acres. By 1830 he had accumulated several hundred more acres and was a respected elder of the Disciples Church in Hiram, serving under the leadership of Sidney Rigdon. Ezra Booth, a friend of Ryder's who had recently become a member of The Church of Jesus Christ of Latter-day Saints, induced Ryder to receive baptism, which he did at the beginning of June 1831. He was ordained an elder at a Church conference that same week.

According to local tradition in Hiram, Joseph Smith wanted part of Ryder's farm on which to build a temple (Garfield, 13, 17). When asked by a close friend if he was going to sell property to Joseph Smith, Ryder responded that he was worried he would be asked to donate it. When Joseph Smith approached Ryder with a written revelation and requested he donate the land, Ryder used the misspelling of his name as an excuse not to comply (Garfield, 32–36). The Latter-day Saint version varies from this account in saying that the revelation called him on a mission, instead of to donate land. No known contemporary documents confirm either story, however, and 52:37 does not specifically call him to serve as a missionary but "to receive the blessing previously bestowed upon [Heman] Basset" (Backman, 93–94). Interestingly, a manuscript of section 52 in the Church History Library in Salt Lake City is in the handwriting of Symonds Ryder; in that manuscript he spells his last name "Rider." Regardless, by September 1831 his zeal as a Church member had decidedly cooled, and he and Ezra Booth renounced their Church membership at a camp meeting at Shalersville, Ohio ("Renunciation," 3). The following March, Ryder led one of the two groups that tarred and feathered the Prophet and Sidney Rigdon at Hiram.

After Ryder's exit from the Church, he reaffiliated with the Disciples, and in 1849, when the Disciples created Hiram College, Symonds

Ryder became the treasurer. He remained one of the most influential and wealthy men of Hiram until his death in 1870.

BIBLIOGRAPHY

Backman, Milton V., Jr. *The Heavens Resound: A History of the Latter-day Saints in Ohio, 1830–1838.* Salt Lake City: Deseret Book, 1983.

Garfield, Abram. "An Episode of the Thirties." Typescript. Hiram College Archives. Hiram, Ohio, 1934, p. 13, 17, as quoted in Richard L. McClellan, "The Battle for Hiram," presentation to Mormon History Association, May 1994.

"Renunciation of Mormonism." *[Hudson, Ohio] Observer and Telegraph,* 29 September 1831, [3].

RJW

Behold, there shall be a record kept among you; and in it thou shalt be called a seer, a translator, a prophet, an apostle of Jesus Christ, an elder of the church through the will of God the Father, and the grace of your Lord Jesus Christ. 21:1

Sabaoth

Hebrew word meaning "hosts," "armies" (Webster, s.v. "Sabaoth"). The term is used in the Doctrine and Covenants four times, always in the context of the Saints' petitions (that is, "prayers," "fastings," "mourning") for help coming "up into the ears of the Lord of Sabaoth" (87:7; 88:2; 95:7; 98:2; cf. Rom. 9:29; James 5:4). Lord of Sabaoth, therefore, means Lord of Hosts, one of the many titles of JEHOVAH. The hosts would include the armies of Israel (1 Sam. 17:45) and the armies of heaven (2 Kgs. 6:16–17). In 95:7 the Lord referred to himself by the title Lord of Sabaoth and added, "which is by interpretation, the creator of the first day, the beginning and the end."

LED

Sabbath, the

The Lord's day, his "holy day"; in modern times, Sunday (59:9–12). The revelations in the Doctrine and Covenants reiterate God's commandment to "observe the Sabbath day to keep it holy" (68:29). Instruction is also given concerning the purpose of the Sabbath and what activities Saints should engage in.

The fundamental purpose of the Sabbath day is to keep oneself "more fully . . . unspotted from the world" (59:9). As such, Saints are instructed to "go to the house of prayer" where they "offer . . . oblations and . . . sacraments unto the Most High" (59:9–12). These offerings may include personal commitment, oaths, testimonies, and private pledges of righteousness, in addition to partaking of the SACRAMENT, which is available to worthy members.

The Sabbath is "a day appointed . . . to rest from your labors" (59:10). While this removes one from the world in a sense, it does not necessarily make him or her holier. Thus, rather than merely a day of rest, the Sabbath is also a day devoted to focusing on the sacred. It is a time to pay "devotions unto the Most High" (59:10) through acts that demonstrate love for God and Christ. It is also a time for correcting oneself by aligning one's life with Christ's will and with one's fellowman and by "confessing thy sins unto thy brethren, and before the Lord" (59:12).

To receive all the blessings of the Sabbath, one must keep all of the commandments associated with the Sabbath (82:10). A fulness of JOY is promised to those who keep the Sabbath holy (59:13; cf. Isa. 58:13–14).

See also Fasting; Historical context and overview of Doctrine and Covenants 59 (p. 765).

MOR

Sackcloth. *See* Appendix E.

Sacrament prayers. *See* Sacrament, the.

Sacraments. *See* Appendix E.

Sacrament, the

A sacred ORDINANCE performed in remembrance of the ATONEMENT of JESUS CHRIST. Bread and water, symbolic of the Savior's body and blood, are partaken of by Church members during sacrament meetings in order to renew covenants they made at their baptism. *See* Baptism by water.

The Doctrine and Covenants contains instructions concerning the sacrament and its administration. The Lord directed that members are to "meet together often" to partake of the sacrament (20:75; cf. 95:16). Administered by worthy PRIESTHOOD holders, the sacrament is blessed and sanctified through solemn prayers (20:76–79), whose prescribed wording was received by revelation and outlines specific promises made by those who partake of the sacrament. The covenant promises include a willingness of those who receive the sacrament to take upon themselves Christ's name, to always remember him, and to keep his commandments. By so doing Church members "may always have [the Lord's] Spirit to be with them" (20:77, 79). Aaronic Priesthood holders have the privilege and responsibility of performing the duties associated with administering the sacrament to the congregation. Usually, Aaronic Priesthood holders prepare the emblems of the sacrament (teachers), which are then blessed (priests) and taken to the congregation (deacons).

Although bread is the emblem typically used to represent Christ's body, and water the emblem of Christ's blood, it was revealed to the Prophet Joseph Smith that it "mattereth not what ye shall eat or what ye shall drink" when partaking of sacramental emblems, as long as they help members in "remembering unto the Father" the body and blood of Christ with an "an eye single" to his glory (27:2).

Partaking of the sacrament is intended for worthy members of the Church; however, bishops are instructed not to announce that the sacrament "will be passed to members only, and nothing should be done to prevent nonmembers from partaking of it" (*Handbook 2*, 173). The Lord commanded his Saints "not to cast any one who belongeth to the church out of . . . sacrament meetings; nevertheless, if any have trespassed, let him not partake until he makes reconciliation" (46:4; cf. 62:4).

In addition to the ordinance of the sacrament, Latter-day Saints are encouraged to offer up "sacraments" on the SABBATH day (59:9). In this context, a sacrament may be understood to be any personal oath, covenant, prayer, devotion, oblation, testimony, and so forth.

BIBLIOGRAPHY

Handbook 2: Administering the Church. Salt Lake City: The Church of Jesus Christ of Latter-day Saints, 2010.

MOR

Sacred treasury. *See* Consecration.

Sacrifice

An essential part of the plan of salvation. From the beginning, Adam and Eve were commanded to offer the firstlings of their flocks as blood sacrifices in "similitude of the sacrifice of the Only Begotten of the Father" (Moses 5:7). Ancient Israel continued to offer blood sacrifice, the first fruits of the field, and a host of other offerings, including tithing, to the Lord at the temple. The ATONEMENT of JESUS CHRIST fulfilled the law of blood sacrifice, and from that time forth the Lord has commanded, "Thou shalt offer a sacrifice unto the Lord thy God in righteousness, even that of a broken heart and a contrite spirit" (59:8; cf. 3 Ne. 9:19–20).

Emblems of the sacrament. "For, behold, I say unto you, that it mattereth not what ye shall eat or what ye shall drink when ye partake of the sacrament, if it so be that ye do it with an eye single to my glory—remembering unto the Father my body which was laid down for you, and my blood which was shed for the remission of your sins" (D&C 27:2).

Thus, just as the Father sacrificed his Son, and the Son sacrificed his own life, Heavenly Father's children are commanded to make sacrifices in their own lives to achieve salvation. Joseph Smith taught, "A religion that does not require the sacrifice of all things never has power sufficient to produce the faith necessary unto life and salvation" (*Lectures*, 69).

The Lord declared, "Now it is called today until the coming of the Son of Man, and verily it is a day of sacrifice, and a day for the tithing of my people" (64:23). In commanding the Saints to build a temple in Jackson County, Missouri, the Lord said, "Behold, this is the tithing and the sacrifice which I, the Lord, require at their hands, that there may be a house built unto me for the salvation of Zion" (97:12). In connection with that requirement, he explained that those "who know their hearts are honest, and are broken, and their spirits contrite, and are willing to observe their covenants by sacrifice—yea, every sacrifice which I, the Lord, shall command— they are accepted of me" (97:8); that explanation was followed with a wonderful promise (97:9). It should be noted that the word *tithing* in these verses, at that time in Church history (1831 and 1833), meant free-will offerings, not "one-tenth of all their interest annually," which did not become a law in the Church until July 1838 (119:4; vv. 1–7).

Though the word *sacrifice* is not used in 128:24, the principle of sacrifice in connection with the temple is present as the Lord directed the Latter-day Saints to "offer unto the Lord an offering in righteousness; and let us present in his holy temple, when it is finished, a book containing the records of our dead, which shall be worthy of all acceptation." That offering includes all aspects of family history and temple work.

In several revelations in the Doctrine and Covenants the Lord acknowledges and commends those who sacrifice through their obedience—Oliver Granger (117:13), Joseph and Emma Smith (132:50–51, 60), and the "spirits of the just, who had been faithful in the testimony of Jesus while they lived in mortality; and who had offered sacrifice in the similitude of the great sacrifice of the Son of God, and had suffered tribulation in their Redeemer's name" (138:12–13).

See also Broken heart and contrite spirit.

BIBLIOGRAPHY

Lectures on Faith. Salt Lake City: Deseret Book Company, 1985.

DRS

Saints

Godly or holy individuals; also used as a designation for members of Christ's Church, ancient and modern. The word *saints* appears dozens of times in the Doctrine and Covenants, almost all of them referring to members of the Restored Church, named officially by the Lord The Church of Jesus Christ of Latter-day Saints (115:4; cf. 127:12; 128:21; 136:2). For example, the Lord directed that "land should be purchased by the saints" (57:4) and said, "I command you, all ye my saints, to build a house unto me" (124:31). Other examples of the Lord referring to members of the Church as Saints are 78:9; 82:13; 89:1; 118:5; 123:1; 125:1. Church members are also called "Latter-day Saints" (121:33; 128:24; 135:3). These terms can be used interchangeably (e.g., OD 1).

The Lord speaks of the gathering of the Saints many times in the Doctrine and Covenants. He states that "Missouri . . . is the land . . . for the gathering of the saints" (57:1), "the city New Jerusalem shall be built by the gathering of the saints" (84:4), and he commands that a house be built "for the gathering together of my saints" (115:8; cf. 84:2; 101:20, 64, 70; 105:15; 115:17; 125:2).

The Doctrine and Covenants also uses the word *saints* to denote righteous individuals in any dispensation (43:18; 45:45–46; 76:29, 102; 87:7; 138:5).

Important considerations in the Doctrine and Covenants concerning Saints are as follows:

• In the last days "the Lord shall have power over his saints, and shall reign in their midst" (1:36).

• Zion, the New Jerusalem, will be "a city of refuge, a place of safety for the saints of the Most High God" (45:66).

• The Saints "shall hardly escape" the wars

and desolations of the last days (63:34). *See* Saints also shall hardly escape.

- SATAN "maketh war with the saints of God, and encompasseth them round about" (76:29).
- At the judgment day, "the saints shall be filled with [Christ's] glory, and receive their inheritance and be made equal with him" (88:107).
- The WORD OF WISDOM is "adapted to the capacity of the weak and the weakest of all saints, who are or can be called saints" (89:2–3).
- Ultimately, "the earth is given unto the saints, to possess it forever and ever" (103:7).
- Nothing can "hinder the Almighty from pouring down knowledge from heaven upon the heads of the Latter-day Saints" (121:33).

JLH

Saints also shall hardly escape

Both a promise and a caution concerning the status of the Saints of God in the midst of the social and political upheavals of the last days, when "the wicked shall slay the wicked, and fear shall come upon every man" before the Lord will eventually "consume the wicked with unquenchable fire" (63:33–34). Joseph Smith "explained concerning the coming of the Son of Man . . . that it is a false idea that the Saints will escape all the judgments, whilst the wicked suffer; for all flesh is subject to suffer, and 'the righteous shall hardly escape;' still many of the Saints will escape, for the just shall live by faith; yet many of the righteous shall fall a prey to disease, to pestilence, etc., by reason of the weakness of the flesh, and yet be saved in the Kingdom of God. So that it is an unhallowed principle to say that such and such have transgressed because they have been preyed upon by disease or death, for all flesh is subject to death; and the Savior has said, 'Judge not, lest ye be judged'" (4:11).

Although some of the Saints will suffer hardships during these troubled times, the Lord promises, "Nevertheless, I, the Lord, am with them" (63:34).

BIBLIOGRAPHY

Smith, Joseph. *History of The Church of Jesus Christ of Latter-day Saints.* Edited by B. H. Roberts. 7 vols. 2d

ed. rev. Salt Lake City: The Church of Jesus Christ of Latter-day Saints, 1932–51.

LED

Salem, Massachusetts

A coastal city about fifteen miles northeast of Boston, Massachusetts. In 1836, upon learning that "a large amount of money would be available to them in Salem," Joseph Smith, Sidney Rigdon, Hyrum Smith, and Oliver Cowdery left Kirtland, bound for the seaport town. Although they did not receive the anticipated money, they transacted Church business and preached the gospel (111, headnote). In addition, on 6 August 1836, Joseph received a revelation informing him that "there are more treasures than one for you in this city" (111:10). He was also told that "it is expedient that you should form acquaintance with men in this city" and to "inquire diligently concerning the more ancient inhabitants and founders" of Salem (111:3, 9). Early and later converts to the Church and an abundance of genealogical records in the area were undoubtedly among the "treasures" spoken of in the revelation.

As a child, Joseph Smith stayed in Salem with his uncle Jesse Smith while he was recuperating from the operation on his leg (Smith, 58). *See* map, p. 447.

See also Historical context and overview of Doctrine and Covenants 111 (p. 820).

BIBLIOGRAPHY

Anderson, A. Gary, Donald Q. Cannon, Larry E. Dahl, and Larry C. Porter. *New England and Eastern Canada.* Vol. 1 of *Sacred Places: A Comprehensive Guide to Early LDS Historical Sites,* edited by LaMar C. Berrett. Salt Lake City: Bookcraft, 1999.

Smith, Lucy Mack. *History of Joseph Smith by His Mother.* Edited by Preston Nibley. Salt Lake City: Bookcraft, 1956.

DQC

Salt Lake City, Utah

Headquarters of The Church of Jesus Christ of Latter-day Saints since the arrival in the Salt Lake Valley of Brigham Young and his company in 1847. The city is nestled between the Wasatch and Oquirrh mountain ranges in the northern part of the state of Utah.

Salt Lake City is named five times in Official

Declaration 1, the announcement that the practice of contracting plural marriages was to stop, and once in Official Declaration 2, the announcement of a revelation extending priesthood to all worthy males. *See* map, p. 857.

LED

Salt of the earth. *See* Covenant people of the Lord.

Salvation

Term used in the Doctrine and Covenants with various meanings. Most often it refers to being saved from sin, death, and hell in the fullest and most complete sense, being synonymous with exaltation and ETERNAL LIFE after mortal probation. For example, being "saved in the kingdom of God" is declared to be "the greatest of all the gifts of God" (6:13), which is exactly the way eternal life is described (14:7). Conversely, "the riches of eternal life" are lost by those who fail to give heed to the Lord's voice. He would have saved them "with an everlasting salvation," but they rejected him (43:25). In addition, four other sections of the Doctrine and Covenants use the phrase *everlasting salvation* to describe the reward of those gospel ministers who thrust in their sickles with their might to reap a harvest of souls for the Lord (6:3; 11:3; 12:3; 14:3). In parallel fashion, faithful missionaries who proclaim "the truth according to the revelations and commandments" which the Lord has given are promised eternal life (75:4–5). They are also described as those who thrust in their sickles with their might to lay up in store that they perish not but bring salvation to their souls (4:4). Thus, the terms *salvation, eternal salvation, everlasting salvation, eternal life,* and *exaltation*—the latter denoting godhood (132:19–20)—are equivalent expressions in many verses in the Doctrine and Covenants.

During the MILLENNIUM, a thousand-year period of peace and righteousness when Satan is bound, the CHILDREN of the righteous "shall grow up without sin unto salvation" (45:57–58). This means these children will receive exaltation.

The term *salvation* is sometimes used to describe the reward of all those who inherit any

kingdom of glory, whether celestial, terrestrial, or telestial. They are all called "heirs of salvation" (7:6; 76:88; 138:59). Here the term *salvation* carries shades of meaning and implies far different eternal realities for different individuals. Thus, the Lord commands that the Saints act "in all holiness of heart, walking uprightly before me, *considering the end of your salvation,*" or the degree of salvation they will inherit (46:7; emphasis added; cf. 38:16).

Employing the symbolism and imagery associated with the ARMOR OF GOD in other scriptures, the Lord commanded his followers to "take the helmet of salvation" (27:18)—*salvation* meaning "deliverance from sin and guilt and all other enemies through the gospel" (Smith and Sjodahl, 138). The Lord commanded the wicked to "take heed," the rebellious to "fear and tremble," the unbelievers to "hold their lips," and warned sign-seekers that they "shall see signs, but not unto salvation" (63:6–10). On the other hand, signs do follow those who believe, but the Lord commanded, "They shall not boast themselves of these things, neither speak them before the world; for these things are given unto you for your profit and for salvation" (84:64–73).

Salvation comes to all through JESUS CHRIST, the premortal Word, "even the messenger of salvation . . . and the Redeemer of the world" (93:8–9). Though he performed "mighty works, and miracles" during his mortal ministry and proclaimed the truth "in great power and authority," few "hearkened to his voice . . . and received salvation at his hands" (138:26). In his name alone can salvation be administered to the children of men (109:4). Jesus Christ gathers his people and will come to his temple "for the salvation of [his] people" (42:36). The keys of salvation have been delegated to Michael (Adam), who acts under the counsel and direction of Jesus Christ (78:16).

Like the "messenger of salvation," salvation itself, including all the ordinances upon which it is predicated, was prepared "from before the foundation of the world" (128:8), meaning in the PREMORTAL EXISTENCE. The Lord associates his GOSPEL with his salvation (18:17); Sidney Rigdon was commanded to "make haste" and proclaim "the gospel of salvation" (93:51). So important is it for the same gospel of salvation, including priesthood and temple ordinances, to be preached to every one of God's children that the salvation of those who enjoy the gospel in this mortal existence depends upon their performing proxy work for those who have died without knowledge of the gospel—"their salvation is necessary and essential to our salvation" (128:15). The proper performance and recording of ordinances "for the salvation of the dead" are necessary to fulfill "the will of God" (128:5).

Salvation in a temporal, physical, or economic sense is also a significant theme in the Doctrine and Covenants. The revelation known as the WORD OF WISDOM was given for the purpose of "showing forth the order and will of God [concerning] the temporal salvation of all saints in the last days" (89:2). The Lord instructed Church leaders regarding their efforts in "the salvation and redemption" of the Saints in Missouri who had been driven and smitten by their enemies (103:1–2). He also said that the United Order was established in the early days of this dispensation for "the benefit of my church, and for the salvation of men until I come" (104:1, 51). The Prophet Joseph Smith received a revelation while incarcerated at Liberty, Missouri, that promised the Saints they would "see the salvation of God" as his arm would be revealed in coming to the rescue of those being persecuted (123:17). This language is reminiscent of the declaration of Moses in the deliverance of the children of Israel from Egypt (Ex. 14:13; cf. 1 Ne. 19:17; Mosiah 12:24; 15:31; 16:1; 3 Ne. 16:20).

The School of the Prophets was to be organized so that leaders might be "perfected in their ministry for the salvation of Zion, and of the nations of Israel, and of the Gentiles" (90:7–8). The Lord commanded the Saints to build a temple also for the salvation of Zion (97:12, 20).

The Doctrine and Covenants boldly declares that the Prophet Joseph Smith has done more for the salvation of men and women in this world than any other person, except Jesus Christ (135:3). Among his prophetic achievements, the Joseph Smith Translation of the Bible, for example, reflects the words of scripture "as they are in mine own bosom," and was

given specifically for "the salvation of mine own elect," said the Lord (35:20).

See also Exalt, exaltation.

BIBLIOGRAPHY

Smith, Hyrum M., and Janne M. Sjodahl. *Doctrine and Covenants Commentary.* Salt Lake City: Deseret Book, 1961.

Smith, Joseph Fielding. *Doctrines of Salvation.* Compiled by Bruce R. McConkie. 3 vols. Salt Lake City: Bookcraft, 1954–56.

ACS

Salvation for the dead

Provision for those who have died to hear and accept the gospel of Jesus Christ in the spirit world. The world offers several responses to the age-old questions: What of those who die without hearing of Jesus Christ and his gospel? Can they be saved? Five such proposals are briefly outlined below and are followed by the response that is clearly explained in the restored GOSPEL of JESUS CHRIST and found in the Doctrine and Covenants and the teachings of the Prophet Joseph Smith.

1. One's eternal fate is sealed at death.

Some believe individuals are saved only if they accept the Lord Jesus Christ here and now, including worshipping the only true God, achieving a union with Christ through full acceptance of his saving GRACE and ATONEMENT, and maintaining a Christian walk that reflects one's membership in the body of Christ. All others will be damned.

> 15 And now, my dearly beloved brethren and sisters, let me assure you that these are principles in relation to the dead and the living that cannot be lightly passed over, as pertaining to our salvation. For their "salvation is necessary and essential to our salvation, as Paul says concerning the fathers—that they without us cannot be made perfect—neither can we without our dead be made *b*perfect.

Doctrine and Covenants 128:15.

2. Universalism.

At the other end of the theological spectrum are those who point out that there is goodness and morality in all religions throughout the world, Christian and non-Christian, none of which has a monopoly on ethical decency. Such people are open to the belief that God will eventually save all of his children.

3. Inclusivism (hopeful equal opportunity).

Justin Martyr, the early Christian apologist (ca. A.D. 100–165), believed that all are partakers of a general revelation through the universal power of God, though in Jesus Christ that power was revealed in its fulness. Likewise, Irenaeus (ca. A.D. 130–200) contended that God has never been completely unknown to any race of people, inasmuch as the universal Spirit of Christ is inherent in the minds of individuals in all times and places.

Christian writer C. S. Lewis pursued a similar inclusive path, reasoning that "those who put themselves in [God's] hands will become perfect, as He is perfect—perfect in love, wisdom, joy, beauty, and immortality. The change will not be completed in this life, for death is an important part of the treatment" (207). On another occasion Lewis remarked: "Here is another thing that used to puzzle me. Is it not frightfully unfair that this new life [in Christ] should be confined to people who have heard of Christ and been able to believe in Him? But the truth is God has not told us what His arrangements about the other people are. We do know that no man can be saved except through Christ; we do not know that only those who know Him can be saved through Him" (64). This perspective does not consider how such opportunity would be afforded or how such thinking accords with scriptural statements requiring ordinances for salvation.

4. "Final option" theory.

This position suggests that all have an opportunity to know of Christ and his salvation, even if that opportunity comes at or near the time of death. Proponents of this view teach that the message may come at the hand of mortals, inspired dreams, angels, or even by open vision or revelation. One view is that Jesus himself appears to every individual at the time of death and allows each one to affirm or deny the faith.

5. Postmortal opportunity.

According to this view, those who die without a knowledge of the gospel are not damned; they have an opportunity to receive the truth in the world to come. "God is resolute," one advocate of this position has pointed out, "never giving up on getting the Word out. In this world God will give us the power to spread the gospel far and wide. But the Word will also be declared to those we can't reach, even if it takes an eternity." He adds that "God's love is *patient* and *persistent*. It outlasts us" (Fackre, 73, 78). Christian writer Donald Bloesch explained: "We do not wish to build fences around God's grace . . . and we do not preclude the possibility that some in hell might finally be translated into heaven. The gates of the holy city are depicted as being open day and night (Isa. 60:11; Rev. 21:25), and this means that access to the throne of grace is possible continuously. The gates of hell are locked, but they are locked only from within" (2:226–27). Again, in this view there is not a comprehensive discussion of scriptural injunctions requiring ordinances, or what, if anything, can be done for the dead by those still living.

The doctrine of salvation for the dead revealed

On Thursday, 21 January 1836, Joseph Smith and several other leaders of the Church, including the First Presidency and the patriarch, Joseph Smith Sr., were gathered together in the upper story of the Kirtland Temple, even while construction was underway. The brethren were involved in what came to be known as a blessing meeting. After blessings had been given to several of the brethren, Joseph's history records, "All of the Presidency laid their hands upon me, and pronounced upon my head many prophecies and blessings" (*History*, 2:380). The heavens were then opened, and the Prophet beheld what is called the vision of the celestial kingdom (137). In this vision Joseph was given a glimpse of the highest heaven, in which he saw such ancient prophets as Adam and Abraham. In addition, he saw his mother, Lucy Mack Smith, and his father, Joseph Smith Sr., but clearly this was a vision of a future celestial world, for Father Smith would live another four years and Mother Smith would live for another twenty.

The Prophet Joseph then beheld someone

whose presence in the celestial kingdom surprised him—his elder brother, Alvin Smith, who had died in 1823 (JS–H 1:56). He was surprised because Alvin had passed away some six years before the priesthood was restored and seven years before the Church was organized; in short, he had gone to his grave without having been baptized by proper authority. The Smith family had grieved his passing, and that grief was only intensified by a strong suggestion on the part of the minister preaching the funeral sermon that Alvin had gone to hell since he had not been baptized (Smith, interview). Thus the great question in the mind of Joseph Smith Jr. was simple: How was Alvin able to inherit the celestial kingdom? The voice of the Lord came to him, saying: "All who have died without a knowledge of this gospel, who would have received it if they had been permitted to tarry, shall be heirs of the celestial kingdom of God; also all that shall die henceforth without a knowledge of it, who would have received it with all their hearts, shall be heirs of that kingdom; for I, the Lord, will judge all men according to their works, according to the desire of their hearts" (137:7–9).

And so the veil was parted, God spoke, and new doctrinal understanding was delivered to the world. The vision of the celestial kingdom opened the door to an understanding of the doctrine of salvation for the dead.

On the afternoon of Tuesday, 8 May 1838, the Prophet Joseph Smith answered a series of questions about the faith and practices of the Latter-day Saints. One of the questions was this one: "If the Mormon doctrine is true, what has become of all those who died since the days of the Apostles?" Joseph responded: "All those who have not had an opportunity of hearing the Gospel, and being administered unto by an inspired man in the flesh, must have it hereafter, before they can be finally judged" (*History*, 3:28–30).

The first public discourse on the subject by Joseph was delivered on 15 August 1840 at the funeral of Seymour Brunson. Simon Baker described the occasion: "I was present at a discourse that the prophet Joseph delivered on baptism for the dead 15 August 1840. He read the greater part of the 15th chapter of Corinthians and remarked that the Gospel of Jesus Christ brought glad tidings of great joy, and then remarked that he saw a widow in that congregation that had a son who died without being baptized, and this widow in reading the sayings of Jesus 'except a man be born of water and of the spirit he cannot enter the kingdom of heaven,' and that not one jot nor tittle of the Savior's words should pass away, but all should be fulfilled. He then said that this widow should have glad tidings in that thing. He also said the apostle [Paul] was talking to a people who understood baptism for the dead, for it was practiced among them. He went on to say that people could now act for their friends who had departed this life, and that the plan of salvation was calculated to save all who were willing to obey the requirements of the law of God. He went on and made a very beautiful discourse" (Ehat and Cook, 49).

In an epistle to the Twelve, dated 19 October 1840, Joseph Smith stated: "I presume the doctrine of 'baptism for the dead' has ere this reached your ears, and may have raised some inquiries in your minds respecting the same. . . . I would say that it was certainly practiced by the ancient churches." Joseph then quoted from 1 Corinthians 15:29 and continued: "The Saints have the privilege of being baptized for those of their relatives who are dead, whom they believe would have embraced the Gospel, if they had been privileged with hearing it, and who have received the Gospel in the spirit, through the instrumentality of those who have been commissioned to preach to them while in prison" (*History*, 4:231).

Further instructions concerning the details of how vicarious baptisms are to be carried out and witnessed were sent in the form of letters from the Prophet Joseph to the Saints in Nauvoo in 1842 (127; 128; cf. 124:29–35). The keys of authority to perform this work had been delivered by the prophet Elijah to Joseph Smith and Oliver Cowdery in the Kirtland Temple on 3 April 1836 (110:13–16), less than three months after the vision of the celestial kingdom was received on 21 January 1836 (137).

Even more clarification about salvation for the dead was revealed to President Joseph F.

Smith in October 1918 in a vision of the Savior's visit to the postmortal spirit world between his death and RESURRECTION. This vision is recorded in Doctrine and Covenants 138. Section 137 addresses the issue of those "who have died *without* a knowledge of [the] gospel" (v. 7; emphasis added). The revelation recorded in section 138 broadens the scope of opportunity to embrace the gospel to "all the spirits of men . . . , even unto *all who would repent of their sins and receive the gospel*," including those who "died . . . in transgression, having rejected the prophets" (vv. 30–32; emphasis added). "These were taught faith in God, repentance from sin, vicarious baptism for the remission of sins, the gift of the Holy Ghost by the laying on of hands, and all other principles of the gospel that were necessary for them to know in order to qualify themselves that they might be judged according to men in the flesh, but live according to God in the spirit" (138:33–34; cf. 1 Pet. 4:6). Giving hope that all the spirits in the postmortal spirit world will be enabled, through the tender mercies of Jesus Christ, to improve their spiritual status, the revelation continues, "the dead who repent will be redeemed, through obedience to the ordinances of the house of God, and after they have paid the penalty of their transgressions, and are washed clean, shall receive a reward according to their works, for they are heirs of salvation" (138:58–59).

The good news, or glad tidings of SALVATION in Christ, is intended to lift the sights of humankind and bring hope to their souls, to "bind up the brokenhearted, to proclaim liberty to the captives, and the opening of the prison to them that are bound" (Isa. 61:1; cf. 128:22).

And so, what of those who never have the opportunity in this life to know of Christ and his gospel? In a world gripped by cynicism and strangled by hopelessness, the restored gospel of Jesus Christ testifies of a God of mercy and vision, whose redemptive power transcends the veil of DEATH. Truly, as Joseph Smith explained, "It is no more incredible that God should *save* the dead, than that he should *raise* the dead" (*History*, 4:425).

See also Celestial kingdom, vision of; Historical context and overview of Doctrine and Covenants 137 (p. 858) and 138 (p. 859); Spirit world, postmortal.

BIBLIOGRAPHY

Anderson, Richard L. *Understanding Paul.* Salt Lake City: Deseret Book, 1983.

Bloesch, Donald G. *Life, Ministry, and Hope.* Vol. 2 of *Essentials of Evangelical Theology.* Peabody, Mass.: Prince Press, 1998.

Ehat, Andrew F., and Lyndon W. Cook, comps. and eds. *The Words of Joseph Smith.* Provo, Utah: Religious Studies Center, Brigham Young University, 1980.

Fackre, Gabriel. "Divine Perseverance." In *What about Those Who Have Never Heard?* edited by John Sanders. Downers Grove, Ill.: InterVarsity Press, 1995.

Kugelman, Richard. "The First Letter to the Corinthians." In Vol. 2 of *Jerome Biblical Commentary*, edited by Raymond E. Brown, Joseph A. Fitzmyer, and Roland E. Murphy. Englewood Cliffs, N.J.: Prentice-Hall, 1968.

Lewis, C. S. *Mere Christianity.* New York: HarperCollins, 2001.

Smith, Joseph. *History of The Church of Jesus Christ of Latter-day Saints.* Edited by B. H. Roberts. 7 vols. 2d ed. rev. Salt Lake City: The Church of Jesus Christ of Latter-day Saints, 1932–51.

Smith, William. Interview by E. C. Briggs and J. W. Peterson. *Deseret News,* 20 January 1894.

RLM

Salvation of little children. *See* Children.

Sanctify, sanctification

The purification and cleansing of the human soul by virtue of the blood of Christ through the power of the HOLY GHOST. Sanctification comes by the GRACE of JESUS CHRIST as a precious gift to "all those who love and serve God with all their mights, minds, and strength" (20:31). Once a person acknowledges his or her sins, repents, and enters into a covenant relationship with God through the ordinances of the GOSPEL of Jesus Christ, he or she can be justified, made right, decreed innocent. Then begins the process of sanctification, a lifelong endeavor. Sanctification is a change in one's inner nature. Those who choose Christ choose to be changed, and that change comes "from the inside out" (Benson, 6). Their hearts become "single to God" (88:68), they abhor sin, and they cherish things of righteousness (124:15; 88:40; Alma 13:12; Mosiah 5:2).

Sanctification is a mighty and merciful gift of grace on the part of a loving Father and Savior, and true disciples are intimately involved in the process. To sanctify is to set apart, to consecrate, to draw a division between, to separate out, to make holy. "Purge ye out the iniquity which is among you," the Master implored, "sanctify yourselves before me" (43:11). Members of the Lord's Church thus sanctify themselves when they choose to sort out the secondary and the sordid, forsake the filthy, ignore the impure, turn their backs on the tainted, and protect themselves from pride.

The Almighty has promised that he will "stay [his] hand in judgment" for those who repent and receive the fulness of his gospel and become sanctified (39:18). Further, those who are instructed and edified by the law of the Church are sanctified by that law, and "shall be endowed with power" (43:9–16). Indeed, "that which is governed by law is also preserved by law and perfected and sanctified by the same," and "that which breaketh a law, and abideth not by law, but seeketh to become a law unto itself, and willeth to abide in sin, and altogether abideth in sin, cannot be sanctified by law, neither by mercy, justice, nor judgment. Therefore, they must remain filthy still" (88:34–35). Those who receive and magnify priesthood callings "are sanctified by the Spirit unto the renewing of their bodies" (84:33). Members of the School of the Prophets were taught both God's role and man's role in this cleansing process: "Sanctify yourselves; yea, purify your hearts, and cleanse your hands and your feet before me, that I may make you clean" (88:74).

God "cannot look upon sin with the least degree of allowance" (1:31), nor will he prevent those who have been sanctified from falling from grace (20:32–34); all must endure faithfully to the end of their mortal lives. But since "all have sinned, and come short of the glory of God" (Rom. 3:23), a loving Heavenly Father has provided a plan for reconciliation, a plan that does not keep one from sin but empowers one to become purified and thus prepared to dwell once again in his presence (76:21; cf. Moses 6:57). Those who abide the celestial law of Christ are sanctified and will inherit the celestial kingdom;

those who are not sanctified by OBEDIENCE to that law will receive a kingdom of lesser glory (88:20–22). Many have been called to serve and labor in the Lord's kingdom, and those who do so, with an eye single to his glory, are chosen, sanctified, and given the assurance of ETERNAL LIFE (88:67; 105:36; McConkie, 270). For that matter, bread and water, emblems of the sacrament (20:77–79); the temple (109:13); the Church (100:15); and the earth itself (77:12; 88:17–18, 25–27) are cleansed, made holy, or sanctified by the power of Christ.

See also Atonement, the; Justification; Forgiveness; Repentance.

BIBLIOGRAPHY

Benson, Ezra Taft. "Born of God." *Ensign* 15 (November 1985): 5–7.

McConkie, Bruce R. *A New Witness for the Articles of Faith.* Salt Lake City: Deseret Book, 1985.

RLM

Sanctuary. *See* Appendix E.

Sarah

Wife of the ancient patriarch Abraham. Sarah's name is found twice in the Doctrine and Covenants, both times in section 132 and in connection with the law of plural MARRIAGE, which God, at certain times, commands his covenant people to live. "God commanded Abraham, and Sarah gave Hagar to Abraham to wife. And why did she do it? Because this was the law; and from Hagar sprang many people. This, therefore, was fulfilling, among other things, the promises." One important aspect of the covenant God made with Abraham was the promise that Abraham and Sarah's seed would be as "innumerable as the stars" or "the sand upon the seashore" (132:34; 29–30, 61–63; cf. Jacob 2:27–34).

The other verse in which Sarah is named is in reference to the "law of Sarah," an expectation that the first wife, after having been taught the law, would give her consent for her husband to take another wife. If the first wife refuses, then she "becomes the transgressor; and he [the husband] is exempt from the law of Sarah." In such a case, the Lord revealed: "Therefore, it shall be lawful in me, if she receive not this law, for him to receive all things whatsoever I, the Lord his God, will give unto him" (132:64–65).

LED

Sarah, law of. *See* Marriage; Sarah.

Satan

Hebrew word meaning adversary. Among many other names in scripture, Satan is also called Lucifer, Perdition, the devil, the "prince of this world," and "that old serpent"; he opposes God and those seeking righteousness (3:8; 76:26–29; 88:110; 127:11). Rather than a mere symbolic representation of EVIL in the world, Satan is presented in the revelations of the Restoration as a real spirit being with real POWER and influence. The Doctrine and Covenants complements other scriptural accounts of Satan's hostility to the Father's plan of happiness with insights into his fall from prominence in the premortal realm, his efforts to bring about human misery in mortality, and his eventual defeat and subjugation at the end of the world.

Past

The revelations unfold the epic struggle that resulted in Lucifer's being cast out of the Father's presence. Satan was "an angel . . . in authority in the presence of God" but having "rebelled against the Only Begotten Son . . . , was thrust down from the presence of God" and "called Perdition, for the heavens wept over him—he was Lucifer, a son of the morning" (76:25–26). Although the accounts of this premortal conflict are fragmentary, it is clear that Lucifer demanded God's "honor, which is [his] power," endeavored "to take the kingdom of our God and his Christ," and sought Christ's throne (29:36; 76:28; 88:115). The book of Moses adds that Satan "sought to destroy the agency of man" (Moses 4:3). A "third part of the hosts of heaven" followed Satan, became "his angels," and, like him, remained spirit beings, never to receive mortal bodies (29:36–37; cf. 129:4–8; 2 Ne. 9:9; Smith, 211).

Present

Since his fall from God's presence, the devil "maketh war with the saints of God, and encompasseth them round about" (76:29). He seeks human misery in myriad ways. Satan, for instance, is the consummate deceiver—a "liar from the beginning"—and he "goeth forth deceiving the nations" (52:14; 93:25; cf. 10:43; 28:11; 50:3, 7). He attempts to disguise himself as "an angel of light" (128:20; 129:8; 2 Ne. 9:8–9). The devil "stirreth . . . up to iniquity against that which is good," "flattereth . . . away to do iniquity," "harden[s] . . . hearts," and "stir[s] up the hearts of the people to contention" and was a pivotal causal factor in the great apostasy in the meridian of time (10:20, 29, 32, 63; 63:28; 78:10; 86:3). Where God's work is to create and redeem, "Satan seeketh to destroy" and "lead . . . souls to destruction" (132:57; 10:22; 64:17).

Satan's power, though, is circumscribed by God in several ways, including the fact that "power is not given unto [him] to tempt little children" until they are accountable for their actions (29:47; cf. 19:1–3; 121:4). Similarly, God's servants have power to "cast out devils" in the name of Christ (35:9; cf. 24:13; 84:67; 124:98). Numbered among the various safeguards against "the fiery darts of the adversary" are faithfulness, PRAYER, and giving heed to the words of God's prophet, OBEDIENCE to God's COMMANDMENTS, and observance of one's covenantal obligations (3:8; 10:5; 21:4–6; 35:24; 46:7). Though "that wicked one cometh and taketh away light and truth, through disobedience . . . and because of the tradition of their fathers," Saints are promised that, by keeping God's commandments, they receive LIGHT and TRUTH sufficient to "forsake that evil one" until they are "glorified in truth and knoweth all things" (93:24–28, 37, 39).

Lucifer's influence, ironically, is also centrally significant to the plan of salvation because temptation actually facilitates moral AGENCY: "It must needs be that the devil should tempt the children of men, or they could not be agents unto themselves" (29:39; 40:2). Only when individuals yield to his temptations of their own free will do they become "subject to the will of the devil" (29:40). Without complementary enticements towards both good and evil, true choice could not exist for mortals (2 Ne. 2:10–16).

Future

After suffering the ill effects of their sins in mortality, unrepentant "liars, and sorcerers, and adulterers, and whoremongers" also suffer for their sins under Satan's power in the afterlife and are not "redeemed from the devil until the last resurrection, until the Lord, even Christ the Lamb, shall have finished his work" (76:85, 103–6). They suffer for their own transgressions, having rejected that portion of the atoning work of Christ, after which they will emerge from those buffetings to inherit a lesser kingdom of glory (19:16–17; 76:81–88). Their suffering is "eternal" or "endless" only in the sense that it is given by a just God, whose name is "Endless" (19:6–12), and stands distinct from the suffering of "sons of perdition," who, after having known and been made partakers of the power of God, "suffered themselves through the power of the devil to be overcome, and to deny the truth and defy my power." SONS OF PERDITION continue to suffer "with the devil and his angels in eternity, where their worm dieth not, and the fire is not quenched, which is their torment." Their final "end," "place," and "torment," however, has not been revealed to man (76:31–38, 43–48). *See* Punish, punished, punishment.

Though Satan will have succeeded in mustering a short-lived "dominion" and "kingdom" and "church" on earth, because of human wickedness, during Christ's thousand-year millennial reign, "Satan shall be bound, that he shall have no place in the hearts of the children of men" (1:35; 10:56; 18:20; 45:55; 82:5; 84:100; 101:28). Near the end of this period of unparalleled peace and righteousness, when "men again begin to deny their God" (29:22), the adversary will be "loosed again" (43:31), though only for "a little season, that he may gather together his armies" (88:111). Thereafter, the devil and "the hosts of hell" will war against Michael (Adam) and his armies in "the battle of the great God." Ultimately, the devil and his angels will be "cast away into their own place, that they shall not have power over the saints any more at all" (88:112–15). Thus, Jesus Christ's power will bring about the "destroying of Satan and his works at the end of the world, and the last great day of judgment" (19:3; 29:28–30).

See also Fiery darts of the adversary/of the wicked; Millennium, the; Premortal existence; Temptation(s); War in heaven.

BIBLIOGRAPHY

Smith, Joseph. *Joseph Smith.* Teachings of Presidents of the Church series. Salt Lake City: The Church of Jesus Christ of Latter-day Saints, 2007.

JSF

Satan, buffetings of. *See* Buffetings of Satan.

Saviors/Savor of men. *See* Covenant people of the Lord.

Scepter. *See* Appendix E.

School in Zion. *See* School(s).

School of the Prophets. *See* School(s).

School(s)

From the beginning of the dispensation of the fulness of times, the Lord has affirmed the importance of schools. In 1831, the Lord called W. W. Phelps to assist Oliver Cowdery in "the work of printing, and of selecting and writing books for schools in this church, that little children also may receive instruction before me as is pleasing unto me" (55:4). Revelations in 1832 and 1833 provided instructions for a school to prepare priesthood officers for their ministry to preach the gospel throughout the world and to prepare for Christ's second coming (88:84, 127; 90:6–11, 13). Students were to study doctrine and to obtain knowledge of "things both in heaven and in the earth, and under the earth; things which have been, things which are, things which must shortly come to pass; things which are at home, things which are abroad; the wars and the perplexities of the nations, and the judgments which are on the land; and a knowledge also of countries and of kingdoms" (88:78–79). They were to "seek learning, even by study and also by faith" (88:118).

A School of the Prophets was to be conducted in a house of God. Sessions were to begin with prayer, and the instructor and students were to exchange a salutation committing themselves to fellowship and obedience to the commandments. The president was to wash the students' feet—an ordinance that would symbolically cleanse them from "the blood of this generation" (88:128–40). Accordingly, a School of the Prophets was established for Church leaders in Kirtland, Ohio, January to April 1833. Unfortunately, "contentions arose in the school of the prophets; which was very grievous unto me, saith your Lord; therefore I sent them forth to be chastened" (95:10). It is not clear what those contentions were.

An August 1833 revelation commended Parley P. Pratt for teaching a "school in Zion" in Jackson County, Missouri, in summer 1833 (97:3–5). Elder Pratt called this "a school of Elders" (Pratt, 75). In Kirtland in the winter of 1834–35, an Elders' School continued some of the work of the School of the Prophets, admitting a broader spectrum of priesthood members. The ordinance of washing of feet was not performed in the Elders' School (Jessee at al., 68, footnote 51).

Joseph Smith announced that a solemn assembly would be convened in autumn 1835

in the Kirtland Temple to organize a School of the Prophets again and to prepare to receive the "endowment with power from on high" that had been promised to faithful members of the priesthood (Jessee et al., 68; cf. D&C 38:32; 105:33). The temple was not completed until several months later, however, and rather than a School of the Prophets, Joseph Smith organized an Elders' School on 2 November 1834 in a building near the temple. A June 1833 revelation directed that space in the upper floor of the Lord's house was to be devoted to "the school of mine apostles" (95:17). The Elders' School was moved to the third floor of the temple as construction progressed. A Hebrew school, organized for Church officers in January 1836, was held concurrently with the Elders' School in an adjacent room of the temple. The two schools concluded before the 30 March 1836 solemn assembly, at which the pentecostal endowment was bestowed in the temple following the ordinance of the washing of feet. This concluded that season's formal preparation

Upper room of the restored Newel K. Whitney Store in Kirtland, Ohio; photograph by Lowell D. Harris. The School of the Prophets was first held here in the winter of 1833.

and empowerment for participating priesthood members. *See* Solemn assembly/assemblies.

From the 1830s onward, numerous other Church-sponsored schools have benefited from revealed directives that originally guided the School of the Prophets.

See also Printing office/schoolhouse.

BIBLIOGRAPHY

Jessee, Dean C., Mark R. Ashurst-McGee, and Richard L. Jensen, eds. *Journals, 1832–1839.* Vol. 1 of the Journals series of *The Joseph Smith Papers,* edited by Dean C. Jessee, Ronald K. Esplin, and Richard Lyman Bushman. Salt Lake City: Church Historian's Press, 2008.

Pratt, Parley P. *Autobiography of Parley P. Pratt.* Edited by Parley P. Pratt Jr. Salt Lake City: Deseret Book, 1985.

RLJ

Scott, Jacob

Birth: date unknown

Death: date unknown

Little is known about Jacob Scott and his place in Church history. Scott joined the Church and was ordained an elder sometime before June 1831. He was ordained a high priest that month during a conference of the Church held on the Isaac Morley farm in Kirtland (Cannon and Cook, 7; Hancock, 33). His name appears in Doctrine and Covenants 52, the revelation received by Joseph during this conference in which certain elders were "appointed to go forth preaching the gospel" (52, headnote). Scott was called to "take [his] journey" from Kirtland to Missouri as a missionary with Edson Fuller (52:28) but struggled with his faith and did not go. Levi Hancock wrote that he was told that at one point Scott, "while preaching, [threw] down the Book of Mormon and jumped on it and said he would go to hell before he would preach it where he was so much persecuted" (35). George A. Smith noted that Scott apostatized, along with Ezra Booth, Symonds Ryder, Eli Johnson, and others, in the fall of 1831 (11:4).

BIBLIOGRAPHY

Cannon, Donald Q., and Lyndon W. Cook, eds. *Far West Record: Minutes of The Church of Jesus Christ of Latter-day Saints, 1830–1844.* Salt Lake City: Deseret Book, 1983.

Hancock, Levi W. Journal. Typescript. L. Tom Perry Special Collections, Harold B. Lee Library, Brigham Young University, Provo, Utah.

Smith, George A. *Journal of Discourses.* 26 vols. London: Latter-day Saints' Book Depot, 1854–86.

ZLL

Scourge

Word related to the verb *excoriate,* meaning "to strip off the hide"; the whip or lash by which flogging was performed as punishment. By the twelfth century *scourge* was used to describe "a thing or person that is an instrument of divine chastisement" (*Oxford,* s.v. "scourge"). It is in this manner that all seven references to *scourge* in the Doctrine and Covenants are used. In 63:31, the term is used to describe the persecution of the Saints by their enemies: "Your enemies are upon you, and ye shall be scourged from city to city." In 84:96, God describes how he has "laid [his] hands upon the nations, to scourge them for their wickedness." The next verse describes the issuing of plagues, which are the means by which God scourges the nations. Similarly, 45:31 speaks of an "overflowing scourge; for a desolating sickness shall cover the land." Again, the sickness is the means by which the scourge is effected. In 84:57–58, Church members are told that if they do not "remember the new covenant, even the Book of Mormon and the former commandments" the Lord had given them, "there remaineth a scourge and judgment to be poured out." This undefined chastisement is also the way in which the term is used in 124:83: "I, the Lord, will build up Kirtland, but I, the Lord, have a scourge prepared for the inhabitants thereof." Earlier, the Lord said, "Vengeance cometh speedily upon the ungodly as the whirlwind; and who shall escape it? The Lord's scourge shall pass over by night and by day" (97:22–23). Perhaps that is a reference to "a desolating scourge" that "shall go forth among the inhabitants of the earth, and shall continue to be poured out from time to time, if they repent not, until the earth is empty, and the inhabitants thereof are consumed away and utterly destroyed by the brightness of my coming" (5:19). The nature of this scourging is not made clear, though we know it will culminate in the destruction associated with Christ's coming.

BIBLIOGRAPHY

Oxford English Dictionary Online.

DLB

Scrip. *See* Appendix E.

Scripture(s)

The spoken or written word of God as revealed through "the Holy Ghost, the voice of God, or the ministering of angels" (20:35). Thus, the inspired utterances by the Lord's appointed servants are considered scripture: "Whatsoever they shall speak when moved upon by the Holy Ghost shall be scripture, shall be the will of the Lord, shall be the mind of the Lord, shall be the word of the Lord, shall be the voice of the Lord, and the power of God unto salvation" (68:4; cf. 21:1–6; 28:1–7; 43:1–7).

Latter-day scripture

The Lord declared that the coming forth of the Book of Mormon, as well as the calling of Joseph Smith and "others" during the restoration of the gospel, "prov[ed] to the world that the holy scriptures are true, and that God does inspire men and call them to his holy work in this age and generation, as well as in generations of old" (20:1–11). The Lord also bore witness of the truthfulness of the Doctrine and Covenants. In his revealed preface to the book, he stated his desire to publish his revelations to all "inhabitants of the earth" and for all to know the source of the revelations and declared: "This is . . . the book of my commandments. . . . I the Lord . . . called upon my servant Joseph Smith, Jun., and spake unto him from heaven. . . . Behold, I . . . have spoken it; these commandments are of me . . . they are true and faithful" (1:6, 17, 24, 37).

Joseph Smith taught that the canon of scripture is not closed. He wrote, "God . . . will yet reveal many great and important things" (A of F 9). An 1831 conference of the Church resolved that the revelations that form "the foundation of the Church" are true and are worth "the riches of the whole Earth speaking temporally" (Cannon and Cook, 32).

Purposes of scripture

Valuable direction and promises concerning scripture are given in the Doctrine and Covenants. For example, the revelations teach that God's laws are found in scripture (42:28, 59) and that "scriptures are given . . . for . . . instruction" of the Saints (33:16). Because of the importance of scripture, the Lord commands that members of his Church not "wrest the scriptures" (10:63) and that "time [should] be devoted to the studying of the scriptures" (26:1). The Lord's servants are to reason, teach, and expound the scriptures (24:5, 9; 25:7; 42:12; 68:1; 71:1; 97:5; 100:11). If a person will "first seek to obtain" the Lord's word, the Lord will enable that person to convince others of the truth (11:21), for those who "treasure up" words of scripture "continually" will be prompted in their "very hour" of need (84:85). Members must manifest faith and works in accordance with the scriptures (20:69). Church procedures are to be conducted in conformity with scripture (20:41, 80).

Joseph Smith Translation of the Bible

Throughout the Doctrine and Covenants the Lord gave directions concerning the importance of Joseph Smith's translation of the Bible. In appointing Sidney Rigdon to be Joseph's scribe in that endeavor, the Lord said, "Thou shalt write for him; and the scriptures shall be given, even as they are in mine own bosom, to the salvation of mine elect" (35:20; cf. 41:7; 42:12–15, 56–60; 45:60–61; 73:3–4; 91:1–6; 93:53; 94:10; 104:58; 124:89).

See also Apocrypha; Doctrine and Covenants and the Joseph Smith Translation of the Bible; Doctrine and Covenants, as capstone scripture; Doctrine and Covenants, what it says about itself; Doctrine and Covenants, what it says about the Bible; Doctrine and Covenants, what it says about the Book of Mormon.

BIBLIOGRAPHY

Cannon, Donald Q., and Lyndon W. Cook, eds. *Far West Record: Minutes of The Church of Jesus Christ of Latter-day Saints, 1830–1844.* Salt Lake City: Deseret Book, 1983.

KRA

Seal, sealed

Terms signifying confirmation, ratification, preservation, and securing. The word *seal* is used in a variety of ways in the Doctrine and

Covenants. Perhaps most familiar to Latter-day Saints today is its use in the context of the doctrine of eternal families, the "sealing of the children to their parents" (138:48) and husbands to wives that enables the continuation of family relationships throughout eternity (132:19–35). The ordinances of sealing, or securing, of families takes place in dedicated temples and are performed through the power of the Melchizedek PRIESTHOOD, through which, the Lord explained to Joseph Smith, "Whatsoever you seal on earth shall be sealed in heaven; and whatsoever you bind on earth, in my name and by my word, . . . shall be eternally bound in the heavens" (132:46; cf. 128:8). Extending to far more than MARRIAGE and family relationships, this promise applies to "all covenants, contracts, bonds, obligations, oaths, vows, performances, connections, associations, [and] expectations" (132:7) performed through the authority of the priesthood and properly recorded—this latter step being an essential prerequisite to the fulfillment of the promise (128:8, 14). While "never but one on the earth at a time"—that is, the president of the Church—is appointed to "hold this power" in its entirety (132:7), he can delegate authority to seal things in heaven and earth to other mortals (124:124). Also, the Doctrine and Covenants indicates that certain angels are given "power to shut up the heavens, to seal up unto life, or to cast down to the regions of darkness" (77:8).

Placing the binding, securing seal on all ORDINANCES (including the promise of ETERNAL LIFE) performed by the proper authority and correctly recorded is a function of the HOLY GHOST as the "Holy Spirit of promise," as he is generally called in this context (e.g., 76:51–62; 88:3–4; 124:124; 132:7, 19, 26). Through "the more sure word of prophecy," individuals can actually know in this life that they have been "sealed up unto eternal life, by revelation and the spirit of prophecy, through the power of the Holy Priesthood" (131:5). See More sure word of prophecy.

The revelations teach that things other than ordinances and individuals can be "sealed"— that is, ratified, confirmed, or secured—in some way. The Lord said: "I have given unto [Joseph Smith] the keys of the mystery of those things which have been sealed . . . from the foundation of the world" to come forth in the latter days (35:18). Similarly, John the Revelator saw a book "sealed on the back with seven seals," with each sealed record containing a portion of the "hidden things of [God's] economy concerning this earth" for the seven thousand-year periods of its "temporal existence" (77:6–7). In this instance, *seal* may refer to an impression stamped or carved upon a surface to certify authenticity and prevent tampering.

The seal spoken of in 77:9 refers to the authority given to ELIAS "to gather together the tribes of Israel and restore all things" and to seal "the servants of our God in their foreheads." The Prophet Joseph Smith taught that to be "sealed in their foreheads . . . signifies sealing the blessing upon their heads, meaning the everlasting covenant, thereby making their calling and election sure" (5:530; cf. D&C 133:18; Rev. 7:3; 9:4; 14:1; 20:4; 22:4).

In 98:2, the Lord tells Joseph and others that their prayers have been recorded with a "seal"— that is, the Lord's sworn promise and decree "that they shall be granted." Moreover, like Abinadi in the Book of Mormon (Mosiah 17:20), Joseph Smith "sealed his mission and his works with his own blood" (135:3; cf. 136:39). As different as these situations are from each other, as well as from the idea of confirming ordinances and sealing up families and individuals to eternal life, the basic idea is the same throughout: when something is "sealed" through the power of the Lord, something of worth is permanently secured or preserved against any influence that might corrupt or destroy it. Like other doctrines or principles of the Church, the truth that something of value can be "sealed," as described in the Doctrine and Covenants, is a testament to God's eternal nature and the extent of his love for his children.

BIBLIOGRAPHY

Smith, Joseph. *History of The Church of Jesus Christ of Latter-day Saints.* Edited by B. H. Roberts. 7 vols. 2d ed. rev. Salt Lake City: The Church of Jesus Christ of Latter-day Saints, 1932–51.

AHH

Sealed by the Holy Spirit of Promise. *See* Holy Ghost, the.

Sealed up unto eternal life. *See* More sure word of prophecy.

Sealing power. *See* Seal, sealed.

Season, little. *See* Millennium, the.

Second Coming of Christ. *See* Jesus Christ, second coming of.

Second death. *See* Death.

Secret combinations

Conspiratorial associations of persons to acquire gain and power, often by unlawful means, including murder. The Lord warned the Prophet Joseph Smith in 1831 that persons in "secret chambers" sought his destruction (38:13, 28; cf. 5:33; 10:5–7; 42:64; 123:13). It is not clear who these persons were in "secret chambers" in 1831; however, there is record of those who engaged in secret combinations "'for the destruction of Joseph Smith and his party'" in Nauvoo in 1844. This secret combination consisted of at least two hundred persons who took the following oath: "'You solemnly swear, before God and all holy angels, and these your brethren by whom you are surrounded that you will give your life, your liberty, your influence, your all, for the destruction of Joseph Smith and his party, so help you God!'" Two witnesses of these proceedings reported to the Prophet Joseph Smith, which resulted in the excommunication of several persons, including Wilson and William Law and Robert D. Foster. These men were deeply involved in the events that soon afterward led to the martyrdom of Joseph and Hyrum Smith (Smith, 297–302).

The prophet Moroni issued a solemn warning that secret organizations will actively exist in the last days among all people of the earth with the specific goal to "overthrow the freedom of all lands, nations, and countries," and they will succeed unless those who know of the intent rise up against them (Ether 8:15–26). Such secret organizations originate with and by the support of SATAN. They began with Cain and his associates as recorded in the Old Testament and Pearl of Great Price (Moses 5:29–33) and were also found among the Jaredites, Nephites,

and Lamanites in the Book of Mormon (Ether 8:20–21). Although the precise term *secret combinations* is not used in the New Testament, the priestcraft of the Jewish leaders who sought for the death of Jesus and obtained it (Mark 14:1–2; John 7:1; 11:53–57; 2 Ne. 10:3–5) and who later plotted to assassinate Paul (Acts 23:12–15; cf. 2 Ne. 26:29) manifests many of the characteristics of a secret organization. Though extremely brutal and wicked, these organizations employed oaths and covenants with perverse religious overtones: swearing by the living God, by heaven and earth, and by one's own head (Ether 8:14–18; Hel. 1:11; Moses 5:29–31, 49–55), which was accompanied by special signs and words of identification and recognition of fellow members (Hel. 2:6–7; 6:22).

BIBLIOGRAPHY

"Secret Combinations." In *Book of Mormon Reference Companion*, edited by Dennis L. Largey et al., 709–10. Salt Lake City: Deseret Book, 2003.

Smith, Joseph Fielding. *Essentials in Church History*. Salt Lake City: Deseret Book, 1953.

RJM

Sectarian. *See* Appendix E.

Sedition. *See* Appendix E.

See, seeing

Terms used in the Doctrine and Covenants in several contexts:

1. To observe with the eyes. Several references are made to seeing with one's eyes (e.g., 1:2; 14:8; 45:37; 129:2). The Three Witnesses of the Book of Mormon plates were commanded to "testify that you have seen them" (17:5). Perhaps the most important references associated with seeing are those pertaining to seeing the Lord himself. Speaking of his second coming, the Lord invites the world to "prepare for the revelation which is to come, when the veil of the covering of my temple, in my tabernacle, which hideth the earth, shall be taken off, and all flesh shall see me together" (101:23; cf. 1:2; 38:8; 88:93). One may also experience a similar personal revelation of the Lord before his second coming, if one remains righteous (67:10; 84:22; 88:68; 97:16). The Lord promised, "It

shall come to pass that every soul who forsaketh his sins and cometh unto me, and calleth on my name, and obeyeth my voice, and keepeth my commandments, shall see my face and know that I am" (93:1).

2. To witness, experience, or understand. The terms *see* and *seeing* are found several times in the Doctrine and Covenants related to one's conscious awareness of truth, or "knowledge of things as they are" (93:24; 10:16; 45:49; 133:3; cf. Jacob 4:13). For instance, "Let him that is ignorant learn wisdom by . . . calling upon the Lord his God, that his eyes may be opened that he may see" (136:32).

3. To attend to or ensure. These words are often used to denote the responsibilities incumbent upon the reader once a truth has been set forth. For instance, after being told that a "marvelous work is about to come forth among the children of men," Joseph Smith Sr. was told, "Therefore, . . . see that ye serve [God] with all your heart, might, mind and strength" (4:1–2). Similarly, 10:3; 20:54–55; 38:38; 41:4; 93:50; 104:63; and 112:27 contain exhortations to "see" to a particular assignment, charge, or instruction.

See also Seer.

DLB

Seed of Abraham

Both literal descendants of the patriarch Abraham and also all who enter into a covenant relationship with God, as Abraham did, becoming Abraham's seed by virtue of the covenant. Abraham's posterity is promised specific blessings, commonly associated with the ABRAHAMIC COVENANT (132:30; 110:12; 124:58). In Genesis, Abraham is repeatedly promised posterity as part of the covenant (Gen. 13:16; 15:5; 17:5–6; 22:17–18). The genetic line of Abraham through the sons of his grandson Jacob was collectively called Israel. It is this definition of "seed of Abraham" that is used in Psalm 105:6 and Isaiah 41:8, referring to the chosen status of his genetic posterity. Paul uses this designation twice to refer to his own genetic heritage (Rom. 11:1; 2 Cor. 11:22), yet he also declared: "For they are not all Israel, which are of Israel: Neither, because they are the seed of Abraham, are they all children" (Rom. 9:6–7). In verse 8

he states, "They which are the children of the flesh, these are not the children of God." This is in keeping with Abraham 2:10: "For as many as receive this Gospel shall be called after thy name, and shall be accounted thy seed, and shall rise up and bless thee, as their father." Thus, the phrase "seed of Abraham" refers to all who have entered into a covenant relationship with God and demonstrated worthiness to receive the same promises given to Abraham because of his righteousness. Because of this designation, it is erroneous to believe that one's genetic relationship to Abraham guarantees the covenant blessings. Indeed, it is those who obtain and then magnify the priesthood(s) who are sanctified and become "the sons of Moses and of Aaron and the seed of Abraham" (84:33–34; cf. Gal. 3:27–29). That one may become the seed of Abraham suggests that this reference is in keeping with the meaning of the term as outlined in Abraham 2.

Following their expulsion from Zion in 1833, the Lord said to the Saints: "For ye are the children of Israel, and of the seed of Abraham, and ye must needs be led out of bondage by power, and with a stretched-out arm. And as your fathers were led at the first, even so shall the redemption of Zion be" (103:17–18). Again, this may refer to blessings of safety given to all who have a covenant relationship with God, not necessarily only those who have a particular literal lineage.

See also Covenant people of the Lord; Sons of Moses and of Aaron.

DLB

Seed(s)

Terms used in the Doctrine and Covenants in at least five ways:

1. Natural biological generation: "fruit of his loins" (29:42; 103:17; 104:22–42; 132:30; cf. 86:8–9).

2. Those who become the children of Abraham, Moses, Aaron, and so forth, through gospel covenants and ordinances (84:34; Abr. 2:9–11; Gal. 3:27–29; cf. Mosiah 5:7).

3. Eternal increase of children after the resurrection: "a continuation of the seeds forever and ever" (132:19; cf. 132:30; 131:1–4).

4. The word of the Lord in "the parable of the wheat and of the tares" (86:1–2).

5. That which produces plants for farming (136:7).

A significant emphasis of the revelations is that blessings flow through natural rights of inheritance to the faithful children, the "literal descendants of the chosen seed, to whom the promises were made" (107:40; 86:8–9). Through the PRIESTHOOD and faithful obedience to the gospel, however, those who are not literal descendants become heirs of the promises and become themselves chosen seed, as though they had been biological seed (84:33–34; cf. Gal. 3:29). *See* Seed of Abraham.

RJM

Seer

One who sees with spiritual eyes things "not visible to the natural eye" (Moses 6:35–36). A seer is "a revelator and a prophet" who can "know of things which are past, and also of things which are to come" (Mosiah 8:16–17). Seers have access to the "interpreters," or the URIM AND THUMMIM (Mosiah 8:13; 28:13–16; JS–H 1:35). The word *seer* appears seven times in the Doctrine and Covenants, five times referring to the Prophet Joseph Smith, one time referring to his brother Hyrum (21:1; 107:92; 124:94, 125; 127:12; and 135:3), and one time referring to President Spencer W. Kimball (OD 2).

The Lord commanded that a record be kept in the Church, and in it Joseph Smith was to be "called a seer" (21:1). As president of the office of the high priesthood he was to preside over the Church and "to be like unto Moses . . . a seer, . . . having all the gifts of God which he bestows upon the head of the church" (107:91–92; cf. 124:125). Joseph Smith was therefore one who could see with spiritual eyes; know of things past, present, and future; and have access to the Urim and Thummin. The Lord also appointed Hyrum Smith to be "a seer, and a revelator unto [the] church, . . . that he may act in concert also with . . . Joseph" (124:94–95). In a letter written to Church members that addressed baptism for the dead, Joseph Smith identified himself as "prophet and seer of the Church of Jesus Christ of Latter-day Saints" (127:12; cf. 135:3).

Today, the president of the Church is sustained "as prophet, seer, and revelator and President of The Church of Jesus Christ of Latter-day Saints . . . [and] the counselors in the First Presidency and the Twelve Apostles as prophets, seers, and revelators" (Eyring, 25).

See also Prophet(s); Revelator.

BIBLIOGRAPHY

Eyring, Henry B. "The Sustaining of Church Officers." *Ensign* 38 (November 2008): 25.

HDG

Seneca County, New York

A county divided from Cayuga County on 29 March 1804 with Ovid as the county seat. In 1817 Waterloo became the shire town. In 1823 it was found desirable to have a half-shire at Ovid. Thus the county court was held alternately in two towns, Waterloo and Ovid, every six months. Peter Whitmer Sr. moved his family from Pennsylvania in 1809 to Fayette Township. Joseph Smith Jr. completed translation of the Book of Mormon in June 1829 and later organized the Church of Christ at the Whitmer home on 6 April 1830. Nineteen revelations, Doctrine and Covenants 14–18, 20–21, 28–36, and 38–40 were received here. *See* Historical context and overview of Doctrine and Covenants 14–18 (pp. 724–27); 20–21 (pp. 728–30); 28–36 (pp. 736–45); and 38–40 (pp. 745–47).

Section 37, closely associated with the Saints at Fayette, was actually received by the Prophet while on a visit to Canandaigua, Ontario County, New York. Joseph Sr. and Lucy Smith went to Seneca County from Palmyra in October or November 1830, locating at the Kingdom, an unincorporated community on the Cayuga-Seneca Canal in Seneca Falls Township, immediately east of the village of Waterloo. From here Lucy Smith led the Fayette branch to Kirtland, mostly by water, in May 1831.

BIBLIOGRAPHY

Jensen, Robin Scott, Robert J. Woodford, and Steven C. Harper, eds. *Manuscript Revelation Books.* Facsimile edition. First volume of the Revelations and Translations series of *The Joseph Smith Papers,* edited by Dean C. Jessee, Ronald K. Esplin, and Richard Lyman Bushman. Salt Lake City: Church Historian's Press, 2009.

McIntosh, W. H. *History of Seneca Co., New York, 1786–1876.* Philadelphia: Everts, Ensign & Everts, 1876.

Porter, Larry C. "A Study of the Origins of The Church of Jesus Christ of Latter-day Saints in the States of New York and Pennsylvania, 1816–1831." Ph.D. dissertation, Brigham Young University, 1971; published, Provo, Utah: Joseph Fielding Smith Institute for Latter-day Saint History and BYU Studies, 2000.

Willers, Diedrich. *Centennial Historical Sketch of the Town of Fayette, Seneca County, New York.* Geneva, N. Y.: W. F. Humphrey, 1900.

LCP

Sensual. *See* Appendix E.

Seraphic, seraphs. *See* Appendix E.

Serve, Service

Assist; meet another's requests or needs. As used in the Doctrine and Covenants, the words *serve* and *service* refer explicitly to service to God, with three exceptions: 24:7 ("service in Zion"), 38:26 ("serve him," referring to the father in a parable), and 57:9 ("his service," referring to clerks in Sidney Gilbert's service); however, any service given to others is also considered service to God (124:103; cf. 24:8; Mosiah 2:17). Many times in the revelations the words *servant* and *servants* carry the same connotation of service to God.

A revelation directed to Joseph Smith Sr. lists at least sixteen attributes that are needed, ideally, in the service of God, beginning with a *desire* to serve and including "faith, hope, charity and love, with an eye single to the glory God" (4:1–7). In the very beginning of man's sojourn on the earth God commanded that "they should love and serve him, the only living and true God, and that he should be the only being whom they should worship" (20:19). Such worship includes taking upon themselves "the name of Jesus Christ, having a determination to serve him to the end" (20:37). Those who "love and serve God with all their mights, minds, and strength" are promised "sanctification through the grace of our Lord and Savior Jesus Christ" (20:31). God delights to honor those who serve him in righteousness (76:5; cf. 100:16), assuring them of both temporal and spiritual blessings, even the "fulness of the earth" as well

as "peace in this world, and eternal life in the world to come" (59:5, 16, 23).

While the specific words *serve* and *service* appear only fourteen times in the Doctrine and Covenants, synonyms appear many times. For example, in each of the references that follow, the words *serve* or *service* could replace the words actually used: work (1:10; 4:5; 6:35; 7:5; 9:4; 77:5), minister (7:6–7; 68:14), assist (12:8; 14:11; 20:52), assistance (69:4; 107:38); succor (81:5), and obey (29:45). Service to others and to God enriches both recipients and the giver. It is one of the ways one can demonstrate love for God and gratitude for blessings received (42:29).

KLA

Seth

HIGH PRIEST, ordained PATRIARCH, and righteous son of Adam and Eve (107:39–42, 53). The Doctrine and Covenants contains interesting details about Seth that were not recorded in the Bible. A "revelation on priesthood" (107, headnote) notes that he was ordained by Adam when he was sixty-nine years old. Described as a "perfect man," Seth's "likeness was the express likeness of his father, insomuch that he seemed to be like unto his father in all things, and could be distinguished from him only by his age" (107:43).

Seth was present at ADAM-ONDI-AHMAN with seven generations of patriarchs and the "residue of [Adam's] posterity who were righteous" three years before the death of Adam (107:53). In that gathering Adam bestowed his last blessing upon those present. Seth was blessed that "his posterity should be the chosen of the Lord, and that they should be preserved unto the end of the earth" (107:42). The Lord appeared, and all those present "rose up and blessed Adam, and called him Michael, the prince, the archangel" (107:53–54). Seth begat Enos and many other sons and daughters, ordained Lamech, and died at 912 years of age (107:51; Moses 6:13–16).

Seth was spoken of as "one of the mighty ones" and was present in the multitude visited by Jesus Christ in the spirit world (138:40).

RJM

Seventy

An office in the Melchizedek Priesthood. All but one reference to this PRIESTHOOD office is found in Doctrine and Covenants 107. This revelation teaches the following:

• "The Seventy are . . . called to preach the gospel, and to be especial witnesses unto the Gentiles and in all the world" (v. 25).

• There is an equality of authority in their respective stewardships existing in the First Presidency, Quorum of the Twelve Apostles, and the Seventy (vv. 26–32). "Every decision made by either of these quorums must be by the unanimous voice of the same; that is, every member in each quorum must be agreed to its decisions, in order to make their decisions of the same power or validity one with the other" (v. 27).

• "The Seventy are to act in the name of the Lord, under the direction of the Twelve or the traveling high council, in building up the church and regulating all the affairs of the same in all nations, first unto the Gentiles and then to the Jews" (v. 34).

• The Twelve are "to call upon the Seventy, when they need assistance, to fill the several calls for preaching and administering the gospel, instead of any others" (v. 38).

• The quorums of seventy are to be organized with seven presidents chosen from the first quorum to preside over that quorum and all other quorums of seventy (to seven times seventy) that may be organized as needed. The seventh president is to preside over the other presidents (vv. 93–96).

• The Seventy are to be "traveling ministers"; those not of the Twelve or the Seventy "are not under the responsibility to travel among all nations" (vv. 97–98).

The other reference to the Seventy, 124:138, lists the names of the seven presidents of "the quorum of seventies" in 1841: Joseph Young, Josiah Butterfield, Daniel Miles, Henry Herriman, Zera Pulsipher, Levi Hancock, and James Foster.

Since its inception early in this dispensation to the present time, the priesthood office of seventy has encompassed a variety of organizational dimensions and responsibilities in the priesthood structure of the Church. The

first ordinations to that priesthood office took place nearly five years after the Church was organized. The Prophet Joseph Smith recorded that on 28 February 1835, the first men were called and ordained to the office of seventy "according to the visions and revelations which I have received. The Seventies are to . . . go into all the earth, whithersoever the Twelve Apostles shall call them" (2:202). Their primary function was to serve as missionaries declaring the gospel message wherever in the world they were called to serve. Leadership for quorums of seventy consisted of seven presidents who presided over all seventies. These seven served as general authorities and were called the First Council of Seventy.

During the next several years more quorums of seventies were organized, with the number of quorums reaching at least thirty-four by the time the Saints left Nauvoo for their trek west. In 1904 there were 146 quorums with approximately ten thousand members. Initially and into the second century of the Church, seventies quorums were distributed geographically and designated numerically, still under the leadership and direction of the First Council of Seventy.

Church growth and expansion throughout the world in the twentieth century necessitated further changes in the roles and organizational structure of the seventies. To facilitate the ability of the leadership to meet the needs of the Church and its members, the Lord has directed changes through his prophets that have adjusted the Church organizational structure and modified some of the roles of the Seventy. The following list illustrates some of the changes:

• In 1961 the seven members of the First Council of Seventy were ordained high priests in order to perform all duties required of them in their role as general authorities.

• In 1967 the First Presidency extended calls to sixty-nine men to serve as "Regional Representatives of the Twelve . . . to be responsible in some aspects of the work to carry counsel to and to conduct instructional meetings in groups of stakes or regions as may be designated from time to time. . . . [They] will not be 'General' Authorities" (Brown, 26). The connection of this new calling to the Seventy would not be apparent for thirty years.

• In 1974 seventies throughout the Church were organized, wherever possible, into quorums within the stakes in which they resided and designated by the name of the stake. Previously, quorums were identified by a number and their membership was determined by the locality or district, or in many cases by the stake, where the member lived. This organizational arrangement remained until 1986 when all stake quorums of seventy were discontinued. During these twelve years of stake quorums, many of the seventies served as stake missionaries and formed the nucleus of organized stake missions. After the discontinuance of local quorums, those who had been ordained seventies became affiliated with elders quorums or high priest groups in their wards.

• On 3 October 1975 the First Quorum of the Seventy was once again organized. It consisted of the seven presidents, no longer called the First Council of Seventy but newly identified as the Presidency of the Seventy, along with three new seventies, all serving as general authorities.

• In 1976 twenty-one general authorities then serving as Assistants to the Twelve were added to the First Quorum of Seventy (Kimball, 9).

• In 1978 the announcement was made that First Quorum members would no longer serve for life but would be granted emeritus status near age seventy, depending on circumstances of health and Church needs. Additional seventies continued to be added to the First Quorum (Tanner, 16).

• In 1989 the Second Quorum of the Seventy was organized. Members of this quorum were also designated as general authorities, to serve for a specified number of years.

• In 1997 the Third, Fourth and Fifth Quorums of the Seventy were organized. All together they consisted of 134 Area Authority Seventies. These brethren had previously been known as Area Authorities, an office that was an outgrowth of the position and role of the Regional Representatives of the Twelve. These new seventies would act in Church service callings within the designated geographical boundaries of the area of the Church where they reside. Many of their assignments are similar to General Authority Seventies.

• In 2004 the Sixth Quorum of the Seventy was organized.

• In 2005 the Seventh and Eighth Quorums of the Seventy were organized. Brethren serving in the Third through Eighth Quorums are called Area Seventies. In August 2005, 195 Area Seventies were serving in the Church worldwide (Tingey, 49).

The revealed scope of the service of a seventy included a sacred worldwide responsibility for sharing gospel teachings. Those called to that office are set apart as general authorities of the Church serving as members of a seventies quorum. They are to act in the name of the Lord under the direction of the First Presidency and the Quorum of the Twelve Apostles with authority equal to that of the apostles, in that they are empowered by them to function as their representatives in building and regulating the affairs of the Church in all nations (107:26, 33–34, 38). Whereas the apostles and seventy are expected to minister worldwide, those ordained to other PRIESTHOOD OFFICES are not expected to do so (107:90, 98). Significant differences exist between the apostles and the seventy. When each apostle is ordained as a member of the Quorum of the Twelve, he functions and is sustained as a prophet, seer and revelator. He also receives the KEYS of the kingdom of God and is thereby empowered, with authorization from the president of the Church, to delegate whatever authority is needed for a member of the seventy to function in behalf of the Twelve. Furthermore, when the First Presidency is dissolved due to the death of the president of the Church, the Quorum of the Twelve holds the keys to preside over the Church with full authority to direct all facets of Church activity, including the ordaining of the presiding senior apostle (president of the Quorum of the Twelve) as the succeeding president of the Church. When the seventy are ordained, they are not recipients of priesthood keys of the kingdom; however, they do receive the sealing power which is exercised in the temples for the living and the dead. They also receive an element of the apostolic power enabling them to stand as special witnesses of the Lord Jesus Christ, in whose name they teach and testify while "building up the church and regulating all the affairs of the same in all nations" (107:34).

See also Church of Jesus Christ of Latter-day Saints, The; Historical context and overview of Doctrine and Covenants 107 (p. 815).

BIBLIOGRAPHY

Brown, Hugh B. Conference Report, October 1967, 24–28.

Kimball, Spencer W. "The Reconstitution of the First Quorum of the Seventy." *Ensign* 6 (November 1976): 4–9.

"Seventy." In *Encyclopedia of Mormonism,* edited by Daniel H. Ludlow et al. 4 vols. New York: Macmillan, 1992.

Smith, Joseph. *History of The Church of Jesus Christ of Latter-day Saints.* Edited by B. H. Roberts. 7 vols. 2d ed. rev. Salt Lake City: The Church of Jesus Christ of Latter-day Saints, 1932–51.

Tanner, N. Eldon. "Revelation on Priesthood Accepted, Church Officers Sustained." *Ensign* 8 (November 1978): 16–17.

Tingey, Earl C. "The Quorums of the Seventy." *Ensign* 35 (August 2005): 48–50.

CMC

Shake off the dust of thy feet

An act symbolic of shedding from oneself the accountability for someone else's sins when that individual rejects the gospel. The Lord clearly lays upon those who have embraced the gospel the responsibility of testifying of the truth and raising a warning voice to the inhabitants of the world. "Behold, I sent you out to testify and warn the people, and it becometh every man who hath been warned to warn his neighbor. Therefore, they are left without excuse, and their sins are upon their own heads" (88:81–82; cf. Ezek. 3:17–21; Jacob 1:19; 2:1–2). Formal actions employing this principle were taught by the Lord and practiced by his servants in both New Testament and Book of Mormon times. They include shaking the dust from the feet (Matt. 10:14; Mark 6:11; Acts 13:51), and shaking the dust off one's garments (Luke 10:11; Acts 18:5–6; 2 Ne. 9:44). In modern revelation the Lord reestablished this practice and gave further insight concerning a witness against those

who reject his gospel, including the additional dimension of "washing" or "cleansing" the feet.

Joseph Smith and Oliver Cowdery, the first and second elders of the newly restored Church, were called in July 1830 to "prune [the Lord's] vineyard with a mighty pruning, yea, even for the last time" (24:19), and were told, "And in whatsoever place ye shall enter, and they receive you not in my name, ye shall leave a cursing instead of a blessing, by casting off the dust of your feet against them as a testimony, and cleansing your feet by the wayside" (24:15).

In the summer of 1831 several elders had traveled to Missouri to participate in the dedication of the land of Zion. In a revelation directing them in their return to Kirtland, Ohio, the Lord chastened some for being reluctant to "open their mouths" (60:2) in testifying of the gospel. They were instructed to preach the gospel "among the congregations of the wicked" on their way home and to "shake off the dust of thy feet against those who receive thee not, not in their presence, lest thou provoke them, but in secret; and wash thy feet, as a testimony against them in the day of judgment" (60:14–15).

In January 1832, "certain elders . . . desired to learn more in detail as to their immediate duties" (75, headnote). The Lord made clear that they were to leave a blessing on those who receive them and "shake off the dust of [their] feet as a testimony against" those who rejected them. The Lord promised, "You shall be filled with joy and gladness; and know this, that in the day of judgment you shall be judges of that house, and condemn them; and it shall be more tolerable for the heathen in the day of judgment, than for that house" (75:19–22).

In a communication designated by the Prophet Joseph Smith as a "revelation on priesthood" (84, headnote), the Lord promised "all the faithful who are called of God in the church unto the ministry" his sustaining influence as they were sent out "to reprove the world of all their unrighteous deeds, and to teach them of a judgment which is to come." Those who received these missionaries were promised great blessings. Concerning those who rejected them, the missionaries were instructed, "He that receiveth you not, go away from him alone by yourselves, and cleanse your feet even with water, pure water, whether in heat or in cold, and bear testimony of it unto your Father which is in heaven, and return not again unto that man" (84:86–92).

In calling John Murdock on a mission to the eastern United States, the Lord promised that he would "have power to declare my word in the demonstration of my Holy Spirit" and that those who received him "as a little child, receiveth my kingdom; and blessed are they." John was further told by the Lord that "whoso rejecteth you shall be rejected of my Father and his house; and you shall cleanse your feet in the secret places by the way for a testimony against them" (99:2–4).

In four of the five times the instruction is given in the Doctrine and Covenants, the Lord cautions his servants to perform these acts "by the wayside" (24:15), "not in their presence, lest thou provoke them, but in secret" (60:15), "away from him alone by yourselves" (84:92), and "in the secret places by the way" (99:4). It is noteworthy that such testimonies against unbelievers are not to be given hastily or casually. Missionaries are instructed to "search diligently and spare not" in their efforts to reach people with the message of the restored gospel (84:94).

Shaking off the dust of one's feet as a testimony against someone is a very serious matter. Elder James E. Talmage wrote: "The responsibility of testifying before the Lord by this accusing symbol is so great that the means may be employed only under unusual and extreme conditions, as the Spirit of the Lord may direct" (345).

See also Curse, cursing; Missionary work; Wash, washed, washing(s).

BIBLIOGRAPHY

Talmage, James E. *Jesus the Christ*. Salt Lake City: Deseret Book, 1916.

RLB

Shakers

United Society of Believers in Christ's Second Coming, commonly known as Shakers because of an ecstatic dance that accompanied their worship services. When Joseph Smith learned of Shaker doctrines and that Leman Copley, a former member of the Shakers who was baptized in March 1831, still held to some of those doctrines, the Prophet inquired of the Lord "in order to have more perfect understanding on the subject" (1:167). The divine answer given was the revelation now recorded in section 49.

The Shaker movement was founded in England in 1747. Later, a charismatic woman, Ann Lee, became its leader. Some of her followers were convinced that Christ would come the second time in the form of a woman (God, in their view, was both male and female) and that Ann Lee was that woman. In 1774 she and a few followers emigrated to America, where several Shaker communities eventually grew. She died ten years later. *See* Lee, Ann.

Shakers revered leaders such as Joseph Meacham, who became their great prophet and apostle in America. They believed in the need to establish a new Zion and to restore New Testament Christianity in preparation for an imminent millennium. The Shaker faith required a simple but rigorous lifestyle that included communal living and sharing all things. Shakers promoted celibacy, a doctrine preached by Ann Lee, who had lost each of her four children in infancy. Not every Shaker was able to live this belief, but for those who could, Joseph Meacham did away with natural families and called the care of children a spiritual, not a natural, obligation. The resulting "'spiritual' families" worked and worshiped together, but men and women lived in separate dormitories (Fluhman, 94–95).

In 1822 a group of Shakers established the North Union community about 15 miles from Kirtland, Ohio. It was there that Leman Copley lived when he joined the Church. Joseph Smith's revelation instructed Copley, Sidney Rigdon, and Parley P. Pratt to go to North Union and preach the gospel to the Shakers. Not surprisingly, the revelation was directed to some of the erroneous beliefs and practices of the Shakers (49, headnote). For example, the revelation directed that after baptism people would receive the gift of the Holy Ghost "by the laying on of the hands of the elders of the church" (49:14), something not practiced by Shakers. The Lord further said that "whoso forbiddeth to marry is not ordained of God, for marriage is ordained of God unto man" (49:15), a direct refutation of Shaker celibacy. The Lord's words, "whoso forbiddeth to abstain from meats, that man should not eat the same, is not ordained of God" (49:18), was another direct refutation of a Shaker belief.

Unfortunately, the mission to the Shakers failed to gain any converts. Leman Copley later reneged on his promise to consecrate his farm as a place where Saints immigrating to the area could settle. He was chastised for his failings in a later revelation (54:4–5). *See* Copley, Leman.

See also Historical context and overview of Doctrine and Covenants 49 (p. 755).

BIBLIOGRAPHY

Black, Susan Easton. *Who's Who in the Doctrine and Covenants.* Salt Lake City: Bookcraft, 1997.

Cook, Lyndon W. *The Revelations of the Prophet Joseph Smith.* Salt Lake City: Deseret Book, 1985.

Fluhman, J. Spencer. "Early Mormon and Shaker Visions of Sanctified Community." *BYU Studies* 44, no. 1 (2005): 79–110.

Smith, Joseph. *History of The Church of Jesus Christ of Latter-day Saints.* Edited by B. H. Roberts. 7 vols. 2d ed. rev. Salt Lake City: The Church of Jesus Christ of Latter-day Saints, 1932–51.

JBA

Sharp, sharpness

Terms used in the Doctrine and Covenants in connection with communicating. To John and Peter Whitmer the Lord said, "I speak unto you with sharpness and with power" (15:2; 16:2; cf. 14:2; 33:1). *See* Sword.

Thomas B. Marsh, president of the Quorum of Twelve Apostles, was told not only to "pray for thy brethren of the Twelve" but to "admonish them sharply for my name's sake . . . for all their sins" (112:12). In setting forth correct principles of priesthood administration, the Lord said it is appropriate to "reprov[e] betimes with sharpness, when moved upon by the Holy Ghost; and then [show] forth afterwards an increase of love toward him whom thou hast reproved, lest he esteem thee to be his enemy;

Drawing of Shakers performing a step dance in New Lebanon, New York. In 1831 the Lord sent three missionaries to a Shaker community near Kirtland, Ohio. "Hearken unto my word, my servants Sidney, and Parley, and Leman; for behold, verily I say unto you, that I give unto you a commandment that you shall go and preach my gospel which ye have received, even as ye have received it, unto the Shakers. Behold, I say unto you, that they desire to know the truth in part, but not all, for they are not right before me and must needs repent" (D&C 49:1–2).

that he may know that thy faithfulness is stronger than the cords of death" (121:43–44).

Many shades of meaning are associated with communicating sharply or with sharpness. They range from "harsh," "biting," "severely rigid," "piercing," and "roughly," to "acutely," "with keen perception; exactly; minutely" (Webster, s.v. "sharp," "sharply"). Clearly, there are times when people need to be admonished sharply or reproved with sharpness. But the spirit in which that is done and the timeliness of the reproof can reflect the more positive meanings of the words—all in the spirit of love and in harmony with the promptings of the Holy Ghost.

BIBLIOGRAPHY

Webster, Noah. *An American Dictionary of the English Language.* 1828.

LED

Sharper than a two-edged sword. *See* Sword.

Sharpness. *See* Sharp, sharpness; Appendix E.

Shedolamak

Geographic location in the ancient world mentioned in connection with Cainan receiving the patriarchal order of the priesthood from Adam (107:39–40, 45).

RJM

Shem

"The great high priest" (138:41), the righteous son of Noah (Gen. 5:32), and ancestor of Abraham (1 Chr. 1:17–27). Shem is mentioned once in the Doctrine and Covenants (138:41), listing him as "among the great and mighty ones who were assembled in [the] vast congregation of the righteous" awaiting the Savior's visit to the postmortal spirit world during the interval between his death and resurrection (138:12–18, 36–49). "These the Lord . . . gave . . . power to come forth, after his resurrection from the dead, to enter into his Father's kingdom, there to be crowned with immortality and eternal life" (138:51).

Tradition, based on the Bible, holds that Shem was Noah's eldest son because he is mentioned before Ham and Japheth in several genealogical lists (Gen. 5:32; 9:18; 10:1; 1 Chr.

1:4). Latter-day revelation and possibly one biblical reference, however, place the birth order as Japheth, Shem, and Ham (Moses 8:12; Gen. 10:21). It is probably because of Shem's prominence that he came to be listed first. Ancient tradition also holds that Shem is Melchizedek, which might be supported by the latter-day declaration that Shem is "the great high priest" (138:41), the same designation given to Melchizedek in the Doctrine and Covenants (107:2; cf. Heb. 7:1–2).

RJM

Sheol

A transliteration of the Hebrew term for the spirit world. *Sheol* is translated as "HELL" in the Old Testament. Found in Doctrine and Covenants 121:4, *sheol* is used by Joseph Smith in the context of his acknowledgment of God's dominion over all things as he pleaded for help while in LIBERTY JAIL. The description of *sheol* as "dark and benighted" fits the biblical view of the underworld as a dark waste. Interestingly, the biblical imagery of *sheol* as a being with an insatiable appetite is found in God's reply where the last event that might overwhelm Joseph is "if the very jaws of hell shall gape open the mouth wide after thee" (122:7; cf. Isa. 5:14).

DLB

Sherman, Lyman

Birth: 22 May 1804, Monkton, Addison County, Vermont

Death: ca. 15 February 1839, Far West, Caldwell County, Missouri

Lyman Sherman married Delcena Didamia Johnson on 16 January 1829. He was converted to the Church and baptized shortly after missionaries began preaching in his area in January 1832. Sherman moved to Kirtland, Ohio, in 1833. On 28 February 1835 he was appointed as one of the presidents of the First Quorum of the Seventy (Cook, 121–22). Sherman came to Joseph Smith on 26 December 1835 and declared, "I have been wrought upon to make known to you my feelings and desires, and was promised that I should have a revelation which should make known my duty" (Smith, 2:345). As promised, Joseph Smith received a revelation directed to Sherman in which the Lord told him, "Your sins are forgiven you, because you have obeyed my voice in coming up . . . to receive counsel" (108:1). The Lord also instructed Sherman to "let your soul be at rest" and "wait patiently until the solemn assembly . . . of my servants," referring to meetings in the Kirtland Temple in which Church leaders, including Sherman, received sacred ordinances and blessings (108:2, 4).

In January 1839 the First Presidency directed that Sherman be called as an apostle (Smith et al.); however, he died in Far West, Missouri, shortly thereafter before being informed and ordained. At the sealing of Sherman's daughter, Susan, to James H. Martineau nearly twenty years later, Heber C. Kimball praised Sherman as "a good man—a noble man—and . . . Joseph's right hand man" (Johnson, 191).

See also Historical context and overview of Doctrine and Covenants 108 (p. 816).

BIBLIOGRAPHY

Cook, Lyndon W. "Lyman Sherman—Man of God, Would-Be Apostle." *BYU Studies* 19, no. 1 (1978): 121–24.

Johnson, Benjamin F. *My Life's Review: Autobiography of Benjamin Franklin Johnson*. Provo, Utah: Grandin Book, 1997.

Smith, Joseph. *History of The Church of Jesus Christ of Latter-day Saints*. Edited by B. H. Roberts. 7 vols. 2d ed. rev. Salt Lake City: The Church of Jesus Christ of Latter-day Saints, 1932–51.

——— et al. Letter to Heber C. Kimball and Brigham Young, 16 January 1839. Photocopy at Church History Library, The Church of Jesus Christ of Latter-day Saints, Salt Lake City, Utah.

SCH

Sherwood, Henry G.

Birth: 20 April 1785, Kingsbury, Washington County, New York

Death: 24 November 1867, San Bernardino, Los Angeles County, California

Henry Sherwood was baptized by 1832. He moved to Kirtland in about 1834, and by 1836 began preaching the gospel in Ohio, Tennessee, and Kentucky. In September 1837 he was appointed to serve on the Kirtland high council. Sherwood moved to Missouri but soon fled the state for Illinois with the rest of the Saints

in 1839. In Commerce, Illinois, he again was called to serve on the high council.

In an 1841 revelation, the Lord said: "Let my servant Henry G. Sherwood [buy] stock" in the Nauvoo House "as seemeth him good" (124:81). The purpose of this boarding house was to create a place where guests could "contemplate the glory of Zion" (124:23–24, 60) and become acquainted with the Church.

In 1847, Sherwood joined the vanguard pioneer company and traveled to Salt Lake City. There he drew the first survey of Salt Lake City on sheepskin, "lacking paper of suitable size" (Black, 264). Some interesting incidents in the life of Henry Sherwood include being healed of malaria by the Prophet Joseph Smith and being present when Joseph declared that he was "going like a lamb to the slaughter" (6:555; 4:4). It was in Sherwood's home that Lorenzo Snow received a revelation regarding "the pathway of God and man" and formed the couplet, "As man now is, God once was: As God now is, man may be" (Snow, 46).

Sherwood moved to San Bernardino in 1852, and after conflicts with Church leaders during the period 1855–56, he evidently left the Church. He died in San Bernardino, California, on 24 November 1867.

BIBLIOGRAPHY

Black, Susan Easton. *Who's Who in the Doctrine and Covenants*. Salt Lake City: Bookcraft, 1997.

Sherwood, Henry Garlie. Record Book. Church Historical Library, The Church of Jesus Christ of Latter-day Saints. Salt Lake City, Utah.

Smith, Joseph. *History of The Church of Jesus Christ of Latter-day Saints*. Edited by B. H. Roberts. 7 vols. 2d ed. rev. Salt Lake City: The Church of Jesus Christ of Latter-day Saints, 1932–51.

Snow, Eliza R. *Biography and Family Record of Lorenzo Snow*. Salt Lake City: Deseret News Company, 1884.

RC

Shod. *See* Appendix E.

Shule. *See* Names, code.

Sickle. *See* Appendix E.

Sign(s)

Events or happenings that mark, represent, symbolize, or point to things that have been prophesied. The Doctrine and Covenants teaches that "faith cometh not by signs, but signs follow those that believe" on Christ's name (63:9; cf. 58:64; 35:8). The performing of "wonderful works," such as casting out of devils, healing the sick, causing the blind to see and the deaf to hear, enabling the dumb to speak, saving from poison, and having powers over poisonous serpents are among the promised signs that "follow them that believe." The Lord cautions, however, that "they shall not boast themselves of these things, neither speak them before the world," for these things are given for spiritual profit and for salvation (84:65–73).

Signs come to mankind as a result of faith and by the will of God, "not by the will of men" (63:10). Those who seek faith from signs do not please God; to them "he showeth no signs, only in wrath unto their condemnation" (63:11–12). It is "an evil and adulterous generation [that] seeketh after a sign" (Matt. 12:38–39). SPIRITUAL GIFTS are to be sought in order to benefit others "and not for a sign that they may consume it upon their lusts" (46:9). Those seeking signs with improper motives "shall see signs, but not unto salvation" (63:7).

Signs prophesied in the Doctrine and Covenants provide a witness to the world of events leading up to the second coming of Jesus Christ. Believers are promised that signs will follow their conversion; to them "it shall be given to know the signs of the times, and the signs of the coming of the Son of Man" (68:9–11; JS–M 1:26, 36). Those who fear the Lord "shall be looking forth for the great day of the Lord to come, even for the signs of the coming of the Son of Man. And they shall see signs and wonders . . . in the heavens above, and in the earth beneath" that will designate the Lord's return (45:39–40; cf. 39:23). Those who "are wise and have received the truth, and have taken the Holy Spirit for their guide, and have not been deceived . . . shall abide the day" (45:57).

See also Jesus Christ, second coming of.

TWC

Signs of the times. *See* Jesus Christ, second coming of; Sign(s).

Similitude. *See* Appendix E.

Sin, transgression

To knowingly act against the will of God. Although *transgression* can have a special meaning (i.e., the transgression of Adam and Eve in the Garden of Eden; *see* Fall of Adam and Eve, the), the meanings of the words *sin* and *transgression* are essentially the same, and none of the five verses in which the words *sin* and *transgression* appear together in the Doctrine and Covenants distinguish any differences between their meanings (24:2; 109:34; 121:17; 132:26; 138:32). Principal contexts in which these words are used include the following: confession and FORGIVENESS of sin, forsaking sin, consequences of sin, baptism for the remission of sin, the special status of children with regard to sin, and redemption of sin through Christ.

The Saints were repeatedly counseled to "confess their sins" (61:2; cf. 19:20; 58:43; 59:12; 64:7) in order to be forgiven. They were also promised multiple times that they could be forgiven of sin (e.g., 25:3; 58:42; 84:61; 90:1; 110:5; 124:76).

The Doctrine and Covenants teaches the importance of forsaking sin. The Saints were told to "sin no more" (6:35; 24:2; 29:3; 82:7; 97:27), and the Lord stated that forsaking sin is a vital part of REPENTANCE (58:43). The Lord commanded them to "repent of all your sins" (49:26) because he "cannot look upon sin with the least degree of allowance" (1:31).

The Lord stated that one of the causes for chastening is sin, saying, "I, the Lord, have suffered the affliction to come upon them . . . in consequence of their transgressions" (101:2; cf. 1:27; 61:8; 95:10; 109:38, 65). The Lord also warned of the consequences of sin, including loss of the Spirit and light, or understanding (1:31–33; 19:17–20; 42:23; 63:16; 93:39); loss of PRIESTHOOD power (121:21, 37–40); loss of PEACE (19:23; 59:23); loss of Church membership (50:8; 52:6; 64:35); experiencing "the buffetings of Satan" (104:10; cf. 78:12; 82:21; 104:9–10; 132:26); and ultimately, the loss of exaltation (132:15–17). *See* Buffetings of Satan; Cast out/cut off; Exalt, exaltation.

The Doctrine and Covenants consistently emphasizes the importance of baptism "for the remission of sins" (13:1; cf. 19:31; 20:37; 33:11; 55:2; 84:27; 107:20; 138:33). *See* Baptism by water.

Little CHILDREN "cannot sin" (29:47), and during the MILLENNIUM "children shall grow up without sin unto salvation" (45:58).

The Doctrine and Covenants teaches that one's sins are redeemed through Christ. Although there was "no sin" (45:4) in Christ, he "was crucified for the sins of the world" (35:2; cf. 27:2; 29:1; 46:13; 54:1; 76:41; 138:7), and his "bowels are filled with compassion towards" the inhabitants of the earth (101:9; cf. 121:3–4).

See also Atonement, the; Wicked, the/wickedness.

JLH

Slothful. *See* Appendix E.

Smith, Alvin

Birth: 11 February 1798, Tunbridge, Orange County, Vermont

Death: 19 November 1823, Manchester, Ontario County, New York

Alvin Smith, oldest brother of the Prophet Joseph Smith, believed Joseph's account of the visitations of Moroni to be true. In his late twenties, Alvin contracted what was diagnosed as the bilious colic. While ill, he spoke with Joseph and urged him to faithfully fulfill his responsibilities. He passed away on 19 November 1823. Of Alvin, Joseph said, "He was a very handsome man, surpassed by none but Adam and Seth, and of great strength" (*History*, 5:247).

On 21 January 1836, Joseph had a vision of the celestial kingdom, in which he saw Adam, Abraham, his parents, and "my brother Alvin, that has long since slept" (137:5). Because Alvin had died before the restoration of the gospel and had not been baptized, the Prophet wondered how he could be saved. He was told that all who died without an opportunity to accept the gospel, "who would have received it if they had been permitted to tarry, shall be heirs of the celestial kingdom of God" (137:7).

Four years after the Prophet's vision of the celestial kingdom, he publicly taught the doctrine of baptism for the dead at the funeral of Seymour Brunson. Wandle Mace recalled the Prophet's words: "Every man who wishes to save father, mother, brothers, sisters, and friends, must go through all the ordinances for each one of them seperately, the same as for himself, from baptism to ordination, washings and anointings, and recieve all the keys and powers of the Preisthood, the same as for himself" (Mace, 74).

Courtesy Scott C. Esplin

Alvin Smith's gravestone in Palmyra, New York. In 1836 the Prophet saw a vision of his brother Alvin in the celestial kingdom and recorded: "The heavens were opened upon us, and I beheld the celestial kingdom of God, and the glory thereof, whether in the body or out I cannot tell. . . . I saw Father Adam and Abraham; and my father and my mother; my brother Alvin, that has long since slept; and marveled how it was that he had obtained an inheritance in that kingdom, seeing that he had departed this life before the Lord had set his hand to gather Israel the second time, and had not been baptized for the remission of sins. Thus came the voice of the Lord unto me, saying: All who have died without a knowledge of this gospel, who would have received it if they had been permitted to tarry, shall be heirs of the celestial kingdom of God" (D&C 137:1–7).

BIBLIOGRAPHY

Durfey Chase Books. Palmyra. Church History Library, The Church of Jesus Christ of Latter-day Saints, Salt Lake City, Utah.

Mace, Wandle. Autobiography (ca. 1890). Church History Library, The Church of Jesus Christ of Latter-day Saints, Salt Lake City, Utah.

Smith, Joseph. *History of The Church of Jesus Christ of Latter-day Saints.* Edited by B. H. Roberts, 7 vols. 2d ed. rev. Salt Lake City: The Church of Jesus Christ of Latter-day Saints, 1932–51.

Smith, Joseph Fielding. Letter, 19 December 1913. Church History Library, The Church of Jesus Christ of Latter-day Saints, Salt Lake City, Utah.

RC

Smith, Don C.

Birth: 25 March 1816, Norwich, Windsor County, Vermont

Death: 7 August 1841, Nauvoo, Hancock County, Illinois

Don Carlos Smith, the youngest brother of the Prophet Joseph Smith, was baptized by David Whitmer on about 9 June 1830. The Prophet stated he was "one of the first to receive my testimony" (*History,* 4:393). Although he passed away at the young age of twenty-five, his life had been filled with service. On 22 January 1836 Oliver Cowdery recorded, "Elder Don Carlos Smith was ordained and anointed president of the high priesthood of the Melchisedek priesthood, by the presidents of the Church" (Journal). In Kirtland, Ohio, he worked on the temple and was editor of the *Elders' Journal.* After moving to Missouri he served a mission in 1838 in both Tennessee and Kentucky "to collect money to buy out land claims of non-Mormons in Daviess County, Missouri" (Cook, 275). Following his missionary service, Don Carlos joined his family in Illinois, where in July 1839 the Prophet sent him and George A. Smith to administer to the sick in Nauvoo. They gave blessings to more than sixty people, who were healed (Smith, *History,* 4:398–99). In Nauvoo Don Carlos was editor and publisher of *Times and Seasons,* a major in the Hancock County militia, a member of the Nauvoo city council, and an officer in the Nauvoo Legion.

In 1841, his name was included among the officers of the Church to be sustained as "president over a quorum of high priests" in a general conference (124:133, 144). Don Carlos died on 7 August 1841. His mother attributed his death to "consumption," a pulmonary or respiratory disease (L. M. Smith, *Revised,* 450). The Prophet Joseph Smith said of him, "He was a lovely, a good-natured, a kind-hearted and a virtuous and a faithful, upright child; and where his soul goes, let mine go also" (*History,* 5:127).

BIBLIOGRAPHY

Cook, Lyndon W. *The Revelations of the Prophet Joseph Smith.* Salt Lake City: Deseret Book, 1985.

Cowdery, Oliver. Journal of Oliver Cowdery, 1 January–27 March 1836. Church History Library, The Church of Jesus Christ of Latter-day Saints, Salt Lake City, Utah.

Smith, Don Carlos, to Agnes M. Smith, 23 October 1838. Church History Library, The Church of Jesus Christ of Latter-day Saints, Salt Lake City, Utah.

Smith, Joseph. *History of The Church of Jesus Christ of Latter-day Saints.* Edited by B. H. Roberts. 7 vols. 2d ed. rev. Salt Lake City: The Church of Jesus Christ of Latter-day Saints, 1932–51.

Smith, Lucy Mack. *The Revised and Enhanced History of Joseph Smith by His Mother.* Edited by Scot Facer Proctor and Maurine Jensen Proctor. Salt Lake City: Bookcraft, 1996.

RC

Smith, Eden

Birth: 1806, Indiana

Death: 7 December 1851, Vermillion County, Indiana

Eden Smith's name appears in the Doctrine and Covenants in connection with two mission calls. In January 1832 Smith was called to "be united in the ministry" with Micah B. Welton (75:30, 36). In March of that same year he was called as a mission companion to Stephen Burnett to "preach the gospel to every creature that cometh under the sound of your voice. . . . Wherefore, go ye and preach my gospel, whether to the north or to the south, to the east or to the west, it mattereth not, for ye cannot go amiss" (80:1–3). On the date of this call Eden Smith became ill, and his father, John Smith (not the Prophet's uncle), went with Burnett for a time. These missions were short but resulted in a number of baptisms (Smith, Journal, 1–4).

In late 1832 Smith was called as a branch

president in Eugene, Ohio. In July 1833 he was reproved by the First Presidency for a lack of humility and being "confederate" with his father in saying "many hard things against the brethren." The First Presidency wrote "to the Church at Eugene," stating that it was "truly painful" to write about "the case of John Smith, and Eden Smith, his son." They stated that the Church did not "hold" Eden and his father in fellowship, that John "has been dealt with, and his authority taken from him," and that the leaders were authorized to call a conference and "sit in judgment on Eden's case" (Smith, *History*, 1:370–71). In consequence, Eden was disfellowshipped on 2 July 1833. After repenting, he returned to full fellowship and served a mission to Pennsylvania with Benjamin Leland. He also gathered with the Saints in Missouri and Nauvoo before moving to Kanesville, Iowa, to the Salt Lake Valley, and then back to Kanesville. He died in December 1851 in Vermillion County, Indiana, at the age of forty-five.

BIBLIOGRAPHY

Smith, Eden. Journal of Eden Smith. Typescript. L. Tom Perry Special Collections, Harold B. Lee Library, Brigham Young University, Provo, Utah.

Smith, Joseph. *History of The Church of Jesus Christ of Latter-day Saints*. Edited by B. H. Roberts. 7 vols. 2d ed. rev. Salt Lake City: The Church of Jesus Christ of Latter-day Saints, 1932–51.

ZLL

Smith, Emma

Birth: 10 July 1804, Harmony, Susquehanna County, Pennsylvania

Death: 30 April 1879, Nauvoo, Hancock County, Illinois

Daughter of Isaac and Elizabeth Hale and wife of the Prophet Joseph Smith. Emma first met Joseph when he was boarding at the Hale home in 1825 in Harmony, Pennsylvania, while he was employed by Josiah Stoal (or Stowell) of nearby Chenango County, New York. On 18 January 1827, Joseph and Emma were married, after which they moved to New York State, where Joseph farmed with his father. There, in September 1827, Joseph received the gold plates, which he began translating as the Book of Mormon. To avoid mounting persecution

Joseph and Emma moved from New York to Harmony, Pennsylvania, and then to the Peter Whitmer Sr. home in Fayette, New York, where the translation was completed. After they returned to Harmony, Emma was baptized on 28 June 1830, just two months after the organization of the Church in Fayette.

Emma is the only woman to whom an entire section of the Doctrine and Covenants is addressed (25). She received the revelation through the Prophet Joseph Smith in July 1830. Its sixteen verses provided Emma with a guide for her relationship to her husband, to the Church, and to the Lord. The Lord's injunction, "This is my voice unto all" (v. 16), gives the revelation universal application.

Emma, wife of a maligned and harassed prophet and mother of eleven children (of whom two were adopted and only five lived to adulthood), received additional spiritual strength from her August 1830 confirmation, which conferred upon her the gift of the Holy Ghost. In the revelation directed to her, Emma was told that her time was to "be given to writing and to learning much" (25:8), including acting as Joseph's scribe on the inspired translation of the Bible when others were unavailable (v. 6), an assignment she had earlier performed during the translation of the gold plates. She was also cautioned to "murmur not because of the things which thou hast not seen" (v. 4), presumably meaning the gold plates, which she had been permitted to feel but not to see. The Lord also commissioned Emma to prepare a hymnbook for the Church (v. 11). She gave herself faithfully to that task, and the hymnbook was published in 1835.

Forgiving her of her sins, the Lord deemed Emma "an elect lady" (v. 3) and instructed her "to expound scriptures, and to exhort the church, according as it shall be given thee by my Spirit" (v. 7). These pronouncements were effected in 1842 in Nauvoo when she became first president of the Relief Society. Joseph explained that the term *elect* meant "to be elected to a certain work . . . and that the revelation was then fulfilled by Sister Emma's election to the Presidency of the Society" (*History*, 4:552–53).

Advising Emma to "beware of pride," the Lord urged her to maintain a "spirit of meekness"

Elect Lady; *painting by Liz Lemon Swindle. "Hearken unto the voice of the Lord your God, while I speak unto you, Emma Smith, my daughter. . . . Behold, thy sins are forgiven thee, and thou art an elect lady, whom I have called"* (D&C 25:1, 3).

(v. 14) and to comfort and console Joseph (v. 5). "Let thy soul delight in thy husband, and the glory which shall come upon him," advised the Lord (v. 14). In turn she was promised Joseph's support in her own ecclesiastical responsibilities (v. 9). As Lucy Mack Smith observed, "Her whole heart was occupied in the work of the Lord and she felt no interest ex[cept] for the church and the cause of truth" (*Book*, 565).

By 1843 the most compelling counsel of the 1830 revelation was verse 2: "If thou art faithful and walk in the paths of virtue before me, I will preserve thy life, and thou shalt receive an inheritance in Zion." The 1843 revelation on plural MARRIAGE (132) instructing Emma to "receive all those [wives] that have been given unto my servant Joseph" (v. 52) tested her faithfulness. The Lord threatened to "destroy" her "if she will not abide this commandment" (v. 54). After this startling directive, the Lord admonished Joseph to "do all things for her, even as he hath said" (v. 55), and instructed Emma to forgive Joseph his trespasses, promising her that her trespasses against the Lord would then be forgiven and she would be blessed (v. 56). It was for Emma and Joseph to forgive each other their trespasses.

From July 1843 until her death, Emma vacillated between acceptance and rejection of the principle of plural marriage. At Joseph's death in 1844, Emma retained her faith in the Restoration but chose not to go west with the Saints under Brigham Young's leadership. She remained in Nauvoo and married Lewis C. Bidamon in 1847. In 1860 she associated with the Reorganized Church of Jesus Christ of Latter Day Saints, led by her son Joseph Smith III.

Emma Smith died denying that Joseph had ever taught or engaged in plural marriage. Perhaps pride, as the Lord had warned (25:14), may have dictated her thoughts and actions regarding this revelation. Her challenge with the principle of plural marriage, however, does not invalidate her many redeeming qualities as a self-sacrificing, steadfast Latter-day Saint, a compassionate and selfless friend to strangers and acquaintances alike, and a loving and loyal companion to Joseph, who wrote that she was "undaunted, firm, and unwavering" (*History*, 5:107).

See also Historical context and overview of Doctrine and Covenants 25 (p. 733).

BIBLIOGRAPHY

Smith, Joseph. *History of the Church of Jesus Christ of Latter-day Saints.* Edited by B. H. Roberts. 7 vols. 2d ed. rev. Salt Lake City: The Church of Jesus Christ of Latter-day Saints, 1932–51.

Smith, Lucy Mack. *Lucy's Book.* Edited by Lavina Fielding Anderson. Salt Lake City: Signature Books, 2001.

CCM

Smith, George A.

Birth: 26 June 1817, Potsdam, St. Lawrence County, New York

Death: 1 September 1875, Salt Lake City, Salt Lake County, Utah

George A. Smith, cousin to the Prophet Joseph Smith, gained a testimony of the Restoration after reading the Book of Mormon. He was baptized on 10 September 1832 (Smith, 5:103). In 1833 he moved with his family to Kirtland, Ohio.

George A. was the youngest member of ZION'S CAMP in 1834. He was ordained a member of the First Quorum of the Seventy 1 March 1835. In 1838 he moved from Kirtland to Missouri, settling in Adam-ondi-Ahman, where he served on the high council.

On 26 April 1839, George A. was ordained an apostle. He was twenty-one years old and not yet married. Shortly thereafter, he left for a mission to England. Although delayed for several months due to sickness, he arrived in England on 6 April 1840, where he labored effectively. In a revelation dated 19 January 1841 he is listed with the Quorum of the Twelve and other Church officers (124:129). Elder Smith arrived in Nauvoo in July 1841 and later served on the city council and as an alderman. He served a short mission in 1843 to solicit donations for the temple and the Nauvoo House, and he campaigned for Joseph Smith's candidacy for president of the United States in 1844.

In 1847, Smith was called to "organize a company" of Saints to travel west (136:14). He traveled with Brigham Young's vanguard company, entered the Salt Lake Valley in July 1847, and actively assisted in the migration of subsequent pioneer companies to Utah. Appointed

George A. Smith, 1817–1875.

historian and general Church recorder in 1854, Elder Smith worked on the Manuscript History of Joseph Smith. In 1855 he became a member of the Supreme Court of Utah Territory. St. George, Utah, founded in 1861, was named in honor of his significant contributions to the settlement of southern Utah.

George A. Smith served as first counselor in the First Presidency to President Brigham Young from 1868 until President Smith's death on 1 September 1875. His grandson and namesake, George Albert Smith, also became an apostle and later the eighth president of the Church.

BIBLIOGRAPHY

Carrington, Albert. Biographical Sketch of G. A. Smith. Church Historical Library, The Church of Jesus Christ of Latter-day Saints, Salt Lake City, Utah.

Smith, George A. *Journal of Discourses.* 26 vols. London: Latter-day Saints' Book Depot, 1854–86.

RC

Smith, Hyrum

Birth: 9 February 1800, Tunbridge, Orange County, Vermont

Death: 27 June 1844, Carthage, Hancock County, Illinois

In May 1829, in a revelation directed to him, Hyrum Smith was told to "keep my commandments, and seek to bring forth and establish the cause of Zion" (11:6). He accepted the counsel and was baptized in June 1829 in Seneca Lake by his brother Joseph. He became one of the Eight Witnesses of the Book of Mormon and was one of the six original members of the Church. In April 1830 he was told by revelation through his brother Joseph, "Thy duty is unto the church forever, and this because of thy family" (23:3). On 9 June 1830 he was ordained a priest and given responsibilities over a branch of the Church at Waterloo, New York. On 31 March 1831 his brother Joseph wrote to him from Kirtland, "My dearly beloved brother Hyrum, I have had much concern about you, but I always remember you in prayers, calling upon God to keep you safe in spite of men or devils. I think you better come to this country immediately" (Corbett, 81).

Hyrum Smith again followed counsel and moved his family to Kirtland, where he was ordained an elder and later a high priest. On 14 June 1831 he left Kirtland to fulfill his first extended mission, traveling through Michigan, Indiana, and Illinois to reach Missouri (52:8). His next missionary journey was with Reynolds Cahoon (75:32). Following this short mission, he and Reynolds Cahoon were called as counselors to Bishop Newel K. Whitney in Kirtland. In 1833 he was appointed as a member of the Church building committee (94, headnote). In 1834 he participated in ZION'S CAMP. Hyrum was called as a member of the Kirtland high council and later as assistant counselor to the First Presidency (September 1837) and then as second counselor in the First Presidency (November 1837). While acting in his office as a counselor in the First Presidency, Hyrum was

Courtesy Church History Library

Hyrum Smith, 1800–1844.

one of those admonished to "arise and shine forth, that thy light may be a standard for the nations" (115:5). From November 1838 to April 1839 he was imprisoned in Missouri until his escape to Illinois. "We endeavored to find out for what cause," wrote Hyrum, "but all we could learn was, that it was because we were 'Mormons'" (Smith, 3:420).

Hyrum, who replaced his father, Joseph Smith Sr., as patriarch to the Church, was promised by the Lord: "Whoever he blesses shall be blessed, and whoever he curses shall be cursed; that whatsoever he shall bind on earth shall be bound in heaven; and whatsoever he shall loose on earth shall be loosed in heaven. And from this time forth I appoint unto him that he may be a prophet, and a seer, and a revelator unto my church, as well as my servant Joseph" (124:91–94).

In this same revelation the Lord said of his servant Hyrum Smith, "I, the Lord, love him because of the integrity of his heart, and

because he loveth that which is right before me" (124:15).

On 27 June 1844, at Carthage, Illinois, Hyrum and his brother Joseph were murdered. John Taylor, a witness to their deaths, wrote that they "will be classed among the martyrs of religion" (135:6). Over seventy years later, the Lord revealed to Hyrum's son Joseph F. Smith that his father had been "reserved to come forth in the fulness of times to take part in laying the foundations of the great latter-day work" (138:53).

See also Martyrdom of Joseph and Hyrum Smith.

BIBLIOGRAPHY

Corbett, Pearson H. *Hyrum Smith, Patriarch.* Salt Lake City: Deseret Book, 1963.

Smith, Joseph. *History of The Church of Jesus Christ of Latter-day Saints.* Edited by B. H. Roberts. 7 vols. 2d ed. rev. Salt Lake City: The Church of Jesus Christ of Latter-day Saints, 1932–51.

SEB

Smith, John

Birth: 16 July 1781, Derryfield, Rockingham County, New Hampshire

Death: 23 May 1854, Salt Lake County, Salt Lake City, Utah

In January 1832 missionaries Joseph Wakefield and Solomon Humphrey met with members of the Smith family. At this time, John, brother of Joseph Smith Sr., agreed to be baptized. According to his son George A. Smith, "my father had been for several years very feeble in health and for about six months previous to his baptism had not been able to visit his barn. The neighbors all believed that baptism would kill him. I cut the ice in the creek and broke a road for 40 rods through the crust of two feet of snow and the day was very cold. The neighbors looked on with astonishment expecting to see him die in the water, but his health continued improving from that moment" (Bates, 80).

In May 1833 Smith moved his family from New York to Ohio. Of the arrival of John and his family, the Prophet Joseph Smith noted: "They were the first of my father's relatives who obeyed the Gospel" (*History,* 1:348). On 17 February 1834 Smith was appointed to serve as a member of the Kirtland high council (102:3). Upon leaving Kirtland, he moved to Missouri with the Saints and served as president of the Adam-ondi-Ahman Stake. Expelled with the Saints from Missouri in 1839, he moved to the Mormon settlements in Iowa, across the river from Nauvoo. There he served as president of the Zarahemla Stake. In 1843 he was directed to move to Ramus, Illinois, where he presided over the branch. In January 1844 he was ordained a patriarch by the Prophet Joseph Smith; in August he was directed to move to Nauvoo, where in October he was appointed president of the Nauvoo Stake. He left Nauvoo in February 1846, and after stopping at Winter Quarters, arrived in the Salt Lake Valley in September 1847. He presided over the settlement in the Salt Lake Valley for the first year until Brigham Young returned in 1848. Smith was called as president of the Salt Lake Stake, and in January 1849 he was ordained patriarch to the Church. He passed away on 23 May 1854.

BIBLIOGRAPHY

Bates, Irene M. "Uncle John Smith, 1781–1854: Patriarchal Bridge." *Dialogue* 20 (Fall 1987): 79–89.

Smith, John, 1781–1854. Papers, 1833–1854. Church History Library, The Church of Jesus Christ of Latter-day Saints, Salt Lake City, Utah.

Smith, Joseph. *History of The Church of Jesus Christ of Latter-day Saints.* Edited by B. H. Roberts, 7 vols. 2d ed. rev. Salt Lake City: The Church of Jesus Christ of Latter-day Saints, 1932–51.

RC

Smith, Joseph, Jr.

Birth: 23 December 1805, Sharon, Windsor County, Vermont

Death: 27 June 1844, Carthage, Hancock County, Illinois

The Lord's chosen prophet to restore the fulness of the gospel in the latter days, holding all the keys of the kingdom of God in the dispensation of the fulness of times, and first president of The Church of Jesus Christ of Latter-day Saints (110:16; cf. 21:1–12; 27:13; 112:30–32; 121:41; 128:9, 18–21; 138:48). Joseph Smith Jr. was one of eleven children born to Joseph Smith Sr. and Lucy Mack Smith. In his fifteenth year he saw GOD THE FATHER and JESUS CHRIST

in what is known as the First Vision (JS–H 1:5–19). In 1823 he was visited by the angel Moroni, from whom he later received the gold plates from which he translated the Book of Mormon by the power of God. In 1829 the Aaronic and Melchizedek priesthoods were restored to him under the hands of John the Baptist and Peter, James, and John, in preparation for the restoration of the fulness of the gospel and the Church of Jesus Christ.

Joseph's roles, identified through revelation

On the day the Church was organized, 6 April 1830, a revelation (21:1; cf. 124:125) outlined Joseph's callings. The revelation recorded in section 21 reflects the actual sequence of the beginning events of the Restoration. The Doctrine and Covenants became a set of milestones in the unfolding drama of the life of Joseph Smith and those who were raised up to assist him. Doctrine and Covenants 21:1 declares of the Prophet:

"Behold, there shall be a record kept among you; and in it thou shalt be called":

"A seer." He beheld the First Vision. Later visions and visitations were shared, witnessed, and recorded (JS–H 1:15–17; D&C 76; 107:93–98; 110; 137).

"A translator." He was the instrument for translating the Book of Mormon and the books of Moses and Abraham and provided an inspired revision of the Bible (3; 5; 45:60–61; 93:53). In the midst of the Book of Mormon project he was told, "This generation shall have my word through you" (5:10).

"A prophet." He was given the gift to foresee and prophesy of many things to come and also to transmit the teachings, authority, and power of Christ (1; 64; 87; 88; 133; 124:125). More than one thousand prophecies are recorded in the Doctrine and Covenants. *See* Prophet(s).

"An apostle of Jesus Christ." He eventually received all the KEYS of the holy PRIESTHOOD, even a fulness (13; 27:12–13; 110:11–16; 128:20–21). He became a special witness of the Savior, holding the keys of all essential ordinances (84:1–5, 32–44; 88:19–22; 107:91–92).

"An elder of the church." He was endowed to participate and administer in all the functions and offices of the Church, including judicial functions (20:1–2; 102:9, 26, 33; 107:78–81).

Undertaking the "marvelous work"

Within two years of the organization of the Church, young Joseph (he was between twenty-five and twenty-seven years old) received daunting and seemingly unattainable assignments from on high. Later he confided to Heber C. Kimball that he was "much tempted [perplexed] about the revelations the Lord gave through him—it seemed to be so impossible for them to be fulfilled" (Whitney, 403).

But Joseph consistently counseled the Saints with inspired direction: "Wherefore, be not weary in well-doing, for ye are laying the foundation of a great work. And out of small things proceedeth that which is great" (64:33; cf. 94:1; 57:6–7; 119:1–2; 123:15–17).

He received many instructions and commandments that led him to plead for guidance:

1. To call, ordain, and bless twelve apostles. "And now, behold, there are others who are called to declare my gospel, both unto Gentile and unto Jew; yea, even twelve; and the Twelve shall be my disciples, and they shall take upon them my name; and the Twelve are they who shall desire to take upon them my name with full purpose of heart" (18:26–29).

2. To build temples where the Lord could manifest himself. "Build a house, in the which house I design to endow those whom I have chosen with power from on high" (95:8); "organize yourselves; prepare every needful thing; and establish a house, even a house of prayer, a house of fasting, a house of faith, a house of learning, a house of glory, a house of order, a house of God" (88:119–20). In Nauvoo the Lord revealed that his covenant people are "always commanded to build" TEMPLES "that I may reveal mine ordinances therein unto my people" (124:39–40; cf. verses 27–55; 57:3; 84:1–5; 115:8–16; 133:1–2).

3. To gather a holy people from the entire world to a center place called Zion. "And ye are called to bring to pass the gathering of mine elect; for mine elect hear my voice and harden not their hearts; wherefore the decree hath gone forth from the Father that they shall be gathered in unto one place upon the face of this land"

Joseph Smith Jr., 1805–1844; portrait by Danquart Anthon Weggeland.

(29:7–8). The "land of Missouri" was designated as the "land of promise, and the place for the city of Zion. . . . Independence is the center place" (57:1–3; cf. 133:4). "Wherefore, prepare ye, prepare ye, O my people; sanctify yourselves; gather ye together, O ye people of my church, upon the land of Zion, all you that have not been commanded to tarry" (133:4; cf. 33:6). *See* Gather, gathering.

4. To establish and extend the Church to fill the whole earth. "The keys of the kingdom of God are committed unto man on the earth, and from thence shall the gospel roll forth unto the ends of the earth, as the stone which is cut out of the mountain without hands shall roll forth, until it has filled the whole earth" (65:2; cf. 1:1–6; 18:28; 107:35).

5. To introduce the law of CONSECRATION. "And behold, thou wilt remember the poor, and consecrate of thy properties for their support" (42:30–42, 53–55, 70–73; 51:3–5, 9; 82:17–20; 105:5).

6. To build a holy city. "Verily this is the word of the Lord, that the city New Jerusalem shall be built by the gathering of the saints, beginning at this place" (84:4; cf. 28:9; 57:1–5). *See* New Jerusalem.

The Lord's mode of address to Joseph Smith

In the Doctrine and Covenants names are often titles, and titles signify roles and attributes. The Lord uses several sacred names for himself in introducing and closing revelations. Along with his characterizations of the Prophet these names communicate much: "Thou art Joseph" (3:9), a "lawful [heir], according to the flesh" (86:9), carries heavy connotations of the ancient Joseph, who became both the spiritual and temporal savior of the family of Jacob.

One can see in other modifiers a pattern of spiritual growth. "My servant Joseph" is used dozens of times (e.g., 93:45). "I called you servants for the world's sake, and ye are their servants for my sake" (93:46). "My friends" ("from henceforth I shall call you friends," 84:77; includes Joseph, the Twelve, and others); this phrase occurs sixteen times. "My son" (121:7) is applied to Joseph and his associates, including Oliver Cowdery, Orson Pratt, and Hyrum Smith. The words *sons* and *daughters* in the sense of reborn sons and daughters unto God occur several times (e.g., 25:1; 76:24).

Zion and destiny

Joseph was instructed not only to establish a city called ZION but to prepare a people of Zion who were "pure in heart" (97:21) and who could live "by the principles of the law of the celestial kingdom" (105:5) and be prepared to meet another Zion, the ZION OF ENOCH, when the Savior comes (84:100; cf. 76:50–70; Moses 7:60–65).

Facing the mammoth tasks ahead, it may have given young Joseph Smith some comfort to learn that Enoch was ordained to the holy priesthood and called to his prophetic responsibility when he was twenty-five years old (107:48; Moses 7:69). Clearly, Joseph's own sense of mission grew as he learned that ancient worthies were foreordained for their crucial roles in the kingdom of God (Abr. 3:22–23; Jer. 1:5), that "every man who has a calling to minister

to the inhabitants of the world was ordained to that very purpose in the Grand Council of heaven before this world was. I suppose that I was ordained to this very office in that Grand Council" (Smith, *History,* 6:364). Joseph Smith is the "servant in the hands of Christ" "on whom there is laid much power," referred to in Isaiah as "the rod" of the "Stem of Jesse" (113:3–4; Isa. 11:1). To him "rightly belongs the priesthood, and the keys of the kingdom, for an ensign, and for the gathering of my people in the last days" (113:6; cf. 86:8–11).

Joseph and the Saints are commanded repeatedly in the revelations, even in the most dire of circumstances, to "lift up thy heart and rejoice" (25:13; 27:15; 31:3; 42:69; 110:5). After having experienced much tribulation from 1820 to 1830, Joseph must have rejoiced in the following assurance, given the day the Church was organized: "For thus saith the Lord God: Him have I inspired to move the cause of Zion in mighty power for good, and his diligence I know, and his prayers I have heard. . . . I will cause that he shall mourn for her no longer" (21:7–8).

Three months later, however, the Lord cautioned the Prophet that his troubles were not over: "Be patient in afflictions, for thou shalt have many" (24:8).

Of weaknesses and growth

"I have sent forth the fulness of my gospel by the hand of my servant Joseph; and in weakness have I blessed him" (35:17). The citing of the weakness and foibles of the Saints, including Joseph Smith, permeates the revelations. Joseph was chastened for yielding to the "persuasions of men" (3:6) and for failing to attend properly to his family (93:47–48). He was admonished to "walk more uprightly" (5:21). Joseph and the whole Church were chastened for postponing the building of the Kirtland Temple (95:2–4). Church members were warned against criticizing Joseph Smith: "There are those who have sought occasion against him [Joseph] without cause; nevertheless, he has sinned; but verily I say unto you, I, the Lord, forgive sins unto those who confess their sins before me and ask forgiveness, who have not sinned unto death" (64:6–7). In another revelation, the Lord said, "Let no one, therefore, set on my servant Joseph; for I will justify him; for he shall do the sacrifice which I require at his hands for his transgressions, saith the Lord your God" (132:60).

Joseph was not rebuked for what some took to be flaws—his jovial banter and good humor, for example. He was not chastened for lack of humility or meekness or for failing to love and forgive, nor for his bold and forthright exposition of scripture, nor for his "native cheery temperament" (JS–H 1:28). His limitations were recognized: "In temporal labors thou shalt not have strength. . . . Attend to thy calling and thou shalt have wherewith to magnify thine office" (24:9). He was cautioned to temper his tendency to overdo: "Do not run faster or labor more than you have strength and means provided" (10:4).

Keys

One can distinguish stages of growth and promise as keys were conferred upon Joseph. At first he was promised the keys "until I shall appoint unto them another in his stead" (28:7, given September 1830 in Fayette). Later he was told that he would hold the keys "*if he abide in me,* and if not, another will I plant in his stead" (35:18, given December 1830; emphasis added). Then, "the keys of the mysteries of the kingdom shall not be taken from my servant Joseph Smith, Jun., through the means I have appointed, while he liveth, *inasmuch as he obeyeth mine ordinances*" (64:5, given 11 September 1831; emphasis added). By 8 March 1833, the promises had become unconditional. "Verily I say unto you, the keys of this kingdom shall never be taken from you, while thou art in the world, neither in the world to come" (90:3).

Among the keys conferred upon him, some of which he shared with other leaders serving with him, include the keys of the kingdom (27:13; 110:16), of the ministering of angels (13), of the mysteries and peaceable things (28:7; 42:61), of discerning false from true spirits (50), of the School of the Prophets (90:7), of all the spiritual blessings of the Church (107:18, 65–66), of the gathering of Israel (110:11), of the power of turning hearts (110:13–16), of the new and last dispensation (27:13; 112:30–32), of asking for answers from the living God and receiving them (124:95; cf. 128:11), and of sealing in the new and everlasting covenant of MARRIAGE (132:7, 19).

Spiritual gifts

As "President of the office of the High Priesthood," Joseph was "to preside over the whole church . . . ; yea, to be a seer, a revelator, a translator, and a prophet, having all the gifts of God which he bestows upon the head of the church" (107:91–92). As that head, he could not only *discern* the gifts of the Spirit but also *have* all those gifts, "in order that every member may be profited thereby" (46:8–29; 50:30).

One would expect to find in Joseph Smith's life evidence of the gifts of the Spirit and the fruits of the Spirit, with power to "chase darkness" from among the people (50:25), and the records amply demonstrate this. In obtaining and magnifying the priesthood, Joseph was taught that each person "ordained of God and sent forth, the same is appointed to be the greatest, notwithstanding he is the least and the servant of all" (50:26), and that "he that exalteth himself shall be abased, and he that abaseth himself shall be exalted" (101:42). Such a humble servant was given a wonderful promise: "Wherefore, he is possessor of all things; for all things are subject unto him, both in heaven and on the earth, the life and the light, the Spirit and the power, sent forth by the will of the Father through Jesus Christ, his Son. But no man is possessor of all things except he be purified and cleansed from all sin. And if ye are purified and cleansed from all sin, ye shall ask whatsoever you will in the name of Jesus and it shall be done" (50:27–29). In this regard, the Prophet Joseph said in March 1844: "The Lord once told me that what I asked for I should have. I have been afraid to ask God to kill my enemies, lest some of them should, peradventure, repent" (*History,* 6:253).

Sealing power

A year before his death Joseph defined the "more sure word of prophecy" as "a man's knowing that he is sealed up unto eternal life, by revelation and the spirit of prophecy, through the power of the Holy Priesthood" (131:5). This blessing is a surety, a seal and prophecy of ETERNAL LIFE. Joseph Smith taught that this blessing is in connection with one's having perfect love: "Until we have perfect love we are liable to fall and when we have a testimony that our

My Servant Joseph; *painting by Liz Lemon Swindle.* "Wherefore, I the Lord, knowing the calam-
*ity which should come upon the inhabitants of the earth, called upon my servant Joseph Smith,
Jun., and spake unto him from heaven, and gave him commandments*" (D&C 1:17).

names are sealed in the Lamb's Book of life we have perfect love & then it is impossible for false Christs to deceive us" (Cannon and Cook, 23). Section 132 affirms that this "seal" was conferred on Joseph: "For I am the Lord thy God, and will be with thee even unto the end of the world, and through all eternity; for verily I seal upon you your exaltation, and prepare a throne for you in the kingdom of my Father, with Abraham your father. Behold, I have seen your sacrifices, and will forgive all your sins; I have seen your sacrifices in obedience to that which I have told you" (132:49–50). *See* More sure word of prophecy; Seal, sealed.

Joseph told the Twelve that God would "feel after [them]" and, to prove them, would "wrench [their] very heartstrings" (Young, 24:197, 199, 264, 267; cf. D&C 101:4–5; 136:31). Such trials he himself endured and, through Christ, overcame. He obeyed all the higher laws of discipleship in full consecration before being promised exaltation. Like Moses, he had dedicated his life (28:2; 103:16); now he had attained the likeness of Abraham (132:32–33, 57).

Unfinished aspirations

As time was running out, Joseph had personal concerns, including the following:

1. He sought to be reassured about his family—Emma and the children. He had prayed at the Kirtland Temple dedication, reaffirming his vows: "Have mercy, O Lord, upon his wife [Emma] and children, that they may be exalted in thy presence, and preserved by thy fostering hand" (109:69, given March 1836). He was clinging to the admonition, "Let mine handmaid [Emma] forgive my servant Joseph his trespasses; and then shall she be forgiven her trespasses, wherein she has trespassed against me; and I, the Lord thy God, will bless her, and multiply her, and make her heart to rejoice" (132:56). In Nauvoo in the late days of his life he said he fervently hoped "that she might share with him the blessings of his exaltation as she had shared with him his sufferings. He rejoiced greatly in the anticipation of these eternal family relations in the future" (Stuy, 5:218).

2. He had been commissioned to write a "proclamation unto the kings of the earth"

(124:1–2, 107; given 19 January 1841). This had to be left to his successors.

3. He wanted to live to see saving ordinances for the dead performed in the Nauvoo Temple.

"That subject seems to occupy my mind, and press itself upon my feelings the strongest, since I have been pursued by my enemies" (128:1; cf. 127, given 1 September 1842). "Brethren, shall we not go on in so great a cause?" (128:22, given 6 September 1842). Stretching his hand toward the temple site, he said, "And if it should be . . . [the] will of God that I might live to behold that temple completed and finished from the foundation to the top stone I will say Oh Lord it is enough Lord let thy servant depart in peace, which is my ernest prayer in the name of the L[ord] Jesus Amen" (Ehat and Cook, 418). That, too, had to be left for others to complete.

4. He had a great desire to lead a vanguard company to the Rocky Mountains.

"The light he had was toward the mountains" (*Southern Star,* 1:117). He had often said, "If I were only in the Rocky Mountains with a hundred faithful men, I would then be happy, and ask no odds of mobocrats" (Young, 11:16). Brigham Young, rather than Joseph Smith, led that pilgrimage. These fond hopes and expectations were denied him as he set his face for Carthage.

Conferring the keys of the kingdom upon the Twelve

Joseph was determined not to leave this earth until all the keys of the kingdom which he had received were conferred upon the Twelve Apostles, so the work of the Lord would continue and fill the whole earth, as he had prophesied it would (65:2). President Wilford Woodruff testified:

"Joseph Smith was what he professed to be, a prophet of God, a seer and revelator. . . . He spent the last winter of his life, some three or four months, with the quorum of the twelve, teaching them. It was not merely a few hours ministering to them the ordinances of the gospel; but he spent day after day, week after week and month after month, teaching them and a few others the things of the kingdom of God. . . . I, Wilford Woodruff, being the last man living in the flesh who was present upon that occasion, feel it a duty I owe to the Church of Jesus Christ of Latter-day Saints, to the House of Israel, and to the whole world, to bear this my last testimony to all nations, that in the winter of 1843–44, Joseph Smith, the Prophet of God, called the Twelve Apostles together in the City of Nauvoo, and spent many days with us in giving us our endowments, and teaching us those glorious principles which God had revealed to him. And upon one occasion he stood upon his feet in our midst for nearly three hours, declaring unto us the great and last dispensation which God had set His hand to perform upon the earth in these last days. The room was filled as if with consuming fire; the Prophet was clothed upon with much of the power of God, and his face shone and was transparently clear, and he closed that speech, never-to-be-forgotten in time or in eternity, with the following language: 'Brethren, I have had great sorrow of heart for fear that I might be taken from the earth with the keys of the kingdom of God upon me, without sealing them upon the heads of other men. God has sealed upon my head all the keys of the kingdom of God necessary for organizing and building up of the Church, Zion, and kingdom of God upon the earth, and to prepare the Saints for the coming of the Son of Man. Now, brethren, I thank God I have lived to see the day that I have been enabled to give you your endowments, and I have now sealed upon your heads all the powers of the Aaronic and Melchizedec priesthoods and apostleship, with all the keys and powers thereof, which God has sealed upon me; and I now roll off all the labor, burden and care of this Church and kingdom of God upon your shoulders, and I now command you in the name of the Lord Jesus Christ to round up your shoulders, and bear off this Church and kingdom of God before heaven and earth, and before God, angels and men; and if you don't do it you will be damned'" (Woodruff, 19–21).

The foundation is laid

Five weeks before his death Joseph Smith said, "I calculate to be one of the Instruments of setting up the Kingdom of Daniel, by the word of the Lord, and I intend to lay a foundation that will revolutionize the whole world" (Ehat

and Cook, 367). After Joseph's death, the Lord, in a revelation to Brigham Young, declared, "Which foundation he did lay, and was faithful; and I took him to myself" (136:38).

"No man knows my history"

In April conference 1844, about three months before he was martyred, Joseph Smith said of himself and his experiences: "You don't know me; you never knew my heart. No man knows my history. I cannot tell it: I shall never undertake it. I don't blame any one for not believing my history. If I had not experienced what I have, I would not have believed it myself. . . . When I am called by the trump of the archangel and weighed in the balance, you will all know me then" (History, 6:317). After the martyrdom, Brigham Young exclaimed: "You did not know who you had amongst you. Joseph so loved this people that he gave his life for them; Hyrum loved his brother and this people unto death. Joseph and Hyrum have given their lives for the church. But very few knew Joseph's character; he loved you unto death—you did not know it until after his death: he has now sealed his testimony with his blood" (Smith, History, 7:240).

Although no one may know the full extent of Joseph Smith's history and mortal ministry, the Doctrine and Covenants contains the following testimony of Elder John Taylor concerning a few of his accomplishments "in the short space of twenty years":

"Joseph Smith, the Prophet and Seer of the Lord, has done more, save Jesus only, for the salvation of men in this world, than any other man that ever lived in it. In the short space of twenty years, he has brought forth the Book of Mormon, which he translated by the gift and power of God, and has been the means of publishing it on two continents; has sent the fulness of the everlasting gospel, which it contained, to the four quarters of the earth; has brought forth the revelations and commandments which compose this book of Doctrine and Covenants, and many other wise documents and instructions for the benefit of the children of men; gathered many thousands of Latter-day Saints, founded a great city, and left a fame and name that cannot be slain. He lived great, and he died great in the eyes of God and his people; and like most of the Lord's anointed in ancient times, has sealed his mission and his works with his own blood" (135:3).

See also Church of Jesus Christ of Latter-day Saints, The; Historical context and overview of Doctrine and Covenants 135 (p. 854); Priesthood, restoration of priesthood and priesthood keys; Martyrdom of Joseph and Hyrum Smith.

BIBLIOGRAPHY

Cannon, Donald Q., and Lyndon W. Cook, eds. *Far West Record: Minutes of The Church of Jesus Christ of Latter-day Saints, 1830–1844.* Salt Lake City: Deseret Book, 1983.

Ehat, Andrew F., and Lyndon W. Cook, comps. and eds. *The Words of Joseph Smith.* Provo, Utah: Religious Studies Center, Brigham Young University, 1980.

Smith, Joseph. *History of The Church of Jesus Christ of Latter-day Saints.* Edited by B. H. Roberts. 7 vols. 2d ed. rev. Salt Lake City: The Church of Jesus Christ of Latter-day Saints, 1932–51.

———. *Personal Writings of Joseph Smith.* Compiled and edited by Dean C. Jessee. Rev. ed. Salt Lake City: Deseret Book, 2002.

Southern Star 1 no. 15 (11 March 1899): 113–20.

Stuy, Brian H., comp. and ed. *Collected Discourses.* 5 vols. B. H. S. Publishing, 1992.

Whitney, Orson F. *Life of Heber C. Kimball.* Salt Lake City: Stevens & Wallis, 1945.

Widtsoe, John A. *The Message of the Doctrine and Covenants.* Salt Lake City: Bookcraft, 1969.

Woodruff, Wilford. *Wilford Woodruff.* Teachings of Presidents of the Church series. Salt Lake City: The Church of Jesus Christ of Latter-day Saints, 2004.

Young, Brigham. *Journal of Discourses.* 26 vols. London: Latter-day Saints' Book Depot, 1854–86.

TGM

Smith, Joseph, Jr., martyrdom of. *See* Martyrdom of Joseph and Hyrum Smith.

Smith, Joseph, Sr.

Birth: 12 July 1771, Topsfield, Essex County, Massachusetts

Death: 14 September 1840, Nauvoo, Hancock County, Illinois

Joseph Smith Sr. married Lucy Mack in January 1896 at Tunbridge, Vermont. From 1796 to 1816, the Smiths lived in a number of places in the area, working at farming and business ventures but finding little success. Finally, after three successive years of crop failures, they moved to Palmyra and then to Manchester, New York, again taking up farming.

It was there that the Restoration began to unfold, beginning with the First Vision, which came to young Joseph Smith Jr. in 1820, and continuing with the coming of Moroni with the Book of Mormon plates, the translation of the Book of Mormon, the restoration of the priesthood, and the organization of the Church. *See* New York period.

In February 1829, Joseph Smith Sr. traveled from New York to Harmony, Pennsylvania, where his son Joseph was living, after he left New York to avoid persecution. The previous summer, the plates were taken from Joseph Jr. for a time because of the loss of the 116 pages of Book of Mormon manuscript. Although the plates had been returned, Joseph recorded: "I did not, however, go immediately to translating, but went to laboring with my hands upon a small farm which I had purchased of my wife's father, in order to provide for my family" (*History,* 1:28). During his father's visit, the Prophet Joseph received a revelation directed to Joseph Smith Sr., recorded in Doctrine and Covenants 4, declaring the marvelous work that was "about to come forth" and outlining the qualifications of those who are "called to the work" (vv. 1–7).

Joseph Smith Sr. was one of the Eight Witnesses who were shown the plates from which the Book of Mormon was translated (Smith, *History,* 1:57–58). He was baptized the day the Church was organized or "shortly after" (Smith, *History,* 1:79). He moved with the Church from New York to Kirtland, Ohio, at the command of the Lord (37) in 1831. Father Smith, as he was affectionately called, was ordained a high priest in June 1831, served on the Kirtland high council in 1834, and worked on the Kirtland Temple. In December 1833, at the age of sixty-two, he was ordained a patriarch and served faithfully as the first patriarch of the Church until his death. He served a mission to the eastern states in 1836 and was appointed as assistant counselor to the First Presidency in September 1837.

He moved from Kirtland to Far West, Missouri, in 1838 but left Missouri with the

Joseph Smith Sr., 1771–1840; portrait by William Whitaker.

Saints and settled in Nauvoo in 1839. From the spring of 1840 until his death in September, Father Smith became progressively ill. Just before he died, Joseph Smith Sr. blessed his beloved wife, Lucy, and each of his children, except Catherine, who was delayed in coming. Addressing Lucy once more, he told her, "Mother, do you not know, that you are one of the most singular women in the world?" and expressed deep appreciation for her role as wife and mother. Sister Smith wrote of his final minutes: "He then paused for some time, being exhausted. After which he said, in a tone of surprise, 'I can see and hear, as well as ever I could.' (*A second pause of considerable length.*) 'I see Alvin.' (*Third pause.*) 'I shall live seven or eight minutes.' Then straightening himself, he

laid his hands together; after which he began to breathe shorter, and in about eight minutes his breath stopped, without even a struggle or a sigh, and his spirit took its flight for the regions where the justified ones rest from their labors" (L. M. Smith, *History*, 313–14).

BIBLIOGRAPHY

Smith, Joseph. *History of The Church of Jesus Christ of Latter-day Saints.* Edited by B. H. Roberts. 7 vols. 2d ed. rev. Salt Lake City: The Church of Jesus Christ of Latter-day Saints, 1932–51.

Smith, Lucy Mack. *History of Joseph Smith by His Mother.* Edited by Preston Nibley. Salt Lake City: Bookcraft, 1958.

LED

Smith, Joseph F.

Birth: 13 November 1838, Far West, Caldwell County, Missouri

Death: 19 November 1918, Salt Lake City, Salt Lake County, Utah

When Joseph Fielding Smith was two months old, mobbers ransacked his family home: "The mob entered the room where I was, the bed on the floor was thrown on to the other [bed] completely smothering me up" (*Life*, 124). Miraculously, he survived. His mother, Mary Fielding Smith, fled with him to Quincy, Illinois, early in 1839 and then moved to Nauvoo. When Joseph was six years old, his father, Hyrum Smith, was assassinated. In the exodus of the Saints from Nauvoo, his mother took Joseph, his sister Martha, and their father's six children from his first marriage (to Jerusha Barden Smith) to Iowa and then on to the Salt Lake Valley.

Joseph's mother died two months before his fourteenth birthday. When he was fifteen, he was called to be a missionary in the Hawaiian Islands. On this mission Smith wrote, "I wish to be humble, prayerful before the Lord, that I may be worthy of the blessings and love of God to protect me at all times" (*Life*, 180–81). His prayer was answered; when he was journeying home to Utah, a drunken man confronted him, asking, "Are you a 'Mormon'?" Without hesitation Smith replied, "Yes, siree; dyed in the wool; true blue, through and through." The ruffian exclaimed, "You are the . . . pleasantest man I ever

Joseph F. Smith, 1838–1918.

met! Shake, young fellow, I am glad to see a man that stands up for his convictions" (*Life,* 189).

After an absence of nearly four years, Joseph arrived in Salt Lake City unharmed. "The day following my arrival home I reported myself to President Young," he wrote, "and immediately enlisted in the legion (militia) to defend ourselves against the encroachment of a hostile and menacing army. From that time until the proclamation of peace . . . I was constantly in my saddle" (*Life,* 195). When the threat of war passed, Smith served as sergeant-of-arms in the territorial legislature and as a high councilor in the Salt Lake Stake.

On 1 July 1866 Brigham Young said, "Shall I do as I feel led? I always feel well to do as the Spirit constrains me. It is my mind to ordain Brother Joseph F. Smith to the Apostleship, and to be one of my counselors" (Smith, *Life,* 227). At age twenty-seven Joseph F. Smith was ordained an apostle and called to the First Presidency. He served as a counselor to Presidents Brigham Young, John Taylor, Wilford Woodruff, and Lorenzo Snow.

Joseph F. Smith became president of the Church in 1901 and served until his death in November 1918. In his opening remarks at the October 1918 general conference, President Smith spoke of receiving "several divine communications during the previous months." He spoke specifically of a vision of the "Savior's visit to the spirits of the dead while his body was in the tomb." His words were written down and "submitted to the counselors in the First Presidency, the Council of the Twelve, and the Patriarch, and it was unanimously accepted by them" on 31 October 1918 (138, headnote). In 1976 this vision was added to the Pearl of Great Price; in 1981 it was moved from the Pearl of Great Price and added to the Doctrine and Covenants as section 138.

President Joseph F. Smith died nineteen days after the unanimous acceptance of the record of his vision by Church leaders. A public funeral was not held due to an influenza epidemic in Salt Lake City at the time, but funeral services were conducted near the open grave. Bishop Charles W. Nibley eulogized, "As a preacher of righteousness, who could compare with him? . . . He was the greatest that I ever heard—strong, powerful, clear, appealing" (Smith, *Life,* 433).

See also Historical context and overview of Doctrine and Covenants 138 (p. 859).

BIBLIOGRAPHY

Smith, Joseph Fielding. *Life of Joseph F. Smith: Sixth President of The Church of Jesus Christ of Latter-day Saints.* Salt Lake City: Deseret News Press, 1938.

SEB

Smith, Lucy Mack

Birth: 8 July 1775, Gilsum, Cheshire County, New Hampshire

Death: 14 May 1856, Nauvoo, Hancock County, Illinois

The mother of the Prophet Joseph Smith. The only reference to Lucy Mack Smith in the Doctrine and Covenants is in section 137. On 21 January 1836, as Joseph Smith was administering "ordinances of the endowment as far as they had then been revealed" in the Kirtland Temple, he had a vision of the celestial kingdom (137, headnote). In that kingdom he saw "Father Adam and Abraham; and my father and my mother; my brother Alvin, that has long

God Bless You, Mother!; *painting by Liz Lemon Swindle. Lucy Mack Smith, bidding farewell to her sons Joseph and Hyrum at their arrest in Far West, Missouri. While they were in Liberty Jail, the Lord promised the Prophet, "Thy friends do stand by thee, and they shall hail thee again with warm hearts and friendly hands" (D&C 121:9).*

since slept" (137:5). At the time, Joseph Sr. and Lucy Smith were still living.

Lucy Mack married Joseph Smith Sr. on 24 January 1796 in Tunbridge, Vermont. The Smiths lived in a number of towns in Vermont, including Sharon, Windsor County, where Joseph Smith Jr. was born 23 December 1805. After a number of crop failures in Vermont, the Smiths moved to Palmyra, New York, about 1816. Lucy experienced firsthand many of the early events of the Restoration. She was baptized shortly after the Church was organized in April 1830. When the Lord instructed the Church to move to Ohio, she led a group of about eighty members from the Fayette, New York, branch to Kirtland, Ohio, in May 1831. She migrated to Far West, Missouri, in the summer of 1838. When the Saints were driven from Missouri in 1839, she fled to Quincy, Illinois, and later to Nauvoo.

Lucy became the mother of eleven children. "My mother also is one of the noblest and the best of all women," wrote Joseph Smith. "May God grant to prolong her days" (5:126). The Lord heard Joseph's plea and extended the mortal life of his mother for many years.

Throughout her days, Lucy was bold in the cause of Christ. For example, when asked, "Is the Book of Mormon true?" without hesitation she replied, "That book . . . was brought forth by the power of God, and translated by the gift of the Holy Ghost; and, if I could make my voice sound as loud as the trumpet of Michael, the Archangel, I would declare the truth from land to land, and from sea to sea, and the echo should reach to every isle, until every member of the family of Adam should be left without excuse. For I do testify that God has revealed himself to man again in these last days" (L. M. Smith, *History*, 204).

At the October 1845 general conference in Nauvoo, seventy-year-old Lucy spoke of being "the mother of eleven children, seven of whom were boys." Since all but one son was dead by 1845, she wished to know whether the congregation still considered her a mother in Israel. Brigham Young arose and said, "All who consider Mother Smith as a mother in Israel, signify it by saying yes!—One universal 'yes' rang throughout" (Smith, *History*, 7:470–71).

Lucy lived the remainder of her days in Illinois. She died in 1856, having spent the last three years of her life with her daughter-in-law Emma Smith Bidamon.

BIBLIOGRAPHY

Smith, Joseph. *History of The Church of Jesus Christ of Latter-day Saints.* Edited by B. H. Roberts. 7 vols. 2d ed. rev. Salt Lake City: The Church of Jesus Christ of Latter-day Saints, 1932–51.

Smith, Lucy Mack. *History of Joseph Smith by His Mother.* Edited by Preston Nibley. Salt Lake City: Bookcraft, 1958.

SEB

Smith, Samuel H.

Birth: 13 March 1808, Tunbridge, Orange County, Vermont

Death: 30 July 1844, Nauvoo, Hancock County, Illinois

Samuel Harrison Smith believed in the visions of his brother Joseph and was baptized on 25 May 1829 by Oliver Cowdery, becoming the third person baptized in this dispensation. He was privileged to be one of the Eight Witnesses of the Book of Mormon and one of the six charter members of the Church. In April 1830 at Manchester, New York, Joseph Smith received a revelation informing his brother Samuel Smith that he was "under no condemnation, and thy calling is to exhortation, and to strengthen the church" (23:4). He is recognized as the first formally called missionary of the Church.

According to commandment, Samuel Smith was called to serve a mission to Missouri with Reynolds Cahoon (52:30). Their missionary labors took them approximately two thousand miles, mostly on foot. On 12 August 1831 he was counseled not to separate from Cahoon "until they return to their homes, and this for a wise purpose in me." The Lord addressed Samuel H. Smith as "my servant . . . with whom I am well pleased" (61:35). His next mission was announced at a conference held in Orange, Ohio, on 25 October 1831. He was called to journey with William E. McLellin "unto the eastern lands, [and] bear testimony in every place" (66:7–8). He also served a mission with Orson Hyde (75:13). It was a challenging mission that lasted eleven months and included travels from Ohio to Maine. Samuel Smith wrote that they "went from House to House and many during that day rejected us we shook off the dust from our feet as a testimony against them" ("Events," in Black, 295–96).

Besides missionary labors, Smith was appointed an agent for the Literary Firm and a member of the Kirtland high council (102:3).

Early in 1838 the Smiths moved to Far West, Missouri, and later, because of the persecution of the Latter-day Saints, left for Illinois, eventually settling in Nauvoo. There, he was an alderman, captain in the Nauvoo Legion, and a regent of the University of Nauvoo. On 19 January 1841 he was presented as a counselor to Bishop Vinson Knight (124:141).

In June 1844, when Samuel learned of the imprisonment of his brothers in Carthage Jail, he attempted to go to their aid. He was chased by a mob before arriving in Carthage. The next day he escorted the bodies of his slain brothers back to Nauvoo, where he told his mother, "Mother, I have had a dreadful distress in my side ever since I was chased by the mob, and I think I have received some injury which is going to make me sick" (L. M. Smith, *History*, 325). He suffered from bilious fever until his death less than five weeks after the martyrdom of his brothers Joseph and Hyrum. His obituary stated, "If ever there lived a good man upon the earth, Samuel H. Smith was that person" (Smith, *History*, 7:222).

BIBLIOGRAPHY

Black, Susan Easton. *Who's Who in the Doctrine and Covenants*. Salt Lake City: Deseret Book, 1997.

"Events in the Life of Samuel Harrison Smith Including His Missionary Journal for the Year 1832." Church History Library, The Church of Jesus Christ of Latter-day Saints, Salt Lake City, Utah.

Smith, Joseph. *History of The Church of Jesus Christ of Latter-day Saints*. Edited by B. H. Roberts. 7 vols. 2d ed. rev. Salt Lake City: The Church of Jesus Christ of Latter-day Saints, 1932–51.

Smith, Lucy Mack. *History of Joseph Smith by His Mother*. Edited by Preston Nibley. Salt Lake City: Bookcraft, 1954.

SEB

Smith, Sylvester

Birth: 28 March 1806, Tyringham, Berkshire County, Massachusetts

Death: 22 February 1880, Council Bluffs, Pottawattamie County, Iowa

Sylvester Smith was baptized into the Church in 1831. Though he served in various capacities in the Church, including as a scribe for the Prophet Joseph, Sylvester Smith is perhaps best known for his struggles in ZION'S CAMP, which included criticism of camp leaders and various confrontations. On one particular occasion, Smith "marched his company" to the music of a fife made by Levi Hancock. As retold by George A. Smith years later, "a dog came out and barked," and Sylvester declared he was going to kill it. The Prophet then reproved Sylvester for his contentious spirit and "predicted that if he did not get rid of [that spirit], the day would come when a dog would gnaw his flesh, and he not have the power to resist it" (*JD*, 11:7).

Sylvester Smith's name appears in the Doctrine and Covenants three times. In the first instance, he was called in 1832 to join with Gideon Carter and preach the gospel, "whether to the east or to the west, or to the north, or to the south" (75:26, 34). Of this experience he stated that he had "travelled about five hundred miles in about six weeks, and held about fifteen meetings" and that he trusted the Lord to continue to "support [him] even to the end" (MH; Smith, *History*, 1:388). In February 1834 Smith was chosen with others to form "a standing council for the church" (102:3, 34) in Kirtland, on which he served for about a year. In August 1834 he was tried for slandering the Prophet Joseph. He confessed his wrongdoing and was forgiven. In February 1835 he was called as a president of the Seventy but was released in April 1837. He became disaffected and left the Church by 1838. Sylvester Smith ultimately moved to Council Bluffs, Iowa, where he practiced law. He died in 1880.

BIBLIOGRAPHY

Manuscript History of the Church, 14 July 1833. L. Tom Perry Special Collections, Harold B. Lee Library, Brigham Young University, Provo, Utah.

Smith, George A. *Journal of Discourses*. 26 vols. London: Latter-day Saints' Book Depot, 1854–86.

Smith, Joseph. *History of The Church of Jesus Christ of Latter-day Saints*. Edited by B. H. Roberts. 7 vols. 2d ed. rev. Salt Lake City: The Church of Jesus Christ of Latter-day Saints, 1932–51.

ZLL

Smith, William

Birth: 13 March 1811, Royalton, Windsor County, Vermont

Death: 13 November 1893, Osterdock, Clayton County, Iowa

William Smith, a younger brother of Joseph Smith, was baptized in June 1830 by David Whitmer. By 1831 he had moved with his family to Kirtland, Ohio. Smith participated in ZION'S CAMP in 1834. In February 1835 he was ordained an apostle. Smith attended the School of the Prophets and the dedication of the Kirtland Temple. He was a charter member of the Kirtland Safety Society, a banking venture. Smith joined other Latter-day Saints in Missouri until they were expelled from that state in 1839. He then moved to Illinois.

William Smith was known for his volatility and stubbornness. He was charged with a rebellious spirit in 1835 and with unchristian conduct in 1836. In both instances he confessed his wrongs and was forgiven. He was disfellowshipped in 1839 but was soon restored to fellowship. He was elected to the Nauvoo city council and also served several missions. The name of William Smith appears in a listing of the members of the Twelve in January 1841 (124:129).

He was serving a mission in the east when his brothers Joseph and Hyrum were murdered on 27 June 1844. With the death of his brother Samuel a month later, William became the only surviving brother of the family. He was ordained as patriarch to the Church in May 1845 but by October 1845 was excommunicated for apostasy. He affiliated with the Strangite movement and the Reorganized Church of Jesus Christ of Latter Day Saints. William Smith died at age eighty-two in Iowa.

William Smith, 1811–1893.

See also Apostles, the first Twelve of latter days.

KD

Snider, John

Birth: 11 February 1800, New Brunswick, Nova Scotia, Canada

Death: 18 December 1875, Salt Lake City, Salt Lake County, Utah

While living in the greater Toronto area, John Snider and others joined with former Methodist preacher John Taylor for religious discussions. When Latter-day Saint missionary Parley P. Pratt attended their discussions and satisfactorily answered their questions, Snider asked for and received baptism in June 1836. In 1837 he was ordained a priest and served his first mission to the British Isles. About a year later, he settled in Far West, Missouri, and was expelled with the Saints in 1839. He then settled in Springfield, Illinois, before taking up residence in Nauvoo by 1840. In 1841 he served on the Prophet Joseph Smith's staff as a guard "and assistant [aide]-de-camp" in the Nauvoo Legion (Smith, 4:296). Subsequently, the Prophet called Snider and others to build the Nauvoo House, "a house for boarding, . . . that the weary traveler may find health and safety while he shall contemplate the word of the Lord" (124:22–23). Snider, George Miller, Lyman Wight, and Peter Haws were directed to "organize themselves, and appoint one of them to be a president over their quorum for the purpose of building [the] house" and to "form a constitution, whereby they may receive stock" to assist them in their building efforts (124:62–63). Strict directives were given concerning the purchase of the stocks (124:64–82).

In a revelation dated 22 December 1841, Snider was called to serve another mission to England, this time to collect money and materials to assist in the building of the Nauvoo House and the Nauvoo Temple (Smith, 4:561). He left in March 1842 and returned in January 1843.

After the Prophet was martyred, Snider helped to guard his remains. He helped dispose of the Saints' property after the exodus from Nauvoo, participated in the California gold rush, and later joined his family in Salt Lake City, where he died in 1875.

BIBLIOGRAPHY

Smith, Joseph. *History of The Church of Jesus Christ of Latter-day Saints.* Edited by B. H. Roberts. 7 vols. 2d ed. rev. Salt Lake City: The Church of Jesus Christ of Latter-day Saints, 1932–51.

KWF

Snow, Erastus

Birth: 9 November 1818, St. Johnsbury, Caledonia County, Vermont

Death: 27 May 1888, Salt Lake City, Salt Lake County, Utah

From the time of his baptism at age fourteen in Derby Lake, Vermont, until his death in 1888, Erastus Snow labored to build up the kingdom of God. He served his first mission at age fifteen and afterwards served multiple missions in the United States and a mission to Scandinavia. He went to Kirtland, Ohio, in December 1835, where he attended the School of Elders and later participated in the dedication of the Kirtland Temple in March 1836. In June 1838, after three missionary excursions to the eastern states, Snow moved to Missouri, intending to help build up Zion there. Forced out of Missouri with the other Saints, Snow eventually

Erastus Snow, 1818–1888.

Courtesy Church History Library

settled with his family in Montrose, Iowa, where he served on the high council in 1839. He then moved to Nauvoo and served several additional missions to the eastern states. Upon learning of the martyrdom of Joseph Smith, he returned from a mission in Massachusetts and helped complete the Nauvoo Temple.

With Ezra T. Benson, Snow was instructed to "organize a company" for the trek west (136:12). He was one of the first to see the Salt Lake Valley, which elicited hat waving and a shout of "hosanna" from him and his companion, Orson Pratt.

Snow became a counselor in the Salt Lake Stake presidency in October 1848 and was ordained an apostle of the Lord Jesus Christ on 12 February 1849. During the next forty years he engaged in missionary work, oversaw emigration, and colonized settlements.

The force of Elder Snow's testimony was felt by those who heard him speak. President Joseph F. Smith stated, "As an orator and profound reasoner, I always felt impressed that he had no superior, especially when he warmed up to his subject, and entered into his discourse with the full force and energy of his active and vigorous mind" (199).

BIBLIOGRAPHY

Smith, Joseph F. *Gospel Doctrine.* Salt Lake City: Deseret Book, 1977.

KWF

Snow, Lorenzo

Birth: 3 April 1814, Mantua, Portage County, Ohio

Death: 10 October 1901, Salt Lake City, Salt Lake County, Utah

Raised on a farm, Lorenzo Snow learned much about hard work and developed a love of reading. As a young man he had been attracted to the military, joining when he was twenty-one. In September 1835 he started out for Oberlin College in Ohio, hoping that further education would enhance his opportunities in the military. He met Elder David W. Patten en route to Oberlin and was deeply impressed with his reasoning about God's purpose for his children on earth. This and other experiences led to Snow's

Lorenzo Snow, 1814–1901; portrait by Frederick Hawkins Piercy.

Courtesy Church History Library

baptism on 23 June 1836 by John Boynton, an apostle.

Over the next two years (1837–39), Lorenzo Snow served missions to Ohio, Missouri, Illinois, and Kentucky. He served a mission to Great Britain from 1840 to 1843, during which time he presented a copy of the Book of Mormon to Queen Victoria and published the pamphlet *The Only Way to Be Saved.* After this mission, he joined the Latter-day Saints in Nauvoo. In 1846 he departed with his family from Nauvoo, arriving in the Salt Lake Valley in the summer of 1848. On 12 February 1849 he was called to the Quorum of the Twelve Apostles. In 1853 Elder Snow was called by Brigham Young to settle the area known at that time as Box Elder and which he later named Brigham City after President Brigham Young.

Lorenzo Snow served as president of the Utah Territorial Legislative Council from 1872 to 1882. He participated in the second dedication of Palestine in March 1873. He was called and sustained as a counselor to Brigham Young in April 1873 and began to establish the United Order in Brigham City; his success in that endeavor was unequaled among all the communities of the Saints.

In 1885 Elder Snow was arrested for practicing plural marriage, and he served an eleven-month prison sentence in 1886–87. After the death of President John Taylor in 1889, he became president of the Quorum of the Twelve at the time Wilford Woodruff was sustained as president of the Church. As president of the Twelve, he called for a sustaining vote following the reading of Official Declaration 1, the Manifesto on the cessation of plural marriage (OD 1). After the dedication of the Salt Lake Temple in 1893, President Snow was set apart as temple president at age seventy-nine. He served in that capacity until the death of President Wilford Woodruff in September 1898.

After President Woodruff's death, Lorenzo Snow petitioned the Lord for direction. The Savior appeared to him in the Salt Lake Temple and instructed him to proceed to reorganize the First Presidency.

As the fifth president of the Church, Lorenzo Snow was known for his famous couplet, "As man now is, God once was; As God now is, man may be" (Williams, 2). President Snow inherited the pressing problems of the Church's financial debt, which had come about in part due to years of persecution and legal expenses incurred by litigation over plural marriage. He prayerfully sought a solution to these financial problems and was directed to emphasize the law of tithing to the Saints. Speaking of the success of President Snow's efforts to bring the Church out of financial despair, President Heber J. Grant said, "[He] came to the presidency of the Church when he was eighty-five years of age, and what he accomplished during the next three years of his life is simply marvelous to contemplate. He lifted the Church from . . . almost financial bankruptcy . . . and made its credit A No. 1. . . . This man, beyond the age of ability in the estimation of the world, this man who had not been engaged in financial affairs . . . took hold of the finances of the Church of Christ, under the inspiration of the living God, and in those three years changed everything, financially, from darkness to light. I know that Lorenzo Snow was God's mouthpiece upon the earth, that he was the representative of the Lord and that he was in very deed a Prophet of God" (847).

On 10 October 1901, just four days after general conference, President Lorenzo Snow died of pneumonia at age eighty-seven.

See also Official Declaration 1.

BIBLIOGRAPHY

Gibbons, Francis M. *Lorenzo Snow: Spiritual Giant, Prophet of God*. Salt Lake City: Deseret Book, 1982.

Grant, Heber J. "Inspiration and Integrity of the Prophets." *Improvement Era* 22 (August 1919): 841–54.

Romney, Thomas C. *The Life of Lorenzo Snow*. Salt Lake City: Deseret Book, 1955.

Williams, Clyde J., comp. *The Teachings of Lorenzo Snow*. Salt Lake City: Bookcraft, 1984.

CJW

Solemn assembly/assemblies

Special gatherings where endowments of power were received, Church leaders were sustained, a house of the Lord (temple) dedicated, and other important Church business conducted. During the Kirtland and Missouri era of the Church (1831–38), particularly, such spiritual manifestations as visions, speaking in tongues, and prophesying were experienced at times in these meetings.

The first reference in the Doctrine and Covenants to such an assembly is in the November 1831 revelation originally designated as an appendix to the Book of Commandments, the first compilation of revelations received by the Prophet Joseph Smith in this dispensation. To prepare for the Savior's second coming, the Saints were instructed to "sanctify yourselves; gather ye together, O ye people of my church, upon the land of Zion. . . . Go ye out from Babylon. Be ye clean that bear the vessels of the Lord. Call your solemn assemblies" (133:4–6; cf. 38:42; 53:2).

The next scriptural reference to such a gathering is in section 88, received in December 1832, wherein the Saints were again commanded to "sanctify yourselves that your minds become single to God, and the days will come that you shall see him . . . and it shall be in his own time, and in his own way, and according to his own will. . . . Tarry ye, tarry ye in this place [Kirtland], and call a solemn assembly" (88:68–70). In that revelation the Lord also commanded the building of the Kirtland Temple and the organization of the School of the Prophets (88:119–20, 127–41). The School of the Prophets, the purposes of which fit the intent of a solemn assembly, was begun early in 1833, and those attending witnessed an abundance of spiritual manifestations, including speaking in tongues (Minute Book 1, vv. 6–8). Letters sent to Missouri in early 1833 prompted the holding of a series of solemn assemblies as times of confession and repentance (Minute Book 2, vv. 3–34; Letter Book, 11 January 1833, 14 January 1833, and 21 April 1833).

In June 1833 the Lord chastened the Saints for delaying the building of the temple, indicating that although many had been called, "but few of them are chosen," and those "not chosen have sinned a very grievous sin, in that they are walking in darkness at noon-day. And for this cause I gave unto you a commandment that you should call your solemn assembly, that your fastings and your mourning might come up into the ears of the Lord of Sabaoth" (95:3–7). The Saints started to build the Kirtland Temple immediately.

By the fall of 1835, the first elders of the Church, "the first laborers in this last kingdom" (88:70), were gathering in Kirtland to attend a solemn assembly at which a promised endowment was to be bestowed. In remarks to the Twelve on 12 November 1835, Joseph Smith explained: "We must have all things prepared, and call our solemn assembly as the Lord has commanded us, that we may be able to accomplish His great work, and it must be done in God's own way. The house of the Lord must be prepared, and the solemn assembly called and organized in it, according to the order of the house of God; and in it we must attend to the ordinance of washing of feet. . . . It is calculated to unite our hearts, that we may be one in feeling and sentiment, and that our faith may be strong, so that Satan cannot overthrow us, nor have any power over us here. . . . I feel disposed to speak a few words more to you, my brethren, concerning the endowment: All who are prepared, and are sufficiently pure to abide the presence of the Savior, will see Him in the solemn assembly" (2:308–10). A solemn assembly was anticipated in a revelation received in December 1835, that

instructed Lyman Sherman to "wait patiently until the solemn assembly shall be called of my servants" (108:4), when he would receive his ordination.

Several preliminary gatherings, at which preparatory ordinances (washings, anointings, and blessings) were performed during the early weeks of 1836, culminated in the dedication of the Kirtland house of the Lord on 27 March. In the dedicatory prayer, the Prophet acknowledged the Lord's instructions: "And as thou hast said in a revelation, given to us, calling us thy friends, saying—Call your solemn assembly, as I have commanded you" (109:6). Many witnessed remarkable spiritual experiences during the dedication. *See* Kirtland Temple dedication.

Undoubtedly, many of these earlier gatherings, both in Missouri and Kirtland, including the dedicatory services of the Kirtland Temple, may be considered solemn assemblies. In addition, a special solemn assembly, held 30 March 1836, three days after the dedication of the temple, seems to fit the description of such a meeting given by the Prophet the preceding November (1835), including the ordinance of washing of feet and the promise of seeing the Lord. The Prophet's history describes that solemn assembly: "At eight o'clock [A.M.], according to appointment, the Presidency, the Twelve, the Seventies, the High Council, the Bishops and their entire quorums, the Elders and all the official members in this stake of Zion, amounting to about three hundred, met in the Temple of the Lord to attend to the ordinance of washing of feet"; "the Presidency proceeded to wash the feet of the Twelve, pronouncing many prophecies and blessings upon them in the name of the Lord Jesus; and then the Twelve proceeded to wash the feet of the Presidents of the several quorums." The meeting continued with the brethren prophesying "upon each other's heads," partaking of the sacrament, and receiving instructions from the Prophet Joseph Smith. At "about nine o'clock in the evening," the Prophet "left the meeting in the charge of the Twelve" and retired for the night. "The brethren continued exhorting, prophesying, and speaking in tongues until five o'clock in the morning. The Savior made His appearance to some, while angels ministered to others, and it was a Pentecost and an endowment indeed, long to be remembered" (2:430–33).

The final reference to solemn assemblies in the Doctrine and Covenants is found in 124:39, which emphasizes that solemn assemblies, along with other sacred ordinances, "are ordained by the ordinance of my holy house, which my people are always commanded to build unto my holy name."

Solemn assemblies are held in the Church when a new First Presidency is sustained, at the dedication of temples, and in special leadership training meetings (Turley, 3:1390–91).

BIBLIOGRAPHY

Haight, David B. "Solemn Assemblies." *Ensign* 24 (November 1994): 14–17.

Joseph Smith Letter Book 1. Church History Library, The Church of Jesus Christ of Latter-day Saints, Salt Lake City, Utah.

Minute Book 2. Church History Library, The Church of Jesus Christ of Latter-day Saints, Salt Lake City, Utah.

Smith, Joseph. *History of The Church of Jesus Christ of Latter-day Saints.* Edited by B. H. Roberts. 7 vols. 2d ed. rev. Salt Lake City: The Church of Jesus Christ of Latter-day Saints, 1932–51.

Turley, Richard E., Jr. "Solemn Assemblies." In *Encyclopedia of Mormonism,* edited by Daniel H. Ludlow et al. 4 vols. New York: Macmillan, 1992.

JFD

Solemn proclamation

A formal, earnest, public declaration of an official position on important matters. In the opening verses of section 124 the Lord enjoined Joseph Smith "to make a solemn proclamation of my gospel, and of this stake [Nauvoo] which I have planted to be a cornerstone of Zion, . . . to all the kings of the world, to the four corners thereof, to the honorable president-elect, and the high-minded governors of the nation in which you live, and to all the nations of the earth scattered abroad" (vv. 2–7). The revelation further directed Robert B. Thompson, general Church clerk and Joseph Smith's secretary, and others (vv. 12, 103–7) to assist in making the proclamation. Thompson helped produce a draft, now in the Church Archives, which was not finished, presumably because of

his death on 27 August 1841. On 21 November 1843 Joseph Smith instructed Willard Richards, Orson Hyde, John Taylor, and William W. Phelps to write a proclamation to the kings of the earth. This effort was interrupted by Joseph Smith's presidential campaign and his assassination.

In 1845 a proclamation, created in response to the Lord's instructions in section 124, was published. It was written by Parley P. Pratt but acknowledged as a *Proclamation of the Twelve Apostles of the Church of Jesus Christ, of Latter-day Saints: To All the Kings of the World; to the President of the United States of America; to the Governors of the Several States; and to the Rulers and People of All Nations.* This 16-page pamphlet, printed at the shop of the New York *Prophet,* a Church-owned newspaper, was advertised in the *Prophet* on 1 March 1845. The advertisement noted that a "few specimen copies" (Crawley, 296) had just been published, but no more would be printed until it was endorsed by the Twelve. Such an endorsement came in a letter to Elder Pratt from Brigham Young, dated 26 May 1845, which spoke approvingly of the proclamation and of Elder Pratt's activities in New York. Elder Pratt stated on the pamphlet's last page that he would endeavor to print one hundred thousand copies at the *Prophet* press for free distribution. The *New-York Messenger,* the *Prophet*'s successor, solicited donations towards the printing costs in August and September 1845. Neither of these endeavors was successful, and no further copies were printed in the United States.

It fell to Wilford Woodruff in England to put the proclamation into wider circulation. He announced in the *Millennial Star,* 15 October 1845, that he had just received a copy of the *Proclamation of the Twelve Apostles* with a request to reprint it for distribution in Europe. In this announcement he made it clear that the pamphlet was published in fulfillment of the revelation (124), that it was necessary to circulate it "in order that the present generation may be left without excuse," and that it would have to be distributed gratis, with the Saints bearing the costs. On 22 October 1845, he received the first of twenty thousand copies from the printer. He sent a copy of the pamphlet to Dan Jones, who translated it into Welsh and two months later published a Welsh edition of four thousand copies.

Dated 6 April 1845, the *Proclamation of the Twelve Apostles* declares that the kingdom of God is again established on the earth, that the authority of that kingdom rests with the Latter-day Saints, and that all people are to repent and be baptized into The Church of Jesus Christ of Latter-day Saints. To the kings and rulers it says, "You are also hereby commanded, in the name of Jesus Christ, to put your silver and your gold, your ships and steam-vessels, your railroad trains and your horses, chariots, camels, mules, and litters, into active use, for the fulfilment of these purposes" (Clark, 1:255).

The American Indians, it asserts, are a remnant of the tribes of Israel and must be educated and civilized, for they are to assist in building the city of the New Jerusalem in America. The proclamation concludes with a series of one-sentence statements summarizing the Church's fundamental positions, each followed by the phrase *"And we know it"* (Clark, 1:263–64).

Section 124 instructed Joseph Smith to write the proclamation "in the spirit of meekness" (124:4), but those outside of Mormonism must have viewed the *Proclamation of the Twelve Apostles* as a rather audacious tract—a fact Woodruff seems to have understood when, in the *Millennial Star*, 15 October 1845, he urged the elders to use wisdom in distributing it "so as not unnecessarily to expose themselves to difficulties and persecution." The full text of the proclamation can be found in *Messages of the First Presidency* (Clark, 1:252–66).

See also Historical context and overview of Doctrine and Covenants 124 (p. 837).

BIBLIOGRAPHY

Clark, James R., comp. *Messages of the First Presidency of The Church of Jesus Christ of Latter-day Saints, 1833–1964.* 6 vols. Salt Lake City: Bookcraft, 1965–75.

Crawley, Peter. *A Descriptive Bibliography of the Mormon Church.* Provo, Utah: Religious Studies Center, Brigham Young University, 1997.

PC

Solemn, solemnity

Serious, earnest, sacred, and reverent (e.g., 124:2, 107; OD 1). *Solemn* is most often used in the Bible in the phrase "solemn assembly," referring to the sacred festivals in ancient Israel (Lev. 23:36; Deut. 16:8, 15) and in the Doctrine and Covenants to the sacred meetings associated with the dedication of temples and spiritual preparation of leaders (88:70, 117; 95:7; 108:4; 109:6, 10; 124:39; 133:6; Smith, 2:308–10). *See* Solemn assembly/assemblies.

Elsewhere in the Doctrine and Covenants the words *solemn* and *solemnity* are also used to describe the proper manner of offering the SACRAMENT prayers (20:76) and of proclaiming the GOSPEL (84:61). The phrase "in solemnity" occurs in passages where the Lord commands his followers to maintain proper reverence in their minds and hearts (84:61; 100:7) and actions (107:84). The Lord commands the elders to "let the solemnities of eternity rest upon your minds" (43:34)—a phrase commonly used in the preaching of the nineteenth century—perhaps impressing upon them that the choices they make in mortality have eternal consequences. A form of the words *solemn/solemnity* also occurs in the phrase "marriages have during that period been solemnized" (OD 1, paragraph 2).

BIBLIOGRAPHY

Smith, Joseph. *History of The Church of Jesus Christ of Latter-day Saints.* Edited by B. H. Roberts. 7 vols. 2d ed. rev. Salt Lake City: The Church of Jesus Christ of Latter-day Saints, 1932–51.

DRS

Solomon

King of Israel, ca. 971–931 B.C. (1 Kgs. 1–11). The only references to Solomon in the Doctrine and Covenants appear in relation to Joseph Smith's inquiry of the Lord about the legitimacy of plural marriages among ancient patriarchs and kings (132:1). *See* Marriage.

The Prophet was told that Solomon and other men in the Bible did not sin in having multiple wives, "save in those things which they received not of me" (132:38).

Solomon succeeded his father, David, to rule Israel in an era of unprecedented material well-being. The Bible presents him as faithful and righteous in his early years—communing with God, building the temple, and being blessed with both wisdom and riches. In his later years, however, Solomon fell into wicked practices, including his marriages to "seven hundred wives" and "three hundred concubines" (1 Kgs. 11:3), who led him into idolatrous practices. The Bible acknowledges Solomon's fall, yet because his reign was characterized by peace, prosperity, and national unity, it was later looked upon as the apex of Israel's earthly glory (e.g., Luke 12:27).

KPJ

Son Ahman

A name-title of JESUS CHRIST in the Adamic language. In the standard works, the term *Son Ahman* is found only in Doctrine and Covenants 78:20 and 95:17 and refers to Jesus Christ. The Book of Commandments and Revelations includes "a Sample of pure Language given by Joseph the Seer" (Jensen et al., 265). In the sample given by Joseph, the name of God is *Awmen* and the name of the Son of God is *Son Awmen*, which W. W. Phelps later spelled as *Ahman* (Jensen et al., 269). The meaning of the word is "the being which made all things in all its parts," or, in short, the Creator. The name of Jesus in that tongue is given as *Son (or San) Awman* or, in other words, the Son of the Creator (Jensen et al., 265, 269; Pratt, 2:342).

See also Son of Man.

BIBLIOGRAPHY

Jensen, Robin Scott, Robert J. Woodford, and Steven C. Harper, eds. *Manuscript Revelation Books.* Facsimile edition. First volume of the Revelations and Translations series of *The Joseph Smith Papers*, edited by Dean C. Jessee, Ronald K. Esplin, and Richard Lyman Bushman. Salt Lake City: Church Historian's Press, 2009.

Pratt, Orson. *Journal of Discourses.* 26 vols. London: Latter-day Saints' Book Depot, 1854–86.

RDD

Son of Man

An English translation of the Adamic name-title of JESUS CHRIST. In "the language of Adam," the name of the Father is "Man of Holiness . . . and the name of his Only Begotten is the Son of Man," or Son of Man of Holiness (Moses 6:57).

There are more than twelve references to

Jesus as the Son of Man in the Doctrine and Covenants. In a revelation to the Prophet Joseph Smith in March 1831, God the Father acknowledged that the Son of Man was indeed his Only Begotten Son whom he sent into the world "for the redemption of the world" (49:5–6). In the dedicatory prayer of the Kirtland Temple, Joseph Smith indicated that the Saints had built the temple so "that the Son of Man might have a place to manifest himself to his people" (109:5). While in Liberty Jail, lamenting his many trials and struggles, Joseph Smith was reminded that "the Son of Man hath descended below them all. Art thou greater than he?" (122:8). Other references to the Son of Man in the Doctrine and Covenants have to do with prophecies and warnings concerning his second coming (e.g., 45:39; 61:38; 64:23; 68:11) and the resurrection (76:16).

See also Son Ahman.

RDD

Songs, singing

Soon after the Church was organized, the Lord instructed Emma Smith to "make a selection of sacred hymns" for the Church, "for my soul delighteth in the song of the heart; yea, the song of the righteous is a prayer unto me, and it shall be answered with a blessing upon their heads" (25:11–12). *See* Historical context and overview of Doctrine and Covenants 25 (p. 733).

Latter-day revelation states that as the righteous are gathered out from among the nations, they will come to Zion "singing with songs of everlasting joy" (45:71). In anticipation of his second coming the Lord declared that even the earth, sun, moon, and stars will join in singing praises (128:23). The Saints also "shall lift up their voice, and with the voice together sing this new song" (84:98). The Lord revealed to Joseph Smith the words of this new song, which emphasize the great work of bringing forth Zion and the glory of God, "for he is full of mercy, / Justice, grace and truth, and peace" (84:102). At the resurrection the risen Saints will express their joy and praise, "and they shall sing the song of the Lamb, day and night forever and ever" (133:56; cf. 109:78–80; Rev. 15:3).

CDG

Sons of God

Those worthy of receiving exaltation in the celestial kingdom. The phrase "sons of God" is found six times in the Doctrine and Covenants. Two of those references equate becoming sons of God with having "eternal life" and being "gods" (45:8; 76:58). Three of the references affirm that those who "believe" on the name of the Savior and "receive" him "may become the sons of God, even one in me as I am one in the Father, as the Father is one in me, that we may be one" (11:30; 34:3; 35:2; cf. 42:52). The sixth reference is found in 128:20–23, wherein Joseph Smith enjoins "all the sons of God" to "shout for joy" in gratitude for the restoration of gospel truths and priesthood authority, providing salvation for the living and the dead.

Although these scriptures speak in terms of sons, the restored gospel makes clear that righteous daughters who believe on the name of the Savior and receive him by way of saving ordinances (e.g., 39:4–6) qualify for the same eternal rewards. They too are designated "gods" who "shall pass by the angels, and the gods, which are set there, to their exaltation and glory in all things, as hath been sealed upon their heads, which glory shall be a fulness and a continuation of the seeds forever and ever" (132:19–23; cf. 76:50–70). *See* Gods. They are among those who, through the Savior's power and atonement, "are begotten sons and daughters unto God" (76:24).

How to become sons of God and receive the attendant blessings is taught in the standard works (e.g., John 1:12; Revelation 21:7; 3 Nephi 9:17; Moroni 7:26, 48; Moses 6:68). The apostle Paul taught, "For as many as are led by the Spirit of God, they are the sons of God. . . . The Spirit itself beareth witness with our spirit, that we are the children of God: and if children, then heirs; heirs of God, and joint-heirs with Christ; if so be that we suffer with him, that we may be also glorified together" (Rom. 8:14–17; cf. D&C 25:1).

See also Jesus Christ, sons and daughters of.

DLB

Sons of Levi

The descendants of the tribe of Levi, who were designated by revelation to be Israel's priesthood bearers under the law of Moses (Ex. 28:1; Num. 3:1–9). The PRIESTHOOD they held is called the Aaronic, or Levitical, Priesthood (107:1, 6). All three occurrences of "sons of Levi" in the Doctrine and Covenants reflect language from Malachi 3:3. In a letter to the Saints, Joseph Smith quoted that verse in its entirety. God will "purify the sons of Levi, and purge them as gold and silver, that they may offer unto the Lord an offering in righteousness" (128:24), foretelling a latter-day restoration of the role of the Levites. The prophecy also points to the restoration of the Jews in general (Mal. 3:4). When John the Baptist ordained Joseph Smith and Oliver Cowdery to the same priesthood that the ancient Levites held, he said that it would remain on earth "until the sons of Levi do offer again an offering unto the Lord in righteousness" (13:1). An 1841 revelation to Joseph Smith teaches that the restoration of temples and temple work was a necessary precursor to the restoration of the sons of Levi to their priesthood (124:37–40).

See also Malachi quotations in the Doctrine and Covenants.

KPJ

Sons of Moses and of Aaron

Worthy males who receive the Aaronic and Melchizedek priesthoods and magnify their calling "become the sons of Moses and of Aaron" (84:33–34). In a PRIESTHOOD context, faithful priesthood holders become adopted sons of Moses and Aaron, regardless of their lineage, much like Gentiles are accounted the seed of Abraham by putting on Christ through baptism (Abr. 2:8–11; Gal. 3:27–29).

Of these priesthood sons of Moses and Aaron, the Lord revealed that they "shall offer an acceptable offering and sacrifice in the house of the Lord" and "shall be filled with the glory of the Lord, upon Mount Zion in the Lord's house" (84:31–32). That house has reference, in part, to the temple which the Lord commanded the Saints to build in Jackson County, Missouri, in 1831–32 (57:1–3). Presumably, the fulfillment of the promises pertaining to the sons of Moses and Aaron in that temple will be realized when it is built at some future time. The Saints were not able to build the temple in Jackson County in their generation because "their enemies" hindered them from "performing that work," and the Lord excused the Saints from that responsibility at that time (124:49–52). Nevertheless, "Zion shall not be moved out of her place, notwithstanding her children are scattered. They that remain, and are pure in heart, shall return . . . to build up the waste places of Zion" and to raise their temple (101:17–18; cf. 101; 103; 105).

REL

Sons of perdition

Willful followers of the devil, who "was called Perdition" (29:36–37; 76:25–29); in Greek *perdition* means "destruction" (cf. John 17:12, "sons of destruction" NIV). Such sons of perdition "know" the power of God, "and have been made partakers thereof, and suffered themselves through the power of the devil to be overcome, and to deny the truth and defy [God's] power . . . having denied the Holy Spirit after having received it, and having denied the Only Begotten Son of the Father, having crucified him unto themselves and put him to an open shame . . . after the Father has revealed him" (76:31–35, 43; cf. 132:26–27). The Prophet Joseph Smith explained that for a man to become a son of perdition, "he must receive the Holy Ghost, have the heavens opened unto him, and know God, and then sin against him. After a man has sinned against the Holy Ghost, there is no repentance for him. He has got to say that the sun does not shine while he sees it; he has got to deny Jesus Christ when the heavens have been opened unto him, and to deny the plan of salvation with his eyes open to the truth of it" (6:314). This most grievous of all sins is not hasty, careless, or accidental. It is knowing, willful, and deliberate. And it is a sin limited to premortality and mortality. The Prophet declared, "No man can commit the unpardonable sin

after the dissolution of the body, nor in this life, until he receives the Holy Ghost; but they must do it in this world" (6:314). In the premortal world, "a third part of the hosts of heaven" became sons of perdition by joining SATAN in his rebellion against God and Christ in the WAR IN HEAVEN. They were "cast out into the earth" and denied the opportunity to obtain physical bodies and receive any level of SALVATION (Rev. 12:7–11; D&C 29:36–37; 76:43–44; cf. Ehat and Cook, 60). Since there can be no salvation without repentance, these "cannot be redeemed from their spiritual fall, because they repent not" (29:44). Having willfully and defiantly forsaken the truth they once embraced, there is no repentance for sons of perdition. The Prophet taught, "You cannot save such persons; you cannot bring them to repentance; they make open war, like the devil, and awful is the consequence" (6:315). Unwilling to repent, they must suffer even as Jesus suffered (19:15–18). They grow dark in mind and experience extreme bitterness of soul. Joseph declared, "A man is his own tormentor and his own condemner. Hence the saying, They shall go into the lake that burns with fire and brimstone. The torment of disappointment in the mind of man is as exquisite as a lake burning with fire and brimstone. I say, so is the torment of man" (6:314; cf. D&C 63:17; 76:36; 2 Ne. 9:16; Mosiah 3:25–27; Alma 15:3). These lost individuals experience no literal flame or piercing knives but suffer the searing pains of mental anguish created by the "consciousness of [their] filthiness" and "nakedness before God" (Morm. 9:4–5). They suffer "eternal punishment, to reign with the devil and his angels in eternity, where their worm dieth not, and the fire is not quenched, which is their torment" (76:44). Because of their open, willful rebellion against God, light, and truth, they are eventually confronted by "the demands of divine justice" and the glory and holiness of Jesus Christ (Mosiah 2:38; Morm. 9:4–5). And their "hell" is of their own making.

Of the ultimate destiny of the sons of perdition, the Lord has revealed, "And the end thereof, neither the place thereof, nor their torment, no man knows; neither was it revealed, neither is, neither will be revealed unto man, except to them who are made partakers thereof; nevertheless, I, the Lord, show it by vision unto many, but straightway shut it up again; wherefore, the end, the width, the height, the depth, and the misery thereof, they understand not, neither any man except those who are ordained unto this condemnation" (76:45–48). Although "no man knoweth *on earth*" the "end" of the sons of perdition, the Lord has indicated that more may be made known at the final judgment (43:33; emphasis added).

Sons of perdition are begotten not in sin and darkness but in virtue and light. There must be a rising before there can be a falling. Only one who has risen to heights of truth and glory can sink to the very depths of error and darkness. Such a one was Lucifer, another name for the devil, whose very name means "light-bearing" (*Webster's*, s.v. "Lucifer"). He was, in the beginning, an angel of light, "an angel of God who was in authority in the presence of God" (76:25). Becoming jealous of the Father's power and the Savior's position as the Firstborn, however, Lucifer "rebelled against God, and sought to take the kingdom of our God and his Christ." He chose to become the archenemy of the Father and the Son and to make "war with the saints of God" (76:28–29). He chose to become the "prince of this world," or "the prince of darkness, who is of this world" (127:11; JST John 14:30). He chose to become the preeminent son of perdition, and the third part of the premortal heavenly hosts, as well as those who become sons of perdition during their mortal lives, did likewise. Sons of perdition are self-made devils.

See also Innocent blood; Judgment(s); Kingdoms of glory and perdition, vision of; Punish, punished, punishment.

BIBLIOGRAPHY

Ehat, Andrew F., and Lyndon W. Cook, comps. and eds. *The Words of Joseph Smith*. Provo, Utah: Religious Studies Center, Brigham Young University, 1980.

Merriam-Webster's Collegiate Dictionary. 11th edition. Springfield, Mass.: Merriam-Webster, 2008.

Smith, Joseph. *History of The Church of Jesus Christ of Latter-day Saints*. Edited by B. H. Roberts. 7 vols. 2d ed. rev. Salt Lake City: The Church of Jesus Christ of Latter-day Saints, 1932–51.

RT

Sorcerer, sorcerers. *See* Appendix E.

Soul

Term used in the Doctrine and Covenants with several distinctions:

1. Both "the spirit and the body" of an individual (88:15), united.

2. Something distinct from the body, that is, one's spirit, as in 59:18–19: "Yea, all things which come of the earth . . . are made for the benefit and the use of man . . . yea, for food and for raiment, for taste and for smell, to strengthen the body and to enliven the soul" (cf. Alma 36:15; 40:18, 21, 23; Abr. 3:22–23).

3. The very center or core of one's emotional/intellectual self or nature (e.g., 56:16; 108:2; 117:11; 121:7; 2 Ne. 4:15–16; Enos 1:9; Hel. 5:30). In this context, the Lord promised Hyrum Smith that the Spirit would enlighten his mind and fill his "soul with joy" (11:13; cf. 25:12). Also, those called to service in the kingdom of God are told to throw their whole selves into the work, to serve "with all your soul" (30:11; 31:5; cf. 4:2–4). And those who exercise the priesthood righteously are promised that the doctrines of the priesthood (121:34–46) would "distil upon [their] soul[s] as the dews from heaven" (121:45).

4. Individuals, whether spirits, mortals, or resurrected beings (e.g., 7:2–4; 18:10–16; 20:77–79; 64:3; 84:64; 87:1; 100:4; 132:63; 138:9, 43, 56).

There are times when the meaning of the word *soul* does not fit uniquely and neatly into just one of the above connotations. A careful look at the context, in such cases, is needed to determine if just one meaning is intended, or if there is more than one possibility (e.g., 33:1; 64:17; 101:37–38).

LED

South Carolina. *See* Historical context and overview of Doctrine and Covenants 87 (p. 791).

Sovereign. *See* Appendix E.

Speaking after the manner of the Lord

A customary or characteristic mode in which the Lord speaks, indicating a difference in the perception of time between God and man. There are two instances in the Doctrine and Covenants where this phrase is found (63:53; 64:23–25). In these references the Lord speaks of events as being "nigh at hand" and "today," whereas from a mortal perspective the events lie in a distant future.

After teaching of events and conditions that will attend the time of the Second Coming, the Lord stated, "These things are the things that ye must look for; and, speaking after the manner of the Lord, they are now nigh at hand, and in a time to come, even in the day of the coming of the Son of Man" (63:49–53). In teaching the principle of tithing and its direct result upon people during the Second Coming, the Lord warned: "Behold, now it is called today until the coming of the Son of Man, and verily it is . . . a day for the tithing of my people; for he that is tithed shall not be burned at his coming. For after today cometh the burning—this is speaking after the manner of the Lord—for verily I say, tomorrow all the proud and they that do wickedly shall be as stubble; and I will burn them up, for I am the Lord of Hosts; and I will not spare any that remain in Babylon" (64:23–24).

BEM

Special witnesses/especial witnesses. *See* Witness, witnesses.

Spirit matter

Substance or element "more fine or pure" than physical matter (131:7). It is real, but mortal eyes cannot perceive it. Although all its properties are not revealed, the Doctrine and Covenants states, "There is no such thing as immaterial matter. All spirit is matter, but it is more fine or pure, and can only be discerned by purer eyes" (131:7–8). The Prophet Joseph Smith stated, "Spirit is a substance; that it is material, but that it is more pure, elastic and refined matter than the body; that it existed before the body, can exist in the body; and will exist separate from the body, when the body will be

mouldering in the dust; and will in the resurrection, be again united with it" (4:575).

It appears that self-existent spirit matter, in an inexhaustible supply in space, is used by God for other purposes in addition to creating the spirit bodies of his own children, as, for example, the spirit bodies of animals (Smith, 5:308–9; D&C 77:2–3; cf. Moses 3:3–5).

See also Man, creation of.

BIBLIOGRAPHY

Smith, Joseph. *History of The Church of Jesus Christ of Latter-day Saints.* Edited by B. H. Roberts. 7 vols. 2d ed. rev. Salt Lake City: The Church of Jesus Christ of Latter-day Saints, 1932–51.

RJM

Spirit of Elias. *See* Elias.

Spirit of Jesus Christ. *See* Light of Christ.

Spirit of prophecy/spirit of revelation. *See* Revelation.

Spirit of truth

A phrase found in the Doctrine and Covenants with two meanings:

1. The power and influence of the HOLY GHOST; the revelatory power of God that fills "the immensity of space" (88:6–13). *See* Light of Christ.

The Lord instructed his servants that if their efforts are to be "of God," both those who preach and those who receive their message must do so by the "Spirit of truth." In this way both parties "understand one another, and both are edified and rejoice together" (50:17–24; cf. 6:15; 107:71).

2. A name title for JESUS CHRIST. John the Baptist bore record "of the Only Begotten of the Father, full of grace and truth, even the Spirit of truth, which came and dwelt in the flesh, and dwelt among us" (93:6–11). The Savior himself said plainly, "I am the Spirit of truth" (93:26).

In the standard works of the Church, the phrase "Spirit of truth" is found only in the Doctrine and Covenants and New Testament. In the New Testament the references to the Spirit of truth refer to the Holy Ghost (John 14:17;

15:26; 16:13; cf. D&C 50:17) and his influence (1 Jn. 4:6; cf. 5:6).

LED

Spirit world, postmortal

Realm of the spirits of deceased mortals and the spirits of the devil and his followers who were cast out of heaven. The revelations in the Doctrine and Covenants contain few references to the postmortal spirit world. In his vision of the redemption of the dead, President Joseph F. Smith saw the Savior's visit to this spirit world. President Smith saw that the spirit world contained both the righteous and the wicked. His vision clarified that Christ "went not in person among the wicked and the disobedient" to teach them but rather "organized his forces" and sent them to proclaim the message of salvation "unto [those to] whom he could not go personally, because of their rebellion and transgression" (138:29–30, 37). His "messengers, clothed with power and authority . . . carry the light of the gospel to them that were in darkness, even to all the spirits of men" (138:30). "The dead who repent will be redeemed, through obedience to the ordinances of the house of God, and after they have paid the penalty of their transgressions, and are washed clean, shall receive a reward according to their works, for they are heirs of salvation" (138:58–59).

Though there are divisions between the righteous and the wicked, all of the spirits of men and women are in one world, just as they are in the flesh. In the postmortal spirit world, the disembodied long for deliverance and seek for relief from their present condition; they look upon the long absence of their spirits from their bodies as a BONDAGE (45:17; 138:50; cf. 138:15–18, 23). In that sense, the entire spirit world, not just that portion designated as HELL or OUTER DARKNESS, is a "prison" (Smith, *History*, 5:425; cf. Pratt, *JD*, 1:289–90).

"In this space between death and the resurrection of the body, the two classes of souls remain, in happiness or in misery, until the time which is appointed of God that the dead shall come forth and be reunited both spirit and body" (Smith, *Gospel*, 448). And so the postmortal spirit world is an intermediate stop for all individuals. It is a place of waiting, of suffering and repentance, of peace and rest, and of instruction and preparation. Those who receive and enjoy the blessings of the GOSPEL or who receive the testimony of Jesus will come forth from the spirit world in the first RESURRECTION (76:51, 74; 88:97–99). Those who continue to assert their own will and refuse the Savior's offer of enlightenment and redemption will remain in the spirit world until the thousand years are ended. Then in that last resurrection they will come forth (76:85; 88:100–101).

Other latter-day scriptures contain additional details about the postmortal spirit world that are not found in the Doctrine and Covenants. For example, at the time of one's entrance into the spirit world, the individual receives a partial JUDGMENT. The righteous are received into a "state of happiness, which is called paradise, a state of rest, a state of peace, where they shall rest from all their troubles and from all care, and sorrow" (Alma 40:12). The wicked on the other hand are received into a state of misery, "a state of awful, fearful looking for the fiery indignation of the wrath of God" (Alma 40:13–14) called hell, or a prison. It is reasonable to suppose that the level of happiness or misery will be commensurate with the level of righteousness or wickedness of each person (76:84, 106; Moses 7:38). Paradise is a place where spirits "expand in wisdom, where they have respite from all their troubles, and where care and sorrow do not annoy" (Smith, *Gospel*, 448). On the other hand, the spirits of the wicked "shall be cast out into outer darkness; there shall be weeping, and wailing, and gnashing of teeth, and this because of their own iniquity, being led captive by the will of the devil" (Alma 40:13).

As to the location of the postmortal spirit world, latter-day prophets have taught that the spirit world occupies the same space as this physical earth. Mortals cannot see that world, however, because it is made of spirit matter which is "more fine or pure, and can only be discerned by purer eyes; we cannot see it; but when our bodies are purified we shall see that it is all matter" (131:7–8). "Is the spirit world here?" Brigham Young asked and then answered, "It . . . is on this earth that was organized for the people that have lived and that do and will live upon it" (Young, 3:372). Parley P. Pratt added that the spirit world "is here on the very planet where we were born" (126).

See also Premortal existence; Salvation for the dead.

BIBLIOGRAPHY

Pratt, Orson. *Journal of Discourses*. 26 vols. London: Latter-day Saints' Book Depot, 1854–86.

Pratt, Parley P. *Key to the Science of Theology*. Salt Lake City: Deseret Book, 1966.

Smith, Joseph. *History of The Church of Jesus Christ of Latter-day Saints*. Edited by B. H. Roberts. 7 vols. 2d ed. rev. Salt Lake City: The Church of Jesus Christ of Latter-day Saints, 1932–51.

Smith, Joseph F. *Gospel Doctrine*. Salt Lake City: Deseret Book, 1963.

Young, Brigham. *Journal of Discourses*. 26 vols. London: Latter-day Saints' Book Depot, 1854–86.

RLM

Spirits, false. *See* Historical context and overview of Doctrine and Covenants 50 (p. 756).

Spirits, ministering. *See* Ministering spirits.

Spiritual

Term denoting various conditions or realms of existence and best understood from the context in each instance. *Spiritual* is generally used in comparison with or in contrast to *temporal*. It is essential to distinguish between *spirit* (noun) and *spiritual* (adjective).

Spirit element and physical element

EARTH was first created, or formed, of spirit element and later clothed with an organization of physical element. At the time of creation, this earth was not subject to DEATH or the characteristics of mortality and can be correctly described as spiritual; this condition prevailed until the Fall brought a TEMPORAL condition (29:30–42; 2 Ne. 2:19–22). *See* Fall of Adam and Eve, the.

Earth's final destiny is to be renewed and become a celestial planet, a permanent spiritual orb (29:22–23, 31–32; 77:1; 88:17–18, 25–26; 130:9). *See* Earth, the.

Each human spirit body was created of spirit element by a birth process as a child of heavenly parents, then later tabernacled in a physical body by birth into the physical world. Adam and Eve, in the Garden of Eden, were spirits housed in physical bodies, which bodies were not subject to death until the Fall. All the remainder of mankind, being born after the Fall, have come directly from the SPIRIT WORLD into mortality and are born temporal.

Likeness of spiritual and temporal

Spirit bodies and physical bodies have a corporeal resemblance of body parts and both were created in the image of God's body (Moses 2:27; Ether 3:16–17). "That which is spiritual being in the likeness of that which is temporal; and that which is temporal in the likeness of that which is spiritual" and "the spirit of man in the likeness of his person." This likeness of spirit and temporal bodies is also true of animals, plants, and all living things which God has created (77:2; Moses 3:1–9). Everything was spiritual when it was created.

Resurrected bodies are spiritual

A resurrected body is physical, tangible flesh and bone and is not subject to death. It is properly defined as spiritual in contrast to its former mortal (temporal) condition (88:27–28; 130:22; Alma 11:45). Without this clarification from the Doctrine and Covenants and the Book of Mormon, Paul's explanation in 1 Corinthians 15:42–45 could be seriously misunderstood to mean that a resurrected body lacks physical and tangible properties. *See* Resurrection, the.

All things unto God are spiritual

God has a tangible, physical, spiritual body of flesh and bones and dwells on a tangible, physical, celestial, spiritual world. Speaking of himself, he said, "All things unto me are spiritual" (29:34–35; 88:17–19, 26; 130:22).

Spiritual life and spiritual death

These terms have reference to levels of individual righteousness or unrighteousness rather than to whether or not the spirit entity and physical body are alive or dead. Spiritual life is to be "alive in Christ" (2 Ne. 25:25; Moro. 8:12, 19, 22; Rom. 6:11), whereas spiritual death is to "die as to things pertaining unto righteousness" (Alma 12:16; cf. D&C 29:41; Alma 40:26; 1 Tim. 5:6). Death means separation. Spiritual death is also called the "second death," the ultimate condition of which is to be a SON OF PERDITION (76:32–37; cf. 29:28).

Divine spiritual perceptions are not discernible to the natural, carnal, mortal mind and are seen only through spiritual eyes (67:10–12; 76:114–17; Moses 1:11).

Additional categories

The language of the Doctrine and Covenants presents other usages of *spiritual* related to the foregoing discussion but of a more general application (e.g., 70:12; 72:14; 107:6–15, 18, 32, 80; 108:2; and 134:6, 9).

RJM

Spiritual Babylon. *See* Babylon.

Spiritual death. *See* Death.

Spiritual gifts

Manifestations given to mankind by the HOLY GHOST. The Doctrine and Covenants provides important information about the purpose and nature of spiritual gifts.

As to the purpose of such gifts, the Lord has said that "all these gifts come from God, for the benefit of the children of God" (46:26); "they are given for the benefit of those who love me and keep all my commandments, and him that seeketh so to do; that all may be benefited that seek or that ask of me, that ask and not for a sign that they may consume it upon their lusts" (46:9); and that the Saints may not be deceived by "evil spirits, or doctrines of devils, or the commandments of men; for some are of men, and others of devils" (46:7–8).

The Lord instructed the Saints that they "should always remember . . . what those gifts are, that are given unto the church," that there are "many gifts," and that though "all have not every gift given unto them . . . to every man is given a gift by the Spirit of God" (46:10–11). He also directed them to seek "earnestly the best gifts, always remembering for what they are given" (46:8). Concerning "best gifts," the Prophet Joseph Smith said, "The greatest, the best, and the most useful gifts would be known nothing about by an observer" (5:30), perhaps

pointing to the quiet gifts of testimony, faith, discernment, wisdom, and so forth.

The Doctrine and Covenants identifies several gifts of the Spirit (46), but an even greater multitude of spiritual gifts is manifested to mankind, given "to enlighten, encourage, and edify the faithful so that they will inherit peace in this life and be guided toward eternal life in the world to come. Their presence is proof of the divinity of the Lord's work" (McConkie, 314; cf. D&C 50:23; 59:23; Moro. 10:19; A of F 7). "The evil one," on the other hand, "ever vigilant in his work of destruction, tries to simulate with an evil purpose every gift of God" (Widtsoe, 98). In that regard, the Prophet Joseph Smith declared that "nothing is a greater injury to the children of men than to be under the influence of a false spirit when they think they have the Spirit of God" (4:573).

Gifts of the Spirit identified in section 46 are as follows:
- "To know that Jesus Christ is the Son of God, and that he was crucified for the sins of the world" (v. 13).
- "To believe" on the words or testimony of those who know, "that they also might have eternal life if they continue faithful" (v. 14).
- "To know the differences of administration" (v. 15). This gift is used when serving in various callings and offices in the Church, receiving guidance about how to carry out one's responsibilities.
- "To know the diversities of operations, whether they be of God" (v. 16). This gift assists individuals to discern whether a teaching, organization, program, or circumstance is "of God."
- "The word of wisdom" (v. 17). This verse refers not to the WORD OF WISDOM (89) but to enlightenment and understanding in applying knowledge.
- "The word of knowledge, that all may be taught to be wise and to have knowledge" (v. 18). Such knowledge includes the content of "all good books," both secular and religious (90:15; 88:78–81, 118; 93:53).
- "Faith to be healed" (v. 19).
- "Faith to heal" (v. 20).
- "The working of miracles" (v. 21).

- "To prophesy" (v. 22; cf. 34:10; Rev. 19:10).
- "The discerning of spirits" (v. 23; cf. 50:31–33; 129:4–9).
- "To speak with tongues" (v. 24).
- "The interpretation of tongues" (v. 25).
- "To discern all those gifts." This gift is given to the "bishop . . . and unto such as God shall appoint and ordain to watch over the church . . . lest there shall be any among you professing and yet be not of God" (v. 27).
- "To have all those gifts, that there may be a head, in order that every member may be profited thereby" (v. 29). The head in this context is the president of the Church (Packer, 96, 104).

"That every member may be profited thereby" is the purpose and function of the spiritual gifts listed in section 46 and all other gifts not mentioned. They are provided by God the Father and the Savior through the power of the Holy Ghost.

BIBLIOGRAPHY

McConkie, Bruce R. *Mormon Doctrine*. Salt Lake City: Bookcraft, 1966.

Packer, Boyd K. *The Shield of Faith*. Salt Lake City: Bookcraft, 1998.

Smith, Joseph. *History of The Church of Jesus Christ of Latter-day Saints*. Edited by B. H. Roberts. 7 vols. 2d ed. rev. Salt Lake City: The Church of Jesus Christ of Latter-day Saints, 1932–51.

Widtsoe, John A. *Evidences and Reconciliations*. Arranged by G. Homer Durham. 3 vols. in 1. Salt Lake City: Bookcraft, 1960.

JC

Spring Hill, Daviess County, Missouri

The location of ADAM-ONDI-AHMAN (116:1). On 29 December 1836, the Missouri legislature passed the bill creating Caldwell and Daviess counties in northwestern Missouri. Alexander W. Doniphan, Clay County's representative in the state legislature and sympathetic to the Latter-day Saints, sponsored the bill. Daviess County was nearly twenty-four miles square and situated north of Caldwell County. It was named after Colonel Joseph H. Daviess, a friend of Doniphan's father and a commander killed in the battle of Tippecanoe in Indiana in 1811. Gallatin was established as the county seat.

A few Church members began settling Daviess County beginning in 1837, but most came in 1838. One of the most prominent Mormon settlers in Daviess County was Lyman Wight. In February 1838 he purchased a farm and established a ferry on the Grand River in the area known as Spring Hill. On 19 May 1838, near Wight's ferry, Joseph Smith received a revelation indicating that Spring Hill was known anciently as Adam-ondi-Ahman, or the former homeland of Adam and his posterity (107:53–56; 116:1; 117:8).

During the summer of 1838 a major settlement was established at Adam-ondi-Ahman (often called Diahman), which soon became the largest settlement in the county. On 28 June 1838, Joseph Smith organized the Adam-ondi-Ahman Stake with John Smith as president and Reynolds Cahoon and Lyman Wight as counselors. Vinson Knight was appointed bishop. A temple site at Adam-ondi-Ahman is also known to have been dedicated. Besides Diahman, other Mormon settlements in Daviess County included Marrowbone (also called Ambrosia), Honeycreek, Lickfork, and Grindstone Fork. In October 1838, the population of Latter-day Saints in Daviess County grew to approximately twelve hundred to fifteen hundred.

A number of conflicts between the Church members and Missourians broke out in Daviess County, beginning 6 August 1838 with the election-day skirmish at Gallatin. Outbreaks between these parties in September led to the calling out of the state militia to quell the fighting. Fearing additional reprisals, in October 1838 Mormon defenders under the leadership of Lyman Wight took control of the region, forcing the non-Mormon inhabitants to leave the county. Church members surrendered to the state militia at Far West on 1 November 1838, and a second surrender occurred at Diahman nine days later. After the surrenders, most of the Saints living in Daviess County abandoned their homes and property and temporarily moved into Caldwell County. They left the state entirely during the first few months of 1839 because of Governor Boggs's extermination order. *See* map, p. 414.

See also Missouri period.

BIBLIOGRAPHY

Baugh, Alexander L. *A Call to Arms: The 1838 Mormon Defense of Northern Missouri.* Provo, Utah: Joseph Fielding Smith Institute for Latter-day Saint History and BYU Studies, 2000.

History of Daviess County, Missouri: An Encyclopedia of Useful Information, and a Compendium of Actual Facts. Kansas City: Birdsall & Dean, 1882.

Jenson, Andrew. "Daviess County, Missouri." *Historical Record* 9 (January 1889): 724–32.

ALB

St. Louis, Missouri

A city named after King Louis IX of France; established as an outpost by the French government in 1763–64. Following the Seven Years' War and the French and Indian War, St. Louis and the region west of the Mississippi River to the Rockies came under Spanish rule. In 1800, Spain ceded the region back to France as part of the treaty of St. Ildefonse. In 1803, as a result of the Louisiana Purchase, St. Louis came under the control of the United States.

By 1830, St. Louis, with a population of about five thousand, had become a commercial center for river traffic on the Mississippi and the major outpost for points farther west. That same year the first Mormon missionaries (the missionaries to the Lamanites, 32:1–5) passed through St. Louis en route to Jackson County, Missouri. During the summer of 1831, Joseph Smith passed through St. Louis while en route to Jackson County (52:1–3) and again while returning to Ohio as instructed in Doctrine and Covenants 60:5–8. In 1832, Joseph Smith again visited St. Louis while on his second journey to Jackson County (82). During the decade of the 1830s, many Latter-day Saints traveling to and from Missouri passed through St. Louis.

Following their forced expulsion from northern Missouri in 1838–39, a number of Latter-day Saints sought temporary refuge and employment in St. Louis. While most members eventually relocated in Illinois, some remained in the city, and a branch of the Church was established in the early 1840s. During the Illinois period (1839–46), many Latter-day Saint converts migrating from Great Britain came by steamboat up the Mississippi River from New

Orleans, stopping briefly at St. Louis before proceeding on to Nauvoo.

During the exodus from Illinois, large numbers of Latter-day Saints went to St. Louis before heading west. In 1847, an estimated fifteen hundred Saints were living in the St. Louis area. For nearly ten years, largely fueled by British emigration, the Mormon population in St. Louis remained constant, leading to the creation of the St. Louis Stake in 1854. After 1857, however, the number of Saints in the city declined, leading to the dissolution of the stake, although a branch of the Church remained for many years.

Church growth in St. Louis swelled during the 1950s, leading to the creation of a new St. Louis Stake in 1958. The dedication of the St. Louis Missouri Temple in 1997 further reflects the growth and sustained presence of the Church in the area. *See* map, p. 355.

BIBLIOGRAPHY

Smith, Joseph. *History of The Church of Jesus Christ of Latter-day Saints.* Edited by B. H. Roberts. 7 vols. 2d ed. rev. Salt Lake City: The Church of Jesus Christ of Latter-day Saints, 1932–51.

Woods, Fred E., and Thomas L. Farmer. *When the Saints Came Marching In: A History of the Latter-day Saints in St. Louis.* Salt Lake City: Millennial Press, 2009.

ALB

Stake(s)

Ecclesiastical organization based on geographical boundaries, directed by a three-man presidency and a twelve-member high council called to oversee Church operations within its jurisdiction. A stake includes approximately five to eight WARDS, all priesthood QUORUMS, and auxiliaries within its geographical boundaries.

Revelations in 1830 and 1831 declared that a holy city known as ZION or the NEW JERUSALEM, patterned after the ancient prophet Enoch's righteous city, was to be built, to which God's people should gather (Moses 7; D&C 28; 42; 57). Branch communities of Zion, termed "stakes of Zion" (119:7), would be added as needed. The Church's first stakes were organized in 1834 in Kirtland, Ohio, and Clay County, Missouri.

At first the restored Church had a simple organizational structure. Based on Articles and

Covenants approved in a 10 April 1830 revelation (now recorded in section 20), the Church soon had functioning deacons, teachers, priests, and elders. In February 1831, Edward Partridge became the first bishop, and in November Newel K. Whitney became the second bishop in the Church. After the first high priests were ordained that year, priesthood councils governed in the Kirtland, Ohio, and Jackson County, Missouri, gathering centers, beyond which small branches formed until members moved to the gathering centers.

The term *stake* is first mentioned in a 3 November 1831 revelation that instructed believers to go forth "unto the land of Zion, that the borders of my people may be enlarged, and that her stakes may be strengthened" (133:9). A 16 December 1833 revelation stated that when Zion was filled by the gathering of Saints, "then I have other places which I will appoint unto them, and they shall be called stakes, for the curtains or the strength of Zion" (101:20–21). "Curtains" and "stakes" reflect a scriptural concept wherein the Lord directed his people to "enlarge the place of thy tent, and let them stretch forth the curtains of thine habitations; spare not, lengthen thy cords, and strengthen thy stakes" (Isa. 54:2–3; 3 Ne. 22:2–5). *See* Curtain(s).

In Doctrine and Covenants 68:25–26 (November 1831) instructions are given for parents to teach children the gospel in Zion and (in an 1835 addition) "in any of her stakes."

Kirtland

In response to increasing membership, the Church's first two stakes were organized in 1834 in Kirtland, Ohio, and Clay County, Missouri, each with a three-man presidency and a high council composed of twelve high priests who resided within the stake's boundaries. Doctrine and Covenants 82:13–14 (26 April 1832) says Kirtland was consecrated to be a stake in Zion, for Zion's "borders must be enlarged." In 96:1 (6 June 1833), the Lord said it was "expedient in me that this stake . . . should be made strong." On 2 August 1833 he instructed the Saints to found "the city of the stake of Zion, here in the land of Kirtland" (94:1). Doctrine and Covenants 104:40 (23 April 1834) discussed the mercantile establishment "for my

stake in the land of Kirtland" and called for forming a "United Order of the Stake of Zion, the City of Kirtland" (v. 48). The Kirtland Temple dedicatory prayer (27 March 1836) mentioned the righteous gathering "to Zion, or to her stakes," and asked God "to appoint unto Zion other stakes besides this one" (109:39, 59). The Kirtland Stake was dissolved in 1838 when Church headquarters moved to Missouri.

Missouri

A stake was created on 3 July 1834 in Clay County, Missouri, with David Whitmer as president. That stake relocated to Far West, Missouri, in 1836. A revelation dated 26 April 1838 instructed that believers must gather to Zion "and upon her stakes" for a defense and refuge and called for "other places" to be "appointed for stakes" in regions near Far West (115:6, 18). In response, a stake was organized at ADAM-ONDI-AHMAN in Daviess County. An 8 July 1838 revelation directed that tithing be a "standing law" for Missouri Saints, serving as "an ensample unto all the stakes of Zion" (119:4, 7). Both Missouri stakes were abandoned in 1838 and 1839 because of the so-called Mormon War and the Saints being forced from Missouri.

Nauvoo

In 1839, the Church's central stake was established at Nauvoo, Illinois. A revelation dated 19 January 1841 affirmed that the stake in Nauvoo was to be a "cornerstone of Zion" and that baptisms for the dead should be performed "in Zion, and in her stakes"; it also mentioned the importance of the Nauvoo Stake presidency (124:2, 36, 142–43). A revelation two months later urged Saints to build up areas around Nauvoo "in all the stakes which I have appointed" (125:1–4). As a result, several stakes were organized nearby in Illinois and Iowa but were discontinued by 1842 (Smith, 4:145, 233, 236, 468, 476, 493).

Stake high councils

Section 102 contains minutes for the 17 February 1834 meeting in Kirtland at which the Church's first HIGH COUNCIL, consisting of twelve high priests, was organized "for the purpose of settling important difficulties which might arise in the church" (v. 2) that could not be settled by a bishop's council or other means. Instructions were provided regarding council vacancies, judicial procedures for handling cases, and the high council's relationship to the "traveling high council" (v. 30), meaning the Twelve Apostles. Since those instructions were given, stake administrations have included high councils in addition to their presidencies. Doctrine and Covenants 20:61–66 contains verses added in 1835 giving high councilors "the privilege of ordaining" and telling how they should be ordained. In 42:34 (February 1831) is an 1835 addition giving high councils a role in deciding how the poor should be cared for. Section 107 (28 March 1835) explains a high council's relationship to the Twelve and Seventy (vv. 36–38). The 1838 revelation on tithing said that tithing should be disposed of by a council that includes "my high council" (120:1). A 19 January 1841 revelation identified and appointed "officers belonging to my Priesthood" (124:123), including a high council, which was to be "the cornerstone of Zion" (124:131). Over time, high councils have served other stake administrative roles in addition to their original assignment to be a stake court (disciplinary council).

Stake priesthood quorums

Although wards became ecclesiastical units in Nauvoo, quorums of elders, priests, teachers, and deacons remained stake quorums. During the late nineteenth century, deacons, teachers, and priests quorums were designated ward instead of stake quorums.

Stake conferences

Doctrine and Covenants 20:61 instructed the Church to hold quarterly conferences. Until 1846, general conferences were held in the Church's gathering centers, so that stake conferences were not yet necessary. Stake conferences became a feature of the Church after the relocation to Utah, and the priesthood reorganization of 1877 caused them to be held quarterly.

Post-Nauvoo stakes

Stakes were formed among exiled Saints living by the Missouri River 1846 to 1852 and in Utah starting in 1847. During the colonizing period in Utah, apostles sometimes served as stake presidents. By then wards, first organized in

Nauvoo, had become the primary local units operating within a stake's boundaries and jurisdiction. Just before Brigham Young died in 1877, he oversaw the total reorganizing of stakes, wards, and quorums, after which the Church had 19 well-established stakes encompassing 241 wards.

See also Church of Jesus Christ of Latter-day Saints, The.

BIBLIOGRAPHY

Hartley, William G. "Nauvoo Stake, Priesthood Quorums, and the Church's First Wards." *BYU Studies* 32 (Winter and Spring 1991): 57–80.

———. "The Priesthood Reorganization of 1877: Brigham Young's Last Achievement." *BYU Studies* 20 (Fall 1979): 3–36.

Smith, Joseph. *History of The Church of Jesus Christ of Latter-day Saints.* Edited by B. H. Roberts. 7 vols. 2d ed. rev. Salt Lake City: The Church of Jesus Christ of Latter-day Saints, 1932–51.

WGH

Stand by the wall

A biblical image also employed in modern revelation (1 Sam. 25:22, 34; 1 Kgs. 14:10; D&C 121:15). To modern ears the Old Testament phrase "pisseth against the wall" seems a vulgar, even offensive, expression. It is, however, a superb illustration of the down-to-earth figures of speech used by ancient Hebrew writers, who were literary artists, painters of powerful mental pictures that conjured up lasting images and impressions. The biblical references have to do with judgments upon a man and his posterity. The same idiom, without the offensive term, occurs with the same meaning in the Doctrine and Covenants: "And not many years hence, that they and their posterity shall be swept from under heaven, saith God, that not one of them is left to stand by the wall" (121:15). This has reference not just to any male but to those who were the persecutors of the Prophet Joseph Smith especially and the Church generally.

DKO

Standard. *See* Ensign.

Standing councils/ministers/presidents

Beginning on 6 April 1830 with only a first and second elder (Joseph Smith and Oliver

Cowdery), the organization of the Church has developed into a complex system of both *standing* and *traveling* presidencies, QUORUMS, and COUNCILS. Even though these appellations are no longer used, those who serve in a particular locale are the *standing* ministers, in contrast to others who serve Churchwide as *traveling* ministers. Stake high councils are *standing* councils that have jurisdiction only within their own stake boundaries (102:3; 107:36), whereas the Quorum of the Twelve Apostles constitutes a *traveling* high council, authorized to function anywhere in the world (102:30). The Church has divided the world into branches, wards, districts, stakes, missions, and areas; thus, those serving within these jurisdictions serve as *standing* ministers and in *standing* quorums, councils, and presidencies.

In another sense, *standing* may also mean "permanent" rather than "temporary." Historically, there were in the 1830s *traveling* high priests, who could organize into temporary, decision-making councils and then disband (102:24–26). Today, in the early part of the twenty-first century, these duties are among the responsibility of area and mission presidencies.

Not only did the Church organization gradually unfold as the Church grew in size and expanded in territory but some of the assigned duties within that organization have also changed over the years. In 1832, high priests, elders, and priests acted as *traveling* ministers while teachers and deacons served as *standing* ministers (84:111). By 1841 high priests and elders were designated *standing* ministers but could travel if needed (124:133–37).

Though the basic foundational organization of "apostles, prophets, pastors, teachers, evangelists, and so forth" (A of F 6; cf. Eph. 2:20) has not changed, provision is made for revealed adaptations to meet the demands of changing circumstances (107:96). Those reading the Doctrine and Covenants must discern between historical and modern application of these instructions as they relate to the ever-expanding Church organization and the designated duties of those who are called to positions within that organization.

See also Traveling high council/bishops/ elders/high priests/ministers/presiding high council; Church of Jesus Christ of Latter-day Saints, The.

RJW

Stanton, Daniel

Birth: 28 May 1795, Manlius, Onondaga County, New York

Died: 26 October 1872, Panaca, Lincoln County, Nevada

On 3 November 1830, Daniel Stanton was baptized in Kirtland, Ohio, by Parley P. Pratt. At the Amherst, Ohio, conference of January 1832, a number of elders received mission calls. Included in this group were Daniel Stanton and his companion, Seymour Brunson (75:33), who served a short mission together.

Following his service as a missionary, Brother Stanton settled his family in Jackson County, Missouri, where he served as a branch president. He later volunteered to serve a mission and labored in Missouri, Illinois, and Indiana. Brother Stanton subsequently served on the high council at Adam-ondi-Ahman, Missouri. In 1840 he was called to preside over the stake in Quincy, Illinois. On 19 July of that year he baptized Ezra T. Benson, a future apostle, in the Mississippi River. Brother Stanton later moved to Lima, Illinois, where he served on the high council. He migrated with the Saints to the Rocky Mountains and passed away in Panaca, Nevada, on 26 October 1872.

BIBLIOGRAPHY

The Evening and the Morning Star 2 (June 1833): 100.

Latter-day Saints' Messenger and Advocate 1 (December 1834): 46.

Smith, Joseph. *History of The Church of Jesus Christ of Latter-day Saints.* Edited by B. H. Roberts. 7 vols. 2d ed. rev. Salt Lake City: The Church of Jesus Christ of Latter-day Saints, 1932–51.

RC

Statute, statutes. *See* Appendix E.

Stay. *See* Appendix E.

Steadfast. *See* Appendix E.

Steward, stewardship

One who has responsibility for something that belongs to another; an assignment or charge. In response to the practice of keeping "common stock" that was brought into the Church by new members in Kirtland, Ohio, in late 1830, Joseph Smith received the revelation recorded in section 42 establishing the law of CONSECRATION, the means by which the temporal needs and wants of each member of the Church would be met. Central to this law is the principle of stewardship, in which the individual participants are responsible for the welfare and upkeep of property or tasks assigned to them (42:32; 70:3–4), giving the excess to the Church to become common goods for the Church as a whole (70:5–12; 82:18). Though it is the economic element of this law that is most often the focus, its true power is that it changes the perception of the participants concerning their relationship both towards property and towards each other (51:9; 82:18–19; 104:11–16). It is rooted in the knowledge that "all things are [God's]" (104:15).

The term *steward* reflects the leadership responsibilities that one has for the welfare of a household, both its possessions and its inhabitants, when the presiding authority or owner is not present. In this manner, the term is also used to describe the proper leadership in Church callings and offices such as priest, teacher, elder, bishop, and missionary over the family of God (42:70; 64:40; 69:5; 72:5), as well as that of political leaders over the inhabitants of the land (101:85–90). Though the position of steward is temporary, the blessings of good stewardship are not. If the steward remains faithful to the responsibilities of his position, caring for and reporting truthfully on his actions, then he inherits all things, becoming a ruler in God's kingdom (72:4; 78:22; 101:61; cf. Luke 12:42). This pattern of stewardship is best represented by Christ himself, who, in 76:106–8, is seen reporting on his stewardship concerning this earth, presenting both himself and the kingdom to the Father, followed by his receiving an eternal crown of glory (cf. 1 Cor. 15:24–28).

See also Accountability.

DLB

Stick of Ephraim

A title for the Book of Mormon. There is only one reference to the "stick of Ephraim" in the Doctrine and Covenants, referring to a future time when Jesus Christ will "drink of the fruit of the vine . . . on the earth" with his disciples, including past leaders who hold keys of various functions and dispensations. The Lord first named "Moroni, whom I have sent . . . to reveal the Book of Mormon, containing the fulness of my everlasting gospel, to whom I have committed the keys of the record of the stick of Ephraim" (27:5). This lone reference verifies that the prophet Ezekiel's prophecy of the stick of Ephraim (Ezek. 37:15–19) is indeed a prophecy of the Book of Mormon (cf. 2 Ne. 3:11–12).

That Moroni holds the keys of this record is also significant for at least two other reasons. First, it links Moroni with the angel whom John the Revelator saw "fly in the midst of heaven, having the everlasting gospel to preach unto them that dwell on the earth, and to every nation, and kindred, and tongue, and people" (Rev. 14:6). Second, in section 133 the Lord stated that the angel "having the everlasting gospel, who hath appeared unto some and hath committed it unto man . . . shall appear unto many that dwell on the earth. And this gospel shall be preached unto every nation, and kindred, and tongue, and people" (133:36–37). Therefore, it seems that Moroni, as the holder of the keys of the stick of Ephraim, will have an important role in taking the Book of Mormon to all people. He may also be the angel who in the last days blows the fifth trump, "the fifth angel who committeth the everlasting gospel—flying through the midst of heaven, unto all nations, kindreds, tongues, and people" (88:103–4; cf. Rev. 14:7).

See also Doctrine and Covenants, what it says about the Book of Mormon.

MSN

Stiffnecked. *See* Appendix E.

Storehouse. *See* Consecration.

Straight, make his paths. *See* Strait, straight.

Strait, straight

Strait generally means narrow or restricted; *straight* can mean, among other things, direct, unobstructed, or not crooked. Because they are homophones (they sound alike but have different meanings), there was a general confusion in the early nineteenth century between the two words, and they were often used interchangeably. A comparison of the occurrences of *strait* and *straight* in various reproductions of revelations of the Prophet Joseph Smith illustrates this interchangeable usage. The occurrence in 22:2, for example, was written as *strait* in Zebedee Coltrin's 1832 journal entry, printed as *straight* in the 1833 Book of Commandments and in the 1835 edition of the Doctrine and Covenants, and later changed to *strait* in the 1981 edition. The occurrences of *strait* in 3:2 and 33:10 (both in the 1833 Book of Commandments), as well as in 65:1 (in the William E. McLellin Collection) and in 133:17 (in *The Evening and the Morning Star*) were all later changed to *straight,* as in the 1981 edition. The occurrences of *strait* in 132:22 and *straight* in 84:28 have remained unchanged.

The 1981 edition of the Doctrine and Covenants uses the word *strait* to modify the word *gate,* and it uses the word *straight* when referring to the paths or way of the Lord. For example, shortly after the organization of the Church in April 1830, some believed and wanted to join with the Saints but felt that they did not need to be baptized again because they had previously received a Christian baptism. The Lord counseled these individuals to "enter in at the strait gate," meaning baptism specifically by the correct authority (22:2; cf. 2 Ne. 31:17). When he revealed to the Prophet Joseph Smith the principle of eternal marriage, the Lord, referring to worthiness to participate in the ordinance of sealing, declared, "Strait is the gate, and narrow the way that leadeth unto the exaltation and continuation of the lives, and few there be that find it" (132:22).

In July 1828, the Lord declared that his "paths are straight," meaning without deviating curves, because he "doth not walk in crooked paths, neither doth he turn to the right hand nor to the left" (3:2). The revelations repeat the declaration three times: "Prepare ye the way of the Lord, and make his paths straight" (33:10; 65:1; 133:17), a reference to the Septuagint (Greek) version of Isaiah 40:3. In this case, the phrase "make straight" can mean "make right" through the restoration of truth and also "to clear away" anything obstructing the path. In September 1832, the Lord applied Isaiah 40:3 to John the Baptist, who was sent "to make straight the way of the Lord before the face of his people, to prepare them for the coming of the Lord" (84:28; cf. Matt. 3:3; Mark 1:3; Luke 3:4; John 1:22–23).

BIBLIOGRAPHY

Hoskisson, Paul Y. "Straightening Things Out: The Use of *Strait* and *Straight* in the Book of Mormon." *Journal of Book of Mormon Studies* 12, no. 2 (2003): 58–71.

Webster, Noah. *An American Dictionary of the English Language,* 1828.

FFJ

Straightway. *See* Appendix E.

Strange act

The Lord's work. The phrase "strange act" appears in two sections of the Doctrine and Covenants (95:4; 101:95; cf. Isa. 28:21). The context for 95:4 is the Lord's scolding the Saints for their delay in building the Kirtland Temple, which they had been commanded to do six months earlier (95:3; 88:119). The Lord said the temple was needed as a place to "endow those whom I have chosen with power from on high" (95:8), to "prepare mine apostles to prune my vineyard for the last time, that I may bring to pass my strange act, that I may pour out my Spirit upon all flesh" (95:4)—a latter-day fulfillment of Joel's prophecy recorded millennia before (Joel 2:28–32; cf. Acts 2:14–21 for Peter's application of Joel's prophecy to the day of Pentecost).

The context of Doctrine and Covenants 101:95 is the Saints' having been driven from Jackson County, Missouri, in 1833. After affirming that he inspired the establishment of the U.S. Constitution and that he is the source of mankind's moral agency and holds "all men" accountable for the exercise thereof, the Lord instructed the Saints to importune at all levels of government for REDRESS for their losses in Jackson County. He followed that instruction with, "What I have said unto you must needs be, that all men may be left without excuse; that wise men and rulers may hear and know that which they have never considered; That I may proceed to bring to pass my act, my strange act, and perform my work, my strange work, that men may discern between the righteous and the wicked" (101:93–95; cf. vv. 76–95).

Both of the Doctrine and Covenants references mention the Lord's great latter-day work, his "strange act," going forward on the earth among his children. The purposes, in part, of his "act" in restoring the gospel of Jesus Christ and having it preached in all the world is to "pour out [his] Spirit upon all flesh" and to enable men and women to "discern between the righteous and the wicked."

The Lord designated his work as his "strange act"—all that the Lord has done and will yet do in these last days: restoring the gospel and sending it worldwide, establishing Zion, coming again to the earth for his millennial reign, his judgments upon the righteous and the wicked, the Resurrection, and so forth. Although these events may seem "strange" to the world, for those who enjoy the Spirit of the Lord, such happenings do not seem strange.

LED

Strangers and pilgrims

Words in Doctrine and Covenants 45:13 that parallel Hebrews 11:9–16 and 1 Peter 2:11, denoting that in this wicked world the righteous are often persecuted and ostracized by, or separated from, the dominant culture.

Stranger denotes one new to an area, unacquainted with and unknown to the established residents. *Pilgrim* denotes one traveling through or to a land not of his or her origin, seeking a better land. Closely related is *sojourned* (Heb. 11:9), denoting one who tarries somewhere for a season as a temporary resident.

The setting for the Doctrine and Covenants passage is that holy men have always sought to establish ZION on this earth but were prevented "because of wickedness and abominations" of the people. Enoch was successful in

this endeavor, and his Zion was "separated" (translated) from the wicked earth. Others, unable to find Zion, "confessed they were strangers and pilgrims on the earth" but obtained the "promise" of the Lord that they would "find it and see it in their flesh," most likely meaning in their resurrected bodies at the beginning of the MILLENNIUM and forever afterwards (45:11–14; Moses 7:62–64; cf. D&C 63:49–54).

RJM

Strength

POWER, force, talent, ability. Contexts in which the term *strength* is used in the Doctrine and Covenants include the following:

1. Strength to accomplish a task. For example, Joseph Smith was told he would have strength in "service in Zion" but he would not have strength in "temporal labors . . . for this is not thy calling" (24:7, 9). Concerning the work of translation, Joseph was cautioned, "Do not run faster or labor more than you have strength and means provided" (10:4). The Lord promised Oliver Cowdery "strength such as is not known among men" if he would be faithful in declaring the gospel "as with the voice of a trump, both day and night" (24:12).

2. Instructions to serve God, to love him, and to keep his commandments with all one's strength (e.g., 4:2; 11:20; 20:31; 59:5).

3. Strengthening the Church. Priesthood holders and leaders are instructed to strengthen Church members by visiting them and exhorting them to faithfulness (e.g., 20:53–55; 23:3–5; 31:8; 37:2; 50:37; 81:5; 108:7). In 1833 the Lord said of the Kirtland Stake, "It is expedient in me that this stake that I have set for the strength of Zion should be made strong" (96:1; cf. 101:21).

4. The Lord is the source of strength. For example, of Joseph Smith: "I have given unto [him] sufficient strength" to translate the Book of Mormon (9:12). Of Oliver Cowdery: "In me he shall have glory, and not of himself, whether in weakness or in strength" (24:11). To David Whitmer: "You have feared man and have not relied on me for strength as you ought" (30:1). And in chastening Joseph Smith in connection with the loss of the 116 pages of Book of Mormon

manuscript, the Lord reminded the Prophet and the Saints that it is "not the work of God that is frustrated, but the work of men; for although a man may have many revelations, and have power to do many mighty works, yet if he boasts in his own strength, and sets at naught the counsels of God, and follows after the dictates of his own will and carnal desires, he must fall and incur the vengeance of a just God upon him" (3:3–4).

5. Members of the Church as "the strength of mine house" (101:55). The phrase "the strength of mine [or my] house" is used eight times in context with Church members being recruited to join ZION'S CAMP. The camp was to assist the Saints who had been driven from their homes in Jackson County, Missouri. Initially, the Lord asked for five hundred volunteers, one hundred being the minimum. As it turned out, two hundred members responded (101:55; 103:22, 30–34; 105:16–17, 27).

6. The PRIESTHOOD. The strength of Zion is the authority of the priesthood. In answer to the question of what is meant by Isaiah 52:1, "Put on thy strength, O Zion," the Lord revealed that "to put on her strength is to put on the authority of the priesthood" (113:7–8).

JLH

Stubble. *See* Appendix E.

Subdue. *See* Appendix E.

Succession, apostolic

The first revealed procedure of succession in the presidency of the Church was established very early in the Restoration, as several men were ordained to succeed Joseph Smith as leader of the Church. One was Oliver Cowdery, a second witness of the restoration of priesthood KEYS, the second elder of the Church, and assistant president of the Church (20:3; Smith, *History,* 2:176; Smith, *Doctrines,* 1:211–13). Another was David Whitmer, who was ordained in 1834 "to be a leader, or a prophet to this Church, which (ordination) was on conditions that he (J. Smith Jr) did not live to God himself," as explained by Joseph Smith in March 1838 (Cannon and Cook, 151; cf. 73–74). Both Oliver Cowdery and David Whitmer apostatized and were excommunicated, losing their right to

lead the Church. The third man ordained to be a possible successor to Joseph was Hyrum Smith. He was appointed by revelation to receive "the same blessing, and glory, and honor, and priesthood . . . that once were put upon him that was my servant Oliver Cowdery" (124:94–96). This calling, as assistant president, was in addition to his appointment as patriarch to the Church (124:91–93).

President Joseph Fielding Smith made it clear that these appointments were legitimate by explaining that "had Oliver Cowdery remained faithful and had he survived the Prophet under those conditions, he would have succeeded as President of the Church by virtue of this divine calling." Moreover, he continued, "President Brigham Young, after the death of Joseph Smith, when they were discussing the matter of succession, said: 'Did Joseph Smith ordain a successor? Who was it? Hyrum Smith. But Hyrum Smith fell martyr before the Prophet did'" (*Doctrines,* 1:213, 220).

These measures, "under those conditions," as President Joseph Fielding Smith stated, were evidently set in place to temporarily secure proper succession and see that the keys of the PRIESTHOOD would not be lost if Joseph Smith were taken. This policy anticipated the time when the Quorum of the Twelve APOSTLES would be prepared to assume their preeminent and presiding role of leading the Church at the death of the president of the Church. From their calling to the apostleship on 21 February 1835, the Twelve experienced a season of preparation, including administering the kingdom in the British Isles, beginning in June 1837; receiving and administering the ordinances of the Nauvoo Temple; and ultimately, in the spring of 1844, when Joseph "rolled" the responsibility of leading the Church "onto the shoulders of the Twelve," giving them "all the keys and authority of the Holy Priesthood which he had received" (Woodruff, 19–21).

Earlier, in 1835, anticipating the time when the Quorum of the Twelve would assume their full responsibilities, the Lord defined their authority and relationship to the First Presidency by noting that the Twelve "form a quorum, equal in authority and power" to the First

Presidency (107:24). And a July 1837 revelation teaches that to both the Twelve and the First Presidency "is the power of this priesthood given, for the last days and for the last time, in the which is the dispensation of the fulness of times. Which power [the Twelve] hold, in connection with all those who have received a dispensation at any time from the beginning of the creation." The Lord declared that these keys had been "sent down from heaven" (112:30–32).

Accordingly, at the death of Joseph Smith, the Twelve became the presiding quorum of the Church and led the Church under the direction of Brigham Young, as president of the Quorum, for three years. Brigham Young was sustained as president of the Church and reorganized the First Presidency on 5 December 1847. From that time to the present, that pattern has been followed—at the death of the president of the Church, the president of the Quorum of the Twelve Apostles becomes the presiding officer of the Church and reorganizes the First Presidency, with the sustaining vote of the Quorum of the Twelve Apostles and members of the Church at a general conference.

BIBLIOGRAPHY

Cannon, Donald Q., and Lyndon W. Cook, eds. *Far West Record: Minutes of the Church of Jesus Christ of Latter-day Saints, 1830–1844.* Salt Lake City: Deseret Book, 1983.

Smith, Joseph. *History of The Church of Jesus Christ of Latter-day Saints.* Edited by B. H. Roberts. 7 vols. 2d ed. rev. Salt Lake City: The Church of Jesus Christ of Latter-day Saints, 1932–51.

Smith, Joseph Fielding. *Doctrines of Salvation.* Compiled by Bruce R. McConkie. 3 vols. Salt Lake City: Bookcraft, 1954–56.

Woodruff, Wilford. *Wilford Woodruff.* Teachings of Presidents of the Church series. Salt Lake City: The Church of Jesus Christ of Latter-day Saints, 2004.

BGS

Succor. *See* Appendix E.

Summum bonum

A term from Latin roots meaning "the highest, or supreme, good" (*Webster's*, s.v. "summum bonum"), or "the end or determining principle in an ethical system" (*Wordfinder*, s.v. "summum bonum"). The term was used

by Joseph Smith in a letter to the Church in September 1842 concerning baptism for the dead. It has reference to the quintessential requirement in effecting the salvation of mankind, for both living and dead—having the keys of the holy priesthood so that things properly recorded and bound (sealed) on earth are recorded and bound in heaven. The "great and grand secret of the whole matter, and the *summum bonum* of the whole subject," Joseph Smith affirmed, "consists in obtaining the powers of the Holy Priesthood. For him to whom these keys are given there is no difficulty in obtaining a knowledge of facts in relation to the salvation of the children of men, both as well for the dead as for the living." The keys referred to are the "keys of the kingdom of heaven," held and exercised in their fulness only by the living prophet, the president of the Church (128:8–11; Smith, 3:134–35).

BIBLIOGRAPHY

Readers Digest Oxford Complete Wordfinder. Pleasantville, N.Y.: Oxford University Press, 1966.

Smith, Joseph Fielding. *Doctrines of Salvation.* Compiled by Bruce R. McConkie. 3 vols. Salt Lake City: Bookcraft, 1954–56.

Webster's New World Dictionary. 3d college edition. New York: Simon and Schuster, 1988.

LED

Sundry. *See* Appendix E.

Supper of the house of the Lord. *See* Marriage of the Lamb.

Supper of the Lamb. *See* Marriage of the Lamb.

Supper of the Lord. *See* Marriage of the Lamb.

Susquehanna County, Pennsylvania

Area near where the Melchizedek Priesthood was restored by Peter, James, and John (128:20). Susquehanna County was divided from Luzerne County on 21 February 1810 by an act of the Pennsylvania legislature. The Borough of Montrose is the county seat. The county derives its name from the Susquehanna River, which enters Pennsylvania through its northeastern limits from the state of New York. Harmony Township, created in 1809 while still part of Luzerne County, occupied the north-eastern corner of Susquehanna County. Isaac Hale and his wife, Elizabeth Lewis, moved from Vermont to the Great Bend of the Susquehanna in about 1790 or 1791. Their daughter Emma met Joseph Smith of Manchester, New York, while he boarded at the Hale family's Harmony home in November 1825. Joseph and Emma were married at South Bainbridge (now Afton), New York, on 18 January 1827.

BIBLIOGRAPHY

Blackman, Emily C. *History of Susquehanna County, Pennsylvania*. Philadelphia: Claxton, Remsen & Haffelfinger, 1873.

Porter, Larry C. "A Study of the Origins of The Church of Jesus Christ of Latter-day Saints in the States of New York and Pennsylvania, 1816–1831." Ph.D. dissertation, Brigham Young University, 1971.

Stocker, Rhamanthus M. *Centennial History of Susquehanna County, Pennsylvania*. Philadelphia: R. T. Peck & Co., 1887.

LCP

Susquehanna River, Pennsylvania

Location where the Aaronic Priesthood was restored by John the Baptist (13:1) and where Michael appeared, "detecting the devil when he appeared as an angel of light!" (128:20). It was "in the wilderness" between Harmony, Pennsylvania, and Colesville, New York, "on the Susquehanna river" that "the voice of Peter, James, and John" declared "themselves as possessing the keys of the kingdom" (128:20). *See* Priesthood, restoration of priesthood and priesthood keys.

One meaning of the Indian name *Susquehanna* is "long crooked river." Otsego Lake, at Cooperstown, Otsego County, New York, is usually assigned as the source of the Susquehanna

The Susquehanna River near Harmony, Pennsylvania; photograph by Welden C. Andersen. "And again, what do we hear? . . . The voice of Michael on the banks of the Susquehanna, detecting the devil when he appeared as an angel of light! The voice of Peter, James, and John in the wilderness between Harmony, Susquehanna county, and Colesville, Broome county, on the Susquehanna river, declaring themselves as possessing the keys of the kingdom, and of the dispensation of the fulness of times!" (D&C 128:20).

River. It flows for approximately 448 miles to its mouth, Havre de Grace, on Chesapeake Bay, Maryland. The North Branch flows from Otsego through Chenango and Broome counties, New York, first entering Pennsylvania in northeastern Susquehanna County, where it becomes the dividing point of today's Harmony and Oakland townships. The Susquehanna then forms the Great Bend, the easternmost portion of which included the old Harmony Township in the period when Emma Hale and Joseph Smith lived in or visited those environs (1825–31). The Susquehanna River has had an influence on those living along its banks. Joseph and Emma's homestead in Harmony bordered the river. Here the Prophet received fifteen revelations contained in the Doctrine and Covenants: sections 3–13 and 24–27. *See* Historical context and overview of Doctrine and Covenants 3–13 (pp. 716–24) and 24–27 (pp. 732–36); map, p. 447.

BIBLIOGRAPHY

Brubaker, Jack. *Down the Susquehanna to the Chesapeake.* University Park: Pennsylvania State University Press, 2002.

Porter, Larry C. "Joseph Smith's Susquehanna Years." *Ensign* 31 (February 2001): 42–51.

Stranahan, Susan Q. *Susquehanna, River of Dreams.* Baltimore and London: Johns Hopkins University Press, 1993.

LCP

Sweet, Northrop

Birth: 1802, New York
Death: Unknown

A few days following Northrop Sweet's baptism in October 1830, Ezra Thayre (or Thayer) and he were "called to lift up your voices as with the sound of a trump, to declare [the] gospel unto a crooked and perverse generation" (33:1–2). Evidently Sweet was faithful and moved with the Saints from New York to Kirtland. He was ordained an elder by 3 June 1831. In that same year, however, Sweet apostatized from the Church. He and five other men, including Wycam Clark, who claimed to receive revelation that he was to be a prophet, formed a new church called "The Pure Church of Christ." Although they held a few meetings, the church failed to grow and was eventually disbanded (Smith, 7:114; 11:4). Sweet moved from Kirtland to Lake County, Ohio. About 1845 he moved to Batavia, Michigan. In 1880, he was living with his son in Bethel, Michigan.

BIBLIOGRAPHY

Smith, George A. *Journal of Discourses.* 26 vols. London: Latter-day Saints Book Depot, 1854–86.

RC

Swine. *See* Appendix E.

Sword

The term is used in the Doctrine and Covenants with several meanings, both literal and figurative:

1. A weapon consisting of a long blade with one or two sharp edges and a pointed end. For example, the sword of Laban; this sword was retained by Nephi after he killed Laban in an effort to obtain the brass plates. From the time of Nephi onward, this sword was passed down by righteous leaders in the Book of Mormon. In June 1829, the Three Witnesses were shown, among other things, the sword of Laban (17:1; cf. 122:6).

2. The word of God is compared to a literal sword. God's word is "quick and powerful, sharper than a two-edged sword, to the dividing asunder of both joints and marrow" (6:2; cf. 11:2). Those who reject the gospel will be divided or separated from the Lord, physically and spiritually, both in this life and in the life to come. Using the imagery of the sword as the word of God, the Lord illustrated that truth tends to divide, or separate, the righteous from the wicked just as a sword divides flesh and bone.

3. A representation for weaponry in general. For example, in the latter days "men will harden their hearts against [the Lord], and they will take up the sword [or other weapon], one against another, and they will kill one another" (45:33, 68; cf. 87:6).

4. "The sword of my Spirit." The Spirit is a critical part of the Lord's "whole armor" that enables the Saints "to withstand the evil day" and "quench all the fiery darts of the wicked" (27:15–18). Great power attends the combining

of the two symbolic swords of the word of God and the Spirit (11:21; cf. Eph. 6:17). "The Lord never intended that his servants, his soldiers, fight only a defensive battle. He desires that we be on the offensive and help overcome evil, free mankind from the terrible effects of evil, and prepare the earth for the return of the Savior. The sword is primarily an offensive weapon" (Millet and Jackson, 130). In the struggle "against spiritual wickedness" (Eph. 6:12), the Saints must be well versed in the scriptures, listen to the living prophets, and obey the promptings of the Holy Spirit if they are "to withstand the evil day" (27:15). *See* Armor of God.

5. A vehicle of the Lord's judgment and destruction, as well as his protection. "I will visit her [Zion] according to all her works, with sore affliction, with pestilence, with plague, with sword, with vengeance, with devouring fire" (97:26; cf. 101:10; 121:5). "[My] sword is bathed in heaven, and it shall fall upon the inhabitants of the earth" (1:13). In contrast to the wicked being destroyed by the sword, the Lord will also protect and preserve the righteous by letting "fall the sword in their behalf" (35:14).

BIBLIOGRAPHY

Millet, Robert L., and Kent P. Jackson, eds. *Studies in Scripture, Vol. 1: The Doctrine and Covenants.* Salt Lake City: Deseret Book, 1989.

AOH

Sword of Laban. *See* Sword.

Synagogue(s)

A religious meetinghouse. *Synagogue* is used in this sense four times in the Doctrine and Covenants. In 63:31, the Saints are told that they may be scourged by their enemies from "city to city, and from synagogue to synagogue." In 66:7 and 68:1, William E. McLellin and Orson Hyde are commanded to bear testimony and proclaim the gospel to all people "in their synagogues."

Although the revelations refer to synagogues in a general sense, synagogues are commonly understood to be buildings of worship in the Jewish religion. Synagogues are mentioned only once in the Old Testament (Ps. 74:8), but they were widely used by the Jews in the New Testament (Luke 4:16; Acts 9:20) as well as by Book of Mormon peoples (e.g., Alma 16:13; 26:29; 31:12). The synagogue is still extensively used by the Jews as a meeting place, specifically for Sabbath worship, which includes scripture, prayer, and song.

DLB

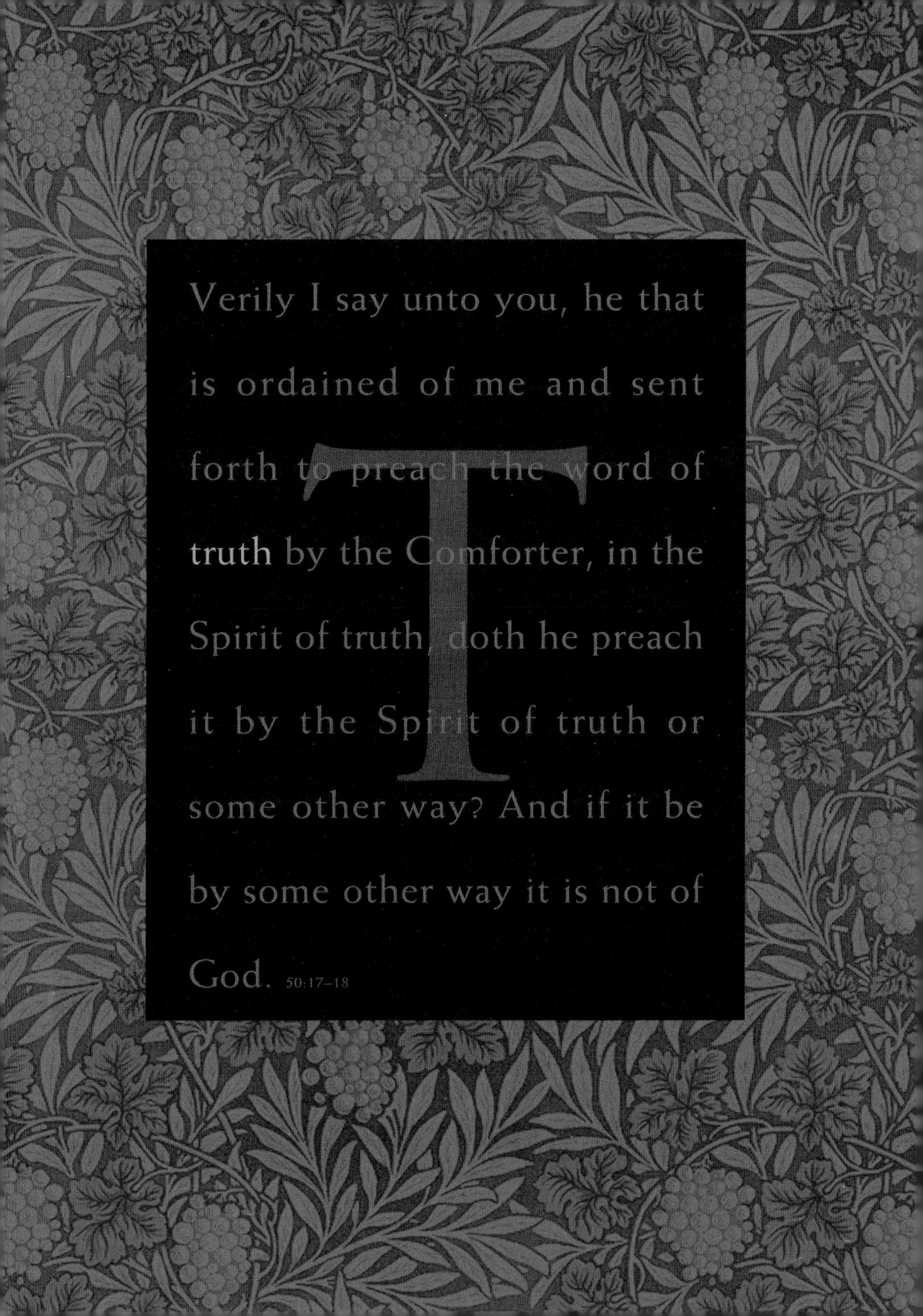

Verily I say unto you, he that is ordained of me and sent forth to preach the word of **truth** by the Comforter, in the Spirit of truth, doth he preach it by the Spirit of truth or some other way? And if it be by some other way it is not of God. 50:17–18

Tabernacle

From the Latin *taberna,* meaning "hut," a temporary shelter or dwelling place. The Doctrine and Covenants uses the term to refer to mankind's mortal bodies as well as to temples, both of which are said to be dwelling places for God. At times, the terms *tabernacle, temple,* and *house of the Lord* are used synonymously (88:119, 137; 93:35; 1 Cor. 3:16–17).

Of his own earthly body Jesus said, "I was in the world and made flesh my tabernacle (93:3–4; cf. Mosiah 15:2–3). In that tabernacle Jesus was "the Only Begotten Son," "yea, even the Son of the Eternal Father," "after the manner of the flesh" (76:23, 35; 93:11; 1 Ne. 11:13–21; Alma 9:26; John 1:14; 3:16).

The mortal bodies of all mankind serve as tabernacles not only of their own spirits but of the Spirit of God. "Man is the tabernacle of God, even temples" (93:35). To qualify to be a tabernacle of the Spirit of God, a mortal must be righteous, because "the Spirit of the Lord doth not dwell in unholy temples" (Hel. 4:24; cf. Mosiah 2:37; Alma 7:21; 34:36).

Using the word *tabernacle* in reference to man-made temples on the earth, the Lord commanded the Saints to build a "house of God," a "house of the Lord," the Kirtland Temple, calling it a "tabernacle of the Holy Spirit" (88:119, 130, 137). To the Saints in Nauvoo the Lord explained that he always commands his people to build temples in which sacred saving ordinances are revealed and administered. That is why he commanded Moses "that he should build a tabernacle [a temporary temple], that they should bear it with them in the wilderness, and to build a house [a permanent temple] in the land of promise." In the same revelation the Lord commanded the Saints to build "a house unto me," the Nauvoo Temple (124:27–40).

Furthermore, the Doctrine and Covenants identifies the Lord's dwelling place in heaven as a tabernacle or temple. The Lord promises that "the veil of the covering of my temple, in my tabernacle, which hideth the earth [prevents the earth from seeing it], shall be taken off, and all flesh shall see me together," referring to the time when Christ will emerge from his heavenly dwelling and manifest himself at his second coming (101:23).

See also Temple(s).

JST

Take up your cross

"To deny himself of all ungodliness, and every worldly lust, and keep my commandments" (JST Matt. 16:26). Just as Jesus paid the ultimate sacrifice on the cross, so his disciples are commanded to sacrifice whatever is needed, even their lives, for the building of the kingdom of God (Mark 8:34–9:1; 10:21; Luke 9:23–27; Matt. 16:24–28). Sacrifices are made in our daily commitment and devotion. In the Doctrine and Covenants the Saints are warned, "He that will not take up his cross and follow me, and keep my commandments, the same shall not be saved" (56:2). For Joseph Knight the Lord's command to take up his cross included the following: "You must pray vocally before the world as well as in secret, and in your family, and among your friends, and in all places. And, behold, it is your duty to unite with the true church, and give your language to exhortation continually, that you may receive the reward of the laborer" (23:6–7). For Thomas Marsh and the Twelve, the Lord's injunction was given in connection with following the Savior and doing missionary work: "Arise and gird up your loins, take up your cross, follow me, and feed my sheep" (112:14).

GS

Talent(s)

Term with two meanings as used in the Doctrine and Covenants:

1. Material or financial resources. Concerning the principles of CONSECRATION, the Lord said that all should improve their talents so "that every man may gain other talents . . . to be cast into the Lord's storehouse, to become the common property of the whole church" (82:18). The use of the word *talents* in these verses could also be interpreted as combining financial resources with the skills and abilities (talents) of the Saints, thus building the Lord's storehouse for the blessing and well-being of the whole Church.

2. Testimony and knowledge of the gospel. The Lord admonished elders returning to the east from Missouri that "with some I am not well pleased, for they will not open their mouths, but they hide the talent which I have given unto them" (60:2). He then commanded: "Thou shalt not . . . bury thy talent that it may not be known" (60:13).

JLH

Tanner, N. Eldon

Birth: 9 May 1898, Salt Lake City, Salt Lake County, Utah

Death: 27 November 1982, Salt Lake City, Salt Lake County, Utah

President N. Eldon Tanner is mentioned in the Doctrine and Covenants in connection with OFFICIAL DECLARATION 2. On 30 September 1978 the First Presidency of the Church—President Spencer W. Kimball, N. Eldon Tanner, and Marion G. Romney—announced that after pleading "long and earnestly" and "supplicating the Lord for divine guidance," it was revealed "that the long-promised day has come when every faithful, worthy man in the Church may receive the holy priesthood" (OD 2).

Long before President Tanner served as a counselor to four presidents of the Church, "the Lord groomed him for . . . Church leadership" (Brown, 13). His first home was a dugout in the Canadian province of Alberta, where he learned to work long hours and complete difficult tasks. He rose from being a teacher to the heights of power in Canadian politics, eventually becoming, simultaneously, minister of Alberta's Department of Mines and Minerals and the Department of Lands and Forests. When he returned to the private sector, he became the executive director of a company that constructed a 2,300 mile trans-Canadian pipeline from Alberta to Montreal.

Known as "Mr. Integrity," President Tanner rubbed shoulders with people from all walks of life and was beloved by all ("President," 8). He lived his life as he encouraged other Church members to live theirs: "The greatest achievement in life," he said, "is not the acquisition of money, position, or power. . . . It is to come to the end of one's day having been true and loyal to his ideals. I can think of no achievement greater than that" ("President," 6).

President Tanner was a devoted advocate of Scouting, promoting the enormous benefits of the program ("President," 9). First and foremost, he was devoted to the gospel of Jesus Christ. He dedicated himself to each calling he had, always striving to go beyond what was asked of him. He served as an assistant to the Quorum of the Twelve Apostles, as an apostle, and as a counselor to four Church presidents from 1963 until his death in 1982.

BIBLIOGRAPHY

Brown, Hugh B. "President N. Eldon Tanner: A Man of Integrity." *Ensign* 2 (November 1972): 13–14.

"President N. Eldon Tanner Dies." *Ensign* 13 (January 1983): 6–9.

KWF

Tannery

A place where animal skins are processed into usable leather through chemical and mechanical means. The tannery in Kirtland is mentioned once in the Doctrine and Covenants in connection with the dividing up of the properties of the United Firm into individual stewardships. The United Firm, sometimes referred to by the code name United Order, was a business organization of about twelve Church leaders who pledged to do their business by the principles of CONSECRATION. In Kirtland the order operated, among other enterprises, a tannery. When the United Firm increasingly accumulated more debts than assets, the Lord instructed them to divide the several holdings into individual stewardships (104:1–46, 53). Concerning the tannery, the revelation says, "Let my servant Sidney Rigdon have appointed unto him the place where he now resides, and the lot of the tannery for his stewardship, for his support while he is laboring in my vineyard" (104:20). Sidney Rigdon had earlier, for a short period of time, made his living as a tanner (Van Wagoner, 34–35). *See* map, p. 345.

BIBLIOGRAPHY

Van Wagoner, Richard S. *Sidney Rigdon.* Salt Lake City: Signature Books, 1994.

HDG

Tares. *See* Appendix E.

Taylor, John

Birth: 1 November 1808, Milnthorpe, West-moreland County, England

Death: 25 July 1887, Kaysville, Davis County, Utah

In 1829 John Taylor migrated from England to York (later Toronto), Upper Canada, where he married Leonora Cannon on 28 January 1833. They were both devout but seeking Methodists (Smith, 3:153–55). On 9 May 1836 Taylor was baptized by Elder Parley P. Pratt. On 8 July 1838 at Far West, Missouri, John Taylor, John E. Page, Wilford Woodruff, and Willard Richards were called by revelation to the Quorum of the Twelve Apostles (118:6). In the same revelation the Twelve were commanded to depart on missions from Far West on 26 April 1839 to the British Isles (118:4–5). The next spring Taylor and others of the Twelve met at the temple site in Far West, as appointed, to begin their historic mission to the British Isles. In a revelation given on 19 January 1841, the Lord named Taylor as seventh in seniority among the apostles of the Church (124:127–30).

On 27 June 1844 John Taylor was with the Prophet Joseph Smith and the Patriarch Hyrum Smith in the upper bedroom of Carthage Jail. Shortly before the mob rushed the jail, Taylor sang "A Poor Wayfaring Man of Grief" for the imprisoned Church leaders. "The song is pathetic, and the tune quite plaintive," he later wrote, "and was very much in accordance with our feelings at the time for our spirits were all depressed, dull and gloomy and surcharged with indefinite ominous forebodings." When Hyrum Smith asked him to sing the song again, Taylor replied, "'Brother Hyrum, I do not feel like singing.'" Hyrum said, "'Oh, never mind; commence singing, and you will get the spirit of it.' At his request I did so," said Taylor (Smith, 7:101–2). The attack commenced soon afterward. The mob murdered Joseph and Hyrum and severely wounded John Taylor (Smith, 7:97–112). Taylor's eyewitness account of the martyrdom and his impassioned tribute to the fallen brothers, canonized as Doctrine and Covenants 135, is a treasure of Church history.

John Taylor, 1808–1887; portrait by Frederick Hawkins Piercy.

John Taylor was set apart as the third president of the Church on 10 October 1880. His motto, "The Kingdom of God or Nothing," helped hold the Church steady and united during a decade of intense persecution against the practice of plural marriage. On 25 July 1887, at age seventy-eight, John Taylor died in Kaysville, Utah, where he had gone into hiding to avoid persecution.

In President Joseph F. Smith's vision of the spirit world, John Taylor is mentioned as being among those spirits President Smith saw in the vast assembly awaiting the glorious resurrection (138:53).

See also Apostles, the Twelve, mission to Great Britain; Historical context and overview of Doctrine and Covenants 135 (p. 854); Martyrdom of Joseph and Hyrum Smith.

BIBLIOGRAPHY

Smith, Joseph. *History of The Church of Jesus Christ of Latter-day Saints.* Edited by B. H. Roberts. 7 vols. 2d ed. rev. Salt Lake City: The Church of Jesus Christ of Latter-day Saints, 1932–51.

RHC

Teach, teaching

Instruct, educate, enlighten, edify. The Doctrine and Covenants offers hundreds of revealing insights about teaching and implications for those who teach. These references address three areas of preparation for teaching: preparing the inner vessel, preparing the message, and communicating the message to others.

Scriptures concerning preparing the inner vessel underline an important truth: what and how one teaches is a reflection of one's personal life. Purifying the inner vessel, therefore, enables the one who is teaching to convey a purer, selfless message, a Savior-centered message.

Scriptures concerning preparing the message instruct those who teach to engage in thoughtful and rigorous preparation. While careful preparation does not ensure effectiveness, its absence leaves listeners wishing they were somewhere else.

Preparing the inner vessel and thorough preparation of the message create the necessary foundation for effectively communicating the message to others. Caring sensitivity, thoughtful interaction, and inspiration of the Spirit enhance teachers' ability to carry the message *unto* the minds and hearts of those being taught (2 Ne. 33:1). Additionally, more formal teaching assignments in the Church require proper authorization (e.g., 5:6; 11:15; 42:11) and then operating within one's assigned stewardship (e.g., 38:23; 81:5; 88:128; 107:99).

Every context in which a teacher works is unique, including the age, attitude, and

PREPARING THE INNER VESSEL

Do not aspire to the honors of men:

- 30:1–3. "But your mind has been on the things of the earth more than on the things of me."
- 58:39. "Let him repent of his sins, for he seeketh the praise of the world."
- 67:5. "You have sought in your hearts knowledge that you might express beyond [Joseph Smith's] language."
- 121:35. "Their hearts are set so much upon the things of this world, and aspire to the honors of men."

Repent daily:

- 66:3. "You are clean, but not all; repent, therefore, of those things which are not pleasing in my sight . . . for the Lord will show them unto you."
- 93:43. "There are many things that are not right in your house."
- 112:33. "Cleanse your hearts and your garments."

Keep the commandments:

- 42:13. "And they shall observe the covenants and church articles to do them, and these shall be their teachings, as they shall be directed by the Spirit."
- 52:14–17. "I will give unto you a pattern in all things, that ye may not be deceived; . . . he that prayeth, whose spirit is contrite, . . . if he obey mine ordinances . . . , whose language is meek and edifieth, the same is of God if he obey mine ordinances

. . . [and] trembleth under my power . . . and shall bring forth fruits of praise and wisdom."
- 63:23. "But unto him that keepeth my commandments I will give the mysteries of my kingdom."
- 97:3–5. "As he continueth to abide in me . . . I will bless him . . . in expounding all scriptures."
- 121:45. "Let virtue garnish thy thoughts unceasingly."

Grow in humility:
- 1:28. "And inasmuch as they were humble they might be made strong."
- 58:41. "Also he hath need to repent, . . . for he seeketh to excel, and he is not sufficiently meek before me."
- 100:7. "But a commandment I give unto you, that ye shall declare whatsoever thing ye declare in my name, in solemnity of heart, in the spirit of meekness, in all things."
- 136:32. "Let him that is ignorant learn wisdom by humbling himself."

Let go of pride:
- 23:1. "But beware of pride."
- 25:14. "Continue in the spirit of meekness."
- 42:40. "Thou shalt not be proud in thy heart; let all thy garments be plain."
- 63:55. "He exalted himself in his heart, and received not counsel, but grieved the Spirit."

PREPARING THE MESSAGE

Pray for inspiration:
- 6:14. "Blessed art thou for what thou hast done; for thou hast inquired of me, and . . . as often as thou hast inquired thou hast received instruction of my Spirit."
- 19:38. "Pray always, and I will pour out my Spirit upon you."
- 42:61. "If thou shalt ask, thou shalt receive revelation upon revelation, knowledge upon knowledge, that thou mayest know the mysteries and peaceable things."
- 75:10. "Calling on the name of the Lord for the Comforter, which shall teach them all things that are expedient for them."

Study the doctrine:
- 1:37. "Search these commandments, for they are true and faithful."
- 11:22. "Study my word which hath gone forth among the children of men, and also study my word which shall come forth among the children of men."
- 26:1. "I say unto you that you shall let your time be devoted to the studying of the scriptures, and to preaching."
- 88:78. "That you may be instructed more perfectly in theory, in principle, in doctrine, in the law of the gospel."
- 88:118. "And as all have not faith, seek ye diligently and teach one another words

of wisdom; yea, seek ye out of the best books words of wisdom; seek learning, even by study and also by faith."

COMMUNICATING THE MESSAGE

Organize a spiritual environment:

- 88:119–20. "Organize yourselves; prepare every needful thing; and establish . . . a house of learning . . . that your incomings may be in the name of the Lord."

Create an atmosphere of respect and caring:

- 43:8. "When ye are assembled together ye shall instruct and edify each other, that ye may know how to act and direct my church, how to act upon the points of my law and commandments."
- 88:122. "Appoint among yourselves a teacher, and let not all be spokesmen at once; but let one speak at a time and let all listen unto his sayings, . . . that all may be edified of all, and that every man may have an equal privilege."
- 88:132–33. "Let the teacher arise, and . . . salute his brother or brethren with these words: . . . I salute you in the name of the Lord Jesus Christ, . . . I receive you to fellowship . . . to be your friend and brother . . . in the bonds of love."
- 121:41–45. "No power or influence can or ought to be maintained . . . only by persuasion, by long-suffering, by gentleness and meekness, and by love unfeigned. . . . Let thy bowels also be full of charity towards all men."

Teach with the Spirit:

- 11:21. "Seek not to declare my word, but first seek to obtain my word, and then shall your tongue be loosed; then, if you desire, you shall have my Spirit and my word, yea, the power of God unto the convincing of men."
- 28:1. "Thou shalt be heard by the church in all things whatsoever thou shalt teach them by the Comforter."
- 42:13–14. "They shall be directed by the Spirit. . . . And if ye receive not the Spirit ye shall not teach."
- 50:14. "Preach my gospel by the Spirit, even the Comforter which was sent forth to teach the truth."
- 100:6–8. "For it shall be given you in the very hour, yea, in the very moment, what ye shall say. . . . The Holy Ghost shall be shed forth in bearing record unto all things whatsoever ye shall say."

knowledge of class members as well as the teacher's personality, background, and testimony. Understanding and applying scriptures in any teaching situation require inspiration. The accompanying table identifies, in three categories, scriptures relevant to effective teaching. Each principle was first given in a unique context in early Church history but can be applied to anyone in any age.

See also Knowledge; Learning; Missionary work.

DCC

Teacher(s)

A term used in two ways in the Doctrine and Covenants:

1. One who instructs others in a classroom (88:122), such as in the School of the Prophets (88:128, 132).

2. An office in the Aaronic, or lesser, PRIESTHOOD (84:30). Like other priesthood offices, an individual is ordained to the office of teacher "according to the gifts and callings of God unto him . . . by the power of the Holy Ghost, which is in the one who ordains him" (20:60). The duties of a teacher include taking the lead of meetings when no elder or priest is present; watching over the Church and seeing that there is "no iniquity . . . neither hardness with each other, neither lying, backbiting, nor evil speaking; and [seeing] that the church meet together often, and . . . that all the members do their duty" (20:54–55; 84:111). Teachers also are "to warn, expound, exhort, and teach, and invite all to come unto Christ" (20:59). They do not "have authority to baptize, administer the sacrament, or lay on hands" (20:58). A teacher belongs to a group (quorum) of up to twenty-four teachers presided over by a president who is "to sit in council with them, teaching them the duties of their office" (107:62, 86). Early in this dispensation, teachers, along with ELDERS, PRIESTS, and DEACONS, were authorized to sign letters certifying that worthy members, moving to areas where they were not previously known, were "regular members . . . in good standing" in the Church (20:84).

In the early Church, in order to keep general Church membership records updated, teachers (who were usually mature men) were sent from the various branches to "conferences held by the elders of the church" to report who had joined the Church and who had been "expelled" (20:81–83).

HDG

Teeth, gnashing of. *See* Gnashing of teeth.

Telestial kingdom. *See* Kingdoms of glory and perdition, vision of.

Temperance. *See* Appendix E.

Temple(s)

An important and unique part of the restored gospel of Jesus Christ, temples are dedicated buildings in which sacred ordinances are performed. President Howard W. Hunter admonished, "I invite the Latter-day Saints to look to the temple of the Lord as the great symbol of your membership" (8). In ancient times, temples served two distinct functions: (1) a place of revelation or contact between God and man (Ex. 25:8, 22), and (2) a place for sacred priesthood ordinances (Talmage, 15; 124:38). Temples that serve both of these functions are part of the latter-day restoration of all things (Acts 3:21; Eph. 1:10).

The building and purposes of temples have been unfolded line upon line in this dispensation by means of revelations now contained in the Doctrine and Covenants.

A forerunner to temple procedures and worship can be seen in the School of the Prophets that began three years before the dedication of the Kirtland Temple. An 1832 revelation instructed Church leaders to convene a "solemn assembly" to prepare those who would go forth to preach. Only worthy brethren were to attend and were told by the Lord to "purify your hearts, and cleanse your hands and your feet before me, that I may make you clean" (88:70, 74–75, 134; cf. 97:15–17). In this same revelation, the Lord commanded the brethren to "establish . . . a house of God" (88:119). This house would be the Kirtland Temple.

In 1833, the following year, the Lord directed that the temple and two other sacred buildings should be planned for Kirtland (94:1–12). That same year, the Prophet drew up a plat for the city of Zion. The plan he envisioned expanded the number of holy buildings at the center of the city from three to twenty-four. These "temples" were to be assigned to the various priesthood quorums and were to serve a variety of functions including "houses of worship, schools, etc." (Smith, 1:358–59). Two years earlier, Joseph Smith had placed a cornerstone for a temple at Independence, Missouri, but persecution during the summer and fall of 1833 led to the Saints being driven from Jackson County before any work on the temple could begin.

Meanwhile, on 1 June 1833, the Lord admonished the Saints to move forward with building the Kirtland Temple, in which he would endow the Saints "with power from on high" (95:8). He specified that the temple was not to be built "after the manner of the world," but according to a plan that he promised to reveal—the main spaces being used for worship and education (95:8, 13–17).

Thus, "the design and construction of the Kirtland Temple was different from that of all other latter-day temples because its purpose was different. While already in 1836 certain ordinances had been introduced in a limited way which later would form part of the regular temple ordinances, the sacred ordinances and ceremonies performed in today's temples were not done in this first temple" (Packer, 129).

Great spiritual blessings and remarkable manifestations followed the period of sacrifice during the temple's construction. On 21 January 1836, at a meeting in the nearly completed Kirtland Temple, "the heavens were opened" and the Prophet saw the glorious celestial kingdom, as recorded in section 137. When he saw his brother Alvin in that kingdom, he "marveled" because Alvin had died before the gospel was restored and so had not been baptized. But the Lord declared: "All who have died without a knowledge of this gospel, who would have received it if they had been permitted to tarry, shall be heirs of the celestial kingdom

The Kirtland Temple; photographer unknown, ca. 1860–1900. "The hearts of thousands and tens of thousands shall greatly rejoice in consequence of the blessings which shall be poured out, and the endowment with which my servants have been endowed in this house. And the fame of this house shall spread to foreign lands; and this is the beginning of the blessing which shall be poured out upon the heads of my people" (D&C 110:9–10).

of God" (137:1, 6–7). This assurance became the foundation for the doctrine of SALVATION FOR THE DEAD, including ordinances performed vicariously in temples. *See* Historical context and overview of Doctrine and Covenants 137 (p. 858).

In the following weeks, many Saints received visions, prophesied, or spoke in tongues (Backman, 285). Joseph Smith recorded, "This was a time of rejoicing long to be remembered" (2:392).

Some of the most memorable spiritual experiences occurred on Sunday, 27 March 1836, the day the temple was dedicated. Hundreds of Latter-day Saints crowded into the temple. In the seven-hour dedicatory service, Sidney Rigdon spoke eloquently, declaring that among all the buildings erected for the worship of God, the temple was unique, having been "built by divine revelation" (Smith, 2:415). *See* Kirtland Temple dedication.

Transcendently important spiritual manifestations occurred on Easter Sunday, 3 April, just one week following the temple's dedication. After the close of the afternoon worship service, Joseph Smith and Oliver Cowdery retired to the Melchizedek Priesthood pulpits in the west end of the lower room of the temple. The veil, a canvas partition, was lowered so that they might pray in private. They then saw a series of remarkable visions. The Lord Jesus Christ appeared, accepted the temple, and promised to manifest himself therein "if my people will keep my commandments, and do not pollute this holy house" (110:8). Three other heavenly messengers then appeared. Moses bestowed "the keys of the gathering of Israel." Elias "committed the dispensation of the gospel of Abraham." Elijah restored KEYS by which priesthood ordinances performed on earth can be bound, or sealed, in heaven for both the living and the dead (110:11–16). *See* Historical context and overview of Doctrine and Covenants 110 (p. 819).

Not long after these glorious occurrences, the forces of persecution increased. In less than two years, the faithful were compelled to flee from their homes in Kirtland. Together with those who had earlier been driven from Jackson County, they gathered at Far West, Missouri, in 1838. Here they were directed to build another temple where they might gather and worship the Lord (115:8). Cornerstones were laid on 4 July 1838, but a few months later the Saints in Missouri were ordered to leave that state without having the chance to build their temple.

By 1839, they had found a new haven in Illinois, where they built the city of Nauvoo. Here the Lord unfolded to their understanding the doctrine of salvation for the dead and restored vital temple ordinances—the second of the two main functions of temples.

Baptism for the dead (1 Cor. 15:29) was first taught in the present dispensation on 15 August 1840 (Ehat and Cook, 49). Almost immediately, Church members began receiving this ordinance in the Mississippi River in behalf of deceased loved ones. By January 1845 more than fifteen thousand baptisms had been performed in behalf of the dead (Black, 39).

In August 1840 the First Presidency declared that the time had come "to erect a house of prayer, a house of order, a house for the worship of our God, where the ordinances can be attended to agreeably to His divine will" (Smith, 4:186).

A revelation received on 19 January 1841 directed the Saints to build a house "for the Most High to dwell therein. For there is not a place found on earth that he may come to and restore again that which was lost . . . , even the fulness of the priesthood." Specifically, the Lord declared that sacred ordinances such as baptism for the dead, washings, anointings, solemn assemblies, memorials, and so forth "belongeth to my house," in temples "which my people are always commanded to build unto my holy name" (124:27–28, 30, 37–40). Hence the Nauvoo Temple was to serve the dual purposes of being a place of revelation from God to man and also a place for sacred priesthood ordinances to be performed.

Anticipating the building of the temple and eager to restore sacred temple rites, Joseph Smith introduced the temple endowment on 4 May 1842 for the first time in this dispensation. It took place with just a few Church leaders in the assembly room above Joseph's Red Brick

Store, arranged for that special purpose (Smith, 5:1–2). By the time of the Prophet's martyrdom, more than fifty individuals had received the blessings of the endowment, which were given in that assembly room or in private homes (Cowan, 55).

The martyrdom of Joseph and Hyrum Smith on 27 June 1844 caused only a temporary halt to the temple construction. Even though the Saints knew they would soon be forced to leave Nauvoo, they were willing to sacrifice to complete the Lord's house. The temple was completed and dedicated a part at a time so that ordinance work could commence as soon as possible.

Endowments were administered in the Nauvoo Temple beginning 10 December 1845. As pressure on the Saints to leave Illinois mounted, Church leaders decided to commence the exodus early in February 1846 rather than wait until spring. This increased the Saints' eagerness to receive their temple blessings before leaving Nauvoo. During the eight weeks before the exodus, approximately 5,500 Saints were endowed. The completed temple was dedicated 1 May 1846, after most of the Saints had left for the West.

Years later, in 1918, President Joseph F. Smith received a remarkable vision that expanded the understanding of how the Lord inaugurated the preaching of the gospel in the spirit world: "From among the righteous, he organized his forces and appointed messengers, clothed with power and authority, and commissioned them to go forth and carry the light of the gospel to them that were in darkness" (138:30). Through "the ordinances of the house of God" those who accept the gospel there can be "redeemed" (138:58). *See* Historical context and overview of Doctrine and Covenants 138 (p. 859).

See also Endow, endowed, endowment; Endowment House; Ordinances; Wash, washed, washing(s).

BIBLIOGRAPHY

Backman, Milton V., Jr. *The Heavens Resound: A History of the Latter-day Saints in Ohio, 1830–1838.* Salt Lake City: Deseret Book Company, 1983.

Black, Susan Easton. "A Voice of Gladness." *Ensign* 34 (February 2004): 35–39.

Cowan, Richard O. *Temples to Dot the Earth.* Springville, Utah: Cedar Fort, 1997.

Ehat, Andrew F., and Lyndon W. Cook, comps. and eds. *The Words of Joseph Smith.* Provo, Utah: Grandin Book Co., 1991.

Hunter, Howard W. "Exceeding Great and Precious Promises." *Ensign* 24 (November 1994): 7–8.

Packer, Boyd K. *The Holy Temple.* Salt Lake City: Bookcraft Publishers, 1980.

Smith, Joseph. *History of the Church of Jesus Christ of Latter-day Saints.* Edited by B. H. Roberts. 7 vols. 2d ed. rev. Salt Lake City: The Church of Jesus Christ of Latter-day Saints, 1932–51.

Talmage, James E. *The House of the Lord.* Salt Lake City: Deseret Book, 1976.

Woodruff, Wilford. *Wilford Woodruff's Journal: 1833–1898.* Typescript. Edited by Scott G. Kenney. 9 vols. Midvale, Utah: Signature Books, 1983–84.

ROC

Temporal

The condition of the earth and all earthly things as a consequence of the fall of Adam, including DEATH, decay, corrosion, aging, and the natural tendency for things to wear out, run down, and become disorganized. Certain aspects of the temporal state have to do with time (*tempo*) and nonpermanency (*temporary*). *Temporal,* which connotes time, death, and change, stands in contrast to *spiritual,* which connotes eternity, life, and constancy (88:110; Alma 40:8).

This earth when first created was physical but not temporal or mortal; that is, no death was attached to it. If there had been no Fall, all things of the earth would "have remained [forever] in the same state in which they were after they were created" (2 Ne. 2:22; Moses 3:9). *See* Fall of Adam and Eve, the.

Temporal state a necessity

The temporal status of the earth is necessary for mankind to "taste the bitter, that they may know to prize the good" (Moses 6:55–56), for "if they never should have bitter they could not know the sweet" (29:39).

Items known as the "temporalities" are the necessities of mortal life: food, drink, sleep, clothing, houses, means of transportation and other material things. These practical items sustain mortal life. But mortal life has a spiritual purpose.

President Howard W. Hunter used the example of a boat to explain the concept of temporal resistance. Water provides resistance to the movement of a boat, but the same water provides necessary resistance to the oars to propel the boat forward. "Resistance creates both the opposition and the forward movement. . . . The law of friction or resistance that we think of as only applying to science seems to find application in our personal lives. . . . We came to mortal life to encounter resistance. It was part of the plan for our eternal progress" (Hunter, 24–25).

The Lord issues no temporal laws

In the temporal condition men's lives are finite and subject to weakness and death; however, God is infinite and SPIRITUAL. To him "all things . . . are spiritual," and "not at any time" has he given unto any man "a law which was temporal." His commandments are not "natural nor temporal, neither carnal nor sensual" (29:34–35). This means more than that everything God does has an ultimate spiritual goal. It also means that it would be contrary to his nature to do only temporal things. The Prophet Joseph Smith seems to be speaking of this distinction when he said, "All things whatsoever God in his infinite wisdom has seen fit and proper to reveal to us, while we are dwelling in mortality, in regard to our mortal bodies, are revealed to us in the abstract, and independent of affinity of this mortal tabernacle, but are revealed to our spirits precisely as though we had no bodies at all" (6:312).

The Lord said that the "first shall be last . . . in all things"; this earth was first spiritual and then temporal and will again be spiritual (29:30–33); and the temporal and the spiritual have their likeness (77:2), meaning they resemble each other in appearance. The temporal experience is an essential part but is neither the beginning nor the end of man's existence.

BIBLIOGRAPHY

Hunter, Howard W. "God Will Have a Tried People." *Ensign* 10 (May 1980): 24–25.

Smith, Joseph. *History of The Church of Jesus Christ of Latter-day Saints*. Edited by B. H. Roberts. 7 vols. 2d ed. rev. Salt Lake City: The Church of Jesus Christ of Latter-day Saints, 1932–51.

RJM

Temporal death. *See* Death.

Temptation(s)

Enticement to make wrong decisions and to sin. *Temptation* and its variants appear more than twenty times in the Doctrine and Covenants. Contexts in which they are used include Satan's role in temptation, not yielding to or entering into temptation, and receiving the Savior's help in overcoming temptation.

A recurring theme in the Doctrine and Covenants is that SATAN is the source of temptation (e.g., 10:15; 29:36–40; 40:2). The Doctrine and Covenants also teaches that Satan's POWER is limited. He does not have power to "tempt little children" (29:47), and during the MILLENNIUM "Satan shall not have power to tempt any man" (101:28), until "the thousand years are ended" and he is "loosed for a little season" (29:22; 88:110–11).

Although facing the temptations of Satan is necessary in order for "the children of men" to be "agents unto themselves" (29:39), the Lord instructs the Saints not only to avoid sinning, that is, to "*yield* to no temptation" (9:13; emphasis added) but to avoid even *entering into* temptation. The Lord told Oliver Cowdery to "beware of pride, lest thou shouldst enter into temptation" (23:1). He also instructed "the church," Thomas B. Marsh, and the missionaries returning to Kirtland from Missouri to "pray always" lest they "fall into" or "enter into" temptation (20:33; 31:12; 61:39). Nephi added holding fast to the iron rod—the word of God—as another safeguard against "the fiery darts of the adversary" (1 Ne. 15:23–24). Avoiding entering into temptation requires constant vigilance, controlling circumstances, thoughts, words, and deeds, and faithfully keeping the commandments of God (cf. Mosiah 4:29–30).

The Lord "knoweth the weakness of man" (62:1) and each individual's temptations (66:10), and because he has suffered "temptations of every kind" (Alma 7:11–13), he knows "how to succor them who are tempted" (62:1). And he has promised, "I prepare a way for their deliverance in all things out of temptation" (95:1).

In 10:15 the word *tempt* is used by the Lord in context with the loss of the 116 pages of Book of Mormon manuscript. Satan put it into the heart of those who stole the manuscript to get Joseph Smith to "tempt the Lord . . . in asking to translate it over again." Here *tempt* means to test or try.

See also Sin, transgression.

JLH

Tenets. *See* Appendix E.

Terrestrial kingdom. *See* Kingdoms of glory and perdition, vision of.

Testify

To make a solemn declaration of the veracity of something; to bear witness of a known truth based on strong evidence and personal experience. For example, the Three Witnesses of the Book of Mormon were commanded by the Lord that after they had obtained a view of the plates, they "shall testify of them, by the power of God" (17:3, 5). The scriptures contain many accounts of prophets, apostles, and disciples who testified of the truths of the GOSPEL they had come to know for themselves through REVELATION, reason, and experience. Likewise, as Saints and others study the Lord's words and receive a witness of their truthfulness, they "can testify that [they] have heard [God's] voice, and know [his] words" (18:36). Moreover, the Lord charged his faithful disciples to do "that which the Spirit testifies unto you" (46:7).

All members of the Church, by virtue of the baptismal covenant, stand "as witnesses of God at all times and in all things" (Mosiah 18:9). Each has the obligation to "testify and warn the people" because "it becometh every man who hath been warned to warn his neighbor" (88:81). Holy prophets testify of Christ "in all things." Christ's mission was not only for "those who believed after he came in the meridian of time, in the flesh, but all those from the beginning, even as many as were before he came, who believed in the words of the holy prophets,

who spake as they were inspired by the gift of the Holy Ghost, who truly testified of him in all things, should have eternal life" (20:26; cf. 138:36, 46–49).

See also Record(s); Testimony.

BLT

Testimony

A witness or declaration concerning something one knows to be true. Though a few references throughout the Doctrine and Covenants use the term to describe legal declarations made in court decisions, including Church disciplinary councils (68:23; 102:26; 107:72), the large majority refer to declarations made by an individual concerning a divine truth. One purpose of such declarations is to establish God's words to the rest of the world. The most familiar use of the term is that in which missionaries and members are exhorted to "bear testimony" of truth, Christ, his name, and revelations they have received (6:31; 58:47; 66:7; 76:22; 84:61–62, 94–95; 109:56; 112:1). *See* Testify.

The seriousness of this exhortation is reflected in the truth that (1) the testimony of the gospel is to be sealed up prior to judgment, condemning the wicked who reject the testimony (5:18; 88:84; 109:38, 46; 133:72), and (2) testimonies are recorded in heaven (62:3). Both the Bible and the Book of Mormon are referred to as testimonies (3:16–18; cf. 88:3, 141).

There are at least two events in which testimony is used to describe a nonverbal witness: (1) The cleansing of one's feet, either by dusting them off or by washing, as a testimony witnessing the rejection of the message of the Lord's servants (24:15; 60:15; 75:20; 84:92; 99:4), and (2) "the testimony of earthquakes [and] the testimony of the voice of thunderings," following the testimony of the missionaries (88:88–90). As the last reference demonstrates, God himself bears testimony. After questions concerning Joseph Smith's revelations, the Lord gave "testimony of the truth of these commandments" (67:4; cf. 124:8). During the Kirtland Temple dedicatory prayer, the Prophet Joseph Smith referred to the Saints' suffering in Missouri, querying, "How long wilt thou suffer this people to bear this affliction . . . and not make a display of thy testimony in their behalf?" (109:49). Demonstrating its importance, the reception of Christ's testimony and valiance in that testimony are distinguishing characteristics between individuals in the kingdoms of glory (76:51, 74, 79, 82).

See also Holy Ghost, the; Knowledge.

DLB

Testimony of Jesus. *See* Kingdoms of glory and perdition, vision of.

Thankfulness, thanksgiving

The celebration, acknowledgment, attitude, or expression of gratitude for God-given gifts, blessings, and kindnesses.

Beginning with a series of "Thou shalt" verses in section 59, the Lord made it clear that supplication and returning thanks to him for "all things" (59:7) is not just a pleasant invitation, but a commandment (59:5–7). God's children are to do "all things with prayer" (46:7; 2 Ne. 9:52), "live in thanksgiving daily, for the many mercies and blessings" bestowed upon them (Alma 34:38–39), and acknowledge "with a thankful heart" his hand as the source of those blessings (62:7). Saints are expected to return thanks to God by obeying his commandments (59:21) and offering "a sacrifice unto the Lord thy God in righteousness, even that of a broken heart and a contrite spirit" (59:7–8). God warned, however, that he is offended and "his wrath kindled" when "his hand in all things" is not acknowledged (59:21).

There is an intrinsic connection between prayer and thankfulness (88:137). When one prays, God is prepared to give "liberally" (46:7). Joseph Smith was taught, "In everything give thanks." In return, the Lord promised with an "immutable covenant" to answer his prayer, but he was to "[wait] patiently on the Lord" (98:1–3). When an answer is received, "ye must give thanks . . . for whatsoever blessing ye are blessed with" (46:32). Prayers of thanksgiving also protect against being "seduced by evil spirits, or doctrines of devils, or the commandments of men" (46:7). The Kirkland Temple was to be a "place of thanksgiving for all saints" (97:13; cf. 109:1).

The attitude and the manner in which one expresses gratitude are important. When addressing the subject of the Sabbath day, the Lord noted that when Saints do "these things with thanksgiving, with cheerful hearts and countenances, . . . the fulness of the earth is yours. . . . And it pleaseth God that he hath given all these things unto man" (59:12–20; cf. 89:11). "And he who receiveth all things with thankfulness shall be made glorious; and the things of this earth shall be added unto him, even an hundred fold, yea, more" (78:19). The beauties of this earth cannot be taken for granted. When one lives in thanksgiving daily, he or she somehow sees with spiritual eyes the many gifts and kindnesses of God and is thankful. President Joseph F. Smith commented: "Where there is an absence of gratitude, either to God or man, there is the presence of vanity and the spirit of self-sufficiency. . . . The grateful man sees so much in the world to be thankful for, and with him the good outweighs the evil. Love overpowers jealousy, and light drives darkness out of his life. Pride destroys our gratitude and sets up selfishness in its place. How much happier we are in the presence of a grateful and loving soul, and how careful we should be to cultivate, through the medium of a prayerful life, a thankful attitude toward God and man!" (262–63).

BIBLIOGRAPHY

Smith, Joseph F. Smith. *Gospel Doctrine.* Salt Lake City: Deseret Book, 1986.

MMM

Thayre (or Thayer), Ezra

Birth: 1793, New York

Death: 6 September 1862, Cass County, Michigan

While listening to Hyrum Smith preach in Palmyra, New York, "tears rolled down" Ezra Thayre's cheeks as he received a spiritual confirmation of the truthfulness of the gospel (in Cook, 47). Consequently, in October 1830, Parley P. Pratt baptized Thayre and Joseph Smith confirmed him.

Shortly following Thayre's baptism, Joseph Smith received a revelation calling Thayre to be a missionary companion to Northrop Sweet

(33:1–2). Thayre responded to his call by preaching at several different homes as he made the journey from New York to Ohio. Many were baptized as a result of his labors.

On 3 June 1831, Thayre was ordained a high priest at the fourth general conference of the Church, held in Kirtland, Ohio. Four days later, he was called to serve a mission with Thomas B. Marsh (52:22). During this time, Leman Copley broke a covenant he had made to consecrate his farm "as a place of inheritance for the Saints arriving from Colesville, New York." Because Thayre became "involved in the controversy," the Lord "revoke[d]" his mission call, and Selah J. Griffin accompanied Marsh in his place (54, headnote; 56:4–5).

As a result of "rebellious" choices, the Lord commanded Thayre to "repent of his pride, and of his selfishness" and to "obey the former commandment . . . concerning the place upon which he lives" (56:4, 8). If Thayre repented, he would still be "appointed" to travel to Missouri (56:9). Shortly thereafter, in a conference setting, he was chastised by W. W. Phelps for his "unwise course" (Cannon and Cook, 15–16). Several months later, on 25 January 1832, Thayre was again called to serve a mission with Thomas B. Marsh (75:31). They faithfully fulfilled this responsibility, serving in New York through the summer and into the early fall. On 1 March 1835 Thayre was ordained a seventy.

In May 1835, Thayre's Church membership was suspended based on a complaint from Oliver Granger (Smith, 2:221). His membership was later restored, and he served on the high council in Adam-ondi-Ahman. At the death of the Prophet Joseph Smith, he did not follow the leadership of the Twelve and on 24 August 1860 was baptized a member of the Reorganized Church of Jesus Christ of Latter Day Saints (now the Community of Christ).

BIBLIOGRAPHY

Black, Susan Easton. *Early Members of the Reorganized Church of Jesus Christ of Latter Day Saints.* 6 vols. Provo, Utah: Religious Studies Center, Brigham Young University, 1993.

Cannon, Donald Q., and Lyndon W. Cook, eds. *Far West Record: Minutes of The Church of Jesus Christ of Latter-day Saints, 1830–1844.* Salt Lake City: Deseret Book, 1983.

Cook, Lyndon W. *The Revelations of the Prophet Joseph Smith.* Salt Lake City: Deseret Book, 1985.

Smith, Joseph. *History of The Church of Jesus Christ of Latter-day Saints.* Edited by B. H. Roberts. 7 vols. 2d ed. rev. Salt Lake City: The Church of Jesus Christ of Latter-day Saints, 1932–51.

RC

They are as grass

A biblical image also employed in modern revelation (124:7) to symbolize the transitory nature of the life of man. For example: "As for man, his days are as grass: as a flower of the field, so he flourisheth. For the wind passeth over it, and it is gone" (Ps. 103:15–16; cf. Isa. 40:6–8; 51:12; 1 Pet. 1:24). With the heavy rains of wintertime, grass flourishes and spreads its velvety green carpet even over the barren wilderness; but with the wisp of the hot desert wind, it is gone. The blades are vivacious and vigorous one day, vanished the next. So is the life of man.

In Doctrine and Covenants 124 the Lord commanded Joseph Smith to "make a solemn proclamation of my gospel. . . . This proclamation shall be made to all the kings of the world . . . to the honorable president-elect, and the high-minded governors of the nation in which you live, and to all the nations of the earth. . . . Call ye, therefore, upon them with loud proclamation, and with your testimony, fearing them not, for *they are as grass,* and all their glory as the flower thereof which soon falleth" (124:2–3, 7; emphasis added).

DKO

Thief in the night. *See* Jesus Christ, second coming of.

Third part of the hosts of heaven. *See* War in heaven.

Thompson, Ohio

A township located about sixteen miles northeast of Kirtland, known today as Madison. In May 1831, when the Saints from Colesville, New York, were arriving in Ohio, it became necessary to make arrangements for their settlement (51, headnote). Church leaders contracted with recent convert Leman Copley to allow the

Colesville Saints to occupy and improve his 759 acres in Thompson. Following that arrangement, the Colesville Saints settled on the Copley property. Newel Knight was appointed president of the Thompson branch. Bishop Edward Partridge implemented the principle of CONSECRATION and stewardship with the Thompson branch members in compliance with a revelation received by Joseph Smith concerning the matter (51). In June 1831, just weeks after the Colesville Saints had settled in Thompson, Copley reneged on his contract and forced the newcomers from his property (54, headnote; vv. 4–5). In response to the broken contract, the Lord instructed the Colesville Saints to "flee the land" and "journey . . . unto the land of Missouri" (54:7–8). Of Copley, the Lord said, "Wo to him by whom this offense cometh, for it had been better for him that he had been drowned in the depth of the sea" (54:5). Leman Copley was disfellowshipped and reinstated twice after this, in 1831 and 1834, but did not later gather with the Saints (Cook, 67). The Colesville Saints, on the other hand, obediently moved from Thompson to western Missouri (Smith, 1:180–81).

It is not known to what extent, if any, the "stiffneckedness of my people which are in Thompson, and their rebellions" (56:6) included the Colesville Saints. Evidently, it did have to do with Ezra Thayre's "pride" and "selfishness" concerning a land deal in Kirtland that delayed him from his assigned mission with Thomas B. Marsh (56:3–5, 8; Cook, 88–89). These attitudes and actions of Thayre made a change in missionary companionships necessary (cf. 52:22, 32; 56:5–6).

Moreover, in consequence of the "stiffneckedness" and "rebellions" at Thompson, Newel Knight was required to forgo his mission with Selah Griffin and instead stay with the Colesville Saints and lead them to Missouri. Knight was told to take "as many as will go . . . that are contrite before me" (56:7), suggesting that there may have been some who were not sufficiently contrite. *See* map, p. 461.

See also Historical context and overview of Doctrine and Covenants 51 (p. 757), 54 (p. 759), and 56 (p. 761).

BIBLIOGRAPHY

Cook, Lyndon W. *The Revelations of the Prophet Joseph Smith.* Salt Lake City: Deseret Book, 1985.

Smith, Joseph. *History of The Church of Jesus Christ of Latter-day Saints.* Edited by B. H. Roberts. 7 vols. 2d ed. rev. Salt Lake City: The Church of Jesus Christ of Latter-day Saints, 1932–51.

MVB

Thompson, Robert B.

Birth: 1 October 1811, Great Driffield, Yorkshire, England

Death: 27 August 1841, Nauvoo, Hancock County, Illinois

Robert Thompson was a Methodist preacher in England before migrating in 1834 to Upper Canada. There in May 1836 he accepted the gospel and was baptized and confirmed by Parley P. Pratt. A year later he moved with his family to Kirtland, Ohio, but soon returned to Canada and served a successful mission. After this mission, increased persecution in Kirtland led him to move to Far West, Missouri. Because of hostilities in Missouri, Thompson fought in the Battle of Crooked River. Later he, with others, suffered exposure and hunger while trying to avoid the enemies of the Church who vowed to "kill every man who had been engaged in the Crooked River battle" (Smith, 4:411).

After being driven from Missouri, Thompson settled in Quincy, Illinois, where he was a reporter for the *Argus* newspaper and a courthouse clerk. He moved to Commerce (later Nauvoo), Illinois in 1839, where he served as a scribe for the Prophet Joseph Smith. He also served as general Church clerk, city treasurer, regent of the University of Nauvoo, and as a colonel and aide-de-camp in the Nauvoo Legion.

In September 1840, Thompson delivered the funeral sermon of Joseph Smith Sr. In a revelation received on 19 January 1841 the Lord directed Joseph Smith to call Thompson to assist in writing a proclamation to the kings and political rulers of the earth. The Lord said he was "well pleased" with Thompson and that hearkening to the Prophet's counsel would bring him a "multiplicity of blessings." The Lord said, "Let him be faithful and true in all things from henceforth, and he shall be great in mine eyes; but let him remember that his stewardship will

I require at his hands" (124:12–14). *See* Solemn proclamation.

Thompson served with Don Carlos Smith as associate editor of the *Times and Seasons* in Nauvoo from May to August 1841. The Prophet Joseph wrote that "Elder Robert Blashel Thompson died of "quick consumption" at his residence in Nauvoo, in the 30th year of his age, in the full hope of a glorious resurrection" (4:411).

BIBLIOGRAPHY

Smith, Joseph. *History of The Church of Jesus Christ of Latter-day Saints.* Edited by B. H. Roberts. 7 vols. 2d ed. rev. Salt Lake City: The Church of Jesus Christ of Latter-day Saints, 1932–51.

KWF

Thoughts

Unspoken ideas conceived in the MIND. Revelations in the Doctrine and Covenants connect thoughts with the "intents of the heart" and make it clear that only God knows one's thoughts and intentions (33:1; cf. 6:16; 88:109). The Lord provided the early Latter-day Saints with much counsel concerning their thoughts. In April 1829, he told Joseph Smith and Oliver Cowdery, "Look unto me in every thought" (6:36). That same month, the Lord instructed Cowdery concerning the process of translation, telling him that after studying the issue and asking for confirmation, "If it be not right . . . you shall have a stupor of thought that shall cause you to forget the thing which is wrong" (9:9). In section 88 the Lord directed those he called "my friends" to "cast away [their] idle thoughts" (vv. 62, 69). The Lord commanded missionaries: "Take ye no thought for the morrow, for what ye shall eat, or what ye shall drink, or wherewithal ye shall be clothed" (84:81), meaning they should not be concerned about their temporal needs while preaching the gospel (84:81–84; cf. 24:18; 3 Ne. 13:25–34; Matt. 6:25–34). In addition, these missionaries were told, "Neither take ye thought beforehand what ye shall say" but instead "treasure up in your minds continually the words of life, and it shall be given you in the very hour" (84:85; cf. 100:5–6). While Joseph Smith and Sidney Rigdon were serving a mission in eastern New York in October 1833, the Lord testified again of his power to inspire their preaching: "Speak the thoughts that I shall put into your hearts" (100:5). When he was imprisoned in LIBERTY JAIL in March 1839, the Prophet Joseph Smith was counseled, "Let virtue garnish [or supply] thy thoughts unceasingly" (121:45). In Nauvoo in January 1841, the Lord promised William Law, a member of the First Presidency at the time, that if he remained faithful "he shall mount up in the imagination of his thoughts as upon eagles' wings" (124:99), meaning that his thought processes would be lofty and inspired. Similarly, Joseph Smith declared, "Thy mind, O man! if thou wilt lead a soul unto salvation, must stretch as high as the utmost heavens" (3:295).

See also Desire(s); Heart(s).

BIBLIOGRAPHY

Smith, Joseph. *History of The Church of Jesus Christ of Latter-day Saints.* Edited by B. H. Roberts. 7 vols. 2d ed. rev. Salt Lake City: The Church of Jesus Christ of Latter-day Saints, 1932–51.

FFJ

Thrash the nations by the power of my/ his Spirit

The word *thrash* or *thresh* has two meanings: (1) to "beat out grain from the husk," and (2) "to beat soundly with a stick or whip; to drub" (Webster, s.v. "thrash"). The phrase "thrash the nations by the power of my [his] Spirit," occurs twice in the Doctrine and Covenants (35:13; 133:59; cf. 1:19) and seems clearly to refer to the first meaning. The second meaning of *thrash* is implicit in 49:9–10 when the Lord says: "Wherefore, I say unto you that I have sent unto you mine everlasting covenant, even that which was from the beginning. And that which I have promised I have so fulfilled, and the nations of the earth shall bow to it; and, if not of themselves, they shall come down, for that which is now exalted of itself shall be laid low of power."

The image portrayed by *thrashing* (or *threshing*) is a process of beating stalks of grain to separate the valuable kernels from the unwanted chaff so the grain can be gathered and used and the chaff burned or blown away. The procedure is one of individual identification and separation similar to the group separation in the parables of the wheat and the tares (86:1–7) and the sheep and the goats (Matt. 25:31–33). *See* Parable of the wheat and the tares.

Thrashing the nations by the power of the Spirit, in this sense, is accomplished by the Lord's humble authorized servants preaching the GOSPEL to the people. As the Spirit bears witness of the truth of the message, the honest in heart rejoice and become converted; the wicked become angry at the truth, reject the message, and separate themselves from the believers. It is not by secular force but by the power of the Spirit that the Lord identifies the grain and gathers it into the garners.

The second meaning is reminiscent of an Old Testament theme that the Lord has a "controversy" with the nations of the earth and will bring JUDGMENTS upon them, because they have forsaken gospel truth (Hosea 4:1; Micah 4:11–13; Jer. 25:13–17).

BIBLIOGRAPHY

Webster, Noah. *An American Dictionary of the English Language.* 1828.

RJM

Time

A measurable portion of eternity, subdivided into such segments as millennia, centuries, decades, years, months, days, and hours. Doctrine and Covenants 130:4–5 teaches that "the reckoning of God's time, angel's time . . . and man's time" is "according to the planet on which they reside." Although "the reckoning" of time (130:4) differs between God and man (Alma 40:8), God works with mortals according to mortal time (e.g., 31:6; 9:3, 11; 20:68).

Together, the words *time* or *times* appears more than two hundred times in the Doctrine and Covenants in several contexts:

1. The probationary state extending from mortality to "all eternity," such as making a marriage covenant "for time and for all eternity" (132:18–19; cf. 132:7; 72:3; 39:22).

2. A particular season or era, such as "the meridian of time" (20:26; 39:3) or "the dispensation of the fulness of times" (112:30; 128:18, 20; 138:48; cf. 27:13).

3. Numbering a sequence of events, such as the first time, second time, and so forth (98:39–44; 137:6).

4. Now, or the present, as in "this time" (29:50; 30:9; 31:4; 35:18; 94:17; 124:19; cf. 48:3).

5. An appropriate moment or period for a particular event to happen, such as "there has been a day of calling, but the time has come for a day of choosing," or "the time speedily cometh that great things are to be shown forth unto the children of men" (105:35; 35:10; cf. 110:14; 120:1; 124:31–35), or in the Lord's "own due time" (42:62; cf. 56:3; 136:18; 138:56).

6. The second coming of Jesus Christ, as in "it shall be a great day at the time of my coming" (34:8; cf. 35:15, 18). In connection with the Lord's coming, 88:110 says, "There shall be time no longer," meaning that mankind's premillennial probationary period and Satan's rule on earth are over.

7. The final dispensation in which the gospel would be declared to the world, as in "thou art called to prune my vineyard . . . yea, even for the last time" (24:19; cf. 27:13; 33:3; 39:17; 43:28; 90:2; 95:4).

RGM

Times of the Gentiles

The period of time in the latter days that began with the restoration of the gospel and will end at or near the second coming of the Savior. There are three references in the Doctrine and Covenants to "times of the Gentiles" (45:25, 28, 30). All are quotations from instructions the Savior gave to his disciples on the MOUNT OF OLIVES shortly before he was crucified (Matt. 24:1–51; JS–M 1:1–55; D&C 45:15–59).

Section 45 identifies when the times of the GENTILES begin: "And when the times of the Gentiles is come in, a light shall break forth among them that sit in darkness, and it shall be the fulness of my gospel" (v. 28), a clear allusion to the restoration of the fulness of the gospel through the Prophet Joseph Smith in the first half of the nineteenth century (cf. JS–H 1:34, 41).

Section 45 affirms that the times of the Gentiles will "be fulfilled" in that generation that "turn their hearts from [God] because of the precepts of men" (vv. 29–31). They will also witness "an overflowing scourge [and] a desolating sickness" which "shall not be stayed until" Christ comes (45:31, 97:22–24; cf. 5:19–20; 84:97). Further, "in the generation in which the times of the Gentiles shall be fulfilled, there shall be signs in the sun, and in the moon, and in the stars . . . and then shall they see the Son of Man coming in a cloud, with power and great glory," and "the generation when the times of the Gentiles be fulfilled, shall not pass away till all be fulfilled" (JST Luke 21:24–32).

Section 45 indicates that the Jews, who were scattered at the time of the destruction of Jerusalem in the first century after Christ, would remain scattered "until the times of the Gentiles be fulfilled" and then "they shall be gathered again" (vv. 24–25). Nephi stated that even before this final gathering, the Jews would "*begin* to believe" and "*begin* to gather" (2 Ne. 30:7–8; emphasis added).

Other terms in the revelations with much the same meaning as the "times of the Gentiles" include "last times" (27:13; 121:27) and "fulness of times" (27:13; 76:106; 121:31; 124:41; 128:18, 20; 138:48, 53). The Book of Mormon employs the phrase "fulness of the Gentiles" to refer to the "times of the Gentiles" (1 Ne. 15:13; 3 Ne. 16:4). The New Testament uses both terms: "times of the Gentiles" (Luke 21:24; JST Luke 21:32) and "fulness of the Gentiles" (Rom. 11:25). All of these scriptural references correspond with the teachings of the Doctrine and Covenants concerning the times of the Gentiles. The first century after Christ, when the Lord made it clear to Peter that the gospel was to be given to the Gentiles (Acts 10) and Paul became a special missionary to the Gentiles (Acts 9:15; 13:46; 18:6), might be considered as the coming in of the times of the Gentiles, but that time period is not the same as the one referred to in the Doctrine and Covenants.

LED

Tithing. *See* Consecration.

Tobacco. *See* Word of Wisdom.

Today, tomorrow. *See* Speaking after the manner of the Lord.

Token. *See* Appendix E.

Tongues/interpretation of tongues. *See* Spiritual gifts.

Torment, endless. *See* Punish, punished, punishment.

Tradition(s) of their fathers

Beliefs and practices inherited from former generations. Such traditions may be considered good or bad. In the Doctrine and Covenants are two references to such traditions, both having a negative context.

The first reference is in section 74, a revelation explaining the meaning of 1 Corinthians 7:14, and speaks of a false tradition "had among all the Jews" through the "*traditions of their fathers*" that little children are unholy without circumcision. The revelation asserts, "But little children are holy, being sanctified through the atonement of Jesus Christ; and this is what the scriptures mean" (74:1–7; emphasis added).

The second reference is in section 93, which testifies that "that wicked one cometh and taketh away light and truth, through disobedience, from the children of men, and because of the *tradition of their fathers*" (v. 39; emphasis added). The implication seems clear—false traditions contribute to the loss of light and truth among men.

LED

Transfiguration

A change from a lower to a higher spiritual state. For mankind, transfiguration is necessary to endure the glorified presence of God. The Doctrine and Covenants reveals that "no man has seen God at any time in the flesh, except quickened by the Spirit of God" (67:11). Moses, after enduring the glory of the presence of God, understood the necessity of this transfiguration when he said, "But now mine own eyes have beheld God; but not my natural, but my spiritual eyes, for my natural eyes could not have beheld; for I should have withered and died in his presence; but his glory was upon me; and

I beheld his face, for I was *transfigured* before him" (Moses 1:11; emphasis added). This may have been the case for Joseph Smith when he described his vision of the celestial kingdom in 1836 as "whether in the body or out I cannot tell" (137:1; cf. 2 Cor. 12:1–4). Examples of persons who were transfigured include Moses (Ex. 34:29–35; Moses 1:11) and Jesus and Peter, James, and John, who were changed to abide the presence of Deity upon the Mount of Transfiguration (Matt. 17:2; Smith, 3:387). Additionally, Paul, Joseph Smith, and others may have been transfigured at various times (76:11–12, 23; JS–H 1:16–17; 2 Cor. 12:1–3).

Transfiguration extends beyond humankind to the earth itself. The scriptures teach of two transfigurations of the earth: one when the earth transitions from a telestial to a terrestrial millennial state at the second coming of Jesus Christ (101:23–34; 2 Ne. 21:6–9), and another at the end of the Millennium when the earth experiences a permanent change through death and resurrection, becoming a celestial sphere (29:22–24; 88:25–28; cf. 130:9). In a revelation received in Kirtland in August 1831, the Lord promised that the person who "endureth in faith and doeth my will, the same shall overcome, and shall receive an inheritance upon the earth when the day of transfiguration shall come; when the earth shall be transfigured, even according to the pattern which was shown unto mine apostles upon the mount; of which account the fulness ye have not yet received" (63:20–21). The language of 63:20–21 indicates that the full account of what took place on the Mount of Transfiguration has not yet been fully revealed and thus seems to anticipate future revelation concerning what the apostles saw.

BIBLIOGRAPHY

Smith, Joseph. *History of The Church of Jesus Christ of Latter-day Saints.* Edited by B. H. Roberts. 7 vols. 2d ed. rev. Salt Lake City: The Church of Jesus Christ of Latter-day Saints, 1932–51.

DMW

Transfiguration, Mount of. *See* Mount of Transfiguration.

Translated beings

Individuals who, through the power of the priesthood, have entered into a "terrestrial order," who are "held in reserve to be ministering angels unto many planets, and who as yet have not entered into so great a fullness as those who are resurrected from the dead" (Smith, *History,* 4:210). The Doctrine and Covenants uses the word *translated* only once as it pertains to translated beings. That single reference is to Enoch (107:49). The entirety of section 7, however, is devoted to clarifying John 21:20–23 and the work of the apostle John, who, as a translated being, was to have "power over death" and be "as flaming fire and a ministering angel . . . for those who shall be heirs of salvation who dwell on the earth" (7:2, 6).

During the Millennium, mortals will live in a state similar to that of translated beings, living to "be as the age of a tree" (101:28–31; Isa. 65:20) until the appointed time when "they shall be changed in the twinkling of an eye" into resurrected beings (63:50–51).

The Book of Mormon adds significantly to our understanding of translated beings (3 Ne. 28:4–9, 25–32). The Three Nephites, for example, were translated in order to "bring the souls of men unto me [Jesus Christ], while the world shall stand." As translated beings they would "never endure the pains of death," and they would be free from both "pain while . . . in the flesh" and sorrow, "save it be for the sins of the world" (3 Ne. 28:8–9).

Documentation of translation first appears in the biblical record of Genesis: "Enoch walked with God: and he was not; for God took him" (Gen. 5:24). Many individuals were translated before the resurrection of Jesus Christ (Smith, *Answers,* 2:44–45), including Enoch (107:48–49; cf. 38:4; Moses 7:21, 69; Heb. 11:5), Elias (meaning, in this case, Elijah) (Matt. 17:1–3), Moses (Matt. 17:1–3), possibly Alma (Alma 45:18–19), and others (Moses 7:24–27; cf. JST Gen. 14:32–34). Individuals translated before Jesus' mortal ministry "were with Christ in his resurrection" (133:55; cf. McConkie, 807).

See also Historical context and overview of Doctrine and Covenants 7 (p. 719); Holy men that ye know not of; Transfiguration.

BIBLIOGRAPHY

McConkie, Bruce R. *Mormon Doctrine*. 2d ed. Salt Lake City: Bookcraft, 1966.

Smith, Joseph. *History of The Church of Jesus Christ of Latter-day Saints*. Edited by B. H. Roberts. 7 vols. 2d ed. rev. Salt Lake City: The Church of Jesus Christ of Latter-day Saints, 1932–51.

Smith, Joseph Fielding. *Answers to Gospel Questions*. Compiled by Joseph Fielding Smith Jr. 5 vols. Salt Lake City: Deseret Book, 1957–66.

DMW

Travail. *See* Appendix E.

Traveling high council/bishops/elders/high priests/ministers/presiding high council

Church officers authorized to function beyond geographically defined stakes, missions, or areas, where *standing* ministers or officers preside (20:66; 107:98). *Traveling* ministers and quorums currently include the First Presidency (107:21–22, 64–67), the Quorum of the Twelve Apostles (102:30–32; 107:23, 33), the Seventy (107:25, 34, 97), and others who are called to churchwide service by these *traveling* ministers.

Historically, there were *traveling* high priests, elders, and priests (84:111), who were designated later to be *standing,* or local ministers (124:134–37). Also, historically, the first two bishops of the Church were, at times, termed regional, or *traveling,* bishops since Bishop Edward Partridge oversaw all the branches of the Church in Missouri and Bishop Newel K. Whitney oversaw the branches in Ohio (41:9–11; 57:7; 58:14–15, 24–25; 72:1–8). During the Nauvoo period there were men called as *traveling* bishops to journey out from Nauvoo to gather Church funds (Hartley, "Bishop," 1:119). *Traveling* bishops were also called to assist in collecting tithes, both in cash and in kind, during the early days of the Utah Territory, from 1851 to 1877 (Hartley, "Brigham Young," 358).

In the Doctrine and Covenants, the Quorum of the Twelve is referred to as "the twelve traveling councilors" or "traveling council" (107:23; 124:127), "the traveling high council" (102:30; 107:34, 36, 38; 124:139), and "a Traveling Presiding High Council" (107:33). The Seventy are referred to as traveling ministers (107:97) to assist the Twelve (107:34). Though these early appellations are not commonly used today, the Quorum of the Twelve and the Seventy still retain their worldwide ministry as given in the Doctrine and Covenants.

These and other adjustments in the organization of the Church have been made in accordance with the will of the Lord. It was revealed to President John Taylor: "Thus saith the Lord unto the First Presidency, unto the Twelve, unto the Seventies and unto all my holy Priesthood, let not your hearts be troubled, neither be ye concerned about the management and organization of my Church and Priesthood and the accomplishment of my work. Fear me and observe my laws and I will reveal unto you, from time to time, through the channels that I have appointed, everything that shall be necessary for the future development and perfection of my Church, for the adjustment and rolling forth of my kingdom, and for the building up and the establishment of my Zion. For ye are my Priesthood and I am your God. Even so. Amen" (Clark, 2:354).

See also Standing councils/ministers/presidents.

BIBLIOGRAPHY

Cannon, Donald Q., and David J. Whittaker, eds. *Supporting Saints: Life Stories of Nineteenth-Century Mormons*. Provo, Utah: Religious Studies Center, Brigham Young University, 1985.

Clark, James R., comp. *Messages of the First Presidency of The Church of Jesus Christ of Latter-day Saints, 1833–1964*. 6 vols. Salt Lake City: Bookcraft, 1965–75.

Hartley, William G. "Bishop, History of the Office." In *Encyclopedia of Mormonism,* edited by Daniel H. Ludlow et al. 4 vols. New York: Macmillan, 1992.

———. "Brigham Young and Priesthood Work at the General and Local Levels." In *Lion of the Lord: Essays on the Life and Service of Brigham Young,* edited by Susan Easton Black and Larry C. Porter. Salt Lake City: Deseret Book, 1995.

RJW

Treasure(s)

Term used in the Doctrine and Covenants with several meanings:

1. Precious possessions, both spiritual and temporal. Spiritual treasure includes the "great treasures of knowledge" mentioned in the WORD

OF WISDOM (89:19). The temporal "treasures of earth" (such as money) are inferior to the spiritual blessings available through the HOLY GHOST (19:38). Saints with temporal means were directed to send their "treasures unto the land of Zion" (63:48). Doctrine and Covenants 111 speaks of treasure that was to be found in the city of Salem and seems to allude to both physical and spiritual treasure (111:2–4, 10). The nature of the "rich treasures" that will be brought to Ephraim by the returning tribes of Israel has not been revealed (133:26–30).

2. Securing a prized reward. The Lord frequently states that those who diligently do MISSIONARY WORK "treasure up . . . everlasting salvation in the kingdom of God" (6:3; 11:3; 12:3; 14:3). The reward of ETERNAL LIFE is "the greatest of all the gifts of God" (14:7; cf. 6:13).

3. Storing or retaining with special reverence or esteem. Several times in the Doctrine and Covenants Saints are commanded to "treasure up" the words of the Lord (6:20; 11:26, 21; 38:30; 84:85; cf. 43:34). Those who "treasure up . . . continually the words of life" will receive "in the very hour that portion that shall be meted unto every man" (84:85).

See also Rich, riches.

JLH

Treasury. *See* Consecration.

Trespass. *See* Appendix E.

Trial, tried, try

Terms used in at least two contexts in the Doctrine and Covenants. "My people must be tried in all things," the Lord revealed to Brigham Young at Winter Quarters in 1847, "that they may be prepared to receive the glory that I have for them, even the glory of Zion" (136:31). Having one's FAITH in God and dedication to his GOSPEL tried and tested is an essential element of the plan of salvation. Numerous scriptures, both ancient and modern, testify of the refining role of trials (cf. Job 23:10; Ps. 66:10; Jer. 9:7; Zech 13:9; 2 Cor. 8:2; Heb. 12:5–11; 1 Pet. 4:12; Mosiah 23:21; Ether 12:6; Abr. 3:25). The Doctrine and Covenants likewise teaches the vital role of trials as tests of faith and as refining experiences that can strengthen spirituality

and OBEDIENCE. "For he will give unto the faithful line upon line, precept upon precept; and I will try you and prove you herewith" (98:12). Such tests and trials may come for a variety of reasons and in diverse ways. Amidst the tribulations and persecutions experienced by the Saints in Missouri the Lord declared: "I, the Lord, have suffered the affliction to come upon them, wherewith they have been afflicted, in consequence of their transgressions; yet I will own them, and they shall be mine in that day when I shall come to make up my jewels. Therefore, they must needs be chastened and tried, even as Abraham, who was commanded to offer up his only son. For all those who will not endure chastening, but deny me, cannot be sanctified" (101:2–5). *See* Chasten, chastening; Persecution(s).

The term *tried* is used in the Doctrine and Covenants in another context. It deals with a specific "trial" or priesthood procedure in which Church disciplinary measures are administered. Today there are disciplinary councils that may be convened on both local and general levels by which a transgressor may be "tried" for his or her fellowship in the Church. In the law of the Lord, it is revealed, "if any man or woman shall commit adultery, he or she shall be tried before two elders of the church, or more" (42:80; cf. 68:22). *See* Church discipline.

BLT

Tribulation. *See* Affliction(s).

Trifle. *See* Appendix E.

Trodden the wine press alone. *See* Winepress.

Trump(s)

A word used many times in the Doctrine and Covenants to symbolize the manner in which the Lord's servants are to proclaim the restored gospel. Trumps, or trumpets, give a penetrating, clear, bright sound that is very difficult to ignore. That is how the message of the gospel is to be preached: "as with the voice of a trump, both day and night" (24:12), lifting up their voices "as with the sound of a trump, both long and loud" (34:6; cf. 30:9; 33:2; 42:6; 75:4).

The Doctrine and Covenants also refers to the use of trumps, or trumpets, to herald the Lord's second coming and the RESURRECTION of the righteous at that time (29:13; 43:17–18; 45:45; 109:75), as well as to announce the final resurrection and JUDGMENT at the end of the MILLENNIUM (29:26–27). *See* Jesus Christ, second coming of.

Trumpets are also mentioned as one means by which the Lord has "called upon" the inhabitants of the earth (43:25) in order to bring them salvation.

Whether figurative or literal, the trumps cited in sections 77 and 88 signal events preceding, at the time of, and after the Savior's appearance to the world. In answer to the question "What are we to understand by the sounding of the trumpets, mentioned in the 8th chapter of Revelation?" modern revelation states, "The sounding of the trumpets of the seven angels are the preparing and finishing of his work, in the beginning of the seventh thousand years—the preparing of the way before the time of his coming" (77:12). The seven trumpets of Revelation 8–10 introduce periods of wickedness, wars, plagues, natural disasters, death, and destruction in the world before the coming of the Lord. Another series of seven trumpets cited in section 88 signals events at the time of the Savior's appearance:

• The first trump: The "mother of abominations . . . is bound in bundles . . . ready to be burned"; there is "silence in heaven for the space of half an hour," followed "immediately" by "the curtain of heaven [being] unfolded . . . and the face of the Lord [being] unveiled." The righteous Saints who are on the earth will be quickened and caught up to meet the Savior, and the resurrection of those who are "Christ's, the first fruits" (celestial candidates) will occur (vv. 94–98).

• The second trump: The resurrection of "those who are Christ's at his coming" (terrestrial candidates) will take place (v. 99).

• The third trump: "The spirits of men who are to be judged, and are found under condemnation" are called up, judged unworthy of resurrection at that time (telestial candidates), and

returned to hell until the end of the Millennium (vv. 100–101; cf. 76:81–85, 103–7).

• The fourth trump: The spirits of those who are "filthy still" (sons of perdition) will "remain until that great and last day, even the end" (v. 102).

• The fifth trump: The message is given to "fear God, and give glory to him who sitteth upon the throne, forever and ever; for the hour of his judgment is come" (vv. 103–4).

• The sixth trump: The announcement of the fall of the mother of abominations (v. 105; cf. 88:94).

• The seventh trump: The heralding of the victory of "the Lamb of God" over "Satan and his works," even "death and hell," with the words, "It is finished; it is finished!" With that conclusion the angels and the Saints receive their "glory" and their "inheritance" (vv. 106–7; 19:1–3; 2 Ne. 9:7–13).

The seven angels who sounded their trumps at the Savior's coming will then sound them again, in order. At the sounding of the first trump, "in the ears of all living," the "secret acts of men, and the mighty works of God in the first thousand years" will be revealed (v. 108). With the sounding of the second trump, "the secret acts of men, and the thoughts and intents of their hearts, and the mighty works of God in the second thousand years" will be made known (v. 109). "And so on, until the seventh angel shall sound his trump"(v. 110); this angel is Michael, the archangel. With the sounding of the seventh trump, he announces the beginning of a new era, the Millennium, that "there shall be time no longer" and that "Satan shall be bound, that old serpent, who is called the devil, and shall not be loosed for the space of a thousand years" (v. 110).

LED

Trust

Reliance or confidence. The Doctrine and Covenants speaks of three different categories of trust:

1. Man's trust in God. The Lord's servants are counseled to trust in God. "Let my servant William [Law] put his trust in me, and cease to fear" (124:87). The Lord commanded Martin

Harris to "declare glad tidings, . . . trusting in me," and was warned that "misery thou shalt receive if thou wilt slight these counsels" (19:29–33). Hyrum Smith was admonished to put his trust "in that Spirit which leadeth to do good" (11:12). Bishop Newel K. Whitney was promised that by trusting the Lord he would "not be confounded; and a hair of his head shall not fall to the ground unnoticed" (84:116).

2. Man's trust in man instead of in God. Trust in man is condemned twice in the Doctrine and Covenants. The Lord commanded his people not to "trust in the arm of flesh" (1:19). He reprimanded Joseph Smith for trusting in Martin Harris, who "sought to destroy you" (10:6).

3. God's approving trust of man. The Doctrine and Covenants contains one reference to God's approving trust in man. The Lord stated about George Miller, "He may be trusted because of the integrity of his heart" (124:20).

See also Faith.

BEM

Truth

"Knowledge of things as they are, and as they were, and as they are to come" (93:24). Truth is eternal (1:39; 88:66; cf. 93:29) and is equated with "light" (84:45). It is a companion of righteousness (50:9; 56:15; 76:5; 107:84; 121:46). The adversary seeks to take away truth "through disobedience" (93:39; cf. 76:31; 78:10; 93:25, 37; 138:29). God is full of truth (66:12; 84:102; 109:77) and his word is truth (84:45). Truth is a constituent of that which glorifies God and humankind (93:28, 36). Christ received a "fulness of truth" and is called the "Spirit of truth" (93:9–11, 23, 26; cf. 88:6–7, 66; 107:71).

"Intelligence" is defined as the "light of truth" and, like truth, is associated with agency (93:29–31). *See* Intelligence; Light.

Truth can help one forsake evil and avoid sin, error, and deception (6:11; 50:25; 66:1; 93:37, 42; cf. 27:16). When one is wise enough to accept and follow truth, it can guide (79:2; 107:71; cf. 49:2), help to overcome prejudice (109:56), lead one to join the Lord's Church (31:2), strengthen, and help one "bring forth fruits of praise and wisdom" (52:17). Christ delights "to honor" those who serve him in truth (76:5). The faithful who "let virtue garnish [their] thoughts" and who have charity are assured that ultimately their scepter will be "an unchanging scepter of righteousness and truth" (121:45–46).

The acquisition of truth is a process and a function of maturity (50:40). Repentance, prayer, humility, obedience, softened hearts, and diligent seeking facilitate the acquisition of truth (6:22; 66:1; 93:26–27; 97:1–2; 124:9, 97). Truth may be learned from the teachings of those who possess it on earth, from scriptures, and through revelation from God, his Son Jesus Christ, and the Comforter, or Holy Ghost (6:15; 19:26; 50:14, 17–21; 52:17; 67:4; 75:4; 91:4; 107:71). God expects those who have obtained the truth to share it with others (6:11; 18:21; 19:37; 23:2; 58:47; 75:4). Parents are especially admonished to "bring up [their] children in light and truth" (93:40, 42).

TBB

Twelve, Council of the. *See* Apostle(s).

Twinkling of an eye. *See* Millennium, the.

This earth, in its sanctified and immortal state, will be made like unto crystal and will be a **Urim and Thummim** to the inhabitants who dwell thereon, whereby all things pertaining to an inferior kingdom, or all kingdoms of a lower order, will be manifest to those who dwell on it; and this earth will be Christ's. 130:9

Unbelief, unbelieving. *See* Belief, believing.

Unfeigned. *See* Appendix E.

United Firm. *See* Consecration.

United Order. *See* Consecration.

Unity

Oneness, harmony, accord. The concept of unity appears in several contexts in the Doctrine and Covenants:

1. The commandment to be unified. "Be one; and if ye are not one ye are not mine" (38:27; cf. 51:9; 61:8). *See* Parable regarding a father and sons.

The Lord warned in a parable that when the people were "at variance one with another they became very slothful, and they hearkened not unto the commandments of their lord" (101:50). *See* Parable regarding a certain nobleman/vineyard.

In 1831 the Lord commanded the Saints, "With one heart and with one mind, gather up your riches that ye may purchase an inheritance which shall hereafter be appointed unto you. And it shall be called the New Jerusalem, a land of peace, a city of refuge, a place of safety for the saints of the Most High God" (45:65–66).

2. The reward of the Saints for being unified in PRAYER. The Lord promised, "Whatsoever ye shall ask in faith, being united in prayer according to my command, ye shall receive" (29:6). As the Saints united themselves in prayer, the Lord responded to their requests by revealing his law (42:3) and the "revelation on priesthood" (84, headnote).

3. The unity of the Father and the Son. The Savior declared, "The Father and I are one. I am in the Father and the Father in me" (50:43; cf. 93:3).

4. The unity of the Saints with the Father and the Son. "As many as will believe on my name . . . may become the sons of God, even one in me as I am one in the Father, as the Father is one in me, that we may be one" (35:2; cf. 29:13; John 17:20–22).

5. Consequences of not being unified. One of the reasons given by the Lord for the Saints being driven out of Jackson County, Missouri,

was that they were "not united according to the union required by the law of the celestial kingdom; and Zion cannot be built up unless it is by the principles of the law of the celestial kingdom; otherwise I cannot receive her unto myself (105:3–5). *See* Law of the celestial kingdom.

6. The uniting of the body and the spirit in the RESURRECTION. "Their sleeping dust was to be restored unto its perfect frame, bone to his bone, and the sinews and the flesh upon them, the spirit and the body to be united never again to be divided, that they might receive a fulness of joy" (138:17; cf. 93:33–34).

7. The United Order. Several early leaders of the Church were instructed by the Lord to organize a United Order wherein they covenanted to do their business by the principles of CONSECRATION (78; 82; 92:1; 104:1, 21, 47, 48, 53).

JLH

Untoward. *See* Appendix E.

Upbraid. *See* Appendix E.

Uriah

A Hittite who lived in the time of David, an Israelite king (ca. 1000 B.C.; 2 Sam. 11). Uriah's name appears one time in the Doctrine and Covenants. Uriah was a valiant and faithful soldier in the Israelite army (1 Chr. 11:41) and the husband of Bathsheba. King David committed adultery with Bathsheba, who conceived a child. To try to cover up his sin, David called Uriah home from the field of battle, thinking that if he were home for a time, the child would be viewed as Uriah's. In the event, however, Uriah refused to go to his own house and enjoy the comforts of life while his fellow soldiers were sleeping in tents on the battlefield. Therefore, King David ordered that Uriah be set "in the forefront of the hottest battle . . . that he may be smitten, and die" (2 Sam. 11:15). Uriah was indeed killed in battle, and the Lord held David accountable for his death. The Lord revealed to Joseph Smith that as a consequence, David "hath fallen from his exaltation" (132:39).

LED

Urim and Thummim

An instrument or object through which information may be revealed. In the revelations included in the Doctrine and Covenants, such an instrument is referenced specifically as the means by which Joseph Smith translated the lost 116 pages (10:1); as one of the objects the Three Witnesses to the Book of Mormon would view (17:1); as the "place where God resides," where all things "past, present, and future . . . are continually before the Lord" (130:7–8); as "this earth, in its sanctified and immortal state, . . . whereby all things pertaining to an inferior kingdom, or all kingdoms of a lower order, will be manifest to those who dwell on it" (130:9); and as the "white stone" referred to in Revelation 2:17, through which "things pertaining to a higher order of kingdoms will be made known" to those who receive one (130:10). In Hebrew, *Urim and Thummim* literally means "lights and perfections," possibly referring to the stones' ability to bring to light hidden things (Alma 37:23–25).

References in other modern scriptures and Church records to the Urim and Thummim are to stones prepared by the Lord for interpreting languages and for other purposes (Mosiah 28:13–14; 8:13, 17). Through these instruments Joseph Smith translated the Book of Mormon (Smith, *Writings*, 234), inquired of the Lord on behalf of various individuals (see headnotes to sections 6; 11; 14–17), learned "whether John, the beloved disciple, tarried in the flesh or had died" (7, headnote), and was able to "ascertain, at any time, the approach of danger" (L. M. Smith, *History*, 110). Such stones, or "interpreters," as the Book of Mormon calls them (Mosiah 8:13; 28:20; Alma 37:21; Ether 4:5), were given to the brother of Jared, who was commanded to seal them up with his record as a means of its future translation (Ether 3:23–24). The Nephite king Mosiah, son of King Benjamin, possessed a Urim and Thummim and used them to translate the twenty-four gold plates containing the history of the Jaredites (Mosiah 28:11–13). Joseph Smith possessed the stones that had been given to the brother of Jared (17:1).

Joseph Smith learned of the stones' existence the night of 21 September 1823 from Moroni—then a resurrected being—who told Joseph that when he should obtain them, he should show them only to those to whom he should be commanded to show them (JS–H 1:42). Joseph first saw the Urim and Thummim the following day (JS–H 1:52) and obtained them and the plates four years later (JS–H 1:59).

Mormon described the Urim and Thummim that Joseph obtained with the plates as "two stones which were fastened into the two rims of a bow" and that they had been "prepared from the beginning, and were handed down from generation to generation, for the purpose of interpreting languages; and . . . discover[ing] to every creature who should possess the land the iniquities and abominations of [the Lord's] people" (Mosiah 28:13–15; cf. Alma 37:23–25). Ammon taught that only select individuals, called "seer[s]," were allowed to use these stones, lest someone "should look for that he ought not and he should perish" (Mosiah 8:13).

Joseph Smith described the Urim and Thummim he used to translate the Book of Mormon as a "curious instrument . . . which consisted of two transparent stones set in the rim of a bow fastened to a breastplate" (*Writings*, 243; cf. JS–H 1:35). Lucy Mack Smith described the instrument as "consist[ing] of two smooth three-cornered diamonds set in glass, and the glasses were set in silver bows, which were connected with each other in much the same way as old fashioned spectacles" (Backman, 73). David Whitmer also compared the Urim and Thummim to a pair of eyeglasses but noted that "the bow between the stones was more heavy, and longer apart between the stones, than we usually find it in spectacles" (Cook, 23). The breastplate upon which this was fastened, Lucy Mack Smith reported, "was concave on one side and convex on the other, and extended from the neck downwards, as far as the center of the stomach of a man of extraordinary size" (L. M. Smith, *History*, 111). The "spectacles" were attached to the breastplate, according to William Smith, "by a rod which was fastened at the outer shoulde[r] edge of the breastplate. . . . This rod was just the right length so that when the Urim and thummim was removed from before the eyes it woul<d> reac<h> to a pocked [pocket?] on the left side of the breast-plate where the instrument was kept when not in use" (Vogel, 1:508–9). As to the manner in which these stones were "set in two rims of a bow," William reported that "a silver bow ran over one stone, under the other, arround [sic] over that one and under the first in the shape of a horizontal figure 8 much like a pair of spectacles. . . . [T]hey were much too large for Joseph and he could only see through one at a time using sometimes one and sometimes the other" (Vogel, 1:508).

Joseph used the Urim and Thummim to translate some of the characters on the plates between December 1827 and February 1828, prior to Martin Harris's taking copies of some of the characters, with their translation, to Professor Charles Anthon (JS–H 1:62–65). After Martin lost the 116 pages of manuscript Joseph had lent him to show his wife and four others, Moroni appeared and took the instrument from Joseph "in consequence of [his] having wearied the Lord in asking for the privilege of letting Martin Harris take the writings" (Smith, *History*, 1:21). Shortly after Martin lost the 116 pages, Moroni returned the Urim and Thummim to Joseph long enough for him to receive what is now Doctrine and Covenants 3 and then again

took the instrument into his custody. Moroni returned the stones to Joseph "in a few days" (Smith, *History*, 1:23), after which time they remained with Joseph until the Book of Mormon was translated. After the Prophet Joseph "had accomplished by them what was required," he again "delivered them up" to Moroni (JS–H 1:60).

See also Revelation.

BIBLIOGRAPHY

Backman, Milton V., Jr. *Eyewitness Accounts of the Restoration.* Orem, Utah: Grandin Book, 1983.

Cook, Lyndon W., ed. *David Whitmer Interviews: A Restoration Witness.* Orem, Utah: Grandin Book, 1991.

Smith, Joseph. *History of The Church of Jesus Christ of Latter-day Saints.* Edited by B. H. Roberts. 7 vols. 2d ed. rev. Salt Lake City: The Church of Jesus Christ of Latter-day Saints, 1932–51.

———. *Personal Writings of Joseph Smith.* Compiled and edited by Dean C. Jessee. Rev. ed. Salt Lake City: Deseret Book, 2002.

Smith, Lucy Mack. *History of Joseph Smith by His Mother.* Edited by Preston Nibley. Salt Lake City: Stevens & Wallis, 1945.

Vogel, Dan, ed. *Early Mormon Documents.* 5 vols. Salt Lake City: Signature Books, 1996–2003.

AHH

Let thy bowels also be full of charity towards all men, and to the household of faith, and let **virtue** garnish thy thoughts unceasingly; then shall thy confidence wax strong in the presence of God; and the doctrine of the priesthood shall distil upon thy soul as the dews from heaven. 121:45

Valiant. *See* Appendix E.

Vanity. *See* Appendix E.

Veil

A word used in the Bible to refer to a piece of clothing (Gen. 24:65; 38:14) or to the woven curtain separating the Holy of Holies from the Holy Place in both the tabernacle and Solomon's temple, much as the curtain in modern temples separates other parts of the temple from the celestial room (Ex. 26:33). The temple veils (also spelled *vails*) were meant to distinguish gradations of holiness within the temple through which individuals who have first proved their worthiness may pass. During the Crucifixion, the veil of the temple rent, perhaps signifying that through Christ's sacrifice all who became worthy could experience that which was beyond the veil, or in other words, could enter into God's presence (Matt. 27:51; Mark 15:38; Luke 23:45; Heb. 6:19).

The revelations in the Doctrine and Covenants consistently use the term *veil* metaphorically to refer to a state of ignorance that is subsequently removed when divine truth is received. This usage can be noted in 110:1, in which Joseph Smith reports that "the veil was taken from our minds, and the eyes of our understanding were opened." Though the term *veil* is not found in 76:12, the same process of enlightenment is described: "Our eyes were opened and our understandings were enlightened, so as to see and understand the things of God" (cf. 137:1). Similarly, in 38:8; 67:10; and 101:23, Christ promises that the veil concealing him from us will be rent and "ye shall see me, and know that I am" (cf. Ether 3:6, 19–20; 12:19, 21; D&C 110:1–2). Importantly, the process by which one experiences this revelatory unveiling reflects the purpose of the physical veil of the temple. Just as the temple veil was not meant to be impassible but to distinguish readiness, so this metaphorical veil is pulled away when one has prepared oneself to receive the revelation, or as Joseph Smith said, "When we understand the character of God, and know how to come to Him, he begins to unfold the heavens to us" (6:308). Finally, the term is also used as a designation for Christ. In Hebrews 10:20 Paul

equates Christ with the veil, emphasizing his position as our intermediary with God. Similarly, in 101:23, Christ prophesies of the time "when the veil of the covering of my temple, in my tabernacle, which hideth the earth, shall be taken off, and all flesh shall see me together," perhaps describing himself as a temple that is hidden from the world and will be revealed (cf. Rev. 21:22–23).

BIBLIOGRAPHY

Smith, Joseph. *History of The Church of Jesus Christ of Latter-day Saints.* Edited by B. H. Roberts. 7 vols. 2d ed. rev. Salt Lake City: The Church of Jesus Christ of Latter-day Saints, 1932–51.

DLB

Vengeance. *See* Appendix E.

Vessels of the Lord

Implements and containers used by ancient Israelite priests in temple service. In the Doctrine and Covenants the phrase "be ye clean that bear the vessels of the Lord" (38:42) conveys the need for those who function in the Lord's name to be pure in every aspect of service.

The Hebrew noun *kēlîm*, translated *vessels*, occurs many times in the Bible to designate a wide range of such items as instruments, weapons, and many types of receptacles and utensils, including those used by Israelite priests in temple rituals (e.g., Jer. 27:16, 18–19, 21). The phrase "vessels of the Lord" occurs only once in the Bible, in Isaiah 52:11: "Depart ye, depart ye, . . . touch no unclean thing; . . . be ye clean, that bear the vessels of the LORD." This passage is generally interpreted to be a reference to the Israelite return from Babylonian exile, ca. 538 B.C. (Isa. 48:20), in which priests returned to Jerusalem with some of the temple "vessels" previously taken by Nebuchadnezzar II in 586 B.C. (2 Kgs. 25:13–15; Ezra 1:7–11). The resurrected Christ later quoted Isaiah 52:11 in prophesying of the latter-day gathering of Israelites (3 Ne. 20:41) and reminding the Nephites of the destiny of their posterity.

The phrase "vessels of the Lord" occurs twice in the Doctrine and Covenants. In section 38 the Lord commanded disciples "without spot"

(v. 31) to gather "to the Ohio" to receive divine law and an endowment of power at the future TEMPLE (v. 32). The revelation concludes with the instruction to "go ye out from among the wicked. . . . Be ye clean that bear the vessels of the Lord" (v. 42), fittingly associating temple and PRIESTHOOD functions with purity. Section 133 opens with the instruction to "sanctify yourselves; gather ye together" to Zion in preparation for Jesus' second coming (v. 4). The Lord then exhorts, "Go ye out from Babylon. Be ye clean that bear the vessels of the Lord" (v. 5). "Babylon" here signifies the corrupting powers and evils of the world, similar to the "wicked" in 38:42. Both of these passages emphasize the need for separation from the unholy world to qualify all Saints, and priesthood holders in particular, to appropriately serve ("bear the vessels of") the Lord.

DMP

Vex. *See* Appendix E.

Vineyard

Literally, an area where grapes are cultivated; symbolically, in scripture, any sphere or area where the work of the Lord functions. In the Doctrine and Covenants the Lord promises successful vineyards to those who keep the Sabbath properly (59:9–17). Both modern and ancient scripture (e.g., 24:19; Jacob 5:1–77), use symbols associated with a vineyard to teach about God's work among his children. Most frequently *vineyard* is used to mean particular areas of the world, such as Kirtland (72:2–19), or Zion (101:43–45; 103:21–23), and even the whole world (e.g., 43:28; 107:96; 135:6). Section 101 contains a latter-day parable concerning the redemption of Zion—that part of the Lord's vineyard located in Jackson County, Missouri (vv. 44–62). *See* Parable regarding a certain nobleman/vineyard.

President Joseph F. Smith's vision of the redemption of the dead teaches that the early leaders of the Restored Church, "before they were born," were "prepared to come forth in the due time of the Lord to labor in his vineyard for the salvation of the souls of men" (138:53–56). Their "labor" in the *vineyard,* and that of all

faithful Saints in this dispensation (38:40–42; 88:80–82), is to "call upon the inhabitants of the earth, and bear record, and prepare the way for the commandments and revelations which are to come" (71:4). In the revelations, the Lord repeatedly testified that this dispensation is "the last time that I shall call laborers into my vineyard" before his second coming and millennial reign (33:3; cf. 24:19; 39:17; 43:28; 95:4).

FFJ

Vipers. *See* Appendix E.

Virtue

In the Doctrine and Covenants the word *virtue* has three meanings: goodness or righteousness, chastity or sexual purity, and spiritual power or authority.

1. Goodness/righteousness. The Lord commands that his Saints "practise virtue and holiness" before him continually (38:24; 46:33; cf. 25:2). Virtue is one of the requirements that qualify a person for the Lord's work (4:5–6). One of the Articles of Faith of The Church of Jesus Christ of Latter-day Saints declares, "We believe in being . . . virtuous, and in doing good to all men; indeed, we may say that we follow the admonition of Paul. . . . If there is anything virtuous, lovely, or of good report or praiseworthy, we seek after these things" (A of F 13; cf. Philip. 4:8). The presiding priesthood quorums of the Church are to make their decisions "in all righteousness, in holiness, and lowliness of heart . . . in faith, and virtue" (107:30). The Prophet Joseph Smith was promised that though fools would have him in derision, "the pure in heart, and the wise, and the noble, and the virtuous, shall seek counsel, and authority, and blessings constantly from under [his] hand" (122:2). Emma Smith was promised by the Lord, "If thou art faithful and walk in the paths of virtue before me, I will preserve thy life, and thou shalt receive an inheritance in Zion." That revelation concluded with the Lord extending the promise "unto all" (25:2, 16).

2. Chastity or sexual purity. Chastity means self-control and purity of thought and deed before marriage and complete fidelity after marriage. To those who hold the priesthood the

Lord said, "Let virtue garnish thy thoughts unceasingly; then shall thy confidence wax strong in the presence of God; and the doctrine of the priesthood shall distil upon thy soul as the dews from heaven. The Holy Ghost shall be thy constant companion" (121:45–46). Those who lust after another, or "commit adultery in their hearts, . . . shall not have the Spirit, but shall deny the faith and shall fear" (63:16). Those who commit ADULTERY and do not repent are to be cast out; those who do repent "with all [their] heart," are to be forgiven (42:22–26). Ancient prophets add their witness that God delights in chastity (Jacob 2:28; cf. Prov. 12:4; 31:10), and that "chastity and virtue" is "most dear and precious above all things" (Moro. 9:9).

3. Spiritual power or authority. The phrase "by virtue of" is used in the scriptures to mean "by the power of," or "by the authority of." The Savior, in his role as an ADVOCATE for believers, said, "By the virtue of the blood which I have spilt, have I pleaded before the Father for them" (38:4; cf. 45:3–5). The Doctrine and Covenants makes clear that "no power or influence can or ought to be maintained by virtue of the priesthood, only by persuasion, by long-suffering, by gentleness and meekness, and by love unfeigned" (121:41). When the Savior healed individuals or groups of people, he indicated that "virtue" had gone out of him (Mark 5:30; Luke 6:19; 8:46). Alma, believing that "preaching of the word . . . had more powerful effect upon the minds of the people than the sword, or anything else," determined "that they should try the virtue of the word of God" (Alma 31:5). The subsequent missionary success of Alma and his sons proved the point—virtue is spiritual power.

WJM

Vision of the celestial kingdom. *See* Celestial kingdom, vision of.

Vision of the kingdoms of glory and perdition. *See* Kingdoms of glory and perdition, vision of.

Vision of the Redemption of the Dead. *See* Salvation for the dead.

Voice of the Lord

The means by which God makes his will known, reveals his plan of salvation to mankind, calls to repentance, exhorts to greater righteousness, and confirms truth. Called the "voice of God" (20:35), the Doctrine and Covenants identifies specific ways in which the "voice of God" is heard: the audible voice of deity (110:3; 128:21; cf. Testimony of the Three Witnesses); through ministering angels (2; 13; 43:25; 128:20–21); the voice of the Spirit (88:66; 97:1; 104:36); the voice of the Lord's anointed servants (1:14, 38; 68:4; 124:45–46); by scriptures (18:33–36); and "by the voice of thunderings, and by the voice of lightnings, and by the voice of tempests, and by the voice of earthquakes, and great hailstorms, and by the voice of famines and pestilences of every kind" (43:25). Whatever the means whereby God "speaks" to man, the command is to "hearken to the voice of the Lord your God, whose word is quick and powerful, sharper than a two-edged sword, to the dividing asunder of the joints and marrow, soul and spirit" (33:1). Heeding God's word and will—hearkening to the voice of the Lord in its many forms—yields the "power of God unto salvation" (68:4). Although "the voice of the Lord is unto all men, and there is none to escape; and there is no eye that shall not see, neither ear that shall not hear, neither heart that shall not be penetrated" (1:2; cf. 133:21–22), only those who have responded to God's voice with sincere repentance and personal righteousness shall be saved in the kingdom of God. "But if they will not hearken to my voice, nor unto the voice of these men whom I have appointed, they shall not be blest, because they pollute mine holy grounds, and mine holy ordinances, and charters, and my holy words which I give unto them" (124:46).

See also Revelation.

BLT

Vote of the Church. *See* Common consent.

Vow. *See* Appendix E.

And thus saith the Lord your God, if you will receive **wisdom** here is wisdom. Behold, the place which is now called Independence is the center place; and a spot for the temple is lying westward, upon a lot which is not far from the courthouse. 57:3

Wakefield, Joseph H.

Birth: 1792, Dublin, Cheshire County, New Hampshire

Death: 1835, Willoughby, Ohio

Joseph Wakefield, a resident of Watertown, New York, was baptized by 1831. The Lord revealed that he was "well pleased" with him and called him to serve a mission with Parley P. Pratt (50:37). Elder Pratt recalled that they set "in order things that were wanting" in different branches of the Church and "rebuk[ed] the wrong spirits which had crept in among them." They baptized those who believed and blessed little children "in the name of Jesus" (Pratt, 51).

Upon returning from this mission, Wakefield was ordained a high priest by Lyman Wight on 3 June 1831. Only four days later, Joseph Smith received another revelation in which Wakefield was called to preach in the East with Solomon Humphrey (52:35). They served in western New York; there, Wakefield baptized a future apostle, George A. Smith.

After completing his eastern mission, he moved to Kirtland and soon after left the Church, joining with dissidents opposed to the Prophet Joseph Smith. George A. Smith stated that Wakefield "having apostatized from the Church," became "convinced" after seeing Joseph Smith play with children after he had completed some translation work "that the Prophet was not a man of God, and that the work was false." "He afterwards headed a mob meeting, and took the lead in bringing about a persecution against the Saints in Kirtland and the regions round about" (JD, 7:112). He was excommunicated by January 1834.

BIBLIOGRAPHY

Mace, Wandle. Autobiography. Church History Library, The Church of Jesus Christ of Latter-day Saints, Salt Lake City, Utah.

Pratt, Parley P. *Autobiography of Parley P. Pratt.* Edited by Parley P. Pratt Jr. Salt Lake City: Deseret Book, 1985.

Smith, George A. "Auto-Biography of George Albert Smith." *Millennial Star* 27 (15 July 1865): 438.

———. *Journal of Discourses.* 26 vols. London: Latter-day Saints' Book Depot, 1854–86.

RC

Ward(s)

The Church's basic ecclesiastical unit; wards first came into use in Nauvoo. Many U.S. cities in the 1800s and still today are divided into political units called wards. In 1839 Commerce (soon to be renamed Nauvoo) was divided into three municipal wards. Then, to manage Church affairs in the growing city, leaders appointed BISHOPS for each municipal ward to handle tithing and care for the poor. As Nauvoo grew, it was subdivided into more wards, finally totaling thirteen, each presided over by a bishop. Nauvoo wards did not hold regular Church meetings or have their own QUORUMS; rather, worship services and deacons, teachers, priests, and elders quorum organizations were Nauvoo Stake matters, which meant citywide.

One reference to wards is found in the Doctrine and Covenants: 128:3 stipulates that in connection with baptisms for the dead, a recorder could be appointed "in each ward of the city" to keep an accurate record of the baptismal proceedings. These records would be turned in to a general recorder who would enter the ward recorder's information into the general Church record. After the Church left Nauvoo and moved to the West, the practice of having a local ecclesiastical unit called a ward, with a bishop assigned to it, became common. Gradually wards became responsible for worship and auxiliary meetings and developed ward-level quorums and auxiliary units, with bishops being responsible for the spiritual as well as temporal well-being of ward members. Wards operate under the direction of STAKES, with a stake typically overseeing five to eight wards. Ward sizes may vary from under two hundred to more than four hundred members, depending upon circumstances.

BIBLIOGRAPHY

Hartley, William G. "Nauvoo Stake, Priesthood Quorums, and the Church's First Wards." *BYU Studies* 32 (Winter and Spring 1991): 57–80.

WGH

War(s)

Conflicts between groups, nations, and peoples. The gospel of Jesus Christ is a gospel of peace, and for that reason Latter-day Saint prophets have viewed wars with dismay. The Book of Mormon teaches that the only justifiable reason for a people to go to war is in defense of "themselves, and their families, and their lands, their country, and their rights, and their religion" (Alma 43:47; cf. D&C 134:11). Nevertheless, the Lord has warned that because of the wickedness and selfishness of mankind, wars are inevitable.

The Doctrine and Covenants contains many passages foreshadowing wars, including war against the Saints themselves. In Fayette, New York, a revelation on 2 January 1831 commanded the Saints to move to Ohio, for enemies in New York sought their lives. "Ye hear of wars in far countries, and you say that there will soon be great wars in far countries," the Lord said, "but ye know not the hearts of men in your own land" (38:29). The foreign wars mentioned may have reference to the recent Napoleonic wars or the conflicts going on at the time in Belgium, Portugal, and Poland. The clear intent of this revelation, however, is to prepare the Saints for possible future problems in their own land.

In a revelation given in Ohio in 1831, the Savior rehearsed a sermon he had given to his disciples in Jerusalem, foreshadowing what would happen before the end of the world. Among other things, he said that "in that day shall be heard of wars and rumors of wars, and the whole earth shall be in commotion," indicating that the only people who will not be at war one with another are those who "flee unto Zion for safety" (45:26, 68–69). His true disciples, however, would "stand in holy places" (45:32), living righteous lives in order to endure the calamities of war with courage, faith, and strength.

Warlike actions against the Saints were presaged in a revelation given in August 1831. The Saints were told that because Satan would kindle anger against them, their enemies would want to shed their blood. The Saints themselves were forbidden to use violence or to shed blood, however (63:31). The Lord also said that he was angry with the wicked and had "decreed wars upon the face of the earth, and the wicked shall slay the wicked, and fear shall come upon every man" (63:32–33). Two years later, alluding to the bitter Missouri persecutions, the Lord

reemphasized his earlier admonition by telling the Saints not to be afraid of their enemies but rather to "renounce war and proclaim peace" (98:16). In 1832, as part of their vision of the three degrees of glory, Joseph Smith and Sidney Rigdon beheld Satan, who "maketh war with the saints of God" (76:29).

On 25 December 1832 Joseph Smith received a "revelation and prophecy on war" (87, headnote), which indicated not only that a civil war would begin in South Carolina but also that "the time will come that war will be poured out upon all nations" (87:1–2). The revelation ended by admonishing the Saints to "stand ye in holy places, and be not moved, until the day of the Lord come" (87:8). Two days later the Prophet received another revelation, which he called the "'olive leaf' . . . the Lord's message of peace to us" (88, headnote). Among other things, the Saints were told that they should be instructed in all things past, present, and future, including "the wars and the perplexities of the nations" so that they would "be prepared in all things when I shall send you again to magnify the calling whereunto I have called you" (88:79–80). A year later the Lord reminded the Saints that the United States CONSTITUTION had been established to protect the rights of the people and, in the only Doctrine and Covenants reference to what might be termed a righteous war, alluded to the American Revolution, implying that through it he had "redeemed the land by the shedding of blood" (101:80).

See also Historical context and overview of Doctrine and Covenants 87 (p. 791).

JBA

War in heaven

The conflict in the premortal life that began when Lucifer, who would become the devil, "rebelled against God, and sought to take the kingdom of our God and his Christ" (76:28).

The Prophet Joseph Smith taught that in heaven "Jesus said there would be certain souls that would not be saved; and the devil said he would save them all, and laid his plans before the grand council, who gave their vote in favor of Jesus Christ. So the devil rose up in rebellion against God" (6:314). Although there are a few references to this rebellion in the Bible (cf. Isa. 14:12–15; Luke 10:17–18; Rev. 12:4–9), the Doctrine and Covenants, as well as the Pearl of Great Price, affords additional and important insights. With clarity the Doctrine and Covenants verifies the historicity of the conflict and its key elements: the devil was prideful, he rebelled, and he was "cast out into the earth" with a "third part" of God's children who followed him (29:36–38; Rev. 12:4, 9). Other latter-day scripture places this story within the larger context of the plan of salvation (cf. Abr. 3:22–27). For example, section 76 contains the description of Joseph Smith's and Sidney Rigdon's vision of the war in heaven, in which they saw not only the key elements of the drama but also, in part, what became of those who followed the devil, those designated as SONS OF PERDITION. This vision of the fate of "the devil and his angels" was given in context with important truths about God's judgments, the "lake of fire and brimstone," the "second death," and the kingdoms of glory (76:25–37). Other scriptures highlight the vital role that AGENCY played in the conflict (29:36–39; cf. Moses 4:1–4). Furthermore, the rebellion in heaven deprived the devil and his premortal followers of mortality with physical bodies of flesh and bone and denied them the opportunity to partake of salvation that comes from the Only Begotten whom they sought to displace (Smith, 5:388). So tragic was the fall of Lucifer that "the heavens wept over him" (76:26).

Known on earth as SATAN, or the devil, Lucifer and his followers still continue the war against the work and people of God. This "war," which began in heaven, will persist until the final judgment day—at the "battle of the great God" that will take place at the end of the Millennium—when Michael, the archangel, and his armies will ultimately triumph, and Lucifer and his followers will be cast out forever (88:111–15).

See also Premortal existence.

BIBLIOGRAPHY

Smith, Joseph. *History of The Church of Jesus Christ of Latter-day Saints.* Edited by B. H. Roberts. 7 vols. 2d ed. rev. Salt Lake City: The Church of Jesus Christ of Latter-day Saints, 1932–51.

BLT

Warn, warned, warning

"To give notice of approaching or probable danger or evil, that it may be avoided; to caution against any thing that may prove injurious" (Webster, s.v. "warn"). The word *warn* and its variations as well as the concept of warning appear numerous times in the Doctrine and Covenants. In his revealed preface to the book, the Lord said, "For verily the voice of the Lord is unto all men, and there is none to escape. . . . And the rebellious shall be pierced with much sorrow . . . and their secret acts shall be revealed. And the voice of warning shall be unto all people, by the mouths of my disciples, whom I have chosen in these last days" (1:2–4).

The Lord has commanded his servants to raise a warning voice to the inhabitants of the world, often identifying the consequences of rejecting his word. Bishop Newel K. Whitney was instructed to warn the people of New York, Albany, and Boston "with the sound of the gospel, with a loud voice, of the desolation and utter abolishment which await them if they do reject these things" (84:114; 98:28–29; cf. 134:12). Warren Cowdery, presiding high priest in Freedom, New York, was told to "lift up his voice and warn the people, not only in his own place, but in the adjoining counties" (106:1–2). Thomas B. Marsh, president of the Quorum of the Twelve Apostles, was commanded, "Day after day let thy warning voice go forth; and when the night cometh let not the inhabitants of the earth slumber, because of thy speech" (112:5). Sidney Rigdon, a counselor in the First Presidency, was told to "lift up his voice as with the sound of a trump, and warn the inhabitants of the earth to flee the wrath to come" (124:103–6). The wrath and indignation to come include "the desolation of abomination which awaits the wicked, both in this world and in the world to come," and the calamities that precede the second coming of the Lord: "earthquakes, . . . thunderings, . . . lightnings, . . . tempests, . . . waves of the sea heaving themselves beyond their bounds," "all things . . . be[ing] in commotion . . . , men's hearts . . . fail[ing] them; [and] fear . . . com[ing] upon all people" (88:85, 87–91).

The Lord commanded not only the leaders

of the Church to raise a warning voice but also "every man, both elder, priest, teacher, and also member, [to] go to with his might . . . and let [his] preaching be the warning voice, every man to his neighbor, in mildness and in meekness" (38:40–41; cf. 20:59; 63:37; 88:71). Indeed, "it becometh every man who hath been warned to warn his neighbor. Therefore, they are left without excuse, and their sins are upon their own heads" (88:81–82; cf. 109:41; 138:21–22). "Those who desire in their hearts, in meekness, to warn sinners to repentance" are to be "ordained unto this power. For this is a day of warning, and not a day of many words" (63:57–58).

In 1833 the Lord warned the Saints about the "evils and designs which do and will exist in the hearts of conspiring men in the last days" (89:4) and revealed the WORD OF WISDOM (89) to help avoid such evils and designs. Those who heed that warning and observe the Word of Wisdom are promised both physical and spiritual health and protection against the "destroying angel" (vv. 18–21).

In addition to the specific use of the word *warn* and its variations, the Doctrine and Covenants contains many commandments with attending blessings for obedience and penalties for disobedience, all of which may be considered a type of warning (e.g., 45:64–71; 68:25–26; 93:40–50; 95:12; 104:11–18; 115:4–6).

See also Accountability; Missionary work; Shake off the dust of thy feet.

BIBLIOGRAPHY

Webster, Noah. *An American Dictionary of the English Language.* 1828.

TWC

Warsaw, Illinois

A town located fifteen miles south of Nauvoo in Hancock County. In 1841 William Law received a missionary call to Warsaw, Carthage, and eastern Iowa (124:88). It is not known whether he served the appointed mission.

In the 1840s, Warsaw was a prominent shipping port and center of political opposition to Joseph Smith and Mormonism. Residents of Warsaw felt challenged by Nauvoo's bustling economy. The two communities competed for

river trade and for business from backcountry farmers. Spearheading the political opposition was Thomas Sharp, editor of the *Warsaw Signal.* Through his newspaper editorials, Sharp criticized Joseph Smith, supported the repeal of the Nauvoo charter, and insisted upon the expulsion of Latter-day Saints from Illinois. He was not alone in his views. Residents of Warsaw were among the "wicked men" (135:7) in the mob that murdered Joseph and Hyrum Smith and celebrated their deaths at a tavern in town. That tavern, now part of a dwelling, still exists, as does the building on the main street where the *Warsaw Signal* was published, although that building is not the one that today is a museum designated *Warsaw Signal.* People of Warsaw were among those who fought against the Latter-day Saints in the September 1846 Battle of Nauvoo (Leonard, 46, 92, 99). *See* map, p. 277.

A town of about seven hundred people in 1847, Warsaw had eleven stores and twenty-three other shops and businesses.

BIBLIOGRAPHY

Leonard, Glen M. *Nauvoo: A Place of Peace, a People of Promise.* Salt Lake City: Deseret Book; Provo, Utah: Brigham Young University Press, 2002.

GML

Wash, washed, washing(s)

To make clean. In the Doctrine and Covenants, w*ash* is used in a number of contexts, both literal and symbolic:

1. Washing away sins. Baptism, by complete immersion in water, is symbolic of washing away one's sins. The Lord instructed James Covill: "Arise and be baptized, and wash away your sins" (39:10; cf. 20:72–73; 76:51–52). In a revelation to President Joseph F. Smith in 1918, the Lord indicated that those in the postmortal spirit world can be "washed clean" and be "redeemed" when they "repent," pay the "penalty of their transgressions," and render "obedience to the ordinances of the house of God," all made possible "through the sacrifice of the Only Begotten Son of God" (138:57–59).

2. Ceremonial washings accompanied by anointings, blessings, and other ordinances in connection with the temple endowment.

In Nauvoo, Illinois, the Lord made clear that these ordinances are to be performed in "my holy house, which my people are always commanded to build unto my holy name" (124:37–40). These instructions in section 124 refer to the temple endowment to be performed in the Nauvoo Temple, which was yet to be built—the same endowment familiar to the Saints in modern temples.

It should be noted that there were washings and anointings in the Kirtland era, sometimes referred to as the Kirtland endowment. These ordinances were preliminary to the more complete temple ordinances revealed to the Prophet Joseph Smith in Nauvoo and instituted there in May 1842 (Smith, 5:1–3). Regarding the Kirtland endowment, the *History of the Church,* under date of 31 January 1836, records: "The Presidency retired to the attic story of the printing office, where we attended the ordinance of washing our bodies in pure water. We also perfumed our bodies and our heads, in the name of the Lord. At early candle-light I met with the Presidency at the west school room, in the Temple, to attend to the ordinance of anointing our heads with holy oil. . . . We then laid our hands upon our aged Father Smith, and invoked the blessings of heaven. I then anointed his head with the consecrated oil, and sealed many blessings upon him" (2:379).

3. Washing of feet. References to washing of feet appear in the Doctrine and Covenants in two contexts. First, it is to be done as a witness against those who reject the gospel and its messengers. The Lord specified that it be done "not in their presence, lest thou provoke them" (60:15), but that the missionaries "go away from him alone by yourselves, and cleanse your feet even with water, pure water . . . and bear testimony of it unto your Father which is in heaven" (84:92; cf. 99:4). *See* Shake off the dust of thy feet.

Second, the washing of feet was an ordinance employed in "the school of the prophets, established for [the] instruction in all things that are expedient . . . for all the officers of the church, . . . those who are called to the ministry in the church, beginning at the high priests, even down to the deacons" (88:127). "And ye shall

not receive any among you into this school save he is clean from the blood of this generation; and he shall be received by the ordinance of the washing of feet, for unto this end was the ordinance of the washing of feet instituted" (88:138–39). Proper procedures are then outlined (88:140–41).

See also Endow, endowed, endowment; School(s); Temple(s).

BIBLIOGRAPHY

Smith, Joseph. *History of The Church of Jesus Christ of Latter-day Saints.* Edited by B. H. Roberts. 7 vols. 2d ed. rev. Salt Lake City: The Church of Jesus Christ of Latter-day Saints, 1932–51.

JFD

Watchman, watchmen

A guard who is stationed on top of a wall or tower and whose responsibility it is to warn the inhabitants of the city of approaching danger (e.g., 2 Sam. 18:24–27; Ezek. 33:2–7). The scriptures sometimes use the symbol of a watchman to refer to the prophet of the Lord, whose responsibility it is to warn people of approaching spiritual danger (Ezek. 3:17; Hosea 9:8). Doctrine and Covenants 101 contains a latter-day parable of the Lord's vineyard concerning the temporal redemption of the Saints in Zion—Jackson County, Missouri. In that parable, the servants of the nobleman failed to build a tower in the midst of the vineyard so that the watchman, representing the leader of the Church in Missouri, could see the enemy approaching and prevent the vineyard from being destroyed (101:45–46, 53–54). *See* Parable regarding a certain nobleman/vineyard.

During the march of ZION'S CAMP in 1834, the Lord, through Joseph Smith, instructed his "warriors" to scatter the watchmen of their enemies, representing those who persecuted the Saints in Missouri (105:16, 30).

In 1841, Joseph Smith received a revelation appointing the Nauvoo House as a resting place where travelers could "contemplate the glory of Zion . . . [and] receive also the counsel from those whom I have set to be as plants of renown, and as watchmen upon her walls," referring to the Prophet Joseph Smith and other Church leaders (124:60–61).

FFJ

Water(s)

Term used with both literal and metaphorical meanings. Literally, *water* refers to the liquid substance (e.g., 35:6; 61:22; 138:9), and examples in the Doctrine and Covenants include references to rivers (61:3, 23), larger bodies called "the waters" (61:14), and the ordinance of baptism by water (e.g., 20:74; 35:5; 39:20; 42:7; 52:10; 128:12).

In the ancient Near East, creation was viewed as the process by which unorganized matter, metaphorically represented as the sea (Gen. 1:2), was transformed through divine manipulation into the cosmos. Baptism, then, may represent a reenactment of this event as the individual demonstrates his or her commitment to the gospel by going under the water and spiritually becoming a new creature who is born again (John 3:2–5; 2 Cor. 5:17). Christ describes himself as the waters of life, which transform the partaker (John 4:14; 7:37–38; D&C 10:66). Similarly, gospel principles are like wells of living water bringing eternal life (63:23). According to 84:92, pure water is required when one of the Lord's servants cleanses his feet as a symbol that his message has been rejected by a man or a city. The voice of Jehovah is characterized "as the sound of the rushing of great waters" (110:3; 133:22). Later, in Liberty Jail, Joseph Smith applied the image of water to the Saints' opposition in Missouri, asking how long "rolling waters [could] remain impure" (121:33). The Prophet compared water to trials, declaring that "deep water is what I am wont to swim in" (127:2).

Though the sea as unorganized matter has been used as a positive symbol for change, the destructive nature of uncontrolled water can be used as a negative symbol of chaos. This negative symbolism of water as chaos may also help in understanding the difficult passages found in section 61, where water is mentioned fifteen times. This revelation was received following a vision by William W. Phelps, who saw the destroyer riding on the waters; similar imagery is used to describe the Lord's adversary that "sitteth upon many waters" (88:94; Rev. 8:11; 17:1). Though the vision implied that Satan has control over the water, the Lord makes it clear that it is he who has that power (61:1, 4–6, 14, 19). The assertion that "no flesh shall be safe upon the waters" in the latter days (61:15) reflects the general increase of chaos across a wide range of phenomena, both physical and social, which will necessitate a new cosmos brought about by the second coming of Christ (133:23; Rev. 21:1). *See* Historical context and overview of Doctrine and Covenants 61 (p. 767).

DLB

Waters of life. *See* Water(s).

Wax. *See* Appendix E.

Weak things of the world

The Lord's chosen servants in the latter days. The Doctrine and Covenants speaks of them as "the weak things of the world" (1:19; 35:13), "the weak things of the earth" (124:1; 133:59), "the weak and the simple" (1:23), or simply "the weak" (133:58). Though generally without worldly influence or acclaim, these weak things of the world are used by the Lord to "break down the mighty and strong." This breakdown is needed so that men will trust in God and not in the "arm of flesh" and "that the fulness of [the] gospel might be proclaimed . . . unto the ends of the world, and before kings and rulers." This is the Lord's stated purpose for restoring his gospel through the instrumentality of Joseph Smith, as affirmed in his revealed preface to the Doctrine and Covenants (1:6, 19, 23; 35:13–14; cf. Jer. 17:5; 2 Ne. 28:31).

In contrasting the values of the Lord and the values of the world, it is important to consider two critical factors. First, the "weak things" of the Lord are weak only in the view of the worldly who know not God. His "weak" servants are strong in faith, spiritual knowledge, and personal purity, though they are often judged by the world as ignorant and naïve. Second, what the world considers wise and even invincible as to the strength of men is not so highly esteemed by the Lord. Man's wisdom and ability are as nothing compared to the perfect character and attributes of God, who "with one glance of his eye . . . can smite you to the dust" (Jacob 2:15; cf. 1 Cor. 1:19–29). In providing for the contingency of losing the 116 manuscript pages of the Book of Mormon translation, the Lord has made clear that "the works, and the designs, and the purposes of God cannot be frustrated, neither can they come to naught. . . . Remember, remember that it is not the work of God that is frustrated, but the work of men" (3:1–3). In order for the "weak" to fulfill their assigned ministries, the Lord, at times, intercedes (e.g., 11:4–6; 101:86–90; 104:78–82). Such divine intervention, exercised "in his time" (101:90), does not make success easy but does make it possible to overcome the world.

In the dispensation of the fulness of times the Lord has worked and will continue to work through "the weak things of the world, those who are unlearned and despised, to thrash the nations by the power of [his] Spirit" (35:13). *See* Thrash the nations by the power of my/his Spirit.

These "weak things" are on the "Lord's errand" and "shall confound the wise" (133:57–59). It started with Joseph Smith, to whom the Lord said, "For unto this end have I raised you up, that I might show forth my wisdom through the weak things of the earth" (124:1; cf. 1:17–19; 35:17–18). The word of the Lord will continue to be proclaimed by "the weak and the simple unto the ends of the world" (1:23), "unto all men, and there is none to escape; and there is no eye that shall not see, neither ear that shall not hear, neither heart that shall not be penetrated" (1:1–2; cf. 138:57).

RJM

Wealth. *See* Rich, riches.

Well of living water. *See* Water(s).

Welton, Micah B.
Birth: 13 August 1792 or 1794, Watertown, Litchfield County, Connecticut
Death: 9 August 1861, Knox County, Illinois
During the 1820s, Micah Welton was a farmer and a millwright living in Ohio. "He was a firm believer in God and a great bible student. If anyone asked him a question he could quote

the bible chapter and verse" (in Black, 325). While residing in Northampton, Ohio, Welton was baptized on 23 June 1831 and ordained a priest and an elder that same year.

On 25 January 1832, after being counseled to be "diligent in all things," a number of elders were called to serve missions, among whom was Micah B. Welton (75:29, 36). Following this mission, he served a series of short missions in Ohio. By 1836, Welton was in Kirtland for the temple dedication and later that same year moved to Clay County, Missouri. When persecution ensued, Welton relocated to Pike County, Illinois. He was ordained a seventy in 1839 and served in the Third Quorum of the Seventy in Nauvoo. Welton was registered there as a property owner between 1839 and 1844 and worked as a carpenter on the temple.

He was appointed to serve a mission to Kentucky in April 1844. On 29 January 1846 he received his endowment in the Nauvoo Temple. He did not travel with the Saints to the West.

BIBLIOGRAPHY

Black, Susan Easton. *Who's Who in the Doctrine and Covenants.* Salt Lake City: Deseret Book, 1997.

KWF

Whit. *See* Appendix E.

White stone
Term used in the Doctrine and Covenants that refers to a phrase in the book of Revelation. Doctrine and Covenants 130:7–11 elaborates on the concept of the white stone with a new name written on it mentioned in Revelation 2:17: "A white stone is given to each of those who come into the celestial kingdom, whereon is a new name written, which no man knoweth save he that receiveth it. The new name is the key word" (130:11). "This earth, in its sanctified and immortal state . . . will be a Urim and Thummim to the inhabitants who dwell thereon, whereby all things pertaining to . . . all kingdoms of a lower order, will be manifest to those who dwell on it. . . . Then the white stone . . . will become a Urim and Thummim to each individual who receives one, whereby things pertaining to a higher order of kingdoms will be made known"

(130:9–10). *See* Historical context and overview of Doctrine and Covenants 130 (p. 846).

DLB

Whitlock, Harvey

Birth: 1809, Massachusetts

Death: ca. 1885, Watsonville, Santa Cruz County, California

Harvey Whitlock was baptized into the Church and ordained an elder prior to June 1831. Joseph Smith ordained him a high priest on 3 June 1831. In a revelation given through the Prophet dated 7 June 1831, addressed "to the elders of the Church, at Kirtland, Ohio" (52, headnote), Whitlock was called to travel to Missouri with David Whitmer and "preach by the way" (52:25). The elders were promised that if they were faithful, they would "be kept and blessed with much fruit" (52:34). Whitlock did go and subsequently relocated his family to Missouri.

In 1833 Whitlock was forced by Missouri mobs to leave Jackson County, and in 1835 he lost his standing in the Church. It was the beginning of a cyclical pattern of faithlessness and penitence that would mark his life. In a heartrending letter he told the Prophet, "When I consider the happy times, and peaceful moments, and pleasant seasons I have enjoyed with you and this people, contrasted with my now degraded state; together with the high and important station I have held before God, and the abyss into which I have fallen . . . I am overwhelmed with feelings that language cannot express. . . . I here beg leave to entreat of those who are still toiling up the rugged ascent, to . . . follow not my example, but steer their course onward in spite of all the combined powers of earth and hell" (Smith, 2:313–14). In a revelation through Joseph Smith, the Lord assured Whitlock, "Return unto me, and unto the bosom of my Church, and forsake all the sins . . . [and they] shall be blotted out" (Smith, 2:315). Whitlock returned to Kirtland, Ohio, and received authorization from the First Presidency to be rebaptized and ordained a high priest on 30 January 1836. In 1838, during the Missouri persecutions, he withdrew from the Church. In 1840 he was living in Cedar County, Iowa,

and by 1850 he had moved to Utah. He was rebaptized in Utah about 1858. By 1864 he had moved to northern California and joined the Reorganized Church of Jesus Christ of Latter Day Saints.

BIBLIOGRAPHY

Smith, Joseph. *History of The Church of Jesus Christ of Latter-day Saints.* Edited by B. H. Roberts. 7 vols. 2d ed. rev. Salt Lake City: The Church of Jesus Christ of Latter-day Saints, 1932–51.

KWF

Whitmer, David

Birth: 7 January 1805, near Harrisburgh, Dauphin County, Pennsylvania

Death: 25 January 1888, Richmond, Ray County, Missouri

David Whitmer first met Joseph Smith in 1829 when he conveyed the Prophet and Oliver Cowdery by team and wagon from Pennsylvania to the Whitmer home in Fayette, New York. Whitmer readily believed in Joseph's prophetic calling, was baptized in June 1829, and was

David Whitmer, 1805–1888; portrait by Charles W. Carter.

Courtesy Church History Library

privileged to be one of the Three Witnesses of the Book of Mormon and one of the six original members of the Church.

In June 1829, ten months before the Church was organized, Joseph Smith received three revelations for David Whitmer. In these revelations Whitmer was told to "seek to bring forth and establish my Zion" (14:6). He was promised a "view of the plates, and also of the breastplate, the sword of Laban, [and] the Urim and Thummim" with Oliver Cowdery and Martin Harris (17:1). He was called with the same calling as "Paul mine apostle," "to cry repentance unto this people" (18:9, 14). By September 1830, through another revelation given to Joseph Smith, the Lord expressed concern that Whitmer thought on "the things of the earth more than on the things of me, your Maker, and the ministry whereunto you have been called" (30:2). Apparently Whitmer repented, for on 7 June 1831, after moving from New York to Kirtland, Ohio, he was called to journey to Missouri—the land of Zion (52:25), where he later settled.

On 3 July 1834 Whitmer was appointed president of the Clay County high council and on 7 July as president of the Church pro tem in Missouri. His leadership of the exiled refugees from Jackson County was laudatory. He became the general agent for the Church's Literary Firm in September 1835 and attended the Kirtland Temple dedication in March 1836. Unfortunately, in 1837 he rebelled against the leadership of Joseph Smith, later declaring that the Prophet had "drifted into error and blindness" (Whitmer, 42). He was excommunicated on 13 April 1838 in Far West, Missouri.

For the next fifty years he resided in Richmond, Missouri. During those years, he was elected to the city council of Richmond several times and served as mayor from 1867 to 1868. For nearly a quarter of a century he operated the "Livery and Feed Stable" of "D. Whitmer & Son" or "Whitmer & Co." of Richmond.

In the 1870s, Whitmer organized the short-lived Church of Christ. In 1887 he wrote the seventy-five-page pamphlet, *An Address to All Believers in Christ*. Though he had been excommunicated, he often bore testimony to the truthfulness of the Book of Mormon. David Whitmer died at age eighty-three. The *Richmond [Missouri] Democrat* eulogized his life: "[N]o man ever lived here, who had among our people, more friends and fewer enemies" (76).

BIBLIOGRAPHY

Cook, Lyndon W., ed. *David Whitmer Interviews: A Restoration Witness*. Orem, Utah: Grandin Book, 1991.

Richmond [Missouri] Democrat, 26 January 1888, in Richard Lloyd Anderson, *Investigating the Book of Mormon Witnesses*. Salt Lake City: Deseret Book, 1981.

Whitmer, David. *An Address to All Believers in Christ*. Richmond, Missouri: n.p., 1887.

SEB

Whitmer, John

Birth: 27 August 1802, Fayette Township, Seneca County, New York

Death: 11 July 1878, Far West, Caldwell County, Missouri

John Whitmer embraced the prophetic calling of Joseph Smith in June 1829. He assisted the young prophet as a scribe for the Book of Mormon translation before being baptized by Oliver Cowdery. By revelation he was told that which "would be of the most worth" to him (15:4): "Declare repentance unto this people, that you may bring souls unto" the Lord (15:6).

Whitmer was one of the Eight Witnesses to the Book of Mormon. He devoted himself to "studying of the scriptures, and to preaching, and to confirming the church at Colesville" (26:1). He strengthened the Colesville Saints and acted as a scribe for Joseph Smith during the early stages of the Bible translation. Whitmer was also the scribe for most of the manuscript revelations recorded in the Book of Commandments and Revelations.

Following a three-day September 1830 conference in Fayette, Whitmer was told "that thou shalt commence from this time forth to proclaim my gospel, as with the voice of a trump" (30:9).

Moving from Fayette to Kirtland, he shared the news of the Restoration as a missionary until he was called to "write and keep a regular history" of the Church (47:1). He wrote ninety-six pages (Whitmer).

John Whitmer, 1802–1878.

Courtesy Church History Library

In November 1831 at Hiram, Ohio, Joseph Smith received a revelation appointing Whitmer to accompany Oliver Cowdery in carrying the revelations to Zion (Jackson County, Missouri) to have them printed as the Book of Commandments (69:1–2). In the revelation, Whitmer was admonished to "continue in writing and making a history of all the important things which he shall observe and know concerning [the] church" (69:3). He was also given a stewardship "over the revelations and commandments" (70:1–3).

Whitmer played a leading role in the Church until 1838, serving as a member of the presidency of the Church pro tem in Missouri. In that year he purchased tracts of land in Caldwell County, Missouri. Financial irregularities in the purchase led to allegations against Whitmer and an investigation into his use of Church funds. Whitmer refused to disclose pertinent records about the matter and was excommunicated on 10 March 1838.

When the Latter-day Saints abandoned their property in Far West, Missouri, Whitmer took

advantage of cheap prices and purchased much of the deserted township. For forty years, he resided in Far West. At his death, at age seventy-five, his estate consisted of 625 acres of prime farmland near Far West, with livestock, farm machinery, and a two-story house.

BIBLIOGRAPHY

Whitmer, John. *An Early Latter Day Saint History: The Book of John Whitmer.* Edited by F. Mark McKiernan and Roger D. Launius. Independence, Mo.: Herald House, 1980.

SEB

Whitmer, Peter, Jr.

Birth: 27 September 1809, Fayette, Seneca County, New York

Death: 22 September 1836, near Liberty, Clay County, Missouri

Peter Whitmer Jr. became acquainted with Joseph Smith in the summer of 1829. The Prophet resided in his family's home, and Whitmer occasionally served as one of his scribes during the Book of Mormon translation. He was also among the Eight Witnesses who handled the gold plates.

In June 1829 the Prophet received a revelation in answer to one of Peter Whitmer's personal questions. The Lord informed him that declaring "repentance unto this people, that you may bring souls unto me" was the thing that would be of "most worth" for him to do (16:6, 4). In that same month, Whitmer was baptized by Oliver Cowdery (Smith, 1:51).

When the Church was organized on 6 April 1830, Whitmer was listed as one of the six original Church members. In September 1830, the Lord called him to preach the gospel with Oliver Cowdery, "for the time has come that it is expedient in me that you shall open your mouth to declare my gospel" (30:5). One month later he was given more specific directions as the Lord requested him to go with Parley P. Pratt, Oliver Cowdery, and Ziba Peterson "into the wilderness among the Lamanites" (32:2).

The four men, who came to be known as the missionaries to the LAMANITES, began their westward journey in October 1830 to share the Book of Mormon with native tribes. They stopped near Buffalo, New York, and preached to the Catteraugus Indians. Then they traveled to Mentor, Ohio, where Frederick. G. Williams joined them. There they baptized Sidney Rigdon and many others from his congregation. They continued their journey to Sandusky and Cincinnati, Ohio, and then to St. Louis, Missouri. They ended their journey in Independence, Missouri.

Whitmer "attended conferences in Hiram, Ohio, November 1831; there [he was] appointed to have [an] inheritance in Zion for assisting Joseph Smith in bringing forth sacred writings, particularly revelations" (Cook, 27). He was driven out of Jackson County to Clay County, Missouri, by mobs in 1833. While in Missouri he supported his family by working as a tailor. On 22 September 1836, Whitmer died of tuberculosis near Liberty, Clay County, nine months after receiving a call to serve on a high council, filling the vacancy created by the death of his brother Christian.

BIBLIOGRAPHY

Cook, Lyndon W. *The Revelations of the Prophet Joseph Smith*. Salt Lake City: Deseret Book, 1985.

Hasley, Lewis. *History of the Seneca Baptist Association with Sketches of Churches and Pastors*. Ithaca, New York: Journal Association Book and Job Printing House, 1879.

Pollard, Lorene Elizabeth Burdick. Whitmer Memoirs, 2003. Church History Library, The Church of Jesus Christ of Latter-day Saints, Salt Lake City, Utah.

Smith, Joseph. *History of The Church of Jesus Christ of Latter-day Saints*. Edited by B. H. Roberts. 7 vols. 2d ed. rev. Salt Lake City: The Church of Jesus Christ of Latter-day Saints, 1932–51.

RC

Whitmer, Peter, Sr.

Birth: 14 April 1773, Pennsylvania

Death: 12 August 1854, Richmond, Ray County, Missouri

The family of Peter Whitmer Sr. lived on a farm in the German-extraction township of Fayette, New York. The farm property was deeded to Whitmer in four different transactions from 1819 to 1827. The one-and-a-half-story log home that Whitmer built for his family on the farm often served as the center of early Church activity. Joseph Smith completed the translation of the Book of Mormon in the Whitmer home

in 1829; Oliver Cowdery, David Whitmer, and Martin Harris obtained their witness of the Book of Mormon near the Whitmer property (Smith, 1:52–56); the Church was organized in the Whitmer home on 6 April 1830; the first three conferences of the Church were held in the Whitmer home (June and September 1830 and January 1831; Smith, 1:84, 110–18, 140); and twenty revelations were received there.

Peter Whitmer embraced the gospel truths that were restored in his small home. Shortly following the Church's official organization, he and his wife, Mary, were baptized by Oliver Cowdery in Seneca Lake on 18 April 1830 (Smith, 1:81). The following year the Whitmer family moved to Kirtland and then to Jackson County, Missouri.

Whitmer remained faithful until 1838, when he joined his sons David, John, and Jacob in rebellion against Joseph Smith. He relocated to Richmond, Missouri, with others who had left the Church. He died there on 12 August 1854.

BIBLIOGRAPHY

Hasley, Lewis. *History of the Seneca Baptist Association with Sketches of Churches and Pastors*. Ithaca, New York: Journal Association Book and Job Printing House, 1879.

Pollard, Lorene Elizabeth Burdick. Whitmer Memoirs, 2003. Church History Library, The Church of Jesus Christ of Latter-day Saints, Salt Lake City, Utah.

Smith, Joseph. *History of The Church of Jesus Christ of Latter-day Saints*. Edited by B. H. Roberts. 7 vols. 2d ed. rev. Salt Lake City: The Church of Jesus Christ of Latter-day Saints, 1932–51.

RC

Whitney, Newel K.

Birth: 5 February 1795, Marlborough, Windham County, Vermont

Death: 23 September 1850, Salt Lake City, Salt Lake County, Utah

In Kirtland, Ohio, as Newel K. Whitney and his wife, Elizabeth, were praying to know how to receive the Holy Ghost, Elizabeth said: "The Spirit rested upon us and a cloud overshadowed the house. . . . We heard a voice out of the cloud saying, 'Prepare to receive the word of the Lord, for it is coming'" (Jenson, 1:223). The word of the Lord came with the missionaries who were called to take the gospel to the Lamanites. In

Newel K. Whitney, 1795–1850.

November 1830 Whitney and his wife were baptized. On or about 1 February 1831, Joseph Smith arrived at the Whitney store in Kirtland. Elizabeth wrote of his arrival: "I remarked to my husband that this was the fulfillment of the vision we had seen of a cloud, as of glory, resting upon our house" (Jenson, 1:224). The Prophet resided with the Whitneys for several weeks.

In August 1831 in a revelation given to the Prophet Joseph Smith, Whitney was admonished to "retain his store" in Kirtland and to "impart all the money which he can impart, to be sent up unto the land of Zion" (63:42–43). One month later, he was again told to retain his store "until the residue of the church, which remaineth in this place, shall go up unto the land of Zion" (64:26). Soon thereafter, Whitney was called to be a bishop (72:1–8). He said to Joseph, "Brother Joseph, I can't see a Bishop in myself." Joseph replied, "Go and ask the Lord about it." Whitney did as directed and heard a voice say, "Thy strength is in me" (Doxey, 2:434). As a bishop, he was told to "travel round about and among all the churches, searching after the poor to administer to their wants" (84:112). He was admonished to "set in order

his family, and see that they are more diligent and concerned at home" (93:50). Whitney was given charge of the French farm in Kirtland—the very land on which the Kirtland Temple was built (96:2). He was also given a stewardship over other lands in Kirtland "for a blessing upon him and his seed after him" (104:40).

On 7 October 1835 Joseph received a revelation advising Whitney that "he shall deal with a liberal hand to the poor and the needy, the sick and afflicted, the widow and the fatherless" (Smith, 2:288). In partial fulfillment of the divine directive, Whitney held a three-day feast in January 1836 for the poor Saints in the vicinity of Kirtland. "This feast was after the order of the Son of God," wrote Joseph, "the lame, the halt, and the blind were invited, according to the instructions of the Savior" (2:362). On 8 July 1838 Whitney was encouraged to settle up his business in Kirtland, journey to Missouri, and repent of "covetous desires, before me, saith the Lord; for what is property unto me?" (117:4). Whitney did as directed and moved to Missouri; from there he went on to Nauvoo and Iowa. In 1848 Whitney journeyed to the Salt Lake Valley. In Salt Lake he served as bishop of the Salt Lake City Eighteenth Ward at the same time he was serving as the presiding bishop of the Church. Within two years of his arrival, he passed away. His obituary stated, "Thus, in full strength, and in mature years, has one of the oldest and most exemplary and useful members of the Church, fallen suddenly."

See also Gilbert and Whitney store in Kirtland, Ohio.

BIBLIOGRAPHY

Doxey, Roy W. *Latter-day Prophets and the Doctrine and Covenants.* 4 vols. Salt Lake City: Deseret Book, 1978.

Jenson, Andrew. *Latter-day Saint Biographical Encyclopedia.* 4 vols. Salt Lake City: Andrew Jenson History Company, 1901–36. Reprint, Salt Lake City: Western Epics, 1971.

Obituary of Newel K. Whitney. *Deseret News,* September 28, 1850.

Smith, Joseph. *History of The Church of Jesus Christ of Latter-day Saints.* Edited by B. H. Roberts. 7 vols. 2d ed. rev. Salt Lake City: The Church of Jesus Christ of Latter-day Saints, 1932–51.

SEB

Whore. *See* Appendix E.

Whoremonger. *See* Appendix E.

Wicked, the/wickedness

Something that is "evil in principle or practice"; a "departure from the rules of the divine law" (Webster, s.v. "wicked," "wickedness"). In the preface of the Doctrine and Covenants (1), the Lord stated that one of the primary purposes of this volume of scripture is to be a "voice of warning" to the inhabitants of the world (v. 4). As a "voice of warning," many revelations in the Doctrine and Covenants condemn wickedness and ungodliness and warn of impending consequences, both physical and spiritual, that will befall the wicked (29:8–9, 11, 17; 43:33; 45:67–68; 63:2, 6, 32–34, 37, 54; 64:24; 88:85; 97:24–26). The revelations also give multiple examples of people with behaviors or practices that can be classified as a "departure from the rules of the divine law," or that are evil, or wicked:

• Those "who will not hear the voice of the Lord, neither the voice of his servants, neither give heed to the words of the prophets and apostles" (1:14).

• Those who have "strayed from [the Lord's] ordinances, and have broken [his] everlasting covenant" (1:15).

• Those who "seek not the Lord to establish his righteousness, but [walk] in [their] own way, and after the image of [their] own god, whose image is in the likeness of the world, and whose substance is that of an idol, which waxeth old and shall perish" (1:16).

• Those who boast "in [their] own strength, and [set] at naught the counsels of God, and [follow] after the dictates of [their] own will and carnal desires" (3:4).

• Those who have "broken the most sacred promises" (3:13).

• Those who "love darkness rather than light, because their deeds are evil" (10:21).

• Those "who do not fear [the Lord], neither keep [his] commandments but build up churches unto themselves to get gain, yea, and all those that do wickedly and build up the kingdom of the devil" (10:56).

• Those who "will not repent" (29:17).

• Those who "observe not to do whatsoever [the Lord has] commanded" (97:26).

• Those who participate in "jarrings, and contentions, and envyings, and strifes, and lustful and covetous desires" (101:6).

• Those who are "slow to hearken unto the voice of the Lord their God. . . . In the day of their peace they esteemed lightly [his] counsel" (101:7–8).

• Those whose "hearts are corrupted . . . and love to have others suffer" (121:13).

• Those who "lift up the heel against [the Lord's] anointed . . . [and] swear falsely against [his] servants" (121:16–18).

The phrase "congregations of the wicked" is a term that is also used in the Doctrine and Covenants but in a somewhat different context from many of the other specific descriptions of wickedness. The Lord commands missionaries from the restored Church to "preach my gospel among the congregations of the wicked" (60:13). From the context of the revelations, "congregations of the wicked" does not appear to mean that all of the inhabitants of that area were guilty of gross wickedness, as defined in the Doctrine and Covenants, but rather that they were living outside the covenant—without knowledge of the saving ordinances and principles of the restored GOSPEL. The missionaries were thus called to invite all to repent of their sins and partake of the ATONEMENT of Christ by baptism into the "only true and living church upon the face of the whole earth" (1:30).

The Doctrine and Covenants, like passages in the Bible and Book of Mormon, specifically associates wickedness, worldliness, and ungodliness with spiritual Babylon (1:16; 64:24; 86:3; 133:14). *See* Babylon.

"Go ye out from Babylon" (133:5) is God's invitation to forsake wickedness in all of its forms and to "sanctify yourselves" through the everlasting gospel (133:4). Forsaking wickedness requires one to "flee unto Zion" (133:12), which is the "pure in heart" (97:21)—the antithesis of wickedness and worldliness—by embracing the principles and ordinances of the gospel and by faithfully living true to the covenants of Church membership.

See also Righteous, the/righteousness; Sin, transgression.

BIBLIOGRAPHY

Webster, Noah. *An American Dictionary of the English Language.* 1828.

BLT

Wight, Lyman

Birth: 9 May 1796, Fairfield Township, Herkimer County, New York

Death: 31 March 1858, Dexter, Medina County, Texas

Lyman Wight was living at the Isaac Morley communal homestead in Kirtland, Ohio, when missionaries first came to the area in 1830. He listened to their message of the Restoration and was baptized on 14 November 1830 by Oliver Cowdery. At a June 1831 conference in Kirtland, he was ordained a high priest by Joseph Smith. He was possibly the first man to be ordained to this priesthood office in this dispensation.

The day following that conference, Lyman Wight and John Corrill were told to "take their journey speedily," with Wight being warned that "Satan desireth to sift him as chaff" (52:7, 12). By September 1831 Wight and his family had moved to the Prairie settlement in Jackson County, where he served as branch president. Mob violence forced him and his family from Jackson County to Clay County, Missouri, in November 1833. From January to February 1834, Wight and Parley P. Pratt journeyed to Kirtland to inform Church leaders of the plight of the Saints in Missouri, and at a high council meeting in Kirtland on 24 February 1834 they gave their report. A revelation received the same day called Wight to assist with the recruitment of volunteers for ZION'S CAMP, an armed effort to assist scattered Saints in Missouri in regaining the lands they had lost to their persecutors (103:30, 38). After recruiting in the East, Wight marched to Missouri with Zion's Camp.

Following a move to Adam-ondi-Ahman, militia involvement, imprisonment with Joseph Smith in LIBERTY JAIL, and a move to Nauvoo, Illinois (Jenson, 1:95), Wight was instructed in a January 1841 revelation that he "should continue in preaching for Zion." The Lord promised Wight that he would "bear him up as on eagles'

Lyman Wight, 1796–1858; portrait by William Whitaker.

wings" and receive him unto himself "when he shall finish his work." Further, he was to serve as a member of the committee to supervise construction of the Nauvoo House, a planned boarding house (124:18–19, 22–24, 56–62, 70). Wight was named an apostle in April 1841 and was campaigning for Joseph Smith's presidential candidacy when he learned of the deaths of Joseph and Hyrum Smith in Carthage, Illinois, on 27 June 1844.

In 1845 Wight led a group of about 150 Saints to the Republic of Texas. As a result of his publishing a pamphlet rejecting the leadership of the Twelve Apostles, he was excommunicated in December 1848. He died in Texas ten years later.

BIBLIOGRAPHY

Jenson, Andrew. *Latter-day Saints' Biographical Encyclopedia.* 4 vols. Salt Lake City: Andrew Jenson History Company, 1901–36. Reprint, Salt Lake City: Western Epics, 1971.

KD

Wilderness

A place or condition that is uncultivated, unproductive, barren, or secluded. The Doctrine and Covenants contains a number of references to *wilderness* in several different contexts.

1. The "wilderness of darkness," of retreat, seclusion, or waiting, into which the Church established in the meridian of time by the Savior was driven by apostasy and the devil, and out of which the Church of Jesus Christ was brought through the restoration of the gospel in the latter days (109:73; 86:1–7; cf. 5:14; 33:5).

2. The wilderness where ancient Israel wandered for forty years with Moses before they were permitted to enter the promised land of Canaan (84:23–24).

3. The wilderness through which Lehi and his family travelled as they journeyed from Jerusalem to the New World (17:1; 33:8).

4. "The wilderness between Harmony, Susquehanna county [Pennsylvania], and Colesville, Broome county [New York], on the Susquehanna river," where Peter, James, and John conferred upon Joseph Smith and Oliver Cowdery the Melchizedek Priesthood, "the keys of the kingdom, and of the dispensation of the fulness of times" (128:20).

5. "The wilderness of Fayette, Seneca county [New York]" where the three witnesses were shown the Book of Mormon plates (128:20).

6. The "wilderness among the Lamanites," the Indian territory immediately west of Missouri to which the Lamanite missionaries were called in 1830 (32:1–4).

7. A wilderness in the ancient world where "God called upon Cainan" (107:45).

8. The wilderness, or the land given to Abraham's descendants, to which Judah will return and where they will "flourish" (49:24; 109:61–64).

9. The wilderness where the Lord is not seen but speaks by the voice of his Spirit (88:66).

In addition, in his revealed appendix, the Lord reminded readers of his power to "dry up the sea" and "make the rivers a wilderness" (133:68).

DFB

Williams, Frederick G.

Birth: 28 October 1787, Suffield, Hartford County, Connecticut

Death: 10 October 1842, Quincy, Adams County, Illinois

Frederick G. Williams had an extensive medical practice and was a respected citizen in the Kirtland community when the four Latter-day Saint missionaries to the LAMANITES began to teach the gospel there in 1830. He and his family accepted the truths presented and were baptized. Williams joined the Missouri-bound missionaries and served with them for approximately ten months.

While Williams was serving in Missouri, Joseph Smith received a revelation regarding the farm owned by Williams in Kirtland. This revelation is not included in the Doctrine and Covenants. In a subsequent revelation, however, the Lord gave specific instructions for Williams not to sell his farm, "for I, the Lord, will to retain a strong hold in the land of Kirtland, for the space of five years." Williams consecrated his farm to

Frederick G. Williams, 1787–1842.

the Lord, and as prophesied it became a "strong hold" for the Church (64:21). Joseph Smith and others lived on this property, the boundaries of which were in effect the limits of the first stake of Zion (94; 95).

Besides being Joseph Smith's medical doctor, Williams became his scribe and counselor in the First Presidency. As Joseph's scribe, Williams penned many important documents, including Joseph's first attempt at recording his own history, which contains an account of the First Vision. Williams also recorded thirty-two of the revelations contained in the Kirtland Revelation Book, twenty-nine of which are published in the Doctrine and Covenants. He drew the plans for the Independence temple and served as one of the scribes for the inspired translation of the Bible. As a counselor to Joseph Smith, Williams was "accounted as equal with [Joseph] in holding the keys of this last kingdom" (90:6). Joseph Smith recorded the following about his counselor, after whom he named a son: "Brother Frederick G. Williams is one of those men in whom I place the greatest confidence and trust, for I have found him ever full of love and brotherly kindness. He is not a man of many words, but is ever winning, because of his constant mind. He shall ever have place in my heart, and is ever entitled to my confidence. He is perfectly honest and upright, and seeks with all his heart to magnify his Presidency in the Church of Christ, but fails in many instances, in consequence of a want of confidence in himself. . . . Blessed be Brother Frederick, for he shall never want a friend, and his generation after him shall flourish" (1:444).

Williams, along with other members of the First Presidency, was chastised by the Lord for not teaching his children light and truth, and he was told to "set in order [his] own house" (93:41–43). Although his testimony and love of the gospel and for Joseph Smith caused him to be persecuted and driven from his homes—and in time cost him all that he owned and broke his health—it was within the Church that he rose to his greatest heights. As a member of the First Presidency he participated in many glorious spiritual experiences, culminating with the dedication of the Kirtland Temple on 27 March

1836, where he was permitted to see a heavenly personage. He lost his position of leadership on 7 November 1837 and his membership in the Church on 17 March 1839. But whatever his personal weaknesses, he had the strength of character to maintain his loyalty to the Prophet. He sought forgiveness for his former wrongdoings at the general conference held in Nauvoo on 6 April 1840 and was received back into the Church. He died in Quincy, Illinois, in full fellowship two years before the martyrdom of Joseph Smith.

BIBLIOGRAPHY

Smith, Joseph. *History of The Church of Jesus Christ of Latter-day Saints.* Edited by B. H. Roberts. 7 vols. 2d ed. rev. Salt Lake City: The Church of Jesus Christ of Latter-day Saints, 1932–51.

Williams, Frederick G. "Frederick Granger Williams of the First Presidency of the Church." *BYU Studies* 12, no. 3 (Spring 1972): 243–61.

———. *The Life of Dr. Frederick G. Williams: Counselor to the Prophet Joseph Smith.* Provo, Utah: BYU Studies, 2012.

FGW

Williams, Samuel

Birth: 22 March 1789, Russell, Hampden County, Massachusetts

Death: 10 November 1855, Ogden, Weber County, Utah

While living in Kirtland, Ohio, Samuel Williams, who was a stonecutter by trade, heard the gospel preached and joined the Church. He went with the Saints to Missouri; he later fled persecution and settled in Nauvoo, Illinois. On 6 October 1839 he was ordained an elder and on 19 January 1841 he was listed as a counselor in the elders quorum presidency in Nauvoo. In addition to presiding over the quorum, members of the presidency were to be "standing ministers to [the Lord's] church" (124:137). Williams was later appointed a temporary member of the Nauvoo high council. He received his endowment on 15 December 1845 in the Nauvoo Temple. When persecution befell the Saints he traveled with others to Iowa. In Winter Quarters, Nebraska, on 24 December 1846 he was ordained a high priest and remained there until 1849. After crossing the plains, he settled in Salt Lake City with his family, where he worked as a stonecutter. He died in Ogden, Utah, at age sixty-six.

KWF

Willing. *See* Appendix E.

Wilson, Calves

Birth: Unknown
Death: Unknown

Little is known about Calves Wilson prior to his baptism and ordination to the office of priest by Oliver Cowdery on 25 October 1831 in Orange County, Ohio. Three months after being ordained, at a conference of the Church in Amherst, Ohio, on 25 January 1832, he and Asa Dodds were directed by revelation to "take their journey unto the western countries, and proclaim my gospel" (75:15). It is not known if they served this mission. Wilson journeyed with Lyman Wight as a missionary to Cincinnati, Ohio, in 1832, where Wight "delivered a series of lectures and built up a branch of the Church and baptized upwards of one hundred" (Jenson, 1:93). Wilson's activities after that date are unknown.

BIBLIOGRAPHY

Jenson, Andrew. *Latter-day Saint Biographical Encyclopedia.* 4 vols. Salt Lake City: Andrew Jenson History Co., 1901–36. Reprint, Salt Lake City: Western Epics, 1971.

KWF

Wilson, Dunbar

Birth: 2 June 1805, Milton, Chittenden County, Vermont
Death: 11 March 1856, Ogden, Weber County, Utah

Dunbar Wilson appears in the Doctrine and Covenants in connection with his calling as a member of the Nauvoo high council (124:132). Historical sources indicate that he was baptized in May 1836, ordained an elder in September 1836, participated in the solemn assembly in the Kirtland Temple in April 1837, and settled in Missouri and then in Nauvoo.

Wilson is perhaps best known for his association with the steamboat *Maid of Iowa*. In July 1843 he and others volunteered to rescue Joseph Smith in case "any persons were running

brother Joseph down the river." There were rumors that an armed militia had chartered a boat to "seize Joseph and kidnap him to Missouri," so Wilson and several others used the *Maid* to patrol the Mississippi and Illinois rivers (MH; Smith, 5:482). Joseph Smith had been arrested by Sheriff Joseph H. Reynolds of Missouri and Harmon T. Wilson of Hancock County, Illinois, but was subsequently discharged in Nauvoo on a writ of habeas corpus (Smith, 5:465–73).

Wilson moved west with the Saints in 1846, settling temporarily in Garden Grove and Pottawattamie County in Iowa. He continued west in 1853 and settled in Ogden, Utah, where he died in 1856 at the age of fifty.

BIBLIOGRAPHY

Manuscript History of the Church, 2 July 1843. L. Tom Perry Special Collections, Harold B. Lee Library, Brigham Young University, Provo, Utah.

Smith, Joseph. *History of The Church of Jesus Christ of Latter-day Saints.* Edited by B. H. Roberts. 7 vols. 2d ed. rev. Salt Lake City: The Church of Jesus Christ of Latter-day Saints, 1932–51.

ZLL

Wine

Term used in the Doctrine and Covenants in two contexts. Wine is, literally, fermented juice from grapes, and symbolically, intoxicating spiritual wickedness.

1. Most references to literal wine in the Doctrine and Covenants are in connection with the SACRAMENT of the Lord's Supper (20:40, 75, 78–79; 27:1–14; 89:5–6).

In 20:40, the sacramental bread and wine are identified as "the emblems of the flesh and blood of Christ." The day the Church was organized, 6 April 1830, the fledgling Church of Christ was instructed to "meet together often to partake of bread and wine in the remembrance of the Lord Jesus" and were given the prayers that were to be said verbatim by the priesthood bearer when blessing the bread and the wine (20:75, 77–79). In August that same year, as Joseph Smith set out to procure some wine to be used in a sacrament meeting where Emma Smith and Sally Knight (wife of Newel Knight) were to be confirmed members of the Church, he was "met by a heavenly messenger" (27, headnote) and received the revelation published as Doctrine and Covenants 27:1–4. In this revelation the Saints were told, "It mattereth not what ye shall eat or what ye shall drink when ye partake of the sacrament, if it so be that ye do it with an eye single to my glory" (27:2). This statement clarifies the symbolic nature of whatever emblems may be used in administering the sacrament. The emblems represent the broken body and the spilt blood of Jesus Christ during the ATONEMENT. Joseph Smith was told not to "purchase wine neither strong drink of your enemies" and to "partake of none except it is made new among you; yea, in this my Father's kingdom which shall be built up on the earth" (27:3–4). Also in section 27, the Lord promises, "The hour cometh that I will drink of the fruit of the vine with you [specifying his prophets and righteous Saints] on the earth" (27:4–14).

Relative to the Lord's instruction on wine consumption, 89:5–6 is both like and unlike 27:1–4. It is like section 27 in that it discusses wine consumption in a sacramental context, that the Saints are to use "pure wine of the grape of the vine, of your own make" when partaking of the sacrament (89:6). It is unlike section 27 in that it instructs the Saints that "it is not good, neither meet in the sight of your Father" to drink wine or strong drink at other times than "assembling yourselves together to offer up your sacraments before him" (89:5–6). It may be argued that "pure wine of the grape of the vine, of your own make," and "made new among you" (27:4) could mean simple grape juice. More likely, it means fermented grape juice with relatively low alcoholic content (Sperry, 448–50).

Although 20:1–4 makes it clear that water may be used for the sacrament, both water and wine were used as sacramental emblems among Church members for some time, until the use of water became the standard. "The first occasion on record where water was used instead of wine" was in a meeting in the Kirtland Temple in April 1837, "but it is possible that water may have been used in the Sacrament before this time" (Smith, 2:480).

2. *Wine* is spoken of in the symbolic sense in Doctrine and Covenants 35:11 and 88:94, 105 (cf. 133:5, 7, 14). In these references the Lord

declared that all who succumb to Babylon's wicked ploys "drink of the wine of the wrath of her fornication," that is, participate in her intoxicating spiritual wickedness. As a result they will experience the "desolations" predicted for such behavior.

See also Historical context and overview of Doctrine and Covenants 27 (p. 736); Word of Wisdom.

BIBLIOGRAPHY

Ford, Clyde. "The Origin of the Word of Wisdom." *Journal of Mormon History* 24 (Fall 1998): 129–54.

Peterson, Paul H. "An Historical Analysis of the Word of Wisdom." Master's thesis, Brigham Young University, 1972.

Smith, Joseph. *History of The Church of Jesus Christ of Latter-day Saints.* Edited by B. H. Roberts. 7 vols. 2d ed. rev. Salt Lake City: The Church of Jesus Christ of Latter-day Saints, 1932–51.

Sperry, Sidney B. *Doctrine and Covenants Compendium.* Salt Lake City: Bookcraft, 1960.

PHP

Wine on the lees

"Well-aged" wines (*Study Bible,* s.v. "Isaiah 25:6") or "wines which have been left to stand upon their lees after the first fermentation is over" (Keil and Delitzsch, 7:286). The word *lees* (Hebrew, *shemer*) refers to "the settlings . . . of wine:–[the] dregs" (Strong, s.v. "lees"). The phrase appears once in the Doctrine and Covenants, where the Lord renews a promise made millennia ago through the prophet Isaiah, that he would invite "all nations," "all people" to a grand "feast of fat things, of wine on the lees well refined." That feast is called "a supper of the house of the Lord," "the supper of the Lamb" (58:8–12; 65:3; Isa. 25:6), a marriage feast celebrating the second coming of the Lord, the BRIDEGROOM, to meet his BRIDE, the Church (33:17; 109:73–74). The sense of such a promise seems to be that no effort will be spared in making the wedding feast at the coming of the Lord an exceptional affair for all who will accept the invitation.

See also Jesus Christ, second coming of; Marriage of the Lamb.

BIBLIOGRAPHY

The HarperCollins Study Bible: New Revised Standard Version. Edited by Wayne A. Meeks et al. New York: HarperCollins, 1993.

Keil, C. F., and Franz Delitzsch. *Commentary on the Old Testament.* 10 vols. Peabody, Mass.: Hendrickson Publishers, 1996.

Strong, James. *The New Strong's Exhaustive Concordance of the Bible.* Nashville, Tenn.: Thomas Nelson Publishers, 1984.

LED

Winepress

"A vat [tub] in which grapes are trodden" (Webster, s.v. "wine press"). Cultivation of vineyards outside the city walls was an important agricultural practice in ancient Israel. Often, a wine press hewed out of stone was located near the vineyard. At harvest, in late summer and early fall, grapes were gathered and placed in the wine press, where they were trodden by foot in preparation for making wine, an important, life-sustaining drink. Three revelations in the Doctrine and Covenants mention "wine-vat" or "wine-press" (133:48, 50; 76:107; 88:106). The earliest instance occurs in section 133, identified as the appendix and received on 3 November 1831. This revelation was purposely placed out of chronological order, emphasizing its important summary of the events of the last days and the second coming of Christ. When the Lord appears, the revelation notes, his apparel will be like "him that treadeth in the wine-vat" (133:48). The revelation also solemnly notes Jesus' declaration, "I have trodden the wine-press alone, and have brought judgment upon all people" (133:50). These verses are rooted in the Bible (Joel 3:13; Isa. 63:1–3), especially in Revelation (Rev. 14:19–20; 19:13, 15).

Specific Bible passages recast the grape harvest as a symbol of the Lord's final harvest at the end of time. The New Testament and the Doctrine and Covenants add to the Old Testament metaphor by specifically identifying Jesus Christ as the One who atoned for sins outside the city walls (Rev. 14:20); thus, his garments are red because of his atoning blood offered at Gethsemane and Golgotha (19:18; cf. Mosiah 3:7; Luke 22:44). Additionally, the Doctrine and Covenants, like the New

Testament, highlights Jesus' return in mighty power to execute the final, complete, inexorable judgment of God upon the nations of the earth, "saying: I have overcome and have trodden the wine-press alone, even the wine-press of the fierceness of the wrath of Almighty God" (76:107; cf. 88:106).

See also Atonement, the.

BIBLIOGRAPHY

Webster Noah. *An American Dictionary of the English Language.* 1828.

RNH

Winevat. *See* Winepress.

Winter Quarters, Nebraska

A Latter-day Saint community built on Omaha and Otoe Indian lands, on the west side of the Missouri River, near where Florence, a suburb of modern Omaha, Nebraska, was later established. It was the headquarters of the Church (1846–48) and the place where Brigham Young presented the "Word and Will of the Lord" about organizing the Saints for the thousand-mile westward trek to the Salt Lake Valley (136:1).

Winter Quarters spread across some six hundred to eight hundred acres. More than four thousand Latter-day Saints resided on that acreage, forming Nebraska's first city (Bennett, 68–69). The city had twenty-three small neighborhoods called wards. A bishop, assigned to each ward, assisted with the temporal needs of the neighborhood. Church leaders, such as Brigham Young, looked after the spiritual needs of the community by holding worship meetings twice a week. To Mormon pioneers, the well-ordered community was not a long-term destination; it was a temporary encampment along the route to the Rocky Mountains. One historian noted, "Nothing in American history—not the ephemeral towns of mining rushes nor the hardier ones of real-estate booms—is like Winter Quarters. An entire people had uprooted itself and, on the way to the mountains, paused here and put down roots" (DeVoto, 435).

Winter Quarters was a staging ground—a place to build and outfit wagons and prepare food and other supplies for the journey west.

And it was a time of sorrow for many, as two thousand Latter-day Saints died in Winter Quarters and in other Mormon encampments on the west side of the river due to inadequate nutrition and shelter, malaria, and fatigue from the arduous journey from Nauvoo to the Missouri River (Bennett, "Winter Quarters," 1568–69).

Brigham Young met with other Church leaders on 11 January 1847 at Winter Quarters, reporting a dream he had the previous night of visiting with the Prophet Joseph Smith. There is some indication in Brigham Young's Manuscript History that in the dream he and the Prophet may have discussed how best to organize the Saints for the move west. In any case, that was the focus of the 11 January meeting (Watson, 501–2). Three days later, Brigham Young presented to the community "The Word and Will of the Lord concerning the Camp of Israel in their journeyings to the West" (136:1). It was accepted as a revelation to the Church by the priesthood councils as well as by members of the Church in Winter Quarters. Emissaries were sent to many settlements of the Saints across the river in Iowa, where the revelation was presented and accepted with gratitude.

In compliance with a U.S. government directive issued over concerns with settlements on Indian lands, the Latter-day Saints abandoned Winter Quarters. Those who did not go west with the advance companies of pioneers to the Salt Lake Valley moved back across the Missouri River and settled with the other Saints in the Council Bluffs area, until they, too, migrated west. Today there is a visitors' center, graveyard, and a temple in the area where Winter Quarters once thrived. *See* map, p. 857.

See also Historical context and overview of Doctrine and Covenants 136 (p. 856).

BIBLIOGRAPHY

Bennett, Richard E. *Mormons at the Missouri, 1846–1853: "And Should We Die . . . ."* Norman: University of Oklahoma Press, 1987.

———. "Winter Quarters." In *Encyclopedia of Mormonism*, edited by Daniel H. Ludlow et al. 4 vols. New York: Macmillan, 1992.

Bryson, Conrey. *Winter Quarters*. Salt Lake City: Deseret Book, 1986.

DeVoto, Bernard. *Year of Decision*. Boston: Little, Brown and Company, 1943.

Watson, Elden J. *Manuscript History of Brigham Young, 1846–1847*. Salt Lake City: Eldon J. Watson, 1971.

SEB

Wisdom, wise

Terms used more than one hundred times in the Doctrine and Covenants to mean good judgment, correct understanding, or the appropriate thing to do or say. When revealing instructions to the Saints through the Prophet Joseph Smith, the Lord often used the phrase, "here is *wisdom*" (10:34; 37:4; 57:3, 9, 12; 58:23, 53; 82:16; 95:13; 96:1; emphasis added) or it is "*wisdom* in me" (9:3, 6; 10:45; 19:21; 25:4; 101:63; 104:11; 105:23; emphasis added) or "this is *wisdom*" (57:5; emphasis added). Analysis of each of these passages provides insights into the kind of wisdom the Lord was imparting to the recipients of his revelations. The revelations speak of God's wisdom, the wisdom of God compared to the wisdom of men and the plans of the devil, and how the Saints can gain wisdom.

1. The wisdom of God. The vision of the kingdoms of glory, given to Joseph Smith and Sidney Rigdon in February 1832, begins with a declaration of the wisdom and power of the Lord: "Hear, O ye heavens, and give ear, O earth, and rejoice ye inhabitants thereof, for the Lord is God, and beside him there is no Savior. Great is his wisdom, marvelous are his ways, and the extent of his doings none can find out. His purposes fail not, neither are there any who can stay his hand" (76:1–3). In the same revelation, the Lord says he delights to honor those who serve him "in righteousness and in truth unto the end" by sharing his wisdom with them, promising that "their wisdom shall be great, and their understanding reach to heaven" (76:5–10). In an invitation to Church members to pay attention as he "reason[s]" with them, and "speak[s] . . . and prophes[ies], as unto men in days of old," the Lord instructed, "Wherefore, hearken ye together and let me show unto you even my wisdom—the wisdom of him whom ye say is the God of Enoch, and his brethren" (45:1, 15, 11).

2. God's wisdom compared to the wisdom of

men and the plans of the devil. Concerning the devil-inspired people who had stolen the 116 pages of Book of Mormon translation, the Lord said, "I will show unto them that my wisdom is greater than the cunning of the devil" (10:43).

Martin Harris, in connection with his role in the loss of the manuscript, was chastened because he "set at naught the counsels of God" and "depended upon his own judgment and boasted in his own wisdom" (3:13).

In section 76 the Lord declared that the wisdom of his faithful, enduring servants would "be great, and their understanding reach to heaven; and before them the wisdom of the *wise* shall perish, and the understanding of the *prudent* shall come to naught" (v. 9; emphasis added). *Wise* and *prudent* in this instance undoubtedly mean those who consider themselves to be wise and prudent or who are considered by others to be wise and prudent but who in reality are not.

Joseph Smith's inspired letter to the Saints in Nauvoo in 1842 affirms that "those things which never have been revealed from the foundation of the world, but have been kept hid from the *wise* and prudent, shall be revealed unto babes and sucklings in this, the dispensation of the fulness of times" (128:18; emphasis added). In November 1831 the Lord revealed that he "sent forth the fulness of his gospel, his everlasting covenant . . . to prepare the weak for those things which are coming on the earth, . . . when the weak shall confound the wise, and . . . shall thrash the nations by the power of his Spirit" (133:57–59; cf. 124:1). Later, in 1833, the beleaguered Saints who had been driven from their homes and lands in Jackson County, Missouri, were instructed to petition all levels of government for redress. If the Saints' pleas were not heeded, the Lord promised to "come forth out of his hiding place, and in his fury vex the nation . . . that wise men and rulers may hear and know that which they have never considered" (101:86–94).

3. How the Saints are to gain wisdom. Several important approaches to gaining wisdom are identified in the revelations:

• Pray. "Therefore, he that lacketh wisdom, let him ask of me, and I will give him liberally and upbraid him not" (42:68).

• Teach one another and study out of the best books. "And as all have not faith, seek ye diligently and teach one another words of wisdom; yea, seek ye out of the best books words of wisdom; seek learning, even by study and also by faith" (88:118). Regarding LEARNING by FAITH, President Harold B. Lee taught: "Let no one think that 'learning by faith' contemplates an easy or lazy way to gain KNOWLEDGE and ripen it into wisdom. From heavenly instructions and added to which are the experiences of almost anyone who has sought diligently for heavenly guidance, one may readily understand that learning by faith requires the bending of the whole soul through worthy living to become attuned to the Holy Spirit of the Lord, the calling up from the depths of one's own mental searching, and the linking of our own efforts to receive the true witness of the Spirit" (10).

• Obey the commandments of God, including the WORD OF WISDOM. "And all saints who remember to keep and do these sayings [obey the word of wisdom], walking in obedience to the commandments . . . shall find wisdom and great treasures of knowledge, even hidden treasures" (89:18–21).

• Listen and attend to the COUNSEL of the Lord. To Joseph Smith and members of the high priesthood of the Church, the Lord said, "Listen to the counsel of him who has ordained you from on high, who shall speak in your ears the words of wisdom, that salvation may be unto you" (78:2).

• Humbly and diligently seek (97:1).

Inherent in all the above approaches is the principle of REVELATION from the Spirit of the Lord (cf. 59:3–4; 76:5–10).

In three instances in the Doctrine and Covenants, *wise* is used as a noun to refer to the way, or manner, in which something is carried out. For example, this use of *wise* appears in section 10 in which the Lord explained to Joseph Smith the evil intentions of those who had stolen the 116 manuscript pages of the Book of Mormon translation: "*On this wise,* the devil has sought to lay a cunning plan, that he may destroy this work" (v. 12; emphasis added; cf. 104:47, 53).

BIBLIOGRAPHY

Lee, Harold B. "The Iron Rod." *Ensign* 1 (April 1971): 5–10.

LED

Withal. *See* Appendix E.

Witness, witnesses

Terms used in the Doctrine and Covenants both as a verb and as a noun, in several contexts:

1. As a verb, *witness* means to declare, certify, or bear TESTIMONY of an event or principle. For example, those who are baptized are to "witness before the church that they have truly repented of all their sins," and the sacramental prayers ask that those who partake of the sacrament will "witness" unto God that they are willing to take upon them the name of Jesus Christ (20:37, 77, 79). This may entail witnessing by action as well as by mental and verbal assent.

2. As nouns, *witness* and *witnesses* are used to refer both to *events* that affirm or give evidence of the truth and to *persons* who, because of their knowledge, assert or testify of events or truths. Examples of *events* that witness of truths include the following:

• The witness that Martin Harris received of the Book of Mormon. He desired to see the Book of Mormon plates as a witness that Joseph Smith had them and was promised "a view of the things which he desires to see" if he would "humble himself in mighty prayer and faith, in the sincerity of his heart" (5:1, 23–24).

• The revelation to Oliver Cowdery concerning Joseph Smith's divine calling to translate the Book of Mormon plates. "I tell thee these things as a witness unto thee—that the words or the work which thou hast been writing are true" (6:17–24).

• The First Vision and the coming forth of the Book of Mormon as "great witnesses" to the world of the restoration of the fulness of the gospel through Joseph Smith (20:1–13).

• The martyrdom of Joseph and Hyrum Smith as a "witness to the truth of the everlasting gospel that all the world cannot impeach" (135:7).

• The deliverance of the Saints from their enemies, which the Lord did as "a witness of [his] name" (136:40).

Examples of *persons* who serve as witnesses are the following:

• Joseph Smith. The Prophet himself was commanded to "stand as a witness" of the fact that he had the Book of Mormon plates (5:2).

• Joseph Smith and Oliver Cowdery. In connection with their receiving the keys of the gift of translation, the Lord declared, "In the mouth of two or three witnesses shall every word be established" (6:25–28; cf. 42:80–81).

• The Three Witnesses of the Book of Mormon. The Lord promised that in addition to the testimony of Joseph Smith, he would send forth his word by the testimony of three witnesses, who would see the plates and other objects, and hear the voice of God declaring the truth of Joseph's claims (5:6–8; 17:1–9; 128:20). (For the fulfillment of this promise see The Testimony of Three Witnesses at the front of the Book of Mormon; cf. Smith, 1:54–56).

• Joseph Smith, Oliver Cowdery, the Twelve Apostles, and the Seventy. All were designated as special, or especial, "witnesses of the name of Christ in all the world" (27:12; 107:23–25).

• The "two witnesses, in the eleventh chapter of Revelation." These witnesses are "two prophets that are to be raised up to the Jewish nation in the last days" (77:15).

• "Two or three witnesses." Witnesses that see with their eyes and hear with their ears the ordinance of baptism for the dead and then certify to the same and deliver their record to the general Church recorder (128:3–4).

• Church members. Everyone who has accepted the gospel of Jesus Christ and entered into a covenant relationship with the Lord through baptism has the responsibility to be "a light unto the world, and to be the saviors of men" (103:9–10). "It becometh every man who hath been warned to warn his neighbor" in the spirit of "mildness and in meekness" (88:81; 38:40–41). By so doing they "stand as witnesses of God at all times and in all things, and in all places . . . even until death" (Mosiah 18:8–10).

BIBLIOGRAPHY

Smith, Joseph. *History of The Church of Jesus Christ of Latter-day Saints.* Edited by B. H. Roberts. 7 vols. 2d

ed. rev. Salt Lake City: The Church of Jesus Christ of Latter-day Saints, 1932–51.

LED

Wo, woe. *See* Appendix E.

Wont. *See* Appendix E.

Woodruff, Wilford

Birth: 1 March 1807, Farmington, Hartford County, Connecticut

Death: 2 September 1898, San Francisco, San Francisco County, California

From his youth Wilford Woodruff longed to find God's true church as it existed in the meridian of time. Therefore, he responded quickly when he heard the message of the Restoration. He was baptized on 31 December 1833 by Zera Pulsipher and soon became one of the greatest missionaries of the Church. As a priest in 1835 he served a mission to Arkansas and Tennessee. In June 1835 he was ordained an elder, and in 1836 he was ordained a seventy. In January 1837 he was called as a member of the First Quorum of the Seventy. He then served a mission to the Fox Islands, off the coast of Maine. He was called to be an apostle in July 1838, and with the rest of the Twelve Apostles he was invested with the KEYS to take the gospel to the "four corners of the earth" (124:128–29; 107:35; 112:21). Wilford Woodruff's missionary work in England from 1840 to 1841 is legendary; he helped to bring about two thousand souls to the restored gospel of Jesus Christ. After returning from England, he served two more short-term missions to the eastern states. When the Saints left Nauvoo, he, with others of the Twelve, was called to organize a company for the journey west (136:13).

Among his many remarkable accomplishments was the writing of his personal journals. "Wilford Woodruff was one of the most prolific record keepers of the nineteenth century, eventually filling thirty-one handwritten volumes with his journal entries" (Monson, 215–16). These journals were an important source of information in compiling the history of the Church.

When President John Taylor passed away on July 1887, Wilford Woodruff became the

Wilford Woodruff, 1807–1898.

Church's fourth president. Of that calling he said, "It is a position I have never looked for. . . . I pray God . . . to give me grace equal to my day." When sustained in the April 1889 conference he said, "I pray God to protect me and give me power to magnify my calling to the end of my days" (Cowley, 560, 565).

President Woodruff enthusiastically promoted temples, temple work and family history. Prior to his call as president of the Church, he served for seven and one-half years as the first president of the St. George Temple, from January 1877 to June 1884. "By the time he was seventy-eight years old 3,188 of his deceased relatives had been baptized vicariously and 2,518 had been endowed" (Monson, 216). The revelation he received when he asked the Lord to whom he should be sealed changed how temple work is done. Prior to this time many Saints had been sealed to prominent Church leaders, but in response to his query, the Lord told President Woodruff that people should be sealed to their own ancestors.

Temple work was so critical that when the Church was threatened by the United States government with the loss of its temples, President Woodruff issued the Manifesto, which stopped the practice of plural marriage (OD 1). On 6 October 1890 he spoke to the assembled Saints in the Salt Lake Tabernacle and said, "I want to say to all Israel that the step which I have taken in issuing this Manifesto has not been done without earnest prayer before the Lord" (Cowley, 570). In a Cache Stake conference in Logan, Utah, on 1 November 1891, he said, "The Lord showed me by vision and revelation exactly what would take place if we did not stop this practice. . . . I saw exactly what would come to pass if there was not something done. . . . The God of heaven commanded me to do what I did do. . . . I went before the Lord, and I wrote what the Lord told me to write" ("Excerpts from Three Addresses by President Wilford Woodruff Regarding the Manifesto," included in the Doctrine and Covenants following Official Declaration 1).

During President Woodruff's term as president several other important events took place, including statehood for Utah and the completion and dedication of the Salt Lake Temple. In addition, members of the Church who had been indicted for practicing plural marriage were given amnesty.

After a brief illness, Wilford Woodruff died at age ninety-two in San Francisco, where he had gone in the hope of improving his health. His body was transported by train from San Francisco to Salt Lake City where he was buried.

See also Apostles, the Twelve, mission to Great Britain; Official Declaration 1.

BIBLIOGRAPHY

Cowley, Matthias F. *Wilford Woodruff, History of His Life and Labors.* Salt Lake City: Bookcraft, 1964.

Monson, Thomas S. "Wilford Woodruff." In *Heroes of the Restoration.* Salt Lake City: Bookcraft, 1997.

KWP

Word of Wisdom

Nearly two dozen men gathered for school in a second-story room of Newel and Ann Whitney's Kirtland, Ohio, store on 27 February 1833. With one of them as scribe and perhaps one or two others present in a nearby room, Joseph Smith received the revelation known as the Word of Wisdom. Besides answering the immediate question of whether the brethren should smoke or chew tobacco, or "the filthy weed and their disgusting slobbering and spitting," as one colorful account put it, the revelation clarified several other issues that were being debated by Joseph's contemporaries (Cook, 204).

Initially, the revelation was given "not by commandment or constraint, but by revelation and the word of wisdom, showing forth the order and will of God in the temporal salvation of all saints in the last days . . . , adapted to the capacity of the weak and the weakest of all saints, who are or can be called saints" (89:1–3).

The revelation was given to warn against conspiracies that "do and will exist" by evil and designing persons in the last days (89:4). Several items were prohibited, including distilled and fermented alcoholic beverages, although WINE could be used for the sacrament, in which case the Saints should make it themselves (27:4). Strong or distilled drinks are for washing or disinfecting the body. Tobacco is not to be ingested but rather used with judgment and skill in treating bruises and sick cattle. The revelation declared hot drinks unfit for ingestion. Soon thereafter, Joseph Smith clarified that tea and coffee "are what the Lord meant when He said Hot drinks" (Johnson, 12). Speaking before the Saints in 1842, Hyrum Smith quoted the Word of Wisdom passage on hot drinks and then interpreted it as Joseph had a decade earlier: "I say it does refer to tea, and coffee" ("Word," 799–801). Considerable evidence attests that Saints in the 1830s understood hot drinks to include tea and coffee and that they struggled to act on this wisdom (Peterson, 22).

A significant part of the revelation includes guidelines for diet. God made wholesome herbs for human intake, each in its season, to be used with "prudence and thanksgiving" (89:11). The meat of animals and birds is to be consumed thankfully and sparingly, particularly in periods of winter, cold, or famine. All grains are to be the staff of life for man and for "beasts of the field, and the fowls of heaven, and all wild animals" (89:14). All grain, fruits, and vegetables are good food for mankind, particularly "wheat for man, and corn for the ox, and oats for the horse, and rye for the fowls and for swine, and for all beasts of the field" (probably meaning domesticated animals). Barley and other grains are good "for useful animals and for mild drinks" (89:17).

All Saints who remember to keep and do the behaviors outlined in this revelation will receive health, wisdom, and great "treasures of knowledge" as a result. They will have health and increased stamina and are promised protection from the destroying angel, similar to the protection the Lord gave to the Israelites anciently (Hinckley, 72–73).

The Word of Wisdom is more than a prohibition on alcohol, tobacco, coffee, and tea. Its doctrinal basis draws on the declaration in section 88 that "the spirit and the body are the soul of man" (v. 15). Whereas some Christians consider the body evil and look forward to leaving it behind at death, Latter-day Saints regard the body as godly and look forward to a literal, glorious resurrection in the image of Heavenly Father and Jesus Christ.

The Word of Wisdom rests on three other important doctrines: AGENCY, stewardship, and accountability. The Word of Wisdom assumes that mankind has agency—the power to act independently and make choices. By communicating his will regarding meat, drinks, tobacco, domesticated and wild animals, and a wide variety of grains, the Lord allowed the Saints their agency to act on those things according to his will or their own. The Word of Wisdom is adapted to the weakest Saint (89:3) and thus is not beyond the power of anyone to obey.

In addition to one's own body being a stewardship, each of the substances mentioned in the revelation is likewise a stewardship, or something God has given mankind to act upon; they are all things God has made and given mankind to use. The revelation tells how to use them in ways that please God. "All these [are] to be used with prudence and thanksgiving," for example, speaking of herbs and fruits (89:11); and "they are to be used sparingly," speaking of meat and poultry (89:12). A seldom-noted aspect of stewardship in the Word of Wisdom is the repeated command to use what God has provided "with thanksgiving" (89:11, 12). In the Word of Wisdom, the Lord is clearly the

owner. Evidence for this is seen in such phrases as "all wholesome herbs God hath ordained for the constitution, nature, and *use* of man"; "flesh also of beasts and of the fowls of the air, I, the Lord, have ordained for the *use* of man," and "these hath God made for the *use* of man" (89:10, 12, 15; emphasis added). The repeated emphasis is on *use*, not *abuse*. God created this earth and its life-sustaining abundance to be used by wise stewards who thankfully acknowledge him, not to be abused by the ungrateful or gluttonous. *See* Steward, stewardship.

The doctrine of ACCOUNTABILITY is also evident in the Word of Wisdom. Good stewards recognize that they are not the owners of the stewardship but that they are accountable to the owner for the way they act in regard to what the owner provides. The last four verses of the revelation describe the promised blessings granted to those who act wisely on the stewardship God has provided. Powerful verbs are used: "All saints who *remember* to *keep* and *do* these sayings, *walking* in obedience to the commandments, shall receive" the promised blessings (89:18–21; emphasis added). In summary, the doctrines of agency, stewardship, and accountability make the Word of Wisdom a "principle with promise" (89:3). If Saints choose to obey God's will as described in the revelation (the principle), then he preserves their lives and endows them with wisdom, stamina, and protection (the promises). Thus, the Word of Wisdom is more than a list of "thou shalt nots." It is more than a simple health code; it is a covenant. President Boyd K. Packer testified that "while the Word of Wisdom requires strict obedience, in return it promises health, great treasures of knowledge, and that redemption bought for us by the Lamb of God, who was slain that we might be redeemed" (19).

Joseph Smith sought the revelation that became the Word of Wisdom because there was in that day no prevailing opinion concerning tobacco or alcohol use or dietary practices. Then, as now, there was much debate but no consensus. The Word of Wisdom sorts out and clarifies the strengths and weaknesses among the variety of opinions, both then and now. By declaring that herbs and fruits should be used in season with prudence and thanksgiving, the Word of Wisdom agreed with the moderate position of the medical profession of the time, as did the revelation's declaration that meat eaten sparingly and especially in winter was healthful. These aspects of the revelation ran counter to the advice of extremists in Joseph Smith's day, who had less in common with the Word of Wisdom than is sometimes assumed. In forbidding the use of alcoholic beverages, as well as coffee, tea, and tobacco, the revelation ran counter to the mainstream culture.

It is important to distinguish the history of transition between the way the Saints originally received the revelation and the way it is applied today. Today's Latter-day Saints are counseled to abstain from drinking anything alcoholic; to abstain from tobacco, coffee, tea, and harmful drugs; and to eat moderately, according to the principles of the Word of Wisdom. Membership in the Church does not depend on keeping this counsel, but generally people are not baptized into the Church or admitted to temples for the highest forms of worship if they choose not to meet these basic requirements. A year after the Word of Wisdom was received, a question arose that led to the establishment of a policy regarding it. Missionaries in Pennsylvania had refused to take the sacrament when they believed that the elder administering it did not obey the Word of Wisdom. When reports of this action reached Kirtland, Ohio, the high council met to decide "whether disobedience to the Word of Wisdom was a transgression sufficient to deprive an official member from holding an office in the Church, after having it sufficiently taught him." Joseph Smith presided at the council, and six members gave their views on the subject; Joseph decided "that no official member in this Church is worthy to hold an office after having the Words of Wisdom properly taught to him, and he, the official member, neglecting to comply with, or obey them." The council sustained this decision (KCMB, 20 February 1834).

The decision meant that one could not hold a calling who chose to disobey the Word of Wisdom. Obeying it in the 1830s meant abstaining generally if not absolutely from alcohol, coffee and tea, and tobacco. The policy did not mean that those who chose to disobey could not belong to the Church, just that they could not represent the Church or officiate in its ordinances if they had been properly taught the Word of Wisdom and chose to disobey it. The Saints were agents for themselves; once they had knowledge to act upon, they were accountable for the choices they made. A choice to disobey resulted in losing the privilege to represent Church and the Savior.

This basic policy has remained in effect, though throughout the years there have been several attempts to enforce the Word of Wisdom more strictly, as well as periods when it was hardly emphasized at all. Since the revelation was given to Joseph Smith in 1833, there has been a wide variety of responses to it within the Church. From the beginning there were, among the Saints, strict advocates and moderates. There was also the occasional libertine who looked for any occasion to indulge excessively. Generally, this remains the pattern today (Harper, 51–64).

The question is asked when exactly the Word of Wisdom became a commandment. The answer depends on what one means by *commandment*. If one means, when did the Lord express his will that the Saints obey the Word of Wisdom, then the answer is, the day he gave it, 27 February 1833. If one means, when did the Church begin forcing the Saints to obey, the answer is never. The Church has never *required* anyone to obey the Word of Wisdom. The Lord revealed wisdom to the Saints and expected them to obey from the beginning as best they could. Some suggest it became binding in 1851, when Brigham Young asked for and received the Saints' sustaining vote to obey it. Some suggest it became binding in the 1880s, when President John Taylor again emphasized OBEDIENCE to it. Still others suggest that it became binding when President Heber J. Grant began making a minimal standard of compliance with the Word of Wisdom a requirement for obtaining a temple recommend.

The Lord's prophets have consistently applied the principle of agency, always urging obedience while making allowances for those who were acted upon by powerful substances before they had enough knowledge to act intelligently for themselves. President Joseph F. Smith believed that if the Word of Wisdom was strictly enforced in the nineteenth century "it would have brought every man, addicted to the use of these noxious things, under condemnation; so the Lord was merciful and gave them a chance to overcome, before He brought them under the law" (CR, 14). President Grant taught that obedience to the Word of Wisdom resulted from love for God rather than from compliance with a constraining command. "If you love God with all your heart, might, mind and strength, does he need to command?" President Grant asked (Peterson, 97).

It is clear that Joseph Smith sought the revelation because of the questions his circumstances generated, but the revelation itself goes far beyond answering questions that were then current. Given because "of evils and designs which do and will exist in the hearts of conspiring men in the last days" (89:4), it forewarns future Saints how to act wisely in the midst of conspiracies designed to temporally and spiritually harm them. The Word of Wisdom is prophetic. Elder Marlin K. Jensen testified that the Word of Wisdom revelation is clear evidence of "Joseph Smith's gifts as a prophet and seer. There is really no other explanation for the origin of that 1833 revelation. It waited until nearly the end of the twentieth century for an almost literal public verification of one of its key passages [the reference to the evils and designs of conspiring men in the last days]. In the hearts of the faithful Saints who have heeded its message for nearly 170 years, however, there has never been any doubt about its authenticity or relevance" (9–10).

See also Historical context and overview of Doctrine and Covenants 89.

BIBLIOGRAPHY

Cook, Lyndon W., ed. *David Whitmer Interviews: A Restoration Witness.* Orem, Utah: Grandin Book, 1991.

Harper, Steven C. *The Word of Wisdom.* Orem, Utah: Millennial Press, 2007.

Hinckley, Gordon B. "Excerpts from Recent Addresses of President Gordon B. Hinckley." *Ensign* 26 (July 1996): 72–73.

Jensen, Marlin K. "May the Kingdom of God Go Forth." In *Out of Obscurity: The LDS Church in the Twentieth Century.* Salt Lake City: Deseret Book, 2000.

Johnson, Joel H. *Voice from the Mountains.* Salt Lake City: Juvenile Instructor Office, 1881.

Kirtland Council Minute Book, 20 February 1834. Church History Library, The Church of Jesus Christ of Latter-day Saints, Salt Lake City, Utah.

Kluger, Richard. *Ashes to Ashes.* New York: Knopf, 1996.

Nelson, Russell M. "Addiction or Freedom." *Ensign* 18 (November 1988): 6–8.

Packer, Boyd K. "The Word of Wisdom: The Principle and the Promises." *Ensign* 26 (May 1996): 17–19.

Peterson, Paul H. "An Historical Analysis of the Word of Wisdom." Master's thesis, Brigham Young University, 1972.

Smith, Hyrum. "The Word of Wisdom." *Times and Seasons* 1 (June 1842): 799–801.

Smith, Joseph F. Conference Report, October 1913, 1–10.

SCH

Works. *See* Obedience.

Workways

"In a working position or manner" (*Webster's*, s.v. "workways"). The term *workways* was used by Joseph Smith in a long letter written from LIBERTY JAIL to the Saints to underscore the importance of keeping a careful record of the persecutions against the Saints. He wrote: "Let no man count them as small things; for there is much which lieth in futurity, pertaining to the saints, which depends upon these things. You know, brethren, that a very large ship is benefited very much by a very small helm in the time of a storm, by being kept workways with the wind and the waves" (123:15–16). A helm is a steering mechanism used to keep a ship directed "workways with the wind," or in such a way as to make the wind "work" in its favor, to help guide it to its proper destination. Clearly, Joseph Smith believed that having an accurate record of the persecutions of the Saints was like a helm benefiting the future course of the Church.

Workways, as one word, is a change from the original manuscript copies of the revelation, where it was written "work ways" (Woodford, 1616, 1619).

See also Historical context and overview of Doctrine and Covenants 123 (p. 836).

BIBLIOGRAPHY

Webster's Revised Unabridged Dictionary. Springfield, Mass.: C. & G. Merriam, 1913.

Woodford, Robert J. "The Historical Development of the Doctrine and Covenants." Ph.D. dissertation. Brigham Young University, 1974.

LED

World(s), world's, worldliness

Term used in the Doctrine and Covenants more than 220 times, with at least ten connotations:

1. The EARTH itself, the planet Earth, which came into existence at a point in time, at the bidding of JESUS CHRIST, and by his power (e.g., 38:1, 3; 49:17; 76:13; 93:7–9).

2. The inhabitants of the earth, or the world (e.g., 1:18, 36; 20:13; 29:17; 45:9; 84:49–53).

3. The earth itself *and* its inhabitants. The earth, as well as those who dwell on it, are to be saved by Jesus Christ (88:18–20, 25–26), who is the source of "the light . . . which giveth life to all things" and is the power by which the earth and the heavens were created (88:5–13). Therefore, when the scriptures speak of Jesus Christ as the "Savior of the world" (1:20) and the "light and the life of the world" (34:2–3), these passages may have reference to the redemption of both the earth and its people (e.g., 10:70; 11:28; 19:1–3; 49:5).

4. The period of time known as mortality, "this world," as distinct from "the world to come" (e.g., 42:18; 76:34; 90:3; 93:52; 101:36; 132:15–18, 27).

5. Evil influences, as in "overcome of the world" (50:8) or keeping oneself "unspotted from the world" (59:9; cf. 127:11).

6. Temporal concerns and institutions, as in "things" (25:10; 121:35), "cares" (39:9; 40:2), "praise" (58:39), "glory" (10:19), "vanities" (20:5), and kingdoms "of the world" (103:7–8; 105:32). The revelations contain admonitions to "forsake the world" (53:2) or to "not . . . live after the manner of the world" (95:13).

7. Worldwide, covering the globe, as in the command to "go into all the world to preach my gospel unto every creature" (e.g., 18:28; 68:8; 84:61–62; 107:23, 25; 112:28; 123:6).

8. Those who are not members of the Restored Church (e.g., 21:12; 31:10; 70:6; 72:14; 103:7–9).

9. Worlds or kingdoms other than this earth in its present state, that is, the telestial world (76:98), the terrestrial world (76:71), and the celestial world (78:7, 14; 88:2).

10. Worlds coexistent with this earth, that is, the premortal spirit world (138:56) and the postmortal spirit world (138:16, 36, 54, 57).

Considering the context inherent in the verses where the word *world* is used will usually point clearly to one of the above listed meanings. There may be occasions where more than one connotation fits. For instance, those verses that speak of overcoming the world (64:2) could include overcoming both the evil influences and temporal concerns of the world.

The plural *worlds* is used six times. Three times it refers to the fact that the Savior has created many worlds (76:24, 39; 93:10); twice it refers to "eternal worlds," meaning realms that follow judgment and resurrection (132:55, 63); and once it refers to "worlds without end," meaning forever (76:112).

World's, the possessive form, appears twice in the Doctrine and Covenants. After calling members of the First Presidency and Bishop Newel K. Whitney his "friends" and assuring them that they would have an inheritance with him, the Lord added, "I called you servants for the world's sake, and ye are their servants for my sake" (93:45–46). The other use of *world's* indicates that religious societies have a right to determine members' fellowship or standing in their organization but do not have the right "to take from them this world's goods" (134:10).

JLH

Worship

Sincere feelings and acts of emulation; homage, reverence, and adoration. A revelation in connection with the organization of the Church on 6 April 1830 states that "all men must repent and believe on the name of Jesus Christ, and worship the Father in his name . . . to the end, or they cannot be saved in the kingdom of God," and that "the only living and true God . . . should be the only being whom they should worship" (20:19, 29; cf. 18:40; 133:39).

Inasmuch as the "Father, Son, and Holy Ghost are one God, infinite and eternal, without end" (20:28), appropriate honor and reverence for all members of the Godhead is in complete harmony with worshiping the Father.

The Lord told the Saints that section 93 was given "that you may understand and know how to worship, and know what you worship, that you may come unto the Father in my name, and in due time receive of his fulness" (v. 19). The revelation teaches that "how to worship" is to follow the example of the Savior in keeping the commandments, receiving "grace for grace" and growing from "grace to grace" until the fulness of the Father is received (vv. 12–13). *See* Grace.

The "everlasting gospel" contains the truths that govern worship. The Lord explained, "It is my will, that all they who call on my name, and worship me according to mine everlasting gospel, should gather together, and stand in holy places" (101:22). A person worships as he learns "words of wisdom out of the best books" and "seek[s] learning even by study, and also by faith" (109:14, 24).

Latter-day Saints "claim the privilege of worshiping Almighty God according to the dictates of [their] own conscience, and allow" others the "same privilege"—to worship "how, where, or what they may" (A of F 11). Section 134, containing the Church's "belief with regard to earthly government and laws" (headnote), declares that as long as one's form of worship does not "infringe upon the rights and liberties of others . . . human law" should not prescribe "rules of worship to bind the consciences of men, nor dictate forms for public or private devotion" (134:4); accountability for proper worship is "to be answered by man to his Maker" (134:6).

To facilitate proper devotion, God commands his children to build "houses of worship," both chapels and temples (42:35; 115:8). He also warns against those who, like Almon Babbitt, may aspire to "establish [their own] counsel instead of the counsel which I have ordained," thereby setting up "a golden calf for the worship of my people" (124:84).

The ultimate objective of true worship is to "come unto the Father" in the name of JESUS

CHRIST "and in due time receive of his fulness" (93:19).

NHW

Worthy of his hire

Phrase indicating that those serving full-time in faithfully administering spiritual things are deserving of having their material needs met, "even as those who are appointed to a stewardship to administer in temporal things" (70:12).

The Lord's law concerning the principles of CONSECRATION provides for the presiding bishop and his counselors "to have their families supported out of the property which is consecrated . . . [or] to receive a just remuneration for all their services" in the Church (42:71–73; cf. 51:13–14). This principle was also in place for others called to engage full-time in various capacities in the work of the Church. Oliver Cowdery, as the second elder in the Church (20:3), was instructed by the Lord, "Thou shalt take no purse nor scrip . . . for the church shall give unto thee in the very hour what thou needest for food and for raiment, and for shoes and for money" (24:18). Others, including Thomas B. Marsh (31:5), early missionaries sent out to "prove the world" (84:79), and Warren Cowdery, the presiding elder in Freedom, New York (106:1–3), were given similar instructions, accompanied by the declaration that "the laborer is worthy of his hire."

The New Testament contains the same doctrine. When the Savior called the seventy, he instructed them to "carry neither purse [money], nor scrip [food bag]" (Luke 10:4). As full-time missionaries, they were to rely upon the generosity of those they contacted, "eating and drinking such things as they give: for the labourer is worthy of his hire" (Luke 10:7), or as stated by Matthew, "the workman is worthy of his meat" (Matt. 10:9–11). The apostle Paul taught, "The Lord ordained that they which preach the gospel should live of the gospel" (1 Cor. 9:11–14), that is, those who are called to preach the gospel full-time, are entitled to receive the necessities of life from those who have accepted the gospel.

FFJ

Wrest. *See* Appendix E.

Exalt not yourselves; rebel not against my servant Joseph; for verily I say unto you, I am with him, and my hand shall be over him, and the keys which I have given unto him, and also to youward, shall not be taken from him till I come. 112:15

Yoke. *See* Appendix E.

Young, Brigham

Birth: 1 June 1801, Whittingham, Windham County, Vermont

Death: 29 August 1877, Salt Lake City, Salt Lake County, Utah

Reading the Book of Mormon, listening to missionaries, and baptism in 1832 brought answers to Brigham Young's search for religious truth. Anxious to learn more about his new religion, he journeyed from his home in New York to Kirtland, Ohio, to meet the Prophet Joseph Smith. Of his initial meeting with Joseph, he recalled, "Here my joy was full at the privilege of shaking the hand of the Prophet of God, and receiving the sure testimony, by the spirit of prophecy, that he was all that any man could believe him to be as a true Prophet" (Roberts, 1:289).

After serving two missions to Upper Canada, Brigham Young moved to Kirtland in 1833. He was a member of ZION'S CAMP in 1834. On 14 February 1835 he was ordained an apostle. By 1838 he had moved to Missouri and became the senior member of the Quorum of the Twelve Apostles after the apostasy of Thomas B. Marsh (cf. 124:127–28). Because Joseph Smith and other Church leaders were incarcerated in LIBERTY JAIL, he directed the evacuation of the Saints from Missouri to Illinois after Missouri governor Lilburn Boggs's extermination order. President Young went on a mission to Great Britain with other members of the Twelve Apostles from 1839 to 1841. In a revelation given to Joseph Smith on 9 July 1841, President Young learned that his sacrifice to preach the gospel to the nations of the earth was "acceptable to [the Lord]" (126:1) and he was no longer required to leave his family. Even so, he served two more short missions in the summers of 1843 and 1844.

After the death of Joseph Smith, the keys for leading the Church, or kingdom of God, rested with the Twelve (Clark, 1:233). Sidney Rigdon challenged the authority of the Twelve on 8 August 1844 "at a special meeting of the Church," proposing that "a guardian for the church" be appointed. President Brigham

Brigham Young, 1801–1877.

Courtesy Church History Library.

Young at a meeting later on the same day testified that "the Quorum of the Twelve have the keys of the kingdom of God in all the world. . . . They stand next to Joseph, and are as the First Presidency of the Church" (Smith, 7:231–33). "It was while delivering this speech that a transformation of President Brigham Young is said to have occurred, that is to say in voice, person and manner. He seemed to be the personification of Joseph Smith, on the testimony of many who were present" (Smith, 7:236). After Brigham Young's address, the Saints sustained the Twelve with a nearly unanimous vote. From 1844 to 1847 Brigham Young led the Church as president of the Quorum of the Twelve. In December 1847 he was ordained president of the Church, fulfilling a prophecy uttered by Joseph Smith in Kirtland: "The time will come when Brigham Young will preside over this church" (Roberts, 1:289).

On 14 January 1847 he received a revelation called "The word and will of the Lord, given through President Brigham Young at the

Winter Quarters of the Camp of Israel, Omaha Nation" (136, headnote). In the revelation, he was instructed to organize the camps of Israel for their journey to the Salt Lake Valley (136:2). Under his direction, thousands of Latter-day Saints journeyed to the valley and settled in the Rockies. Under Brigham Young's direction, the Saints built hundreds of settlements to colonize the West.

President Young died at 4 P.M. on 29 August 1877, calling "Joseph, Joseph, Joseph" (Nibley, 533). In a revelation given to President Joseph F. Smith, President Smith was told that Brigham Young was "among the noble and great ones who were chosen in the beginning to be rulers in the Church of God" (138:55).

See also Apostles, the first Twelve of latter days; Apostles, the Twelve, mission to Great Britain; Historical context and overview of Doctrine and Covenants 136 (p. 856).

BIBLIOGRAPHY

Clark, James R., comp. *Messages of the First Presidency of The Church of Jesus Christ of Latter-day Saints, 1833–1964.* 6 vols. Salt Lake City: Bookcraft, 1965–75.

Nibley, Preston. *Brigham Young: The Man and His Work.* Salt Lake City: Deseret Book, 1965.

Roberts, B. H. *A Comprehensive History of The Church of Jesus Christ of Latter-day Saints, Century One.* 6 vols. Salt Lake City: The Church of Jesus Christ of Latter-day Saints, 1930. Reprint, Provo, Utah: Brigham Young University Press, 1965.

Smith, Joseph. *History of The Church of Jesus Christ of Latter-day Saints.* Edited by B. H. Roberts. 7 vols. 2d ed. rev. Salt Lake City: The Church of Jesus Christ of Latter-day Saints, 1932–51.

SEB

Young, Joseph

Birth: 7 April 1797, Hopkinton, Middlesex County, Massachusetts

Death: 16 July 1881, Salt Lake City, Salt Lake County, Utah

In June 1830 Joseph Young, older brother of Brigham Young, traveled to Canada with their brother Phineas. On their way they stopped at the home of their brother-in-law, J. P. Greene, in Lyons, New York. Joseph Young recalled that he saw the Book of Mormon there for the first time: "Nothing could have been more acceptable to my famishing soul. I hailed it as my Spiritual

Joseph Young, 1797–1881.

Jubilee a deliverance from a long night of darkness and bondage" (5–6).

After returning from Canada to his family's home in Mendon, New York, Joseph, along with his brother Phineas and their father, traveled to a small branch of the Church in Pennsylvania. They were baptized on 6 April 1832 and subsequently moved to Kirtland, Ohio (Young, 6–7). In 1834 Joseph marched with ZION'S CAMP to Missouri. On 8 February 1835 Joseph Smith invited Joseph and Brigham Young to his home. The Prophet addressed Brigham, who had also been converted and baptized, and informed him of the upcoming formation of the Quorum of the Twelve Apostles. The Prophet "then turned to Elder Joseph Young with quite an earnestness, as though the vision of his mind was extended still further, and addressing him, said, 'Brother Joseph, the Lord has made you President of the Seventies'" (2:181). He was ordained to that office 1 March 1835 and served faithfully in this position for forty-six years. One of his first assignments included helping the Kirtland poor move in the summer of 1838 to Far West, Missouri. He was expelled from Missouri with the Saints in 1839, and after a short stay in Quincy, Illinois, he settled in Nauvoo. His appointment as a president of the Seventies was confirmed in a revelation given to the Prophet Joseph Smith in Nauvoo in 1841 (124:138). Joseph Young left Nauvoo in 1846, residing for a time in Iowa and Winter Quarters, Nebraska, before journeying to the Salt Lake Valley in 1850. One of his assignments in Salt Lake City included visiting settlements of the Saints in Utah, Idaho, Arizona, and New Mexico, organizing quorums of the seventy. In 1870 he served a mission to the British Isles. He passed away on 16 July 1881.

BIBLIOGRAPHY

Biographical Sketch of Joseph and Jane B. Young. Church History Library, The Church of Jesus Christ of Latter-day Saints, Salt Lake City, Utah.

Smith, Joseph. *History of The Church of Jesus Christ of Latter-day Saints*. Edited by B. H. Roberts. 7 vols. 2d ed. rev. Salt Lake City: The Church of Jesus Christ of Latter-day Saints, 1932–51.

Young, Joseph. Autobiographical Sketch. Church History Library, The Church of Jesus Christ of Latter-day Saints, Salt Lake City, Utah.

RC

Youward

Term meaning "toward you" or "to you." In early manuscript copies of Doctrine and Covenants 112:15 the term was rendered as a hyphenated word, "you-ward," and as two words, "you ward" (Woodford, 1486, 1488). The Lord promised, "The keys which I have given unto him [Joseph Smith], and also to youward [the Twelve], shall not be taken from him till I come" (112:15). Those KEYS are the "keys of the kingdom of God" (65:2), that is, all priesthood keys pertaining to "the dispensation of the fulness of times" (112:16, 30–32; cf. 110:16).

BIBLIOGRAPHY

Woodford, Robert J. "The Historical Development of the Doctrine and Covenants." Ph.D. dissertation. Brigham Young University, 1974.

LED

And behold, and lo, this shall be their cry, and the voice of the Lord unto all people: Go ye forth unto the land of Zion, that the borders of my people may be enlarged, and that her stakes may be strengthened, and that Zion may go forth unto the regions round about. 133:9

Zacharias

A priest "of the course of Abia" (Luke 1:5), husband of Elisabeth, and father of John the Baptist. His name is found in one verse of the Doctrine and Covenants, which says that ELIAS, the angel Gabriel (Luke 1:19), visited Zacharias "and gave promise that he should have a son, and his name should be John, and he should be filled with the spirit of Elias" (27:7; cf. Luke 1:5–25, 57–79).

LED

Zarahemla

A town, branch, and stake of the Church in Lee County, Iowa, located on the west side of the Mississippi River across from Nauvoo. Zarahemla was founded and named in 1841 as directed by revelation (125:3–4). The Iowa Stake, first organized in October 1839 with John Smith as president, was renamed the Zarahemla Stake in August 1841 (Cannon, 32–33). The name refers to the "great city Zarahemla" (Hel. 1:18) and to the Mulekite leader Zarahemla named in the Book of Mormon (Omni 1:13–18; Mosiah 25:2). The Zarahemla Stake, once consisting of nine branches and 750 members living in Lee and Van Buren counties, "was discontinued," and "a branch was organized in place thereof" on 6 January 1842 (Smith, 4:493). The insufficient number of members to sustain a stake was largely due to the Saints moving across the river to Nauvoo (Kimball, 132–42).

BIBLIOGRAPHY

Cannon, Donald Q. "Mormon Satellite Settlements in Hancock County, Illinois, and Lee County, Iowa." In *The Iowa Mormon Trail: Legacy of Faith and Courage,* edited by Susan Easton Black and William G. Hartley. Orem, Utah: Helix Publishing, 1997.

Kimball, Stanley B. "Nauvoo West: The Mormons of the Iowa Shore." *BYU Studies* 18 (Winter 1978): 132–42.

Smith, Joseph. *History of The Church of Jesus Christ of Latter-day Saints.* Edited by B. H. Roberts. 7 vols. 2d ed. rev. Salt Lake City: The Church of Jesus Christ of Latter-day Saints, 1932–51.

GML

Zion

The society of the pure in heart; the city of God (97:19, 21). Conversion to JESUS CHRIST and his GOSPEL is an individual undertaking. At the same time, heaven on earth and heaven hereafter are brought to pass through the establishment of unity and love within a community of holy people of covenant.

In December 1830, the Prophet Joseph Smith received additional knowledge concerning the patriarch Enoch and his ancient city of Zion (see Moses 7). Enoch's Zion became the pattern, the scriptural prototype for the Latter-day Saints. In the months that followed, several revelations in the Doctrine and Covenants spoke of the ancient ZION OF ENOCH, providing the broad framework whereby the Latter-day Saints could lay the foundation for a modern society of Zion. Zion is defined or described in several ways.

The Restoration/Restored Church

Among the earliest revelations was the repeated command, "Now, as you have asked, behold, I say unto you, keep my commandments, and seek to bring forth and establish the cause of Zion" (6:6; 11:6; 12:6; 14:6). Zion thus came to be associated with the restored Church and the work of the Restoration.

Zion as a specific location

On 20 July 1831, the Latter-day Saints learned that the land of Missouri was "the land which I have appointed and consecrated for the gathering of the saints. Wherefore, this is the land of promise, and the place for the city of Zion. . . . The place which is now called Independence is the center place" (57:1–3). And one month later the Lord said, "Behold, the land of Zion—I, the Lord, hold it in mine own hands" (63:25). In the words of Elder Bruce R. McConkie, the center place is "where the chief temple shall stand, a place to which the Lord shall come, a place whence the law shall go forth to govern all the earth . . . and that center place is what men now call Independence in Jackson County, Missouri, but which in a day to come will be the Zion of our God and the City of Holiness of his people. The site is selected; the place is known; the decree has gone forth; and the promised destiny is assured" (*New Witness,* 595). When the future city of Zion is established, it will be called "the New Jerusalem, a land of peace, a city of refuge, a place of safety for the saints of the Most High God" and "there shall be gathered unto it out of every nation under heaven" (45:66–69). Enoch's city and people will be united with the latter-day Zion: "Then shalt thou [Enoch] and all thy city meet them there . . . and there shall be mine abode, and it shall be Zion," and for a "thousand years the earth shall rest" (Moses 7:62–64). During the millennial period "out of Zion shall go forth the law, and the word of the Lord from Jerusalem" (Isa. 2:3).

Although the Church will establish a significant presence in Missouri, at the present time the Saints are counseled to gather to stakes of Zion in their own lands and build up the Church there (101:17–21; 109:59; cf. Isa. 54:2; McConkie, "Come," 115–18).

North and South America

Joseph Smith taught that "the whole of America is Zion itself from north to south" (6:318–19). Brigham Young added, "What is Zion? In one sense Zion is the pure in heart. But is there a land that ever will be called Zion? Yes, brethren. What land is it? It is the land that the Lord gave to Jacob, who bequeathed it to his son Joseph, and his posterity, and they inhabit it, and that land is North and South America. That is Zion as to land, as to Territory, and location" (2:253).

An ensign, banner, or standard

Zion is spoken of in scripture as a "standard" (ensign or banner) around which God's covenant people can rally "for a defense, and for a refuge from the storm, and from wrath when it shall be poured out without mixture upon the whole earth" (115:5–6). It is also to be "like unto a judge sitting on a hill, or in a high place, to judge the nations" (64:37–38).

A state of the soul

Zion is a state of being, a purity of heart (97:21) that characterizes the household of faith. "As to the spirit of Zion, it is in the hearts of the Saints, of those who love and serve the Lord with all their might, mind, and strength" (Young, 2:253). On another occasion President Brigham Young affirmed: "Zion will be redeemed and built up, and the Saints will rejoice. This is the land of Zion; and *who are Zion? The*

pure in heart are Zion; they have Zion within them. Purify yourselves, sanctify the Lord God in your hearts, and have the Zion of God within you" (8:198; emphasis added). President Stephen L Richards observed: "There is no fence around Zion or the world, but to one of discernment, they [Zion and Babylon] are separated more completely than if each were surrounded with high unscalable walls. Their underlying concepts, philosophies, and purposes are at complete variance one with the other. . . . The philosophy of Zion is humility, not servility, but a willing recognition of the sovereignty of God and dependence on his providence" (110).

Conclusion

Zion is a place. Zion is a people. Zion is a holy state of being. Zion is the "highest order of priesthood society" (Kimball, 78). It is the heritage of the Saints. "The building up of Zion," Joseph Smith declared, "is a cause that has interested the people of God in every age; it is a theme upon which prophets, priests and kings have dwelt with peculiar delight" (4:609). This is the destiny and abode of those who endure faithfully to the end. Consequently Joseph Smith stated, "We ought to have the building up of Zion as our greatest object" (3:390).

See also Curtain(s); Gather, gathering; Historical context and overview of Doctrine and Covenants 57 (p. 761); New Jerusalem; Stake(s); Zion, redemption of.

BIBLIOGRAPHY

Kimball, Spencer W. "Welfare Services: The Gospel in Action." *Ensign* 7 (November 1977): 76–79.

McConkie, Bruce R. *A New Witness for the Articles of Faith.* Salt Lake City: Deseret Book, 1985.

———. "Come: Let Israel Build Zion." *Ensign* 7 (May 1977): 115–18.

Richards, Stephen L. Conference Report, October 1951, 109–18.

Smith, Joseph. *History of The Church of Jesus Christ of Latter-day Saints.* Edited by B. H. Roberts. 7 vols. 2d ed. rev. Salt Lake City: The Church of Jesus Christ of Latter-day Saints, 1932–51.

Young, Brigham. *Journal of Discourses.* 26 vols. London: Latter-day Saints' Book Depot, 1854–86.

RLM

Zion, city of. *See* New Jerusalem.

Zion of Enoch

The scriptural prototype of a society that meets every temporal and spiritual need of its members. The phrase is used once in the Doctrine and Covenants, where the Lord says, "I am the same which have taken the Zion of Enoch into mine own bosom" (38:4).

Because of their unity and consummate righteousness, Enoch and his people were translated, elevated to a terrestrial state (Moses 7:18–21; Smith, 4:209–10, 425). Concerning "Enoch, and his brethren," the Lord explained that they were "separated from the earth, and were received unto myself—a city reserved until a day of righteousness shall come" (45:11–14). That day of righteousness will be at the second coming of the Lord when Enoch and his people will return to the earth to meet the righteous inhabitants of "an Holy City," even "Zion, a New Jerusalem," "the city of Zion" to be built in Jackson County, Missouri (Moses 7:60–64; D&C 57:1–3; 57, headnote).

See also Book of Enoch; New Jerusalem; Order of Enoch; Translated beings; Zion.

BIBLIOGRAPHY

Smith, Joseph. *History of The Church of Jesus Christ of Latter-day Saints*. Edited by B. H. Roberts. 7 vols. 2d ed. rev. Salt Lake City: The Church of Jesus Christ of Latter-day Saints, 1932–51.

RLM

Zion, redemption of

The individual and corporate effort to purify men and women, establish ZION, and prepare the earth for the second coming of Jesus Christ, "the King of Zion" (Moses 7:53).

As the head of the dispensation of the fulness of times, Joseph Smith was charged to "move the cause of Zion in mighty power for good" (21:7) and to devote "all [his] service in Zion" (24:7). When the Latter-day Saints were driven from Jackson County, Missouri, in 1833, there was a great sense of loss among the people—the followers of Joseph Smith felt the pain of not being able to establish and maintain the "center place" (57:3). They were instructed that they had been driven from their land of promise partly because of their transgressions, because they were not ready and prepared to dwell there

(101:1–8; 105:9, 13). Although ZION'S CAMP was organized in 1834 to help restore the Saints to their lands in Jackson County, Missouri, it was not the right time for that to happen. But, the Lord assured the Saints, Zion would indeed be redeemed (reclaimed or recovered) in a time to come when the Saints were truly prepared, sanctified, and greatly increased in numbers (101:16–20; 103; 105:10, 11, 31). Thus the revelations spoke of a future time, a day of glory and power when Zion would be redeemed. In a literal sense, the Saints will in the future once again establish a significant physical and spiritual presence in Independence and its environs: property will be purchased, land will be developed, meetinghouses and even a great temple will be erected, as prophesied (84:1–5; cf. 124:49–54).

In a broader sense, however, the redemption of Zion is taking place as the members of The Church of Jesus Christ of Latter-day Saints throughout the earth are learning to be obedient and loyal to their covenants; as they hearken to the words of the Lord's anointed spokesmen; as they purify their lives and separate themselves from worldly influences. The redemption of Zion, in other words, entails the gradual sanctification and glorification of a people who will then be eager and ready to welcome the King of kings and Lord of lords for his millennial reign.

The redemption of Zion will come as the number of full-time missionaries increases, as members become more directly involved in sharing the message of the Restoration with their friends and associates, and as the marvelous work and a wonder foreseen by prophets from ages past (Isa. 29:13–14) spreads to all corners of the globe. "For Zion must increase in beauty, and in holiness; her borders must be enlarged; her stakes must be strengthened; yea, verily I say unto you, Zion must arise and put on her beautiful garments" (82:14; cf. 133:4–5, 14). Thus, after the Lord has chastened and "contend[ed]" with his people sufficiently to purify them, he will, in his own time, redeem Zion (90:36–37; 100:13; 136:18).

The redemption of Zion in Jackson County is but the type, the shadow of what will exist in the stakes of Zion throughout the earth. Elder

Bruce R. McConkie explained that "every gathering place, for the scattered remnants who there assemble, becomes to them as a New Jerusalem. It becomes a City of Holiness, a place where they can worship the Father in spirit and in truth, a place where temples are available in which they may receive the fulness of the priesthood, a place where no blessing is denied them" (586). Such redemption will not come without significant opposition, but the Lord has promised, "Concern not yourselves about Zion, for I will deal mercifully with her" (111:6). He has also assured the Saints that he will fight their battles for them (105:14).

See also Historical context and overview of Doctrine and Covenants 101 (p. 806), 103 (p. 808), 104 (p. 810), 105 (p. 812); Missouri period.

BIBLIOGRAPHY

McConkie, Bruce R. *A New Witness for the Articles of Faith*. Salt Lake City: Deseret Book, 1985.

RLM

Zion's Camp

A military-religious organization of Latter-day Saints that marched from Ohio to Missouri, intending to assist exiled Church members to regain their lands in Jackson County from which they had been unlawfully driven (101; 103; 105).

Following the expulsion of Latter-day Saints from Jackson County in November 1833, Joseph Smith received a revelation (103), in which the Lord called for volunteers "of the strength of my house" (v. 34); Zion's Camp was the result. The call was for five hundred volunteers (v. 30), but that number was not forthcoming because many of the Saints refused to "go up unto Zion" and contribute money to the cause (105:8). The camp, which had two divisions or groups, was composed of 207 men, 11 women, and 11 children. In May and June 1834, Joseph Smith led the larger of the two groups from Kirtland, Ohio, to Missouri, a journey of nearly nine hundred miles. Hyrum Smith led the second division from Pontiac, Michigan, to Missouri, also

Zion's Camp; *painting by Judith Mehr. In June 1834, while the members of the expedition were encamped between two branches of the Fishing River in western Missouri, the Lord protected them from an approaching mob with a severe storm.*

in May and June 1834. The two groups met at Salt River about one hundred miles east of Independence, Missouri, in early June (Bradley, 29).

Most camp members lacked military training. Although sham battles and military exercises were held during the march, a battle for ownership of lands in Jackson County did not ensue. Governor Daniel Dunklin of Missouri had previously promised to help reinstate the Saints on their lands with the assistance of the state militia, but he refused to honor his word. He encouraged displaced Latter-day Saints to sell their lands and settle elsewhere or to seek REDRESS through the courts. With the refusal of the governor to call out the militia to enforce the law, a military initiative by Zion's Camp was not a reasonable measure. At Fishing River, the Lord revealed to Joseph Smith that "Zion" would not be redeemed because of the Saints' lack of unity, their refusal to care for the poor, and the need for further preparations to establish a Zion society (105:2–12). The camp was disbanded

without military action, but the experience of Zion's Camp taught important lessons:

1. The Lord wants men who are willing to offer their lives for his kingdom. From such men, he chooses his leaders. Nine members of the original Quorum of the Twelve Apostles and seventy members of the original Quorum of the Seventy marched with Zion's Camp.

2. Those in the camp gained valuable experience that prepared them for future journeys to Illinois and the Salt Lake Valley (Richards, 136).

3. Camp members learned firsthand the importance of the calling and power of a prophet. Wilford Woodruff said, "We gained an experience that we never could have gained in any other way. We had the privilege of beholding the face of the prophet, and we had the privilege of travelling a thousand miles with him, and seeing the workings of the Spirit of God with him, and the revelations of Jesus Christ unto him and the fulfilment of those revelations" (Woodruff, 13:158).

Brigham Young summarized the experience of Zion's Camp when he was asked what he had

March of Zion's Camp, 1834.

gained from his journey to Missouri. He replied, "Just what we went for" (Young, 2:10).

See also Historical context and overview of Doctrine and Covenants 101 (p. 806), 103 (p. 808), and 105 (p. 812).

BIBLIOGRAPHY

Bradley, James L. *Zion's Camp 1834: Prelude to the Civil War*. Logan, Utah: James L. Bradley, 1990.

Richards, Franklin D. Conference Report, October 1965.

Smith, Joseph. *History of The Church of Jesus Christ of Latter-day Saints*. Edited by B. H. Roberts. 7 vols. 2d ed. rev. Salt Lake City: The Church of Jesus Christ of Latter-day Saints, 1932–51.

Woodruff, Wilford. *Journal of Discourses*. 26 vols. London: Latter-day Saints' Book Depot, 1854–86.

Young, Brigham. *Journal of Discourses*. 26 vols. London: Latter-day Saints' Book Depot, 1854–86.

TLG

Zoramites

Descendants of Zoram, a man who lived in Jerusalem about 600 B.C. Zoram was a servant of Laban, from whom Nephi and his brothers were commanded to obtain the plates of brass (1 Ne. 3–4). Zoram accompanied Lehi and Ishmael and their families from Jerusalem to the New World. He married Ishmael's oldest daughter (1 Ne. 16:7) and their offspring became known as Zoramites. They went with the righteous Nephites when they separated from the Lamanites and remained faithful to God and his people (2 Ne. 5:6).

Another group called Zoramites appears much later in the Book of Mormon (Alma 30:59). They were an apostate Nephite group (Alma 31) who "became Lamanites" (Alma 43:4). There is no apparent connection in the record between the two groups of Zoramites.

In any event, the Doctrine and Covenants lists the Zoramites with the righteous descendants of Lehi called "the Nephites, and the Jacobites, and the Josephites," who are to come to "the knowledge of [the] Savior" in the last days through the Book of Mormon (3:16–19).

LED

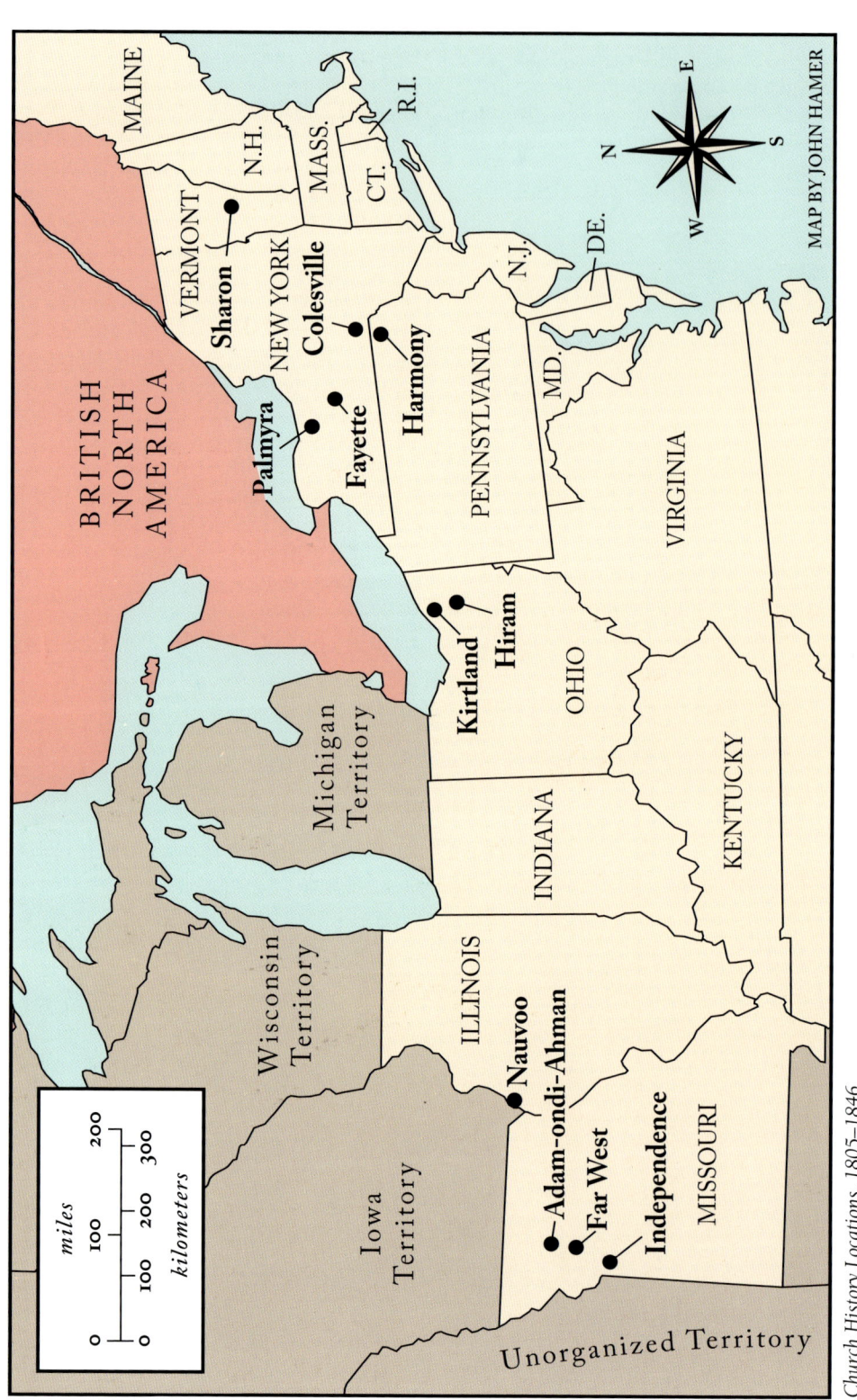

Church History Locations, 1805–1846.

HISTORICAL CONTEXT AND OVERVIEW OF DOCTRINE AND COVENANTS 1–138

Historical context and overview of Doctrine and Covenants 1

Historical context

By 1831 many religious and political groups were publishing newspapers and books, reaching wider audiences than ever before through the medium of print. How could the Saints follow suit? The growing number of missionaries was to strictly apply the revelations in their ministry, but copies of them were scarce and could be obtained only by copying them by hand or by crossing paths with an elder who had a copy.

The Lord had called experienced editor William W. Phelps to be a printer for the Church (57:11). Then the Prophet Joseph Smith convened a council at the Johnson home in Hiram, Ohio, in early November 1831 and laid a manuscript called the Book of Commandments and Revelations before Church leaders; it was time for the revelations in it to be published. The council voted that the revelations should "be prized by this Conference to be worth to the Church the riches of the whole Earth" (Cannon and Cook, 32). Oliver Cowdery asked "how many copies of the Book of commandments it was the will of the Lord should be published in the first edition of that work." The council voted to publish ten thousand copies, a number later reduced to three thousand in a meeting of the Literary Firm (Cannon and Cook, 27, 46). A committee of the Church's best writers drafted a preface for the book, but the Lord revealed his own preface through Joseph Smith. Joseph spoke the words of the revelation slowly as Sidney Rigdon wrote them down, and the Lord called his words in section 1 "*my* preface unto

the book of *my* commandments" (1:6; emphasis added).

Content overview

Section 1 performs the work of a preface. The Doctrine and Covenants is the Lord's book, and though section 1 was not the first section to be revealed, it sets forth his purposes for the subsequent sections.

The revelation in section 1 contains a prophecy of the imminent coming of the Savior and the just punishments awaiting the "unbelieving and rebellious" before and at the Savior's coming (1:8). The revelation separates mankind into two categories: repentant and unrepentant. It outlines the Lord's rationale for opening the last dispensation. The first premise of that rationale is that the world is apostate. As the Lord is omniscient, he saw the devastating potential of such apostasy. He provided a solution by calling Joseph Smith and giving him revelations, called "commandments" (1:17). Obedience to these commandments resulted in the translation of the Book of Mormon and the restoration of the Church, the ONLY TRUE AND LIVING CHURCH, the only one with the fulness of the GOSPEL and PRIESTHOOD authority through which God still speaks. Men were also led to serve missions to spread the restored gospel as a means of fulfilling God's promises to restore his covenant and offer the fulness of the gospel to all mankind. Consequently, each individual can choose

17 Wherefore, I the Lord, *a*knowing the calamity which should come upon the *b*inhabitants of the earth, *c*called upon my *d*servant Joseph Smith, Jun., and *e*spake unto him from heaven, and gave him *f*commandments;

Doctrine and Covenants 1:17.

37 "Search these *b*commandments, for they are true and *c*faithful, and the prophecies and *d*promises which are in them shall all be fulfilled.
38 What I the Lord have spoken, I have spoken, and I excuse not myself; and though the heavens and the earth pass away, my *a*word shall not pass away, but shall all be *b*fulfilled, whether by mine own *c*voice or by the *d*voice of my *e*servants, it is the *f*same.

Doctrine and Covenants 1:37–38.

repentance or destruction according to his or her own free will. The revelation emphasizes the Lord's intent to make the gospel known universally: he is no respecter of persons, and he does not play favorites or predetermine the destiny of souls. Instead, he warns everyone, enabling each to choose. He will speak until every ear hears and every heart is penetrated. "The voice of the Lord is unto the ends of the earth, that all that will hear may hear" (1:11).

The revelation in section 1 introduces the author of the book, the Lord Jesus Christ, and acquaints readers with his literary voice. He framed the book in a typology of opposites: Babylon (or the world) strays from God's order, breaks covenants, and does things its "own way" (1:16); the restored Church is the way out of Babylon. It reestablishes broken covenants, facilitates repentance, increases faith, and proclaims

the gospel to all mankind. The Lord was pleased with his restored Church, if not with all of its members. He will forgive and save all those who repent. Babylon, however, is doomed to destruction (1:16). The entire Doctrine and Covenants is framed by the conflict between Zion and Babylon. This revelation informs mankind of the inevitable choice to be made between them: Repent and be saved at the Lord's imminent coming, or rebel and be damned. It authoritatively establishes that those who are repentant embrace the Lord's covenants (which are fully available only in his restored Church) as the only alternative to impending calamities. "I am God and have spoken it," the Lord declared. "These commandments are of me" (1:24).

The Lord warned that before his second coming "the devil shall have power over his own dominion" on the earth, but the Lord also

Courtesy Alex L. Baugh.

Upstairs room of John Johnson's farm home. In this home on November 1, 1831, the Lord revealed his preface to the Book of Commandments: "Behold, this is mine authority, and the authority of my servants, and my preface unto the book of my commandments, which I have given them to publish unto you, O inhabitants of the earth" (D&C 1:6).

promised that he "shall have power over his saints, and shall reign in their midst" (1:35–36). He instructed his Saints to "search these commandments, for they are true and faithful, and the prophecies and promises which are in them shall all be fulfilled" (1:37). *See* Appendix D.

The revelation ends with his own testimony of the truth of his words, which "shall all be fulfilled, whether by mine own voice or by the voice of my servants, it is the same" (1:38–39).

BIBLIOGRAPHY

Cannon, Donald Q., and Lyndon W. Cook, eds. *Far West Record: Minutes of the Church of Jesus Christ of Latter-day Saints, 1830–1844.* Salt Lake City: Deseret Book, 1983.

Harper, Steven C. *Making Sense of the Doctrine and Covenants: A Guided Tour through Modern Revelations.* Salt Lake City: Deseret Book, 2008.

Smith, Joseph. *History of The Church of Jesus Christ of Latter-day Saints.* Edited by B. H. Roberts. 7 vols. 2d ed. rev. Salt Lake City: The Church of Jesus Christ of Latter-day Saints, 1932–51.

SCH

Historical context and overview of Doctrine and Covenants 2

Historical context

After the First Vision in the spring of 1820, Joseph Smith and his family continued to live in a small log house on the one-hundred-acre farm they had contracted to buy near Palmyra, New York. Joseph later wrote concerning this time period, "I was left to all kinds of temptations; and, mingling with all kinds of society, I frequently fell into many foolish errors, and displayed the weakness of youth, and the foibles of human nature" (JS–H 1:28). Retiring to bed in an upstairs room of the log house on the evening of 21 September 1823 and feeling "condemned for [his] weakness and imperfections," Joseph prayed for forgiveness of his sins and asked for a "manifestation" indicating his "state and standing" before God (JS–H 1:29). While he prayed, a heavenly messenger identifying himself as Moroni appeared to him. After informing him of the existence of the gold plates from which Joseph later translated the Book of Mormon,

The rebuilt log home of Joseph Smith Sr. in Palmyra, New York. Moroni appeared to the Prophet here on the evening of 21 September 1823, telling him of the Book of Mormon and instructing him with the words found in Doctrine and Covenants 2.

Moroni then quoted scriptures from the Old and New Testaments, beginning with part of Malachi 3 (JS–H 1:30–41).

Content overview

Moroni quoted Malachi 4, "though with a little variation," Joseph reported, "from the way it reads in our Bibles" (JS–H 1:36). These variations included verses 5 and 6, which prophesy of Elijah revealing "the Priesthood" and the restoration of the sealing keys, which would provide a "welding link . . . between the fathers and the children" and between dispensations "from the days of Adam even to the present time" (2:1–3; 110:13–16; 128:14–18). Emphasizing dispensations, ancient covenants, and family history work, Moroni's version of Malachi 4:5–6 helps clarify the relationship between the keys that Elijah would restore and temple work in the latter days, witnessing the importance of that work in saying, "If it were not so, the whole earth would be utterly wasted at his [the Lord's] coming" (2:3). Section 2 was added to the Doctrine and Covenants in 1876 just before the completion of the St. George Temple in 1877 and the commencement of endowments and sealings for the dead.

See also Malachi quotations in the Doctrine and Covenants; Priesthood, restoration of

He Called Me by Name; *painting by Liz Lemon Swindle.* "*While I was thus in the act of calling upon God, I discovered a light appearing in my room, which continued to increase until the room was lighter than at noonday, when immediately a personage appeared at my bedside, standing in the air, for his feet did not touch the floor. . . . When I first looked upon him, I was afraid; but the fear soon left me. He called me by name, and said unto me that he was a messenger sent from the presence of God to me, and that his name was Moroni; that God had a work for me to do; and that my name should be had for good and evil among all nations, kindreds, and tongues, or that it should be both good and evil spoken of among all people*" (JS–H 1:30–33)

© Liz Lemon Swindle

priesthood and priesthood keys; Salvation for the dead; Seal, sealed.

AHH

Historical context and overview of Doctrine and Covenants 3

Historical context

In mid-April 1828, Martin Harris began serving as Joseph Smith's scribe as he translated the Book of Mormon in Harmony, Pennsylvania. Harris had written 116 pages of manuscript by 14 June 1828, which he wanted to take to Palmyra and show to his wife and others. The Lord, through the URIM AND THUMMIM, denied Joseph's first and second requests on Harris's behalf for permission to do so. At the third request the Lord finally allowed Harris to take the manuscript on the condition that he show it to only five specific people. Once in Palmyra, however, he broke his promise and showed the manuscript to others. Later, Harris discovered the manuscript was missing from the drawer of the dresser where he had kept it (Smith, *Papers,* 1:286; L. M. Smith, *Biographical,* 144–45).

Meanwhile, in Harmony, the Urim and Thummim had been taken from Joseph "in consequence of [his] having wearied the Lord in asking for the privilege of letting Martin Harris take the writings" (Smith, *Papers,* 1:287; cf. *History,* 1:21–22). Joseph had been nursing his wife, Emma, back to health after the birth of their first child, a boy, who died shortly after being born. After about three weeks, with Emma's health improving and having heard nothing from Harris, Joseph traveled to Palmyra, where, his mother recorded, he "pac[ed] backwards and forwards weeping and grieving like a tender infant" upon learning that Martin had lost the manuscript (Smith, *Book,* 419). Remaining at his parents' house "for a short season," Joseph returned to Harmony. Immediately after his arrival there, while "walking out a little distance" from his house, he was met by Moroni, who returned the Urim and Thummim to him just long enough to receive the revelation contained in section 3, after which both the PLATES and the Urim and Thummim were taken from him (Smith, *Papers,* 1:287; cf. *History,* 1:21–23).

Content overview

Reminding Joseph in this revelation that his work will not be frustrated (3:1–3, 16), the Lord chastened the Prophet for having "transgressed the commandments and the laws of God, and [having] gone on in the persuasions of men" (3:6). "Thou hast suffered the counsel of thy director to be trampled upon from the beginning," the Lord continued (3:15) and warned Joseph that "because of transgression, if thou art not aware thou wilt fall" (3:9). Softening his rebuke, the Lord reminded the Prophet that "God is merciful" and that if Joseph repented, he would "again [be] called to the work" (3:10). The revelation ends with the Lord reaffirming for Joseph the importance of the Nephite record and the "very purpose" (3:19) for which the plates have been preserved, which is "that the Lamanites might come to the knowledge of their fathers, and that they might know the promises of the Lord, and that they may believe the gospel and rely upon the merits of Jesus Christ" (3:20).

See also Book of Mormon, lost manuscript (116 pages); Doctrine and Covenants, what it says about the Book of Mormon; God's works cannot be frustrated; Historical context and overview of Doctrine and Covenants 5 (p. 717) and 10 (p. 720).

BIBLIOGRAPHY

Smith, Joseph. *History of The Church of Jesus Christ of Latter-day Saints.* Edited by B. H. Roberts. 7 vols. 2d ed. rev. Salt Lake City: The Church of Jesus Christ of Latter-day Saints, 1932–51.

———. *The Papers of Joseph Smith.* Edited by Dean C. Jessee. 2 vols. Salt Lake City: Deseret Book, 1989–92.

Smith, Lucy Mack. *Biographical Sketches of Joseph Smith the Prophet and His Progenitors for Many Generations.* Vol. 6 of Prominent Works in Mormon History. Lamoni, Iowa: The Reorganized Church of Jesus Christ of Latter-day Saints, 1912.

———. *Lucy's Book: A Critical Edition of Lucy Mack Smith's Family Memoir.* Edited by Lavina Fielding Anderson. Salt Lake City: Signature Books, 2001.

AHH

Historical context and overview of Doctrine and Covenants 4

Historical context

Sometime in the late summer or early fall of 1828, Moroni returned the URIM AND THUMMIM and the PLATES of the Book of Mormon to Joseph Smith. They had been taken from him in consequence of the loss of the 116-page manuscript. *See* Historical context and overview of Doctrine and Covenants 3 (p. 716).

The need to provide for his family, however, prevented Joseph from doing much, if any, translating for the next several months. In February 1829, Joseph's father, Joseph Smith Sr., visited Joseph and his wife, Emma, in Harmony, Pennsylvania, where they had been living since December 1827. It was during this visit that Joseph received this revelation directed to his father (Smith, *Papers,* 1:288; cf. *History,* 1:28).

Content overview

Given the year before the organization of the Church, the revelation indicates that those who have "desires to serve God" with all their "heart, might, mind and strength" (4:2–3) are called to the "marvelous work [that] is about to come forth among the children of men" (4:1). The revelation then lists several personal and spiritual qualities that those who "embark in the service of God" need to develop in order to be successful in their callings (4:2, 5–6). The revelation ends with the promise, "Ask, and ye shall receive; knock, and it shall be opened unto you" (4:7).

See also Missionary work.

BIBLIOGRAPHY

Smith, Joseph. *History of The Church of Jesus Christ of Latter-day Saints.* Edited by B. H. Roberts. 7 vols. 2d ed. rev. Salt Lake City: The Church of Jesus Christ of Latter-day Saints, 1932–51.

———. *The Papers of Joseph Smith.* Edited by Dean C. Jessee. 2 vols. Salt Lake City: Deseret Book, 1989–92.

AHH

Historical context and overview of Doctrine and Covenants 5

Historical context

Joseph Smith received the revelation recorded in section 5 at the request of Martin Harris in Harmony, Pennsylvania, sometime in March 1829. Nine months earlier, through transgression, Martin had lost 116 pages of the Book of Mormon manuscript. This is the first known communication between these two men since that event. Joseph mentioned none of the circumstances leading up to the reception of this revelation in his history, although it is clear from the revelation itself that Martin asked Joseph for some sort of "witness" from the Lord that he, Joseph, actually had the PLATES containing the Nephite record in his possession. Moroni had taken the plates and the URIM AND THUMMIM from Joseph in consequence of the loss of the 116-page manuscript, and it is understandable that the former scribe and benefactor would inquire of Joseph if he was again in possession of "these things" (5:1–2).

Content overview

The Lord instructed Joseph to inform Martin that he, Joseph, had made a covenant with the Lord to show the plates only to those whom the Lord told him to show them (5:2–3). In addition, the Lord revealed that he would "show these things" to three witnesses who would "behold and view these things as they are" (5:11, 13–15). With apparent reference to Martin becoming one of these witnesses of the Book of Mormon plates, the Lord told Joseph to inform Martin that if he would "humble himself in mighty prayer and faith, in the sincerity of his heart," the Lord would "grant unto him a view of the things which he desires to see" (5:24). The Lord then put strict parameters around the words Martin could use in testifying to the world of what he had seen (5:25–26).

The Lord also revealed to Joseph that unless Martin humbly confessed his transgressions and exercised faith, Joseph was to tell Martin that "he shall do no more, nor trouble [the Lord] any more concerning this matter" (5:29). This warning was an apparent reference to Martin previously asking again and again to take the 116-page manuscript after being told he could not. The Lord then commanded Joseph to stop translating "for a season" until the Lord provided him with further means to do so (5:30, 34; at that time the Lord was preparing Oliver Cowdery to become Joseph's scribe). Martin did eventually see the plates as one of the Three Witnesses later in the summer (Smith, *Papers,* 1:235–37; cf. *History,* 1:52–57; D&C 17; Book of Mormon, Testimony of the Three and Eight Witnesses).

In this revelation the Lord also gave a solemn warning to the people of the world that his word was to be revealed in this day and age through Joseph Smith, and acceptance of his word could not be based on the physical evidence of gold plates and the Urim and Thummim. "If they will not believe my words, they would not believe you, my servant Joseph, if it were possible that you should show them all these things which I have committed unto you" (5:6–10).

See also Book of Mormon, lost manuscript of (116 pages); Historical context and overview of Doctrine and Covenants 3 (p. 716) and 10 (p. 720); Doctrine and Covenants, what it says about the Book of Mormon; Witness, witnesses.

BIBLIOGRAPHY

Smith, Joseph. *History of The Church of Jesus Christ of Latter-day Saints.* Edited by B. H. Roberts. 7 vols. 2d ed. rev. Salt Lake City: The Church of Jesus Christ of Latter-day Saints, 1932–51.

———. *The Papers of Joseph Smith.* Edited by Dean C. Jessee. 2 vols. Salt Lake City: Deseret Book, 1989–92.

AHH

Historical context and overview of Doctrine and Covenants 6

Historical context

Joseph Smith went through a season of contrition and repentance following the loss of the 116-page manuscript of the Book of Mormon, after which Moroni returned the PLATES and the URIM AND THUMMIM to him and the Lord gave him permission to translate once again. *See* Book of Mormon, lost manuscript of (116 pages).

Without a scribe to write for him, however, he accomplished little during the winter of 1828–29. On 5 April 1829, Oliver Cowdery arrived at Joseph and Emma's home in Harmony, Pennsylvania (Smith, *Papers,* 1:288; cf. *History,* 1:32–33)—two or three days, according to Lucy Mack Smith, after Joseph had prayed for the Lord to send him a scribe and had been told that one would be arriving shortly (Smith, *Biographical,* 155). Oliver had spent the winter teaching school in Palmyra, New York, during which he had boarded for a time with Joseph's parents and heard from them about the gold plates and Joseph's efforts to translate them. "Delighted with what he had heard," Lucy

wrote, Oliver had it "impressed upon his mind, that he should . . . have the privilege of writing for Joseph" and "determined to pay him a visit at the close of the school" (Smith, *Biographical,* 152). Oliver began to write for Joseph while the latter translated on 7 April 1829; having "continued for some time" on the translation, Joseph "enquired of the Lord through the Urim and Thummin" and received this revelation for Oliver later in the month (Smith, *Papers,* 1:288–89; cf. *History,* 1:32–33).

Content overview

In this revelation, the Lord informed Oliver of the "great and marvelous work . . . about to come forth unto the children of men" (6:1) and the things he was to do to help "bring forth and establish the cause of Zion" (6:6). *See* Great and marvelous work.

Oliver was commanded to "seek not for riches but for wisdom" (6:7); to "say nothing but repentance unto this generation" (6:9); not to trifle with sacred things (6:12); and to not only "stand by . . . Joseph, faithfully, in whatsoever difficult circumstances he may be for the word's sake" but also to "admonish him in his faults, and also receive admonition of him" (6:18–19).

The Lord also informed Oliver of a sacred "gift" that he possessed (6:10)—later identified as the gift of REVELATION (8:3–4)—through which he might "find out mysteries" and "bring many to the knowledge of the truth" (6:10–11). Further, the Lord told Oliver that if he desired it, he would also be allowed "to translate, even as . . . Joseph" (6:25). And he was given the keys conjointly with Joseph to "bring to light this ministry" (6:28). Helping Oliver to better recognize the spirit of revelation, the Lord also reminded him of a certain night he had asked for, and received, a witness from God that what he had heard about Joseph Smith and the plates was true. "Did I not speak peace to your mind concerning the matter?" the Lord asked. "What greater witness can you have than from God?" (6:23). As a result of this verse, Oliver told Joseph later, he "knew that the work was true, because that no . . . being living knew of the thing alluded to in the revelation but God and himself" (Smith, *Papers,* 1:289; cf. *History,* 1:35; D&C 6:14–17).

Addressing his "little flock" (that is, the Church), the Savior closed the revelation with the admonition to "perform with soberness the work which I have commanded you. Look unto me in every thought; doubt not, fear not. Behold the wounds which pierced my side, and also the prints of the nails in my hands and feet; be faithful, keep my commandments, and ye shall inherit the kingdom of heaven" (6:34–37).

BIBLIOGRAPHY

Smith, Joseph. *History of The Church of Jesus Christ of Latter-day Saints.* Edited by B. H. Roberts. 7 vols. 2d ed. rev. Salt Lake City: The Church of Jesus Christ of Latter-day Saints, 1932–51.

———. *The Papers of Joseph Smith.* Edited by Dean C. Jessee. 2 vols. Salt Lake City: Deseret Book, 1989–92.

Smith, Lucy Mack. *Biographical Sketches of Joseph Smith the Prophet and His Progenitors for Many Generations.* Vol. 6 of Prominent Works in Mormon History. Lamoni, Iowa: The Reorganized Church of Jesus Christ of Latter-day Saints, 1912.

AHH

Historical context and overview of Doctrine and Covenants 7

Historical context

In April 1829, shortly after Oliver Cowdery began serving as Joseph Smith's scribe during the translation of the Book of Mormon, "a difference of opinion" arose between the two men regarding John 21:22 and whether or not John the apostle had died or been allowed to tarry on the earth. Joseph and Oliver received this revelation after having "mutually agreed" to settle the question through the URIM AND THUMMIM (Smith, *Papers,* 1:289; cf. *History,* 1:35–36). Unique among the revelations contained in the Doctrine and Covenants, this section is a translation of a brief statement John the apostle himself had written on parchment and then hidden (Smith, *Papers,* 1:289; cf. *History,* 1:36). Nothing Joseph recorded about the incident suggests that he had the parchment in his possession; most likely, he either saw the parchment in vision and was able to translate it, or he simply received the translation of it with a brief explanation of its origin.

Content overview

The revelation recorded in section 7 makes it clear that John was allowed to live on the earth until the second coming of the Savior to the earth (7:3) and that he would "prophesy before nations, kindreds, tongues and people" (7:3) and be "as flaming fire and a ministering angel . . . for those who shall be heirs of salvation who dwell on the earth" (7:6). Reference is also made to Peter's concern over John's request (7:4; cf. John 21:22) and the Lord's explanation that Peter and John "shall both have according to your desires, for ye both joy in that which ye have desired" (7:8)—Peter to come quickly to the Lord in his kingdom and John to stay on the earth and do "a greater work yet among men than what he [had] before done" (7:4–5). The Lord also promised Peter, James, and John the "keys of this ministry until I come," which KEYS these three apostles conferred upon Joseph Smith and Oliver Cowdery in this DISPENSATION (7:7; 27:12–13).

See also John the Beloved/Revelator quotations in the Doctrine and Covenants; Translated beings.

BIBLIOGRAPHY

Smith, Joseph. *History of The Church of Jesus Christ of Latter-day Saints.* Edited by B. H. Roberts. 7 vols. 2d ed. rev. Salt Lake City: The Church of Jesus Christ of Latter-day Saints, 1932–51.

———. *The Papers of Joseph Smith.* Edited by Dean C. Jessee. 2 vols. Salt Lake City: Deseret Book, 1989–92.

AHH

Historical context and overview of Doctrine and Covenants 8

Historical context

Oliver Cowdery "became exceedingly anxious to have the power to translate bestowed upon him" (Smith, *Papers,* 1:289; cf. *History,* 1:36–37) after he received the Lord's promise that he would be able to "translate, even as . . . Joseph," if he desired to do so (6:25). *See* Historical context and overview of Doctrine and Covenants 6 (p. 718).

The revelation recorded in section 8 was received "in relation to this desire," sometime during April 1829 while the two men were working on the translation of the Book of Mormon at Joseph's home in Harmony, Pennsylvania (Smith, *Papers*, 1:289–90; cf. *History*, 1:36).

Content overview

In this revelation, Oliver is told that he has the "spirit of revelation" and the Lord would tell him in his mind and heart by the Holy Ghost "concerning the engravings of old records, which are ancient," if he would "ask in faith, with an honest heart" (8:1–3). Further, supplementing this gift of revelation, Oliver had "another gift, which is the gift of Aaron"—a gift that had already told him "many things" and through which he could do "marvelous works" while holding it in his hands (8:6, 8). While this "gift of Aaron" possibly refers to an actual instrument Oliver was allowed to use (Just as Moses' brother Aaron used a rod) to receive revelation, the Lord reminded Oliver that the real power lay in faith (8:10) and that only "according to [his] faith" would he be able to "translate and receive knowledge from all those ancient records which have been hid up" (8:11). Joseph's history is silent regarding what happened following the reception of this revelation, and only in Doctrine and Covenants 9 do we learn that Oliver actually "began to translate" but was not able to continue to do so (9:5).

See also Gift of Aaron; Rod(s); Revelation.

BIBLIOGRAPHY

Smith, Joseph. *History of The Church of Jesus Christ of Latter-day Saints*. Edited by B. H. Roberts. 7 vols. 2d ed. rev. Salt Lake City: The Church of Jesus Christ of Latter-day Saints, 1932–51.

———. *The Papers of Joseph Smith*. Edited by Dean C. Jessee. 2 vols. Salt Lake City: Deseret Book, 1989–92.

AHH

Historical context and overview of Doctrine and Covenants 9

Historical context

Soon after Oliver Cowdery began serving as Joseph Smith's scribe during the translation of the Book of Mormon, the Lord told Oliver that if he desired it and exercised faith, he would be able to translate like Joseph. *See* Historical context and overview of Doctrine and Covenants 6 (p. 718) and 8 (p. 719).

Oliver expressed an interest in doing so and

> 8 But, behold, I say unto you, that you must *a*study it out in your *b*mind; then you must *c*ask me if it be right, and if it is right I will cause that your *d*bosom shall *e*burn within you; therefore, you shall *f*feel that it is right.

Doctrine and Covenants 9:8.

began to translate. Because he did not "continue as [he] commenced," the Lord took away "this privilege" from him (9:5), after which Joseph received this revelation in April 1829 on Oliver's behalf.

Content overview

The Lord explained to Oliver that the gift to translate was taken away because he "took no thought save it was to ask" the Lord for the translation, rather than having studied it out in his mind first—the latter step being an essential prerequisite to receiving the REVELATION necessary to translate the PLATES (9:7–9). Oliver had failed to do this partly out of apparent ignorance about how revelation worked and partly out of fear or anxiety rather than faith (9:7–11; cf. 8:1, 10). Telling Oliver that it was "expedient" that he translate "when [he] commenced" but "it is not expedient now," the Lord assured Oliver that he had given Joseph "sufficient strength, whereby it is made up" (9:10–12). With the Lord strengthening Joseph, Oliver was told to continue to serve as the scribe until the translation was completed, after which he "may assist" in translating "other records" (9:1–2).

AHH

Historical context and overview of Doctrine and Covenants 10

Historical context

After the loss of the 116 pages of Book of Mormon manuscript in June 1828, Moroni took both the PLATES and the URIM AND THUMMIM from Joseph Smith. It is unclear how long he waited until they were returned and he was given permission to translate again. His own record indicates it was simply "in a few days" (Smith, *Papers*, 1:287; cf. *History*, 1:23), while his mother, Lucy Mack Smith, recorded that it was not until 22 September of that year (L. M. Smith, *Biographical*, 147). In any event, Joseph "enquired of the Lord" and received the revelation contained in section 10 (Smith, *Papers*, 1:287–88; cf. *History*, 1:23).

Historians have attached three different dates to this revelation—summer 1828, circa April 1829, and May 1829. Editors of *The Joseph Smith Papers* have dated it circa April 1829 based on the incomplete manuscript of the revelation in the Book of Commandments and Revelations (Jensen et al., 13). It was dated May 1829 in the Book of Commandments and all editions of the Doctrine and Covenants until the 1921 edition. It was first dated summer 1828 by Elder Brigham H. Roberts in the *History of the Church* when it was published in 1902 (Smith, *History*, 1:23 footnote). It was then changed to that date in the 1921 edition of the Doctrine and Covenants and in all later printings, even though it is located among the April and May 1829 revelations in that volume.

Content overview

The Lord instructed the Prophet to "continue on unto the finishing of the remainder of the work of translation as you have begun" (10:3). The Lord also told Joseph that "wicked men" had the 116-page manuscript (10:8) and that "Satan hath put it into their hearts to alter the words" (10:10). Satan had also "put it into their hearts" to persuade Joseph to retranslate the portion that he lost (10:15), after which they would produce the original, but altered, manuscript, point out the discrepancies between the two, and use that as evidence to convince people that Joseph "has lied in his words, and that he has no gift, and that he has no power" (10:18, 31–32). The Lord commanded Joseph to "not translate again those words which have gone forth" (10:30) but rather to translate that portion of the plates—that is, the "first part of the engravings of Nephi" (10:45)—that contains a second, "more particular" account of the things he had translated earlier and lost (10:38–42). This second account, the Lord informed Joseph, "throw[s] greater views" on the gospel than the

account which had been lost, which was "only . . . an abridgment" of Nephi's record (10:44–45). "Thus I will confound those who have altered my words," the Lord says (10:42), as well as bring forth "all those parts of my gospel which my holy prophets, yea, and also my disciples, desired in their prayers should come forth unto this people" (10:46).

From the Book of Mormon, readers learn that the second, "more particular" account to which the Lord referred in this revelation is the small plates of Nephi (1 Nephi–Omni). These plates contain the words of the prophets from Nephi through Amaleki (a contemporary of King Benjamin), and were written in an effort to focus on the "ministry" of the Nephites rather than their secular history (1 Ne. 9:2–3). The 116-page manuscript that was stolen was part of Mormon's abridgment of the large plates of Nephi, these being a set of plates kept by the Nephites on which "an account of the reign of the kings, and the wars and contentions" of the people was kept (1 Nephi 9:4). Specifically, the stolen manuscript recorded the first part of Mormon's abridgment of this record—that is, the part dealing with Nephite history from the time of Lehi down to the time of King Benjamin—which is precisely the same period of time covered by the small plates of Nephi. Mormon, when making his abridgment of the secular-oriented large plates, was impressed to put the unabridged, spiritually focused small plates with his abridgment, thereby providing Joseph Smith with two separate, somewhat different accounts for the period from Lehi to King Benjamin (W of M 1:3–7).

In section 10 the Lord explained that the coming forth of the Book of Mormon fulfills the desires, faith, and prayers of Book of Mormon prophets and disciples that the gospel would be brought to their descendants and "other nations" that would come to the Americas. He further said that the Book of Mormon does not "destroy" the Bible but is to "build it up, and shall bring to light the true points of my doctrine," thereby putting down contention (10:46–70; cf. 1 Ne. 15:14; 2 Ne. 3:12).

See also Book of Mormon, lost manuscript of (116 pages); Doctrine and Covenants, what it says about the Book of Mormon; Historical context and overview of Doctrine and Covenants 3 (p. 716) and 5 (p. 717); God's works cannot be frustrated.

BIBLIOGRAPHY

Jensen, Robin Scott, Robert J. Woodford, and Steven C. Harper, eds. *Manuscript Revelation Books.* Facsimile edition. First volume of the Revelations and Translations series of *The Joseph Smith Papers,* edited by Dean C. Jessee, Ronald K. Esplin, and Richard Lyman Bushman. Salt Lake City: Church Historian's Press, 2009.

Smith, Joseph. *History of The Church of Jesus Christ of Latter-day Saints.* Edited by B. H. Roberts. 7 vols. 2d ed. rev. Salt Lake City: The Church of Jesus Christ of Latter-day Saints, 1932–51.

———. *The Papers of Joseph Smith.* Edited by Dean C. Jessee. 2 vols. Salt Lake City: Deseret Book, 1989–92.

Smith, Lucy Mack. *Biographical Sketches of Joseph Smith the Prophet and His Progenitors for Many Generations.* Vol. 6 of Prominent Works in Mormon History. Lamoni, Iowa: The Reorganized Church of Jesus Christ of Latter-day Saints, 1912.

AHH

Historical context and overview of Doctrine and Covenants 11

Historical context

Shortly after his own baptism on 15 May 1829, Oliver Cowdery baptized Joseph Smith's younger brother Samuel in Harmony, Pennsylvania, after which Samuel "returned to his father's house greatly glorifying and praising God, being filled with the Holy Spirit." Joseph's brother Hyrum, apparently intrigued by what he heard from Samuel, visited Joseph and Oliver in Harmony "not many days afterwards." At Hyrum's "earnest request," Joseph later recorded, he received the revelation contained in section 11 through the URIM AND THUMMIM (Smith, *Papers,* 1:292; cf. *History,* 1:44–45).

Content overview

In the revelation recorded in section 11, the Lord instructed Hyrum concerning the role he was to play in the "great and marvelous work" that "is about to come forth" (11:1). *See* Great and marvelous work.

Like Oliver Cowdery before him (6:1–9), Hyrum was told to seek for wisdom rather than riches, to preach nothing but repentance, and to

keep the commandments (11:1–9). To aid him in this, the Lord promised him a gift, the gift of REVELATION: "I will impart unto you of my Spirit, which shall enlighten your mind, which shall fill your soul with joy . . . by this shall you know, all things whatsoever you desire of me, which are pertaining unto things of righteousness, in faith believing in me that you shall receive" (11:10–14). Before attempting to teach the gospel, Hyrum was told to study the scriptures until he had "obtained all which [the Lord] shall grant unto the children of men in this generation." Only then would his "tongue be loosed" and he be able to teach with "the power of God unto the convincing of men" (11:21–22, 26).

The revelation extended the instructions given to Hyrum to "all who have good desires, and have thrust in their sickle to reap" (11:27).

BIBLIOGRAPHY

Smith, Joseph. *History of The Church of Jesus Christ of Latter-day Saints.* Edited by B. H. Roberts. 7 vols. 2d ed. rev. Salt Lake City: The Church of Jesus Christ of Latter-day Saints, 1932–51.

———. *The Papers of Joseph Smith.* Edited by Dean C. Jessee. 2 vols. Salt Lake City: Deseret Book, 1989–92.

AHH

Historical context and overview of Doctrine and Covenants 12

Historical context

Toward the end of May 1829, "about the same time" that Hyrum Smith visited Joseph Smith in Harmony, Pennsylvania (Smith, *History,* 1:47–48), Joseph Knight Sr. from Colesville, New York, went to Joseph Smith's house.

Joseph Knight Sr. did not arrive empty-handed but carried with him "a quantity of provisions, in order that we might not be interrupted in the work of translation, by the want of such necessaries of life" (Smith, *Papers,* 1:293; cf. *History,* 1:47–48). Knight contributed "money and food on several occasions" and "at a particularly desperate time" provided "a barrel of mackerel and some lined paper for writing, . . . nine or ten bushels of grain and five or six bushels of taters [potatoes]" (*Joseph Smith,* 115). Joseph Smith received the revelation recorded in section 12 on behalf of Joseph Knight Sr., the latter being "very anxious to know his duty as to this work" (Smith, *Papers,* 1:293; cf. *History,* 1:48).

Content overview

The Lord told Joseph Knight Sr. that his role in the "great and marvelous work" about to begin on the earth was to keep the commandments and "seek to bring forth and establish the cause of Zion" (12:1, 6)—the very same instructions given earlier to Oliver Cowdery (6:1–7) and Hyrum Smith (11:1–7) and later to David Whitmer (14:1–7). *See* Great and marvelous work.

The Lord reminded Joseph Knight that "no one can assist in this work except he shall be humble and full of love, having faith, hope, and charity, being temperate in all things" (12:8). The Lord closed the revelation by saying, "Behold, I am the light and the life of the world, that speak these words, therefore give heed with your might, and then you are called" (12:9).

BIBLIOGRAPHY

Smith, Joseph. *History of The Church of Jesus Christ of Latter-day Saints.* Edited by B. H. Roberts. 7 vols. 2d ed. rev. Salt Lake City: The Church of Jesus Christ of Latter-day Saints, 1932–51.

———. *Joseph Smith.* Teachings of Presidents of the Church series. Salt Lake City: The Church of Jesus Christ of Latter-day Saints, 2007.

———. *The Papers of Joseph Smith.* Edited by Dean C. Jessee. 2 vols. Salt Lake City: Deseret Book, 1989–92.

AHH

Historical context and overview of Doctrine and Covenants 13

Historical context

Joseph Smith recorded that on 15 May 1829 he and Oliver Cowdery "went into the woods to pray and inquire of the Lord respecting baptism for the remission of sins, that we found mentioned in the translation of the plates. While we were thus employed, praying and calling upon the Lord, a messenger from heaven descended in a cloud of light, and having laid his hands upon us, he ordained us, saying: 'Upon you my fellow servants, in the name of Messiah I confer the Priesthood of Aaron, which holds the keys of the ministering of angels, and of the Gospel of repentance, and of baptism by immersion for the remission of sins; and this shall never be taken again from the earth, until the sons of Levi do offer again an offering unto the Lord in righteousness'" (1:39).

Joseph said the messenger "who visited us on this occasion, and conferred this priesthood upon us, said that his name was John, the same that is called John the Baptist in the New Testament, and that he acted under the direction of Peter, James and John who held the keys of the Priesthood of Melchizedek, which Priesthood he said would in due time be conferred on us" (1:40).

After they received Aaronic PRIESTHOOD, Joseph baptized Oliver Cowdery, then Oliver baptized Joseph. After the baptism, Joseph ordained Oliver to the Aaronic Priesthood, and then Oliver ordained Joseph to the same, "for so we were commanded," wrote the Prophet (JS–H 1:71). Joseph reported that after this event the Holy Ghost fell upon them in great measure and both prophesied (JS–H 1:73–74).

Joseph was "forced to keep secret the circumstances of having received the Priesthood and [their] having been baptized, owing to a spirit of persecution which had already manifested itself in the neighborhood" (Smith, 1:43–44). Being cautious, he did not even write the circumstances of the event at that time, and he did not do so until he began to dictate his history in 1838. By that time the Book of Commandments and the 1835 edition of the Doctrine and Covenants had both been published. This section was finally included in the 1876 edition of the Doctrine and Covenants.

Oliver Cowdery also wrote an account of the restoration of the Aaronic Priesthood; it is found in the Pearl of Great Price (JS–H, Note, par. 4–6).

Content overview

John the Baptist conferred the Aaronic Priesthood on Joseph and Oliver and enumerated the KEYS and powers circumscribed in that priesthood. He also stated that this priesthood "shall never be taken again from the earth, until the sons of Levi do offer again an offering unto the Lord in righteousness" (13:1). *See* Sons of Levi.

See also Law of carnal commandments;

Preparatory gospel; Priesthood, restoration of priesthood and priesthood keys.

BIBLIOGRAPHY

Smith, Joseph. *History of The Church of Jesus Christ of Latter-day Saints*. Edited by B. H. Roberts. 7 vols. 2d ed. rev. Salt Lake City: The Church of Jesus Christ of Latter-day Saints, 1932–51.

JMB

Historical context and overview of Doctrine and Covenants 14

Historical context

During the time Oliver Cowdery had been serving as the Prophet's scribe (April 5 to June 1829), he had also been corresponding with an acquaintance, David Whitmer of Fayette, New York. He and Whitmer had previously discussed what Cowdery knew about Joseph and the Book of Mormon record, and Cowdery promised he would keep Whitmer informed about the work once he (Cowdery) arrived in Harmony, Pennsylvania. Whitmer shared these letters from Cowdery with his parents and siblings, and they all became intensely interested in the translation. In the latter part of May 1829, opposition by antagonists (including the Prophet's father-in-law, Isaac Hale) was interrupting the work of translation. Cowdery wrote to Whitmer asking if he and Joseph could move to the Whitmer farm to finish the translation, sheltered from these foes. The family agreed to the proposal, and Whitmer promptly traveled to Harmony in a wagon and returned with them to Fayette in early June. Of the five sons of Peter Whitmer Sr., the two oldest, Christian and Jacob, were married and not living in the home. Joseph recorded that the other three, John, David, and Peter Jr., "became our zealous friends and assistants in the work; and being anxious to know their respective duties, and having desired with much earnestness that I should inquire of the Lord concerning them, I did so, through the means of the Urim and Thummim, and obtained for them in succession the following revelations: [sections 14–16]" (1:49). Section 14 was received in behalf of David Whitmer.

Content overview

The counsel to David Whitmer in the beginning of the revelation recorded in section 14 is the same given to Oliver Cowdery (6:1–6), Hyrum Smith (11:1–6), and Joseph Knight (12:1–6). The Lord told him that a GREAT AND MARVELOUS WORK was about to come forth and he must "give heed to my word" (14:1–2). The Lord explained that "the field is white already to harvest" and he who will "thrust in his sickle with his might, and reap while the day lasts" will "treasure up for his soul everlasting salvation in the kingdom of God" (14:3). The Lord then called David to "seek to bring forth and establish my Zion" and "keep my commandments" (14:6). If he would do as counseled, he would "have eternal life, which gift is the greatest of all the gifts of God" (14:7). In order for him to succeed in his calling, the Lord instructed him to pray (14:5, 8) so that he might receive the Holy Ghost, "which giveth utterance, that you may stand as a witness of the things of which you shall both hear and see, and also that you may declare repentance unto this generation" (14:8). He then promised David both spiritual and temporal blessings if he was faithful (14:11).

BIBLIOGRAPHY

Smith, Joseph. *History of The Church of Jesus Christ of Latter-day Saints*. Edited by B. H. Roberts. 7 vols. 2d ed. rev. Salt Lake City: The Church of Jesus Christ of Latter-day Saints, 1932–51.

JMB

Historical context and overview of Doctrine and Covenants 15

Historical context

Beginning in the early part of June 1829, Joseph Smith and Oliver Cowdery lived temporarily in the home of Peter Whitmer Sr. in order to complete the translation of the Book of Mormon. *See* Historical context and overview of Doctrine and Covenants 14 (p. 724).

Joseph Smith later wrote that "John Whitmer, in particular, assisted us very much in writing during the remainder of the work" (1:49). John and his brothers David and Peter were "anxious to know their respective duties," and Joseph received this revelation in behalf of John (Smith, 1:49).

Content overview

The Lord revealed the secret desire of John Whitmer, known only to John and the Lord, which was "to know that which would be of the most worth unto" him (15:3–4). The Lord told him, "The thing which will be of the most worth unto you will be to declare repentance unto this people, that you may bring souls unto me, that you may rest with them in the kingdom of my Father" (15:6).

BIBLIOGRAPHY

Smith, Joseph. *History of The Church of Jesus Christ of Latter-day Saints.* Edited by B. H. Roberts. 7 vols. 2d ed. rev. Salt Lake City: The Church of Jesus Christ of Latter-day Saints, 1932–51.

JMB

Historical context and overview of Doctrine and Covenants 16

Historical context

Beginning early in June 1829, Joseph Smith and Oliver Cowdery lived temporarily in the home of Peter Whitmer Sr. in order to complete the translation of the Book of Mormon. *See* Historical context and overview of Doctrine and Covenants 14 (p. 724).

Joseph Smith recorded that Peter Whitmer Jr. and his brothers John and David "became our zealous friends and assistants in the work; and [were] anxious to know their respective duties" (1:49). Joseph received this revelation in behalf of Peter Jr.

Content overview

This revelation is the same as the revelation recorded in section 15 to John Whitmer, with the exception of the name change. The Lord revealed the secret desire of Peter, known only to Peter and the Lord, which was "to know that which would be of the most worth unto" him (16:4). The Lord told him, "The thing which will be of the most worth unto you will be to declare repentance unto this people, that you may bring souls unto me, that you may rest with them in the kingdom of my Father" (16:6).

BIBLIOGRAPHY

Smith, Joseph. *History of The Church of Jesus Christ of Latter-day Saints.* Edited by B. H. Roberts. 7 vols. 2d ed. rev. Salt Lake City: The Church of Jesus Christ of Latter-day Saints, 1932–51.

JMB

Historical context and overview of Doctrine and Covenants 17

Historical context

Joseph Smith learned from the scriptures he was translating that the Lord would call "three special witnesses . . . to whom He would grant that they should see the plates from which this work (the Book of Mormon) should be translated" (Smith, *History*, 1:52–53; cf. 2 Ne. 27:12–13; Ether 5:2–4). Martin Harris had already received a tentative promise that he could be one of the witnesses (5:23–24; cf. 5:11–15), but now, as the translation was nearing completion, Oliver Cowdery, David Whitmer, and Martin Harris (who had recently arrived from Palmyra) pressed Joseph to "inquire of the Lord to know if they might not obtain of him the privilege to be these three special witnesses." Joseph recorded, "They became so very solicitous, and urged me so much to inquire that at length I complied; and through the Urim and Thummim, I obtained of the Lord for them the following [section 17]" (*History*, 1:53).

Shortly after the revelation was received, these three men and Joseph Smith, in a wilderness setting, were shown the sacred record and other artifacts by an angel, and they "heard a voice from out of the bright light above . . . saying, 'These plates have been revealed by the power of God, and they have been translated by the power of God. The translation of them which you have seen is correct, and I command you to bear record of what you now see and hear'" (Smith, *History*, 1:54–55). When they returned to the house following the experience, Lucy Mack Smith, who was there, later wrote, "Martin Harris . . . seemed almost overcome with joy, and testified boldly to what he had both seen and heard. And so did David and Oliver, adding that no tongue could express the joy of their hearts, and the greatness of the things which they had both seen and heard" (L. M. Smith, *History*, 152–53).

For reasons unknown, this revelation was not included in the Book of Commandments but was first published in the 1835 edition of the Doctrine and Covenants.

Content overview

The Lord promised the Three Witnesses that they would see "the plates, and also . . . the breastplate, the sword of Laban, the Urim and Thummim . . . and the miraculous directors" (17:1). The Lord commanded that after they had seen them, they were to "testify of them, by the power of God" (17:3). Then, with a solemn oath, the Lord testified, "He [Joseph Smith] has translated the book, even that part which I have commanded him, and as your Lord and your God liveth it is true" (17:6). The Lord also promised that if these witnesses were true to the commandment to testify of the book, "the gates of hell shall not prevail against you; for my grace is sufficient for you, and you shall be lifted up at the last day" (17:8). *See* Gates; Lifted up at the last day.

All three of the witnesses left the Church for a time: Oliver Cowdery and Martin Harris returned and died in full fellowship; David Whitmer did not return. Nevertheless, to their dying day, all three remained faithful to their testimony of the truthfulness of the Book of Mormon and of their having seen the gold plates.

See also Doctrine and Covenants, what it says about the Book of Mormon; Witness, witnesses.

Courtesy Richard Crookston.

Replicas of objects seen by the Three Witnesses. "Behold, I say unto you, that you must rely upon my word, which if you do with full purpose of heart, you shall have a view of the plates, and also of the breastplate, the sword of Laban, the Urim and Thummim, which were given to the brother of Jared upon the mount, when he talked with the Lord face to face, and the miraculous directors which were given to Lehi while in the wilderness, on the borders of the Red Sea" (D&C 17:1).

BIBLIOGRAPHY

Smith, Joseph. *History of The Church of Jesus Christ of Latter-day Saints.* Edited by B. H. Roberts. 7 vols. 2d ed. rev. Salt Lake City: The Church of Jesus Christ of Latter-day Saints, 1932–51.

Smith, Lucy Mack. *History of Joseph Smith by His Mother.* Edited by Preston Nibley. Salt Lake City: Bookcraft, 1958.

JMB

Historical context and overview of Doctrine and Covenants 18

Historical context

Joseph was counseled to focus on the translation of the Book of Mormon and nothing else (5:4), even though in previous revelations the Lord had informed him that he would soon reestablish his Church (5:14; 10:53–55). By the end of June 1829, the priesthood had been restored and the translation was coming to an end; however, the organization of the Church was still months in the future, awaiting the publication of the Book of Mormon. During the interim, much work needed to be done to prepare for that organization, and it was in this setting that these "instructions relative to building up the church of Christ, according to the fulness of the gospel" were given (Book of Commandments, xv, introduction). At the same time, Oliver Cowdery, who held the keys conjointly with Joseph Smith to "bring to light this ministry" (6:28), was preparing a document listing the major ordinances and their associated covenants that were to be included in the restored Church (Cowdery, 1–3). The early part of this revelation instructed Oliver to use the Book of Mormon as his source for gathering this information (18:1–5).

Content overview

Oliver Cowdery and David Whitmer, as apostles were called to "cry repentance unto this people" because "the worth of souls is great in the sight of God" (18:9–16). After specifying the preparation these two men needed in order to perform the labor to which they were called (18:17–21), the Savior proclaimed that "as many as repent and are baptized . . . and endure to the end . . . shall be saved" (18:22). He then announced that twelve other apostles were to be called to supervise the preaching

of the gospel in the world (18:26–36). Oliver Cowdery and David Whitmer were assigned to "search out the Twelve," and they were given instructions on how to recognize them and how to train them in their duties, the most important of which was preaching the GOSPEL in all the world (18:37–47). Martin Harris was later appointed to help with that assignment (Smith, 2:185–87).

BIBLIOGRAPHY

Cowdery, Oliver. "Articles of the Church of Christ." Manuscript Revelation Collection, Church History Library, The Church of Jesus Christ of Latter-day Saints, Salt Lake City, Utah.

Smith, Joseph. *History of The Church of Jesus Christ of Latter-day Saints.* Edited by B. H. Roberts. 7 vols. 2d ed. rev. Salt Lake City: The Church of Jesus Christ of Latter-day Saints, 1932–51.

JMB

Historical context and overview of Doctrine and Covenants 19

Historical context

During the winter of 1830, the citizens in and around Palmyra, New York, held a mass meeting and agreed to boycott the sale of the Book of Mormon (Smith, 1:166–67). When the book was made available for sale in the latter part of March, cooperation among the people of Palmyra was such that sales were minimal in the area. Martin Harris, who had the financial obligation to pay for the printing of the book, was frustrated in his efforts to persuade people to buy it. Joseph Smith, just arriving in Palmyra from Harmony, Pennsylvania, in company with Joseph Knight, encountered Martin with an armload of copies of the Book of Mormon. Joseph Knight later wrote: "He Came to us and after Compliments he says, 'The Books will not sell for no Body wants them. Joseph says, 'I think they will sell well.' Says he, 'I want a Commandment.' 'Why,' says Joseph, 'fullfill what you have got.' 'But,' says he, 'I must have a Commandment.' Joseph put him off. But he insisted three or four times he must have a Commandment." No commandment was forthcoming when it was requested, but the next day, Joseph Smith did receive this revelation, which was directed to Martin Harris (Jessee, 36–37).

Content overview

Jesus Christ identified himself as the one giving the revelation (19:1–3). After declaring that "every man must repent or suffer, for I, God, am endless," he defined the terms *endless* and *eternal* with respect to God's punishment, indicating they were "more express than other scriptures, that it might work upon the hearts of the children of men" (19:4–12). *See* Punish, punished, punishment.

The Savior then commanded Martin Harris to repent and told him in great detail what he would suffer if he failed to do so. The Lord compared the sufferings of those who do not repent to his suffering when he atoned for the sins of all mankind, saying that Martin had "tasted" such suffering "in the smallest, yea, even in the least degree . . . at the time I withdrew my Spirit" (19:13–20). *See* Atonement, the.

Martin was then given several commandments concerning what and how he was to preach and concerning his own personal preparation. Furthermore, he was commanded to fulfill his obligation to pay E. B. Grandin for the publication of the Book of Mormon (19:21–38). After admonishing Martin to "be humble and meek, and [to] conduct [himself] wisely," the Lord concluded with the invitation to "come unto me thy Savior" (19:41).

BIBLIOGRAPHY

Jessee, Dean. "Joseph Knight's Recollection of Early Mormon History." *BYU Studies* 17 (Autumn 1976): 29–39.

Smith, Joseph. *History of The Church of Jesus Christ of Latter-day Saints.* Edited by B. H. Roberts. 7 vols. 2d ed. rev. Salt Lake City: The Church of Jesus Christ of Latter-day Saints, 1932–51.

JMB

Historical context and overview of Doctrine and Covenants 20

Historical context

Read and sustained at a general conference on 9 June 1830 and at other early conferences, section 20 was originally titled "The Articles and Covenants of the Church of Christ." It was the first revelation of the Doctrine and Covenants to be canonized. Although the earliest extant manuscript of this section is dated 10 April 1830,

its roots go back several months earlier. In June 1829, as the translation of the Book of Mormon was drawing to a close, Oliver Cowdery, who held the keys conjointly with Joseph Smith to "bring to light this ministry" (6:28), desired further instructions regarding how the Church should be built up. The Lord responded by directing him to "rely upon the things which are written [a reference to the Book of Mormon]; for in them are all things written concerning the foundation of my church, my gospel, and my rock" (18:3–4). Consequently, Oliver produced a document entitled "Articles of the Church of Christ," of which about half was drawn from the Book of Mormon. This document may be regarded as a "forerunner" to section 20 (Faulring, 67): both list the same instructions, ordinances, and covenants Oliver gleaned from the Book of Mormon. Joseph Smith testified, "In this manner did the Lord continue to give us instructions from time to time, concerning the duties which now devolved upon us; and among many other things of the kind, we obtained of Him the following, by the spirit of prophecy and revelation [section 20]" (*History,* 1:64). This section provided a summary of basic doctrines and organizational procedures in the restored Church similar to formal statements being distributed by other religious bodies at the time. The italicized words in verses 37, 38, and 68 can be seen as subheadings in the Church's statement.

Content overview

Verses 1 to 4 record events that took place four days before this document was written. The Church was organized on 6 April (a Tuesday), "one thousand eight hundred and thirty years since the coming of our Lord and Savior Jesus Christ in the flesh" (20:1). This pronouncement of the year has led to a belief among some members of the Church that Jesus was born precisely on 6 April 1 B.C. Others, citing difficulties in calendaring and early documents, see it as a more general reference using the current calendar system (McConkie, 1:349–50, notes).

At this organizational meeting of the Church, Joseph Smith and Oliver Cowdery were sustained by those assembled to be their leaders and the First and Second Elders of the Church. They then ordained each other to these offices.

Verses 5 to 16 review the events leading up to the Church's organization, including Joseph Smith's early dealings with God; the coming of Moroni; and the translation of the Book of Mormon, which is a "record of a fallen people" and contains "the fulness of the gospel" (20:9). A testimony of the Book of Mormon strengthens faith in the Bible and in the reality of latter-day revelation (20:11–12). The Book of Mormon will be one of the books out of which people will be judged (20:13–16). This fact having been stated, the verses that follow (17–36) teach the essential truths from the Book of Mormon that "we must know" and by which one must live (Benson, 7).

They testify of the Father, Son, and Holy Ghost, "the creation of man, the Fall, the Atonement, the ascension of Christ into heaven, prophets, faith, repentance, baptism, the Holy Ghost, endurance, prayer, justification and sanctification through grace, and loving and serving God" (Benson, 7). *See* Doctrine and Covenants, what it says about the Book of Mormon.

The connection between passages from the Book of Mormon included in Oliver Cowdery's "Articles of the Church of Christ" and section 20 concerning the requirements of baptism is apparent (cf. Moro. 6:1; D&C 20:37); however, 20:37 adds the requirement that candidates for baptism must "truly manifest by their works that they have received of the Spirit of Christ unto the remission of their sins." Oliver Cowdery was upset at how 20:37 expanded on the requirements for baptism as written in his "Articles of the Church of Christ," and he wrote the Prophet commanding him "in the name of God" to delete the requirement. In response, Joseph asked "by what authority he took upon him to command me to alter or erase, to add or diminish to or from a revelation or commandment from the Almighty God" (Smith, *Papers*, 1:260). Joseph came from Harmony, Pennsylvania, to Fayette, New York, a few days later to visit Cowdery. After a lengthy discussion, which also involved the Whitmer family, Oliver saw that he was in error: the dispute was settled, and the verse remained unchanged.

Verses 38–67 delineate the various duties of those receiving the PRIESTHOOD offices of ELDER, PRIEST, TEACHER, and DEACON. All of these offices share the essential role of teaching and expounding the GOSPEL. Priesthood responsibilities are cumulative, with each successive office adding to the duties of those given before. The requirement for elders "to conduct the meetings as they are led by the Holy Ghost" (20:45) is the same as that given to the Book of Mormon people recorded in Moroni 6:9. Similarly, the counsel that those who are ordained are "to be ordained by the power of the Holy Ghost" (20:60) reflects Moroni 3:4.

Conferences were to be held every three months to transact Church business (20:61–62). "Church business" included the issuance of licenses to preach and certificates of ordination (20:63–64). *See* License/certificate(s).

Verses 65–67, which reflect revelation received later and which were added to this section in the 1835 edition of the Doctrine and Covenants, provide instruction on priesthood ordinations. They also explain the principle of COMMON CONSENT (20:65; cf. 26:2; 28:13).

Verses 68–70 list duties of members following baptism. Converts should be carefully taught and demonstrate faithfulness before they receive such ordinances as baptism and confirmation, or partake of the sacrament. Members of the Church are to have their CHILDREN blessed by the elders (20:70). The mode of baptism (20:71–74) in this dispensation is the same as that of the Book of Mormon people, and these verses reflect 3 Nephi 11:23–26. Only those who have reached "the years of accountability" are to be baptized into the Church (20:71); this age was specified later as eight years old (68:25). *See* Baptism by water; Baptism of fire and the Holy Ghost.

Instructions concerning the SACRAMENT are given next. Partaking of the sacrament often (20:75) reflects Moroni 6:6; how the priesthood administers it (20:76) reflects Moroni 4:1–2; and the sacrament prayers (20:77, 79) reflect Moroni 4:3 and Moroni 5:2.

Members guilty of serious transgressions are to be "dealt with as the scriptures direct" (20:80; cf. 102 and 107:69–84). *See* Church discipline. This discipline is patterned after that of the Book of Mormon people (Moro. 6:7). Membership records are to be maintained so that individuals may be remembered and "nourished by the good word of God" (Moro. 6:4); the procedures for handling these records (20:83–84) have been superseded as the Church has grown larger and as new technology, such as computers, have become available.

See also Church of Jesus Christ of Latter-day Saints, The.

BIBLIOGRAPHY

Benson, Ezra Taft. "A New Witness for Christ." *Ensign* 14 (November 1984): 6–7.

Faulring, Scott H. "An Examination of the 1829 'Articles of the Church of Christ' in Relation to Section 20 of the Doctrine and Covenants." *BYU Studies* 43, no. 4 (2004): 57–91.

McConkie, Bruce R. *The Mortal Messiah: From Bethlehem to Calvary.* 4 vols. Salt Lake City: Deseret Book, 1979–81.

Smith, Joseph. *History of The Church of Jesus Christ of Latter-day Saints.* Edited by B. H. Roberts. 7 vols. 2d ed. rev. Salt Lake City: The Church of Jesus Christ of Latter-day Saints, 1932–51.

———. *The Papers of Joseph Smith.* Edited by Dean C. Jessee. 2 vols. Salt Lake City: Deseret Book, 1989–92.

ROC

Historical context and overview of Doctrine and Covenants 21

Historical context

On Tuesday, 6 April 1830, about fifty people crowded into Peter Whitmer's log home near Fayette, New York. To satisfy the New York State requirement for founding a new religious society, six men officially signed the certificate of incorporation: Joseph Smith, Oliver Cowdery, Hyrum Smith, Peter Whitmer Jr., Samuel H. Smith, and David Whitmer. After an opening prayer, the group unanimously voted to organize the Church and to accept Joseph Smith and Oliver Cowdery as first and second elders, respectively. Joseph and Oliver then ordained one another to these offices. After the congregation had partaken of the sacrament, Joseph and Oliver laid hands on all who had previously been baptized, confirming them members of the new Church and bestowing upon them the gift of the Holy Ghost. The Prophet recorded, "The Holy Ghost was poured out upon us to a very great degree—some prophesied, whilst we all praised the Lord, and rejoiced exceedingly" (1:78).

Content overview

The first commandment given to the Church was to keep a record; in the record, Joseph Smith was to be known as "a seer, a translator, a prophet, an apostle of Jesus Christ, an elder of the church" (21:1). At a conference of the Church in June 1830, Oliver Cowdery was the first man called to keep this record; this was the genesis of the Church's massive record-keeping programs of today.

The Lord admonished Church members to receive the Prophet's words "as if from mine own mouth, in all patience and faith" (21:4–5; cf. 1:38), and if they did, he promised "the gates of hell shall not prevail against you; yea, and the Lord God will disperse the powers of darkness from before you, and cause the heavens to shake for your good, and his name's glory" (21:6–9). The revelation concluded with instructions to Oliver Cowdery to ordain Joseph Smith. Oliver was to be "an elder unto [the] church of Christ" and "the first preacher of this church unto the church, and before the world" (21:11–12), both to the Gentiles and the Jews. Consistent with his appointment as "first preacher," Oliver Cowdery "preached the first public discourse that was delivered by any of our number . . . at the house of Mr. Peter Whitmer, Sen." (Smith, 1:81).

See also Church of Jesus Christ of Latter-day Saints, The.

BIBLIOGRAPHY

Smith, Joseph. *History of The Church of Jesus Christ of Latter-day Saints.* Edited by B. H. Roberts. 7 vols. 2d ed. rev. Salt Lake City: The Church of Jesus Christ of Latter-day Saints, 1932–51.

ROC

4 Wherefore, meaning the church, thou shalt give *a*heed unto all his words and *b*commandments which he shall give unto you as he receiveth them, walking in all *c*holiness before me;

5 For his *a*word ye shall receive, as if from mine own mouth, in all patience and faith.

Doctrine and Covenants 21:4–5.

Revelation Given to Joseph Smith at the Organization of the Church; *painting by Judith Mehr.* "*Wherefore, meaning the church, thou shalt give heed unto all his words and commandments which he shall give unto you as he receiveth them, walking in all holiness before me; for his word ye shall receive, as if from mine own mouth, in all patience and faith*" (*D&C 21:4–5*).

Historical context and overview of Doctrine and Covenants 22

Historical context

People who had been baptized in other churches wanted to know whether they needed to be rebaptized in order to join the recently organized Church. The accepted Protestant practice at that time was that the baptism of a person into one faith was sufficient when seeking admission into another faith if that person was decent and God-fearing. Orson Pratt identified those making this request as members of the "Baptist denomination, very moral and no doubt as good people as you could find anywhere" (Pratt, 16:293–94).

In New Testament times, the GOSPEL of Jesus Christ superseded the LAW OF MOSES. Similarly, in the latter days, this revelation (dated 16 April 1830 in a manuscript written by William E. McLellin [McLellin, 236]), affirmed that "all old covenants" had been "done away" and that "a new and an everlasting covenant," the fulness of the gospel, had been established (22:1; cf. 66:2).

Content overview

The Lord announced "that all old covenants have I caused to be done away in this thing; and this is a new and an everlasting covenant, even that which was from the beginning," referring to the restored gospel of Jesus Christ (22:1). Therefore even a hundred baptisms performed without priesthood authority are considered "dead works" and do not constitute admission through the "strait gate" (22:2–3; cf. Matt. 7:13–14). Those who might question this were admonished to "seek not to counsel your God" (22:4; cf. Jacob 4:10).

Section 22 has often been linked to section 20 as part of "The Articles and Covenants of the Church" sustained at early conferences. The first edition of *The Evening and the Morning Star* in June 1832 did make this association, but other early sources did not include section 22 in the "Articles." For example, the Book of Commandments placed the present section 22 ahead of section 20, while only section 20 was given the title of "Articles and Covenants" (Book of Commandments, chapters 23, 24).

See also Baptism by water; Baptism of fire and the Holy Ghost; Dead works; Gate(s); Strait, straight.

BIBLIOGRAPHY

McLellin, William E. *The Journals of William E. McLellin, 1831–1836.* Edited by Jan Shipps and John W. Welch. Urbana: University of Illinois Press; Provo, Utah: BYU Studies, 1994.

Pratt, Orson. *Journal of Discourses.* 26 vols. London: Latter-day Saints' Book Depot, 1854–86.

ROC

Historical context and overview of Doctrine and Covenants 23

Historical context

In the days following the organizational meeting of the Church, 6 April 1830, Oliver Cowdery, Hyrum Smith, Samuel Smith, Joseph Smith Sr., and Joseph Knight came to the Prophet Joseph Smith "anxious to know of the Lord what might be their respective duties in relation to this work" (Smith, *History*, 1:80). The Lord's answer to their petitions is recorded in section 23. Four of the five individuals named had previously received counsel from the Lord through Joseph Smith; however, now that the Church was formally organized, they sought further direction. This section, originally published as five separate revelations in the Book of Commandments, has been united as one section since the publication of the Doctrine and Covenants in 1835. The misdating of these revelations in the Book of Commandments—*6 April 1830* —was corrected to *April 1830* beginning with the 1835 edition (cf. Jensen et al., 28–31).

Content overview

Oliver Cowdery, the second elder of the Church and the first named in the section, was told that he was under no condemnation but to beware of PRIDE. He was promised his heart would "be opened to preach the truth" (23:1–2), a promise partially fulfilled when he delivered the first public sermon of the Church on Sunday, 11 April 1830, and continued to be fulfilled throughout his ministry as long as he had the Spirit with him. Wilford Woodruff said, "I have seen Oliver Cowdery when it seemed as though the earth trembled under his feet. I never heard a man bear a stronger testimony than he did when under the influence of the Spirit" (Woodruff, 391).

Hyrum Smith was told that he had a duty to the Church "because of [his] family" (23:3) and "to strengthen the church continually." This may be a reference to his later role as Church patriarch (Smith, *Doctrines*, 3:164). Samuel Smith, the only individual mentioned who had not previously received a written revelation from the Lord through the Prophet, was told his calling was to "exhortation, and to strengthen the church," as he was "not as yet called to preach before the world" (23:4). After proper authorization, however, he is generally credited with being the first formally called missionary of the Church, preaching in the New York area in June 1830. Joseph Smith Sr. was called to "exhortation, and to strengthen the church . . . from henceforth and forever" (23:5). He later served as Church patriarch until his death. Joseph Knight, unlike the others, who were all told they were "under no condemnation" (23:1, 3, 4, 5), was commanded to "take up your cross . . . pray vocally . . . unite with the true church, and give your language to exhortation" (23:6–7). Knight had known Joseph Smith for a number of years and had provided temporal aid to the Prophet during the translation of the Book of Mormon; however, he had not yet been baptized because he "had not re[a]d the Book of Morman and . . . wanted to oxeman [examine] a little more" (Jessee, 37). Obedient to the command recorded in section 23, Joseph Knight entered the waters of baptism later in June 1830 (Jessee, 37).

BIBLIOGRAPHY

Jensen, Robin Scott, Robert J. Woodford, and Steven C. Harper, eds. *Manuscript Revelation Books*. Facsimile edition. First volume of the Revelations and Translations series of *The Joseph Smith Papers*, edited by Dean C. Jessee, Ronald K. Esplin, and Richard Lyman Bushman. Salt Lake City: Church Historian's Press, 2009.

Jessee, Dean. "Joseph Knight's Recollection of Early Mormon History." *BYU Studies* 17 (Autumn 1976): 29–39.

Smith, Joseph. *History of The Church of Jesus Christ of Latter-day Saints*. Edited by B. H. Roberts. 7 vols. 2d ed. rev. Salt Lake City: The Church of Jesus Christ of Latter-day Saints, 1932–51.

Smith, Joseph Fielding. *Doctrines of Salvation*. Compiled by Bruce R. McConkie. 3 vols. Salt Lake City: Bookcraft, 1954–56.

Woodruff, Wilford. *Deseret News*, 23 March 1889.

SCE

Historical context and overview of Doctrine and Covenants 24

Historical context

The summer of 1830 was a difficult time for Joseph Smith and his associates. Opposition to the work had intensified, especially in the

Colesville, New York, area. Seeking to strengthen the newly formed Church, the Prophet journeyed frequently from his home in Harmony, Pennsylvania, to Fayette and Colesville, New York. Joseph Knight observed, "Soon after the Church Began to gro the People Began to Be angry and to persecute and Cald them fools and said they ware Decived" (Jessee, 38).

In early July, Joseph was arrested and taken to South Bainbridge "on the charge of being a disorderly person, of setting the country in an uproar by preaching the Book of Mormon" (Smith, 1:88). He was ably defended by James Davidson and John Reid, neighbors of Joseph Knight whom the Prophet called "respectable farmers, men renowned for their integrity, and well versed in the laws of their country." The Prophet was acquitted of the charges, only to be immediately arrested and tried again in Colesville (Smith, 1:88–96). Again he was acquitted.

In both cases, Joseph and his associates narrowly escaped mob attacks as they shuttled between trials. Shortly thereafter, Joseph and Oliver again tried to visit the Saints in Colesville, only to be rebuffed once more. "Our enemies pursued us," the Prophet recalled, "and it was oftentimes as much as we could do to elude them. However, we managed to get home, after having traveled all night, except a short time, during which we were forced to rest ourselves under a large tree by the wayside, sleeping and watching alternately" (1:97). Safely home in Harmony, the Prophet observed, "Although we this time were forced to seek safety from our enemies by flight, yet did we feel confident that eventually we should come off victorious" (1:101). Upon their return, Joseph and Oliver received this section as well as sections 25 and 26.

Content overview

Several portions of section 24 reflect the challenges that Joseph and the Church faced in July 1830. The Lord reminded Joseph that he had been "lifted . . . up out of [his] afflictions . . . [and] delivered from all [his] enemies" (24:1). Though preserved for a season, the Prophet was warned, "Be patient in afflictions, for thou shalt have many; but endure them, for, lo, I am with thee, even unto the end of thy days" (24:8). Reflective of their recent legal challenges in South Bainbridge and in Broome County, Joseph and Oliver were promised, "Whosoever shall go to law with thee shall be cursed by the law" (24:17).

In this section, the Lord also emphasized the balance Joseph was to maintain throughout his life. In spite of the lateness of the season, he was reminded to take care of his fields before visiting Church members in Colesville, Fayette, and Manchester (24:3). The Lord reminded him, however, that "in temporal labors thou shalt not have strength, for this is not thy calling" (24:9). Instead, Church members were to support Joseph, for which they would be blessed (24:3, 18; cf. 41:7; 43:12–14).

Oliver Cowdery, a fellow recipient of much of the opposition in the summer of 1830, also received counsel in section 24. As the second elder, he was reminded to "continue in bearing [the Lord's] name before the world, and also to the church" (24:10), with the promise that God would give him "strength such as is not known among men" (24:11–12). The last few verses may apply to both Oliver and Joseph and other authorized servants of the Lord. "Require not miracles, except I shall command you," "casting off the dust of your feet . . . as a testimony" against those who reject the gospel message and "prune my vineyard with a mighty pruning, yea, even for the last time" (24:13–19).

BIBLIOGRAPHY

Jessee, Dean. "Joseph Knight's Recollection of Early Mormon History." *BYU Studies* 17 (Autumn 1976): 29–39.

Smith, Joseph. *History of The Church of Jesus Christ of Latter-day Saints.* Edited by B. H. Roberts. 7 vols. 2d ed. rev. Salt Lake City: The Church of Jesus Christ of Latter-day Saints, 1932–51.

SCE

Historical context and overview of Doctrine and Covenants 25

Historical context

At the time of the revelation in July of 1830 now recorded in section 25, Emma Hale Smith and her husband, the Prophet Joseph Smith, had suffered much persecution, humiliation, and harassment over several months. As Joseph devoted his full attention to the Church (24:3, 7), Emma was concerned over their temporal security. The Prophet received this section to instruct and strengthen her concerning her temporal and spiritual welfare. President Gordon B. Hinckley described this as "a great and remarkable revelation" and noted that its teachings are "applicable to every woman in the Church" ("Daughters," 99; cf. D&C 25:16).

Content overview

The Lord addressed Emma, who had been baptized the previous month, as "my daughter," explaining that "all those who receive my gospel are sons and daughters in my kingdom" (25:1; cf. Mosiah 5:7). On condition of her faithfulness, Emma was assured "an inheritance in Zion" and was described as an "elect lady" (25:2–3). The word *elect* meant "chosen" (Webster, s.v. "elect"), particularly for a special service or blessing. *See* Elect, election.

In 1842, the Lord, through Joseph, called Emma to be the first president of the Relief Society. On that occasion Joseph explained that "the elect meant to be elected to a certain work, . . . and that the revelation was then fulfilled by Sister Emma's election to the Presidency of the Society" (Smith, 4:552–53).

Emma was admonished not to murmur about the things she had not been able to see (25:4). President Hinckley explained that the Lord "was speaking of the plates which her husband was translating, she serving at the time as his scribe." This must have been of great concern to her since the plates had been returned to Moroni a year earlier. Joseph did not determine who could see the plates, President Hinckley continued, "nor have we set the rule concerning those who should receive the priesthood. That was established by him whose work this is, and he alone could change it" (Hinckley, "Faithful," 91).

The first specific assignment given to Emma was to be "a comfort" unto her husband (25:5). In the spirit of meekness and avoiding pride, she was to "delight" in her husband and "the glory which shall come upon him" (25:14). She was also to serve as Joseph's scribe, relieving Oliver Cowdery for other duties (25:6).

Emma was to be "ordained" to teach the scriptures (25:7). Today the word *ordain* is used in reference to receiving priesthood offices, but in the early years of the Restoration this word was used more broadly. One definition of *ordain* given in a dictionary published at that time was "set apart for an office; to appoint" (Webster, s.v. "ordain"). In the 1830s, such a calling was highly unusual because women in most other churches were under the injunction to remain "silent," as 1 Corinthians 14:34–35 was interpreted to mean.

Persecution at Colesville had prevented Emma's confirmation at the time of her baptism (on 28 June 1830). In this revelation the Lord informed her that she was to receive the Holy Ghost under the hands of her husband. She was then to devote time "to writing, and to learning much" (25:8). She and Sally Knight were confirmed by Joseph Smith and Newel Knight early in August 1830 (Smith, 1:108).

Emma was told that she need not fear for her

Emma Smith, 1804–1879. "Hearken unto the voice of the Lord your God, while I speak unto you, Emma Smith, my daughter; for verily I say unto you, all those who receive my gospel are sons and daughters in my kingdom" (D&C 25:1).

well-being but was assured that her husband would support her. She was reminded that his duty was to the Church and was counseled to "lay aside the things of this world, and seek for the things of a better" (25:9–10).

Emma was assigned to "make a selection of sacred hymns" for use in the Church. The Lord stated that "the song of the righteous is a prayer unto me, and it shall be answered with a blessing upon their heads" (25:11–12). With the help of W. W. Phelps, Emma published the Church's first hymnal in Kirtland in 1835; it included 90 hymns, 36 of which were written by Latter-day Saint authors.

The Lord concluded this revelation by encouraging Emma to "rejoice, and cleave unto the covenants which thou hast made. Continue in the spirit of meekness, and beware of pride." She was promised, if obedient, "a crown of righteousness"; she was also warned, "And except [you] do this, where I am you cannot come." This instruction was made applicable to everyone when the Lord declared, "This is my voice unto all" (25:13–16).

BIBLIOGRAPHY

Hinckley, Gordon B. "Daughters of God." *Ensign* 21 (November 1991): 97–101.

———. "'If Thou Art Faithful.'" *Ensign* 14 (November 1984): 89–91.

Smith, Joseph. *History of The Church of Jesus Christ of Latter-day Saints*. Edited by B. H. Roberts. 7 vols. 2d ed. rev. Salt Lake City: The Church of Jesus Christ of Latter-day Saints, 1932–51.

Webster, Noah. *An American Dictionary of the English Language*. 1828.

ROC

Historical context and overview of Doctrine and Covenants 26

Historical context

Joseph Smith and his associates faced significant opposition during the summer of 1830. *See* Historical context and overview of Doctrine and Covenants 24 (p. 732) and 25 (p. 733).

Before the revelation recorded in section 26 was received, efforts to strengthen newly baptized members, especially those in Colesville, New York, had been severely hindered by mob actions. One such incident followed the baptism of thirteen individuals in Colesville. On that occasion, an evening confirmation meeting was broken up when the Prophet Joseph was arrested "on the charge of being a disorderly person, of setting the country in an uproar by preaching the Book of Mormon, etc." (Smith, 1:88). After his acquittal, Joseph and Oliver returned to Colesville a few days later "for the purpose of confirming those whom [they] had been forced to leave for a time" (Smith, 1:97). Unfortunately, as on the previous occasion, a mob again assembled to oppose them. The Prophet remembered, "Our enemies pursued us, and it was oftentimes as much as we could do to elude them" (1:97). After safely returning to Harmony, Pennsylvania, the Prophet received this revelation from the Lord.

Content overview

Parts of section 26 reflect the challenging historical context in which the revelation was received. In spite of the opposition they faced, Joseph Smith, Oliver Cowdery, and John Whitmer were told to devote their time "to preaching, and to confirming [i.e., strengthening] the church at Colesville" (26:1), something they had tried to do on a number of occasions. In response, the Prophet, with John and David Whitmer, visited Colesville again in August 1830, where they "assembled the Church, and confirmed them, partook of the Sacrament, and held a happy meeting" (Smith, 1:109). This successful visit was due to the miraculous protection of the Lord, who hid their identity from the mob (Smith, 1:108–9). The Lord further counseled them to continue studying the scriptures, an apparent reference to the work Joseph had recently begun on the translation of the Bible. Reference is also made to traveling "to the west to hold the next conference" (26:1). Accordingly, the second conference of the Church was held in Fayette, New York, in September 1830 (Smith, 1:110). Finally, the doctrine of COMMON CONSENT was reiterated, with the command that all things in the Church follow this procedure, "by much prayer and faith" (26:2; cf. 20:65). The concept of "common consent," which is the practice of seeking the agreement of Church members for a particular course of action, was introduced to the Prophet during the summer of 1829 (Smith,

1:60–62) and first exercised 6 April 1830, the day the Church was organized (Smith, 1:74–79).

BIBLIOGRAPHY

Smith, Joseph. *History of The Church of Jesus Christ of Latter-day Saints*. Edited by B. H. Roberts. 7 vols. 2d ed. rev. Salt Lake City: The Church of Jesus Christ of Latter-day Saints, 1932–51.

SCE

Historical context and overview of Doctrine and Covenants 27

Historical context

Parts of the revelation recorded in section 27 were given on at least two separate occasions. The first four verses were given at the time of a confirmation meeting for Sally Knight and Emma Smith in Harmony, Pennsylvania, early in August 1830. The 1833 Book of Commandments included these verses, together with the first half of verse 5, verse 14, the first half of verse 15, and the phrase "and be faithful until I come" in verse 18. There is uncertainty about the date the remaining part was received. According to the 1851 edition of the Pearl of Great Price, it was received in July 1830, but Newel Knight said it was received in September 1830 at Fayette, New York, in connection with a Church conference (JH, August 1830). The complete text was first published in the 1835 Doctrine and Covenants, and what it records about the ancient prophets reflects better an 1835 understanding of them and their roles in ancient history and the Restoration. This section of the Doctrine and Covenants is a prime example of Joseph Smith enriching original revelation with later insights also gained by revelation.

Content overview

Emma Smith and Sally Knight were baptized 28 June but had not yet been confirmed. Joseph Smith desired all to partake of the SACRAMENT prior to their confirmations. He left to buy WINE for the service when a heavenly messenger appeared and gave him these instructions from the Lord: "It mattereth not what ye shall eat or what ye shall drink when ye partake of the sacrament, if it so be that ye do it with an eye single to my glory." Nevertheless, the Church was commanded not to purchase wine or strong drink

for use in partaking of the sacrament but to use only that which was "made new among you" (27:2–4). Gradually water became the emblem used by the Church in the sacrament.

In verse 5, echoing remarks he made to his apostles at the Last Supper (Matt. 26:29), the Lord referred to a time associated with his second coming in which he will partake of the sacrament with ancient prophets and apostles and "with all those whom my Father hath given me out of the world" (27:5–14). *Elias,* as used in this list, refers to Gabriel, who appeared to Zacharias (27:7; cf. Luke 1:19). *See* Elias.

One of the first references in the Doctrine and Covenants to the restoration of the Melchizedek PRIESTHOOD is made in verse 12 (cf. 128:20). *See* Priesthood, restoration of priesthood and priesthood keys.

The restoration of the higher priesthood included a bestowal of "the keys of my kingdom" (27:13), the key to "the knowledge of God" (84:19), and "the keys of all the spiritual blessings of the church" (107:18). *See* Key(s).

In verses 15–18, gospel principles and righteous practices are compared to items of armor which Saints are to "take upon" themselves as a protection against "the fiery darts of the wicked" (cf. Eph. 6:11–18). *See* Armor of God.

BIBLIOGRAPHY

Journal History of the Church, August 1830. Church History Library, The Church of Jesus Christ of Latter-day Saints, Salt Lake City, Utah.

ROC

Historical context and overview of Doctrine and Covenants 28

Historical context

As the Church's second conference approached in September 1830, Hiram Page, one of the Eight Witnesses of the Book of Mormon plates, began receiving revelations through a stone "concerning the upbuilding of Zion the order of the Church and so forth, but which were entirely at variance with the order of Gods House, as it is laid down in the scriptures. and our own late revelations" (Smith, 1:263). Newel Knight wrote that Page "had quite a roll of papers full of these revelations, and many in the Church were led astray by them," including

Oliver Cowdery and many of the Whitmer family (Knight, 63–66). Distressed, Joseph worried how he could help the Saints understand that each of them was entitled to direct REVELATION but that the order of revelation for the Church had been given in April when it was organized (21:1–6), namely that Joseph would receive the commandments from the Lord for the whole Church. Joseph spent most of a sleepless night prayerfully seeking direction and receiving section 28.

Content overview

In section 28, the Lord directed his instructions to Oliver Cowdery, the second elder of the Church, clarifying that his role was to "speak or teach" by the Comforter and to "declare faithfully the commandments and the revelations" given to Joseph, but he was not to "write by way of commandment" or to command Joseph (28:3–6). The Lord also directed Cowdery to go on a mission "unto the Lamanites" or Native Americans in the West, hinting that Hiram Page's predictions for the location of ZION were wrong: "It shall be on the borders by the Lamanites" (28:8–9). See Lamanites.

But first Cowdery was to assist in settling the controversy, in part by visiting Page privately to "tell him that those things which he hath written from that stone are not of me and that Satan deceiveth him" (28:11). The Lord reminded Cowdery that Page had not been appointed to receive commandments on Church government; he was out of order. "For all things must be done in order, and by common consent in the church, by the prayer of faith" (28:13).

By speaking through Joseph to Cowdery, the Lord illustrated the order in which revelation flows for the Church. By countering the information in Page's revelation with accurate details about Zion, the Lord helped Cowdery recognize that either Joseph or Hiram Page was a true revelator, not both. By commanding Cowdery to teach Hiram Page these principles, the Lord reinforced them in Cowdery's mind and illustrated the order of the Church at work at a critical moment. Cowdery obeyed the revelation and "after much labor with these brethren they were convinced of their error, and confessed the same, renouncing the revelations as not being of God,

but acknowledged that Satan had conspired to overthrow their belief in the true plan of salvation" (Knight, 65).

BIBLIOGRAPHY

Knight, Newel. "Newel Knight's Journal." *Classic Experiences and Adventures*. Salt Lake City: Bookcraft, 1969.

Smith, Joseph. *The Papers of Joseph Smith*. Edited by Dean C. Jessee. 2 vols. Salt Lake City: Deseret Book, 1989–92.

SCH

Historical context and overview of Doctrine and Covenants 29

Historical context

About the same time that the second conference of the Church was held at Fayette, New York, in September 1830, six elders and three members differed concerning the transgression of Adam. The discussions may have come about through the work Joseph Smith had begun on the translation of the first several chapters in Genesis. They united in prayer with Joseph Smith that they might "see eye to eye" on the matter (Jensen et al., 43). As a result, the revelation recorded in section 29 was received, and it included much more than a response to their question—information was given on the gathering of Israel, apocalyptic judgments upon the wicked, and the ultimate triumph of the Saints in the last days. Since it is not known what specific differences these people had concerning the transgression of Adam, it is not known what specific verses in this revelation addressed the issues in question.

Content overview

The opening verses of the revelation contain one of the earliest references to the latter-day gathering of ISRAEL. See Gather, gathering.

In connection with the Second Coming, the elect are to be "gathered in unto one place upon the face of this land . . . and be prepared in all things against the day when tribulation and desolation are sent forth upon the wicked" (29:8). See Jesus Christ, second coming of.

From several revelations it seems clear that the "one place" to which the Lord has reference is the "center place," the city of Zion, the NEW

JERUSALEM, in Jackson County, Missouri (57:1–3; 84:2–4; cf. 49:25; 90:36–37; 100:13), "until the day cometh when there is found no more room for them; and then I have other places which I will appoint unto them, and they shall be called stakes, for the curtains or the strength of Zion" (101:21–23). *See* Curtains.

Inasmuch as the early Saints of this dispensation were not able to establish ZION because of their own "transgressions" and because of the persecution of their enemies, the Lord said, "It is expedient in me that mine elders should wait for a little season for the redemption of Zion," that the Saints may be "taught more perfectly," "have experience, and know more perfectly concerning their duty," be "endowed with power from on high," become greater in numbers, and "be sanctified" (105:9–11, 31). Zion will yet be redeemed, and inhabited by the Lord's elect (101:10–20). "But gathered Israel cannot be confined to the 'center place,' nor to the region immediately adjacent; other places have been and will be appointed, and these are called Stakes of Zion . . . to be permanent possessions" (Talmage, 353).

Because the people of the world will not repent, calamities will sweep the EARTH before Christ comes (29:14–21). His coming, which is "nigh," will be a time of JUDGMENT when the wicked will be destroyed and the righteous will reign with Christ during the MILLENNIUM (29:9–11). The original Twelve "shall stand at [the Lord's] right hand at the day of [his] coming . . . to judge the whole house of Israel" (29:12). "When the thousand years are ended, and men again begin to deny their God," the earth will be spared "but for a little season" (29:22). Then there will be another time of judgment when Michael, or Adam (27:11), will usher in the last RESURRECTION, and there shall be "a new heaven and a new earth"— the earth itself will come into its celestial state (29:22–30; cf. 88:16–20, 25–28).

Although, ultimately, all things are SPIRITUAL unto the Lord, he speaks of things spiritual and TEMPORAL that mankind can "naturally understand" (29:33–34). Section 29 explains that the Lord created "all things both spiritual and temporal (29:31). In "the beginning," God's children were in a spiritual state before they entered

the present, mortal temporal condition. In the future, however, after their temporal existence, mortals will return to a spiritual condition. The effects of God's commandments are not limited to this temporal existence (29:31–34).

AGENCY existed during the PREMORTAL EXISTENCE. This enabled SATAN to lead astray "a third part of the hosts of heaven" (29:36). Satan's temptations, which test how one uses his or her agency, are an essential part of God's plan (29:39). Still, the only power the devil has over God's children is what they choose to give him (29:40); he cannot tempt people beyond their power to resist (1 Cor. 10:13), if they would humble themselves before the Lord and continue in prayer (Alma 13:28; 34:39). Because of his transgression, Adam was cast out of God's presence, thus suffering spiritual DEATH; this is the same kind of death as the second death (29:41). Even after the Fall, Adam and his posterity are given the opportunity to repent and qualify for eternal life or to refuse redemption and receive damnation (29:42–45). *See* Fall of Adam and Eve, the.

Satan is not permitted to tempt little CHILDREN, who cannot sin "until they begin to become accountable" (29:46–48); the age of this accountability was later defined as eight years (68:25). Similarly, those who are without understanding cannot sin and are not accountable (29:49–50).

BIBLIOGRAPHY

Jensen, Robin Scott, Robert J. Woodford, and Steven C. Harper, eds. *Manuscript Revelation Books.* Facsimile edition. First volume of the Revelations and Translations series of *The Joseph Smith Papers,* edited by Dean C. Jessee, Ronald K. Esplin, and Richard Lyman Bushman. Salt Lake City: Church Historian's Press, 2009.

Talmage, James E. *Articles of Faith.* Salt Lake City: Deseret Book, 1964.

ROC

Historical context and overview of Doctrine and Covenants 30

Historical context

Section 30 is composed of three revelations given to David, Peter, and John Whitmer. They were originally published as three separate chapters in the 1833 Book of Commandments but were combined in the 1835 edition of the Doctrine and Covenants.

The Whitmers were among those who had accepted Hiram Page's claim to be receiving revelations through a seer stone (28), and the confusion this caused was settled at the Church conference in September 1830. The Prophet's only statement concerning this revelation is that "before we separated [from the conference] we received the following: [section 30]" (1:115).

Content overview

The Lord cautioned both David Whitmer and John Whitmer not to fear man more than God (30:1, 11) and specifically chastised David because he had paid more attention to those whom the Lord had not authorized (30:2).

The Lord's observation that David's mind had "been on the things of the earth more than on the things of [the Lord]" (30:2) and the counsel to reside at his father's home (30:4) may be interrelated. David, a farmer, was contemplating marriage to Julia Ann Jolley, which marriage took place less than four months later on 9 January 1831. It would be natural for him to be looking for a place of his own to farm. By the time he married, however, he and the other members of the Church had been counseled to leave New York and move to Ohio (37 and 38).

Previously, Oliver Cowdery had been called to go among the LAMANITES (28:8), and the Lord now appointed Peter Whitmer Jr. to join him, reminding Peter to follow the direction of Oliver, who in turn would receive direction from Joseph Smith as the head of the Church (30:5–7). John Whitmer was also called to preach (30:9–10) but was assigned to labor at "Philip Burroughs,' and in that region round about" (30:10); his "whole labor shall be in Zion . . . from henceforth" (30:11). John was called to be the Church historian in March 1831 (47:1–4; cf. 69:2–8), and served in that capacity until his apostasy and excommunication in March 1838.

BIBLIOGRAPHY

Smith, Joseph. *History of The Church of Jesus Christ of Latter-day Saints.* Edited by B. H. Roberts. 7 vols. 2d ed. rev. Salt Lake City: The Church of Jesus Christ of Latter-day Saints, 1932–51.

ROC

Historical context and overview of Doctrine and Covenants 31

Historical context

Thomas B. Marsh, a native of Massachusetts, had been seeking the true Church and traveled to Palmyra, New York, in 1829 to investigate a story he had heard about a "gold bible." "His search to learn more about the matter led him to E. B. Grandin's printing office in Palmyra." As reported in the *Millennial Star*, 11 June 1864, Marsh said that he was "highly pleased with the information I had obtained concerning the new found book." He "took sixteen pages of the text and returned to Boston. Within the year he had moved his family to Palmyra" (Black, 186). He was baptized at the time of the restored Church's second conference in September 1830. A few days later, Joseph Smith received this revelation in his behalf.

Content overview

In this revelation the Lord called Thomas B. Marsh to preach the gospel and also offered counsel to him and his family. Although Marsh had experienced some problems in his family (he ran away from home at age fourteen), he was promised that his "little ones" would be blessed and become united with him in the Church (31:2). He was counseled to be patient and to "govern [his] house in meekness, and be steadfast" (31:9). He was told to "declare glad tidings of great joy unto this generation" and was promised that his tongue would be loosed (31:3). The urgency of his call was reflected in the Lord's declaration that the field was "already to be burned" (31:4) rather than to be harvested.

The Lord also called Marsh to be "a physician unto the church" (31:10). While this could be a call to heal moral sicknesses, there are two accounts of Marsh medically treating Church members: one with cholera and the other with the "bloody flux" [severe dysentery] ("History," 18).

Marsh was admonished to "pray always" lest he lose his reward (31:12). In 1835, Thomas B. Marsh became the senior apostle, being the oldest of those called into the original Quorum of the Twelve. Unfortunately, persecution and a disagreement involving his wife and a neighbor contributed to Marsh's apostasy and his loss of membership in the Church and in the Twelve; he was excommunicated 17 March 1839 (Smith, 3:284). Even though he was rebaptized in 1857 and traveled to rejoin the Saints in Utah, he never regained his standing in the Twelve.

BIBLIOGRAPHY

Black, Susan Easton. *Who's Who in the Doctrine and Covenants.* Salt Lake City: Deseret Book, 1997.

"History of Thos. Baldwin Marsh." *Deseret News,* 24 March 1858.

Smith, Joseph. *History of The Church of Jesus Christ of Latter-day Saints.* Edited by B. H. Roberts. 7 vols. 2d ed. rev. Salt Lake City: The Church of Jesus Christ of Latter-day Saints, 1932–51.

ROC

Historical context and overview of Doctrine and Covenants 32

Historical context

Members of the Church understood from the Book of Mormon that the American Indians were among the descendants of the LAMANITES and that they were of the house of Israel. As part of the gathering in the latter days, Oliver Cowdery and Peter Whitmer Jr. were called in September 1830 as missionaries to the Lamanites (32:2–3; cf. 28:8; 30:5). Other elders manifested a "great desire" concerning the Lamanites, and the desire was "so great, it was agreed that we should inquire of the Lord respecting the propriety of sending some of the Elders among them . . . and received the following: [section 32]" (Smith, *History,* 1:118–19). In this revelation, Parley P. Pratt and Ziba Peterson were called as missionary companions with Oliver Cowdery and Peter Whitmer Jr.

Content overview

This revelation was given in October 1830, a month following Pratt's baptism and only six months after Peterson's. These brethren were directed to go with Elders Cowdery and Whitmer "into the wilderness among the Lamanites." The Lord promised to "go with them and be in their midst" if they would pray always, heed the scriptures they already had, and "pretend to no other revelation" (32:2–5).

Concerning this revelation, Lucy Mack Smith recorded, "Emma Smith, and several other sisters, began to make arrangements to furnish those who were set apart for this mission, with the necessary clothing, which was no easy task, as the most of it had to be manufactured out of the raw material" (L. M. Smith, *History,* 190).

The four missionaries departed in October 1830, the same month this revelation was received. They preached to the Cattaraugus Indians in western New York and the Wyandot tribe in Ohio but with little success. Their main contribution was teaching and baptizing Sidney Rigdon and many of his followers whom they met in the Kirtland area on their way to the western border of Missouri, where more of the Lamanites were located. They also experienced the Church's first contact with Jackson County, Missouri, which would figure prominently in future Latter-day Saint history.

Before leaving on their mission to the Lamanites, the four brethren signed their names to two statements (Cook, 43–44):

"Manchester, New York, Oct. 17, 1830
"I Oliver, being commanded by the Lord God, to go forth unto the Lamanites, to proclaim glad tidings of great joy unto them, by presenting unto them the fullness of the Gospel, of the only begotten Son of God; and also, to rear up a pillar as a witness where the temple of God shall be built, in the glorious new Jerusalem; and having certain brothers with me, who are called of GOD TO ASSIST ME, whose names are Parley, and Peter and Ziba, do therefore most solumnly covenant with God that I will walk humbly before him, and do this business, and this glorious work according as he shall direct me by the Holy Ghost; ever praying for mine and their prosperity, and deliverance from bonds, and from imprisonment, and whatsoever may befall us, with all patience and faith.
"Amen

"Oliver Cowdery"

"We, the undersigned, being called and commanded by the Lord God, to accompany our brother Oliver Cowdery to go to the Lamanites and to assist in the above mentioned glorious work and business, we do, therefore, most solumnly covenant before God, that we will assist him faithfully in this thing, by giving heed to all

Go into the Wilderness; *painting by Robert Barrett. Oliver Cowdery, Peter Whitmer Jr., Parley P. Pratt, and Ziba Peterson journeyed to preach the gospel to the Lamanites in the winter of 1830–1831. Regarding their labors, the Lord promised, "And I myself will go with them and be in their midst; and I am their advocate with the Father, and nothing shall prevail against them" (D&C 32:3).*

his words and advise, which is, or shall be given him by the spirit of truth, ever praying with all prayer and supplication, for our and his prosperity, and our deliverance from bonds, and imprisonments and whatsoever may come upon us, with all patience and faith.

"Amen.

"Signed in the presence of Joseph Smith jun.,

"David Whitmer   Parley P. Pratt
                       "Ziba Peterson
                       "Peter Whitmer"

See map, p. 355.

BIBLIOGRAPHY

Cook, Lyndon W. *The Revelations of the Prophet Joseph Smith*. Salt Lake City: Deseret Book, 1985.

Smith, Joseph. *History of The Church of Jesus Christ of Latter-day Saints*. Edited by B. H. Roberts. 7 vols. 2d ed. rev. Salt Lake City: The Church of Jesus Christ of Latter-day Saints, 1932–51.

Smith, Lucy Mack. *History of Joseph Smith by His Mother*. Edited by Preston Nibley. Salt Lake City: Bookcraft, 1958.

ROC

Historical context and overview of Doctrine and Covenants 33

Historical context

In this revelation, the Lord called recent converts Ezra Thayre and Northrop Sweet "to the ministry" (Jensen et al., 59–60) and expounded in broad terms the urgent need for them to labor in this, "the eleventh hour" (33:3). As in other revelations of this period, the Lord emphasized that the gathering of Israel had begun and that people needed to repent; the kingdom of God was at hand, and they needed to prepare for the coming of Christ.

Content overview

In his preface to this revelation, the Prophet declared: "The Lord, who is ever ready to instruct such as diligently seek in faith, gave the following revelation at Fayette, New York" (*History*, 1:126). The Lord called Thayre and Sweet to preach and bring others unto the gospel: "For verily, verily, I say unto you that ye are called to lift up your voices as with the sound of a trump, to declare my gospel unto a crooked and perverse generation" (33:2).

They were both informed that "the field is white already to harvest; and it is the eleventh hour, and the last time that I shall call laborers into my vineyard" (33:3). The millennial note added urgency to their call. These two men were not being called as missionary companions to serve in a particular area or time frame. In all but one of the revelations given to individuals in the Doctrine and Covenants (126 being the exception) the Lord counsels the individual to actively preach the gospel. Thus, one of the important messages in the revelations is "every member a missionary." In one or two cases, formal missionary calls are given to individuals in revelations directed to them, but such calls are generally found in revelations given at conferences, such as those found in sections 52 and 75.

Historical records indicate that Thayre and Sweet both stayed faithful to their covenants up to the point of obeying the command to "go to the Ohio" (38:32). Northrop Sweet left the Church shortly thereafter and in 1831 helped organize the first break-off movement from the Church, the Pure Church of Christ, with four other men (Smith, *JD*, 11:4). Ezra Thayre was later ordained a high priest, participated with Zion's Camp, served on a high council, and helped campaign for Joseph Smith's presidency; however, he did not support the Twelve after the death of the Prophet and by 1860 had joined with the Reorganized Church of Jesus Christ of Latter Day Saints.

BIBLIOGRAPHY

Jensen, Robin Scott, Robert J. Woodford, and Steven C. Harper, eds. *Manuscript Revelation Books.* Facsimile edition. First volume of the Revelations and Translations series of *The Joseph Smith Papers,* edited by Dean C. Jessee, Ronald K. Esplin, and Richard Lyman Bushman. Salt Lake City: Church Historian's Press, 2009.

Smith, George A. *Journal of Discourses.* 26 vols. London: Latter-day Saints' Book Depot, 1854–86.

Smith, Joseph. *History of The Church of Jesus Christ of Latter-day Saints.* Edited by B. H. Roberts. 7 vols. 2d ed. rev. Salt Lake City: The Church of Jesus Christ of Latter-day Saints, 1932–51.

MAG

Historical context and overview of Doctrine and Covenants 34

Historical context

Orson Pratt inquired of the Prophet Joseph Smith as to the Lord's will concerning him. He had been baptized on his nineteenth birthday, 19 September 1830, by his brother Parley P. Pratt. Joseph petitioned the Lord and received what is now known as Doctrine and Covenants 34 (November 1830). Almost thirty years later, Orson spoke of this revelation: "I went forth from a farming occupation in the eastern part of the State of New York, and traveled alone between two hundred and three hundred miles, for the purpose of beholding the Prophet Joseph Smith. I found him in Fayette, Seneca County, New York, at the house of father Whitmer, where this Church was organized with only six members. In that house I found not only Joseph, the Prophet, but David Whitmer, John Whitmer, Christian Whitmer, and many of those witnesses whose names are recorded in the Book of Mormon. Those were happy days to me. To see a prophet of the living God, to look on a man whom the Lord had raised up to bring forth one of the most glorious records that ever saluted the ears of mortal man, was to me almost equal to beholding the face of an holy angel!" (12:85).

Content overview

The Lord declared that Orson Pratt, through the Atonement, and as one who "believed" (34:4), had become one of "the sons of God." *See* Sons of God.

The Lord also testified of his love for mankind, demonstrated by giving his own life in their behalf (34:1–3; cf. John 3:16). Pratt was called "blessed" because he believed, and "more blessed" because of his call to preach the gospel (34:4–5). The Lord then called Pratt to the ministry with almost the same wording as that given to Ezra Thayre and Northrop Sweet (cf. 33:2–3): "Lift up your voice as with the sound of a trump, both long and loud, and cry repentance unto a crooked and perverse generation, preparing the way of the Lord for his second coming" (34:6). Pratt was ordained an elder by Joseph Smith on 1 December 1830 and served his first mission to Colesville, New York, at the end of the same year

(1830). He would go on to serve in many capacities and many more missions. In 1859 he said of his missionary service: "I have not only borne testimony to my own nation on this continent, baptizing believers, building up churches, travelling on foot thousands and tens of thousands of miles without purse or scrip, being mobbed and driven to-and-fro, and hunted by the enemy; but I have also had the privilege of crossing the Atlantic Ocean ten times for the word of God and the testimony of Jesus, to bear his name among the nations afar off; and I have endeavoured in those distant lands, as well as on this continent, to bear my testimony faithfully among the people" (7:180). Elder Pratt lived until 1881 and crossed the Atlantic six more times to preach the gospel (Jenson, 1:90).

Finally, the Lord commanded him to "prophesy" (34:10). From Pratt's writings and sermons, it is evident he understood this to mean he was to speak under the inspiration of the Holy Ghost. He said this mandate caused him "oftentimes to tremble and shrink, for fear I never should be able to fulfil and accomplish so great a work. . . . How few of us have obtained a message beforehand by the Spirit of the living God to deliver to the people" (7:311).

BIBLIOGRAPHY

Pratt, Orson. *Journal of Discourses*. 26 vols. London: Latter-day Saints' Book Depot, 1854–86.

Jenson, Andrew. *Latter-day Saints' Biographical Encyclopedia*. 4 vols. Salt Lake City: The Andrew Jenson History Company, 1901–36. Reprint, Salt Lake City: Western Epics, 1971 .

MAG

Historical context and overview of Doctrine and Covenants 35

Historical context

In December 1830, recent converts Sidney Rigdon and Edward Partridge made the long journey from Ohio to Fayette, New York, to meet the Prophet Joseph Smith. One month before Oliver Cowdery, Parley P. Pratt, Peter Whitmer Jr., and Ziba Peterson had passed through Ohio on their way to teach the Lamanites in Missouri. Pratt, who had previously lived in the area, called on Sidney Rigdon, his "former friend and instructor, in the Reformed Baptist Society." Pratt had studied with Rigdon and was eager to share the news of the restoration of the gospel with his former teacher. Rigdon received him and the other Mormon missionaries "cordially and entertained [them] with hospitality" (Pratt, 47). He agreed to read the Book of Mormon and even allowed the missionaries to address his congregation. After two weeks of study, Rigdon was convinced of the truthfulness of the Book of Mormon and was baptized by Pratt on 14 November 1830. Ultimately, more than a hundred followers of Sidney Rigdon were converted and baptized into the Church. Before they left the area, the missionaries also ordained Rigdon to the office of elder.

Edward Partridge had also listened to the missionaries but had not yet been baptized; however, he was interested enough that he wanted to meet Joseph Smith. That is why, in early December 1830, Partridge and Rigdon traveled to Manchester and then to Fayette, New York. In

Orson Pratt, 1811–1881. "My son Orson, hearken and hear and behold what I, the Lord God, shall say unto you, even Jesus Christ your Redeemer. . . . And blessed are you because you have believed; and more blessed are you because you are called of me to preach my gospel—To lift up your voice as with the sound of a trump, both long and loud, and cry repentance unto a crooked and perverse generation, preparing the way of the Lord for his second coming" (D&C 34:1, 4–6).

Fayette, they asked the Prophet to inquire of the Lord on their behalf. The revelation Joseph received for Sidney Rigdon on 7 December was recorded in section 35, and the revelation received for Edward Partridge on 9 December in section 36 (Jensen et al., 63–67).

Content overview

Similar to the initial words to Orson Pratt in section 34, the Lord declared that through the Atonement, those who "believe" on his name "become the sons of God" (35:1–2). *See* Sons of God.

After commending Rigdon for the work he had done, "even as John" (meaning John the Baptist) in preparing the way for others to accept the gospel, the Lord called him to "tarry" with Joseph and serve as his scribe (35:3–4, 20–22). Rigdon began that month to serve as a scribe for the translation of the Bible and continued as the main scribe throughout the translation. The importance of Joseph Smith's translation of the Bible is made clear in the Lord's statement that "the scriptures shall be given, even as they are in mine own bosom" (35:20). *See* Doctrine and Covenants and the Joseph Smith Translation of the Bible.

Additionally, now that Rigdon had received the "fulness of my gospel" (35:12, 17), the Lord called him to preach, baptize, and confer the Holy Ghost (35:6). The Lord then expounded on "a great work" to be accomplished through the restoration of the gospel and spoke of miracles, healings, signs and wonders (35:7–12). He also called upon the elders to "thrash the nations by the power of [his] Spirit . . . for even now already summer is nigh" (35:13–16). Rigdon was then given the assignment to "watch over" the Prophet Joseph Smith and assist him in his work (35:17–27).

BIBLIOGRAPHY

Jensen, Robin Scott, Robert J. Woodford, and Steven C. Harper, eds. *Manuscript Revelation Books*. Facsimile edition. First volume of the Revelations and Translations series of *The Joseph Smith Papers*, edited by Dean C. Jessee, Ronald K. Esplin, and Richard Lyman Bushman. Salt Lake City: Church Historian's Press, 2009.

Pratt, Parley P. *Autobiography of Parley P. Pratt*. Edited by Parley P. Pratt Jr. Salt Lake City: Deseret Book, 1976.

MAG

Historical context and overview of Doctrine and Covenants 36

Historical context

Before moving to Ohio, Edward Partridge lived in New York and apprenticed as a hatter. At the time he met the Mormon missionaries, he belonged to a congregation whose members sought to emulate the church that Christ established in the meridian of time. Partridge was impressed with the message of the Restoration as taught by the missionaries; however, he was not ready to be baptized. He did agree to travel with Sidney Rigdon to New York to meet the Prophet Joseph Smith. *See* Historical context and overview of Doctrine and Covenants 35 (p. 743).

In early December 1830, Partridge and Rigdon journeyed to Manchester and then to Fayette, New York. The day they arrived in Fayette they attended a meeting at which the Prophet Joseph Smith addressed the Saints. Partridge was so impressed he immediately requested baptism at the hands of Joseph Smith (Smith, 1:129). The Prophet baptized him the following day.

The earliest manuscript of this revelation dates it 9 December 1830 (Jensen et al., 67).

Content overview

The *History of the Church* contains the following entry introducing the revelation given to Edward Partridge: "In December Sidney Rigdon came to inquire of the Lord, and with him came Edward Partridge; the latter was a pattern of piety, and one of the Lord's great men. Shortly after the arrival of these two brethren, thus spake the Lord" (Smith, 1:128). Partridge had been baptized for the remission of sins, and in this revelation, the Lord attested that his sins were forgiven (36:1). Then the Lord declared, "I will lay my hand upon you by the hand of . . . Sidney Rigdon, and you shall receive . . . the Holy Ghost . . . which shall teach you the peaceable things of the kingdom" (36:2). Like many new converts, Partridge was also called to "preach [the] gospel as with the voice of a trump" (36:1). The Lord established this as a pattern for all who accept the gospel: "And this commandment shall be given unto the elders of my church, that every man which will embrace [the gospel] with singleness of heart may be ordained and sent forth, even as I have spoken" (36:4–8).

BIBLIOGRAPHY

Jensen, Robin Scott, Robert J. Woodford, and Steven C. Harper, eds. *Manuscript Revelation Books*. Facsimile edition. First volume of the Revelations and Translations series of *The Joseph Smith Papers*, edited by Dean C. Jessee, Ronald K. Esplin, and Richard Lyman Bushman. Salt Lake City: Church Historian's Press, 2009.

Smith, Joseph. *History of The Church of Jesus Christ of Latter-day Saints*. Edited by B. H. Roberts. 7 vols. 2d ed. rev. Salt Lake City: The Church of Jesus Christ of Latter-day Saints, 1932–51.

MAG

Historical context and overview of Doctrine and Covenants 37

Historical context

In September 1830 the Lord revealed that the Church had the mandate to bring about the gathering of ISRAEL in the latter days (29:7–10) and that the initial gathering was to take place on what was then the western frontier of the United States (28:9; 52:2; 57:1–2). Oliver Cowdery and three others were sent to the frontier to preach to the native American Indians and "also, to rear up a pillar as a witness where the temple of God shall be built, in the glorious New-Jerusalem," where the gathering was to begin (Booth to Eddy, 1; D&C 28:8; 30:5–8; 32:1–5). *See* Gather, gathering; Historical context and overview of Doctrine and Covenants 32 (p. 740); Lamanites.

As they traveled west, these four men were instrumental in the conversion of Sidney Rigdon in Ohio. Rigdon came to New York and promptly became Joseph Smith's scribe in his work of translating the Bible (35:20). Toward the end of December, conditions existed in New York which prompted this revelation to temporarily suspend the translation and begin the gathering (37:1; 38:13). This was to be accomplished by moving the members of the Church in New York to an interim gathering place in Ohio until Oliver Cowdery could return with further information.

Content overview

The Lord told Joseph Smith and Sidney Rigdon to go to Ohio in order to escape "the enemy," which was the immediate threat of persecution beginning to mount against the Church, and "for [their] sakes" (37:1). First, they were to preach to and strengthen the members of the Church in New York "and more especially in Colesville; for . . . they pray unto me in much faith" (37:2). The command was then extended to all members of the Church to "assemble together at the Ohio" (37:3) to await the return of Oliver Cowdery from Missouri. The revelation closes with the Lord affirming the principle of agency: "Let every man choose for himself until I come" (37:4).

BIBLIOGRAPHY

Booth, Ezra, to Ira Eddy, 29 November 1831. In *Ohio Star* (8 December 1831): 1.

GLD

Historical context and overview of Doctrine and Covenants 38

Historical context

Section 38 is the record of a revelation received by the Prophet Joseph Smith during a conference of the Church in Fayette, New York, on 2 January 1831. The Church, officially organized nine months earlier, had been commanded in December 1830 to gather to "the Ohio" (37:3). *See* Historical context and overview of Doctrine and Covenants 37 (p. 745).

In November and December, Joseph Smith had also received revelations concerning Enoch and the gathering of his people to their city of ZION (Moses 6–7). *See* Zion of Enoch.

At the conference in January 1831, John Whitmer recorded: "The solemnities of eternity rested on the congregation, and having previously received a revelation to go to Ohio, they desired to know somewhat more concerning this matter. Therefor the Seer . . . enquired of the Lord in the presence of the whole congregation, and thus came the word of the Lord" (6).

After the conference, most of the Saints were determined to obey the commandment to relocate to Ohio. This move, however, required much of the Saints. Newel Knight of the

Colesville branch stated: "It was at this conference that we were instructed as a people, to begin the gathering of Israel, and a revelation was given to the prophet on this subject. Having returned home from conference, in obedience to the commandment which had been given, I, together with the Colesville Branch, began to make preparations to go to Ohio. . . . As might be expected, we were obliged to make great sacrifices of our property" (*Scraps*, 68).

Content overview

In this revelation the Lord instructed the Saints that it was he who was commanding the move, even the "same which looked upon the wide expanse of eternity, and all the seraphic hosts of heaven, before the world was made" (38:1, 32). He referred to the account of the translation of the "Zion of Enoch" (which Joseph Smith had just received by revelation), explaining that it was by the Lord's power that Enoch's Zion was redeemed in his day (38:4). The revelation instructed the Saints to begin living the ideals of Zion by remembering the poor and seeking to be "one" (38:16–17, 24–27, 34–35). *See* Parable regarding a father and sons.

The Lord encouraged them in their removal to Ohio by revealing that their "enemy," in "secret chambers," was seeking to destroy them, indicating that the Saints could learn "these things" either by "wisdom" and obedience or by sad experience (38:13, 28–31). He also promised that in Ohio he would "give unto [them his] law" and that they would there "be endowed with power from on high" (38:32). This power from on high was realized again and again through spiritual manifestations before, during, and after the dedication of the Kirtland Temple in the late winter and spring of 1836 (Backman, 284–309). The endowment of power would also include the priesthood ordinances of washing and anointing. It should be understood that the priesthood ordinances of washing and anointing performed in the Kirtland Temple constituted a preparatory endowment to the full endowment revealed later in Nauvoo. *See* Endow, endowed, endowment; Kirtland Temple dedication; Temple(s).

The Lord also enumerated the rich blessings he had in store for the righteous in Zion (38:18–22). With these blessings, he also gave the solemn warning to "beware of pride, lest ye become as the Nephites of old" (38:39).

Pertaining to the need for the Saints to gather, the Lord taught that corrupt persons and the "powers of darkness" had caused revelation to cease ("silence to reign") and that angels would ultimately "reap down the earth, to gather the tares ["the children of the wicked one"; Matt. 13:38] that they may be burned": "Behold, the enemy is combined" (38:11–12; 87:1–8).

The Lord concluded the revelation with a call for all the Saints to work together to accomplish what the Lord commanded them to do in this revelation. Moreover, the Saints were to raise a "warning voice, every man to his neighbor," and to come "out from among the wicked. . . . Be ye clean that bear the vessels of the Lord" (38:37–42).

BIBLIOGRAPHY

Backman, Milton V., Jr. *The Heavens Resound: A History of the Latter-day Saints in Ohio, 1830–1838*. Salt Lake City: Deseret Book, 1983.

Scraps of Biography: The Tenth Book of the Faith-Promoting Series. Salt Lake City: Juvenile Instructor Office, 1883. Reprinted as part of *Classic Experiences and Adventures*. Salt Lake City, Utah: Bookcraft, 1969.

Smith, Joseph. *History of The Church of Jesus Christ of Latter-day Saints*. Edited by B. H. Roberts. 7 vols. 2d ed. rev. Salt Lake City: The Church of Jesus Christ of Latter-day Saints, 1932–51.

Whitmer, John. "The Book of John Whitmer Kept by Commandment." Ca. 1835–46, Community of Christ Library-Archives, Independence, Mo.

GLD

Historical context and overview of Doctrine and Covenants 39

Historical context

This revelation was directed to James Covill through the Prophet Joseph Smith at Fayette, New York, on 5 January 1831. Joseph Smith stated, "Not long after this conference of the 2d of January closed [the conference at which the Prophet had received section 38], there was a man came to me by the name of James Covill, who had been a Baptist minister for about forty years, and covenanted with the Lord that he would obey any command that the Lord would give to him through me, as His servant, and I received the following: [section 39]" (1:143). Recent discoveries indicate that Covill was a Methodist minister of forty years' experience, not a Baptist. In Methodist records, the only man who fits this profile is James Covel (1770–1850).

Content overview

Covill was taught in this revelation that he could become one of the SONS OF GOD through "repentance and baptism by water," followed by the reception of the HOLY GHOST, which could teach him the "peaceable things of the kingdom" (39:4–6). The Lord indicated to him that his heart was right at that time, although he was reminded that in the past he had "rejected [the Lord] many times because of pride and the cares of the world" (39:8–9). He was commanded to be baptized, with a promise of great blessings if he obeyed. Contingent upon his baptism, he was also called to labor in the Lord's vineyard, build up the Church, and bring forth Zion. This he was to do in Ohio, where he was to go forth baptizing and giving the GIFT OF THE HOLY GHOST in preparation for the Lord's coming, which was imminent (39:10, 13–16, 20–23). Because of his membership in the Church, he would now be able to teach "the fulness of [the] gospel," whereas before he had only known a portion of it (39:11).

The Lord teaches a vital principle in verses 16–18: prayer, even if done "in much faith," cannot overrule the decrees of God concerning his "judgment upon the nations." For the Lord to withhold his judgments, the people must repent and accept "the fulness of [the] gospel."

BIBLIOGRAPHY

Smith, Joseph. *History of The Church of Jesus Christ of Latter-day Saints.* Edited by B. H. Roberts. 7 vols. 2d ed. rev. Salt Lake City: The Church of Jesus Christ of Latter-day Saints, 1932–51.

GLD

Historical context and overview of Doctrine and Covenants 40

Historical context

Section 40 is the record of a revelation given to Joseph Smith and Sidney Rigdon in Fayette, New York, on 6 January 1831 concerning James

Covill. Joseph had received section 39 the day before, which commanded a Methodist minister named James "Covel" to repent and be baptized so that he could take an active part in the Lord's latter-day kingdom. *See* Historical context and overview of Doctrine and Covenants 39 (p. 746).

Content overview

Covill was not obedient, and the Lord explained to Joseph and Sidney Rigdon in this revelation that although Covill's heart "was right" earlier and he had "received the word with gladness," he had been tempted by Satan, and "the fear of persecution and the cares of the world caused him to reject the word" (40:1–2). There are no Church records indicating whether James was baptized. In this revelation the Lord said that he "broke my covenant, and it remaineth with me to do with him as seemeth me good" (40:3).

GLD

Historical context and overview of Doctrine and Covenants 41

Historical context

Section 41 is the first of the sixty-five revelations given to Joseph Smith in Ohio that are recorded in the Doctrine and Covenants. It was received on 4 February 1831, just days following the Prophet's arrival in the area. Joseph's wife, Emma, had also traveled to Ohio with him. She was in the last trimester of a pregnancy with twins. Also accompanying him were Sidney Rigdon and Edward Partridge. One of the most pressing needs for Joseph and Emma was finding suitable quarters. A recent convert, Leman Copley, who owned a large farm in Thompson, Ohio, a little over fifteen miles from Kirtland, offered both "houses & provisions" there for the Smiths and the Rigdons (Jensen et al., 93). Joseph Smith learned from this revelation, however, that a house would be built for him to live in and accomplish the Lord's work (41:7).

The Prophet also seemed to have on his mind the necessity of fulfilling the promise the Lord had made a month earlier that he would give to the Saints his "law" (38:32). The conditions under which the Lord's law would be revealed are outlined in this revelation. Finally, a person was needed to help administer certain aspects of the law, and Edward Partridge was called to the position of "a bishop unto the church" (41:9). (The historical material in this article draws from a prepublication draft of a volume to be published in the Documents series of *The Joseph Smith Papers*.)

Content overview

Section 41 begins with the Lord's declaration that he delights to bless with "the greatest of all blessings" those that "hear" him and a warning that those who profess his name but do not "hear" him will receive "the heaviest of all cursings" (41:1).

One purpose of this revelation was to prepare the Saints for the "law" (42:2), which was revealed a few days after this revelation was received. The Saints in Kirtland were to assemble in order to "agree upon my word; and . . . receive my law" so that they could know how to govern the Church (41:2–3). They were instructed that discipleship is defined by obedience to the Lord's law, and those who do not obey the law are to be "cast out from among you" (41:5). In further preparation for the revelation of the "law," the Lord commanded that Edward Partridge "should be appointed by the voice of the church, and ordained a bishop unto the church . . . to see to all things as it shall be appointed unto him in my laws" (41:9–10). The Lord stated that this call was given because Edward's heart was pure and he was like Nathanael of old, without guile (41:11).

In order for Joseph Smith to accomplish his work, the Lord counseled the Saints in Kirtland to build Joseph a house "in which to live and translate" (41:7). The Smiths were provided with a small cabin on the Morley farm, where they lived until the fall of 1831. *See* Morley, Isaac, farm.

In the meantime the Saints were instructed to meet all of Joseph Smith's temporal needs so that he could accomplish the work he was commanded to do (43:13).

The Lord closed this revelation by stating that the words which he had given were "pure before me" and cautioned all who received them to be careful "how you hold them," for they would

"be answered upon your souls in the day of judgment" (41:12).

BIBLIOGRAPHY

Jensen, Robin Scott, Robert J. Woodford, and Steven C. Harper, eds. *Manuscript Revelation Books*. Facsimile edition. First volume of the Revelations and Translations series of *The Joseph Smith Papers*, edited by Dean C. Jessee, Ronald K. Esplin, and Richard Lyman Bushman. Salt Lake City: Church Historian's Press, 2009.

GLD & RJW

Historical context and overview of Doctrine and Covenants 42

Historical context

Section 42, the "law of the Church" (42, headnote), is a composite of revelations received on 9 and 23 of February 1831. A little over a month earlier, on 2 January, the Lord promised to reveal his law once the members of the Church in New York had moved to Ohio (38:32). Joseph Smith and those traveling with him arrived in Kirtland early in February. This revelation was received a few days later. Pursuant to the instructions given in section 41 (41:2–3), on 9 February twelve elders "were called together, and united in mighty prayer, and were agreed, as touching the reception of the Law" (Whitmer, 12). The Lord revealed on that occasion what is now verses 1 to 73.

The disciples in Ohio were novices in the gospel compared to those from New York who had been tutored for months by the Prophet Joseph Smith, and questions arose on implementing the law. Consequently, on 23 February Joseph Smith and seven elders met to determine "how the Elders of the church of Christ are to act upon the points of the Law" (Woodford, 561). The Lord revealed the remaining verses of section 42 (vv. 74–93) at that time.

Content overview

The Lord first commanded the brethren to preach the gospel "two by two," bearing the name of Christ and declaring the word with their voices "as with the sound of a trump" (42:4–6). After they received the appropriate ordination, they were to teach the principles of the gospel from the Bible and the Book of Mormon as they were directed by the Spirit (42:11–14).

The Lord instructed the brethren to "observe the covenants and church articles" (20) and stated that if they received not "the Spirit," they were not to teach (42:13–17).

In verse 18 the Lord instructed not just the elders but all of the members of the Church. He reiterated the moral COMMANDMENTS given to ancient Israel and to those he taught in New Testament times, concluding with the injunction: "If thou lovest me thou shalt serve me and keep all my commandments" (42:18–29). The Lord then introduced the law of CONSECRATION with both its temporal and spiritual facets. The Saints were to "remember the poor," to consecrate their properties to the Lord, and to receive stewardships governed by humility, frugality, and honest labor. Consecrated means ("substance") were to be "laid before the bishop . . . and his counselors," who would administer them to the poor. Members were told to be simple in their dress, to be clean, and to not be idle (42:30–31, 40–42, 53–55). An essential part of the law of consecration was the Lord's admonition to "live together in love," caring for and administering to the sick and dying (42:43–52).

The Lord then addressed several issues related to the scriptures and revelations to the Church. He discussed the new translation of the Bible, which the Prophet was then working on, and revelations concerning the mysteries of the kingdom, the gathering, future commandments, and the site of the NEW JERUSALEM (42:56–69). He also revealed the law of remuneration, in which all those laboring in full-time Church service were to receive temporal support from the surplus property consecrated to the Lord (42:70–73).

In response to questions that had arisen about how to implement the "law," the Lord revealed the remainder of this section on 23 February 1831. Regulations governing the discipline of members were given regarding DIVORCE, ADULTERY, and law breaking (42:74–87). *See* Church discipline.

The Lord also outlined what to do when one is offended in the Church (42:88–93).

BIBLIOGRAPHY

Hedges, Andrew H., J. Spencer Fluhman, and Alonzo Gaskill, eds. "'The Laws of the Church of Christ' (D&C 42): A Textual and Historical Analysis." *The Doctrine and Covenants: Revelations in Context.* Provo, Utah: Religious Studies Center, Brigham Young University; Salt Lake City: Deseret Book, 2008.

Whitmer, John. "The Book of John Whitmer Kept by Commandment." Ca. 1835–46, Community of Christ Library-Archives, Independence, Mo.

Woodford, Robert J. "The Historical Development of the Doctrine and Covenants." Ph.D. dissertation. Brigham Young University, 1974.

GLD & RJW

Historical context and overview of Doctrine and Covenants 43

Historical context

Soon after section 42, known as the "law," had been received, a problem surfaced presenting a challenge to Joseph Smith's authority. John Whitmer wrote: "About these days there was a woman by the name of Hubble [possibly Laura Fuller Hubbell, older sister of Edson Fuller cited in 52:28] who professed to be a prophetess of the Lord and professed to have many revelations, and knew the Book of Mormon was true; and that she should become a teacher in the Church of Christ. She appear[ed] very sanctimonious and deceived some, who were not able to detect her in her hypocracy: others however had a spirit of discernment and her folies and abominations were made manifest. The Lord gave Revelation that the saints might not be deceived [section 43]" (18).

Content overview

This revelation reiterated the principle given earlier in section 28 that the prophet of the Church is the only one authorized to receive REVELATION for the Church. The Lord reminded the elders that they had received the law "through him whom I have appointed unto you to receive commandments and revelations," and that there was "none other appointed . . . to receive commandments and revelations" (43:2–3). The Lord stated that they were to "receive not the teachings of any that shall come before you as revelations or commandments . . . that you may not be deceived" (43:5–6). He reminded the Saints that they knew the "gate" through which these ordained servants would come (43:7), which was a reference to proper ordination and sustaining by Church members (cf. 42:11). See Deception.

The Lord commanded the Saints that they were to "instruct and edify" one another "that ye may know how to act and direct my church." He instructed them to "bind [themselves] to act in all holiness" and to purge out iniquity and sanctify themselves (43:8–11). He told the elders that they were sent out to teach, not to be taught (43:15). He also gave the members of the Church the responsibility to take care of the temporal needs of the Prophet so that he might give his full effort to the work of the Lord (43:12–14).

The Lord reminded them that "the great day of the Lord is nigh at hand" and that they had a responsibility to warn others to prepare for that day (43:17–20; 28). He then lamented how often he called upon the nations of the earth by his own voice, by the mouth of his servants, and by the catastrophic events of the earth, such as tempests, earthquakes, and famine; and they would not listen (43:21–26). See Disasters, calamities.

The Lord then spoke of the events that would take place at the end of this last DISPENSATION before the MILLENNIUM, when Christ will reign on the earth, SATAN will be bound, and the JUDGMENTS will take place (43:29–33). At the end of the revelation, the Lord counseled the Saints to "hearken . . . to these words," "treasure these things up in your hearts," "let the solemnities of eternity rest upon your minds," and "keep all my commandments" (43:34–35).

This revelation seemed to have a profound effect upon the Saints. John Whitmer noted, "After this commandment was received, the saints came to understanding on this subject, and unity and harmony prevailed throughout the church of God: and the Saints began to learn wisdom, and treasure up knowledge which they learned from the word of God, and by experience as they advanced in the way of eternal life" (21).

BIBLIOGRAPHY

Whitmer, John. "The Book of John Whitmer Kept by Commandment." Ca. 1835–46, Community of Christ Library-Archives, Independence, Mo.

GLD

Historical context and overview of Doctrine and Covenants 44

Historical context

The first commandment in section 42, known as the "law" (headnote), which was received on 9 February 1831, directed the elders of the Church to "go forth for a little season . . . preaching my gospel . . . [and] baptizing with water" (42:4–8). Later in the month, the word of the Lord to the elders was as follows: "Labor ye, labor ye in my vineyard for the last time—for the last time call upon the inhabitants of the earth" (43:28). Then the revelation recorded in section 44 was received, in which the Lord called for a meeting of all the elders of the Church, even those still getting ready to leave New York, to ensure they would be united as they went forth to preach the gospel. On 22 February, Joseph Smith wrote to Martin Harris in New York: "The work is here breaking forth on the east west north and south, you will also inform the Elders which are there that all of them who can be spared will come here without delay if possable this by Commandment of the Lord [section 44] as he has a great work for them all" (Smith, Letter, 1).

In connection with verse 4 of the revelation, it was imperative for the missionaries to build up congregations wherever possible in Ohio, because the laws of that state at the time did not recognize a central headquarters of any church, only local congregations. In order to be legally organized, a congregation had to have, along with a few other requirements, at least twenty members. It also had to have an official leader, and the name of the leader as well as the name of the church had to be registered with the county clerk (Acts, Chapter LIV).

Content overview

The Lord called for a general meeting of the elders of the Church and stated they were to be contacted for that meeting by mail "or some other way" (44:1). He promised that if they would exercise faith he would "pour out [his] Spirit" upon them when they assembled (44:2). After they met, the Lord told them that they were to "go forth into the regions round about, and preach repentance unto the people" (44:3). He promised that by organizing according to the "laws of man," their enemies would have no power over them (44:4–5). The Lord ended this revelation by reminding the early Saints to "visit the poor and the needy and administer to their relief" (44:6) as they had been instructed earlier in "the law" (42).

Correspondence did go out from Kirtland calling for the elders to assemble, and they did meet on 9 April 1831. After transacting the business of the meeting, they "adjourned until the first Saturday in June next" (Cannon and Cook, 5).

BIBLIOGRAPHY

Acts Passed at the First Session of the Seventeenth General Assembly of the State of Ohio. Chapter LIV of vol. XII. Chillicothe, Ohio: Office of the Supporter, 1819.

Cannon, Donald Q., and Lyndon W. Cook, eds. *Far West Record: Minutes of The Church of Jesus Christ of Latter-day Saints, 1830–1844.* Salt Lake City: Deseret Book, 1983.

Smith, Joseph. Joseph Smith Collection (bx 2, fd 3). Church Historical Library, The Church of Jesus Christ of Latter-day Saints, Salt Lake City, Utah.

———. Kirtland, Ohio, to Martin Harris, Palmyra, New York, 22 February 1831. Letter, LS, 1 p., in handwriting of Sidney Rigdon. Endorsed "Kirtland Mills 0/23 Feby/ 18¾ [cents postage]."

GLD

Historical context and overview of Doctrine and Covenants 45

Historical context

The Prophet Joseph Smith stated: "At this age of the Church . . . many false reports, lies, and foolish stories, were published in the newspapers, and circulated in every direction, to prevent people from investigating the work, or embracing the faith." He added, "But to the joy of the Saints who had to struggle against every thing that prejudice and wickedness could invent, I received the following [section 45]" (1:158). Embedded in this revelation (45:16–59, except for the parenthetical comment in v. 34 and the first five words of v. 35) is a version

of the Savior's prophetic sermon given on the MOUNT OF OLIVES (Matt. 24). It adds important information not included in Matthew 24 or Joseph Smith–Matthew. It clarifies which events happened shortly after the Savior's death and those that will happen just before the Savior comes again (note the transition in 45:24, which shifts focus from the A.D. 33 era to the last days). The message of the revelation reinforced to the Saints the truth that these are, indeed, the last days.

This revelation is also associated with Joseph Smith's work on the translation of the Bible. Until the day this revelation was received, 7 March 1831, he had been working on the Old Testament, but as instructed in 45:60–61, he began work on the New Testament the very next day, March 8.

Content overview

The Lord identified himself as the Creator and as mankind's Advocate before the Father (vv. 1–5). He further identified himself as the Savior and the one who restored the "everlasting covenant" to be a "light" and a "standard" for all people (vv. 6–10). He then instructed members of the Church to "hearken" to his words and, after reviewing events in the life of Enoch and his people, as well as those who sought for ZION, he again asked them to "hearken" and he would speak to them and "prophesy, as unto men in days of old" (vv. 11–15). Quoting from his prophetic sermon on the Mount of Olives shortly before the Crucifixion, the Lord explained which of his prophecies given at that time were fulfilled shortly after his death (vv. 16–23). He then recounted those events foretold in the same sermon that will occur in the latter days (vv. 24–59). He prophesied concerning SIGNS and wonders that would take place at the time of the Second Coming, including the miracle of the RESURRECTION (vv. 39–47). Citing from the book of Zechariah (Zech. 14:4), he stated that he would stand upon the Mount of Olives and that the conversion of the JEWS as a nation would take place at that time (vv. 48–53). He then told of some of the events that would occur during the MILLENNIUM, including the binding of SATAN and the fulfillment of the PARABLE OF THE TEN VIRGINS (vv. 54–59).

The Lord then instructed Joseph Smith to begin the translation of the New Testament (vv. 60–62) in which he would reveal more concerning events spoken in the previous verses. Returning to the theme of Zion, he told Church members to gather together and create the latter-day city of Zion as a "city of refuge, a place of safety for the saints of the Most High God" (vv. 63–75).

See also Doctrine and Covenants and the Joseph Smith Translation of the Bible; Jesus Christ, second coming of; Times of the Gentiles.

BIBLIOGRAPHY

Smith, Joseph. *History of The Church of Jesus Christ of Latter-day Saints.* Edited by B. H. Roberts. 7 vols. 2d ed. rev. Salt Lake City: The Church of Jesus Christ of Latter-day Saints, 1932–51.

GLD

Historical context and overview of Doctrine and Covenants 46

Historical context

The revelation recorded in section 46 answered several pressing needs in connection with the administration of the Church. Concerning one issue, John Whitmer wrote: "In the beginning of the church, while yet in her infancy, the disciples used to exclude unbelievers, which caused some to marvel, and converse about this matter because of the things that were written in the Book of Mormon [3 Nephi

O Jerusalem; *painting by Greg Olsen. "And now ye behold this temple which is in Jerusalem, which ye call the house of God, and your enemies say that this house shall never fall. But, verily I say unto you, that desolation shall come upon this generation as a thief in the night, and this people shall be destroyed and scattered among all nations. And this temple which ye now see shall be thrown down that there shall not be left one stone upon another" (D&C 45:18–20).*

18:22]. Therefore the Lord deigned to speak on this subject, that his people might come to understanding" (Whitmer, 23). Before this revelation was received, some of the members of the Church had been exhibiting the extravagant spiritual phenomena often seen at camp meeting revivals, believing that these were true gifts from God. The Lord explained that they needed to seek the gifts of the Spirit that they be not deceived.

This revelation was received on 8 March 1831 and followed by just one day the revelation known as section 45. Joseph Smith wrote, "The next day after [D&C 45] was received, I also received the following revelation, relative to the gifts of the Holy Ghost" (1:163).

Content overview

The Lord admonished the Saints to avoid developing a spirit of exclusivity in their sacrament and confirmation meetings (Jensen et al., 124–25). The Saints were commanded "never to cast any one out from your *public meetings*," "not to cast any one who belongeth to the church out of your *sacrament meetings*," and to allow "any that are not of the church, that are earnestly seeking after the kingdom" to attend *confirmation meetings* (46:3–4, 6; emphasis added). Thus, officers of the Church were admonished to avoid alienating those who were sometimes characterized as unbelievers or simply as nonmembers.

The Lord then set forth the pattern and purposes of true SPIRITUAL GIFTS, which he instructs "are given for the benefit of those who love me and keep all my commandments, and him that seeketh so to do" (46:9).

Rather than setting forth all possible gifts, examples of gifts enumerated in this revelation are illustrative of the diverse nature of spiritual gifts (cf. Moro. 10:8–18; 1 Cor. 12:1–12). Spiritual gifts may be withdrawn from the earth because of "wickedness and unbelief" (Morm. 1:13–14; 9:7–21).

In the modern Church, the Lord instructed that not every member is given every spiritual gift; however, the Saints are promised, "To every man is given a gift by the Spirit of God. To some is given one, and to some is given another, that all may be profited thereby" (46:11–12).

In order to protect the Saints against false spiritual gifts, the Lord designated "the bishop of the church, and unto such as God shall appoint and ordain to watch over the church and to be elders unto the church, are to have it given unto them to *discern* all those gifts lest there shall be any among you professing and yet be not of God" (46:27; emphasis added). In addition, "unto some it may be given to *have all those gifts,* that there may be a head" (46:29; emphasis added).

A review of the gifts mentioned in this revelation makes it clear that spiritual gifts serve primarily to strengthen and unify the Church and its members. Much of this purpose is accomplished as those who possess such gifts develop them for the betterment of the human family.

BIBLIOGRAPHY

Jensen, Robin Scott, Robert J. Woodford, and Steven C. Harper, eds. *Manuscript Revelation Books.* Facsimile edition. First volume of the Revelations and Translations series of *The Joseph Smith Papers,* edited by Dean C. Jessee, Ronald K. Esplin, and Richard Lyman Bushman. Salt Lake City: Church Historian's Press, 2009.

Smith, Joseph. *History of The Church of Jesus Christ of Latter-day Saints.* Edited by B. H. Roberts. 7 vols. 2d ed. rev. Salt Lake City: The Church of Jesus Christ of Latter-day Saints, 1932–51.

Whitmer, John. "The Book of John Whitmer Kept by Commandment." Ca. 1835–46, Community of Christ Library-Archives, Independence, Mo.

RCF

Historical context and overview of Doctrine and Covenants 47

Historical context

"There shall be a record kept among you" (21:1), the Lord declared when the Church was organized on 6 April 1830. Accepting the command, Oliver Cowdery continued the duty previously given him to "write for my servant Joseph" (9:4), including beginning a record of the history of the Church. In the June 1830 conference of the Church, Oliver Cowdery was "appointed to keep the Church record and Conference minutes until the next conference," which was planned for the following September (Cannon and Cook, 2). In September 1830, however, Cowdery was "appointed to another office" (47:3) as head of the mission to the Lamanites (cf. section 28).

Thus, at the September conference "Br. David Whitmer [was] appointed to keep the Church records until the next Conference," scheduled for 1 January 1831 (Cannon and Cook, 3). Since no minutes were taken at the January conference (Cannon and Cook, 5), it is not known if he kept the records until this revelation was received in March 1831.

In March 1831, Joseph Smith selected John Whitmer, who had previously served as scribe on part of the Book of Mormon translation as well as on the Prophet's work on the Bible, "to keep the church record" (47:3). Not having sought the office of historian, John recorded, "I was appointed by the voice of the Elders to keep the Church record. Joseph Smith Jr. said unto me You must also keep the Church history. I would rather not do it but observed that the will of the Lord be done, and if he desires it, I desire that he would manifest it through Joseph the Seer" (Whitmer, 24). In answer to Whitmer's request for the Lord's will on the matter, the revelation recorded as section 47 was given to Joseph Smith.

Content overview

In this revelation the Lord directed that John Whitmer "keep a regular history . . . continually" (47:1, 3). He was promised that if he did so, "it shall be given him, inasmuch as he is faithful, by the Comforter, to write these things" (47:4). Accordingly, John Whitmer replaced Oliver Cowdery as historian. Whitmer recorded that Cowdery had "written the commencement of the church history, commencing at the time of the finding of the plates, up to June 12, 1831" (25). Whitmer continued, "From this date I have written the things that I have written, and they are a mere sketch of the things that have transpired, they are however all that seemed to me wisdom to write" (25). His manuscript is 96 pages in length, a few pages of which were written after he was excommunicated. He included the complete text of some revelations but referred to the published versions for others. After Whitmer's disaffection from the Church in March 1838, Joseph Smith asked him for his "notes on the history of the Church" but was denied them (Smith, 171). The manuscript was first published in 1908 by

the reorganized church in its periodical, *Journal of History*. In 1980 Herald House published a new version edited by F. Mark McKiernan and Roger D. Launius.

Joseph Smith, with the aid of several scribes, began dictating the *History of the Church* in 1838, which begins with the origins of the Smith family. It includes all the major events of the Restoration, including the martyrdom and the beginning of the Brigham Young administration. This is the version published by the Church: first serially in the *Times and Seasons* in Nauvoo, the *Millennial Star* in England, and the *Deseret News* in Utah, and then as seven volumes at the beginning of the twentieth century.

BIBLIOGRAPHY

Cannon, Donald Q., and Lyndon W. Cook, eds. *Far West Record: Minutes of The Church of Jesus Christ of Latter-day Saints, 1830–1844.* Salt Lake City: Deseret Book, 1983.

Smith, Joseph. *An American Prophet's Record: The Diaries and Journals of Joseph Smith.* Edited by Scott H. Faulring. Salt Lake City: Signature Books, 1989.

Whitmer, John. "The Book of John Whitmer Kept by Commandment." Ca. 1835–46, Community of Christ Library-Archives, Independence, Mo.

SCE

Historical context and overview of Doctrine and Covenants 48

Historical context

Three months prior to the reception of this revelation on 10 March 1831 (Jensen et al., 130–31), the Lord had directed the Saints in western New York and Pennsylvania to gather to Ohio (37:3). In response to this direction, the Prophet Joseph Smith moved to northeastern Ohio, arriving at Kirtland on 1 February 1831. A week later, he received a revelation "embracing the law of the Church" (42, headnote), including the principles of CONSECRATION and stewardship (42:30–42). By the following month, Joseph and the Saints in Kirtland were preparing for the anticipated influx of Saints from the East. They must have wondered how lands should be secured in order to create stewardships for the newcomers. Furthermore, in September 1830, another revelation indicated that while the location of the city of ZION had not been revealed, it would be "given hereafter"; and it would be "on the borders by the Lamanites" (28:9). *See* Borders of the Lamanites.

Still, the Saints wondered whether Zion was to be built in Ohio or elsewhere. The Prophet recorded: "Upon inquiry how the brethren should act in regard to purchasing lands to settle upon, and where they should finally make a permanent location, I received the following: [D&C 48]" (1:166).

There appears to be an anachronism in verse 6 of this revelation because there was no "presidency" when this revelation was received. Until it was published in the 1835 edition of the Doctrine and Covenants, "presidency and the bishop of the church" read "bishop and the elders of the church." Such adjustments of the revelations by Joseph Smith demonstrate how the Lord revealed his will, "line upon line, [and] precept upon precept" (128:21; cf. 2 Ne. 28:30) as the Church grew in numbers and the organizational structure expanded.

Content overview

The Lord instructed the Saints in Kirtland to make their lands available to their brethren coming from the East and to save money in order to purchase additional land for them (48:2–4). He also indicated that the location of the city (Zion) still had not been revealed, but it would be made known to "certain men" who were to be "appointed" to identify the location of the city and to "purchase the lands, and to make a commencement to lay the foundation of the city" (48:4–6). Those in Kirtland should "remain for the present time in [their] places of abode" (48:1). On 20 July 1831, the Lord finally declared by revelation the site of the city of Zion (57:1–3).

BIBLIOGRAPHY

Jensen, Robin Scott, Robert J. Woodford, and Steven C. Harper, eds. *Manuscript Revelation Books*. Facsimile edition. First volume of the Revelations and Translations series of *The Joseph Smith Papers,* edited by Dean C. Jessee, Ronald K. Esplin, and Richard Lyman Bushman. Salt Lake City: Church Historian's Press, 2009.

Smith, Joseph. *History of The Church of Jesus Christ of Latter-day Saints.* Edited by B. H. Roberts. 7 vols. 2d ed. rev. Salt Lake City: The Church of Jesus Christ of Latter-day Saints, 1932–51.

ROC

Historical context and overview of Doctrine and Covenants 49

Historical context

North Union, not far from Kirtland, Ohio, was home to a religious group: The United Society of Believers in Christ's Second Appearing, also known as the SHAKERS.

In the fall of 1830 Oliver Cowdery and a few other elders visited North Union, told the Shakers of the coming forth of the Book of Mormon and of Cowdery's role in translating it, and left several copies of the book with them. Most rejected the missionaries' message, but sometime later one of their number, Leman Copley, accepted the gospel. He was baptized and ordained an elder by March 1831.

After his conversion Copley was eager to take the gospel to his Shaker friends. Though apparently honest in heart, he still believed that the Shakers were right in some aspects of their faith. Accordingly, the Prophet inquired of the Lord "in order to have more perfect understanding on the subject" and received the revelation known as section 49 (Smith, 1:167).

The manuscript of this revelation dates it 7 May 1831 (Jensen et al., 132–33).

Content overview

The revelation called Sidney Rigdon, Parley P. Pratt, and Leman Copley to take the gospel to the Shakers, who, it said, "desire to know the truth in part, but not all, for they are not right before me" (49:2). Elders Rigdon and Copley arrived in North Union on a Saturday night and met with Ashbell Kitchell, organizer and first elder of the Shaker Community in North Union, who recorded the story in his journal. The missionaries spent the evening talking with Kitchell, who was completely nonresponsive. He thought the life of self-denial led by the Shakers was more in tune with the life of Christ than what he saw in Mormonism. He concluded, in fact, that Copley had left the Shakers only because he saw Mormonism as an "easier plan" than the Shaker practice of celibacy, which they referred to as "the cross" ("Mormon Interview," 96–97).

The next morning, Sunday, Parley P. Pratt arrived and the three missionaries attended a Shaker worship service. At the end of the meeting Rigdon received permission to deliver a message, whereupon he read section 49 to the congregation and then asked for a response. The people completely rejected the message. Pratt then spoke, somewhat emotionally, and then returned to Kirtland early in the day. Rigdon remained until evening, carrying on a warm and friendly dialogue, and Copley spent another night in North Union after receiving a strong rebuke from Ashbel Kitchell for abandoning the Shakers.

Section 49 is one of those revelations that, at least in part, confirmed for others certain principles that Joseph Smith was already well aware of. It was intended specifically to inform Leman Copley and others of certain Shaker doctrines that were incorrect. It begins by calling Elders Rigdon, Pratt, and Copley on their mission to the Shakers (49:1–4). Since the Shakers believed that the second coming of Christ "had already occurred and that he had appeared in the form of a woman, Ann Lee" (49, headnote), the Lord assured these men that Christ was the Only Begotten and that he was yet to return to the earth, although "the hour and the day no man knoweth" (49:5–11). See Lee, Ann.

Additional corrections of errant Shaker beliefs included the need for repentance, baptism, and the laying on of hands to receive the gift of the Holy Ghost; that marriage, rather than the practice of celibacy, was ordained of God; that eating meat should not be prohibited; and that "the Son of Man cometh not in the form of a woman" (49:12–22). The Lord assured them that before the coming of the "great day of the Lord," the "Lamanites shall blossom as the rose" and "Zion shall flourish" (49:23–25).

In conclusion, the Lord promised the missionaries that he would be with them in their work (49:26–28). None of the Shakers accepted the gospel message.

BIBLIOGRAPHY

"A Mormon Interview. Copied from Brother Ashbel Kitchell's Pocket Journal.—(By E.D.B.) [Elisha D. Blakeman]." *BYU Studies* 20 (Fall 1979): 95–99.

Jensen, Robin Scott, Robert J. Woodford, and Steven C.

Harper, eds. *Manuscript Revelation Books.* Facsimile edition. First volume of the Revelations and Translations series of *The Joseph Smith Papers*, edited by Dean C. Jessee, Ronald K. Esplin, and Richard Lyman Bushman. Salt Lake City: Church Historian's Press, 2009.

Smith, Joseph. *History of The Church of Jesus Christ of Latter-day Saints.* Edited by B. H. Roberts. 7 vols. 2d ed. rev. Salt Lake City: The Church of Jesus Christ of Latter-day Saints, 1932–51.

JBA

Historical context and overview of Doctrine and Covenants 50

Historical context

Parley P. Pratt reported in his autobiography that in the spring of 1831 "as I went forth among the different branches . . . some very strange spiritual operations were manifested, which were disgusting rather than edifying" (in Smith 1:170n). He described some of them as "very strange." "Some persons would seem to swoon away, and make unseemly gestures, and be drawn or disfigured in their countenances. Others would fall into ecstacies, and be drawn into contortions, cramp, fits, etc. Others would seem to have visions and revelations, which were not edifying," because they were out of harmony with the truths of the gospel. "In short," he concluded, "a false and lying spirit seemed to be creeping into the Church" (Pratt, 61–62). Elder Pratt and others asked Joseph Smith "to inquire of the Lord concerning these spirits or manifestations" so they would not "err in judgment" (Pratt, 61–62).

Content overview

In this revelation the Lord instructed Joseph Wakefield and Parley P. Pratt to "go forth among the churches and strengthen them by the word of exhortation" (50:37). Pratt recorded: "In obedience to the foregoing, Joseph Wakefield and myself visited the several branches of the Church, rebuking the wrong spirits which had crept in among them, setting in order things that were wanting" (65–66). After acknowledging that there were many false and deceiving spirits in the world and hypocrites in the Church (50:2, 6–9), the Lord reminded the elders that they had been called to "preach my gospel by the Spirit, even the Comforter" and that attempting to do so in any other way "is not of God" (50:13–18). Those who teach and those who listen by the Spirit "understand one another, and both are edified and rejoice together." Those who are edified receive increasing light, "and that light groweth brighter and brighter until the perfect day." The Lord reminded them: "that which doth not edify is not of God, and is darkness," and he admonished them to "chase darkness from among you" (50:19–25). *See* Edify, edification.

He promised worthy priesthood holders power to discern by the HOLY GHOST whether or not spiritual manifestations were from God, and if they were not, to rebuke them (50:26–27, 31–32). They were also counseled to avoid abrasive confrontations or boasting (50:33). In connection with these things the Lord held out the possibility that one could become "purified and cleansed from all sin" and that when this has been accomplished, "ye shall ask whatsoever you will in the name of Jesus and it shall be done" (50:28–29).

Even though Jesus likened his servants to little children who needed to grow, he assured them: "You are of them that my Father hath given me; and none of them that my Father hath given me shall be lost" (50:41–42). Rather, they would be united with him, the "good shepherd, and the stone of Israel," even as he is one with the Father (50:43–44).

See also Historical context and overview of Doctrine and Covenants 129 (p. 843).

BIBLIOGRAPHY

Pratt, Parley P. *Autobiography of Parley P. Pratt.* Edited by Parley P. Pratt Jr. Salt Lake City: Deseret Book, 1966.

Smith, Joseph. *History of The Church of Jesus Christ of Latter-day Saints.* Edited by B. H. Roberts. 7 vols. 2d ed. rev. Salt Lake City: The Church of Jesus Christ of Latter-day Saints, 1932–51.

ROC

41 ^aFear not, little ^bchildren, for you are mine, and I have ^covercome the world, and you are of them that my Father hath ^dgiven me;

Doctrine and Covenants 50:41.

Historical context and overview of Doctrine and Covenants 51

Historical context

In February 1831 the Lord directed the bishop to receive consecrations of properties and to provide stewardships for worthy members of the Church (42:32–33). The following month he instructed the Saints at Kirtland to share their lands with those members who would soon begin arriving from New York (48:2–3). By May members of the branch from Colesville had arrived at Fairport, Ohio, and were directed to settle collectively in nearby Thompson on land consecrated for that purpose by Leman Copley (54, headnote). Edward Partridge, the Church's bishop, requested that the Prophet Joseph Smith ask the Lord for further instructions.

Content overview

The Lord instructed Bishop Partridge to assign stewardships to "every man equal according to his family, according to his circumstances and his wants and needs" (51:3). *See* Consecration.

The bishop was to appoint ownership of these stewardships by legal deed. If the individual should apostatize, he could retain his stewardship that was legally deeded to him but would have no claim on any additional property originally consecrated (51:4–5). Conversely, people who were faithful in their stewardships were promised "the joy of [their] Lord" and "eternal life" (51:19). Bishop Partridge was also to appoint an agent to receive money with which he would supply food and clothing to the needy (51:8). The following month, Algernon Sidney Gilbert was called to be this agent (53).

The Lord commanded that each branch of the Church be economically independent from other Church branches and instructed them that the property of one branch was not to be given to another without proper financial arrangements (51:10–11). Furthermore, the Lord reiterated the command that the bishop have a storehouse for the present and future needs of the people (42:34; 51:13). Because the bishop's assignment would essentially demand his full time, his family was to receive their support from this storehouse (51:14). Finally, the Lord consecrated Kirtland as the Saints' inheritance "for a little season"; however, the Saints were to establish themselves as if they would be there "for years" (51:16–17). Thus, the Lord stated: "I grant unto this people a privilege of organizing themselves according to my laws" (51:15).

ROC

Historical context and overview of Doctrine and Covenants 52

Historical context

In February 1831 the Lord had declared that it was "expedient" that the elders who were preaching the gospel convene in a conference. The Lord promised: "I will pour out my Spirit upon them in the day that they assemble themselves together" (44:1–2). This conference convened in Kirtland on 9 April 1831. After transacting the business of the meeting, they "adjourned until the first Saturday in June next" (*FWR*, 3). Few of the elders from New York were in Kirtland for the April meeting, but by 4 June, the first Saturday in June, a substantially greater number were able to attend. The conference actually began on 3 June, and Parley P. Pratt, one of those in attendance, recorded that Joseph Smith "spake in great power, as he was moved by the Holy Ghost; and the spirit of power and of testimony rested down upon the Elders in a marvelous manner" (68). According to John Whitmer, among other things Joseph "prophesied that John the Revelator was then among the ten tribes of Israel" (27). Whitmer added: "Joseph Smith, Jr., prophesied the day previous that the man of sin should be revealed. While the Lord poured out his spirit upon his servants, the devil took a notion, to make known his power, he bound Harvey Whitlock and John Murdock so that they could not speak, and others were affected but the Lord showed to Joseph the Seer, the design of the thing, he commanded the devil in the name of Christ and he departed to our joy and comfort" (28–29).

Of great significance during this three-day conference was that brethren were ordained to the office of HIGH PRIEST for the first time in this dispensation. Joseph Smith commented that "great harmony prevailed" (1:176). At the conclusion of this conference, the revelation recorded in section 52 was received, in which the Lord gave directions to the elders on "what to do" (Whitmer, 29). The earliest manuscript of this revelation dates it 6 June 1831 (Jensen et al., 147). Joseph Smith later wrote that he received this revelation "by an heavenly vision" (*MA*, 179).

Content overview

The Lord directed that the next conference be held in Missouri, where, if Joseph Smith and Sidney Rigdon were faithful, the land of the elders' inheritance would "be made known unto them" (52:1–5, 42). Their destination was Independence, Missouri, where Oliver Cowdery and other missionaries to the Lamanites awaited them. Joseph Smith and those traveling with him were to go directly to Independence, but the other elders were to go "preaching the word by the way" (52:3–10, 22–32, 41–42). Specifically, the Lord instructed the elders to go "two by two" in companionships designated in the revelation and to preach "none other things than that which the prophets and apostles have written, and that which is taught them by the Comforter through the prayer of faith" (52:9–10). The Lord revealed a "pattern" by which the elders could avoid deception: those who were "contrite" and professed spiritual gifts were acceptable before God only if they "obey mine ordinances [commandments and laws]" and "bring forth fruits of praise and wisdom, according to the revelations and truths which I have given you" (52:14–19). In this missionary journey the elders were not to "build upon another's foundation, neither journey in another's track" (52:33).

In addition to those going to Missouri, Joseph Wakefield and Solomon Humphrey were directed to preach in the "eastern lands" (52:35). "The residue of the elders" were to "labor with their own hands," "watch over" the branches, and preach "in the regions round about them" (52:39–40).

BIBLIOGRAPHY

Far West Record. Church History Library, The Church of Jesus Christ of Latter-day Saints, Salt Lake City, Utah.

Jensen, Robin Scott, Robert J. Woodford, and Steven C. Harper, eds. *Manuscript Revelation Books*. Facsimile edition. First volume of the Revelations and Translations series of *The Joseph Smith Papers*, edited by Dean C. Jessee, Ronald K. Esplin, and Richard Lyman

Bushman. Salt Lake City: Church Historian's Press, 2009.

Messenger and Advocate 1 (October 1834–September 1835).

Pratt, Parley P. *Autobiography of Parley P. Pratt.* Edited by Parley P. Pratt Jr. Salt Lake City: Deseret Book, 1966.

Smith, Joseph. *History of The Church of Jesus Christ of Latter-day Saints.* Edited by B. H. Roberts. 7 vols. 2d ed. rev. Salt Lake City: The Church of Jesus Christ of Latter-day Saints, 1932–51.

Whitmer, John. "The Book of John Whitmer Kept by Commandment." Ca. 1835–46, Community of Christ Library-Archives, Independence, Missouri.

ROC

Historical context and overview of Doctrine and Covenants 53

Historical context

Recent convert and Kirtland citizen, Algernon Sidney Gilbert came to Joseph Smith requesting to know what the Lord would have him do as a member of the Church. On 8 June 1831 Joseph Smith received this revelation (Jensen et al., 151) in which the Lord called Gilbert to specific duties.

Content overview

The Lord counseled Gilbert to "forsake the world," be ordained an elder, and accept a calling "to be an agent unto this church" (53:1–4). In May 1831 the Lord had directed that an agent be appointed to assist Bishop Edward Partridge in handling the Church's consecrated funds (51:8). In this revelation, Algernon Sidney Gilbert, a business partner of Newel K. Whitney with extensive commercial experience, was called to that position (53:4). Although there is some discrepancy in early records, it appears that Gilbert was ordained an elder by Joseph Smith about eight days after this revelation was received.

During a conference held in Kirtland beginning 3 June 1831, Joseph Smith and others were directed to go to Missouri (52). In this revelation, Gilbert was now instructed to accompany them (53:5). In Missouri a later revelation reaffirmed Gilbert's appointment as agent and specifically instructed him to establish a store in Missouri (57:6–8); as a result, the Gilbert and

Whitney store was organized in Independence. *See* Gilbert and Whitney store in Kirtland, Ohio.

BIBLIOGRAPHY

Jensen, Robin Scott, Robert J. Woodford, and Steven C. Harper, eds. *Manuscript Revelation Books.* Facsimile edition. First volume of the Revelations and Translations series of *The Joseph Smith Papers,* edited by Dean C. Jessee, Ronald K. Esplin, and Richard Lyman Bushman. Salt Lake City: Church Historian's Press, 2009.

ROC

Historical context and overview of Doctrine and Covenants 54

Historical context

The Saints from Colesville, New York, arrived at Thompson, Ohio, in the spring of 1831, where they received stewardships of property. They settled and made improvements on land that Leman Copley had consecrated for that purpose. At the urging of Copley, a former member of the United Society of Believers in Christ's Second Appearing (SHAKERS), missionaries were sent to a nearby community of that church (49). When this mission failed, Copley's faith wavered, and he evicted the Colesville Saints from his land. Somewhat divided and wondering what to do next, the evicted Saints sent their leader, Newel Knight, to seek guidance from Joseph Smith. The Prophet inquired of the Lord and received the revelation in section 54.

Content overview

The Lord directed Newel Knight to "stand fast" in his calling as their leader and admonished the Colesville Saints at Thompson to "repent . . . and become truly humble before me and contrite" (54:2–3). The Lord noted that their covenant of consecration was "void and of none effect" and that those responsible for its being broken would be held accountable, while those who had attempted to honor it would be "blessed" (54:4–6). He instructed the Saints to "flee the land" in Ohio and journey to Missouri, there to "seek ye a living like unto men" until the Lord prepared "a place for you," presumably under the law of CONSECRATION (54:7–9). The Lord told them to be "patient in tribulation," promising that those who seek him "early shall find rest to their souls" (54:10).

ROC

Historical context and overview of Doctrine and Covenants 55

Historical context

William Wines Phelps had purchased a copy of the Book of Mormon from Parley P. Pratt in the spring of 1830 and met Joseph Smith in December of that year (Black, 223; Cook, 87). In June 1831 Phelps, an editor and printer from Canandaigua, New York, moved to Kirtland, Ohio; it was his desire "to do the will of the Lord" (Smith, 1:184–85), and he hoped Joseph would receive a revelation on his behalf. "The Prophet sought the Lord for information concerning him," and received the revelation contained in section 55 in June 1831 (55, headnote). Shortly after he received this revelation he was baptized, ordained an elder, and traveled with Joseph to Missouri.

Content overview

In this revelation, the Lord informed Phelps that he was "called and chosen," and that after his baptism he would receive a remission of his sins, receive the Holy Ghost, and become an elder in the Church. This would enable him to preach repentance to others (55:1–2), and also empower him to bestow the "Holy Spirit" on the "contrite" (55:2–3). The Lord also told Phelps to assist Oliver Cowdery with selecting, writing,

Courtesy Alex L. Baugh

Leman Copley's farm in Thompson, Ohio. Following Copley's disappointing mission to a nearby Shaker community, division erupted about his consecrated farm. In response to Newel Knight's questions about the matter, the Lord revealed: "As the covenant which they made unto me has been broken, even so it has become void and of none effect. And wo to him by whom this offense cometh, for it had been better for him that he had been drowned in the depth of the sea. But blessed are they who have kept the covenant and observed the commandment, for they shall obtain mercy" (D&C 54:4–6).

and printing books for the schools of the Church (55:4), a calling which required Phelps and his family to move to Missouri (55:5). The Lord also instructed Joseph Coe, a convert from New York, to travel with Joseph Smith, Sidney Rigdon, and W. W. Phelps to Missouri (55:6). They subsequently left on 19 June 1831 (Smith, 1:356).

BIBLIOGRAPHY

Black, Susan Easton. *Who's Who in the Doctrine and Covenants.* Salt Lake City: Deseret Book, 1997.

Cook, Lyndon W. *The Revelations of the Prophet Joseph Smith.* Salt Lake City: Deseret Book, 1985.

Smith, Joseph. *The Papers of Joseph Smith.* Edited by Dean C. Jessee. 2 vols. Salt Lake City: Deseret Book, 1989–92.

MOR

Historical context and overview of Doctrine and Covenants 56

Historical context

In early June 1831, Thomas B. Marsh and Ezra Thayre were called to Missouri to preach the word (52:22). Before the missionary companions could leave for Missouri, however, Ezra Thayre demanded reimbursement for money he had consecrated in exchange for land on Frederick G. Williams's farm. Thayre was vexed by the circumstances and refused to fulfill his missionary call until the problem was resolved. As a result, Thomas B. Marsh, who was ready to leave for Missouri, visited Joseph Smith, seeking guidance and direction (Smith, 1:186–87). The earliest manuscript of this revelation dates it 15 June 1831 (Jensen et al., 155–56).

Content overview

The Lord expressed great displeasure with the rebellious and those who fail to "take up [the] cross," warning that they will be cut off in due time (56:1–3). The Lord emphasized that he has the power to "command and revoke, as it seemeth [him] good" (56:4). Therefore, considering Ezra Thayre's and the Saints' disobedience in Thompson, Ohio, the Lord revoked some previous callings and made new arrangements. Among other changes, he revoked Ezra Thayre's call to be companions with Thomas B. Marsh and commanded that Selah J. Griffin take his place (56:5–6). Griffin had been assigned

as a companion to Newel Knight, who could no longer travel with him because of difficulties in the branch at Thompson, Ohio (54). Ezra Thayre was further chastised and called to repent of his pride and selfishness. He was also warned that if he persisted with his demands for remuneration, he would receive the money, but he would be cut off from the Church (56:8–10).

While Ezra Thayre was the focus of this revelation, the Lord told the Saints in general that they have "many things to do and to repent of." They were chastised because they sought "to counsel in [their] own ways," "obey not the truth," and "have pleasure in unrighteousness" (56:14–15). The Lord pronounced a "wo" upon the selfish rich for not sharing with the poor. While they may have great possessions, their riches would ultimately canker their souls. He also condemned the lazy poor because they "will not labor with [their] own hands" but lust after other men's possessions (56:16–17). On the other hand, however, "the poor who are pure in heart, whose hearts are broken, and whose spirits are contrite," he promised, "shall inherit the earth . . . forever and ever" (56:18–20).

BIBLIOGRAPHY

Jensen, Robin Scott, Robert J. Woodford, and Steven C. Harper, eds. *Manuscript Revelation Books.* Facsimile edition. First volume of the Revelations and Translations series of *The Joseph Smith Papers,* edited by Dean C. Jessee, Ronald K. Esplin, and Richard Lyman Bushman. Salt Lake City: Church Historian's Press, 2009.

Smith, Joseph. *History of The Church of Jesus Christ of Latter-day Saints.* Edited by B. H. Roberts. 7 vols. 2d ed. rev. Salt Lake City: The Church of Jesus Christ of Latter-day Saints, 1932–51.

MOR

Historical context and overview of Doctrine and Covenants 57

Historical context

Obedient to the commandment of the Lord to hold the next conference of the Church in Missouri, Joseph Smith and those traveling with him left Kirtland on 19 June 1831 and arrived at Independence, Jackson County, Missouri, "about the middle of July" (Smith, 1:188). There Joseph Smith united once again with Oliver Cowdery, Peter Whitmer Jr., and Ziba Peterson, who had come to Independence the previous January as missionaries to the LAMANITES and to find the site for the gathering to ZION. Parley P. Pratt, the fourth missionary, had been sent by the other missionaries to report their progress to the Prophet and had arrived in Kirtland about the beginning of March. On 20 July 1831 the Prophet lifted his voice in prayer, asking, "When will the wilderness blossom as the rose? When will Zion be built up in her glory, and where will Thy temple stand, unto which all nations shall come in the last days?" (Smith, 1:189). In answer to his prayer, the Lord gave this revelation unveiling the site of the latter-day Zion.

In earlier scriptures, the Lord revealed only partial information concerning the location of the city of Zion, the NEW JERUSALEM. For example, members of the Church had read in the Book of Mormon about the "New Jerusalem" which would be located in America (3 Ne. 20:22; 21:23–24; Ether 13:2–10). In September 1830, the Lord had revealed to the Saints that the city of Zion would "be on the borders by the Lamanites" (28:9). On 9 February 1831 the Lord informed them that when the time was right, they would be told where the New Jerusalem would be built (42:62). During the following month, the Lord announced he would reveal the location after the Saints from New York arrived in Ohio (48:4–5). In early June 1831, he commanded that the next conference of the Church be "held in Missouri, upon the land which I will consecrate unto my people" (52:2).

John Whitmer attached the following notation to the manuscript of this revelation at the time the Book of Commandments was being typeset: "[Not to be printed at present]" (Jensen et al., 158). Hence, this revelation was not included in the Book of Commandments but was first published in the 1835 edition of the Doctrine and Covenants.

Content overview

The Lord revealed that Missouri is "the place for the city of Zion" and that Independence, Missouri, is the "center place" where the temple will be built (57:1–3). He instructed members of the Church to buy land there (57:4–5), which

the United States government made available at $1.25 per acre for unsettled property (Parkin, 7).

Further, the Lord gave specific commandments to Sidney Gilbert, Edward Partridge, William W. Phelps, and Oliver Cowdery. He appointed Sidney Gilbert as Church agent to receive money from contributors to purchase land (57:6). Bishop Edward Partridge, the first bishop to the Church (41:9), was commanded to divide the purchased land among the gathering Saints as "their inheritance" (57:7). The Lord further instructed Brother Gilbert, a skilled businessman and merchant, to establish a store so that he could "sell goods without fraud" (57:8). This store was to be a commercial enterprise as well as a local storehouse under the law of CONSECRATION. Also, Sidney Gilbert was instructed to obtain a license to do business according to the laws of the land (57:9).

William W. Phelps, a printer by trade, was instructed to establish a printing business, with Oliver Cowdery assisting him (57:11–13). This counsel superseded earlier instructions that he was to assist Oliver Cowdery (55:4). It took almost a year before he was able to begin operations, but in June 1832 he began publishing a monthly newspaper for the members of the Church in Missouri, *The Evening and the Morning Star*. At the same time he published a weekly community newspaper called the *Upper Missouri Advertiser*. Because the Mormon press was located "about 120 miles west of any press in the state" (*EMS*, 6), the *Advertiser* was the sole locally published source of news. Phelps also helped prepare revelations for printing the Book of Commandments and published some of them in *The Evening and the Morning Star*.

The Lord concluded section 57 by emphasizing the importance of "the bishop," Edward Partridge, and "the agent," A. Sidney Gilbert, making preparations for others to come to Zion (57:14–16).

BIBLIOGRAPHY

The Evening and the Morning Star 1 (June 1832): 6.

Jensen, Robin Scott, Robert J. Woodford, and Steven C. Harper, eds. *Manuscript Revelation Books*. Facsimile edition. First volume of the Revelations and Translations series of *The Joseph Smith Papers,* edited by Dean C. Jessee, Ronald K. Esplin, and Richard Lyman

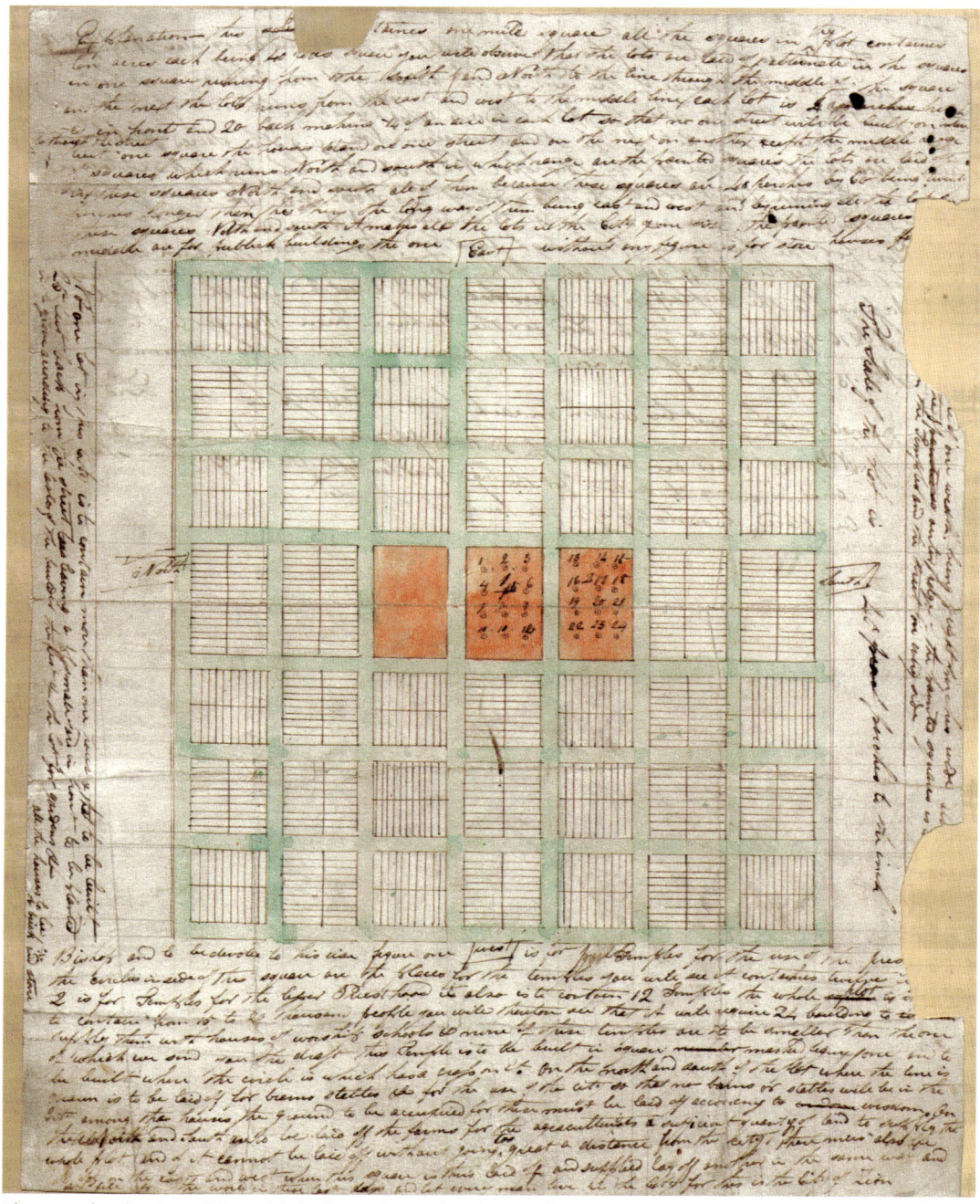

Plat map for the City of Zion, likely drawn by Frederick G. Williams, sent by Joseph Smith to Church leaders in Missouri in June 1833. The design contains large city blocks, divided into lots, with twenty-four temple structures at the city's center. Concerning the location of Zion, the Lord revealed, "Behold, the place which is now called Independence is the center place; and a spot for the temple is lying westward, upon a lot which is not far from the courthouse" (D&C 57:3).

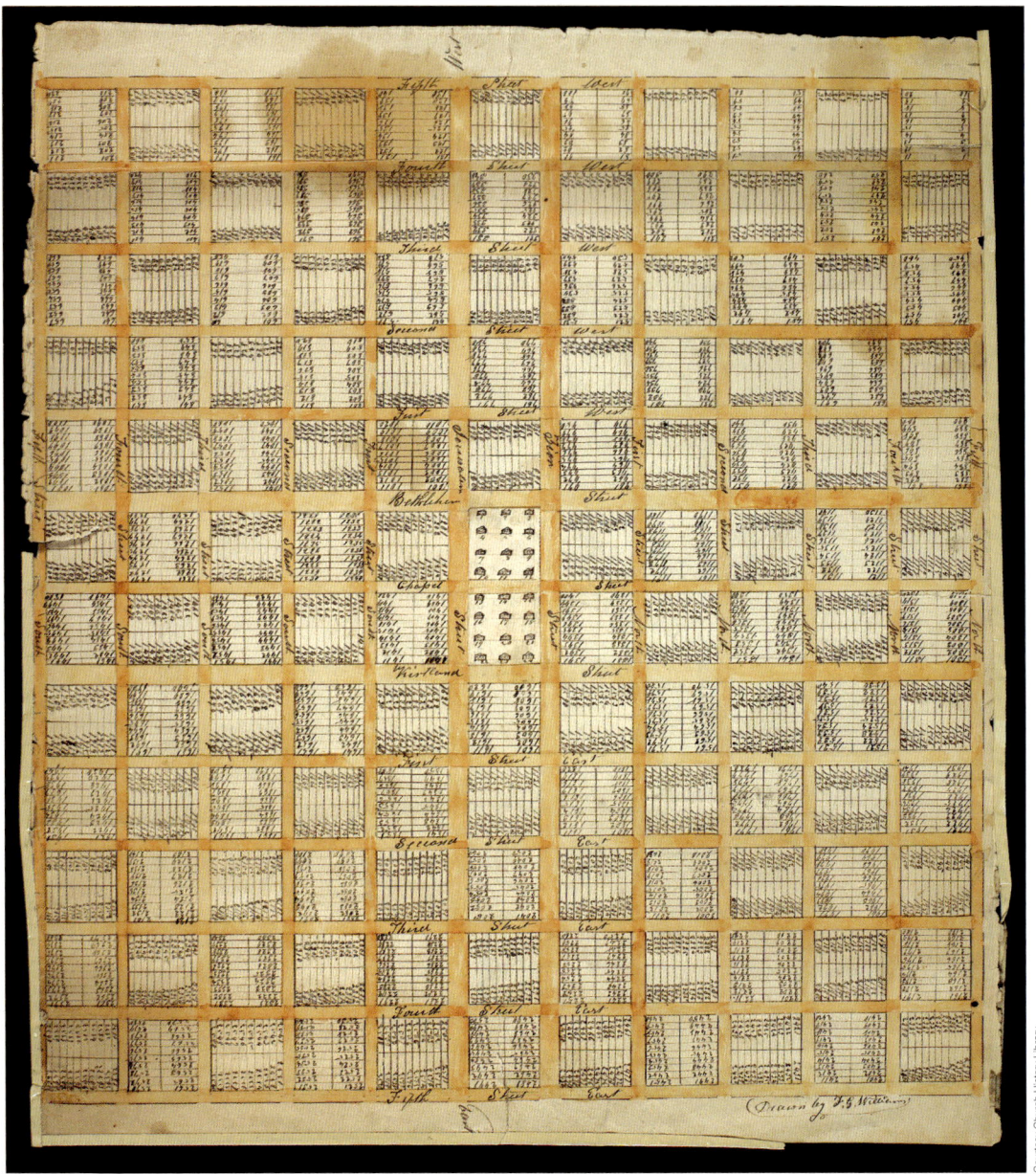

Revised plat map for the City of Zion drawn by Frederick G. Williams and sent to Church leaders in Missouri in August 1833. Prominent additions to the earlier map include the expansion of blocks, the naming of streets, and the numbering of lots. Twenty-four structures continue to dominate the center of the city.

Bushman. Salt Lake City: Church Historian's Press, 2009.

Parkin, Max. *Missouri*. Vol. 4 of *Sacred Places: A Comprehensive Guide to Early LDS Historical Sites*, edited by LaMar C. Berrett. Salt Lake City: Deseret Book, 2004.

Smith, Joseph. *History of The Church of Jesus Christ of Latter-day Saints*. Edited by B. H. Roberts. 7 vols. 2d ed. rev. Salt Lake City: The Church of Jesus Christ of Latter-day Saints, 1932–51.

DJR

Historical context and overview of Doctrine and Covenants 58

Historical context

In June 1831 the Lord commanded that the next conference of the Church should be held in Missouri (52:2). Already on the site at Independence, Jackson County, were the three missionaries to the LAMANITES named in section 32, given in October 1830: Oliver Cowdery, Peter Whitmer Jr., and Ziba Peterson (cf. 28:8; 30:5; and 32), as well as Fredrick G. Williams, who joined them in this missionary effort after he was baptized and ordained an elder in November 1830. Those traveling to Missouri that summer went in three groups: (1) Joseph Smith and those traveling with him (cf. 52:3, 24; 53:5; 55:5–6), who arrived about the middle of July; (2) more than two dozen elders, who traveled by different routes and preached along the way (52) and arrived at various times in July and August; and (3) about sixty members of the Church originally from Colesville, New York, who had most recently been residing in Thompson, Ohio (54:8), arrived during the last week of July. On 1 August 1831, those who had already arrived in Jackson County, Missouri, were eager to learn more about the gathering place for the Lord's people. *See* Gather, gathering.

Content overview

The Lord's opening remarks in this revelation included a solemn and prophetic warning to those Saints gathered in Missouri concerning the "tribulation" they would suffer before they experienced "the glory which shall follow" (58:1–5). Also prophetic was his statement that they were honored in only "laying the foundation" of ZION, to which his people, in a great future day, would

gather. He would then come and "partake of the supper of the Lord" with them (58:6–12). *See* Marriage of the Lamb.

The Lord then turned to matters of immediate concern. First, he taught Bishop Edward Partridge and his counselors their duties as administrators of the law of CONSECRATION in Zion (58:13–18). In a very forthright manner, he directed the members of the Church to keep his law "on this land" and to obey "the laws of the land, for he that keepeth the laws of God hath no need to break the laws of the land" (58:19–23). In remarks directed to Edward Partridge, which he also addressed to all members of the Church, the Lord taught that men should use the agency which he had given them to bring about much good (58:24–29). He also censured those who do not obey his commandments and then claim "this is not the work of the Lord, for his promises are not fulfilled" (58:30–33). He counseled Martin Harris and William W. Phelps to repent, and he also declared that "if a man repenteth of his sins—behold, he will confess them and forsake them" (58:34–43). The Lord then gave counsel on various matters related to the Saints purchasing their inheritance in Missouri, including a commandment that Sidney Rigdon write a description of the land to be read to the congregations in Ohio, urging them to send money to Bishop Partridge to purchase land, and for Rigdon to dedicate the land and the temple site (58:44–57).

The Saints had been obedient to the instructions to hold the next conference of the Church in Missouri (52:2), and the Lord now directed them to make further decisions concerning Zion. He also told them to hold a second conference when the rest of the elders who were preaching the gospel on the way had arrived (58:58–63). The revelation closed with a call for "the sound" to "go forth from this place," that the gospel "be preached unto every creature" (58:64–65).

DJR

Historical context and overview of Doctrine and Covenants 59

Historical context

Two previous revelations had given the location of the latter-day ZION as Independence,

Missouri, and the mechanics of laying "the foundation" of the city (57; 58). Now the Lord revealed the standard of moral conduct he expected of his people in Zion, with emphasis on keeping the SABBATH holy, fasting, and praying. This revelation was received on the Sabbath, 7 August 1831, and tacitly addressed the lack of Sabbath observance among people on the frontier. A missionary located in Independence for both the Presbyterian and the Congregational faiths reported: "Christian Sabbath observance here appears to be unknown. It is a day for merchandising, jollity, drinking, gambling, and general anti-Christian conduct. When the Santa Fe wagon trains return here, or pass through on their way eastward, there is a multiplication of sin beyond the usual amount. There appears to be an over abundance of females here practicing the world's oldest profession. . . . Gouging and more serious forms of violence are common. The sheriff has little support from the populace, except to prevent burglars breaking into the merchants' shops. He confided to me that the citizens do not care to have the lawless punished" (Lyon, 16). This revelation set a standard for the members of the Church that, to even a casual observer, set them apart from their neighbors.

Content overview

The Lord blessed those who had traveled to Missouri "with an eye single" to his glory. These blessings included being "crowned with blessings from above, yea, and with commandments not a few, and with revelations in their time—they that are faithful and diligent before me" (59:1–4). The Lord then reiterated some of the fundamental commandments, including the two great commandments in the law: to love and serve the Lord and to love one's neighbor as oneself. Moreover, "thou shalt not steal . . . commit adultery, nor kill" (59:5–8; cf. Matt.

> 6 Thou shalt *a*love thy *b*neighbor as thyself. Thou shalt not *c*steal; neither commit *d*adultery, nor *e*kill, ==nor do anything *f*like unto it.==

Doctrine and Covenants 59:6.

22:36–40). He emphasized the importance of proper Sabbath observance, "that thou mayest more fully keep thyself unspotted from the world," and detailed the temporal and spiritual blessings for those who keep the Sabbath holy (59:9–20). The revelation ended with the wonderful promise: "But learn that he who doeth the works of righteousness shall receive his reward, even peace in this world, and eternal life in the world to come" (59:23).

BIBLIOGRAPHY

Lyon, T. Edgar. "Independence, Missouri, and the Mormons, 1827–1833." *BYU Studies* 13, no. 1 (Autumn 1972): 10–19.

DJR

Historical context and overview of Doctrine and Covenants 60

Historical context

Within a month after arriving in Zion, Jackson County, Missouri, from Kirtland, Ohio, Joseph Smith and several elders were preparing to return to the Kirtland area, as commanded by the Lord (58:46, 58, 63). They had dedicated the land of Zion for the eventual gathering of the Lord's people, dedicated the temple site, and established a foundation for gathering as instructed in sections 57 and 58. They desired instruction from the Lord for their return journey to Kirtland, including the route and means of travel.

In section 52, some twenty-four of these men were called to travel to Missouri, taking different routes and preaching the gospel on the way. At the time this revelation was received, not all of the elders had arrived. Those who had taken the most direct routes and those who had done the least preaching were the first to arrive at Independence. In this revelation the Lord chastised those who had been lax in preaching the gospel on their way to Missouri. He also gave counsel for those elders who had not yet arrived.

Content overview

In answer to their supplication, the Lord confirmed that they were to return "speedily" to Kirtland but not so fast that they failed to preach the gospel along the way (60:1–4). At that time travel between Independence and

St. Louis could be accomplished on land, the Missouri River, or a combination of the two. The Lord instructed those journeying on the river: "Let there be a craft made, or bought, as seemeth you good" (60:5). Several, including Joseph Smith, chose to travel by canoe. The Lord then told Joseph Smith, Oliver Cowdery, and Sidney Rigdon that after they arrived in St. Louis they were to go directly to Cincinnati, where they were to preach the gospel (60:6–7). The "superhighway" to Cincinnati took them by boat down the Mississippi River to the confluence of the Ohio River and then up the Ohio River to Cincinnati. The remaining elders were to travel overland, two by two, preaching the gospel (60:8–9). Next, the Lord directed Edward Partridge and agent A. Sidney Gilbert to make a distribution of resources to enable the elders to return home (60:10–11; cf. 57:6–8). The Lord then concluded the revelation with counsel to those elders who were yet on their way to Independence (60:12–17). "Congregations of the wicked" (60:8, 13) in this revelation refers to those who have yet to receive the gospel and have their sins remitted (84:49–53).

DJR

Historical context and overview of Doctrine and Covenants 61

Historical context

After obeying the Lord's command to journey to Missouri from Kirtland, Ohio (52) and learning that the center place for the city of Zion is Independence, Missouri (57), Joseph Smith and several elders began the return journey to Kirtland, as commanded by the Lord (58:46, 58, 63). On 9 August 1831, Joseph and ten elders started down the Missouri River in canoes, and on the third day of their journey, they encountered "many of the dangers so common upon the western waters" (Smith, *History,* 1:203). Ezra Booth, who was one of the elders, recorded a detailed account of the event. The canoe in which Joseph Smith was riding "ran foul of a sawyer, and [was] in danger of upsetting" (Booth, 1; a sawyer was a half-submerged tree or log that had fallen into the river and was a hazard even to large paddle wheel boats navigating the river). Booth also reported dissensions and arguments

among the men. Brigham H. Roberts wrote: "During the three days upon the river some disagreements and ill feeling had developed among the brethren and explanations and reconciliations had become necessary" (1:262–63). Having survived a harrowing day on the river, they camped on the banks of the Missouri River at a place called McIlwaine's Bend. *See* McIlwaine's Bend, Missouri River.

The Prophet recorded that "Brother Phelps, in open vision by daylight, saw the destroyer in his most horrible power, ride upon the face of the waters; others heard the noise, but saw not the vision" (Smith, *History,* 1:203). The next morning, 12 August 1831, Joseph Smith received this revelation. Section 61 contains much that is specific to certain rivers and the travel of the Saints in Joseph Smith's day, as well as some general prophecy regarding WATER and land in the present day.

A major theme of this revelation is that "there are many dangers upon the waters" (61:4). Besides wrecked or sunken boats and drowning, there was cholera and dysentery, which afflicted many on the rivers in the early 1830s. In an editorial the following year in *The Evening and the Morning Star,* entitled "THE WAY OF JOURNEYING FOR THE SAINTS OF THE CHURCH OF CHRIST," the editor wrote: "FEELING a great anxiety for the welfare of the disciples . . . , it is thought proper to give some instruction upon the subject of journeying to the land of Zion. Fulfilling the commandment [section 61], and experience, have already shown, that, to come by land, especially from the state of Ohio, and this side, is the safest, and generally the quickest, and cheapest. Besides the saving of time and money, you save risks and many dangers: Firstly, of disasters upon the waters, and secondly, in some degree, the fear and trouble of the Cholera, which the Lord has sent into the world, and which may, without repentance, ravage the large towns near the waters, many years, or, at least, till other judgments come" (EMS, 53). A worldwide epidemic of cholera was raging at that time, killing millions, and Joseph Smith noted in a letter to W. W. Phelps, "Frequent cases of the cholera occures on steem boats and other water crafts" (Smith, *Writings,* 275).

Content overview

The Lord assured the elders that their sins were now forgiven because they had reconciled their differences and become "one" (61:2, 8, 20). The Lord then stated that there will be many dangers associated with water in the last days but promised protection to the "faithful" (61:4–6). He instructed Sidney Gilbert and William Phelps to make haste to complete their mission to return to Ohio, evidently to collect supplies they needed for the store and the printing office, gather their families, and return to Missouri (61:7–12; cf. 57:8–11). At an early November conference in Hiram, Ohio, Phelps was also instructed to purchase a press in Cincinnati and take it with him to Independence (Smith, *History*, 1:217).

The Lord then explained a significant reason for warning them about travel on the water. "In the beginning," he said, he had "blessed the waters," but through the apostle John, he later "cursed the waters," and "the destroyer rideth upon the face thereof" (61:13–22; cf. Gen. 1:20; Rev. 8:8–11). The Lord specified, however, that the recently completed Ohio Canal connecting Cleveland with the Ohio River was a safe means of travel (61:23–26). He also indicated that the faithful would know by the Spirit how to travel, "whether upon the land or upon the waters" (61:27–29).

The Lord instructed Sidney, Joseph, and Oliver to wait to preach until they arrived at Cincinnati. The people of Cincinnati (population about thirty thousand) were described as "well-nigh ripened for destruction" (61:30–31), but somewhat like the people of ancient Nineveh, enough of them became members of the Church that a branch was established there before the end of 1831. This branch gathered to Missouri in 1833. Joseph and Sidney were also commanded to labor among the "congregations of their brethren," or members of the Church, where these labors were needed (61:32). The other elders were to continue preaching along the way home to Kirtland in order to "rid their garments" (61:34), or in other words, shift the burden of accountability for the souls of the people from the missionaries to the people themselves. The Lord ended the revelation by instructing all the brethren to "be of good cheer," to "gird up your loins and be watchful and be sober," and to "pray always that you enter not into temptation, that you may abide the day of his coming, whether in life or in death" (61:36–39).

BIBLIOGRAPHY

Booth, Ezra. "Mormonism—No. VII." *Ohio Star*, 24 November 1831.

The Evening and the Morning Star (December 1832): 53.

Roberts, B. H. *A Comprehensive History of The Church of Jesus Christ of Latter-day Saints, Century One.* 6 vols. Salt Lake City: The Church of Jesus Christ of Latter-day Saints, 1930. Reprint, Provo, Utah: Brigham Young University Press, 1965.

Smith, Joseph. *History of The Church of Jesus Christ of Latter-day Saints.* Edited by B. H. Roberts. 7 vols. 2d ed. rev. Salt Lake City: The Church of Jesus Christ of Latter-day Saints, 1932–51.

———. *Personal Writings of Joseph Smith.* Compiled and edited by Dean C. Jessee. Rev. ed. Salt Lake City: Deseret Book, 2002.

DJR

Historical context and overview of Doctrine and Covenants 62

Historical context

On 13 August 1831, Joseph Smith and the ten elders traveling with him from Independence to Kirtland met Hyrum Smith, John Murdock, Harvey Whitlock, and David Whitmer at Chariton, Missouri (Murdock, 10). These four elders were among those called to travel to Missouri to hold a conference of the Church and to preach the gospel along the way (52:1–2, 8, 25). They were still journeying to Independence, having preached in several places and being delayed because of the illness of John Murdock (Murdock, 10). After a joyful reunion, the Prophet received this revelation.

Content overview

Even though the land of Zion and temple site had been dedicated and many of the elders were returning to Kirtland, the Lord informed these men that their mission was not yet complete. After expressing gratitude for the work they had already accomplished, he told them they were to continue their journey to Independence, attend the second conference of the Church to be held there, and then return home, preaching the gospel along the way (62:1–5; cf. 58:61–64). The Lord then approved of various means of conveyance as preferred by the elders. In that regard, John Murdock, because of his illness, was provided a pony to ride upon. Murdock recorded that they had waded through rivers and swamps, and he "took a violent cold by which [he] suffered near unto death." He also seems to have been experiencing symptoms of malaria. The brethren put their "money together and bought a pony" on which he rode (62:6–7; Murdock, 9–11). The Lord concluded the revelation by counseling them to work out the details of their calling "according to judgment and the directions of the Spirit" (62:8–9).

BIBLIOGRAPHY

Murdock, John. Journal. L. Tom Perry Special Collections, Harold B. Lee Library, Brigham Young University, Provo, Utah.

DJR

Historical context and overview of Doctrine and Covenants 63

Historical context

On Saturday, 27 August 1831, Joseph Smith and others arrived in Kirtland, Ohio, ending their journey from Missouri. John Whitmer recorded: "And now when the Elders had returned to their homes in Ohio, the churches needed much exortation in the absence of the Elders many apostitized. but many have returned again to the fold from whence they have strayed" (33). Nonetheless, the faithful Saints felt "a great anxiety to obtain the word of the Lord upon every subject that in any way concerned our salvation" (Smith, 1:207). The news that Missouri was the land of ZION, with Independence as the "center place" (57:2–3) caused many members to desire to know more about it and the gathering to Jackson County. Three days after his return to Ohio, 30 August 1831, the Prophet received this revelation.

Content overview

The Lord first issued a warning to the "wicked," the "rebellious," and the "unbelieving," who seek SIGNS, commit ADULTERY (either in fact or "in their hearts"), lie, seduce others, and engage in sorcery. Those who commit these sins will "not have part in the first resurrection" if they do not repent (63:1–18). *See* Judgment(s); Resurrection, the.

But the Lord promised great blessings for those who "overcome" and "him that keepeth my commandments"—"an inheritance upon the earth when the day of transfiguration shall come," and in the meantime; "the mysteries of my kingdom" that shall be "a well of living water, springing up unto everlasting life" (63:19–23). *See* Transfiguration.

The Lord then counseled the members of the Church concerning the establishment of Zion, including specific directions for raising the money needed to purchase property in Missouri. His counsel also included a warning to avoid any conflict with others in obtaining property there (63:24–46). He enumerated the blessings that would flow to those who followed his counsel in this revelation concerning Zion (63:47–54). The Lord then censured Sidney Rigdon, informing him that the description of Zion the Lord had commanded him to write (58:50–51) was not acceptable, and he was to rewrite it (63:55–56). The Lord instructed the missionaries to preach repentance, "for this is a day of warning, and not a day of many words," and the Lord is "not to be mocked in the last days" (63:57–60). The revelation ends with a caution for men to "beware how they take my name in their lips" (63:61–66).

See also Jesus Christ, second coming of; Millennium, the.

BIBLIOGRAPHY

Smith, Joseph. *History of The Church of Jesus Christ of Latter-day Saints.* Edited by B. H. Roberts. 7 vols. 2d ed. rev. Salt Lake City: The Church of Jesus Christ of Latter-day Saints, 1932–51.

Whitmer, John. "The Book of John Whitmer Kept by Commandment." Ca. 1835–46, Community of Christ Library-Archives, Independence, Mo.

DJR

Historical context and overview of Doctrine and Covenants 64

Historical context

Joseph Smith received this revelation on 11 September 1831, a little over two weeks after returning to Kirtland from Missouri. The brethren "who were commanded to go up to Zion" were preparing to leave for Missouri (Smith, 1:211). This revelation included instructions to many of them and informed the other members of the Church that the gathering to ZION was to be gradual and orderly.

Content overview

The Lord had previously revealed that his people were to be of "one heart and one mind" and dwell "in righteousness" in Zion (Moses 7:18; cf. D&C 45:65), yet arguments and dissensions among the elders had punctuated their return travel from Missouri. The Lord chastised this behavior in the beginning of the revelation, and included an injunction for these men to forgive one another, declaring that "he that forgiveth not his brother his trespasses standeth condemned before the Lord; for there remaineth in him the greater sin" (64:1–19). The Lord then disclosed that he intended "to retain a strong hold in the land of Kirtland, for the space of five years" (64:21) and gave specific instructions to some of the elders and the Church at large in the gradual settlement of Zion. Specifically, Newel K. Whitney and Sidney Gilbert were instructed to not sell their store in Kirtland until the Saints moved from Kirtland to Zion. As "agents" of the Lord, "on the Lord's errand," they were "set . . . to provide for his saints" (64:20–32). Since the gathering was not to be immediate, the Lord counseled the brethren to "be not weary in well-doing" and to be "willing and obedient" (64:33–34). The Lord then warned that

> 33 Wherefore, be not ªweary in ᵇwell-doing, for ye are laying the foundation of a great work. And out of ᶜsmall things proceedeth that which is great.
> 34 Behold, the Lord ªrequireth the ᵇheart and a ᶜwilling mind; and the willing and ᵈobedient shall ᵉeat the good of the land of Zion in these last days.

Doctrine and Covenants 64:33–34.

rebelliousness was not to be tolerated in Zion and gave instructions for disciplining those who were guilty (64:35–36). He concluded the revelation by confirming Zion's role "to judge the nations" in the "last days" and of her future glory (64:37–43).

BIBLIOGRAPHY

Smith, Joseph. *History of The Church of Jesus Christ of Latter-day Saints.* Edited by B. H. Roberts. 7 vols. 2d ed. rev. Salt Lake City: The Church of Jesus Christ of Latter-day Saints, 1932–51.

DJR

Historical context and overview of Doctrine and Covenants 65

Historical context

On 12 September 1831 Joseph Smith moved his family to the John Johnson home in Hiram, Ohio, about 30 miles southeast of Kirtland, in response to a revelation received about two weeks before (63:65). Sidney Rigdon likewise moved to a small log home on the Johnson farm. A major reason for removing from Kirtland was to resume work on the translation of the Bible, the results of which are now known as the Joseph Smith Translation of the Bible (JST). *See* Doctrine and Covenants and the Joseph Smith Translation of the Bible.

As early as June 1830, the Prophet had begun his inspired revision of the Bible, but because of his recent journey to Missouri, that important work had been temporarily set aside (Smith, 1:215).

This section is the first of several revelations that Joseph Smith received while residing with the John Johnson family in Hiram, Ohio. Though the Prophet's history records he received this "in the fore part of October" 1831 (1:218), the two surviving manuscripts date it 30 October 1831, one of which also has the heading "the 6th Matthew 10 verse" (McLellin, 242–43). Matthew 6:10 is that part of the Lord's Prayer that includes the phrase "Thy kingdom come," thus giving the context of this revelation (65:5–6).

Content overview

The Lord confirmed that the restored Church is the kingdom of God on the earth and has the

KEYS to take the gospel "unto the ends of the earth" in fulfillment of Daniel's prophecy (65:1–2; cf. Dan. 2:34–45). Its express purpose is to "prepare . . . the way of the Lord" for his return (65:3). The Lord invited the elders to "pray unto the Lord, call upon his holy name, make known his wonderful works among the people" and "call upon the Lord, that his kingdom may go forth upon the earth" (65:4–5). The earth will then be prepared for the "kingdom of heaven" or the millennial reign of Christ (65:6).

BIBLIOGRAPHY

McLellin, William E. *The Journals of William E. McLellin, 1831–1836*. Edited by Jan Shipps and John W. Welch. Urbana: University of Illinois Press; Provo, Utah: BYU Studies, 1994.

Smith, Joseph. *History of The Church of Jesus Christ of Latter-day Saints*. Edited by B. H. Roberts. 7 vols. 2d ed. rev. Salt Lake City: The Church of Jesus Christ of Latter-day Saints, 1932–51.

DJR

Historical context and overview of Doctrine and Covenants 66

Historical context

For many years it appeared that the Lord gave this revelation on 25 October 1831 at a conference in Orange, Ohio, but the manuscript "Book of Commandments and Revelations" and the rediscovered journals of William McLellin clarify that the Lord gave this revelation to Joseph Smith in Hiram, Ohio, on 29 October 1831 (Jensen et al., 194–95; McLellin, 46). After copying the revelation in his entry for that day, McLellin wrote that it "[gave] great joy to my heart because some important questions were answered which had dwelt upon my mind with anxiety yet with uncertainty" (McLellin, 46). Previous to meeting Joseph, McLellin secretly prayed that God would "reveal the answer to five questions through his Prophet, and that too without his having any knowledge of my having made such request." In 1848, ten years after bitterly parting ways with Joseph Smith, McLellin wrote: "I now testify in the fear of God, that every question which I had thus lodged in the ears of the Lord of Sabbaoth, were answered to my full and entire satisfaction. I desired it for a testimony of Joseph's inspiration. And I to this

day consider it to me an evidence which I cannot refute" (McLellin, 57).

McLellin's questions are unrecorded, but the revelation he wrote as Joseph dictated expresses the Lord's will for him (66:4). The revelation therefore compelled McLellin to act either in obedience or disobedience to the Lord's will. His subsequent journal is an accountability report with the revelation in mind. It and related documents reveal his inconsistent effort to obey the Lord's many specific commands (McLellin, 61–129).

Content overview

The revelation commended McLellin for turning from his iniquities to truth and receiving the fulness of the gospel. Still, the Lord told McLellin that he was not completely clean and needed to repent of sins the Lord would show him. The Lord specifically warned McLellin to "commit not adultery—a temptation with which thou hast been troubled" (66:10), and commanded him to serve a mission to the East with Samuel Smith until the Lord sent word for them to return. McLellin was to bear testimony everywhere he went, and his journal testifies that he did. He went about "reasoning with the people" (66:7) while Samuel Smith bore his simple, powerful testimony as a witness of the Book of Mormon plates. Commanded to "lay your hands upon the sick, and they shall recover," McLellin did so and the sick were healed. He tried to "be patient in affliction" (66:9), but as rejections mounted and winter approached, McLellin's resolve to obey the revelation faltered. He forsook Samuel Smith and returned to Kirtland in late December 1831 of his own volition. The Lord rebuked McLellin a few weeks later (75:6–8).

Humbled, McLellin started on another mission but again forsook his companion and calling, attributing his disobedience to poor health and lack of faith. He took a job to accumulate cash and married Emiline Miller, perhaps in disobedience to the command "seek not to be cumbered" (66:10) with family obligations while called to serve as a missionary. Then the newlyweds set out for Zion in Jackson County, Missouri, where McLellin circumvented the law of CONSECRATION. Rather than meeting with Bishop Partridge to consecrate his property and receive an inheritance, McLellin purchased two lots on Main Street, all in disobedience to specific commands that he "go not up unto the land of Zion as yet; but inasmuch as you can send, send; otherwise, think not of thy property" (66:6). McLellin's disobedience to the revelation did not diminish his belief in it or its revelator. He wrote in August 1832 that "Joseph Smith is a true Prophet or Seer of the Lord and that he *has* power and *does* recieve revelations from God, and that these revelations when received are of divine Authority in the church of Christ" (McLellin, 84). Upset by McLellin's response to the revelations, Joseph wrote that his "conduct merits the disapprobation of every true follower of Christ" (Smith, *Writings,* 265).

Section 66 left McLellin's future in his own hands. If he chose to do the Lord's will continually, he could "have a crown of eternal life" (66:12). He was at times humble and obedient, sufficient to be called as a member of the original Quorum of Twelve Apostles in 1835. But on 11 May 1838 McLellin confessed that he had "quit praying and keeping the commandments of God, and indulged himself in his lustful desires" (Smith, *History,* 3:31). He was apparently excommunicated from the Church and spent the rest of his long life struggling to resolve the tension between his sure testimony and his unwillingness to repent.

BIBLIOGRAPHY

Jensen, Robin Scott, Robert J. Woodford, and Steven C. Harper, eds. *Manuscript Revelation Books.* Facsimile edition. First volume of the Revelations and Translations series of *The Joseph Smith Papers,* edited by Dean C. Jessee, Ronald K. Esplin, and Richard Lyman Bushman. Salt Lake City: Church Historian's Press, 2009.

McLellin, William E. *The Journals of William E. McLellin, 1831–1836.* Edited by Jan Shipps and John W. Welch. Urbana: University of Illinois Press; Provo, Utah: BYU Studies, 1994.

Smith, Joseph. *History of The Church of Jesus Christ of Latter-day Saints.* Edited by B. H. Roberts. 7 vols. 2d ed. rev. Salt Lake City: The Church of Jesus Christ of Latter-day Saints, 1932–51.

———. *Personal Writings of Joseph Smith.* Compiled and edited by Dean C. Jessee. Rev. ed. Salt Lake City: Deseret Book, 2002.

SCH

Historical context and overview of Doctrine and Covenants 67

Historical context

In November 1831, Joseph Smith convened a conference at the Johnson home in Hiram, Ohio, and laid before the Church leaders the manuscript Book of Commandments and Revelations, a copy book into which John Whitmer and Oliver Cowdery had transcribed his revelations. Joseph indicated that "the Lord has bestowed a great blessing upon us in giving commandments and revelations" (Cannon and Cook, 27). It was time to publish the revelations that had been copied by hand into the book. Oliver Cowdery asked, "How many copies of the Book of commandments it was the will of the Lord should be published in the first edition of that work." The council eventually voted for ten thousand (Cannon and Cook, 27). At the conference the Lord revealed a preface for the book, Doctrine and Covenants 1, in which he said, essentially, that though he was a divine being, he communicated to mortals "in their weakness, after the manner of their language," so that they could understand (1:24; Smith, *History,* 1:223–24).

Joseph's history records that a discussion followed "concerning revelations and language" (*History,* 1:224). The manuscript book itself evidences that the revelation texts were not properly punctuated, the spelling was not standardized, and the grammar was inconsistent.

Though acknowledging the limitations of his own literary skills, Joseph knew that his revelations were divine, even though the language in which they were written was imperfect. Just a few days earlier Joseph had predicted that if the Saints could all "come together with one heart and one mind in perfect faith the vail might as well be rent to day as next week or any other time" (Cannon and Cook, 20). The brethren sought a special divine confirmation of the truth of the revelations but were not successful in this instance; section 67 explains why.

Content overview

The revelation begins with the Lord's command that the assembled Church leaders hear and obey him. He had heard their prayers and knew their "hearts" and their "desires," but "there were fears in [their] hearts," and "this is the reason that [they] did not receive" (67:1–3). He then told them he would give them a testimony of the revelations lying before them (67:4). They had been watching Joseph, listening to him talk and observing his imperfections and had secretly wished, or perhaps even assumed, that they could do better than he had done. The Lord offered them the opportunity. He invited them to have the wisest man in the council (or any of them who cared to) duplicate what they considered to be the "least" of the revelations. The Lord told the elders that if they succeeded in composing a text equal to the least of Joseph's, then they could justifiably say that they did not know that the revelations were true (67:5–7). But if they failed, they would be "under condemnation if [they did] not bear record that they are true" (67:8).

Knowing their hearts (67:1), the Lord then reminded them that they already knew there was no "unrighteousness" in any of the revelations (67:9).

The Lord then promised the brethren that *if* they would strip themselves of jealousy and fear and choose to be humble, *then* the veil between him and them would be "rent," and they would see him and know he exists with their most reliable senses—their spiritual senses. The Lord explained that no mortal has ever seen God "except [ne be] quickened by the Spirit of God" (67:10–11). For these reasons the members of the council were not able to endure God's presence then, nor even the presence of a ministering angel. But he encouraged them to "continue in patience until ye are perfected. Let not your minds turn back," he urged, "and when ye are worthy, in mine own due time, ye shall see and know that which was conferred upon you by the hands of my servant Joseph Smith" (67:13–14).

Section 67 provided the brethren with the Lord's own testimony of the revelations, even though it was not the dramatic one they had hoped for (67:13–14).

Joseph's history and other sources indicate how the brethren acted out the instructions in section 67 and became willing to testify before the world that the revelations were indeed true. William McLellin "endeavored to write a commandment like unto one of the least of the Lord's, but failed" (Smith, *History,* 1:226). Joseph asked the men present "what testimony they were willing to attach to these commandments which should shortly be sent to the world. A number of the brethren arose and said that they were willing to testify to the world that they knew that they were of the Lord." Joseph provided a statement to be signed by those who were willing to testify of the truth of the revelations (Cannon and Cook, 27; Smith, History, 1:226). The only known manuscript of that statement is "The Testimony of the witnesses to the Book of the Lord's commandments which he gave to his church through Joseph Smith Jr," copied into the Book of Commandments and Revelations. It reads, "We the undersigners feel willing to bear testimony to all the world of mankind to every creature upon all the face of all Earth <&> upon the Islands of the Sea that god hath born record to our souls through the Holy Ghost shed forth upon us that these commandments are given by inspiration of God & are profitable for all men & are verily true we give this testimony unto the world the Lord being my <our> helper" (Jensen et al., 215). McLellin and several others signed this statement. John Whitmer copied the revelation and their signatures into the manuscript copy of the Book of Commandments and Revelations and subsequently entered the revealed instructions for him to accompany Oliver Cowdery to Missouri with the manuscript revelations and money to print them (69). Thirteen more elders signed the statement in Missouri when the book arrived there for printing (Harper, 33–35). A similar testimony appears in current editions of the Doctrine and Covenants and lists the names of the original Twelve Apostles of this dispensation as witnesses to the truth of the revelations. *See* Doctrine and Covenants, testimony of the Twelve Apostles to the truth of.

Joseph undoubtedly appreciated these witnesses. He was not, by his own acknowledgment, an accomplished writer. He felt imprisoned by what he called the "totel dark-ness of paper pen and ink and a crooked bro-ken scattered and imperfect language" (Smith, *Writings*, 287). He testified that it is "an awful responsibility to write in the name of the Lord" (Smith, *History*, 1:226), yet he knew the respon-sibility was his (1:17; 5:10). As section 67 ac-knowledged, these witnesses knew the limits of Joseph's imperfect language. It was a striking vote of confidence in Joseph and in the reve-lations he received that men who knew him well declared their testimonies that the revelations were true. The discussion about revelations and language concluded as "the brethren then arose in turn and bore witness to the truth of the Book of Commandments. After which br. Joseph Smith jr arose & expressed his feelings & gratitude" (Cannon and Cook, 28). At the con-clusion of the conference Joseph reported that "the conference voted that they prize the reve-lations to be worth to the Church the riches of the whole earth, speaking temporally" (Smith, *History*, 1:235).

The information in section 67 was thus a key component in the bold project of publishing the revelation texts.

BIBLIOGRAPHY

Cannon, Donald Q., and Lyndon W. Cook, eds. *Far West Record: Minutes of The Church of Jesus Christ of Latter-day Saints, 1830–1844*. Salt Lake City: Deseret Book, 1983.

Harper, Steven C. "The Making of Modern Scripture: Latter-day Saints and the Book of Commandments and Revelations." *Mormon Historical Studies* 10, no. 2 (Spring 2009): 30–39.

Jensen, Robin Scott, Robert J. Woodford, and Steven C. Harper, eds. *Manuscript Revelation Books*. Facsimile edition. First volume of the Revelations and Trans-lations series of *The Joseph Smith Papers*, edited by Dean C. Jessee, Ronald K. Esplin, and Richard Lyman Bushman. Salt Lake City: Church Historian's Press, 2009.

Smith, Joseph. *History of The Church of Jesus Christ of Latter-day Saints*. Edited by B. H. Roberts. 7 vols. 2d ed. rev. Salt Lake City: The Church of Jesus Christ of Latter-day Saints, 1932–51.

———. *Personal Writings of Joseph Smith*. Compiled and edited by Dean C. Jessee. Rev. ed. Salt Lake City: Deseret Book, 2002.

SCH

Historical context and overview of Doctrine and Covenants 68

Historical context

In a conference at the home of Sirenes Burnett in Orange, Ohio, on 25 October 1831, Oliver Cowdery ordained fifteen men to the high priesthood, including Orson Hyde, Luke Johnson, and William E. McLellin. Cowdery also ordained Lyman Johnson an elder, and Hyde was "appointed & ordained" with five other men to visit branches of the Church, "setting them in order" and informing them of the finan-cial needs of Joseph Smith and Sidney Rigdon (Cannon and Cook, 24–25, 17). At the confer-ence that day, Joseph Smith taught, "It is the privilege of every Elder to Speak of the things of God" and that high priests received power "to seal up the Saints unto eternal life" (Cannon and Cook, 20–21).

Four of the men in attendance that day—Hyde, McLellin, and Luke and Lyman Johnson—attended another conference one week later at the John Johnson home in Hiram to endorse plans to publish the Book of Com-mandments (Cannon and Cook, 26–27). At that time they "were desirous to know the mind of the Lord concerning themselves" (Smith, 1:227). Joseph Smith received a revelation that laid out their responsibilities (68:1–12). The Lord also revealed more about the ordination and disci-pline of BISHOPS (68:13–24) and specified paren-tal duties regarding the teaching of their children (68:25–35).

Verses 16–21 were not part of the original revelation; they were added when it was pub-lished in the 1835 edition of the Doctrine and Covenants. These verses reflect a later under-standing of the calling of bishops and the privi-leges of "literal descendants of Aaron" (68:15–16). This same information was added in 1835 to another revelation received on 11 November 1831 (107:59–100) as verses 69–70, 73, 76.

An additional anachronism in this revelation is found in verses 15, 22–23. There was no First Presidency until months later. According to the earliest manuscript of this revelation, bish-ops were to be chosen by "[a council] of high priests," and they could only be tried before a similar council (Jensen et al., 200, 201).

These later additions to the revelation are an example of the Lord revealing his will "line upon line, [and] precept upon precept" (128:21) as the Church grew in numbers and as the organizational structure developed.

Content overview

The Lord called the four men and "all the faithful elders" to "preach the gospel to every creature," acting in "authority" and "by the Spirit of the living God" (68:1, 7–8). Consistent with the Prophet's remarks on 25 October, the Lord promised that what they said when "moved upon by the Holy Ghost shall be scripture," or in other words the Lord's "will" or "mind" or "word" or "voice," and "the power of God unto salvation" (68:2–5). Those who believed their words and accepted baptism would receive spiritual gifts and be saved, while those who rejected their testimony would be damned (68:6–10). The Lord also promised the men power to recognize the signs of the times and to seal up believers unto eternal life (68:11–12).

The Lord then revealed that "other bishops" would be called to "minister" in the same way Edward Partridge had been called (68:14; cf. 41:9). These men should be worthy high priests, "appointed by the First Presidency of the Melchizedek Priesthood" (68:15). Worthy firstborn descendants of Aaron could claim this office by virtue of lineage but would still need to be called by the First Presidency (68:15–21). Church discipline of a presiding bishop, not ward bishops, requires the participation of the First Presidency (68:22–24).

The final part of the revelation called on parents "in Zion, or in any of her stakes" to teach their CHILDREN to "understand the doctrine" of repentance, faith in Christ, baptism, and the gift of the Holy Ghost by the age of eight, specified as the age of accountability (68:25–27; cf. 18:42; 20:71). The Lord also commanded parents to "teach their children to pray, and to walk uprightly before the Lord" (68:28). He called on the "inhabitants of Zion" to keep the Sabbath day holy and to "labor, in all faithfulness," reproving the idle, the greedy, and those who neglected regular prayer (68:29–34).

BIBLIOGRAPHY

Cannon, Donald Q., and Lyndon W. Cook, eds. *Far West Record: Minutes of The Church of Jesus Christ of Latter-day Saints, 1830–1844.* Salt Lake City: Deseret Book, 1983.

Jensen, Robin Scott, Robert J. Woodford, and Steven C. Harper, eds. *Manuscript Revelation Books.* Facsimile edition. First volume of the Revelations and Translations series of *The Joseph Smith Papers,* edited by Dean C. Jessee, Ronald K. Esplin, and Richard Lyman Bushman. Salt Lake City: Church Historian's Press, 2009.

Smith, Joseph. *History of The Church of Jesus Christ of Latter-day Saints.* Edited by B. H. Roberts. 7 vols. 2d ed. rev. Salt Lake City: The Church of Jesus Christ of Latter-day Saints, 1932–51.

JCT

Historical context and overview of Doctrine and Covenants 69

Historical content

At a special conference on 1 November 1831, Church leaders agreed to publish the Book of Commandments. Oliver Cowdery was appointed to carry the manuscript revelations to Independence, Missouri, for printing (Smith, *History,* 1:229). The conference resolved on 8 November 1831 that Joseph Smith should first review and correct the manuscripts (Cannon and Cook, 28–29). Prior to another conference at the John Johnson home in Hiram, on 12–13 November 1831, Joseph Smith received this revelation calling John Whitmer to accompany Cowdery on the journey to Missouri.

Content overview

After appointing him to journey with Oliver Cowdery (69:1–2), the Lord reiterated Whitmer's responsibilities as Church historian and recorder. He was to "travel many times from place to place . . . preaching and expounding, writing, copying, selecting, and obtaining all things which shall be for the good of the church" (69:3–8; cf. 47:1–4).

On 12 November, the Prophet prayed in conference for the Lord to "dedicate & consecrate these brethren & the sacred writings & all they have entrusted to their care" (Cannon and Cook, 32). Whitmer wrote that the two men left for Missouri on 20 November 1831 and arrived in Jackson County on 5 January

1832 (Whitmer, 102). En route they convened and recorded the proceedings of a series of conferences in Winchester, Indiana (Cannon and Cook, 33–38). Joseph Smith subsequently reminded Whitmer of his duties in part of a long letter to William W. Phelps, July 1832: "I exhort Bro John also to remember the commandment to him to keep a history of the church & the gathering and be sure to shew him self approoved whereunto he hath been called" (Smith, *Writings*, 276; cf. 85:1). The third number of *The Evening and the Morning Star* reminded elders of the revealed injunction to send "accounts of their stewardships to the land of Zion" (69:5–6), and subsequent issues of the newspaper reprinted extracts from missionaries' letters containing these reports.

BIBLIOGRAPHY

Cannon, Donald Q., and Lyndon W. Cook, eds. *Far West Record: Minutes of The Church of Jesus Christ of Latter-day Saints, 1830–1844.* Salt Lake City: Deseret Book, 1983.

The Evening and the Morning Star 1, no. 3 (August 1832): 17–24; 1, no. 8 (January 1833): 57–64.

Smith, Joseph. *History of The Church of Jesus Christ of Latter-day Saints.* Edited by B. H. Roberts. 7 vols. 2d ed. rev. Salt Lake City: The Church of Jesus Christ of Latter-day Saints, 1932–51.

———. *Personal Writings of Joseph Smith.* Compiled and edited by Dean C. Jessee. Rev. ed. Salt Lake City: Deseret Book, 2002.

Whitmer, John. *From Historian to Dissident: The Book of John Whitmer.* Edited by Bruce N. Westergren. Salt Lake City: Signature Books, 1995.

JCT

Historical context and overview of Doctrine and Covenants 70

Historical context

Several conference sessions were held at the John Johnson farm in Hiram, Ohio, from 1 through 12 November 1831. At these meetings, the Preface (1), sections 67–70, and the Appendix (133) were received by revelation, as well as the "Testimony of the Book of Commandments." At the last conference, Joseph Smith discussed the importance of the "sacred writings . . . now going to the Church for their benefit." He proposed that he and a handful of brethren who had "labored with [him] from the beginning" or "for a considerable time" should "have claim on the Church for recompense" when the scriptures were published. The members of the conference agreed that "the book of Revelation now to be printed [was] the foundation of the Church & the salvation of the world" and that it was "worth . . . the riches of the whole Earth" to the Church. They also agreed that Joseph Smith, Oliver Cowdery, John Whitmer, and Sidney Rigdon should be "appointed to manage" proceeds from the publication of the revelations, "according to the Laws of the Church & the Commandments of the Lord" (Cannon and Cook, 31–32). After these deliberations and "in answer to an inquiry" (Smith, 1:236), Joseph received further instruction through this revelation.

Content overview

The revelation named two more men, Martin Harris and William W. Phelps, to join the four previously nominated as "stewards over the revelations and commandments." The Lord said that he would require all six men to give "an account of this stewardship . . . in the day of judgment" (70:1–4). They would "manage" the "concerns" and the "benefits" of the Church's literary labors, drawing income from the proceeds. If they received "more than is needful for their necessities," they should give the surplus to the storehouse, like other stewards (70:5–11). The Lord taught that those who labor in "spiritual things" are "worthy of [their] hire" even as those who labor in temporal things (70:12–14). The Lord described their stewardship as "a reward of their diligence" and a means to provide for their material needs (70:15–16).

The Lord soon revealed that the "stewards over the literary concerns of my church" (labeled "The Literary Firm") could call on the bishops for funds or other assistance needed to publish the revelations or "benefit the church" in other ways (72:20–23). In the spring of 1832 this arrangement was formalized by creating an organization that came to be called the "United Firm," sometimes referred to as "united order" (92:1; 104:1, 47, 48, 53), or "mine order" (96:4), or simply "the order" (96:8; 104:5, 10, 19, 21, 36), which linked the literary business of the Church to the "mercantile establishment" of the bishops in Ohio and Missouri, named "Gilbert, Whitney & Company in Zion" and "Newel K. Whitney & Company in Kirtland," Ohio, providing needed access to capital (Cannon and Cook, 45–48; D&C 78:3–4, 8, 11, 14; 82:11–19; Parkin, 12–16; Smith, 1:365–66). *See* Consecration.

The United Firm added other members as needed to "[bring] forth my word unto the children of men" (96:8; cf. 92:1), and its literary concerns included "the translation of [the] scriptures" (94:10) as well as periodicals and a hymnbook. The expense of publishing these important records, compounded by violence against the Church's printing operation in Missouri, created a burden of debt for the handful of members that neither the literary nor mercantile revenues could cover. In April 1834, the Ohio and Missouri firms were separated and the properties of the United Firm were divided into individual stewardships (104; Cook, 112–17, 146–48; Parkin, 37–39).

BIBLIOGRAPHY

Cannon, Donald Q., and Lyndon W. Cook, eds. *Far West Record: Minutes of The Church of Jesus Christ of Latter-day Saints, 1830–1844.* Salt Lake City: Deseret Book, 1983.

Cook, Lyndon W. *The Revelations of the Prophet Joseph Smith.* Salt Lake City: Deseret Book, 1985.

Parkin, Max H. "Joseph Smith and the United Firm: The Growth and Decline of the Church's First Master Plan of Business and Finance, Ohio and Missouri, 1832–1834." *BYU Studies* 46 (2007): 5–66.

Smith, Joseph. *History of The Church of Jesus Christ of Latter-day Saints.* Edited by B. H. Roberts. 7 vols. 2d ed. rev. Salt Lake City: The Church of Jesus Christ of Latter-day Saints, 1932–51.

JCT

Historical context and overview of Doctrine and Covenants 71

Historical context

From 13 October to 8 December 1831, the *Ohio Star* published nine letters from Ezra Booth denouncing Joseph Smith's prophetic claims and the restored Church as "pernicious" and "destructive" delusions (*Ohio Star,* 13 October 1831). Booth had joined the Church earlier that year, attended conference at Kirtland in June, and journeyed to Missouri with several other priesthood holders. On that journey, his faith

failed and he began opposing the work (Smith, 1:215–16). Upon his return from Missouri in early September, he was "silenced from preaching as an Elder in this Church" (Cannon and Cook, 11–12). Later the same month, he and Symonds Ryder, another dissenter, renounced their Church membership at a camp meeting at Shalersville, Ohio ("Renunciation," 3). Having been a prominent minister in the area before he became a member of the Church, his public critique created enough negative publicity that Joseph Smith inquired about what should be done.

Content overview

On 1 December 1831 the Lord revealed that Joseph and Sidney Rigdon should interrupt their work on the translation of the Bible to serve a mission "for the space of a season" to "proclaim" the gospel message "unto the world in the regions round about, and in the church also" (71:1–4). The Lord told Joseph and Sidney to "call upon [your enemies] to meet you both in public and in private" (71:7). He promised that "no weapon . . . formed against you shall prosper" and that any who should "lift his voice against you . . . shall be confounded in mine own due time" (71:9–10). In response, Joseph and Sidney preached in Kirtland, Shalersville, Ravenna, and other places from 3 December 1831 until about 10 January 1832 (Smith, 1:239, 241). On 15 December 1831, Sidney Rigdon published a notice in the *Ohio Star* that he would rebut Booth's letters publicly in Ravenna on 25 December. Booth failed to appear, and so Rigdon preached to those who had assembled to hear the debate. Rigdon also proposed a public debate on the Book of Mormon with another dissenter named Symonds Ryder, a challenge Ryder declined (*Ohio Star,* 15 December 1831, 29 December 1831).

Joseph Smith reported that his and Sidney Rigdon's effort "did much towards allaying the excited feelings which were growing out of the scandalous letters then being published in the *Ohio Star,* at Ravenna, by . . . Ezra Booth (Smith, 1:241).

BIBLIOGRAPHY

Cannon, Donald Q., and Lyndon W. Cook, eds. *Far West Record: Minutes of The Church of Jesus Christ of Latter-day Saints, 1830–1844*. Salt Lake City: Deseret Book, 1983.

The Ohio Star, 13 October 1831, 15 December 1831, 29 December 1831.

"A Renunciation of Mormonism." *Observer and Telegraph,* 29 September 1831, [3], Hudson, Ohio.

Smith, Joseph. *History of The Church of Jesus Christ of Latter-day Saints*. Edited by B. H. Roberts. 7 vols. 2d ed. rev. Salt Lake City: The Church of Jesus Christ of Latter-day Saints, 1932–51.

JCT

Historical context and overview of Doctrine and Covenants 72

Historical context

In response to the revelation recorded in section 71, Joseph Smith and Sidney Rigdon left Hiram, Ohio, on 3 December 1831 to preach "in the regions round about" in order to "allay the unfriendly feelings that had developed against the Church as a result of the publication of some newspaper articles by Ezra Booth, who had apostatized" (71:2; headnote). The next day, a Sunday, they met with "several elders and members" in Kirtland and spent "some time . . . in conversing about our temporal and spiritual welfare." As these members wished "to learn their duty," the Prophet inquired and received two revelations (vv. 1–8 and vv. 9–26) that compose section 72 (headnote; Smith, 1:239).

Content overview

In the first revelation the Lord indicated the need for a bishop in the Kirtland area and called Newel K. Whitney to serve in that capacity (72:1–2, 8). He also affirmed that "every steward" is to "render an account of his stewardship, both in time and in eternity," to be recorded for eventual transmission to Bishop Edward Partridge, the bishop in Zion (Missouri) (72:3–6).

In the second revelation the Lord detailed some of Whitney's responsibilities as the bishop in Kirtland. As keeper of "the Lord's storehouse," he should expect elders to "pay for that which they receive" in order to generate funds for "the good of the church" and "the poor and

needy." If they lacked means to pay, he should grant them credit, forwarding their account to the bishop in Zion, "who shall pay the debt out of that which the Lord shall put into his hands" (72:10–13). Upon receiving the account of an elder's stewardship, he should write a certificate for the bishop in Zion to endorse the man "as a wise steward and as a faithful laborer" (72:16–18). The Lord also specified what aid should be given those who were "stewards over the literary concerns" of the Church (72:19–23).

The Lord directed Whitney (or three elders) to similarly certify the worthiness of any members "appointed" or "privileged to go up unto Zion" (72:24–26). In the first number of *The Evening and the Morning Star,* Bishop Partridge reminded readers of the need to be certified by the bishop in Ohio before gathering to Zion so that "order and not confusion may be produced," and subsequent issues of the newspaper repeated and amplified that revealed counsel (*EMS,* June 1832, July 1832, December 1832).

BIBLIOGRAPHY

The Evening and the Morning Star (June 1832); (July 1832); (December 1832).

Smith, Joseph. *History of The Church of Jesus Christ of Latter-day Saints*. Edited by B. H. Roberts. 7 vols. 2d ed. rev. Salt Lake City: The Church of Jesus Christ of Latter-day Saints, 1932–51.

JCT

Historical context and overview of Doctrine and Covenants 73

Historical context

Having traveled intermittently for about five weeks in response to divine command (71:1–3), Joseph Smith and Sidney Rigdon returned to the John Johnson home in Hiram, Ohio. A conference had previously been appointed for Amherst, Ohio, on 25 January 1832, and the question arose as to what they and others should do for the next two weeks in anticipation of the conference.

Content overview

The Lord commanded Joseph and Sidney to resume work on the translation of the Bible and preach in the area "inasmuch as it is practicable"

(73:3–4). *See* Doctrine and Covenants and the Joseph Smith Translation of the Bible.

Other priesthood officers should continue "preaching the gospel, and in exhortation to the churches" until the conference, when more specific calls would be issued (73:1–2).

JCT

Historical context and overview of Doctrine and Covenants 74

Historical context

Joseph Smith said that he "received [this revelation] as an explanation of the First Epistle to the Corinthians, 7th chapter, 14th verse" while he "labored diligently" on the new translation of the Bible before the scheduled conference at Amherst on 25 January 1832 (1:242; 74, headnote). The manuscripts of the translation indicate that he and Sidney Rigdon were studying the Gospels (most likely Luke) rather than Paul's epistles at this point of their work (Faulring et al., 58). Thus it is unclear what prompted the Prophet to inquire about this passage. One possibility is that a member of the Church who was married to an unbeliever asked about the meaning of Paul's counsel.

Content overview

According to the section heading, this revelation was given as "an explanation of 1 Corinthians 7:14. It deals with a controversy that existed in the ancient Church over the fulfillment of the LAW OF MOSES and its implications regarding CIRCUMCISION. When unbelieving husbands (those who did not believe in the gospel as taught by Christ and the apostles but who held to the law of Moses) insisted that their sons be circumcised "and become subject to the law of Moses," there was danger that their CHILDREN would heed "the traditions of their fathers" instead of the "gospel of Christ," thereby becoming "unholy" (74:1–4). Contrary to the "tradition . . . that little children are unholy," the Lord restated the truth that "little children are holy, being sanctified through the atonement of Jesus Christ" (74:6–7; cf. 29:46–48). The revelation indicates that the apostle Paul "wrote unto the church [at Corinth], giving unto them a commandment, not of the Lord, but of himself, that

a believer should not be united to an unbeliever; except the law of Moses should be done away among them" (74:5).

See also Paul quotations in the Doctrine and Covenants.

BIBLIOGRAPHY

Faulring, Scott H., Kent P. Jackson, and Robert J. Matthews, eds. *Joseph Smith's New Translation of the Bible: Original Manuscripts*. Provo, Utah: Religious Studies Center, Brigham Young University, 2004.

Jensen, Robin Scott, Robert J. Woodford, and Steven C. Harper, eds. *Manuscript Revelation Books*. Facsimile edition. First volume of the Revelations and Translations series of *The Joseph Smith Papers*, edited by Dean C. Jessee, Ronald K. Esplin, and Richard Lyman Bushman. Salt Lake City: Church Historian's Press, 2009.

Smith, Joseph. *History of The Church of Jesus Christ of Latter-day Saints*. Edited by B. H. Roberts. 7 vols. 2d ed. rev. Salt Lake City: The Church of Jesus Christ of Latter-day Saints, 1932–51.

JCT

Historical context and overview of Doctrine and Covenants 75

Historical context

At the conclusion of their meetings in Orange, Ohio, on 26 October 1831, Church officers scheduled the next "General Conference" for 25 January 1832 in Amherst, Ohio (Cannon and Cook, 26). As many as eighty priesthood holders from various states assembled at Amherst, about twice as many as had attended the October conference (McLellin, 81–82). Those present sustained Joseph Smith as "President of the High Priesthood," and Sidney Rigdon ordained him to that office. This was done in fulfillment of the revelation received 11 November 1831 but added to section 107 (vv. 59–100). Part of the revelation was given in March of 1835, in which the Lord directed: "Wherefore, it must needs be that one be appointed of the High Priesthood to preside over the priesthood, and he shall be called President of the High Priesthood of the Church" (107:65; cf. headnote). In his history, Joseph emphasized that at the conference the "Elders seemed anxious" that he inquire of God to learn how they might "bring men to a sense of their condition" (*History,* 1:243). These men were aware of the revelation received two weeks earlier, in which the Lord said he would make "known unto them, by the voice of the conference, their several missions" (73:2). Joseph Smith received and dictated two revelations in the midst of the conference; today they compose section 75 (JH, 25 January 1832, 2). Orson Pratt, who attended the conference, recorded in his journal: "At this conference, by the request of the priesthood, the Prophet inquired of the Lord, and a revelation was given and written in the presence of the whole assembly, appointing many of the elders to missions" (12). In all, the revelations called twelve pairs of men to serve.

Content overview

The first revelation (75:1–22) called ten elders to journey and preach in various areas—four in "the south countries"; four in "the eastern countries"; and two in the "western countries" (75:8–17). The Lord called these men, who had "given [their] names," to "go forth and not tarry," working hard to declare "the truth according to the revelations and commandments" they had received (75:2–4). The Lord promised the faithful among them "many sheaves," saying that the faithful would "overcome all things, and be lifted up at the last day" (75:5, 16, 22). He counseled them to bless receptive households but to "depart speedily" from those who rejected them "and shake off the dust of your feet as a testimony against them" in "the day of judgment" (75:19–22).

The second revelation (75:23–36) called on Church members to "open their hearts" and provide "support" and "places" when a diligent missionary was unable to provide for his family (75:24–29). The elders who were not able to provide for their families in this way were excused from travelling and were assured that they would "in nowise lose [their] crown," but they were still to "labor in the church" locally (75:28). The revelation also named seven pairs of elders to "be united in the ministry," without specifying their fields of labor, except to say that they could go to "the east or to the west, or to the north, or to the south" and promised the Comforter would make known "whither they shall go" (75:24–27, 30–36).

As counseled by the Lord the previous November (69:5), some of the men named in the revelation—Reynolds Cahoon, Gideon Carter, Orson Hyde, William E. McLellin, Orson Pratt, Eden Smith, Samuel H. Smith—created a personal record of their travels that year that remains extant (McLellin, 408–12). These journal accounts were sent to the land of Zion to become part of the permanent record of the Church (69:6) and are in the Church archives today.

William E. McLellin, chastened in the revelation "for the murmurings of his heart" (75:7), wrote that he "was sorely tempted of [the] Devil" in the succeeding day but "made a hard struggle a[nd] shook him off my back." Within a month, however, he ceased "traveling to preach," taking a job and marrying soon after (McLellin, 70, 73, 82). Joseph Smith complained that McLellin had "disobayed the voice of him who is altogether Lovely for a woman" and said that his "conduct merits the disapprobation of every true follower of Christ" (*Writings*, 265).

BIBLIOGRAPHY

Cannon, Donald Q., and Lyndon W. Cook, eds. *Far West Record: Minutes of The Church of Jesus Christ of Latter-day Saints, 1830–1844.* Salt Lake City: Deseret Book, 1983.

Journal History of the Church, 25 January 1832. Church History Library, The Church of Jesus Christ of Latter-day Saints, Salt Lake City, Utah.

McLellin, William E. *The Journals of William E. McLellin, 1831–1836.* Edited by Jan Shipps and John W. Welch. Urbana: University of Illinois Press; Provo, Utah: BYU Studies, 1994.

Pratt, Orson. *The Orson Pratt Journals.* Edited by Elden J. Watson. Salt Lake City: E. J. Watson, 1975.

Smith, Joseph. *History of The Church of Jesus Christ of Latter-day Saints.* Edited by B. H. Roberts. 7 vols. 2d ed. rev. Salt Lake City: The Church of Jesus Christ of Latter-day Saints, 1932–51.

———. *Personal Writings of Joseph Smith.* Compiled and edited by Dean C. Jessee. Rev. ed. Salt Lake City: Deseret Book, 2002.

JCT

Historical context and overview of Doctrine and Covenants 76

Historical context

Doctrine and Covenants 76 is an account of a vision Joseph Smith and Sidney Rigdon had on 16 February 1832 in John Johnson's farm home in Hiram, Ohio. Joseph and Emma Smith had been living with the Johnsons since the previous September; Sidney Rigdon's family lived in a cabin not far from there. Joseph and Sidney had been engaged for several months in a "translation of the Scriptures" (Smith, 1:245), and returning to Hiram from a Church conference in Amherst, Ohio, they resumed that activity. From Joseph Smith's introduction of the revelation, it seems clear that he had been pondering the probability of there being "more kingdoms than one" in heaven "if God rewarded every one according to the deeds done in the body" (76, headnote). Receiving section 76 confirmed Joseph's understanding that there must be eternal rewards commensurate with different levels of obedience or disobedience.

Content overview

The Lord prefaced this vision of the eternities with a statement that he was revealing it because he is "merciful and gracious" to those who "fear" him and delights "to honor those who serve [him] in righteousness and in truth unto the end" (76:5–10). While marveling and meditating upon the translation of John 5:29, dealing with the RESURRECTION of the just and the unjust, which was "given unto [them] of the Spirit . . . the Lord touched the eyes of [their] understandings and they were opened, and the glory of the Lord shone round about" (76:15–19). "By the power of the Spirit" they were able to "see and understand the things of God." They saw and conversed with the Savior and bore solemn testimony "that he lives" (76:12–22). They saw Jesus on the right hand of the Father and angels worshipping God. They heard "the voice" bearing witness that Jesus is the Only Begotten of the Father and that "by him, and through him, and of him, the worlds are and were created, and the inhabitants thereof are begotten sons and daughters unto God" (76:20–24). They then saw the WAR IN HEAVEN, Lucifer becoming SATAN because he rebelled against God, and his being cast out (76:25–30). Other scriptures teach that "a third part of the hosts of heaven" rebelled and were cast out with him (29:36–37; cf. Rev. 12:7–9). They also saw the misery of all those who "suffered themselves through the power of the devil to be overcome, and to deny the truth

and defy my power," those who become "sons of perdition" (76:30–49). A voice from heaven declared to Joseph and Sidney that all mankind are saved through JESUS CHRIST except the SONS OF PERDITION (76:40–44). There followed a vision of the qualifications and blessings pertaining to those who come forth in the Resurrection to inherit the celestial kingdom (76:50–70, 92–96), the terrestrial kingdom (76:71–80, 91, 97), and the telestial kingdom (76:81–90, 98–112). The Lord likened the differences in glory of the three kingdoms to the differences in glory of the sun, moon, and stars. Interestingly, the word *telestial* is unique to the Doctrine and Covenants. Though the apostle Paul spoke of a glory of the sun, moon, and stars, and named the celestial and terrestrial glories, he did not label the glory of the stars as telestial (1 Cor. 15:40–41).

Joseph and Sidney were told what to write and what not to write concerning the vision. Some things they saw "are not lawful for man to utter; neither is man capable to make them known, for they are only to be seen and understood by the power of the Holy Spirit, which

Upstairs room of John Johnson's home in Hiram, Ohio; photograph by Craig Dimond. "While we were doing the work of translation, which the Lord had appointed unto us, we came to the twenty-ninth verse of the fifth chapter of John. . . . And while we meditated upon these things, the Lord touched the eyes of our understandings and they were opened, and the glory of the Lord shone round about" (D&C 76:15, 19).

God bestows on those who love him, and purify themselves before him" (76:113–16, 28, 49, 80; cf. 76:5–10). In May 1843 Joseph Smith said, "I could explain a hundred fold more than I ever have of the glories of the kingdoms manifested to me in the vision, were I permitted, and were the people prepared to receive them" (5:402).

According to Philo Dibble, there were as many as twelve other men in the room when the vision was received. He said he was there for over an hour, for the last two-thirds of the time. If his recollections are correct, the vision would have lasted for about an hour and a half. He reported that throughout the vision Joseph and Sidney would alternately say, "What do I see?" then describe what he was looking at, whereupon the other would say, "I see the same." Others in the room said nothing. Philo Dibble's account indicates that "Joseph sat firmly and calmly . . . but Sidney sat limp and pale . . . observing which, Joseph remarked, smilingly, 'Sidney is not used to it as I am.'" Dibble said, "I saw the glory and felt the power, but did not see the vision" (303–4). It is not known whether any of the others in the room left a record of their experience.

Five months after the revelation was received, it was published in the July 1832 issue of *The Evening and the Morning Star,* the Church newspaper printed in Independence, Missouri. It was included as section XCI (91), under the title "A Vision," in the first edition (1835) of the Doctrine and Covenants.

The doctrines in the vision were not immediately embraced by the whole Church. Brigham Young's reaction is representative of what some were experiencing. "After all, my traditions were such, that when the Vision came first to me, it was so directly contrary and opposed to my former education, I said, wait a little; I did not reject it, but I could not understand it. I then could feel what incorrect traditions had done for me . . . I used to think and pray, to read and think, until I knew, and fully understood it for myself, by the visions of the Holy Spirit" (Young, *News,* 52; cf. *JD,* 16:42). Although some may have struggled in the beginning, the Prophet Joseph Smith exulted over the vision. "The sublimity of the ideas; the purity of the language;

the scope for action; the continued duration for completion, in order that the heirs of salvation may confess the Lord and bow the knee; the rewards for faithfulness, and the punishments for sins, are so much beyond the narrow-mindedness of men, that every honest man is constrained to exclaim: '*It came from God*'" (Smith, 1:252–53). That expresses the feelings of the Saints today who treasure the distinctive, merciful doctrines of salvation contained in the vision. *See* Kingdoms of glory and perdition, Vision of; Appendix A, "The Vision."

BIBLIOGRAPHY

Dibble, Philo. "Recollections of the Prophet Joseph Smith." *Juvenile Instructor* 27 (15 May 1892): 303–4.

Smith, Joseph. *History of The Church of Jesus Christ of Latter-day Saints.* Edited by B. H. Roberts. 7 vols. 2d ed. rev. Salt Lake City: The Church of Jesus Christ of Latter-day Saints, 1932–51.

Young, Brigham. *Deseret News* —Extra (Salt Lake City), 14 September 1852, as quoted in Robert J. Woodford, "The Historical Development of the Doctrine and Covenants." Ph.D. dissertation, Brigham Young University, 1974.

———. *Journal of Discourses.* 26 vols. London: Latter-day Saints' Book Depot, 1854–86.

LED

Historical context and overview of Doctrine and Covenants 77

Historical context

On 8 March 1831, while in Hiram, Ohio, Joseph Smith began his inspired work of translating the New Testament. Approximately one year later, just before 24 March 1832, he was working in the book of Revelation. As he prepared for the translation work, he had questions about certain images described by John, and he turned to God for answers. His history records simply: "In connection with the translation of the Scriptures, I received the following explanation of the Revelation of St. John" (1:253). The explanation came in response to direct questions, and in recording the inspired answers, Joseph Smith retained the question-and-answer format, making this section unique.

By March 20, Joseph Smith had finished translating through Revelation 11, and on that day he received the following unpublished revelation in answer to a question he put to the

Lord: "Shall we finish the translation of the New Testament before we go to Zion or wait till we return It is expedient saith the Lord that there be no delays and thus saith the Lord for the greatest good and benefit of the church Wherefore omit the translation for the present time" (Whitney, 20 March 1832 revelation). Shortly after he returned from Missouri the following June, he resumed the translation, beginning with Revelation 12. Thus Doctrine and Covenants 77 offers help only in understanding the first eleven chapters of the book, and there is no other comparable revelation for the remainder.

Content overview

The section touches on the future celestialization of the earth (77:1; cf. 88:17–20, 25–26), the salvation of animals and their immortal nature (77:2–4), the identification of the twenty-four elders who worship God (77:5), the content of the book in the hand of God and the meaning of its seals (77:6–7), the nature of the four destroying angels and how they operate (77:8), the work of the angel ascending from the east (77:9), the timing of the events covered in the seventh chapter of Revelation (77:10), the work of the 144,000 and the meaning of their sealing (77:11), the meaning of the trumpet blasts recorded in Revelation 8 and 9 and the timing of the events recorded there (77:12–13), the content of the little book eaten by John (77:14), and the work of the two prophets raised up to the Jews in the last days (77:15).

This revelation broke with scholarly thinking of Joseph Smith's day, most of which placed the events in chapters seven through nine and eleven in the past (Hedges, 84–89). The revelation clearly places them in the future and, therefore, broke a long-standing point of view. The spirit of prophecy infused within the revelation can be seen in the current fulfillment of two events mentioned: one is the reference to a Jewish nation that did not exist until the twentieth century (77:15); and the other is the gathering of the tribes of Israel, a work now being realized through worldwide missionary efforts (77:9).

See also John the Beloved/Revelator quotations in the Doctrine and Covenants.

BIBLIOGRAPHY

Hedges, Andrew H. "John's Revelation and the Restoration of the Gospel." Sydney B. Sperry Symposium. Salt Lake City: Deseret Book, 1998.

Smith, Joseph. *History of The Church of Jesus Christ of Latter-day Saints.* Edited by B. H. Roberts. 7 vols. 2d ed. rev. Salt Lake City: The Church of Jesus Christ of Latter-day Saints, 1932–51.

Whitney, Newel K. Manuscript Revelations. Newel K. Whitney Collection, Brigham Young University Library, Provo, Utah.

RDD

Historical context and overview of Doctrine and Covenants 78

Historical context

Beginning in 1831, Joseph Smith had received considerable instruction dealing with the financial affairs for the Saints, including establishing a storehouse for the needy (42:34; 70:7; 72:10). In March 1832, Joseph received this additional revelation concerning "an organization" for establishing and regulating a storehouse in both Ohio and Missouri (78:3). This organization is specifically deemed in all of the prepublication manuscript versions of this revelation as being the "litterary and the Mercantile establishments of my Church" (Jensen et al., 267). The Literary Firm, responsible for the publication of the revelations (Book of Commandments) and several other Church publications, was already established in November 1831 (70:1–3). This revelation urged the establishment of the United Firm (still code named "united order" in the Doctrine and Covenants), which would function as a corporation based upon principles of CONSECRATION, thus uniting the mercantile and literary concerns of the Church under one organization.

Content overview

The organization was designed to promote equality among the Saints in both heavenly and temporal things (78:4–6). The Lord called Joseph Smith, Newel K. Whitney, and Sidney Rigdon to the United Firm by covenant and instructed them to "sit in council with the saints which are in Zion" in order to complete the organization at both Church centers (78:9–11). Even though tribulation would test the faithful, the providence of the Lord would prepare the

Saints to be independent of all earthly things. As such, thankful, faithful, and wise stewards inherit all things pertaining to the kingdom of God, the riches of the eternities, as well as the "things of this earth" (78:14–19).

The Lord indicated that his Saints did not understand the promised blessings of the Father and that they could not "bear all things now; nevertheless," he encouraged, "be of good cheer, for I will lead you along. The kingdom is yours and the blessings thereof are yours. . . . Wherefore, do the things which I have commanded you, saith your Redeemer, . . . who prepareth all things before he taketh you," and who delivers to every Saint his or her appointed portion (78:18–21).

This revelation is the first instance where the phrase "Adam-ondi-Ahman" occurs in the Doctrine and Covenants. The latter part of 78:15—"who hath established the foundations of Adam-ondi-Ahman"—and all of verse 16, however, are not part of the text of the manuscripts of this revelation, and were added in the 1835 edition of the Doctrine and Covenants. By that time Doctrine and Covenants 107:53–54 had been received, in which the information found in these verses was initially included. *See* Adam-ondi-Ahman; Historical context and overview of Doctrine and Covenants 107 (p. 815).

When this revelation was first published in 1835, "Son Ahman" replaced "Jesus Christ" in verse 20. "Jesus Christ" was in the handwritten manuscript copy of the revelation. Even though Joseph Smith received a revelation at the same time as Doctrine and Covenants 78 (March 1832), wherein the Lord revealed that the name of God in the "pure Language" was Ahman, and the name of the Savior was "Son Ahman" (Jensen et al., 264–65), "Son Ahman" was first incorporated into this revelation in the 1835 edition of the Doctrine and Covenants. As "Son Ahman," Christ has power to claim those faithful in his Church (the "church of the Firstborn") so they may "inherit all things" (78:20–22). *See* Church of the Firstborn.

BIBLIOGRAPHY

Jensen, Robin Scott, Robert J. Woodford, and Steven C. Harper, eds. *Manuscript Revelation Books*. Facsimile edition. First volume of the Revelations and Translations series of *The Joseph Smith Papers*, edited by Dean C. Jessee, Ronald K. Esplin, and Richard Lyman Bushman. Salt Lake City: Church Historian's Press, 2009.

MOR

Historical context and overview of Doctrine and Covenants 79

Historical context

From September 1831 to February 1832, Jared Carter had been serving a mission in Pennsylvania, New York, and Vermont. On 12 March 1832, he sought Joseph Smith in Hiram, Ohio, to inquire about his ministry for "the ensuing season" (Carter, 53).

Content overview

The Lord instructed Jared Carter to return "in the power of [his] ordination" to the eastern countries and proclaim the glad tidings of the everlasting gospel from "city to city" (79:1). Carter was promised that through the Holy Ghost, his course would be directed and he would teach the truth and bring forth many converts (sheaves). In the revelation Jared Carter was given no companion, so he went to Kirtland to find someone to go with him. A conference of elders appointed Calvin Stoddard, the husband of Joseph Smith's sister Sophronia. He also traveled part of the time with his brothers Gideon and Simeon Carter and with Sylvester Smith, all three of whom had also received missionary calls (75:30, 34). Jared Carter began serving this mission on 25 April 1832, where he found much success. Through his instrumentality ninety-eight people were brought into the gospel while on this mission (Cook, 169–70).

BIBLIOGRAPHY

Carter, Jared. Journal. Church History Library, The Church of Jesus Christ of Latter-day Saints, Salt Lake City, Utah.

Cook, Lyndon W. *The Revelations of the Prophet Joseph Smith*. Salt Lake City: Deseret Book, 1985.

MOR

Historical context and overview of Doctrine and Covenants 80

Historical context

Stephen Burnett was first called to preach the gospel on 25 January 1832 with Ruggles Eames, and Eden Smith was called at the same time to preach with Micah B. Welton (75:35–36). Just six weeks later, on 7 March 1832, Burnett and Smith were called by this revelation to be missionary companions. Eden Smith, the son of John Smith (not the Prophet's uncle), was an elder in his mid-twenties. Stephen Burnett was still in his teenage years and a high priest.

Content overview

Unlike the calling of many missionaries at that time, the Lord did not specify a geographical region where Burnett and Smith should serve. Instead, they were told "it mattereth not" where they serve, for they "cannot go amiss" if they would "preach the gospel to every creature that cometh under the sound" of their voices (80:1–3). Unfortunately, on 7 March 1832, the date this revelation was received, Eden Smith recorded in his journal that he was taken "sick and was verry sick for sometime" (7 March 1832). John Smith, Eden's father, recorded in his journal that he traveled with Stephen Burnett for a short time, beginning 22 March 1832 (22 March–14 April 1832).

BIBLIOGRAPHY

Smith, Eden. Journal. Church History Library, The Church of Jesus Christ of Latter-day Saints, Salt Lake City, Utah.

Smith, John. Journal. Church History Library, The Church of Jesus Christ of Latter-day Saints, Salt Lake City, Utah.

MOR

Historical context and overview of Doctrine and Covenants 81

Historical context

The formal progress towards organizing and defining key leadership bodies of the Church began with the reception of Doctrine and Covenants 107:59–100 on 11 November 1831. In 107:65 the Lord instructed the Church that "it must needs be that one be appointed of the High Priesthood to preside over the priesthood, and he shall be called President of the High Priesthood of the Church." This president was "to preside over the whole church, and to be like unto Moses" (107:91). Joseph Smith was sustained in that position by members of the Church who attended the Amherst conference held on 25 January 1832. He was ordained at the same time by Sidney Rigdon. On 8 March 1832, Joseph chose Jesse Gause and Sidney Rigdon as counselors in the Presidency of the High Priesthood (Jensen et al., 432–35), and one week later, 15 March, Joseph received section 81, which informed Jesse Gause concerning his duties (Jensen et al., 254–57). After Gause's defection from the Church, Joseph Smith received a revelation (unpublished) on 5 January 1833 in which the Lord said: "Verily verily I say unto you [Frederick G. Williams] thou art called to be a councillor & scribe unto my servant Joseph" (Smith, Revelation). On 8 March 1833, Joseph received section 90, in which the Lord stated that Sidney Rigdon and Frederick G. Williams, as counselors in the Presidency, "are accounted as equal with thee [Joseph Smith] in holding the keys of this last kingdom" (90:6). Ten days later, 18 March 1833, at a meeting of the School of the Prophets, these two men were ordained (Smith, *History,* 1:334). Frederick G. Williams's name was then attached to section 81, as could the name of any other man who has served as a counselor to the president of the Church, since it describes the duties of one called to that position. Shortly thereafter the presidency of the high priesthood gradually began to be known as the First Presidency of the Church.

Content overview

The Lord first called Jesse Gause and then Frederick G. Williams, as "a counselor" to Joseph Smith (81:1). He admonished Williams to be "faithful in counsel . . . in prayer always . . . and . . . in proclaiming the gospel" (81:3). The Lord then gave powerful instruction to his new leader: "Succor the weak, lift up the hands which hang down, and strengthen the feeble knees" (81:5). This instruction has come to epitomize the work of members of the "Presidency of the High Priesthood," which presidency holds the "keys of the kingdom" (81:2).

See also Church of Jesus Christ of Latter-day Saints, The.

BIBLIOGRAPHY

Jensen, Robin Scott, Robert J. Woodford, and Steven C. Harper, eds. *Manuscript Revelation Books.* Facsimile edition. First volume of the Revelations and Translations series of *The Joseph Smith Papers,* edited by Dean C. Jessee, Ronald K. Esplin, and Richard Lyman Bushman. Salt Lake City: Church Historian's Press, 2009.

Smith, Joseph. *History of The Church of Jesus Christ of Latter-day Saints.* Edited by B. H. Roberts. 7 vols. 2d ed. rev. Salt Lake City: The Church of Jesus Christ of Latter-day Saints, 1932–51.

———. Revelation, Kirtland, Ohio, 5 January 1833, in handwriting of Frederick G. Williams, F. G. Williams Papers, Church History Library, The Church of Jesus Christ of Latter-day Saints, Salt Lake City, Utah.

RCF

Historical context and overview of Doctrine and Covenants 82

Historical context

The Lord instructed Joseph Smith and others in earlier revelations to form an organization to administer the temporal affairs of the Church, including printing Church publications and assisting the poor. The leaders of the Church first created the Literary Firm for Church publications (70) and then four months later the United Firm for all other temporal concerns (78). The Literary Firm was incorporated into the later organization and received its funding through it. The Church at the time was located in two centers—Kirtland, Ohio, and Jackson County, Missouri, but the original United Firm functioned only at Kirtland. To include the members of the Church in Missouri in the United Firm, the Lord counseled the original officers of the Firm—Newel K. Whitney, Joseph Smith, and Sidney Rigdon—to "sit in council with the saints which are in Zion" (78:9). They left Kirtland on 1 April 1832 and arrived at Independence, Missouri, on 24 April. Two days later, at a council meeting, Joseph Smith received section 82, in which the Lord further explained details of the organization and called additional men to be officers of the Firm. The United Firm later became referred to as the United Order, or simply "the

order," or "mine order" (92:1; 96:4, 8; 104:1, 5, 10, 19, 40, 47–48). *See* Consecration.

Content overview

There had been disagreements between the leaders of the Church at Kirtland and those in Missouri that had been amicably settled at the council meeting before this revelation was received. The Lord acknowledged the situation and forgave them for their trespasses but warned them of the serious nature of ignoring the commandments he had given them (82:1–4). He enhanced the warning by counseling them to "sin no more" and warning them that unto the "soul who sinneth shall the former sins return" (82:7). He then promised, "I, the Lord, am bound when ye do what I say; but when ye do not what I say, ye have no promise" (82:10).

The Lord then named nine men, five of whom lived in Missouri (Partridge, Gilbert, Whitmer, Cowdery, and Phelps), to be officers in the United Firm and explained some of their duties (82:11–12). He concluded the revelation by explaining the purposes of the organization and the consequences of disobedience (82:13–24). The Lord had previously stated to the original officers of the Firm, "If ye are not equal in earthly things ye cannot be equal in obtaining heavenly things" (78:6), and now, to all of the officers, he declared "every man" was to seek "the interest of his neighbor, and [do] all things with an eye single to the glory of God" (82:19).

RJW

Historical context and overview of Doctrine and Covenants 83

Historical context

In April 1832, Joseph Smith visited the Saints settling in Missouri, hoping "to so organize the Church, that the brethren might eventually be independent of every incumbrance beneath the celestial kingdom, by bonds and covenants of mutual friendship, and mutual love" (Smith, 1:269). After receiving warm fellowship and rejoicing with the Saints in Kaw Township, Joseph returned to Independence for further organizational meetings. While sitting in council with the brethren, Joseph received this revelation which gave additional instruction to what had already been given concerning temporal provisions for the Saints (42; 51; 78; 82).

Content overview

The Lord instructed husbands to provide for their wives and families until their children are able to provide for themselves. Under the principles of CONSECRATION revealed in the early 1830s, faithful "widows and orphans . . . , as also the poor" could rely on the Church for support (83:2–6; cf. 42:30–34; 82:17–24). If parents did not have the resources to give their children inheritances, the children were to receive a stewardship from the Lord's storehouse (83:5). Those leaving the fellowship of the Church could retain the land deeded to them but would not have claim on that which was originally consecrated to the bishop (83:3; cf. 51:4–5).

BIBLIOGRAPHY

Smith, Joseph. *History of The Church of Jesus Christ of Latter-day Saints.* Edited by B. H. Roberts. 7 vols. 2d ed. rev. Salt Lake City: The Church of Jesus Christ of Latter-day Saints, 1932–51.

MOR

Historical context and overview of Doctrine and Covenants 84

Historical context

Identified by the Prophet Joseph Smith as a "revelation on Priesthood" (1:287), the revelation recorded in Doctrine and Covenants 84 was given on 22 and 23 September 1832 and is of considerable doctrinal significance. The historical beginnings for this revelation came many months earlier as the Prophet engaged in his translation of the Bible. Undoubtedly, the doctrines of PRIESTHOOD in antiquity and the establishment of a latter-day ZION were upon his mind. In January 1832, the Lord called at least twenty-four elders on missions to various areas in the United States (75). By late September of that year, these missionaries returned to Kirtland with reports of their successes. It was in the joyful setting of these missionaries reporting "the histories of their several stewardships in the Lord's vineyard" (Smith, 1:286) that the Prophet sought and received this revelation. Historical evidence confirms that the revelation as it is now recorded in the Doctrine and

Covenants was three separate but interrelated revelations received on consecutive days—22 and 23 September. The first was received in the presence of six elders of the priesthood and is recorded in verses 1 to 41 or 42. The second, verses 41 or 42 through 102, was received in the presence of ten high priests on 23 September, and the third, verses 103 through 120, on the same day (Jensen et al., 274–75, 278–79, 286–87).

Content overview

In the first part of the revelation recorded in section 84 (vv. 84:1–41), the Lord reaffirmed his will concerning the establishment of the NEW JERUSALEM in Jackson County, Missouri. This city, Zion, was to be a gathering place for the Saints, and a temple was to be built there wherein the glory of the Lord would prevail. In this revelation, the Lord declared that "this generation shall not all pass away until an house shall be built unto the Lord" (84:5); however, because antagonists caused the Saints to withdraw from Jackson County, the Lord, at least temporarily, modified the plan. In a later revelation, he said: "Verily, verily, I say unto you, that when I give a commandment to any of the sons of men to do a work unto my name, and those sons of men go with all their might and with all they have to perform that work, and cease not their diligence, and their enemies come upon them and hinder them from performing that work, behold, it behooveth me to require that work no more at the hands of those sons of men, but to accept of their offerings. . . . Therefore, for this cause have I accepted the offerings of those whom I commanded to build up a city and a house unto my name, in Jackson county, Missouri, and were hindered by their enemies, saith the Lord your God" (124:49, 51).

> 19 And this greater *a*priesthood administereth the gospel and holdeth the *b*key of the *c*mysteries of the kingdom, even the key of the *d*knowledge of God.

Doctrine and Covenants 84:19.

The doctrine of the priesthood is a primary focus of section 84. The revelation contributes greatly to the understanding of the difference between the "lesser" (Aaronic) and the "greater" (Melchizedek) priesthoods. The historical information contained in the revelation concerning the history of the priesthood reflects Joseph's involvement in the translation of both the Old and New Testaments. The Lord revealed Moses' priesthood line of authority through his father-in-law, Jethro (84:6–17) and the origin of the Aaronic Priesthood as given when the children of Israel hardened their hearts and the greater priesthood was taken from them (84:18–27). In addition, specific instruction was given concerning the purposes and powers of the greater and lesser priesthoods: the "greater priesthood administereth the gospel and holdeth the key of the mysteries of the kingdom" (84:19); the "lesser" priesthood holds the keys of the "preparatory gospel," which is the "gospel of repentance and of baptism" (84:26–27). Also revealed is knowledge concerning the priesthood and ministry of John the Baptist (84:27–28). This "revelation on priesthood" (84, headnote) provides an important link between ancient and modern practices and promises of the priesthood, which "is without beginning of days or end of years" (84:17). The Lord identified those "whom I have called and sent forth to build up my church" as modern-day "sons of Moses and of Aaron," who have taken upon themselves, as did the ancients, solemn responsibilities and who will receive the promised blessings for their faithfulness, even "all that my Father hath shall be given unto him . . . according to the oath and covenant which belongeth to the priesthood" (84:32–39). Verses 33–44 outline the conditions of this "oath and covenant" of the priesthood, and contain the Lord's command to "live by every word that proceedeth forth from the mouth of God."

The Lord began the second part of the revelation (84:42–102) with an explanation that the Spirit of Jesus Christ is given to "every man that cometh into the world," and that following the promptings of that Spirit will lead one to the gospel covenant that was "renewed and confirmed" upon Joseph Smith (84:45–48). How people respond to the Spirit of Jesus Christ determines the righteous from the wicked (84:49–51). Proclaiming the GOSPEL to the world is a major theme in this section. Specific counsel regarding how to teach the gospel was given along with promises of success, protection, and power for laborers in the kingdom (84:61ff). Within the context of this counsel to missionaries, one aspect of the revelation is of particular importance to the Church. The Lord declared that "vanity and unbelief have brought the whole church under condemnation" (84:55). Specifically the "vanity and unbelief" of which the Lord spoke that had caused members' and missionaries' "minds in times past [to become] darkened" was the failure to "remember the new covenant, even the Book of Mormon and the former commandments which I have given them, not only to say, but to do according to that which I have written" (84:54–57). In the April 1986 general conference, President Ezra Taft Benson specifically commented on this passage as it relates to the Book of Mormon:

"Unless we read the Book of Mormon and give heed to its teachings, the Lord has stated in section 84 of the Doctrine and Covenants that the whole Church is under condemnation: 'And this condemnation resteth upon the children of Zion, even all.' (D&C 84:56.) The Lord continues: 'And they shall remain under this condemnation until they repent and remember the new covenant, even the Book of Mormon and the former commandments which I have given them, not only to say, but to do according to that which I have written.' (D&C 84:57.)

"Now we not only need to *say* more about the Book of Mormon, but we need to *do* more with it. Why? The Lord answers: 'That they may bring forth fruit meet for their Father's kingdom; otherwise there remaineth a scourge and judgment to be poured out upon the children of Zion.' (D&C 84:58.) We have felt that scourge and judgment! . . .

"The Book of Mormon has not been, nor is it yet, the center of our personal study, family teaching, preaching, and missionary work. Of this we must repent" (5).

In the third part of the revelation (84:103–20), the Lord called for unity in the work. "Let every man stand in his own office, and labor in his own calling" (84:109). The Church has need of each member, "that all may be edified together, that the system may be kept perfect" (84:110). The Lord's servants are to faithfully "go . . . forth as your circumstances shall permit, in your several callings . . . reproving the world in righteousness" (84:117). The Lord also promised to "exert the powers of heaven" in rending the "kingdoms" of the world (84:118–19). He closed the revelation with a sure promise: "Ye cannot see it now, yet a little while and ye shall see it, and know that I am, and that I will come and reign with my people" (84:119).

BIBLIOGRAPHY

Benson, Ezra Taft. "Cleansing the Inner Vessel." *Ensign* 16 (May 1986): 4–7.

Jensen, Robin Scott, Robert J. Woodford, and Steven C. Harper, eds. *Manuscript Revelation Books*. Facsimile edition. First volume of the Revelations and Translations series of *The Joseph Smith Papers*, edited by Dean C. Jessee, Ronald K. Esplin, and Richard Lyman Bushman. Salt Lake City: Church Historian's Press, 2009.

Smith, Joseph. *History of The Church of Jesus Christ of Latter-day Saints*. Edited by B. H. Roberts. 7 vols. 2d ed. rev. Salt Lake City: The Church of Jesus Christ of Latter-day Saints, 1932–51.

BLT

Historical context and overview of Doctrine and Covenants 85

Historical context

Joseph Smith had received correspondence from some of the brethren in Missouri and in response wrote to William Phelps on 27 November 1832. Section 85 is part of the letter added to the Doctrine and Covenants in 1876. The call to migrate to Missouri and build Zion according to the law of CONSECRATION and stewardship created a need to keep accurate records. Some of the Missouri Saints would not keep the law of consecration, and Joseph Smith supposed their leaders were asking themselves, "What shall becom[e] of all these who are assaying to come up unto Zion in order to keep the commandments of God and yet rec[e]ive not there inheritance by consecration by order or deed from the bishop the man that God has appointed in a legal way agreeable to the law given to organize and regulate the church[?]"

(Smith to Phelps). Joseph Smith discerned these needs and questions by "the still small voice" (85:6) and wrote the revealed answers. Though Frederick G. Williams wrote down the first part of the letter, most of what is now section 85 is in the handwriting of Joseph Smith.

Content overview

There is a mixture of Joseph's voice and the Lord's in this section (cf. 85:6–7). The letter clarified the duties of the Lord's clerk, namely, to keep a history of righteousness and unrighteousness in Zion, including accurate records "of all those who consecrate properties, and receive inheritances legally from the bishop" (85:1). Those who did not receive their inheritance by living the law of consecration, together with their ancestors and descendants, were to be excluded from the Church record referred to as "the book of the law of God" (85:3–5). Verse 7 contains the prophecy that the Lord would send someone to arrange inheritances for those whose names were recorded in the book, but those who were not in the book were to receive no inheritance in Zion. Verse 8 warned that those who steady the ark, a clear reference to the Old Testament account of Uzzah reaching out to steady the ark of the covenant (2 Samuel 6:6–7), would be smitten.

This revelation inspired Joseph with the importance of keeping records. He started writing his first history, minute book, journal, and letterbook following his reception of section 85. In the Book of the Law of the Lord he entered the names of many who consecrated their lives to Zion. The revelation makes clear that those "whose names are not found written in the book of the law . . . shall not find an inheritance among the saints of the Most High" (85:11).

The prophecy about the "one mighty and strong" (85:7) has caused much speculation. In 1905 the First Presidency officially explained that either Edward Partridge, as bishop in Zion in 1832, was that man, or that the prophecy may yet be fulfilled. In the latter case, "Let the Latter-day Saints know that he will be a future bishop of the Church who will be with the Saints in Zion. . . . He will be designated by the inspiration of the Lord, and will be accepted and sustained by the whole Church" (in Clark, 4:118–19).

Oliver Cowdery sought clarification from Joseph Smith about the warning that the man who steadied the ark would be smitten (85:8). Joseph replied that the prophecy "does not mean that any had" steadied the ark "at the time, but it was given as a caution to those in high standing to beware, lest they should fall by the vivid shaft of death as the Lord had said" (Cowdery to John Whitmer). Church leaders in Missouri failed to heed the warning fully. Joseph subsequently wrote to them that "men should not attempt to steady the ark of God!" (Smith to Partridge and others). Edward Partridge repented. President Joseph F. Smith stated that the Lord "forgave Edward Partridge his sins, and withheld the execution of the judgment pronounced against him" (in Clark, 4:118).

See also Ark of God, steady the.

BIBLIOGRAPHY

Clark, James R., comp. *Messages of the First Presidency of The Church of Jesus Christ of Latter-day Saints, 1833–1964.* 6 vols. Salt Lake City: Bookcraft, 1965–75.

Cowdery, Oliver, to John Whitmer, 1 January 1834. Huntington Library, San Marino, California.

Smith, Joseph, to Edward Partridge and others, 30 March 1834. *Oliver Cowdery Letterbook,* 30–36, Huntington Library, San Marino, California. In Jessee, *Personal Writings of Joseph Smith,* 333–39.

Smith, Joseph, to William W. Phelps, 27 November 1832. Joseph Smith Letterbook 1, 7–10, Church History Library, The Church of Jesus Christ of Latter-day Saints, Salt Lake City, Utah. In Jessee, *Personal Writings of Joseph Smith,* 285.

SCH

Historical context and overview of Doctrine and Covenants 86

Historical context

In December 1832, as Joseph Smith was "reviewing and editing the manuscript of the translation of the Bible" (86, headnote), he received this revelation, interpreting the PARABLE OF THE WHEAT AND THE TARES in a latter-day context.

Content overview

While the New Testament identifies the sower of the wheat (the wheat meaning "the children of the kingdom") as "the Son of man" (Matt. 13:37–38), in Doctrine and Covenants 86 "the apostles" are said to be "the sowers of the seed" (86:2). Obviously, the apostles would be "sowing" under the direction of the Savior. In both the New Testament and the Doctrine and Covenants, the devil is identified as the sower of the tares (the tares being "the children of the wicked one"), which "tares chok[ed] the wheat," according to this revelation, and drove "the church into the wilderness" (86:3; Matt. 13:38–39). This occurred during the time of the great apostasy, beginning toward the end of the first century A.D. With the restoration of the gospel in the latter days, the Church is coming forth out of the wilderness (5:14; 33:5; 109:73). The wheat has been resown, and the tares continue to be sown and grow along with the wheat. This revelation affirms that in 1832, "even now . . . the angels are crying unto the Lord day and night, who are ready and waiting to be sent forth to reap down the fields." But because the wheat plants are yet tender and pulling up the tares might uproot the wheat as well as the tares, the harvest was to be postponed until the plants were "fully ripe" (86:4–7; cf. Matt. 13:27–30). Evidently that time has come. President Wilford Woodruff stated in 1894 that "God has held the angels of destruction for many years, lest they should reap down the wheat with the tares. But I want to tell you now, that those angels have left the portals of heaven . . . and are hovering over the earth waiting to pour out the judgments. And from this very day they shall be poured out." Further, he said, "It's by the power of the Gospel that we shall escape" (512–13). In this harvest of the wheat and the tares, section 86 clarifies the sequence of the gathering, agreeing with the Joseph Smith Translation of Matthew: "First gather out the wheat from among the tares, and after the gathering of the wheat, behold and lo, the tares are bound in bundles, and the field remaineth to be burned" (86:7; cf. Matt. 13:30; JST Matt. 13:29). Missionaries of The Church of Jesus Christ of Latter-day Saints are currently in the process of gathering the wheat. Concerning the gathering of the tares, President Marion G. Romney, in the October 1966 general conference, said, "Even now the tares are binding themselves in bundles, making ready for the field to be burned" (53).

The Lord closed the revelation linking the

parable of the wheat and the tares with the importance of the PRIESTHOOD restored through the Prophet Joseph Smith and his associates. The Lord declared: "Through the lineage of your fathers . . . ye are lawful heirs" of the priesthood, "according to the flesh," and that the priesthood "must needs remain through you and your lineage until the restoration of all things spoken by the mouths of all the holy prophets since the world began" (86:8–10). Thus is fulfilled, in part, the Lord's ancient promise to Abraham that his posterity would bear the priesthood and that through them "shall all the families of the earth be blessed, even with the blessings of the Gospel, which are the blessings of salvation, even of life eternal" (Abr. 2:11). *See* Abrahamic covenant.

See also Apostasy, the great.

BIBLIOGRAPHY

Romney, Marion G. Conference Report, October 1966, 50–54.

Woodruff, Wilford. *The Young Woman's Journal.* Vol. 5. Salt Lake City: George Q. Cannon and Sons Co., 1894.

ROC

Historical context and overview of Doctrine and Covenants 87

Historical context

From the time the CONSTITUTION of the United States went into effect there were serious questions about how it should be interpreted and how inclusive it was. One of the most serious issues was states' rights. How much power did the national government have over the states? Could individual states nullify within their borders laws of Congress that they found offensive? Did the Constitution create an indissoluble union, or was it merely a compact between the states that could be dissolved if one party broke the terms of the contract? Was secession a viable option?

Tensions between the states, and particularly between North and South, flared up frequently, and at times American statesmen commented with alarm at the prospect of disunion and civil war. Such a tragedy, they thought, could easily be related to the issue of slavery, which was closely tied to states' rights. In 1820, for

example, Thomas Jefferson looked with dismay at the "Missouri Compromise," which temporarily solved one crisis, predicting that the slavery question would rise again, like a "firebell in the night," and be the death-knell of the Union. (Allen, 75).

Various crises over the next forty years fueled the fear of civil war, but one of the most serious came in 1832, after the state of South Carolina defiantly declared that the hated American tariff laws of 1828 and 1832 were unconstitutional and forbade the collection of the tariff within the state after 1 February 1833. The tariff, South Carolinians believed, would hurt their slave-supported economy by increasing the expense of cotton goods imported from England and, in turn, diminish England's demand for southern cotton.

President Andrew Jackson was horrified at what he considered an act of rebellion, and he was ready to use armed force, if necessary, to enforce the collection of the tariff in the ports of South Carolina. He sent reinforcements to federal garrisons in the state, a warship, and seven revenue cutters to Charleston Harbor. Only a compromise tariff, which passed Congress on 1 March 1833, averted civil war at that time.

Joseph Smith was very much aware of all that was going on and looked at it with deep concern. He was dismayed and disgusted at the actions of South Carolina which, he believed, threatened the nation with "immediate dissolution." "President Jackson," he said, "issued his proclamation against this rebellion, called out a force sufficient to quell it, and implored the blessings of God to assist the nation to extricate itself from the horrors of the approaching and solemn crisis" (1:301).

It was in this atmosphere of national crisis

8 Wherefore, *ª*stand ye in holy places, and be not moved, until the day of the Lord come; for behold, it cometh *ᵇ*quickly, saith the Lord. Amen.

Doctrine and Covenants 87:8.

that, on Christmas day 1832, the Prophet prayed about the subject. As a result, his fears were turned to solemn assurance when he received the revelation that is known as section 87.

Content overview

This revelation confirmed, in no uncertain way, the worst fears of the times: a division between the states, the efforts of the South to enlist the aid of Great Britain, and the rising of slaves against their masters. Ten years later Joseph told some close friends that on the day he received this revelation he was also told that eventually WAR would begin in South Carolina and would probably arise over the question of slavery (130:12–13; Ehat and Cook, 172). The war did not immediately happen, but it came in 1861.

The revelation foretold that beginning with the conflict between the states, "war shall be poured out upon all nations" (87:3), which together "with famine, and plague, and earthquake" will make "a full end of all nations" (87:6). "A full end of all nations" can be interpreted to mean that when the Lord returns to the earth there will be no laws but his laws governing the nations (38:22; 58:22; cf. Smith, 5:64). The Lord ended the revelation with an important message to all: "Wherefore, stand ye in holy places, and be not moved, until the day of the Lord come; for behold, it cometh quickly, saith the Lord" (87:8). This revelation not only contains a prophecy of war but a reaffirmation of the approaching MILLENNIUM, or "day of the Lord." If there was hope in America that political compromise had avoided civil war, there was a sense of surety among the Saints that no such thing had happened. For them, war and great natural calamities could not be avoided; they were only precursors to the coming of the Lord. Joseph Smith's prophecy became well known among them and was even carried in manuscript form by missionaries. It was first published in England, in 1851, as part of the first edition of the Pearl of Great Price. Additionally, Church leaders often preached about it from the pulpit, and the Saints were not the least surprised when civil war finally came in 1861. The revelation was first added to the Doctrine and Covenants in the 1876 edition.

BIBLIOGRAPHY

Allen, James B. "Joseph Smith vs. John C. Calhoun: The States' Rights Dilemma and Early Mormon History." In *Joseph Smith Jr.: Reappraisals After Two Centuries.* New York: Oxford University Press, 2008.

Ehat, Andrew F., and Lyndon W. Cook, comps. and eds. *The Words of Joseph Smith.* Provo, Utah: Religious Studies Center, Brigham Young University, 1980.

Smith, Joseph. *History of The Church of Jesus Christ of Latter-day Saints.* Edited by B. H. Roberts. 7 vols. 2d ed. rev. Salt Lake City: The Church of Jesus Christ of Latter-day Saints, 1932–51.

JBA

Historical context and overview of Doctrine and Covenants 88

Historical context

The Prophet Joseph Smith received most of the revelation known as "The Olive Leaf," Doctrine and Covenants 88, on 27 and 28 December 1832. This was a season of unrest for the Saints as they dealt with increasing persecution in Kirtland, Ohio, and in Missouri. More importantly, there were the lingering disagreements between the leaders of the Church in Missouri and those in Ohio. Joseph Smith and others had traveled to Missouri the previous March and thought the problems had been resolved, but in the ensuing months, they had resurfaced. Joseph Smith convened a conference of ten high priests in the upper room of the Gilbert and Whitney store in Kirtland on 27 December 1832. Frederick G. Williams, who was clerk of the conference, recorded: "Bro Joseph arose and said, to receive revelation and the blessings of heaven it was necessary to have our minds on god and exercise faith and become of one heart and of one mind therefore he recommended all present to pray seperately and vocally to the Lord for to reveal his will unto us concerning the upbuilding of Zion, & for the benefit of the saints and for the duty and employment of the Elders. Accordingly we all bowed down before the Lord, after which each one arose and spoke in his turn his feelings, and determination to keep the commandments of God. And then proceded to receive a revelation concerning the duty [not legible] of our above stated 9 o clock P.M. the revelation not being finished the conference adjourned . . . and commenced by Prayer thus proceded to receive the residue of the above revelation and it being finished and there being no further business before the conference closed the meeting by prayer in harmony with the brethren and gratitude to our heavenly Father for the great manifestation of his holy Spirit during the setting of the conference" (KCMB, 3–4).

The revelation received in the conference consisted of Doctrine and Covenants 88:1–126. Verses 127–37 were received by Joseph on 3 January 1833 as the leadership of the Church in Kirtland prepared to begin the School of the Prophets. The Prophet combined these two separate revelations, along with verses 138–41, which were also received in connection with the School of the Prophets, when the 1835 edition of the Doctrine and Covenants was published. The title "Olive Leaf" was given to the revelation by Joseph Smith in a 14 January 1833 letter he sent to William W. Phelps, one of the presiding officers of the Church in Missouri. In that context he stated: "I send you the 'olive leaf' which we have plucked from the Tree of Paradise, the Lord's message of peace to us; for though our brethren in Zion indulge in feelings towards us, which are not according to the requirements of the new covenant, yet, we have the satisfaction of knowing that the Lord approves of us, and has accepted us" (1:316). In the same packet with this letter and the revelation was another letter commissioned by a conference of high priests in Kirtland on 13 January. It was written in response to an earlier revelation wherein the Lord counseled the leaders in Ohio to upbraid "your brethren in Zion for their rebellion against you at the time I sent you [the previous March]" (84:76). Hyrum Smith and Orson Hyde were selected to write the letter, which they did. It was then read to the conference and approved (KCMB, 5–6; cf. Smith, 1:317–21). The revelation and the two letters of reproof had the desired effect: the brethren in Missouri repented, and the difficulties were resolved (Smith, 1:327; cf. FWR, 34).

Content overview

In the opening verses the Lord assured the brethren gathered that their prayers had been heard and recorded in the "book of the names of the sanctified" (88:1–2). He promised them "another Comforter . . . even the Holy Spirit of promise; which other Comforter is the same that I promised unto my disciples, as is recorded in the testimony of John. This Comforter is the promise which I give unto you of eternal life, even the glory of the celestial kingdom" (88:3–5; cf. John 14:16).

The revelation provided early Church leaders a sweeping vista of the grandeur of the Lord and his role in the governance of all things through his light, even the "light of Christ" (88:6–13, 40–50) and his law. Through the redemption of Christ, all of God's children will be resurrected and will receive a reward commensurate with the level of their obedience to his laws while on the earth; those who abide in sin will "remain filthy still" and will not receive a kingdom of glory (88:14–17, 20–40). The earth abides "the law of a celestial kingdom" and will become the habitation of those who live that same law (88:25–26, 18–20). The Lord further revealed that all his creations are governed by law and if men will obey his law "the day shall come when [they] shall comprehend even God, being quickened in him and by him" (88:41–50). In the parable of the man sending his servants into the field, the Lord explained that his law extends beyond this earth and that he visits each of his creations in their turn (88:51–61). *See* Parable regarding the Lord's visits to kingdoms.

Following this extensive explanation of his law and power, the Lord turned his attention to the brethren to whom the revelation was given. If they would "draw near" to him, he would "draw near" to them, and they would eventually "see . . . his face" (88:62–73). To receive such a blessing, they were to "sanctify" themselves and teach each other the "doctrine of the kingdom" (88:74–80). In the remainder of the revelation the Saints were instructed concerning the need to teach and be taught "things both in heaven and in the earth" so that they could be prepared to go out to the world and teach the gospel (88:78–83). The brethren were told to remain in Kirtland that they could be "perfected in [their] ministry to go forth among the Gentiles for the last time . . . and to prepare the saints for the hour of judgment which is to come" (88:84–86). The Lord then enumerated events that will precede and accompany his second coming: the testimony of the elders followed by great natural disasters (88:87–91); angels declaring the coming of Jesus, the BRIDEGROOM, followed by a "great sign in heaven" and the appearance of the Lord (88:92–95; cf. 65:3); angels sounding TRUMPS signaling the RESURRECTION of various groups (88:96–102); more angels heralding Christ's victory through the ATONEMENT and that "every knee shall bow, and every tongue shall confess" his sovereignty (88:103–7); and a series of seven more angels sounding trumpets revealing "the secret acts of men, and the mighty works of God" through the seven thousand years of its "temporal existence" (88:108–10; 77:6–7). Also included is an account of SATAN being bound for one thousand years, then being "loosed for a little season" in preparation for "the battle of the great God," the last great battle of the war that began in heaven, at the end of which battle "the devil and his armies shall be cast away into their own place" (88:110–16). *See* Jesus Christ, second coming of; Millennium, the.

"Therefore," the Lord told the Saints, "call your solemn assembly . . . and teach one another words of wisdom . . . even by study and also by faith" (88:117–18). *See* Solemn assembly/assemblies.

The Saints were also instructed to build the Kirtland TEMPLE. The Lord said, "Organize yourselves; prepare every needful thing; and establish a house, even a house of prayer, a house of fasting, a house of faith, a house of learning, a house of glory, a house of order, a house of God" (88:119). This was to be not only a place of worship but a house of learning where they could fulfill the commission given them to teach each other. The learning here was to be done "by study and also by faith" (88:118). They were instructed to prepare to be worthy to learn in the temple (88:121–24) as well as in the School of the Prophets (88:127), which was to be established in Kirtland. *See* Schools.

The purpose of the ordinance of the washing of feet was that participants would be "clean from the blood of this generation" (88:138–41). *See* Wash, washed, washing(s).

This revelation steadied the early leaders,

established the beginning of temple building, and opened the way for the members of the Church to prepare themselves for the greater blessings of the Lord.

BIBLIOGRAPHY

Far West Record. Church History Library, The Church of Jesus Christ of Latter-day Saints, Salt Lake City, Utah.

Kirtland Council Minute Book. Church History Library, The Church of Jesus Christ of Latter-day Saints, Salt Lake City, Utah.

Smith, Joseph. *History of The Church of Jesus Christ of Latter-day Saints.* Edited by B. H. Roberts. 7 vols. 2d ed. rev. Salt Lake City: The Church of Jesus Christ of Latter-day Saints, 1932–51.

GLD

Historical context and overview of Doctrine and Covenants 89

Historical context

In the nineteenth century there was much talk in America about the negative influence of liquor. Crusaders against consumption of liquor and other alcoholic beverages formed a popular temperance movement. As a result of its popularity in the greater Kirtland area, some critics of Joseph Smith claim the WORD OF WISDOM was no more than a "product or logical result of contemporary experience and more particularly the temperance movement" (Peterson, 17). Joseph Smith countered such thinking when he wrote on 27 February 1833, "I received the following revelation" (1:327).

The revelation is known as the Word of Wisdom, for it sets "forth the order and will of God in the temporal salvation of all saints in the last days" (89:2). It was a revelation given to Joseph Smith after the School of the Prophets was organized in Kirtland. Brigham Young, in a discourse given on 8 February 1868, recalled how the revelation came to be received:

"The first school of the prophets was held in a small room situated over the Prophet Joseph's kitchen, in a house which belonged to Bishop Whitney. . . . The brethren came to that place for hundreds of miles to attend school in a little room probably no larger than eleven by fourteen. When they assembled together in this room after breakfast, the first they did was to light their pipes, and, while smoking, talk about the great things of the kingdom, and spit all over the room, and as soon as the pipe was out of their mouths a large chew of tobacco would then be taken. Often when the Prophet entered the room to give the school instructions he would find himself in a cloud of tobacco smoke. This, and the complaints of his wife at having to clean so filthy a floor, made the Prophet think upon the matter, and he inquired of the Lord relating to the conduct of the Elders in using tobacco, and the revelation known as the Word of Wisdom was the result of his inquiry" (12:158).

The Word of Wisdom, unlike other revelations given to Joseph Smith, was not given "by commandment or constraint." It was "given for a principle with promise, adapted to the capacity of the weak and the weakest of all saints, who are or can be called saints" (89:2–3). As a result, the revelation has met with varied responses and interpretations. From the beginning, some viewed it as binding, others as sound advice, and still others as a matter of little consequence.

In February 1834 a resolution concerning the revelation was adopted: "No official member in this Church is worthy to hold an office, after having the Word of Wisdom properly taught him, and he, the official member, neglecting to comply with or obey it" (Smith, 2:35). The resolution, however, was not generally made a test of fellowship. For example, when the Mormon pioneers trekked west, tea and coffee were considered staples. Not until 9 September 1851, after a discourse on the Word of Wisdom by patriarch John Smith, did Brigham Young propose that the Latter-day Saints covenant to abstain from the negative substances "mentioned in the Word of Wisdom" ("Minutes," 35). The motion was accepted and became binding as a commandment, but again, there were no particular consequences for failure to comply.

In 1908, "President Joseph F. Smith read section 89" in its entirety to those assembled in the Salt Lake Tabernacle during a general conference of the Church. Several discourses on the subject by Church leaders followed. A vote was called for, and once again the Word of Wisdom was accepted as binding upon Church membership (Packer, 26). The difference, when compared to other occasions, was that this time there was added emphasis given to the Word of Wisdom at all levels of the Church. Today, observance of the Word of Wisdom is a requirement for baptism, priesthood ordination, and entrance into holy temples. Living the health code in the Word of Wisdom has become one of the most recognized characteristics of The Church of Jesus Christ of Latter-day Saints.

Content overview

The Lord did not begin by discussing the obvious health benefits derived from living the principles found in the Word of Wisdom (89:18, 20), but by warning members of the Church about the "evils and designs which do and will exist in the hearts of conspiring men" (89:4). These "conspiring men" are the purveyors of the habit-forming and addictive products proscribed in the revelation—fermented and distilled alcoholic beverages (89:5–7), tobacco products (89:8), and "hot drinks" (89:9). From the beginning the term "hot drinks" has been interpreted to mean tea and coffee. Though the abuse of harmful drugs is not mentioned in the revelation, it is certainly implied, and the Brethren have counseled repeatedly to not abuse them in any form.

The Lord then taught that herbs and fruits "in the season thereof" are for man's use "with prudence and thanksgiving" (89:10–11). He also counseled that the flesh of "beasts and of the fowls of the air" is "to be used sparingly" (89:12–13) and that "all grain is ordained for the use of man and of beasts, to be the staff of life" (89:14).

The Lord ended the revelation by promising great physical and spiritual blessings to those who obey the Word of Wisdom and walk "in obedience to the commandments" (89:18–21).

See also Wine.

> **3** Given for a principle with "promise, adapted to the capacity of the ᵇweak and the weakest of all ᶜsaints, who are or can be called saints.

Doctrine and Covenants 89:3.

BIBLIOGRAPHY

"Minutes of the General Conference." *Millennial Star* 14, no. 3 (1 February 1852): 35.

Packer, Boyd K. "The Spirit of the Tabernacle." *Ensign* 37 (May 2007): 27–29.

Peterson, Paul H. "An Historical Analysis of the Word of Wisdom." Master's thesis, Brigham Young University, August 1972.

Smith, Joseph. *History of The Church of Jesus Christ of Latter-day Saints.* Edited by B. H. Roberts. 7 vols. 2d ed. rev. Salt Lake City: The Church of Jesus Christ of Latter-day Saints, 1932–51.

Young, Brigham. *Journal of Discourses.* 26 vols. London: Latter-day Saints' Book Depot, 1854–86.

SEB

Historical context and overview of Doctrine and Covenants 90

Historical context

The Lord revealed the final step in the organization of the First Presidency of the Church in this section of the Doctrine and Covenants. When the Church was organized in 1830, Joseph Smith and Oliver Cowdery were named as the first apostles and served as first and second elders, respectively, of the infant Church (20:1–4; 21). At that time little indication of an organizational framework for the newly founded Church was provided. As the Church grew in numbers and expanded in territory the Lord began to shed further light on this matter. *See* Historical context and overview of Doctrine and Covenants 81 (p. 785).

In section 90, the Lord stipulated that the counselors in the presidency "are accounted as equal with [the president] in holding the keys of this last kingdom" (90:6). When the "Presidents Church Council" was organized in February 1834, the minutes state: "The president of the church, who is also the president of the council, is appointed by revelation, and acknowledged in his administration by the voice of the church. And it is according to the dignity of his office that he should preside over the council of the church; and it is his privilege to be assisted by two other presidents, appointed after the same manner that he himself was appointed. And in case of the absence of one or both of those who are appointed to assist him, he has power to preside over the council without an assistant;

and in case he himself is absent, the other presidents have power to preside in his stead, both or either of them" (102:9–11). Ten days after receipt of section 90, on 18 March 1833, Joseph Smith set apart Sidney Rigdon and Frederick G. Williams to serve as his counselors.

Content overview

This section provides essential information about the character and role of the presidency, including the duty to see that "the word may go forth unto the ends of the earth," anticipating a time when "every man shall hear the fulness of the gospel in his own tongue" (90:8–12). Of primary importance, the Lord revealed that the keys of the kingdom given to Joseph Smith would remain with him even in "the world to come," an apparent reference to Joseph presiding over this latter-day dispensation, even after his death (90:3). Nevertheless, Joseph would give to another the KEYS of the kingdom to preside over the earthly Church (90:4). The Lord also set forth the governing role of the First Presidency in directing the manner in which others are to exercise their PRIESTHOOD authority. In the latter portion of the revelation the Lord gave counsel to several individuals (90:19–35). Included is the instruction to "search diligently, pray always, and be believing," with the promise that "all things shall work together for your good, if ye walk uprightly" (90:24). The counsel to Joseph Smith Sr. that his family "be small" was not referring to the size of his biological family but rather was a caution about using the resources of the Church for "those that are not worthy," thus hindering the work of the kingdom (90:25–27).

In the first organized First Presidency, three individuals were called to serve. This pattern has continued to the present day, although on occasion the number of members in the presidency has exceeded three (for example, Thorpe B. Isaacson and Alvin R. Dyer served as additional counselors to President David O. McKay). Several apostles served for a period as counselors in the First Presidency before their call as president of the Church, including David O. McKay, Gordon B. Hinckley, and Thomas S. Monson.

See also Church of Jesus Christ of Latter-day Saints, The.

BIBLIOGRAPHY

Black, Susan Easton. *Who's Who in the Doctrine and Covenants.* Salt Lake City: Deseret Book, 1997.

McConkie, Joseph F., and Craig Ostler. *Revelations of the Restoration: A Commentary on the Doctrine and Covenants and Other Modern Revelations.* Salt Lake City: Deseret Book, 2000.

Robinson, Stephen E., and H. Dean Garrett. *A Commentary on the Doctrine and Covenants.* 4 vols. Salt Lake City: Deseret Book, 2000–2005.

Turley, Richard E. "First Presidency." In *Encyclopedia of Latter-day Saint History,* edited by Arnold K. Garr, Donald Q. Cannon, and Richard O. Cowan. Salt Lake City: Deseret Book, 2000.

RCF

Historical context and overview of Doctrine and Covenants 91

Historical context

The APOCRYPHA is a collection of ancient writings that are placed between the Old Testament and New Testament in some editions of the Bible. Martin Luther's Bible of 1534 was the first to print the Apocrypha as a separate intertestamental section. The books in the Apocrypha provide some historical and ecclesiastical information during the approximately four-hundred-year gap between the Old and New Testaments. It also includes information found in the books of Daniel and Esther. These writings are regarded as canonical by members of the Catholic and Eastern Orthodox churches but are not accepted by most Protestants. When Joseph Smith came to these writings as he proceeded with his "translation" of the Bible, he wondered whether or not to include them. *See* Doctrine and Covenants and the Joseph Smith Translation of the Bible.

Content overview

The Lord told the Prophet that the Apocrypha contained "many things . . . that are true" but that there were many other things "that are not true, which are interpolations by the hands of men." He therefore instructed the Prophet not to include these writings in his translation (91:1–3), acknowledging, however, that a person reading these books could "obtain benefit" if "enlightened by the Spirit" (91:5).

ROC

Historical context and overview of Doctrine and Covenants 92

Historical context

In 1831, a group of Church leaders was organized into a corporation known as the United Firm (cf. 78; 82. The Firm is named the "united order" in the Doctrine and Covenants; 92:1). *See* Consecration.

Content overview

On 15 March 1833, Joseph Smith received the revelation recorded in section 92. The Prophet was instructed to include Frederick G. Williams as a "lively member" in the United Firm. Williams was promised that if he was "faithful in keeping all former commandments," he would be blessed forever (92:2).

MOR

Historical context and overview of Doctrine and Covenants 93

Historical context

Little is written about the historical context for this important revelation. Joseph Smith simply recorded in his history for 6 May 1833: "I received the following." The revelation contained in Doctrine and Covenants 93 is then recorded (1:343). The Prophet did not give any indication as to what prompted the revelation. Of the three prepublication manuscripts of this revelation, only one is endorsed: "Revelation to Joseph, Sidney, Frederick & Newel by chastisement & also relative to the Father & Son 6 May 1833" (Revelation, Whitney Collection).

At the time of this revelation, Joseph and his family were living in quarters above the Newel K. Whitney store in Kirtland, Ohio. Verse 53 directed Joseph to "hasten to translate my scriptures." The translation of the New Testament had been essentially completed in February of that year, and work on the Old Testament continued into July (Smith, 1:324). Perhaps some of this revelation is a fruit of the previous New Testament translation work. *See* Doctrine and Covenants and the Joseph Smith Translation of the Bible.

APOCRYPHA.

¶ I. ESDRAS.

CHAPTER I.

1 Josias' charge to the priests and Levites....7 A great passover is kept....22 His death is much lamented....34 His successors....55 The temple, city, and many people are destroyed....56 The rest are carried unto Babylon.

AND Josias held the * feast of the passover in Jerusalem unto his Lord, and offered the passover the fourteenth day of the first month ;

2 Having set the priests according to their daily courses, being arrayed in long garments, in the temple of the Lord.

3 And he spake unto the Levites, the holy ministers of Israel, that they should hallow themselves unto the Lord, to set the holy ark of the Lord in the house that king Solomon the son of David had built :

4 *And said,* Ye shall no more bear the ark upon your shoulders : now therefore serve the Lord your God, and minister unto his people Israel, and prepare you after your families and kindreds.

5 According as David the king of Israel prescribed, and according to the magnificence of Solomon his son : and standing in the temple according to the several dignity of the families of you the Levites, who minister in the presence of your brethren the children of Israel.

6 Offer the passover in order, and make ready the sacrifices for your brethren, and keep the passover according to the commandment of the Lord, which was given unto Moses.

7 And unto the people that was found there Josias gave thirty thousand lambs and kids, and three thousand calves : these things were given of the king's allowance, according as he promised to the people, to the priests, and to the Levites.

8 And Helkias, Zacharias, and ‖ Syelus, the governors of the temple, gave to the priests for the passover two thousand and six hundred sheep, and three hundred calves.

9 And Jeconias, and Samaias, and Nathanael his brother, and Assabias, and Ochiel, and Joram, captains over thousands, gave to the Levites for the passover five thousand sheep, and ‖ seven hundred calves.

10 And when these things were done, the priests and Levites having the unleavened bread, stood in very comely order according to the kindreds.

11 And according to the several dignities of the fathers before the people, to offer to the Lord, as it is written in the book of Moses : b and thus did they in the morning.

12 And they roasted the passover with fire, as appertaineth : as for the sacrifices, they sod them in brass pots, and pans, ‖with a good savour,

13 And set them before all the people : and afterward they prepared for themselves, and for the priests their brethren, the sons of Aaron.

14 For the priests offered the fat until night : and the Levites prepared for themselves, and the priests their brethren, the sons of Aaron.

15 The holy singers also, the sons of Asaph, were in their order, according to the appointment c of David, to wit, Asaph, Zacharias, and Jeduthun, who was d of the king's retinue.

16 Moreover, the porters were at every gate ; it was not lawful for any to go from his ordinary service ; for their brethren the Levites prepared for them.

17 Thus were the things that belonged to the sacrifices of the Lord accomplished in that day, that they might hold the passover,

18 And offer sacrifices upon the altar of the Lord, according to the commandment of king Josias.

19 So the children of Israel which were present held the passover at that time, and the feast of sweet bread seven days.

20 And such a passover was not kept in Israel since the time of the prophet Samuel.

21 Yea, all the kings of Israel held not such a passover as Josias, and the priests, and the Levites, and the Jews, held with all Israel that were found dwelling at Jerusalem.

22 In the eighteenth year of the reign of Josias was this passover kept.

23 And the works of Josias were upright before his Lord, with a heart full of godliness.

24 As for the things that came to pass in his time, they were written in former times, concerning those that sinned, i and did wickedly against the Lord above all people and kingdoms, and how they grieved him ‖ exceedingly, so that the words of the Lord rose up against Israel.

25 e Now after all these acts of Josias it came to pass, that Pharaoh the king of Egypt came to raise war at Carchamis upon Euphrates : and Josias went out against him.

26 But the king of Egypt sent to him, saying, What have I to do with thee, O king of Judea ?

27 I am not sent out from the Lord God against thee ; for my war is upon Euphrates : and now the Lord is with me, yea, the Lord is with me hasting me forward : depart from me, and be not against the Lord.

28 Howbeit Josias did not turn back his chariot from him, but undertook to fight with him, not regarding the words of the prophet Jeremy, spoken by the mouth of the Lord :

29 But joined battle with him in the plain of Megiddo, and the princes came against king Josias.

30 Then said the king unto his servants, Carry me away out of the battle ; for I am very weak. And immediately his servants took him away out of the battle.

31 Then gat he up upon his second chariot ; and being brought back to Jerusalem died, and was buried in his father's sepulchre.

32 And in all Jewry they mourned for Josias, yea, Jeremy the prophet lamented for Josias, and the chief men with the women made lamentation for him unto this day : and this was given out for an ordinance to be done continually in all the nation of Israel.

33 These things are written in the book of the stories of the kings of Judah, and every one of the acts that Josias did, and his glory, and his understanding in the law of the Lord, and the things that he had done before, and the things now recited, are reported in the book of the kings of Israel and Judea.

34 f And the people took Joachaz the son of Josias, and made him king instead of Josias his father, when he was twenty and three years old.

35 And he reigned in Judea and in Jerusalem three months : and then the king of Egypt deposed him from reigning in Jerusalem.

36 And he set a tax upon the land of a hundred talents of silver and one talent of gold.

37 The king of Egypt also made king Joacim his brother king of Judea and Jerusalem.

38 And he bound Joacim and the nobles : but Zaraces his brother he apprehended, and brought him out of Egypt.

39 Five and twenty years old was g Joacim when he was made king in the land of Judea and Jerusalem ; and he did evil before the Lord.

40 Wherefore against him Nabuchodonosor the king of Babylon came up, and bound him with a chain of brass, and carried him into Babylon.

41 (Nabuchodonosor also took of the holy vessels of the Lord, and carried them away, and set them in his own temple at Babylon.)

42 But those things that are recorded of him, and of his uncleanness and impiety, are written in the chronicles of the kings.

43 And Joacim his son reigned in his stead : he was made king being eighteen years old ;

44 And reigned but three months and ten days in Jerusalem, and did evil before the Lord.

45 So after a year Nabuchodonosor sent and caused him to be brought into Babylon with the holy vessels of the Lord,

46 And made Zedechias king of Judea and Jerusalem, when

A

The Apocrypha in an 1828 Bible published by the H. and E. Phinney Company in Cooperstown, New York. An edition of this Bible was used by Joseph Smith while he was translating the Bible. The Lord said, "Verily, thus saith the Lord unto you concerning the Apocrypha—There are many things contained therein that are true, and it is mostly translated correctly; There are many things contained therein that are not true, which are interpolations by the hands of men. Verily, I say unto you, that it is not needful that the Apocrypha should be translated" (D&C 91:1–3).

Content overview

The revelation begins with a promise that "every soul who forsaketh his sins and cometh unto me, and calleth on my name, and obeyeth my voice, and keepeth my commandments, shall see my face and know that I am" (93:1). That promise will be fulfilled either in this life or in the life to come. *See* God, man seeing.

The Lord revealed contents of a record written by John the Baptist (and probably used by John the apostle as source material for his Gospel) that testifies of the premortal and earthly ministry of the Savior (93:6–18). *See* Record of John.

John's record testifies that Jesus Christ as the Son of God obtained the fulness of his Father "grace for grace." *See* Grace.

The Lord promised that the fulness of John's record would someday be revealed "if you are faithful" (93:18).

With John's testimony of the Savior's receiving the fulness of the Father as the foundation, the Lord gave his purpose for this revelation: that the Saints may know how and what to worship, "that you may come unto the Father in my name, and in due time receive of his fulness" (93:19). The revelation not only illuminates the Son's relationship to the Father but also man's relationship to God and his potential to become like God by following the Savior's example. Receiving the fulness of the Father requires receiving a fulness of truth, which cannot be obtained without obedience to the commandments of God (93:26–28). In the context of worship, the Lord revealed that just as he was with the Father in the PREMORTAL EXISTENCE, so too was mankind (93:29). The revelation provided important insights concerning man's premortal

existence, specifically that there is an eternal component of man known as "intelligence, or the light of truth" (93:29). *See* Intelligence.

Another meaning of "intelligence" given in section 93 is "light and truth," an attribute of those seeking righteousness, purity, spiritual enlightenment, and knowledge; also designated as "the glory of God," which "forsake[s] that evil one" (93:36–37).

The revelation contains a chastisement of the First Presidency (Joseph Smith, Sidney Rigdon, and Frederick G. Williams) and the bishop in Kirtland (Newel K. Whitney) for failing to adequately "set in order" things at home. They were commanded to bring up their "CHILDREN in light and truth," teach their families to "give more earnest heed unto [their] sayings," be more diligent at home, and "pray always" (93:40–50).

The revelation ends with instructions to the First Presidency to "obtain a knowledge of history, and of countries, and of kingdoms, of laws of God and man, and all this for the salvation of Zion" (93:51–53).

BIBLIOGRAPHY

Cook, Lyndon W. *The Revelations of the Prophet Joseph Smith*. Salt Lake City: Deseret Book, 1985.

Revelation in the handwriting of Frederick G. Williams, Newel K. Whitney Collection, L. Tom Perry Special Collections, Harold B. Lee Library, Brigham Young University, Provo, Utah.

Smith, Joseph. *History of The Church of Jesus Christ of Latter-day Saints*. Edited by B. H. Roberts. 7 vols. 2d ed. rev. Salt Lake City: The Church of Jesus Christ of Latter-day Saints, 1932–51.

BLT

Historical context and overview of Doctrine and Covenants 94

Historical context

Since the 1835 edition of the Doctrine and Covenants, when the revelation recorded in section 94 was misdated, writers have attempted to make historical events conform to the May 1833 date attached to this revelation. All three contemporaneous manuscripts of the revelation agree, however, that it was actually received immediately after section 97 on 2 August 1833. The revelations in the 1835 edition were not placed in chronological order and somehow

> 19 I give unto you these sayings that you may understand and know how to worship, and "know what you worship, that you may come unto the Father in my name, and in due time receive of his fulness.

Doctrine and Covenants 93:19.

what is now section 93 was placed between these two August 1833 revelations (D&C 81–83, 1835 ed.). In that edition, section 81 (now 97) is dated "August 1833"; section 82 (now 93), "May, 1833"; and section 83 (now 94), "Revelation given same date." "Revelation given same date" refers to August 1833 and not to May 1833, but in the 1876 edition of the Doctrine and Covenants "Revelation given same date" was changed to "May 6, 1833." This error has been perpetuated in all later editions of the Doctrine and Covenants and, relying on these early editions, in the *History of the Church* as well.

On 23 March 1833, "a council was called for the purpose of appointing a committee to purchase land in Kirtland, upon which the Saints might build a Stake of Zion" (Smith, 1:335). The plans for a stake of Zion in Kirtland included the TEMPLE to serve as a chapel and a schoolhouse. As the efforts to procure lands progressed, another conference of Church leaders was held on 4 May 1833, where a Church building committee was appointed. It was composed of Hyrum Smith, Jared Carter, and Reynolds Cahoon. They were given the responsibility to raise money and supervise the construction of needed Church buildings (Smith, 1:342–43). In August the Prophet received this revelation in which the members of the Church were instructed to build two additional buildings—a house for the presidency of the Church and a house for the printing operations of the Church.

On 6 August 1833, four days after this revelation was received, the presidency of the Church copied this revelation and the revelations now recorded in sections 97 and 98 into a letter sent to the leaders of the Church in Zion (Jackson County, Missouri), informing them they were to construct three similar buildings. The temple was built in Kirtland, but time and finances prevented the construction of the other two buildings specified in this revelation. One 30-by-38-foot, two-story building was built to serve as both an office building and a printing office. *See* Printing office/schoolhouse.

None of the three similar buildings was constructed in Zion.

Content overview

The revelation sets forth a pattern for the building up of Kirtland, with the temple as the central feature. In addition to the reaffirmation of the commandment to build the temple, section 94 commands that additional buildings be erected. A house (office) for the First Presidency was to be built "for the work of the presidency, in obtaining revelations; and for the work of the ministry of the presidency, in all things pertaining to the church and kingdom" (94:3). It was to be a sacred, dedicated edifice wherein the Lord's Spirit and glory could abide. A printing house was also to be built for the general purpose of printing Church materials, including the "printing of the translation of my scriptures," the Prophet's translation of the Bible (94:10; cf. 35:20; 104:58). *See* Doctrine and Covenants and the Joseph Smith Translation of the Bible.

The revelation also designated "inheritances" (94:13–14), or building lots, for the three members of the building committee.

BIBLIOGRAPHY

Smith, Joseph. *History of The Church of Jesus Christ of Latter-day Saints*. Edited by B. H. Roberts. 7 vols. 2d ed. rev. Salt Lake City: The Church of Jesus Christ of Latter-day Saints, 1932–51.

BLT

Historical context and overview of Doctrine and Covenants 95

Historical context

On 27 December 1832, a revelation received by the Prophet Joseph Smith commanded the Saints to build a TEMPLE in Kirtland to serve as "a house of prayer, a house of fasting, a house of faith, a house of learning, a house of glory, a house of order, a house of God" (88:119). Despite the divine command, little was done to fulfill this charge in the months immediately following the revelation. In May 1833, a conference was held to discuss plans for constructing a place for the elders to "come together to receive instruction preparatory for their missions, and ministry," an important purpose for building the temple. Hyrum Smith, Jared Carter, and Reynolds Cahoon were chosen at that conference to be a Church building committee (Smith, *History*, 1:342–43; cf. D&C 88:119–27). Yet by

June there had still been virtually no progress on the temple. The delay was caused by the extreme poverty in which the members of the Church found themselves at the time. Not only was cash scarce for individuals but the Church as an institution was deeply in debt. These concerns are evident in Lucy Mack Smith's account of the discussions that took place in June 1833 regarding the temple: "Some thought that it would be better to build a frame house. Others said that a frame house was too costly, and the majority concluded upon putting up a log house and made their calculations about what they could do towards building it. Joseph rose and reminded them that they were not making a house for themselves or any other man, but a house for God. 'And shall we, brethren, build a house for our God of logs? No, I have a better plan than that. I have the plan of the house of the Lord, given by himself. You will see by this the difference between our calculations and his idea of things'" (L. M. Smith, *History*, 321).

Content overview

The Lord rebuked the members of the Church for their failure to obey the commandment to build the temple. He reminded them that this rebuke was a chastening that evidenced his love and desire to "endow those whom I have chosen with power from on high" (95:8). The Saints were promised that if they would be obedient to the previous command, the Lord would open the way whereby they would "have power to build it" (95:11). On the other hand, if they continued to disobey, instead of being endowed with power, they would "walk in darkness" (95:12; cf. v. 6). He then reminded them that he had sent members of the School of the Prophets

"forth to be chastened" because of their sin of contention (95:9–10). The revelation ends with specific instructions concerning the construction of the temple. "Let the house be built, not after the manner of the world, for I give not unto you that ye shall live after the manner of the world; therefore, let it be built after the manner which I shall show unto three of you, whom ye shall appoint and ordain unto this power" (95:13–14). The First Presidency of the Church were those three who saw in vision the divine plan. Truman Angell, a contemporary of the Prophet Joseph Smith who helped with the construction of the Kirtland Temple and later served as architect of the Salt Lake Temple, recorded in his journal that President Frederick G. Williams related how this manifestation occurred: "Joseph [Smith] received the word of the Lord for him to take his two counselors, Williams and Rigdon, and come before the Lord and He would show them the plan or model of the house to be built. We went upon our knees, called on the Lord, and the building appeared within viewing distance, I being the first to discover it. Then all of us viewed it together. After we had taken a good look at the exterior, the building seemed to come right over us, and the makeup of this hall seemed to coincide with what I there saw to a minutia" (Angell, 4).

The members of the Church went to work immediately after this revelation was received and built the temple. Even in their poverty they completed it in less than three years and dedicated it 27 March 1836 (109).

BIBLIOGRAPHY

Angell, Truman O. Journal, MS. L. Tom Perry Special Collections, Harold B. Lee Library, Brigham Young University, Provo, Utah.

Smith, Joseph. *History of The Church of Jesus Christ of Latter-day Saints*. Edited by B. H. Roberts. 7 vols. 2d ed. rev. Salt Lake City: The Church of Jesus Christ of Latter-day Saints, 1932–51.

Smith, Lucy Mack. *The Revised and Enhanced History of Joseph Smith by His Mother*. Edited by Scot Facer Proctor and Maurine Jensen Proctor. Salt Lake City: Bookcraft, 1996.

1 VERILY, thus saith the Lord unto you whom I love, and whom I *a*love I also chasten that their sins may be *b*forgiven, for with the *c*chastisement I prepare a way for their *d*deliverance in all things out of *e*temptation, and I have loved you—

Doctrine and Covenants 95:1.   BLT

Historical context and overview of Doctrine and Covenants 96

Historical context

As the Saints gathered to Kirtland, it was necessary for the Church to purchase additional land. On 18 April 1833, the Church purchased 103 acres from Peter French, a local farmer. A council of Church leaders met with the Prophet in early June to decide how best to use the land. When they could not agree, they petitioned the Prophet to inquire of the Lord to resolve the matter (Smith, 1:352). This revelation came as a result.

The process of obtaining the French farm began with a committee meeting in March 1833. At that time, those present reviewed the land available for purchase in the Kirtland region. Several members of the committee recommended that the Church purchase 103 acres from Peter French for five thousand dollars (KCMB, 18–19). They recognized that the farm provided suitable building lots close to the crest of the hill near the business and industrial area of Kirtland, as well as additional land that met a variety of Church needs.

Content overview

The revelation assigned the responsibility for developing the land to Bishop Newel K. Whitney (96:2). He was to divide the farm into building lots for the Saints gathering to Kirtland and sites for erecting Church structures (96:3–4). The crest of the hill on the south of the French farm became the site of the Kirtland Temple. In addition, the French farm property became home to the Kirtland Safety Society building, a print shop, several Church businesses, and a number of individual residences. The revelation also invited John Johnson, a wealthy Church member, to join the United Firm, a Church business

Building the Kirtland Temple; *painting by Walter Rane.* "Now here is wisdom, and the mind of the Lord—let the house be built, not after the manner of the world, for I give not unto you that ye shall live after the manner of the world; Therefore, let it be built after the manner which I shall show unto three of you, whom ye shall appoint and ordain unto this power" (D&C 95:13–14).

venture, and to assist in the plans to develop Kirtland (96:6–9). As a result, he donated funds to help pay the mortgage on the French farm. The land then belonged to the United Firm and became available for Church use (Backman, 144–45). *See* map, p. 345.

See also Consecration.

BIBLIOGRAPHY

Backman, Milton V., Jr. *The Heavens Resound: A History of the Latter-day Saints in Ohio, 1830–1838.* Salt Lake City: Deseret Book, 1983.

Kirtland Council Minute Book. Council of High Priests, 23 March 1833, Minute Book 1. Church History Library, The Church of Jesus Christ of Latter-day Saints, Salt Lake City, Utah.

Smith, Joseph. *History of The Church of Jesus Christ of Latter-day Saints.* Edited by B. H. Roberts. 7 vols. 2d ed. rev. Salt Lake City: The Church of Jesus Christ of Latter-day Saints, 1932–51.

DAW

Historical context and overview of Doctrine and Covenants 97

Historical context

Joseph Smith received this revelation 2 August 1833 in response to questions from Church leaders in ZION. The Prophet had sent them the revelation recorded in section 88, the Olive Leaf, earlier in the year, and consistent with the counsel in that revelation, they had organized a "school of Elders" in Zion (88:127–41), and Parley P. Pratt was called to preside over it (Pratt, 75–76). *See* School(s).

In a letter now lost, those attending the school wrote to the Church presidency desiring to know God's will "as relates to the school in Zion." The First Presidency replied on 6 August 1833: "According to your request we inquired of the Lord and send in this letter the communication which we received from the Lord concerning the school in Zion. It was obtained August 2d and reads thus [section 97]" (Smith et al., 6 August 1833, 1). The letter also included sections 94 and 98.

It is important to note that during the summer of 1833 the Prophet finished his translation work on the Bible and turned his attention to the construction of the Kirtland Temple. The cornerstone of this building was laid on 23 July.

While the Saints in Kirtland rejoiced, during that same week the Missouri Saints faced a mob ultimatum to leave Jackson County. Though the Prophet and others at Kirtland were aware of growing opposition in Missouri (cf. section 98, headnote), it is unlikely that the Prophet was aware of the specific events, including the destruction of the printing press and attacks on Church members. Given this context, the warning in section 97 regarding chastening and "sore affliction" (v. 26) promised to a disobedient people was most timely.

Content overview

The Lord addressed the brethren in Zion as "friends" and commended Parley P. Pratt for his labors "to preside over the school in the land of Zion" (vv. 1, 4), but he also chastened those whose "works" were less than the covenants they had made with him, indicating that to be accepted of the Lord the Saints must be "willing to observe their covenants by sacrifice—yea, every sacrifice which I, the Lord, shall command" (vv. 6, 8). During the summer Joseph Smith and others had sent to Zion a letter dated 25 June 1833 that included a pattern for the "house of the Lord." The Lord instructed the members in Zion to commence construction of the house of the Lord immediately. If they would do as instructed, "Zion—THE PURE IN HEART" would rejoice (v. 21) and escape future judgments. If they refused to be obedient, the Lord promised he would "visit" them "with sore affliction, with pestilence, with plague, with sword, with vengeance, with devouring fire" (v. 26). Unfortunately, circumstances in Jackson County were such that the members of the Church were driven out by their antagonists before the end of the year.

BIBLIOGRAPHY

Pratt, Parley P. *Autobiography of Parley P. Pratt.* Edited by Parley P. Pratt Jr. Salt Lake City: Deseret Book, 1985.

Smith, Joseph, Sidney Rigdon, and Frederick G. Williams. Letter to Brethren in Zion, 6 August 1833. Church History Library, The Church of Jesus Christ of Latter-day Saints, Salt Lake City, Utah.

Smith, Joseph, Sidney Rigdon, Frederick G. Williams, Martin Harris. MS, Letter to Brethren in Zion, 25 June

1833. Church History Library, The Church of Jesus Christ of Latter-day Saints, Salt Lake City, Utah.

DAW

Historical context and overview of Doctrine and Covenants 98

Historical context

Conditions in both Ohio and Missouri during the summer of 1833 were not favorable for the peace and happiness members of the Church were hoping to obtain. In Kirtland, recent excommunicant Doctor Philastus Hurlbut was fomenting strife, and Joseph Smith wrote to the leaders in Zion that Hurlbut was "lieing in a wonderful manner and the peopl are running after him and giveing him mony to brake down mormanism which much endangers <our lives> at preasnt." He also wrote, "We <are> no safer here in Kirtland then you are in Zion the cloud is gethering around us with great fury and all pharohs host or in other words all hell and the comb[ined] powrs of Earth are Marsheling their forces to overthrow us" (*Writings*, 311, 309). Through correspondence, Joseph was also kept abreast of the maneuvers of the Church's antagonists in Missouri, even as late as eleven days before a mob attack on 20 July. On that day, in an effort to pressure the members of the Church to leave Jackson County, they destroyed the printing office, tarred and feathered Edward Partridge and Charles Allen, and publicly announced that "Mormons were the common enemies of mankind, and ought to be destroyed" (Smith, *History,* 1:392), .

Oliver Cowdery left Missouri the last week in July to inform the Prophet of the actions of the mob to force the expulsion of the Saints from Jackson County. He arrived in Kirtland in mid-August, as reported by the *Painesville [Ohio] Telegraph* on 16 August 1833: "We learn from the Mormon colony in Missouri, that a great riot took place there about the 20th ult. We understand that O. Cowdery, one of the principal men among the pilgrims, has just arrived at the headquarters of the Prophet in this country. . . . An attack [was made] upon a brick building containing the printing establishment, and the family of the editor, and razed it to the ground—scattering the type, revelations, translations

and commandments, printed or in manuscript, to the four winds" (3). It was at this time that the Kirtland Saints learned the specifics of the events in Missouri.

The Prophet received section 98 on 6 August 1833, more than a week before Cowdery's arrival. He included this revelation with sections 97 and 94 in a 6 August 1833 letter written in response to questions posed by leaders of the Church in Missouri. *See* Historical context and overview of Doctrine and Covenants 97 (p. 803) and 94 (p. 799).

The letter gives little indication that Joseph knew the gravity of the situation in Missouri, yet the revelation provides instructions that are specifically relevant to how the Saints should respond to PERSECUTION. Whether this revelation came as a result of the events in Kirtland or Missouri, or both, it is certain Joseph Smith knew that anti-Mormon antagonists were plotting the Church's destruction, and he was meditating on how the Church should respond.

Content overview

The Lord counseled the Saints to wait "patiently on the Lord" in their afflictions (98:1–3) and, by implication, to appeal to the law of the land for relief. The Lord also explained that the members of the Church are to support the

> **1** VERILY I say unto you my friends, *a*fear not, let your hearts be comforted; yea, rejoice evermore, and in everything give *b*thanks;
> **2** *a*Waiting patiently on the Lord, for your prayers have entered into the ears of the Lord of Sabaoth, and are recorded with this seal and testament—the Lord hath sworn and decreed that they shall be granted.
> **3** Therefore, he giveth this promise unto you, with an immutable covenant that they shall be fulfilled; and all things wherewith you have been *a*afflicted shall work together for your *b*good, and to my name's glory, saith the Lord.

Doctrine and Covenants 98:1–3.

constitutional law of the land and uphold honest and wise men in their elected offices (98:4–10). He then advised them that their ultimate safety is found in abiding in his covenants (98:11–15), and they were to "renounce war and proclaim peace," assuring them that he has prepared a place for them in the mansions of the Father (98:16–18).

Acknowledging that the Saints in Missouri were not the only ones needing correction, the Lord pointed out that the Saints in Kirtland needed to repent of their "sins" and "pride," but he promised that if they would repent, he would "turn away all wrath and indignation" from them (98:19–22). He then revealed the laws governing the Saints in responding to the persecutions and afflictions imposed on them—the same law he gave to the prophets and patriarchs in ancient Israel and in the Americas (98:23–46). In that law, the Lord makes clear that war is justified only when he commands it (98:33–38). The revelation ends with conditional promises to both the Saints and their enemies. The Saints were promised that if they would forgive their enemies, even after repeated trespasses, the Lord would "avenge thee of thine enemy an hundredfold" (98:44–46). Mercifully, however, the enemies are promised that if they or their descendants repent "and turn to the Lord their God, with all their hearts . . . vengeance shall no more come upon them" (98:47–48).

BIBLIOGRAPHY

Painesville [Ohio] Telegraph, 16 August 1833.

Smith, Joseph. *History of The Church of Jesus Christ of Latter-day Saints.* Edited by B. H. Roberts. 7 vols. 2d ed. rev. Salt Lake City: The Church of Jesus Christ of Latter-day Saints, 1932–51.

Smith, Joseph. *Personal Writings of Joseph Smith.* Compiled and edited by Dean C. Jessee. Rev. ed. Salt Lake City: Deseret Book, 2002.

DAW

Historical context and overview of Doctrine and Covenants 99

Historical context

This revelation for John Murdock was received 29 August 1832, calling him to serve a mission in the eastern states. Correctly dated in the 1835 to 1869 printings of the Doctrine and Covenants, the date of this section was erroneously changed to 29 August 1833 in the 1876 edition. It was in this edition that the revelations were put in chronological order, and this revelation was placed among those received in 1833. Though the dating error was corrected in the 1981 edition, its position in the book and its section number were not changed; thus, all previous references to it by section number in other publications remain valid.

Content overview

The Lord called John Murdock to preach the gospel in the eastern part of the United States. He then enumerated the blessings attending those who accepted the gospel message and the warnings to those who did not (99:1–5). Murdock was a widower with three small children. Because the revelation directed Murdock to send his children to Missouri (99:6), he arranged for Caleb Baldwin to transport them to Bishop Partridge, who was to care for them. John was told that "after a few years," if he desired, he could go to Zion, "otherwise thou shalt continue proclaiming my gospel until thou be taken" (99:7–8).

DAW

Historical context and overview of Doctrine and Covenants 100

Historical context

Freeman Nickerson, a recent Canadian convert to the Church, traveled with Joseph Smith and Sidney Rigdon on a mission to the East. After joining the Church at Dayton, New York, in April 1833, Nickerson came to Kirtland, Ohio. While there he met the Prophet Joseph Smith and encouraged him to visit Nickerson family members in Perrysburg, New York, and Ontario, Canada. Joseph and Sidney Rigdon agreed to this proposal, and with Nickerson they left Kirtland on 5 October. Along the way, they preached the gospel to those who would listen. On the evening of 11 October, Joseph recorded a personal concern: "Very well in my mind. The Lord is with us, but have much anxiety about my family" (1:419). It is apparent from the contents of the revelation that Joseph was concerned not only about the welfare of his family but also about the situation in Jackson County, Missouri. The next day they arrived at the Nickerson home in Perrysburg, New York. It was on this day that the Prophet received the revelation recorded in section 100.

The importance of this mission must not be underestimated. Rigdon successfully preached to a large group gathered at the Nickerson home, and the three brethren then continued north to Ontario, where they preached to a congregation at Brantford and another at Mt. Pleasant. In spite of opposition, many accepted the testimony of Joseph and his companions. The missionaries baptized sixteen individuals and organized a branch of the Church. Some time later, Parley P. Pratt visited this branch as he began his mission in Canada. Moses Nickerson, a convert from the 1833 mission, introduced Pratt to John Taylor, whose conversion proved critical to the success of the 1837–40 missions to Great Britain, which dramatically affected the course of Church history.

Content overview

After assuring Joseph Smith and Sidney Rigdon that their families were well, the Lord told them to listen to the counsel he was about to give them (100:1–2). He explained he had "much people" in the area, and Joseph and Sidney were to open "an effectual door" for the "salvation of souls" (100:3–5). He then promised he would give them "in the very moment, what [they] shall say," and the Holy Ghost would bear record of what they taught (100:6–8). After issuing a call for Sidney Rigdon to be a spokesman for Joseph Smith and Joseph to be "revelator" to Sidney (100:9–12; cf. 2 Nephi 3:17–18), the Lord informed them that "Zion shall be redeemed, although she is chastened for a little season" (100:13). He then advised them that Orson Hyde and John Gould, whom Joseph sent to Jackson County with counsel to the Saints in their current troubles, were under the Lord's protective care (100:14). The Lord concluded with comforting words concerning the work in which these men were engaged, reassuring them that "all things shall work together for good to them that walk uprightly, and to the sanctification of the church," and that he would

raise up unto himself "a pure people, that will serve [him] in righteousness" (100:15–17).

BIBLIOGRAPHY

Smith, Joseph. *History of The Church of Jesus Christ of Latter-day Saints.* Edited by B. H. Roberts. 7 vols. 2d ed. rev. Salt Lake City: The Church of Jesus Christ of Latter-day Saints, 1932–51.

DAW

Historical context and overview of Doctrine and Covenants 101

Historical context

Beginning 31 October and continuing through 8 November 1831, Missouri militia and armed civilians carried out attacks against the Mormon settlers living in Jackson County, forcing their removal. Most of the Saints sought refuge in Clay County, situated north of Jackson County across the Missouri River, although some members temporarily settled in Ray and Lafayette counties. When news of the expulsion reached Joseph Smith in Kirtland, the Prophet sought for divine understanding regarding why the calamities had come upon Zion and what course of action should be taken to assist the exiled Missouri Saints.

Content overview

The Lord revealed that many of the persecutions experienced by the Missouri Saints were, at least in part, because of their own spiritual transgressions (101:1–2, 6, cf. verses 41–42). Yet, in spite of their disobedience, they were still promised an eternal reward (101:3, 9). The revelation clearly teaches that the Saints of all dispensations "must needs be chastened and tried, even as Abraham" to enable them to be sanctified (101:4–5). Some Saints may even be required to sacrifice their lives for the restored gospel but are given the promise that if they

4 Therefore, they must needs be *chastened and tried, even as* *Abraham*, who was commanded to offer up his only son.

Doctrine and Covenants 101:4.

"endure in faith," they will be partakers of the Lord's glory (101:35–38).

The Lord also informed the Church that although the Saints no longer occupied land and property in Zion (Jackson County), "Zion shall not be moved out of her place, notwithstanding her children are scattered" (101:17; cf. verses 18–21). *See* Be still and know that I am God.

Furthermore, the Lord instructed the Saints to continue to gather to Missouri, to purchase land in the region, to refrain from selling their Jackson County property, and to seek legal REDRESS through the courts at all levels of government (101:63–101). Significantly, each of these injunctions was carried out by Missouri Church leaders. With assistance from David R. Atchison, Alexander W. Doniphan, Amos Rees, and William T. Wood—attorneys from Liberty, Missouri—legal proceedings were undertaken in both Clay and Jackson counties in behalf of the Saints but without success. Additionally, Church officials addressed letters to Missouri governor Daniel Dunklin and U.S. president Andrew Jackson outlining the difficulties experienced by the Saints in Jackson County and requesting assistance in their behalf, none of which ultimately proved successful.

The revelation includes a unique parable, the parable of the nobleman and his vineyard, illustrative of the situation of the Missouri Saints (101:43–62). *See* Parable regarding a certain nobleman/vineyard.

> **16** Therefore, let your hearts be comforted concerning Zion; for all flesh is in mine ᵃhands; be still and ᵇknow that I am God.
> **17** ᵃZion shall not be moved out of her place, notwithstanding her children are scattered.
> **18** They that remain, and are pure in heart, shall return, and come to their ᵃinheritances, they and their children, with ᵇsongs of everlasting joy, to ᶜbuild up the waste places of Zion—

Doctrine and Covenants 101:16–18.

Significantly, the parable clearly indicated the Church would respond to the Jackson County difficulties with an organized military body. The revelation summoned "all the strength of mine house, which are my warriors, my young men, and they that are of middle age also among all my servants, who are the strength of mine house . . . [to go] straightway unto the land of my vineyard, and redeem my vineyard; for it is mine" (101:55–56). The expedition of ZION'S CAMP to western Missouri in 1834 was the fulfillment of this directive (103).

In addition to addressing the situation of the Missouri Saints, the revelation contains a number of doctrinal teachings regarding the physical changes that the EARTH will undergo after the Savior's coming when the earth returns to its paradisiacal state, and the conditions that will exist during the MILLENNIUM (101:22–34).

See also Hiding place, the Lord's; Missouri period; Parable of the woman and the unjust judge; Zion, redemption of.

BIBLIOGRAPHY

Smith, Joseph Jr. *History of The Church of Jesus Christ of Latter-day Saints.* Edited by B. H. Roberts. 7 vols. 2d ed. rev. Salt Lake City: The Church of Jesus Christ of Latter-day Saints, 1932–51.

ALB

Historical context and overview of Doctrine and Covenants 102

Historical context

By revelation, the Prophet Joseph Smith was directed to organize the "Presidents Church Council" which he said was patterned after "the order of councils in ancient days . . . as shown to him by vision." He added that "Jerusalem was the seat of the Church Council in ancient days" and "the apostle, Peter, was the president of the Council" (KCMB, 29–30; cf. Cook, 207). This council in Kirtland, Ohio, was unique in that the president of the Church presided over the council, but it was the pattern for councils wherever the Church was organized in stakes of Zion. This council consisted of twelve high priests, presided over by a presidency. It was appointed for the purpose of performing the functions of a duly constituted Church court (now called a disciplinary council) (102:1–2). On 17

February 1834, the council was organized, and the minutes of that first organizational meeting were adopted as a constitution for high councils within stakes when functioning as Church disciplinary councils. Those minutes form section 102. This organization took place about a year before the Quorum of the Twelve was called. Once that quorum was established, the president's Church council was reorganized with the First Presidency of the Church as the presidency of the council and the Quorum of the Twelve as the council members. It then became known as the "high council of the seat of the First Presidency of the Church" (v. 26) and the "traveling high council" (v. 30) and had Churchwide jurisdiction. A separate high council was then organized for the Kirtland Stake.

Content overview

When a high council functions as a disciplinary council, the members are equally divided into two groups. One group represents the interests of the Church and the other group represents the interests of the accused. This process is unique in that neither of these groups constitutes a prosecution, defense, or jury element. Instead, their function is to prevent insult and injustice to either the Church or the accused (102:12–18).

After the high councilors have spoken, the responsibility for rendering a decision rests with the stake president, assisted by his two counselors. The high councilors are then called upon to sustain the decision (102:19). An appeal process is also provided (102:27–33).

See also Bishop(s); Common council of the church; Church discipline; Repentance.

> 2 The *ᵃ*high council was appointed by revelation for the purpose of *ᵇ*settling important difficulties which might arise in the church, which could not be settled by the church or the *ᶜ*bishop's council to the satisfaction of the parties.

Doctrine and Covenants 102:2.

BIBLIOGRAPHY

Cook, Lyndon W. *The Revelations of the Prophet Joseph Smith*. Provo, Utah: Seventy's Bookstore, 1981.

Kirtland Council Minute Book. Church History Library, The Church of Jesus Christ of Latter-day Saints, Salt Lake City, Utah.

Otten, Leaun G., and C. Max Caldwell. *Sacred Truths of the Doctrine and Covenants*. Vol. 2. Salt Lake City: Deseret Book, 1993.

Smith, Joseph. *History of The Church of Jesus Christ of Latter-day Saints*. Edited by B. H. Roberts. 7 vols. 2d ed. rev. Salt Lake City: The Church of Jesus Christ of Latter-day Saints, 1932–51.

CMC

Historical context and overview of Doctrine and Covenants 103

Historical context

Following the expulsion of some twelve hundred Latter-day Saints from their communities in Jackson County, Missouri, in October and November 1833, Missouri Church leaders and their attorneys petitioned Governor Daniel Dunklin to intercede in their behalf. Writing to Oliver Cowdery in December, John Corrill, a counselor to Bishop Edward Partridge, reported that Dunklin had indicated he would take some sort of action in their behalf. "The Governor . . . manifested a willingness to restore us back, and will if we request it," Corrill wrote, "but this will be of but little use unless he could leave a force there to help protect us" (to Cowdery, 126). In February 1834 the governor reiterated this position in a formal reply. He fully acknowledged the Mormons had a right to organize a military body; "indeed it is [your] duty to do so," he wrote. "As to the request for keeping up a military force to protect your people, and prevent the commission of crimes and injuries," however, he believed such a request did not warrant the use of state troops (Smith, 1:476). Based upon these reports, Church leaders in Missouri believed that: (1) the state of Missouri would render assistance by mustering a militia force that would help reinstate the displaced Saints in Jackson County; (2) the Saints were authorized to organize their own independent military unit, which body would join forces with the state militia in helping restore the Saints to their lands; and (3) after the Jackson County Saints were reinstated, the Mormon contingent would remain for a time to provide protection and maintain order until peace was restored.

A revelation given to the Prophet Joseph Smith the previous December 1833 (101) intimated the Church would respond to the Missouri difficulties with an organized military body. The revelation summoned "all the strength of mine house, which are my warriors, my young men, and they that are of middle age also among all my servants, who are the strength of mine house . . . [to go] straightway unto the land of my vineyard, and redeem my vineyard; for it is mine" (101:55–56). When Parley P. Pratt and Lyman Wight arrived in Kirtland on 22 February 1834, following a lengthy midwinter journey from Missouri, the two men informed Joseph Smith of the latest developments in connection with the exiled members. They likely delivered a letter written by William W. Phelps informing the Prophet, "The Governor is willing

to restore us, but . . . the constitution gives him no power to guard us when [we come] back" (Smith, 1:457). On 24 February, two days after the arrival of Pratt and Wight, the Prophet received the revelation recorded in section 103, officially calling for the formation and organization of a military body known as ZION'S CAMP.

Content overview

The Lord identified two reasons why he had suffered the Saints to be driven from their homes in Jackson County: to permit the enemies of the Church to "fill up the measure of their iniquities" and to chasten the Saints for their failure to "hearken altogether" to his commandments (103:3–4). The Lord called for five hundred recruits, but no fewer than one hundred men were to make up the company that was to travel to Missouri to assist the Saints (103:32–34). This revelation instructed that the camp be organized in companies of tens, fifties, and hundreds

Zion's Camp Arrives in Missouri. *This engraving shows the company marching through a town while its citizens watch.*

(103:30) and called for Joseph Smith to take command of the entire operation (103:21–22, 35). In addition to the Prophet, seven men—Parley P. Pratt, Lyman Wight, Sidney Rigdon, Hyrum Smith, Frederick G. Williams, Orson Hyde, and Orson Pratt—were instructed to obtain supplies and money, recruit volunteers, and organize the companies (103:29–34, 37–40). The Lord assured them that the expedition would be successful: "Your brethren which have been scattered shall return to the lands of their inheritances" (103:11). The promise was conditional upon the obedience of the expedition's members and the entire Church at large, however: "Inasmuch as they [the Church] keep not my commandments, and hearken not to observe all my words, the kingdoms of the world shall prevail against them" (103:8). Although not specified in the revelation, a departure date of 1 May 1834 was set for the company. *See* Historical context and overview of Doctrine and Covenants 105 (p. 812); map, p. 708.

BIBLIOGRAPHY

Corrill, John, to Oliver Cowdery, December 1833, in *The Evening and the Morning Star* 2, no. 16 (January 1834): 124–26.

Smith, Joseph. *History of The Church of Jesus Christ of Latter-day Saints.* Edited by B. H. Roberts. 7 vols. 2d ed. rev. Salt Lake City: The Church of Jesus Christ of Latter-day Saints, 1932–51.

ALB

Historical context and overview of Doctrine and Covenants 104

Historical context

The revelation recorded in Doctrine and Covenants 104 is associated with the United Firm—the Church's commercial and mercantile institution, organized to manage the business interests of the Church between March 1832 and April 1834, a period of just over two years. The United Firm had two branches—the first established in Kirtland in March 1832 (78), and the second established in April of that year in Jackson County, Missouri (82). Officers and members of the United Firm included Joseph Smith, Sidney Rigdon, Jesse Gause (his name does not appear in the published revelation because of his excommunication in December

1832), Newel K. Whitney, and Martin Harris, residents of Kirtland; and Oliver Cowdery, William W. Phelps, Edward Partridge, John Whitmer, and Algernon Sidney Gilbert, residents of Independence (82:11). Later, Frederick G. Williams and John Johnson were called by revelation to be additional members of the United Firm in March and June 1833, respectively (cf. 92; 96:6–9). The United Firm should not be confused with the Literary Firm established in November 1831 to oversee the printing and publication enterprises of the Church (70). After the establishment of the United Firm, however, the Literary Firm became integrated into the United Firm.

The United Firm is frequently identified as the "United Order" or simply "order," and it is this name or title that appears in the published revelations dealing with the United Firm (78; 82; and 104). United Firm is the correct title, however, and it is this name that appears in earliest manuscripts of the revelation. The terms "United Order" or "order" are actually code names for the United Firm, or the "firm."

It is important to note that the United Firm operated primarily in a management capacity, and individuals continued to hold title to their property and businesses. Under this arrangement, in Missouri the Firm's officers managed the W. W. Phelps and Company (*The Evening and the Morning Star* printing establishment), the Gilbert, Whitney and Company store and storehouse, and the purchase and distribution of Church property in Jackson County. In

13 For it is expedient that I, the Lord, should make every man ^aaccountable, as a ^bsteward over earthly blessings, which I have made and prepared for my creatures.
14 I, the Lord, stretched out the heavens, and ^abuilt the earth, my very ^bhandiwork; and all things therein are mine.
15 And it is my purpose to provide for my saints, for all things are mine.

Doctrine and Covenants 104:13–15.

Kirtland, the Firm oversaw the operations of the N. K. Whitney and Company store and ashery, the Frederick G. Williams and Peter French farms, a tannery, and beginning in September 1833, after the destruction of the Independence printing establishment, the F. G. Williams and Company publishing firm.

Content overview

By April 1834, mounting debt and internal dissonance threatened the United Firm's financial stability (104:1–10, 78–86). By revelation (104), the two orders (Kirtland and Missouri) were separated (vv. 47–48) and members were assigned individual stewardships and properties (vv. 11–14, 49–50). In short, the United Firm was permanently dissolved. The individuals who were appointed specific property included only the former members of the United Firm living in Kirtland, namely, Sidney Rigdon (vv. 20–23), Martin Harris (vv. 24–26), Frederick G. Williams (vv. 27, 29–33), Oliver Cowdery (vv. 28, 29–33),

John Johnson (vv. 34–38), Newel K. Whitney (vv. 39–42), and Joseph Smith (vv. 43–46). No mention is made regarding the distribution of property of the members of the Firm living in Missouri, but that is understandable considering that just a few months previous (November 1833), Church members living in Jackson County had been expelled from their property and the county.

Instructions in section 104 also called for the establishment of two monetary accounts or treasuries—a "sacred treasury of the Lord" used to fund the printing operations of the Church (vv. 60–66) and a second treasury containing the profits generated from the individual stewardships of the former members of the Firm (vv. 67–77). In addition, a treasurer was to be appointed to manage each treasury, but historical records do not indicate who the persons were who were chosen for either of these positions. It is likely that Newel K. Whitney, bishop

The rebuilt ashery in Kirtland, Ohio; photograph by Welden C. Andersen. "And again, let my servant Newel K. Whitney have appointed unto him the houses and lot where he now resides, and the lot and building on which the mercantile establishment stands, and also the lot which is on the corner south of the mercantile establishment, and also the lot on which the ashery is situated" (D&C 104:39).

of Kirtland, filled at least one of the two treasurer positions.

Although the revelation primarily deals with instructions to the members of the United Firm, several verses have relevance to the present-day reader. Verse 14 reiterates the doctrine that Jesus Christ created the heavens and the earth and that all things are his. Verses 16 and 17 indicate that the earth contains an abundance of natural resources, even "enough and to spare." Simply put, the earth is equipped to sustain all of God's children who have or will be born into mortality. Finally, verses 13 and 15 instruct that each person has a temporal earthly stewardship for which he or she will be accountable to God. Furthermore, verse 18 teaches that those who have an abundance of temporal means are expected to give a portion of that abundance, "according to the law of my gospel," to the poor and needy or be counted among "the wicked." *See* map, p. 345.

See also Consecration.

BIBLIOGRAPHY

Parkin, Max H. "Joseph Smith and the United Firm: The Growth and Decline of the Church's First Master Plan of Business and Finance, Ohio and Missouri, 1832–1834." *BYU Studies* 46, no. 3 (2007): 5–66.

ALB

Historical context and overview of Doctrine and Covenants 105

Historical context

During a period of nearly two months (early May to late June 1834), Joseph Smith led the Mormon military expedition known as ZION'S CAMP, composed of over two hundred volunteers, from Ohio to Missouri. The company's primary objective was to provide additional military manpower to Missouri state militia forces in assisting nearly twelve hundred displaced Church members, most of whom were residing in Clay County, Missouri, to reclaim their homes and property in Jackson County.

On 5 May 1834 the main company of Zion's Camp left Kirtland, Ohio. Coincidentally, that same day a smaller group under the direction of Hyrum Smith and Lyman Wight left Pontiac, Michigan, to join the main body en route. On 7 June, following a month of travel through Ohio,

Indiana, and Illinois, picking up recruits along the way, the Mormon army arrived at a small branch of the Church known as the Salt River or Allred settlement (named after James Allred, an early convert), situated in present-day Monroe County, Missouri. The following day, the company from Michigan arrived, bringing the total number of men in Zion's Camp to just over two hundred.

At the Allred settlement Joseph Smith dispatched Parley P. Pratt and Orson Hyde to Jefferson City, the state capital, to meet with Missouri governor Daniel Dunklin, expecting to receive orders concerning the role Zion's Camp would play in conjunction with the troops called out by the state. The governor reneged on his agreement to lend military assistance, stating that "he dare not attempt the execution of the laws in that respect, for fear of deluging the whole country in civil war and bloodshed"; but he believed the Saints should continue their efforts through the courts (Pratt, 94). Immediately following their meeting with the governor, Pratt and Hyde returned to the main company to report to Joseph Smith. Dunklin's change of position came as devastating news. Without the immediate support of state troops, the return and reinstatement of the displaced Missouri Saints to Jackson County—the primary object of Zion's Camp—could not take place. Despite the report, the Prophet decided to march to Clay County to meet and confer with Missouri Church leaders and members, and hope that a revelation would be received giving additional direction.

Content overview

On 22 June 1834, while Zion's camp was near a branch of the Fishing River just over the county line in Clay County, the hoped-for revelation was received. In the revelation (sometimes

> 5 And *ᵃ*Zion cannot be built up *ᵇ*unless it is by the *ᶜ*principles of the *ᵈ*law of the celestial kingdom; otherwise I cannot receive her unto myself.

Doctrine and Covenants 105:5.

called the "Fishing River revelation"), the members of Zion's Camp were informed that the redemption of Zion would yet be future (105:9). The Lord declared that Zion could not be built up "unless it is by the principles of the law of the celestial kingdom" (105:5) and that the Saints need to be chastened and better prepared to establish Zion (105:6, 10–11, 30–34, 37). Furthermore, the members of Zion's Camp were assured that their journey and sacrifice were not in vain. "I have heard their prayers, and will accept their offering," the Lord declared, indicating that it had been expedient that the journey be undertaken "for a trial of their faith" (105:19). Meanwhile, most of the men were instructed to return to Ohio, where they would receive "a great endowment and blessing to be poured out upon them" (105:12, 33)—a promise fulfilled with the blessings associated with the Kirtland Temple. To the Missouri Saints who had lost their homes and property in Jackson County, the Lord promised they would find "peace and safety" living among the citizens of Clay County (105:25–27).

On 3 July, a general meeting for Church members living in Clay County and the members of Zion's Camp was held on the property owned by Michael Arthur about three miles south of Liberty. Arthur, who was not a Latter-day Saint, had befriended the Saints and employed a number of them. During the meeting, Joseph Smith officially disbanded Zion's Camp, instructing them that they were free to return to their homes in Ohio and elsewhere. In this meeting the Prophet organized the Missouri presidency and high council with David Whitmer as president and William W. Phelps and John Whitmer as assistant presidents, or counselors.

Zion's Camp members did not return to Ohio together in one large body but made their way home in smaller groups. Joseph Smith spent a few more days in Clay County counseling and instructing Church leaders before beginning the return trip; he left on 9 July, arriving back in Kirtland around 1 August after nearly a three-month absence.

In mid-August, a little more than two weeks after his return to Kirtland following Zion's Camp, Joseph Smith dictated a letter to several of the Church leaders in Missouri. In the letter the Prophet indicated that he fully expected that during the months ahead, the Saints would continue to gather to western Missouri (particularly Clay County) in sufficient numbers that they could return to Jackson county and reclaim their lands. Joseph even set a date for the return: "Use every effort to prevail on the churches to gather to those regions and locate themselves, to be in readiness to move into Jackson county in two years from the eleventh of September next, which is the appointed time for the redemption of Zion." In other words, the Prophet anticipated that on 11 September 1836, the Church would make another attempt— a second Zion's Camp—to return to Jackson County. He counseled them further: "Let not this be noised abroad; let every heart beat in silence, and every mouth be shut" (Smith, 2:145; cf. Smith to Wight et al.). During the next two years, Latter-day Saint migration to western Missouri continued, and expectations that the Saints would make another attempt to return to Jackson persisted. By the summer of 1836, however, some of Clay's citizens became concerned with the ever-increasing number of Saints in the region, resulting in isolated outbreaks of violence. These hostilities led Missouri Church leaders to search for another place for the Saints to settle. In August, W. W. Phelps and John Whitmer purchased a plot of land one-mile square in a relatively uninhabited portion of Ray County, and there they established Far West as the new place of gathering. In short, despite the Prophet's expectation to return to Jackson County in September 1836, conditions at the time necessitated that the Saints relocate rather than reoccupy, and the Jackson plan, or second Zion's Camp, was abandoned. By the fall of 1838 greater hostilities had broken out, Governor Boggs had issued the infamous extermination order, and the Saints were driven from the state of Missouri to settle in Illinois. *See* map, p. 708.

See also Historical context and overview of Doctrine and Covenants 101 (p. 806) and 103 (p. 808); Missouri period; Parable regarding a certain nobleman/vineyard.

BIBLIOGRAPHY

Baugh, Alexander L. "Joseph Smith and the Redemption of Zion." In *Joseph Smith: The Prophet & Seer,* edited by Richard Neitzel Holzapfel and Kent P. Jackson, 151–94. Provo, Utah: Religious Studies Center, Brigham Young University; Salt Lake City: Deseret Book, 2010.

———. "Joseph Smith and Zion's Camp." *Ensign* 35 (June 2005): 42–47.

Crawley, Peter, and Richard Lloyd Anderson. "The Political and Social Realities of Zion's Camp." *BYU Studies* 14, no. 4 (Summer 1974): 406–20.

Launius, Roger D. *Zion's Camp: Expedition to Missouri, 1834.* Independence: Herald House, 1984.

Manscill, Craig K. "'Journal of the Branch of the Church in Pontiac, . . . 1834': Hyrum Smith's Division of Zion's Camp." *BYU Studies* 39, no. 1 (2000): 167–88.

Pratt, Parley P. *Autobiography of Parley P. Pratt.* Edited by Parley P. Pratt Jr. Salt Lake City: Deseret Book, 1985.

Smith, Joseph. *History of The Church of Jesus Christ of Latter-day Saints.* Edited by B. H. Roberts. 7 vols. 2d ed. rev. Salt Lake City: The Church of Jesus Christ of Latter-day Saints, 1932–51.

Smith, Joseph, to Lyman Wight, Edward Partridge, John Corrill, Isaac Morley and others, 16 August 1834. Joseph Smith Letter Book 1. Church History Library, The Church of Jesus Christ of Latter-day Saints, Salt Lake City, Utah.

ALB

Historical context and overview of Doctrine and Covenants 106

Historical context

In 1834 Joseph Smith visited the Latter-day Saints residing in New York. On 9 March 1834, he preached in a schoolhouse to "a few disciples who were firm in the faith; and, after meeting found many believing and could hardly get away from them, and appointed a meeting in Freedom [Cattaraugus County] for Monday the 10th" (Smith, 2:42). He stayed that night with Warren A. Cowdery, Oliver Cowdery's older brother and a successful farmer, physician, and apothecary entrepreneur in Freedom. Warren Cowdery had been baptized three years earlier. Of his baptism the Lord said, "There was joy in heaven when my servant Warren bowed to my scepter, and separated himself from the crafts of men" (106:6).

Joseph continued to reside at the Cowdery home during his stay in Freedom and wrote of being "blessed with a full enjoyment of temporal and spiritual blessings, even all we needed, or were worthy to receive" (2:42). After meetings were held in the home, some "thirty or forty" persons were baptized and "a branch of the Church—called the Freedom branch—[was organized] from which nucleus the light spread and souls were gathered into the fold in all the regions round." To Parley P. Pratt, these conversions showed how the word of God, "or the seed sown by that extraordinary personage, the Prophet and Seer of the nineteenth century," grew (Pratt, 89).

Content overview

Nine months after the Prophet's visit to New York, he received a revelation about Warren Cowdery. In the revelation, Joseph was told that Cowdery should be "appointed and ordained a presiding high priest over my church, in the land of Freedom and the regions round about" (106:1). He was to preach the "everlasting gospel, and lift up his voice and warn the people" in Freedom and the adjoining counties (106:2). He was to "devote his whole time to this high and holy calling, which I now give unto him, seeking diligently the kingdom of heaven and its righteousness" (106:3). For such labors, Cowdery was promised that "all things necessary shall be added thereunto; for the laborer is worthy of his hire" (106:3). He was warned concerning the "vanity of his heart," but assured "a crown . . . in the mansions of [the] Father" if he continued to be "a faithful witness and a light unto the church" (106:7–8).

After moving to Kirtland, Ohio, in 1836, Warren A. Cowdery served in several capacities: as a scribe recording historical events and patriarchal blessings, as a member of the Kirtland high council, and eventually as editor of *The Messenger and Advocate.* After his brother Oliver was excommunicated in 1838, Warren also became disaffected from the Church but continued to live in Kirtland until his death in 1851.

BIBLIOGRAPHY

Pratt, Parley P. *Autobiography of Parley P. Pratt.* Edited by Parley P. Pratt Jr. Salt Lake City: Deseret Book, 1985.

Smith, Joseph. *History of The Church of Jesus Christ of Latter-day Saints.* Edited by B. H. Roberts. 7 vols. 2d

ed. rev. Salt Lake City: The Church of Jesus Christ of Latter-day Saints, 1932–51.

Sperry, Sidney B. *Doctrine and Covenants Compendium.* Salt Lake City: Bookcraft, 1960.

SEB

Historical context and overview of Doctrine and Covenants 107

Historical context

On 14 February 1835, the Quorum of the Twelve Apostles was organized—the first time in this dispensation. As directed by an earlier revelation (18:37), Oliver Cowdery and David Whitmer, two of the Three Witnesses of the Book of Mormon, were given the responsibility to call and ordain those men who would stand as "special witnesses of the name of Christ in all the world" (107:23). Martin Harris, the third of the Three Witnesses of the Book of Mormon, was subsequently assigned to assist the others in this important task (Smith, 2:186). After the apostles were ordained, Oliver Cowdery gave them charge regarding this sacred calling and the solemn responsibility that rested upon them. Among other things, Cowdery declared: "You are as one; you are equal in bearing the keys of the Kingdom to all nations. You are called to preach the Gospel of the Son of God to the nations of the earth; it is the will of your heavenly Father, that you proclaim His Gospel to the ends of the earth and the islands of the sea" (Smith, 2:196).

Over the next several weeks the Prophet Joseph Smith met periodically with the newly called APOSTLES and instructed them concerning their duties. At one such meeting, held in Kirtland on 12 March 1835, the Prophet announced that the time had arrived for the Twelve to go forth on their "first mission through the Eastern States, to the Atlantic Ocean, and hold conferences in the vicinity of the several branches of the Church for the purpose of regulating all things necessary for their welfare" (Smith, 2:209). The reality of their apostolic responsibility and the sacrifices required to fulfill it must have struck them deeply with this call to leave home and family and embark on their mission. At a meeting held on 28 March 1835, the newly ordained apostles felt a need to confess

their sins and seek forgiveness. "We have not realized the importance of our calling to [the] degree that we ought," the statement of the Quorum read, as recorded in the minutes of the meeting by Elders Orson Hyde and William E. McLellin. "We have been light-minded and vain, and in many things have done wrong. For all these things we have asked the forgiveness of our heavenly Father." Further, they called upon the Prophet to seek a revelation from the Lord "that we may look upon it when we are separated, that our hearts may be comforted." The "Revelation on Priesthood," as Joseph Smith described section 107, came as a result (Smith, 2:209–10; 107, headnote).

Section 107, as found today in the Doctrine and Covenants, is a composite of revelations received over a period of three and one-half years. Verses 59–100 were received on 11 November 1831, declaring some of the duties of various offices in the PRIESTHOOD, including those of the Twelve (Jensen et al., 216–19). The latter half of verse 69 and verses 70, 73, 76–77, and 88 were revealed sometime after November 1831. In them the Lord enumerated the duties assigned to BISHOPS and the special privileges given bishops who are direct descendants of Aaron. Verses 53–55 are quoted from part of the patriarchal blessing Joseph Smith gave his father on 18 December 1833 (MH, 18 December 1833). Verses 25–26, 90, and 93–98 address the calling of the SEVENTY, which Joseph Smith first spoke of to Brigham Young and Joseph Young in January 1835 (Smith, 2:180–81). The remaining verses appear to have been revealed at the time the request was made by the Twelve. How much of the final version of section 107 was revealed to the Prophet by March is not known, but the revelation as published today was printed five months later in the first edition of the Doctrine and Covenants. Underscoring the importance of this "Revelation on Priesthood," it appeared as section 3 in all editions of the Doctrine and Covenants until the sections were arranged chronologically in the 1876 edition.

Content overview

Section 107 identifies "two priesthoods, namely, the Melchizedek and Aaronic, including the Levitical Priesthood" (107:1). The lesser priesthood "is called the Priesthood of Aaron, because it was conferred upon Aaron and his seed" (107:13). The greater priesthood, *"the Holy Priesthood, after the Order of the Son of God,"* "is called the Melchizedek Priesthood . . . to avoid the too frequent repetition" of the name of God and because Melchizedek "was such a great high priest" (107:2–4). The revelation provides instruction concerning the KEYS and specific offices associated with each priesthood, clarification concerning the organization of the presiding QUORUMS of the Church, and their relationship to each other. The Melchizedek Priesthood is presided over by the First Presidency, identified as the "Presidency of the High Priesthood" (107:9) and the "three Presiding High Priests" (107:22). The Melchizedek Priesthood "holds the right of presidency" and "to administer in spiritual things" (107:8). The Presidency of the High Priesthood is the "highest council of the church" and administers "the most important business of the church" and judges "the most difficult cases" (107:78–80). The Aaronic Priesthood is presided over by a "bishopric" or "presidency" (107:15), known today as the Presiding Bishopric. They administer, under the direction of the First Presidency, all of the temporal matters of the Church. The bishop is also a "judge in Israel, to do the business of the church, to sit in judgment upon transgressors" (107:72). An extension of this role in Church discipline, the revelation instructs that the Presiding Bishopric, "assisted by twelve counselors of the High Priesthood," would constitute a "common council of the church" to sit in judgment if a member of the First Presidency were to be found in transgression (107:81–84; cf. Smith, 7:268). *See* Common council of the church.

The Aaronic Priesthood, also known as the "lesser priesthood" (107:14) or "preparatory" priesthood, administers the "outward ordinances" and temporal matters of the Church (107:14, 20; 84:26–27).

In addition to the roles and responsibilities of these "two priesthoods" generally, the revelation identifies specific duties of the Twelve Apostles (107:21–24), the Seventy (107:25–26, 90, 93–98), ELDERS (107:11–12, 89–90), the

Aaronic Priesthood (107:85–88) and their respective quorum presidents (107:85–96), including PRIESTS, TEACHERS, and DEACONS. It also identifies a priesthood office of "evangelical ministers" who are to be ordained by the Twelve (107:39). The Prophet explained, "An Evangelist is a Patriarch" (3:381). *See* Patriarch(s).

This revelation provides a priesthood genealogy, or line of authority, regarding priesthood authorities back to Adam (107:39–57). Moreover, readers learn of the principle of unanimity and the power attending decisions thus rendered by the presiding quorums of the Church (107:27–32). The revelation concludes with an admonition from the Lord to those Twelve Apostles called in 1835 and to "every man" today to learn his priesthood duties "and to act in the office in which he is appointed, in all diligence" (107:99–100).

BIBLIOGRAPHY

Cook, Lyndon W. *The Revelations of the Prophet Joseph Smith.* Salt Lake City: Deseret Book, 1985.

Jensen, Robin Scott, Robert J. Woodford, and Steven C. Harper, eds. *Manuscript Revelation Books.* Facsimile edition. First volume of the Revelations and Translations series of *The Joseph Smith Papers,* edited by Dean C. Jessee, Ronald K. Esplin, and Richard Lyman Bushman. Salt Lake City: Church Historian's Press, 2009.

Manuscript History of the Church, 18 December 1833. Church History Library, The Church of Jesus Christ of Latter-day Saints, Salt Lake City, Utah.

Smith, Joseph. *History of The Church of Jesus Christ of Latter-day Saints.* Edited by B. H. Roberts. 7 vols. 2d ed. rev. Salt Lake City: The Church of Jesus Christ of Latter-day Saints, 1932–51.

BLT

Historical context and overview of Doctrine and Covenants 108

Historical context

Joseph Smith was studying his Hebrew lesson on 26 December 1835 when Lyman Sherman, who was serving as one of the presidents of the Quorum of the Seventy, went to his home and said he had been "wrought upon to make known to you my feelings and desires and was promised that I should have a revelation which should make known my duty." Joseph received the revelation now recorded in Doctrine and Covenants 108 and recorded it in his journal (Jessee et al., 137–38).

Content overview

By exercising faith to obey the Lord's revelation to him, Sherman obtained forgiveness and comforting counsel as well as instructions relative to his calling and future responsibilities in the Church. When Sherman said he was "wrought upon," he meant that he was unsettled, even disturbed. "Let your soul be at rest," the Lord counseled him in response, and "wait patiently until the solemn assembly . . . of my servants," referring to the meetings in the house of the Lord in which Church leaders, including Sherman, received sacred ordinances and blessings in March or April 1836 (108:2, 4; Smith, 2:410–33).

The way the revelation recorded in section 108 came to Lyman Sherman reveals much about the order of revelation. Joseph Smith taught that revelations were universally available to individuals directly but that there was also an order to revelation. Sherman's role as a general authority and in the upcoming SOLEMN ASSEMBLY were matters to be revealed through Joseph Smith. In verse 1, the Lord forgave Sherman because he had repented and acknowledged and followed this order. He was a loyal, devoted Saint. In January 1839 the First Presidency called Lyman Sherman as an apostle, but he died before he was ordained to the position (Whitney, 238–39).

BIBLIOGRAPHY

Jessee, Dean C., Mark Ashurst-McGee, and Richard L. Jensen, eds. *Journals, 1832–1839.* Vol. 1 of the Journals series of *The Joseph Smith Papers,* edited by Dean C. Jessee, Ronald K. Esplin, and Richard Lyman Bushman. Salt Lake City: Church Historian's Press, 2008.

Smith, Joseph. *History of The Church of Jesus Christ of Latter-day Saints.* Edited by B. H. Roberts. 7 vols. 2d ed. rev. Salt Lake City: The Church of Jesus Christ of Latter-day Saints, 1932–51.

Whitney, Orson F. *Life of Heber C. Kimball.* Salt Lake City: Kimball Family, 1888.

SCH

Historical context and overview of Doctrine and Covenants 109

Historical context

On 27 December 1832, the Lord revealed to Joseph Smith the importance of building "a house, even a house of prayer, a house of fasting, a house of faith, a house of learning, a house of glory, a house of order, a house of God"—a TEMPLE in Kirtland, Ohio (88:119; cf. 95:8–9). The plan for building the temple was given to Joseph by the Lord (L. M. Smith, *History,* 230). The plan was intricate in detail and magnificent in design but well beyond the financial reach of Joseph and his followers. On 1 June 1833 the Lord rebuked the Saints for not having begun to build the temple (95:1–4). "Notwithstanding the Church was poor," Joseph observed, work on the temple began on 5 June 1833 (*History,* 1:349, 353). By summer, nearly every able-bodied follower had caught the spirit of building a temple to God and was engaged in cutting stones, felling trees, milling, and carpentry. Lucy Mack Smith recorded: "There was but one mainspring to all our thoughts and actions, and that was, the building of the Lord's house" (L. M. Smith, *History,* 231).

Three years later, as the temple neared completion, Sunday, 27 March 1836 was set as the date for dedicatory services. The day before, Joseph Smith, Oliver Cowdery and his brother Warren, Sidney Rigdon, and Warren Parrish "united in writing a prayer for the dedication of the house" (Cowdery, 21). Details as to how the prayer was received are lacking except that it "was given by Revelation to Joseph, the Seer" (Smith, *History,* 2:420). About seven o'clock in the morning of 27 March, hundreds congregated outside the temple, many coming from "regions round about." Within the hour, Joseph Smith and other Church leaders, acting as doorkeepers and stewards, seated the assembly and welcomed donations to help "defray the expense of building the House of the Lord" (Smith, *History,* 2:410). At nine o'clock President Sidney Rigdon began the day's service by praying and reading Psalms 96 and 24. He then spoke of many houses of worship throughout the land but of only one house—the Kirtland Temple—built by divine revelation. At the close of his lengthy discourse, he "called upon the several quorums, commencing with the Presidency, to manifest, by rising, their willingness to acknowledge" Joseph Smith as "a Prophet and Seer, and uphold [him] as such, by their prayers" (Smith, *History*, 2:416). Each quorum and then the congregation as a whole witnessed their assent by rising.

After a singing interlude, Joseph Smith asked the quorums and congregation "to acknowledge the Presidency as Prophets and Seers, and uphold them by their prayers." Again witnessing their assent, the quorums and congregation arose. The same pattern was followed as Joseph asked acknowledgment of the Twelve Apostles, presidents of the seventies, high council of Kirtland and Zion, the bishoprics of Kirtland and Zion, and the presidencies of the elders, priests, teachers, and deacons. The vote was

"unanimous in every instance" (Smith, *History*, 2:417–18). Joseph said, "I prophesied to all, that inasmuch as they would uphold these men in their several stations, (alluding to the different quorums in the Church), the Lord would bless them; yea, in the name of Christ, the blessings of heaven should be theirs" (*History*, 2:418).

With hands raised toward heaven, Joseph read the dedicatory prayer—a prayer given by revelation. In the prayer, he petitioned the Lord: "And we ask thee, Holy Father, that thy servants may go forth from this house armed with thy power, and that thy name may be upon them, and thy glory be round about them" (109:22).

After the prayer, the choir sang:

The Spirit of God like a fire is burning!
The latter-day glory begins to come forth;
The visions and blessings of old are returning,
And angels are coming to visit the earth. (Phelps)

Interior of the Kirtland Temple. Church leaders and members filled the hall for the dedication of the temple on 27 March 1836. Pictured are the Melchizedek Priesthood pulpits, located at the west end of the main floor.

Joseph then asked the quorums and congregation if they accepted the dedicatory prayer and could acknowledge that the Kirtland Temple had been dedicated.

Following a unanimous vote, the sacrament was administered by Don Carlos Smith and distributed to the congregation by the elders. Afterwards, Joseph spoke on the ministration of angels, Don Carlos Smith on the "truth of the work of the Lord," Oliver Cowdery on the Book of Mormon, Frederick G. Williams on an angel being present, David Whitmer on seeing angels, and Hyrum Smith on appreciation for those "who had endured so many toils and privations to build the house." Sidney Rigdon gave closing remarks and a benediction on the proceeding. The congregation shouted "hosanna, hosanna, hosanna to God and the Lamb, three times, sealing it each time with amen, amen, and amen" (Smith, *History*, 2:427–28).

Although it was nearly four o'clock and most of those in attendance had been in the temple for eight hours, few were eager to leave, especially when Brigham Young stood and gave a short address in tongues. The address was interpreted by David W. Patten, who gave an "exhortation in tongues himself." Joseph Smith concluded by blessing "the congregation in the name of the Lord" (Smith, *History*, 2:428). After the blessing, the dedicatory services ended.

Content overview

In the initial verses of the prayer, Joseph recounted the revelations and instructions to build "the House of the Lord" (109:1–10). The Prophet pleaded that the members of the Church would receive the blessings promised to those who were worthy and who worshipped God in his house (109:11–28). He next asked the Lord to mollify the influence of their enemies and to deliver the Saints "from under this yoke" of oppression (109:29–33). He prayed that God would "forgive the transgressions of [his] people" and give them the testimony necessary to proclaim his word and "seal up the law" (109:29–46) wherever the Lord would send them. He made particular mention of those Saints who were driven from Jackson County, Missouri, and pleaded that their antagonists "may repent of their sins if repentance is to be

found"; otherwise, he prayed "that the cause of thy people may not fail before thee may thine anger be kindled, and thine indignation fall upon them" (109:47–52). He then prayed that the nations of the earth would be receptive to the message of the Lord's servants and that the Lord would "appoint unto Zion other stakes" in order "that the gathering of [his] people may roll on in great power and majesty, that [his] work may be cut short in righteousness" (109:53–59). He concluded the prayer by dedicating the building and pleading for mercy upon the Saints, their leaders and their families. He asked the Lord to bless the members of the Church "with glory, honor, power, majesty, might, dominion, truth, justice, judgment, mercy, and an infinity of fulness, from everlasting to everlasting, that they would be clothed with salvation" (109:60–80). *See* Palms in our hands.

See also Endow, endowed, endowment; Endowment house; Kirtland Temple dedication.

BIBLIOGRAPHY

Cowdery, Oliver. Journal, 1 January–27 March 1836. Church History Library, The Church of Jesus Christ of Latter-day Saints, Salt Lake City, Utah.

Launius, Roger D. *The Kirtland Temple: A Historical Narrative*. Independence, Mo.: Herald House, 1986.

Phelps, William W. "The Spirit of God Like a Fire Is Burning." *Hymns of The Church of Jesus Christ of Latter-day Saints*, no. 2. Salt Lake City: The Church of Jesus Christ of Latter-day Saints, 1985.

Smith, Joseph. *History of The Church of Jesus Christ of Latter-day Saints*. Edited by B. H. Roberts. 7 vols. 2d ed. rev. Salt Lake City: The Church of Jesus Christ of Latter-day Saints, 1932–51.

Smith, Lucy Mack. *History of Joseph Smith by His Mother*. Edited by Preston Nibley. Salt Lake City: Bookcraft, 1958.

SEB

Historical context and overview of Doctrine and Covenants 110

Historical context

On Easter Sunday, 3 April 1836, one week after the dedication of the Kirtland Temple, Joseph Smith and Oliver Cowdery experienced an outpouring of spiritual blessings. Joseph, Oliver, other members of the First Presidency, and priesthood quorum presidents seated about a thousand people who had come to worship

God in the Kirtland Temple. Thomas B. Marsh and David W. Patten preached sermons in the forenoon to what was reported to be "an attentive audience" (Smith, 2:434–35). "In the afternoon," Joseph wrote, "I assisted the other Presidents in distributing the Lord's Supper to the Church, receiving it from the Twelve, whose privilege it was to officiate at the sacred desk this day" (110, headnote).

After the sacrament service, while a few worshipers remained in various sections of the temple, Joseph and Oliver retired to the pulpits reserved for the presiding officers of the Melchizedek Priesthood on the west end of the building. There they pulled down a canvas curtain to separate themselves from those still in the building. They then bowed themselves before the Lord in a "solemn and silent prayer" (110, headnote).

Content overview

Joseph later recorded, "The veil was taken from our minds, and the eyes of our understanding were opened" (110:1). Joseph and Oliver saw on the breastwork of the pulpit the resurrected Lord Jesus Christ. "Under his feet was a paved work of pure gold, in color like amber. His eyes were as a flame of fire; the hair of his head was white like the pure snow; his countenance shone above the brightness of the sun; and his voice was as the sound of the rushing of great waters, even the voice of Jehovah" (110:2–3). The Lord said to his servants Joseph and Oliver, "Let the hearts of all my people rejoice, who have, with their might, built this house to my name. . . . I have accepted this house" (110:6–7). His acceptance was a direct answer to the dedicatory prayer offered by Joseph on 27 March 1836 (109:4).

When this vision had closed, the heavens were again opened. Moses, Elias, and Elijah appeared to Joseph and Oliver, committing to them "the keys of this dispensation" (110:16). "Elias was the representative of the Patriarchal dispensation; Moses, of the Mosaic, and Elijah of the dispensation preparatory to the coming of the Lord" (Smith and Sjodahl, 727). Each ancient prophet bestowed priesthood KEYS upon Joseph and Oliver. Moses bestowed "keys of the gathering of Israel from the four parts of the

earth, and the leading of the ten tribes from the land of the north" (110:11). Elias "committed the dispensation of the gospel of Abraham," and Elijah, in fulfillment of the words of Malachi, bestowed the keys of turning "the hearts of the fathers to the children, and the children to the fathers" (110:12, 15; cf. Mal. 4:5–6). These PRIESTHOOD keys gave Joseph and Oliver the right to exercise all the power and authority of the Melchizedek Priesthood, which they had already received, to gather Israel, administer the fulness of the GOSPEL, and to perform all the saving ordinances for the living and the dead in holy temples. *See* Salvation for the dead.

Section 110 was recorded in Joseph Smith's 1835–36 journal by Oliver Cowdery's older brother, Warren A. Cowdery, and it was added to the Doctrine and Covenants in the 1876 edition. These sacred events were known to the general membership of the Church prior to 1876 because they had been published in the *Deseret News* on 6 November 1852 and in the *Millennial Star* the following year.

See also Priesthood, restoration of priesthood and priesthood keys.

BIBLIOGRAPHY

Anderson, Karl Ricks. *Joseph Smith's Kirtland: Eyewitness Accounts.* Salt Lake City: Deseret Book, 1989.

Smith, Hyrum M., and Janne M. Sjodahl. *Doctrine and Covenants Commentary,* Salt Lake City: Deseret Book, 1961.

Smith, Joseph. *History of The Church of Jesus Christ of Latter-day Saints.* Edited by B. H. Roberts. 7 vols. 2d ed. rev. Salt Lake City: The Church of Jesus Christ of Latter-day Saints, 1932–51.

SEB

Historical context and overview of Doctrine and Covenants 111

Historical context

In order to understand the revelation received at Salem, Massachusetts, and now recorded in Doctrine and Covenants 111, one must have some knowledge of the financial situation of the Church in 1836. The Church was in DEBT, some of which had been incurred during the construction of the Kirtland Temple. This building project had severely taxed the resources of the members. Another source of financial distress was the aid rendered to the Saints in Missouri— both directly and indirectly in paying for ZION'S CAMP (Backman, 142–46, 153–57, 161).

Given this situation, Church leaders were anxious to find ways to relieve the debt and increase the amount of usable money. When Jonathan Burgess came to Kirtland telling of a large amount of money that had belonged to a widow, now deceased, hidden in the cellar of a house located in Salem, he found believing listeners.

Joseph Smith, Sidney Rigdon, Hyrum Smith, and Oliver Cowdery left Kirtland 25 July 1836 and arrived in Salem on 4 August. They were joined later by Brigham Young and his brother Joseph. They rented a house on Union Street, not far from the Salem Custom House made famous by American author Nathaniel Hawthorne.

Burgess met them there, but because of changes in the town, he could not identify the house, thus ending their attempt to find the money. Apparently they then divided their time between preaching and sightseeing. Meanwhile, the Prophet Joseph Smith received the revelation recorded in section 111. On 6 August 1836, Oliver Cowdery, Sidney Rigdon, and Hyrum Smith went to visit the East India Marine Society Museum, leaving Joseph Smith in the solitude of the rented house. It was in this setting that he received the revelation (Cannon, 433–35). Joseph was in Salem from "early in August" until he "returned to Kirtland, some time in the month of September" (Smith, 2:464, 466).

Content overview

The Lord informed Joseph and the other brethren, "I, the Lord your God, am not

Jesus Christ Appears to Joseph Smith and Oliver Cowdery; *painting by Walter Rane. "We saw the Lord standing upon the breastwork of the pulpit, before us; and under his feet was a paved work of pure gold, in color like amber. His eyes were as a flame of fire; the hair of his head was white like the pure snow; his countenance shone above the brightness of the sun; and his voice was as the sound of the rushing of great waters, even the voice of Jehovah"* (D&C 110:2–3).

displeased with your coming . . . notwithstanding your follies" (111:1). Supposedly, their follies included "trying to solve their financial problems on their own, without seeking the help of the Lord" (Cannon, 435). In the revelation the Lord said, "Concern not yourselves about your debts, for I will give you power to pay them" (111:5).

The Lord revealed to these men that there was real TREASURE in Salem, not gold or silver but "many people in this city, whom I will gather out in due time for the benefit of Zion, through your instrumentality" (111:2). In response, the brethren began the task of preaching to the people in Salem in 1836 and in a major missionary effort in the 1840s when Erastus Snow baptized about one hundred people there (Cook, 221, 331).

The Lord mentioned another kind of treasure when he instructed the elders: "Inquire diligently concerning the more ancient inhabitants and founders of this city" (111:9). Perhaps the Lord was challenging the Prophet and his associates to learn of their ancestors while in the area—possibly as an introduction to genealogical research (family history). Salem is only a few miles from Topsfield, the ancestral home of the Prophet Joseph Smith. Salem had then, and still has today, excellent library facilities for genealogy. It should also be noted that the Prophet's uncle, Jesse Smith, had resided in Salem and that Joseph lived in his home for an extended period of time while recuperating from his leg operation as a young boy.

Section 111 is the record of a revelation that shows the follies of men, the goodness of God, and the eventual triumph of the Lord's work through the faith and efforts of his Saints (Cannon, 435–36). It was first included in the Doctrine and Covenants in the 1876 edition.

BIBLIOGRAPHY

Backman, Milton V., Jr. *The Heavens Resound: A History of the Latter-day Saints in Ohio, 1830–1838.* Salt Lake City: Deseret Book, 1983.

Cannon, Donald Q. "Joseph Smith in Salem." In *The Doctrine and Covenants.* Vol. 1 of Studies in Scripture series, edited by Robert L. Millet and Kent P. Jackson. Sandy, Utah: Randall Book, 1984.

Cook, Lyndon W. *The Revelations of the Prophet Joseph Smith.* Salt Lake City: Deseret Book, 1985.

Smith, Joseph. *History of The Church of Jesus Christ of Latter-day Saints.* Edited by B. H. Roberts. 7 vols. 2d ed. rev. Salt Lake City: The Church of Jesus Christ of Latter-day Saints, 1932–51.

Walker, Ronald W. "The Persisting Idea of American Treasure Hunting." *BYU Studies* 24 (Fall 1984).

DQC

Historical context and overview of Doctrine and Covenants 112

Historical context

This revelation was directed to Thomas B. Marsh, president of the Quorum of the Twelve Apostles. It was received by the Prophet Joseph Smith on 23 July 1837 in Kirtland, Ohio. Several factors seem to have led up to this revelation being received. Two years earlier, February 1835, the Quorum of the Twelve had been organized, and a subsequent revelation had designated the quorum as equal in authority to the First Presidency but subject to their direction (107:27, 33). Yet, since their first mission to the eastern states in 1835, the quorum had not completely fulfilled their divine mission. There was confusion in the minds of some concerning the relationship between the Quorum of the Twelve, the First Presidency, the presidency of the Church in Missouri, and the high councils in Kirtland and Zion. In addition, there was disunity and a lack of communication among the Twelve. Some of the Twelve, including Thomas B. Marsh, president of the Twelve, and David W. Patten, second in seniority in the quorum, lived in Missouri, making coordination and communication difficult. Others of the apostles had fallen into the spirit of apostasy that plagued the Church in 1837. Compounding the problems, Parley P. Pratt announced that he was planning a mission to Great Britain. When Thomas B. Marsh heard of his intentions, he wrote to Pratt informing him that such a mission needed to be planned by the whole quorum if they expected God to bless them in their labors. Marsh asked Pratt to postpone his mission to England and called for a general meeting of the Twelve to be held in Kirtland on 24 July 1837 (Smith, Letterbook, 62–63).

In late spring 1837, the apostasy in Kirtland reached such a point that a conspiracy to overthrow the Prophet, renounce certain doctrines, and establish a new church was concocted by some. Amidst this unrest, Joseph Smith said, "God revealed to me that something new must be done for the salvation of His Church." That "something new" was to call Heber C. Kimball to open the door of salvation and preside over a mission to the nation of Great Britain—the first foreign mission of the Church. Heber C. Kimball was set apart for that mission 1 June 1837. On 13 June 1837, he, along with Orson Hyde of the Quorum of the Twelve, Willard Richards, an elder, and Joseph Fielding, a priest, departed for England (Smith, *History*, 2:489, 492–93).

When Thomas B. Marsh arrived in Kirtland in July, he learned of the mission to England. He was deeply upset by the news and disappointed that his efforts to unify the quorum with a meeting of all the apostles would not now be realized. Marsh wanted clarification of his role as the leader of the quorum. On 23 July, one day before the quorum meeting was to occur, the Prophet Joseph Smith received this revelation, and Thomas B. Marsh served as scribe (Cook, 222, 224). Coincidentally, on that same day, the missionaries to England preached the first sermons on British soil, having arrived in that land on 20 July. *See* Apostles, the Twelve, mission to Great Britain.

Content overview

There are two main dimensions of the revelation recorded in section 112: individual counsel to Thomas B. Marsh and counsel to the collective Quorum of the Twelve Apostles. The Lord counseled Marsh to be humble (112:2, 3, 10), to lead the quorum in love, and to call them to repentance (112:11–13) the Lord reminded Marsh of his relationship, and that of the quorum, to the First Presidency (112:16–20, 30–32). The Lord admonished the Twelve to "arise and gird up your loins, take up your cross, follow me, and feed my sheep"; not to exalt themselves; and not to rebel against Joseph Smith (112:14–15). He further reemphasized the sacredness and significance of their calling, the power they possessed "inasmuch as they shall humble themselves before me, and abide in my word, and hearken to the voice of my Spirit" (112:19–22). The Twelve were told to cleanse their "hearts" and their "garments" and be faithful (112:33–34).

Along with this counsel came a warning concerning "vengeance [that] cometh speedily upon the inhabitants of the earth, a day of wrath, a day of burning, a day of desolation, of weeping, of mourning, and of lamentation" (112:24). Concerning these evidences of God's wrath upon the wicked prior to the Second Coming, the Lord declared that the vengeance would begin first "upon my house" and "among those among you . . . who have professed to know my name and have not known me, and have blasphemed against me in the midst of my house" (112:25–26). While the rebuke was given specifically because of the apostasy in Kirtland at the time, this warning serves to remind all who belong to his house, the Church, of the need to purify their hearts, cleanse their garments, and faithfully look to that day when the Lord will return "to recompense every man according as his work shall be" (112:34).

See also Apostles, the first Twelve of latter days.

BIBLIOGRAPHY

Cook, Lyndon W. *The Revelations of the Prophet Joseph Smith*. Salt Lake City: Deseret Book, 1985.

Smith, Joseph. *History of The Church of Jesus Christ of Latter-day Saints*. Edited by B. H. Roberts. 7 vols. 2d ed. rev. Salt Lake City: The Church of Jesus Christ of Latter-day Saints, 1932–51.

———. Letterbook 2. Church History Library, Salt Lake City, Utah.

BLT

Historical context and overview of Doctrine and Covenants 113

Historical context

Because of internal dissension caused by Mormon apostates and concerns over legal entanglements, Joseph Smith and Sidney Rigdon were instructed by revelation on 12 January 1838 to make a hasty departure from Kirtland and take up permanent residence in Missouri (Jessee et al., 283). Following a tedious midwinter journey of over two months, the Smith and Rigdon families arrived in Far West, Missouri, on 14 March 1838. With their arrival, Far West became the official headquarters of the Church.

At Far West, the Smith family resided temporarily with George W. Harris, a member of the Missouri high council, and his wife, Lucinda. Within just a few days of his arrival, probably during an informal meeting with perhaps several men, Joseph Smith was asked to clarify passages from Isaiah. His explanations regarding verses in Isaiah 11 and 52 were noted in his "Scriptory Book" by his secretary, George W. Robinson (Jessee et al., 239). The revelation illustrates that on occasion, Joseph Smith considered his explanations of scriptural texts significant enough to warrant inclusion in his personal record or in the official history of the Church.

Content overview

The revelation gives keys to understanding Isaiah 11:1–5, 10–11, and Isaiah 52:1–2. It is significant that in his 1839 history, Joseph Smith indicated that on the occasion of the visit of the angel Moroni on 21 and 22 September 1823, the heavenly messenger "quoted the eleventh chapter of Isaiah, saying that it was about to be fulfilled" (JS–H 1:40). Regarding Isaiah 11:1–5, the general interpretation among Christian scholars is that the passage is a prophetic allusion to the life and ministry of Jesus. While Latter-day Saints also believe this interpretation, since the angel Moroni indicated that the fulfillment of Isaiah 11 was yet future, some Latter-day Saints believe that portions of the passage also refer to Joseph Smith himself. As indicated in Doctrine and Covenants 113:3–4, the "rod" spoken of in Isaiah 11:1 would be "a servant in the hands of Christ, who is partly a descendant of Jesse as well as of Ephraim, or of the house of Joseph, on whom there is laid much power." On 9 December 1834 Joseph Smith Sr. pronounced a patriarchal blessing on Joseph Smith Jr., in which he declared that the Prophet was a lineal descendant and birthright heir to the patriarchal fathers Abraham, Isaac, and Jacob, particularly through Joseph of Egypt (Blessing Book, 3). Furthermore, Brigham Young declared, Joseph Smith was a descendant of Joseph through Ephraim (2:269). Additionally, Doctrine and Covenants 113:5–6 states that the "root of Jesse" as spoken of in Isaiah 11:10 is "a descendant of Jesse, as well as of Joseph, unto whom rightly belongs the priesthood, and the

keys of the kingdom, for an ensign, and for the gathering of my people in the last days." Such wording suggests the individual to be Joseph Smith who had received these keys from earlier angelic ministers (cf. 27:12; 110:11).

The passages in Isaiah 52 refer to the strength of Zion being the priesthood, and loosing the bands upon the neck of Zion as the Israelites returning to the Lord after being scattered among the Gentiles (113:7–10).

See also Isaiah quotations in the Doctrine and Covenants.

BIBLIOGRAPHY

Jessee, Dean C., Mark Ashurst-McGee, and Richard L. Jensen, eds. *Journals, 1832–1839*. Vol. 1 of the Journals series of *The Joseph Smith Papers*, edited by Dean C. Jessee, Ronald K. Esplin, and Richard Lyman Bushman. Salt Lake City: Church Historian's Press, 2008.

Ludlow, Victor L. *Isaiah: Prophet, Seer, Poet*. Salt Lake City: Deseret Book, 1982.

Nyman, Monte S. *Great Are the Words of Isaiah*. Salt Lake City: Bookcraft, 1980.

Smith, Joseph, Jr. Patriarchal Blessing Book. Joseph Smith Jr. Papers. Church History Library, The Church of Jesus Christ of Latter-day Saints, Salt Lake City, Utah.

Young, Brigham. *Journal of Discourses*. 26 vols. London: Latter-day Saints' Book Depot, 1854–86.

ALB

Historical context and overview of Doctrine and Covenants 114

Historical context

David W. Patten and his wife, Ann, moved from Kirtland, Ohio, to Far West, Missouri, in late 1836 or early 1837. Patten, a member of the original quorum of the Twelve, was second in seniority in the Quorum to Thomas B. Marsh, who also resided in Far West. On 17 April 1838 Joseph Smith received a revelation in Patten's behalf.

Content overview

Though brief, the revelation instructed Patten and the other members of the Twelve to begin to settle their affairs so that they could embark on a collective mission the following spring (1839). Although the revelation does not mention where the Twelve would be sent, reports had been received regarding the success of fellow apostles Heber C. Kimball, Orson Hyde, and five other missionaries then serving in north-central Great Britain. The revelation to Patten clearly implied that the entire Twelve were to perform a follow-up mission to the British Isles the next year. Tragically, Patten was unable to personally fulfill the revelation due to his death on 25 October 1838 from wounds he received during the conflict between Mormon and Missouri militia at the Battle of Crooked River in northern Ray County.

At the time this revelation was received, four members of the quorum were in a state of apostasy: William E. McLellin, Luke and Lyman Johnson, and John Boynton. The Lord clearly stated that they would be replaced because they "deny [the Lord's] name" (114:2). Three months later, by revelation to Joseph Smith, John Taylor, John E. Page, Wilford Woodruff, and Willard Richards were chosen to "fill the places of those who [had] fallen" (118:6).

BIBLIOGRAPHY

Whiting, Linda S. *David W. Patten: Apostle and Martyr.* Springville, Utah: Cedar Fort, 2003.

ALB

Historical context and overview of Doctrine and Covenants 115

Historical context

With the establishment of the Mormon settlement of Far West, Caldwell County, Missouri, in 1836–37, Missouri Church leaders made plans to build a TEMPLE similar in design and function to the one in Kirtland, Ohio. In April 1837, the Missouri presidency, high council, and bishopric were appointed to oversee construction of the building (Cannon and Cook, 103–4). A site was chosen in the northeast corner of the Far West public square, and on 3 July work began. W. W. Phelps noted on that day some fifteen hundred Saints assembled and broke ground, creating an excavation 110 feet long by 80 feet wide (Phelps, 529). Although the digging of the foundation marked an important beginning, further construction was suspended until revealed instruction and direction could be given by Joseph Smith. During a visit by Joseph Smith

to Far West the first week of November 1837, a council was held in which it was decided that "the building of the House of the Lord be postponed until the Lord shall reveal it to be His will to have it commenced" (Smith, 2:521). On 26 April 1838, less than six weeks after the Prophet relocated to Far West, he received the revelation recorded in Doctrine and Covenants 115 outlining instructions regarding how construction on the temple should proceed and declaring that the city of Far West was to be "holy" and a "refuge from the storm" that was soon to descend on the earth (115:6–7).

Content overview

The Lord commanded the Church to officially dedicate the temple foundation on 4 July 1838 and then to make preparations so that actual construction could begin "in one year from this day," namely, 26 April 1839 (115:7–11). Furthermore, the Lord instructed the Saints not to incur any debt for the temple's construction. Finally, the building was to be built after the pattern which the Lord would reveal to the First Presidency (115:13–15). It is not known whether Joseph Smith actually received any divine instruction regarding the design of the temple at Far West. According to John Wyckliffe Rigdon, son of Sidney Rigdon, however, the temple was to have been similar in design and function to that of the Kirtland Temple, including a lower hall or auditorium and an upper hall to be used for a school (Rigdon, 31).

> 5 Verily I say unto you all: *a*Arise and shine forth, that thy *b*light may be a *c*standard for the *d*nations;
> 6 And that the *a*gathering together upon the land of *b*Zion, and upon her *c*stakes, may be for a defense, and for a *d*refuge from the storm, and from wrath when it shall be *e*poured out without mixture upon the whole earth.

Doctrine and Covenants 115:5–6.

In addition to detailing plans for building the Far West temple, the Lord also established the official name of his Church. When the Church was organized on 6 April 1830, it bore the name "Church of Christ" (20:1). Then, on 3 May 1834, Church leaders officially adopted the title "The Church of the Latter Day Saints." Soon, however, the Lord specified that his Church should be called "The Church of Jesus Christ of Latter-day Saints" (115:3–4), which name has continued to the present day. *See* Church of Jesus Christ of Latter-day Saints, The.

The Lord instructed the entire Church to gather to northern Missouri (115:17–19); however, the anticipated influx of Latter-day Saints into the region would necessarily require additional settlements to be established. The Lord instructed Joseph Smith to search out other settlement locations. Pursuant to these instructions, from 18 May to 5 June 1838, the Prophet conducted three expeditions, primarily north of Caldwell County in Daviess County, in search of possible Mormon settlement sites. Additional exploratory expeditions were also conducted throughout the summer. A settlement of Saints in ADAM-ONDI-AHMAN followed.

BIBLIOGRAPHY

Baugh, Alexander L. "The Mormon Temple Site at Far West, Caldwell County, Missouri." In *The Missouri Mormon Experience,* edited by Thomas M. Spencer. Columbia: University of Missouri Press, 2010.

Cannon, Donald Q., and Lyndon W. Cook, eds. *Far West Record: Minutes of The Church of Jesus Christ of Latter-day Saints, 1830–1844.* Salt Lake City: Deseret Book, 1983.

Phelps, W. W. 7 July 1837 letter. In *Latter Day Saints' Messenger and Advocate* 3, no. 10 (July 1837): 529.

Rigdon, John Wyckliffe. "The Life and Testimony of Sidney Rigdon." In "'I Never Knew a Time When I Did Not Know Joseph Smith': A Son's Record of the Life and Testimony of Sidney Rigdon," edited by Karl Keller. *Dialogue: A Journal of Mormon Thought* 1, no. 4 (Winter 1966): 15–42.

Smith, Joseph. *History of The Church of Jesus Christ of Latter-day Saints.* Edited by B. H. Roberts. 7 vols. 2d ed. rev. Salt Lake City: The Church of Jesus Christ of Latter-day Saints, 1932–51.

ALB

Historical context and overview of Doctrine and Covenants 116

Historical context

On 18 May 1838, Joseph Smith, in company with several others, left Far West, Missouri, on the first of three exploratory expeditions to Daviess County "for the purpose of . . . making Locations & laying claims for the gathering of the saints for the benefit of the poor" (Jessee et al., 270). The following day, 19 May, the company arrived at the home of Lyman Wight, a Church member who had secured a property claim about 23 miles north of Far West on the Grand River in Grand River Township, Daviess County, where he farmed and operated a ferry during the high-water season. On this occasion, the first time Joseph Smith visited the region, George W. Robinson, Joseph Smith's clerk, recorded the following significant entry in the Prophet's journal (sometimes referred to as the "Scriptory Book"): "Spring Hill a name appropriated by the bretheren present, But after wards named by the mouth of [the] Lord and was called Adam Ondi Awmen [Adam-ondi-Ahman], because said he it is the place where Adam shall come to visit his people, or the Ancient of days shall sit as spoken of by Daniel the Prophet" (Jessee et al., 271).

In the 1870s, as Orson Pratt was editing and revising the revelations for publication in what became the 1876 edition of the Doctrine and Covenants, he included, as a new section, the part of the text from Joseph Smith's 19 May 1838 journal that discussed Adam-ondi-Ahman. Pratt also composed an introduction, or headnote, to the revelation, which reads: "Revelation to Joseph, the Seer, given near Wight's Ferry, at a place called Spring Hill, Davis [Daviess] County, Missouri, May 19th, 1838, wherein Spring Hill is named by the Lord." He then included as the text of the revelation: "ADAM-ONDI-AHMAN, because, said he, it is the place where Adam shall come to visit his people, or the Ancient of days shall sit, as spoken of by Daniel the Prophet" (D&C, 379, 1876 ed.). A comparison of Pratt's text with the original from Joseph Smith's journal shows that the wording is precisely the same; the only changes made by Pratt were in spelling, punctuation, and capitalization. In 1921, while revising the revelations and headings for yet another edition, the Scripture Committee added a portion of Pratt's heading to the revelation, "Spring Hill is named by the Lord," to the original manuscript text.

Content overview

Doctrine and Covenants 116 clarifies and identifies the location of the fulfillment of a prophecy made anciently by the prophet Daniel (Dan. 7:9–10, 13–14). That prophecy describes a latter-day event in which the resurrected Jesus and the resurrected Adam, the "Ancient of Days," will visit and preside at an assemblage of Adam's posterity at Adam-ondi-Ahman prior to the second coming of Christ to all the world. The Prophet Joseph Smith taught that the purpose of the meeting is to "prepare them for the coming of the Son of Man. He (Adam) is the father of the human family, and presides over the spirits of all men, and all that have had the keys must stand before him in this grand council. . . . Adam delivers up his stewardship to Christ"

(Smith, 3:386–87). This is the same location where Adam met with his righteous posterity three years before his death and "predicted whatsoever should befall his posterity unto the latest generation" (107:50–56).

BIBLIOGRAPHY

"History of Joseph Smith." *Deseret News* 3, no. 10 (2 April 1853), 1.

Jessee, Dean C., Mark Ashurst-McGee, and Richard L. Jensen, eds. *Journals, 1832–1839.* Vol. 1 of the Journals series of *The Joseph Smith Papers,* edited by Dean C. Jessee, Ronald K. Esplin, and Richard Lyman Bushman. Salt Lake City: Church Historian's Press, 2008.

McConkie, Bruce R. *The Millennial Messiah: The Second Coming of the Son of Man.* Salt Lake City: Deseret Book, 1982.

Smith, Joseph. *History of The Church of Jesus Christ of Latter-day Saints.* Edited by B. H. Roberts. 7 vols. 2d ed. rev. Salt Lake City: The Church of Jesus Christ of Latter-day Saints, 1932–51.

———. Journal, May 19, 1838, 43–44. Church History

Lyman Wight's home near Spring Hill, Missouri, in the valley of Adam-ondi-Ahman; photograph by George Edward Anderson, 1907. The Prophet was visiting Wight, who had settled near Spring Hill and was operating a ferry on the Grand River when section 116 was received on 19 May 1838.

Library, The Church of Jesus Christ of Latter-day Saints, Salt Lake City, Utah.

ALB

Historical context and overview of Doctrine and Covenants 117

Historical context

Doctrine and Covenants 117 is a revelation containing directions and instructions to three men—William Marks, Newel K. Whitney, and Oliver Granger. The revelation was included in an 8 July 1838 letter by the First Presidency (Joseph Smith, Sidney Rigdon, and Hyrum Smith) written from Far West and addressed specifically to Marks and Whitney, both of whom had remained in Kirtland, Ohio, after most of the Saints had moved to Missouri. The revelation was also transcribed by George W. Robinson, Joseph Smith's clerk, into the Prophet's journal (Jessee et al., 289–90).

Following Joseph Smith's departure from Kirtland in January 1838, William Marks was appointed to preside over the Ohio Saints. Newel K. Whitney, the bishop in Kirtland, also remained to oversee the temporal operations of the Church. It was fully expected, however, that both Marks and Whitney would very soon settle their affairs and relocate in Missouri. By July 1838, when the two men continued to reside in Kirtland, Joseph Smith sought revelatory understanding of their situation.

Content overview

The Lord made clear that Marks and Whitney were to relocate to Missouri before winter (117:1–2). Once in Missouri they would preside over the Saints in their respective callings—Marks as president in the Missouri presidency and Whitney as a bishop (117:10–11). To expedite their move, the Lord instructed that Oliver Granger be dispatched to Kirtland to act as an agent for the First Presidency in settling some of their business affairs. The Lord also praised Oliver Granger, saying "his name shall be had in sacred remembrance from generation to generation, forever and ever" (117:12–15).

Pursuant to the instructions given in the revelation, Newel K. Whitney and his family left Kirtland in the fall of 1838. In St. Louis, after learning of Governor Lilburn W. Boggs's order

to exterminate the Saints from Missouri, the Whitneys located temporarily in Greene County, Illinois, later moving to Commerce (subsequently named Nauvoo) in 1839. Whitney became one of the first four bishops in Nauvoo. After leaving Ohio, the Marks family settled for a short time in Quincy, Illinois, before their move to Commerce. Marks later became the Nauvoo Stake president. Oliver Granger labored to resolve the Church's unpaid debts in Kirtland until his death in August 1841. He succeeded in settling the affairs of the First Presidency to the satisfaction of their creditors. One of them wrote, "Oliver Granger's management in the arrangement of the unfinished business of people that have moved to the Far West, in redeeming their pledges and thereby sustaining their integrity, has been truly praiseworthy, and has entitled him to my highest esteem, and every grateful recollection" (Smith, 3:174).

BIBLIOGRAPHY

Jessee, Dean C., Mark Ashurst-McGee, and Richard L. Jensen, eds. *Journals, 1832–1839.* Vol. 1 of the Journals series of *The Joseph Smith Papers,* edited by Dean C. Jessee, Ronald K. Esplin, and Richard Lyman Bushman. Salt Lake City: Church Historian's Press, 2008.

Smith, Joseph. *History of The Church of Jesus Christ of Latter-day Saints.* Edited by B. H. Roberts. 7 vols. 2d ed. rev. Salt Lake City: The Church of Jesus Christ of Latter-day Saints, 1932–51.

ALB

Historical context and overview of Doctrine and Covenants 118

Historical context

Doctrine and Covenants 118 is one of four canonized revelations received by Joseph Smith on 8 July 1838 (including 117; 119; and 120).

Content overview

The revelation is directed to the Twelve Apostles and contains three distinct instructions—Thomas B. Marsh, the President of the Twelve, was to remain for the time being in Missouri to assist in the printing operations of the Church (that is, printing the *Elders' Journal*) (118:2); the Twelve were to prepare to serve a mission to Great Britain, which mission was to commence from Far West on 26 April 1839

(118:4–5); and John Taylor, John E. Page, Wilford Woodruff, and Willard Richards were to be ordained members of the Quorum of the Twelve to fill the vacancies created by the excommunication of apostles John F. Boynton, Luke S. Johnson, Lyman E. Johnson, and William E. McLellin (118:6).

Later that summer, hostilities broke out between the Missourians and the Mormons, culminating in Governor Lilburn W. Boggs issuing the Extermination Order on 27 October 1838. Joseph Smith and several other Church leaders were imprisoned, and the main body of the Saints was forced to evacuate to Quincy, Adams County, Illinois, during the early winter months of 1839.

On 17 March 1839, in Quincy, Illinois, Brigham Young presided over a council meeting that included several apostles. During the meeting it was decided that the Twelve would return to Far West to fulfill the instructions called for in two revelations—to "re-commence" laying the temple cornerstones (115:11) and to take leave for their appointed mission to Great Britain (118:5). At this same meeting Thomas B. Marsh, among others, was excommunicated from the Church for his apostasy in Missouri. With the excommunication of Marsh and the death of David W. Patten the previous fall, Brigham Young became the senior apostle in the Quorum.

During the third week of April, five of the ordained apostles—Brigham Young, Heber C. Kimball, Orson Pratt, John Taylor, and John E. Page—in company with Wilford Woodruff, who had been appointed in section 118 to fill one of the vacancies in the Twelve, and George A. Smith, who was subsequently called to the Twelve—made their way back to Far West. Despite threats to their safety, during the early morning hours of 26 April 1839 the apostles and a small number of other Saints assembled at the temple site. Wilford Woodruff recorded the proceedings of the private meeting:

"At a Council held at Far West by the Twelve, High Priests, Elders, & Priests on the twenty Sixth of April 1839 The following resolutions were adopted:

"Resolved that the following persons should

be no more fellowshiped in the Church of Jesus Christ of Latter Day Saints but excommunicated from the Same [Elder Woodruff listed the names of thirty men and women who had apostatized from the Church and were cut off by the Twelve].

"The Council then proceded to the building spot of the Lords house when the following business was transacted: Part of a Hymn was sung on the mission of the Twelve. Elder [Alpheus] Cutler the Master workman of the house then recommenced laying the foundation of the LORD'S house agreeable to revelation by rooling [rolling] up a large stone near the South east corner.

"The following of the Twelve were present: Brigham Young, Heber C. Kimble, Orson Pratt, John E. Page, & John Taylor, who proceded to ordain (on the chief corner stone of the building) Willford Woodruff & George A. Smith, (who had been previously nominated by the first Presidency, accepted by the Twelve, & acknowledged by the Church,) to the office of the Twelve to fill the place of those who had fallen. Darwin Chase & Norman Shearer (who had Just been liberated from Richmond prison whare they had been confined for the cause of Jesus Christ) were then Ordained to the office of the Seventies.

"The Twelve then offered up vocal Prayer in the following order: Brigham Young, Heber C Kimble, Orson Pratt, John E. Page, John Taylor, Willford Woodruff & George A. Smith, after which we Sung Adamondi ahmon [Adam-ondi-Ahman] & then the Twelve took (the parting hand) their leave of the following Saints agreeable to revelation. . . . [Elder Woodruff listed the names of eighteen other Latter-day Saints who were also present].

"Elder Alpheus Cutler then placed the stone before alluded to in its regular position after which in consequence of the peculiar situation of the Saints he thought it wisdom to adjourn untill some future time when the Lord should open the way expressing his determination then to procede with the building" (1:326–27).

The meeting complete and the revelation fulfilled, the Twelve and other Latter-day Saints present on the occasion hastily departed from the state, most arriving back at Quincy the first part of May. After settling their families in Montrose, Iowa, and Commerce (later named Nauvoo), Illinois, the Twelve departed for Great Britain in August and September 1839. *See* map, p. 33.

See also Apostles, the Twelve, mission to Great Britain.

BIBLIOGRAPHY

Baugh, Alexander L. "The Mormon Temple Site at Far West, Caldwell County, Missouri." In Thomas M. Spencer, ed., *The Missouri Mormon Experience.* Columbia: University of Missouri Press, 2010.

Woodruff, Wilford. *Wilford Woodruff's Journal, 1833–1898, Typescript.* Edited by Scott G. Kenney. 9 vols. Midvale, Utah: Signature Books, 1983–84.

ALB

Historical context and overview of Doctrine and Covenants 119

Historical context

In September 1837, recognizing the need to bring about a more systematic means to encourage membership contributions to the Church, the bishopric in Kirtland issued a letter proposing that the Saints be tithed (Smith, 2:515–18; cf. Mal. 3:8–12). The Missouri bishopric also proposed and adopted a similar but more definitive measure in December 1837, recommending that the Saints be tithed two percent annually (Cannon and Cook, 129–30). It appears, however, that no attempt was made at any time to make the payment of tithes obligatory for a member to be considered in good standing.

Joseph Smith was clearly aware of both tithing proposals issued by the Kirtland and Missouri bishoprics, but he took no action regarding either proposal. By July 1838, however, the projected growth and expenses of the Church in Missouri created the need for immediate capital and property. On 8 July 1838, the Prophet sought revelatory direction. "O Lord!" he asked, "show unto thy servant how much thou requirest of the properties of thy people for a tithing?" whereupon the revelation was received and recorded in Joseph Smith's journal by his secretary, George W. Robinson (Smith, 3:44; Jessee et al., 288).

Content overview

The Lord instructed the Saints to consecrate what surplus property or assets they had so that the Church could immediately obtain financial resources (119:1–2). Thereafter, Church members would be expected to consecrate a tithe, or one-tenth of their annual increase, as a "standing law unto them forever" (119:4). The Lord further directed that if the Saints gathering to Zion "observe not this law, to keep it holy . . . it shall not be a land of Zion unto you" (119:6). The revelation ends with the directive that "this shall be an ensample unto all the stakes of Zion. Even so. Amen" (119:7).

See also Consecration.

BIBLIOGRAPHY

Cannon, Donald Q., and Lyndon W. Cook, eds. *Far West Record: Minutes of The Church of Jesus Christ of Latter-day Saints, 1830–1844.* Salt Lake City: Deseret Book, 1983.

Jessee, Dean C., Mark Ashurst-McGee, and Richard L. Jensen, eds. *Journals, 1832–1839.* Vol. 1 of the Journals series of *The Joseph Smith Papers,* edited by Dean C. Jessee, Ronald K. Esplin, and Richard Lyman Bushman. Salt Lake City: Church Historian's Press, 2008.

Smith, Joseph. *History of The Church of Jesus Christ of Latter-day Saints.* Edited by B. H. Roberts. 7 vols. 2d ed. rev. Salt Lake City: The Church of Jesus Christ of Latter-day Saints, 1932–51.

ALB

Historical context and overview of Doctrine and Covenants 120

Historical context

On 8 July 1838, the same day the revelation recorded in section 119 was received, the Lord gave the revelation recorded in section 120, "making known the disposition of the properties tithed" (headnote).

Content overview

The Lord specified that Church funds were to be overseen by a council composed of (1) the First Presidency, then composed of Joseph Smith Jr., Sidney Rigdon, and Hyrum Smith, with Joseph Smith Sr. and John Smith as assistant presidents in the First Presidency; (2) the "bishop and his council," namely, Edward Partridge and his two counselors, Isaac Morley and John Corrill; and (3) the "high council," who at the time consisted of the Missouri presidency, Thomas B. Marsh, David Patten, and Brigham Young (the three senior members of the Twelve) and twelve high priests (councilors). Although initially the Missouri high council was directed to assist in the expenditure of the tithes, that role was later given to the Council of the Twelve Apostles. Therefore, the "council" referred to in the revelation that is responsible for all Church expenditures is currently known as the "Council on the Disposition of the Tithes," and "is composed of the First Presidency, the Quorum of the Twelve Apostles, and the Presiding Bishopric" ("Church Auditing," 28). The revelation makes clear that the Lord's "own voice unto them" is to be followed in their decisions (120:1).

See also Consecration; Historical context and overview of Doctrine and Covenants 119 (p. 830).

BIBLIOGRAPHY

"Church Auditing Department Report, 2010." *Ensign* 41 (May 2011): 28.

Jessee, Dean C., Mark Ashurst-McGee, and Richard L. Jensen, eds. *Journals, Volume 1: 1832–1839.* Vol. 1 of the Journals series of *The Joseph Smith Papers,* edited by Dean C. Jessee, Ronald K. Esplin, and Richard Lyman Bushman. Salt Lake City: Church Historian's Press, 2008.

ALB

Historical context and overview of Doctrine and Covenants 121

Historical context

From 31 October 1838 until 16 April 1839, a period of over five and one-half months, Joseph Smith was held in custody by Missouri state officials. Following his initial arrest, the Prophet and six other Mormon leaders were taken to Independence, where they remained for a few days (4–8 November 1838) before being transferred to Richmond (8–9 November 1838) for a preliminary hearing before circuit court judge Austin A. King. After more than two weeks of testimony against a total of 64 Mormon defendants, King found probable cause against Joseph Smith, Sidney Rigdon, Hyrum Smith, Lyman Wight, Alexander McCrae, and Caleb Baldwin

on the charge of treason and ordered them to be taken to Liberty Jail in Clay County to await their court appearance scheduled for the following spring. The six men arrived in Liberty on 1 December to begin their incarceration, which would last until 6 April 1839 (Sidney Rigdon secured an early release in January 1839 because of serious illness). The hearing for Joseph Smith and the remaining prisoners convened in Gallatin in early April (9–11 April 1839), at which time a change of venue was granted that resulted in their intended transfer to Columbia, Missouri. En route, Sheriff William Morgan and the guards allowed the prisoners to escape.

Eight letters, written or dictated by Joseph Smith during his confinement in Liberty Jail, have survived. The letter dated 20 March 1839 has received the most attention. This is due primarily to Orson Pratt, who, under the direction of Brigham Young and while editing and revising the revelations for publication in what became the 1876 edition of the Doctrine and Covenants, extracted excerpts from the letter between 20 and 25 March 1839 to form sections 121–23. *See* Historical context and overview of Doctrine and Covenants 122 (p. 833) and 123 (p. 836).

The day before he dictated the letter, the Prophet received letters from his wife, Emma, his younger brothers Don Carlos and William, and Bishop Edward Partridge, prompting his reply. The letter is addressed to "the church of Latterday saints at Quincy Illinois and scattered abroad and to Bishop Partridge in particular" (Smith, 430) and consists of twenty-nine manuscript pages. Twenty-seven pages are in the

> 33 How long can rolling waters remain impure? What *a*power shall stay the heavens? As well might man stretch forth his puny arm to stop the Missouri river in its decreed course, or to turn it up stream, as to *b*hinder the *c*Almighty from pouring down *d*knowledge from heaven upon the heads of the Latter-day Saints.

Doctrine and Covenants 121:33.

handwriting of Alexander McRae. Caleb Baldwin acted as scribe for the other two pages.

Content overview

Orson Pratt was selective in the five passages he extracted from the letter to form section 121. The first excerpt (121:1–6) reflects the Prophet's knowledge of the physical hardships encountered by the Saints as they made their way out of Missouri during the winter season of February and early March 1839. Let "thine heart . . . be softened . . . and thy bowels be moved with compassion toward them" (121:3) was his heartfelt plea, with the hope that God would "remember thy suffering saints" (121:6). At the same time, he asked that vengeance be poured out upon those who caused the suffering: "Let thine anger be kindled against our enemies" (121:5).

In the second excerpt (121:7–25), the Lord revealed to Joseph Smith that his incarceration would come to an end (121:7) and that his friends would "hail thee again with warm hearts and friendly hands" (121:9). Furthermore, the Lord assured him that in due time his enemies, both apostates from the Church and other persecutors, would incur God's judgment and punishment and "shall not escape the damnation of hell" (121:23).

In the third and fourth excerpts (121:26–32, 33) the Lord clarified that the Restoration was not yet complete—that there were doctrines and teachings associated with the eternal world that he would yet reveal, that there was "a time to come in the which nothing shall be withheld."

Finally, the fifth excerpt (121:34–46) provides poignant counsel regarding those called to exercise PRIESTHOOD authority. Of critical importance is the fact that "the rights of the

Liberty Jail; *painting by Greg Olsen. "My son, peace be unto thy soul; thine adversity and thine afflictions shall be but a small moment; and then, if thou endure it well, God shall exalt thee on high; thou shalt triumph over all thy foes"* (D&C 121:7–8).

priesthood are inseparably connected with the powers of heaven, and that the powers of heaven cannot be controlled nor handled only upon the principles of righteousness" (121:36). The problems experienced by the Saints in Missouri resulted not only from outside persecution but from a number of prominent Church leaders exercising unwarranted and unauthorized control and dominion in the Church, leading to their apostasy. Some of the Church leaders in Missouri who were disfellowshipped or excommunicated during this period include Oliver Cowdery, David Whitmer, John Whitmer, William E. McLellin, William W. Phelps, Frederick G. Williams, Thomas B. Marsh, Orson Hyde, and Sampson Avard.

The revelation makes clear that those who exercise the priesthood unrighteously lose the Spirit of the Lord and then proceed to "kick against the pricks, to persecute the saints, and to fight against God" (121:37–38). Although such individuals may have been "called," they are not "chosen" (121:40).

To guard against improper use of priesthood authority, priesthood leaders are instructed to continually exercise the Christlike virtues of persuasion, long-suffering, gentleness, meekness, love, kindness, charity, and virtue. With charity and virtuous thoughts they are promised that the "doctrine of the priesthood shall distil upon [their souls] as the dews from heaven," the Holy Ghost will be their "constant companion," and their scepter (a symbol of priesthood authority) will be "an unchanging scepter of righteousness and truth" (121:41–46). *See* Priesthood, proper exercise of.

BIBLIOGRAPHY

Baugh, Alexander L., "'We Took Our Change of Venue to the State of Illinois': The Gallatin Hearing and the Escape of Joseph Smith and the Mormon Prisoners from Missouri, 1939." *Mormon Historical Studies* 2, no. 1 (Spring 2001): 59–82.

Jessee, Dean C. "'Walls, Grates, and Screeking Iron Doors': The Prison Experience of Mormon Leaders in Missouri, 1838–1839." In *New Views in Mormon History: A Collection of Essays in Honor of Leonard J. Arrington,* edited by Davis Bitton and Maureen Ursenbach Beecher, 19–42. Salt Lake City: University of Utah Press, 1987.

Jessee, Dean C., and John W. Welch. "Revelations in Context: Joseph Smith's Letter from Liberty Jail,

March 20, 1839." *BYU Studies* 39, no. 3 (2000): 125–45.

Smith, Joseph. *Personal Writings of Joseph Smith.* Compiled and edited by Dean C. Jessee. Rev. ed. Salt Lake City: Deseret Book, 2002.

ALB

Historical context and overview of Doctrine and Covenants 122

Historical context

Section 122 is the second of three sections in the Doctrine and Covenants taken from Joseph Smith's 20–25 March 1839 letter written from LIBERTY JAIL. *See* Historical context and overview of Doctrine and Covenants 121 (p. 831).

Content overview

Section 122 contains some of the most eloquent prose in modern or ancient scripture, demonstrating a divine voice of assurance and peace. The Lord acknowledged that in spite of Joseph Smith's present circumstances, he was still called and chosen as the prophet-leader to the Latter-day Saints (122:1–4) and taught Joseph Smith (and Latter-day Saints in general) that there is a cost for one's discipleship. In short, the true disciple must be willing to suffer as did Christ for the cause of truth, and that such suffering would "give thee experience, and shall be for thy good" (122:5–8). In conclusion, the Lord assured Joseph Smith that the days of his mortal probation were known and that the Prophet would not die until his work was completed (122:9).

It is interesting to note that the wording in the revelation alludes to two experiences of Joseph Smith that transpired a short time after his arrest by Missouri militia authorities on 31 October 1838. One incident mentioned (122:6) took place on 2 November on the occasion when the Prophet was separated and taken from his family. That day, Joseph Smith, Sidney Rigdon, Hyrum Smith, Parley P. Pratt, Lyman Wight, Amasa Lyman, and George W. Robinson were taken from the militia encampment south of Far West, where they had been held, and were escorted to their homes to procure clothing and other personal effects and to say good-bye to their family members before being taken to Independence. Joseph Smith III recalled: "When [my father] was brought to the house by an armed guard I ran out of the gate to greet him, but was roughly pushed away from his side by a sword in the hand of the guard and not allowed to go near him." Joseph III remembered that his mother, Emma, received similar treatment. "My mother, also, was not permitted to approach him and had to receive his farewell by word of lip only" (Smith, 2).

The second incident alluded to in the revelation (122:4) occurred sometime between 9 and 29 November 1838 when Joseph Smith and the six other prisoners were in custody at Richmond during the time their preliminary hearing was being held before circuit court judge Austin A. King. In reminiscing about their imprisonment in the jail at Richmond, Missouri, Parley P. Pratt

noted that on one occasion during the late evening hours he and the other Latter-day Saint prisoners were trying to get some sleep but were unable to do so due to the vile language and repulsive conversation of their guards. After this had gone on for some time, Elder Pratt stated that Joseph Smith arose "and in a voice of thunder, or as the roaring lion" (179) rebuked the guards for their disgusting talk and behavior. The passage in verse 4, which states that for a moment Joseph's voice would be more terrible that that of a "fierce lion," probably has reference to that incident.

BIBLIOGRAPHY

Pratt, Parley P. *Autobiography of Parley P. Pratt.* Edited by Parley P. Pratt Jr. Salt Lake City: Deseret Book, 1985.

Smith, Mary Audentia Smith Anderson, ed. "The

The reconstructed Liberty Jail; photograph by Richard Crookston. "And if thou shouldst be cast into the pit, or into the hands of murderers, and the sentence of death passed upon thee; if thou be cast into the deep; if the billowing surge conspire against thee; if fierce winds become thine enemy; if the heavens gather blackness, and all the elements combine to hedge up the way; and above all, if the very jaws of hell shall gape open the mouth wide after thee, know thou, my son, that all these things shall give thee experience, and shall be for thy good. The Son of Man hath descended below them all. Art thou greater than he?" (D&C 122:7–8).

Of One Heart: Joseph in Liberty Jail; *painting by Liz Lemon Swindle. "Fear not what man can do, for God shall be with you forever and ever" (D&C 122:9).*

Memoirs of President Joseph Smith (1832–1914)." *Saints' Herald*, 6 November 1834.

ALB

Historical context and overview of Doctrine and Covenants 123

Historical context

Section 123 is the third of three sections in the Doctrine and Covenants taken from Joseph Smith's 20–25 March 1839 letter written from LIBERTY JAIL. *See* Historical context and overview of Doctrine and Covenants 121 (p. 831).

Content overview

During his confinement in Liberty Jail, Joseph Smith came to the conclusion that the persecutions by the Missourians against the Latter-day Saints should be brought to the attention of the American people, and more particularly to that of the federal government. In his 20–25 March letter he counseled the Saints, most of whom had temporarily relocated in Adams County, Illinois, to "[gather] up a knowledge of all the facts, and sufferings and abuses put upon them by the people of this State; and also of all the property and amount of damages which they have sustained, both of character and personal injuries, as well as real property; and also the names of all persons that have had a hand in their oppressions, . . . that we may not only publish [this] to all the world, but present them to the heads of government" (123:1–6). "[This] should then be attended to with great earnestness" (123:14), he concluded. He also recommended, "A committee can be appointed to find out these things" (123:4). Accordingly, at a conference of the Church held on 4 May 1839 at Quincy, Illinois, with Joseph Smith presiding, "it was Resolved That Almond Babbit [Almon Babbitt], Erastus Snow and Robert B. Thompson be appointed a traveling committee to gather up and obtain all the libelous reports and publications which have been circulated against our Church—as well as other historical matter connected with said church which they can possibly obtain" (Smith, Letterbook, 47). Later, Joseph Smith counseled that Babbitt and Snow should do the field work and Thompson the writing and compiling.

Church members responded to Joseph Smith's directive by preparing formal affidavits, sworn before civil authorities (clerks of the circuit court, justices of the peace, and notary publics) to ensure legal validity. Most of these affidavits were prepared in 1839 and 1840, but a few were written as late as 1845. More than 770 affidavits are known to exist, most of which are archived in the LDS Church History Library in Salt Lake City. Some 218 affidavits are located in the National Archives in Washington, D.C. In addition to the affidavits written and signed by individual Latter-day Saints, several petitions outlining Mormon grievances were signed by literally hundreds of Latter-day Saints.

Although Joseph Smith's attempts to secure REDRESS or reparation from the federal government proved unsuccessful, the petitions they wrote provide historical documentation and evidence of the civil injustices perpetrated by the Missourians against the Latter-day Saints. The petitions have proven to be a valuable resource for historians in their efforts to accurately interpret and reconstruct the history of the Church during the Missouri period (1831–39). Perhaps this is what Joseph Smith had in mind when he wrote, "Let no man count them as small things; for there is much which lieth in *futurity,* pertaining to the saints, which depends upon these things" (123:15; emphasis added).

The Prophet identified the main cause of opposition and persecution as "the influence of that spirit which hath so strongly riveted the creeds of the fathers, who have inherited lies, upon the hearts of the children, and filled the world with confusion, and has been growing stronger and stronger, and is now the very mainspring of all corruption, and the whole earth groans under the weight of its iniquity." These creeds, he wrote, were "urged on and upheld" by Satan (123:7–8). The Prophet also wrote that it is "an imperative duty" given the Church in their generation and for future generations to bring to light the truth, and to help other people not be deceived by false religious creeds (123:8–14).

BIBLIOGRAPHY

Johnson, Clark V. "Government Responses to Mormon Appeals." In *Regional Studies in Latter-day Saint Church History: Illinois,* edited by H. Dean Garrett,

183–204. Provo, Utah: Department of Church History and Doctrine, Brigham Young University, 1995.

———, ed. *Mormon Redress Petitions: Documents of the 1833–1838 Missouri Conflict.* Provo, Utah: Religious Studies Center, Brigham Young University, 1992.

Smith, Joseph. *History of The Church of Jesus Christ of Latter-day Saints.* Edited by B. H. Roberts. 7 vols. 2d ed. rev. Salt Lake City: The Church of Jesus Christ of Latter-day Saints, 1932–51.

———. Letterbook, 6 November 1838–9 February 1843. Church History Library, The Church of Jesus Christ of Latter-day Saints, Salt Lake City, Utah.

ALB

Historical context and overview of Doctrine and Covenants 124

Historical context

After the Latter-day Saints were driven from Missouri in early 1839, most found temporary refuge in Quincy, Adams County, Illinois. Between April and August, however, Latter-day Saint leaders negotiated several land purchases in Lee County, Iowa, and Hancock County, Illinois, which included the small Mississippi riverfront village of Commerce. As a result of these acquisitions, significant numbers of Church members began to relocate in Lee and Hancock counties during the spring and summer of 1839. Joseph Smith purchased a small, two-story, square-cut log home that was named the Homestead and was situated on the outskirts of Commerce proper. Commerce (later renamed Nauvoo by Joseph Smith) subsequently became the principal place of Latter-day Saint settlement and the headquarters of the Church.

In late October 1839, the Prophet journeyed to Washington, D.C., to seek REDRESS from federal government officials for the Missouri persecutions. President Martin Van Buren denied their petitions and turned a deaf ear, and U.S. Senate leaders determined that the reparation in behalf of the Saints could be secured only in Missouri's courts. After an absence of four months, Joseph Smith returned to Illinois, where he turned his attention from the past to moving ahead to the future. His agenda became that of community builder, and thereafter he sought to establish Nauvoo as the new gathering place, the "city . . . set on an hill" (Matt. 5:14),

the Zion that the Saints were unable to establish in western Missouri.

By early 1841, Nauvoo was bustling with home construction and mercantile and business development. In addition, plans for a temple and a hotel (the Nauvoo House) were already underway. The Nauvoo Charter, establishing Nauvoo as a state-sanctioned municipality with a city council, a university, and an independent militia, had been approved by the state legislature and signed by Governor Thomas Carlin in December 1840 and was set to go into effect on 1 February 1841. Nauvoo—a Hebrew word meaning "beautiful"—was on the rise and the Saints' optimism ran high.

It was under these circumstances that Joseph Smith received the revelation recorded in section 124 on 19 January 1841. It is the longest canonized revelation (5,529 words, 145 verses) and the first revelation of the Illinois period included in the Doctrine and Covenants. The revelation provides practical directives to specified individuals and to the Church in general.

Content overview

1. Official Church Proclamation to political and government leaders (124:1–11). On 15 January 1841, just three days prior to the reception of this revelation, the First Presidency issued a formal proclamation detailing the rise and progress of Nauvoo and the call for all the Latter-day Saints to gather there. The Lord called for another proclamation to be written and sent to the "kings of the world . . . to the honorable president-elect [William Henry Harrison], and the high-minded governors of the nation" (v. 3). Joseph Smith and Robert B. Thompson received the charge to draft the document (v. 12), but the Prophet did not complete it during his lifetime. The proclamation was eventually completed and issued on 6 April 1845 under the authority of the Twelve Apostles. *See* Solemn proclamation.

Parley P. Pratt wrote the proclamation, which declared that the true gospel has been restored, and that Zion, the NEW JERUSALEM, will be established by the Church before the second coming of Christ. (Givens and Grow, 237–38).

2. Instructions concerning the building of the Nauvoo House (vv. 22–24, 56–82, 111–12, 117, 119–22). The revelation commanded the

Saints to build a boarding house or hotel for the "weary traveler" (vv. 23, 60). It was also to have been the home for Joseph Smith's family (vv. 56–59). The L-shaped, multistoried building was to have been 120 feet at its longest dimension and 80 feet wide. George Miller, Lyman Wight, John Snider, and Peter Haws received appointments to oversee the building's construction (vv. 22, 62). Funding for the structure was to come from stock purchases (vv. 63–71), and specific individuals were instructed to purchase stock (vv. 72–82, 117, 119). In March 1844, the Prophet suspended work on the Nauvoo House so that more resources and manpower could be directed toward constructing the Nauvoo Temple. At the time of the martyrdom, the Nauvoo House remained uncompleted. On 29 June 1844, the bodies of Joseph and Hyrum Smith were secretly interred beneath the ground floor of the unfinished building at the direction of Emma Smith. A few months later the bodies were removed and interred in a site a short distance south of the Homestead. In 1869, Lewis C. Bidamon, Emma's second husband, reconfigured the structure and built a home, called the Riverside Mansion, on the southwest corner of the foundation. Emma died in this home on 30 May 1879. The building is owned and maintained by the Community of Christ (formerly the Reorganized Church of Jesus Christ of Latter Day Saints). The instructions concerning the Nauvoo House compose one-fourth (thirty-seven verses) of the revelation.

3. Instructions concerning the Nauvoo TEMPLE (vv. 25–28, 37–55, 145). At the time of the exodus from Missouri in 1839, Joseph Smith and the Saints fully expected that the new main gathering place would include a temple, and plans for the temple's construction began long before the receipt of the revelation recorded in section 124 in January 1841. The revelation *confirmed* much of what they had already decided: "And ye shall build it [the temple] on the place where you have contemplated building it, for that is the spot which I have chosen for you to build it" (v. 43). The revelation gave many beautiful promises: "Let this house be built unto my name, that I may reveal mine ordinances therein unto my people; for I deign to reveal unto my

church things which have been kept hid from before the foundation of the world, things that pertain to the dispensation of the fulness of times. And I will show unto my servant Joseph all things pertaining to this house, and the priesthood thereof" (vv. 40–42).

4. Procedures regarding the ordinance of baptism for the dead (vv. 29–36). On 15 August 1840, Joseph Smith preached the funeral sermon of Seymour Brunson, during which he declared for the first time the doctrine of baptism for the dead. It is not known precisely when the first proxy baptism or baptisms were performed; however, the first documented baptism for the dead was performed on 12 September 1840, when Jane Neyman requested that Harvey Olmstead baptize her in behalf of her deceased son Cyrus Livingston Neyman. Vienna Jacques (Jaques) witnessed the proxy baptism by riding into the Mississippi River on horseback to hear and observe the ceremony. A short while later, upon learning the words Olmstead used in performing the baptism, Joseph Smith gave his approval of the ordinance. Later, instructions were given concerning proper procedures for performing and recording baptisms for the dead (127; 128), and it was clarified that "females should be baptised for females, and males for males" (Woodruff, 5:85). Doctrine and Covenants 124 (given five months after the first baptisms for the dead were performed) instructed that the practice of baptizing for the dead outside the Nauvoo Temple would be temporary. "For a baptismal font there is not upon the earth, that they, my saints, may be baptized for those who are dead—for this ordinance belongeth to my house, and cannot be acceptable to me, only in the days of your poverty, wherein ye are not able to build a house unto me" (vv. 29–30; see also vv. 31–34). During the October 1841 general conference Joseph Smith announced, "There shall be no more baptisms for the dead, until the ordinance can be attended to in the Lord's House. . . . *For thus saith the Lord!*" (4:426). Allowance for the practice of performing proxy baptisms outside the temple lasted approximately thirteen and one-half months (15 August 1840 to 3 October 1841). With the announcement that the practice must cease,

the Saints in Nauvoo moved quickly to comply with Joseph Smith's directive. On 8 November 1841, Brigham Young dedicated a temporary wooden baptismal font in the basement of the unfinished temple, and less than two weeks later, on 21 November, the first baptisms for the dead were performed in the temple by Brigham Young, Heber C. Kimball, and John Taylor. They performed the ordinance for approximately forty deceased persons. Willard Richards, George A. Smith, and Wilford Woodruff performed the confirmations. *See* Salvation for the dead.

5. The reorganization of the First Presidency and Hyrum's appointment as patriarch and assistant president of the Church (vv. 91–96). On 5 December 1834, Oliver Cowdery was ordained assistant President of the Church holding the priesthood keys of presidency jointly with Joseph Smith. Cowdery's appointment remained in place until his excommunication on 12 April 1838. Following his disaffection from the Church, this office of assistant president remained unfilled for nearly three years. Then the receipt of section 124 directed that Hyrum Smith receive the office and keys "that once were put upon him that was my servant Oliver Cowdery" (v. 95), thus appointing Hyrum to the office of assistant president. Additionally, on 14 September 1840, four months previous, Joseph Smith Sr. had died, thus vacating the office of patriarch to the Church. Because Hyrum was the eldest surviving son of Joseph Sr., the revelation instructed that Hyrum also be ordained to the office of patriarch, "which was appointed unto him by his father, by blessing and also by right" (v. 91). Since November 1837, Hyrum had been serving as second counselor to his brother Joseph Smith in the First Presidency. His appointment as assistant president left a vacancy in the First Presidency, which vacancy was filled by William Law (v. 91).

6. A list of the general officers, Melchizedek and Aaronic Priesthood quorum presidencies, and the Nauvoo Stake high council (vv. 123–44). During the years following the conflicts in Missouri (1839–41), leadership among the various offices and quorums of the Church had changed, some of it dramatically, due to apostasy, disaffection, and death. But during this same time the Church had also been strengthened by new converts, many of whom had already proven to be capable and competent leaders. The closing verses of section 124 set forth a list of the presidencies of the various priesthood quorums then serving or being called to serve in the following quorums or councils: (1) the First Presidency (vv. 123–26); (2) the members of the Quorum of the Twelve (vv. 127–30); (3) the Nauvoo high council (vv. 131–32); (4) the presidency of the high priests (vv. 133–36); (5) the presidency of the elders (v. 137); (6) the presidents of the seventy, including their responsibilities (vv. 138–40); (7) the presiding bishopric (v. 141); and (8) the remainder of priesthood officers (vv. 142–44).

7. Commendation and counsel to specified individuals. A number of verses in section 124 include approbation and instruction given to specific individuals regarding their spiritual status and responsibilities, and include the following (listed alphabetically by last name): Almon Babbitt (v. 84), John C. Bennett (vv. 16–17), Amos Davies (vv. 111–14), Robert D. Foster (vv. 115–18), William Law (vv. 82–83, 87–91, 97–102, 107), George Miller (vv. 20–22), Sidney Rigdon (vv. 103–10), John Snider (v. 22), Hyrum Smith (vv. 15, 91–96, 102), Robert B. Thompson (vv. 12–14), and Lyman Wight (vv. 18–19, 22). *See* map, p. 440.

See also Illinois period; Nauvoo, Illinois.

BIBLIOGRAPHY

Baugh, Alexander L. "'Blessed Is the First Man Baptised in This Font': Reuben McBride, First Proxy to be Baptized for the Dead in the Nauvoo Temple." *Mormon Historical Studies* 3, no. 2 (Fall 2002): 253–61.

———. "'For This Ordinance Belongeth to My House': The Practice of Baptism for the Dead Outside the Nauvoo Temple." *Mormon Historical Studies* 3, no. 1 (Spring 2002): 47–58.

Clark, James R., ed. *Messages of the First Presidency of The Church of Jesus Christ of Latter-day Saints, 1833–1864.* 6 vols. Salt Lake City: Bookcraft, 1965.

Givens, Terryl L., and Matthew J. Grow. *Parley P. Pratt: The Apostle Paul of Mormonism.* New York: Oxford Press, 2011.

Leonard, Glen M. *Nauvoo: A Place of Peace, a People of Promise.* Salt Lake City: Deseret Book; Provo, Utah: Brigham Young University Press, 2002.

Perkins, Keith W., and Donald Q. Cannon. *Ohio and*

Illinois. Vol. 3 of *Sacred Places: A Comprehensive Guide to Early LDS Historical Sites,* edited by LaMar C. Berrett. Salt Lake City: Deseret Book, 2002.

Smith, Joseph. *History of The Church of Jesus Christ of Latter-day Saints.* Edited by B. H. Roberts. 7 vols. 2d ed. rev. Salt Lake City: The Church of Jesus Christ of Latter-day Saints, 1932–51.

Woodruff, Wilford. *Journal of Discourses.* 26 vols. London: Latter-day Saints' Book Depot, 1854–86.

ALB

Historical context and overview of Doctrine and Covenants 125

Historical context

On 27 October 1838, Missouri governor Lilburn W. Boggs issued an executive order calling for the removal of Latter-day Saints from the state. During the winter of 1839, most Church members temporarily relocated to Adams County, Illinois, until a permanent location for resettlement was decided upon.

Between late April and mid-August 1839, Church leaders negotiated with Isaac Galland, a land speculator living in Commerce (later Nauvoo), Illinois, for the purchase of nearly 18,000 acres of land in Lee County, Iowa, located in the extreme southeast portion of the territory bordering the Mississippi River, and for 700 acres situated in the vicinity of Commerce, Hancock County, Illinois, situated on the opposite side of the Mississippi River directly to the east.

The property acquired by the Church in Lee County had been part of the Half-Breed Tract, a parcel of land consisting of some 119,000 acres once set aside for half-breed Sac and Fox Indians, who had sold to white settlers during the 1830s. In 1839, when the Saints began arriving, two principal settlements had already been established—Montrose and Keokuk.

Near Montrose was Fort Des Moines, a United States military post that had been abandoned in 1837. During the summer of 1839, the deserted fort became the home for a number of Latter-day Saint families, including those of several members of the Twelve; namely, Brigham Young, Orson Pratt, Wilford Woodruff, and John Taylor. Three significant Mormon settlements soon emerged: Nashville (three miles south of Montrose), Ambrosia (three miles west

of Montrose), and Zarahemla (immediately west of Montrose).

To accommodate the Saints living on the Iowa side of the Mississippi River, the Iowa Stake was created on 5 October 1839 during a general conference of the Church. John Smith, the Prophet's uncle, was appointed stake president, with Reynolds Cahoon and Lyman Wight as counselors (these three men had also served as the stake presidency at Adam-ondi-Ahman). A stake high council was also organized, and Alanson Ripley was called as bishop (Smith, 4:12).

Content overview

In March 1841, Joseph Smith received the revelation recorded in Doctrine and Covenants 125. In it the Saints were specifically instructed to build up the Mormon settlement of Zarahemla and to settle also "in the city of Nashville, or in the city of Nauvoo, and in all the stakes" which the Lord had appointed (125:3–4).

In August of that year, during a conference of the Church held at Zarahemla and presided over by apostles George A. Smith and John Taylor, the name of the Iowa Stake was officially changed to the Zarahemla Stake. John Smith was retained as stake president, but two new counselors were appointed—David Pettigrew and Moses Nickerson. The former counselors were "removed by appointment" (Smith, 4:352). Lyman Wight had been ordained an apostle the previous April, and Reynolds Cahoon was serving on the committee to build the temple in Nauvoo. At that time the stake in Iowa was composed of nine branches—five in Lee County, two in Van Buren County, one in Des Moines County, and one in Brown County—with a total membership of approximately seven hundred. The Zarahemla Stake was relatively short-lived, however; during a conference held on 6 January 1842, the stake was discontinued and replaced by a branch (Smith, 4:493). After the dissolution of the stake, the number of Saints in Lee County and the surrounding area declined, primarily because of the encouragement given by Church leaders for members to build up Nauvoo. *See* map, p. 277.

BIBLIOGRAPHY

Baugh, Alexander L. "Remembering the Mormons in Lee County, Iowa: Marking the Past in Montrose and Keokuk." *Mormon Historical Studies* 4, no. 2 (Fall 2003): 175–84.

Cook, Lyndon W. "Isaac Galland—Mormon Benefactor." *BYU Studies* 19, no. 3 (Spring 1979): 261–84.

Kimball, Stanley B. "Eastern Iowa." In *Historical Atlas of Mormonism,* edited by S. Kent Brown, Donald Q. Cannon, and Richard H. Jackson, 58. New York: Simon and Schuster, 1994.

———. "Nauvoo West: The Mormons of the Iowa Shore." *BYU Studies* 18, no. 2 (Winter 1978): 132–42.

Smith, Joseph. *History of The Church of Jesus Christ of Latter-day Saints.* Edited by B. H. Roberts. 7 vols. 2d ed. rev. Salt Lake City: The Church of Jesus Christ of Latter-day Saints, 1932–51.

ALB

Historical context and overview of Doctrine and Covenants 126

Historical context

Brigham Young, president of the Quorum of the Twelve Apostles, had been away from his family and the main body of the Church from 14 September 1839 to 1 July 1841, laboring with other members of his quorum on an extended mission to Great Britain. Nine days after his return, Joseph Smith visited with him at his home in Nauvoo, where the revelation recorded in Doctrine and Covenants 126 was given on his behalf.

Although not specified in the revelation, Brigham Young's Church missions until this time included journeys to New York (summer, 1832); Canada (December 1832–February 1833); Canada (April–August 1833); Missouri (Zion's Camp, May–August 1834); the eastern states and New England (May–September 1835); a second mission to the eastern states and New England (summer, 1836); New York and Massachusetts (March–May 1837); and Great Britain (1839–41) (cf. Arrington, 30–61, 79–112; Cook, 279–80).

Content overview

The wording of the revelation may indicate that Brigham Young had experienced concerns about the amount of time he had spent away from his family. "It is no more required at your

Brigham Young, 1801–1877; portrait by Charles DeForest Fredericks. "Dear and well-beloved brother, Brigham Young, verily thus saith the Lord unto you: My servant Brigham, it is no more required at your hand to leave your family as in times past, for your offering is acceptable to me. I have seen your labor and toil in journeyings for my name" (D&C 126:1–2).

hand to leave your family as in times past," the revelation reads, "for your offering is acceptable to me. . . . Therefore . . . send my word abroad, and take especial care of your family from this time, henceforth" (126:1–3).

Although the revelation indicated he would not be required to leave his family "as in times past" (126:1), President Young served three short-term missions during the Nauvoo period. In 1842 he traveled throughout parts of Illinois to counteract accusations made by the apostate John C. Bennett against Joseph Smith. In 1843 he traveled to the eastern states to collect funds for the Nauvoo Temple and the Nauvoo House. Finally, in late May 1844 he again went east, this time to promote the campaign of Joseph Smith for president of the United States. It was while he was on this latter mission that Joseph Smith and his brother Hyrum were killed in Carthage Jail.

BIBLIOGRAPHY

Arrington, Leonard J. *Brigham Young: American Moses.* New York: Alfred A. Knopf, 1985.

Cook, Lyndon W. *The Revelations of the Prophet Joseph Smith.* Salt Lake City: Deseret Book, 1985.

ALB

Historical context and overview of Doctrine and Covenants 127

Historical context

Joseph Smith introduced the subject of baptism for the dead on 10 August 1840, while speaking to the Saints during the funeral of Seymour Brunson. The first proxy baptisms for the dead in this dispensation were performed the following month in the Mississippi River. The ordinance continued to be performed out-of-doors until October 1841, when Joseph instructed the Saints to discontinue the practice until such baptisms could be performed in a TEMPLE. On 21 November 1841, the ordinance was resumed in a temporary baptismal font in the basement of the unfinished Nauvoo Temple. While Church members appear to have kept records of these early baptisms for the dead, they did not systematically use witnesses in the process—the need for which had become apparent to Joseph by 31 August 1842, when he addressed the Relief Society in Nauvoo on the topic (Minutes, 82, 31 August 1842). Joseph wrote the letter that is now recorded in Doctrine and Covenants 127, which also addresses the issue, the following day (1 September), either while working "in the large room over the [red brick] Store" in the morning or "at home attending to business" in the afternoon (Smith, 2:448).

Joseph had been in and out of hiding since 8 August 1842, when state officials in both Missouri and Illinois tried to arrest him on the charge of being an "accessory before the fact" in an assassination attempt on former governor of Missouri Lilburn W. Boggs. Joseph was formally cleared of the charge the following January. In the meantime he was in constant danger of unlawful arrest. Two days after recording this letter Joseph fled his home for safety (Smith, 2:448–50)—the possible need for which he had apparently seen coming (127:1), and which accounts for his having written the letter in the

first place rather than delivering its contents in a discourse (127:10). Following Joseph's instructions, the letter was "read before the saints when assembled at the Grove near the Temple" on Sunday, 4 September 1842, in his absence (Smith, 2:455).

Content overview

Considering his persecution "but a small thing" (127:2), Joseph encouraged the Saints to continue work on the Nauvoo Temple and redouble their efforts to live the gospel (127:4). Because the Saints had been keeping somewhat haphazard records of baptisms for the dead, without noting any witnesses, Joseph stressed the importance of having the "recorder" be an "eye-witness" of the baptisms he records (127:6) and of having the records kept "in order" (127:9). Forced to close his letter "for the want of more time" (127:11), Joseph promised to "write the word of the Lord from time to time" on this subject "as well as many other things" (127:10), referring to the restoration of things "pertaining to the priesthood," presumably in connection with the temple (127:8; cf. 124:28).

See also Salvation for the dead.

BIBLIOGRAPHY

Minutes of the Female Relief Society of Nauvoo, 31 August 1842. Church History Library, The Church of Jesus Christ of Latter-day Saints, Salt Lake City, Utah.

Smith, Joseph. *The Papers of Joseph Smith.* Edited by Dean C. Jessee. 2 vols. Salt Lake City: Deseret Book, 1989–92.

AHH

Historical context and overview of Doctrine and Covenants 128

Historical context

On Wednesday, 7 September 1842, while in hiding to avoid unlawful arrest, Joseph Smith "dictated a long Epistle to the Saints" (Smith, 2:458, 461) on the subject of keeping records of baptisms for the dead, a topic he had recently addressed in an earlier letter under similar circumstances. *See* Historical context and overview of Doctrine and Covenants 127 (p. 842).

This "long Epistle," misdated in a later entry as 6 September 1842 in Joseph's journal and in the headnote to section 128, was "read to the saints at the Grove near the Temple" the following Sunday, 11 September, in Joseph's absence (Smith, 2:468).

Content overview

Among other things, this 7 September letter provides "a few additional views" on the importance of having records for baptisms for the dead kept by a "recorder" who is an "eye-witness" to the ordinance, "that he might make a record of a truth before the Lord" (128:2). Observing that it would be "very difficult for one recorder to be present at all times, and to do all the business," Joseph directed that each ward in Nauvoo appoint its own recorder who could be eyewitness to the baptisms performed by members of that ward and who would be "very particular and precise" in creating his record, "giving the date, and names, and so forth, and the history of the whole transaction; naming also some three individuals that are present, . . . who can at any time when called upon certify to the same" (128:3). These records were then to be forwarded to a "general recorder," who would enter them and their accompanying certificates into the general Church record. By following these steps, Joseph wrote, the resulting record "shall be just as holy, and shall answer the ordinance just the same as if he [the general recorder] had seen with his eyes and heard with his ears, and made a record of the same on the general church book" (128:4).

Joseph affirmed the importance of the doctrine of baptism for the dead and the necessity of creating proper records of the ordinance. He noted that "the Lord ordained and prepared" the ordinance of baptism for the dead "before the foundation of the world, for the salvation of the dead who should die without a knowledge of the gospel" (128:5). Further, he explained that something bound on earth is bound in heaven only when it is properly recorded (128:8–9), and that the earth "will be smitten with a curse unless there is a welding link of some kind or other between the fathers and the children" (128:18). Joseph reminded the Church that the proper performance and record keeping of proxy baptisms for the dead "are principles in relation to the dead and the living that cannot be lightly passed over, as pertaining to our salvation"

(128:15). He explained that the work of baptism for the dead is "mercy from heaven" and "a voice of gladness for the living and the dead" (128:19). Briefly recounting important events of the Restoration, the coming forth of the Book of Mormon, and the appearance of "divers angels, from Michael or Adam down to the present time" bringing "keys . . . and the power of their priesthood" (128:20–21), Joseph closed his letter by encouraging Church members to "go on in so great a cause" (128:22), that at some future time they might be able to present in the temple "the records of our dead, which shall be worthy of all acceptation" (128:24).

In an effort to obey the instructions they had received, Church members drew up two different certificates shortly after this letter was read—one to be used to identify ward recorders, and the other, listing names of witnesses, to be used to record the actual ordinance. This information was then used by the general Church recorder at the time, James Sloan, to create an official Church record (Baptisms).

See also Salvation for the dead.

BIBLIOGRAPHY

Baptisms for the Dead, 1840–45. Church History Library, The Church of Jesus Christ of Latter-day Saints, Salt Lake City, Utah.

Smith, Joseph. *The Papers of Joseph Smith.* Edited by Dean C. Jessee. 2 vols. Salt Lake City: Deseret Book, 1989–92.

AHH

Historical context and overview of Doctrine and Covenants 129

Historical context

During the late spring and summer of 1839, Joseph Smith spent considerable time instructing the Twelve preparatory to their departure for Great Britain in August and September. During one such meeting, held at Commerce (later Nauvoo), Illinois, on 27 June 1839, Wilford Woodruff recorded the Prophet giving the following instructions regarding how to distinguish a resurrected heavenly messenger from one sent by SATAN:

"In order to detect the devel when he transforms himself nigh unto an angel of light. When an angel of God appears unto man face to face in personage & reaches out his hand unto the man & he takes hold of the angels hand & feels a substance the same as one man would in Shaking hands with another he may then know that it is an angel of God, & he should place all Confidence in him. Such personages or angels are Saints with there resurrected Bodies.

"But if a personage appears unto man & offers him his hand & the man takes hold of it & he feels nothing or does not sens any substance he may know it is the devel, for when a Saint whose body is not resurrected appears unto man in the flesh he will not offer him his hand for this is against the law given him & in keeping in mind these things we may detec the devil that he decieved us not (Woodruff, 341)."

Joseph Smith gave similar instructions again in 1840 and makes an additional point:

"A Key by Joseph Smith Dec 1840—W[illiam]. C[layton]. If an Angel or spirit appears offer him your hand; if he is a spirit from God he will stand still and not offer you his hand. If from the Devil he will either shrink back from you or offer his hand, which if he does you will feel nothing, but be deceived. *A good spirit will not decieve.* Angels are beings who have bodies and appear to men in the form of a man" (Clayton, 44).

When Joseph Smith first gave instructions regarding the appearance of resurrected beings and unembodied evil spirits in June 1839, not all of the Twelve were present, most notably Parley P. Pratt, who at the time was incarcerated in Columbia, Boone County, Missouri. He escaped and arrived in Commerce around 12 July. A month and a half later (29 August), Parley and his brother Orson were the first of the apostles to embark on the mission of the Twelve to Great Britain (118). During the six weeks Parley was in the Commerce-Montrose area, he may have learned from other members of the Twelve about Joseph Smith's teachings in regard to distinguishing heavenly versus satanic messengers, but that does not appear to have been the case. More than likely, Parley learned about Joseph Smith's teachings on the subject while laboring with the Twelve in England. This was the case with Willard Richards, who was in Great Britain at the time of his calling to the Twelve and made a brief entry in his journal in 1840 about the appearance of resurrected beings and evil spirits. Note the similarities between Elder Richards's journal entry with that of Elder Woodruff's journal (e.g., "substance," "deceive us not"), suggesting that it was Elder Woodruff who provided Elder Richards with the information:

"As there are many Keys to the Kingdom of God the following one will detect Satan when he transforms himself nigh unto an Angel of Light. When Satan appears in the form of a personage unto man & reaches out his hand unto him & the man takes hold of his hand & feels no substance he may know it is Satan for an angel of God (which is an angel of light) is a Saint with his resurrected body & when he appears unto man and offers him his hand & the man feels a substance when he takes hold of it as he would in shaking hands with his neighbor he may know it is an Angel of God. & should a Saint appear unto man whose body is not resurrected he will never offer him his hand for it would be against the law by which they are governed & by observing this Key we may detect Satan that he deceive us not" (Richards, *Journal,* 1840).

In April 1841, most members of the Twelve left Great Britain to return to the States. Elder Parley P. Pratt remained until October 1842 to preside over the British Mission. He did not arrive back in Nauvoo until 7 February 1843. On 9 February, only two days after his return, Elder Pratt, apparently eager to learn firsthand from Joseph Smith what he had taught the Twelve in 1839, requested that the Prophet give additional explanation regarding the "keys" of detection. William Clayton, Joseph Smith's personal secretary, recorded the following in the Prophet's journal:

"Parley Pratt & others came in & Joseph explained the following there are 3 administrter [administrators] Angels. Spirits Devils one class in heaven Angels the spirits of Just men made perfect.—innumerable co of angels & spirits of Just men made perfect.

"An angel appears to you how will you prove him. ask him to shake hands if he has flesh & bones he is an Angel, "spirit hath not flesh & bones"

"spirit of a Just men made perfect. Person in its tabernacle could hide its glory.

"if David Patten or the Devil come, how would you determine should you take hold of his [Patten's] hand you would not feel it. if it were a false adminestrter [administrator] he would not do it.

"true spirit will not give his hand the Devil will. 3 Keys—"

One will observe that the text found in Doctrine and Covenants 129 only vaguely resembles the material recorded in Joseph Smith's journal as recorded by Clayton. This is because the text for Doctrine and Covenants 129 is taken from the Manuscript History of the Church under the date of 9 February 1843, which material was written by individuals working in the Church historian's office in the 1850s, including Willard Richards, George A. Smith, and Wilford Woodruff. Thus, in putting together the Manuscript History, the compilers no doubt examined Clayton's 9 February 1843 entry and, possibly using additional sources (such as Woodruff's and Richards's journals, and the published 1841 writings of Joseph Smith), then made an amalgamated summary of the Prophet's teachings on the subject.

The text for Doctrine and Covenants 129 first appeared in the *Deseret News* on 23 April 1856, and was included as section 129 in the 1876 edition of the Doctrine and Covenants.

Content overview

In heaven there are both resurrected beings and those awaiting resurrection (129:1–3). KEYS are given to determine if a messenger from heaven is resurrected or not (129:4–7). Satan can also appear as "an angel of light," and a key is given whereby a person can detect him in his deception (129:8–9; cf. 50:31–33).

There are several cautions one must consider when trying to understand or interpret this section of the Doctrine and Covenants. When Wilford Woodruff wrote about these keys in 1839, he also wrote: "Among the vast number of the Keys of the Kingdom of God Joseph presented the following one to the Twelve *for [their] benefit in [their] experience & travels in the flesh*" (Woodruff, 341; emphasis added). Since it is "by the power of the Holy Ghost" that members of the Church "may know the truth of all things"

(Moro. 10:5), angelic visits are rather rare in comparison. Such events would be expected to be more frequent to members of the Twelve and the First Presidency than to other Church members and that such visits would occur in relation to their callings. These keys were originally presented to the Twelve for their benefit, but since the counsel in section 129 does not answer every situation in which an angelic being appears and in the vast literature of the Church only a few of the Brethren other than Joseph Smith have ever spoken about this section (and in doing so, they have only made brief reference to it), it must be remembered "that that which cometh from above is sacred, and must be spoken with care, and by constraint of the Spirit" (63:64).

BIBLIOGRAPHY

Baugh, Alexander L. "The Final Episode of Mormonism in Missouri in the 1830s: The Incarceration of the Mormon Prisoners in Richmond and Columbia Jails, 1838–1839." *John Whitmer Historical Association Journal* 28 (2008): 1–34.

Clayton, William. Journal, December 1840. In Andrew F. Ehat and Lyndon W. Cook, comps. and eds., *The Words of Joseph Smith*. Provo, Utah: Religious Studies Center, Brigham Young University, 1980.

Cook, Lyndon W. *Revelations of the Prophet Joseph Smith*. Salt Lake City: Deseret Book, 1985.

Manuscript History of the Church, D-1, 1665. Church History Library, The Church of Jesus Christ of Latter-day Saints, Salt Lake City, Utah.

Richards, Willard. Journal, 1840, 9–10. Church History Library, The Church of Jesus Christ of Latter-day Saints, Salt Lake City, Utah. In Woodford, "Historical Development of the Doctrine and Covenants," 1702.

Smith, Joseph. *History of The Church of Jesus Christ of Latter-day Saints*. Edited by B. H. Roberts. 7 vols. 2d ed. rev. Salt Lake City: The Church of Jesus Christ of Latter-day Saints, 1932–51.

———. *The Papers of Joseph Smith*. Edited by Dean C. Jessee. 2 vols. Salt Lake City: Deseret Book, 1989–92.

Woodford, Robert J. "The Historical Development of the Doctrine and Covenants." Ph.D. dissertation, Brigham Young University, 1974.

Woodruff, Wilford. *Wilford Woodruff's Journal, 1833–1898, Typescript*. Edited by Scott G. Kenney. 9 vols. Midvale, Utah: Signature Books, 1983–84.

ALB

Historical context and overview of Doctrine and Covenants 130

Historical context

Joseph Smith visited Ramus, Illinois, on several occasions to instruct Church members and to visit friends and family. His sister Sophronia Smith McCleary and her family resided there, and another sister, Katherine Smith Salisbury, and her family lived nearby in Fountain Green. The information contained in Doctrine and Covenants 130 and 131 was recorded during two separate visits to the area.

On 1 April 1843, Joseph Smith, Orson Hyde, and William Clayton traveled to Ramus. After spending the night at the home of Benjamin F. Johnson, a meeting was held the following morning, during which Orson Hyde offered some remarks. Later, at a midday meal at his sister Sophronia's home, the Prophet indicated that in the afternoon meeting he would make corrections to Hyde's sermon. Clayton, one of Joseph Smith's secretaries, took detailed notes, which compose the material in Doctrine and Covenants 130:1–17. Later that evening Joseph spoke at another meeting; Clayton's notations from that sermon now compose 130:18–23 (Smith, 5:323–25).

Content overview

Joseph Smith identified two points from Hyde's teachings earlier that day that he considered to be incorrect. First, Hyde stated that at the Second Coming the Savior would appear as a warrior on a white horse, to which Joseph Smith replied, "When the Savior shall appear we shall see him as he is" (130:1). Second, referring to John 14:23, Hyde taught that the appearance of the Father and the Son in that verse had reference to "the Father and the Son dwelling in our hearts." To this Joseph Smith replied, "The appearing of the Father and the Son, in that verse, is a personal appearance; and the idea that the Father and the Son dwell in a man's heart is an old sectarian notion, and is false" (130:3).

The following is a summary of the remaining doctrinal teachings given by Joseph Smith in the 2 April 1830 afternoon meeting:

During the course of his remarks, he responded to a question about the reckoning of God's time to that of man's. This question probably arose from the fact that the year previous, beginning in March 1842, Joseph Smith began publishing his translation of the Book of Abraham in the *Times and Seasons*. The book of Abraham teaches that a day on the planet where God resides is a thousand years of earth time (Abr. 3:4). Hence, God's time (and angels' time) is calculated differently from man's or earth's time. It appears that some of the Saints living in Ramus may have not been entirely familiar with the teachings from the book of Abraham, and thus the question was raised (130:4).

In explaining God's time versus man's time, the Prophet elucidated the doctrine about angels, declaring that all angelic ministrants who have appeared to man on earth have lived or will live on this earth (130:5–7).

In his role as a seer, Joseph Smith was privileged to see many of God's creations, including the celestial world where God himself resides (76:19–23; 137:1–4). The Prophet described the celestial realm as "like unto crystal" (130:9) or "like a sea of glass" (130:7; 77:1; Rev. 4:6). Furthermore, Joseph Smith explained that the celestialized earth serves a revelatory purpose, providing those who inhabit it with knowledge about lesser worlds or planets. Additionally, individuals who inherit a celestial glory also receive a WHITE STONE whereby information may be received "pertaining to a higher order of kingdoms" (130:8–11).

While addressing the Ramus Saints, Joseph Smith reflected upon the revelation that he received on Christmas day 1832, reiterating his understanding that a great civil conflict associated with the institution of black servitude would take place in the future and would commence in South Carolina (87). Clayton's notes reveal that Joseph Smith indicated the 1832 revelation was received by an audible voice (130:12–13). *See* Historical context and overview of Doctrine and Covenants 87 (p. 791).

Verses 14–17 describe Joseph Smith's desire to know with some specificity the time when the second advent of Jesus would take place. Perhaps because he had already received a number of revelations that included scores of specific SIGNS associated with the last days and Jesus' final return (e.g., 29; 43; 88; 133), and having been instructed that only the Father knows the "day, and hour," of the Savior's coming (JS–M 1:40), Joseph was told to "trouble" the Lord no more on the matter. At this time Americans, including many Latter-day Saints, were caught up in "Second Coming" hysteria, primarily due to the teachings of William Miller, a nationally known Seventh-Day Adventist preacher who predicted that Jesus would return sometime between 21 March 1843 and 21 March 1844. In fact, the Prophet's remarks on this occasion may have been prompted by someone in the meeting voicing questions and concerns regarding Miller's predictions (130:14–17). See Jesus Christ, second coming of.

The Prophet planned to travel to Carthage following the meeting, but bad weather prevented it, so another meeting was scheduled for the evening, at which he spoke. In a previous revelation Joseph Smith had learned that "the glory of God is intelligence, or, in other words, light and truth" (93:36). Spiritual knowledge and INTELLIGENCE come from gaining an understanding of eternal gospel truths and requires "diligence and obedience" to God's laws and commandments. Individuals who acquire spiritual intelligence and live the principles associated with that knowledge are promised that they will have "so much the advantage in the world to come" (130:18–19).

Joseph summarized the law of OBEDIENCE and disobedience. The person who obeys a divine directive or law will receive a positive blessing, reward, or consequence as a result of keeping that commandment (130:20–21).

The Prophet Joseph Smith taught throughout his ministry that the Father, Son, and Holy Ghost were separate and distinct personages. To the Saints in Ramus he made it clear that the Father and the Son have bodies of flesh and bone, and that the Holy Ghost is a personage of spirit (130:22–23). See God, nature of.

BIBLIOGRAPHY

Cannon, Donald Q. "Spokes on the Wheel: Early Latter-day Saint Settlements in Hancock County, Illinois." *Ensign* 16 (February 1986): 62–68.

Dick, Everet N. *William Miller and the Advent Crisis.*

Berrien Springs, Michigan: Andrews University Press, 1994.

Hartley, William G., and Alexander L. Baugh. "Ramus/Macedonia (Illinois) Markers Dedicated." *Mormon Historical Studies* 1 (Spring 2000): 143–46.

Rugh, Susan Sessions. "Conflict in the Countryside: The Mormon Settlement at Macedonia, Illinois." *BYU Studies* 32 (Winter and Spring 1991): 149–74.

Smith, Joseph. *History of The Church of Jesus Christ of Latter-day Saints.* Edited by B. H. Roberts. 7 vols. 2d ed. rev. Salt Lake City: The Church of Jesus Christ of Latter-day Saints, 1932–51.

ALB

Historical context and overview of Doctrine and Covenants 131

Historical context

In mid-May 1843, Joseph Smith, in company with a few friends and associates, traveled to visit and instruct the Saints residing in the eastern part of Hancock County, Illinois, particularly those living in Ramus. The text comprising Doctrine and Covenants 131 is taken from notes transcribed by William Clayton, the Prophet's secretary, who accompanied Joseph Smith on the occasion and who wrote down, in abbreviated form, a few of the doctrinal teachings elucidated by the Prophet.

Content overview

On 16 May, Joseph Smith's party arrived in Ramus. That evening, before retiring, the Prophet personally instructed Clayton and Benjamin F. Johnson and his wife regarding a major principle associated with eternal MARRIAGE. Clayton recorded Joseph Smith's statement that in the celestial or highest kingdom of glory "there are three heavens or degrees" (131:1). The concept of three divisions or degrees within the celestial realm was not revealed in Doctrine and Covenants 76 and had not been taught by the Prophet previously. This concept, if taken to its logical conclusion, implies that within both the two lower heavens—the terrestrial and telestial kingdoms—there are also divisions or "degrees" (76:98). Additionally, and most important, Joseph Smith revealed that to obtain the highest degree of the celestial kingdom a man and woman must receive the eternal marriage covenant or they "cannot have an increase" (131:1–4). In clarifying what Joseph Smith meant by "increase," Clayton wrote: "Except a man and his wife enter into an everlasting covenant and be married for eternity . . . by the power and authority of the Holy Priesthood, they will cease to increase when they die; that is, they will not have any children after the resurrection" (Smith, 5:391).

The following morning, 17 May, Joseph Smith preached a sermon in Ramus, taking 2 Peter 1 as his text. Some of his remarks focused on the meaning of Peter's declaration that he, the senior apostle, along with James and John, had received a "more sure word of prophecy." Clayton's notes indicate that the Prophet stated this term had reference to being "sealed up unto eternal life," it having been made known to the individual by "revelation and the spirit of prophecy, through the power of the Holy Priesthood" (131:5). While preaching to the Saints in the Mormon settlement of Yelrome in southern Hancock County just three days earlier (14 May), the Prophet had expounded this same principle while also discoursing on the texts from 2 Peter. Speaking of the manifestation to the three apostles on the MOUNT OF TRANSFIGURATION, Joseph Smith said: "And though they had heard an audible voice from heaven bearing testimony that Jesus was the Son of God, yet he [Peter] says we have a more sure word of prophecy. . . . Though they might hear the voice of God and know that Jesus was the Son of God, this would be no evidence that their election and calling was made sure. . . . They then would want that more sure word of prophecy, that they were sealed in the heavens and had the promise of eternal life in the kingdom of God." In other words, even after their transcendent theophany, Peter, James, and John had not yet received the unconditional guarantee of ETERNAL LIFE. Hence, Joseph concluded, "I would exhort you to go on and continue to call upon God until you make your calling and election sure for yourselves, by obtaining this more sure word of prophecy, and wait patiently for the promise until you obtain it" (Smith, 5:388–89).

After expounding upon the principles associated with the MORE SURE WORD OF PROPHECY, Joseph Smith taught, "It is impossible for a man to be saved in ignorance" (131:6). This statement suggests that a knowledge of the principles and ordinances of the GOSPEL is essential for SALVATION.

The Prophet's explanations on this occasion (in addition to his remarks given to the Saints in Yelrome a few days earlier) led him to conclude that Peter "penned the most sublime language of any of the apostles" (Smith, 5:392). Interestingly, Samuel A. Prior, a Methodist minister who was visiting Ramus at the time, heard Joseph preach and reported that he delivered "a very interesting and elaborate discourse," evidence to him that the Latter-day Saint leader "was well worthy to be styled 'a workman rightly dividing the word of truth'" (Prior, 198; see 2 Tim. 2:15).

Later that night (17 May) arrangements were made for Reverend Prior to address the Saints. "In the evening I was invited to preach, and did so," he wrote. "The congregation was large and respectable—they paid the utmost attention." At the conclusion of the minister's remarks, Joseph Smith asked if he could share his thoughts on a few points in which they differed. The minister reported that the Prophet responded "mildly, politely, and affectingly; like one who was more desirous to disseminate truth and expose error, than to love the malicious triumph of debate over me. I was truly edified with his remarks" (Prior, 198). Clayton's transcription of Joseph's brief comments on this occasion indicate that he pointed out that spirit substance is composed of material matter. "All spirit is matter, but it is more fine or pure, and can only be discerned by purer eyes; we cannot see it; but when our bodies are purified we shall see that it is all matter" (131:7–8). Simply stated, the Prophet taught that spirit element and spirit bodies have physical, tangible, corporeal properties not generally distinguishable to mortals but discernible to more glorified personages.

BIBLIOGRAPHY

Prior, Samuel A. "A Visit to Nauvoo." *Times and Seasons* 4, no. 13 (15 May 1843): 197–99.

Smith, Joseph. *History of The Church of Jesus Christ of Latter-day Saints.* Edited by B. H. Roberts. 7 vols. 2d ed. rev. Salt Lake City: The Church of Jesus Christ of Latter-day Saints, 1932–51.

ALB

Historical context and overview of Doctrine and Covenants 132

Historical context

Though the principles of eternal and plural MARRIAGE were revealed to Joseph Smith in the 1830s, the text of section 132 was not written until 12 July 1843. Even then, it was not written with the intent to publish it at that time. Joseph F. Smith, sixth president of the Church, explained: "When the revelation was written, in 1843, it was for a special purpose, by the request of the Patriarch Hyrum Smith, and was not then designed to go forth to the church or to the world. It is most probable that had it been then written with a view to its going out as a doctrine of the church, it would have been presented in a somewhat different form. There are personalities contained in a part of it which are not relevant to the principle itself, but rather to the circumstances which necessitated its being written at that time. Joseph Smith, on the day it was written, expressly declared that there was a great deal more connected with the doctrine which would be revealed in due time, but this was sufficient for the occasion, and was made to suffice for the time. And, indeed, I think it much more than many are prepared to live up to even now" (JD, 20:29–30; cf. 132:66).

William Clayton, who acted as scribe when Joseph dictated the revelation, testified years later that it was done at Hyrum Smith's request. When Joseph and Hyrum entered the office in which Clayton was working that morning they were discussing plural marriage. Hyrum wanted to show the revelation to Joseph's wife, Emma, believing he could "convince her of its truth." In this he failed. "The revelation was read to several of the authorities during the day. Towards evening Bishop Newel K. Whitney asked Joseph if he had any objections to his taking a copy of the revelation; Joseph replied that he had not, and handed it to him. It was carefully copied the following day by Joseph C. Kingsbury." A day or two later Emma Smith burned the original of this revelation, and so the Kingsbury copy, which was a "true and correct copy of the original in every respect," was the only one remaining (Smith, History, 5:xxxii–xxxiii). After the Prophet's death, Bishop Whitney gave this copy to Brigham Young, and it was the one used when the revelation was finally published. It was printed in a Deseret News Extra, 14 September 1852 and later included in the Doctrine and Covenants, beginning with the 1876 edition. In that edition, an article attributed to Oliver Cowdery and William W. Phelps advocating monogamy (101 and 109 in previous editions) was removed.

Content overview

Section 132 begins with the Lord acknowledging Joseph's question about the polygynous relationships of Old Testament patriarchs. (Technically, polygyny refers to a man having more than one wife, while polygamy refers to either marriage partner having more than one spouse.) He soon left that ultimately tangential question to set forth a fundamental premise in verse 4: "For behold, I reveal unto you a new and an everlasting covenant." One must make

> 7 And verily I say unto you, that the ᵃconditions of this law are these: All covenants, contracts, bonds, obligations, ᵇoaths, ᶜvows, performances, connections, associations, or expectations, that are not made and entered into and ᵈsealed by the Holy Spirit of promise, of him who is ᵉanointed, both as well for time and for all eternity, and that too most holy, by ᶠrevelation and commandment through the medium of mine anointed, whom I have appointed on the earth to hold this ᵍpower (and I have appointed unto my servant Joseph to hold this ʰpower in the last days, and there is never but one on the earth at a time on whom this power and the ⁱkeys of this priesthood are conferred), are of no efficacy, virtue, or force in and after the resurrection from the dead; for all contracts that are not made unto this end have an end when men are dead.

Doctrine and Covenants 132:7.

and keep this covenant to obtain a fulness of God's glory, as verses 4–6 explain, but this covenant is referring not to *plural* marriage but to marriage according to the law of God, the law set forth in verses 7–8 and again in verses 15–21. The discussion of plural marriage resumes at verse 29. Meanwhile, Joseph Smith answered the question many raise from Matthew 22:23–30: will a married couple live as husband and wife after the resurrection and on what terms? The answer was yes, and the terms and conditions are very specific. They are set forth in verse 7 as one long if-then statement, which signals that it is a covenant. The verse indicates that any kind of marriage agreement is temporary unless a covenant "for time and for all eternity" is "made and entered into," "sealed by the Holy Spirit of promise," and "that too most holy, by revelation and commandment through the medium of mine anointed"—the one man "on the earth at a time on whom this power and the keys of this priesthood are conferred." *See* Key(s); Priesthood.

All these requirements must be met, because "all contracts that are not made unto this end have an end when men are dead" (v. 7). That is the Lord's law. This world's legal codes do not endure in the resurrection; marriages that do not meet the conditions the Lord has set forth do not endure eternally. People who are going to be married forever will participate in the new and everlasting covenant of marriage; otherwise they will remain "separately and singly, without exaltation, in their saved condition, to all eternity" (v. 17).

Verses 19–20 describe more explicitly the terms and conditions of exaltation. "*If* a man marry a wife by my word, which is my law, and by the new and everlasting covenant, and it is sealed unto them by the Holy Spirit of promise" (meaning the Holy Ghost in his role as verifier of faithfulness), "and it shall be said unto them—Ye shall come forth in the first resurrection; and if it be after the first resurrection, in the next resurrection; and shall inherit thrones, kingdoms, principalities, and powers, dominions, all heights and depths—*then* shall it be written in the Lamb's Book of Life" (emphasis added). If neither partner commits "murder whereby

to shed innocent blood," and if they "abide in my covenant, . . . it shall be done unto them in all things whatsoever my servant hath put upon them, in time, and through all eternity; and shall be of full force when they are out of the world; and they shall pass by the angels, and the gods, which are set there, to their exaltation and glory in all things, as hath been sealed upon their heads, which glory shall be a fulness and a continuation of the seeds forever and ever. Then shall they be gods, because they have no end." *See* Exalt, exaltation; Gods.

Verses 21–28 restate the Lord's law concerning the new and everlasting covenant of marriage and explain that committing "murder wherein ye shed innocent blood" and assenting unto the death of the Savior, after having received the new and everlasting covenant, constitutes "blasphemy against the Holy Ghost, which shall not be forgiven in the world nor out of the world." *See* Innocent blood; Sons of perdition.

Having established the terms and conditions of exaltation, the Lord returned in verse 29 to Joseph's concerns about plural marriage as practiced in Old Testament times. He began by setting forth three premises: Abraham received and obeyed revelation and is now exalted (v. 29), God promised Abraham an endless posterity (v. 30), and Joseph Smith has the same promise as Abraham (v. 31). The last premise indicated that Joseph should do as Abraham did—that is, he should receive and obey revelation, whatever it may be (v. 32). Beginning in verse 34, the Lord reviewed instances when he commanded plural marriage, teaching that he justifies plural marriage in cases where he commands it, as he did with Abraham, Isaac, and Jacob. Conversely, the Lord does not justify a plural marriage entered without his approval: "in those things which they received not of me." He illustrated by citing David as one who entered a plural marriage without justification and lost his exaltation as a consequence (vv. 38–39). To answer Joseph's concern about whether polygyny is adulterous, the Lord explained in some detail the cases in which it is not adulterous (vv. 41–44 and 58–63). Adulterers will be destroyed (v. 63), but their actions will not ruin their innocent partner's potential for exaltation.

Joseph had the power and authority to seal the innocent wife of an adulterous husband to another man, even as a plural wife (v. 44). This power and authority is inherent in the "keys and power of the priesthood" conferred upon Joseph Smith as part of the restoration of "all things," and by which power things sealed on earth are sealed in heaven (vv. 45–48).

Because of Joseph's obedience and sacrifice, the Lord sealed him to exaltation and forgave his sins (vv. 49–50). The details of Joseph's promised "escape" and Emma's not "partak[ing]" (vv. 50–51) of that which Joseph was commanded to offer her are not made clear in the revelation and are not known. The revelation does make clear that Emma is to receive Joseph's plural wives, cleave to him, forgive his trespasses (with the promise that then her own trespasses would be forgiven), and "abide this commandment" (vv. 52–54).

The revelation ends with a brief explanation of the "law of Sarah," evidently directed to Emma, indicating that she, having been taught the doctrine of plural marriage, should facilitate Joseph's taking plural wives as Sarah facilitated Abraham's receiving Hagar as his wife (vv. 64–65). See Sarah, law of.

The central focus of section 132 is that marriages performed by proper authority and sealed by the Holy Spirit of promise endure in time and for all eternity (132:7). This involves not only husbands and wives but children sealed to them, creating an eternal family.

See also Seal, sealed.

BIBLIOGRAPHY

Deseret News Extra [Salt Lake City], 14 September 1852.

Smith, Joseph. *History of The Church of Jesus Christ of Latter-day Saints.* Edited by B. H. Roberts. 7 vols. 2d ed. rev. Salt Lake City: The Church of Jesus Christ of Latter-day Saints, 1932–51.

Smith, Joseph F. *Journal of Discourses.* 26 vols. London: Latter-day Saints' Book Depot, 1854–86.

RJW

Historical context and overview of Doctrine and Covenants 133

Historical context

At the November 1831 conference at Hiram, Ohio, the leading elders of the Church decided to publish ten thousand copies of the revelations given to Joseph Smith as *A Book of Commandments for the Government of the Church of Christ.* Joseph then began to edit the revelations and Oliver Cowdery made plans to take them to Independence, Missouri, for publication by William Phelps on the Church's press. Joseph's history recorded that "at this time there were many things which the Elders desired to know relative to preaching the Gospel to the inhabitants of the earth, and concerning the gathering; and in order to walk by the true light, and be instructed from on high, on the 3rd of November, 1831, I inquired of the Lord and received the following important revelation, which has since been added to the book of Doctrine and Covenants, and called the Appendix" (1:229; cf. MH, 166–72; *EMS,* 12). In early editions of the Doctrine and Covenants, all of the revelations to Joseph Smith were placed between the Preface (1) and the Appendix (now 133).

Content overview

Section 133 continues and even increases the apocalyptic tone of section 1. Echoing themes of Isaiah and the Revelation of John, the Lord clarified what the Saints were to learn from the revelations. Christ will dramatically return to the earth to judge all who forget God, including ungodly Latter-day Saints; therefore they should prepare for his coming by sanctifying their lives and becoming worthy to live in Zion (133:4). "Go ye out from Babylon," the Lord warned again and again (133:5, 7, 14), solidifying the dualistic ZION versus BABYLON typology he chose to frame the entire Doctrine and Covenants. Zion will be rescued when the Lord comes. Babylon will be destroyed. "Hearken and hear, O ye inhabitants of the earth. Listen, ye elders of my church together, and hear the voice of the Lord; for he calleth upon . . . all men everywhere to repent" (133:16). Angels had already been sent to announce that the hour of his coming nears. Indeed, that was the beginning of the Restoration. The "everlasting gospel" has been committed unto man, and the servants of God shall be sent forth to preach that GOSPEL to "every nation, and kindred, and tongue, and people" (133:36–38). Subsequently the Lord will answer the prayers of his people, who have long pleaded, "O that thou wouldst rend the heavens, that thou wouldst come down, that the mountains might flow down at thy presence" (133:38–40). He will answer "as the melting fire that burneth, and as the fire which causeth the waters to boil" (133:41).

The Lord emphasized that the Saints must get themselves out of Babylon before it is destroyed, and "flee unto Zion" for safety (133:12). The elders were to be sent into the world to rescue any who would repent—first to the Gentiles and then to the Jews (133:8). "By the weak things of the earth the Lord shall thrash the nations by the power of his Spirit" (133:59) and gather to Zion any who will repent to be endowed with priesthood power and the blessings promised to the house of Israel (133:32–35). "And unto him that repenteth and sanctifieth himself before the Lord shall be given eternal life. And upon them that hearken not to the voice of the Lord shall be fulfilled that which was written by the prophet Moses, that they should be cut off from among the people" (133:62–63).

Other revelations give more detailed instructions about how to preach the gospel and gather Israel. Section 133 emphasizes why and when. To a group of fledgling Latter-day Saints gathered in a private home, it set forth a bold scope of covering the globe with the restored gospel. It reiterated Christ's great commission to take the gospel to every creature so that each can decide whether to repent or not. Moreover, there is no time to lose. The revelation's urgent tone emphasizes that Christ will soon come to judge an apostate world—Babylon. He will come in vengeance to some, wearing robes stained with the blood of the unrepentant (133:50–51; cf. v. 64). Nevertheless, he will also come in "loving kindness" to the redeemed (133:52–53). The revelation closes with the Lord's reminder that the wicked rejected him when he came to live on earth and again when he called "to [them] out of the heavens" through his servants, perhaps a reference to the restoration of the gospel through Joseph Smith (133:66–74; cf. 1:17).

BIBLIOGRAPHY

The Evening and the Morning Star 1, no. 12 (May 1833): 12.

Manuscript History of the Church. Book A, in the

handwriting of Willard Richards. Church History Library, The Church of Jesus Christ of Latter-day Saints, Salt Lake City, Utah.

Smith, Joseph. History of The Church of Jesus Christ of Latter-day Saints. Edited by B. H. Roberts. 7 vols. 2d ed. rev. Salt Lake City: The Church of Jesus Christ of Latter-day Saints, 1932–51.

SCH

Historical context and overview of Doctrine and Covenants 134

Historical context

On 17 August 1835, Church priesthood leaders and quorum members convened a special conference in Kirtland, Ohio, for the purpose of approving "the Book of Doctrine and Covenants." It appears that another purpose of the August 1835 meeting was to consider the inclusion of two additional documents in the Doctrine and Covenants, neither of which was a revelation. Since the publication of the book was nearing completion and neither of the two documents being presented was a revelation, Church leaders felt the need to receive official approval from the respective quorums. Furthermore, the fact that Joseph Smith and Frederick G. Williams (second counselor in the First Presidency) were in Michigan and not present at the time further necessitated the need for priesthood endorsement. The first document presented to the conference, titled "Marriage" and numbered "SECTION CI," was read by William W. Phelps. The second, titled "Of Governments and Laws in General," and numbered "SECTION CII," was read by Oliver Cowdery and included a preamble that stated: "That our belief with regard to earthly governments and laws in general, may not be misinterpreted, nor misunderstood, we have thought proper to present, at the close of this volume, our opinion concerning the same" (D&C, section CII, 1835 ed.). Following the reading of these documents, both were "accepted and adopted and ordered to be printed in said book" (Smith, 2:246–47). In the final printed version, the articles on marriage and GOVERNMENT appear after the appendix (D&C, 247–54, 1835 ed.), and are followed by a document titled "General Assembly," which included the proceedings of the August 1835 meeting and the testimony of the Twelve concerning the book's truthfulness (D&C, 255–57, 1835 ed.). There is also an index and a list of contents at the end of the book.

Oliver Cowdery is generally credited with the authorship of both the article on marriage and the article on government; however, W. W. Phelps deserves at least equal credit, if not more, for his literary contribution to these two documents, especially in connection with the article on government. Previous to his affiliation with the restored gospel, Phelps had considerable political experience. Given that experience and Phelps's distinguished career as a newspaper editor and writer, he may have had a heavier hand in the drafting of the document than did Cowdery.

The impetus behind writing the document regarding the relationship of the Church (and religion in general) with that of government may have come from activities perpetrated against the Latter-day Saints in Jackson County in 1833 and the failure on the part of government officials to uphold the civil and political rights of the Saints. Both Phelps and Cowdery had experienced firsthand the Jackson County persecutions. Furthermore, Phelps had played a leading role in negotiations with Missouri officials in the Saints' attempts to seek just retribution in the courts. In the end, however, the legal appeals exercised by Missouri Church leaders were struck down. Thus, Cowdery's and Phelps's intentions of securing authorization of an official policy statement regarding the Church and its relationship to government was intended not only to promote the principle of free exercise of religion but also to explain the responsibility that rested on governments to protect its citizens in matters of belief and religious practice.

Content overview

A significant part of the article relates directly to the proper role and purpose of government in general, affirming the principle that not only are governments necessary but that they are "instituted of God" for the "safety of society" and to secure to individuals the inherent rights of man—freedom of conscience (that is, belief), the right to own and control property, and the "protection of life" (vv. 1–2). Because governments require officers and magistrates, such persons should execute and enforce the laws judiciously and fairly (v. 3) "for the protection of the innocent and the punishment of the guilty" (v. 6). Furthermore, all citizens have a responsibility to "owe respect and deference" to the rule of law (v. 6; cf. A of F 12), while those found guilty of criminal activity "should be punished according to the nature of the offense" (v. 8).

A poignant issue discussed in the article is the right to the free exercise of conscience, particularly that of religious belief and worship—a right guaranteed by the First Amendment. The First Amendment states that "Congress shall make no law respecting an establishment of religion" and has generally been interpreted to mean that (1) there would be no state church, or in other words, no national religion; and (2) government is prohibited from favoring one religious denomination over that of another. The article on government discusses the second aspect of the clause: "We do not believe it just to mingle religious influence with civil government, whereby one religious society is fostered and another proscribed in its spiritual privileges, and the individual rights of its members, as citizens, denied" (v. 9).

The second phrase in the First Amendment regarding religion or religious worship states that government cannot prohibit "the free exercise thereof." With obvious reference to the "free exercise" clause, the article on government states: "We do not believe that human law has a right to interfere in prescribing rules of worship to bind the consciences of men, nor dictate forms for public or private devotion" (v. 4). Also, governments "are bound to enact laws for the protection of all citizens in the free exercise of their religious belief . . . , so long as a regard and reverence are shown to the laws and such religious opinions do not justify sedition nor conspiracy" (v. 7; cf. A of F 11). Additionally, verse 8 states that "all men should step forward and use their ability in bringing offenders against good laws to punishment."

Three additional aspects of religious privileges are explained in the last three verses: the right of religious societies to excommunicate their members (v. 10); the right to defend oneself and one's community "in times of exigency"

(v. 11); and the right of the Latter-day Saints to preach the gospel to the nations of the earth, except to those in slavery without the consent of their masters (v. 12).

BIBLIOGRAPHY

Doctrine and Covenants, 1835 edition.

Smith, Joseph. *History of The Church of Jesus Christ of Latter-day Saints.* Edited by B. H. Roberts. 7 vols. 2d ed. rev. Salt Lake City: The Church of Jesus Christ of Latter-day Saints, 1932–51.

ALB

Historical context and overview of Doctrine and Covenants 135

Historical context

Section 135 is an eloquent eulogy to the life and contributions of the Prophet Joseph Smith and his brother Hyrum, the patriarch, who were cruelly killed by a band of armed vigilantes on 27 June 1844 while incarcerated in Carthage Jail. The section first appeared as section 111 in the 1844 Nauvoo edition of the Doctrine and Covenants, which was completed sometime in the late summer of that year.

While the authorship of Doctrine and Covenants 135 is not given, several historical factors point to John Taylor as the writer. First, he had personally witnessed the deaths of Joseph and Hyrum Smith. Second, as editor of both the *Times and Seasons* and *Nauvoo Neighbor,* in the weeks immediately following the martyrdom he included four accounts of the Carthage killings in the two newspapers—one of which he co-authored and one which he personally wrote. Third, Taylor had also overseen the editing and printing of the 1844 Doctrine and Covenants and included the statement on the martyrdom as the last section in the book. And fourth, the writing style and prose reflect those of John Taylor.

In composing section 135, it appears that Elder Taylor drew from previously published accounts of the martyrdom. The 1 July 1844 headline article of the *Times and Seasons* read: "Awful assassination of JOSEPH AND HYRUM SMITH!—The pledged faith of the state of Illinois stained with innocent blood by a Mob!" The report bore the names of Willard Richards and John Taylor, eyewitnesses of the tragedy,

and Samuel H. Smith, one of the first persons to appear on the scene after the event. The next number of the paper, issued two weeks later, included another article titled "The Murder," and provided an expressive and eloquent tribute to the Prophet, interspersed with important details about the assault. No authorship is given; however, the wording and expressions in the narrative and the fact that Taylor was also the editor of the paper (newspaper editors often did not subscribe their names to their own pieces) strongly suggest that Taylor was the sole author. A third account, written solely by Richards and detailing the specifics of the attack at the jail titled "Two Minutes in Jail," appeared in the 24 July 1844 issue of the *Nauvoo Neighbor*; it was reprinted in the 1 August issue of the *Times and Seasons.* A close comparison of each of these narratives with that of the wording and phrasing used in section 135, it becomes apparent that John Taylor relied on these narratives (as well as his memory and firsthand knowledge) as "sources" for his composition.

Content overview

Section 135 is composed of the following four segments: (1) a brief account of the facts surrounding the attack at Carthage Jail (vv. 1–2); (2) an appraisal of Joseph Smith's most significant accomplishments and contributions (v. 3); (3) evidence that both Joseph and Hyrum could foresee that they would die at Carthage (vv. 4–5); and (4) Joseph and Hyrum's innocence, and the failure on the part of the state (particularly Illinois governor Thomas Ford) to secure their legal rights and safety (vv. 6–7).

Perhaps the passage cited most frequently from section 135 is verse 3: "Joseph Smith, the Prophet and Seer of the Lord, has done more, save Jesus only, for the salvation of men in this world, than any other man that ever lived in it." While this sentence clearly represents the Latter-day Saint position regarding the divinity of JESUS CHRIST as the literal Son of God, who as the one and only sinless being carried out the eternal ATONEMENT, some might conclude that Joseph Smith was "second" only to Christ and therefore the next greatest prophet (or man) who ever lived—greater than Adam, Enoch, Noah, Abraham, Moses, John the Baptist,

Carthage Jail with statues of the Prophet Joseph Smith and patriarch Hyrum Smith. "In life they were not divided, and in death they were not separated!" (D&C 135:3).

Nephi, Mormon, Moroni, or a host of other ancient righteous men. That, however, is not the meaning the author intended to convey. Rather, the emphasis of the text is on what *resulted* from Joseph Smith's ministry, such as the translation and publication of the Book of Mormon, the introduction and preaching of the restored gospel in foreign lands, the receipt of new revelations (including those found in the Doctrine and Covenants), and building the city of Nauvoo (the author mentions only a few accomplishments, and could have given many more)—not the Prophet's "level" of greatness. In short, Joseph Smith's importance and prominence are on account of the restoration of the everlasting gospel through his instrumentality, in this dispensation—the dispensation of the fulness of times—and through the work for the dead, which will eventually reach into all dispensations, the blessings and opportunity for salvation and exaltation will be extended to more of God's children than by the work of any previous prophet.

See also Martyrdom of Joseph and Hyrum Smith.

BIBLIOGRAPHY

Jensen, Robin Scott, Richard E. Turley Jr., and Riley M. Lorimer, eds. *Published Revelations.* Vol. 2 of the Revelations and Translations series of *The Joseph Smith Papers,* edited by Dean C. Jessee, Ronald K. Esplin, and Richard Lyman Bushman. Salt Lake City, UT: Church Historian's Press, 2011.

"Murder." *Times and Seasons* 5, no. 13 (15 July 1844): 584–86.

Richards, Willard. "Two Minutes in Jail." *Nauvoo Neighbor* 2, no. 13 (24 July 1844): 265; *Times and Seasons* 5, no. 14 (1 August 1844): 598–99.

Richards, Willard, John Taylor, and Samuel H. Smith. "Awful assassination of Joseph and Hyrum Smith." *Times and Seasons* 5, no. 12 (1 July 1844): 560–61.

ALB

Historical context and overview of Doctrine and Covenants 136

Historical context

Section 136, "The Word and Will of the Lord concerning the Camp of Israel" (136:1), Brigham Young's only canonized revelation, was proclaimed on 14 January 1847 in the depths of a very cold winter and at a most trying moment in Church history. Having been driven from their comfortable homes and their glorious temple in Nauvoo, some twelve thousand Latter-day Saints huddled in various makeshift settlements, including Winter Quarters in Nebraska Territory on Indian lands just west of the Missouri River; Council Bluffs (Kanesville), Iowa Territory; other communities stretching along the Missouri River as far south as St. Louis; and temporary settlements such as Mt. Pisgah and Garden Grove, along the trail from Winter Quarters to the Salt Lake Valley. Some five hundred of the Saints' most able men had been called into service by the United States Army of the West and were then marching to the Pacific coast as the Mormon Battalion. Church members were largely uprooted and spread out on their way west in a full-scale exodus of man and beast to a new ZION in some valley of the Rocky Mountains.

During the winter of 1847, the Quorum of the Twelve and others counseled together on how best to move the large body of Saints to the Great Basin. While they were discussing how they should travel in companies with presidencies over each company and captains of hundreds, fifties, and tens (as did the ancient Israelites under Moses; Deuteronomy 1:15), Brigham Young received this revelation. It was read to each quorum in the area and sustained as the word of the Lord to them. Copies were made and members of the Twelve and the local high councils traveled to all the other camps, read the revelation, and obtained sustaining votes. Thus, the revelation was canonized by the Saints within days of its reception and is evidence that these people were committed to the leadership of Brigham Young and the other members of the Quorum of the Twelve (JH; Woodruff; Snow).

Furthermore, the revelation transformed their travels and travails from a mere westward departure into an exodus of modern Israel with divine design and purpose. Spelling out the revised organization by which they would begin to travel west of the Missouri through hostile Indian country, the revelation was at once a resolution and an explanation, a vindication and a promise—in short, "The Word and Will of the Lord" (136:1).

Content overview

More than a statement on travel organization, this revelation was, first, about Church leadership. The Church, those who had "received my kingdom" (136:41), was to go west "under the direction of the Twelve Apostles" (136:3). Second, it was a message of redemption. The death of Joseph Smith was shown to be purposeful; it was "needful that he should seal his testimony with his blood" (136:39). So, too, their own sufferings and death would be redemptive, for "my people must be tried in all things" (136:31). Third, it was an exhortation for the Saints to be obedient. Counseled to cease contention, drunkenness, stealing, and to refrain from other sins, the Saints would find their Zion if they would follow their God. Though they did not know for sure the ultimate physical destination of their travels, much was given concerning their spiritual preparation and obedience

(136:20–29). Fourth, it was a statement of prophecy that great judgments would soon come upon "the nation that has driven you out" and killed the prophets (136:34–36). It was not, however, a call for vengeance or retribution, for, said the Lord, "Zion shall be redeemed in mine own due time," even if the Church was driven far away to the West (136:17–18, 30).

In addition to instruction concerning the companies that would include the women and children, flocks and herds, and all their possessions, the revelation directed that a company of "able-bodied and expert men" take "teams, seeds, and farming utensils, [and] go as pioneers to prepare for putting in spring crops" (136:7). This was the group that arrived in the Salt Lake Valley in July 1847. The revelation also directed that "each company bear an equal proportion . . . in taking the poor, the widows, the

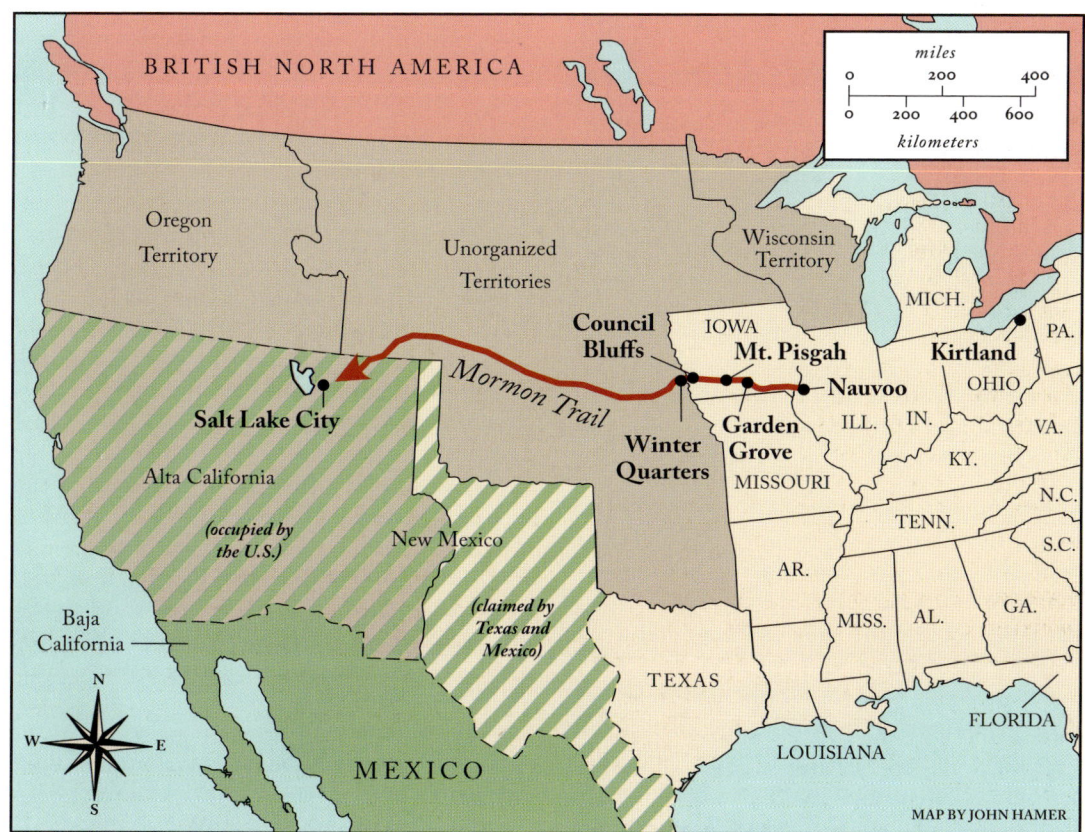

The Exodus from Nauvoo to the West, 1846–1847.

fatherless, and the families of those who have gone into the army" (136:8).

The pioneering Latter-day Saints took great faith and inspiration from this revelation and doctrinal anthem of the exodus, knowing that it was God's mind and will to them. They followed the Twelve and the "Camp of Israel" to the Salt Lake Valley. After arriving in July 1847, Brigham Young returned to Kanesville, Iowa, and was there officially sustained as president of the Church in December 1847. *See* map, p. 857.

BIBLIOGRAPHY

Bennett, Richard E. *Mormons at the Missouri: Winter Quarters, 1846–1852*. Norman: University of Oklahoma Press, 2004.

Hartley, William G. "Pushing on to Zion: Kanesville, Iowa, 1846–1853." *Ensign* 32 (August 2002): 14–24.

Holmes, Gail G. "A Prophet Who Followed, Fulfilled and Magnified: Brigham Young in Iowa and Nebraska." In *Lion of the Lord: Essays on the Life and Service of Brigham Young*, edited by Susan Easton Black and Larry C. Porter. Salt Lake City: Deseret Book Company, 1995.

Journal History of the Church, 11 and 14–18 January 1847. Church History Library, The Church of Jesus Christ of Latter-day Saints, Salt Lake City, Utah.

Snow, Erastus, 1841–47, 84–87. Journal. Church History Library, The Church of Jesus Christ of Latter-day Saints, Salt Lake City, Utah.

Woodruff, Wilford. Journal, 16 January 1847. Church History Library, The Church of Jesus Christ of Latter-day Saints, Salt Lake City, Utah.

REB

Historical context and overview of Doctrine and Covenants 137

Historical context

Section 137 is taken from an entry in Joseph Smith's journal for 21 January 1836 and describes a vision Joseph saw that evening in the temple at Kirtland, Ohio, of the future celestial kingdom and its heirs. It was added to the Doctrine and Covenants in the 1981 edition.

On 21 January 1836, Joseph met on the top floor of the nearly finished house of the Lord with the other members of the First Presidency; his father, the Church patriarch; Joseph's secretary; and the bishoprics from Missouri and Ohio. In adjacent rooms were the high councils from Missouri and Kirtland, who joined the others later in the evening.

"Sanctify yourselves," had been the admonition of the Lord in previous revelations to the brethren of the Church (43:11, 16; 88:68; 133:4), and this they were to do in preparation for being "endowed with power from on high" as promised by the Lord (38:32; 38; 43:16). The brethren came to the meeting after attending to the ordinance of "washing [their] bodies in pure water," symbolizing their efforts to repent and present themselves in the temple clean before the Lord (Smith, *History*, 2:379). The First Presidency consecrated oil, then anointed and blessed Father Smith, who in turn anointed and blessed Joseph. In the course of the evening, all the men in the room were similarly anointed. Oliver Cowdery wrote that "the glorious scene is too great to be described. . . . I only say, that the heavens were opened to many, and great and marvelous things were shown." Bishop Edward Partridge affirmed that some of the brethren "saw visions & others were blessed with the outpouring of the Holy Ghost." Joseph was the only one present who described in his journal in detail some of what he experienced (Harper, 338, 344).

Content overview

Following a short description of the celestial kingdom and the throne of God (137:1–4), Joseph told of seeing his parents and brother Alvin in that kingdom (137:5). Since his parents were both still alive, he was seeing things in the future. Alvin died on 19 November 1823, not long after Moroni first appeared to Joseph and taught him of the Book of Mormon plates. Nearly twenty years later Joseph dictated an entry in the manuscript entitled "Law of the Lord," a blessing and record book he kept near the end of his life. "I remember well the pangs of sorrow that swelled my youthful bosom and almost burst my tender heart, when he died," Joseph said of Alvin. "He was the oldest, and the noblest of my fathers family. He was one of the noblest of the sons of men" (Smith, *Papers*, 2:440). Even so, at Alvin's funeral the Reverend Benjamin Stockton "intimated very strongly that [Alvin] had gone to hell, for Alvin was not a church member." Understandably, Joseph's father "did not like it"

(Smith, *MS*, 133). Joseph translated the Book of Mormon, which clarified that infants who died would not be damned, but it said nothing of accountable adults who died before accepting the gospel. Not until the Kirtland Temple was nearly finished did the Lord reveal a clarification. In this vision in 1836 Joseph saw the Father and the Son on their heavenly throne, as well as Adam and Abraham, his own parents, and his brother Alvin (137:1–5). He did not expect to see Alvin, for he had died before the restoration of the gospel, and he had never been baptized. Consequently, Joseph marveled how Alvin could be an heir of celestial glory. The Lord explained that "all who have died without a knowledge of this gospel, who would have received it if they had been permitted to tarry" will inherit celestial glory (137:7–8). Death is not a deadline that determines salvation, "for I, the Lord, will judge all men according to their works, according to the desire of their hearts" (137:9). Individual desire and works (137:9), not the time of one's death, are determining factors in whether one is saved by Christ or not.

Joseph later revealed the ordinance of baptism for the dead, which enables all mankind to make and keep gospel covenants (127–28). Joseph taught the doctrine to his father on his deathbed, and Father Smith asked Joseph to attend to the ordinance for Alvin. Joseph and his brother Hyrum fulfilled their father's dying wish (Turley). "I see Alvin," Father Smith said just a few minutes before his own passing (Smith, *Biographical*, 265–70). By beginning to explain the Lord's answer to the question about those who do not have the opportunity to receive the fulness of the gospel in mortality, section 137 solved a persistent theological problem faced by Joseph's family and many, many others.

See also Celestial kingdom, vision of; Historical context and overview of Doctrine and Covenants 138; Salvation for the Dead.

BIBLIOGRAPHY

Harper, Steven C. "'A Pentecost and Endowment Indeed': Six Eyewitness Accounts of the Kirtland Temple Experience." In *Opening the Heavens: Accounts of Divine Manifestations, 1820–1844*, edited by John W. Welch and Erick B. Carlson. Provo, Utah: Brigham Young University Press; Salt Lake City: Deseret Book, 2005.

McDermott, Gerald R. *Jonathan Edwards Confronts the Gods: Christian Theology, Enlightenment Religion, and Non-Christian Faiths.* New York: Oxford University Press, 1999.

Smith, Joseph. *History of The Church of Jesus Christ of Latter-day Saints.* Edited by B. H. Roberts. 7 vols. 2d ed. rev. Salt Lake City: The Church of Jesus Christ of Latter-day Saints, 1932–51.

———. *The Papers of Joseph Smith.* Edited by Dean C. Jessee. 2 vols. Salt Lake City: Deseret Book, 1989–92.

Smith, Lucy Mack. *Biographical Sketches of Joseph Smith, the Prophet and His Progenitors for Many Generations.* London: Published for Orson Pratt by S. W. Richards, 1853.

Smith, William. In *Millennial Star* 56, no. 9 (26 February 1894): 133.

Turley, Richard E., Jr. "The Latter-day Saint Doctrine of Baptism for the Dead." Unpublished address given at BYU Family History Fireside, Brigham Young University, 9 November 2001.

SCH

Historical context and overview of Doctrine and Covenants 138

Historical context

Section 138 describes a series of visions of the postmortal spirit world seen by President Joseph F. Smith on 3 October 1918. President Gordon B. Hinckley called it "a document without parallel" and said, "There is nothing quite like it in all of our sacred literature" (4).

DEATH haunted mankind in 1918. The Great War, or World War I, was in the process of claiming more than 9 million lives. That staggering figure paled in comparison with the number of those who died in even less time due to a global influenza pandemic. Worldwide, the virus reaped a grim harvest of perhaps 50 million souls. It killed more than 195,000 Americans in October 1918 alone, the deadliest month in American history—the month the Lord gave the visions recorded in section 138.

Joseph F. Smith was president of the Church during a time of widespread intense suffering. His life's experiences equipped him to grasp the enormity of death and its implications. His father, Hyrum, had been brutally shot to death when Joseph was five. "I lost my mother, the sweetest soul that ever lived," he wrote, "when I was only a boy" ("Status," 5:92). His first child, Mercy Josephine, died at age two, leaving Joseph "vacant, lonely, desolate, deserted" (Smith, *Life,* 456). His beloved eldest son, Hyrum Mack Smith, died unexpectedly in January 1918, creating what President Smith called his "overwhelming burden of grief." In between these untimely deaths, President Smith buried a wife and eleven other children (Smith, *Life,* 476). Few people have tasted the bitterness of death more frequently.

As general conference approached in October 1918, President Smith himself was less than two months from the end of his own mortal life. Very ill, he surprised the Saints by appearing at conference on 4 October. He spoke briefly, saying, "I have dwelt in the spirit of prayer, of supplication, of faith and of determination; and I have had my communication with the Spirit of the Lord continuously" (CR, 2). Indeed he had; the Lord had revealed to him this vision of the redemption of the dead just the day before. After conference he dictated it to his son Joseph Fielding Smith.

Content overview

Section 138 is a Christ-centered text from beginning to end. President Smith related that he had been pondering the ATONEMENT of JESUS CHRIST and Christ's entry into the postmortal spirit world. The vision opened with the GOSPEL of Jesus Christ being preached to departed spirits and concluded in the name of Jesus Christ. Section 138 is written in the language of testimony. President Smith's words emphasize his witness of Christ. "I saw" (138:11), "I beheld" (138:15, 57), "I understood" (138:25), "I perceived" (138:29), "I observed" (138:55), "I bear record, and I know that this record is true," he declared (138:60).

Section 138 begins with a recipe for revelation. President Smith used powerful verbs to describe what he did to receive the sublime series of visions. "I sat in my room *pondering* over the scriptures; and *reflecting* upon the great atoning sacrifice that was made by the Son of God, for the redemption of the world" (138:1–2; emphasis added). He intellectually *"engaged"* (v. 5) one of the deepest theological questions known to man, as well as the most terrible questions of his time, in which "the sheer, overwhelming quantity of death awakened individual

and communal grief on an unprecedented scale. With loss came questions: What is the fate of the dead? Do they continue to exist? Is there life after death?" (Tate, 21). He turned to relevant Bible passages and "pondered over these things which are written" (138:11).

In the vision, Joseph F. Smith saw an innumerable gathering of the righteous dead, those who had been faithful Christians in life. "I beheld that they were filled with joy and gladness, and were rejoicing together because the day of their deliverance was at hand" (138:15). They were waiting for Christ to come and deliver them from the bondage of being disembodied (cf. 45:17; 93:34). The Savior arrived and preached the law of the gospel. He did not preach to the ungodly or to the spirits of those who in life had rejected the warnings of prophets (138:20–22).

President Smith related that this vision led him to marvel, to wonder, and to inquire further. Christ's three-year mortal ministry, full of miracles and power, resulted in relatively few converts. How then could his comparatively short ministry among the dead be effective? What did Peter mean when he wrote that the Savior preached to the spirits in prison who had been disobedient in the days of Noah? The revelation answers these questions: "The Lord went not in person among the wicked and the disobedient," but "he organized his forces and appointed messengers, clothed with power and authority, and commissioned them to go forth and carry the light of the gospel to them that were in darkness, even to all the spirits of men; and thus was the gospel preached to the dead" (138:29–30; Tate, 34). This vision made plain God's just plan of offering the same opportunities and blessings to all mankind, making each individual responsible to receive or reject "the sacrifice of the Son of God" (138:35).

President Smith named many of the "great and mighty ones" (138:38) whom the Lord taught personally "and gave them power to come forth, after his resurrection from the dead, to enter into his Father's kingdom, there to be crowned with immortality and eternal life" (138:51). He saw faithful Saints from all dispensations, among them his own martyred father, Hyrum Smith, together with Hyrum's brother

Joseph, and President Smith's own predecessors in the Church presidency "among the noble and great ones who were chosen in the beginning to be rulers in the Church of God" (138:55). In a unique and heartening aspect of the vision, President Smith saw "our glorious Mother Eve, with many of her faithful daughters who had lived through the ages and worshiped the true and living God" (138:39). He "beheld that the faithful elders of this dispensation, when they depart from mortal life, continue their labors in

Joseph F. Smith, 1838–1918. "On the third of October, in the year nineteen hundred and eighteen, I sat in my room pondering over the scriptures; and reflecting upon the great atoning sacrifice that was made by the Son of God, for the redemption of the world; and the great and wonderful love made manifest by the Father and the Son in the coming of the Redeemer into the world. . . . As I pondered over these things . . . , the eyes of my understanding were opened, and the Spirit of the Lord rested upon me, and I saw the hosts of the dead, both small and great" (D&C 138:1–11).

the preaching of the gospel of repentance and redemption, through the sacrifice of the Only Begotten Son of God, among those who are in darkness and under the bondage of sin in the great world of the spirits of the dead" (138:57). As both an orphaned son and a grieving father, President Smith undoubtedly appreciated the vision's confirmation of "the redemption of the dead, and the sealing of the children to their parents" (138:48).

The revelation declares in verse 58 that the dead can repent and be redeemed through the same gospel of Jesus Christ that saves the repentant living. The determining factor was not death but AGENCY. Individuals were not saved or damned based on when they lived or died but on what they decided to do with Christ's offer of salvation when they learned about it.

Section 138 restored and expanded Bible doctrine. In doing so it reinforced the Bible's wholeness and truthfulness and its compatibility with the Book of Mormon and the Restoration. President Smith saw Adam, Eve, and Old Testament patriarchs and prophets, Book of Mormon prophets, Joseph Smith and others from the last dispensation, all unified by the Savior and his unbounded gospel. The vision gives coherence to God's perfect plan for the redemption of his children; a wholeness that is lacking from most theologies. The devastating toll of death at the time the visions recorded in section 138 were given had people understandably looking for answers. This vision of the redemption of the dead answered that need to know.

On 31 October 1918, an ailing President Smith sent his son Joseph Fielding Smith to read the revelation to a meeting of the First Presidency and Quorum of the Twelve Apostles. They "accepted and endorsed the revelation as the Word of the Lord" (Talmage). The *Deseret Evening News* published the revelation about a month later. In the meantime, President Joseph F. Smith passed from life to death, knowing what he could expect on the other side of the veil.

See also Celestial kingdom, vision of; Historical context and overview of Doctrine and

Covenants 137; Resurrection, the; Salvation for the dead; Spirit world, postmortal.

BIBLIOGRAPHY

Hinckley, Gordon B. "Remarks at the Dedication of the Joseph F. Smith Building at Brigham Young University." Address given at Brigham Young University, Provo, Utah, September 20, 2005.

Lund, Anthon H. Journal, 31 October 1918. Church History Library, The Church of Jesus Christ of Latter-day Saints, Salt Lake City, Utah.

Smith, Joseph F. Conference Report, October 1918, 2–7.

———. "Status of Children in the Resurrection." In *Messages of the First Presidency of The Church of Jesus Christ of Latter-day Saints, 1833–1964,* comp. by James R. Clark. 6 vols. Salt Lake City: Bookcraft, 1965–75.

Smith, Joseph Fielding. *Life of Joseph F. Smith: Sixth President of The Church of Jesus Christ of Latter-day Saints.* Salt Lake City: Deseret News Press, 1938.

Talmage, James E. Journal, 31 October 1918. Church History Library, The Church of Jesus Christ of Latter-day Saints, Salt Lake City, Utah.

Tate, George S. "'The Great World of the Spirits of the Dead': Death, the Great War, and the 1918 Influenza Pandemic as Context for Doctrine and Covenants 138." *BYU Studies* 46 no. 1 (2007): 4–40.

SCH

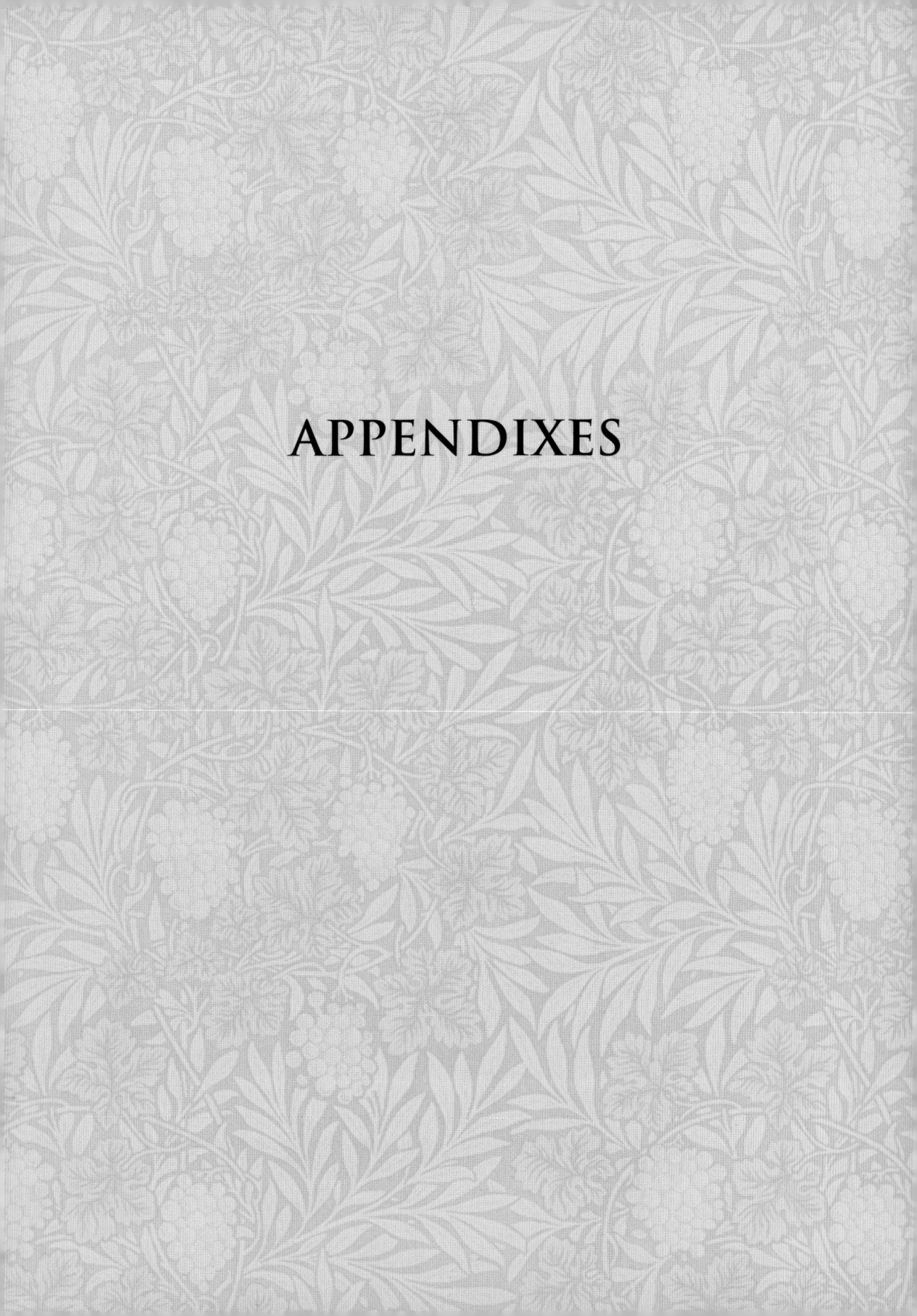

APPENDIXES

Appendix A

The Vision

On 1 February 1843 there appeared in the *Times and Seasons* a short poem by W. W. Phelps addressed to Joseph Smith, entitled "Go with Me." Accompanying it was a much longer response by the Prophet, a poetic rephrasing of Doctrine and Covenants 76, with some interpretive commentary. It is instructive to compare the verses in section 76 with Joseph Smith's poetic version of the vision. The verse numbers from section 76 are given in brackets following the corresponding verse in the poem.

FROM W. W. PHELPS TO JOSEPH SMITH:
THE PROPHET.

VADE MECUM, (TRANSLATED.) GO WITH ME.

Go with me, will you go to the saints that have
  died,—
To the next, better world, where the righteous re-
  side;
Where the angels and spirits in harmony be
In the joys of a vast paradise? Go with me.
Go with me where the truth and the virtues prevail;
Where the union is one, and the years never fail;
Not a heart can conceive, nor a nat'ral eye see
What the Lord has prepar'd for the just. Go with
  me.
Go with me where there is no destruction or war;
Neither tyrants, or sland'rers, or nations ajar;
Where the system is perfect, and happiness free,
And the life is eternal with God. Go with me.
Go with me, will you go to the mansions above,
Where the bliss, and the knowledge, the light, and
  the love,
And the glory of God do eternally be?—
Death, the wages of sin, is not there. Go with me.

  Nauvoo, January, 1843.

THE ANSWER.

TO W. W. PHELPS, ESQ.

A Vision.

1. I will go, I will go, to the home of the Saints,
     Where the virtue's the value, and life the re-
       ward.
     But before I return to my former estate
     I must fulfil the mission I had from the Lord.
2. Wherefore, hear, O ye heavens, and give ear O
     ye earth;
     And rejoice ye inhabitants truly again;
     For the Lord he is God, and his life never ends,
     And besides him there ne'er was a Saviour of
       men. [v. 1]
3. His ways are a wonder; his wisdom is great;
     The extent of his doings, there's none can un-
       veil;
     His purposes fail not; from age unto age
     He still is the same, and his years never fail.
       [vv. 2–3]
4. His throne is the heavens, his life time is all
     Of eternity now, and eternity then;
     His union is power, and none stays his
       hand,—
     The Alpha, Omega, for ever: Amen. [v. 4]
5. For thus saith the Lord, in the spirit of truth,
     I am merciful, gracious, and good unto those
     That fear me, and live for the life that's to
       come;

My delight is to honor the saints with repose;
[v. 5]

6. That serve me in righteousness true to the end;
Eternal's their glory, and great their reward;
I'll surely reveal all my myst'ries to them,—
The great hidden myst'ries in my kingdom
stor'd—[v. 6]

7. From the council in Kolob, to time on the
earth.
And for ages to come unto them I will show
My pleasure & will, what my kingdom will do:
Eternity's wonders they truly shall know. [v. 7]

8. Great things of the future I'll show unto them,
Yea, things of the vast generations to rise;
For their wisdom and glory shall be very great,
And their pure understanding extend to the
skies: [v. 8]

9. And before them the wisdom of wise men shall
cease,
And the nice understanding of prudent ones
fail!
For the light of my spirit shall light mine elect,
And the truth is so mighty 't will ever prevail.
[vv. 9–10]

10. And the secrets and plans of my will I'll reveal;
The sanctified pleasures when earth is
renew'd,
What the eye hath not seen, nor the ear hath
yet heard;
Nor the heart of the natural man ever hath
view'd. [v. 10]

11. I, Joseph, the prophet, in spirit beheld,
And the eyes of the inner man truly did see
Eternity sketch'd in a vision from God,
Of what was, and now is, and yet is to be.
[vv. 11–12]

12. Those things which the Father ordained of old,
Before the world was, or a system had run,—
Through Jesus the Maker and Savior of all;
The only begotten, [Messiah] his son. [v. 13]

13. Of whom I bear record, as all prophets have,
And the record I bear is the fulness,—yea even
The truth of the gospel of Jesus—the Christ,
With whom I convers'd, in the vision of
heav'n. [v. 14]

14. For while in the act of translating his word,
Which the Lord in his grace had appointed to
me,
I came to the gospel recorded by John,
Chapter fifth and the twenty ninth v., which
you'll see. [v. 15]
Which was given as follows:

"Speaking of the resurrection of the dead,—
"Concerning those who shall hear the voice of
the son of man—
"And shall come forth:—
"They who have done good in the resurrection
of the just.
"And they who have done evil in the resurrec-
tion of the unjust." [vv. 16–17]

15. I marvel'd at these resurrections, indeed!
For it came unto me by the spirit direct:—
And while I did meditate what it all meant,
The Lord touch'd the eyes of my own intel-
lect:—[vv. 18–19]

16. Hosanna forever! they open'd anon,
And the glory of God shone around where I
was;
And there was the Son, at the Father's right
hand,
In a fulness of glory, and holy applause. [v. 20]

17. I beheld round the throne, holy angels and
hosts,
And sanctified beings from worlds that have
been,
In holiness worshipping God and the Lamb,
Forever and ever, amen and amen! [v. 21]

18. And now after all of the proofs made of him,
By witnesses truly, by whom he was known,
This is mine, last of all, that he lives; yea he
lives!
And sits at the right hand of God, on his
throne. [v. 22]

19. And I heard a great voice, bearing record from
heav'n,
He's the Saviour, and only begotten of God—
By him, of him, and through him, the worlds
were all made,
Even all that career in the heavens so broad,
[vv. 23–24]

20. Whose inhabitants, too, from the first to the
last,
Are sav'd by the very same Saviour of ours;
And, of course, are begotten God's daughters
and sons,
By the very same truths, and the very same
pow'rs. [v. 24]

21. And I saw and bear record of warfare in heav'n;
For an angel of light, in authority great,
Rebell'd against Jesus, and sought for his
pow'r,
But was thrust down to woe from his Godified
state. [v. 25]

22. And the heavens all wept, and the tears drop'd like dew,

    That Lucifer, son of the morning had fell!

    Yea, is fallen! is fall'n, and become, Oh, alas!

    The son of Perdition; the devil of hell! [vv. 26–27]

23. And while I was yet in the spirit of truth,

    The commandment was: write ye the vision all out;

    For Satan, old serpent, the devil's for war,—

    And yet will encompass the saints round about. [vv. 28–29]

24. And I saw, too, the suff'ring and mis'ry of those,

    [Overcome by the devil, in warfare and fight,]

    In hell-fire, and vengeance, the doom of the damn'd;

    For the Lord said, the vision is further: so write. [v. 30]

25. For thus saith the Lord, now concerning all those

    Who know of my power and partake of the same;

    And suffer themselves, that they be overcome

    By the power of Satan; despising my name:— [v. 31]

26. Defying my power, and denying the truth;—

    They are they—of the world, or of men, most forlorn,

    The Sons of Perdition, of whom, ah! I say,

    'T were better for them had they never been born! [vv. 31–32]

27. They're vessels of wrath, and dishonor to God,

    Doom'd to suffer his wrath, in the regions of woe,

    Through the terrific night of eternity's round,

    With the devil and all of his angels below: [v. 33]

28. Of whom it is said, no forgiveness is giv'n,

    In this world, alas! nor the world that's to come;

    For they have denied the spirit of God,

    After having receiv'd it: and mis'ry's their doom. [vv. 34–35]

29. And denying the only begotten of God,—

    And crucify him to themselves, as they do,

    And openly put him to shame in their flesh,

    By gospel they cannot repentance renew. [v. 35]

30. They are they, who must go to the great lake of fire,

Which burneth with brimstone, yet never consumes,

    And dwell with the devil, and angels of his,

    While eternity goes and eternity comes. [v. 36]

31. They are they, who must groan through the great second death,

    And are not redeemed in the time of the Lord;

    While all the rest are, through the triumph of Christ,

    Made partakers of grace, by the power of his word. [vv. 37–39]

32. The myst'ry of Godliness truly is great;—

    The past, and the present, and what is to be;

    And this is the gospel—glad tidings to all,

    Which the voice from the heavens bore record to me: [v. 40]

33. That he came to the world in the middle of time,

    To lay down his life for his friends and his foes,

    And bear away sin as a mission of love;

    And sanctify earth for a blessed repose. [v. 41]

34. 'Tis decreed, that he'll save all the work of his hands,

    And sanctify them by his own precious blood;

    And purify earth for the Sabbath of rest,

    By the agent of fire, as it was by the flood. [v. 42]

35. The Savior will save all his Father did give,

    Even all that he gave in the regions abroad,

    Save the Sons of Perdition: They're lost; ever lost,

    And can never return to the presence of God. [v. 43]

36. They are they, who must reign with the devil in hell,

    In eternity now, and eternity then,

    Where the worm dieth not, and the fire is not quench'd;—

    And the punishment still, is eternal. Amen. [v. 44]

37. And which is the torment apostates receive,

    But the end, or the place where the torment began,

    Save to them who are made to partake of the same,

    Was never, nor will be, revealed unto man. [vv. 45–46]

38. Yet God shows by vision a glimpse of their fate,

    And straightway he closes the scene that was shown:

So the width, or the depth, or the misery thereof,
Save to those that partake, is forever unknown. [vv. 47–48]

39. And while I was pondering, the vision was closed;
And the voice said to me, write the vision: for lo!
'Tis the end of the scene of the sufferings of those,
Who remain filthy still in their anguish and woe. [v. 49]

40. And again I bear record of heavenly things,
Where virtue's the value, above all that's pric'd—
Of the truth of the gospel concerning the just,
That rise in the first resurrection of Christ. [v. 50]

41. Who receiv'd and believ'd, and repented like-wise,
And then were baptis'd, as a man always was,
Who ask'd and receiv'd a remission of sin,
And honored the kingdom by keeping its laws. [v. 51]

42. Being buried in water, as Jesus had been,
And keeping the whole of his holy commands,
They received the gift of the spirit of truth,
By the ordinance truly of laying on hands. [v. 52]

43. For these overcome, by their faith and their works,
Being tried in their life-time, as purified gold,
And seal'd by the spirit of promise, to life,
By men called of God, as was Aaron of old. [v. 53]

44. They are they, of the church of the first born of God,—
And unto whose hands he committeth all things;
For they hold the keys of the kingdom of heav'n,
And reign with the Savior, as priests, and as kings. [vv. 54–56]

45. They're priests of the order of Melchisedek,
Like Jesus, [from whom is this highest reward,]
Receiving a fulness of glory and light;
As written: They're Gods; even sons of the Lord. [vv. 57–58]

46. So all things are theirs; yea, of life, or of death;
Yea, whether things now, or to come, all are theirs,
And they are the Savior's, and he is the Lord's,

Having overcome all, as eternity's heirs. [vv. 59–60]

47. 'Tis wisdom that man never glory in man,
But give God the glory for all that he hath;
For the righteous will walk in the presence of God,
While the wicked are trod under foot in his wrath. [v. 61]

48. Yea, the righteous shall dwell in the presence of God,
And of Jesus, forever, from earth's second birth—
For when he comes down in the splendor of heav'n,
All these he'll bring with him, to reign on the earth. [vv. 62–63]

49. These are they that arise in their bodies of flesh,
When the trump of the first resurrection shall sound;
These are they that come up to Mount Zion, in life,
Where the blessings and gifts of the spirit abound. [vv. 64–66]

50. These are they that have come to the heavenly place;
To the numberless courses of angels above:
To the city of God; e'en the holiest of all,
And the home of the blessed, the fountain of love: [v. 67]

51. To the church of old Enoch, and of the first born:
And gen'ral assembly of ancient renown'd.
Whose names are all kept in the archives of heav'n,
As chosen and faithful, and fit to be crown'd. [v. 68]

52. These are they that are perfect through Jesus' own blood,
Whose bodies celestial are mention'd by Paul,
Where the sun is the typical glory thereof,
And God, and his Christ, are the true judge of all. [vv. 69–70]

53. Again I beheld the terrestrial world,
In the order and glory of Jesus, go on;
'Twas not as the church of the first born of God,
But shone in its place, as the moon to the sun. [v. 71]

54. Behold, these are they that have died without law;
The heathen of ages that never had hope.

And those of the region and shadow of death,
The spirits in prison, that light has brought up.
[vv. 72–73]

55. To spirits in prison the Savior once preach'd,
And taught them the gospel, with powers
afresh;
And then were the living baptiz'd for their
dead,
That they might be judg'd as if men in the
flesh. [v. 74]

56. These are they that are hon'rable men of the
earth;
Who were blinded and dup'd by the cunning
of men:
They receiv'd not the truth of the Savior at
first;
But did, when they heard it in prison, again.
[vv. 74–75]

57. Not valiant for truth, they obtain'd not the
crown,
But are of that glory that's typ'd by the moon:
They are they, that come into the presence of
Christ,
But not to the fulness of God, on his throne.
[vv. 76–79]

58. Again I beheld the telestial, as third,
The lesser, or starry world, next in its place.
For the leaven must leaven three measures of
meal,
And every knee bow that is subject to grace.
[v. 81]

59. These are they that receiv'd not the gospel of
Christ,
Or evidence, either, that he ever was;
As the stars are all diff'rent in glory and light,
So differs the glory of these by the laws. [v. 82]

60. These are they that deny not the spirit of God,
But are thrust down to hell, with the devil, for
sins,
As hypocrites, liars, whoremongers, and
thieves,
And stay 'till the last resurrection begins.
[vv. 83–85]

61. 'Till the Lamb shall have finish'd the work he
begun;
Shall have trodden the wine press, in fury
alone,
And overcome all by the pow'r of his might:
He conquers to conquer, and save all his own.
[vv. 85 and 107]

62. These are they that receive not a fulness of
light,

From Christ, in eternity's world, where they
are,
The terrestrial sends them the Comforter,
though;
And minist'ring angels, to happify there.
[v. 86]

63. And so the telestial is minister'd to,
By ministers from the terrestrial one,
As terrestrial is, from the celestial throne;
And the great, greater, greatest, seem's stars,
moon, and sun. [vv. 86–88]

64. And thus I beheld, in the vision of heav'n,
The telestial glory, dominion and bliss,
Surpassing the great understanding of men,—
Unknown, save reveal'd, in a world vain as
this. [vv. 89–90]

65. And lo, I beheld the terrestrial, too,
Which excels the telestial in glory and light,
In splendor, and knowledge, and wisdom, and
joy,
In blessings, and graces, dominion and might.
[v. 91]

66. I beheld the celestial, in glory sublime;
Which is the most excellent kingdom that
is,—
Where God, e'en the Father, in harmony
reigns;
Almighty, supreme, and eternal, in bliss.
[vv. 92–93]

67. Where the church of the first born in union
reside,
And they see as they're seen, and they know as
they're known;
Being equal in power, dominion and might,
With a fulness of glory and grace, round his
throne. [vv. 94–95]

68. The glory celestial is one like the sun;
The glory terrestr'al is one like the moon;
The glory telestial is one like the stars,
And all harmonize like the parts of a tune.
[vv. 96–98]

69. As the stars are all different in lustre and size,
So the telestial region, is mingled in bliss;
From least unto greatest, and greatest to least,
The reward is exactly as promis'd in this.
[v. 98]

70. These are they that came out for Apollos and
Paul;
For Cephas and Jesus, in all kinds of hope;
For Enoch and Moses, and Peter, and John;
For Luther and Calvin, and even the Pope.
[vv. 99–100]

71. For they never received the gospel of Christ,
Nor the prophetic spirit that came from the Lord;
Nor the covenant neither, which Jacob once had;
They went their own way, and they have their reward. [vv. 100–101]

72. By the order of God, last of all, these are they,
That will not be gather'd with saints here below,
To be caught up to Jesus, and meet in the cloud:—
In darkness they worshipp'd; to darkness they go. [v. 102]

73. These are they that are sinful, the wicked at large,
That glutted their passion by meanness or worth;
All liars, adulterers, sorc'rers, and proud;
And suffer, as promis'd, God's wrath on the earth. [vv. 103–4]

74. These are they that must suffer the vengeance of hell,
'Till Christ shall have trodden all enemies down,
And perfected his work, in the fulness of times:
And is crown'd on his throne with his glorious crown. [vv. 105–8]

75. The vast multitude of the telestial world—
As the stars of the skies, or the sands of the sea;—

The voice of Jehovah echo'd far and wide,
Ev'ry tongue shall confess, and they all bow the knee. [vv. 109–10]

76. Ev'ry man shall be judg'd by the works of his life,
And receive a reward in the mansions prepar'd;
For his judgments are just, and his works never end,
As his prophets and servants have always declar'd. [v. 111]

77. But the great things of God, which he show'd unto me,
Unlawful to utter, I dare not declare;
They surpass all the wisdom and greatness of men,
And only are seen, as has Paul, where they are. [vv. 114–18]

78. I will go, I will go, while the secret of life,
Is blooming in heaven, and blasting in hell;
Is leaving on earth, and a budding in space:—
I will go, I will go, with you, brother, farewell.

JOSEPH SMITH.

Nauvoo, Feb. 1843.

BIBLIOGRAPHY

"*Vade Mecum*" and "*The Vision.*" *Times and Seasons* 4, no. 6 (1 February 1843): 81–85.

APPENDIX B

SECTION NUMBERS FOR THE SIX PRINCIPAL EDITIONS OF THE DOCTRINE AND COVENANTS/ BOOK OF COMMANDMENTS

Each column shows the section or chapter numbers for each edition of the Doctrine and Covenants. For example, section 4 from the 1981 edition appeared as section 4 in the 1921 and 1876 editions, as section 31 in the 1844 and 1835 editions of the Doctrine and Covenants, and as chapter 3 in the 1833 Book of Commandments. Items in the Doctrine and Covenants that are not in the chart below include Official Declaration 1, which has been published in the Doctrine and Covenants since 1908, and Official Declaration 2, which was first published in the Doctrine and Covenants in 1981.

1981	1921	1876	1844	1835	1833	1981	1921	1876	1844	1835	1833
1	1	1	1	1	1	18	18	18	43	43	15
2	2	2				19	19	19	44	44	16
3	3	3	30	30	2	20	20	20	2	2	24
4	4	4	31	31	3	21	21	21	46	46	22
5	5	5	32	32	4	22	22	22	47	47	23
6	6	6	8	8	5	23	23	23	45	45	17–21
7	7	7	33	33	6	24	24	24	9	9	25
8	8	8	34	34	7	25	25	25	48	48	26
9	9	9	35	35	8	26	26	26	49	49	27
10	10	10	36	36	9	27	27	27	50	50	28
11	11	11	37	37	10	28	28	28	51	51	30
12	12	12	38	38	11	29	29	29	10	10	29
13	13	13				30	30	30	52	52	31–33
14	14	14	39	39	12	31	31	31	53	53	34
15	15	15	40	40	13	32	32	32	54	54	
16	16	16	41	41	14	33	33	33	55	55	35
17	17	17	42	42		34	34	34	56	56	36

1981	1921	1876	1844	1835	1833
35	35	35	11	11	37
36	36	36	57	57	38
37	37	37	58	58	39
38	38	38	12	12	40
39	39	39	59	59	41
40	40	40	60	60	42
41	41	41	61	61	43
42	42	42	13	13	44, 47
43	43	43	14	14	45
44	44	44	62	62	46
45	45	45	15	15	48
46	46	46	16	16	49
47	47	47	63	63	50
48	48	48	64	64	51
49	49	49	65	65	52
50	50	50	17	17	53
51	51	51	23	23	
52	52	52	66	66*	54
53	53	53	67	66*	55
54	54	54	68	67	56
55	55	55	69	68	57
56	56	56	70	69	58
57	57	57	27	27	
58	58	58	18	18	59
59	59	59	19	19	60
60	60	60	71	70	61
61	61	61	72	71	62
62	62	62	73	72	63
63	63	63	20	20	64
64	64	64	21	21	65
65	65	65	24	24	
66	66	66	75	74	
67	67	67	25	25	
68	68	68	22	22	
69	69	69	28	28	
70	70	70	26	26	
71	71	71	91	90	
72	72	72	90	89	

1981	1921	1876	1844	1835	1833
73	73	73	29	29	
74	74	74	74	73	
75	75	75	88	87	
76	76	76	92	91	
77	77	77			
78	78	78	76	75	
79	79	79	77	76	
80	80	80	78	77	
81	81	81	80	79	
82	82	82	87	86	
83	83	83	89	88	
84	84	84	4	4	
85	85	85			
86	86	86	6	6	
87	87	87			
88	88	88	7	7	
89	89	89	81	80	
90	90	90	85	84	
91	91	91	93	92	
92	92	92	94	93	
93	93	93	83	82	
94	94	94	84	83	
95	95	95	96	95	
96	96	96	97	96	
97	97	97	82	81	
98	98	98	86	85	
99	99	99	79	78	
100	100	100	95	94	
101	101	101	98	97	
102	102	102	5	5	
103	103	103	101		
104	104	104	99	98	
105	105	105	102		
106	106	106	100	99	
107	107	107	3	3	
108	108	108			
109	109	109			
110	110	110			

1981	1921	1876	1844	1835	1833
111	111	111			
112	112	112	104		
113	113	113			
114	114	114			
115	115	115			
116	116	116			
117	117	117			
118	118	118			
119	119	119	107		
120	120	120			
121	121	121			
122	122	122			
123	123	123			
124	124	124	103†		
125	125	125			

1981	1921	1876	1844	1835	1833
126	126	126			
127	127	127	105		
128	128	128	106		
129	129	129			
130	130	130			
131	131	131			
132	132	132			
133	133	133	108	100	
134	134	134	110	102	
135	135	135	111		
136	136	136			
137					
138					
			109	101‡	

* In the 1835 edition, two sections were mistakenly numbered as section 66.

† In the 1844 edition, the revelation now known as section 124 was not numbered. However, it seems that it was intended to be section 103, as sections numbering 102 and 104 immediately preceded and succeeded this revelation in the text.

‡ An article entitled "Marriage" was originally included as section 101 in the 1835 edition of the Doctrine and Covenants and reprinted as section 109 in the 1844 edition. It was replaced by a revelation on marriage, known today as section 132, in the 1876 edition.

CDT

Appendix C

First Publication of the Doctrine and Covenants in Languages Other Than English

Following is an alphabetical listing of all the languages into which the Doctrine and Covenants has been translated, up to August 2012. Also shown is the date when the Doctrine and Covenants was first published in a triple combination with the Book of Mormon and the Pearl of Great Price.

Language	First Published	First Inclusion in a Triple Combination
Welsh	1851 (out of print)	
Danish	1852	Triple 1965
German	1876	Triple 1924
Spanish	1887 (selected sections)	Triple 1957
Swedish	1888	Triple 1956
Dutch	1908	Triple 1954
French	1908 (selected sections)	Triple 1958
Hawaiian	1914 (out of print)	
Maori	1919 (out of print)	
Norwegian	1934 (selected sections)	Triple 1992
Czech	1939	Triple 2004
Armenian-West	1941	
Portuguese	1950	Triple 1998
Finnish	1955	Triple 1957
Japanese	1957	Triple 1957
Tongan	1959	Triple 2007
Samoan	1963	Triple 2011
Tahitian	1965	
Italian	1965	Triple 1982
Korean	1968	Triple 1974
Indonesian	1979	Triple 2010
Thai	1979	Triple 2010
Vietnamese	1981	Triple 2003

Language	First Published	First Inclusion in a Triple Combination
Afrikaans	1982	
Croatian	1982	
Icelandic	1982	Triple 1999
Fijian	1984	
Polish	1984	
Kekchi	1985	Triple 2011
Greek	1986	
Arabic	1989	
Hungarian	1995	Triple 2005
Ilokano	1995	Triple
Russian	1996	
Cebuano	1998	Triple
Raratongan	1998	
Tagalog	1998	Triple
Catalan	1999	
Fante	2003	Triple
Romanian	2004	Triple
Bulgarian	2004	Triple
Albanian	2005	Triple
Ukrainian	2005	Triple
Swahili	2005	Triple
Armenian	2006	Triple
Latvian	2006	Triple
Lithuanian	2006	Triple
Malagasy	2006	Triple
Haitian	2007	Triple
Cambodian	2007	Triple
Chinese, Trad. Char.	2007	Triple
Igbo	2007	Triple
Mongolian	2007	Triple
Shona	2007	Triple
Chinese, Simp. Char.	2008	Triple
Estonian	2011	Triple

Spanish, Norwegian, and French editions of the Doctrine and Covenants, originally published as selected sections, were published in 1948, 1957, and 1958, respectively.

BIBLIOGRAPHY

Information courtesy of the Church History Department and Priesthood Department of The Church of Jesus Christ of Latter-day Saints, August 2012.

Lambert, A. C. "The Editions of the Doctrine and Covenants of The Church of Jesus Christ of Latter-day Saints in All Languages, 1833–1950." Mimeograph, 1950.

CDT

APPENDIX D

PROPHECIES AND PROMISES IN THE DOCTRINE AND COVENANTS

The Doctrine and Covenants is laden with prophecies and promises from the Lord. In his revealed preface to his revelations, the Lord admonished readers to "search these commandments, for they are true and faithful, and the prophecies and promises which are in them shall all be fulfilled" (1:37). Although many promises are also prophecies and, in a sense, all prophecies are promises, there are occasions when a distinction may be made. For the purposes of this treatment, prophecies are defined as declarations concerning what will occur in the future, and promises relate to blessings, or the loss of blessings, based on faithfulness or the lack thereof. Following is a list of prophecies and promises contained in the Doctrine and Covenants in order of first appearance, according to subject.

PROPHECIES IN THE DOCTRINE AND COVENANTS

These prophecies give hope for the future to all the faithful. Faith leads the Saints to trust in the fulfillment of these prophecies, according to the time and means the Lord prescribes, and through faith the Saints are prepared to receive further truths as they are revealed through his prophets.

PROPHECIES	SCRIPTURE REFERENCES
The wicked, rebellious, and unrepentant	
• Their sins will be revealed, and they will be pierced with sorrow.	1:3
• The anger of the Lord will be kindled, and his sword will fall upon them.	1:13
• They will be cut off from among the Lord's people.	1:14; 133:63
• The testimony of the Three Witnesses will condemn them.	5:18
• A desolating scourge, including sword, famine, bloodshed, and natural disasters of every kind, will be poured out upon the wicked and will utterly consume them until the Lord's work is done and he comes.	5:19; 63:6; 84:97; 87:6; 97:22–23, 26; 101:10–11
• The scourge will begin at the Lord's house among those who have professed to know his name but have blasphemed against him in the midst of his house.	112:24–26
• The Lord will disturb them and cause them to tremble and shake to the center.	10:56
• Woes, weeping, wailing, and gnashing of teeth will go forth to those found on the Lord's left hand.	19:5
• Those who profess the Lord's name but will not hear him will be cursed with the heaviest of all cursings.	41:1

PROPHECIES	SCRIPTURE REFERENCES
• Sign seekers will see signs but not unto salvation.	63:7
• The rebellious are not of Ephraim, will be cut out of the land of Zion, will have no inheritance, and will be plucked out.	64:35–36
• Those who break the law, seek to become a law unto themselves, and abide in sin cannot be justified or sanctified by the law, mercy, justice, or judgment and therefore will remain filthy still.	88:35, 39
• Those who exalt themselves will be abased.	49:10; 101:42; 136:19
• The blood of innocent martyrs will cry unto the Lord until he has avenged them on the earth.	135:7
• The Lord's enemies are in his hands, and he will do with them according to his will and pleasure.	136:30

The Lord's words

• Will all be fulfilled and verified.	1:7, 37–38; 5:20; 29:30; 42:39; 49:10; 58:31–33; 62:6; 64:31
• Will go to all people, and they will come to a knowledge of the Savior.	3:16–20
• Will come to this generation through Joseph Smith.	5:10
• Will be taught to all nations in their own tongue by those who are ordained to teach.	42:58; 90:10–11
• Will be uttered by his voice and will be obeyed.	63:5

The Lord's faithful servants

• Will have the sealing power.	1:8–9
• Will break down the mighty and strong and thrash the nations by the power of the Spirit.	1:19; 35:13; 133:59
• Will fight valiantly for the Lord; their enemies will be under their feet, and the Lord will preserve them by the fire of his indignation.	35:14
• Will be sent forth to the east, west, north, and south.	42:63
• Will be considered lawful heirs of the priesthood, which will remain in their lineage until the restoration of all things.	86:8–10
• Will have an effectual door opened for them.	100:3
• Will hear his voice, see him, abide the day of his coming, and be purified even as he is pure.	35:21

Devil

• The devil will have power over his dominion.	1:35
• The Lord will show his wisdom is greater than the cunning of the devil.	10:43
• Satan and his works will be destroyed.	19:3

Millennium (*See* Millennium, the)

• The Lord will reign in the midst of his Saints, have power over them, and come down in judgment on the world.	1:36

The Restoration

• The priesthood will be revealed by the hand of Elijah.	2:1

PROPHECIES	SCRIPTURE REFERENCES
• The promises made to the fathers will be planted in the hearts of the children, and their hearts will turn to their fathers.	2:2
• A great and marvelous work will come forth.	3:16; 4:1; 6:1; 11:1; 12:1; 14:1
• The Lord has reserved things that will be shown to future generations.	5:9
• The Lord will build his Church upon the rock of the restored gospel.	33:13
• The Restoration will make known the folly of the Gentiles.	35:7
• Great things will soon be shown to the children of men.	35:10
• Church covenants will be given sufficient to establish the Saints.	42:67
• The keys of the kingdom of God will be restored, and the stone cut without hands will roll forth to fill the whole earth.	65:2
• The testimony of things written in the book of Enoch will be given in due time.	107:57
• The Lord will show Joseph Smith all things pertaining to the Nauvoo Temple, the priesthood, and the place where the temple will be built.	124:42
• The Lord will restore many things to the earth pertaining to the priesthood.	127:8
• The Lord will restore all things and make all things known in due time through the keys conferred upon Joseph Smith.	132:45

The Book of Mormon

• The testimony of three witnesses will go forth with it.	5:11–15
• The Lord will confound those who altered its words.	10:42–43
• It will go to the Lord's people.	10:52
• It will bring to light true points of doctrine.	10:60–62
• It will go to the Jews, including the Lamanites.	19:26–27; cf. 3:19–20

The Lord's work

• The Lord will not suffer the wicked to destroy his work.	10:43; 136:17
• The Lord will gather his elect from the four quarters of the earth.	29:2, 8; 33:6
• The Lord will hasten his work in its time.	88:73

New Jerusalem, Zion, Missouri

• The Lord will reveal in due time where the New Jerusalem is to be built.	28:9; 42:62; 52:5
• Zion shall rejoice upon the hills and flourish.	35:24
• There will not be a curse upon Zion when the Lord comes.	38:18
• New Jerusalem will be a city of refuge and safety for the Saints; the glory and terror of the Lord will be there; the wicked will not come to it; those in Zion will be the only people not at war one with another; New Jerusalem will be called Zion and will be an ensign to all people.	45:66–71; 64:37–43
• Certain men will have the place revealed to them, and they will proceed to purchase lands and lay the foundation of the city.	48:5–6
• Before the Second Coming, Jacob will flourish in the wilderness, the Lamanites will blossom as a rose, and Zion will flourish and be gathered to the place the Lord has appointed.	49:24–25

PROPHECIES	SCRIPTURE REFERENCES
• The Lord will hasten the city in its time and will redeem Zion.	52:43; 136:18
• It will be said in a future day that only the upright in heart will be able to go to Zion on the water.	61:16
• New Jerusalem and its temple will be built in this generation.	84:3–5
• The sons of Moses and Aaron will offer sacrifices at the temple in New Jerusalem in this generation; they will be filled with the Lord's glory.	84:31–32
• The Lord has heard the prayers concerning Zion and has sworn an immutable decree that they will be granted.	98:2–3
• Zion will be redeemed after she is chastened for a little season.	100:13
• The Lord will raise up a pure people (Zion) who will serve him in righteousness.	100:16
• The Lord will own them (Zion), and they will be his when he makes up his jewels.	101:3
• Zion will not be moved out of her place; those who have been scattered will be gathered; those who have mourned will be comforted; the Lord will not cast them off but will remember mercy in the day of wrath; those who are found on the watchtower will be saved; the pure in heart will return and build up the waste places of Zion.	101:9–18
• The Lord will raise up a man like unto Moses, who will lead them out of bondage with power; the Lord's presence and his angels will go before them.	103:15–20
• Not many years hence the Lord's enemies will not be left to pollute the land he has consecrated for the gathering of the Saints.	105:15

Second Coming of Jesus Christ (*See* Jesus Christ, second coming of; Signs)

• Behold, I come quickly.	33:18; 34:12; 35:27; 39:24; 41:4; 49:28; 51:20; 54:10; 58:65; 68:35; 87:8; 88:126, 99:5; 112:34

Rich and poor

• The gospel will be preached to the poor and the meek.	35:15
• The riches of gentile converts will be consecrated for the poor of the house of Israel.	42:39
• The poor will inherit the earth from generation to generation.	56:19–20
• The poor will be exalted, the rich will be made low.	104:16

Wars and destruction

• Wars and secret combinations will be heard of in America.	38:29; 42:64; 45:63
• The Lord decreed much destruction upon the waters; in a future day, no flesh will be safe upon the waters.	61:4–5; 61:15–16
• Wars will come, beginning with the rebellion of South Carolina (probably over the slave question), and will be poured out upon all nations; in future wars the wicked will slay the wicked, and the Saints will hardly escape.	63:33–34; 87:1–5; 130:12–13

PROPHECIES	SCRIPTURE REFERENCES
Ohio	
• The Lord will send servants to all nations, he will tell them what they should do, and he will lead them; no power shall stay them.	38:32–33
• The Lord will consecrate unto his people this land for a little season until he shall provide for them otherwise and command them to go hence.	51:16
• The Lord will retain a stronghold in Kirtland, Ohio, for five years, in which he will not overthrow the wicked so that some might be saved.	64:21
• The hearts of many will rejoice because of the endowment and blessings poured out in the Kirtland Temple; the fame of this house will spread to foreign lands; this is the beginning of the blessings which will be poured out upon the people.	110:9–10
• Moneychangers will be overthrown in the Lord's own due time.	117:16
• The Lord will build up Kirtland, but he has a scourge prepared for the inhabitants thereof.	124:83
Earth; celestial kingdom	
• The poor and meek will inherit the earth; the earth will become the celestial kingdom.	88:17–20, 25–26; 130:4–11
Resurrection and final judgment (*See* Judgment[s]; Kingdoms of glory and perdition, vision of; Resurrection, the)	
• All will be resurrected and inherit a kingdom of glory or a kingdom of no glory based on the law they kept.	88:21–24, 28–32
Salem, Massachusetts	
• Many will be gathered out of this city in the Lord's due time; they will have power over this city and its wealth pertaining to gold and silver.	111:2, 4
Nauvoo	
• The Nauvoo stake is a cornerstone in Zion and will be polished with the refinement of a palace.	124:2

PROMISES IN THE DOCTRINE AND COVENANTS

The Lord encourages his children to righteousness by extending promised blessings based on obedience, despite his foreknowledge of whether or not they will obey. His loving kindness and tender mercies are clearly revealed when comparing his promised blessings to the acts of obedience that are rewarded by them. The justice of God is also manifest by the cursings pronounced upon unrepentant sinners. All have the opportunity and responsibility to learn and embrace the word of God and so order their lives to be the grateful beneficiaries of these promises

PROMISES	SCRIPTURE REFERENCES
To the unrepentant	
• Those who fail to listen to the Lord and obey his commandments will be cast out/cut off from among his people.	1:14; 41:5; 42:20–21, 23–24, 26, 28, 37, 74–75; 45:44; 50:8; 51:2; 52:6; 56:3; 63:63; 64:35; 85:11; 101:90; 133:63

PROMISES	SCRIPTURE REFERENCES
• Those who are unrepentant will lose the light and the Spirit; if they sin against greater light, they receive greater condemnation and walk in darkness.	1:33; 82:3; 95:12
• The unrepentant will suffer even as he did and will encounter perils.	19:15–17; 29:3
• Those who have made sacred covenants and then broken them will be delivered over to the buffetings of Satan.	78:12; 82:21; 104:9–10; 132:26
• Those who break covenants and deny the Lord's name will lose office and standing in the Church.	60:2–3; 78:12; 114:2
• The disobedient and the unrepentant will not be saved.	18:46; 20:29; 56:2
• Those who receive the law but don't keep it will not be the Lord's disciples.	41:5; 52:40; 84:91
• Those who are idle shall not eat the food or wear the clothes of the laborer.	42:42
• The rich who will not give to the poor will not be saved but will experience torment in hell.	56:16; 104:18
• Those who sin will have their former sins return.	82:7
• Those who do not obey the Lord will have no promise.	82:10
• Those priesthood holders who break the oath and covenant of the priesthood and turn from it will lose their exaltation.	84:41
• Those children of Zion who treat lightly the Book of Mormon and the Lord's "former commandments" will be under condemnation, and judgment will be poured out upon them.	84:54–58
• Those things that are asked for but are not expedient will turn to one's condemnation.	88:65
• Those who do not bring forth good fruit will be hewn down and cast into the fire.	97:7
• Those who will not endure chastening and deny the Lord cannot be sanctified.	101:5
• Those who are slothful, undutiful, and unapproved will not be counted worthy to stand.	107:100
• Those who are enemies of the Church will receive promised cursings.	121:11–25; 124:50, 52
• Those who will not hearken to the Lord's voice or his servants' voices will be cursed.	124:46–48
• Those who commit the unpardonable sin cannot enter the Lord's presence.	132:27

To the repentant and forgiving

• Those who repent and obey will be forgiven.	1:32; 50:39; 64:17; 68:24
• The Lord will stay his hand in judgment for those who repent, receive the fulness of the gospel, and become sanctified.	39:18
• Those who forgive others will be forgiven by the Lord.	82:1
• Those who remain steadfast in bearing testimony of the things they have received will be forgiven.	84:61
• The scattered remnants of Zion will receive revelation upon returning to the Lord.	113:10

PROMISES	SCRIPTURE REFERENCES
• Those who repent and sanctify themselves will receive eternal life.	133:62
Spiritual gifts	
• Asking and receiving.	4:7; 6:5; 6:7; 6:11; 11:5; 11:7; 12:5; 14:5; 42:61, 68; 46:28; 49:26; 66:9; 88:63–64; 103:31
• Receiving manifestations of the Spirit and being born of God.	5:16
• Revealing of mysteries.	6:7; 11:7; 63:23; 76:5–10; 121:26–33
• Receiving revelation in one's heart and mind.	8:2
• Receiving enlightening of the mind, filling the soul with joy; asking in faith, knowing all things pertaining to righteousness.	11:13–14
• Being given the Spirit by the prayer of faith and receiving attendant blessings.	19:38; 41:3; 42:14; 44:2
• Being shown when and where to go, what to do, where to stay; being led by the Lord.	28:15; 31:11; 42:5; 52:2, 4; 78:18; 79:2; 111:8; 112:10
• Being united in prayer when assembled together and receiving the promise of revelation.	29:6; 42:3
• Receiving gifts of the Spirit, which are given for the benefit of all: the gift to heal and be healed, faith, wisdom, knowledge, miracles, prophecy, tongues, diversity of operations, differences of administration.	35:8–9; 42:48–52; 46:9–26; 66:9; 68:10; 84:65–72
• Seeing the Lord, knowing him, and having his face unveiled.	35:21; 50:45; 67:10; 88:49–50, 67–68; 93:1
• Being taught the peaceable things of the kingdom by the Holy Ghost.	36:2
• Speaking and prophesying as directed by the Spirit.	42:16
• Discerning gifts of the Spirit by those holding keys.	46:27
• Giving all of the gifts of the Spirit to the head of the Church that all might be profited.	46:29
• Receiving light and continuing in God, receiving more light that will grow brighter and brighter until the perfect day.	50:24; 93:28
• Asking in the Spirit according to the will of God.	46:30; 50:29–32
• Receiving future revelation.	55:6; 57:16; 63:22; 66:4
• Seeing and knowing that which has been conferred upon you.	67:14
• Knowing the signs of the Second Coming.	68:11
• Withholding of abundant spiritual manifestations unless the Saints are equal in temporal things.	70:14
• Calling on the Lord and receiving the Comforter, which teaches all things that are expedient.	75:10
• Receiving wisdom and great and hidden treasures of knowledge.	89:19
• Receiving revelation line upon line, precept upon precept.	98:12
• Discerning of spirit matter by purified bodies.	131:7–8

PROMISES	SCRIPTURE REFERENCES
The faithful and obedient	
• Will be lifted up at the last day.	5:35; 9:14; 17:8; 27:18; 75:16, 22
• Will be given the kingdom.	6:13; 10:55; 35:27; 38:9, 15; 50:35; 62:9; 78:18; 82:24
• Will have the Lord's Church established among them.	10:53
• Will not have the gates of hell prevail against them.	10:69; 17:8; 18:5; 21:6; 33:13; 98:22
• Will have power to become the sons of God.	11:30; 39:4; 42:52
• Will inherit eternal life and all the Father has.	14:7; 20:25–28; 39:22; 50:5; 56:20; 59:2, 23; 66:12; 72:4; 78:22; 81:6; 84:38; 88:26; 132:19
• Will have the Lord shake the heavens for their good, and Satan will tremble.	21:6; 35:24
• Will abide the day of his coming.	27:15; 35:21; 61:39; 64:23
• Will be with him in eternal worlds.	27:18; 39:22
• Will have the Lord to be with them until he comes/the end.	31:13; 34:11; 75:11–14; 100:12; 105:41; 108:8
• Will not be overcome but will overcome all things.	38:9; 50:35; 75:16, 22; 76:60
• Will not be confounded.	35:25; 49:27; 84:116; 100:5
• Will be his disciples.	41:5; 52:40; 84:91
• Will die unto the Lord, and death will be sweet.	42:44, 46
• Will be saved.	42:60; 100:14, 17
• Will be endowed with power.	38:32; 43:16
• Will receive increase.	43:10; 52:13, 34; 71:6; 75:5; 78:19; 79:3; 97:9
• Will be accepted of God.	52:15; 97:8
• Will be made strong.	52:17; 66:8
• Will have their desires granted unto them according to their faith.	10:47, 52
• Will find peace and rest to their souls.	54:10; 59:23
• Will be blessed after tribulation.	58:3–4; 98:3; 101:35; 112:13; 121:7–8; 122:7
• Will receive temporal blessings.	59:16–19; 64:34; 111:5
• Will not perish by water.	61:6

PROMISES	SCRIPTURE REFERENCES
• Will be blessed with a multiplicity of blessings for their faithfulness.	82:10; 92:2; 104:2, 31–33, 38, 42, 46
• Will be preserved, perfected, and sanctified by the law.	88:34
• Will have all things work together for their good.	90:24; 100:14–15
• Will receive the full record of John the Baptist.	93:18
• Will receive of his fulness, grace for grace.	93:20, 27

Lord's servants

PROMISES	SCRIPTURE REFERENCES
• Will be the means of doing much good, help many understand the error of their ways, and be blessed for bringing forth this work.	6:8–9, 11; 11:8–9; 18:44–45
• Will have the Lord with them, on their right hand and their left, in their midst, before their face; the Spirit in their hearts and angels round about them.	32:3; 49:27; 84:88
• Will have their mouths filled, be given what to say, and not be confounded.	33:8–10; 49:27; 84:85; 93:52; 100:5–6
• Will convert many by their preaching.	44:4
• Will have power over their enemies.	71:7–10; cf. 44:5; 136:17
• Will speak scripture: the will, mind, word of the Lord, power of God unto salvation, when moved upon by the Holy Ghost.	68:3–5
• Will be filled with joy despite rejection and will judge those who reject them.	75:20–21
• Will be counted as sons of Moses and Aaron, seed of Abraham, church and kingdom, and elect of God.	84:33–34
• Will have physical needs provided; those who sustain them will be blessed.	84:80, 89–90
• Will have the Holy Ghost bear record of their words.	100:7–8
• Will be united; righteous quorums will be fruitful in the knowledge of the Lord.	107:27, 30–31
• Will have effectual door opened if they are faithful and hearken to the voice of his Spirit.	112:19, 21–22; 118:3
• Will have families provided for by the Lord.	118:3
• Will not be accountable when hindered by their enemies from keeping the Lord's commandments; offering will be accepted.	124:49, 51; 84:3–5, 31–32
• Will have actions justified by the Lord when they act according to his word and law.	132:59

To those who sustain the prophet

PROMISES	SCRIPTURE REFERENCES
• The Lord will overcome the adversary and cause the heavens to shake for their good.	21:5–6
• They will be blessed temporally and spiritually and receive the mysteries of the kingdom.	24:3–4, 6; 43:12–14
• They can faithfully follow the prophet Joseph Smith, knowing if he fails he will be replaced.	35:18
• They will not be moved out of their place if they listen to the voice of the Lord and his servants.	124:45

PROMISES	SCRIPTURE REFERENCES
Obedient to first principles	
• Receive the Holy Ghost.	33:15; 35:6; 39:23; 49:12–14; 84:64
• Receive remission of sins.	55:1
• Be saved through belief and baptism; unbelievers will be damned.	68:9; 84:74; 112:29
Mercy	
• The Lord will be merciful unto the weak; the weak will be made strong.	50:16; 135:5
• The Lord will have compassion and mercy.	64:2–3; 70:18
• The Lord shows mercy to the meek.	97:2
• The Lord will be merciful to those who receive his servants.	99:2–3
Zion, or the New Jerusalem	
• Zion is a land of promise for current and future generations when sought with full purpose of heart.	38:19–20
• Faithful Saints will assemble and rejoice in Missouri, the land of their inheritance.	52:42
• The land can only be obtained by shedding of blood if not purchased with money; if by blood, Saints will be scourged and few will receive an inheritance.	58:51–53; 63:29–31
• The faithful who come to Zion will inherit the earth; they will receive a crown in the mansions of the Father, good things of the earth, commandments, and revelations in their time.	59:1–4
• Those who send treasures to Zion receive an inheritance in this world and a reward in the world to come.	63:48
• The Lord will not hold any guilty who go to Zion from Ohio with an open heart after five years from September 1831.	64:21–22
• The bishop and counselors will be replaced if they are not faithful.	64:40
• Zion will prosper, spread, become glorious, great and terrible, and escape judgment if they are obedient.	97:18–19, 25, 27–28
• After much tribulation, Saints will live there, eat the fruit thereof, prevail against the world, be established and restored if they are faithful.	101:100–101; 103:5–8, 11–14
• Obedient Saints will receive the people's favor; they will rest in peace and safety while the Saints seek redress and the army of the Lord gathers strength and numbers.	105:23–27
• The Saints will be held guiltless in recovering land by force after the land is purchased.	105:29–30
• If they follow counsel, the Saints will have power to redeem Zion "after many days."	105:37
• The Lord will deal mercifully with Zion.	111:6
• The inhabitants of Zion will observe the law of tithing or "it shall not be a land of Zion" unto them.	119:5–6
Ohio	
• The Saints are commanded to go to Ohio, where they will be given the law, an endowment of power, and blessings not known among men.	38:32; 39:15

PROMISES	SCRIPTURE REFERENCES
• The Lord's servants will go forth to all nations from Ohio.	38:33; 39:15

Men who provide for their families

• Those unable to serve missions in order to provide for their families will in nowise lose their crown.	75:28

Physical health

• Bodies will be renewed if callings are magnified.	84:33
• Health, endurance, and the destroying angel will pass by if obedient to the Word of Wisdom.	89:18, 20–21

Temple/Temples

• If undefiled, the Lord's glory and presence will be there; he will appear to his servants and speak to them in his own voice.	94:8–9; 97:15–17; 110:7–8
• If obedient, the Saints will have power to build it.	95:11
• If the Saints labor with their might, the Lord will consecrate the site of the Nauvoo Temple and it will be made holy.	124:44
• If the Saints persist in laboring on the Nauvoo temple despite persecution, they will receive a reward in heaven.	127:4

Those who lay down their life for Christ's cause

• Will receive eternal life.	98:13
• Will be crowned and partake of his glory.	101:15, 35
• Will be saved.	124:54

Patience with injustice

• If Saints bear injustice patiently, they will be rewarded; if they bear it twice, rewarded 100 fold; if they bear it three times, their reward will be doubled to them 4 fold; if they spare enemies a fourth time, they will be rewarded for their righteousness, as will their children to the fourth generation.	98:23–30, 34–37
• If Saints raise the standard of peace, the Lord will fight their battles and avenge them of their enemies to the fourth generation.	98:34, 44–48; 103:25–26; 105:14; 127:3

Government officials

• The Lord will curse them if they reject the testimonies of his servants, withhold help from the Saints, and do not repent.	101:86–92; 124:8; 136:34–35
• The Lord's will concerning them will be given by the Holy Ghost.	124:5
• The Lord will soften the hearts of many.	124:9

For being chaste, virtuous, and charitable

• Confidence will wax strong in the presence of God.	121:45
• Doctrine of the priesthood will distill upon the soul.	121:45
• The Holy Ghost will be a constant companion.	121:46
• Priesthood power and dominion will flow without compulsory means forever.	121:46

PROMISES	SCRIPTURE REFERENCES

Nauvoo/Nauvoo House

- The Nauvoo House will be a healthful, holy place where the Lord can dwell if it is not polluted. — 124:24
- Joseph and his seed will have place in the Nauvoo House forever. — 124:56–57, 59
- Misappropriation of stock in the Nauvoo House will result in offenders being accursed. — 124:71
- The sickness of the land will redound to the glory of those who love and obey the Lord. — 124:86–87

Intelligence

- Intelligence gained in life will provide advantage in the Resurrection. — 130:18–19

Eternal covenants, including marriage

- Covenants not entered into according to the Lord's laws will end at death. — 132:7, 13–18
- Those who marry in the temple and keep covenants will come forth in first resurrection, inherit all things, have their names written in the Lamb's book of life, will be gods and enter into exaltation, and will be forgiven of their sins if they repent (except the unpardonable sin). — 132:19–23, 26
- Those who are of Abraham will receive the promises made to him if they do the works of Abraham and the Father. — 132:30–33
- The Lord will reveal more pertaining to the law of plural marriage. — 132:66 (cf. OD 1)

Judgment and accountability

- Those who die without a knowledge of the gospel, who would have received it, will be exalted. — 137:7–8
- Children who die before the age of accountability will be saved. — 137:10

Promises to individuals

- Joseph Smith
  - He will lose the gift to translate and become as other men if he is not "aware." — 3:9–11
  - This generation will have the Lord's word through him. — 5:10
  - He will receive a multiplicity of blessings and eternal life if obedient. — 5:22; 104:46
  - He will never lose priesthood keys if faithful. — 35:17–18; 64:5; 90:3; cf. 6:25–28
  - He will mourn no longer for Zion but will rejoice for remission of his sins and for his blessings. — 21:8
  - He will be supported by the Colesville Saints. — 24:3
  - He will not have strength in temporal labors but will be able to magnify his calling. — 24:8–9
  - The Lord will smite all his enemies. — 24:16–17; 127:2
  - If he fails, another will be placed in his stead. — 35:18; 43:4
  - He will have the gift of prophecy. — 35:23
  - Personal money spent will be repaid. — 56:12–13
  - He will have power to discern who should go to Zion. — 63:41

PROMISES	SCRIPTURE REFERENCES
○ He will know by the Spirit who are chosen.	105:36
○ The Lord will be with him and sanctify him.	115:19; 122:9; 132:49
○ He will receive the blessings of Abraham.	124:58; 132:31
○ If he lives to the age of eighty-five, he will "see the face of the Son of Man."	130:15
○ If he rejects the covenant of plural marriage, he will not be permitted to enter the Lord's glory.	132:3–6
○ He will be given the sealing power.	132:46–48
○ Exaltation will be sealed upon him.	132:49
○ He will be forgiven of all his sins and a way for his escape will be prepared.	132:50
○ He will be blessed and multiplied an hundredfold with fathers, mothers, brothers, sisters, houses, lands, wives, children, and crowns of eternal lives.	132:55
• Martin Harris	
○ He will see and bear testimony as one of the Three Witnesses.	5:24–25, 28
○ He will be destroyed, along with his property, unless he gives a portion of it for the publication of the Book of Mormon; commanded to pray vocally and in secret and to share gospel with all.	19:28–38
○ He and his posterity will receive a multiplicity of blessings, if he is faithful.	104:25
• Oliver Cowdery	
○ He will be given the key to translate ancient records, along with Joseph Smith.	6:25–28; 8:1, 11; 9:2
○ The Holy Ghost will deliver him from his enemies who otherwise would kill him and destroy his soul.	8:4
○ He will be given the gift of Aaron.	8:6–8
○ Not a hair of his head will be lost and he will be lifted up at the last day if he is faithful.	9:14
○ He will be given strength such as is not known to man.	24:12
○ The Lord will smite his enemies.	24:16–17
○ He will be heard by the Church as he teaches by the Spirit concerning revelations and commandments given by the Lord.	28:1
○ The Lord will make known concerning him by the mouth of Joseph Smith.	60:17
• Hyrum Smith	
○ He will be given the gift of the Spirit if he asks in faith.	11:10
○ He will act in concert with Joseph as a prophet, seer, and revelator; be given the sealing power and keys of patriarchal blessings; and be crowned with the blessings that were formerly Oliver Cowdery's; his name will be had in honorable remembrance from generation to generation.	124:92–96
• David Whitmer	
○ He will receive the Holy Ghost and be one of the Three Witnesses.	14:8

Promises	Scripture References
○ He will receive spiritual and temporal blessings—a great reward if he will assist in the work.	14:11
• Three Witnesses	
○ They will view sacred objects if they have faith.	17:1–2
○ They will know who to call as the Twelve by their desires and works.	18:37–38
• Emma Smith	
○ The Lord will preserve her life, and she will have an inheritance in Zion if she is faithful and virtuous.	25:2
○ She will have a crown of righteousness, based on obedience; otherwise she cannot come where God is.	25:15
○ She will be destroyed if she will not abide the covenant of plural marriage.	132:54
○ If she forgives Joseph, she will be forgiven, and the Lord will bless her, multiply her, and make her heart to rejoice.	132:56
• Thomas B. Marsh	
○ His family will join the Church.	31:2
○ His tongue will be loosed; he will preach Joseph Smith's revelations; people will receive him; with the Prophet, he will establish a church.	31:3–4, 7–8
○ He will be laden with sheaves; his family will live and a place will be prepared for them.	31:5–6
○ He will be a physician to the Church but not to the world.	31:10
○ He will send the Lord's words to the ends of the earth; his path lies in the mountains and among many nations; many will repent because of his preaching.	112:4–9
• Orson Pratt	
○ He will prophesy by the power of the Holy Ghost.	34:10
• Sidney Rigdon	
○ He will be blessed and will do great things.	35:4
○ The Lord will make known concerning him by the mouth of Joseph Smith.	60:17
○ He will receive a multiplicity of blessings if he is humble.	104:23
○ If he will offer an acceptable offering and remain with the Lord's people , he will be healed, be a spokesman, and it shall be well with him.	124:104, 108–10
• James Covill	
○ He will receive the Spirit and a great blessing; preach the gospel and be sent to recover the house of Israel; have great faith and power; and the Lord will be with him and will go before his face, if he accepts the fulness of the gospel.	39:10–12
• John Whitmer	
○ The Comforter will enable him to write the history of the Church if he is faithful.	47:3–4

PROMISES	SCRIPTURE REFERENCES

- Leman Copley
  - He will be blessed if he reasons with the Shaking Quakers according to the teachings of the Lord's servants. — 49:1, 4

- William W. Phelps
  - He will be ordained an elder, preach the gospel, give Holy Ghost to others, and help Oliver Cowdery write and print books. — 55:2–4

- Ezra Thayre
  - He will be appointed to go to Missouri, if faithful; if not, he will be cut off. — 56:8–11

- Newel K. Whitney
  - If he trusts in the Lord, he will not be confounded and a hair of his head will not go unnoticed. — 84:116
  - He will receive a multiplicity of blessings if he is faithful. — 104:42
  - It will not be well with him if he tarries in Kirtland. — 117:1–3

- John Johnson
  - He will receive eternal life if he is obedient. — 96:6
  - He will be given a multiplicity of blessings if he is faithful. — 104:35, 38

- Parley P. Pratt
  - If faithful, he will preside over the school in Zion until the Lord gives him other commandments; he will receive a multiplicity of blessings in expounding scripture and mysteries for edification of the school. — 97:4–5

- Warren Cowdery
  - If humble, the Lord will have mercy, lift him up, give him grace and assurance, make him a light to the Church, and prepare him a crown. — 106:7–8

- Lyman Sherman
  - He will receive great blessings, ordination, and the right to preach the gospel and will be remembered with the first elders. — 108:3–6

- William Marks
  - It will not be well with him if he tarries in Kirtland. — 117:1–3

- Oliver Granger
  - His name will be had in sacred remembrance from generation to generation, forever and ever; the blessings of the people will be upon him forever and ever. — 117:12–15

- Robert Thompson, John C. Bennett, Lyman Wight, Vinson Knight, Isaac Galland, William Law, Amos Davies, Robert Foster
  - They will be given great blessings according to their faithfulness. — 124:13–19, 75–76, 78–79, 86–87, 90, 97–100, 113, 118

RB

Appendix E

Definitions from
Webster's 1828 American Dictionary
of the English Language

Behold, I am God and have spoken it; these commandments are of me,
and were given unto my servants in their weakness, after the manner
of their language, that they might come to understanding.

—*Doctrine & Covenants 1:24*

Abbreviations

a.	stands	for	adjective.
adv.	"	"	adverb.
def.	"	"	definition.
defs.	"	"	definitions.
n.	"	"	or name or noun.
obs.	"	"	obsolete.
pp.	"	"	participle passive.
ppr.	"	"	participle of the present tense.
prep.	"	"	preposition.
pret.	"	"	preterit tense.
v.i.	"	"	verb intransitive.
v.t.	"	"	verb transitive.

The number associated with each definition coincides with that found in Webster's 1828 *American Dictionary of the English Language.*

Definitions

Abase, *v.t.* [as in 101:42; 112:3; 124:114] 2. To cast down; to reduce low; to depress; to humble; to degrade; applied to the passions, rank, office, and condition in life.

Abridgment, *n.* [as in 10:44] An epitome; a compendium, or summary of a book.

Affrighted, *pp.* [as in 101:51] Suddenly alarmed with fear; terrified.

Amen, [as in 1:39; 121:37; 138:60] As a *verb,* it signifies to confirm, establish, verify; to trust, or give confidence; as a *noun,* truth, firmness, trust, confidence; as an *adjective,* firm, stable. In English, after the oriental manner, it is used at the beginning, but more generally at the end of declarations and prayers, in the sense of, *be it firm, be it established.*

Amenable, *a.* [as in 134:4] 2. Liable to answer; responsible; answerable; liable to be called to account.

Antiquit[ies], *n.* [as in 124:26] 5. The remains of ancient times. In this sense it is usually or always plural. *Antiquities* comprehend all the remains of ancient times; all the monuments, coins, inscriptions, edifices, history and fragments of literature, offices, habiliments, weapons, manners, ceremonies; in short, whatever respects any of the ancient nations of the earth.

Appendage, *n.* [as in 84:29–30; 107:5, 14] Something added to a principal or greater thing, though not necessary to it, as a portico to a house.

Avail[eth], *v.t.* [as in 22:2] 2. To assist or profit; to effect the object, or bring to a succesful issue.

Avails, *n. plu.* [as in 104:64–65] Profits or proceeds.

Avenge, *v.t.* [as in 87:7; 98:37] 1. To take satisfaction for an injury by punishing the injuring party; to vindicate by inflicting pain or evil on the wrong doer. 3. To revenge. To *avenge* and *revenge,* radically, are synonymous. But modern usage makes a valuable distinction in the use of these words, restricting *avenge* to just punishment and *revenge* to the infliction of pain or evil, maliciously, in an illegal manner.

Behoov[eth], *v.t.* [as in 21:10; 61:9; 124:49] To be necessary for; to be fit for; to be meet for, with respect to necessity, duty, or convenience.

Benighted, *pp.* [as in 121:4] Involved in darkness, physical or moral; overtaken by the night.

Bespeak[eth], *v.t.* [as in 60:4] 4. To betoken; to show; to indicate by external marks or appearances.

Betimes, *adv.* [as in 121:43] Seasonably; in good season or time; before it is late.

Box, *n.* [def. 6 of "box" refers to "box-tree," as in 124:26] 6. a tree or shrub, constituting the genus *buxus,* used for bordering flower-beds.

Breastwork, *n.* [as in 110:2] In *fortification,* a work thrown up for defense; a parapet ["Literally, a wall or rampart to the breast or breast high," s.v. "parapet"].

Buckler, *n.* [as in 35:14] A kind of shield, or piece of defensive armor, anciently used in war.

Calamity, *n.* [as in 1:17; 45:50; 109:46; 136:35] Any great misfortune, or cause of misery; generally applied to events or disasters which produce extensive evils, as loss of crops, earthquakes, conflagrations, defeat of armies, and the like. But it is applied also to the misfortunes which bring great distress upon individuals.

Chaff, *n.* [as in 52:12] 1. The husk, or dry calyx of corn, and grasses. In common language, the word is applied to the husks when separated from the corn by thrashing, riddling or winnowing. 2. Refuse; worthless matter; especially that which is light, and apt to be driven by the wind. In *scripture,* false doctrines, fruitless designs, hypocrites and ungodly men are compared to chaff.

Chariot[s], *n.* [as in 62:7] A half coach; a carriage with four wheels and one seat behind, used for convenience and pleasure.

Cleave, *v.i.* [def. 1 as in 25:13; 98:11; def. 3 as in 11:19; 42:22] 1. To stick; to adhere; to hold to. 3. To unite or be united closely in interest or affection; to adhere with strong attachment.

Cleave, *v.i.* [as in 45:48] To part; to open; to crack; to separate, as parts of cohering bodies.

Concatenation, *n.* [as in 123:5] A series of links united; a successive series or order of things connected or depending on each other.

Condemnation, *n.* [def. 1 as in 5:18; 10:23; def. 3 as in 93:31] 1. The act of condemning; the judicial act of declaring one guilty, and dooming him to punishment. 3. The cause or reason of a sentence of condemnation.

Consumption, *n.* [as in 87:6] 1. The act of consuming; waste; destruction by burning, eating, devouring, scattering, dissipation, slow decay, or by passing away, as time. 2. The state of being wasted, or diminished.

Contrite, *a.* [as in 20:37; 21:9] *Literally,* worn or bruised. Hence, broken-hearted for sin; deeply affected with grief and sorrow for having offended God; humble; penitent.

Corner-stone, *n.* [spelled "cornerstone" as in 124:2, 23, 60, 131] The stone which lies at the corner of two walls, and unites them; the principal stone, and especially the stone which forms the corner of the foundation of an edifice.

Creed[s], *n.* [as in 123:7] 1. A brief summary of the articles of Christian faith; a symbol. 2. That which is believed; any system of principles which are believed or professed.

Cumber[ed], *v.t.* [as in 66:10] 1. To load, or crowd. 2. To check, stop or retard, as by a load or weight; to make motion difficult; to obstruct. 4. To trouble; to be troublesome to; to cause trouble or obstruction in, as any thing useless. Thus, brambles *cumber* a garden or field.

Deign, *v.i.* [as in 38:18; 124:41] To think worthy; to vouchsafe; to condescend.

Devotion[s], *n.* [def. 1 as in 24:7; 26:1; defs. 2, 3, 5 as in 134:4; defs. 3, 4, 5 as in 59:10] 1. The state of being dedicated, consecrated, or solemnly set apart for a particular purpose. 2. A solemn attention to the Supreme Being in worship; a yielding of the heart and affections to God, with reverence, faith and piety, in religious duties, particularly in prayer and meditation; devoutness. 3. External worship; acts of religion; performance of religious duties. 4. Prayer to the Supreme Being. 5. An act of reverence, respect or ceremony.

Diabolical, *a.* [as in 123:5] Devilish; pertaining to the devil; hence, extremely malicious; impious; atrocious; nefarious; outrageously wicked; partaking of any quality ascribed to the devil.

Diligence, *n.* [as in 4:6; 21:7] 1. Steady application in business of any kind; constant effort to accomplish what is undertaken; exertion of body or mind without unnecessary delay or sloth; due attention; industry; assiduity. 2. Care; heed; heedfulness.

Divers, *a.* [as in 45:33; 128:21] 1. Different; various. 2. Several; sundry; more than one, but not a great number.

Dog[s], *n. To give* or *throw to the dogs* [as in 41:6], is to throw away, as useless.

Dominion, *n.* [defs. 1, 2 as in 76:95; 109:77; def. 2 as in 121:37; def. 3 as in 1:35; 76:111; 82:5; 121:4, 46; 132:19] 1. Sovereign or supreme authority; the power of governing and controlling. 2. Power to direct, control, use and dispose of at pleasure; right of possession and use without being accountable. 3. Territory under a government; region; country; district governed, or within the limits of the authority of a prince or state.

Effectual, *a.* [as in 100:3; 112:19] Producing an effect, or the effect desired or intended; or having adequate power or force to produce the effect.

Emblem[s], *n.* [as in 20:40] 4. That which represents another thing in its predominant qualities.

Enjoined, *pp.* [as in 123:6] Ordered; directed; admonished with authority; commanded.

Enmity, *n.* [as in 101:26] 1. The quality of being an enemy; the opposite of friendship; ill will; hatred; unfriendly dispositions; malevolence. 2. A state of opposition.

Escutcheon, *n.* [as in 135:7] The shield on which a coat of arms is represented; the shield of a family; the picture of ensigns armorial.

Essaying, *ppr.* [as in 124:85; 125:2] Trying; making an effort; attempting.

Exhort, *v.t.* [as in 19:37; 20:42; 25:7] 1. To incite by words or advice; to animate or urge by arguments to a good deed or to any laudable conduct or course of action. 2. To advise; to warn; to caution. 3. To incite or stimulate to exertion.

Exigency, *n.* [as in 134:11] 2. Pressing necessity; distress; any case which demands immediate action, supply or remedy.

Expound, *v.t.* [as in 20:42; 24:9] To explain; to lay open the meaning; to clear of obscurity; to interpret.

Extortion, *n.* [as in 59:20] The act of extorting; the act or practice of wresting any thing from a person by force, duress, menaces, authority, or by any undue exercise of power; illegal exaction; illegal compulsion to pay money, or to do some other act. *Extortion* is an offense punishable at common law. 2. Force or illegal compulsion by which any thing is taken from a person.

Feigned, *pp.* [as in 104:4, 52] Invented; devised; imagined; assumed.

Felicity, *n.* [as in 77:3] 1. Happiness, or rather great happiness; blessedness; blissfulness; appropriately, the joys of heaven. 2. Prosperity; blessing; enjoyment of good.

Fellowship, *n.* [as in 83:2–3; 134:10; 88:133; 104:75] 1. Companionship; society; consort; mutual association of persons on equal and friendly terms; familiar intercourse. 2. Association; confederacy; combination. 3. Partnership; joint interest. 4. Company; a state of being together. 7. Communion; intimate familiarity.

Fetter[s], *n.* [as in 123:8] 1. A chain for the feet; a chain by which an animal is confined by the foot, either made fast or fixed, as a prisoner, or impeded in motion and hindered from leaping, as a horse whose fore and hind feet are confined by a chain. 2. Any thing that confines or restrains from motion.

Folly, *n.* [as in 45:49; 63:15; 136:19; 35:7; 124:116] 1. Weakness of intellect; imbecility of mind; want of understanding. 3. An absurd act which is highly sinful; any conduct contrary to the laws of God or man; sin; scandalous crimes; that which violates moral precepts and dishonors the offender.

Garnish, *v.t.* [as in 121:45] 1. To adorn; to decorate with appendages; to set off. 3. To furnish; to supply.

Guile, *n.* [as in 41:11; 121:42; 124:20, 97] Craft; cunning; artifice; duplicity; deceit; *usually in a bad sense.*

Hearken, *v.i.* [as in 1:1; 61:1; 81:1; 103:4–5, 8] 1. To listen; to lend the ear; to attend to what is uttered, with eagerness or curiosity. 2. To attend; to regard; to give heed to what is uttered; to observe or obey. 3. To listen; to attend; to grant or comply with.

Heed, *v.t.* [as in 101:87–89] To mind; to regard with care; to take notice of; to attend to; to observe.

Heed, *n.* [def. 2 as in 20:33–34; def. 3 as in 1:14] 2. Caution; care; watch for danger; notice; circumspection; usually preceded by *take.* 3. Notice; observation; regard; attention; often preceded by *give.*

Herb, *n.* [as in 42:43; 59:17; 89:8, 10–11] 1. A plant or vegetable with a soft or succulent stalk or stem, which dies to the root every year, and is thus distinguished from a tree and a shrub, which have ligneous or hard woody stems. 2. In *the Linnean botany,* that part of a vegetable which springs from the root and is terminated by the fructification, including the stem or stalk, the leaves, the fulcra or props, and the hibernacle. The word *herb* comprehends all the grasses, and numerous plants used for culinary purposes.

Heritage, *n.* [as in 58:13, 17; 105:15] 1. Inheritance; an estate that passes from an ancestor to an heir by descent or course of law; that which is inherited. 2. In *Scripture,* the saints or people of God are called his *heritage,* as being claimed by him, and the objects of his special care.

High-minded, *a.* [as in 90:17; defs. 1, 2 as in 124:3] 1. Proud; arrogant. 2. Having honorable pride; magnanimous; opposed to *mean.*

Hoar-frost, *n.* [spelled "hoar frost" as in 121:11] The white particles of ice formed by the congelation of dew or watery vapors.

Hosanna, *n.* [as in 19:37; 109:79; 124:101] An exclamation of praise to God, or an invocation of blessings. In the Hebrew ceremonies, it was a prayer rehearsed on the several days of the feast

of tabernacles, in which this word was often repeated.

Idolatry, *n.* [as in 52:39] 1. The worship of idols, images, or any thing made by hands, or which is not God. Idolatry is of two kinds; the worship of images, statues, pictures, &c. made by hands; and the worship of the heavenly bodies, the sun, moon and stars, or of demons, angels, men and animals. 2. Excessive attachment or veneration for any thing, or that which borders on adoration.

Immutable, *a.* [as in 98:3; 104:2] Unchangeable; invariable; unalterable; not capable or susceptible of change.

Imposition[s], *n.* [as in 123:5] 5. Constraint; oppression; burden. 6. Deception; imposture.

Inalienable, *a.* [as in 134:5] Unalienable; that cannot be legally or justly alienated or transferred to another.

Inculcate, *v.t.* [as in OD 1] To impress by frequent admonitions; to teach and enforce by frequent repetitions; to urge on the mind. Our Savior *inculcates* on his followers humility and forgiveness of injuries.

Integrity, *n.* [as in 124:15, 20] 2. The entire, unimpaired state of any thing, particularly of the mind; moral soundness or purity; incorruptness; uprightness; honesty. *Integrity* comprehends the whole moral character, but has a special reference to uprightness in mutual dealings, transfers of property, and agencies for others.

Interpolation[s], *n.* [as in 91:2] 1. The act of foisting a word or passage into a manuscript or book. 2. A spurious word or passage inserted in the genuine writings of an author.

Inviolate, *a.* [as in 134:2] Unhurt; uninjured; unprofaned; unpolluted; unbroken.

Laden, *pp.* [as in 31:5; 33:9; 75:5] Loaded; charged with a burden or freight.

Lightminded, *a.* [appears as "light-mindedness" as in 88:121] Unsettled; unsteady; volatile; not considerate.

Magnify, *v.t.* [def. 1 as in 24:3, 9; 66:11; 84:33; defs. 2, 3 as in 132:64] 1. To make great or greater; to increase the apparent dimensions of a body. A convex lens *magnifies* the bulk of a body to the eye. 2. To make great in representation; to extol; to exalt in description or praise.

3. To extol; to exalt; to elevate; to raise in estimation.

Mantle, *n.* [as in 88:125] 1. A kind of cloke or loose garment to be worn over other garments. 2. A cover.

Measure, *n.* [def. 3 as in 49:17; 58:61; 103:3; def. 4 as in 103:3; defs. 5, 9 as in 1:10 ; def. 15 as in 88:19, 25] 3. A limited or definite quantity. 4. Determined extent or length; limit. 5. A rule by which any thing is adjusted or proportioned. 9. Portion allotted; extent of ability 15. Means to an end; an act, step or proceeding towards the accomplishment of an object. *Without measure,* [as in 1:9; 101:11; 103:2; 109:45] without limits; very largely or copiously.

Memorial, *n.* [as in 112:1; 124:39] That which preserves the memory of something; any thing that serves to keep in memory. A monument is a *memorial* of a deceased person, or of an event. The Lord's supper is a *memorial* of the death and sufferings of Christ.

Mete, *v.t.* [as in 84:85; 98:24; 127:3] To measure; to ascertain quantity, dimensions or capacity by any rule or standard.

Might, *n. pret.* of *may,* [as in 1:18, 95:7; 101:19; def. 2 as in 101:49] 2. It sometimes denotes *was possible,* implying ignorance of the fact in the speaker.

Might, *n.* [defs. 1, 5, 6, 7 as in 4:2, 4; 84:102; defs. 5, 8 as in 76:95; 109:77] 1. Strength; force; power; primarily and chiefly, bodily strength or physical power. 5. Ability; strength or application of means. 6. Strength or force of purpose. 7. Strength of affection. 8. Strength of light; splendor; effulgence.

Millstone, *n.* [as in 121:22] A stone used for grinding grain.

Minister, *n.* [as in 84:111; 107:39, 97; 109:35; 124:137] 1. Properly, a chief servant; hence, an agent appointed to transact or manage business under the authority of another; *in which sense, it is a word of very extensive application.*

Minister, *v.i.* [as in 7:6–7; 68:14; 132:16] 1. To attend and serve; to perform service in any office, sacred or secular. 2. To afford supplies; to give things needful; to supply the means of relief; to relieve.

Ministering, *ppr.* [as in 13:1; 132:16] 1. Attending and serving as a subordinate agent; serving under superior authority. 2. Affording aid or supplies; administering things needful.

Mocked, *pp.* [as in 63:58] Imitated or mimicked in derision; laughed at; ridiculed; defeated; illuded.

Mote, *n.* [as in 29:25] A small particle; any thing proverbially small; a spot.

Municipal, *a.* [appears as "municipals" *n.* in 124:39] A person who enjoys the rights of a free citizen. 1. Pertaining to a corporation or city. 2. Pertaining to a state, kingdom or nation.

Murmur, *v.i.* [as in 9:6; 25:4] 2. To grumble; to complain; to utter complaints in a low, half articulated voice; to utter sullen discontent.

Naught, *n.* [as in 3:1, 4, 7, 13; 19:21; 76:9; 109:30] Nothing. *To set at naught,* to slight, disregard or despise.

Nefarious, *a.* [as in 123:5] Wicked in the extreme; abominable; atrociously sinful or villainous; detestably vile.

Nowise, *adv.* [as in 33:12; 58:28; 132:27] Not in any manner or degree.

Oath[s], *n.* [as in 84:39–40; 124:47; 132:7] A solemn affirmation or declaration. . . . If the declaration is false, or if the declaration is a promise, the person invokes the vengeance of God if he should fail to fulfill it. A false oath is called perjury.

Oblation[s], *n.* [as in 59:12] Any thing offered or presented in worship or sacred service; an offering; a sacrifice.

Obviate, *v.t.* [as in 128:3] Properly, to meet in the way; to oppose; hence, to prevent by interception, or to remove at the beginning or in the outset.

Pavilion, *n.* [as in 121:1, 4] A tent; a temporary movable habitation.

Perverse, *a.* [as in 33:2; 34:6] 1. Literally, turned aside; hence, distorted from the right. 2. Obstinate in the wrong; disposed to be contrary; stubborn; untractable.

Prevail, *v.i.* [def. 1 as in 6:34; 10:69; 109:26; def. 3 as in 38:11; defs. 1, 6 as in 103:7] 1. To overcome; to gain the victory or superiority; to gain the advantage. With *over* or *against.* 3. To be predominant; to extend over with force or effect. 6. To succeed.

Priestcraft[s], *n*. [as in 33:4] The stratagems and frauds of priests; fraud or imposition in religious concerns; management of selfish and ambitious priests to gain wealth and power, or to impose on the credulity of others.

Principalit[ies], *n*. [as in 121:29; 128:23; 132:13, 19] 1. Sovereignty; supreme power. 3. The territory of a prince; or the country which gives title to a prince.

Promulgate, *v.t.* [as in 118:4] To publish; to make known by open declaration; as, to *promulgate* the secrets of a council. It is particularly applied to the publication of laws and the gospel. The moral law was *promulgated* at mount Sinai. The apostles *promulgated* the gospel. Edicts, laws and orders are *promulgated* by circular letters, or through the medium of the public prints.

Proscribe, *v.t.* [as in 89, headnote; 134:7, 9] 5. To interdict; as, to *proscribe* the use of ardent spirits. **Proscribed**, *pp*. Doomed to destruction; denounced as dangerous, or as unworthy of reception; condemned; banished.

Prudent, *a*. [as in 76:9; 128:18] 1. Cautious; circumspect; practically wise; careful of the consequences of enterprises, measures or actions; cautious not to act when the end is of doubtful utility, or probably impracticable. 5. Wise; intelligent.

Quickened, *pp*. [as in 67:11; 88:26; 138:7, 29] Made alive; revived; vivified; reinvigorated. 3. Stimulated; incited.

Railing, *a*. [as in 50:33] Expressing reproach; insulting; as a *railing* accusation.

Rascality, *n*. [as in 123:5] 2. Mean trickishness or dishonesty; base fraud.

Rearward, *n*. [as in 49:27] 1. The last troop; the rear-guard. 2. The end; the tail; the train behind.

Recompense, *v.t.* [as in 1:10; 112:34] To compensate; to make return of an equivalent for any thing given, done or suffered.

Recompense, *n*. [def. 1 as in 56:19; 124:121; def. 2 as in 127:3] 1. An equivalent returned for any thing given, done or suffered; compensation; reward; amends. 2. Requital; return of evil or suffering or other equivalent; as a punishment.

Reconciliation, *n*. [as in 46:4] 1. The act of reconciling parties at variance; renewal of friendship after disagreement or enmity. 2. In *Scripture*, the means by which sinners are reconciled and brought into a state of favor with God, after natural estrangement or enmity; the atonement; expiation.

Redound, *v.i.* [as in 124:87] 2. To conduce in the consequence; to contribute; to result. 3. To proceed in the consequence or effect; to result.

Rend, *v.t.* [def. 2 as in 84:118; 133:40] 2. To separate or part with violence. *To rend the heavens*, to appear in majesty.

Reproachfully, *adv*. [as in 42:92] 1. In terms of reproach; opprobriously; scurrilously. 2. Shamefully; disgracefully; contemptuously.

Revile, *v.t.* [as in 31:9; 98:23, 25] To reproach; to treat with opprobrious and contemptuous language.

Rill[s], *n*. [as in 128:23] A small brook; a rivulet; a streamlet.

Sackcloth, *n*. [as in 133:69] Cloth of which sacks are made; coarse cloth. This word is chiefly used in Scripture to denote a cloth or garment worn in mourning, distress or mortification.

Sacrament[s], *n*. [as in 59:9, 12; 20:46, 58, 68; 46:4–5] 2. An oath; a ceremony producing an obligation. 3. An outward and visible sign of inward and spiritual grace; or more particularly, a solemn religious ceremony enjoined by Christ, the head of the christian church, to be observed by his followers, by which their special relation to him is created, or their obligations to him renewed and ratified. Thus baptism is called a *sacrament*, for by it persons are separated from the world, brought into Christ's visible church, and laid under particular obligations to obey his precepts. The eucharist or communion of the Lord's supper, is also a *sacrament*, for by commemorating the death and dying love of Christ, christians avow their special relation to him, and renew their obligations to be faithful to their divine Master. When we use *sacrament* without any qualifying word, we mean by it, 4. The eucharist or Lord's supper.

Sanctuary, *n*. [as in 88:137] 1. a sacred place; particularly among the Israelites, the most retired part of the temple at Jerusalem, called the *Holy of Holies*, in which was kept the ark of the covenant, and into which no person was permitted to enter except the high priest, and that only once a year to intercede for the people. The same name was given to the most sacred part of the tabernacle. 3. A house consecrated to the worship of God; a place where divine service is performed. 5. A place of protection; a sacred asylum. 6. Shelter; protection.

Scepter, *n.* [def. 1 as in 85:7; defs. 1, 2, 3 as in 106:6; 121:46;] 1. A staff or batoon borne by kings on solemn occasions, as a badge of authority. 2. The appropriate ensign of royalty; an ensign of higher antiquity than the crown. 3. Royal power or authority; as, to assume the *scepter*.

Scrip, *n.* [as in 24:18; 84:78, 86] A small bag; a wallet; a satchel.

Sectarian, *a.* [as in 130:3] Pertaining to a sect or to sects; as *sectarian* principles or prejudices. ["A body or number of persons united in tenets, chiefly in philosophy or religion, but constituting a distinct party by holding sentiments different from those of other men," s.v. "sect"].

Sedition, *n.* [as in 134:5, 7] A factious commotion of the people, or a tumultuous assembly of men rising in opposition to law or the administration of justice, and in disturbance of the public peace.

Sensual, *a.* [defs. 1, 4 as in 29:35; defs. 4, 5 as in 20:20] 1. Pertaining to the senses, as distinct from the mind or soul. 4. In *theology*, carnal; pertaining to the flesh or body, in opposition to the spirit; not spiritual or holy; evil. 5. Devoted to the gratification of sense; given to the indulgence of the appetites; lewd; luxurious.

Seraphic, *a.* [as in 38:1] 1. Pertaining to a seraph; angelic; sublime.

Seraph[s], *n.* [as in 109:79] An angel of the highest order.

Sharpness, *n.* [as in 15:2; 16:2; 121:43] 6. Severity of language; pungency; satirical sarcasm. 7. Acuteness of intellect; the power of nice discernment; quickness of understanding; ingenuity. 8. Quickness of sense or perception. 9. Keenness; severity.

Shod, [as in 27:16; 112:7] for *shoed,* pret. and pp. of *shoe.*

Sickle, *n.* [as in 4:4; 31:5] A reaping hook; a hooked instrument with teeth; used for cutting grain.

Similitude, *n.* [def. 1 as in 124:2; 138:13; def. 2 as in 128:13] 1. Likeness; resemblance; likeness in nature, qualities or appearance. 2.≈Comparison; simile.

Slothful, *a.* [as in 58:26; 101:50; 107:100] Inactive; sluggish; lazy; indolent; idle.

Sorcerer[s], *n.* [as in 63:17; 76:103] A conjurer; an enchanter; a magician.

Sovereign, *n.* [as in 134:3] 1. A supreme lord or ruler; one who possesses the highest authority without control. 2. A supreme magistrate; a king.

Statute[s], *n.* [as in 119:6; 124:39; 136:2] 1. An act of the legislature of a state that extends its binding force to all the citizens or subjects of that state, as distinguished from an act which extends only to an individual or company; an act of the legislature commanding or prohibiting something; a positive law. *Statutes* are distinguished from *common law.* The latter owes its binding force to the principles of justice, to long use and the consent of a nation. The former owe their binding force to a positive command or declaration of the supreme power. 2. A special act of the supreme power, of a private nature, or intended to operate only on an individual or company.

Stay, *v.i.* [as in 43:18; 58:46; 122:6;] To remain; to continue in a place; to abide for any indefinite time.

Stay, *v.t.* [def. 1 as in 56:17; 132:51; 133:26; defs. 1, 2 as in 1:5; 29:19; 38:22; 97:23; def. 3 as in 1:5; 133:26] 1. To stop; to hold from proceeding; to withhold; to restrain. 2. To delay; to obstruct; to hinder from proceeding. 3. To keep from departure.

Steadfast, *a.* [as in 31:9; 49:23; 84:61] 1. Fast fixed; firm; firmly fixed or established. 2. Constant; firm; resolute; not fickle or wavering.

Stiffnecked, *a.* [as in 5:8] Stubborn; inflexibly obstinate.

Straightway, *adv.* [as in 40:2; 76:47] Immediately; without loss of time; without delay.

Stubble, *n.* [as in 29:9; 64:24; 133:64] The stumps of wheat, rye, barley, oats or buckwheat, left in the ground; the part of the stalk left by the sythe or sickle.

Subdue, *v.t.* [defs. 1, 2, 3, 4 as in 19:2; 58:22; defs. 5, 7 as in 96:5; def. 8 as in 58:22; 76:61; 103:7] 1. To conquer by force or the exertion of superior power, and bring into permanent subjection; to reduce under dominion. 2. To oppress; to crush; to sink; to overpower so as to disable from further resistance. 3. To tame; to break by conquering a refractory temper or evil passions; to render submissive. 4. To conquer; to reduce to mildness. 5. To overcome by persuasion or other mild means. 7. To soften; to melt; to reduce to tenderness. 8. To overcome; to overpower and destroy the force of.

Succor, *v.t.* [as in 62:1; 81:5] Literally, to run to, or run to support; hence, to help or relieve when in difficulty, want or distress; to assist and deliver from suffering.

Sundry, *a.* [as in 76, 107, headnotes; 128:21] Several; divers; more than one or two.

Swine, *n.* [as in 41:6; 89:17] A hog; a quadruped of the genus Sus. . . . The fat or lard of this animal enters into various dishes in cookery. The swine is a heavy, stupid animal, and delights to wallow in the mire.

Tare[s], *n.* [as in 38:12; 86:1, 3, 6–7, headnote] A weed that grows among corn [grain].

Temperance, *n.* [as in 4:6; 6:19; 107:30] Moderation; particularly, habitual moderation in regard to the indulgence of the natural appetites and passions; restrained or moderate indulgence.

Tenet[s], *n.* [as in 19:31] Any opinion, principle, dogma or doctrine which a person believes or maintains as true.

Token, *n.* [as in 88:131, 133, 135; 104:75] A sign; something intended to represent or indicate another thing or an event. Thus the rainbow is a *token* of God's covenant established with Noah. The blood of the paschal lamb, sprinkled on the doors of the Hebrews, was a *token* to the destroying angel of God's will that he should pass by those houses.

Travail, *v.i.* [as in 84:101] 1. To labor with pain; to toil. 2. To suffer the pangs of childbirth; to

be in labor. **Travail**, *n.* [as in 136:35] 2. Labor in childbirth.

Trespass, *v.i.* [as in 46:4; 98:40–44, 47; 132:56] 2. To commit any offense or to do any act that injures or annoys another; to violate any rule of rectitude to the injury of another. 3. In *a moral sense*, to transgress voluntarily any divine law or command; to violate any known rule of duty. 4. To intrude; to go too far; to put to inconvenience by demand or importunity.

Trespass, *n.* [as in 64:9; 82:1; 98:40, 47–48; 132:56] 1. In *law*, violation of another's rights, not amounting to treason, felony, or misprision of either. 2. Any injury or offense done to another. 3. Any voluntary transgression of the moral law; any violation of a known rule of duty; sin.

Trifle, *v.i.* [as in 6:12; 8:10; 32:5] 1. To act or talk without seriousness, gravity, weight or dignity; to act or talk with levity. 2. To indulge in light amusements. *To trifle with*, to mock; to play the fool with; to treat without respect or seriousness. *To trifle with*, *To trifle away*, to spend in vanity, to waste to no good purpose.

Unfeigned, *a.* [as in 121:41] Not feigned; not counterfeit; not hypocritical; real; sincere.

Untoward, *a.* [as in 36:6, 109:41] Froward; perverse; refractory; not easily guided or taught.

Upbraid, *v.t.* [def. 1 as in 84:76; defs. 2, 5 as in 42:68] 1. To charge with something wrong or disgraceful; to reproach; to cast in the teeth; followed by *with* or *for*, before the thing imputed; as, to *upbraid* a man *for* his folly or his intemperance. 2. To reproach; to chide. 5. To treat with contempt.

Valiant, *a.* [as in 76:79; 121:29] 2. Brave; courageous; intrepid in danger; heroic.

Vanity, *n.* [as in 20:5; 84:55; 20:5; 84:55, 106:7] 1. Emptiness; want of substance to satisfy desire; uncertainty; inanity. 4. Emptiness; untruth. 5. Empty pleasure; vain pursuit; idle show; unsubstantial enjoyment. 6. Ostentation; arrogance. 7. Inflation of mind upon slight grounds; empty pride, inspired by an overweening conceit of one's personal attainments or decorations.

Vengeance, *n.* [as in 3:4; 29:17; 76:105; 97:22] The infliction of pain on another, in return for an injury or offense. Such infliction, when it proceeds from malice or mere resentment, and is not necessary for the purposes of justice, is revenge, and a most hainous crime. When such infliction proceeds from a mere love of justice, and the necessity of punishing offenders for the support of the laws, it is *vengeance,* and is warrantable and just. In this case, vengeance is a just retribution, recompense or punishment. In this latter sense the word is used in Scripture, and frequently applied to the punishments inflicted by God on sinners.

Vex, *v.t.* [as in 87:5; 97:23; 101:89] 1. To irritate; to make angry by little provocations. 2. To plague; to torment; to harass; to afflict. 3. To disturb; to disquiet; to agitate. 4. To trouble; to distress.

Viper[s], *n.* [as in 121:23] 2. A person or thing mischievous or malignant.

Vow, *n.* [as in 59:11; 108:3; 132:7, 43–44] 1. A solemn promise made to God, or by a pagan to his deity. A *vow* is a promise of something to be given or done hereafter. 2. A solemn promise; as the *vows* of unchangeable love and fidelity. In a moral and religious sense, *vows* are promises to God, as they appeal to God to witness their sincerity, and the violation of them is a most hainous offence.

Wax, *v.i.* [as in 1:16; 45:27, 58; 121:45] 2. To pass from one state to another; to become.

Whit, *n.* [as in 33:4] A point; a jot; the smallest part or particle imaginable. It is used without a preposition.

Whore, *n.* [as in 29:21; 86:3] A harlot; a courtesan; a concubine; a prostitute.

Whoremonger, *n.* [as in 63:17; 76:103] The same as *whoremaster:* One who practices lewdness.

Willing, *a.* [as in 1:34; 64:34; 88:32] Free to do or grant; having the mind inclined; disposed; not averse. 3. Ready; prompt.

Withal, *adv.* [as in 46:16] With the rest; together with; likewise; at the same time.

Wo, [woe], *n.* [as in 5:5; 10:28; 11:25; 19:5; 38:6; 56:16–17; 60:2] 1. Grief; sorrow; misery; a heavy calamity. 3. *Wo* is used in denunciation, and in exclamations of sorrow.

Wont, *a.* [as in 127:2; 128:13] Accustomed; habituated; using or doing customarily.

Wrest, *v.t.* [as in 10:63] 3. To distort; to turn from truth or twist from its natural meaning by violence; to pervert.

Yoke, *n.* [as in 109:32, 47, 63; 123:8] 1. A piece of timber, hollowed or made curving near each end, and fitted with bows for receiving the necks of oxen; by which means two are connected for drawing. From a ring or hook in the bow, a chain extends to the thing to be drawn, or to the yoke of another pair of oxen behind. 2. A mark of servitude; slavery; bondage.

INDEX